Eastern Europe

GEOGRAPHIES FOR ADVANCED STUDY

Edited by Professor S. H. Beaver, M.A., F.R.G.S.

The Tropical World
The Soviet Union
Malaya, Indonesia, Borneo and the Philippines
West Africa
The Scandinavian World
A Regional Geography of Western Europe
The British Isles—A Geographic and Economic Survey
Central Europe
Geomorphology
Statistical Methods and the Geographer
The Polar World
An Historical Geography of South Africa
North America
Land, People and Economy in Malaya
The Western Mediterranean World
Human Geography
Geography of Population
Urban Geography
An Historical Geography of Western Europe before 1800
Eastern Europe

Eastern Europe

NORMAN J. G. POUNDS

University Professor of Geography and History,
Indiana University

LONGMAN

LONGMAN GROUP LIMITED
London

Associated companies, branches, and representatives throughout the world

© Longman Group Ltd.
(formerly Longmans, Green & Co. Ltd.) 1969

First published 1969
Second impression 1969

SBN 582 48143 0

PRINTED IN GREAT BRITAIN BY
SPOTTISWOODE, BALLANTYNE & CO. LTD.
LONDON AND COLCHESTER

Preface

My interest in Eastern Europe was first aroused many years ago by the lectures of Harriet Wanklyn (Mrs. J. A. Steers) at Cambridge University and was several years later sharpened by association with colleagues in the Institute of East European Studies at Indiana University. The concept of Eastern Europe was changed radically, between these two dates by the events of the Second World War and its aftermath. Previously it had been the 'Eastern Marchlands' of Europe; afterwards, it became the territory of the People's Democracies. It is in this latter sense that Eastern Europe is defined in this book. Only in this way can one justify the inclusion of the German Democratic Republic, and the exclusion of Greece, to whose civilisation much of Eastern Europe owes far more than it does to the Germans.

This book was begun under the shadow of Stalin; it was completed at a time when the unity of the bloc had become an illusion, and some of its members were consciously and openly departing from Marxist-Leninist orthodoxy. The intervening years were a period of revolutionary change and rapid economic growth. This growth is continuing, so that the qualitative and quantitative discussions of these changes contained in the following pages may date quite rapidly. Fortunately all the countries discussed publish statistical yearbooks, some of which are of a high quality, as well as a considerable literature on the field of geography, both academic and popular.

The author has been able to travel extensively in the area from 1956 onwards, and has visited most parts of seven out of the eight countries. Only Albania has eluded him, and he has so far been obliged to content himself with a Pisgah-view of the promised land from hilltops in Greece and Yugoslavia.

All photographs used were taken by the author in the course of these travels, with the exception only of *. All maps were drawn by him but he gratefully acknowledges the help of John M. Hollingsworth and Brian C. Goodey in printing the lettering on them.

East European place-names have presented a problem. The practice was adopted of using the forms of these names that were current

* See p. xv.

locally, with the exception only of a few names, such as Warsaw and Danube, which are too well-established to be avoided. This has necessarily led to the use of two or even three forms, according to the context, for a single feature. The Polish *Odra* and Czech Labe, for example, become the East German Oder and Elbe respectively, while the Drim changes to the Drin as it crosses the boundary from Yugoslavia to Albania. Alternative forms are in the more important cases given in the text, and a fuller list of variant forms of place-names is given in the appendix.

He is greatly indebted to many friends both within and outside of Eastern Europe who have helped him on his travels and given him the benefit of their knowledge and experience. In particular he would like to mention: Doctors Kostrowicki, Kosziński, Kukliński, Leszczicki and Dziewoński of the Instytut Geografii, Polish Academy of Science; Professor George W. Hoffman of the University of Texas, Professor Robert N. Taaffe of the University of Wisconsin, and his friends and colleagues, past and present, of Indiana University especially Professors Václav L. Beneš, Lowell C. Bennion, Gretchen Buehler, Barbara Jelavich, Charles Jelavich, James Scott, Denis Sinor, and Barbara Zakrzewska. He would also like to acknowledge the help of many of his students, especially Hristo Hristov and Béla Ováry, and of Professor Stanley Beaver who edited this book, and of his wife who accompanied him on many arduous journeys in Eastern Europe.

Bloomington
Indiana

N. J. G. POUNDS

Contents

Maps and Diagrams

1*

Photographs

All photographs are the author's, except those facing page 140,
which are by Plan und Karte, Münster, West Germany

List of Abbreviations

Abh. K. K. geogr. Ges. Wien	*Abhandlungen der K. K. Geographischen Gesellschaft in Wien*
Am. Anthrop.	*American Anthropologist*
Am. anthrop. Ass. (Bull.)	*American Anthropological Association, Bulletin of*
Ann. Ass. Am. Georgr.	*Annals of the Association of Américan Geographers*
Annls geogr.	*Annales de géographie*
C. r. Congr. int. Geogr.	*Compte rendu du Congrès international de Géographie*
Deutsch. Verlag. d. Wissen, Berlin	*Deutscher Verlage der Wissenschaften, Berlin*
Econ. Geogr.	*Economic Geography*
Geogr. Annlr	*Geografiska annaler*
Geogrl J.	*Geographical Journal*
Geogrl Rev.	*Geographical Review*
Geogr. Ber.	*Geographische Berichte*
Geogr. Rdsch.	*Geographische Rundschau*
Geogr. Z.	*Geographische Zeitschrift*
Geogr. Anz.	*Geographischer Anzeiger*
Geography	*Geography*
J. Geogr.	*Journal of Geography*
Mber.	*Monatsbericht*
Mem. soc. Serbe Géogr.	*Mémoires de la Société Serbe de Géographie*
Mitt. geogr. Ges. Wien	*Mitteilungen der Geographischen Gesellschaft in Wien*
Petermanns Mitt.	*Petermanns geographische Mitteilungen*
Petermanns geogr. Mitt.	*Petermanns geographische Mitteilungen*
Population, Lond.	*Population*
Population, Paris	*Population*

Pr. geogr.	*Prace geograficzne*
Prof. Geogr.	*Professional Geographer*
Przegl. geogr.	*Przegląd geograficzny*
Scott. geogr. Mag.	*Scottish Geographical Magazine*
Tijdschr. econ. soc. Geogr.	*Tijdschrift voor economische en sociale geographie*
Trans. Inst. Br. Geogr.	*Transactions of the Institute of British Geographers*
Z. WirtGeogr.	*Zeitschrift für Wirtschaftsgeographie*
Przegl. zach.	*Przegląd Zachodni (Poznań)*

CHAPTER ONE

The Physical Geography

Eastern Europe, like all such divisions of the continent of Europe, is an arbitrary one. It owes everything to the contingencies of past history and contemporary politics, and little or nothing to the facts of physical geography. Eastern Europe can be defined in many ways. It is the area within which have lived for over a thousand years most of the non-Russian Slavs; it is one where the Russian and German, Turkish and Austro-Hungarian empires struggled for mastery; it is the eastern 'marchland' of Europe, within which an essentially European or Western civilisation merges gradually into a culture which is in many ways non-European and non-Western; it is a 'shatter-zone' in which fragments of broken nations have been laboriously pieced together to make the nation-states of this division of Europe. Above all, Eastern Europe may be defined as the sphere of Soviet domination, or at least of Communist control since the end of the Second World War (Fig. 1.1).

None of these descriptions or definitions of Eastern Europe has any precision, except the last, and it is this which is used to define the scope of this book. The validity or otherwise of other definitions that have been suggested will be examined in the course of the next six chapters. Eastern Europe is here defined as the territory of the eight states which fell under Soviet political domination—only temporary in the case of Yugoslavia—at the end of the Second World War. These states include the German Democratic Republic, more often known as East Germany, which had not previously existed as a separate state and indeed only gradually separated itself from the rest of Germany. All eight of these states adopted the state-controlled economic system which is commonly described as Communistic, as listed in Table 1.

Taken together, these countries extend from the Baltic Sea to their boundaries with Turkey and Greece, through almost 1,200 miles and over 15 degrees of latitude. Their most westerly point lies on the border between Hesse and Thuringia, only 75 miles from Frankfurt-am-Main. Their most easterly, 1,000 miles and 20 degrees of longitude away, lies where the Black Sea laps against the marshes of the Danube delta.

As defined by its present political boundaries, Eastern Europe comprises just over a quarter of the area of Europe, excluding the Soviet Union, and its total population, estimated in 1965 to have been about

Fig. 1.1. Eastern Europe.

Table 1. Eight states of Communist Eastern Europe

	Area in square kilometres	Population, 1965 est.
East Germany (incl. East Berlin)	107,431	16,000,000
Poland	311,370	31,496,000
Czechoslovakia	127,859	14,159,000
Hungary	93,030	10,148,000
Romania	237,500	19,027,000
Yugoslavia	110,669	19,508,000
Bulgaria	255,804	8,200,000
Albania	28,748	1,865,000
	1,272,411	120,403,000

Source: *United Nations Statistical Yearbook, 1966* (pub[d]. 1967).

120,500,000, is about 27 per cent of the European total. The importance of this region to the rest of the continent has never been in doubt.
It lies astride and to the west of the narrow 'waist' of Europe, where the
Black and Baltic Seas approach within 800 miles of each other. It is in
a sense an isthmus linking Western Europe with its continental base in
Eurasia, and since the time of early prehistoric migrations it has provided corridors for peoples entering Europe from the east. It has
served no less to guide European peoples who have moved eastward
into the vaster land mass of Eurasia.

Mackinder claimed, in words that have become all too familiar,
that:

> 'Who rules East Europe commands the Heartland.'

Not everyone today is willing to accept the logic of Mackinder's argument, and it is by no means certain that Germany's attempts to control
the region were ever inspired by such broad geopolitical considerations. Nevertheless, it cannot be denied that both the German and
Austrian empires to the west and the Russian and Turkish to the east
sought at different times to control this strategic region both to gain
access to its resources and to threaten or invade the territories of their
enemies.

In the 1930s Germany acquired an economic domination over much
of this area, which contained much needed resources, and in the war
which followed, German military power overran almost the whole of
it and came within striking distance of the Suez Canal and the oilfields
of the Middle East. Since the closing stages of that war, the same area
has fallen under Soviet domination and control, and a significant part
of its territory has been annexed to the Soviet Union. Before the
Communist Revolution, Russian imperialism had extended quite
deeply into Eastern Europe, but no earlier penetration was as extensive and as profound as that which followed the Second World War.
Eastern Poland was annexed by the Soviet Union; Bessarabia was
stripped from Romania, and Sub-Carpathian Russia from Czechoslovakia. The Soviet Union broadened its base on the Baltic and Black
Sea coasts, and if it had succeeded in maintaining its political hold on
Yugoslavia and Albania, it would have been able to command a broad
frontage on the Mediterranean Sea, extending from the Italian border
to the Greek. In East Germany Soviet forces are only 400 miles from
Paris and within 500 miles of London, and a Soviet soldier examines
the travel documents of German citizens who travel from one part of

their own country to the other. It is this pervasive Soviet influence, diminishing though it is, which in the last analysis, gives unity to this area.

Compared with other major divisions of Europe, Eastern Europe has only a short frontage on the sea. On the north, from near the West German city of Lübeck to the Soviet city of Kaliningrad (*Germ*: Königsberg) the plains of East Germany and Poland look out on the Baltic Sea for almost 400 miles. Yugoslavia has a coastline which, if its minor indentations are ignored, extends for 450 miles from the suburbs of Trieste to the Albanian border, and Albania itself has a straighter and more regular coastline of about 175 miles. Bulgaria and Romania together border the Black Sea for 320 miles. A total of some 1,400 miles of coastline, less in fact than that of France, is little for a region which embraces a quarter of the area of Europe. Much of this coastline, furthermore, is either harbourless or has such imperfect communications with its hinterland that its harbours can have but little value. In modern times the countries which now make up Eastern Europe have had to rely heavily for their seaborne commerce on ports outside the region, notably on Trieste in Italy; on Hamburg and Lübeck in West Germany, and on Thessaloníki in Greece. Those countries which have ports on the Black Sea coast—Bulgaria and Romania—must gain access to the world's shipping lanes through the territorial waters of Turkey.

Although no place within the territory of Eastern Europe, as defined in this chapter, is much more than 400 miles from the sea,[1] the region as a whole has a strongly continental character. This is most clearly shown in its climate, but its landforms, more expansive and less varied within small areas than those of much of Western Europe, share also the general character of continental Eastern Europe. To these facts of physical geography we now turn.

STRUCTURE AND RELIEF

Physically, as in almost every other respect, Eastern Europe is intermediate between Central Europe and the greater Eurasian land mass. Its geological structures are continuous from the one to the other, and the landform regions, which, in general, parallel the geological structures, extend across Eastern Europe and are common to both Central Europe and the Soviet Union.

[1] The place farthest from the sea is near Košice, in eastern Slovakia.

Palaeozoic Europe

A feature of the geological structures of Eastern Europe is their great variety and their great range of geological age, from early Palaeozoic

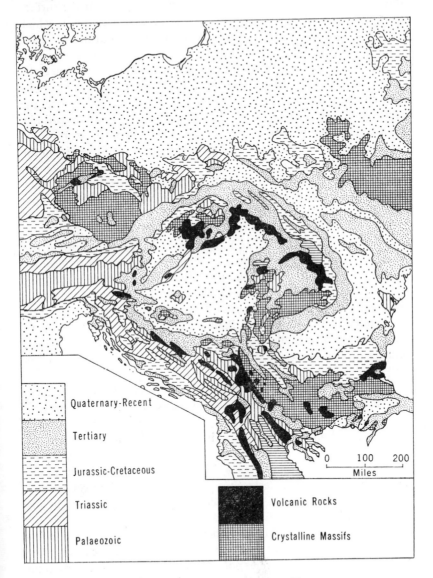

Fig. 1.2. Geological map of Eastern Europe.

to Recent. Eastern Europe, in fact, presents a cross-section through Europe, from which only the Scandinavian Shield is missing. The foundation on which Eastern Europe is built is a mass of ancient rock, undoubtedly much folded and faulted, but appearing at the surface over only a small fraction of the area. Time and the pressures to which these rocks have been exposed have converted many of them to hard metamorphic rocks. Within the Palaeozoic period they were subjected to two periods of earth movement and mountain building, the Caledonian and the Hercynian. Though the former is not readily recognisable among the folds of the Palaeozoic rocks of Eastern Europe, the Hercynian gave rise to a mountain system of considerable magnitude. It extended from west to east across the region, and its worn-down remains are present today in the hills and plateaus of Bohemia, in the Holy Cross Mountains (Świętokrzyskie Góry) of southern Poland, and the Ore Mountains of Slovakia (Slovenské rudohorie). They constitute the core of much of the Carpathian and Balkan Mountains; they compose the isolated Bihor Massif of Romania, the Rhodope Mountains of Bulgaria and the hill-country of southern Serbia and and Macedonia (see Fig. 1.2). Elsewhere in Eastern Europe the Palaeozoic platform lies unseen, sometimes only a short distance below the surface. It underlies south-eastern Poland and neighbouring parts of the Soviet Union, where the more deeply etched valleys of the Bug, Dnepr and their tributaries have revealed its presence. It also underlies the Hungarian Plain, where it constitutes a resistent mass around which the Alpine mountain system was later folded, and its presence is revealed locally by small inliers in the Bakony and Mecsek hills.

Long after they were folded the rocks of these Hercynian mountains were intruded by igneous rocks, which today give rise to hill masses, often of more rugged relief than the surrounding areas, in Bohemia and Slovakia, and in parts of Transylvania, Serbia and the Rhodope mountains. More recently, renewed igneous activity led to volcanic action and the formation of volcanic cones and even small lava flows. The highly picturesque České Středohoří of Czechoslovakia are volcanic, and lava flows of fairly recent geological age occur in the Carpathian Mountains of Romania.

Among the more recent of the Palaeozoic deposits is the Carboniferous series, which includes in its upper levels the coal measures. The Carboniferous, being more exposed to post-Hercynian erosion than beds of greater age and depth, has been stripped from much of Eastern

Europe. Though deeply buried beneath later deposits over some parts of the area, it occurs significantly only in southern Poland, Bohemia and Moravia. Small pockets of Carboniferous age, sometimes including part of the coal series, occur in Hungary, Romania and the Balkan peninsula.

The period which followed the Carboniferous and the building of the Hercynian mountain system was marked first by widespread semi-arid conditions, when salt deposits were formed as the shallow lakes and seas slowly evaporated. In this way originated the potash, sulphur and common-salt deposits of East Germany and Poland. More extensive seas spread over Europe, and in them were laid down beds, frequently relatively thin, of limestone, intercalated with beds of clay and sandstone. In the central and southern parts of the East European region these beds accumulated to a far greater thickness than in the northern, as if the seas in which they formed, collectively known as the Tethys, were becoming deeper and so allowing far greater quantities of sediment to accumulate.

Alpine folding
This sedimentation process was but the prelude to the most recent of the mountain-building phases which Europe has experienced, the Alpine. The beds which had accumulated in the deepening Tethys were raised into a series of highly complex folds. The fold mountains which resulted continue eastward the general features and the direction of those of Switzerland and Austria. They lack however the complex *nappes*, or overfolds, which characterise the latter, and on the map the ranges are narrower and their course more serpentine than those of Central Europe. In fact, they have been built or folded against the relatively stable masses of Hercynian Europe, more especially the Bohemian Massif; the submerged Pannonian Massif, which underlies the Hungarian Plain; the massifs which underlie the Ukraine and Walachia, and the Pelagonian Massif which centres in Macedonia and the northern basin of the Aegean Sea.

The Alpine system thus diverges as it enters Eastern Europe. The more northerly ranges of the Alps of Austria become narrower and lower as they reach out towards the Danube in the vicinity of Vienna. They terminate in cliffs, which drop to the south bank of the river. Beyond its northern bank, this line of folding is continued in the Carpathian ranges of Slovakia. These curve in an immense arc north-eastward, then east and south-eastward, until in southern Romania they swing back toward the west as the narrower and more rugged Transylvanian Alps. Again turning to the south, the line of folding regains the Danube, where the river crosses it in the sequence of gorges frequently, though incorrectly, called the Iron Gate. South of the Danube the range is continued to the east as the Stara Planina, or Balkan Mountains. These mountains become lower and are at last

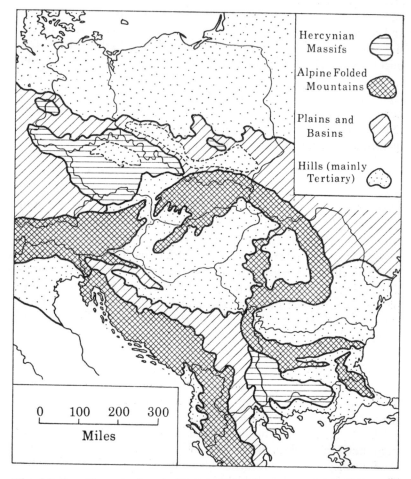

Hercynian Massifs

Alpine Folded Mountains

Plains and Basins

Hills (mainly Tertiary)

0   100   200   300

Miles

Fig. 1.3. Landform regions in Eastern Europe; these regions are further elaborated in the maps of landform regions which accompany the chapters on individual countries.

truncated by the Black Sea, but are continued 300 miles away in the ranges of the southern Crimea and yet farther in the Caucasus Mountains.

The more southerly branch of the Alpine system diverges from the main mass of the Alpine system near the boundary of Austria with north-eastern Italy, and extends south-eastward, parallel with the coast of the Adriatic Sea. It broadens as it is traced in this direction until it culminates in a vast dissected plateau, built mainly of limestone. This is the Dinaric mountain system. Beyond the boundary of Yugoslavia the lines of folding turn toward the south, and are continued through mountains of Albania into the Píndhos Mountains of northern Greece.

The Alpine mountain-building occurred so recently in the geological history of Europe, that the resulting relief forms are still fresh and sharp. Nevertheless, erosion of the mountains has led to the deposition of the later Tertiary deposits over large areas of lowland in Central and Eastern Europe. These include the plains of Hungary, Walachia, and Moldavia, and of the Marica valley and Macedonia. These regions are today characterised by beds of soft sandstone, marls, and clays, and by a gentle, rolling relief.

Ice Age

The latest phases in the geological history of Europe, the Pleistocene and Recent, are characterised by the Quaternary Ice Age and its aftermath. Only the northern part of Eastern Europe was greatly influenced by the glaciation. Ice sheets extended southward from Scandinavia, reaching at their maximum extent the northern foothills of the Sudeten and Carpathian Mountains. There appear to have been four major advances of the ice, separated by prolonged periods when the ice melted away and a dry and perhaps very cold climate prevailed over much of northern Europe. With each advance and subsequent melting and disappearance of the ice, a spread of boulder clay was laid down and was to some degree graded by the torrential rivers that discharged from the melting ice sheet itself. The deposits left by the first and even by the second advance of the ice were to a large extent removed by erosion during the ensuing interglacial periods. The boulder clay laid down by the later advances of the ice, however, remains, but has been modified in some measure by erosion during post-glacial times. As they are traced northward toward the Baltic Sea, the glacial landforms become fresher and more similar to what they must have looked like when the ice finally melted from this region.

South of the plains of East Germany and Poland there was no extensive glaciation. Ice sheets formed only in the higher mountains and sent valley glaciers down toward the lower ground. But these were very small, except in the Tatra Mountains, the culminating mountain mass of the Carpathian chain. Only the Tatra Mountains today show on any considerable scale the sharp peaks and arêtes, the cirques and steep-sided valleys of the typical glaciated mountain landscape.

The remaining mountain regions of Eastern Europe were too low even to have had extensive ice fields. At most there were snow patches, which led to the erosion of cirques on slopes shielded from the sun. Such glaciated forms are found today in the Krkonoše range, in north-eastern Bohemia; at numerous points in the Carpathian Mountains, and in the Rhodope Massif.

The dry and probably cold interglacial periods were characterised by strong winds which blew outward from what must then have been a pronounced high pressure system over northern Europe. The bare expanses of boulder clay were dried out by the wind, and the pulverised dust blown outward in clouds. It was laid down as deposits of loess, some of them of great thickness, along the northern margin of the mountains of Bohemia and of the Carpathians. The dust was also carried across the mountains to be deposited in parts of the plains of Bohemia and Moravia, in the Hungarian Plain, and in Walachia and Moldavia.

While the ice sheets were melting away the great rivers, swollen with melt-water, carried immense quantities of silt down toward the sea, building their deltas forward into the water and forming alluvial plains along the coasts. The greatest volumes of water were liberated in the plain of northern Europe. At one phase in the melting process water was ponded between the Carpathian Mountains and the margin of the ice sheet. Unable to escape laterally, it overflowed southward between the Bohemian Massif and the Carpathians to join the Danube. In this way the rushing waters cut the Moravian Gate, a gap which to-day links the plain of Poland with that of the Danube valley. During a later phase of the glacial retreat the waters made their way north-westward toward the North Sea, excavating the broad valleys—*Urstromtäler* or *pradoliny*—which, with their marshy floors and misfit streams, are so conspicuous and important a feature of the plains of Poland and East Germany.

Landform regions

On the basis of relief and type of rock it is possible to delimit a small number of major physiographic regions in Eastern Europe. Several of these extend beyond the boundaries of the region as a whole into Central or Southern Europe or into the Soviet Union. In this chapter they are described and their relationship to one another explained only in general terms. A more detailed regional analysis is deferred to the eight chapters on individual countries, which make up the second part of this book. It must be emphasised that the regions described here are defined primarily in terms of relief and landforms, not of geological structure and age.

North European Plain. Most of East Germany and Poland belong to the North European Plain. This is by definition a region of gentle relief, rarely rising to more than 500 feet above sea-level, and exceeding 1,000 feet in altitude only in the moraine region of north-eastern Poland. By and large it is a region of Secondary rocks, ranging in geological age from the Triassic to the Cretaceous, with occasional small deposits of Tertiary age. Over much of the plain, however, this 'solid' geology is covered and hidden by the deposits left by the Quaternary Ice Age, and on the basis of these glacial deposits the plain as a whole can be divided into three sub-regions.

1. Across the north is a region of the most recent glacial deposits. It is characterised by terminal moraines and drumlins, by outwash sands and gravels, and by depressions, formed either by the irregular deposition of glacial material or by the slow melting of masses of ice left embedded in the boulder clay itself, and now filled with lake or marsh. On the south this sub-region is bounded by the outwash deposits, formed during the relatively long period of time when the ice halted in the course of its retreat along this line. To the north, its level sinks toward the alluvium and coastal marshes which fringe the Baltic Sea.

2. The second region, sometimes known as the region of the 'Former River Valleys' or *Urstromtäler* (*P: pradoliny*), is characterised by a series of parallel or sub-parallel valleys, formed by the escape north-westward to the North Sea of the vast quantities of water that flowed from the melting ice front. These rivers excavated wide valleys whose flat floors even today are occupied in part by marsh and damp meadowland. The rivers, frequently diminutive, which today flow through them from south-east to north-west bear little resemblance to the torrents which excavated them during the Quaternary period. Nor

is any one of them today occupied throughout its length by a single river. The largest and most continuous of them, the so-called Toruń-Eberswalde valley, is occupied in turn by the Bug and the middle Vistula, by the Noteć, Warta and middle Oder, and by the Havel and lower Elbe. Another valley diverges from this one near Warsaw and takes a more southerly course. In different segments of its course it is drained by the Bzura, the upper Warta, the Oder and the Spree, before it merges into the Elbe valley below Magdeburg. The most southerly of these great valleys is occupied in turn by the upper Oder, the upper reaches of the Black Elster, the middle Elbe, the Aller and the lower Weser. In some places these valleys have no river in them at all, only damp bottom-land, drained by small streams, where the drainage pattern has even reversed itself since the later phases of the Ice Age.

Between these great valleys of the northern plain the land is generally flat or gently rolling, and generally forms a series of low plateaus. Worn-down morainic ridges, patches of gravel and wind-blown sand, and small, marshy or even lake-filled depressions, relics of a formerly more extensive system of glacial lakes, break the evenness of these plains. In East Germany the valleys become wider, and in some areas, particularly to the west and east of Berlin, are laced by a maze of small waterways. Here the plateau-like regions which separate the valleys support vast hills and ridges of morainic and outwash sands and gravels. These include the recently afforested heaths of Fläming and Lausitz.

3. The third division of the northern plain lies south of the maximum of all except the earliest advance of the ice, and its most south-easterly extension in Romania goes far beyond the glacial limit. The remaining boulder clay deposits are visible to the trained eye of the geologist but are not significant in either the landscape or the soil. Instead, over much of this region the solid geology is hidden either by alluvium or by the loess that was spread here during the cold, dry inter- and post-glacial periods. Locally the 'solid' geology shows through at the surface, and is never far beneath it. Along the southern margin of this region it emerges sometimes gradually and almost imperceptibly, as in southern Poland, sometimes abruptly, as where the Harz Mountains and the northern bastions of the Bohemian Massif lift their steep faces from the drift and alluvium of the nearby plains. Relief in this region of the northern plain is, in general, gentle or rolling, but toward the south-east, in Moldavia, the surface rises into rounded, loess-covered hills, cut from the soft Tertiary beds by

the many rivers which flow south-eastward toward the Danube delta or the Black Sea.

Hills and plains of Central Europe. The term 'Central Europe' is here used for a region lying from west to east, intermediate between the northern plain and the Alpine mountain system. This is a region of great variety and complexity. Broadly speaking, it consists of a series of low mountain or hill ranges, composed of hard Palaeozoic rocks and separated by lowlands, sometimes formed by erosion, sometimes by the downfaulting of segments of the massifs themselves, but generally floored by Tertiary or later deposits and often covered by a dusting of loess. The hills of Central Europe are typically steep-sided with flat or rounded summits, which rise to heights of between 2,500 and 4,500 feet. These higher surfaces are generally taken to represent an early Tertiary peneplain. The hills themselves, with their intervening valleys and plains, can be divided into (1) a western group, consisting of the Harz Mountains and the Thuringian Forest (Thüringer-wald) and the intervening Thuringian Basin; (2) Bohemia, consisting of an interior region of lowland, surrounded by a frame of mountains and hills, and (3) the hills of south-central Poland. The Thuringian and Bohemian regions belong to Hercynian Europe, and the mountains and hills are composed of Palaeozoic rock. The third region consists of a core of rocks of similar date, forming the Holy Cross Mountains (Świętokrzyskie Góry), but flanked on west and east by younger rocks —Jurassic and Cretaceous in age—which make up the Kraków Jura and the Lublin Plateau. The latter is continued eastward into the hills of the northern Ukraine. To these should be added on structural grounds the more rugged Bihor Massif of Romania, which lies to the south of and is partially enclosed by the Carpathian Mountain system.

The Alpine system: Carpathian Mountains–Transylvanian Alps. The more northerly ranges of the Austrian Alps reach down to the Danube, becoming lower and less formidable, until they overlook the river in high bluffs. Beyond the Danube and its bordering plain they again emerge from the lowlands as the White and Little Carpathians (*C-s: Bílé* and *Malé Karpaty*). A series of parallel mountain ranges emerges. At first they trend to the north-east, then swing round to the east. The mountains become higher, broader and more complex. Masses of older rock are caught up in the mountain folds, which were also intruded during the concluding phases of the Alpine mountain building by igneous rocks. The Western Carpathians are the highest and most impressive segment of the whole range, and only here are

2

typically glaciated Alpine landforms to be found. The Central Carpathians of eastern Slovakia and the Ukraine are narrower, lower, and more broken up by transverse valleys, and are thus more easily crossed. But beyond them, near the boundary of Romania, the mountain chain broadens again into the rugged and in places almost inaccessible Eastern Carpathians.

The mountains then swing abruptly to the west for 200 miles as the Transylvanian Alps, before making another of those abrupt turns, which appear to characterise the eastern Alpine system, and passing into Yugoslavia and Bulgaria. The Balkan Mountains, or Stara Planina, with the parallel range of the Sredna Gora, or Middle Mountains, to the south, are lower and constitute a far less formidable barrier than the Carpathian and Transylvanian mountains themselves. As they extend eastward toward the Black Sea, they become lower, narrower, and less conspicuous, until they appear only as ridges rising above the plains of eastern Bulgaria and terminate in low cliffs along the shores of the Black Sea.

This serpentine range, over 1,200 miles in length from the castle-crowned hill of Bratislava, where the Little Carpathians overlook the Danube, to the Black Sea coast near Burgas, encloses two distinct and separate regions within its embrace. Almost encircled by the Carpathians and Transylvanian Alps is Transylvania itself, a hilly, upland basin, floored largely with the material eroded from the Carpathians and partially covered with loess. It is drained mainly westward toward the Hungarian Plain, but on this side is largely shut in by the Bihor Mountains. These are a rounded massif made up mainly of Palaeozoic and igneous rock, rising steeply from the surrounding lowlands and culminating in a wide and in parts almost level summit. The Bihor Mountains resemble such Hercynian massifs of Central Europe as the Harz Mountains, and they are in fact just such a mass, cut off from others by the fold mountains of the Alpine system.

Pannonian–Walachian Plain. The two branches of the Alpine system in Eastern Europe are separated from one another by an extensive, low-lying and generally level area, the Pannonian or Hungarian Plain. Despite its prevailingly gentle relief, it represents, in fact, a hidden massif, not unlike the Bihor Mountains in its geological composition, around which the mountains have been folded. The upper surface of this massif lies below sea-level, but the roots of the fold mountains go very much deeper, so that the folds themselves were forced up against this relatively stable and resistant mass. Locally, as in the western part of the Pannonian Basin, the underlying Palaeozoic rocks show through the cover of Tertiary and later deposits, producing small areas of stronger relief and reminding one of the very different rocks and structures which lie in some areas only a few hundred feet below the surface of the plain.

The Pannonian Plain, which extends in most directions beyond the present boundaries of Hungary, is divided into two by the ridge of hills known as the Bakony Forest. To the north-west lies the smaller plain, known as the Little or *Kiss*alföld; to the south-east, the Great or *Nagy*alföld. The Great Alföld is itself divisible into a low-lying and over large areas quite level region, to the east of the Danube, and a somewhat more hilly region lying between the Danube and the Bakony Forest. The plain itself is enclosed by mountains. Its drainage is exclusively to the Danube, which enters the region by cutting across the mountain spurs which link the Alps with the Carpathians, and leaves by way of the far more formidable gorges known as the Iron Gate.

In late Tertiary times the plain contained a lake, held back by the barrier formed by the Transylvanian Alps and Balkan Mountains. Water escaped across these mountains, and gradually incised its course across them at the Iron Gate, at the same time permitting the Pannonian Basin to be drained of its lake and the land surface to be lowered by erosion. The gorges of the Danube still constitute the base-level of erosion for the plain as a whole. The silt formed by the hard rocks of the gorge tract of the river has led to sedimentation upstream and increases the flood problem on the middle course of the Danube and along its tributaries.

The Walachian Plain similarly represents a deeply buried massif of resistant rock, but differs from the Pannonian in its lack of any enclosing barrier to the east. It is low-lying, its Secondary and Tertiary deposits have been cut up by the rivers which flow down from the Transylvanian Alps and Balkan Mountains, and its 'solid' geology has been largely obscured by one of the most extensive areas of loess in the whole of Europe.

After it escapes from the gorges of the Iron Gate, the Danube flows eastward toward the Black Sea, but when only about 40 miles from the coast at Constanţa it turns sharply to the north to pass around the low tableland of the Dobrogea before again turning to the east, breaking up into the distributaries of its delta and so reaching the sea. On the north the lower Danube is bordered for much of its course by lakes, marshes and extensive deposits of alluvium; on the right by low bluffs which constitute the margin of the platform of northern Bulgaria. The plain lying between the Transylvanian Alps and the Danube is, in fact, a slip-off slope, where the Danube, eroding the bluffs along its right bank and depositing alluvium along its left, is very slowly shifting towards the south. The platform whose margin the river is slowly eroding, is built mainly of Cretaceous and Tertiary rocks, covered with the ubiquitous loess. In Dobrogea, however, the Palaeozoic foundation shows through, a reminder that here, as in the Pannonian Plain, it is nowhere far below the surface, and that it is its unseen presence which is chiefly responsible for the violent contortions in the course of the folded mountains of the Carpathian system.

The Alpine system: the Dinaric Mountains. The high central ranges of the Austrian Alps end abruptly on the margin of the Pannonian Plain; the more southerly are continued into Yugoslavia. The Karawanken Alps, which bear along their ragged crest the boundary between Austria and Yugoslavia, are continued in a series of ridges, lower, narrower and more broken, which extend eastward between the Drava and Sava rivers, diminishing gradually in height until they fade into the plain of Slavonia.

The Julian Alps branch from the Karawanken close to where Italy, Austria and Yugoslavia meet. Near their northern extremity they rise, in the sharp, pointed peak of Triglav, to 9,394 feet; they then sink to a dissected plateau, known as the Dinaric Mountains, which rarely rises much more than 5,000 feet above sea-level. This plateau, low and narrow in the north-west, where it is crossed with relative ease, expands and becomes higher toward the south-east. In southern Yugoslavia it reaches a width of over 150 miles, and at its highest point, Durmitor in Montenegro, attains a height of 8,272 feet. Beyond this point the plateau narrows to less than 100 miles as it is continued into Albania and Greece.

The Dinaric Mountains consist primarily of limestone of Cretaceous age. They are not acutely folded, like most other parts of the Alpine system, and the limestone itself provides a dry surface, in parts almost devoid of vegetation, over large areas. This is, in fact, the most extensive area in Europe of karst, and perhaps one of the most extensive and spectacular in the world.

This southern extension of the Alpine region is divisible into three distinct sub-regions. In the extreme north-west is the small Alpine zone, coterminous very roughly with the Yugoslav province of

Slovenia and containing the Karawanken and Julian Alps The western Dinaric region constitutes a zone from 40 to 70 miles in width and bordering the Adriatic Sea from the Istrian peninsula in the north-west to the boundary of Greece in the south-east. On the south-west it drops steeply and in places precipitously to the *ria* coast of the Adriatic Sea. Offshore is a fringe of islands, most of them narrow and elongated, strung out parallel to the fold-lines of the Dinaric system. This region is predominantly karst, and its inland boundary follows very roughly the interior margin of the limestone.

The eastern Dinaric region is lower and more dissected by the rivers which, rising within or on the margin of the limestone region, have here carved deep and in places narrow and gorge-like valleys across it toward the Sava and Danube. Geologically it is far more complex than the more south-westerly Dinaric region. The limestone cover is still extensive in some areas, notably in the Raška region of Old Serbia, but over much of the area it has been eroded to expose underlying Triassic and Palaeozoic beds. The greater variety of rock, the broader range of hardness, and the more complex structures exposed here are reflected in the very much more accidented relief of this region.

On the north this eastern Dinaric region sinks gently toward the Sava valley and the southern margin of the Pannonian Plain. On the east, however, it is impossible to differentiate it on the basis of the physical map alone from the last important physical region of Eastern Europe, the Rhodope region.

Rhodope region. Although the Rhodope Mountains cover only a restricted part of this region, their name is used here to designate a very much broader area which in geological age and structure may be said to resemble the Rhodope. The whole area extending eastward from the Dinaric region to the Black Sea and southward from the Pannonian Basin and the Stara Planina to the Aegean Sea is made up of Palaeozoic and even older rocks, many of them strongly metamorphosed and crystalline. The whole has been extensively intruded by more recent igneous rocks. The region must have been much eroded before the end of Palaeozoic times, for numerous basins and plains were formed, in which were laid down not only small deposits of the Carboniferous series, but also Secondary and Tertiary deposits. Some of these were also folded during the Alpine mountain-building, and the whole region was further eroded in later Tertiary and subsequent times.

On the basis of existing relief it is possible to divide the whole region into three sub-regions.

1. First is a western region which extends from the margin of the Pannonian Plain southward to the Aegean. Its northern part is drained northward to the Danube by the Morava and its tributaries, and its more southerly extension southward by the Vardar and Struma to the Aegean. These rivers and their tributaries have dissected the whole region, so that it is now one of small plains and basins, some of them lake basins in Tertiary and Quaternary times, and most of them today covered with lacustrine deposits separated from one another by steep-sided and frequently isolated mountain and hill masses. These mountains rise at their highest points to over 6,500 feet in the Kopaonik Mountains and to nearly 8,500 feet in the Šar Planina. Between them, however, are interlinked valleys which afford a variety of routeways between the Danubian plains and the Mediterranean coast.

2. The second division of the Rhodope region is made up of the Rhodope itself. This is, like the Kapaonik and Šar mountains, a massif of ancient crystalline rocks, but is very much larger in extent, as well as higher and less dissected by rivers into subsidiary masses. It rises at its highest point, Musala, to 9,610 feet, the highest point in the whole Balkan peninsula. On the south it drops to the narrow broken plains of Macedonia and Thrace, where the ancient rocks, much eroded, are partly covered by recent alluvial deposits.

3. To the north and north-east lies the third division of the Rhodope region. This is the valley of the Marica River, a rather hilly lowland, underlain by ancient rocks similar to those which compose the Rhodope itself, but here deeply covered with Tertiary lacustrine deposits and more recent alluvium. The Marica River, which rises on the northern flanks of the Rhodope, takes a curving course around the mountain mass to the east and then to the south, before entering Thrace and reaching the Aegean Sea. Beyond the Marica to the east and north-east, the same ancient rocks, covered here and there with deposits of Secondary and Tertiary date, reach out through the Strandža Mountains to the Black Sea.

Drainage

Eastern Europe is drained northward to the Baltic and North Seas, eastward to the Black Sea and also southward to the Mediterranean. The greater part of the area, however, lies within the basin of the Black Sea drainage, and the rivers which flow to the Mediterranean

Sea are mostly short and drain only a small part of the area (Fig. 1.4).

Rivers of the northern plain. The courses of the northern rivers, the Elbe, Oder, Vistula and their tributaries are largely post-glacial in origin. They developed as the ice sheets melted away, and their courses

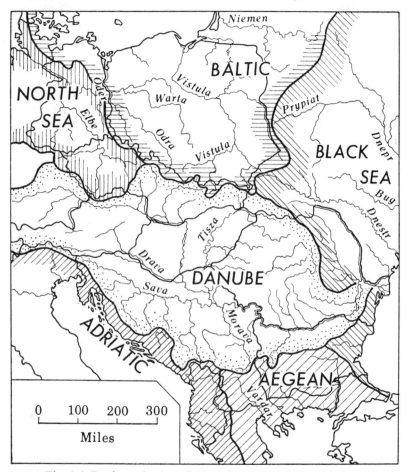

Fig. 1.4. Drainage basins of the major rivers of Eastern Europe.

are still in the main those followed by the flood waters of the Quaternary period as they made their ways to the sea. But the northern rivers today rise within the mountains and hills of Thuringia and Bohemia, and in the Carpathian Mountains. They are fed by the heavy rains of the mountains and the springtime melting of the snows of both mountain and plain. As they cross the northern plain to the sea, their discharge is increased by the heavy summer rains. The northern rivers thus have a sharply seasonal regime. The river Odra, which is typical of the rivers of the plain, has its greatest average monthly flow in the period from February to June, with its maximum in April. The lowest

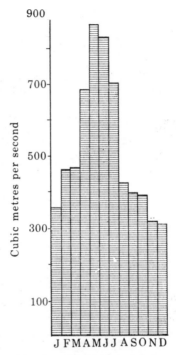

Fig. 1.5. Regime of the river Odra in Lower Silesia. After *Monografia Odry*, Poznań, 1948.

rate of discharge is between September and January. This accords with the climatic regime of northern Europe, which has generally a relatively dry late summer and autumn. The graph (Fig. 1.5) shows the variations in flow through the year.

Danube system. The Danube and its tributaries together make up a river system a good deal more complex than those of the northern plain. The Danube itself rises in the Black Forest of south-west Germany, and flows eastward through Bavaria and Austria to enter the limits of Eastern Europe, as defined in this book, between Vienna and Bratislava. From this point the Danube flows across the Little Alföld, cuts across the Bakony Forest and then traverses the Great Alföld. It crosses the Transylvanian Alps and Balkan Mountains by the gorges of the Iron Gate, and finally makes its way along the southern margin of the Walachian Plain to the sea. In its course of 1,725 miles the Danube flows from Western, across Central to Eastern Europe; from the relatively mild and rainy climate of Western Europe to the dry, continental climate of Eastern. Its tributaries drain

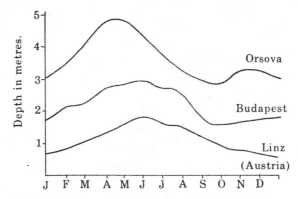

Fig. 1.6. Regime of the Danube, After Pardé, *Fleuves et Rivières*, Paris, 1933.

much of Moravia, the Carpathian Mountains and Transylvania on the north, and the Alps of Austria and north-western Yugoslavia, and the Dinaric and Balkan Mountains on the south. The tributaries flow from Central European regions of summer rain and from the borderland of the Mediterranean region with its summer drought; from the Hungarian and Moldavian plains with their low rainfall, and from the Alps and Carpathians, where the snows melt and the rivers flood in spring. All these influences combine to produce a regime as complex as any in Europe. The graph (Fig. 1.6) shows the level of the river's flow at four points along its course. In its upper course the Danube has high water in late winter and spring associated with winter rains of Western Europe and the melting of the snows of early spring in the Alps. At Linz, in Austria, a late spring and early summer maximum becomes apparent, as the contribution from the melting snow and ice of the Alps is felt more strongly. Lower downstream, at Budapest, the

2*

maximum is pushed later into the summer, partly by the lapse of time
needed for the waters to reach this point, partly by the heavy summer
rains. But as the Danube approaches the south-west of the Pannonian

Fig. 1.7. Navigable rivers and canals in Eastern Europe. After Jerzy
Kostrowicki, Mihail Haşeganu, Marton Pecsi and Bela Sárfalvi, Gerhard
Schmidt-Renner, and Vladimir Blaškovic.

Plain, it picks up rivers, notably the Sava and the Serbian Morava,
which, with their tributaries, drain much of the Balkan peninsula.
Rainfall in the mountains south of the Danube is heavy in winter, and

tributaries from this quarter restore to the river's flow a winter maximum which over the greater part of the river's course had been disguised by the heavy summer maximum of Central Europe.

Mediterranean rivers. The rivers which flow from the Balkan peninsula to the Mediterranean Sea are small and unimportant compared with the Danube and the northern rivers. The rivers that drop from the Dinaric Mountains to the Adriatic Sea are short and only the Naretva and the Drin can be regarded as permanent rivers. The others are little more than torrents, in spate in winter and their courses often dry and rock-strewn for the rest of the year.

The rivers of Macedonia and Thrace are larger and more permanent than those which flow to the Adriatic, but are nevertheless subject to great fluctuations of level, and are navigable only in the lowermost courses and then only for very small vessels. Yet these rivers have an importance that is out of all relation to their size, because their valleys open routes through this intractable mountain country from the interior to the sea. The Vardar of Serbia and Macedonia is in this respect the most important, because its valley constitutes part of the most important routeway between the Pannonian Plain and the Aegean Sea. The Struma and Mesta drop steeply from the Rhodope to the plains of Thrace; the Marica, from its source in the northern Rhodope, flows out around the north-eastern flanks of the massif, cuts across its eastern foothills, and enters the Aegean on the borders of Greece and Turkey. These Mediterranean rivers show the greatest variation in the volume of their discharge of any rivers in Eastern Europe, ranging as they do from winter floods to dried out, stony river beds in summer.

Inland navigation. The rivers of all except the Mediterranean region are potentially important for navigation, and some among them are much used. The Oder, now regulated and in part canalised, is an important avenue of communication, especially for bulky commodities between the industrial centres of Silesia and the port of Szczecin. The Elbe is navigable from the ocean port of Hamburg upstream to the heart of Bohemia, but the fact that within this course the river crosses two international boundaries does nothing to facilitate navigation or to increase the volume of trade.

The Vistula was formerly of great importance in the internal trade of Poland, but today the lower course of the river, from Warsaw to the sea, is little used, and above Warsaw there is practically no navigation. The river is shallow, and improvements have been hindered by the vast quantities of sand and silt which form shifting banks within its course.

A few of the tributaries of the northern rivers are navigable in their natural state for small barges. Thanks to the channels cut by the great rivers of the closing phases of the Ice Age, these rivers can be easily enlarged and supplemented by canals. Canals today link the Vistula with the Noteć and the Warta, and the Oder with the Elbe. It is theoretically possible to navigate a small barge from the western territories of the Soviet Union to the Atlantic Ocean entirely by inland waterways.

Present plans are to enlarge existing waterways and to supplement them by canals. The improvement of river and canal connections between the Dnepr and the Vistula is planned by way of the Prypeć and Bug, and work has already begun to improve parts of this waterway system. The upper Oder is now linked with the Upper Silesian industrial region by a modern canal, the Gliwicki Canal, built in the 1930s along the approximate line of the small and out-of-date Kłodnica Canal, which had been begun before the end of the eighteenth century. Plans have now been prepared for the most ambitious project of all, the joining of the Odra and Vistula with the Danube by means of a canal cut through the Moravian Gate and the plains of Moravia.

The Danube is considered a navigable river from near Ulm, in Bavaria, to the sea, but above Vienna it can be used by only small craft. There are nevertheless many obstacles to navigation throughout the river's course. The speed of the current in summer, especially along its upper course, makes the upstream movement of ships slow and difficult. In winter ice forms, and the river may have a broken cover of ice for several months. In autumn the river is sometimes too shallow for navigation, and in its course across the Hungarian Plain it breaks up into a multitude of shallow channels which reunite and again divide enclosing islands which change their shapes with each flood. Where it leaves the Pannonian Plain the Danube plunges into that 80-mile series of gorges commonly known as the Iron Gate. The stream deepens and the speed of the current increases to the point where upstream traffic is almost impossible without some kind of traction from the bank. Below the gorges, the river broadens and flows more gently between the high bluffs of Bulgaria and the low and marshy banks of Romania. Then, flowing to the north around the platform of Dobrogea, it breaks up into the distributaries of the delta and enters the Black Sea. Of the many channels of the Danube mouth, three—the

Kilia, Sulina and St. Gheorghe—carry most of the water and almost all the traffic, and of these the Sulina Channel is the one most used by ships.

The great potentialities of the Danube as a highway of East European commerce have never been fully realised. The reasons are partly political—the fragmentation of the Danube basin between no less than eight states, and its division between the Western and the Eastern blocs—and partly technical. Immense works are needed along the river before it can be made easily navigable at all times. Much has been done on the upper river in Germany and Austria both to improve navigation and to generate power by building dams and locks. In the Iron Gate gorges the navigable channel has been deepened and improved, and a light railway established for a short distance along the southern bank for the purpose of towing vessels upstream (see page 652). In the delta, the most used channels have been straightened and deepened. Elsewhere minor improvements have been made both in the main stream of the Danube and in those of its tributaries, such as the Tisza and Sava, that are considered navigable. Nevertheless much remains to be done on the technical side alone if the Danube is ever to become a navigable river comparable in importance to the Rhine. A start has been made with the construction of dams across the Danube at the Iron Gate and at the great bend of the river above Budapest. These will not only serve to drive electric generators, but will also improve the conditions of navigation for a considerable distance upstream from each of them.

Most of the projected improvements on the river cannot be carried through within the limits of a single country in this politically-fragmented region. They necessitate river management over a large area, and hitherto the much publicised though rather nebulous TVA for the Danube has been held up as much by political as by economic and technical considerations. Lastly, the Danube river links the riverine states with the Black Sea, which for most of them holds little commercial attraction, and serves today mainly to transport bulk goods from the Soviet Union to certain of the East European countries.

Much of the Balkan peninsula is drained to the Danube. Its rivers, however, are navigable for only very small craft, and then only along their lowermost courses. Those that discharge towards the Mediterranean Sea are mostly short and all of them are seasonal in their flow, and, except in the last few miles before they enter the sea they are incapable of being used for navigation. The irregularity of their flow, which does much to render them useless for navigation, also reduces their value as sources of hydro-electric power.

CLIMATE, VEGETATION AND SOILS

In respect of climate, vegetation and soils Eastern Europe is not clearly distinguishable from Central or even Western Europe. It is rather a transition zone between peninsular Europe, and the Eurasian base from which that peninsula extends.

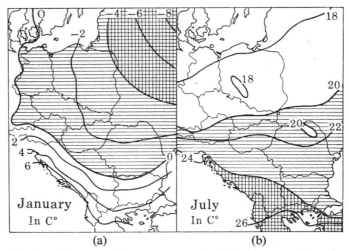

Fig. 1.8. Mean monthly temperatures in (a) January and (b) July.

Climate
Eastern Europe lies at all seasons of the year in the path of the 'lows' which move into the continent of Europe from the Atlantic. Their intensity and frequency vary with the season. They take more northerly courses in summer, when a high-pressure area may develop over the southern part of the region for prolonged periods. In winter the 'high', which covers intermittently much of the Soviet Union, extends westwards over part of Eastern Europe, and forces the 'lows' to move around its margins, particularly across the southern Balkans and Greece.

Although the 'lows' carry oceanic influences deep into the continent, much of Eastern Europe is too far removed from the ocean to benefit greatly from the moderating influence of the Atlantic. The climate over most of it is continental; Köppen classified it as 'microthermal'. Its average temperature in the coldest month is below 0°C (32°F) and in the warmest below 22°C (72°F) in the northern part of Eastern Europe, but rises to over 22°C (72°F) in summer in the southern. In Köppen's symbols the climates of most of the region are Dbf and Daf.

Only towards the coastal margin of the Balkan peninsula does a mesothermal climate occur, with the coldest month above freezing, the warmest above 22°C (72°F) (Caf). The southern part of the region

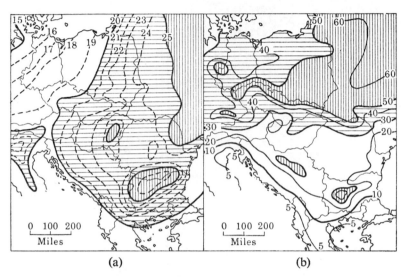

(a)   (b)

Fig. 1.9. (a) The annual range of temperature in Eastern Europe, in degrees centigrade. After B. F. Dobrynin. (b) The average duration of snow-cover, in days. After B. F. Dobrynin.

is truly Mediterranean, with mild winters and hot, dry summers. The main climatic regions of Eastern Europe are shown in Fig. 1.11.

Temperature. The isothermal maps for January and July demonstrate that, in Eastern Europe no less than in Western, the chief influence on the winter temperatures is the proximity of the ocean, and on those of summer, direct insolation. The winter isotherms run almost directly north and south in the area north of the Danube, and in the Balkans they generally lie parallel with the coast. In summer they trend approximately from west to east. The highest temperatures of summer are recorded in Macedonia and southern Bulgaria, and the coldest of winter, in north-eastern Poland.

The annual range of temperature increases to the east, but reaches its greatest extent—over 25°C (45°F)—in the eastern parts of the Pannonian Plain and in the lowermost tracts of the Danube valley. The annual range diminishes in each direction toward the coast; it is 18°C (32·5°F) on the coast of north-western Poland and only 16°C (29°F) on the islands that fringe the Dalmatian coast.

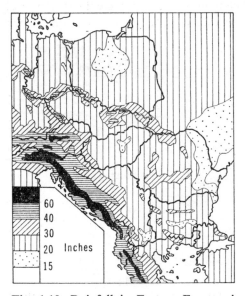

Fig. 1.10. Rainfall in Eastern Europe, in inches. After *Agricultural Geography of Europe and the Middle East*, U.S. Department of Agriculture, Washington, DC, 1948. Rainfall maps of the individual countries, given in Chapters 7 to 14, were based upon national sources, and give totals in millimetres.

Rainfall. The amount of precipitation ranges from less than 400 millimetres (16 inches) in the region of the Danube delta and under 500 millimetres (20 inches) in the lower Vistula valley to over 1,000 millimetres (40 inches) in the Carpathian Mountains and Transylvanian Alps and over 1,500 millimetres (60 inches) in parts of the Dinaric range. The volume tends to diminish from west to east, and the driest regions of the whole of Eastern Europe lie in the rainshadow of the Carpathian mountains.

Over Eastern Europe as a whole, the rainfall tends to come mainly in the summer half year, with June or July as the wettest months. In general, two-thirds of the total rainfall can be expected in the half-year period from April to September. Much of it comes in heavy, convectional storms and is accompanied not infrequently by thunder.

The predominantly summer rainfall of most of Eastern Europe changes rather suddenly to a predominantly winter rainfall as the

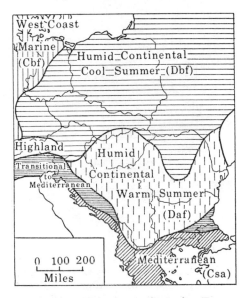

Fig. 1.11. Climatic regions in Eastern Europe. Based on the adaptation of the Köppen System made by Glenn T. Trewartha.

coast of the Balkan peninsula is approached. The three stations: Beograd, Sarajevo, and Dubrovnik, in Table 2, illustrate this transition.

Over a large area of Eastern Europe much of the winter precipitation is in the form of snow, and snow covers the ground for prolonged periods in the north of the region and for some part of the year in the remainder. Fig. 1.9(b) shows the average duration of the snow cover. Related to the duration of snow cover is of course the winter freeze on the rivers. All rivers of the northern plain are impeded by ice in winter. The Odra, for example, has ice sufficiently thick to prevent navigation

The Physical Geography

for on average a month in the year in its upper course, and for two months in its lower. Broken ice may persist a great deal longer. The freeze is somewhat more prolonged on the relatively still waters of canals and lakes.[1] The Danube has a somewhat shorter freeze, and the speed of the current commonly breaks up the ice, so that it ceases to be

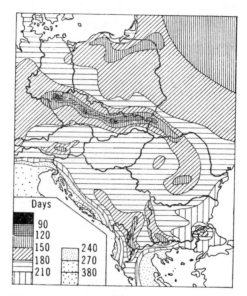

Fig. 1.12. Length of the growing season in Eastern Europe, in days. After *Agricultural Geography of Europe and the Middle East*, U.S. Department of Agriculture, Washington, DC, 1948.

Table 2. *Average rainfall 1950–58 in millimetres at Beograd, Sarajevo and Dubrovnik*

	Jan.	Feb.	Mar.	Apr.	May	June	July	Aug.	Sept.	Oct.	Nov.	Dec.
Beograd	42	49	43	51	80	111	67	48	53	54	58	55
Sarajevo	60	81	57	63	91	57	59	53	72	97	87	98
Dubrovnik	133	146	98	94	79	52	21	26	103	153	215	153

Source: *Statistički Godišnjak FNRJ*, Beograd.

[1] *Monografia Odry*, eds. A. Grodek, M. Kiełczewska-Zaleska and A. Zierhoffer, Poznań, 1948, pp. 254–9.

an absolute barrier to navigation. Nevertheless, the twin cities of Buda and Pest were, before the bridges were built across the Danube, completely cut off from one another for a period sometimes of several weeks each winter, because the ice-floes were such as to prevent the river from being crossed either on foot or by boat.

South of the Danube the period of the winter freeze is of short duration, and the rivers flowing to the Mediterranean are not as a general rule, subject to a winter freeze.

Vegetation

The natural or primeval vegetation of Eastern Europe survives over only a very small part of the area. To primitive man, as he spread into this region from the south and south-east, it must have seemed predominantly forested. Dense forest covered the northern plains. Coniferous forest covered the mountains, and lighter woodland the loess soils of Germany and Poland and the plains of the middle and lower Danube valley. Broadleaved forest spread through the Balkan peninsula, giving way, near the coasts of the Adriatic and Aegean, to the drought-resistant Mediterranean vegetation of scrub and xerophytic trees.

This 'natural' vegetation has been so modified by man that scarcely anywhere can it still be recognised. The Białowieża Forest, which spans the boundary between north-east Poland and the Soviet Union, is commonly regarded as the only surviving example of the primeval forest which once covered the clay-lands of the northern plain. The vegetation of most of the northern plain was mixed woodland: broadleaved, among which the oak, ash and elm must have predominated on the clay, and coniferous in all probability on the sand, gravel and outwash. The conifers faded out toward the south, to produce broadleaved forest, dense over the heavy soils, more open on the lighter.

The belt of mountains which extends from Bohemia in the west to the Transylvanian Alps of Romania is characterised mainly by forest, coniferous on the higher ground, mixed in the valleys. The mountains themselves are commonly forested over their rounded summits. Sometimes the forest gives way to grassland, either natural or man-made, which provides summer grazing for cattle and sheep brought up from the valleys. Over only very restricted areas are truly Alpine or tundra conditions met with. Hill forest is very much less extensive south of the Danube than to the north. Here it is predominantly broadleaved, and in the Mediterranean region of the southern Balkans, the former cover of light woodland has largely disappeared, to be replaced by drought-resistant scrub or maquis.

The primitive vegetation of the Pannonian Plain and of the lowlands which border the lowermost course of the Danube is a matter of

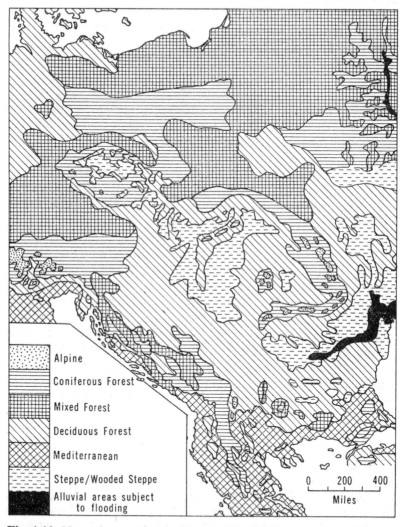

Alpine

Coniferous Forest

Mixed Forest

Deciduous Forest

Mediterranean

Steppe/Wooded Steppe

Alluvial areas subject to flooding

0   200   400

Miles

Fig. 1.13. Natural vegetation in Eastern Europe. After *Agricultural Geography of Europe and the Middle East*, U.S. Department of Agriculture, Washington, DC, 1948.

dispute. On the one hand, the Pannonian Plain is regarded by some as a region of natural grassland, 'a detached area of steppes'.[1] On the other it is treated as man-made steppe, a region from which the woodland or forest cover has been removed by the hand of man and prevented either by human or natural agencies from regenerating. The steppes of eastern and south-eastern Romania are almost certainly the extreme extension of the grassland belt of the Ukraine, but the Pannonian Plain has a rainfall, between 482 and 660 millimetres (19 and 26 inches) on average, which, combined with its temperature range, should bring it within the belt of deciduous forest. The evidence[2] is that in early historic times most of the plain was highly wooded; that the trees were destroyed in the course of war, to establish settlements and to clear land for grazing, and that changes in the water table (see page 500) have prevented forest from recovering. In fact, much of the Pannonian Plain is today characterised by trees, frequently planted for shade, in the villages and along the roads.

Over most of Eastern Europe the natural vegetation has disappeared at the hand of man. Although the area as a whole remains fairly well wooded, with 29 per cent of its total area under forest, much of this woodland has been planted by man or so modified by human agency that it can in no sense be described as natural. Almost half—about 45 per cent—of the total area is actually cultivated, and grazing land—much of it in Hungary and Romania—covers about 17 per cent of the total area. Table 3 shows the distribution of the main categories of land-use.

The distribution of the principal categories of cultivated plants is discussed later; the distribution of only a few which may be regarded as climatically critical is mentioned here. The olive occurs only within a few miles of the Adriatic and Aegean littoral. The grape vine is widely distributed in the Danube valley and Balkan peninsula, but north of this limit is found in only a few particularly favoured localities, such as the Melník district of Bohemia, to the north of Prague, and the morainic hills of Zielona Góra, in western Poland, the most northerly occurrence of commercial viticulture in Eastern Europe.

[1] H. J. Mackinder, 'The Geographical Pivot of History', *Geogrl J.*, **23** (1904). 421–37.
[2] The argument is summarised in N. J. G. Pounds, 'Land Use on the Hungarian Plain', in *Geographical Essays on Eastern Europe*, ed. N. J. G. Pounds, Indiana University Publications, 1961, pp. 54–75.

Table 3. Land use in Eastern Europe

(in square kilometres)

	Cropland	Meadow and pasture	Forest	Unused but potentially pro- ductive	Built-on waste, etc.	Total land area
East Germany	5,053	1,406	2,954	85	1,131	10,649
Poland	16,068	4,194	7,786	—	3,125	31,173
Czechoslovakia	5,412	1,825	4,420	—	1,130	12,787
Hungary	5,622	1,390	1,368	—	923	9,303
Romania	10,491	4,197	6,397	—	2,665	23,750
Yugoslavia	8,363	6,500	8,702	—	2,015	25,580
Bulgaria	4,538	1,147	3,599	—	1,809	11,093
Albania	479	753	1,282	—	361	2,875

Source: *FAO Production Yearbook*, 1963, p. 3.

Rye is heavily cultivated in East Germany, Poland and Czecho-slovakia, and is of some importance in Hungary, but to the south is scarcely grown at all. Wheat is widely cultivated on the better soils, and the divide between a predominantly autumn-sown and spring-sown wheat lies approximately from north-west to south-east, across Hungary and Romania.

Soils

The soil is the association of rock waste and organic material which forms a thin cover over most of the land. Its actual composition is dependent partly on the nature of the rock from which in part it is formed, partly on the nature and amount of its organic constituents. Of no less importance is the actual arrangement of these elements within the soil profile. This organisation of organic and mineral con-stituents is the work of nature, of rainfall, percolation and solution, but is always being modified by man, who drains and irrigates, ploughs deep or shallow, and modified the vegetation and thus the supply of humus to the soil, and the behaviour of the moisture which comes from rain and snow.

The soils of Eastern Europe may be divided roughly into those of the cool and humid north, those of the drier plains of the middle and lower Danube valley, and those of the mountains (Fig. 1.14). These geographical types are far from being mutually exclusive, but, based as they are on climate and relief, they afford a rough classification which may be used to gain a general view of the nature and range of soil types in Eastern Europe.

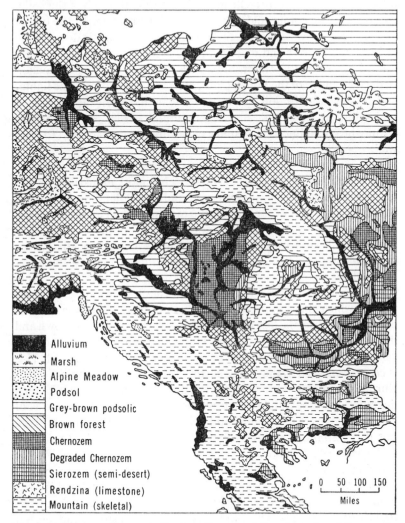

Alluvium
Marsh
Alpine Meadow
Podsol
Grey-brown podsolic
Brown forest
Chernozem
Degraded Chernozem
Sierozem (semi-desert)
Rendzina (limestone)
Mountain (skeletal)

0   50 100 150

Miles

Fig. 1.14. Major soil types in Eastern Europe. After *Agricultural Geography of Europe and the Middle East*, U.S. Department of Agriculture, Washington, DC, 1948. This map differs in detail from the larger-scale soil maps given in Chapters 7 to 14, as the latter were based upon different sources and used slightly differing methods of classification.

Forest soils. The soils of the northern plains, together with those of Bohemia and Moravia and of parts of the margin of the Pannonian Plain, have evolved under a forest cover. The annual leaf-fall has supplied humus which, if present in sufficient quantities gives the soil a chestnut-brown colour and a loose, crumby structure. In the cooler and moister areas, however, the humus tends to break down fairly quickly into simpler and more soluble substances, and thus to be removed by percolating water. Such soils, partially leached or podzolised, cover much of the Polish plain, and, as a general rule, the lighter and more sandy the soil, the more extreme has been the process of podzolisation. Such soils are not naturally fertile, and commonly require heavy additions of manure or fertiliser to enable them to yield well.

This *grey-brown podzolic soil* merges locally into a less leached and more fertile *brown forest soil*, which occurs most noticeably on the loess-covered areas of East Germany, southern Poland, Bohemia and Moravia. Such soils occur around the margin of the Pannonian Plain, in valleys and basins within the mountains and in parts of the Moldavian and Walachian plains. They are, however, comparatively rare in the Balkan peninsula, except over the floors of some of the once-forested basins of the interior.

Grassland soils. Natural grassland is usually a response to lower rainfall which does not permit the growth of trees. The same climatic conditions restrict the loss of humus through chemical breakdown and dispersion by percolating waters. Humus tends therefore to be concentrated near the surface, and to give a dark colour to the soil. This is *chernozem*, such as the 'black earth' of the Ukraine. Within Eastern Europe chernozem occurs only in the driest areas, and here it is often degraded, merging into brown forest soils. The most extensive area of chernozem covers the eastern and drier part of the Pannonian Plain, but it is also found over considerable areas in Walachia, Moldavia, and south-east Poland and over very much smaller areas in the Thuringian Basin of East Germany and in Bohemia and Moravia.

Mountain soils. The mountain ranges of Czechoslovakia and Romania, together with most of the Balkan peninsula, are characterised by *lithosolic* soils. These are very shallow and stony, and, even if the climate were suitable, they would have very little agricultural value. Over large areas of the Dinaric Mountains soil is completely lacking, or occurs only in the cracks and joints of the rock. The soil is usually severely leached, and is sometimes also eroded. On the other hand, the soil removed from the mountain slopes is commonly deposited as alluvium in the nearby basins and along the valley floors.

The Dinaric Mountains are characterised also by basins—*doliny* and *polja*—produced by the solution of the karstic limestone. These are usually floored by a heavy, often reddish, residual clay, formed from residual materials from limestone which has been dissolved and removed in solution.

The low fertility of the lithosolic soils, reinforced by the roughness of the terrain, has made much of the Balkan peninsula a region of low agricultural value. Exceptions are found in the alluvial basins ensconced in the Karst, in the alluvial lowlands which border the larger rivers, and over the narrow coastal plains.

Alluvial soils. In their total extent, the alluvial soils of Eastern Europe cover an area larger by far than that of the chernozem and probably as extensive as that of the brown forest soils. Wide belts of alluvium border all the larger rivers of the northern plain, they cover extensive areas of the Pannonian Plain, and border the lower Danube, widening downstream until they pass into the delta. Patches of alluvium, individually too small in most instances to be shown in Fig. 1.14, lie scattered through all the mountain regions and they form a series of interrupted and generally small coastal plains bordering the shores of the Mediterranean. Much of the alluvial soil, especially that which borders the lower Danube, needs drainage before it can have any agricultural value. In the northern plain it is more important for its meadowland than for crop-farming. In the Balkan peninsula, where rainfall in general is smaller and problems of land-drainage less acute, the patches of alluvium are intensively cultivated and constitute the most valuable cropland in the whole area.

The most extensive of all the soil regions of Eastern Europe are the lithosolic and the grey-brown podzolic, the soil-types of the lowest agricultural value. This is a factor, but by no means the only one, in the rural poverty and agricultural backwardness which have for so long characterised Eastern Europe. Primitive agricultural techniques and an excessive concentration on a small number of subsistence crops are no less significant. The roots of East European poverty and backwardness, relative to most other parts of the continent, lie in social rather than physical conditions. To these social conditions, in their widest sense, we turn in the next five chapters.

Bibliography

CVIJIC, JOVAN, *La Péninsule Balkanique*, Paris, 1918.

DOBRYNIN, B. F. Физиуеская Географря Западной Европы, Moscow, 1948.

GARNETT, ALICE, 'The Loess Regions of Central Europe in Prehistoric Times', *Geogl. J.* **106** (1945), 132–43.

GEORGE, PIERRE, *Géographie de l'Europe Centrale*, Paris, Presses universitaires de France, 1964.

GEORGE, PIERRE and JEAN TRICART, *L'Europe Centrale*, Paris, Presses Universitaires, 1954, Vol 1.

JARANOFF, DIMITRI, 'Les zones morphologiques dans les parties centrales et orientales de la Péninsule Balkanique', *C.r. du IV Congrès des Géographes et Ethnographes Slaves*, Sofia, 1936.

KIROV, K. T. 'Les limites des influences climatiques dans la Péninsule Balkanique', *C.r. du IV Congrès des Géographes et Ethnographes Slaves*, Sofia, 1936, 1938, 119–25.

PARTSCH, JOSEPH, *Central Europe*, London, William Heinemann, 1903.

PAWŁOWSKI, STANISŁAW, 'Les Karpates à l'époque glaciaire', *C.r. Congr. int. Géogr.*, Warsaw, 1934, 1936, **2**, 89–141.

SHACKLETON, MARGARET R. *Europe: A Regional Geography*, 7th edn., London, Longmans, 1964.

SINNHUBER, KARL A. 'Central Europe–Mitteleuropa–Europe Centrale: An Analysis of a Geographical Term', *Trans. Inst. Br. Geogr.*, **20** (1954), 15–39.

See also bibliographies following chapters 7 to 14.

CHAPTER TWO

The Peoples of Eastern Europe

Eastern Europe is today inhabited predominantly by Slavs. Out of a total population of about 120 million, inclusive of that of East Germany, about 70 million, or 60 per cent of the total are Slav. The Slavs are today more numerous than the German-speaking peoples and considerably more numerous than the French-speaking population of Europe. If we include the Slav-speaking peoples of the Soviet Union we have a linguistic group which ranks in size next after only the Chinese and the English. Politically united, as it seemed at one time that they might have been, the Slav peoples of Eastern Europe alone would be a major force in the councils and balances of the continent.

The Slavs

Yet there are few people whose origins are at the same time more shrouded in mystery and enveloped in controversy. The former homeland and the geographical expansion of the Slavs have acquired a contemporary political significance out of all relation to the real importance of these far-off events.

The Slavs are distinguished from other groups by their language. Aside from significant dialects, they have between them eight[1] important languages, in addition to Russian, which are so closely related as to be in several instances mutually intelligible. Their closeness in syntax and vocabulary suggests that they began to diverge from their parent Slavic root only in comparatively recent times.

The Slavic languages belong to the Indo-European family, though the gulf between them and their neighbouring languages—Lithuanian, German, Italian and Greek—is far greater than that which separates the individual Slav tongues from one another. This indicates, on the other hand, that the Slav languages began to emerge and to become distinguishable from the non-Slavic languages of Central and Eastern Europe at a relatively early date.

[1] These are Polish, Czech, Slovak, Slovene, Serb, Croat, Bulgar and Macedonian. In their spoken forms Serb and Croat are nearly identical.

It must not be forgotten that in this chapter we are dealing primarily with language groups, not with races, nor are we at present considering the distribution of material cultures. We are concerned with speech, the chief means of social communication, and the chief force holding political societies together in the modern world.

The pre-Slavs. The Slavs were by no means the earliest inhabitants of Eastern Europe. Over part of the area Germanic tribes had migrated and had occasionally settled; the Celts had formerly inhabited the middle Danube basin, and also Bohemia, to which one of their tribes, the Boii, had given its name. In classical times the Thracian and Illyrian peoples, from the latter of whom the Albanians appear to have derived, inhabited the Balkan peninsula, and in late prehistoric times, the Hellenic tribes, ancestors of the Greeks, migrated from this region towards the Aegean Sea. North of the Danube there lived the Dacians, related probably quite closely to the Thracians, whose early conflicts with invading Celts are vaguely mentioned in the earliest histories. To the east, beyond the curve of the Carpathians, were the Scythian peoples, pastoralist and predominantly nomadic, who in their forays reached south-west to the Danube and west through the mountains into the Hungarian Plain. Scythian burials have been found as far away from the usual habitat of the Scythians as northern Poland, but nothing of their language has survived.

The southern half of this region was conquered by the Romans. In the later years of the Roman Republic they had occupied Greece and the mountainous province of Epirus, across the Adriatic Sea from the 'heel' of Italy, as well as Macedonia and Thrace, which lay to the north of the Aegean Sea. During the Principate of Augustus (27 B.C. to A.D. 14) much of the Balkan peninsula was loosely annexed, and later during the first century A.D. the frontier of the Empire was advanced to the Danube. A line of fortresses guarded the river crossings, and the ruins of two of them: *Aquincum*, near Budapest, and *Carnuntum*, near Petronell in Lower Austria, are not unimpressive even today.

The territory lying south of the river must have been in some degree Romanised. Roads were built, cities established, legionary camps laid out, and time-expired legionaries were settled here. These settlers must have come from the ends of the Empire. Their speech may not have been Ciceronian, but at least they introduced some form of Latin into the region. In A.D. 101 the Emperor Trajan set out to subdue the territory lying beyond the Danube, between the Tisza River to the

west and the Carpathian crest to the east. The Dacian Wars dragged
on until A.D. 107 before the region was at last subdued, and Trajan
could erect the column in the Roman Forum which bears his name and
records both his triumph and the chief events of the campaigns.

But Dacia was lightly held, and was readily abandoned by the
Emperor Aurelian (A.D. 270–275). Romanisation can only have been
superficial. Few settlers came, and trade was inconsiderable
in this remote and unvalued province of the Empire. And when
Roman rule ended, one must presume that such Romans as still lived
here either withdrew to more secure regions of the Empire or were submerged beneath the tide of Slavic and Tatar invaders.

Historians are accustomed to represent the movements of peoples
during these and succeeding centuries by arrows which dart and curve
across the continent and suggest a picture of violent and rapid movement. There was movement in plenty, but such maps distort the true
picture. The movements were in most instances the slow creep on a
broad front of tribes, with women and children, flocks and herds.
Sometimes they paused and cultivated the soil for a year or two before
resuming their migrations; only rarely did they conduct an incisive,
military operation.

While the Romans were occupying Dacia, the Scythian and Sarmatian tribes, Indo-European in their speech and distantly related to the
Iranians, had established a loose empire over the Russian Steppe,
extending their influence if not also their authority northward into the
forest belt. Merchants had carried their artistic products by way of the
great Russian rivers to the Baltic region, and there the artifacts of the
Scythians had served as models for the artwork of the Scandinavians
who were in turn to bring these designs to the British Isles.

Germanic peoples—the Goths—filtered eastward, settling among
the Scythians and serving also as intermediaries in the westward
spread of Scythian artforms. But this generally peaceful and certainly
constructive and creative association was terminated by the appearance of another wave of peoples from the remote interior of the Eurasian continent. These were the Huns, first of that 'cloud of ruthless and
idealess horsemen, who came sweeping over the unimpeded plain'.[1]
The reality was probably less dynamic than Halford Mackinder
appears to suggest. Like the Scythians, the Huns were horse-riding,
nomadic and pastoral, but here the similarity ends. In race they were

---

[1] H. J. Mackinder, 'The Geographical Pivot of History', *Geogrl J.*, **23** (1904),
421–37.

Mongoloid. Contemporaries wrote with fear and horror of their savage appearance and even more barbaric practices. In speech they were Ural-Altaic, and their language, modified by time, survives today among the Bashkir and related tribes of the Ural region. The Huns broke up the trading patterns that had begun to emerge in the Russian Steppe; they scattered the Goths westward into Central and Southern Europe, and themselves broke through the ring of mountains into the plain which today by a linguistic accident perpetuates their name. Then, west of the Rhine, they met their end at the battle of Châlons (A.D. 451), and melted into the pages of history.

Huns were by no means the last of the Mongol invaders of Eastern Europe, though later invaders from Asia appeared only after the Slavs had moved southwards into the Balkans. Within a century of the Hunnish invasions, the Bulgars, also immigrants from the Asiatic Steppe, passed to the north of the Black Sea and then southward to the Danube delta. Crossing the river, they settled within the limits of the Byzantine Empire and, unlike the Huns, took up agriculture and soon were merged with the local and predominantly Slavic population, whose language they assumed, preserving only to a slight degree the influence of their original Ural-Altaic tongue.

After the Bulgars came the Avars, like them establishing a loosely-knit empire over the Slav agriculturalists whom they found in the Danube basin. The rule of the Avars lasted little longer than that of the Huns. They succumbed to the Germanic Franks, and they too disappeared from history. The last of the Uralic invaders of Europe, the Magyars, are too important and their imprint too enduring for their movements to be briefly dismissed. But before we turn to the Magyar settlement of the Danubian Plain, we must deal with the Slavs themselves, the most numerous and the most important of all the peoples of Eastern Europe.

Migrations of the Slavs. As was noted earlier, the early movements of the Slavs are enveloped in controversy. One of the earliest positions was adopted by the Polish botanist Rostafiński in 1908. His views were paraphrased by the Austrian historian, T. Peisker,[1] in these words: 'The Balto-Slavs have no expression for beech, larch and yew, but they have a word for hornbeam. Therefore their original home must have been within the hornbeam zone but outside the three other tree-zones, that is within the basin of the middle Dnieper. Hence Polesie—the marshland traversed by the Prypeć but the area not south

[1] T. Peisker, 'The Expansion of the Slavs', *Camb. Med. Hist.*, vol. 2, pp. 418–58.

or east of Kiev—must be the original home of the Slavs.' To a geographer the Prypeć Marshes seem particularly unconvincing as the homeland of the Slavs, and the suppositions of Rostafiński have found no support in archaeology. Nevertheless, the Polesian origin of the Slavs has found special favour among German writers, presumably because its effect would be to weaken Slav claims to territory on which the Germans have laid eager eyes and greedy hands.

At the opposite extreme are the views widely held, especially in Poland, and currently expressed by Konrad Jażdżewski,[1] that the homeland of the Slavs lay at least 400 miles to the west, in the valley of the Oder, near enough where the medieval state of Poland originated. This supposition is based on an identification of the Slav peoples with the bearers of the so-called Lusatian culture, which emerged in this region during the Middle Bronze Age. But the Lusatian pots and burials cannot speak to us; we have no means of knowing how the Lusatian people communicated with one another, only what artifacts they made, and the evidence which links them with the later bearers of the Slav languages is wholly circumstantial and far from generally acceptable. Unquestionably a peasant culture spread during the late Neolithic and the ensuing Bronze Ages from the Elbe river in the west almost to the Niemen in the north-east, and southward to the Danube.[2] There can be little doubt that the peoples represented by these cultures were Indo-European, and that from them emerged the Germanic and Slavic languages. Yet it is extraordinarily difficult to date the development of these languages. The classical writers were vague in the extreme both in their geographical location of the Central and East European peoples, and also in their attempts to distinguish the languages which they spoke. Nevertheless it seems reasonable to identify the Venedi, mentioned by Pliny and Tacitus, with the proto-Slavs, and to locate their homeland toward the east of the region of Bronze Age peasant cultures and north of the Carpathian Mountains.

The Romans seem never to have come into contact with the Slavs. The period of vigorous southward expansion of the Slavs did not begin until perhaps the third century A.D. The reasons for this movement are difficult, if not impossible, to discover. Perhaps overpopulation played a role; perhaps the Scytho-Sarmatians were driven by the Huns into the Slav lands, or perhaps the Goths, moving south-eastward through

[1] Konrad Jażdżewski, *Atlas do Pradziejów Słowian*, Łódź, 1948.
[2] Marija Gimbutas, *The Prehistory of Eastern Europe*, American School of Prehistoric Research, Peabody Museum, Cambridge, Mass., 1956.

their area, destroyed their villages, disrupted their husbandry, and set them in motion. The Slavs spread south-eastward approximately along the loess belt, into the South Russian Steppe, mixing with Goth and Sarmatian, until this perhaps none too peaceful coexistence was broken up by the onslaught of the Huns.

At about the same time they reached the arc of the Carpathians and the mountains which border Bohemia. At what date they penetrated the present territory of Czechoslovakia and Hungary is far from clear. That they were there before the arrival of the Huns is apparent from the narratives of the early historians Jordanes and Priscus, though it is also probable that their numbers were small, and consisted perhaps only of sporadic family groups. Procopius, for example, wrote of the Slavic *Antae* that they 'lived apart one man from another, they inhabited their country in a sporadic fashion. And in consequence of this very fact they hold a great amount of land'.[1] But after the collapse of the power of the Huns, Slav settlement unquestionably intensified in the middle lower Danube valley. Then, in the later years of the sixth century, Slav groups crossed the Danube and invaded the Balkans. They pressed into the Dinaric Mountains and threatened the cities which remained in imperial hands along the Dalmatian coast. They invaded the Balkan Mountains and, following the routes already traced by the Romans, they went up the Serbian Morava and down the Vardar and Marica valleys towards the Aegean Sea. Soon there was a scattered pattern of Slav settlements over much of Greece. From the southern capes of Peloponnesus to the base of the Danish peninsula; from the Elbe eastward to the headwaters of the Volga, Europe was predominantly, though not exclusively Slav (Fig. 2.1).

The non-Slav peoples
Within this Slav area, however, there were not a few regions where the earlier peoples survived. Many of these were regions of refuge, into which they had retreated before the pressure of invaders and where the latter had been deterred from following by the lack of resources and the small opportunity for gain.

Vlachs and Romanians. Among these regions were unquestionably the mountains of the Balkan peninsula. Here a latinised population, diminishing in numbers and living in continual fear, existed along the Dinaric coast. To the south-east, in the mountains which make up most of Albania and neighbouring Greek Epirus, the descendants of

[1] Procopius, *Gothic Wars*, vol. 7, pp. xiv, 29–30.

the ancient Illyrians preserved their old language and something of their ancient ways. Elsewhere in the Balkan peninsula, the romanised population retreated into the hills where the invaders had little desire

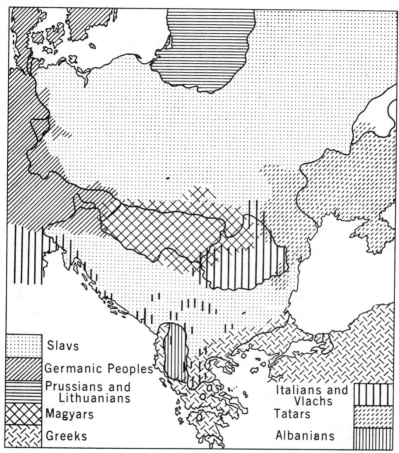

Fig. 2.1. The peoples of Eastern Europe, about 1100. After K. Jażdżiewski, *Atlas do Pradziejów Słowian, Łódź*, 1949.

to follow them. Their language degenerated with the incorporation of Slavic and other words and economically they reverted to an almost wholly pastoral society. These became the Vlachs, the nomads of the Balkans who continued their transhumant life into modern times, wintering in the valleys and spending summers on the mountain pastures, in the Píndhos Mountains of northern Greece, the Rhodope and

3

in other mountain regions of the Balkans. Such groups were formerly widely distributed over the region; today they are represented only by the Vlachs of northern Greece.[1] With them, however should be associated the Karakatschan of Bulgaria, similar in their way of life and ethnic history, but speaking a debased Greek.

This raises the vexed question of the origin of the Romanians. The Romanian people are clearly related to the Vlachs. Until recently they were known to travellers as Walachs; one of their provinces is known as Walachia and modern Romanian is very closely related to the language of the surviving Vlach communities in the Balkans. The view of their origins that is most commonly accepted in Romania is that they too are the descendants and the bearers of the cultural legacy of the Roman provincials of the imperial period. This may well be so, but the further claim that 'they are the true descendants of Trajan's colonists, that Transylvania is the cradle of their race and that historic continuity, has never been lost',[2] is indeed more difficult to substantiate. As we noted earlier, Roman occupation of Dacia lasted only 163 years; the romanisation of the province was superficial in the extreme, and can hardly be expected to have left an imprint deep enough to have long endured after connection with its fountainhead in Rome had been severed. The alternate view is that the Romanian people derive from invaders of this region, who came in from south of the Danube during the middle ages, perhaps during the period of the first Bulgarian Empire of the ninth century which extended into the Walachian Plain and perhaps beyond.

Some light is thrown on the movement of the Vlachs by their appearance in modern times in the northern Carpathians, which they appear to have reached by following the arc of the mountains as they curve around to the north of the Hungarian Plain.[3] Similar in origin perhaps were small groups of romance-speaking peoples who lived until recently in the Dinaric Mountains of Croatia and Slovenia.

Bulgars and Magyars. Other non-Slav peoples who today live within the limits of Central and Eastern Europe were later immigrants. Foremost among these are the Hungarians, who, according to their own tradition, entered the plain of the Middle Danube in the year 897. The Magyar or Hungarian people belonged to the Ural-Altaic language group. Linguistically and possibly also ethnically they were related to

[1] A. J. B. Wace and M. S. Thompson, *The Nomads of the Balkans*, London, 1914.
[2] R. W. Seton-Watson, 'Romanian Origins', *History*, 7 (1922–3).
[3] See Stanislas Łukasik, *Pologne et Roumanie*, Paris and Warsaw, 1938.

the Huns, the Bulgars and the Avars, who had preceded them into Europe. The Bulgars first appeared late in the fifth century, a generation after the defeat and dispersion of the Huns. At this latter time they lived to the north of the Black Sea, where they were located by Byzantine historians. They broke up into tribal groups, one of the larger of which moved south-westward into the Balkans during the sixth century. They settled first in the region of the Danube delta, then, in the seventh century, they moved into the territory between the Danube and the Balkan Mountains. This became the core of the Bulgar state from which, during the periods of their greatest power, they extended south into Thrace and Macedonia, and west into Serbia and Albania.

But the Bulgars never drove out the agricultural Slav tribes which they found here, and over most of their territory they constituted only a landowning and ruling aristocracy. Even this situation did not last. Linguistically and racially they came to be absorbed by the Slav peoples among whom they settled, bequeathing only their name and a few elements of vocabulary and syntax to the modern Bulgarian language.

Their successors, the Avars, have left even less evidence of their sojourn in the Danubian Plain. They had been neighbours of the Bulgars, and appear to have swept up in the course of their westward movement some fragments of the Bulgarian people. They crossed the Carpathians in the seventh century, destroying some of the Slav tribes who lived in their path, and doubtless gathering up and assimilating others. The Avar empire was extensive, but short-lived. The Avar armies, penetrating South Germany by the Danube valley route, were completely destroyed by Charlemagne, and the Avar peoples already ethnically and culturally mixed, melted into the ground mass of middle Danubian peoples.

The Magyars have been in all respects the exception among the Ural-Altaic invaders of Eastern Europe. They were settled along the river Don, in southern Russia, about the middle of the ninth century, and from this base they raided the Danube plains, and late in the year 895 they invaded the Hungarian plains *en masse*, subduing the ethnically mixed and possibly polyglot peoples whom they found. 'It is proof', in the words of C. A. Macartney,[1] 'of the astonishing vitality of the race that it has absorbed them and impressed its language upon them.' Not only did the Magyars impose their culture on the peoples

[1] C. A. Macartney, *The Magyars in the Ninth Century*, Cambridge University Press, 1930, p. 122.

who had preceded them into the Hungarian Plain; they also absorbed the Turkic Cumans, who came in the thirteenth century and even the Turks themselves.

The Magyars were not wholly nomadic and pastoral. Some of their number seem already to have developed agriculture and to have practised it from the time of their arrival in the Hungarian Plain. But nomadic pastoralism remained important. There is good evidence that the pastoral Magyars developed a transhumant way of life, passing the winters with their flocks and herds in the plains, and the summers in the surrounding mountains, especially those of Slovakia. Not until the time of King Stephen (997–1038), did this seasonal movement begin to weaken, and the agriculturalist begin to triumph over the whole plain.

In this process, the Magyars became essentially a plain people. Political control over the surrounding hills was not accompanied by cultural domination, except in parts of Transylvania and the nearby Carpathians, where the closely related Szekély people settled. These latter were Magyars, whose language was almost identical with that of the Hungarian spoken in the plain. Opinions differ on how they came to be located thus far from the main body of the Magyar people. Perhaps, in the course of their migration from the Russian steppe they never got as far as the Hungarian Plain; perhaps, as they themselves claim, they derive from communities deliberately sent out from the plain in order to hold the mountain passes across the Carpathians and, like a marcher state, to protect Hungary itself from later waves of invaders. Perhaps, again, their presence here derives from the ancient transhumance of the Hungarian, the Szekély having made their homes near the summer rather than the winter grazing.

By the end of the tenth century the linguistic-cultural pattern of Eastern Europe had in its main features been established. It consisted of a northern or western Slav group, embracing the Poles, Czechs, and Slovaks, as well as a number of lesser peoples who have not survived as distinct national groups, and a southern Slav group, which extended from the Danube river to the southern peninsulas of Greece. Between them lay a belt of non-Slav peoples, consisting primarily of the Magyars, the Germans who had pressed down the valley from southern Germany, and whatever peoples had survived or found refuge in the mountains of Romania.

In the course of the last 900 years this pattern has changed only in detail. It has contracted along its western border; its internal boundaries have shifted, but newcomers to the area have been few.

Among these latter, however, we must count, in the order of their appearance, the Gypsies, the Germans, the Turks and the Jews. The Gypsies—the Egyptians of European folklore—came in fact from India. In the ninth century they were living in Armenia. Then they

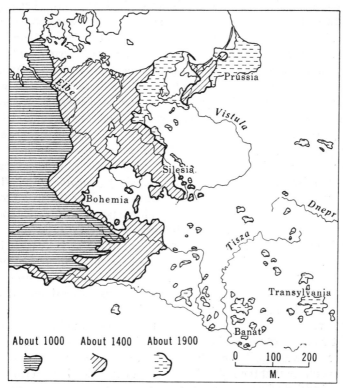

Fig. 2.2. Eastward expansion of the German peoples. Based on F. W. Putzger, *Historischer Schul-Atlas* and Hermann Schreiber, *Land im Osten*, Düsseldorf, 1961.

moved, driven perhaps by the Seljuk Turks, into the territory of the Byzantine Empire. In the mid-eleventh century, there were Gypsies in Constantinople; from here they spread into Thrace and up through the Balkans, apparently in advance of the Turks. In the fifteenth century they reached the Danube valley and spread thence over Western Europe.[1] They were noted for their knowledge of the occult; they were outcasts from Byzantine society, despised, feared and

[1] George C. Soulis, 'The Gypsies in the Byzantine Empire and the Balkans in the Late Middle Ages', *Dumbarton Oaks Papers*, **15** (1961), 143–65.

obliged constantly to move and to live by their wits. Thus during the Middle Ages they acquired the reputation which they have never wholly lost.

German settlers. Next to come into the region were the Germans. The German migration into lands which had previously been Slav took two related forms. First there was a steady eastward pressure on a broad front. In this way the territory between the Elbe and the Oder and then parts of that lying east of the Oder were Germanised. The mountainous borderland of Bohemia together with the Danube valley lying to the south of it, which was later to become Austria, were settled by Germans. This region was the scene of bloody battles between the Slav tribes and the invading Germans. The struggles which took place in the Elbe valley are described for us for the eleventh century by the chronicler, Adam of Bremen.[1]

The German colonists themselves moved eastward in small, carefully organised communities, each directed by a *locator* who had already inspected the land and had contracted to move the group to its new home and to see it settled in. Not all the peoples who later spoke German were descended from such German settlers. In time, the surrounding Slavs came to be Germanised and intermarried with neighbours of Germanic origin. This process of Germanisation continued until late in the nineteenth century, when it encountered a stiffening resistance from the Slavs, among whom a sense of nationhood was rapidly developing. At first this opposition seems to have been a natural reaction of the local peoples to a higher immigrant culture, but later the Germans tried to impose their language, especially in the territory of western Poland. It was in resisting this pressure from a foreign culture that the Poles discovered a new pride in fostering and developing their own.

It is commonly assumed that in these lands the city was a peculiarly German institution, that it was laid out with its streets on a regular grid pattern, equipped with a market, surrounded by walls, and made a focus of German influence in a land in which urban life had hitherto been unknown. This is, however, far from the truth. The city as a legal entity may well have owed its origin to German example, but there were functional cities in the Slav lands long before the arrival of the Germans. It cannot be doubted, however, that the number of cities was immensely increased as a result of German settlement.

[1] Adam of Bremen, *History of the Archbishops of Hamburg-Bremen*, trans. Francis J. Tschan, Columbia University Press, 1959.

In addition to this eastward increment on a broad front, smaller groups of Germans ventured far ahead of the main body, establishing themselves as farmers, miners, and traders far to the east even of this East European region. In this way originated the German colony in the Spiš region of Slovakia; the Transylvanian Germans, or Saxons, in Romania; Dutch and Frisian groups in the marshy regions of northern Poland that needed draining, and small groups—merchants and artisans—in every important city north of the Balkans.

The eastward advance of the Germans has been interpreted as a response to the agricultural opportunities which the lands of Eastern Europe offered to land-hungry peoples from western Germany and the Rhineland. Three eastward prolongations of the German-settled area stand out: the Baltic coast, the loess belt, and the Danube valley. The loess belt was unquestionably a region of easy movement and fertile and tempting soil; its course was marked out by merchants' routes and dotted with cities. But the Germans also settled the morainic country of East Prussia, which bordered the Baltic Sea and offered little scope to the farmer, and the infertile mountain ring which encircled Bohemia, without venturing in more than inconsiderable numbers into the richer plain of the interior. German eastward movement was conditioned more by the ability of the Slavs to resist them than by the actual distribution of good farm land. Not until the eighteenth century did they conquer and in some degree Germanise the core-areas of the Polish, Czech and Hungarian states.

Turkish invasion and conquest. The Turks first entered Europe in 1345 in support of a claimant to the Byzantine throne. The pretext is unimportant; they would have come anyway. They swept through Thrace and, at a high price, helped the Emperors against their Balkan enemies, before returning to Asia Minor. In 1354 they came to Europe again, this time with the intention of staying. Thrace and southern Bulgaria were occupied. Constantinople was cut off from contact with the rest of Europe but stubbornly resisted the Turks until its capture in 1453. The Bulgarian state was defeated. The Serbs offered a fiercer resistance, but they too were overcome by the all-powerful Turks in the battle of Kosovo, in 1389. Yet the Turks made little progress for almost a century after this. In the mid-fifteenth century they overran Bosnia and Hercegovina, and invaded the Romanian province of Walachia, but it was not until 1521 that the Sultan Suleiman captured Beograd. Then began a rapid northward advance. In 1526, the Turks invaded Hungary, defeating the Hungarian army at Mohács, beside the Danube. They occupied Buda soon afterwards, and advanced to an unsuccessful siege of Vienna in 1529.

The Turks retained possession of the Hungarian Plain until the closing years of the seventeenth century and the beginning of the eighteenth. In 1683 they again attacked Vienna, and were again driven from its walls, this time by the Polish army of Jan Sobieski. The Turks extended their rule over Transylvania and later the Romanian provinces of Walachia and Moldavia, and their armies, following the grassland route that lies outside the curve of the Carpathians, came into conflict with the Poles.

The Turks were never as numerous as their vast empire might have suggested. Very few ever came to the Balkans or Danubian valley merely to settle. Turkish armies were stationed at strategic points and maintained order in their own peculiar and heavy-handed way. Turkish merchants and tax-collectors exploited and oppressed, but the Turkish civil service contained large numbers of Greeks and Jews, and the flower of the Turkish army, the Janissaries, was continuously supplied by the tribute of children levied on the Christian subjects of the Empire.

The Turkish impact on the lands which they occupied was almost wholly negative. They tolerated the Christian, as they did the Jew, but their corrupt and oppressive rule for a period which ranged from 200 to 500 years, inhibited almost all economic development. When at last Turkish rule withdrew from the Balkans it left only a few, small Turkish-speaking communities. But the Turks did succeed in converting to Islam a part of the population of Bosnia, Macedonia and Bulgaria.

East European Jewry. The most recent of the immigrant groups into the Balkans was the Jews. Their history has been far more confusing than that of any other of the smaller ethnic groups of the Balkans and Eastern Europe. The main body of the Jewish people remained in the Middle East from the time of the Diaspora until the eleventh century. From here they spread both northward into the lands around the Black Sea and westward, beyond the Mediterranean Sea, to Spain. These movements gave rise to Sephardic, or southern Jewry, and Askanazim, or northern. But the distinction was never clear-cut. As persecution drove the Jews out of southern Europe, some moved eastward into the lands of the more tolerant Turks; others filtered northward and then eastward to Germany and Poland, as the wave of intolerance and inhumanity spread outward from its Christian source. Jewish communities from southern Europe reinforced the northern or Askanazim Jews. Debarred by Christian prejudice from holding land and from the knightly pursuit of war, the Jews were obliged to find a livelihood in trade; they discovered the commercial possibilities inherent in the Germans' eastward movement, and, in the words of H. G. Wanklyn,[1] 'they took part unconsciously in the medieval period of the German "Drang nach Osten".'

The greater part of the Jewish population of Europe thus came to inhabit a broad belt of territory extending from the Baltic Sea in the north-west to the Black Sea in the south-east. The heaviest concentration was in the area which now comprises Poland, White Russia and the western Ukraine. Unable to go farther to escape their oppressors, they had gathered here, under Russian rule, the object of hatred as virulent and of persecution as cruel, though more capricious, as any they had experienced in the West. Within this 'Pale' of Jewish settlement, they were excluded from the larger towns, and, as their numbers grew, they came to dominate the smaller. Many of these came to be more than two-thirds Jewish in population.

During the eighteenth century a more tolerant attitude developed in the West and slowly communicated itself eastward. Many of the German states, including Prussia, which was for its time one of the more enlightened in Europe, and the Austro-Hungarian Empire, were willing to receive, if not also to welcome the Jews. There was thus a return movement from the 'Pale' toward the west and south-west.

Hungary and the Danubian lands were at this time a new frontier for them, as eastern Germany had been during the Middle Ages. Here the Jewish immigrants had renewed opportunities to exhibit their traditional talents and to open up trade in the lands newly recovered from the Turks. Travellers in Hungary and Romania in the later years of the eighteenth century and early in the nineteenth described with a mixture of pity and scorn the newly-arrived Jewish immigrants, who had crossed the Carpathian Mountains and filtered down into the Danubian plains. It was this frontier character of the Hungarian Plain at this time which gave them their opportunity. South of the Danube they found little to attract them; few came this far, and the Jewish communities of the Balkan countries remained small.

It is nevertheless true that some of the West European Jews found

[1] H. G. Wanklyn, 'Geographical Aspects of Jewish Settlement East of Germany', *Geogrl J.*, **95** (1940), 175–90.

3*

employment under the rule of the Turkish Sultan. Islam was always tolerant of Judaism as well as of Christianity. It was also continually short of skilled labour, and the Jews could perform a very useful role. 'Jewish traders and craftsmen were to be found in almost every city in the (Turkish) empire. Jewish physicians, interpreters, and financiers made themselves indispensable to Ottoman officials.'[1] That intrepid English traveller, Lady Mary Wortley Montagu, wrote in 1717 that 'I observed most of the rich tradesmen were Jews. . . . Every pasha has a Jew, who is his *homme d'affaires*; he is let into all his secrets, and does all his business. No bargain is made, no bribe received, no merchandise disposed of, but what passes through their hands. They are the physicians, the stewards, and the interpreters of the great men.[2] Nevertheless, Stavrianos claims that these Balkan Jewish communities may have numbered no more than 100,000, only a fraction of the number of Jews in northern Europe.

Ethnic pattern of Eastern Europe

By the end of the Middle Ages, the main elements in the population of Eastern Europe had been assembled. The role of the succeeding centuries was to rearrange them and to combine them into the national groups which we know today. We have already noted the northward drift of the Vlachs and Gypsies, the eastward movement of the Jews and their later return movement toward the west and south-west. In parts of the region where two or more peoples were living intermixed with one another there was usually a tendency for one to absorb or assimilate the other. This process was accelerated by public authorities, in whose interest it was that certain groups should be submerged and others dominate. In Greece, the Slav invaders were assimilated during the Middle Ages by the Greek peoples without the application of any particular governmental pressure by the Byzantine authorities. The assimilation of the western Slavs to the language and culture of the Germans was achieved by forceful methods, which became more oppressive in the nineteenth century, as Slav resistance became more coordinated and vigorous.

Migration within Eastern Europe. Actual movements of peoples over considerable distances usually accompanied and followed the destruction and depopulation of war. Two areas stand out as the scene of

---

[1] L. S. Stavrianos, *The Balkans since* 1453, New York, 1958, p. 90.
[2] *Letters and Works of Lady Mary Wortley Montagu*, London, George Bell, 1898, **1**, p. 197; the letter is dated Adrianople, 1717.

such changes: the borderland of Albanian, Slav and Greek settlement, and the southern margin of the Hungarian Plain.

The mountainous terrain which had allowed the Albanians to preserve, without too great a contamination from without, the ancient speech of the Illyrians, also served to safeguard them from the worst aspects of Turkish rule. They multiplied in their infertile mountain home, and as the power of the Byzantine emperors weakened, they spread into Thessaly and southward through the Greek peninsula, until they became an important element in the population of Arcadia and Argolis and of many of the Greek islands of the Aegean Sea.[1] The Albanian population of Greece has, to a very large degree, been assimilated, like the earlier Slav invaders, by the prevailing Greek.

A later and, from our present point of view, more important Albanian migration occurred in the later years of the seventeenth and early eighteenth century, and was a result of the evacuation of the Metohija region by the Serbs during the wars between the Austrians and the Turks. When in 1688 the Austrian armies invaded the Turkish Empire south of the Danube and Sava rivers, they called upon the Serbs to rise in revolt against the Turks. They did so, and when, a few years later, the Austrians streamed back across the rivers into Hungary, there were many in Serbia who rightly feared the vengeance of the Turks. In 1690 a large body of them from the Raška region, formerly the centre of the medieval Serbian state, responded to an invitation from the Austrian Emperor and migrated northward to Hungary. They were led by their Patriarch, and may have numbered as many as 100,000.[2] In Hungary they were settled along the exposed southern border, where their military services were of great value in protecting the Habsburg Empire from Turkish incursions. Most of the Serbs continued to live here though some drifted northwards. Travellers in the later eighteenth century often referred to the 'Rascians' in and around Budapest, who seem to have formed an underprivileged proletariat, living as much by its wits as its labour. In the meantime their original homeland was occupied by Albanians who came down from their mountains to occupy the more fertile plains of Kosovo and Metohija.

In the course of the military campaigns of the early years of the

[1] F. W. Hasluck, 'Albanian Settlements in the Aegean Islands', *The Annual of the British School at Athens,* **15** (1908–9), pp. 222–8.
[2] Robert Lee Wolff, *The Balkans in Our Time,* Harvard University Press, 1956, p. 64. This estimate seems high. Stavrianos, *op. cit.,* 174, suggests 30,000.

eighteenth century, the southern and south-eastern parts of the Hungarian Plain had been utterly devastated and its population largely dispersed or destroyed. So empty a land invited renewed invasion from the south, and it became the policy of the Austrian government to re-populate it from whatever source was available. To some extent, the Serbs from Raška fulfilled this need, but other colonists: German, Czech, Slovak, Romanian, even French, were brought in. New villages were laid out, compact and regularly planned, with straight streets intersecting at right angles, and were settled with foreign communities, whose descendants still speaking their native languages, are in many instances still to be found there.

The later years of the eighteenth century and the whole span of the nineteenth saw few migrations of importance. A stable pattern had been achieved, and the imperial powers which had riveted their authority on the area for most of this period permitted few movements of peoples which they did not themselves deliberately promote. Indeed, the only conspicuous movement was one of migration from Eastern Europe, as opportunities developed to emigrate to the New World. The greatest numbers came from the densely peopled lands of Poland, both Russian and Austrian. But Hungarians and the southern Slavs also took part in this movement, In all, it is estimated that some eight million people left these regions of Eastern Europe during the nineteenth and early twentieth centuries.

The peace treaties which concluded the First World War brought about few migratory movements of peoples. Indeed, a settlement predicated upon the political self-determination of peoples might be expected to result in few changes of this kind. The exchange of part of the Turkish population in Bulgaria and Greece for the Greek population living within Turkey and Bulgaria was, in fact, the only large scale population movement at this time. Between 1922 and 1924 about 800,000 Greeks left Asia Minor, most of them from the Smyrna region, and were settled in Thrace, Macedonia and other parts of Greece. At the same time 388,000 Turks living in Greece were returned to Turkey. The exchange between Bulgaria and Greece was on a smaller scale. Beginning in 1923, about 250,000 Bulgarians moved from northern Greece to Bulgaria, and some 40,000 Greeks left Bulgaria for Greece.

The ethnic pattern of Eastern Europe in 1918. It is time to take stock of the geography of the ethnic groups of Eastern Europe as it presented itself to those who gathered at Paris in the closing months of 1918 to write the treaties which, it was confidently hoped, would be the basis of a lasting peace. In detail, this picture was by no means clear, but certain broad features stood out from a mass of uncertain detail. There were three western Slav groups, Poles, Czechs and Slovaks, each of which demanded and deserved political recognition. To the east lay the White Russians and the Ukrainians, or little Russians. The geographical division between them and the Poles, never clear-cut, had been made yet more obscure by the superposition of the heavy

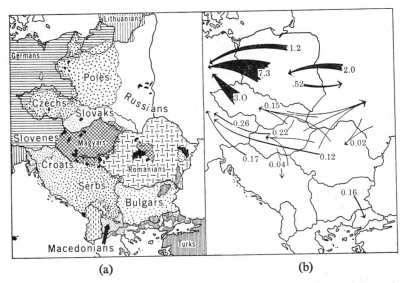

(a)   (b)

Fig. 2.3. (a) Ethnic map of Eastern Europe between the First and Second World Wars. (b) Migration of ethnic groups after 1944. Based on data in Leszek Kosiński, *Geographia Polonica*, **2** (1964). Figures are in millions.

Jewish population of this area. In the west the line between the Slavs and the Germans was somewhat more distinct, but even here the Allied Powers had to resort to the device of a plebiscite in three areas (see page 100)—and could justifiably have done so in more—in an attempt to discover the loyalties and desires of the people.

The Jewish population, which in Poland alone amounted to about three million, was too dispersed and intermixed too intimately with the non-Jewish population for political aspirations within Eastern Europe even to have been seriously entertained. On the other hand the establishment in the British mandated territory of Palestine of a National Home for the Jews failed to attract many immigrants from East European Jewry.

At this time there were about 23 million Poles most of whom were included in the newly created Polish state. A few lived in Czechoslovakia, and larger numbers remained in eastern Germany. The number of the latter was difficult to determine. Estimates were coloured by political considerations, and those given by Polish and German sources were in flagrant contradiction.

Czechs numbered about 6,800,000,[1] and Slovaks, about 2,000,000 and, in addition, small groups of both peoples lived in Austria and Hungary.

The settlement area of the German-speaking Austrians, the Hungarians and the Romanians separated the western from the southern Slavs. The Austrians are excluded from this discussion, though attention must be given to the German-speaking communities which were scattered through Hungary and Romania.

The total number of Hungarians (Magyars) at this time, is also somewhat difficult to establish. In the state of Hungary there were about 7,147,000. In Czechoslovakia, about 745,000; in Romania, a further 1,464,000, including the Szekély of Transylvania, and in Yugoslavia some 468,000, most of whom lived in scattered communities resulting from the resettlement of this region during the eighteenth century. In addition, a handful of Hungarians was left in Austria. In all, there was a population of about 9,825,000 Hungarians. Their settlement area was pre-eminently the Hungarian Plain, and as a general rule, they were not found in the surrounding hill country, with the exception of the Szekély of Transylvania. The limits of their settlement area were, however, far from distinct, and, as on the eastern border of Poland, the ethnic transition was masked by a heavily Jewish settlement in the cities, especially those of northern Hungary.

In Romania the ethnic situation was even more confused than in the other countries of Eastern Europe. The Szekély and the 'Saxons', whose homeland in the Middle Ages had been almost certainly Luxembourg and the Mosel region rather than Saxony, occupied the heart of the country. The 'Saxons' at this time numbered about 400,000; the Szekély, about 800,000. To the east and south, in the provinces of Moldavia and Walachia, the population was mainly

---

[1] Czechoslovak statistics did not list the two peoples separately, but gave their combined total in February 1921, as 8,760, 937.

Romanian, with however a large Jewish population which increased in proportion to the Romanian as the former Russian Pale of Settlement was approached. Beyond the River Prut, the province of Bessarabia was so confused ethnically as to have no clear-cut national majority. There were Romanians from the south and Ukrainians from the east. A few Poles made their appearance toward the north, and there were relict communities left by Turkish invaders and by the Tatars from the Steppe. Along its western boundary, the new Romania embraced a continuous belt of Hungarian population, and in the Dobrogea, the Romanian province lying south of the Danube river, there were communities of Bulgars who had been here since the time of the Second Bulgarian Empire (1185–1330).

The population south of the Danube was dominated by the southern Slavs. Indeed, if Greece and European Turkey are excluded, the population was at this time over 80 per cent Slav. But this is misleading. The region is in fact intensely divided. It is now customary to speak of five southern Slav peoples: the Slovenes, Croats, Serbs, Macedonians and Bulgars, though within each of these groups there are dialect differences which, in different circumstances, could have developed into distinct languages.

The Slovene language was spoken by about 1,100,000 people in the extreme north-west of this region. A few Slovenes lived north of the Karawanken Alps, in the Austrian Province of Kärnten, and more numerous groups in the hinterland of Trieste in northern Italy. Croats and Serbs scarcely differed in their spoken language, only in their calligraphy and in habits of life and thought, which, however superficial the differences, have served to hold them apart and make them rivals if not enemies for centuries. The Croats use the Latin alphabet which they derived from their contacts with the west; the Serbs, the Cyrillic which emphasises their former links with the Byzantine Empire. The Croats, furthermore, are predominantly Roman Catholic and the Serbs, Orthodox.

The Bulgarian language is, however, quite distinct, and is probably closer to the protoslavic root than all the others that have derived from it. Macedonian presents peculiar problems. In certain respects it is intermediate between Serb and Bulgar, but it also has certain affinities with Greek, and it has absorbed some Turkish elements. Linguistically, Macedonian is so confused that a case can be made out for its affiliation to either Serb or Bulgar. Today, more for political than for narrowly linguistic reasons, it is recognised as a separate language, and those who speak it constitute one of the 'nations' of Yugoslavia.

The numbers of the southern Slavs in 1919 were estimated to have been as follows:

Slovenes: 1,020,000, with about 302,000 in Austria and Italy in addition.

Croats: 2,600,000, with about 93,000 in Italy and 36,800 in Hungary in addition.

Serbs: 6,000,000, with 52,500 in Romania and 17,000 in Hungary in addition.

Macedonians: 500,000.

Bulgars: 5,200,000, with about 68,000 in Yugoslavia and 351,000 in Romania in addition.

The non-Slav communities, as we have seen, were few. They included Germans, Italians, Albanians and Turks, and very small groups of Romanians and Hungarians. The Germans were represented by compact and coherent communities in the Vojvodina, where they had been settled by Maria Theresa in the eighteenth century, and by smaller and more scattered groups in Slovenia and Croatia. They never settled in significant numbers in the more southerly parts of the Balkans.

The Italians continued to live after the First World War along the Dalmatian coast, where their ancestors had settled during the medieval period of Italian commercial supremacy. They formed merely a string of settlements, expanding into larger Italian nuclei in such cities as Pola (Pula), Fiume (Rijeka), Spalato (Split), Zara (Zadar), Sibenico (Šibenik) and Ragusa (Dubrovnik). In addition very small groups of Italians had even penetrated Albania. If we exclude Trieste and the Istrian peninsula, which passed under Italian rule after the First World War, the total Italian population of the Dalmatian and Albanian coastlands did not exceed 15,000 persons.

The Albanians formed, apart from the Greeks, the most numerous of the non-Slav peoples of the Balkan peninsula. We have already seen something of their origin and history, and of their need, induced by the poverty of their mountains, to spread into neighbouring lands. Their language is quite distinctive, deriving, it is commonly supposed, from the speech of the ancient Illyrians, although it has absorbed elements from many of the later invaders of the Balkans. It is distinguished by two dominant dialects, Geg, spoken to the north of the

Shkumbî River, and Tosk which prevails to the south. This linguistic division roughly corresponds with slight physiological differences between the population of north and south and also with certain differences in temperament. This serves to emphasise the fact that there has been very little intermixture between the northern and southern Albanian communities.

When Albania held its first census, in 1930, there were about a million Albanians. A decade earlier there were probably slightly fewer, perhaps 900,000. Albanian communities outside Albania were almost as numerous. In Serbia there were 750,000 and in Northern Greece, about 30,000.[1]

The Turks are the last significant ethnic group in the Balkans. A distinction must be made, however, between Slavs who had accepted Islam (see page 669) and were numerous in particular in Bosnia and parts of Bulgaria, and the Turks themselves. The mosques and minarets, which form so conspicuous a feature in the landscape of Sarajevo or Travnik, are indicative only of the former. The Turks themselves lived in small communities, especially in southern Romania and Bulgaria and above all in Greece, but most were returned to Turkey in the population exchanges of the 1920s or in the more recent expulsion of Turks from Bulgaria.

To these communities, each of which can be described as a national group with political aspirations of some sort, must be added those groups, few in number and scattered over most of the region, who lacked such aspirations. These included the Vlachs and Gypsies. The former were becoming fewer in the Balkan peninsula, as the smaller communities gave up their nomadic or transhumant life and became assimilated in language and way of life to the rest of the local population. The most numerous communities lived in fact outside the limits set for Eastern Europe in this book, in the Grammos and Píndhos Mountains of north-western Greece. Within Eastern Europe proper, there were at this time possibly no more than 100,000 Vlachs, most of them living in the Rhodope Mountains of Bulgaria and in neighbouring parts of Serbia. Those Vlachs who had migrated north-westward through the Dinaric chain and had come to live in Croatia and Slovenia had by the time of the First World War almost entirely lost their identity.

---

[1] Estimates differ widely. Earlier Yugoslav estimates are certainly too low, and Albanian authorities claimed 900,000 Albanians in Yugoslavia. See Stavro Skendi, ed., *East-Central Europe under the Communists: Albania*, London, 1958, p. 50.

The Gypsies proved to be a more tenacious group than the Vlachs with whom they were so often confused. They continued to wander in their small family groups, to speak their 'Romany' language intermixed with the local vernacular, and to live by their traditional occupations. There may have been as many as half a million Gypsies in the Balkans and Romania, and perhaps 750,000 in Eastern Europe as a whole, relatively few of whom managed to survive the Second World War and Nazi occupation.

The ethnic pattern after the Second World War. For 20 years there was little change in this pattern of peoples in Eastern Europe. The boundaries established by the Paris Conference and by later decisions of its continuing organisations did not in every instance respect the rights of national groups. In some instances these were so intermixed that violence of some kind had to be done in order to draw a boundary. Nevertheless, the rights of minority groups were in some way guaranteed by the Minority Treaties. The period of relative stability lasted until the Second World War destroyed the uneasy balance established at the end of the First, and precipitated the biggest and cruellest movement of peoples known in human history.

It was the alleged injustices of the 1919–20 settlement that formed the pretext both for the stormy prelude to the Second World War and for its actual outbreak. Ethnic realities in Eastern Europe were soon submerged beneath more momentous issues, but it is with the former that we are here concerned. The Second World War, together with its prelude and its immediate aftermath, changed the ethnic pattern of large parts of Europe, reduced the total population by perhaps ten million, and went far toward extinguishing two of the ethnic groups, the Jews and the Gypsies.

The 'solution' of the Jewish 'problem' was one of the declared aims of the German rulers in Eastern Europe. We can never know how many Jews perished. The gas chambers of Oświęcim (Auschwitz) accounted for over three million, and large numbers perished also at Majdanek and at other extermination centres. The Jewish population of Poland was reduced from about three million to not more than 100,000. The Czechoslovak Jews were decimated; the Hungarian, almost obliterated. Romanian Jewry suffered less, and the small Jewish communities of the Balkans scarcely at all.

The Gypsies were to be disposed of in the same way, and the German campaign against them was relatively successful in the northern part of the area. In the Balkans, however, it was as ineffective as the campaign against the Jews. The rugged terrain, the relative smallness of the German forces, and the almost continuous guerrilla fighting combined to give them a considerable degree of protection.

As the war drew to its close, and the German armies which had proudly advanced as far as Leningrad, Stalingrad and the Caucasus, limped slowly home, there began what was probably the greatest movement of peoples the world has known. It lasted for a period of from five to six years, but it was most intense in 1945 and 1946. Most Germans and all who had sided openly with the Germans in Eastern Europe were in danger; almost all found refuge in Germany, and most of those who tried to remain were expelled soon after. It is difficult to form an estimate of the numbers of the German-speaking population who trekked westward out of Czechoslovakia and the new Poland, as well as from Hungary, Romania and Yugoslavia. In some of these areas the population had recently been increased by an eastward movement of refugees from the bombed cities of Central and Western Germany. The peace-time population of the area taken over by Poland had been about 8,900,000. Of these about 1,260,000 had been Poles. In all, it is admitted by the Polish authorities, about 150,000 Germans were allowed to remain. This suggests, after making an allowance for wartime casualties and the evacuation to this area of people from Central Germany in order to escape the Allied bombing, that about seven million Germans either fled or were driven to the west of the newly established boundary.

In the Sudetenland of Czechoslovakia there had been a German-speaking population of over three million. Almost all fled or were driven out, leaving only a handful, whose numbers are currently estimated to be about 165,000. This total must be assumed to include also the German-speaking people who have been allowed to remain in other areas, such as Prague and the Spiš region of Slovakia.

German communities had been insignificant in Hungary, but they had been numerous and important in Yugoslavia and Romania. In both their number has been drastically reduced by violence and expulsion either during or immediately after the war. In Romania, it is claimed that only about 150,000 of the former Saxon community remain, and the German colonies in Yugoslavia have been reduced yet more drastically. Thus it may be said that of the former German communities in the area that now comprises Eastern Europe, only about a sixth remain, as Table 4 shows.

A similar fate has befallen the small Italian communities which

Table 4. German-speaking population in Eastern Europe

	1939 estimates	1955–56 estimates
Poland	765,000[1]	150,000
Czechoslovakia	3,300,000	165,000
Hungary	400,000	200,000
Romania	535,000	365,000
Yugoslavia	500,000	65,000

[1] Boundaries of 1938.

Based on *East Europe*, 8 (March 1959), pp. 3–14.

formerly lived along the Dalmatian coast of Yugoslavia. Before the Second World War, there cannot have been more than about 15,000 Italians living along this coast between Trieste and the Albanian border. The cities, notably Fiume (Rijeka) and Zara (Zadar) had a considerable Italian population, and Italian-speakers were numerous in most of the others. The political consequences of the concentration of the Italian community along this coast are examined in Chapter 4.

In 1945, the Italian communities, like the German, fled or were expelled, leaving only a handful behind, and the almost exclusively Italian cities of Pola, Fiume and Zara passed into Yugoslav possession and control.

The recoil of German and Italian settlement in the west was paralleled by a retreat of Polish settlement in the east in the face of the Russian peoples. In 1939 the western boundary of the Soviet Union was advanced from the line established in 1920 at Riga to one which accorded closely with the Curzon Line of 1919. The population thus incorporated into the Soviet Union was predominantly Ukrainian (Ruthene) and White Russian. Poles had constituted only a minority, which had included nevertheless a significant part of the small land-owning and middle-class element. Both the land and the people suffered severely from the Soviet, then the German and again the Soviet occupation, and from the twofold passage of the battlefront through this region. After 1945 the Polish elements in the population were moved to Poland, the intention being to use them to re-people the lands of western Poland vacated by the Germans. The eastern Poles were, however, very much less numerous than the expelled Germans, and their total number did not in all probability exceed 1,700,000.

Ethnic changes within Eastern Europe as a consequence of the war were few. The policy of the Communist governments was, in general, to minimise such cultural differences as existed within their territory, but at the same time to tolerate their expression, provided this was done without political overtones. In Czechoslovakia, the separateness of Czechs and Slovaks was reduced by deliberately mixing them together, taking Slovak peasants to work in Czech factories and sending Czech industrial workers to the factories newly built in Slovakia. At the same time the Czechoslovak government permitted a Polish language newspaper to be published in Ostrava to serve the needs of the minority which still lives in Ostrava and Těšin.

Only Yugoslavia has set out to give greater cultural and political autonomy to the several ethnic groups which make up its population. Its federal system is based in the separateness of Slovenes, Croats, and Serbs. It recognised the ethnically mixed nature of the population of the Vojvodina and of Kosovo-Metohija, and itself contributed to the rise of Macedonian as a distinct language, erecting Macedonia into a separate and co-equal member of the federation.

An exchange of the Czechoslovak minority in Hungary for the Hungarian minority in Slovakia was arranged by their respective governments in 1946. A beginning was made, and about 155,000 persons were exchanged; but the operation was never completed. The small cities of southern Slovakia have all the appearances of being bilingual, though Czechoslovak statistics show a steadily diminishing Magyar minority. It is to be presumed that more and more Magyars become bilingual and then find it politically advisable to call themselves as Slovaks.

Eastern Europe today is more ethnically homogeneous and the pattern of its peoples more simple probably than at any time in the past. The most significant change has been, of course, the withdrawal of the Germans and Italians. To a lesser degree the ethnic boundaries have been simplified and made to conform more closely with the political by means of small scale, controlled migration. It might be assumed that the national claims and counter claims which have for so long bedevilled relations between the states of Eastern Europe would gradually become less rancorous and then terminate. But they have not yet done so. The Communist system has not readily tolerated any rift in its once monolithic façade. But there are rifts, and it would not take any great relaxation of present controls to let loose a flood of claims and disputes of the old and long familiar kind. Indeed, such old and almost tribal disputes have been enlisted in the course of the cold war, as is apparent from any consideration of the boundary question between Yugoslavia on the one hand and Albania and Bulgaria on the other.

Race in Eastern Europe

The previous pages have suggested a remarkably unstable picture throughout the historical period, as invaders followed one another into the region and in doing so, set others in motion. Yet this does not accord with the facts of physical anthropology. These suggest a stability which is far from apparent in the historical record. The population of Europe is very broadly divisible into a northern group—commonly described as Nordic—in which long (dolichocephalic) heads, tall stature, and a predominantly light skin and hair colouration tend to prevail; a Mediterranean group, characterised also by long heads, but also darker colouration, and by an intermediate belt of 'alpines', whose predominant characteristics are a pronounced broad-headedness (brachycephaly), a shorter stature, and medium to dark colouration. These distinctions can be recognised only in the broadest sense; they are 'no more than small differences between averages'.[1] Within them, however, are small pockets or 'islands' of peoples who in some significant respect differ from their neighbours. The important feature of this racial distribution is that it was established very early in human history, and, despite tribal movements and invasions, has remained relatively stable.

Certain conclusions derive from the most superficial examination of the racial composition of Europe. In the first place the linguistic and cultural differences are in no way paralleled by any racial contrasts. There is no such entity as a Polish or even a Magyar 'race'. A second conclusion is that there are virtually no abrupt transitions or changes in the distribution of racial characteristics. 'The languages indicate marked distinctions and discontinuity, whereas the physical characters show no corresponding hiatuses, but gradual transitions and continuity throughout the region.'[2] The only exception to this generalisation found by Morant was provided by the German and Magyar settlers in Romania, who are clearly distinguished from the surrounding Romanians.

[1] G. M. Morant, *The Races of Central Europe*, London, 1939, p 142.
[2] *Ibid.*, p. 138..

A third conclusion, supported by the first two, is that in the movements of peoples which have occupied the past three millenia, only a minority moved, that the ground-mass of the people remained relatively stable, merely taking on and putting off its cultural colour with each wave of conquerors. The invasion of the Bulgars and their assimilation by the Slavs is merely the best documented example of a process which must have been continuous through prehistoric and historic times.

The northern Poles are more or less Nordic. The Slavic culture spread southward to the Danubian basin and beyond, but the racial characteristics of the Neolithic and Bronze Age Danubian peasants moved in the contrary direction from the south into and across Poland. Southern Poland is more 'alpine' than northern, and the Gorals, Huzuls and other mountain peoples of the Polish and Czechoslovak Carpathians show almost no northern racial influence. In the words of C. S. Coon, 'the Slavicisation of these mountaineers was more a linguistic than a racial phenomenon.'[1] In a similar way, the Slavic language of the Byelorussians was imposed upon a ground-mass with strong East Baltic affinities and racially but little different from the ancient Prussians and the modern Lithuanians.

The Czechs and Slovaks are, by and large, 'alpines', and it is impossible to draw any clear racial distinction between them and the Germans who entered and settled among them. The Magyars are culturally and linguistically one of the most distinctive peoples in Europe. It might be supposed that they would show some racial individuality, but their racial composition, though it is, in detail, extraordinarily complex, does not, when expressed in terms of averages, stand out from that of its neighbours. A racial analysis, quoted by C. S. Coon,[2] suggested that about 15 per cent of the Hungarian people are true 'alpines'; about 35 per cent appear to derive from the Neolithic Danubian Peasant substratum, and 20 per cent are Dinarics, with Mediterranean affinities. Of the remainder, only 5 per cent have any recognisably Mongoloid characteristic and 20 per cent show some trace of Turkish, Tatar, or other non-European racial elements. This would certainly tend to emphasise the relative permanence of the ancient substratum and the fewness of those mongoloids whose exploits have echoed for centuries through history.

The history of the lands south of the Danube has probably been

[1] Carleton S. Coon, *The Races of Europe*, New York, 1939, p. 572.
[2] *Ibid.*, p. 586.

more catastrophic than that of lands lying to the north; the devasta-
tion and depopulation of one area after another has been more drastic,
and changes in racial complexion through both space and time, more
far-reaching. This has tended to produce distinctive communities, but
the Balkans as a whole are characterised by blends and combinations
of the main proto-European types—'alpine' in the west and north;
neo-Danubian in the north-west; and Mediterranean in the south. It
probably did not differ greatly when this region was inhabited by
Illyrians, Thracians and Hellenised Greeks.

Then, as now, the Dinaric mountain-belt was characterised by very
tall people with broad, high heads—the so-called Dinarics. These
characteristics have survived in their extreme form in the mountains of
Montenegro. The Montenegrins are linguistically Serb, but 'there can
be no question that they are to a large extent Slavicized Albanians',[1]
as the characteristics which they exhibit are continued beyond the
boundary into Albania.

A further conclusion, which must be expressed in more guarded
terms than the others, is that, whereas racial composition bears no
relationship to language, it is more clearly related to the quality of the
terrain. The ruggedness of the Montenegrin and Albanian mountains,
and the 'alpine' quality of the Carpathians are instances which can
surely be correlated with certain ethnic traits. It would almost seem
that freedom of movement and of access to neighbouring communities
is a major factor in the modification of pronounced racial traits, and
that, by contrast, where the terrain is more accidented, racial peculiarities are intensified by intermarriage.

A discussion of race in Eastern Europe should not end without some
examination of the racial composition of two distinctive and widespread peoples, the Gypsies and the Jews. Both have a long history of
segregation—only partially involuntary—from other peoples, and
both have been victims of a policy of extermination, directed against
their race as such. The racial statistics which make little distinction
between most of the peoples of Eastern Europe, nevertheless show
some degree of separation between these peoples and others.

The characteristics of the Gypsies are the most pronounced and
show the highest degree of correlation between themselves. These
people are darker in skin and hair colouration, have a higher percentage of brown eyes and of wavy and curly hair than any of other
European people. This accords closely with the historical facts, since

[1] C. S. Coon, *op. cit.*, p. 591.

the Gypsies derive from an immigrant group which came originally from southern Asia. Their social aloofness and resulting in-breeding has preserved the racial characteristics which they brought with them.

The separateness of the Jews is a great deal less marked than that of the Gypsies. They are commonly regarded as slightly darker and their hair as a little less straight than that of most non-Jewish peoples. At the time of their dispersion the Jews can have shown relatively little racial homogeneity, and since this time their stock has become even more diversified. They have in many areas taken on the racial characteristics of the peoples among whom they have lived for centuries. Thus the Askanazim Jews are 'physically . . . much like the northern Slavs', and the Sephardic 'tend to approach the Mediterranean type'.[1] Nevertheless, many, perhaps a majority, show some physical characteristic, commonly regarded as Jewish, which they derive from the Palestinian Mediterraneans who in some indeterminate degree constitute their common ancestry.

Bibliography

ANCEL, JACQUES, *Peuples et Nations des Balkans*, Paris, Colin, 1926.

AUTY, ROBERT, 'Community and Divergence in the History of the Slavonic Languages', *The Slavonic and East European Review*, **42** (1963) 257–73.

CHADWICK, H. MUNRO, *The Nationalities of Europe and the Growth of National Ideologies*, Cambridge University Press, 1945.

CHILDE, V. GORDON, *The Danube in Prehistory*, Oxford University Press, 1929.

— *Prehistoric Migrations in Europe*, Oslo, Instituttet for Sammenlignende Kulturforskning, 1950.

COON, CARLETON S. *The Races of Europe*, London, Macmillan, 1939.

CORNISH, VAUGHAN, *Borderlands of Language in Europe*, London Sifton Praed and Company, 1936.

CROSS. SAMUEL HAZZARD, *Slavic Civilization through the Ages*, New York, Russell & Russell, 1963.

DVORNIK, FRANCIS, *The Slavs: Their Early History and Civilization* Boston, American Academy of Arts and Sciences, 1956.

— *The Slavs in European History and Civilization*, New Brunswick N.J., Rutgers University Press, 1962.

FILIP, JAN, *Keltska civilizace a jeji dédictvi*, Prague, 1963.

[1] Julian S. Huxley and A. C. Haddon, *We Europeans*, 1935 edn, p. 184; also C. S. Coon, *op. cit.*, pp. 638–6.

FLEURE, H. J. *The Peoples of Europe*, Oxford University Press, 1922.

GIMBUTAS, MARIJA, *The Balts*, London, Thames and Hudson, 1963.

— *The Prehistory of Eastern Europe*, Peabody Museum, Harvard University, 1957.

— 'On the Origin of the North Indo-Europeans', *Am. Anthrop.*, **54** (1952), 602–11.

HASLUCK, F. W. 'Albanian Settlements in the Aegean Islands', *Annual of the British School at Athens*, **15** (1908–09), 222–8.

HENCKEN, HUGH, *Indo-European Languages and Archaeology*, Am. anthrop. Ass., Memoir No. 84 (1955).

HUXLEY, JULIAN S. and A. C. HADDON, *We Europeans: A Survey of 'Racial' Problems*, London, Jonathan Cape, 1935.

JAŻDŻEWSKI, KONRAD, *Atlas do Pradziejów Słowian*, Łódź, 1948 (text and atlas).

ŁUKASIK, STANISLAS, *Pologne et Roumanie*, Paris, 1938.

MAYER, ANTON, *Die Sprache der alten Illyrier*, Schriften der Balkankommission, Linguistische Abteilung, **15**, Vienna, 1954.

MEYER, PETER, B. D. WEINRYB, E. DUSCHINSKY and N. SYLVAIN, *The Jews in the Soviet Satellites*, Syracuse University Press, 1953.

MORANT, G. M. *The Races of Central Europe: A Footnote to History*, London, Allen & Unwin, 1939.

NIEDERLE, LUBOR, *Manuel de l'Antiquité Slave*, 2 vols., Paris, 1926.

PALLIS, A. A. 'Racial Migrations in the Balkans during the Years 1912–1924', *Geogrl J.*, **66** (1925), 315–31.

PEISKER, T. 'The Expansion of the Slavs', in *Cambridge Medieval History*, Cambridge University Press, 1913, vol. 2, pp. 418–58.

PITTARD, EUGÈNE, *Les Peuples des Balkans*, Paris, n.d.

PRIBICHEVICH, STOYAN, *Living Space*, Heinemann, 1940.

RIPLEY, W. Z. *The Races of Europe*, New York, Appleton, 1899.

SCHÖPFLIN, GEORGE A. 'National Minorities under Communism in Eastern Europe', in *Eastern Europe in Transition*, ed. Kurt London, Baltimore, Johns Hopkins Press, 1966, pp. 115–41.

SKENDI, STAVRO, ed. *Albania*; *East-Central Europe under the Communists*, London, Atlantic Press, 1957.

STAVRIANOS, L. S. *The Balkans since 1453*, New York, Holt Rinehart, 1958.

WANKLYN, H. G. *The Eastern Marchlands of Europe*, London, G. Philip, 1941.

WILKINSON, H. R. *Maps and Politics: A Review of the Ethnographic Cartography of Macedonia*, Liverpool, University Press, 1951.

CHAPTER THREE

States and Empires

Against this background of language and race must be set the changing map of empires and states. For over 2,000 years empires have succeeded one another, and the extent of Eastern Europe is definable in terms of these political vicissitudes. The scope of this book, territorially at least, is the area which became subject after the Second World War to the latest 'empire'—the Soviet—to intrude into this area.

Very broadly, one may say that periods of external and imperial control over the region have alternated with periods when the peoples of Eastern Europe were free to pursue their own destinies. Each period during which the nations of Eastern Europe were able to assert themselves, was followed by one when imperial control was again extended from one direction or another over the region. This cycle of nationalism and imperialism, of freedom and oppression, began in classical times. The Greeks established control over a few small toeholds around the southern periphery of the region. The Romans extended their empire over the whole area lying south of the Danube, and also, for a period of more than a century and a half, over the province of Dacia lying to the north.

The Byzantine Empire was heir to the eastern provinces of the Roman Empire, but under Byzantine rule its boundaries contracted, and long before the sceptre fell from the faltering hands of the last of the Palaeologi emperors, states had arisen to the north which in some way reflected the aspirations of their peoples: the Bulgars, Serbs, Magyars, Czechs and Poles.

Another period of imperial domination began with the eastward movement of German settlers and the extension of German and Austrian political control over part of Poland and all the Czech and Magyar lands as well as those of the Slovenes and Croats. It continued with the Turkish advance through the Balkans and into the Danubian valley, and culminated with the Russian annexation of the lion's share of the territory of the Polish state. From 1795, when, with its final partition, Poland disappeared from the European map, until the Greek revolt a generation later, no part of Eastern Europe, with the possible exception only of the rugged and diminutive state of Montenegro, continued sovereign and independent.

During the nineteenth century a wave of nationalism ran through Eastern Europe, and there was not a single people that did not rebel in some way against its oppressors. Early in the century the Serbs achieved an effective independence, though they had to wait half a century before it was generally recognised. Then the states of Romania and Bulgaria were established; Serbia expanded, and Hungary became independant of Austria. This was the 'springtime of the nations'. It was followed by the rapid recession of the imperial powers. First the Turkish empire, rotten at the core, was eroded and reduced to European Turkey. Then the Russian, the Austro-Hungarian and the German empires, each defeated suddenly and catastrophically in the First World War, were rolled back from Eastern Europe, and the whole region, for the first time in its history, was subject in no part to an outside power.

The boundaries of the Eastern Europe in the years following the First World War differed in detail from those of today. They included substantial areas now within the Soviet Union. They excluded territory which has since been taken from Germany and Italy. For a short period of barely 20 years, from the end of 1918 until 1938, Eastern Europe again experienced the joys and hazards of independence. But the clouds had again begun to form before this period ended. Germany incorporated Austria in 1938; cut Czechoslovakia into fragments, and went on to partition Poland with the Soviet Union and to invade the Balkans.

The Second World War, unlike the First, did not end in the defeat of all the imperial powers of continental Europe. Germany suffered a defeat more complete than any great power had previously known, and this was reflected in the westward recoil of German power and authority. The Italians were driven in defeat from the Balkans, but the Soviet Union, though weakened by the ordeal, nevertheless had the resilience to spring back and to dominate Eastern Europe in the wake of the retreating Germans.

Yet there was a brief interval between the collapse of Germany and the reassertion of Soviet authority in this area, long enough for free institutions to appear and a new era of political freedom to dawn. But the bright dawn of 1945 only ushered in a stormy day. The Soviet empire over most of Eastern Europe differed in its mechanism of control from the earlier empires. It was more ruthless and incomparably more efficient, and it established a system of Communist control over the whole area and of a Soviet political supremacy over the greater part of it. Herein lies another of the unifying features of this otherwise fragmented region, and the only reason for including Eastern Germany within the scope of this book.

The ancient empires

The impact of the ancient empires on Eastern Europe proved in the end to be slight. The Greeks established a few maritime cities around its coasts, but the Romans carried out no plan of urban development in the areas which they controlled comparable in any way with their urbanisation of Western Europe. The road net which they built was an open one, which left many areas untouched. The number of settlers from the Mediterranean coastlands was trifling and their cultural influence was in most respects small.

Greek and Hellenistic civilisations. Greek civilisation was essentially Aegean, and although Greek city-states were founded on the coast of Macedonia, Thrace and the Hellespont, they were mostly small; their orientation was southward to the Aegean world, and the Balkan peninsula was merely a back-country, in which they traded their pots and pans and wines for skins and furs and metals.

Even after the kingdom of Macedonia, in the fourth century B.C., had gained control over the declining Greek cities, the civilisation of Greece was carried eastward to the Middle East rather than northward into the Balkan peninsula. A few cities were built by the Thracian and Illyrian tribes, pale imitations of those of Greece, but the influence of the Hellenistic world diminished rapidly north of the Rhodope Mountains.

The Roman Empire. The Greek world was to influence profoundly the Balkan peninsula, but only after the Romans had conquered it, built cities within it and laid out roads. During the second century B.C. the Romans, whose rule had been extended over the peninsula of Italy and had spread to Spain, North Africa and the Mediterranean islands, now found it necessary to interfere in the affairs of the Greek peninsula. After over half a century of intermittent conflict, Macedonia was conquered and made a Roman province in 146 B.C., and Greece was reduced to subjection. Already the Romans had gained control of the Dalmatian coastal region, between the limestone mountains and the sea. But the karst formed no permanent frontier, though it served this function until the whole of the region south of the Danube was annexed to the Empire during the principate of Augustus.

North of Macedonia, the provinces of Thrace, Moesia, Illyricum and Pannonia were then organised. Along the river, frontier cities were established both for commerce and also defence, and the ruins of *Carnuntum*, between Vienna and Bratislava, and of *Aquincum*, upstream from Budapest, witness to their size and the massive scale of their construction.

Within the Balkans, roads were built inland from the few coastal cities which served as gateways to the peninsula: from Tergeste (Trieste), Dyrrachium (Durrës), Thessaloníki and Constantinople, an open network of routes was established, which still, in the twentieth century, forms the basic pattern of communication in the peninsula.

But the Danube was difficult to guard and easy to cross, and soon proved to be inadequate as a boundary. At the beginning of the second century, between A.D. 101 and 107, the Emperor Trajan conquered the mountain fastnesses of the Carpathians, and handed on to his successors the imperial province of Dacia. But the Romans held Dacia for little more than a century and a half. Under the Emperor Aurelian (A.D. 270–275) the Roman legions were withdrawn. How deep and lasting was the Roman influence in Dacia has since been a matter of bitter controversy.

It was the Romans who conquered the Balkan peninsula, but the dominant cultural influences over much of the area were Greek. Under the Emperor Diocletian (A.D. 284–305) the Roman Empire was divided. A line running from Sirmium, on the Sava above Beograd, up the Sava valley for a short distance, and then south to the Adriatic Sea near Kotor, divided the Western from the Eastern Empire. The area to the west, was nominally ruled from Rome or from one of its successors as capital of the Western Empire. To the east, the Eastern Empire, ruled from Constantinople, merged gradually into the Byzantine. The weakness of imperial rule and the invasion of the Balkan peninsula by the Bulgar, Slav and other peoples, made the precise line of division an entirely academic question; nevertheless, its approximate course has since been an important cultural divide in the Balkan peninsula. To the west lay Rome's field of missionary activity; to the east, that of the Eastern Church. On one side the people are Croat and Catholic, and use a Latin script; on the other, Serb and

Orthodox, and their Cyrillic script was derived in the ninth century from Greek.

Rome quickly lost effective control of the territory lying to the north-west of Diocletian's line of division. It was occupied first by Germanic tribes—Goths and Gepids—and then by Slavs, and Rome itself, abandoned by its emperors, fell prey to barbarian invaders. But it was the Empire's ghostly successor, the Papacy, that in a sense regained the lost territory for the west. Its missionaries coming from Italy and from Austria, attached the Croats and Slovenes to the Church of Rome just as their territory had once belonged to the emperors of the West.

The Byzantine Empire. To the east of Diocletian's line of division, the fortunes of the Byzantine Empire fluctuated for over a thousand years, but, with a tenacity that was little short of miraculous the Empire itself lingered on until its capital at last succumbed to the Turks in 1453.

For much of its history the Byzantine Empire was under pressure from the Slavs and Avars to the north and from the Arabs to the east. The Slav invasions had brought an alien people into the Balkan peninsula, and, despite the claims to theoretical sovereignty over the whole area made by the Emperors, most of the Slav settlers lived beyond the range of effective Byzantine rule. The rise of the First Bulgarian Empire placed a formidable barrier between the core-area of the Byzantine Empire and its remote, Danubian provinces. In the eleventh century the Byzantine emperors reasserted themselves, overthrew the Bulgar state and again broadened the limits of their Empire. But in the twelfth century external pressures again mounted. The attacks of the Bulgars brought about a gradual disintegration of the Empire.

Bulgaria and Serbia became independent kingdoms; quasi-independent principalities arose in the mountains of Albania and Epirus, and fragments of the Empire, strategically placed near the sea, were occupied by the commercial republic of Venice. In 1204 the Fourth Crusade was diverted to an attack on Constantinople, and for over half a century the Eastern Empire was ruled by a Latin prince, and its policy was made subservient to the commercial interests of the West.

Early in the fourteenth century the first Turkish landings had taken place on the Balkan peninsula; the Byzantine state was soon reduced to little more than the coastal lands of the Sea of Marmara. The Byzan-

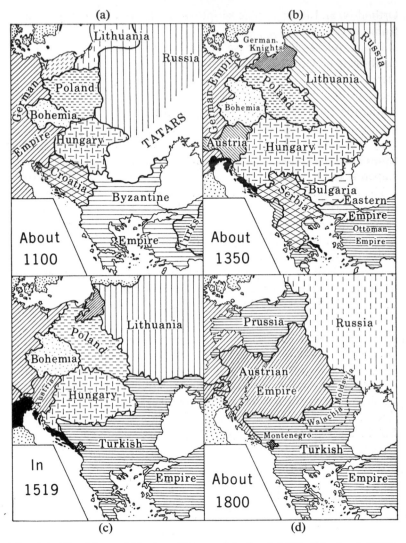

Fig. 3.1. The Map of Eastern Europe (a) about 1100, (b) about 1350, (c) in 1519, (d) about 1800.

tine Empire had been replaced by that of the Ottoman Turks, and in 1453 it came to a formal end with the siege and capture of Constantinople.

Yet Byzantine influence on the Balkan peninsula was not wholly negative. It is true that the road system ceased to be much used; that many of the cities were abandoned during this period, and that even the sites of some are not even known today; that even in areas under direct Byzantine rule, a rigid, quasi-feudal system evolved, and that the best energies of the Byzantine bureaucracy were given to the defence of the Empire. Yet, at the same time, cultural influences spread northward from the Aegean. Cyril and Methodius, missionaries to the Danubian valley, came from Thessaloníki, and the Emperors saw to it that missions permeated the region and converted the majority of the southern Slavs to Christianity and to a spiritual dependence upon Constantinople. Church architecture and monastic organisation in most of the Balkan peninsula and Romania derived from the southeast rather than from the west. And calligraphy followed the faith. Over most of the Balkan peninsula, the Greek or its derivative, the Cyrillic alphabet prevailed, and in Romania it has been replaced by Roman characters only within the last century.

The emergence of the tribal kingdoms
Both within and beyond the rather theoretical limits of the Byzantine Empire, immigrant peoples began to create states of their own. Earliest to emerge was that of the Bulgars, created by a Bulgar aristocracy and a Slav peasantry. The nucleus around which it took shape lay on the undulating, fertile plateau which slopes from the Danube up to the Balkan Mountains. Its limits fluctuated, extending north of the Danube and west of the Serbian Morava during periods of prosperity and power. But to the south of the Bulgarian state there lay the power of the Byzantine emperors, always hostile to the Bulgars. The Byzantine Empire blocked Bulgarian expansion to the south and ultimately destroyed the First Bulgarian Empire. The Bulgars had also to contend with the Serbian tribes to the west and the Avars and later the Magyars to the north.

Despite the hostility between Bulgar and Byzantine, the former came to be attached firmly to the Greek civilisation of the Byzantine Empire. Such an attachment was not, however, implicit in the geography of the Balkan peninsula. The Bulgarian emperors welcomed missionaries from Rome, and it was only the coming of the Magyars, who severed the landward connections with Italy, that ended this flirtation, and exposed the Bulgars to the Christianising influences of Byzantium.

The line which came to divide the region of Europe subjected to the

4

Church of Rome from that which accepted the authority of the Eastern or Orthodox Patriarch ran through the area covered by this book. The forces which shaped it were as much social and political as they were geographical, but the course which it assumed became ultimately one of the most divisive of all boundaries in Eastern Europe. It must be remembered, however, that for several centuries the hostility with which the Patriarch and the Pope viewed one another was more diplomatic than it was doctrinal. There was no formal schism between them until the late eleventh century, and the rupture did not become absolute until after attempts to heal it had failed in the fifteenth.

The Slavs, whose social organisation at the time of their invasion was tribal, began at a relatively early date to build broader political organisations, in which we may recognise their earliest states. After the Bulgar state, the next to arise was the little known Slav state of Samo. Samo may himself have been a Frankish adventurer, but the area over which he exercised a short-lived rule lay on the western margin of the Pannonian Plain, and embraced Lower Austria and Moravia. It was terminated by the attacks of the Avars in the late seventh century. But Avar power also did not long endure. The Avars, a conquering aristocracy, like the Bulgars with whom they were at one time closely associated, succumbed to the Franks in the 790s, and disappeared from recorded history.

A second Slav State arose to fill the vacuum left by the Avars. This, the state of Great Moravia, held greater promise, or at least its promise is better known to us today. Like its predecessor, it embraced the western parts of the Pannonian Plain, and was ruled for much of the ninth century from its capital of Nitra, in Slovakia. Great Moravia was converted to Christianity by the missionaries—Cyril and Methodius—from the Byzantine Empire. They were Greeks from Thessaloníki, who had learned the Slav language from the invaders of the Balkans and had invented a script—first the Glagolitic and then the Cyrillic—in which to express it.

The schism between the Eastern and Western churches had not yet arisen, but the two competed in far from friendly rivalry for the souls of the Slavs of Great Moravia. The Western church won this spiritual struggle not, as might have been supposed, because of Great Moravia's closer proximity to Italy and Rome than to Byzantium, but rather because the Magyar invasion cut the Moravians off from their more easterly spiritual fountain-head.

The Byzantine missionaries withdrew south of the Danube and there completed the conversion of the Bulgars and Serbs. It was at this time that the Cyrillic alphabet and the church liturgy in the Slavonic language became general over the south-eastern Balkans and from here spread northward into Romania.

Italian missionaries, reinforced by German, Frankish and even Irish, entered the East European region from the west, attaching most of it to the Roman Church. Conversion came at an early date south of the Danube; the Czechs and Poles began to be converted in the tenth century but the Hungarians not until the beginning of the eleventh; in the remote and mountainous regions conversion to Christianity was doubtless delayed very much longer, and the Lithuanians did not succumb until the late fourteenth century. The line which came ultimately to divide affiliation with the Orthodox Church from that with the church of Rome bears in part a certain similarity to the division of the Roman Empire under Diocletian. Both, in some degree, reflect the relative ease and difficulty of communication and access from Rome and Constantinople. But it must not be forgotten, especially by those who perceive a kind of geographical inevitability in this development, how nearly the missionaries from the east came to controlling the minds of the Moravians, ancestors of many of the Czechs and Austrians.

The Serb state. During the period of its greatness the Bulgarian Empire had embraced the Serbs, but with its decline the Serb tribes grew more restless and more united among themselves. In the twelfth century the Serbs gained their independence and created a state with its focus in the hills and upland basins of Raška, in part the present Kosovo-Metohija Autonomous Region. For a time the Serbian Empire overshadowed the Bulgarian, until both were eclipsed by the coming of the Turks in the fourteenth century.

The neighbours of the Serbs to the west and north-west were the closely related Croats and Slovenes. Throughout their history they had been exposed to Western influences. Surviving Roman settlements along the Dalmatian coast were reinforced by later Italian immigrants. Venice established colonies here, and the Frankish Empire of Charlemagne and its successor, the Holy Roman Empire of the German Nation, asserted its supremacy but never succeeded in enforcing its authority.

A somewhat amorphous Croatian state was formed under its native dukes and later kings. Lying between the Franks and the Bulgars, its

opportunities of expansion were limited, and early in the twelfth
century Croatia was overwhelmed by the Hungarians, under whose
control it was to remain until the defeat and humiliation of the
Hungarian kingdom in the First World War.

The Hungarian state. The Magyar tribes came out of the Russian
Steppe and settled in the Hungarian Plain in the closing years of the
ninth century. The tribes of which they were composed gradually
merged to form a nation; their transhumant and nomadic practices
became restricted, and were then abandoned, and about a century
after their arrival the Hungarians accepted Christianity. For over six
centuries the Hungarian state was one of the more stable elements in
the political geography of Eastern Europe. Its boundaries fluctuated
with its relations with the Slav peoples which bordered it, and for most
of the period from its foundation, about 900, to its overthrow by the
Turks in 1526, Hungary embraced the Slavs of Slovakia and Croatia
as well as most of the miscellaneous peoples of the Transylvanian
basin of Romania.

The Czech state. For most of their history the Slovaks were under
the rule of the Hungarians, but the Czechs, escaping this servitude,
were able to create one of the more illustrious of the states of medieval
Europe. Like most other Slav states, that of the Czechs was created by
the fusion of groups of continuous and related tribes. In Bohemia
this was accomplished in two stages, first the unification of western
Bohemia under the Přemysl family and of eastern under the Slavnici,
and then, with the extermination of the latter in the tenth century, the
whole region became united under the Přemyslids. From the beginning German influences were strong in Bohemia. The territory became
a kind of march, or border state, helping to guard the eastern approaches to the Reich. After the extinction of the Přemyslids, German
kings alternated with native Czech princes on the throne of Bohemia,
and the most illustrious of them, Charles IV (1346–78), was not only
Holy Roman Emperor, but also the son of that blind King John whose
devotion to all things French led him to his death against the English
on the battlefield of Crécy.

It is possible to see in the Hussite revolt and the religious wars of the
fifteenth century a popular rising against this growing German infiltration into Bohemia. The exploits of the Czech leader, Jan Žiška,
have never ceased to inspire Czech nationalism, and the outcome of
the struggle was the election to the throne of Bohemia of a native
Czech, George of Poděbrady. But this success was shortlived, reflecting

mainly the weakness of Germany at this time. During the sixteenth and seventeenth centuries, the Germans, under Habsburg leadership, established their control on the Czech people.

The Polish state. The Polish state originated in the region still called Wielkopolska or 'Great Poland'.[1] The Slav tribes inhabiting the area enclosed on most sides by the wide, marshy valleys of the Warta and Noteć, united in the middle years of the tenth century. The state which they created at this time extended its authority westward to the Oder, southward into Silesia and southward into Małopolska, or 'Little Poland', the rich farmland that stretches from Kraków eastward.

During the early centuries of its existence Poland expanded its territory eastward into what is today Byelorussia and the Ukraine. Until the seventeenth century, it met with little resistance. The Russians were remote and the Lithuanians ill-organised. The dynasty which had ruled Poland since the tenth century became extinct in the male line in 1370, with the death of Kazimierz I. After an interval of a few years, his heiress carried the Polish crown to Jagiełło, prince of Lithuania. The Jagiełłos ruled Poland and Lithuania until their line ended in 1572, first as two separate states and after 1569 as a united Polish–Lithuanian 'republic'.

Despite encroachments by the Germans from the west, the Polish–Lithuanian state reached at this time its greatest extent, extending eastward to beyond the Dnepr and north-east into present-day Latvia.

For a period of several centuries, from about the tenth century until the Turkish invasions, much of Eastern Europe was made up, in the main, of a series of independent states. It would be anachronistic to call them nation-states, though they did tend to reflect the existence of individual nations. Nationalism certainly had no mass appeal at this time, though the landed and educated classes were beginning to conceive of themselves as members of distinct national groups.

Empires in Eastern Europe

Scarcely had these native states appeared on the map of Eastern Europe when they began to be eroded by the encroachment of the empires which lay around their borders. The German sphere to the west encroached gradually and slowly on the Slavic and did not reach its maximum extent until the end of the eighteenth century; the

---

[1] The medieval name was *Polonia Major*, 'Greater Poland'.

Russian to the east even seemed for centuries to be at the mercy of the western Slavs; Moscow was occupied by the Poles early in the seventeenth century. But later in this same century the tide turned, and the flood-tide of Russian conquest flowed westward, stemmed the advance of the Germans and absorbed most of the Polish state.

The Turks descended on the Balkans in the fourteenth century, and quickly overran most of the region lying to the south of the Danube. Then, subjugating Hungary, they attacked Vienna for the first time in 1529. For a century and a half the Turkish forces occupied the Hungarian Plain, their advanced lines only a few miles downstream from the Austrian capital. In 1683 the Turks again besieged Vienna. It is symbolic of the unity of the whole region in the face of Turkish attack that it was Polish forces, under their king, Jan Sobieski, who came to the rescue of the beleaguered city. But this was not the only point of contact between the Poles and the Turks. They had met and had fought protracted and cruel campaigns along the loess belt that curves around the outer foothills of the Carpathian Mountains.

The defeat of the Turks before the walls of Vienna was the prelude to their retreat across the Hungarian Plain, beyond the Danube and down through the Balkans. They were followed by the advancing Austrians, who created over much of the area, formerly occupied by the Turks, the wide, polyglot empire of the Habsburgs. To each of these empires we must now turn.

The Turkish Empire. The Ottoman Turks came out of Central Asia, across the mountains of Armenia and into Anatolia in the thirteenth century. Here they mingled with the Seljuk Turks who had emerged from Asia several centuries earlier. The Byzantine Empire, weakened by long wars, a bureaucratic government, and the depredations of Christian crusaders from the west, was in no position to resist them. In 1345 the Turks first set foot on European soil; a few years later they came to settle and soon had occupied Thrace and the mountainous south of Bulgaria, known as Rumelia. The massive fortifications and the easily defended site of Constantinople deterred them, but they pushed up through the Balkans, occupied Sofia and at Kosovo, in 1389, overthrew the Serbian state.

The Turks were not numerous; they settled few of their own peoples in the Balkans, and recruited their army from the tribute of children which they exacted at intervals from their conquered subjects. After the subjugation of Serbia their advance was checked, though it was the assault of Tamurlane on their rear in Asia Minor, rather than the resistance of the Balkan peoples that halted them. By the mid-fifteenth century they were again ready to advance their frontier in Europe. Bosnia and Hercegovina fell before them; they reached the Danube along a broad front, from Beograd to the Black Sea, perhaps driving before them the Vlachs of Bulgaria who went to reinforce those already living across the river in Walachia. Then they occupied Walachia itself, while, back on the Bosporus, their armies besieged and captured the city of Constantinople, which they had long cut off from the rest of the Balkan peninsula.

The Turks as rulers were generally tolerant and always inefficient, and, although they welcomed conversion to Islam, they did little to encourage it. Indeed, their coming was sometimes even welcomed by the common peasantry. Among those who gladly received the Turks were the Bogomils, a heretical group in Bosnia, which had been savagely persecuted by the kings of Hungary and the Catholic Church. Indeed, those that remained of the puritanical Bogomils tended to embrace the equally austere creed of Islam. Today these areas of Bosnia and Hercegovina, in which the Bogomil funeral monuments are most common, are no less noteworthy for their mosques and their Islamic faith.

Under Turkish rule Western catholicism disappeared from much of the Balkan peninsula, where it had never been particularly strong. But beyond the limit of medieval Turkish conquest, Roman catholicism entrenched itself, and from the regions of the north—Croatia, Slovenia, Hungary—it was never dislodged by the subsequent and short-lived Turkish invasions. It was not until a century after the Serbian collapse that the Turks again prepared to advance. Croatia was overrun, the Hungarian Plain invaded, and in 1526 the Hungarian state overthrown at the Battle of Mohács. Buda was captured, and Vienna threatened. At about the same time the Turks advanced northward from the Danube delta in Moldavia and Bessarabia, and extended their authority around the shores of the Black Sea until it met that of the Tatar Khans of the Crimea.

But Turkish authority was not felt equally in all parts of the vast empire of the Turks. Their numbers were too small for effective control over all of it. They maintained garrisons and controlled the routeways, but the more rugged areas escaped their control. The mountains of Montenegro were never effectively conquered and formed an independent principality under their prince-bishops until they were incorporated into Yugoslavia in 1919. The mountains of Albania were only theoretically a part of the Turkish Empire, and the Albanian tribesmen remained in most respects a law to themselves throughout this period. In Romania also the authority of the Turks was at times little more than nominal, and consisted in sending periodic expeditions to levy taxes and exact promises of obedience.

The Austro-Hungarian Empire. The Turkish assault on Vienna in 1683 marked the high tide of military success for the Turkish Empire. But it failed, and with the retreat of the Turkish armies from the city the true weakness of the Ottoman Empire lay revealed. The Austrians in alliance with Poles and Russians prepared for an all-out attack on the Turks. Three years later Buda was taken, after having been in the hands of the Turks for over a century and a half. Before the end of the century, the Hungarian Plain was cleared of Turks, with the exception of the Banat at its south-eastern extremity, and Transylvania and Croatia were brought under Austrian rule. A few years later, by the Treaty of Passarowitz of 1718, the rest of the Hungarian Plain and a small part of Walachia were occupied. The frontier of the Turkish Empire had been forced back approximately to the line which it had followed in the fifteenth century, and here, with but little modification it was to remain until the nineteenth century.

During the sixteenth and seventeenth centuries the Austrian Habsburgs succeeded in creating a vast empire mainly in the Danube valley. This they did in part by inheriting the Czech lands, in part by driving back the Turks and taking over the lands which they vacated. The Czech lands passed under Habsburg rule in 1526, when the Austrian Archduke Ferdinand was elected by the Czech nobles to occupy the throne of Bohemia in succession to Lewis, who had fallen at Mohács. Rather less than a century later the Czech nobles, clinging to the principle that the crown of Bohemia was elective, attempted to switch their loyalty from the house of Habsburg to a ruler more tolerant of their religious heterodoxy. It was the suppression of this Czech revolt which precipitated the Thirty Years' War. In the course of the struggle the Czech aristocracy was virtually destroyed, and an Austrian ruling and landowning class was imposed upon the Czech lands, where it remained in power until 1918. The other Austrian territorial gains were at the expense of the Turks. They embraced the Hungarian Plain, with Transylvania to the east and Croatia to the south-west. To these were added in the late nineteenth century the provinces of Bosnia and Hercegovina.

Drang nach Osten. Unlike other forms of domination and control of Eastern Europe, that of the Germans began with the slow, un-recorded eastward creep of German peasants. Land hunger, rein-forced perhaps by the desire to escape feudal restrictions in the west, drove them on. The limits of sovereignty were ill-defined at this time, and the Slav lands were thinly peopled. It was not difficult for German farming communities to infiltrate the Polish area, and, with the lapse of time, to intermarry with, and impose their language upon, their Slav neighbours. It was in ways such as this that the frontier of German settlement moved eastward from the Elbe to the Oder, and from the Oder eastward into Pomerania, Prussia and Silesia.

Not all the area embraced within the frontier of German settlement was Germanised in this way. Islands of Slavs remained. Some, like the Polabians along the lower Elbe, have disappeared by assimilation only in recent years; others, like the Lusatian Sorbs, who live in the marshy country to the south-east of Berlin, still retain many elements including language, of their ancient culture. Nor was this eastward movement of the German language achieved only by peasants. At all periods, from the twelfth century to the eighteenth, it was accompanied by the organised creation of German colonies and the foundation of commercial cities as a part of public policy. The settlement of the Baltic coastlands east of the Vistula by the German military orders—the Teutonic Knights and the Knights of the Sword—and their penetration of the East Prussian hinterland is a medieval example of a more ambitious programme of conquest and colonisation. Similarly, in the eighteenth century Frederick the Great established agricultural colonies in the newly-conquered province of Silesia, not so much to Germanise as simply to develop its resources.

The map, Fig. 2.2, shows in a simple and highly generalised form this eastward progress of German settlement and culture. It must always be remembered that at no time were the two cultural worlds, the Germanic and the Slav, sharply divided. The one merged into the other through a region of mixed language and divided loyalties, where governmental pressure could tip the balance in either direction, as in fact, it did in the late nineteenth and early twentieth centuries. National loyalties were rarely as strongly felt or as clear-cut as many who took part in the Paris Conference of 1919 tended to assume.

The partial settlement and Germanisation of the lands of the western Slavs was followed by their political absorption into the German realm. The lands between the Elbe and Oder were brought under German control long before the Middle Ages ended. Silesia,

4*

transferred from Poland to Bohemia in the fourteenth century, passed with the latter under Austrian rule. In 1741 it was conquered by Frederick the Great, and was annexed to the Kingdom of Prussia, of which most of it remained a part until 1945.

Prussia, in origin the lands of the Teutonic Order, was secularised by its last Grand Master during the Reformation, and in 1618 passed into the hands of the Hohenzollerns of Brandenburg. At the end of the Thirty Years' War much of Pomerania was also acquired by Prussia, and in the course of the Partitions of Poland, between 1772 and 1795, Prussia advanced her boundary to include much of present-day Poland, including its capital city of Warsaw.

The Russian Empire. The Russian Empire was the last to encroach on the territory of Eastern Europe, but its influence has been more profound than that of any. Unlike the other imperial peoples who have at times dominated and controlled Eastern Europe, the Russians were themselves Slavs, deriving their language and culture from the same Slavic ancestors as the Poles, Czechs and Yugoslavs. Intermittently, and for their own profit, they furthered the ideals of Slav unity, or Panslavism. Yet the cultural gulf that in fact separated the Russian peoples from their Polish neighbours was no less deep than that which divided the Poles from the Germans. The traditions of both peoples were those of mutual hostility. Early in the seventeenth century Polish armies had occupied Moscow; the two peoples had fought for control of the Ukraine, and large areas of White Russia and the Ukraine had been carved up into great estates where a Polish aristocracy ruled harshly and cruelly over a Slav, but non-Polish peasantry.

The Poles had extended their authority and control through this area during the later Middle Ages, and reached their farthest limits in the seventeenth century. The government of Poland had been either wise or fortunate during the sixteenth and seventeenth centuries. The country had escaped involvement in any major wars and had thus avoided the destruction that had fallen upon Germany. During the second half of the seventeenth century this changed. We have already noted how a revived and revitalised Prussia encroached on Poland. Now the Swedes, Russians, and Turks, in a combined assault on Poland (1655–1667), known appropriately as *Potop*—the 'Deluge'—brought Poland to her knees. Russia first occupied the parts of the Polish-Lithuanian kingdom lying beyond the Dnepr, and a century later participated in the series of Partitions of Poland which netted for the Tsars well over half the total area of this vast country.

When the last Partition was concluded in 1795 by an agreement between the three rapacious powers and forced upon the representatives of the Polish nation, the last internationally recognised state disappeared from Eastern Europe. Only in the mountains of Montenegro and neighbouring Albania was any semblance preserved of independence and autonomy. Elsewhere the peoples of Eastern Europe: Slav, Hungarian, Romanian, Greek, lived under the rule of Prussian or Austrian, Russian or Turk.

The extinction of the last independent state in Eastern Europe did not terminate the period of boundary conflicts and claims to territory. Russia continued to press against Turkish territory to the north of the Black Sea. In 1812 the Russians occupied Bessarabia, thus beginning a movement toward the Balkan peninsula which was to dominate the history of this region during the nineteenth century. But already Eastern Europe was beginning to experience that wave of nationalism which was, in the early years of the twentieth century to complete the overthrow of all four of the old-style empires, and to create in their place a tier of weak and quarrelsome, but sovereign and independent states.

Bibliography

CAHNMAN, WERNER J. 'Frontiers between East and West in Europe', *Geogrl J.* **49** (1949), 605–24.

CONDURACHI, EMILE, 'Les influences grecques et romaines dans les Balkans en Hongroie et en Pologne,' *Le Rayonnement des Civilisations Grecques et Romaines sur les Cultures Périphériques*, 8ᵉ Congrès International d'Archéologie Classique, Paris, 1965, 317–32.

DROZ, JACQUES, *L'Europe Centrale*, Paris, Payot, 1960.

DVORNIK, FRANCIS, *The Slavs: Their Early History and Civilization*, Boston, American Academy of Arts and Sciences, 1956.

— *The Slavs in European History and Civilization*, New Brunswick, N.J., Rutgers University Press, 1962.

ERICKSON, JOHN, *Panslavism*, London, Historical Association, 1964.

HALECKI, OSCAR, *Borderlands of Western Civilization*, New York, Ronald Press, 1952.

IONESCU, GHITA, *The Break-up of the Soviet Empire in Eastern Europe*, Harmondsworth, Penguin Books, 1965.

JELAVICH, CHARLES, *Tsarist Russia and Balkan Nationalism: Russian Influence in the Internal Affairs of Bulgaria and Serbia, 1879–1886*, University of California Press, 1958.

JELAVICH, CHARLES and BARBARA JELAVICH, *The Balkans*, Englewood Cliffs, NJ, Prentice-Hall, 1965.

JELAVICH, BARBARA, *A Century of Russian Foreign Policy 1814–1914*, Philadelphia, J. B. Lippincott Co., 1964.

LEWIN, PERCY EVANS, *The German Road to the East*, London, Doran, 1917.

LUKACS, JOHN A. *The Great Powers and Eastern Europe*, New York, American Book Co., 1953.

MARRIOTT, J. A. R. *The Eastern Question: An Historical Study in European Diplomacy*, Oxford University Press, 1924.

NAUMANN, FRIEDRICH, *Central Europe*, London, P. S. King, 1916.

NEWBIGIN, MARION L. *Geographical Aspects of Balkan Problems*, London, Constable, 1915.

OBOLENSKY, DMITRI. *The Bogomils: a Study in Balkan neo-Manichaeism*, Cambridge University Press, 1948.

OSTROGORSKY, G. 'Byzantium and the South Slavs', *The Slavonic and East European Review*, **42** (1963), 1–14.

SHEPHERD, GORDON, *Russia's Danubian Empire*, London, Heinemann, 1954.

STAVRIANOS, L. S. *The Balkans since 1453*, New York, Rinehart & Co., 1958.

TAYLOR, A. J. P. *The Hapsburg Monarchy*, 1815–1918, London, Macmillan, 1941.

WOLFF, ROBERT L. *The Balkans in Our Time*, Oxford University Press, 1956.

CHAPTER FOUR

The Nation-State in Eastern Europe

The nineteenth century was in Eastern Europe the century of national-ism, when new states were created and old long vanished states, re-appeared on the European map. It was a century when the sense of nationhood, the feeling of belonging to the linguistic and cultural group, spread downward from the intelligentsia and middle classes which first experienced it, to the mass of the common people. It was the 'Springtime of the Nations', when hopes welled high among the peoples of Eastern Europe for freedom and independence. The Paris settlement of 1919–20 marked the summer time of these nations. They then reached their fullest territorial expansion; they discovered that independence from imperial control does not necessarily bring har-mony, and that a petty Ruritanian boss can be as oppressive as a Turkish Sultan or a Russian Tsar. They then passed into their autumn, when new empires developed to west and east of them. They fought and survived the German and the Russian attacks to enjoy a short St Martin's summer, and were then swallowed up into a new winter of Soviet occupation and control. Only in the last year or two has a new spring begun to break.

This chapter is concerned with the political geography of Eastern Europe during this period of the rise, flowering and decline of the nation-states of Eastern Europe. It will trace the emergence of the states-system of this area and will examine the changing patterns of political influence and control.

THE NINETEENTH CENTURY

The states of the Balkans
In 1795 Poland disappeared from the map. Only eight years later revolt broke out in the Šumadija, in the Turkish province of Serbia. It was led by Karageorge, himself an itinerant dealer in pigs which were raised in the oak-woods of Serbia and sold to the Austrians. The rising was very far from being an unqualified success, but the Turks never

afterwards really regained control of all Serbia, and in 1833 acknowledged the autonomy of the Serbian state, now under the rule of Miloš
Obrenovič.

The Greek revolt began later than the Serbian, and ended sooner,
with the creation in 1829 of the Greek state. In 1858 the Romanian
principalities of Walachia and Moldavia elected the same prince and
merged to form the nucleus of modern Romania. Twenty years later
the Principality of Bulgaria was created, but only after the spirited
revolt of the Bulgars had stimulated both the Russian Tsar and the
rulers of the western states to aid them. All these states had been
created at the expense of the decadent and moribund empire of the
Turkish Sultans.

'*The sick man of Europe*'. The legend of the 'noble Turk' had evaporated, and travellers in the Balkans during the nineteenth century were
loud in their condemnation of the evils of Turkish rule. The Turks, it is
true, made little attempt to obliterate the native Balkan cultures; but
the grinding Turkish tax-collector; the tribute of children to supply the
Janissaries, at least until the bloody suppression of the latter in 1826;
the heavy-handed Turkish bureaucracy and its opposition to all progress and change, prepared the people for revolution.

The geographical location of the Balkan peninsula insured that the
problems of the Balkans could never be left to be settled between the
native peoples and the Turks themselves. The decline in Turkish power
created a power vacuum into which others among the Great Powers
attempted to move, so that the Balkans became, and remained for
much of the nineteenth century, the focus of a power struggle between
them.

Briefly, Tsarist Russia had long cast envious eyes on the Turkish
Straits. Since Russia had in 1739 acquired the port of Azov, the right
to navigate Turkish waters had been important to her. In 1774, by the
Treaty of Kuchuk Kainarji, the Russians gained the right to navigate
the Straits freely, and at the same time, assumed the obligation to protect the Christian subjects of the Sultan. Given the anarchic and oppressive conditions that generally prevailed, this was an open invitation to the Tsar to intervene in the affairs of the Turkish Empire
whenever he wished. At the same time, however, the Turks maintained
fortifications along the shores of the Bosporus, and claimed—and
after 1841 were allowed by their allies to exercise—the right to exclude
warships of other nations from the Straits even in time of peace.

Strategic requirements made it necessary for the Russians to interest themselves in the affairs of the Balkans. Their policy was to have friendly and, if possible, subservient states in this area who would look after Russia's interests. At the same time, Austria which had advanced into the Balkan peninsula in the wake of the retreating Turks, also saw this as a route-way leading to the Mediterranean, to the Middle East, and on to India. Austria by herself might not have been particularly effective, but, backed by the military power and commercial influence of Germany, she could play an important role in the Balkans. Lastly there were Great Britain and France, important in the Mediterranean even before the opening of the Suez Canal, and thereafter dedicated to keeping the Mediterranean open for their commerce. Both had reason to fear the southward-driving power of both Russia and Austria, and, however distasteful such a policy might be, both aimed to support the decadent Turks as a barrier against both.

The Balkan states. With the exception of the creation of the Kingdom of Greece, there was, in fact, little change in the political geography of the area south of the Danube between the Serbian revolt and the year 1876, when the Bulgarian revolt broke out. A generation before this a Russian bid to increase her influence in the region of the Straits met with strong Anglo-French resistance, and culminated in the Crimean War (1853–56). This held the Russians back from the gates of Constantinople, but the uneasy equilibrium could not last much longer. In 1875 revolt broke out in Bulgaria and further to the west in the mountains of Bosnia and Hercegovina. It was suppressed with a savagery which, as reported in the West, outraged public opinion. W. E. Gladstone, the leader of the Liberal opposition in the British Parliament, called for the expulsion of the Turks 'one and all, bag and baggage . . . from the province they have desolated and profaned'. But it was the Russian Tsar who came to the aid of the Bulgars. His armies crossed the Danube, defeated the Turkish army and dictated the Treaty of San Stefano. By the terms of this treaty a Bulgarian state was created that did more than justice to the most ambitious of Bulgarian claims (Fig. 4.1). It stretched from the Danube to the Aegean, and from the Black Sea to Lake Ohrid and the mountains of Albania, and in area rivalled the medieval Bulgarian Empire at its greatest extent. This territorial claim reflected the Bulgarian—and the Russian—thinking on the area of the Bulgarian ethnic group. But this latter certainly included a number of Serbs, many Greeks, Turks and Albanians, and assimilated to the Bulgars the whole group which we now know as Macedonian.

An overriding factor in the creation of 'Great' Bulgaria at this time was Russia's determination to control as wide an area as possible on the route to Constantinople. It was this, rather than any ethnic considerations, which led the Western powers to protest with such vigour, that the Russians were obliged to abandon their extreme position. A conference met at Berlin in 1878, with, amongst other tasks, the obligation to cut 'Great' Bulgaria down to size and at the same time to do justice to the legitimate claims of the Bulgars. A principality

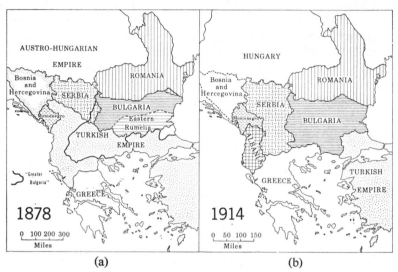

(a)   (b)

Fig. 4.1. (a) The Balkans after the Berlin Congress of 1878, showing the extent of the Bulgarian state created by the Treaty of San Stefano. (b) The Balkans after the conclusion of the Balkan Wars, and before the outbreak of the First World War. Both maps are based mainly on C. Grant Robertson and J. G. Bartholomew, *An Historical Atlas of Modern Europe*, Oxford, 1924.

of Bulgaria was established stretching from the Danube southward to the crest of the Balkan Mountains, and thus including the core-area of the first Bulgar state. Toward the west, however, it stretched south of the mountains to include the whole of the Iskâr valley, with the city of Sofia, and the headwaters of the River Struma. It excluded the Marica valley which was established as an autonomous province, known as Eastern Rumelia, within the Ottoman Empire.

At the same time Serbia was conciliated by a small accession of territory, including the city of Niš, and the extent of Montenegro was increased—both changes at the expense of Turkey. An important clause also was that which allowed Austria-Hungary to garrison and govern the provinces of Bosnia and Hercegovina. The rivalry between Austria and Russia required that any concession to the one should be compensated by a concession to the other. But this was not the chief reason; as a result of the Berlin agreement, the area under Turkish rule between Serbia and Montenegro was narrowed to a corridor, only forty miles wide. This was the Sanjak, or county, of Novi Pazar. It contained the upper Ibar valley, through which the Austrians and their German backers hoped to build a railway from Central Europe through the Balkans to the Middle East. Austria did not at this time gain possession of the Sanjak, though she did obtain the right to station a garrison in Novi Pazar and thus to hold the route-way open until she should be ready to use. it. At the same time Serbia was held back from joining up with the fellow-Serb state of Montenegro and thus from creating a great southern Slav state that might indefinitely block Austrian ambitions in this direction.

The Berlin settlement of 1878 did not contain the elements of permanence. The Serbian and Bulgarian peoples remained divided, and a considerable number of each lived still under Turkish rule. To the south, the Greeks aimed to extend their territory by incorporating Thessaly and even Macedonia, and at the same time the Russians and Austrians pursued their schemes for greater political control of the Balkans.

Gladstone had prophesied that the strongest bulwark against Russian imperialism in the Balkans would be 'the breasts of free men'. The Bulgars, once they had achieved independence, proved to be far from subservient to the Russians who had assisted them. In 1885 a revolt broke out in Eastern Rumelia, aiming to unite this province with the Principality of Bulgaria. It was successful. The Great Powers objected to this change in the delicate balance which they had been at such pains to establish in the Balkans, but nevertheless they recognised this extension of the boundaries of Bulgaria.

There followed a lull of over 25 years, interrupted only when Austria in 1908 turned her occupation of Bosnia and Hercegovina into absolute sovereignty over these areas. The railway from Vienna was completed to Constantinople, but by way of Beograd and Sofia, and German railway imperialism was intensified in the Balkans and Middle East. The Slavs, Greeks and Albanians who still lived under Turkish rule became more restless, and the 'Young Turk' movement, which aimed at reforming the government of the Ottoman Empire only increased their alarm lest an efficient administration replace the incompetent rule of the Sultan. Bulgars and Greeks aimed to drive the Turks from the territory which they claimed for themselves. The Serbs hoped not only to gain the Raška area and much of Macedonia and Albania from the Turks, but also to drive the Austrians from Bosnia and Hercegovina, and thus to build up a great Serb state which in area might rival the medieval kingdom of Stefan Dušan. All these hopes and ambitions culminated in the events of 1912–14.

The Balkan wars. In 1912 the four Balkan states of Serbia, Bulgaria, Greece and Montenegro combined for a grand attack on the Turks. They were remarkably successful, and the Turks were left with only a small foothold in Europe, when peace was made in 1913. The unity which inspired the Balkan states at once evaporated as their individual ambitions came into sharp conflict.

Foremost among these was Serbia's ambition to gain access to the coast, to establish a port and to engage in seaborne trade. From the southern borders of the region inhabited by Serbs two rivers flowed to the sea: the Vardar southward to the Aegean near the port of Thessaloníki, and the Drin westward across the mountains of Albania to the Adriatic Sea near Shkodër in present-day Albania. The former was a wide and open route, but at its extremity the port of Thessaloníki was Greek in sympathy and was now also in Greek possession. Furthermore, it traversed Macedonia to which the Bulgars had laid claim in 1875 and to which they now renewed their pretentions.

The route to the west was technically far more difficult. It had been opened up by the Romans, and its course was in part followed by their road from the Adriatic coast to Thrace. It was then abandoned, and to this day has never been used regularly. Nevertheless, it was upon this route that the Serbs placed their hopes. Politically it seemed to present fewer difficulties. The Albanian tribesmen showed little cohesiveness and their national ambitions had barely been made articulate. Turkish control was feeble and ineffective, and the Serbs confidently expected to drive down to the sea. They ran, however, not into the resistance of the Turks, but into that of the Western Powers. Italy had ambitions to control the area opposite the heel of Italy; the Austrians and Hungarians, who had access to the head of the Adriatic Sea, had no desire to have their enemies, the Serbs, on one shore of its narrow southern entrance. The result was the Conference of London of 1913, at which it was agreed to confer independence upon the territory which none of them could willingly see occupied by any other.

It should not, however, be assumed that there was no reason, other than the contemporary political balance, for the creation of Albania. The Albanians were a distinctive people, in fact one of the most individual in all Eastern Europe. They had a long history and a great oral tradition; they had little love for any of their neighbours, and they had produced a number of national leaders who had tried, generally unsuccessfully, to rouse their national ambitions. The chief criticism of the creation of the Albanian state was, not that it did not reflect the aspirations of a national group, but that this group lacked cohesion and was politically immature.

Thus was solved the question of a Serbian outlet westward. There remained the questions of Macedonia, Thrace and access to the Aegean Sea. The Turks had been driven out, and their fortresses captured, but the victors had abundant reason to dispute among themselves the possession of the newly conquered territory. The conflicts arose in part from the confused ethnic pattern of the territory in question, in part from claims based on the extent of medieval empires, and in part also on claims of a more technical order, such as the demand for access to the sea and possession of a port.

The Second Balkan War broke out within a few weeks of the conclusion of the First. Ostensibly it resulted from the territorial claims of Bulgaria; it culminated in a struggle between Bulgaria and all her neighbours, including Romania, and in Bulgaria's loss of a considerable area that she had gained during the First Balkan War.

The map that emerged in 1914, after the conclusion of the Second Balkan War showed a remarkable change (Fig. 4.1). European Turkey was reduced to an area of only 9,120 square miles, which today remains as Turkey-in-Europe. Serbia had advanced southward to include much of Macedonia. Bulgaria, despite her losses, ended the struggle with north-eastern Macedonia and eastern Thrace in her possession, together with a foothold on the Aegean Sea and the indifferent port of Dede Agach. Greece occupied western Thrace, the rest of Macedonia and a large tract of mountainous country near the Albanian border, and Montenegro, lastly, rounded off her small territory. But none were satisfied. Serbia aimed to incorporate at least the Serb lands of Bosnia and Hercegovina, lying within the limits of the Austro-Hungarian Empire, and Bulgaria still nourished her ambitions in Macedonia and Thrace. Out of these grievances was to grow the First World War.

North of the Danube

Change came slower to the north of the Danube, not because the forces of nationalism were less strong, but because the rule of the Prussian, Austrian and Russian empires was more rigorous and able to suppress an incipient revolt before it got out of hand. Nevertheless, the western Slavs and Hungarians possessed a greater political maturity than the turbulent southern Slavs, and a larger capacity for orderly self-government.

During the years between the extinction of the Polish 'Republic' in 1795 and the outbreak of the First World War, only three changes in the political geography of this region call for comment. One was the attempt to revive a Polish state; the second, the creation of a Hungarian kingdom within the Habsburg monarchy, and the third, the formation of Romania.

Poland. A Polish state was re-created by Napoleon in 1807 from the territory occupied by Prussia and Austria in the Partitions. This was the Grand Duchy of Warsaw, whose chief purpose was to win for Napoleon the support of the Polish people. It was however short-lived. The Polish question presented difficulties at the Vienna Conference in 1815, just as it was to do at the Paris Conference a century later. And at the former, just as at the latter, the settlement reflected the power balance in Central Europe, rather than the justice of Polish claims. Russia was politically dominant in 1815, and the Grand Duchy of Warsaw was entrusted to the Russian Tsar to rule as a Polish principality, separate and distinct from the Russian Empire. But this distinction was a finer one than the Russians were able to draw. In 1831 'Congress' Poland was absorbed into the Russian Empire, where, despite risings, protests and discontent, it remained until that Empire collapsed in 1917.

Hungary. Hungary had been, as we have seen, an independent state throughout the Middle Ages. In the sixteenth century it succumbed to the attacks of the Turks, from whom, in the late seventeenth and eighteenth centuries, it was reconquered by the Austrians and made part of the Habsburg Empire. The Hungarians maintained their language and traditions through these vicissitudes, and were particularly restless under Austrian rule. In 1848 the rising of Louis Kossuth was suppressed only when Austria called in Russia to her aid. It was not until Austria had been weakened by conflict with Prussia that she at last made concessions to the Hungarians. By the *Ausgleich,* or 'Compromise', of 1867, Hungary was politically separated from Austria, but continued to share as its ruler the person of the Habsburg emperor, who was subjected to a separate coronation ceremony with the crown of St Stephen.

The boundaries of Hungary were drawn with more regard to the limits of medieval Hungary than to the realities of the ethnic situation. They included within the Hungarian kingdom not only the province of Slovakia, but also Transylvania and the currently Yugoslav regions of the Vojvodina, Slavonia and Croatia, including much of the Dalmatian coast and the port city of Fiume (Rijeka). Magyars were a minority in the state as thus constituted, but their political domination was undisputed. Magyar repression of Slovaks, Croats and other minority groups was one of the many causes that contributed to the collapse of the Austro-Hungarian monarchy in 1918.

Romania. The third development during these years was the rise of Romania. Turkish supervision over the Romanian principalities of Walachia and Moldavia had never been close. The Romanian nobles had been accustomed to elect their own governors, or *hospodars,* but any greater degree of unity or independence on the part of the Romanian leaders was objectionable to the Western Powers because it would be held to weaken the authority of the Turkish Empire, which they aimed to support against Russia. Nevertheless, in 1859, the two provinces elected the same *hospodar,* and the united Romanian principality was created.

The Romanian leaders at once turned their attention to the Romanians or Walachs living under Austro-Hungarian, Russian and Bulgarian rule. Each of these groups suffered from varying degrees of discrimination, and at a time when a national government was cultivating specifically Romanian characteristics, these were being destroyed beyond the boundaries of Moldavia and Walachia. The Romanian government showed great interest in the Vlach groups of the Balkans as well as in the Romanians of Transylvania and Bessarabia. But the strength of the Austro-Hungarian and Russian empires made any change of boundary in these directions impossible. Change was easier to accomplish to the south, where in 1878 and 1913, Romania annexed areas in the southern Dobrogea. In this direction a few Romanians were brought within the limits of the state at the expense of including also a large number of Bulgars and some Turks.

THE TWENTIETH CENTURY

When the First World War began in 1914, Eastern Europe was strewn with unresolved problems. The legitimate political aspirations of the western Slavs and of many of those of the southern were left unsatisfied; elsewhere boundary problems between the young nation-states were left unresolved. In these difficulties lay both the spark which set off the First World War and also fuel to add to the conflagration.

The Paris settlement

In the Paris settlement of 1919–20 and in later agreements which derived from it, the nations of Eastern Europe reached the high tide of their fortunes. This they owed, on the one hand, to the simultaneous defeat and collapse of the empires of Germany, Austria-Hungary and Russia, and on the other, to the policies of the United States and of the West European countries.

On 8 January 1918, President Woodrow Wilson of the United States proposed certain conditions, the *Fourteen Points*, on which, he suggested, a lasting peace might be based. Among these were:

10. The peoples of Austria-Hungary, whose place among the nations we wish to see safeguarded and assured, should be accorded the freest opportunity of autonomous development.
11. Rumania, Serbia and Montenegro should be evacuated, occupied territories restored, Serbia accorded free and secure access to the sea, and the relations of the several Balkan States to one another determined by friendly counsel along historically established lines of allegiance and nationality, and international guarantees of the political and economic independence and territorial integrity of the several Balkan States should be entered into.
13. An independent Polish State should be erected which should include the territories inhabited by indisputably Polish populations, which should be assured a free and secure access to the sea, and whose political and economic independence and territorial integrity should be guaranteed by international covenant.

In general the allies of the United States, notably France, concurred in these conditions, and the treaties concluded at Paris attempted to implement them.

Woodrow Wilson probably underrated the complexity of the territorial problems, and 'friendly counsel' was a thing in which some of the countries of Eastern Europe were incapable of engaging. We must, however, examine the political map which emerged from the Paris treaties and consider to what extent it satisfied the conditions predicated by Wilson.

Poland. There was no question that the Polish state, partitioned finally in 1795 and revived temporarily by Napoleon, had to be

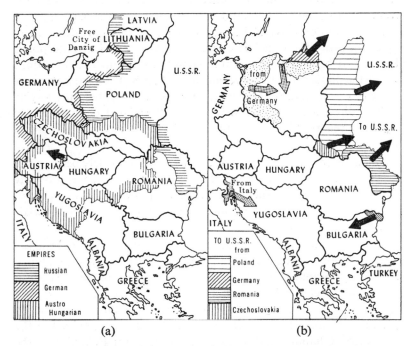

Fig. 4.2. (a) The territorial settlement in Eastern Europe made at the end of the First World War, by the treaties of Versaille, St-Germain, Trianon and Neuilly. (b) The territorial changes made in Eastern Europe during and after the Second World War.

brought back on to the political map of Europe. It lay within the competence of the allies to determine the new boundaries on the north, west and south, but the newly created Union of Soviet Socialist Republics was not represented at the Conference, and the eastern boundary of Poland was thus not a matter for negotiation at Paris. The boundaries determined at the Paris Conference were based in the main on ethnic considerations. The ethnic boundary was nowhere clearcut and in two areas, the Olsztyn (Allenstein) and Kwidzyń

(Marienwerder) districts of East Prussia and the highly industrialised region of Upper Silesia, was the subject of a plebiscite.

A curving line was drawn from the Baltic coast, west of Danzig, to Upper Silesia, leaving Pomerania and Silesia within Germany. The province of East Prussia, its boundaries somewhat modified, was also retained within Germany. The effect of this was to create a 'corridor' from the main body of Poland to the Baltic coast, separating East Prussia from Pomerania. The establishment of this 'corridor' was in agreement with the principle expressed in Wilson's thirteenth point, but it also accorded with ethnic conditions within the 'corridor', where the population was predominantly Polish. The Germans never ceased to assert that the so-called 'corridor' was created only to give Poland direct access to the sea and that it violated German ethnic rights. In reality this was not the case. In the words of Haskins and Lord:

> Poland needs an access to the sea, but it was not solely because she needed it that she obtained it. The Peace Conference probably would not have satisfied this desire if ethnical reasons had not authorized it to do so. The Conference did not invent the 'Corridor': it existed already.[1]

This did not end the question. A corridor to the sea was of little use without a port on the coast, and the only port here was the almost exclusively German city of Danzig (Gdańsk). To hand Danzig over to Poland would clearly have been a violation of German ethnic rights; to leave it in East Prussia would have made the 'corridor' economically useless to Poland. The matter was exacerbated by the refusal of the Danzigers to handle military supplies destined for Poland, and the Polish government resolved that, as soon as the time was opportune, they would build a new port on Polish territory. The solution of the Danzig problem was to separate the city and its immediate environs from both Germany and Poland and to establish it as a 'Free City', under the sovereignty of the League of Nations and the administrative control of a high commissioner appointed by the League, and in customs union with Poland. This compromise pleased no one. The Poles built the rival port of Gdynia, and the Danzigers hoped for reunion with Germany. The division of Germany by the 'corridor' raised technical problems in transport and communications and was highly offensive to the Germans.

[1] C. S. Haskins and R. H. Lord, *Some Problems of the Peace Conference*, Cambridge, Mass., 1920, p. 153.

The port of Memel (Klaipeda) on the other side of East Prussia, fulfilled a similar function to that of Danzig. It was a German city serving a Lithuanian hinterland. Like Danzig, it was given an international status, until, in 1923, Lithuanian forces occupied and incorporated the city.

At the opposite extremity of the German–Polish boundary lay the highly industrialised region of Upper Silesia. Ethnic groups were intermixed here on a scale found in few other areas of Eastern Europe. It was, in fact, impossible to separate German from Pole, and their division tended to follow social rather than geographical lines. The professional people, administrators and technicians were commonly German; the miners, farmers and workers, generally Polish. The region was occupied by an international force; two Polish risings were suppressed and a plebiscite held in 1921, on the basis of which the Council of Ambassadors, to whom the task had been delegated by the Paris Conference, partitioned the region.

The Geneva Line did what justice was possible to ethnic claims at the expense of playing havoc with public utilities and factory installations. Again neither side was satisfied, and, although an international commission continued for fifteen years to facilitate cooperation between the German and Polish portions of the region, neither side ceased to hope for the incorporation of the whole within its boundaries.

The eastern boundaries of Poland presented far more difficult problems, and these were intensified by the absence of a Soviet delegation from the Paris Conference. The ethnic boundary in the west was far from clear, but in the east the Polish-settled region faded gradually into that of the Lithuanians, White Russians or Ukrainians. The division was more social than geographical. The peasantry belonged to one of the latter groups, while the landowners and the small professional class tended to be Polish, and much of the local commerce was in the hands of the Jews.

The problem in the east was, in reality, twofold: the question of a boundary with Lithuania and that with the Soviet Union. The two proved in fact to be closely connected. At the end of 1919 the Supreme Council of the Allied Powers had suggested that Poland might accept a boundary corresponding approximately with the eastern limit of the area of predominantly Polish speech. But the Polish army, flushed with its first successes in conflict with the Russian, went on to invade the Ukraine and Byelorussia. An allied conference, meeting at Spa in Belgium, sent a telegram strongly urging a boundary that would accord with the ethnic realities. The line proposed has been erroneously attributed to Lord Curzon, who was, in fact, not its author, and knew very little about the area. Some of the Poles, on the other hand, claimed nothing less than the boundary of 1772. In the event, the Poles accepted, by the Treaty of Riga, a boundary intermediate between the 1772 line and the Curzon Line. The result was to include about 989,900 Byelorussians and 4,441,600 Ukrainians (1931 Census) within the Polish state.

Lithuania. The territory of Lithuania had been, from the Union of Lublin in 1569 to the Partitions (1772–95), part of the Polish state. Thereafter it had been incorporated in Tsarist Russia. In 1920, the independence of the new Lithuanian state was recognised by the Soviet Union, though its boundaries were left in part undetermined. The Lithuanians had set their eyes on Vilna as their capital, but in April 1919 this was occupied by the Poles, and was held by them until the Soviet offensive of the summer of 1920. After the failure of this attack, the Soviet forces withdrew far to the east of the city, handing it over as they did so to the Lithuanians. The League of Nations urged upon the Poles a compromise arrangement, whereby the Lithuanians would keep the city of Vilna and surrender to the Poles the Suwałki region. This reasonable arrangement was at once reversed by a *fait accompli*, whereby Polish forces, secretly ordered to do so by their government, seized the city. Although the resulting boundary line was unwillingly accepted, Lithuania refused until 1938 to reopen diplomatic relations with Poland, and their mutual border remained closed to communication and commerce.

Czechoslovakia. Less serious difficulties were presented by Czechoslovakia, if only because her territory was taken from Germany, Austria and Hungary, and the transfer could thus be legalised by the Paris Conference and embodied in the treaties which were imposed on the defeated powers. The creation of a Czecho-Slovak state had been predetermined by the representatives of these two peoples; its existence had been proclaimed, and a provisional agreement already reached on at least its western boundaries. Czechoslovakia was to embrace the two historic provinces of Bohemia and Moravia. The Czechs, it is true, made certain additional claims to German and Austrian territory, in part for strategic reasons, especially near Kładzko (Glatz) and Racibórz (Ratibor). Some small concessions were made here, but substantially Czechoslovakia inherited the historic boundaries of Bohemia.

The only reluctance at the Paris Conference to admit the Czech claims to the ancient boundaries sprang from the fact that they would include a substantial German-speaking population, which came subsequently to be known as Sudeten Germans. Their numbers according to the Austrian census were about 3,200,000, of whom over half lived in western Bohemia. They had been citizens of Austria, not of Germany, but their inclusion in the Czechoslovak state was held by many to be not only a grave violation of the ethnic principle, but also a source of danger and disharmony within the Czech state itself. On the other hand, to separate the German-settled area from the Czech— while not technically impossible—would have presented even graver difficulties. It would have cut the central Bohemian region and the city of Prague off from the fuel and power resources of the Ohře (Eger) valley, from the industrial cities of the Krkonoše range, and even from much of the heavy industry of northern Moravia. Furthermore, it was held that the historic boundaries, traversing as they did, a mainly mountainous area, gave a certain natural protection to Czechoslovakia, which a purely ethnic boundary could not possibly have done. There was, in fact, no real alternative to the historic boundaries; the Czech crisis of 1938 was implicit in the settlement of 1919.

Slovakia presented difficulties that were less acute than those present in the western boundaries only because they concerned countries less powerful than Germany. The configuration itself of Slovakia raised problems. The province was elongated along the Carpathian Mountains; very roughly, it conformed with the mountains because the mountains had provided a refuge for the Slovak peoples. But such a mountain zone was difficult to traverse, and the mountain valleys were tied economically to small market centres along the margin of the plain to the south, where mountain and plain peoples had been accustomed since time immemorial to meet and to exchange their products. The determination of the boundary here, just as in Bohemia and Moravia, necessitated some form of compromise between ethnic, technical and economic claims.

To be more specific, the territorial disputes concerned three small territories on the northern border of Slovakia, where Czechoslovak and Polish claims came into conflict, and much larger areas along the northern margin of the Pannonian Plain.

The former territories were Těšín (Cieszyń; Teschen), Orava and Spiš. The basis of the dispute was only partly ethnic. Těšín contained valuable coal deposits and a developed iron and steel industry. Orava and Spiš were feudal entities to which both Poland and Czechoslovakia could lay some kind of historic claim. Ultimately all three were partitioned by agreement between the two countries involved. But this did not close the matter. In 1938, at the time of the German annexation of the Sudetenland, the Poles laid claim to and annexed that part of Těšín which had eluded them in 1920. It was formally restored to Czechoslovakia in 1945.

Hungary had long enjoyed a poor press in the West. In the mid-nineteenth century, the Magyars were admired for their resistance to the Austrians; now they were condemned for their oppression of their own Slav minorities, and there was a disposition to favour Czecho-Slovak pretensions at their expense. An ethnic boundary would have given Slovakia very little of the Pannonian Plain and probably no access to the River Danube. Czecho-Slovak claims were from the first more extensive and more ambitious. A boundary along the Danube from above Bratislava to approximately the great bend above Budapest was a demand which admitted of no compromise. Without it Czechoslovakia could not satisfy her ambition to become an important Danubian power. East of the Danube a boundary was claimed running through the Mátra and Bükk hills as far as the Tisza. The French supported Czechoslovak claims here as elsewhere; the British were critical, and the Americans apparently had no desire to see so numerous a body of Hungarians pass under Czechoslovak rule. In the end a compromise was accepted. Czechoslovakia acquired the Žitný Ostrov, a large area of alluvium, surrounded by branches of the Danube, lying downstream from Bratislava. But the Czechoslovaks failed to obtain the bridgehead on the south bank of the Danube, opposite Bratislava, which they had originally claimed. This small area was acquired in 1946. The boundary east of the Danube was made to run to the north of the Mátra and Bükk hills, and, in the opinion of the Commission appointed by the Peace Conference to report on the matter, only 850,000 Hungarians were included in the new state, instead of 1,300,000 who would otherwise have passed under Czechoslovak rule.

A final difficulty in delimiting the boundaries of Czechoslovakia was presented by Ruthenia. The Carpathian Mountains of Slovakia become narrower and more broken towards the east, and their population changes about the longitude of Uzhgorod from predominantly Slovak to predominantly Ruthene. The Ruthenes are part of the Ukrainian people, and one must explain their appearance here within the Pannonian basin in terms of the easy routes across the mountains to the north. The Ruthene-settled territory was less than a hundred miles from west to east, and on the south it ended where the mountains gave place to the Hungarian-settled plain.

These Ruthenes had been since the earlier Middle Ages under Hungarian rule. Their condition was even more backward than that generally prevailing in Slovakia, and their organs for self-expression were non-existent. Under these conditions the initiative was taken by a group of *émigrés* in the United States. These met at Pittsburgh, and urged the Czech government to incorporate their homeland. This the Czechs were not unwilling to do. They were concerned that the Ukrainian Republic, which had been recently proclaimed, or the Soviet Union itself would incorporate this Ruthene territory. In either event, Russian influence would be introduced into the Pannonian Plain, and Czechoslovakia would find itself separated by a Russian- or Ukrainian-held corridor, from Romania.

And so the boundaries of Czechoslovakia were drawn in the Treaty of Trianon (4 June 1920) to include the Ruthenian mountains, together with a tract of the Pannonian Plain, with its predominantly Hungarian population.

Hungary. In the eyes of the Peace Conference, Hungary was no less imperialist and no less guilty of making war than Austria had been. Its population of about twenty million contained no more than ten million Magyars. The rest were Slavs and Romanians, with a sprinkling of Germans. The self-determination for the subject peoples of the Austro-Hungarian empire, advocated by Wilson, was possible only by the dismemberment of Hungary. Few, however, expected the surgical operation to be as drastic as in fact it was.

The Hungarians, as we saw in Chapter 2, were in the main a plains people dominating and controlling the upland people of the encircling arc of mountains. This imperialism was rationalised by the Hungarians themselves. The mountains, they said, constituted a 'natural' divide, imposing a kind of unity on the territory that lay inside them. The fact that the rivers discharged toward the Hungarian Plain further emphasised this unity. These specious arguments were reinforced by more practical considerations. Mountain and plain came to complement one another and to constitute a functional unity. In the words of Paul Teleki:

> Between lowlands and highlands, commercial centers sprang up wherever rivers made openings in the mountain chains. A line,

which the Hungarian geographers called the 'market line', connects all these towns as the line of exchange between the highland region and the lowlands. . . . The co-operation of the different regions so widely diverging as to natural conditions of production, and of the products themselves, formed together the greater economic energy of old Hungary.[1]

The railway net reflected this orientation of Old Hungary towards the centre of the plain; it consisted of a system of lines radiating from Budapest. There is much reason in the Hungarian claim as to the complementary nature of the peripheral and central areas of Old Hungary; they could also have added the very important question of river management and flood control, which, as has now been learned, can be handled only on the basis of whole river basins. Yet in Hungary in 1919–20, as in India in 1947 and in many other countries in recent years, the spirit of nationalism triumphed over economic considerations. An Hungarian state was created, with only 29 per cent of the area and just over 40 per cent of the population of its predecessor, deprived of outlet to the sea and dependent upon the goodwill of its neighbours for the supply of many essential materials as well as for all its foreign trade.

The boundary problems of the new Hungary can be grouped according to the four cardinal points of the compass. The northern boundary, that with Czechoslovakia, has already been discussed. Somewhat similar problems were raised by the eastern boundary with Romania. Since the middle years of the nineteenth century, Romania had consisted of the two principalities of Walachia and Moldavia, whilst Hungary since the Middle Ages, had held the Transylvanian Basin and the Bihor mountain massif. The ethnic pattern in this area had become confused and complex. Magyars had settled the plain and the valleys along its western margin. The Szekély and 'Saxons' constituted compact and distinct communities in the rolling plateau country which constitutes the heart of Transylvania. In the Carpathian and Bihor mountains lived communities of Romanians.

It was thus impossible for Romania to embrace within her territory the Walachs of Transylvania without at the same time taking in about half a million Hungarians or Szekély. But Romania went further than this and, like Czechoslovakia, demanded and obtained by the terms of the Treaty of Trianon the eastern periphery of the Hungarian Plain

[1] Paul Teleki, *The Evolution of Hungary and its Place in European History*, New York, 1923, pp. 108–9.

together with a number of predominantly Hungarian cities and their connecting railway lines.

Old Hungary had contained most of modern Croatia and had extended to the Dalmatian coast. Croatia now became a part of the new southern Slav state, and a boundary was established, following in part the River Drava and in part cutting across the northern Vojvodina and Banat to meet the Romanian boundary about ten miles to the south-east of Szeged. For the Drava section of the boundary there was a certain historical sanction, but from the point where it left the Drava the boundary cut across an ethnically confused area. It could not avoid doing violence to some ethnic claims though it cannot be doubted that here, as also along other boundaries, the scales of justice were weighted against Hungary.

It might have been supposed that the boundary between Hungary and Austria, hallowed by centuries of use and revived in the 'Compromise' of 1867, might be allowed to stand. In 1098, according to William of Tyre, the Crusaders crossed the Leitha river from Austria into Hungary, and until 1920 this river continued to form the boundary of historic Hungary. But to the east of it there lived in 1918 a considerable German-speaking population, as well as a number of Croats. Before the First World War the question of transferring part of the area lying east of the Leitha to Austria had been raised, only to be dismissed by the Austrian and, of course, the Hungarian governments. Now the question was revived; the Paris conference became aware of the inequities of the accepted boundary, and a plebiscite was ordered. The plebiscite was held in the city and district of Sopron in West Hungary, and resulted in the cession to Austria of the Burgenland, but the retention of Sopron itself in Hungary. Austria was thus the only power defeated in the First World War, which benefited at its conclusion by an accession of territory. Burgenland had an area of 1,529 square miles and a population in 1920 of 294,850, 75 per cent of it German-speaking; 15 per cent Croat, and only 8 per cent Magyar.

Hungary felt outraged by the onerous terms of the Treaty of Trianon, which seemed to the Hungarians to ignore both historical and ethnic argument and to be based largely on the economic or technical needs of the new states. In retrospect, it does seem that the territorial clauses of the Treaty of Trianon did less than justice to Hungary and that ethnic considerations, interpreted so rigidly along, for example, the German–Polish boundary, were here almost ignored. On the other hand, Hungary's treatment of her minorities from 1867 to 1918 had been harsh and had left a legacy of hatred. In their desire to allow none of these minorities to remain under Hungarian rule, the allies were obliged to include many Hungarians in neighbouring states. Table 5 illustrates the resulting fragmentation of the Hungarian nation by the Treaty of Trianon.

Table 5. Hungarian peoples in neighbouring countries after the Treaty of Trianon (1920)

In Hungary	7,147,053 (1920 census)
In Czechoslovakia	745,431 (1921 census)
In Romania (including Székély)	1,463,500 (estimated)
In Yugoslavia	467,652 (1921 census)
In Austria	25,071 (1923 census)

Lastly, the Hungarian claim that the boundary settlement did as much harm to the economy as to the ethnic pattern has surely been overstated. The new boundary did not completely sever the older trading connections, and elements of the former pattern of trade continued. Hungary never ceased to be a viable unit, and new trading partnerships were soon established to supplement or replace the old. As far as access to the sea was concerned, Hungary acquired a free zone in the port of Fiume (Rijeka) together with the necessary right of transit across Yugoslavia.

Yugoslavia. The southern Slavs had gained their independence in part from the Turks, in part from the Austro-Hungarians. Those who had lived under Austria–Hungary had, despite a rule that was at times capricious and unenlightened, been exposed to Western influences which manifested themselves in a more advanced agricultural technique, the beginnings of modern industry, better roads, more extensive public utilities and a higher literacy level. By contrast, Turkish rule had been corrupt, venal and ineffective, and those who had lived under it had received little tutelage in democratic or in any other form of government. They earned their political freedom earlier only because the Turks proved to be incompetent to control them any longer.

The two most numerous peoples of the new southern Slav state, the Serbs and the Croats, derived respectively from the Turkish and Austro-Hungarian empires. Despite an almost complete identity in

Farmhouse of the "long-house" type, set at right angles to the road; west of Budapest

Fortified farmhouse (*kula*), near Dečane, Kosmet, Yugoslavia

Shingle-roofed, wood-built cottages of Alpine type; the Karavanke Mountains, north-west of Kranj, Yugoslavia

Isolated farm settlement in the Pannonian Plain, near Szolnok Hungary

Ploughing in the traditional way in the northern foothills of the Stara Planina, Bulgaria. This photograph was taken in 1963

Isolated settlement, in the Prokletije, Montenegro

language, these two peoples were in most respects strongly contrasted. The Serbs possessed a long tradition of revolt and independence, whereas the Croats and their neighbours the Slovenes had not known independence since the Middle Ages. The latter had on the other hand undergone a greater degree of economic development and had acquired a level of education and sophistication not generally found among others of the southern Slavs. By contrast, the Serbs were relatively poor and backward. Each of these peoples had the vices associated with its particular virtues; the Croats despised the more backward Serbs, and the latter derived satisfaction from their rugged history of resistance to invaders and conquerors. Their differences made harmony between them almost impossible. Nevertheless, at the Corfu Conference in 1917, their leaders had agreed to make common cause against the Austro-Hungarians and to form a united southern Slav state at the end of the war. The structure of the future state was left vague, and it was this issue that was, a decade later, to split the Yugoslav state wide open. The Serbs hoped to establish a unitary state, a sort of Greater Serbia, built around their existing dynasty and institutions. The Croats and, of course, other and less numerous peoples who might find themselves included in the southern Slav state, looked for a federal constitution, in which their cultural autonomy would be assured. The basic internal struggle in Yugoslavia was that between a unitary and a federal constitution, and this conflict was implicit in the cultural geography of the country.

In the meanwhile, the weakening of the Habsburg power had allowed the Slovenes to press their claims for recognition, and for inclusion amongst the southern Slavs. But of necessity the southern Slavs were forced together more by external pressures and threats— from Italy, Hungary and Bulgaria—than by any internal feelings of cohesion. The Montenegrins deposed their old prince, and, with Serbs, Croats and Slovenes, joined on 1 December 1918, to proclaim the Kingdom of the Serbs, Croats and Slovenes. It was a unitary state; its ruling family of Karageorgevich was also the royal house of Serbia; its prime minister was the Serb, Pašič.

At this point we are more concerned with the political map than with essentially political problems. On all sides the new state was beset with territorial problems, and on most it faced potential enemies which resented the appearance of a potentially powerful state in the place of the relatively weak Serbia and Montenegro. These problems may be grouped according to the countries with which they were

5

shared: Austria, Hungary, Romania, Bulgaria, Greece, Albania, and Italy.

The north-western province of Slovenia with part of Croatia had previously been part of Austria. The Karawanken Alps, straight, steep, with few passes and a crestline generally above 5,000 feet seemed to offer a desirable boundary between the new state and Austria. But its barrier character was deceptive. In the Klagenfurth Basin to the north lived Slovene communities, cut off by the mountain barrier of the Karawanken from the rest of their people. Their number is difficult to estimate. In recent years Kardelj, President of the Yugo-slav Federal Assembly, has claimed that they number 130,000, but Austrian authorities admit to only 26,000. A British estimate, made at the time of the British occupation of this Zone of Austria (1945–55), put their number at about 70,000. These were what remained of a far more numerous Slav community in Austrian Carinthia and Styria. The Croats of Austrian Burgenland, who in 1920 numbered about 45,000 and thirty years later, about 34,500, are the descendants of eighteenth-century immigrants from the south. The Yugoslavs demanded the inclusion of part of the Klagenfurth Basin in the new state; the Peace Conference ordered a plebiscite, which went convinc-ingly in favour of Austria, and the boundary was established along the crest of the Karawanken Alps. The question may be raised whether the Slovenes of Carinthia may not in fact have tended to vote in favour of Austria and against their own ethnic group because of their fears and suspicions of a new state centralised under Serb rule as against the attractions of the relatively stable Austria.

The boundary between Yugoslavia and Hungary has already been described. Its continuation between Yugoslavia and Romania is made up of 140 miles across the plains of the Banat, and a rather shorter distance along the Danube. The former is traced through an ethnically confused region, but, although it occasioned grievances among the local people, it did not cause strife between the states which it separated.

Yugoslavia's relations with Bulgaria were probably more critical than those with any other of its neighbours. During the period of the First Bulgarian Empire and again for a brief period after 1875, Bul-garia had extended westward and southward across Macedonia and into territory inhabited by Albanians and Greeks, and Bulgars were now unwilling to forego these ancient claims, which conflicted directly with those of Yugoslavia. The Yugoslavs were justifiably suspicious of their neighbour, but suspicion could not be held to condone the annexation by Yugoslavia of four segments of territory on the western border of Bulgaria. These territories with a combined area of about 600 square miles and an estimated population of nearly 75,000, overwhelmingly Bulgar or Macedonian, were held to threaten the main railway communication, along the Morava and Vardar valleys, from Beograd to Thessaloníki.

The dispute over Macedonia was, in a sense more legitimate, because the affiliation of the Macedonian people was itself indefinite. Bulgaria lost the argument because it had lost the war, and Macedonia continued to be divided between Yugoslavia and Greece along the line established after the Balkan Wars and the expulsion of the Turks.

Macedonia is, after the Vojvodina, ethnically the most diversified area in Eastern Europe. It lay at the crossing of two of the most important routeways in the whole of the Balkans: the west–east route through Macedonia and Thrace and the south–north Vardar valley route. We have seen also how Bulgars and Serbs; Greeks, Turks and Albanians converged on this area. Here there evolved a Macedonian dialect of Slav, resembling in some respects both Serb and Bulgar. Some neutral linguistics described it as *Macedo-Slav*; others, more biased, asserted that it was a dialect of either Serb or Bulgar. The division of the area had been determined by the fortunes of war, and bore no close relationship to ethnic realities. It left unsolved two significant problems: Yugoslav access to the Aegean Sea and Bulgarian claims to Greek and Yugoslav Macedonia.

The Yugoslavs laid no claim to any part of the Aegean littoral, and recognised Thessaloníki as a Greek port. This recognition made it easier for the Greeks to make concessions to Yugoslav commercial interests and to agree to concede a free zone in the port of Thessaloníki to Yugoslavia.

Less tractable was Bulgaria's claim to Macedonia. The term 'Macedonia' defied definition, and Bulgaria's territorial claims were by no means precise. As early as 1895, while Macedonia was still under Turkish rule, a revolutionary body, the Internal Macedonian Revolutionary Organisation (IMRO) had been formed. Though founded and directed by Macedonians, it was from the start under Bulgarian influence, and after 1918 became an unofficial agent of Bulgarian policy. During the 1920s, the IMRO exercised a virtual reign of terror in Yugoslavia and Greek Macedonia, and the Yugoslavs retailated by denying that the Macedonian language was anything more than a dialect of Serb.

The boundary between Yugoslavia and Albania also derived from the settlement which in 1914 ended the Balkan wars, though the new boundary was not in fact demarcated until after the First World War. Yugoslavia inherited a boundary which included within her territory as many as half a million Albanians.[1] Conditions long remained unsettled along the Albanian boundary, but Albania herself remained powerless to press any territorial claim against Yugoslavia. Yugoslavia would have liked to annex northern Albania in order to assure herself of a technically manageable route to the Adriatic Sea, but this claim also was not pressed.

The most determined opposition to the creation of the Yugoslav state—at least within the limits which it came ultimately to assume—was from Italy. The Adriatic littoral had since the period of the Roman Empire been dominated by Italy. During the Middle Ages it was dotted with Italian settlements, and the most important of its commercial cities, Dubrovnik, was in close alliance with Venice. The coastal cities, from Trieste in the north to Dubrovnik and even beyond, were inhabited partly by Italians, and in style they were more Italian than Balkan. To this coastline Italy laid claim, and in the Treaty of London of 1915, whose terms were for the time being kept secret, the Western allies agreed to allow Italy to annex much of the coast and most of the islands at the end of the war. In the final settlement, however, Italy acquired the Istrian peninsula, with the ports of Trieste and Pola (Pula) and, on the mainland to the south-east only the small port city of Zara (Zadar), with the offshore islands of Lagosta, Pelagosa and a few others of smaller size and importance. Italy acquiesced unwillingly and ungraciously in this decision which was, however, fairly based on ethnic considerations. The dispute then focused on the city of Fiume (Rijeka), which in character and function bore a close similarity to Danzig. The city was partly Italian, but its immediate hinterland was Croat. On ethnic grounds it should have been assigned to Italy, but behind the city lay one of the few easy crossings of the Dinaric chain, and the only crossing adequately equipped with both road and rail communications. It could be argued that possession of Fiume was essential to the foreign trade of Yugoslavia, which would otherwise, despite its long coastline, have no port which it could really use. The secret Treaty of London had provisionally left Fiume in Yugoslav hands, but in September 1919, the city and port were seized

---

[1] The Yugoslav census of 1921 gave only about 250,000, but this figure was certainly too low.

by the Italian freebooter, Gabriele d'Annunzio, and his following of ill-armed adventurers. The Italian troops remained, although by the Treaty of Rapallo of November 1920, Fiume acquired the status of a Free City.

In 1922 Benito Mussolini came to power in Italy. He refused to acquiesce in this independent status for what he regarded as an Italian city. A new Italo-Yugoslav agreement was reached in 1924, which recognised Fiume as Italian, while its south-east suburb, Sušak, with an indifferent harbour, went to Yugoslavia, for whose seaborne commerce it was entirely inadequate.

Bulgaria. In both the Second Balkan War and also in the First World War Bulgaria gambled and lost, and the price which she paid both in territory and in the ill-will of all her neighbours was heavy. By the Treaty of Neuilly (November 1919), which ended Bulgaria's participation in the First World War, she ceded not only the four small areas along her western boundary, already mentioned, but also Eastern Thrace, and with it her access to the Aegean Sea. The Bulgaria that remained was small, compact and ethnically homogeneous. It was also jealous and resentful, fomenting discord among its neighbours, and, like Hungary, anxiously awaiting the opportunity to fish again in the troubled waters of Balkan politics. Unhappily the opportunity came when in 1941 Hitler attacked Yugoslavia.

Romania was one of those countries that benefited greatly from the peace settlement. After its formation in 1859, Romania had been able to increase her territory only by the annexation of southern Dobrogea from Bulgaria in 1913. In 1916 Romania entered the First World War, suffered almost immediate defeat, and was obliged to surrender the whole of Dobrogea to Bulgaria and a thin strip of territory around the margin of the Transylvanian Basin to Hungary. These transfers of territory were annulled on the defeat of Germany in 1918, and Romania went on to expand her territory to more than twice its area in 1914.

Such an accession of territory was not wholly deserved and, it gave Romania a kind of indigestion from which it never really recovered. The north-eastern boundary of Romania was formed by the River Prut and the northern branches of the Danube delta. From 30 to 100 miles to the north-east of the Prut, the River Dnestr also flowed down from the steppes of the Ukraine to the Black Sea. Between lay the province of Bessarabia, named from its medieval rulers the Bassarabs. In 1812, it had been taken from the feeble hand of the Turks by the Russians. Its population was made up of some segment of almost every people that had passed through this troubled land. The most numerous were the Romanians, though they constituted little more than a third of the population. After them came, roughly in declining order of numerical importance, the Ukranians, Germans, Jews, Poles, Turks and Tatars.

During the anarchy that followed the collapse of Russian rule in 1917, the Bessarabians organised a Moldavian-Bessarabian Republic, whose unstable government dissolved itself by voting for incorporation in Romania. The Soviet Union never recognised Romania's title to Bessarabia, and only slowly and reluctantly did Romania's Western allies do so.

Bukovina lies to the north-west of Moldavia and Bessarabia, which it separated from south-eastern Poland. Before the war it had been in Austrian possession, and formed in fact, the most easterly extension of the Austrian Empire. Its population was mixed. The largest group —though not a majority—was Ruthene or Ukrainian; the rest were Romanian, German and Jewish. A large part of the Ruthene population had been recent immigrants from the Ukraine. By the terms of the Treaty of St Germain of 1919, all Bucovina was incorporated into Romania.

On the west, Romania had brashly demanded a boundary along the Tisza river. This was unrealistic, but Romania had no difficulty in gaining recognition of her claim to Transylvania, including its compact German and Szekély communities. She also got, as we have already seen, a strip of land along the eastern margin of the Hungarian Plain, with its market cities, strategic railway, and predominantly Hungarian population. Romania was unquestionably overextended, more so perhaps than even Poland.

From the First to the Second World War
From Poland to the borders of Greece seven states had now come into existence primarily to express the will to nationhood of their dominant peoples. Two, Hungary and Bulgaria, had been grossly penalised. Partly in consequence of this, other countries were faced with minority problems. Poland, Romania and Yugoslavia embarked on a new imperialism, aimed against the minority groups unfortunate enough to have got caught up within their boundaries.

Unquestionably boundaries could have been drawn more fairly, but not even a plebiscite was an infallible guide to ethnic loyalties. Too many people voted in favour of a government that was tested, tried and stable, and thus against their own ethnic group; some had been bribed or intimidated. But, above all, the question was complicated by the intrusion into Eastern Europe of the rivalries of the Great Powers. In particular the Western democracies looked here for two things: allies in the event of a revival of German militarism, and states able to hold the line in the event of a westward thrust of Soviet Communism. They thus tended to favour those that they thought they could trust most fully to accomplish these ends—Poland, Czechoslovakia, Romania and Yugoslavia, and to penalise and, it was hoped, weaken those—Hungary and Bulgaria—that might be expected to side with Germany. In this way the peacemakers created more problems than they solved, and in the end hastened the evils which they had tried to forestall.

The architect of this new power-balance was France, which laboured to give additional territory and power to its allies, and then negotiated treaties of mutual aid and assistance with them. Within Eastern Europe, the problems of Hungary and Bulgaria which were, at least in part, of the allies' creation, led respectively to the Little and Balkan Ententes, designed to keep them in a permanent state of submission. Such stability as resulted could only last until the power-balance was disturbed. The rise of Hitler and the rearmament of Germany effected just this change.

Germany's new order. The tragedy of the 1919–20 settlement was that, of necessity, it gave Germany potential allies in every country of Eastern Europe. Hungary and Bulgaria came inevitably to hitch their destinies to the rising star of Nazism. In Poland dissident Germans and Ruthenes; in Czechoslovakia, the Sudeten Germans, Magyars and to some extent the Slovaks; in Yugoslavia, the Macedonians and Germans, and in Romania, the Szekély, Germans and Bulgars all became the willing or unwilling tools of Hitler's Third Reich.

It is impossible to chronicle here the acts of aggression which broke up most of the states of Eastern Europe. The latter had made themselves too vulnerable. First came the disintegration of Czechoslovakia, in many ways the most stable of the group; then the partition—the fourth—of Poland between Germany and the Soviet Union. Yugoslavia realised too late the mistakes as well as the dangers of its own highly centralised and Serb-oriented system of government. In 1940 Romania collapsed like a pack of cards, and no less than 40 per cent of its population passed under Soviet, Hungarian or Bulgarian rule.

The boundaries within Eastern Europe were redrawn. The limits of

Germany were extended to include much of Poland and Czecho-slovakia. Hungary was rewarded with parts of Transylvania, Vojvo-dina and Slovenia; Bulgaria, with Macedonia and Dobrogea; Italy, with the hinterland of Fiume and parts of the Dalmatian coast, and Albania, with neighbouring areas of Serbia. Germany herself added much of Slovenia to her Austrian provinces. To some degree these changes could be justified on ethnic grounds, but, by and large, they reflected the new power-balance in Eastern Europe—the domination of the whole region by Germany and her Hungarian and Bulgarian allies.

Soviet domination. Simultaneously with Germany's encroachment on this area from the west, the Soviet Union occupied parts of it from the east. Soviet aggression began with the Molotov–Ribbentrop Pact of August, 1939, by which Germany agreed that the Soviet Union should occupy the area of Poland, lying east of approximately the Curzon Line. This was followed by the annexation from Romania of the province of Bessarabia, to whose loss the Soviet Union had never been reconciled, and by Soviet demands on the Baltic states for military bases. This was followed by their absorption into the Soviet Union. In June 1945, by agreement with the government of Czecho-slovakia, which it was in a position to influence, the Soviet Union annexed the predominantly Ruthene area of Sub-carpathian Russia.

The Soviet Union has relinquished none of this territory, and has instead extended its control farther to the west by its political influence over the governments of the 'bloc' countries and by the maintenance of military garrisons within their territory of some of them.

The Second World War and its aftermath saw the extinction of the short-lived independence of the countries of Eastern Europe. They could exist and flourish only under political conditions which from their nature could not occur frequently or last long. They were predi-cated upon a Germany and Russia that were politically and militarily weak. It was under such conditions that the medieval kingdoms arose in this area. They were extinguished by the eastward pressure of the Germans and the rise of Russian imperialism, reinforced, as it hap-pened, by the Turkish invasions. The First World War achieved the unique result of defeating all the Central and East European imperial-ists, but their condition of weakness could not last indefinitely, and inevitably the integrity and independence of the East European states was threatened first and only temporarily by Germany and then by the Soviet Union.

Only one consideration remains in this discussion of the political geography of Eastern Europe—the effect of political pressures from west and east on the area. The collapse of Germany in 1944–45 led to the westward shift of Poland, and to the inclusion within its boundaries of all the territory lying to the east of the rivers Oder and Neisse. Similarly, the defeat of Italy allowed Yugoslavia to annex the Julian region and the Istrian peninsula. The westward shift of Eastern Europe, as defined in political terms, was made possible because the region was more readily accessible to the forces of the Soviet Union than to those of the West. Indeed, the zonal boundary across Germany, which has become the 'Iron Curtain', was delimited originally in terms primarily of logistics. The only exception to this picture of a Soviet-dominated Eastern Europe has been for 20 years provided by Yugoslavia which made good its bid for independence of action in 1948, in part because it was directly accessible from the west and, if the Soviet Union should press too strongly, could receive aid and consolation from the Western Powers. Hungary in 1956 could receive no such aid, and, even if its revolt had been more skilfully handled, still it probably could not have succeeded. The Communist heterodoxy of Albania also can largely be explained in terms of its remoteness from Soviet control and its hostility to Yugoslavia. The more recent intransigence of Romania and Czechoslovakia, however, is explicable only in terms of the general weakening in the mid-sixties of the cohesiveness of the bloc and the resurgence of nationalism.

Much of this chapter has been given to the geography of disputes *between* the East European countries. These were essentially territorial disputes, concerned with ethnic groups, transit rights, and access to ports and the sea. The conditions which gave rise to these disputes are still present though the disputes themselves are obscured by the apparatus of consultation and cooperation between the countries of the bloc. Only when such a dispute arises along the borderland of the Communist bloc itself, as it does in Macedonia and as it did, until it was resolved, in the territory of Trieste, is it allowed to sharpen and ferment. The Communist leadership has not readily tolerated bourgeois and nationalist disputes within the area under its control, except when these happen to coincide with its own needs and policies.

Bibliography
ANCEL, JACQUES, *Manuel Géographique de Politique Européenne*, **1**, *L'Europe Centrale*, Paris, 1936.
BOWMAN, ISAIAH, *The New World*, London, Harrap, 1929.

5*

118   *The Nation-State in Eastern Europe*

BROWN, J. F. *The New Eastern Europe: the Krushchev Era and After*, London, Pall Mall Press, 1966.

BURGHARDT, ANDREW, *Borderland*, University of Wisconsin Press, 1962.

DUROSELLE, JEAN-BAPTISTE, *Les Frontières Européennes de L'URSS 1917–1914*, Paris, Colin, 1957.

Eastern Europe in Transition, ed. Kurt London, Baltimore, The Johns Hopkins Press, 1966.

FEIS, HERBERT, *Between War and Peace*, Princeton University Press, 1960.

GEORGE, PIERRE, and JEAN TRICART, *L'Europe Centrale*, Paris, 1954, vol. 2, *Les États*.

HASKINS, CHARLES H. and R. H. LORD, *Some Problems of the Peace Conference*, Harvard University Press, 1920.

HOFFMAN, GEORGE W. *The Balkans in Transition*, Princeton, N.J.; Van Nostrand Company, 1963.

JELAVICH, CHARLES and BARBARA JELAVICH, *The Balkans*, Englewood Cliffs, N.J., Prentice-Hall, 1965.

KAECKENBEECK, G. *The International Experiment of Upper Silesia*, Oxford University Press, 1942.

KOLARZ, WALTER, *Myths and Realities in Eastern Europe*, London, Lindsay Drummond, Ltd., 1946.

MACARTNEY, C. A. *Hungary and Her Successors*, Oxford University Press, 1937.

MOODIE, A. E. F. *The Italo-Yugoslav Boundary: a Study in Political Geography*, London, G. Philip, 1945.

MORROW, I. F. D. *The Peace Settlement in the German–Polish Borderland*, Oxford University Press, 1936.

NEWBIGIN, M. I. *Geographical Aspects of the Balkan Problem*, Constable, 1915.

POUNDS, N. J. G. 'Fissures in the Eastern Bloc,' *Annals of the American Academy of Political and Social Sciences*, **372**, (1967), 40–58.

WHEELER-BENNETT, JOHN W. *Brest-Litovsk, The Forgotten Peace*, March 1918. London, Macmillan, 1938.

SCHLESINGER, RUDOLF, *Federalism in Central and Eastern Europe*, London, Routledge & Kegan Paul, 1945.

SETON-WATSON, HUGH, *Neither War nor Peace*, London, Methuen, 1960.

— *Eastern Europe Between the Wars* 1918–1914, Cambridge University Press, 1945.

STAVRIANOS, L. S. *The Balkans since 1453*, Holt, Rinehart & Winston, 1958.

WAMBAUGH, SARAH, *Plebiscites since the World War*, Washington, D.C., Carnegie Endowment for International Peace, 1953.

— *A Monograph on Plebiscites*, New York, Oxford University Press, 1920.

WANDYCZ, PIOTR S. *France and Her Eastern Allies*, 1919–1925, University of Minnesota Press, 1962. Oxford University Press, 1962.

WANKLYN, H. G. *The Eastern Marchlands of Europe*, London, G. Philips, 1941.

WISKEMANN, ELIZABETH, *Germany's Eastern Neighbours*, Oxford University Press, 1956.

— *Czechs and Germans*, Oxford University Press, 1938.

WOLFF, ROBERT LEE, *The Balkans in Our Time*, Harvard University Press, 1956.

WILKINSON, H. R. *Maps and Politics*, Liverpool University Press, 1951.

WALLIS, B. C. 'The Rumanians in Hungary', *Geogrl J.*, **6** (1918), 156–71.

— 'The Slavs of Northern Hungary', *Geogrl J.*, **6** (1918), 268–81.

CHAPTER FIVE

Population and Settlement

In the eight countries of East-Central and Eastern Europe that are described in this book there was in 1965 an estimated population of about 120,500,000. These people inhabited an area of 491,290 square miles, with an average density of 243 persons per square mile.

Table 6. Population and Density—1965

	Population, in thousands; 1965 estimate	Density per square mile
East Germany	16,000	388
Poland	31,496	261
Czechoslovakia	14,159	287
Hungary	10,148	284
Romania	19,027	209
Yugoslavia	19,508	196
Bulgaria	8,200	194
Albania	1,865	165
	120,403	243 av.

Source: *UN Statistical Yearbook, 1965.*

Despite a sharp rise throughout most of the nineteenth century and the early years of the twentieth, the density had still not reached that found in most of Western Europe. Nor had the countries achieved the degree of urbanisation and level of industrialisation met with in the West. Nevertheless, most of Eastern Europe was, by common consent, over-populated.

Population growth

It is difficult owing to lack of census data to estimate the rate of population growth during the nineteenth century. The area had, within its present boundaries, a population of about 111·6 million in 1938. In

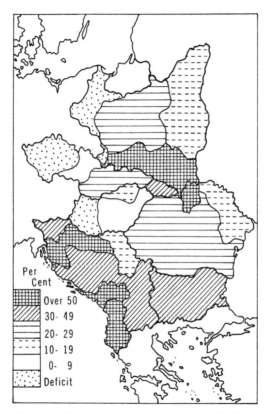

Fig. 5.1. The extent of overpopulation in Eastern Europe before the Second World War. After Wilbert E. Moore, *Economic Demography of Eastern and Southern Europe*, Geneva, League of Nations, 1945.

1920 the total was about 90 million; in 1850, it may have been about 55 million, and for any date earlier than this it would be rash to hazard a guess. Throughout this period the birth-rate remained high and population growth was rapid. In the absence of any major industrial development, a large part of the increase was obliged to emigrate.

Between the First and Second World Wars the population continued to increase. Despite continuing migration—Poland alone recorded a net outmigration of about a million between 1918 and 1931—the total for the whole of Eastern Europe had risen by about 20 million when the Second World War began. When it ended the population was at least eight million smaller; official estimates put it at 103,666,000 in 1947. Losses in combat, the deliberate attempts to exterminate the Jewish and Gypsy population, the premature deaths caused by the hardships of these years, expulsion at the end of the war, and flight must together have accounted for almost one person in twelve. These were compensated in part by people moving west from the Soviet Union and by others returning home.

There may still be flight from the East European countries, but there is no longer migration. The forced industrialisation of recent years has created almost everywhere an acute shortage of labour. Countries which only a generation ago were happy to see their citizens migrate to the New World, have recently denied them a passport to leave the country or have secured a hostage for their eventual return. The population, meanwhile, continues to increase. But the birth-rate has dropped and, even without the safety valve of migration, the rate of population increase is considerably slower than in the years before the Second World War. By 1975, the total for the whole area is expected to be about 137·5 million.

Rural and urban settlement. Until recent years the population of Eastern Europe has been overwhelmingly rural and agricultural. Only in Czechoslovakia and East Germany, for which it is impossible to compute precise figures, did agriculture before 1939 employ less than half the total population. Elsewhere the greater part of the labour force was in agriculture and contributed a disproportionately small part of the gross national product of each country, as Table 7 shows.

Manufacturing was important locally in 1939, and the industrially employed outnumbered those in agriculture, for example, in Western Poland and in parts of Czechoslovakia and Hungary. But the Balkan peninsula, Romania and the eastern provinces of Czechoslovakia were almost destitute of modern factory industry.

The change from rural to urban living, from agricultural to industrial and tertiary employment was slow before the First World War. It was intensified during the period of national development between

Table 7. Pre-1939—Percentage of population in agriculture and of national income from agriculture

	Percentage of population in agriculture	Percentage of national income from agriculture
Poland	n.d.	n.d.
Czechoslovakia	39·7 per cent	36·0 per cent
Hungary	53·2	33·9
Romania	78·1	49·0
Yugoslavia	76·1	48·3
Bulgaria	81·8	53·5

Source: *Agrarian Problems from the Baltic to the Aegean*, Royal Institute of International Affairs, London, 1944, p. 50.

the two world wars, but not until after the Second World War did Eastern Europe begin to lose its heavily rural and agricultural character. Table 8 for 1964 points the contrast with the pre-1939 years.

Table 8. 1964—Percentage of population in agriculture and of gross national product from agriculture

	Percentage of population in agriculture	Percentage of gross national product from agriculture
East Germany	18	11
Poland	48	22
Czechoslovakia	38	14
Hungary	38	21
Romania	70	30
Yugoslavia	57	28
Bulgaria	64	n.d.
Albania	n.d.	n.d.

Sources: *UN Statistical Yearbook, 1965; FAO Production Yearbook, 1965.*

How this revolution has been achieved is left until the next chapter.

Distribution of population. In an area so heavily dependent on farming the distribution of population must bear a close relationship to agricultural potentialities. Even the distribution of urban population is related to agricultural conditions, because, until the planned industrial growth of recent years, most towns were primarily market and service centres for their surrounding countryside, and were larger and more closely spaced in areas of high agricultural production. The resulting population distribution is today being changed by the decision of governments which locate new industries in areas hitherto poorly developed and only weakly urbanised. At the same time there are in most of the countries examined certain optimum areas for industrial development. The advantages of intensifying industrial development in these areas are such that the governments cannot avoid adding to the size and range of their industrial growth. Industrial regions are thus emerging that have no relationship to the agricultural base upon which the older settlements were founded.

Though the density of population varies greatly within quite small areas according to soil fertility, relief and exposure, rainfall and temperature, it is nevertheless possible to generalise and to indicate broad regions of high, medium and low density.

In general, the northern plain is an area of moderately dense rural population and is furthermore the most highly urbanised part of Eastern Europe. The regions of glacial sands and clays are the least productive and the most sparsely settled. The loess belt, extending along the southern margin of the plain, is the most intensively cultivated and populous region in all Eastern Europe. In fact, Galicia became one of the classical areas of small and fragmented farms and rural overcrowding.

The cities of the northern plain are both numerous and large. They tend to form a series of lines or belts extending from west to east across the region. There is, first, a line of ports and coastal cities. Inland, a number of cities has developed at focal points in the *Urstromtäler* which extend across the region from Magdeburg in the west to Warsaw in the east. The last alignment follows the loess belt and borders the hills, from Hannover, through Leipzig, Dresden, Wrocław and Kraków to L'vov in the Ukraine.

The mountains and hills, both those which enclose Bohemia and also the arc of mountains which extends from western Slovakia through Romania to the Danube, are thinly populated, except where minerals or power resources or recent governmental decision have led

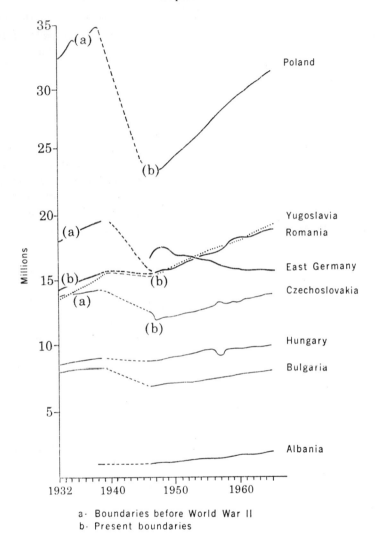

Fig. 5.2. Population changes in Eastern Europe during and since the Second World War. Based on *Demographic Yearbooks*, UN.

to small concentrations of people. The interior of Bohemia and the plain of Moravia are, on the other hand, distinguished by good soil, favourable climate and ease of movement, and have developed populations which are amongst the densest in Eastern Europe.

The Pannonian Plain resembles the North European in its moderate density of population. In general it is a well-settled, intensively cultivated region, with, nevertheless, some extensive areas, such as the Bakony Forest, the sandy region of Kecskemét and the dry Hortobágy, of low population density. The plains of southern and eastern Romania have a fairly dense rural population though here also the intensity of land use is restricted by the low rainfall and the climatic extremes of the region. The upland basin of Transylvania, with its sunny and more humid climate, surrounded by sparsely peopled mountains, forms a kind of population oasis in the heart of Romania.

The Balkan peninsula is more sparsely peopled than the area to the north of the Danube. It is more mountainous than the rest of Eastern Europe, and a larger proportion of its area lies at too high an altitude or is too steep for agriculture. Furthermore, toward the south the summers become drier until they merge into the nearly rainless summers of the Mediterranean climate. Physical conditions of agriculture deteriorate and cropland makes up a diminishing proportion of the area in this direction.

Until well into the present century manufacturing industries were not well developed even in the more northerly parts of Eastern Europe. They were scarcely developed at all in the Balkans, and there are today no industrial and urban complexes south of the Danube even on the scale met with in Bohemia, Moravia and southern Poland. Nor has the coast attracted more than a sparse population, partly because of its aridity and lack of large areas of level, cultivable land; partly on account of the barrier which the mountains present to communications with the hinterland. On the whole extent—almost a thousand miles—of the Mediterranean coast of the Balkans, excluding peninsular Greece, there were in 1964 only two port cities of over 100,000 inhabitants: Rijeka and Thessaloníki.

The distribution of total population in Eastern Europe is shown in somewhat generalised form in Fig. 5.3, and the distribution of cities with a current population of over 50,000 in Fig. 5.5. Theoretically the town, however small, exists to perform urban functions; it is a centre of local commerce and may contain a small industrial plant, often serving to process local agricultural products. In recent years the improvement of communication and means of transport has tended to focus these activities on cities of regional rather than of local importance and of intermediate rather than small size. The small town thus tends to revert to the function of a large village. The map (Fig. 5.5.)

emphasises the relatively high degree of urbanisation of the northern and north-western parts of Eastern Europe in contrast with the relatively low level in the rest of the area.

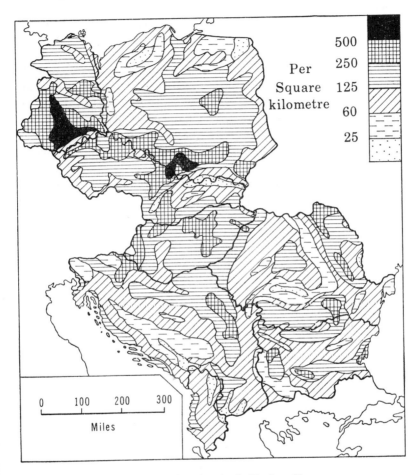

Fig. 5.3. Population density in Eastern Europe.

The peasant
Throughout Eastern Europe agriculture has for centuries been organised very largely on a peasant basis, and until recently the peasantry made up the greater part of the population. A peasantry is not easy to define. E. E. Evans defines the peasant thus: 'I take the peasant to be

the self-employed farmer . . . who is largely dependent on the labour of his family; and we may expect the contribution of his labour to be more important than the contribution of capital.'[1] But there is more to it than this. The under-capitalisation is accompanied usually by an extreme conservatism and a reluctance to change or to adopt new farming methods. The life of the peasant is commonly, though by no means invariably, dominated by customary folk-ways; by traditional costume and design, architecture, tools and equipment. To some the peasant is the repository of all virtues, cheerful, industrious and frugal; to others, mean and grasping, ignorant and unenterprising, churlish and uncouth. The peasant can, in fact, be all this, and all these qualities are present in the peasants described in Reymont's novel *Chłopi*, perhaps the most important and revealing novel of peasant life in Eastern Europe.[2]

In the context of this chapter the most important aspects of peasant life are the smallness of his holding, his lack of equipment, and of all except the most rudimentary technical skills. Everywhere in Eastern Europe the peasant is poor, and the *kulak* is rich only in relation to the mass of the peasantry. The intense industry, which commonly characterises the peasant, springs from his poverty and from the overriding need to extract from his meagre holding all that it is capable of yielding.

The peasant problem, which existed in all the countries of Eastern Europe, as well as in parts of Central, Southern and even Western Europe, was essentially that of farm holdings that were too small to support a family and capital and skill that were inadequate to work the land properly. It is difficult to tabulate and compare the sizes of farm holdings in all eight countries owing to the lack of strictly comparable statistics. In Poland however, about 65 per cent of all holdings before the Second World War were of under 5 hectares (12·4 acres); in Czechoslovakia, 71 per cent; in Romania, 75 per cent, and in Bulgaria. 62 per cent. In Hungary, where the unit of areal measurement is the cadastral hold, 85 per cent of all holdings were of less than ten holds— about 4·45 hectares (about 11 acres). This is eloquent of the extreme

[1] E. Estyn Evans, 'The Ecology of Peasant Life in Western Europe', in *Man's Role in Changing the Face of the Earth*, ed. William L. Thomas, Univ. Chicago Press, 1956, p. 220.

[2] Władisław Reymont's *Chłopi* was published in 1904–09, and an English translation, *The Peasants*, appeared in 1925–26. The novel describes the life of the peasants of the village of Lipce, 60 miles south-west of Warsaw, Poland, through the course of a single year.

smallness of the majority of farm holdings, but it relates to the number of holdings, not the proportion which they bore to the total area of agricultural land. For example, the 65 per cent of Polish farm holdings covered only 15·3 per cent of the land; the 85 per cent of the Hungarian, only 19·1 per cent of the agricultural area. In Czechoslovakia, Romania and Bulgaria also the great majority of the farm holdings covered only a small part of the farm land. The extremes were reached in Hungary and Poland. In the former, 30 per cent of the land was in holdings of over 1,000 holds, or about 445 hectares (about 1,100 acres); in Poland, 43 per cent of the area was in farms of over 100 hectares, or 247 acres.

Land reform. The existence of great estates served to intensify the peasant problem, by restricting the amount of land available for the peasants and thus limiting the size of peasant holdings. The problem was least in the Balkans, where such land-owning aristocracy as may once have existed had long since perished at the hands of the Turks. It was most serious in Poland and in 'greater' Hungary, where Austrian, Prussian and Russian rule had tended to insulate and preserve the outworn feudalism of these countries. In the Czech lands the ancient Czech aristocracy had largely perished during the wars of the seventeenth century, and had been replaced mainly by German and Austrian landowners.

Land reform was in the programme of all the new states of Eastern Europe, and was made all the easier in some by the fact that the landowners belonged to the former imperial powers and could thus without compunction be expropriated or expelled. Romanian land reform was probably the most thorough-going, especially as, in the newly acquired provinces at least, it was the non-Romanians who suffered most. In Czechoslovakia, the German, Austrian and Hungarian-owned estates were broken up. Land reform, as is evident from figures already quoted, made less progress in Hungary and Poland. In Hungary, in particular, the old land-owning aristocracy remained in political control and did little that would prejudice their own class interests. The Polish programme was theoretically more liberal, but its implementation was delayed and postponed, mainly for political reasons, and never completed before the outbreak of the Second World War. In Yugoslavia, there were Muslim-owned estates in Bosnia, and German and Hungarian in the north. These were broken up and the land distributed to the peasants, but the lands formerly ruled by the Turks were not in general characterised by large estates. Thus, when the outbreak of the Second World War shattered the short-lived hegemony of the nation-state in Eastern Europe, the peasantry owned most of the land in five of them, and Hungary alone still remained, a land of large estates. Hungary had no significant programme of land reform. In the other countries a total of about 11 million hectares (about 27·5 million acres), taken from the estates and large farms, had been distributed to the peasantry by 1938:

Poland	2,500,000 hectares (6,175,000 acres)
Czechoslovakia	1,790,000 hectares (4,421,300 acres)
Hungary	271,000 hectares (669,370 acres)
Romania	4,000,000 hectares (9,884,000 acres)
Yugoslavia	2,485,000 hectares (5,975,000 acres)
Bulgaria	45,000 hectares (111,150 acres)

This redistribution of land neither solved the peasant problem nor did it appease the demands of the peasants themselves. Their number was increasing; the technical level of their agriculture was improving only very slowly, and there was not enough land in most parts of Eastern Europe either to employ them fully or to feed them adequately.

The peasant problem was exacerbated by the practice, sanctioned by law and custom, of dividing the peasant holding between heirs, which prevailed over most of Slav Europe, with the exception of Bohemia, where the law of primogeniture obtained. Only such a practice in an area of high peasant birth-rate could explain the extreme fragmentation of farm holdings in, for example, Galicia and parts of Croatia.

The end of the Second World War, the Soviet military occupation, the flight of the old landowning class, and the accession to power of governments more clearly dedicated to social welfare, prepared the way for another round of land reform. There was a hasty parcelling out of what remained of the great estates. In Poland and Czechoslovakia this was facilitated in the one case by the incorporation of former German territory from which the previous population had fled or been expelled, and in the other by the expulsion of the Sudeten Germans. In both, the land thus made available was used to establish medium-sized peasant farms.

In Hungary, which had experienced only a very modest land reform during the period between the two world wars, the situation was quite different. Here almost all large estates, irrespective of ownership, were confiscated. It was reported that 3·2 million hectares (7·9 million acres) were affected by the new reform, and almost overnight Hungary became a land of small peasants. But a peasant problem remained. Many of those who had worked for hire on the great estates, were now without both land and employment. The effect of the Hungarian land reform was to satisfy the demands of a large body of the peasants, but also to produce a minority of landless and unemployed peasants.

This second round of land reform had only a minor impact south of the Danube, because here there were very few large holdings to be dismembered. Land reform here took the form of shaving a little off the larger peasant farms and adding even less to the area of the small, except in the few areas where land was made available through the expulsion of German or other minorities.

Collectivisation. Land reform had alleviated, but never removed the agrarian problem. Over the whole region, the majority of farms were still of less than 5 hectares (12·3 acres), and in Hungary and Romania, more than half were under 2 hectares (under 4·9 acres). The structure of agriculture had not been improved; indeed, the breakup of the large estates meant that the average size of fields and of parcels of land became smaller; and the scope for the use of machines and introduction of improved methods diminished. The ultimate solution envisaged in Eastern Europe was collectivisation. The process of collectivising agriculture had actually begun before the second phase of land reform was completed. Some lands confiscated by the government were not redistributed among the peasants, in some instances because of the quality of the land itself; in others, such as the Sudetenland and the Polish recovered provinces, because the problems of peasant migration and resettlement seemed at the time to be insuperable.

A further motive for collectivisation arose when the governments embarked on a planned development of heavy industry, and a demand arose for labour both in the factories and in construction work, which could only be supplied at the expense of agriculture. The collectives established ranged from peasant cooperatives to the thorough-going kolkhoz, in which the private sector was reduced to a small vegetable plot.

Progress towards collectivisation was erratic. The movement was in general opposed by the peasantry. After the death of Stalin it ceased for a time and was even reversed in some countries. Not until the later 1950s was it resumed, and this time carried to completion in the 1960s. This progress is examined in the next chapter.

Rural settlement

The East European peasantry was formed when a feudal mode of land tenure and exploitation gradually disintegrated. The villages and farms in which the peasant lived and worked dated in many instances from the medieval expansion of settlement. Village patterns have changed in detail through the centuries, but in their general plans they have been remarkably permanent. The organisation of the homes and farms within the hamlet or village is, in some respects, a reflection of local conditions of terrain and water-supply and of local sources of building materials; in some respects, also, it was adjusted to the social order, and may have represented ideas of social organisations and artistic expression carried over by immigrant peoples from other regions.

The village. The late nineteenth-century student of human settlement, August Meitzen, related the plan of the settlement to the ethnic origins of the people who created it. He regarded the compact or nucleated village as indicative of Germanic settlement; a pattern of scattered farms as typical of the Celts, and the 'street' village and the village arranged in a ring or circular pattern, with a central open space, as the creation of the Slavs. All these types of settlement are present in Eastern Europe, along with others that did not make their appearance in Meitzen's classification. All these peoples to whom he attributed specific patterns of settlement have inhabited at some time or other extensive areas of Eastern Europe, but it is utterly impossible to associate particular village types with any of these particular groups. Tribal custom and practice must have been a factor shaping the layout of the village, but so also were technology and terrain, social organisation, soil and crops. In most instances it is impossible to explain exactly why a village assumed the shape and size which it did. It seems probable, however, that some of the village patterns which we recognise today are separate stages in an evolutionary process from the small, open cluster of huts to the large, compact village, and that the pressure of increasing population was the principal factor in the change.

Fig. 5.4 shows in a highly simplified fashion the types of village found in Eastern Europe; detailed examinations of particular countries will follow in the second part of this book. This map, with the explanation which follows, is intended only to give a general survey of the region as a whole. Its most conspicuous feature is its tendency to reproduce in the different types of settlement the geographical pattern of the main physiographic regions of Eastern Europe itself.

About a third of the region is characterised by the 'street' village. This consists of houses—most of them small peasant farms—arranged somewhat irregularly along both sides of a road. The institution is an

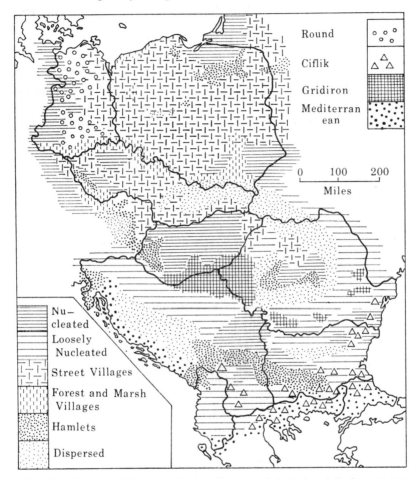

Round

Ciflik

Gridiron

Mediterranean

0   100   200

Miles

Nu—cleated

Loosely Nucleated

Street Villages

Forest and Marsh Villages

Hamlets

Dispersed

Fig. 5.4. Types of villages in Eastern Europe. Adapted mainly from J. M. Houston, *A Social Geography of Europe*, Duckworth, 1953, with detail from J. Cvijic, B. Zaborski, V. Michailescu (see bibliography).

old one, however recent the individual houses may be themselves. It derives probably from the original settlement of medieval farmers along a trackway through the forest—for the 'street' village is limited in its distribution to the formerly forested areas of northern Europe.

It is found over most of the East German and Polish Plain, as well as in the plains of Bohemia and Moravia, and along the northern margin of the Pannonian Plain.

A variant of the street village shows a widening of the street to enclose an elongated open space or 'green'—the so-called *Angerdorf.* Another variant is the forest village, or *Waldhufendorf*, similar in its general features to the 'street' village, though less regular, as if built along the sides of a winding forest path. In the mountains which border East Germany and Poland and extend over much of Czechoslovakia and Romania the irregularity of the forest village tends to replace the greater rigidity of the street village, and in this it is easy to perceive the influence of terrain as the village twists along a winding mountain valley.

A nucleated village pattern, in which the houses form a compact and more or less rounded cluster, is conspicuous in East Germany, parts of southern Poland, Bohemia, parts of the Pannonian Plain and of the Balkan peninsula. The nucleated village occurs widely in West Germany, where it is the commonest type of village plan, and it seemed reasonable to associate its appearance in Eastern Europe with German settlement. It is probably more correct to relate it to physical conditions and to regard it as the limiting case of a broad type of settlement, of which the small, open hamlet is the other extreme.

The size of such a village will be limited, since its function is almost exclusively agricultural, by the potentialities and the extent of the surrounding cropland. It will be largest in areas where the land within a given distance of the village centre is most productive. The settlement is likely to remain a hamlet in those, such as the Carpathian regions of Romania, where it is least, and secondary settlements, remote or nearby, will be established to take the population surplus.

The small building plots of the nucleated village probably arise from the subdivision of larger between heirs, just as the multi-patterned strips in the village fields arose from progressive division of the units of cultivation. Such a system tends to be cemented by custom and by techniques, especially of ploughing, reaping, fallowing, and by that mutuality which characterises simple communities.

The mountains which make up the Carpathian system, together with the Balkan Mountains, the Rhodope and the whole Dinaric system is characterised in general by a dispersed pattern of settlement, made up of isolated farmsteads or hamlets or by very small groups of farms. The primitive economy of such areas was predominantly pastoral, and pastoral activities almost necessitate a scattered pattern of settlement, because each requires a relatively large area of land. To some extent the scattered settlements of these regions represent the summer dwellings of a transhumant society which customarily spent its winters in the valleys or lowlands. In the Hungarian Plain, isolated settlements, or *tanyák*, have grown up in fairly recent years in the wide empty spaces which formerly surrounded and separated the over-great villages of the plain. Here they result, not from pastoralism or poor soil, but from the greater security of life and the technological changes in agriculture which make the family group increasingly independent of its neighbours.

In parts of the Hungarian Plain, as well as in the Danubian valley in Romania, are villages which, in their careful, almost mathematical organisation, clearly derive from government planning. These include the villages established in the Banat and Bačka by the Austrians after the expulsion of the Turks had left the region depopulated and devastated. They are square in plan, and made up of streets, evenly spaced and intersecting at right angles. In general, their distribution coincides with that of ethnically extremely mixed areas, into which population, conscripted for the purpose, was brought from many different areas. In the southern Balkans a not dissimilar type of settlement—the *čiflik* —has arisen, though here it derives from the Turkish imperialists, rather than from the Austrian. It is square in plan, with straight streets intersecting regularly, and the whole is not infrequently protected by a defensive wall.

The Mediterranean coastline, lastly, from the Istrian peninsula to the Albanian border and around the northern shore of the Aegean Sea, presents physical conditions which are exceptional for Eastern Europe. The climate is characterised by hot, dry summers; the terrain is rough, and settlements tend to be restricted to areas where water is available. The exposure of the whole coastline to piracy for a period of many centuries has served to reinforce the Mediterranean tendency to form compact settlements, walled if near the coast, and, if inland, situated on hilltops, in the best positions for defence.

House types. The design of rural houses and the materials of which they are built also show a distinct geographical pattern. Commonly, though by no means invariably, design is adjusted to local materials and to the physical—especially climatic—conditions. They may—and often do—incorporate elements that are far from functional, and which represent, in a certain sense, cultural borrowings.

In a peasant society, houses must in general be built of local materials, and over most of the area covered in this book, timber is the most abundant. Indeed, it may be said that wood construction is normal in rural communities except in some areas of the northern plain and of Bohemia and Moravia, where brick and stone may replace it. In these areas, the use of masonry reflects a higher level of wealth and sophistication than is general in Eastern Europe. In some of the mountain areas stone of building quality is relatively abundant and is much used, and in the region of Mediterranean climate, the lack of usable timber makes it necessary to use stone almost exclusively.

In the north and north-west of the region the strong German influence is reflected in the 'Saxon' house, a massive building, commonly of brick and timber, designed to house the family, together with much of its farm equipment and some at least of its farm animals under a single roof. A similar type of house appears in the Alpine region, where in winter conditions of heavy snow it is desirable that as much as possible of the farmstock be gathered under a single roof together with the farmer's family. Commonly in such houses both the angle and the material of the roof and the size of the overhang show an adjustment to winter conditions of heavy snow.

To the south, especially in Bohemia and Moravia, the farmhouse, substantially built of wood and masonry, is separated from the farm buildings, and the whole grouped around a courtyard. Such complex courtyard farms are not infrequently closely spaced along a street, presenting to the road a wall with few openings except the high arched entrance gate, through which the farm wagons pass.

Over most of Poland and much of Slovakia and Romania the peasant house is simple in design and construction. It has a single floor, not infrequently still of beaten earth, with walls of wooden beams; it is usually elongated in plan and divided into two rooms, with sometimes a kind of porch at one end. The roof is either thatched or of wooden shingles, and is steeply pitched. A small and roughly fenced yard may contain a stall for a few animals, storage for farm equipment and a heap of manure. The basic style is almost uniform; its degree of elaboration, endlessly varied. Sometimes the wooden beams of which it is built are plastered over and coloured. The colours, like the pale blue in the cottages of Galicia, are usually traditional. Gable ends and porticoes are often carved and decorated. The cottage is very much a status symbol among the peasantry, which is as conscious of fine social distinctions as any more sophisticated group. In some of the poorer regions, especially in Romania, cottages of this type sink to a level of crudeness in construction that is difficult to describe. In extreme cases the village may be a loose cluster of such cottages, with steeply-pitched, thatched roofs and without fence, yard or any form of external adornment.

Over the Hungarian Plain and parts of the Balkan peninsula, the common type of cottage is a variant of this pattern. The use of masonry is more widespread because in many areas it is more readily available than timber. Against the long side of the cottage is commonly a kind of verandah, its roof supported on pillars. Usually it faces into the courtyard, and its aspect as often as not is more or less southerly. The verandah is probably an indication of generous sunshine, and it provides shade on a hot summer's day. Such houses, with varying degrees of elaboration and decoration, are found over much of the Balkans.

Three significant house types, found south of the Danube, should be mentioned. These are the so-called 'Turkish' house, the Albanian house and the Mediterranean house. The 'Turkish' and Albanian houses show strongly the influence of cultural factors. The former, found most commonly in the cities, is a courtyard house, with few or no external windows on the ground floor and an upper floor which usually overhangs the lower. The Albanian house is such as would be built in an area marked by banditry and the blood-feud. It is mainly built of rough masonry; it is often a tower of two or more storeys, not unlike the peel-towers of the Scottish Border, and has a minimum of openings for windows and doors. It is, in effect, a small castle.

The distinctive character of the Mediterranean region extends to its domestic architecture. The scarcity of timber for construction purposes necessitates a more widespread use of stone than in most other areas; the nature of the predominant crops and the character of their products—wine and olive oil—necessitates cool storage spaces. At least since the time when Xenophon wrote his *Oekonomikos*, the need to store oil and wine has influenced the architecture of the Mediterranean house. It is commonly of two or more storeys; its basement serves as a cool storage place, and may also contain the wine press; its roof is made of curved pantiles, which serve to shed the sometimes heavy winter rains, and at the same time, allow the breeze to pass through, and thus to cool the attic and keep it fit for storage purposes. The windows of the Mediterranean house are adjusted rather to an excess of sunshine than to its deficiency. The cool, dim light of the

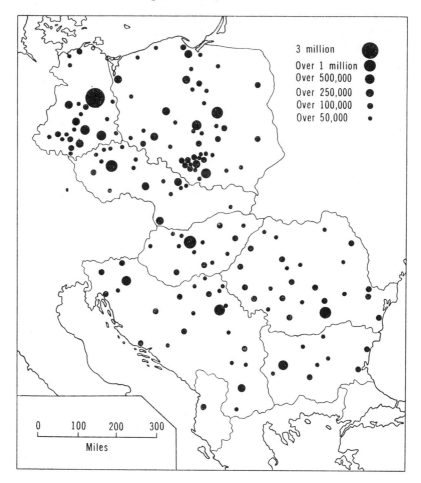

Fig. 5.5. Urban development in Eastern Europe; the map shows the distribution of all cities of more than 50,000 inhabitants; for names see the corresponding maps in Chapters 7 to 14. Data from the statistical yearbooks of the respective countries for 1964 or 1965.

Mediterranean home, as of the Mediterranean church, is a refreshing change from the glare outside.

Urban settlement

The map, Fig. 5.5, suggests that the city in Eastern Europe spread from the north-west and west and was of German or Italian origin.

Such a conclusion, though often drawn, would not be wholly warranted. In some ways the town owed much to German example and
experience, but it is too complex an institution to be ascribed to any
single origin. The town serves many functions, of which specialised
industries and crafts and the pursuit of commerce are probably the
most important and certainly the most widespread. But towns have
also important administrative and governmental functions; they serve
as centres of church organisation and in earlier centuries acted as
places of refuge in times of trouble.

Towns may be studied from the points of view of their morphology
and of their function. To some extent these are related, because their
layout was in most cases made to further the purposes which the cities
themselves were designed to serve. Towns were founded in classical
times around the periphery of the Balkan peninsula, from Trieste and
Pula in the north-west to Tomi and Olbi on the shore of the Black Sea.
They combined many functions: administrative, commercial, industrial and residential. In general, they were built of masonry, and
were planned with straight streets and regular city blocks. Some served
also as garrison towns, especially in the interior of the Balkan peninsula.
As if in imitation of the classical cities, the native peoples of the
Balkans and Eastern Europe themselves built towns, which served the
same range of function, though with differences of emphasis. The
Thracians and Illyrians and, farther to the north, the early Slavs built
towns, sometimes of considerable size, mainly as defensive points.
Such were the hilltop capital of the Dacians, Sarmizegetusa; the
Great Preslav of the early Bulgars; the so-called 'burgwalls' of the
Czechs and Slovaks, and the ninth- and tenth-century towns of Poland.
In some instances these Dark Age cities have been occupied continuously until today; at Poznań and Gniezno there has probably
been some kind of urban life without interruption for a thousand
years.

The East European town. With the emergence of the medieval states
of Eastern Europe, a capital city developed in each and began to
distinguish itself both in its function and its architecture from other
cities. The close association of the earliest royal families with the
Church is apparent. The Church played a role in selecting the kings;
it bestowed on them the unction of coronation, and afterwards continued to supply them with the only skilled administrative staff that
was available in those times. The capitals of the early East European
states constitute an interesting group of cities because of the close

association of the organs of Church and state. Kraków, Prague and Budapest constitute the best examples, but with these might be associated Nitra, Zagreb, Warsaw, and Poznań. Typically, the city crowns a defensible hill, such as the Wawel at Kraków, the Hradčany at Prague, and the hill of Buda in Budapest, and in this it shows its derivation from the prehistoric city of refuge. Within the fortifications is the castle of the king and the cathedral of the archbishop or bishop. Only the Wawel at Kraków retains with any degree of completeness its medieval appearance. The Hradčany preserves its Gothic cathedral of St. Vitus, but most of that monumental pile of building which crowns the hill above the Vltava belongs to the eighteenth century. Buda has also suffered from repeated destruction and rebuilding; at Zagreb, the ecclesiastical sector was almost wholly rebuilt in the eighteenth and nineteenth centuries.

All these cities were autonomous developments within Eastern Europe, owing nothing to German precedent. But two types of town nevertheless did owe their inspiration to Central European example: the feudal city and the merchant city.

The former was by no means as common in Eastern Europe as it became in Central and Western. It consisted essentially of a castle which served as a nucleus for an urban development, attracted to it by the degree of protection which it could afford. In its typical development, castle and town merged to form an organic whole, such as one finds, for example, at Meissen, in Saxony. Their small number is due to the fact that feudalism was a relatively late development in Eastern Europe and that there were some areas to which, in fact, it never came at all. The majority of the cities of Central and Western Europe derive from nuclei—usually castle or monastery— around which they crystallised. The East European town, at least in the area lying to the north of the Danube, was most often established by merchants for the purposes of trade. It was regular and compact in plan and was usually surrounded by walls. Its streets were straight, and focused on the market-place, scene of the most important of the activities of its citizens.

The town plan. In a few instances the merchants' city grew up without any preconceived plan. Usually, however, it was planned as a number of straight streets, intersecting at right angles and creating rectangular town blocks. One or more such blocks was left as an open market place. The town-hall, *Rathaus,* or *Ratusz,* commonly overlooked the square, or stood free within it, as at Wrocław. Such towns contained parish

Wrocław, showing the islands in the Odra on which the early medieval city grew up. The cathedral is seen bottom right

Wrocław, town square and town hall. This rather old photograph illustrates the rectangular planning of the late medieval town

Split, the Palace of Diocletian, the decorative pilasters of which are clearly visible along the water front. The tower marks the site of the mausoleum of the emperor, which was subsequently converted into the cathedral

Plovdiv, Bulgaria. In the foreground is the old city, clinging to the slopes of the granite hills; in the distance, beyond the Marica, is the new post-war development

churches, but very rarely did they have cathedrals, as the seats of most bishops had already been chosen when they were established. The churches were not commonly obtrusive. The merchants commonly set more store by a pretentious town- or guild-hall than by gothic churches. However carefully planned the original layout may have been, the town plan came in time to be distorted. Bends and constrictions appeared in the streets, as property owners encroached on the roads or the houses were rebuilt on slightly different ground plans after their not infrequent fires and catastrophes. The diagrams of such planned towns as Plzeň and Wrocław show how much the earlier plan has been warped by time. Some, Kalisz for example, have become so twisted that from the map alone it is difficult to say whether or not they began as rectilinear planned cities.

The types of town discussed here are not mutually exclusive. There are examples of planned towns which grew up before the walls of a feudal castle; the city of Kraków developed in the shadow of the Wawel on a rectilinear plan. There are, conversely, commercial towns, such as Lublin, which did not have a castle as nucleus and show little evidence of ever having been planned; the merchants' cities in Prague, the Staré Město on the right bank of the Vltava, and in Pest on the left bank of the Danube, were planned very imperfectly, if at all.

We turn lastly to the Turkish town of the Balkans and the agricultural town of the Hungarian Plain. The former derived usually from a Hellenistic, Roman or Byzantine city, but its original plan and appearance have been distorted to accord with the prescriptions of Muslim religion and the practice of Muslim law. 'The mark of Islam,' wrote Xavier de Planhol, 'has been impressed on the life and appearance of its cities more indelibly than anywhere else.'[1] The Muslim city was dominated by the mosque, around which revolved many aspects of Muslim life. The lack of public parks and large open spaces accords with Islam's opposition to public recreation and entertainment. In the Islamic city, petty commerce is concentrated in the bazaar, unlike the western town, where shop and home are virtually synonymous. Most of the city is thus residential, and the homes have that secretive look, already mentioned, designed to protect its interior from the casual glance of the passer-by. Such were the towns which the Turks either created, or occupied and modified in Bosnia, Serbia, Macedonia and Bulgaria. The more recent development of all these towns has,

[1] Xavier de Planhol, *The World of Islam*, Cornell Univ. Press, Ithaca, N.Y., 1959, p. 1.

6

however, been in the direction of bringing them, at least in outward appearance, into closer accord with those of Central Europe.

The coastal town, whether Baltic or Mediterranean, was primarily a merchants' settlement. The few that grew up along the straight, flat and generally harbourless Baltic coast, bear the stamp of the Hanseatic trader. Their elongated town blocks, their tall, richly decorated, merchants' houses, and their warehouses along the water-front—as at Gdańsk (Danzig) for example—are in the tradition of Hamburg and Lübeck. Those of the Mediterranean coast derive their inspiration from Italy. Rijeka (Fiume) was in origin a Roman settlement; Split grew around the palace built here by the Emperor Diocletian for his retirement. Dubrovnik originated in a small offshore island settlement of Italian merchants, which, by filling in the narrow channel that separated it from the coast, was joined up with a small Slav settlement on the mainland. Thessaloníki and Durrës were Roman in origin, and most of the few other coastal towns are small, irregular agglomerations of medieval date.

The towns of the Pannonian Plain—at least those lying to the east of the Danube—differ in form and function from those in almost every other part of Eastern Europe. Despite their sometimes considerable size, most of them were originally agricultural in function, and many remain predominantly so today. These overgrown villages, entirely devoid of order or planning, grew up for security reasons amid a society still largely pastoral, and only in recent years have these tightly agglomerated settlements begun to break up.

The modern town. Most towns of Eastern Europe originated during the Middle Ages. They grew little during the first two or three centuries of modern times; then more rapidly during the nineteenth century. Today their early core is usually clearly separated from the areas of nineteenth-century development. The line of the ancient walls is commonly marked today by public parks, like the *Planty* at Kraków, or by boulevards, as at Prague and Budapest. In a few instances they survive in part, as at Zagreb and Warsaw. The area which was built up in the nineteenth century has generally wider streets and buildings that are taller and stylistically distinct. Interspersed with residential and commercial buildings are the factories, which were the cause of this urban growth, and the railways and marshalling yards which for obvious reasons had failed to penetrate the older urban core.

Few towns in Eastern Europe owed their origin entirely to the industrial and commercial growth of the nineteenth century, but among them are Łódź, Katowice, Chorzów and Zabrze in Poland; Ostrava in Czechoslovakia, and Miskolc in Hungary. In general, these towns resemble the contemporary and peripheral growth of the older cities, with their wider streets, their functional architecture and their complete lack of character and taste.

The socialist town. The planned economic development of recent years has led to the foundation of yet other industrial cities. The 'socialist' town of today is in general more homogeneous and better planned than the nineteenth-century town. The former, with its huge apartment blocks, its state-run shops, its children's playgrounds, and its community centre, is monotonous and egalitarian, but incomparably more comfortable and hygienic than the crowded alleys of the nineteenth century towns. Such are Nowa Huta and Nowy Tychy in Poland; Havířov in Czechoslovakia, Dunaújváros in Hungary, and Victoria in Romania.

The ghetto. The medieval town was commonly divided into sectors, in each of which there was some specialisation in occupation or trade. In the Turkish Empire, the sectors were characterised more by uniformity of faith or ethnic group than by occupation, though the latter sometimes served also as a basis of segregation within the city. In the Balkans, where the Turks were never more than a small minority, they segregated themselves into a certain quarter in each city. The diminution of their numbers led ultimately to the infiltration of non-Turks into their reserved areas and to the breakdown of the system. Such voluntary segregation is commonly the act of a minority, whether a ruling minority or not. It reflects a social and religious need for its members to live together, but it also suggests that the group lives in fear of the majority. This latter situation was particularly characteristic of the most widely distributed urban minority in all Eastern Europe, the Jews. In Tsarist Russia the segregation of the Jewish population into ghettos was legally enforced. In the East European countries, with the exception of parts of Eastern Poland which had fallen within the Pale of Jewish Settlement when under Russian rule, this was not so. Nevertheless, many towns of Eastern Europe came to be characterised by ghettos, generally small in area and overbuilt, in which all except the wealthier members of the Jewish community lived, partly from their own desire to be together, partly from social pressures exerted against them. But for the virtual extermination of the Jewish population during the Second World War, this kind of voluntary ghetto would probably have survived as part of the urban geography of many—especially the larger—East European towns. The Warsaw ghetto, comprising the Muranów sector of the city, was the scene of the Jewish rising against the Germans in 1943 and of its savage suppression. Here and also at Łódź the Jewish sectors were deliberately destroyed. In many of the Polish towns, as well as in Prague and a number of other Czechoslovak and some Hungarian cities, there was also a predominantly Jewish quarter.

Bibliography

Agrarian Problems from the Baltic to the Aegean, London, Royal Institute of International Affairs, 1944.

BLANC, ANDRÉ, 'Communautés rurales et structures agraires dans les pays sud-slaves', *Géographie et Histoire Agraires*, Annales de l'Est, Memoire 21, Nancy, 1959.

COMBS, JERRY W. 'Demographic Changes in Eastern Europe', *Population Trends in Eastern Europe, the USSR and Mainland China*, 11–34, New York, Milbank Memorial Fund, 1960.

HOUSTON, J. M. *A Social Geography of Europe*, London, Duckworth, 1953.

KOSIŃSKI, L. 'Les problèmes démographiques dans les territoires occidentaux de la Pologne et les régions frontières de la Tchécoslovaquie', *Annls Géog.* **71** (1962), 79–98.

MEYER, PETER, BERNARD D. WEINRYB, EUGENE DUSCHINSKY and NICOLAS SYLVAIN, *The Jews in the Soviet Satellites*, Syracuse University Press, 1953.

'Minorities in Eastern Europe', *East Europe*, **8** (1959), March, 3–14.

MOORE, WILBERT E. *Economic Demography of Eastern and Southern Europe*, Geneva, League of Nations, 1945.

SCHECHTMAN, JOSEPH B. *Postwar Population Transfers in Europe*, 1945–55, University of Pennsylvania Press, 1962.

SCHULMAN, ELIAS, 'The Jews in Eastern Europe', *East Europe*, **11**, April, 1962, 3–7.

STEERS, MRS. J. A. (H. G. WANKLYN), 'The Artisan Element in the Slav Countries', *Geogrl J.* **103** (1944), 101–19.

WANKLYN, H. G. 'Geographical Aspects of Jewish Settlement East of Germany', *Geogrl J.* **95** (1940), 175–90.

WILHELMY, HERBERT, 'Völkische und Koloniale Siedlungsformen der Slawen', *Geogr. Z.* **42**, (1936), 81–97.

CHAPTER SIX

Resources and Development

Both the agricultural and the industrial revolutions came late to Eastern Europe, and even at the outbreak of the Second World War their impact had not been felt in all parts of the area. The planned development of resources which began in the late 1940s and has continued until today has changed this. Development was rapid but uneven. Pre-industrial techniques continued to be used alongside the most modern, and many of the aspects of the economy which have not been modernised have continued to lower the effectiveness of those which have. The resources of the area, as the East European writers never cease to tell us, had formerly been under-used or misused. This, we are told, is now changed. A more rational use is now being made of all natural resources of the region, and in some instances a larger development is predicated upon them than their extent would appear to justify.

The resources for agriculture and manufacturing in Eastern Europe differ from those in Western, and in many ways they are smaller. The attempt to build in Eastern Europe an industrial structure similar to that found in the West has been possible only by importing many raw materials which Western Europe possessed in abundance. Indeed, the natural endowment of Eastern Europe is in some respects so weak that it is difficult to conceive of a thorough-going industrialisation—such as that which has taken place—without political support by the Soviet Union and strong ideological inspiration. In short, without the creation of socialist states, development could not have taken place on its present scale.

AGRICULTURE

The agricultural resources of Eastern Europe appear to be more generous than the industrial. For almost a century before the Second World War, the East European countries enjoyed the reputation of being a storehouse of agricultural products for the nourishment of the

West. Such a reputation was not wholly deserved. Expanding population and a small rise in living standards have absorbed most of the former surplus, and the East European countries are today only a small net exporter of food-stuffs.

Agricultural resources

Table 9 shows that cropland today makes up only 45 per cent of the total area, and the agriculturally employed population has sunk from

Table 9. Agricultural area and percentage of total area—1965

Country	Total area (hectares)	Cropland (hectares)	Percentage	Meadow and pasture (hectares)	Percentage
East Germany	10,789	4,995	46·9	1,434	12·7
Poland	31,173	15,682	52·0	4,264	13·4
Czechoslovakia	12,787	5,387	42·4	1,773	14·8
Hungary	9,303	5,647	61·3	1,304	15·4
Romania	23,750	10,475	43·6	4,316	17·7
Yugoslavia	25,580	8,306	32·6	6,450	25·7
Bulgaria	11,093	4,563	41·7	1,230	9·4
Albania	2,875	501	16·4	729	27·0

Source: *FAO Production Yearbook, 1966.*

considerably over half of the labour force when the plans began to about 40 per cent today. Cropland is far from evenly distributed, as Table 9 shows, and is particularly restricted in the Balkan countries. The area of high quality farmland is small. Over much of Eastern Europe the climate is moist enough for extensive podzolisation of the soil to have taken place, and in the hilly and mountainous areas a thin and sometimes only a skeletal soil is in general to be found. The plain of East Germany and Poland has been glaciated, and the soils range from heavy and poorly-drained clay to light sands and gravels, both of which form highly intractable farmland. Good soils occur in parts of Polish Silesia and Galicia, where drier conditions, a hard winter, and loess deposits have encouraged the formation of a chernozem-type soil. Not dissimilar conditions occur in northern Bohemia, parts of Moravia and of the Pannonian Plain. In the latter, however, although the climate may favour the formation of chernozem, the high water-table under the lowland areas of the plain and its extensive areas of

Table 10. Percentage of labour force in agriculture

	Percentage of labour force in agriculture	
	1930–44	*1965 est.*
East Germany	23 (1952)	19
Poland	60	42
Czechoslovakia	33	16
Hungary	49	31
Romania	61	59
Yugoslavia	76	53
Bulgaria	73	59
Albania	80	58

Source: *FAO Production Yearbook, 1966.*

wind-blown sand very greatly reduce the agricultural value of the region.

On the outer side of the curving arc of the Carpathian Mountains, are good chernozem soils, developed in many instances on loess, in Moldavia, Walachia and of parts of the platform of northern Bulgaria and the Dobrogea. A low and somewhat unreliable rainfall, sets limits to their agricultural usefulness. In the Balkan peninsula the large area of rough terrain, much of it with at best a skeletal soil, greatly reduces the areal extent of agriculture and in fact restricts it to the river valleys and the intramontane basins—many of them former lake floors—which are characteristic of the region.

Large areas of Eastern Europe need drainage if their agricultural potential is to be realised. Elsewhere irrigation, particularly by the use of sprinklers, is necessary if the maximum use is to be made of cropland. These improvements are costly, and are being made only when high-value crops, such as garden vegetables and cotton can be grown. Industrialisation is creating a demand for technical crops, such as flax, hemp, sugar-beet, oil seeds and, where it can be grown, cotton, and these crops are tending to cut into the area formerly sown with bread crops. In Czechoslovakia, for instance, the import of wheat has increased as sugar-beet has taken over land formerly sown with grain.

Agricultural resources are thus severely limited, and it has been the policy of the East European governments to make the greatest possible use of them by increasing the capital investment in farming and by improving the technical level of agriculture.

Collectivisation

In all countries of Eastern Europe there was, as we have seen, a measure of land reform directly after the Second World War, so that by about 1948 most of the land was in the hands of the peasantry. This was but the prelude to the drive towards collectivisation. Producer co-operatives began to be formed before the land reform was everywhere completed, and in the early 1950s considerable progress was made, in the face of a strong resistance by the peasantry. The period immediately following the death of Stalin was followed by a reversal of the process; collectives were broken up, and reverted to independent peasant farms. In Poland and Yugoslavia this has continued to be the state of affairs, but elsewhere a renewed pressure by the government has led to the collectivisation of virtually all land capable of being exploited in this way. The process was for practical purposes complete in the early 1960s and in all countries of Eastern Europe, except Poland and Yugoslavia, the socialised sector embraces more than 90 per cent of all agricultural land.

In Poland and Yugoslavia collectivisation is declared to be the ultimate goal of the governments, but fear of alienating the peasantry has caused them to postpone—apparently indefinitely—its attainment.

Collectivisation has followed closely the Soviet model, with the creation of state farms for scientific and plant-breeding purposes, of collective farms to which in theory the peasants contribute their land and labour voluntarily, and of machine and tractor stations. The collectives at first assumed a variety of organisational patterns, in part at least to conciliate the peasants who were obliged to join them. In theory peasants are still free in most cases to leave the collectives and to take back their share of land and equipment. In practice this freedom is about as real as that enjoyed by the Soviet Socialist Republics under the constitution to withdraw from the Soviet Union.

The collectivisation of agriculture has proved in recent years to be a one-way process. The replacement of horses and oxen by machines, the installation of land-drainage and irrigation equipment, and the establishment of government-controlled channels for the supply of seed and fertiliser and the marketing of the farm produce, has made

Table 11. *Percentage of agricultural land in socialised sector*

	Percentage of agricultural land in the socialised sector
East Germany	89·1
Poland	14·0
Czechoslovakia	*c.* 90·0
Hungary	*c.* 97·0
Romania	95·0
Yugoslavia	13·0
Bulgaria	*c.* 95·0
Albania	*c.* 93·0

any reversion to small-scale peasant agriculture technically impossible. In almost all forms of collectivisation the peasant retains a small plot, where he can grow a few crops, commonly vegetables and potatoes, for his family, and keep a cow, a few pigs and some poultry. One still sees in most parts of Eastern Europe, the tethered cow being led out to graze by the roadside in the evening, and the peasant is still accused of lavishing more care on his privately-owned pigs than on the animals of the collective farm.

Collectivisation has everywhere brought changes in the physical landscape. Except in Poland and Yugoslavia, the patchwork pattern of small and irregular strips, separated by unseen boundaries, known only to the peasants who cultivate them, has disappeared, and with it much of the variety and colour from the landscape. As a general rule, fields are very large, for combines and large tractors cannot operate in confined spaces. Now, instead of the multi-coloured plots of land, one sees gangs of brightly clothed women working their way across vast, uniform fields, indicative of the disharmony that has arisen in the technological equipment of agriculture.

Collectivisation has also necessited the erection of new farm buildings. The clustered stables, cow-sheds, barns and equipment parks, generally built of masonry, roofed with tiles and surrounded by paddocks and feed-lots for the animals, make an impressive sight, and in many areas are the dominant feature of the landscape.

6*

Agricultural production

Changes in the structure and organisation of agriculture have resulted in an overall increase in agricultural production. This increase has been uneven. It is pointless to criticise the social ownership of land for the difficulties in the supply of bread crops, when this is due, in fact, to the new order of priorities that has been imposed on agriculture by the planning authorities. Some of these changes make good sense. It is, for example, better to grow high-value industrial crops on the good soil of northern Bohemia than the lower-priced bread crops, which can be imported without difficulty. Only in Romania is the traditional East European export of bread-grains still of any great importance. Elsewhere the shift to more sophisticated crops, such as sugar-beet in Czechoslovakia, fruit and early vegetables in Bulgaria, tobacco in Yugoslavia is becoming increasingly important.

Table 12. Agricultural production for 1964 and 1965 (1957–59 = 100)

	1964	1965
East Germany	102	103
Poland	118	122
Czechoslovakia	106	94
Hungary	105	106
Romania	116	121
Yugoslavia	118	109
Bulgaria	118	109
East Europe	116	111

Source: *East Europe*, **15**, no. 11, November 1966.

This changing structure of agriculture makes comparisons of productivity, both between the present and the past and also between different countries at the present time, extremely difficult. Nevertheless, some of them publish statistics which purport to show the increase in crude agricultural production. How these figures have been computed, and how comparable they are is not known. They suggest, however, that the increase in agricultural production has been greater than western critics of the system have been ready to admit, and that, in relation to the labour input, this growth has been not inconsiderable.

MANUFACTURING INDUSTRY

It is in manufacturing, and particularly in the heavy or capital goods industries, that the most ambitious plans have been made and advances achieved. A region which had been predominantly agricultural, with only a few centres of modern industrial development, has, within the space of 20 years, become a truly significant producer of basic industrial goods. 'This half-enforced and half-spontaneous industrialisation of the mid-European area,' wrote Jan Wszelaki, 'is a major event in European history. The Communist system may endure or perish, but what has already been done can hardly be undone: (Eastern) Europe will not return to its pastoral era.'[1]

Many factors combined to make possible this industrial development. Among them was the far from gentle persuasion of the Soviet Union, anxious to see a developed Eastern Europe that would present a barrier of friendly and powerful states to any possible aggression from the West, and at the same time provide a supplementary source of manufactured goods to satisfy its own needs. Then, too, there were the ideological considerations defined by Lenin and Stalin and thoroughly learned by the Communist leaders who had spent much of their exile in the Soviet Union: the factory worker was more amenable to party discipline than the peasant, and in the steelworks and machine-shops was forged not only the spirit of socialism, but also the means to defend the socialist state. This kind of argument, so outdated and threadbare today, was not without its effect in the early days of planned development. Lastly, this movement towards the planned growth of socialised industry received, unwittingly perhaps, a measure of support from that 'bourgeois nationalism' which it was its purpose to replace.

The nations of Eastern Europe, in becoming 'People's Democracies', had lost little of their former national spirit. This was blanketed by a monolithic Communist organisation with control exercised in Moscow over the national Communist parties, but sooner or later it would emerge again. Poles, Czechs and others were taught to prepare themselves against a resurgence of German nationalism. In doing so they prepared themselves also for reviving the feuds which had long divided them from one another.

These quarrels and claims have in recent years come to be expressed more and more overtly, until Romania even dares to challenge Soviet

[1] Jan Wszelaki, in *Foreign Affairs*, 30 (1951–52), pp. 123–134.

control of Bessarabia. Such playing with fire may be somewhat premature; Hungarians and Bulgarians have their own claims against Romania, and may be tempted to press them. When one read on a

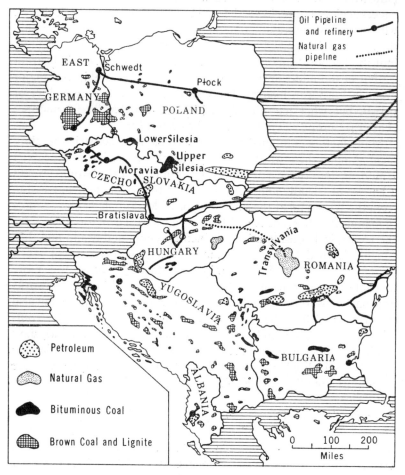

Fig. 6.1. Map of fuel resources in Eastern Europe. The pipelines were based on *Statesman's Yearbook, 1966*.

banner stretched across a main street in Warsaw, that 'the whole nation is building Nowa Huta' there must have been many who secretly hoped that the hardware which it produced would be used against their neighbours, both German and Slav.

The programme of industrialisation has been adopted not without some enthusiasm in many quarters. Is it matched, one may ask, with commensurate industrial resources in fuel, metalliferous ores and minerals for the chemical industries?

Fuel resources
It is difficult to conceive of industrial growth in Western Europe having taken place without abundant reserves of high-grade fuel. It was an industrialisation which spread outwards from the coal-fields. Eastern Europe has no such abundance. It has one large coal-field, that of Silesia and Moravia, and a multitude of very small coal-fields of indifferent quality; it contains a large part of the world's brown coal resources, which cannot, for reasons of cost, be transported far. It has Europe's largest oilfield, which nevertheless produces only about 1 per cent of the world's crude oil, and it has a considerable though hitherto little developed hydro-electric power potential.

Bituminous coal. Estimates of the total reserves of bituminous coal are conflicting, and geological surveying in recent years has tended to raise them somewhat. The basis for formulating estimates is not consistent between countries, and it is by no means easy to arrive at a figure for Eastern Europe as a whole. Table 13 has been compiled mainly from United Nations statistics, which are significantly lower than those announced by some of the more sanguine East European writers. Total estimates are about a quarter of that attributed at the same time to West Germany. It should be added that whereas demand for coal is declining in Western Europe, it is still rising in every one of the Eastern countries, and is likely to continue to do so for a very considerable period.

It is apparent that only two countries have large reserves, and that most of these come in fact from different parts of the same coal basin, that of Upper Silesia and Moravia. The problem of distribution of coal from this field is a serious one. A large part of East Germany's supply of coking coal, is in fact sent by barge down the Odra from the Polish sector of the field. The Czechoslovak sector similarly supplies coking coal to works in Bohemia and Eastern Slovakia by rail, and there is some exchange of coal of differing qualities between Poland and Czechoslovakia. Both Romania and Hungary import coal, including coking coal, from outside the region, and in East Germany, Bulgaria and Yugoslavia a low-grade metallurgical coke is being produced from sub-bituminous coal which is not included in the totals given

Table 13. Estimates of total reserves of bituminous and coking coal
(millions of metric tons)

	Estimated reserves	Estimated reserves of coking coal
East Germany	225	—
Poland	60,000	18,200
Czechoslovakia	6,000	4,000
Hungary	210	20
Romania	48	10
Yugoslavia	39	—
Bulgaria	1	—
Albania	n.d.	n.d.
	66,298	22,230

Sources: *European Steel Trends in the Setting of the World Market*, Steel Division Economic Commission for Europe, Geneva, 1949; *World Iron Ore Resources and Their Utilization*, Department of Economic Affairs, UN, 1950.[1]

above. It seems certain that the coal reserves of Bulgaria have been very seriously underestimated, and it is probable that coking coal is less abundant in the Polish field than is indicated.

The graph (Fig. 6.2) shows the expansion of coal production since prewar years. It is unfortunately impossible to say how much of this was coking coal, since it has become the practice to blend coals from different sources before putting them into the coke ovens. Coke technology now allows coals, once regarded as non-coking, to be used for this purpose, and the category of coking coal is no longer as clearcut as it once was. Table 14 shows the production, export, import and apparent consumption of coal in the countries of Eastern Europe in 1964.

The coal exports appear to have been in the main to countries within the East European bloc, and the excess of imports over exports for the region as a whole was largely represented by coal from the Soviet Union.

[1] There are very considerable discrepancies between these two works. The more conservative estimates have been accepted as being more realistic.

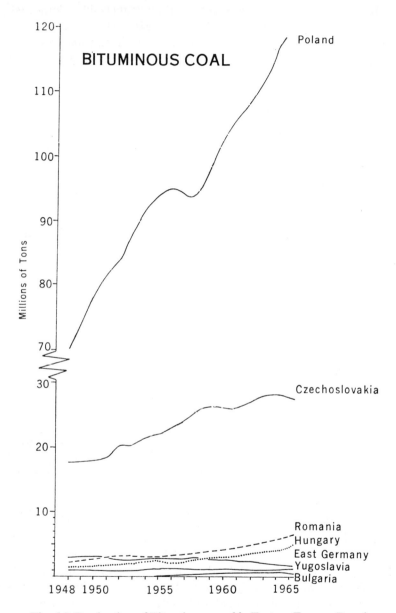

Fig. 6.2. Production of Bituminous coal in Eastern Europe. Based on *Statistical Yearbooks*, UN.

It seems certain that increasing quantities of fuel will be imported. Even if the productivity of the Upper Silesian–Moravian coal-field were expanded sufficiently, it would still be difficult and costly to supply the whole region from this source. Two of the largest users of

Table 14. Production, export, import, apparent consumption of coal (thousands of metric tons) in 1965

	Production	Export	Import	Apparent consumption
East Germany	2,212	—	9,464 3,205[1]	16,000
Poland	118,831	21,045·1 2,323·5[1]	1,209·6	95,000
Czechoslovakia	27,731	2,378 1,835	4,538	27,500
Hungary	4,362	—	2,665·3[2] 1,082	8,400
Romania	6,036	—	706·3 929·8	7,500
Yugoslavia	1,192	130·5[4]	2,185·6 110·9[3]	3,400
Bulgaria	552	—	2,600[1] 264[1]	1,000
Albania	n.d.		10·4[2]	10·4

[1] Coke.   [2] Coal and lignite.   [3] Coke and semi-coke.   [4] Coal, coke and briquettes.

Source: *UN Yearbook of International Trade Statistics, 1965.*

imported fuel, the Dunaújváros and Galați iron and steel works, were located on the Danube for the greater convenience of the import and handling of fuel and other materials. The completion, perhaps by the early 1970's, of the Rhine–Main–Danube waterway, could allow at least the Danubian countries to obtain West German coal by barge. At present their imported coal comes from the Soviet Union mainly by ship to the lower Danube, where it is trans-shipped at Brăila and taken upstream by barge, but in part also by rail, either by way of Przemyśl in south-eastern Poland, or of Uzhgorod in Ruthenia.

Sub-bituminous coal. In contrast with the shortage—in some countries acute—of bituminous coal, one finds in Eastern Europe a quite exceptional abundance of the sub-bituminous variety. Most is of Tertiary geological age, and accumulated in lake basins which were numerous during the period following the Alpine earth-movements. It varies greatly in quality; that with the highest carbon content, known as brown coal can even be made to yield a usable coke. At the opposite extreme is lignite, low in carbon content and high in ash. Eastern Europe has all these varieties, occurring sometimes at different levels in the same pit.

Most sub-bituminous coals occur at only a shallow depth, and can be worked by strip-mining methods. Only rarely today is a sub-bituminous coal found to be worth the cost of sinking a shaft. Usually the overburden is stripped, the coal removed, and the overburden restored by giant machines which are capable of handling immense quantities of material in a short period of time (see page 261). Conditions of working, however, vary greatly within the region. The highly mechanised operations are found in the large coal deposits of East Germany, Poland and Czechoslovakia. Elsewhere, deposits are generally smaller; the resources would not justify the investment, even if the country were capable of making it, in heavy earth-moving equipment, and here we often find the coal being extracted by means of shafts, inclined planes, adits and small, quarry-like excavations.

Sub-bituminous coal is rarely transported far from its source without some form of processing. Most often it is briquetted and its high moisture content removed. Part is then burned close to the pits from which it has been extracted to raise steam and generate electric power; a smaller part is used directly, especially in East Germany and Czechoslovakia, for distillation and the manufacture of certain chemicals.

The map, Fig. 6.1, shows the distribution of brown coal and lignite reserves. Exploitation of these reserves, which constitute the chief source in much of Eastern Europe of industrial power, has become increasingly important, and one may expect the volume of lignite and brown coal extracted to increase. Already Czechoslovakia, which is far from being the least well-endowed of the East European countries, is hastening its construction of a nuclear-powered generating station in order to supplement its production of the more traditional fuels. The output of brown coal and lignite in 1965 is shown in Table 15.

Petroleum. Europe is not rich in either petroleum or natural gas, and most of the known deposits, apart from the newly discovered field in north-west Germany, the Netherlands and under the North Sea, are found in close association with the Carpathian Mountains. Oil is

Table 15. Output of brown coal and lignite in 1965 (thousands of metric tons)

	Brown coal and lignite production
East Germany	251,301
Poland	22,626
Czechoslovakia	73,216
Hungary	27,075
Romania	6,059
Yugoslavia	28,788
Bulgaria	24,490
Albania	350

Source: *UN Statistical Yearbook, 1966.*

obtained in southern Moravia, where the field is an extension of the richer deposits of Zistersdorf, in Austria, and in parts of western Hungary (see Fig. 6.1). In the past a small amount of oil was won from bores in the Carpathian foot-hills of southern Poland, but this is now of negligible importance. It has been from the eastward continuation of this latter field in Romania that the greater part of Europe's oil production has come.

Until after the Second World War, Romanian oil came mainly from the Transylvanian foot-hills in northern Walachia. More recently exploratory work has revealed large reserves farther to the east and north-east. Romanian production increased sharply during the 1950s, but a peak seems to have been reached, and Romania is now looking with some forboding to the time when its large petrochemical industry will be supplied in part at least with imported crude oil.

Yugoslavia, Bulgaria and Albania all have oil reserves which, on present evidence, appear to be quite small. Their oil production is inadequate for their domestic needs, and is likely to remain so. The more northerly countries of Eastern Europe have come to depend upon the Soviet Union for the supply of crude oil. A pipeline, one of the few tangible results of the Council for Mutual Economic Cooperation (Comecon), has been constructed from the Urals oilfield through

Poland to East Germany, with branches across the Carpathians to Hungary and also to Most in western Bohemia. Refineries have been built on the pipeline at Płock, on the Vistula, and at Schwedt, to the north of Frankfurt-on-Oder, and receive apparently all their crude oil by way of the 'Friendship' pipeline from the Soviet Union. This dependence on Soviet crude oil is expected to increase. Deliveries in 1964 and planned deliveries for 1970 are shown in Table 16.

Table 16. Deliveries of Soviet crude oil in 1964 and those planned for 1970 (thousands of metric tons)

Delivered to:	1964	1970 (plan)
East Germany	4,414	8,500
Poland	3,815	9,000
Czechoslovakia	5,138	9,600

Source: *Economists Intelligence Unit.*

Crude oil has been prominent amongst the cargoes carried by barge up the Danube. It is to be expected that here, as on the Rhine, the tanker fleet will be replaced by the cheaper and more direct pipeline.

Natural gas is found in northern Yugoslavia and western Hungary and neighbouring parts of Czechoslovakia, but the largest reserves by far are those of Transylvania. A pipeline net has been constructed to deliver the gas to a number of industrial centres in Romania, and it is also exported by pipeline to Budapest.

The current volume of production of crude oil within Eastern Europe is shown in Table 17.

Hydro-electric power. The hydro-electric potential of Eastern Europe is considerable, but has hitherto been little used. The mountain regions have not only a sufficient rainfall, but the relief is in very many places highly suitable for the construction of dams and the formation of reservoirs. On the other hand, hydro-electric power installation requires more capital per unit of capacity than thermal, and, as a general rule, the potential is at a distance from consuming centres.

The hydro-electric potential of the northern plain is relatively small, and is, in fact, not used. There are a few installations in the hills which

Table 17. *Production of crude oil and natural gas in 1965*

	Crude petroleum[1]	Natural gas[2]
East Germany	—	133
Poland	340	1,378
Czechoslovakia	192	943 (1964)
Hungary	1,802	1,107
Romania	12,571	17,281
Yugoslavia	2,063	330
Bulgaria	229	—
Albania	764 (1964)	—

[1] Thousands of metric tons.   [2] Millions of cubic metres.

Source: *UN Statistical Yearbook, 1966.*

border it on the south, but the relative cheapness of solid fuel has discouraged the development of hydro-electricity. The most ambitious projects completed hitherto are in Czechoslovakia, where a series of dams has been built along the Vltava, above Prague, and the Vah. The installations along the course of the latter are a major source of power for the industrialisation of Slovakia. A similar, though somewhat smaller development has taken place along the Bistriţa River in eastern Romania, but in Yugoslavia and Bulgaria undertakings, as on the Neretva and Iskâr rivers, have only a relatively small capacity.

The largest hydro-electric undertakings not merely in Eastern but in all Europe are those which have been commenced on the Danube at Vác and Kladovo. The latter, which is making unusually rapid progress and is expected to be completed by 1970, consists of a dam at the lower end of the Iron Gate, which will lift the water-level within the gorge by about 177 feet. Locks will allow the passage of shipping, and the generators are expected to produce 10·7 billion kilowatt-hours per year. The project is a joint enterprise of Yugoslavia and Romania, and on its completion is predicated a considerable expansion of manufacturing industry in Serbia and Walachia.

The Vác dam will be built on the Danube 25 miles to the north of Budapest, where the river cuts across the Bakony-Börzsöny line of hills. Water will back up over part of the Danubian Plain of Slovakia, but the dam will have a very much smaller generating capacity than the Iron Gate. The map, Fig. 6.4, shows the location of the more important hydro-electric stations in the area. Altogether, they pro-

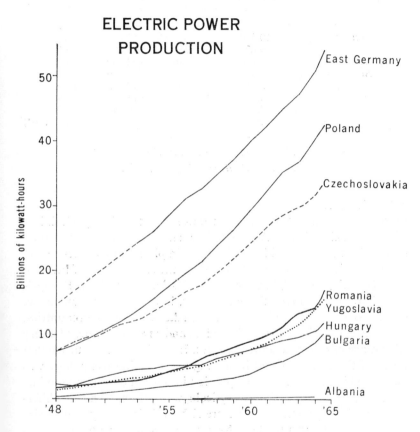

Fig. 6.3. Production of electric power in Eastern Europe. Based on *Statistical Yearbooks*, UN.

duce only 8 per cent of the electric power generated, but one may expect that the overall shortage of solid fuel will ultimately lead to hydro-electric power playing a larger role in the economy. Table 18 (page 162) shows the amount of hydro-electric power generated in 1965 and its relationship to the total.

Table 18. Amount of hydro-electricity generated and its relationship to total in 1965

	Installed capacity[1]	of which hydro-electric	Generated power[2]	of which hydro-electric
East Germany	10,350	430	53,611	785
Poland	9,672	350	43,801	913
Czechoslovakia	8,186	1,540	34,190	4,456
Hungary	1,998	21	11,176	75
Romania	3,258	461	17,215	1,005
Yugoslavia	3,700	2,265	15,523	8,985
Bulgaria	2,155	768	10,244	2,000
Albania	n.d.	n.d.	288	203(1964)

[1] Thousand kilowatts.   [2] Million killowatt-hours.

Source: *UN Statistical Yearbook, 1966.*

Mineral resources

Eastern Europe has played an illustrious role in the history of mining. Here the prehistoric Iron Age took shape; here was mined and smelted much of the metals used in the Roman Empire; many a fortune, besides that of the Függer, was founded on the silver mines of Přibram and Kremnica, and the Bihor mountains have long been Europe's most important source of gold. Copper, lead and zinc; manganese, chrome and bauxite are all obtained from the East European countries, as well as the earliest supply of uranium and small quantities of a very wide range of other metalliferous ores. It was in Eastern Europe that much of the early progress in mining and smelting technology was made, and in East Germany the earliest important treatise on mining, the *De Re Metallica* of Georg Agricola, was written.[1] The metalliferous deposits of Eastern Europe are rich in their variety, but in size they are not abundant. Many have been exhausted; others are too small to justify the installation of modern mining equipment.

Ferrous ores. At its present stage of development Eastern Europe is most in need of iron-ores. It has many ore deposits, many of them low-grade and most of them small. The result is that the present development of the metallurgical industries is based in the main on imported materials. The largest reserves are in Bohemia, where they have long supplied a smelting industry. There are also reserves of moderate size

[1] Georg Agricola, *De Re Metallica*, Basel, 1556.

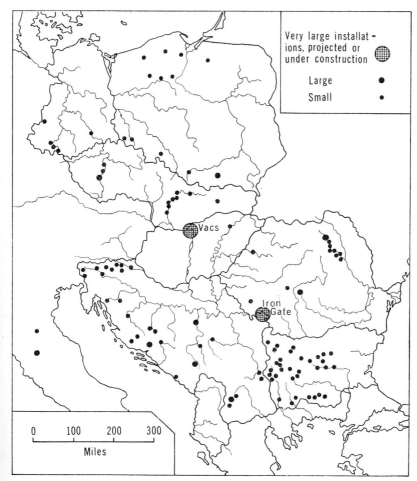

Fig. 6.4. Distribution of the major hydro-electric installations in Eastern Europe. Based on G. Schmidt-Renner, Stanislaw Berezowski, *Poznavame Svet: Československo*, M. Pecsi and B. Sarfalvi, *The Geography of Hungary*, V. Blaškovic, *Geografski Atlas Jugoslavije*, *Atlas Geografic Republica Socialista Romania*, A. C. Beškov and E. B. Valev.

in central Yugoslavia where they support the present industrial developments at Sisak and Zenica, and in the Kraków Jura of Poland. At no other place in Eastern Europe is there an ore-body, large and rich enough to justify the location there of a modern smelting industry without consideration of alternative sources of supply.

Table 19 showing the estimated size of the ore reserves is based on data that are now somewhat dated. The figures are unquestionably on the conservative side, though in few cases can exploratory work in recent years have increased the figures by a factor of more than two.

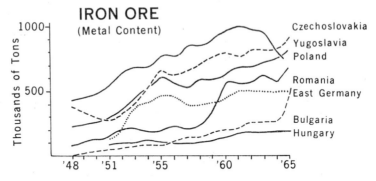

Fig. 6.5. Production of iron ore in Eastern Europe. Based on *Statistical Yearbooks*, UN.

Table 19. *Estimated iron-ore reserves and production*

	Iron-ore: probable and potential reserves in millions of tons	Average metal content, per cent	Iron-ore production, 1965: iron content (thousands of tons)
East Germany	n.d.	—	489
Poland	234	35	788
Czechoslovakia	250	32–35	723
Hungary	160	40	187
Romania	20	45	748
Yugoslavia	485	46	904
Bulgaria	1	63	585
Albania	40	50	—
	1,190		4,424

Sources: *World Iron Ore Resources and their Utilization*, UN Department of Economic Affairs 1950; *UN Statistical Yearbook, 1966*.

By contrast the six countries of the European Common Market were estimated at the same time to have a total of 24,660 million tons, of which only a third was 'probable'.

The situation in individual countries is described in the following chapters. It can be stated here that ore-mining within Eastern Europe supplies no more than about 20 per cent of the metal content required, and that this proportion, with the exhaustion of ore-bodies and the expansion of the industry, is tending to fall.

Non-ferrous ores. In marked contrast with the iron-bearing minerals, the non-ferrous ores occur in richer variety and greater abundance in Eastern Europe than in Central and Western, and have been worked in all probability for a greater period of time. They are associated in particular with the Palaeozoic massifs which occur in many parts of the area, and actually underlie others at a shallow depth. Yet others occur as secondary or replacement deposits in Triassic and later limestone. Such has been the origin of the lead-zinc ores of Upper Silesia, probably the most important single non-ferrous ore deposit worked today. Even more recent are the bauxite deposits, formed as a weathering product in Secondary limestone.

The more important of these ore-bodies are mentioned in the regional chapters which follow. Table 20 summarises the production of the more important of the non-ferrous ores in the East European countries; the statistics relate to 1965.

Table 20. Production of major non-ferrous ores in 1965 (thousands of tons of metal content, except for bauxite, which is crude tonnage)

	East Germany	Poland	Czecho-slovakia	Hungary	Romania	Yugo-slavia	Bulgaria	Albania
Bauxite	—	—	—	1478	12	1,574	—	—
Copper	22	15·1	—	0·3	—	62·6	20·9	2·6
Chrome	—	—	—	—	—	22·6	—	—
Lead	10	41·2	14·0	1·4	15·0	106·3	100·1	—
Manganese	—	—	12·7	45·0	31·4	2·5	11·8	—
Zinc	10	152·1	—	3·3	—	67·0	79·6	—

Source: *UN Statistical Yearbook, 1966.*

Other minerals and earths. There are very few countries of the world in which the non-metallic minerals do not occur in both variety and quantity. Clay for pottery, bricks and tiles; silica sand, building-stone and stone for both concrete and road-making are widely found. Limestone and clay for cement manufacture are found less frequently in close proximity to one another, but the industry has never been impeded by scarcity of materials in any of the eight countries.

Other and more valuable minerals are less widespread, and some familiar deposits are unique in the area. The potash salts which occur

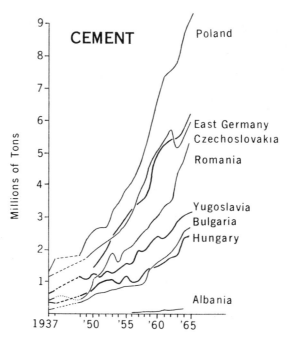

Fig. 6.6. Production of cement in Eastern Europe.
Based on *Statistical Yearbooks*, UN.

in the Trias, and underly parts of the Saxon and Thuringian basins of East Germany, have no rival, and are the foundation of important branches of the East German chemical industry. The same is true of the sulphur deposits discovered more recently near Tarnobrzeg, in southern Poland. Rock salt is more common, but is nevertheless restricted enough for the more important deposits, such as Wieliczka and Bochnia in southern Poland and Tuzla in Bosnia to have a great deal more than local importance. Kaolin, a superior type of clay for use in insulators; quartz sand of high purity for the manufacture of quality glass—all occur in only limited areas and have in many instances given rise to processing industries, especially in Czechoslovakia.

Such minerals are not transported far. Most are processed or refined very close to the quarry or mine, and the individual works commonly serves only a small area. Eastern Europe is dotted with small brick and tile, pottery and glass works. Only a few products of the mineral industries, such as sulphur, potash salts, glass and cement, for example, have markets which are national in extent, and in some of these there is, in fact, a small international trade.

Other industrial raw materials

Apart from the food-processing industries, only the woodworking and textile industries can be said to rely to any great extent on local raw materials. Lumber is abundant in all countries of the area except Hungary. In all others forest covers from a quarter to a third of the total area (see page 34). Coniferous forest predominates in the Carpathians and Rhodope and on the light and acid soils of many parts of the northern plain. Elsewhere hardwoods are the most extensive. The latter supply materials for furniture and other woodworking industries, and for the manufacture of veneer and pre-fabricated builders' materials. The softwood forests supply sawn lumber for the building industries as well as large quantities of pulpwood for paper and cellulose manufacture. The manufacture of the latter has recently been greatly extended in or near the forested regions of Czechoslovakia and Romania.

Before the period of planned industrial growth food processing was the most important branch of industry, and it remains of great importance in all parts of Eastern Europe, though it is now exceeded in terms of value added by the metal industries. The raw materials of the food industries are in the main produced domestically, though the processing of imported fats and the milling of imported grain is significant in some of the countries.

Industrial growth

Soon after the end of the Second World War all industrial enterprises above a certain very small size, were nationalised. The completion of the short-lived plans for restoration and rehabilitation was followed by the introduction of more radical plans for economic development. These were based upon the Soviet model and in the first round of plans each country was treated as an autonomous and autarchic unit. Co-operation between the countries and international division of labour became important only after 1953, and have still made no great progress.

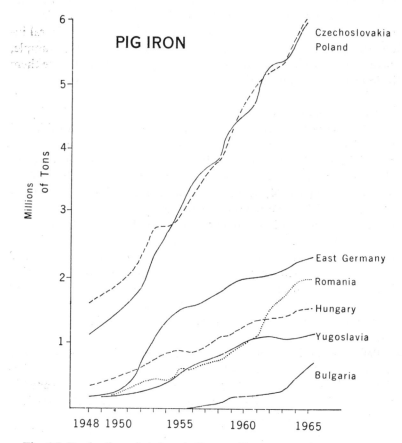

Fig. 6.7. Production of pig iron in Eastern Europe. Based on *Statistical Yearbooks*, UN.

Investment in all eight countries went largely into manufacturing industries, and within manufacturing, heavy or basic industries received the lion's share. The light and consumer goods industries received only a small amount of investment capital in the whole period of planned growth. This emphasis on the heavy industries springs rather from Communist ideology and the practical needs of the Soviet Union, than from any realistic appraisal of the resources and requirements of Eastern Europe. The shape assumed by the Soviet plans had been predicated on the relationship of capital to consumer goods production outlined by Marx. Lenin had claimed that 'the sole material base possible for socialism is large-scale machine industry', and Stalin had echoed this sentiment: 'The core of industrialisation, its very basis, consists of the development of heavy industry.'[1]

Table 21. Percentage contribution of manuacturing to the GNP and machinery production's share in manufacturing

	1950	Contribution of manufacturing to the GNP 1964	Share of machinery production in manufacturing 1964
East Germany	57·0	65·0	35·6
Poland	52·0	52·0	24·6
Czechoslovakia	62·0	65·7	31·4
Hungary	48·0	63·6	27·5
Romania	44·0	47·8	28·2
Yugoslavia	42·0	38·0(1965)	n.d.
Bulgaria	34·0	46·2	15·5

Source: *East Europe, 15,* no. 11, November 1966, and *Statistical Yearbooks,* UN, 1966.

It was the Stalinist doctrine that all the countries of the bloc should develop their own iron, steel and engineering industries at whatever cost in economic terms. The extraordinary thing was that this somewhat unrealistic doctrine was in fact eagerly adopted by all except Albania, which found such a programme far beyond its resources, both natural and financial.

[1] Quoted in Michael Kaser, *Comecon: Integration Problems of the Planned Economies,* Oxford University Press, 1965, p. 18.

Resources and Development

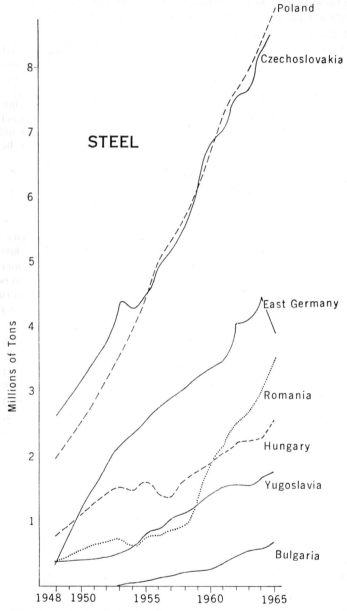

Fig. 6.8. Production of steel in Eastern Europe. Based on *Statistical Yearbooks*, UN.

The programme was realistic only to the extent that the Soviet Union could not supply mechanical equipment for the mechanisation of agriculture and the expansion of manufacturing, and the countries of the bloc were not permitted for ideological reasons to turn to the West for investment goods, as the Soviet Union had itself turned thirty years earlier.

The most spectacular growth was recorded in steel and mechanical engineering, chemicals and electric power generation. The graphs, Figs. 6.3 and 6.8 show the growth in power and steel, but in the other branches of the basic industries the units of measurement and the variety of product make comparisons between countries and through time too difficult to be illustrated in this way. Table 21, however, illustrates the large and increasing contribution of manufacturing to the GNP of all East European countries, with the exception only of Albania. It shows also how important is the role of machinery construction in most of these countries. The expansion of iron and steel production is illustrated by Table 22.

Table 22. Iron and steel production (in tons)

| | Pig iron | | Steel | |
	1948	1965	1948	1965
East Germany	182	2,338	305	3,890
Poland	1,134	5,760	1,955	9,088
Czechoslovakia	1,645	5,927	2,621	8,598
Hungary	384	1,588	770	2,520
Romania	186	2,019	353	3,426
Yugoslavia	183	1,176	368	1,769
Bulgaria	1	695	—	588
Albania	—	—	—	n.d.

Source: *UN Statistical Yearbooks, 1966.*

Industrial regions. Before the initiation of the industrial plans heavy industry had been located in only a few restricted areas. Most important of these by far were the brown coal regions of Saxony which produced heavy chemicals, the Upper Silesian-Moravian iron- and steel-producing region, and western Bohemia, with its steel and

engineering industries. There were centres of the heavy industries elsewhere: in Slovenia, in northern Hungary, near Zagreb, and in south-
western Romania. But these were small in output and in most instances
outdated in their equipment.

These older centres of heavy industry have in every instance been
modernised and extended, and to them have been added a number of
large industrial 'combines'. Some of these have necessarily gone to the
older centres of production, but many have been established on virgin
sites, like the Nowa Huta, Košice, Dunaújváros, Zenica and Galaţi
steel plants, and the new chemical works at Kędzierzin and Tarnów.
There has been a tendency to establish large factories in areas that had
not hitherto been significantly industrialised. To some extent this was
part of a deliberate policy to bring industry to areas, such as Slovakia,
Moldavia and Macedonia which had hitherto been relatively backward.

Light industries. There has been little growth in the light industries,
and little change in their geographical pattern. In most countries
some rationalisation of production took place. A large number of uneconomically small factories and workshops have been either closed
or merged; this has been the case particularly in the textile centres of
Bohemia. Where new light industries have been established, this has
been at least in part in order to bring factory industry to areas basically
unsuited to the heavy sector or to take advantage of an export market.

The Council for Mutual Economic Cooperation (Comecon)
It was noted above that the first round of development plans envisaged
no international specialisation or division of labour. All members of
the bloc were expected to span the whole industrial spectrum. The
defects of such a programme became apparent long before the death
of Stalin, but it is doubtful whether steps would have been taken to
remedy it if the West European countries had not agreed to collabor-
ate, in response to Marshall's offer of American aid, in establishing
the Organisation for European Economic Cooperation (OEEC). The
formation of the European Coal and Steel Community five years
later, in 1952, was yet another object lesson, if such were still needed,
in the benefits of international collaboration and specialisation.

Comecon was established in 1949 for purposes which contradicted
the essential theory of Lenin and Stalin regarding industrial growth.
It is not surprising, then, that it made little headway until after Stalin's
death, nor that few meetings were held until after 1956. For many

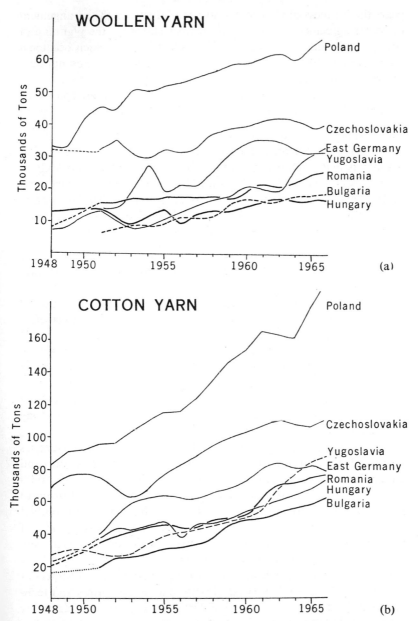

Fig. 6.9. Production of typical consumer goods in Eastern Europe: (a) woollen yarn, (b) cotton yarn. Based on *Statistical Yearbooks*, UN.

7

years the business of Comecon consisted largely in the arrangement of barter agreements between its member states; in the planning of such joint facilities as an international electric grid, which became a reality only in 1962, and a few very tentative agreements on national priorities and fields of specialisation.

In the summer of 1957 Krushchev announced to a group of East European journalists visiting the Soviet Union that

> it is impossible to develop everything everywhere simultaneously. ... As regards tractor or motor vehicle production ... the situation today is that tractors and motor vehicles are produced not only in the Soviet Union but by Poland, Czechoslovakia, Hungary, and Romania. Thus production is not always profitable. The sooner and the better we develop the division of labour between our countries, the stronger will our economies be.[1]

The Communist parties had taken a long time to learn so elementary a principle, but having learned it, they found that reversing their previous policy was by no means easy.

In 1956 commissions were established to supervise the international division of labour within each of a number—eventually thirteen—of separate fields. From 1957 Yugoslavia began, largely as a result of its interest in technical and power developments along the Danube, to participate in the work of certain commissions. It was within the framework of Comecon that technical agreements were reached on the Iron Gate and Vác projects on the Danube, and also on the 'Friendship' Pipeline. Joint investments were arranged in this way in developments in mining and manufacturing.

The allocation of fields of specialisation between the countries aroused fears and jealousies. Albania left the organisation, and Romania made no secret of its resentment at being allocated a relatively small role in heavy industry. Trade between the East European members of Comecon remained small, and each continued to conduct most of its trade with the Soviet Union. There was no development of multilateral trade, and exchanges between pairs of countries were organised in practice on a basis of barter.

On the other hand, technical co-operation between the members of Comecon was greatly increased. Scientific data, blueprints and technically trained personnel circulated among them, and must inevitably have contributed to increasing the speed and efficiency of economic

[1] Quoted by M. Kaser, *op. cit.*, p. 59.

growth. Comecon is not—and never set out to become—a common market, but it does appear, after several years of feeble and ineffective activity, to have achieved some very modest successes.

TRANSPORT AND COMMUNICATIONS

Travel between the countries of Eastern Europe remains strangely inhibited. The boundary of Albania is for practical purposes closed. All other countries have only a very restricted number of crossing points, at each of which the volume of movement, both of travellers and of freight, appears to be very small.

The means of modern transport and communication were conceived and first established by the empires which formerly extended over the whole area. Route systems were made to converge on the imperial capitals or the centres of imperial administration; on Berlin, Vienna, Budapest or Constantinople. The countries of Eastern Europe were faced between the First and the Second World Wars with the task of creating road and rail systems to serve national ends. In this, by and large, they succeeded. They now face the need to create a system of international routes, and with this task they have scarcely begun to cope.

One still finds in most of the countries of Eastern Europe that the roads deteriorate as the boundary is approached; the international road from Niš to Sofia was, until very recently, notoriously bad, primarily because the Yugoslavs saw no reason to help the Bulgarians by improving what is for the latter the main routeway to the West.

The relief of Eastern Europe tends to hinder transport and communication within the region as a whole; movement is obliged at present to make use of a certain number of gates or passageways, because only here are the means of travel adequately maintained: the Moravian Gate, the saddle behind Rijeka, the Predeal Pass across the Carpathians, and the Serbian Morava, Marica and Vardar valleys.

At the same time the complex political pattern of the region, with two inland states and a third with somewhat limited access to the sea, has necessitated a large and growing transit traffic by river as well as by road and rail. For the riverine states the Danube itself provides a highway of great importance. But the Danube flows eastwards to the Black Sea. Bulgaria and Romania are developing trade with Central and Western Europe, and, unless they use the long and tedious sea route—impossible for Bulgaria's export of fruit and vegetables—they must ship their goods across Yugoslavia and Hungary and even Czechoslovakia.

Czechoslovakia uses the East German port of Rostock, in which at one time it had a free zone; Czechoslovakia and Hungary both use the Adriatic ports of Yugoslavia, and Yugoslavia itself enjoys considerable privileges in the Greek port of Thessaloníki.

River and canal navigation

Internal waterways are very much less important in Eastern than in Central and Western Europe. For this there are many reasons, apart from the late economic development of the region: winter freeze in the north and summer drought in the south; the smallness of rivers, with only a few exceptions, and the great fluctuations in their discharge; the strong relief in many parts of the region, which has prevented the construction of canals linking the river systems, and international rivalries which in the past have prevented agreement on policies and collaboration in carrying them out.

Elbe–Oder–Vistula system. Only in the North European Plain have physical conditions been propitious for the construction of a *system* of internal waterways. The Elbe (Labe) and Oder (Odra) are both navigable for the greater part of their courses, though only after a considerable amount of work had been done to deepen and improve the channel. Both are used, especially for heavy, bulk cargoes, such as coal and iron ore, and both furthermore have important ports, Hamburg and Szczecin (Stettin), at their respective mouths. The Vistula, though used formerly for the shipment of wheat and lumber downstream to the Baltic Sea, is now very little used below Warsaw and not at all above. Its channel is shallow and shifting, and in its present condition quite unsuitable for modern barges.

These rivers are not only interlinked by their navigable tributaries and supplementary canals, but are further connected westwards to the Rhine and eastwards to the Dnepr. The canal and river system across East Germany, roughly from Magdeburg to Frankfurt-on-Oder, is well engineered, large in scale and intensively used. Indeed, one might say that the recent industrial development of greater Berlin would have been impossible without it. Within Poland, however, the waterways are smaller; many vital links can take only the smallest barges, and as a system it is of very little value. The same may be said also of the Bug river and its canal links with the Soviet Union. Their economic role is negligible, and plans to enlarge and modernise them have not been put into effect.

Danube system. The Danube is considered to be navigable at Regensburg in Bavaria, though small craft ascend the river as far as Ulm. For Czechoslovakia, Hungary, Yugoslavia, Romania and Bulgaria it is an important commercial highway. Its tributaries are, in general, not considered to be navigable, and within Eastern Europe only the Sava and Tisza are in fact much used. Though in all respects the largest river in Europe, the Danube is not without its difficulties and limitations. The low water-level of autumn and winter; high water and swift current in summer, ice-floes and sand-banks, and the rush of water at Vác and the Iron Gate have all combined to make navigation difficult at times and occasionally hazardous. Over the past century a great deal of work has been done to regulate and improve the channel, and the completion of the Iron Gate and Vac projects will remove two of the more serious of the present navigational hazards. The Sulina channel in the delta has been straightened and regulated (see page 553) and most of the shipping from the Black Sea to Brăila, the effective limit of ocean-shipping, is by this waterway.

The volume of shipping using the river is now greater than at any time in its history, and has in fact doubled within the past ten years. A large part of this traffic does not cross international boundaries, and is between one Hungarian, Yugoslav or Romanian port and another. The most used sectors are the Hungarian and Romanian–Bulgarian, and here the river is very significant in internal as well as foreign trade (Fig. 6.10).

The Danube at present has no effective link with any other waterway system. The existing canal from the river near Regensburg to the Regnitz and so to the Main is very small and, in fact, is little used. It is at present being replaced by a larger and more up-to-date waterway, the *Rhein–Main–Donau Grossschiffahrt*, which will allow large barges to travel from the Rhine to the Danube systems. At present only a very small part of West Germany's commerce with the Danubian countries is waterborne. One might expect the completion of the waterway to be followed by an expansion of this commerce and, in particular, for fuel and iron-ore to become an important part of it.

Another long awaited waterway is the Moravian Canal, from the upper Odra, near Bohumín, to the lower Morava and thus to the Danube. This has long been in the planning stage, but work has not been begun. Not only would it facilitate the exchange of bulky industrial materials between Poland and Czechoslovakia, but would also allow both to participate more fully in Danubian commerce. In conjunction with the Main–Danube canal, it could greatly increase the area of distribution of Ruhr coal and even of West European iron-ore. Water transport is really significant only for bulky and low-value goods, and the importance of extending the Danube system is to be seen largely in the greater ease of supplying scarce raw materials, notably fuel and ore, to the riverine countries.

Danube Commission. The potential importance of the Danube as a commercial avenue was recognised early in the nineteenth century, and in 1856 an international commission was established to supervise navigation on the deltaic tract of the river. In 1921 the commission was reconstituted and its scope broadened. The Danube was declared an 'international river', open without restriction to the flags of all nations, but international friction combined with the trade recession to prevent the planned improvements on the river from being carried out.

After 1945 political conditions changed radically. The Soviet Union became a riparian state, and hence forward played a dominant role in the deliberations of the Danubian Commission. The latter was reconstituted, the instrument of 1921 abrogated, and membership limited to the bloc countries with the addition of Yugoslavia. This commission, with its headquarters in Budapest, continues to control navigation on the longer and more important part of the river. Indeed, it was not until 1954 that Austria was able to resume commercial navigation on the Communist-controlled section of the river.

Railway system

The greater part of the traffic both within and between the countries of Eastern Europe is by rail, and in most of the countries the railway system is fully used. It was constructed in the late nineteenth and early years of the present century. The railways of Russian Poland were built on a broad gauge which was converted to standard gauge soon after 1918, and, apart from a few lengths of narrow-gauge track— most extensive in Yugoslavia—standard gauge was adopted throughout the rest of the area from the first.

The individual railway systems were built to serve the needs of the empires which controlled most of the area during the nineteenth century, and in the case of that of Russian Poland, the primary consideration in its planning and construction appears to have been strategic. Between the two world wars new lines were laid to make existing railways serve the interest of the national states; Poland, for example, had to construct a north–south line to link its chief industrial region with Gdańsk–Gdynia; Czechoslovakia was obliged to improve the rail links between Moravia and Slovakia; Romania, those between Walachia and Transylvania, and Yugoslavia its connections with the Adriatic.

The railways built may, however, be regarded as minimal, and numerous additional lines have been built since the Second World War to serve the new industrial needs and to bring the more remote areas of some of the countries into the stream of their national life. One of the most important of the new projects is the conversion of the Bosnia–Neretva valley railway of Yugoslavia to standard gauge and the extension of the Lim valley railway to the Adriatic coast at Bar.

Considerable progress has been made in the electrification of the main lines or their conversion to diesel operation. The main west to east line in Czechoslovakia and the Warsaw–Upper Silesian line are now electrified, and on other main lines, such as those of the Morava, Nišava and Marica valleys diesel locomotives are increasingly common. But to some extent on the main lines and usually on the minor and branch lines one still finds the fussy, smoky but nonetheless fascinating steam locomotives. Most of the lines, including some of the most important and most used, are single track. Even a line of such vital importance as that from Cheb in Czechoslovakia, through Prague and Olomouc to Ostrava and Slovakia, has no more than one track for a very great deal of its distance.

Road system

A road system is more quickly built and more cheaply maintained than a railway net. Viewed merely as a system of roads, without regard to quality, the net might appear adequate over the region as a whole. It is in fact difficult to find any routes newly opened up during the present century, because, in general there has been no need. On the other hand, most of the existing roads began as tracks to serve local, village or market needs, and many have not been raised above this technical level, though now used for purposes of which their unknown creators could never have dreamed.

In all countries a significant part of the road system still consists of 'macadam', a euphemistic term for a loose spread of irregularly crushed stone, torn into potholes by passing lorries and liberally laced with mud. It is a system adjusted to the needs and the technical demands of peasants and their horse- or ox- drawn carts. It is unfit for heavy motor traffic though used by lorries and the few passenger cars. On this primitive road net has been imposed a very open pattern of modern, engineered and surfaced roads. This more recent net is adequate in East Germany and parts of Poland and Czechoslovakia. In Romania and the Balkan countries it is quite inadequate. Slow progress is, however, being made in extending it. Yugoslavia, the country least well provided with modern roads, now has a good highway, the *Autoput*, which follows the valleys of the Sava, Morava and Vardar from Ljubljana to the Greek border; it also has a good road, built to trap the tourist's D-mark or dollar, along the coast from Rijeka to Bar. The axial routes of Bulgaria and Romania are now in satisfactory condition, and the network of main roads which radiates from Budapest is good.

Ports
Six of the eight countries of Eastern Europe have coastlines, however short, and these have all established ports, developed seaborne commerce and, with the exception of Albania, built a merchant marine. Czechoslovakia and Hungary, with neither coastline nor ocean port, are obliged to exercise transit rights across the territory of their neighbours if they are to engage in ocean commerce.

Collectively the Eastern European countries have about 400 miles of Baltic coastline; 625 miles of Adriatic, without following the intricacies of the coast, and 320 miles on the Black Sea. They thus border on enclosed seas, and their ports, at a distance from the world's main shipping lanes, are at some disadvantage.

Czechoslovakia, East Germany and even parts of Poland and Hungary could be regarded as lying formerly within the hinterland of Hamburg. Today they are cut off from this port by the international boundary and the zonal division of Germany, and very little commerce in fact takes this route. Nor is Trieste, formerly a port serving much of the needs of the Austro-Hungarian Empire, now used to any significant degree by the commerce of East European countries. These countries have, at no small cost, built alternative ports under their own control. East Germany has developed Wismar and Rostock from relatively small ports to be the country's major outlets, though neither has the advantage of river and canal links with its hinterland. Poland, formerly heavily dependent on Gdynia, now, with the acquisition of Gdańsk and Szczecin, has an almost embarrassing wealth of port facilities, but this is unusual. Romania has expanded the facilities of its only sea port, Constanţa, and also those of its river ports of Galaţi and Brăila, which serve as points of trans-shipment for part of the seaborne commerce of Bulgaria, Yugoslavia, Hungary and Czechoslovakia. Bulgaria has greatly increased the facilities at Varna and Burgas, and Yugoslavia, finding Rijeka, Split and its own free zone in the port of Thessaloníki inadequate for its needs, is now building commercial ports at Ploče and Bar (see page 726).

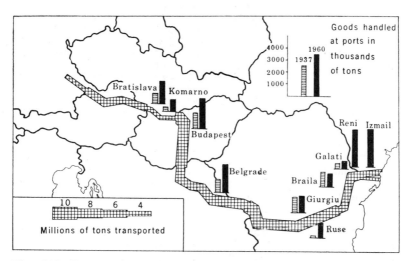

Fig. 6.10. Ports and waterborne commerce of the Danube. After *Die Wirtschaftliche Bedeutung und Entwicklung der Donauschiffahrt*, Vienna, 1962.

COMMERCE

In all countries of Eastern Europe foreign commerce has expanded *pari passu* with the growth of industry. And at the same time there has been, during the period of planned development, a gradual shift of emphasis away from a simple exchange of imported manufactures for exported primary goods, and towards a more complex pattern in which the export of agricultural and mineral products is exceeded by that of the mechanical and chemical industries. Table 23 shows the present break down of the aggregate foreign trade of the eight countries according, as nearly as possible, to the accepted international code.

7*

Table 23. Foreign trade for 1955 and 1965 (in percentages of total trade)

	Machinery and equipment 1955 1965	Fuels, raw materials and other materials 1955 1965	Foodstuffs (including raw and semi-manufactured) 1955 1965	Consumer goods 1955 1965

Exports (per cent)

	1955	1965	1955	1965	1955	1965	1955	1965
East Germany	55·7	48·4	31·8	33·1	1·8	3·5	10·7	15·0
Poland	13·1	34·4	64·5	35·1	15·2	18·2	7·2	12·3
Czechoslovakia	43·5	48·5	39·3	30·4	6·1	4·6	11·1	16·5
Hungary	29·7	32·7	23·8	24·1	30·7	21·9	15·8	21·3
Romania	6·1	18·5	69·7	49·2	22·9	21·3	1·3	11·0
Yugoslavia	1·4	17·2	61·4	42·0	31·6	24·1	5·6	16·7
Bulgaria	2·6	24·8	49·7	25·3	35·2	36·3	12·5	13·6
Albania	0·5	0	96·9	71·7	2·6	23·1	0	5·2

Imports (per cent)

	1955	1965	1955	1965	1955	1965	1955	1965
East Germany	3·4	12·3	59·1	58·7	31·7	23·6	5·8	5·4
Poland	30·9	32·8	51·7	47·3	13·1	13·2	4·3	6·7
Czechoslovakia	13·3	29·9	53·6	48·8	29·0	15·9	4·1	5·4
Hungary	12·3	28·1	67·7	57·0	17·0	9·6	3·0	5·3
Romania	37·2	39·0	46·6	51·2	12·0	3·1	4·2	6·7
Yugoslavia	19·8	19·7	51·1	62·1	27·1	12·1	2·0	6·1
Bulgaria	57·4	43·6	40·9	44·2	4·3	7·2	3·4	5·0
Albania	41·5	49·6	33·9	27·8	10·1	15·8	14·5	6·8

Source: *Foreign Trade of the European Satellites in 1965: A Statistical Summary*, Central Intelligence Agency, Washington, DC, 1966.

A feature of Table 23 is the sharp increase within a period of only ten years in the export of machinery and other manufactured goods, the overall diminution in the export of raw materials, and the small increase in the import of factory products. These statistics show how close the East European countries have come to the pattern of trade which has long been considered normal in the West.

In all instances the value of total exports was approximately equal to that of imports. Manufactured goods have in recent years constituted an increasing proportion of a rising volume of trade. This is a measure of the extent to which the countries of Eastern Europe have ceased to be dominated by a nearly self-sufficing peasant economy, and have adopted that specialisation and mechanisation of production which have been the mainspring of West European progress.

The trade of the East European countries is a controlled trade, in which individual initiative and the play of market conditions have no role. It is organised by government missions, and the trade resolves itself into simple barter. In consequence the value of the exports of country A to country B are approximately equal in value to its imports from country B, and discrepancies, as a general rule, are due to the varying increments of value represented by the costs of handling and freight. Marked differences arise only with those Western countries which are free to grant credits to the East European countries.[1]

These countries, then, have had no multilateral pattern of trade, and this has placed severe restrictions on their industrial and commercial growth. If country A must import a given commodity from country B then it is obliged to produce something that B wants in order to import it. At the present time there is good evidence that these countries are feeling their way towards a less rigid commercial pattern and are looking for the mechanism whereby some form of multilateral trading might be instituted.

Direction of trade

These considerations have made it inevitable that the countries of the Communist bloc should trade primarily with one another, since only in this way have they in general been able to carry on the kind of barter which their economic system makes necessary. Their governments have shown a certain reluctance to doing business with the representatives of Western private and commercial companies, not only because these represent an economic system which they oppose but also—and perhaps more importantly—because the channels have not been established for such a dialogue.

The foreign trade of every country of Eastern Europe, with the exception only of Albania, is dominated by the Soviet Union. In all, about 55 per cent of the total trade of the Comecon countries is with the USSR, and, despite the attempts of recent years to achieve an international division of labour within Eastern Europe, the intra-trade amounts to only 38 per cent of the total. Trade with other Communist countries—Cuba and the Communist states of Asia—remains, again

---

[1] The United States has not been free to make such credits, and this is one of several reasons why its trade with the bloc countries has suffered.

Resources and Development

with the exception of Albania, very small both in the aggregate and in relation to the total trade. Trade with non-Communist countries remains relatively small but is increasing as a percentage of total trade. The foremost trading partners in the capitalist world are West Germany, which has made a serious effort to recapture its former markets in Eastern Europe, France, Italy and the United Kingdom. Canada has been important in some countries, but the role of the United States has hitherto been negligible. This was due to the formal policy, legislatively enacted, to refuse to have regular commercial relations with the East European countries. This policy was expected, by an extraordinary piece of reasoning, to enable the peoples of these countries to assert themselves against their alleged oppressors.

There are signs of change even in American policy. The Department of State is trying to liberalise its own outmoded policy, and in this is

Table 24. Eastern European pattern of trade, 1965
(in millions of US dollars)

	With USSR		With other East European countries (including Albania and Yugoslavia)		With other Communist countries		With industrial West (including USA and Canada)		With the under-developed world	
	Ex-ports	Im-ports	Ex-ports	Im-ports	Ex-ports	Im-ports	Ex-ports	Im-ports	Ex-ports	Im-ports
East Germany	1,310·8	1,205·8	918·4	777·7	67·7	63·7	554·9	557·0	215·0	198·0
Poland	781·4	728·4	587·4	775·0	38·5	44·0	604·6	545·2	214·6	247·6
Czecho-slovokia	1,022·8	954·7	866·8	932·2	76·2	73·2	433·5	479·2	289·6	232·0
Hungary	525·4	553·3	499·6	444·3	32·8	20·6	321·5	381·2	130·2	120·9
Romania	438·4	406·2	279·1	225·2	38·3	28·2	254·5	347·2	91·1	70·4
Yugo-slavia	56,275	32,380[2]	81,135	77,910[2]	1,486	1,598[2]	130,072	206,883[2]	58,484	67,614[2]
Bulgaria	613·6	588·4	298·1	253·9[1]	22·1	n.a.	156·6	n.a.	85·4	n.a.
Albania	—	—	28·4	26·1	n.a.	n.a.	n.a.	n.a.	n.a.	n.a.

[1] Excludes trade with Albania.   n.a. = Not available.
[2] In millions of old dinars.

Source: *Foreign Trade of the European Satellites in 1965*, CIA, Washington, DC, and *Yearbook of International Trade Statistics, 1965* (for Yugoslavia only).

fighting a not unfamiliar struggle with reactionary members of Congress.[1]

The present pattern of trade is indicated in Table 24, where the value of the trade of each of the East European countries with each of the major countries or groups of countries is shown. Intra-bloc trade is included in the totals.

There is evidence that this pattern may change; that trade with non-Communist countries will increase and that within the bloc diminish as a percentage of the total. On the other hand, much has been done, not merely by way of agreements to specialise in production and to standardise equipment, but also in the installation of hardware, like pipelines, to preserve the present pattern. One hopes for a greater flexibility in commercial policy, but any radical change within the near future would not be in the interests either of Eastern Europe or the world.

Bibliography

General

BASCH, ANTONÍN, *The Danube Basin and the German Economic Sphere*, London, Routledge & Kegan Paul, 1944.

Economic Development in S.E. Europe, London, Political and Economic Planning, 1945.

Economic Plans of Six European Satellite Countries through 1965: A General Appraisal, Washington DC, Central Intelligence Agency, 1965.

Economic Bulletin for Europe, Economic Commission for Europe, United Nations, quarterly.

European Steel Trends in the Setting of the World Market, Steel Division, Economic Commission for Europe, Geneva, 1949.

Economic Survey of Europe, Economic Commission for Europe, UN, Geneva, annually.

HOFFMAN, GEORGE W., 'The Problem of the Undeveloped Regions in Southeast Europe: A Comparative analysis of Romania, Yugoslavia, and Greece,' *AAAG* **57** (1967), 637–666.

KULA, WITOLD, 'Some Observations on the Industrial Revolution in Eastern European Countries,' *Ergon*, **1** (1958), 239–48.

---

[1] See 'East-West Trade Relations Act of 1966', *Department of State Bulletin*, 30 May and 25 July, 1966.

POUNDS, N. J. G. and SPULBER, N. *Resources and Planning in Eastern Europe*, Indiana University Press, 1956.

Some Factors in the Economic Growth of Europe during the 1950s, Economic Commission for Europe, United Nations, Geneva, 1954.

South-Eastern Europe: A Political and Economic Survey, London, Royal Institute of International Affairs, 1939.

SPULBER, NICOLAS, *The Economics of Communist Eastern Europe*, London, Chapman & Hall, 1957.

— 'The Development of Industry', *Annals, American Academy of Political Science*, 317 (1958), 36–43.

WARRINER, DOREEN, *The Economics of Peasant Farming*, 2nd edn. London, F. Cass, 1964.

World Iron Ore Resources and their Utilization, United Nations, Department of Economic Affairs, New York, 1950.

ZAUBERMAN, ALFRED, *Industrial Progress in Poland, Czechoslovakia and East Germany*, Oxford University Press, 1964.

Agricultural Development

FÖLDES, LASZLO, ed., *Viehzucht und Hirtenleben in Ostmittelleuropa*, Academy of Sciences, Budapest, 1961.

Food Balances for Eight East European Countries, 1959–61, Economic Research Service, US Dept. of Agriculture, Washington, 1965.

HOFFMAN, GEORGE W. 'Problems of Agricultural Change in South-eastern Europe', *Geogrl Rev.* 55 (1965), 428–431.

KARCZ, JERZY F., *Soviet and East European Agriculture*, Cambridge University Press, 1967.

MORGAN, O. S., *Agricultural Systems of Middle Europe*, New York, 1933. 'The Party and the Peasant', *East Europe*, 7, May, 1958, 17–28.

SANDERS, IRWIN T. ed., *Collectivization of Agriculture in Eastern Europe*, University of Kentucky Press, 1958.

STRUŻEK, BOLESŁAW, *Rolnictwo Europejskich Krajów Socjalistycznych*, Ludowa Społdzielnia Wydawnicza, Warsaw, 1963.

TOMASEVICH, JOZO, 'Agriculture in Eastern Europe', *Annals of the American Academy of Political Science*, 317 (1958), 44–52.

ZAGOROFF, S. D., J. VÉGH and A. D. BILIMOVICH, *The Agricultural Economy of the Danubian Countries 1935–45*, Oxford University Press, 1956.

Transport and Trade

ALEXANDERSON, GUNNAR and GÖRAN NORSTRÖM, *World Shipping*, London, Wiley, 1963.

BEAVER, S. H. 'Railways in the Balkan Peninsula', *Geogrl J.* 97 (1941), 273–94.

Die Donau als Grossschiffahrtsstrasse, Wirtschaftskammer Wien, Vienna, 1941.

'Die wirtschaftliche Bedeutung und Entwicklung der Donauschiffahrt', *Mber. des Österreichischen Institutes für Wirtschaftsforschung*, Vienna, 1962.

Foreign Trade of the European Satellites in 1965: A Statistical Summary, Central Intelligence Agency, Washington, DC, 1966, and annually.

HOLZMANN, GUSTAV, 'Die Zukunft der Donauschiffahrt', *Z. Wirt-Geogr.* 8 (1964), 18–25.

KASER, MICHAEL, *Comecon: Integration Problems of the Planned Economies*, Oxford University Press, 1965.

KORBONSKI, ANDRZEJ, 'Comecon', *International Conciliation*, No. 549, Sept., 1964.

KOSTROWICKI, JERZY, 'An attempt to determine the geographical types of agriculture in East-Central Europe on the basis of the case studies on land utilization, *Geographica Polonica*, 5, 1965, 453–498.

MANCE, SIR OSBORNE, *International River and Canal Transport*, Oxford University Press, 1944.

OTREMBA, E., 'Die Rhein-Main-Donau Linie', *Geogr. Rdsch.*, 16 (1964), 56–63.

PIGRADA, ANTHONY, *Danube Waterways*, Mid-European Studies Center, mimeographed series, No. 5, New York, 1953.

POPPER, OTTO, 'The International Regime of the Danube', *Geogrl J.* 102 (1943), 240–53.

RUDZKI, ADAM, *Organization of Transportation in Captive Europe*, New York, Mid-European Studies Center, 1954.

— *Roads, Waterways and Seaports of Captive Europe*, New York, Mid-European Studies Center, New York, 1954.

SMETANA, J., 'Le canal Elbe-Oder-Danube et la navigabilité des fleuves,' *Przegl. Zach.*, 1 (1948), 189–214.

The Europe and Soviet Union Agricultural Situation, Economic Research Service, US Dept. of Agriculture. Washington, 1967, and annually.

The USSR and Eastern Europe Agricultural Situation, US Department of Agriculture, Economic Research Service, Washington DC, 1966.

SINNHUBER, K. A. 'Inland Waterway Projects in East Central Europe', *Geography*, **40** (1955), 269–71.

VAS, OSKAR, 'Die Donau als Energieträger', *Der Donauraum-Zeitschrift des Forschungsinstitutes für Fragen des Donauraumes*, **3** (1958), Heft 1, 29–40.

CHAPTER SEVEN

East Germany

The seven countries which make up the greater part of Eastern Europe have come into being through the national aspirations of their peoples. The German Democratic Republic is different. It continues to exist probably in violation of the wishes of a majority of its people; it is a fragment of a greater Germany, cut off from the rest by the accident of war and the contingencies of postwar politics. East Germany came into being in 1945 in order to satisfy the Soviet demand to occupy some part of the territory of defeated Germany, and it continues to exist because the powers which had triumphed in the Second World War have found no mutually agreeable way to terminate its existence, In the course of over 20 years its separation from the rest of Germany has become complete. Its economic organisation has been brought into line with that of the other East European countries; it is a member of the Council for Mutual Economic Cooperation and of the Warsaw, Pact, and as the years pass, the chance of its re-unification with West Germany recedes.

THE EAST GERMAN STATE

The separation of East Germany from the German Federal Republic is denounced in West Germany and criticised by West Germany's allies. It has not been accepted even by the Soviet Union as the ultimate solution of the problem of Germany's future. And yet this uneasy compromise has begun to acquire some of the elements of permanence. Though most people in West Germany and East would like to see an end to their separate political existence, and many well-wishers outside Germany give their support to the ideal of a unified Germany, no political avenue seems to be at present open for its realisation.

Boundaries of East Germany
East Germany is an arbitrary creation. Long before the Second World War came to an end it had been realised that the territory of Germany

would have to be occupied by the victorious powers for a period of a year or two. After it had been agreed that Poland should be compensated at Germany's expense for the territory which the Soviet Union had seized in 1939, plans were made to divide the area which remained into zones of occupation. Not a great deal of thought appears to have been given to the matter. Indeed, in Churchill's words, 'the occupational zones were decided rather hastily at Quebec in September 1944. . . .'[1] It was impossible to deny the Soviet claim to Eastern Germany as an occupation zone, even though it would embrace Berlin, however the boundary might be drawn. Zonal boundaries were drawn along the lines of existing administrative divisions, and the western boundary of the Soviet Zone was defined in an allied protocol of 12 September 1944, as:

> . . . a line drawn from a point on Lübeck Bay where the frontiers of Schleswig-Holstein and Mecklenburg meet, along the western frontier of Mecklenburg to the frontier of the province of Hanover, thence, along the eastern frontier of Hanover, to the frontier of Brunswick, thence along the western frontier of the Prussian province of Saxony to the western frontier of Anhalt; thence along the western frontier of Anhalt; thence along the western frontier of the Prussian province of Saxony and the western frontier of Thuringia to where the latter meets the Bavarian frontier; then eastwards along the northern frontier of Bavaria to the 1937 Czechoslovakian frontier. . . .[2]

This boundary has undergone no changes. Its divisive qualities have merely been intensified, so that it is now an 'Iron Curtain', demarcated by a barrier of wire and steel, protected by mine-fields, and crossable by road only at three points.

The eastern boundary of East Germany sprang also from the decisions made during the closing year of the war. It had been decided at the Yalta Conference (February 1945) that Poland should be compensated for the loss of the territory which the Soviet government had occupied in September 1939, in fulfilment of the Ribbentrop–Molotov agreement of the previous month. Churchill had himself suggested such a step: 'Personally, I thought Poland might move westward, like soldiers taking two steps "left close". If Poland trod on some German

[1] Winston S. Churchill, *The Second World War*, Cassell, 1954, vol. 6, p. 448.
[2] 'Protocol . . . on the Zones of Occupation in Germany and the Administration of "Greater Berlin"', *Selected Documents on Germany and the Question of Berlin 1944–1961*, Cmd. 1552, HMSO, 1961, pp. 27–9.

toes that could not be helped. . . .'[1] At Yalta Molotov had proposed that the boundary should lie along the Oder, with Stettin (Szczecin), which lay on the west bank, going to Poland.

Final decision on this boundary was postponed to the Potsdam Conference of July–August 1945. The Protocol of the Potsdam Conference stated:

> that, pending the final determination of Poland's western frontier, the former German territories east of a line running from the Baltic Sea immediately west of Swinemünde, and thence along the Oder River to the confluence of the western Neisse River and along the western Neisse to the Czechoslovak frontier. . . .[2]

The whole eastern boundary of East Germany was thus defined in terms of rivers, so that no demarcation was necessary, except that to the west of Stettin. By a subsequent agreement between the Soviet Union and Poland, this boundary was delimited. Poland received the eastern extremity of the island of Usedom, together with the city of Swinemünde (Świnoujście) and the channel, the Swine, by which the Oder and the Stettiner Haff communicate with the sea. West of Stettin a boundary was demarcated running from the coast at Neuwarp approximately southward to reach the Oder at Greifenhagen.

Since 1871 Berlin had been the capital of Germany. Though devastated by bombing and gutted by street fighting, no one doubted that it would be rebuilt, and most expected that within a few years of the armistice it would again become the capital of a Germany, reduced perhaps in area, but chastened by the experiences of war, educated by the precept and example of the Allies, and again sovereign and independent. However the zonal boundaries might be devised, Berlin lay within the Soviet Zone of occupation. Though entirely acceptable to the Russians, this situation scarcely recommended itself to the Western allies. They could not leave a city so politically sensitive and, to the Germans, so emotionally significant entirely in Soviet possession. So Berlin also came to be divided, like Germany as a whole, into sectors, each to be occupied and administered by one of the allied powers.

The sector lines in Berlin were drawn at the same time as the zonal boundaries in Germany as a whole. Greater Berlin itself was that area of 289 square miles (882 square kilometres), most of it urbanised,

---

[1] Winston S. Churchill, *op. cit.*, vol. 5, p. 319.
[2] *Protocol of the Proceedings of the Berlin (Potsdam) Conference*, Cmd. 7087, HMSO, 1945, sect. VIII, B.

which had been defined by German public law in April 1920. Its sectors were each made up of groups of municipal districts. These were essentially the towns from which Berlin had been formed in 1920. They had retained until the allied occupation of the city very considerable rights of self-government, and their mutual boundaries were well known.

Thus in 1944 the Soviet Sector of the city was defined as the 'districts of Pankow, Prenzlauerberg, Mitte, Weissensee, Friedrichshain, Lichtenberg, Treptow, Köpenick'.[1] At the same time two other zones were defined, but were not specifically allocated to particular powers. During the following spring sector lines in West Berlin were redrawn in order to establish a third sector to be occupied by the forces of France.

The use of German administrative boundaries as both zonal and sector lines indicated that the role of the allied occupation was to serve as a kind of local government. These were boundaries of convenience; they separated jurisdictions which were viewed as only temporary. No one at the time was pessimistic enough to think that they might ever acquire international status.

Deutsche Demokratische Republik. During the years of the Second World War the partition of Germany into two or more separate and sovereign states had been contemplated, but the allied leaders wisely favoured the maintenance of German unity within somewhat narrower political limits. This decision was reiterated at the Potsdam Conference: 'During the period of occupation Germany shall be treated as a single economic unit. To this end common policies shall be established in regard to . . . .'[2] agriculture, mining and industry; wages, prices, the internal movement of commodities and foreign trade. The decentralisation of economic control; the break-up of 'the present excessive concentrations of economic power, as exemplified in particular by cartels, syndicates, trusts, and other monopolistic arrangements'; the encouragement 'of agriculture and peaceful domestic industries', and the prevention of Germany from again developing a war potential: these were the declared intentions of the allies. Within two years allied unity of purpose had been forgotten, and most of the allied objectives in Germany abandoned.

Supreme authority in Germany was, according to the terms of the

---

[1] *Protocol on the Zones of Occupation and the Administration of 'Greater Berlin'*, Section 2.
[2] *Protocol of Berlin (Potsdam) Conference*, Section II, B, 14.

Potsdam Protocol, to be vested in a Control Council, made up of the commanders-in-chief of the armed forces of each of the occupying powers. The Control Council made very little progress in its assigned tasks. Early in 1946 an agreement was reached with difficulty on industrial production as a means of paying for the imports of food and raw materials so desperately needed. Agreed levels of industry could not be reached as long as the exchange 'of commodities, persons and ideas' within Germany was restricted. The American Secretary of State complained that 'the barriers between the four zones of Germany are far more difficult to surmount than those between normal, independent states',[1] and called for the merging of the American with the other zones of occupation. The British agreed and were joined later, and somewhat reluctantly, by the French, but the Soviet government refused, and the zonal boundary which separated the Soviet-occupied zone from the rest of Germany rapidly hardened into the most divisive in Europe. Behind it the Soviet Union was systematically despoiling German industry in the name of reparations, and was using German agriculture to supply the deficiencies of the Soviet. Early in 1947 an attempt was made at a foreign ministers' meeting in Moscow to reach agreement on the terms of a constitution for a united Germany. Little progress was made, and the conference ultimately broke down on the question of the economic unity of Germany, which, in the view of the Western Powers, was prerequisite to political unity. From this failure it has become customary to date the beginning of Cold War.

An agreement was quickly reached on the political unification of the three Western zones. In 1948, a provisional constitution—the so-called Basic Law—was drawn up by the *Landtäge*, the elected bodies in each of the West German *Länder*. In 1949 it was approved by the military governors of the western zones, and in September of that year the German Federal Republic came into being. The sovereignty of West Germany was not, however, complete. An Occupation Statute defined the rights and obligations of the three occupying powers, but in 1954 the latter declared their intention to terminate even this limited control over the German Republic. West Germany was invited to become a member of NATO; the occupation statute was terminated, and on 5 May 1955, almost ten years after the unconditional surrender of Hitler's *Reich*, West Germany became an independent and sovereign state.

[1] James F. Byrnes, 6 September 1946.

In the meanwhile, attempts to draw East Germany into the framework of a united Germany had not been abandoned. These were, however, rebuffed by the Soviet Union, which proceeded instead to develop East Germany into a sovereign state, closely linked with the Eastern bloc and cut off completely from West Germany. The Peoples' Council of East Germany, following the example of the West German *Länder*, drew up a constitution, transformed itself into a parliament, and on 7 October 1949, declared the Soviet Zone to be the German Democratic Republic.

The change was in fact little more than in name, but it had serious consequences. The Soviet Union now recognised a government of East Germany, which had, like the Bonn government, a restricted sovereignty. In September 1955, following the Western agreement with West Germany, the Soviet Union and the German Democratic Republic entered into a treaty which recognised the complete sovereignty of the latter.

> The Contracting Parties solemnly reaffirm that the relations between them are based on full equality, respect for each other's sovereignty, and non-intervention in each other's domestic affairs. The German Democratic Republic is accordingly free to take decisions on all questions pertaining to its domestic and foreign policy, including its relations with the Federal Republic of Germany and the development of relations with other states.[1]

Both the Bonn government and its Western allies have refused to recognise the new East German republic, which, they considered, not only violates the Potsdam Agreement, but is calculated to prevent the formation of a united Germany at a later date. Although the government of the Federal Republic had recently entered into formal diplomatic relations with the Soviet Union, it refused to entertain such relations with any other country which recognised the government of East Germany. An exception has had to be made for the countries of the East European bloc, but this so-called 'Hallstein Doctrine', though not rigorously applied, until recently still called for the severance by West Germany of diplomatic relations with any country which establishes such relations with East Germany.

That such a policy can become embarrassing is obvious. A dialogue between East and West Germany is necessary if reunification is to be

---

[1] Article 1, *Treaty concerning relations between the USSR and the German Democratic Republic*, 20 September 1955, in *Selected Documents*, pp. 226–8.

achieved, and, in the absence of formal diplomatic recognition, such a dialogue has to be carried on by devious means.

The Berlin Question. In no matter is non-recognition more serious than in that of Berlin. West Berlin, made up of the three Western sectors, lies, by the shortest route, 108 miles within East Germany, and all traffic reaching the city, except that by air, has to pass East German check points. In the Western view these must be manned by Soviet forces and officials, since they consider that political power in the Eastern Zone is vested in the Soviet occupying forces. A Soviet official continues to be stationed at all points of entry into East Germany from the west, but not from the east. This scrutiny of passes and check on goods is at most perfunctory, and the work of issuing passes and controlling traffic is in fact done by the East German authorities themselves.

The status of Berlin itself is in theory still governed by the agreements reached at the end of the Second World War. The sectors themselves were established for purposes of a relatively low level of administration. The city itself, under a quadripartite control, exercised by the commandants of the four occupying forces, was to be administered as a whole. There was to be freedom of movement within the city, and it was not to be separated for purposes of commerce and economic development from the zone within which it lay or from the rest of Germany.

The quadripartite Control Council had never functioned well, and, in March 1948, the Soviet representative withdrew. The Council never met again. Berlin was breaking into two politically separate units. In June the western powers introduced their reformed West German currency, the D-Mark, into West Berlin. The Soviet authorities retaliated by closing all surface access routes to the city from the west. This ground blockade, which lasted from 24 June 1948 until 12 May 1949, was broken by an air-lift on a gigantic scale, and ended when the Soviet Union indicated its willingness to enter into discussions once again on the future of Germany. These discussions failed, as their predecessors had done. The uneasy compromise in Berlin remained, and access to West Berlin continued to be harrassed at intervals by Soviet and East German authorities.

The three Western sectors of the city, though garrisoned independently by Western forces, have since 1950 been administered as a single municipality, while East Berlin has, in defiance of earlier agreements, been absorbed for most purposes into the zone which encloses it. It has indeed become the political capital of the German Democratic Republic. West German authorities have at times acted as if West Berlin were part of West Germany. In approving the constitution for West Berlin in 1950, the allied commanders in the city pointed out that 'Berlin shall possess none of the attributes of a twelfth *Land*', and 'furthermore, the provisions of any Federal law shall apply to Berlin only after they have been voted upon by the House of Representatives (of Berlin) and passed as a Berlin law'.[1]

This is in accord with the agreements reached with the Soviet Union at the end of the Second World War. Berlin has, however, been represented in the West German *Reichstag* by non-voting observers; the *Reichstag* has itself held a somewhat provocative meeting in Berlin, and a former *Burgermeister* of the city was at the same time leader of one of the two main political parties in West Germany. Many West Germans act as if West Berlin were already part of the *Bundesrepublik*.

The position taken by the Soviet Union and East Germany is no less extreme. They admit that the western occupying forces have a legal right to be in West Berlin. 'These rights flow,' in the words of Krushchev, 'from the fact of German surrender. . . . But fourteen years have elapsed since the end of the war, and there is no need for the further occupation of West Berlin.'[2] Krushchev had reason on his side. The occupation of Berlin was designed to anticipate the transfer of power to an all-German government with its seat in the city. This has not taken place, and prospects for its realisation are at present remote. The allied occupation of the Western sectors of Berlin no longer fulfills its original function. This does not mean that other good reasons have not emerged for the retention of allied forces in West Berlin. This in effect the Russians admitted when they proposed 'to transform Western Berlin into a demilitarised free city, with its independence and the necessary business, cultural, and other ties with the countries of West and East protected by firm international guarantees'.[3] The West was distrustful of Soviet intentions toward a demilitarised and defenceless city which it could surround and isolate. It replied that 'Berlin is one city, and belongs to all Germany', and that 'the freedom and integrity of the united city of Berlin and access thereto [should]

---

[1] *Kommandatura Letter approving Berlin Constitution of 1950*, 29 August 1950. At present there are only ten *Länder* in West Germany.
[2] Krushchev, 19 March 1959.
[3] Soviet note to the United Kingdom Government, 2 March 1959.

be guaranteed by the four Powers who would continue . . . to station troops in Berlin'.[1]

Discussions which followed made no progress toward the unification of Berlin or of Germany. Instead, tensions mounted; the flow of refugees from East Berlin into West increased to the point where it posed a severe threat to the economic well-being of East Germany, and on 12 August 1961, the East German authorities began to seal off the sector boundary separating West Berlin from East. The accompanying decree of the East German government claimed that it was only introducing 'such control . . . on the borders of the German Democratic Republic, including the border with the Western Sectors of Greater Berlin, which is usually introduced along the borders of every sovereign State'. Unfortunately it was a far more stringent control than most sovereign states find it necessary to adopt. East Berlin was henceforward a part of East Germany, and West Berlin an enclave within it, maintaining a precarious hold on its lines of communication with the West.

LANDFORM REGIONS

East Germany is a section cut across the territory of the former German *Reich*. On the north is the Baltic Sea; to the south, the Czechoslovak Republic. Its western boundary, made up of former German provincial boundaries, runs from the Lübeck Bay to the Elbe, follows this river upstream for 60 miles, and then takes a circuitous course southward across the Lüneburg Heath, the damp valley of the Aller, and the loess-covered Börde, to reach the Harz Mountains. Crossing the high plateau of the Harz just to the west of the Brocken, the boundary very roughly separates the Göttingen basin from that of Thüringen. Then, crossing and recrossing the Werra river, it winds its way southward to the Rhön Massif, and thence eastward, across the Thüringerwald and Frankenwald to reach the north-western extremity of Czechoslovakia.

A boundary less logical than this would have been hard to devise, and its very absurdity shows that those who shaped it considered it to be only temporary. The boundary with Czechoslovakia, on the other hand, has not only a certain logic, but also the sanction of history. As a political boundary it has been in existence since the Middle Ages, and in physical terms it follows the flattened summit of the Erzgebirge.

[1] Western Peace Plan, presented at the Geneva Conference of Foreign Ministers, 14 May 1959.

The eastern boundary, the Oder-Neisse line, was proposed during the wartime conferences of the allied leaders, and confirmed as the 'temporary' boundary of East Germany at the Potsdam Conference. It had never previously served as a boundary, if we exclude the tenth century frontier of Poland which lay astride this valley. It was adopted because it seemed clear and unambiguous, and appeared to give Poland as much territory as, in the eyes of the allies, Poland seemed to deserve.

Drainage

These boundaries embrace an area, inclusive of the city of Berlin, of 42,000 square miles (108,780 square kilometres). Most of it is drained by the Elbe and its tributaries, and a feature of its drainage pattern is that the rivers discharge north-westward. Only a very small area is drained eastward to the Oder. This is due in large measure to erosion and deposition during and immediately after the Ice Age. The Elbe rises in Bohemia (see page 411), crosses the Erzgebirge by a deep, rugged and picturesque valley between Ústi nad Labem and Dresden. Its upper course, and that of its left-bank tributaries, were not greatly influenced by the glaciation. Above Wittenberg the Elbe receives the Schwarzer Elster, which occupies as a misfit stream the most southerly of the 'former river valleys', or *Urstromtäler*. This valley continues north-westward into West Germany, but near Magdeburg, the Elbe leaves it, flows north-east and then northward, to reach the next such valley. This valley is followed in its south-eastward extension by the upper Oder, but west of the Oder it breaks up into the maze of narrow marshy valleys, separated by the gravel heathland, which lies around Berlin. The Havel and its principal tributary, the Spree, drain much of this region north-westward, to join the Elbe near Havelberg. From this point the Elbe continues its course in a north-westerly direction. Below Hamburg it broadens into its long estuary, and at Cuxhaven it enters the North Sea.

North of the Elbe–Havel valley lies the Baltic End-Moraine of Mecklenburg. A number of short streams descend the southern slopes of this moraine-country to the Elbe and Havel, and one, the Elde, rises in the lake-country beyond, and crosses the end-moraine to reach the Elbe. None is large enough for navigation, but the lower courses of several are linked by the elaborate system of canals that encircles Berlin and links the Elbe with the Havel.

Above Magdeburg the Elbe receives two significant left-bank

tributaries, the Mulde and the Saale, which rise respectively in the Erzgebirge and Thuringian Basin. Only in the extreme south-west of its territory does East Germany extend beyond the drainage basin of the Elbe to embrace part of that of the Werra, one of the headstreams of the Weser. The Saale by contrast rises in the Frankenwald of northern Bavaria, and enters East Germany below Hof as a developed river.

North of the great end-moraine of Mecklenburg a boulder clay plain extends to the Baltic coastline. It is dotted with lakes which are linked by the rivers which make their way, usually by routes which are anything but direct, to the Baltic Sea. Of these the Warnow, Peene and Ücker are the most developed river systems.

The Northern Plain
Seven-eighths of East Germany lies within the plain of Northern Europe, and most of it is within the area that was glaciated during the Quaternary period. The simplest division of the plain is into that part where the imprint of the glaciation is fresh and glacial landforms are conspicuous, and the more southerly region where either the ice never came or its deposits have been eroded away. The boundary separating them is far from distinct. In general, however, it may be said to lie along the valley of the Schwarzer Elster and middle Elbe, and to be continued south-eastward through the Hoyerswerda depression into Poland and north-westward along the Ohre to the Aller valley.

North of this line, the glaciated landscape is divisible into a northern region characterised by ground-moraine, and a more southerly and more varied region in which outwash alternates with boulder clay and with alluvial valleys scoured by the glacial rivers as they made their way to the sea. The glacial forms belong to the closing phases of the Central European glaciation, when the ice front was in rapid retreat towards the north-north-east. Its withdrawal was punctuated by periods when the balance between the movement of the ice on the one hand and melting on the other was fairly stable. At these times terminal moraine accumulated. They were followed by periods of more rapid melting and the quick recession of the ice. At these times ground-moraine, interrupted only by fragments of terminal moraine, was laid down. It was during the temporary standstill of the ice that the vast aprons of outwash sands (*Sandr*) were formed, and the *Urstromtäler* were cut by the melt-water. The result is the pattern of landform regions illustrated in Fig. 7.1 and described below.

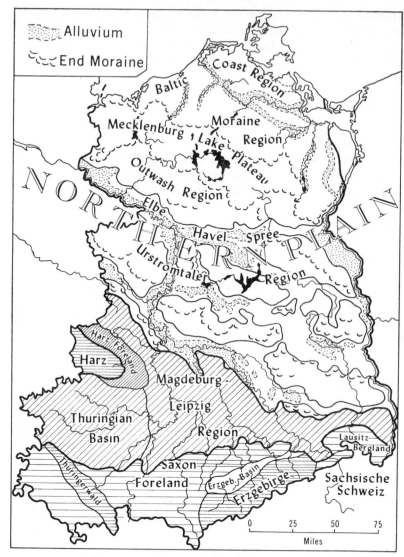

Fig. 7.1. Landform regions of East Germany.

The Baltic coast. From the Bay of Lübeck to the Stettin Bay lies a low, flat, but at the same time irregular coast. It is a product in part of the complex changes that have taken place in and around the Baltic Sea since the retreat of the ice sheets, in part of recent changes brought about by wind and the action of the waves. The most recent major change has been one of uplift of the land relative to the sea. The outlets from the Baltic Sea between the Danish islands were made narrower and shallower; the inflow of salt water was restricted, and the Baltic Sea itself became gradually more fresh. At present, the western Baltic has a salinity of 10 to 12 per thousand, while off the East German island of Rügen this drops to 8 to 9 per thousand.

As a result a coastal plain, broad in the west, but narrowing eastwards, was formed by the uplift of the Baltic Sea floor. Its surface was broken by fragments of moraine as well as by outcrops of more resistant rock such as chalk. Recently, however, the coastline has sunk, and part of this coastal plain now lies beneath a shallow sea. Along much of the coast this most recent change has brought the sea up against the ground- and end-moraine, which in some places form low cliffs. The coastal region meanwhile survives chiefly in the offshore islands. The channels which cut them off from the sea were in several instances the valleys of post-glacial rivers. All are narrow; those separating Rügen and Usedom from the German mainland are crossed by bridges, and the growth of sandbars has linked others both to one another and also to the coast. Rügen itself is a complex group of islands, at least 15 in number, which have been linked in this way.

The soft morainic deposits make large quantities of sand available for transport by the waves. The winds, both the prevailing and the predominant, are from the south-west or west. Sandbars have been drawn out generally towards the north-east or the east, and sand dunes have been piled up on west-facing coasts.

Ground-moraine of Mecklenburg. From the lower Oder to Lübeck Bay lies a region of ground-moraine cut across from south-east to north-west by the so-called Mecklenburgisch-Pommersches Grenztal, an *Urstromtal* now occupied in different parts by segments of the Tollense, Trebel and Recknitz rivers. The region as a whole is low-lying and rolling. A number of lakes and marshy hollows dot its surface, and fragments of end-moraine twist across it. The region of ground-moraine rises gently toward the south, and merges imperceptibly into the lake plateau.

Mecklenburg Lake plateau. This region, one of the most distinctive in East Germany, lies between the ramparts formed by the Inner or Pomeranian, and the Outer or Brandenburg moraines of the Great Baltic End-Moraine. These lie in general about 25 miles apart, but approach to within 10 miles of one another to the east of the region, in the Ückermark. The region is true end-moraine country. Fragments of moraine form low but often steep-sided hills, whose gravelly soil is usually left under forest. In between, the marshy depressions are linked and imperfectly drained by a number of somewhat indeterminate rivers, which discharge, some through the more northerly morainic barrier to the Baltic Sea; some across the more southerly to the Havel and the Elbe. The Schweriner See has, indeed, outlets in both directions. Sand has been spread by the late-glacial rivers or left after the finer particles had been sifted and removed from the boulder clay, so that the region as a whole is agriculturally less valuable though scenically more attractive than the region of ground-moraine lying to the north.

Above all, this is a lake region. A larger proportion of the area is covered by water than in any other province of Germany, and its only rival in this respect is the closely similar Masurian region of north-eastern Poland. Lakes vary greatly in size from the small ponds which occupy 'kettle-holes' in the moraine, to the Müritz See which covers 44 square miles (114 square kilometers), and the Plauer See, 15 square miles (38·8 square kilometres). The lakes are of every shape, though most tend to be relatively long and narrow, merely expansions of the water bodies in the course of the small, twisting rivers of the region. Very broadly it may be said that the south-eastern third of the region is characterised by a multitude of small lakes, and the remainder by a smaller number of lakes of very much greater size. The lakes vary greatly in depth; most are shallow, and some have in fact been filled by sedimentation and accumulation of peat. Others reach depths of more than 100 feet.

Outwash region. South of the Outer Moraine lies a strongly contrasted region. Relief is more gentle as the land drops southward toward the west–east valleys of the *Urstromtäler* region. The region is furrowed by the shallow valleys of the many small rivers which rise, some within the Lake Plateau, some on the outer face of the more southerly belt of end-moraine. Between these valleys, ground-moraine from an older glaciation forms level or rolling country. Along the valleys themselves lie narrow strips of alluvium, but over much of the region lies sand. To the north coarse sand, not unmixed with gravel and boulders, forms an almost continuous border to the morainic region itself. Toward the south the sand becomes finer, as a result of the natural grading process of the glacial rivers, and at the same time its deposits become discontinuous, until they terminate at the margin of the alluvium of the Eberswalde—Lower Elbe *Urstromtal*. In the nineteenth century, parts of this region were even known for their moving sand dunes. Today the sands are largely forested, and this is a region of little agricultural value, except where the boulder clay of the earlier glaciation shows through along the interfluves, framed by the sands.

Elbe–Havel–Spree Urstromtäler region. Stretching from west to east across East Germany is a complex region of twisting, marshy valleys, like a gigantic braided stream, whose channels enclose and separate flat-topped islands of boulder clay and outwash sands. Three separate and distinct advances of the Scandinavian ice sheet across North Germany have been recognised, corresponding with the Mindel, Riss and Würm glaciations of the Alpine region.[1] The massive end-moraines of Mecklenburg belong to the last of these advances of the ice, known in Germany as the Weichsel glaciation. The allocation of the glacial landforms which occur to the south of the Mecklenburg moraines to specific glaciations is far from clear, and it is even possible that all the moraines and boulder clay deposits of this region represent phases in the retreat of the second North German, or Saale, glaciation.

Fragmentary end-moraines are found as far south as the valley of the middle Elbe and locally even beyond it. In general they do not link up into an extensive system comparable to those of the Weichsel glaciation. There is, however, one conspicuous exception, the belt of end-moraines and accompanying outwash which begins to the south of Hamburg, and extends south-eastwards as the Lüneburg, Fläming and Lausitz Heaths.

The Elbe, after pursuing a generally north-westerly course through Saxony, makes an abrupt turn at Magdeburg and cuts across this belt of heath country. West of this transverse valley is the Altmark. This is the south-eastern extremity of the Lüneburg region. It is characterised by gentle relief and soils which range from sandy loam in the north to coarse sands in the south, where the barrier of terminal moraine over-looks the depression now occupied by the Aller and Ohre (Eyer) rivers.

East of the transverse course of the Elbe landforms are more complex. The terminal moraines of the Wartha phase lie roughly parallel with the middle Elbe, and with their accompanying outwash and ground-moraine, give rise to a region of considerable variety in both

[1] Johannes F. Gellert, *Grundzüge der Physischen Geographie von Deutschland*, Berlin, 1958, vol. 1, pp. 222–9.

relief and soil. This is the Fläming Heath. Much of it is covered, like the Altmark, with a sandy loam, which passes on the one hand into sterile sands and on the other into loess-like deposits of not inconsiderable fertility.

There is no conspicuous divide, only the valley of the small River Dahme, to separate the Fläming from the Lausitz Heath. The latter is somewhat lower and has a more gentle relief than the Fläming region. The glacial deposits are spread more thinly. The underlying Tertiary deposits come close enough to the land surface for their immense reserves of brown coal to be exploited in vast open-cast workings. The terminal moraine itself gives rise to a narrow line of steep-sided hillocks, to the north of which lies ground-moraine strongly admixed with sand washed down from the ice margin during later pauses in its retreat. To the south of the Lausitz moraine lie small alluvial basins such as that which lies around Finsterwalde and also along the course of the Schwarze Elster, interspersed with areas of outwash sands and gravels.

South of the valley of the middle Elbe, and between the latter and the course of its left-bank tributary, the Mulde, lie the most southerly of the glacial landforms. Like much of the area to the north of the Elbe, it is primarily a region of sandy outwash, interrupted by fragmentary segments of terminal moraine, indicative of pauses in the glacial retreat earlier and probably less prolonged than the Warthe stadium.

The primary outlet for glacial melt-water during the Warthe pause was the valley of the Schwarze Elster and the middle Elbe, prolonged south-eastwards by a damp depression to the headwaters of the Spree and on to the Neisse, Bóbr and upper Odra (Oder). North-westwards, below Magdeburg, the waters escaped by the Ohre and Aller toward the North Sea. The route which the escaping waters thus traced forms the most southerly of the *Urstromtäler*, today a broad, alluvial valley floor. It is a damp, but fertile region, with a high water table and levées to protect it from the river, and it is always at the mercy of floods.

The ice withdrew irregularly and unevenly from the Warthe stage. Tongues of dead ice must have lain for long periods in hollows in the ground-moraine of Brandenburg, and temporary lakes occupied its valleys before the further retreat of the ice opened up routes by which they discharged to the sea. North of the Fläming and its continuation, the Lausitz Heaths, is another such elongated marshy depression.

Toward the north-west it is occupied in part by the lower Havel, but towards the south-east it is drained in succession by the Nuthe, the Dahme, and the Spree, all of which discharge northwards across the low plateaus of Brandenburg to the Havel. This depression, sometimes known as the Baruthertal, is marshy and ill-drained. The alluvium is too damp for cultivation, and the areas of sand that have been spread over parts of it are too infertile. It is a region of forest and meadow, which, toward the south-east, passes into the Spreewald. Here is a basin, almost surrounded by low plateaus (*Platten*) of drift, drained, if that expression does not exaggerate its functions, by the Spree. The river itself breaks up into a maze of narrow waterways, separated by damp and generally wooded islands of alluvium. It is in the recesses of this somewhat forbidding region that the Slavic Sorbs have been able to preserve their folkways and a certain national identity.

Between the Baruth-Spree depression and the most northerly of the *Urstromtäler*, which extends from the Oder westward by way of Eberswalde and the Rhin valley, to the lower Havel and the Elbe, lies the complex region of central Brandenburg. This consists very broadly of low plateaus built of thick deposits of ground-moraine. Across these have accumulated fragments of end-moraine, resulting from pauses in the glacial retreat, and a thin veneer of glacial sand. But the region owes its peculiar quality to the channels which were cut by the ice water. These constitute an intricate pattern. Foremost is the valley which takes off from the Oder near Fürstenberg, runs north-westward, picking up the Spree and continuing by way of Fürstenwalde, the centre of Berlin, and Spandau, until it merges with the valley of the Rhin and the Elbe. Toward the south a series of valleys, narrower than the *Urstromtäler* themselves, and partially closed by natural dams of moraine to give a series of lakes, breaks the glacial plateau into a number of segments: the Nauen, Taltow, Lehnin, Beelitz, Luckenwalde, Zossen, Buchholz and Lieberose plateaus. The latter have a certain similarity. Where the underlying boulder clay comes to the surface the land is likely to be cultivated, but over much of the area what soil there is derives from end-moraine and sandy outwash. In the past much was heathland (*Heide*); today most of it is under coniferous forest. Agricultural land-use is really important only along the valleys which separate and encircle the sandy plateaus.

North of the Berlin-Spree depression the landscape is similar; the glacial landforms are sharper, but the lakes which characterise the

8

region to the south are largely absent. Instead, the Barnim and Lebus plateaus extend from the Havel to the Oder with little break or interruption.

The northern boundary of this Brandenburg region of *Urstromtäler* and sandy, heath and forest-covered plateaus is the Elberswalde-Rhin-Elbe depression. This is the newest, the most extensive, and the most clearly marked of all the glacial river channels. It is clearly traceable from the Vistula valley east of Toruń to the sea below Hamburg, and its origins lie even farther to the east. For much of this distance it constitutes a broad, damp flood plain, within which the river has often to be confined between levées. Only in East Germany is this depression not occupied by a major river. The dominant river of central Brandenburg, the Havel, follows it for only a short distance, before pursuing its twisting course across the plateaus which lie to the west of Berlin. East of the Havel the Elberswalde depression narrows between the Barnim plateau and the outwash region which borders southern Mecklenburg, before broadening into the marshy floodplain of the Oder. West of the Havel, its course is traced only by the Ruppin Canal, until the Rhin, descending from the Mecklenburg moraines, enters the great valley and carries its drainage west to the Elbe.

Such is the region in which, in the twelfth century, German settlers established the March of Brandenburg. It was no great agricultural wealth that attracted them, but rather the need for protection against the Slavs. The city of Brandenburg had been a Slavic stronghold amid the marshes by the Havel. Early in the eighteenth century, the government of the March, which had by now become the nucleus of the kingdom of Prussia, was shifted 22 miles to the east to Potsdam, also beside the Havel and between the Templiner and the Havel Lakes. In the later nineteenth century Potsdam was in turn forsaken for the new capital of the German Empire, Berlin. The new site lay on the Spree, in the Berlin-Spree *Urstromtal*. But here the sandy plateaus to the north and south of the depression approached close to one another. Not only did the Spree and Havel offer the facilities for water transport between west and east; the ease of north–south movement, where the valley was narrowest, made land transport no less practicable.

The political rise of Brandenburg and the development of Berlin, the largest city in continental Europe, in so unpropitious an environment has not been easy to explain. To Toynbee, this region with 'its starveling pine-plantations and its sandy fields',[1] could only offer the

[1] A. J. Toynbee, *A Study of History*, vol. 2, p. 58.

stimulus of hardship. To others the need to combine to resist the Slavs was thought to have brought about a craving for order and discipline and devotion to hard work. These explanations are at best partial. The Havelland was the section of Germany's eastern borderland to which Frederick of Hohenzollern was sent by his Emperor in 1411. It became, as it were, the cradle of the dynasty, but it was from other regions of Germany that the Brandenburg Electors drew their wealth and the manpower to serve in their armies. As a result of marriage and inheritance, their possessions were extended north-east to Prussia and west to the Rhineland. In the seventeenth century Brandenburg acquired possession of the rich loess lands which bordered the Harz mountains, and in the mid-eighteenth, the fertile plain of Silesia. It was thus a varied and extensive territory which became dependent politically on Brandenburg, and to some of these regions of superior fertility we must turn.

Saxon–Thuringian Plain
The effective limit of glacial deposits and *Urstromtäler* lies along the Elbe to the south-east of Magdeburg, the Mulde and the southern margin of the Lausitz heathlands. The earliest advance of the ice extended far to the south-west of this line. Fragments of end-moraine and of boulder clay are recognisable; erratics occur in the soil, but the landscape shows little of the direct influence of the glaciation. Instead, the loess, distributed by the wind probably in the cold, dry interglacial periods, covers part of the low-lying regions, imparting soft, rounded outlines to the land surface, and to the soil a lightness and fertility not found farther north. Landforms, however, are carved in large measure from the 'solid' geology, which is here of considerable complexity.

The dominant relief features of the southern part of East Germany are the regions of old (Palaeozoic) rock, folded during the Hercynian mountain-building period and represented today by regions of high, steep-sided plateaus. Within East Germany itself these hills form two separate masses: the Harz Mountains, to the south-west of Magdeburg, and the Erzgebirge, through which runs the boundary with Czechoslovakia, and their extension toward the west and north-west, the Frankenwald and Thüringerwald. Before the end of Palaeozoic times these mountain masses had not only been folded, but their surface was eroded to form the widely separated masses which we have today.

In early Secondary times these mountainous areas formed islands in a Triassic sea. Triassic beds were laid down around and between them, and were succeeded by the Jurassic, here developed on only a feeble scale, and the Cretaceous. In the course of the Tertiary period these beds were lightly faulted and forced into broad folds. Depressions were invaded from the north by a Tertiary sea, and shallow water deposits were laid down, including the immense reserves of brown coal, for which this part of Germany is well known.

It is to this great range of geological structures that the region in large measure owes the variety of its landforms, soils and mineral resources. Similar structures and landforms extend northward beneath the glacial deposits. In a few areas the latter are thin enough for the underlying minerals to be reached without difficulty, but toward the north of the Republic, the thickness of glacial deposits becomes so great that the costs of prospecting and developing the underlying mineral resources are prohibitive. In the following pages the landform regions south approximately of the Lüneburg–Fläming–Lausitz heaths are examined.

Magdeburg–Leipzig region. Between the valley of the Elbe and the foothills of the Harz Mountains lies a low, rolling plateau. It is made up of gently folded beds of Secondary geological age. It was covered by ice during its earlier and more extensive advances, but of this there is little evidence beyond traces of terminal moraine. The terrain is rolling, and outcrops of the harder beds give rise to scarp-like ridges of slight elevation. The region is crossed by the Saale, Weisse Elster and Bode rivers. Much of it is covered by loess, which gives rise to a light, fertile soil, easily cleared and brought under the plough. It is today an open, intensively cultivated and treeless region, traditionally one of easy movement and prosperous agriculture, in and near which have grown up some of the largest and most important cities in East Germany, including Magdeburg, Halle and Leipzig.

The northern part of the region is the Magdeburg Börde, a region long known for its fertility. Loess deposits are also extensive and thick to the south-east in the direction of Köthen and Bitterfeld, but over the low, level plateau that encircles Halle and Leipzig the loess gives place to glacial deposits and the loess is here intermixed with sands. But to the south-west and south the loess plateau again appears, and around Querfurt and Weissenfels is again among the most fertile and productive regions in Germany.

Harz Foreland. Between the low rolling Börde of Magdeburg and the Harz Mountains lies the Harz Foreland. It is composed, like the

Börde, of gently flexed secondary strata, but here the harder beds give rise to ridges and small areas of hill which rise steeply from the plain. Though aligned roughly parallel with the Harz, these scarps and hogsbacks are rarely continuous for more than a few miles. The geological structures upon which they are partially dependent lie from west to east, and the ridges are themselves cut into short segments by the fanlike pattern of rivers which radiates from the Harz. In the extreme west of the region these flow to join the West German Oker, a tributary of the Aller. The rest join the Bode or the Saale and thus the Elbe.

The hilly ridges become higher as the Harz is approached, and the steep, forested slopes of the highest rise almost a thousand feet above sea level. Between them the land is loess-covered, with alluvium along the valleys. The soil at its best is as light and fertile as that of the Börde, but deteriorates southward with increasing altitude. Nevertheless, the region is one of early human settlement and intensive cultivation on the lower ground. In the east it wraps around the extremity of the Harz Mountains, and here merges into the Thuringian Basin.

Thuringian Basin. This region of hilly lowland lies framed between the Harz and the Thüringerwald and Frankenwald. Structurally it resembles the Harz Foreland, but its lines are drawn on a larger scale. Its geological structure is more complex; its hilly ridges, higher and more continuous, and its lowlands more extensive. Structurally the region is a basin trending in a north-west to south-east direction, made up of Triassic beds and bordered by Palaeozoic deposits to the north-east and south-west. Its dominant landforms conform with the general direction of folding, and extend from north-west to south-east. Relief does not, however, result entirely from the outcrop of Triassic beds of varying hardness. South of the Harz Mountains lies another and structurally similar massif of Palaeozoic rock, the Kyffhäuser Gebirge. It is a small, fault-bounded and steep-sided massif, which, with its subterranean extensions, divides the Thuringian basin into a smaller north-eastern and a larger south-western section. In each the geological components are:

    d. Keuper.
    c. Muschelkalk (shelly limestone).
    b. Buntsandstein (Bunter sandstone).
    a. Zechstein.

The more northerly basin is floored by the limestone of the Zechstein series, which outcrops around the rim of the basin, against the

Harz and Kyffhäuser Massifs. The basin, framed by this narrow out-crop, is filled with the Buntsandstein series. The Zechstein gives rise to a small but strongly developed area of karst, but the Buntsandstein, which occupies the whole of the central part of the basin, forms a level plain, intensively cultivated and of great fertility: the *Goldene Aue*.

South of the Kyffhäuser the bleached, dry limestone of the Zech-stein again comes to the surface, and is again succeeded by the Bunt-sandstein, with its accompanying gentle relief and good soils. This is the *Diamantene Aue*. This basin—the main Thuringian Basin—is deeper as well as more extensive. The Buntsandstein is succeeded southward by Muschelkalk, which here forms a conspicuous north-facing scarp which at its highest points rises over 1,640 feet above sea-level. It begins beside the Unstrut, extends north-westwards as the Hainleite, and is continued as the Dün and the Eichsfeld, where its high, flat-topped hills overlook the deep meanders of the Werra along East Germany's western border. Then the Muschelkalk curves back toward the south-east in the rolling Hainich plateau, which ends against the Gera valley near Erfurt.

East of the Gera river the Muschelkalk continues as a rolling and in some parts almost level plateau. The Olm and other tributaries of the Saale are sunk into its surface. Soils are light and calcareous, locally intermixed with loess.

Within this circle of limestone uplands lies the central basin of Thuringia, a lower but nonetheless hilly region developed in the varied marls and limestones of the Keuper. Along the axis of the basin flows the Unstrut, before turning to the north and in turn cutting across the Hainleite and flowing around the eastern flank of the Kyffhäuser. Its fan-shaped pattern of tributaries drains the whole interior section of the Thuringian Basin. To the natural richness of soils derived from the Keuper has been added extensive deposits of loess. Alluvium derived from these sources has been spread over the valleys, and over higher ground is a light and predominantly loess soil. This is a region of generally low rainfall; soil nutrients are removed less readily than in most other parts of Germany, and in some areas the soil even approxi-mates to a black earth.

The soils of the inner basin are amongst the best in East Germany. It is a region of early human settlement, and the close pattern of cities, almost all of which are of medieval origin, marks it as one of the more precocious in the development of urban society. Around the margin of the inner basin lie Gotha, Erfurt and Weimar, and only a few miles across the Muschelkalk plateau to the east of the latter, is Jena.

It was in this environment that Goethe lived, and through this landscape he took his periodic drives nearly a century and a half ago. He must often have driven from Erfurt northwards into the Unstrut valley, and Eckermann thus described the view which met him from the valley's southern rim.

The view from this spot, in the clear morning light of the autumn sun, was magnificent: on the south and south-west, the whole range of the Thüringerwald . . .; on the west, beyond Erfurt, the towering Castle Gotha and the Inselberg;[1] farther north, the mountains behind Langensalza and Mühlhausen,[2] until the view was bounded on the north by the blue Harz Mountains.[3]

South of this outcrop of the Muschelkalk the Buntsandstein and Zechstein beds abut directly against the older rocks enclosing the basin. This is a strongly dissected region, intermediate in terms of relief between the Muschelkalk plateau and the rougher terrain of the Thüringerwald. In part it is drained northward toward the centre of the basin by the Gera and its tributaries, but toward the west this region forms the basin of the Nesse. This river, rising near Erfurt, keeps outside the curving perimeter of the Muschelkalk plateau, then, swinging around the northern extremity of the Thüringerwald, it flows beneath the castled crag of the Wartburg, passes by the walls of Eisenach and enters the Werra on the West German boundary.

East of the Gera the Buntsandstein region broadens into the Saale plateau. Much of its undulating surface lies at an altitude of about 1,600 feet. The Saale and its tributary, the Orla, occupy broad valleys, and the Weisse Elster a very much narrower and steeper valley. This is in general a region of poor, sandy soil, especially short in lime. It is in consequence one of small agricultural value and forests are more extensive than in any other part of the Thuringian Basin. Rural settlement is less dense than in most other parts of the basin, and it lacks the scatter of small towns, such as characterise the inner basin of Thuringia.

Saxon Foreland. East of the valley of the Schwarze Elster, the hilly foreland of the Erzgebirge extends eastward to the Neisse river and so

[1] Probably Seeberg, 3 miles south-east of Gotha.
[2] The Eichsfeld and Hainich in the Muschelkalk ridge.
[3] J. P. Eckermann, *Gespräche mit Goethe*. This passage is from J. Oxenfords' translation, Dent, Everyman's Library, p. 228.

into Poland. Its geological structure, however, undergoes an abrupt change. The ancient Palaeozoic massif of Bohemia which, as we have seen, sends a long finger towards the north-west in the Frankenwald and Thüringerwald, here extends northward as a broad, uneven plateau dropping gradually in altitude, until it disappears beneath the Trias, the Tertiary deposits, and the glacial drift.

A second ridge of the older rocks links the Harz and Kyffhäuser with the Lausitz Mountains, which form the northern bastion of the Bohemian Massif. It does not reach the altitude of the Thüringerwald, and for much of its length it lies hidden beneath the Triassic and later deposits. It nevertheless comes to the surface along the Elbe to the north-west of Dresden; gives rise to isolated basaltic hills between the Elbe and the Mulde, and appears again to the east of Halle.

Between these inliers of the Palaeozoic massif which underlies the whole region lie the well differentiated beds of the Trias. The lower-most of these is, as in the Thuringian Basin, the Zechstein, with its endowment in natural and potash salts. Above it lie the Bunter sandstone, the Muschelkalk and the Keuper, all of them eroded and far from continuous in their occurrence. Their distribution, however, is hidden firstly by the Tertiary deposits and later by the Quaternary. This region became a shallow sea early in the Tertiary period, and along with the clay swept down by the rivers—ancestors to the present Elbe and Saale system—were deposited immense beds of organic matter which now constitute some of the most extensive deposits of brown coal in the world. These brown-coal basins were never continuous; they occupied hollows in the surface of the Triassic beds, but they were spread over an immense area. They extend north-westward along the Harz Foreland, and so into West Germany, near Braunschweig. They spread through the Nieder Lausitz region and into Lower Silesia, northward into Brandenburg, and north-easward into central Poland.

The Tertiary beds—mostly Eocene and Oligocene—come to the surface over only small areas; they are covered by immense deposits of glacial moraine, outwash, diluvium and loess. Over extensive areas these are too thick for the underlying brown coal to be worked economically, but where they are thin and easily removed, the brown coal is being quarried from enormous opencast workings (see page 261).

The geological complexity of the Saxon Foreland is hardly visible in its relief. As a whole this is a rolling plateau region, ranging from

1,000 to 2,000 feet above sea-level. Ridges of gneiss and isolated basaltic hills raise their forested slopes above it. The valleys of the Pleisse, the Zwickaue Mulde, Flöha, Feirberge Mulde, Elbe and of the headwaters of the Schwarze Elster and Spree flow deeply entrenched across it, and between the plateaus it is covered with loess which smooths its rough surfaces and produces a region that is rarely paralleled for fertility and ease of communication'

Like the Thuringian Basin to the west it was a region of early settlement. It formed from an early date part of the west to east routeway which traced out the loess belt from Central Europe into the Russian Steppe. Cities developed at frequent intervals, and although the modern centres of industry have moved either southward into the Erzgebirge or northward to the salt deposits and brown coal-fields, some, like Dresden and Meissen, remain of more than local importance.

The northern part of this foreland is characterised by hills of crystalline rock and by the larger Palaeozoic inlier of the Collmberg. Toward the south the rolling, loess-covered, and deeply dissected plateau rises gradually toward the Erzgebirge. The Elbe valley is the broadest and deepest of the region. Near Pirna the river emerges from its gorge-like passage through the Erzgebirge, and broadens into the Dresden Basin, which extends downstream to Meissen, where the Lausitz granites encroach and again narrow the valley.

East of the Elbe valley the gentle relief of the foreland is continued, but becomes more irregular and higher as the granite highlands of northern Bohemia are approached. Forested hills rise to heights of 1,500 feet above the loess-covered plateau. Curving northward around the higher ground of northern Bohemia, this region reaches the Neisse and the boundary with Poland.

Thüringerwald–Erzgebirge

From the Wartburg, overlooking the deep valley of the Werra, the Hercynian massif of central Germany extends eastward in a shallow curve to the granite massif of Oberlausitz and northern Bohemia. It is part of a more extensive area of hills, the German *Mittelgebirge*. It is continued westward beneath and beyond the Triassic hills of Hesse in the Rhineland massif. Toward the north these older and harder rocks sink beneath the Thuringian Basin to reappear in the Harz Mountains, and southward they are continued without interruption in the hills of Bohemia.

8*

In terms of relief this region is comparatively simple. It is an undulating tableland, planated in Tertiary times, which drops sometimes steeply, sometimes in broad steps to the lowland areas which border it. Its geological structure, by contrast, could not easily be more complex.

Thüringerwald. This is a long, narrow and tapering ridge, which points finger-like from its base bear the Schwarza river north-westward to the Werra valley, a distance of 50 miles. Its width between its steep, fault-bounded flanks is at most about 10 miles, and diminishes near its extremity to less than half. Its undulating surface lies at from 2,500 to 3,000 feet, dropping to below 1,500 feet in the north-west, and for the whole of its distance constitutes a divide between the upper Werra drainage and the rivers of the Thuringian Basin. These rivers have from both sides cut back into the ridge in a series of deep and narrow valleys which in fact dissect the narrow plateau.

The Thüringerwald is made up essentially of much folded lower Palaeozoic gneisses in the south-east, and of no less strongly folded Permian beds to the north-west. These have, however, been extensively intruded by granite and porphyry. It is these crystalline rocks which form the rounded summits of the range. Of these the highest is the Grosser Beerberg, an igneous mass which rises to 3,221 feet.

The summits of the Thüringerwald are open and grassy, though too high for any form of agriculture except rough summer grazing. There are villages and patches of cultivation in the valleys, but elsewhere the region lives up to its name; it is forested with conifers.

Thuringian slate plateau. The direction of the Thüringerwald is continued to the south-east in the Bavarian Frankenwald and the Bohemian Forest. Beyond the Schwarza river, however, the mountainous platform from which the Thüringerwald rises is continued eastward between the Erzgebirge proper and the Thuringian and Saxon basins. It forms a rolling plateau, rising in the south-west, along the West German border to over 2,000 feet, but dropping toward the north to less than 1,600 feet. To the south this plateau passes into the Frankenwald; to the south-east it rises to the Elstergebirge, which lie along the Czechoslovak border and drop steeply along their fault-bounded southern face to the Cheb Basin (the Egerland) of Czechoslovakia. This area has long been known as the Vogtland.

The plateau is built in the main of lower Palaeozoic slates and gneisses, intruded extensively by granite and other igneous rocks. These appear as scattered small outcrops, and give rise to hills which rise steeply perhaps some 650 feet above the plateau surface. The plateau on the other hand is steeply trenched by the Saale and Weisse Elster and their tributaries. Their valleys are usually deep and always narrow and forested. They are followed by the few railways which penetrate this plateau, and the Saale is dammed at two places for the generation of hydro-electric power. Slate is quarried, but agricultural resources are slender in the extreme. The soil is poor and podzolised; rye is the chief field crop, and forests of spruce and birch are extensive.

The Erzgebirge. East of the valley of the Weisse Elster the Thuringian plateau passes into the Erzgebirge. Landforms do not greatly differ, but their altitude and local relief become greater. For nearly 140 miles the Erzgebirge forms a high, dissected plateau. Its slope toward the north-west is gentle, though the discerning eye will detect in the huge interfluves, between the north-flowing rivers, a series of faint steps, cut by the higher marine levels of the earlier Tertiary. Toward the south-east, the flat or gently rounded summits end abruptly along an immense fault-line. Beyond it are the Bohemian lowlands drained by the Ohře or Eger river and floored with Tertiary deposits— clay and brown coal—corresponding with those of the Saxon Basin to the north. The Czechoslovak boundary follows this high plateau leaving its highest summits and also the divide between the Elster-Mulde and the Ohře drainage systems a mile or two within Czechoslovakia. The greatest altitude in the range is Klinovec, 4,080 feet, above Jáchymov. The highest point within Germany is the Fichtelberg, 3 miles to the north and only a few feet lower.

The shales and slates of the Vogtland give place to schists and gneisses of indeterminate but generally pre-Cambrian age. These have been intruded by granites and basalts which usually give rise, when they come to the surface, to isolated hills which may rise several hundred feet above the general level of the plateau. Relief is stronger than in the Thuringian plateau to the west. Valleys are deeper and the hills steeper. Soils are even poorer; most are strongly podzolised, and some are merely skeletal. Agriculture is here of negligible importance. Much of the land is covered with forest, mixed in the valleys and spruce on higher ground, while the rounded summits bear only a sub-arctic plant association.

The wealth of the Erzgebirge lies in its minerals. Their formation was associated with the intrusion of the granite. They arose from the latter as fluids which passed upwards through joints and faults in the prevailing gneisses. Here the ores condensed to form lodes. The latter tend to occur in two areas. Toward the east in the Freiberg area the ores are predominantly of lead, zinc and silver. To the west, in close association with the granite mass of Eibenstock, are lodes in which cobalt, nickel, silver and uranium occur. The most important source of uranium actually lies on the southern flanks of this high granite area, at Jáchymov (Joachimstal). In addition to these two major concentrations of ore deposits, metalliferous lodes are distributed through the whole length of the Erzgebirge.

It is not improbable that ores were worked here in prehistoric times. The Erzgebirge are one of the very few European sources of tin, and may thus have contributed to the early bronze industry. Mining on a more significant scale began in the Freiberg area in the twelfth century. Silver was in greatest demand, and in the fourteenth century silver mines were opened up in the more westerly area. This became, under the direction of the Függer family, one of the chief sources of silver supply until cheaper silver from the New World forced the closing of the mines in the Erzgebirge. It was at this time that silver minted from the metal of Joachimstal, began to circulate under the name of *Täler* or Dollars.

Saxon Switzerland. The Bohemian Basin is drained by the river Labe (Elbe) to Saxony and the North Sea. The Elbe cuts across the line of the Erzgebirge–Lausitz Bergland by a deep and narrow valley of great beauty. This is the *Sächsische Schweiz*, a small but distinctive region within the mountain chain.

In late Palaeozoic times (Hercynian) the south-west to north-west line of the Erzgebirge was disturbed by faulting. Two groups of faults, lying roughly at right angles to the range itself, led to the sinking of a block of territory, between the Bohemian and the Saxon basins. The Secondary sea which covered Saxony, extended through the gap thus formed into Bohemia, and deposited here a narrow belt of Cretaceous sandstones no more than 16 miles across.

Through this depression, between the higher ground of the Erzgebirge and the Lausitz Bergland, the Elbe cut its incised valley. Short tributary streams have cut back into the sandstone on each side of the river, breaking it up into a series of flat-topped buttes. Some of the 'table mountains' (*Tafelberge*) stand isolated; others are grouped in clusters. Their steep sides, clothed with conifers and mixed woodland, rise from an undulating valley plain that is mainly under cultivation to their dry, flat, heath-covered summits.

Lausitz Bergland. Beyond the more north-easterly of the Elbe faults the Lausitz granite comes to the surface to form a rounded upland which extends southward into northern Bohemia. Its rounded hills, separated by broad open valleys, rise to over 1,600 feet and, beyond the Czechoslovak boundary, to over 2,000 feet. Yet this is a region of gentler relief than the Erzgebirge. Its soils, derived principally from the granite, have, at least locally, been improved by the loess that has been swept up on to this plateau, and this is agriculturally one of the best endowed of the Thüringerwald–Erzgebirge regions.

East of the granite lies a small basin, drained by the Neisse and centering in Zittau. The alignment of the German–Polish boundary along the Neisse river divided this basin politically and gave East Germany the larger western part. The basin itself constitutes a depression between the Lausitz granite region and the Jizerské Hory and Krkonoše of Bohemia (page 407), and, like a wider version of the Elbe trough, it too was occupied by the late Tertiary sea and received thick deposits of Cretaceous sandstone. Erosion has here, however, taken a different course from that in the Elbe sandstone region. The sandstone has been stripped from the Neisse Basin, but preserved in the Lužické Hory (Lausitzer Gebirge) and their continuation in Bohemia, the Krkonoše. Germany territory extends into the Lausitzer Gebirge. In the Zittau Basin itself the Lausitz granite is almost completely masked by Tertiary and later deposits. Among these is a thick deposit of brown coal which occupies a depression in the surface of the granite.

Erzgebirge Basin. North of the Erzgebirge, and parallel with its crest lies a basin—more geological than orographical—in which Carboniferous and Permian beds have been preserved. This region is somewhat lower and more dissected than the Erzgebirge which bound it on the south, and to a slight degree it has served to orient the courses of rivers in a south-west to north-east direction. Its distinction, however, is primarily geological; the upper Carboniferous beds here contain East Germany's only significant reserves of bituminous coal: the two small coal basins of Zwickau and Karl-Marx-Stadt (Chemnitz). Their combined output is less than a quarter of a million tons a year, but they served to locate here during the nineteenth century the industrial complexes of Zwickau and Karl-Marx-Stadt.

Harz Mountains
Last of the mountainous regions of Palaeozoic rock to be described is the small, compact and complex massif known as the Harz. It forms,

with its small outlier, the Kyffhäuser, the northern boundary of the Thuringian Basin. Westward it extends into the territory of the German Federal Republic; south-eastward a buried continuation (above, page 213) links it with the Lausitz region. The Harz Mountains as a whole cover an area of 784 square miles, of which about two-thirds lies in East Germany. They lie in a west-north-west to east-south-east direction for about 50 miles, and for much of this distance maintain a width of from 15 to 20 miles. On all sides except the south-east the boundaries of the Harz are clear and distinct, rising steeply from the surrounding Trias. Towards the south-east, however, the Palaeozoic massif sinks more gradually in altitude until it passes beneath the Zechstein and Bunter sandstone beds without any conspicuous change in the relief.

The Harz is built mainly of Silurian and Devonian slates, gneisses and quartzites, which were intensely folded and faulted during the Variscan phase of mountain-building. Among the faults which developed were those which bound the massif on all sides except the south-east and are in large measure responsible for the extraordinary abruptness of its flanks. The Harz is the ideal horst. Its slopes have, however, been greatly modified by erosion. As in the Erzgebirge, they have been cut during the high sea-levels of the Tertiary into a series of steps, and the flattened summit of the massif is made up in part of such erosion platforms at altitudes of about 2,900 and 3,300 feet.

The mountains were, subsequent to their formation, intruded by granite and related igneous rocks, and then by mineral-bearing lodes. The highest point in the Harz, the Brocken (3,747 feet), is merely a rounded upland which rises inconspicuously above the high plateau. The many rivers which rise in the Harz have cut back their valleys, so that most are now deep, narrow gashes, almost completely forested, in the flanks of the massif. The most extensive and probably the most picturesque of these is the Bode valley, which commences to the east of the Brocken and flows north-eastward to the Saale (page 208). The Harz rises so suddenly from the North Germain Plain, and presents a landscape so wild and so different from the gentle contours of the plain that it has almost inevitably entered strongly into German folklore, legend and literature. Here was set the *Walpurgisnacht* in Goethe's *Faust*, and the *Hexentanzplatz* in the Bode valley is shown to the credulous tourist. Heinrich Heine walked across the Harz, climbed the Brocken, and noted in his *Harzreise*, a classic of the literature of travel, how in the Ilsetal:

The mountains gradually rise higher and higher, and are covered to their very base with beeches, oaks, and similar broad-leaved trees. . . . For the common lowland timber prevails in the Lower Harz, as the east side of the Harz is called, in contradistinction to the west side, or Upper Harz, which is actually much higher, and better adapted to the growth of conifers. . . . The higher one ascends, the more dwarfed become the fir-trees. They seem to shrink and shrivel up until nothing is left but bilberries, raspberries, and mountain vegetation. . . . Here you first get a proper view of the wonderful groups of granite blocks. Some of them are of astounding size, and one can easily fancy them the balls that the evil spirits play at catch with on Walpurgis night, when the witches troop in.[1]

Heine's regional division of the Harz was correct. The *Oberharz* is the high granite plateau in the west, bordered on the east by the lower and more dissected *Unterharz*. Beyond the latter, where the Harz ridges pass under the Trias, is the Mansfeld Bergland, a hilly rather than mountainous region, where the tributaries of the Saale have cut indiscriminately across Palaeozoic and Triassic beds. The latter increase in size and depth to the east and south and merge into the Saxon and Thuringian basins.

The wealth of the Harz lay formerly in its minerals, which occurred in lodes which extended outwards from its granitic core. The most highly mineralised region lay to the west, where the fortunes of Goslar were founded upon the silver-lead deposits of the Rammelsberg, Klaustal and St Andreasberg. Mining is still of some small importance here, but the lodes, never as numerous or rich as in the west, have been abandoned in the eastern Harz. Iron-ore was formerly smelted in small, stone-built furnaces over much of the region, but the only mineral industry, other than quarrying, which remains important in the eastern Harz is copper-mining. The copper deposits of Mansfeld, which now constitute the most valuable reserve of non-ferrous metals in East Germany, are not associated with the Palaeozoic and intrusive rocks. They are a bedded deposit, occurring in the Zechstein series which lines the Triassic basins of the Mansfeld Bergland, and are mined near Mansfeld.

[1] This translation is from Heine's *Travel-Pictures*, trans. F. Storr, London, 1887, pp. 47, 69.

CLIMATE, VEGETATION AND SOILS

East Germany comes between Lübeck and the river Elbe to within 70 miles of the shores of the North Sea. Its southern boundary lies nearly 300 miles from the ocean. The climate of East Germany ranges in consequence from the mild and humid conditions of north-western Europe to the drier and more continental conditions of eastern Europe. Indeed, the state is almost bisected by the boundary between the mesothermal and microthermal climates of Köppen's classification.

Climate
There is in fact a gradual transition from the mild, damp winters and cool, cloudy summers of the north-west to the frosty winters and the bright, hot and stormy summers of the south-east. Any line drawn to divide this climatic spectrum must inevitably be arbitrary. The map of climatic regions (Fig. 1.11) shows it running from the lower Oder somewhat irregularly to the Elbe near the point where the latter is joined by the Havel, and thence south-westward to the zonal boundary.[1] The two contrasted climates which together span most of East Germany lie one on each side of this line. But the abrupt changes in the terrain themselves bring about accidents in the climate. The Harz Mountains and their hilly foreland form a distinct climatic region. They are far enough from the sea to show the continental features characteristic of eastern Europe, while their greater relief brings a larger and better distributed rainfall. Rising from this intermediate region are the mountainous massifs discussed earlier in this chapter: the Thüringerwald and Erzegebirge, in which the lower temperatures, greater precipitation and shorter growing season are even more pronounced. The Börde and Thuringian basins are further distinguished by their somewhat colder winters, their longer duration of sunshine and above all their lower rainfall.

Rainfall. In the first of these climatic regions the average annual rainfall generally ranges from about 550 to 650 millimetres (22 to 26 inches) dropping below this level only in eastern Mecklenburg and the Oder valley. Already a summer maximum has appeared, and the wettest months are July and August, but there is a secondary maximum in early winter, a reminder as it were that we are still within the

[1] *Klima-Atlas für das Gebiet der Deutschen Demokratischen Republik*, Berlin, 1953, Blatt 1/5.

climatic region of north-western Europe. Over much of the second region the average rainfall drops below 609 millimetres (24 inches), and, along the Elbe valley, below 550 millimetres (22 inches). At the same time the proportion of this rainfall which falls in the months of June to September increases. Near Lübeck it has been about 32 per cent; in Saxony it rises to 36; in Bohemia to 38, and in Silesia to 40 per cent.

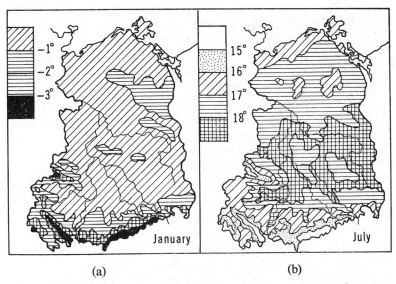

(a)   (b)

Fig. 7.2. Mean monthly temperatures in East Germany in (a) January, (b) July. After *Klima-Atlas für das Gebiet der DDR.*

The hills which border East Germany on the south-west and south are wetter at all seasons. The Harz Mountains and parts of the Harz Foreland have over 810 millimetres (32 inches); most of this hilly area has over 1,015 millimetres (40 inches) and the meteorological station on the summit of the Brocken records an average 1,190 millimetres (47 inches).

The Thuringian Basin, ringed except on the east by hills and mountains, is one of the driest areas in all Germany. In the central parts of the Basin the average annual rainfall sinks to well below 508 millimetres (20 inches); steppe vegetation begins to appear and a black-earth soil is formed over small areas.

Temperature. The changing pattern of temperatures conforms closely with that of rainfall. Increasing distance from the ocean brings with it colder winters and hotter summers. In no part of East Germany does the January average rise above freezing, though in the north-west it is less than half a degree Fahrenheit (about 0·3°C) below. At Berlin, the January temperature drops to −4°C (25°F); at Erfurt, to −7°C (19°F), and at Leipzig to −8°C (17·5°F). The increase in summer temperatures is no less marked. Hamburg, only 28 miles beyond the East German boundary, has a July average of 17·2°C (63°F). In Berlin, this rises to 18·9°C (66°F); in Stettin (Szczeczin) to 18·4°C (65°F); in Erfurt to 17·7°C (64°F), and in Leipzig, to 18·2°C (64·5°F). Temperatures are clearly reduced with altitude. The Brocken, the only summit for which there are reliable recordings for a long period of time, has a July average of 10·8°C (51·5°F) and a January average of −4°C (25°F). The depression of its summer temperature by 6·9°C (12·5°F) below that of Hanover, which is about 3,500 feet lower, is normal. The January temperature is lowered, however, by only 4·4°C (8°F). This reflects the temperature inversions which occur on still winter days, and give an unexpected warmth to some mountain sites.

Snow lies for prolonged periods in the east and south-east and on the mountains. Where the climate is mildest, in the extreme north-west, up to 40 days in the year may be marked by snow cover. This may increase to 70 as the Oder valley is approached, and in the hills of the south and south-east snow may in extreme cases lie for almost half the year. At the same time ice hinders navigation on the rivers. On the Elbe ice is normally thick enough to impede movement for over 20 days, and on the still waters of the canals for even longer.

In the coastal waters of the Baltic Sea, the low salinity and the movement of the waves hinders the formation of ice. In most years it does not form over the open sea, but lagoons are usually frozen over and the offshore islands linked with one another and to the mainland by ice. In more severe winters pack-ice may form along much of the Baltic coast, and an exceptional winter, such as that of 1946–47, may see the extension of pack-ice all the way to the Danish islands.

The average period that is free of damaging frost ranges from over 200 days in the year in the coastal region of the north-west and in certain sheltered valleys, such as that of the Elbe at Dresden, and of the Saale at Halle, down to 100 days and even less in the mountains. Freedom from frost is, however, so heavily dependent upon the accidents of local relief that generalisation is difficult. Over most of the lowland regions the frost-free period is of from 165 to 190 days. There is a tendency for field-work to begin somewhat earlier and for harvest to be a little earlier in the valley of the upper Elbe and of its tributaries, the Unstrut, Saale and Mulde, than in either the hilly regions or in the northern plain. Growth is, in fact, most forward in the Fläming and Lausitz regions, where the sandy soils make for earlier cultivation than the heavier soils of the valleys and of the northern plain. The rye harvest is a full month earlier in these regions than in the hilly regions and comes more than a fortnight before that in Mecklenburg.

River regimes. The rivers of East Germany all rise within its borders or at no great distance beyond them, and their seasonal regime thus reflects primarily local climatic conditions. The excess of summer rain over that for each of the other seasons is by no means strongly marked, and is not reflected in the flow of the rivers. Indeed, owing to the high rate of evaporation the discharge in some summer months may not be much more than half the average monthly flow. Autumn rains begin to increase the rate of flow somewhat, but a volume of discharge approaching the average is not often experienced before December. The next five months are generally characterised by a rate of flow above or even considerably above the average. By this time of the year the water table is high; the soil has absorbed as much moisture as it is capable of doing, and the evaporation rate is at its lowest. On the other hand, much of the precipitation is as snow which may lie and accumulate, especially in the hills for a period of months. In the west of East Germany, the winter maximum is felt early; toward the east the more intense and prolonged winter freeze tends to postpone the period of high water until the snows melt, commonly in March.

Obstruction by ice is normally most severe in January and February, and, but for the relatively high level and considerable speed of flow, might be more serious and prolonged than it is. Barge traffic is usually held up on the navigable rivers for a period of not more than two or three weeks. Equally serious is the low level of late summer which sometimes hinders, if it does not actually prevent, navigation on some sections of the Elbe and Oder.

Soils

Quality of the soils of East Germany is dependent primarily on the parent materials, and in these, as we have seen, there is great range and variety. The surface materials range from the heavy clays of Mecklenburg and the alluvium of the *Urstromtäler* to the sands of the Fläming

Heath and the loess of the Börde. In the Thuringian Basin, the Zechstein and Muschelkalk frequently support only a thin calcarous soil,
and the Buntsandstein gives rise to a sandy, porous soil. But over
much of the lower ground the soil-forming material is not the rock

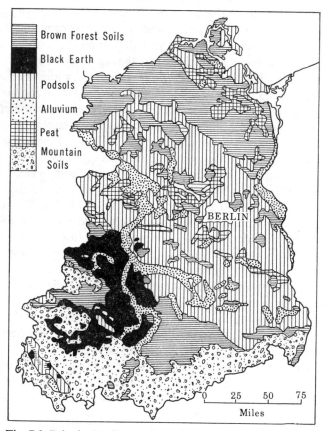

Fig. 7.3. Principal soil-types in East Germany. After Gerhard
Schmidt-Renner.

itself, but a superficial deposit: loess over much of the south; peat,
alluvium and outwash materials in the rest of the country.

Climate has operated within the limitations imposed by the nature of
the parent materials, to produce the present soils. The distribution of
soil-types conforms very approximately with the variations in climate.
In the moister, milder north-west soils are moderately podzolised,

though alluvium and the small areas in which peat has formed display no clear soil structure. Towards the south-east the degree of podzolisation becomes less, and the soils are more often classified as forest soils, weakly podzolised. In the driest areas of all, the central parts of the Thuringian Basin an opposite kind of soil structure begins to appear. A degraded chernozem has developed around the margin of the basin and passes into small areas of true Black Earth, or Steppe soil, toward its centre.

The mountain areas, the Harz and the Thüringerwald-Erzgebirge, like the alluvium along the valleys, usually display no clearly developed soil structure. Their soils are most often classified as lithosols. The soil is very thin, usually intermixed with stones, and is underlain at only a shallow depth by rock in various stages of decomposition. Rainfall is heavy and soil particles are readily removed. The formation of humus is on the one hand slowed by the low temperatures and on the other offset by the solution and removal of soil chemicals by the heavier rainfall. Where a soil structure is developed it is usually found to be strongly podzolised.

East Germany is but poorly endowed agriculturally. Almost a third of its area is on soils which are more or less sandy, and much of this area is strongly podzolised. The glacial clays of the north yield a heavy, poorly-drained soil, interspersed with patches of moraine and outwash, which resemble the heathlands of Brandenburg in their generally low level of fertility. The alluvium, which is extensive along all the 'great river valleys', is potentially fertile but often too damp for regular cultivation. One is left with the lithosols, much of which is incultivable, and the loess, on which most of the Black Earth and much of the better brown forest soils are developed. Soils of high agricultural value cover no more than about 7 per cent of the area of East Germany.

Agriculture has in the past been practised almost as widely as physical circumstances have permitted. It has been customary in East Germany to cultivate large areas with but a small return. The area has never been a great source of food, though its industrial development, until comparatively recent years, has been so slight that a small exportable surplus remains for shipment to other parts of Germany. Today, only 47 per cent of the total area is cropland, while a further 13 per cent is under meadow or pasture. No less than 27 per cent is forest, a higher percentage than that of any other East European member of the bloc.

Vegetation

In very few areas does the vegetation of East Germany even remotely resemble that which met the eyes of primitive man. It was always a forested country, though the forest was rarely as dense or as continuous as it is often reputed to have been. There were always openings in the forest cover. The damp valley floors must have had a broken cover of willow, aspen and poplar. The loess belt was but lightly wooded, and may even have had only a cover of light scrub, and over the Harz, Thüringerwald and Erzgebirge the short and twisted conifers probably abandoned the struggle against wind, weather and thin soil before reaching the rounded summits.

The forest varied from beechwoods on the clays of Mecklenburg, with pine woods on the light soil and alder over the damp valley floors, to open woodlands of birch, dry oak, and hornbeam on the sands of the Lüneburg and Fläming heaths, and from natural meadow (*Aue*) along the river valleys to marshland (*Flachmoore*) in the *Urstromtäler*. Much of the ground moraine between the Elbe and Spree must have been covered, though far from continuously, by mixed woodland, dominated by the pine and the oak. In the Saxon and Thuringian basins, with their drier climate and superior soil mixed woodland gave place to oak and hornbeam, with beech woods on the limestone and a steppe plant association (*Steppenheide*) in areas where soil moisture was particularly deficient.

Mixed woodland, mainly fir, spruce and beech, reappeared on the slopes of the mountains of the south-east and south, passing upward into forests of spruce, before these yielded to high peat moorland or to coarse grassland.

This landscape began to be modified by man long before the historical period began. The better soils were among the least thickly wooded, and were therefore the easiest to clear and settle. At the beginning of the historical period, cleared, settled and cultivated land was extensive only on areas of light soil. Most important of such areas by far was that rolling, loess-covered lowland, the Börde, which bordered the Harz and was continued into the central region of the Thuringian Basin. Smaller areas of open land extended eastward through Saxony into the Lausitz region. In Mecklenburg, with its variable soils and prevailing forest, clearings were numerous, but small and separated from one another by lake and marsh. In the Altmark and Brandenburg, however, man had made but little impression. Clearings were few and small and restricted to areas where the soil was light and dry. The broad damp valleys remained uninhabited, and were passable only with difficulty.

Forest clearance. Such must have been the vegetation cover of East Germany at the time when Tacitus described it. It is difficult to say to what extent human settlement was then fixed in permanent villages; probably a shifting cultivation was practised over much of the area, with clearings made and cultivated for a period of years before being abandoned. During the early Middle Ages population was increasing, necessitating not only the permanent occupation and cultivation of cleared lands, but also the extension of cultivation on to areas of heavier soil.

This was made possible by the introduction of a heavier plough than prehistoric man had been able to command. It was often supported by wheels, and was drawn by a team of oxen. It could plough a deep furrow even in the heavy clays and made possible a more continuous cultivation of any given area.

The heavy plough probably reached the Slav lands—and East Germany was at this date settled by Slavs—in the early Middle Ages.[1] Its revolutionary influence soon became apparent. Society became more stable. The greater wealth which accrued from agriculture not only supported the petty princes who arose in these lands but also yielded the surplus which went into the building of castles and cathedrals, parish churches and monasteries. It was no accident that Europe began to put on 'its white robe of churches' soon after the heavy plough had replaced the light, and permanent cultivation the earlier practice of assarting.

During the medieval period of population increase, which lasted approximately until the fourteenth century, settlements multiplied and woodland and waste receded. The loess areas were completely settled. The intermediate soils of Saxony and Mecklenburg were cleared. Only in the mountains and on the sands and in the marshes of Brandenburg was there little advance. The latter remained on the whole unsettled and unused until the valleys were drained and the rivers regulated in the eighteenth century and later. The sandy heaths proved yet more intractable. Cultivation has at times crept onto their infertile soils, but in the main the only change that much of their area has undergone has been the substitution of neat, orderly rows of conifers, with

[1] See Henryk Łowmiański, 'La Genèse des états slaves et ses bases sociales et économiques', *La Pologne au Xe Congrès International des Sciences Historiques*, Warsaw, 1955, pp. 29–53.

regular fire-breaks, for the irregular and uneven mixture of heath flora and pine trees.

The mountainous areas remain forested, as in fact they have always been, but this does not mean that they have not been cut over and the trees replaced. Quite apart from local needs for construction timber, the smelting of metals has at times severely strained the forest resources of these areas. The Erzgebirge was for a long period one of the major sources of the non-ferrous metals; the Harz and Thüringerwald were at one time dotted with small iron-furnaces and refineries, which used charcoal in extravagant quantities. The whole of these areas has at some time been cleared, but over much of it trees have been replanted. The tendency was, in general, to cut the hardwoods, which made the better charcoal, and to replace them with the quicker growing softwoods. Thus, over a period of centuries, there has been a gradual change in the character of the forests, with the elimination in some areas of the hardwood oak and beech.

The 27 per cent of the area of East Germany that is now forested, lies mainly on the light soils of the outwash regions and in the mountains of the south and south-west. It is now predominantly coniferous, as a result of past cutting and recent and current programmes of re-afforestation. The seemingly endless forests, that one drives through in Brandenburg owe nothing to the forests of the early Germans. The ordered rows of spruce and fir are the creation of the Prussian government.

POPULATION AND SETTLEMENT

East Germany today has the unique characteristic of a declining population. This, however, is a phenomenon of recent years, and is due to the circumstances which surround the Soviet occupation of the territory. During previous centuries the population of this area had been increasing at a rate above the normal for Central Europe. This had been a 'frontier' area, where land, admittedly of indifferent quality, was available, where labour was cheap, and the market for industrial products expanding.

Germanic settlement
During the earlier centuries of the Middle Ages this area had been thinly occupied by Slavic tribes. The eleventh century chronicler, Adam of Bremen, had described it as 'very rich in arms, men and

crops . . . shut in on all sides by fast barriers of wooded mountains and rivers', and extending 'from the Elbe river to the Scythian Sea'.[1] He then listed the Slavic peoples and their tribal capitals, in many of which we can recognise the modern place-names. Into this area Germanic settlers penetrated during the Middle Ages. This was an organised movement. Groups of settlers from West Germany, which was beginning to seem overpopulated, were led eastward by promoters, known as *locatores*, and were settled on lands taken from the Slavs. The latter were either exterminated in the fighting which accompanied the German colonisation or were reduced to some servile status and employed in the service of their new masters. The areas of German settlement were not without large, nucleated settlements that might be called cities, like Rethra, on an island in the Tollensee, which had 'nine gates and is surrounded on all sides by a deep lake. A wooden bridge . . . affords a means of crossing'.[2]

Such primitive towns, if such they may be called, were taken over by the Germans, who added to them. Some became the seats of bishops; in most the feeble commercial development of the Slavs was intensified. Beside these older settlements, the Germans established new cities of their own. Many of these grew up under the protection of a castle. In most, the streets were laid out on a gridiron pattern; a large and usually rectangular market-place was established, and walls and towers were built around the whole.

Important as long-distance trade may have been, most medieval cities were dependent upon their local regions for which they formed a market. The size, or at least the number of such cities, was directly related to local agricultural resources. The heaths of Brandenburg could support with their agricultural surplus only a few small market centres. The Börde and the Thuringian Basin, where the labour input was more generously rewarded, had a close network of cities. Some of these grew to be places of great size and importance, such as Magdeburg. In this way an irregular belt of cities came into existence. It wound its way around the Harz Foreland, where cities such as Halberstadt and Quedlinburg were founded; through the Börde of Saxony and into the fertile and highly organised Thuringian Basin. From here it extended eastward along the northern margin of the Erzgebirge and so into Silesia.

[1] Adam of Bremen, *The History of the Archbishops of Hamburg-Bremen*, ed. F. J. Tschan, Columbia University Press, 1959, p. 65.
[2] *Ibid.*, p. 66.

Not until the nineteenth century did this urban pattern undergo significant change. The modern industrial city is dependent more upon resources for its factories and upon ease of communications than upon agricultural land. The small coal-fields of the Erzgebirge and the larger resources in brown coal of Lausitz have led in the last century to an intensive industrial development. To some extent this has been in the older urban centres, such as Meissen and Pirna, but primarily it has been at sites which in the Middle Ages had been inconspicuous and un-important. These included Berlin itself, Karl-Marx-Stadt, the im-portant centres of the chemical industry, such as Merseburg, and the burgeoning industrial complexes of Schwarze Pumpe and Lauch-hammer.

The eastward expansion and settlement of the Germans submerged the native Slavs over much of the territory of East Germany. Only in the marshy and unattractive region of the Spreewald have the latter been able to survive. Four centuries ago a wide area extending south-ward from near Frankfurt-on-Oder to the Lausitz mountains was in-habited by Slav-speaking Sorbs. This has gradually contracted until today it consists of a number of small and separate areas, some of them consisting of nothing more than a village or two. The more northerly of these groups, located near Cottbus, speaks a Slav lan-guage related to Polish. The more southerly is found over a rather larger area between Spremberg and Bautzen, and speaks a dialect more closely related to Czech. All, however, are said now to be bi-lingual. Their numbers, never at any time very great, have been diminishing steadily. Over a century ago they are said to have num-bered over 141,000. In 1900, their numbers had fallen to 106,000; in 1934 to 57,000, and in 1946 the census allowed them only 32,000.[1]

The Sorb-settled region of Lausitz has in the past not proved par-ticularly attractive to German settlers. Now, however, its extensive brown coal resources are being exploited. Many Sorb farms have been overwhelmed by the spread of open-cast mining, and the Sorbs them-selves are fast disappearing beneath the wave of immigrant workers from other parts of East Germany.

Population

The population of the area of East Germany was never as great or as dense as that of the Federal Republic. For a period immediately after

[1] Roy Mellor, 'A Minority Problem in Germany', *Scott. geogr. Mag.* **79** (1963), 49–53.

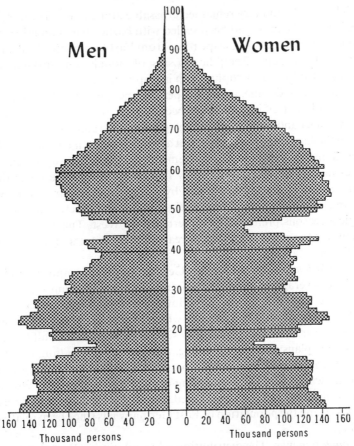

Fig. 7.4. The structure of the East German population. After *Statistisches Jahrbuch der DDR, 1964.*

the end of the Second World War, the immigration of refugees from Eastern Europe raised its total population to:

East Germany	17,700,000	(1947 est.)
Berlin (all Sectors)	3,197,000	,,
	20,897,000	,,

Some of these were in slow transit toward the West. The sharpening of the ideological conflict, the worsening political situation in East Germany, and prosperity and full employment in West Germany, led to an efflux of dangerous proportions.

The zonal boundary remained crossable at many points for a time, and, even when this had been sealed with barbed wire and minefields, there still remained the escape route from East Berlin into West and by air to the Federal Republic. Losses of population through these avenues led to a catastrophic drop in population.

This rate of decline, about 0·5 per cent per year, was the highest in the world. In itself it would have been serious, but it affected primarily the younger and more vigorous age-groups, who could not only escape from the East Zone more easily but also find employment and establish new homes in the West. The movement of population was not entirely one-way. There was a small flow from the West to the East: those whose families had been broken by the zonal boundary; some who desired to return to the home of their youth, and a few who for ideological reasons preferred East Germany to West. This return movement was too small to influence greatly either the total or the structure of the population.

Population structure. The East German population appears to have a higher average age than that of any other political unit in Europe. Its crude birth rate is one of the lowest, and its population pyramid today resembles that of a country which has lost the flower of its manhood in war. This is an unhealthy situation. It made the fulfilment of economic plans almost impossible, and created a situation which the East German government had to end at all cost. The closing of the Berlin escape route by the building of the 'Wall' in August 1961, was regrettable, but was not unexpected. It reduced the flow of refugees to a trickle, and the population of East Germany has since been relatively stable.

Population map. The distribution of population in East Germany is a function, on the one hand, of agricultural development and, on the other, of urbanisation and industrialisation. The northern half of the country offered little in either respect. The region lying to the north of the zone of *Urstromtäler* remains thinly peopled. In the area of the great river valleys themselves population is greater. Not only is Berlin itself the largest urban concentration in the area covered by this book; it is furthermore surrounded by lesser cities, which are manufacturing and commercial centres in their own right.

South of the greater Berlin area lies another region of sparse population which coincides roughly with the Altmark and the Fläming and Lausitz Heaths. In the extreme south-east of this region, however, in the areas of Cottbus, Spremberg and Senftenberg, population is greater and has in recent years been increasing. This growth has been dependent upon the working of the brown coal resources and their attendant industries. But south-west and south of the line of the Ohre, middle Elbe, and Schwarze Elster rivers there is an abrupt change in

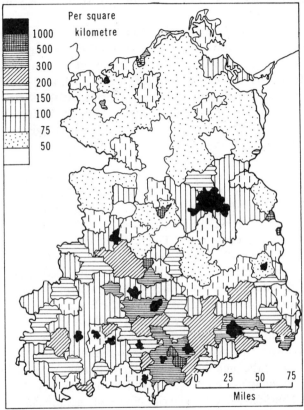

Fig. 7.5. Distribution of population in East Germany. After Gerhard Schimdt-Renner and *Statistisches Jahrbuch der DDR.*

population density. Agricultural resources are greater and farm population larger; the Börde, the central parts of the Thuringian Basin, and the Erzgebirge and Lausitz Forelands have a dense rural population. To this is added the larger population of the industrial towns of Thuringia and Saxony. Industry extends up valleys of the southern borderland of East Germany, where small manufacturing or mining cities are found amid the hills where agriculture is unimportant.

Rural settlement

It is difficult to estimate the fraction of the population which may be described as rural. In 1961, no less than 18 per cent lived in *Gemeinden* (parishes) of less than a thousand inhabitants, and 28 per cent in *Gemeinden* of less than two thousand. Most of these were village dwellers.

Rural settlement in East Germany is undergoing a more rapid change than it has seen for many centuries. The formation of collectives has removed from the individual groups of farm buildings many of the functions which they formerly performed, and the village is ceasing to be a closely spaced group of farms. At the same time the agricultural worker, in accordance with Marxist doctrine, is being assimilated to the status of the industrial. In some villages even blocks of apartments are being constructed to house the employees of the neighbouring collective.

Nevertheless, the traditional villages are still to be seen over most of East Germany. Their plan derives from the conditions of the original Germanic or even Slavic settlement, and has been little modified until recent years. Over most of East Germany (Fig. 5.4.) the street-village, or *Strassendorf*, predominates. The farms, each made up usually of a dwelling house, a cattle shed, a barn and sometimes other subordinate buildings, grouped around a small courtyard, are lined up side by side along both sides of a road. Other village patterns are present, and locally they predominate. In the areas of the Erzgebirge and the Vogtland that had remained densely forested until late in the Middle Ages, a closely analogous village type, the *Waldhufendorf*, made its appearance. It is also a street village, but its layout is less regular. The road is more winding; the buildings less regularly spaced. Along the western border, especially in the lower Elbe valley and in most of Saxony and much of Thuringia, is found the ring-fence village, *Runddorf* or *Rundling*. This consists essentially of a rounded open space, sometimes containing a church or other public building, and surrounded by the buildings of the village which form, as it were, a ring around it. This type of village has been sometimes attributed to a pastoral people, on account presumably of its kraal-like character. In his study of village settlement in Central Europe, Albrecht Meitzen ascribed it to the Slavs. Neither opinion bears serious scrutiny. Most are certainly of German origin, and their location in and to the east of the Elbe valley makes it probable that they were established by medieval German settlers in the east-Elbian Slav lands. It is at least possible that their

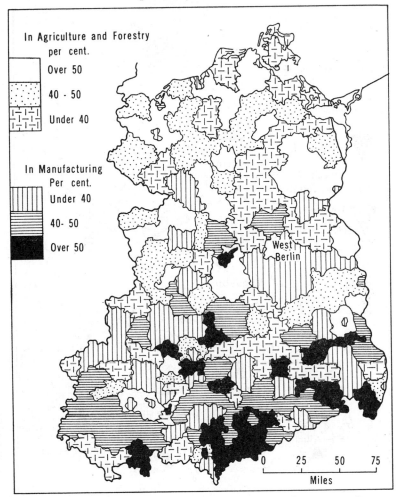

Fig. 7.6. Proportion of population in agriculture and forestry, and manufacturing. After *Statistisches Jahrbuch der DDR, 1966*.

ring-like pattern was to allow them to be defended against the frequently hostile people among whom they were established.

East Germany, lastly, is characterised by the irregularly nucleated village, the 'thrown together' village or *Haufendorf*. It predominates in all except the north-west and parts of the south, and between the Harz Mountains and the Thüringerwald it intrudes from the Hills of Hesse into the Thuringian Basin.

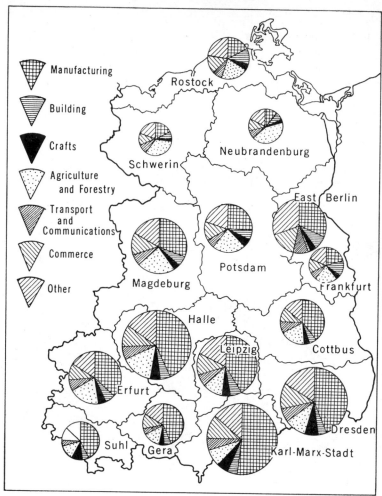

Fig. 7.7. Distribution of working population, by employment classification. After *Statistisches Jahrbuch der DDR, 1964*.

House types. Farmhouses also show in plan and architectural style regional characteristics that are as distinctive as those of the villages themselves. Architectural style, however, for all its idiosyncracy and ornament, is more closely related to climate and building materials than the village appears to be to its physical environment.

Across the north, from Lower Saxony into Pomerania, is found the *Saxon house*. It is a large building, commonly built of *Fachwerk*, a wooden frame filled in with wickerwork and plaster. The roof is steeply pitched and covers at one end the living quarters of the farm family and at the other, the stables, the storage for farm implements and also for fodder and grain. Such a style reflects not only the absence of building stone but also the snowy winter when outdoor activities are restricted. To the south approximately of the Elbe, the *Middle German* farmhouse begins to appear. It is a courtyard house; living quarters are separated from barn and stable, and masonry is far more prominent in the construction, though wood and plaster may continue to predominate in the construction of the upper storeys. The whole, furthermore, is often surrounded by a masonry wall and entered through an archway high enough for farm wagons to pass.

Urban settlement
East Germany is a highly urbanised country. If West Berlin is excluded, it has 11 cities with over 100,000 inhabitants and a total population of 3,696,000, and a further 13 with over 50,000. In all, no less than 51 per cent of the population lives in cities of over 10,000. The map (Fig. 7.8) on page 238 shows the distribution of the latter. Their concentration in the south-western third of the country is overwhelming. Many of these, such as Merseburg,[1] Bitterfeld and Karl-Marx-Stadt are the product of industrial development in the nineteenth and early twentieth centuries. Others, like Lauchhammer and Hoyerswerda, result from the planned industrial growth of the last two decades. The following pages make no attempt to present an urban geography of East Germany; only to describe the salient features of the location and function of the larger and more important of the cities.

   Berlin. Foremost of these is Berlin itself, which grew before its destruction and division to be a city of 4·35 millions (1939). Yet it is very much a *parvenu* among German cities, and its growth has largely been since 1871, when it became the capital of the German Empire. Berlin lies in the Spree valley, which here follows a south-east to north-west direction along one of the flat and marshy valleys left by the glacial rivers. It grew up during the Middle Ages, partly on an island, known as Kölln, in the Spree; partly on the opposite north bank of the river. This small area of considerably less than a square mile was the city of Berlin until the seventeenth century. Then it began to spread out over the low sandy platforms, separated by the

---

[1] The nucleus of Merseburg was, however, an early medieval monastic settlement.

9

East Germany

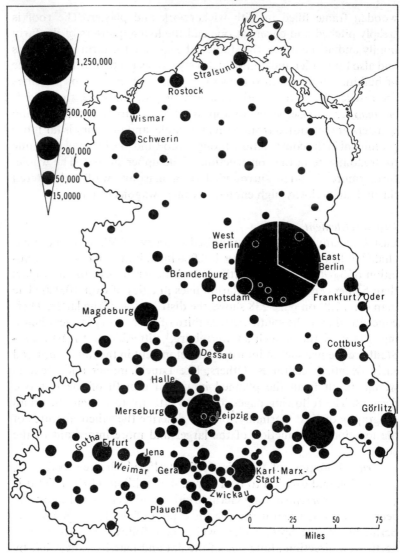

Fig. 7.8. Distribution of cities, by size; only cities of over 50,000 are named.
Based on *Statistisches Jahrbuch der DDR, 1966.*

interlacing channels of the *Urstromtäler*. By the mid-eighteenth the
Customs Wall (*Zollmauer*) of the city enclosed over 5 square miles.
This is approximately the area which subsequently developed into the
city's business and administrative core.

The next limit set to the spread of the city was the Ringbahn, the elliptical railway which encircled the whole city at an average distance of 3 to 4 miles from the centre, and linked the main railway terminals. In the latter half of the nineteenth century, Berlin began to spread beyond the *Ringbahn*. Villages became dormitories for the city, and then grew into suburbs. Industries which had grown up within the *Ringbahn* moved to the more spacious area without. The most intensively industrialised areas came to lie to the north-west in Siemensstadt and Spandau, where factories gathered along the Spree near its junction with the Havel, and up the Spree valley to the south-east of the city, where Köpenick and Neukölln grew up as industrial suburbs of the city. Between lay an untidy urban sprawl, much of it made up of tall dwellings with stuccoed fronts of the late nineteenth and early twentieth centuries, which reached out with long distended fingers into the pine-woods of Brandenburg.

Almost a hundred *Gemeinden* (parishes or villages) thus came within the reach of the city. In 1921 administrative organisation at last caught up with reality. A city of Greater Berlin was formed, with boundaries which have remained unchanged until today. It covered an area of 289 square miles and was itself divided into districts or 'boroughs'. It was on the basis of the latter that the current sector division of the city was made.

Before the Second World War, the city bore unmistakably the stamp of its period of growth—that of the German Empire. The somewhat heavy, baroque-style architecture of the *Altstadt*; the tall house fronts of the residential areas which enclosed it; the small shops of the suburban market centres; the acres of market-garden and allotment. The war, bombing and partition have ended this. The *Altstadt* suffered severely; the Wilhelmsstrasse no longer focuses the government of a populous and powerful country, and, above all, the city is now divided into two functionally separate entities.

The legal unity of Berlin is now only a fiction. The *Altstadt*, with its shops, museums, and places of entertainment, even when rebuilt, still lie beyond the reach of two-thirds of the population of Berlin. East Berlin is now the capital of East Germany, but the immense governmental apparatus of the former *Reich* is no longer necessary, and part of it still lies in ruins. Around the periphery, however, factories have been rebuilt, and East Berlin is today the largest single industrial centre in the country. The only obstacle to the supply of fuel, power and materials is distance. No political barriers intervene. The most important industries today are much the same as those which dominated before the Second World War: electrical and mechanical engineering, clothing and consumer goods industries and food processing. Despite the shabby appearance which the *Altstadt* presents to the visitor today, in contrast with the brittle brilliance of West Berlin, economic growth has been faster—perhaps as much as twice as fast—in East Berlin than in West.

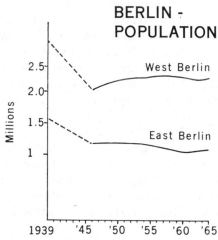

Fig. 7.9. Population of West and East Berlin, 1939–65. Based on *Wirtschafts-zahlen aus der SBZ*, Bundesministerium für Gesamtdeutsche Fragen, Berlin, 1964, and *Demographic Yearbooks*, UN.

Northern cities. The growth of Berlin and, with it, of communications with all parts of Germany brought with it the development of many small towns of the Berlin region. Foremost among these was Potsdam, a city of about 115,000, lying on the Havel, which here widens into the Templiner See. The city is of medieval origin, but was unimportant until the Electors of Brandenburg established their residence here in the seventeenth century. The city was greatly enlarged by Frederick the Great, who left to it a legacy of baroque architecture. The seat of government moved, with the creation of the German Empire in 1871, to Berlin, but Potsdam has remained not only a residential city but also a centre of light and consumer goods industries.

North of Berlin all cities are small, and their primary function is that of market centres for their surrounding agricultural regions. The only exceptions are the port cities of Wismar, Rostock and Stralsund. *Rostock*, with a population of about 170,000, is the largest. It is a Hanseatic city, regularly laid out, dominated by its brick gothic churches, and is typical of those North German cities, though severely damaged during the Second World War. It lies on the Warnow, 10 miles from its outport on the coast, Warnemünde. Its fortunes had declined in modern times with the competition of Hamburg, but it is now being developed as the chief port of East Germany.

Across the centre of the state lies a belt of towns, all associated in some way with the east–west communications by water, road and rail. In addition to Berlin and the ring of cities which encloses it, are Brandenburg, Frankfurt and Magdeburg. *Brandenburg*, with a population of about 89,000, lies on the Havel, which provided protection to the medieval city and divided it into a number of islands. It was capital of the march-state of Brandenburg, and contains more memorials of its earlier history than most other cities of this region. It is now an industrial centre, with steel-making, mechanical engineering and light industries.

Frankfurt-an-der-Oder lies at an ancient crossing of the Oder river, and to its early routeways it has now added the convenience of the Oder-Spree canal, which joins the river a few miles above the city. Like Rostock, it was a Hanseatic city, and its early fortunes were based on riverborne commerce with areas lying to the south-east. Its buildings spread over a steep valley terrace, dominated by the towers of its medieval brick church. It is now a city of about 58,000, with metal, chemical and other industries, but the Oder here forms the boundary with Poland, and now cuts the city off from an important part of its former hinterland.

Magdeburg, with 268,000 citizens, is one of the oldest and largest cities in East Germany. A commercial settlement existed here in the ninth century. It was made the seat of an archbishop whose diocese reached far to the east, and became a centre not only for the conversion but also for the conquest and settlement of Slav lands. In this the location of the city at a bend of the Elbe helped by providing, with its tributaries, easy routes to the east. In modern times canals have reinforced the value of its position, and it is now a leading inland port of East Germany (page 285). The city was built on the steep west bank of the Elbe. Although it has suffered severely in wars from the seventeenth century to the twentieth, some of its ancient buildings have survived, and it is dominated by the tall medieval towers of its cathedral and churches. It has become one of the principal centres in East Germany of the heavy engineering and chemical industries. The surrounding country, the Börde, is one of the most fertile and productive in Europe, thus contributing greatly to the city's wealth and prosperity. Food processing and in particular, sugar-refining, are important.

Southern cities. In the southern half of East Germany the river Elbe constitutes a boundary between a highly urbanised south-western region and a south-eastern in which cities are few and many of those which do occur are of recent origin. The south-western region had a close urban net at the end of the Middle Ages. To this has been added the considerable number of cities which owe their origin to modern industrial development. The Börde of *Bz.* Magdeburg and Halle, the Thuringian Basin and the belt of open country which followed the northern margin of the Erzgebirge were all characterised by their cities. These were small and walled; many are quaint and picturesque and a few are extraordinarily beautiful. Such are Quedlinburg and Halberstadt, on the margin of the Harz, and Meissen and Pirna on the Elbe. Some have grown into modern industrial cities, like Erfurt and Dresden, without losing all of their early charm. In others, such as Halle, Leipzig and Karl-Marx-Stadt, the ancient has been smothered beneath the nineteenth-century growth.

The ancient routeway across the southern part of East Germany ran from Eisenach in the west, through Gotha, Erfurt and Naumburg to Leipzig. Here it was joined by the route which had come by way of Halle from the Harz foreland. To the east it continued, along the fairly narrow belt of open country which separated the hills of the Erzgebirge from the heaths of Lausitz. Another routeway entered from Bavaria; crossed the Frankenwald and the Vogtland, and followed the foothills through Zwickau and Dresden. These routeways strongly influenced the growth of the cities which lay on or near them. They helped to determine which were to become commercial cities of wide importance and which were to remain market centres for their local areas.

A second, selective influence has been the development of mining and industry. Johanngeorgenstadt, for example, was developed in the seventeenth century as a mining town in the western Erzgebirge. Industrial cities, however, sprang up in the greatest number in the nineteenth century, when the small coal-fields of Saxony began to be exploited, and villages along the mountain valleys turned into mill-towns.

The most recent urban development is inseparable from the working of brown coal. In the nineteenth century this mining was not intensive enough to give rise to large settlements, but in the twentieth, the coke furnaces and chemical industries based upon it have led to the rapid expansion of a few old cities, such as Merseburg and Cottbus, and to the foundation of new ones, such as Hoyerswerda and Leuna.

Leipzig-Halle-Dresden. The largest city in the southern half of East Germany is *Leipzig*, with about 588,000 inhabitants. Many factors have conspired to favour its growth. The small medieval city which formed its nucleus lay on a terrace to the east of the damp valley of the Elster. It did not have the advantage of river navigation, and has never become an inland port. But around it stretched the rolling, loess-covered Börde, which not only supplied food for the city, but facilitated movement across its dry surface. To this Leipzig added its focal position in the route system of Central Europe. Its fairs began to be held during the later Middle Ages, and, though their importance declined in modern times, they have been revived in recent years as an international exhibition of industrial products.

Leipzig, lastly, found itself on the edge of the Elbe–Saale brown coal field, from which it has derived power for its factories and raw materials for its chemical industries. The city has spread to the north, east, and south, and beyond the wide belt of water-meadows which border the Elster, to the west. It is the most important route centre after Berlin, and more goods pass through its freight yards than through those of any other city. And yet, despite its growth, it has retained many of the features of its medieval core: the narrow streets, the *Rathaus*, and its medieval churches, in one of which, the *Thomaskirche*, J. S. Bach was organist.

Only 20 miles to the north-west lies *Halle*, a more specialised city of only half Leipzig's size. Its site and situation are similar to those of Leipzig. It lies on the terraces which here come close to the east bank of the Saale. It lay on both the medieval routeway which followed the loess-belt eastwards, and on the brown coal field, and to these assets added the possession of salt-springs from which it derived both its early prosperity and its name. Halle is now a city of about 279,000. From its medieval nucleus it has grown mainly toward the north and south, and has still not spread across the water-meadows of the Saale. Its chief industries include the processing of the agricultural products of its local region, paper-making, printing, textile manufacture and mechanical engineering.

The urban geography of Saxony is dominated by a line of towns of considerable size and importance: Plauen, Zwickau, Karl-Marx-Stadt, Freiberg and Dresden. Each was of medieval origin, though their present size bears no relationship to their medieval significance. The biggest then was Freiberg, which is today the least. *Dresden,* with a population of 499,000, is now the largest. The small, walled town grew up on a small hillock that rose above a bend of the Elbe, approximately where the river escapes from the hills. From the first it was a crossing point of the river route and of the west-to-east routeway along the loess belt. The city was of no great importance until in the sixteenth century it became the capital of the Electorate of Saxony. In the late seventeenth and eighteenth the Electors rebuilt Dresden as a baroque city, which, despite its disastrous bombing, it has in part remained. Dresden, backed by the hills, with its wide river and impressive eighteenth-century buildings, has long been one of the most beautiful cities of Germany. It is also a city of art, with museums and art galleries. It has given its name to the foremost porcelain made in Germany, though the manufacture has for two and a half centuries been in nearby Meissen. Dresden has sought to preserve its unique character by restricting the foundation and expansion of factories. Most of its industries remained small-scale and were interspersed with the residential areas of the city. A consequence has been the great variety of industrial activity in Dresden. It is, however, predominantly a manufacturer of light goods, especially precision machinery, printing, and leather goods. Dresden serves also as a focal point for a number of small industrial towns spread along the Elbe valley from Pirna in the south-east to Riesa in the north-west.

Freiberg, to the south-west of Dresden, has still its non-ferrous smelting industries, though the ores which once gave the city its importance are almost exhausted, and mining is now of negligible importance.

Karl-Marx-Stadt–Zwickau–Plauen. Karl-Marx-Stadt, in which we recognise the medieval town of Chemnitz, is now the fourth largest in East Germany, with about 289,000 inhabitants. It lies well within the hills of the Erzgebirge Foreland, in the valley of the Chemnitz, where the latter, joined by several small streams, suddenly widens. The manufacture of textiles became important in the fourteenth century, and has since dominated the city's activities. In the early nineteenth the domestic industry gradually gave place to spinning and weaving sheds. At first these clustered round the old city; then spread up the valleys of the small streams that are tributary to the Chemnitz. Here water-power was available, and at no great distance (page 260) was bituminous coal, which was to replace the power of the streams. Early in the nineteenth century the manufacture of textile machinery was introduced. Even today in the older mills of Łódź one meets with looms with 'Chemnitz' moulded into their cast-iron frames. From the manufacture of textile machinery the workshops of Chemnitz went on to the manufacture of other types of machinery, including steam-locomotives and machine tools. Today industrial production in Karl-Marx-Stadt is shared between textiles—woollen, cotton, linen and now to an increasing extent synthetic—and light engineering, with chemicals—primarily fibres and dyestuffs—a poor third.

Zwickau. Twenty miles to the south-west of Karl-Marx-Stadt, Zwickau is a smaller city of 129,000, but, like its neighbour, developed the textile industry at an early date, and is now the second largest centre of the spinning and weaving industries in East Germany. The Zwickau coal-field is the chief source of East Germany's small output of bituminous coal. Zwickau is the commercial focus of a large number of small mill-towns which line the valleys of the Zwickauer Mulde and its tributaries.

Plauen is the last of the industrial cities of the Erzgebirge. It lies on the Weisse Elster, in the midst of the region of small, scattered industries, known as the Vogtland. Textile manufacture is the chief pre-occupation of its 79,000 inhabitants, and Plauen is an important centre of the knitwear, hosiery and clothing industries. It is also important for the manufacture of machinery and machine-tools. The small towns of the Vogtland are engaged mainly in textile industries and in manufactures related to textiles. Carpet manufacture, for example, is the chief industry of the small town of Oelspitz. Furniture and other wood products are also important branches of industry in the Vogtland.

Thuringian towns. The south-western *Bezirke* of Gera, Erfurt and Suhl are less urbanised, and indeed less industrialised than those which lie along the Elbe and in the Erzgebirge. A line of medium-sized towns extends westward along the southern margin of the Thuringian Basin, including Gera, Jena, Weimar, Erfurt, Gotha and Eisenach. Most other cities, as is apparent from Fig. 7.6, are small, and their industrial functions are very restricted. The city of *Gera* itself marks in reality the western extremity of the Erzgebirge textile region but has

9*

also important engineering industries. It is a city of 104,000 inhabitants, situated in the valley of the Weisse Elster, 28 miles to the north of Plauen and close to the margin of the hills. Placed as it is centrally within the curving line of the Thüringerwald–Frankenwald–Erzgebirge, it has become one of the chief route centres of the whole region, commanding the railways which radiate across the mountains to Bavaria and Bohemia.

Jena, 22 miles to the west on the Saale river, is, with 83,000 inhabitants, a smaller and more specialised town than Gera. Indeed, its industrial structure is dominated by the *Zeisswerke*, and Jena has a world-wide reputation for the quality of its optical and precision instruments.

Next towards the west is Weimar, former seat of the Dukes of Saxony, home of Goethe and Schiller and for a brief period after the First World War, the seat of the German government. It had been primarily a residential and handicraft city; recently engineering industries have been established, notably the manufacture of agricultural machinery.

Next in this line of cities is *Erfurt*, which with its 190,000 inhabitants is the largest in this south-western region of the Republic. It was a small, walled city, almost surrounded by the Wilde Gera, and is still dominated by its medieval churches, with their associations with Luther, and by its ancient fortresses on the hills to the west of the old city. The wealth which accrued from trade and from its agricultural region gave it at an early date an importance which it has since retained. In addition to leather, food-processing and woodworking industries, which may be said to derive from its agricultural surroundings, Erfurt now has important electro-technical and instrument manufactures.

Gotha and *Eisenach* are smaller and more specialised, and the chief industries of each are associated primarily with the transport industries. Gotha is a centre of the manufacture of railway equipment and rolling stock, and Eisenach of automobiles. The 'Wartburg' car is made in this small city overlooked from the summit of the crags which form the end of the Thüringerwald, by the castle of the Wartburg.

AGRICULTURE

The discussion earlier in this chapter of the land forms, climate and soil of East Germany has demonstrated that agricultural resources are somewhat slender over most of the country and that the area of first-class farmland is relatively small. This is reflected in the land use of East Germany. Only about two-thirds of the total area is used agriculturally and over a quarter is under forest.

Land use

Table 25 shows the chief categories of land use in 1965.

Table 25. Land use in East Germany in 1965

	Area (hectares)	Percentage
Used agriculturally	6,429	59·6
Forest	2,942	27·3
Waste, built-up, etc.	1,418	13·1
	10,789	100·0

Source: *FAO Production Yearbook, 1966.*

Much of the land which is used agriculturally is under crops, with meadow and pasture coming a poor second. The chief categories of agricultural land are shown in Table 26.

Table 26. Categories of agricultural land, 1966

	Area (hectares)	Percentage
Cropland	4,703,724	73·9
Fallow	13,035	—
Gardens	129,016	2·0
Orchards	75,099	1·2
Vineyards	315	—
Meadow	868,003	13·6
Pasture	570,949	8·9
Other	5,773	—
Total	6,365,915	

Source: *Statistisches Jahrbuch der DDR, 1967.*

There are conspicuous variations both in the proportion borne by agricultural land to the total and also in the relationship between cropland and grazing. The importance of cropland is greatest on the light, loess soils which make up much of the *Bezirke* of Magdeburg, Halle, Leipzig and Erfurt, and least in the sandy regions of Potsdam and Cottbus and the hills of Suhl and Gera.

Collectivisation

East Germany had long been known for its great estates and farms that were far above the average size for Central Europe. In this Mecklenburg was outstanding, though in Brandenburg and the whole Oder valley small peasant holdings were rare.[1] Little progress was made after the First World War in breaking up the larger holdings and over much of East Germany large farms and estates, worked with hired labour, continued to predominate until the end of the Second World War.

The war had been over for only a few months when the first steps were taken to break up holdings which were judged to be excessive and to distribute them to poor and landless peasants. All estates of more than 100 hectares (247 acres) were expropriated, and a Land Fund of 3·22 million hectares (7·95 million acres)—nearly a third of the total area of East Germany—was established. Of this 2,165,602 hectares (about 5,000,000 acres)—a third of the total cropland—was divided among farmers whose holdings were uneconomically small or allocated to agricultural workers who had possessed none. The size of the newly established farms was small; the average seems to have been less than 10 hectares (24·7 acres), and in the village of Stresow, in Mecklenburg, the size ranged from 5 to 7 hectares (12 to 17 acres) (Fig. 7.10).[2] In 1950, when some collectivisation had already begun, 888,245 farm units possessed 6,528,371 hectares (15,000,000 acres) of cropland, an average of 7·3 hectares (18·3 acres) per farm. The new farms were in most instances born divided. Each consisted usually of two or more strips in the open-fields, or *Gewanne*, and a fragment of enclosed meadow. Again in the twentieth century one sees efficiency being sacrificed on the altar of equality: but not for long.

The land reform eliminated the richer landowners and in some measure won over the peasants to the support of the regime. In 1952

[1] Wilhelm Abel, *Geschichte der deutschen Landwirtshaft vom frühen Mittelalter bis zum 19. Jahrhundert*, Stuttgart, 1962, pp. 187–93.

[2] Bruno Benthien, 'Karten zur Entwicklungsgeschichte des Vollgenossenschaftlichen Dorfes Stresow (Kreis Greifswald)', *Geogr. Ber.* 8 (1963), 1–9.

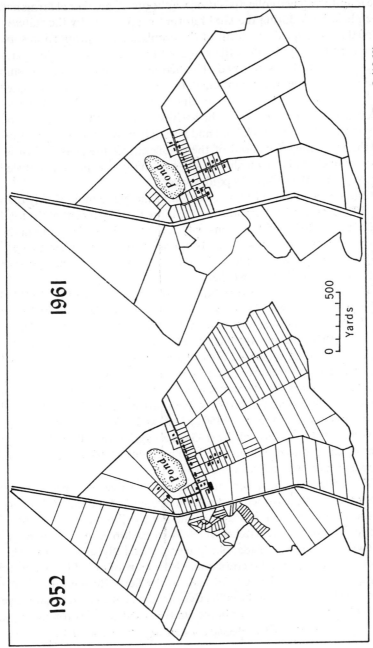

Fig. 7.10. The village of Stresow, before and after collectivisation. After B. Beuthien, in *Geogr. Ber.*, **8** (1963).

the long-threatened collectivisation was begun. A number of farms had been held back during the land reform for operation by the state. In 1950 these occupied 5 per cent of the cropland. This proportion soon increased sharply. In 1952 the so-called Land Production Co-operatives[1] began to be established. The fiction of voluntary membership and profit-sharing was maintained, though every means was adopted to insure that in each community all farmers were members of the co-operative. The co-operatives themselves varied in their organisation and in the extent to which land and initiative were left to the peasants. In the most fully socialised of the co-operatives the peasant lost all control over the land which was still nominally his, and was reduced once again to the status of a paid worker.

State-owned farms (*Volkseigene Güter*) increased more slowly than the LPGs, and in 1961 embraced little more than 7 per cent of the total socialised sector. In these farms, which are very much larger than the co-operatives, the land is owned by the state; the peasant has not even a theoretical interest in the soil, and is a wage earner, analogous in every way to the factory worker.

The size of the collective farms has increased steadily. In 1950 their average size was 76 hectares (187 acres); by 1955, this had risen to 180 hectares (444 acres), and by 1960 to 200 hectares (494 acres). By now (1966) the average has risen to over 380 hectares (920 acres). At the same time socialised farms have absorbed more and more of the total agricultural area. After a rapid rate of growth in the early 1950s, the increase in the number and size of collectives was halted in the middle fifties, and many were even broken up and re-distributed to the peasants. In the late 1950s a renewed effort was made by the government to socialise all East German agriculture. By 1961, 88 per cent of the economically usable land and almost 93 per cent of all cropland had been collectivised.

The collectives, whether euphemistically called co-operatives or recognised as state-owned farms, have wrought a fundamental change in the East German landscape. Gone are the long, narrow strips of cropland and the tiny patches of enclosed meadow. In their place are a few large, compact fields. No longer, in the fully socialised village, does the peasant milk his cows under his own roof or in his own farmyard, and drive his draught animals to the fields through the village streets. The activities of the collectives are concentrated in a new range of buildings, which may embrace stalls for cattle, sties for the pigs,

[1] *Landwirtschaftlicheproduktionsgenossenschaften*, or LPGs.

barns for fodder and grain, and a machine and tractor station. Sometimes the old home farm of an estate could be adapted to these purposes; more often a new building has been erected.[1]

Crop yields have not been commensurate with the large investment which collectivisation has made necessary. There has been a net decline in the area under grain crops, which the slight overall improvement in yields has been too small to offset. On the other hand the area under fodder crops has increased somewhat, and that under industrial crops, such as sugar beet and oil seeds, to a rather larger degree. Yields per hectare have varied very greatly both from year to year and from one region of East Germany to another. In general the yield of grain crops has been somewhat above the average in the same area for the years 1934–38; that of potatoes and sugar beet generally somewhat below.

The soil had been neglected during the Second World War, and the supply of fertiliser has not been sufficient for the loss sustained to be made good. The country's important basic chemical industries are not able to supply in quantity all the varieties of fertiliser needed. The use of fertiliser is still inadequate, and is very far below the level usual in West Germany. The soil is particularly deficient in phosphates for which East Germany is dependent primarily upon imports.

The rapidly increasing use of machines seems to have contributed little to output, though it has permitted agriculture to be continued with a diminishing labour force. The number employed in agriculture and forestry has declined from 1,666,998 in 1952 to 1,222,233 in 1966.[2] The increase in the number of farm machines has been more spectacular. That of tractors rose from about 14,500 in 1950 to 132,761 in 1966, and the increase in other types of machine has been in proportion.

It is evident that East German agriculture has failed to respond either to the territorial reorganisation of farms or to the large investment that has been made in it. The reason probably lies in the lack of motivation of the farm-worker; in the flight of the younger and more energetic to the cities or to the West, and the predominantly untrained and heavily female labour force that is at present available. External factors, notably the weather and the failure of the chemical industries to provide adequate supplies of certain fertilisers, have no doubt

[1] K. H. Schröder, 'Der Wandel der Agrarlandschaft in ostelbischen Tiefland seit 1945', *Geogr. Zeitschr.*, **52** (1964), 289–316.
[2] *Statistisches Jahrbuch der DDR*, 1967.

contributed greatly to the poor performance of East German agriculture.

Crops. The dominant crops in eastern Germany have traditionally been rye and potatoes, and these have for centuries provided a large part of the diet of a majority of the population. There has been little change. Rye is still the most cultivated crop, and is sown on almost 20 per cent of all cropland, and about 37 per cent of the land given over to grain crops. Next in importance among the cereals comes barley, used primarily for brewing but also as a fodder, closely followed by wheat and oats. Buckwheat and mixed grains are grown on a small area, but maize is of minor importance. The grain crops are fairly evenly divided between autumn- and spring-sown, with the former predominating over East Germany as a whole, and the latter in the north of the country and in the hills.

The area under grain crops has diminished steadily during the past 15 years. Both the area under potatoes and the total crop have been maintained at approximately their prewar level. Potatoes are now grown on about 15 per cent of the area, and in terms of the quantity of food produced are by far the most important crop.

The so-called industrial crops have increased in importance, and have taken over much of the area no longer planted with cereals. Most important of these are rapeseed and other oleaginous plants, and sugar beet. The latter, in particular, has shown a very considerable expansion over the prewar level in the same area. The growing of fodder crops has also expanded, although cereals, such as oats, which were usually fed to the animals, are of diminished importance. The smaller need for oats reflects the displacement of horses by tractors and lorries in East German agriculture. The increase in the area under clover and other crops, often used for silage, results from the increasing importance of animal husbandry.

A feature of East German agriculture has been the sharp increase in the number of pigs and cattle. In part this has been due to the fact that even in fully collectivised villages, the peasants have been able to retain a cow and a few pigs; almost half the dairy cattle are privately owned. The volume of milk and meat production has been increasing steadily through the fifties, but has not always been reflected, however, in the standard of living of the predominantly urban population.[1]

In a country with such widely differing soil types as those of East

[1] Jacques M. May, *The Ecology of Malnutrition in Five Countries of Eastern and Central Europe*, New York, 1963, pp. 27–35.

Germany one would expect considerable local variation in crop patterns. Rye, the dominant crop, is grown almost everywhere and on almost every type of soil. On the best soils, such as the 'black earth' of the Halle and Magdeburg *Bezirke*, it yields place to the more demanding wheat, but on the sands of Potsdam and Frankfurt and the clays of Neubrandenburg and Schwerin it has no rival amongst the grains. Wheat is essentially the crop of the good soils of the Thuringian Basin and Saxony, and covers only a relatively small area in other *Bezirke*. Oats are a crop of the poorest soil, where, however, they are of diminishing importance owing to the replacement of horses with machines. Barley is widely grown as a winter crop for cattle feed, but for malting purposes is planted as a spring crop only on relatively good, dry soil. This means, in fact, that a great deal of the crop grows in the Börde region and in Thuringia.

Among the root crops the potato is outstanding. Like rye, it is grown everywhere, and forms an essential part of the human diet. It is also used in starch manufacture, for distillation, and is fed to the farm animals. Heaviest yields are obtained from the good loess soils, but it is also grown on the poorest, where it may cover almost as large an area as rye. Sugar-beet, second in importance to potatoes, has been growing in importance in recent years, and is the only product of East German agriculture that contributes significantly to the export trade. In 1963 it was grown on more than 15 per cent of the cropland, and was most intensively grown on the best soils of Magdeburg and Halle, where yields are heaviest. Very recently sugar-beet cultivation has been expanded in the northern *Bezirke* of Rostock and Neubrandenburg, where lack of processing factories has necessitated the shipment of beet to the Magdeburg region.

Industrial crops, especially those which produce an oil-seed, such as rape, flax and sunflower, are widely cultivated, but account for no more than about 3 per cent of the cultivated area. Flax is grown in the moist soils of the north and the even wetter hills of the south and south-west. Tobacco is grown in the Oder valley in the north-east, and in Saxony, and hops in Thuringia and Saxony, in the same general area as most of the malting barley.

The cultivation of garden vegetables is carried on in the close vicinity of every city, and there are in addition a number of areas where the production of vegetables for distant markets and also of seed is a specialised branch of agriculture. Among these are the Erfurt region of Thuringia and the Spreewald. The cultivation of vegetables is mainly organised in socialised *Produktionsgenossenschaften,* which are particularly numerous in the *Bezirke* of Potsdam, Dresden and Erfurt.

Fruit, like vegetables, is grown in most parts of East Germany, but its heaviest concentration is close to the larger cities which constitute the most important market. The grape vine is cultivated in Saxony, especially on south-facing valley slopes of the Saale and Unstrut and in the Elbe valley, near Dresden. But this is at the climatic margin for the grape vine, and wine-making is of negligible importance in East Germany.

Animal husbandry. Animal farming is of great and increasing importance. Almost 60 per cent of the cultivated area is said to be given over to pasture and fodder crops. This includes over 10 per cent of the total area of farmland which is under permanent or rotation meadow, much of it over the damp floors of the former river valleys. Maize has recently attracted much attention as a fodder crop. It does not ripen well in the German climate, but can be used for green silage, and has the further advantages of cropping heavily and making small demands on labour. But hay, roots, cereals and the waste from the sugar beet and dairy industries all contribute to feeding the farm animals.

The intensity of animal husbandry is much greater than before the Second World War. Only draught animals have diminished in importance. Cattle are widely maintained, with a tendency for dairy cattle to be relatively more important in the vicinity of the larger towns. Pig rearing is similarly distributed, with concentrations near the cities and in the richer agricultural areas, in each of which the greater volume of food waste is used as feed. The number of sheep has increased less than that of most other animals. They are most numerous in the richer farmlands of the Magdeburg, Halle and Erfurt *Bezirke.* The East German economy needs all the wool that can be produced domestically, but attempts to foster sheep-rearing have not met with great success. Sheep do not fit well into the pattern of East German agriculture.

Poultry, lastly, have increased very sharply and egg production has almost doubled within the last ten years. This is in part because many —though not a majority—are kept privately, and form no part of the socialised farm economy.

Summary. East Germany has usually been thought of as predominantly an agricultural region with a considerable food surplus for export. Such was the view expressed by Churchill when he complained to Truman about the hurried way in which the occupational zones of Germany were established. 'As it stands at present,' he wrote, 'the Russian occupational zone has the smallest proportion of people and grows by far the largest proportion of food . . . and we poor British are to take over all the ruined Ruhr and large manufacturing districts, which are, like ourselves, in normal times large importers of food.'[1] Such is to exaggerate the efficiency and productivity of East Germany. In a period of less intensive urbanisation and industrial development than the present, the territory of East Germany could in fact have broken even in the essential food-stuffs and have had an exportable surplus in a few, such as rye and potatoes. It must be emphasised that neither the soil nor the *latifundia* of East Germany made for efficient farming; that a surplus was available in only a few commodities, and that industrial expansion has now made East Germany on balance a food deficit area.

Postwar changes in the structure and the geographical pattern of agriculture have done nothing to improve production. The expansion of industrial crops has cut into food production, and that of dairy and animal products has improved the quality of the diet at the expense of volume of food-stuffs. At the same time collectivisation of agriculture has reduced incentives. The land is now less carefully managed than it was while in private ownership, though it must be added that re-organisation and mechanisation have reduced considerably the labour needs.

East Germany has become a net food importer. The only food-stuffs exported regularly and in quantity are eggs and refined sugar. These are greatly exceeded in value by imported food-stuffs. In addition to goods, such as coffee, cocoa and subtropical fruits, which East Germany is incapable of producing, there is a large import of wheat, equivalent to about 40 per cent of the total consumption. Even rye, oats, barley and potatoes are imported in small quantities. Exchange considerations have tended to restrict this trade to the Soviet Union and other countries of the Eastern bloc, and it does not seem likely, at least in the near future, that East Germany will escape dependence on this source for at least part of its food supply.

Forestry

Over a quarter of the total area of East Germany is forested, and three-quarters of it is coniferous. The fir is dominant in the hills of the

[1] Winston S. Churchill, *The Second World War*, vol. 6, London, 1954, p. 448.

south; the pine, on the sands of the centre and north. Beechwoods are extensive in the south-west, and the birch graces much of the heathland of the centre and north. The widespread deforestation which accompanied the spread of medieval settlement and the development of mining and smelting denuded much of the broadleaved woodland. In modern times, when the demand was heavily for softwoods, which

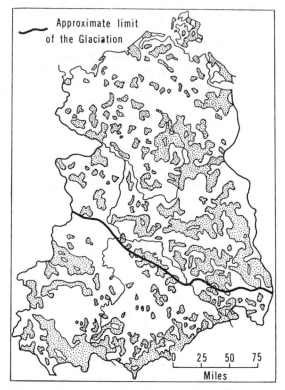

Fig. 7.11. Areas under forest in East Germany.
After Gerhard Schmidt-Renner.

yielded in any event quicker profits to the landowners, very extensive plantations, particularly of pine, were established. Forest resources were depleted by the end of the Second World War, but there has since been extensive replanting. The forests are carefully worked and replanting accompanies cutting. The lumber is used primarily for pitprops and constructional use and as raw material for paper and synthetic fibre manufacture.

Fisheries

Before the Second World War most of Germany's extensive ocean fishery was conducted from North Sea ports, and only a minute fraction of the total catch was landed at Baltic Sea ports. Thus East Germany inherited no important fishing docks and fish processing plant and no significant fishing fleet. The fishing fleet which has been built up since the Second World War is not large, and its activities are principally on the North Atlantic fishing grounds. The Baltic fisheries, owing to the low salinity of the waters, are of only minor importance.

The most important Baltic fishing port is Rostock-Marienehe, which is suitably equipped not only with docking and packing facilities, but also with good communications with the interior. Other fishing ports are Wismar, Stralsund and Sassnitz, on the island of Rügen. In each the operation of the fishing industry is concentrated in the *Fischkombinat*, a socialised undertaking which owns the boats and processing plant and employs the fishermen. The total catch of German sea-fisheries has increased very sharply, but started in the late 1940s from a very low base. From 26,600 tons in 1950 it has risen to 211,150 tons in 1966, which does not make the fisheries an important industry or a significant contributor to East Germany's food supply.

INDUSTRIAL DEVELOPMENT

East Germany has always been regarded as less industrialised than West. Its industrial growth came later than that of West Germany; it differed in its fields of concentration, and it operated under the disadvantages of distance from ocean ports and lack of high quality fuel. East Germany was also less well endowed with iron-ore, with the consequence that, although it once had an important charcoal-iron industry, it has had difficulty in building up a modern iron and steel industry. On the other hand, East Germany possessed an abundance of low-grade fuel as well as of mineral salts stored in the beds of the Zechstein series. East German industrial growth has in large measure been shaped by these considerations. The metal industries have emphasised the finishing processes and the fabrication of machinery; there has been a greater emphasis on 'light' goods than in West Germany, and there has been a very considerable development of the basic chemical industries and of thermal-electric power generation, both encouraged by the abundance of their respective raw materials.

Mineral and fuel resources

The resources of East Germany in these respects are closely related to the geological history of the area. They belong, in fact, to three geological horizons. Oldest are those associated with the Palaeozoic rocks of the south-west and south. These include the iron-ore of the Thüringerwald, the non-ferrous resources of the Harz and the Erzgebirge, and the bituminous coal, which occurs only in a few basins in the Erzgebirge Foreland.

Second are the rocks of Secondary age. These include the lower Triassic (Zechstein) with its deposits not only of potash salts and rock salts but also of bedded copper ores. Higher in the Secondary series are the bedded iron ores of Jurassic age, which occur in the Harz Foreland. Lastly, Tertiary beds cover much of East Germany, but are generally covered by glacial and diluvial deposits. Early in the Tertiary a series of shallow lakes was formed in the central parts of East Germany, extending locally into West Germany and more broadly into Poland. In these lakes accumulated the vegetable matter which has given rise to the very extensive brown coal deposits, the richest source of fuel and power in East Germany.

Metalliferous mining. Parts of East Germany have a long and notable history of metalliferous mining and of metal-working. The Erzgebirge, Vogtland, Thüringerwald and Harz were highly mineralised. Copper and iron were worked in prehistoric times. During the later Middle Ages the silver mines of the Erzgebirge, under the control primarily of the Fuggers, dominated the mining industry. Silver yielded place to lead, copper and zinc, but the region as a whole has retained its importance into the present century. Georg Agricola, who wrote one of the earliest treatises on mining, was born near Zwickau, spent much of his life around the mining camps of Altenberg, Annaberg and Schneeberg, and wrote his book in Karl-Marx-Stadt, which to him was just Chemnitz.[1] His descriptions and diagrams must have been taken from mining practice in the Erzgebirge. The Freiberg School of Mining (*Bergakademie*) was one of the most famous in Europe, where in the late eighteenth century Abraham Gottlob Werner, 'father of German geology' and himself a Lausitzer, taught the sciences of geology and mining.

At the opposite end of that arc of mineralised Palaeozoic rock which extends from the Lausitz to the Harz, lay the silver-lead mines of Clausthal and the Rammelsberg (now in West Germany) upon

[1] Georg Agricola, *De Re Metallica*, first published at Basel, 1556.

which were based in part the fortunes of the early Saxon emperors. Here too was a *Bergakademie* second only to that of Freiberg.

The metalliferous minerals of these areas consisted largely of lodes in the granite and metamorphic rocks. The ore deposits occupied usually only a narrow zone, and gave place in depth to other minerals which were not necessarily of economic value. Many have been exhausted, and the non-ferrous metals are today of very slight importance. Silver mining, once the mainstay of the region, has ceased. A small amount of tin is obtained in the Erzgebirge, and lead-zinc mines are active near Freiberg and in the mineralised granite of Lausitz. The only active mines in the Harz region lie just within the boundary of West Germany. Only the production of uranium ore continues to be pursued in the older mining areas with customary vigour. It has long been worked at Jáchymov (Joachimstal), on the Czech side of the range, but in recent years deposits have been opened up near Johanngeorgenstadt, Aue and Annaberg in the western Erzgebirge, and near Gera. Volume of production is unknown, but it is claimed that the output from this area, which is managed by a joint Soviet–East German undertaking, is the largest in Europe.

Apart from uranium, the most important non-ferrous metal production in East Germany is from the copper deposits of the eastern Harz. These are bedded deposits of lower Triassic age. The ore is low-grade and disseminated through copper shales, which occur in thin beds and lie at depths of up to 1,200 metres (3,940 feet). The oldest mines are near Mansfeld, where copper has been worked for many centuries. In recent years, extensions of these deposits have been opened up at Sangerhausen and Niederröblingen. Other small but geologically related deposits have been discovered on the flanks of the Kyffhäuser and at other points around the margin of the Thuringian Basin, where the Zechstein beds come close to the surface.

Even before the Second World War, the Mansfeld copper deposits furnished over 90 per cent of the copper mined in Germany. Since 1945 the demand for copper in East Germany has increased, with the intensification of the electrical industries, while overseas sources of supply have in general been cut off owing to difficulties with foreign exchange. Copper mining has therefore been greatly expanded from 804,000 tons (8,300 tons of metal content) in 1950, to 1,433,000 tons (22,000 tons) in 1965.

The copper is reduced to a matte by a crude smelting process at Eisleben, close to both Mansfeld and Sangerhausen, and further refined, rolled or drawn at nearby Hettstedt. The largest consumers of Mansfeld copper are the electrical industries of greater Berlin, where part of the final processing of the copper and its fabrication is located.

Mineral fuels. Industrial development in East Germany has long been hindered by the poverty and the poor quality of its bituminous coal resources. The coal beds now found in the Ruhr and in Hanover were formerly continued eastwards into Saxony. Most have, however, been removed by erosion, and the coal which survives lies in a few faulted and folded basins on the northern edge of the Erzgebirge. Most important of these is near Zwickau, where the seams are not only much folded but also very deep. Before the Second World War it was difficult for this coal to compete with that from the Ruhr, and production had been diminishing. Now, with a heavy demand for coal and West German sources for practical purposes cut off, the exploitation of the Zwickau coal basin has again been emphasised, and it now produces almost half the East German coal production.

The other coal basins are smaller, but are geologically related to that of Zwickau. They stretch out towards the north-east; the Lugau-Oelsnitz field near Karl-Marx-Stadt, and the Freital-Gittersee field, near Dresden. An inlier of Palaeozoic rocks near Halle also contains bituminous coal, but reserves are small and output negligible. This does, however, serve to emphasise the fact that bituminous coal may occur more widely in Central Germany beneath the thick cover of Secondary, Tertiary and later deposits.

Bituminous coal production in East Germany has fluctuated in recent years. In 1958, it reached 2,903,000 tons but has usually fallen considerably short of this total. The failure of the East German authorities greatly to stimulate bituminous coal mining reflects primarily the small size of the reserves and the technical difficulties of mining them. About four-fifths of the bituminous coal used has to be imported.

Brown coal. East Germany's resources in brown coal are, by contrast, the largest in the world, and it is claimed that they contain approximately a third of all known reserves. East Germany accounts at present for about 36 per cent of world production. The deposits are mostly thick, from 30 to 45 feet, and near enough to the surface for opencast mining to be practicable. The deposits are also large enough for mechanical extraction of the coal to be practicable on the largest possible scale. As mined the brown coal has a high moisture content of 46 to 62 per cent, and a low calorific value. Briquetting, which is done at the pits, more than doubles the calorific value of the coal, and makes it economic to transport it considerable distances.

There is a very great number of separate deposits, not all of which are worked. The greater part of the resources are, however, concentrated in two areas. The first surrounds the city of Leipzig, and extends from Köthen in the north to Zeitz and Borna in the south, and from Halle and Merseburg on the west to Torgau on the east. The second and larger deposit underlies the sandy wastes of Nieder Lausitz in

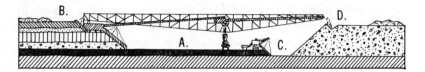

A. Brown Coal

B. Removing Overburden

C. Removing Coal

D. Replacing and levelling overburden

Fig. 7.12. Cross-section through a brown coal working, near Halle. After Hellmuth Barthel, in *Petermanns Geogr. Mitt. Erganzugsheft*, No. 270, (1962).

Bezirk Cottbus. It extends, with interruptions from Finsterwalde and Lauchhammer on the west to the Neisse River, where it extends into Poland, and from Eisenhüttenstadt south almost to the outskirts of Bautzen.

There is no long history of the mining of brown coal. Although peasants had occasionally dug the fuel for their own use, the first mining undertakings date from the early nineteenth century. These were small, opencast workings which soon exhausted the coal that could be obtained from such shallow pits. The overburden, which was too thick to be removed with the equipment then available, forced miners to sink shafts, and the second half of the nineteenth century and early years of the twentieth were characterised by a large number of shaft-mines. Though these penetrated to no great depth, they were a comparatively expensive way of obtaining what was in reality a very low-grade fuel. It is not surprising that, with the development of large earth-moving equipment, deep-mining was gradually abandoned in favour of opencast. The present practice is to move across the coal basin, stripping the overburden, extracting the coal and replacing the former, all in virtually one operation. A large *Förderbrücke* takes the waste from in front of the coal-face, transports it *over* the worked coal, and deposits it behind (Fig. 7.12) Deep-mining of brown coal has not entirely disappeared from East Germany, but is now of negligible importance. The immense opencast workings have great advantages: the cost of mining per ton of coal extracted is much reduced; they permit a rapid expansion of production, and they remove all the coal in the beds being worked. On the other hand, opencast mining is destructive of the countryside. Present-day writers in East Germany blame the exploitative operations of the years between the two World Wars, when little care was taken to restore the land surface after mining had been completed. Greater efforts are now being made to make good the destruction which necessarily accompanies this kind of mining. Waste heaps are levelled, topsoil replaced and trees planted. Nevertheless the agricultural value of the land is necessarily reduced, the soil profile is disturbed and the surface lowered so much that the water table is often made dangerously high. A very careful study of mining and reclamation in the Zeitz–Weissenfelser and Borna–Meuselwitz districts of the Leipzig coal-field shows that out of a total area of 13,385 hectares (33,462 acres) which had been or was currently being worked, rather less than 30 per cent had been restored to agricultural use, and over a half was occupied by the actual workings or by waste which had not yet been restored to any form of agricultural use.[1] A permanently reduced agricultural output is part of the price which has to be paid for the increased production of brown coal.

There are marked variations in the quality of brown coal, just as in that of bituminous. The water content ranges widely, and variations in the chemical composition of the coal determine the uses to which it can most profitably be put. The low calorific value of the coal as it comes from the pit restricts the distance over which it may be transported with profit. It is said that raw brown coal cannot be moved more than 30 miles. For this reason the coal is usually compressed into briquettes at the pit-side, thus reducing the water content and more than doubling the calorific value per ton.

There are small but important variations in the chemical composition of the coal. The most valuable, but also the most restricted is the

[1] Hellmuth Barthel, '*Braunkohlenbergbau und Landschaftsdynamik*', *Petermanns geogr. Mitt., Ergänzungsheft* Nr. 270, Gotha, 1962.

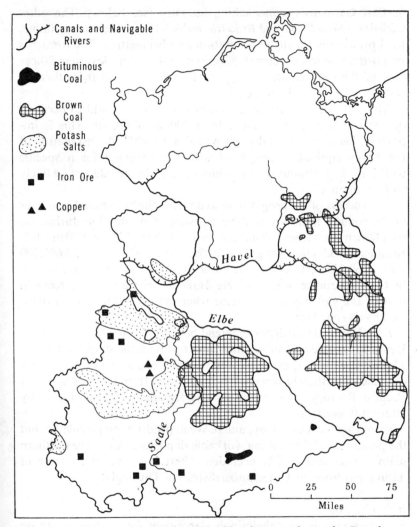

Fig. 7.13. Mineral resources, navigable rivers and canals. Based on *Statistisches Jahrbuch der DDR.*

so-called *Schwelkohle*, which, on heating in a retort, yields by-products of significance in the chemical industry. Next is a *Kokskohle* which can be made to yield a metallurgical coke. This is inferior to the coke obtained from the coking-coal of the Ruhr and can be used only in a specially constructed furnace. It nevertheless plays an important part in East Germany's iron-smelting industry (see below). The other varieties—*Kesselkohle* and *Brikettierkohle*—are, as their names imply, used principally for steam generation and briquetting. The former is by far the heaviest consumer of brown coal, and no less than 90 per cent of the total electric energy generated is derived from thermal stations which burn brown coal.

Almost three-quarters of the known reserves are said to occur in deposits each containing more than 200 million tons. This is important, because a small deposit would not justify the installation of the heavy equipment—much of which is designed for a specific working—and without such machines extraction would not be likely to be economic.

The success of the programme to develop the brown coal resources of the country is shown by the expansion of production during the past fifteen years from 137 million tons in 1950 to 254,219,000 in 1963. Briquette production has grown in the same period from 37,697,000 tons to 60,256,000. At the same time there has been a relative decline in the importance of the Leipzig–Halle district and an increase in that of the Cottbus mining area, where much of the recent expansion has taken place.

Peat. If brown coal deposits extend beneath the northern part of the Republic they lie at depths which are at present too deep for mining. There are, however, extensive deposits of peat, a fuel of even lower calorific value than brown coal. It is extracted from the peat moors of *Bezirke* Rostock, Schwerin and Neubrandenburg, and is locally important as a fuel.

Petroleum. East Germany, unlike West, produces no petroleum, but the possibility of discovering workable deposits beneath the northern plain can certainly not be excluded. There is a small production of natural gas from the Langensalza district of Thuringia.

Industrial Power

East Germany is overwhelmingly dependent for motive power on brown coal, and since this is a bulky and low-grade fuel, it is first transformed into electrical energy. Bituminous coal is produced in quantities too small to be significant in this respect, and there is, in fact, only one power-station—Klingenberg, in East Berlin—which uses this fuel. In 1963 only 3·8 per cent of the generated power derived from bituminous coal. On the other hand, almost 90 per cent was derived from burning brown coal or brown coal by-products.

There is little scope in East Germany for the development of water-power. The only developed sites of importance are on the upper Saale at Hohenwarte and Bleiloch in the Harz Mountains at Bodetal, and on the Elbe near Dresden. Altogether, however, they yielded only 1·2 per cent of the total power. Natural gas, obtained from wells in Thuringia, is also used for the generation of electric power, as well as directly for heat processes in industry.

Most of the electric power is produced in some 20 large generators established on the brown coal field. Considerably over three-quarters of the total electric energy is generated in the five *Bezirke* of Halle, Cottbus, Leipzig, Dresden and Magdeburg. Power generation is being greatly expanded in this area, not only to satisfy the immense demands of the chemical industries, but also because the energy of brown coal can be most economically transported as electric power. This is an important reason for the electrification of the railways.

The processing of brown coal yields large quantities of gas, and with the expansion of the coking industry at Schwarze Pumpe the amount available will be increased. It is at present transmitted by a pipeline network through the industrial south-west. New pipelines are being built by way of Eisenhüttenstadt to Berlin, and extensions are planned to Rostock and the north coast. Much of the gas is used at electric generating stations. Over 4 per cent of the power is actually obtained by burning gas, either natural or derived from brown coal.

Metallurgical industries
The iron and steel industry is at the same time one of the oldest and yet one of the youngest industries in East Germany. Until the middle years of the nineteenth century, the small, scattered deposits of iron-ore and the abundant forests were a sufficient resource. But lack of large deposits of high-grade ore and above all the absence of coking coal, restricted its development. Modern technology could not easily be applied to the East German industry, and the region as a whole came to supply its metal-using industries from the Ruhr and Upper Silesia. Indeed, the Berlin engineering firm of Borsig A.G. actually built and operated an iron and steel works near Bytom, in Upper Silesia, to supply its needs. Yet the earlier pattern of industry has not entirely disappeared. There remains the small, but fully integrated *Maxhütte*, at Unterwellenborn, on the edge of the Thüringerwald, which had been an important centre of the charcoal-iron industry. This works

has, however, been modernised in recent years. Other works per-
petuate the sites of undertakings of the eighteenth and nineteenth
centuries. Most of the older iron and steel works in East Germany

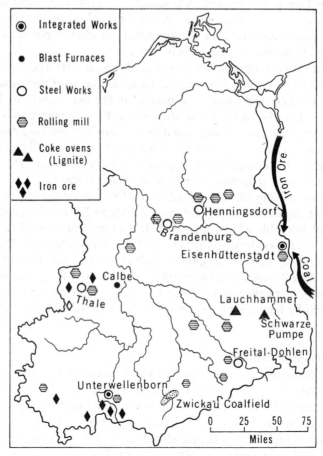

Fig. 7.14. Iron and steel industry of East Germany. Based
mainly on H. Smotkine, in *Annls Géogr.* **70** (1961).

passed into the possession of the Flick Concern in the 1930s, a steel
'empire' which spanned much of Germany. By the end of the Second
World War most works were either damaged or in need of thorough
modernisation.

Other iron and steel works are of recent origin. The smelting works
at Calbe, the *Eisenwerke West*, to the south of Magdeburg, was built

in the course of the implementation of the first Five-Year Plan (1951–55). It smelts the low-grade iron-ore of the Harz Foreland with coke obtained at the Lauchhammer (*Bz*. Cottbus) works from brown coal. The shafts were designed for the use of this fuel, and are very much lower than blast-furnaces built elsewhere at this time. This was in part because the rather soft nature of the coke used prevented it from withstanding the weight of a tall furnace charge.

The largest and most recent undertaking of this kind has been the *Eisenhüttenkombinat Ost*, commenced under the first Five-Year Plan and extended under subsequent plans. It was located on a terrace above the river Elbe 14 miles to the south of Frankfurt-on-Oder. Across the river lay Poland. The construction of a fully integrated plant on this site is evidence both of the confidence of the East German planning authorities in a continuance of good relations with Poland, and also of the overriding need to import raw materials. The site is the most easterly that could have been chosen; it has the advantage of water transport on the River Oder, and obtains most of its coking coal by river barge from Upper Silesia (see page 284). Iron-ore has also to be imported. Some comes by rail from Krivoi Rog in the Ukraine and the rest by barge upstream from the Polish port of Szczecin (Stettin). Six blast furnaces of large capacity and modern design have been constructed. Though the local brown coal field can contribute to the power requirements of the works by the supply of thermal electric power, there is no possibility whatever of using coke from brown coal in the furnaces.[1]

Steelworks, using pig-iron from the iron-smelting works already mentioned, have been established at Riesa, Gröditz and Döhlen, all in *Bz*. Dresden; at Thale in *Bz*. Halle, and at Brandenburg and Hennigsdorf in *Bz*. Potsdam. All these works are semi-integrated.

East Germany is very far indeed from being one of the world's more important producers of crude iron and steel. But the volume of output has increased very greatly above the level obtaining before the Second World War. The objective of the government to produce domestically all the steel required by the engineering and other metal using industries has not however been realised. The import of iron for castings and for steel-making has nearly doubled within the last ten years, and the import of crude steel and rolled steel goods has more than trebled. The current (1965) import of steel and rolled steel goods is almost

---

[1] Gerhard Mohs, *Die Industrie im Bezirk Frankfurt (Oder)*, Verlag d. Wissen., Berlin, 1962.

equal to the domestic steel output. A small part of the latter (about 14 per cent) is also made from the imported pig-iron (*Stahleisen*). Domestic production of pig-iron has risen from 337,200 tons in 1950, which was considerably above the small prewar output,[1] to 2,447,700 tons in 1966. Steel output has risen from 998,700 in 1950 to 4,084,500 tons in 1966.

Metal industries. These constitute the most important branch of manufacturing industries in East Germany. They are very varied in their nature and are important in all *Bezirke* except Schwerin and Neubrandenburg. The primary fabrication of steel is in general integrated with the steel-making process, although rolling mills with attached steelworks are to be found at Olbernbau (*Bz*. Karl-Marx-Stadt), Ilsenburg (*Bz*. Magdeburg), Burg (*Bz*. Potsdam) and Finow (*Bz*. Frankfurt). From these and from the steelworks previously named metal is supplied for the very numerous centres of the mechanical engineering, construction and instrument industries.

Before the Second World War the territory of the Democratic German Republic had been significant for some only among the metal-using industries. These included the electro-mechanical industry, the construction of textile machinery and machine-tools, and the manufacture of precision machinery, office equipment and optical instruments. Most other branches of the metal-using industries were concentrated in the western provinces of Germany. Since 1960 East Germany has strengthened those branches in which it was already significant, remedied many of the shortages which resulted from the division of Germany, and has built up the others which had hitherto been of slight importance. Among the latter have been the ship-building industry and the building of heavy machinery and steel-construction.

It is not easy to group the metal-using industries for a summary discussion. In range and volume of production they come second only to those of the Soviet Union within the Communist sphere. In the following pages those branches of industry which were already well established before the Second World War are first discussed. Those which have been introduced or greatly expanded since 1950 are examined next. It is impossible to catalogue the many widely scattered manufacturing centres some of which contribute only components for larger works. Industrial regions will however be defined, and the general character of their industrial production discussed.

Agricultural machinery. Although the manufacture of farming

[1] This was all from the Maxhütte at Unterwellenborn (*Bz*. Gera).

The navigable Spree in East Berlin

EAST GERMANY

Meissen, East Germany. The cathedral and the castle of the medieval dukes of Meissen lie on top of the rock, the Albrechtsburg, overlooking the Elbe. The town lies on lower ground to the left

The restored *Zwinger*, the palace of the former Kings of Saxony, in Dresden, East Germany

The rebuilt quarter of Magdeburg, East Germany. To the right lie the ruins of one of the several romanesque churches of the medieval city

Dresden, the main street of the rebuilt city

equipment was an important industry before the Second World War, it has been greatly expanded to meet the needs of a collectivised agriculture. The factories are widely scattered and, in general, highly specialised. The chief sources of such heavy equipment as combine-harvesters are Neustadt, in Oberlausitz, and Weimar. Ploughs are made in Leipzig; tractors built in Gotha and near Magdeburg, and spreaders, drills, harrows, milking-machines constructed in factories scattered all the way from Stralsund to Eisenach.

Railway equipment. The territory of East Germany had been important for the manufacture of railway locomotives and rolling-stock long before the Second World War. The chief centre had been Berlin itself, and the Berlin region remains the chief source of locomotives, including electric locomotives, with factories in Hennigsdorf and Babelsberg. The building of railway wagons and carriages is, however, more widespread. Its chief centres are in Saxony and Thuringia, at Dessau, Halle, Werdau (*Bz.* Karl-Marx-Stadt), and Gotha, and at Görlitz and Bautzen in the extreme south-east of the Republic.

Automobile manufacture. Almost a third of the prewar manufacture of automobiles had been in the present East German territory, but a number of important components had been manufactured in the West. The manufacture of components has been established in East Germany, but remains widely scattered. The actual manufacture of cars is carried on principally at Eisenach, very close to the zonal boundary, and at Zwickau. Lorries and other heavy vehicles are built at Zwickau and Zittau, and motorcycles at Suhl.

Textile machinery. Saxony is one of the oldest centres of the textile manufacturing industry in Germany, and the manufacture of looms and spinning machines came early. Today the manufacture of equipment for the spinning of thread, the weaving and knitting of fabrics, and the dyeing and finishing of cloth is of great importance in Karl-Marx-Stadt and neighbouring towns, and these goods play an important role in East Germany's foreign trade. Indeed, it is claimed that from 60 to 80 per cent of the production of some lines is for export.

Electro-technical industry. Berlin has long been the chief centre in Germany for the manufacture not only of heavy electrical equipment such as dynamos and transformers, but also of light articles of everyday use such as batteries and light bulbs. East Berlin and the smaller towns of the greater Berlin complex continue to dominate the industry in East Germany, and to produce almost every type of electrical machine, wire, cable and components. Though more narrowly

10

concentrated than any other major branch of East German industry, electrical equipment is nevertheless manufactured in a number of other places. Electric motors are made in Wernigerode and Oschersleben on the northern margin of the Harz Mountains, and in Dresden and some of its surrounding towns in Saxony. Radio and television equipment is made in Dresden, Stassfurt and Rochlitz (*Bz.* Karl-Marx-Stadt); radio valves in Erfurt, and electric light bulbs in Plauen, Zwickau and Dresden.

Precision and optical engineering. This branch of manufacturing has long been one of the most distinguished in East Germany, and one for which Germany had a worldwide reputation. It includes the manufacture of typewriters, calculating machines and similar office equipment at Erfurt, Sömmerda, Karl-Marx-Stadt, Dresden and Leipzig; clock and watch manufacture at Ruhla and Glashütte, south of Dresden; photographic equipment at Dresden and Berlin; medical instruments and equipment at Potsdam and also Berlin, and optical and precision equipment and machines at Rathenau and above all at Jena. The latter, founded in 1846 by Carl Zeiss, has become almost legendary. Although much of its equipment was taken to the West in 1945, followed by a large number of its skilled operatives, the works have been rebuilt, re-equipped and modernised to become perhaps the world's leading producer of all optical equipment.

Other branches of industry which relied heavily on iron and steel were relatively undeveloped in East Germany before 1945, and their present level is the result of planned development under the present regime.

Ship-building. Foremost amongst these is ship-building. Before the Second World War, Germany's ship-building industry, like its ports, was concentrated in the north-west, where its chief centres lay along the lower Elbe and lower Weser. East Germany inherited neither a merchant marine nor a tradition in ship-builidng. Both have been developed in recent years. Shipyards have been established at Wismar and Rostock, and at Warnemünde, on the coast to the north of Rostock, where the largest vessels are built. At Wolgast, on the Peene, one of the outlets of the Stettiner Haff, small coastal craft are built. Fishing-craft had long been built for the Baltic fisheries; now this industry has been greatly expanded chiefly at inland sites, such as Brandenburg and Eisenhüttenstadt, which have good connections by water with the sea.

Heavy machinery. Like shipbuilding, the construction of large-scale mechanical equipment makes heavy demands on the steel industry, and primarily for this reason had been concentrated in western Germany. Large advances, however, have been made in the past 15 years, and there is today a significant export of certain types of machines. Indeed, the very great expansion of brown coal production would have been impossible without the means to build the *Förderbrücken* and excavators. At the present time there is a large and expanding manufacture of such heavy mechanical tools as lathes, drills, presses and assembly-line equipment. This type of manufacture is widespread in the south-western half of the country, where its chief centres of production are in Magdeburg, Leipzig, Erfurt, Karl-Marx-Stadt and Dresden, as well as in Berlin and a number of smaller industrial towns.

Castings and forgings. When an iron-smelting and steel-making industry is obliged by shortage of materials or technological change to close down, it often leaves as a legacy to the later industrial pattern a number of foundries, forges and press-works. This has been so in northern Hungary and Bohemia, and also in parts of East Germany. Along the Oder-Havel Canal near Eberswalde and in the Erzgebirge such small industrial undertakings remain like ghosts of the vanished smelting and refining industry.

The newly developed ship-building, machine and tool industries, however, make heavy demands for iron and steel castings, for forgings and for pressed or stamped goods. The older centres were not equipped to supply these, and new factories have been built close to the centres of heavy machine construction. They are found in Rostock, where they produce components for the ship-building industry; in Berlin, near Halle and Leipzig, in Eisenach and Erfurt, and a number of other industrial centres of Saxony and Thuringia.

Machine construction. The industrial expansion which has characterised East Germany in recent years would have been inconceivable without the motive power to operate the machines. The manufacture of machines had already been important in Berlin, where the Borsig concern had built turbines, generators, steam-engines and pumps. This industry has been expanded, and extended to other cities, notably Halle, Dresden and Gera. Halle produces the pumps necessary to evacuate water from the brown coal workings; Meissen makes turbines; pumps and winding-gear for mines are made in Magdeburg, Leipzig and in a number of small towns of the Thuringian Basin, where the potash and salt mines create a local demand for such equipment.

Chemical industries

In East Germany the chemical industries are second in importance only to the metal industries, and in 1966 contributed 17 per cent of the total value of manufactures and employed 10 per cent of the industrially employed population. In relation to the size of the population, East Germany's chemical industry is one of the largest in the world. This has long been one of the principal branches of industry in East Germany, and one in which productivity greatly exceeded that in Western Germany. This supremacy of East Germany—specifically the supremacy of *Bz*. Halle—is attributable in large measure to the extensive deposits of rock and potash salts, which provide the raw materials for the manufacture of basic chemicals.

The chemical industry was formerly engaged primarily in producing finished articles: fertilisers, drugs and pharmaceutical goods. This has changed; most of the products of the chemical industry are now the raw materials of other manufacturing industries, such as the textile and automobile. The development of the chemical industry has become basic to a great deal of the industrial structure of East Germany. It was possible also to conceive of separate and distinct branches of the industry, carried on separately from one another and serving different markets. While one can group the products of the industry, as the *Statistisches Jahrbuch* does, for statistical purposes, it is no longer possible to separate their places and processes of manufacture. They are almost all interrelated and interdependent.

The so-called basic chemicals account for about 38 per cent by value of the total production. These include caustic soda and potash and the common acids and their basic derivatives. Among the latter are the fertilisers and high explosives which were among the earliest chemical products of the area. In part they derive ultimately from the local reserves of common and potash salts, of anhydrite and pyrites.

From this base the more sophisticated chemical products are produced, many of them at the same works that produce the basic chemicals; others at distant and more specialised factories. These commodities at present make up to about 20 per cent by value of the industry's production. Plastics and synthetic fibres form separate categories with about 6 and 5 per cent respectively of the total. The remaining categories are the large synthetic rubber and asbestos manufacture, with about 18 per cent; the petrochemical and tar derivatives industry, with about 15 per cent, and the manufacture of pharmaceuticals.

The chemical industry is dominated by five major works, which are said between them to produce some 40 per cent of the total production within the chemical sector. All lie within *Bz*. Halle and within 35 miles of the city of Halle itself. The largest of these and in fact the largest works in the Republic, is the *Leuna-Werke*, situated on the Saale River, near Merseburg. It was established during the First World War for the manufacture of explosives, but was converted shortly after to the manufacture of nitrogenous fertiliser. The plant was damaged during the Second World War, but was not dismantled, and early in the 1950s its capacity began to be expanded. Its basic manufacture is of ammonia and the common acids, to which has been added the production of motor fuel synthesised from brown coal. The range of derivatives from these products is almost endless; they include plastics and synthetic fibres; varnishes, preservatives and glues; drugs and pharmaceutical goods. At present a second plant, known as Leuna II, is under construction; its range will include the petrochemical products.

Some 6 miles to the north, at Schkopau, is the second largest chemical plant, the *Buna-Werke*. Its nucleus, built before the Second World War, was a factory for the manufacture of synthetic rubber, the ultimate source of which is carbon and calcium. These were synthesised electrically to make calcium carbide, which was in turn the source of acetylene, the primary ingredient of buna. The process required very large quantities of electric power, which was obtained from nearby thermal-electric stations using brown coal as a fuel. The range of products at the *Buna-Werke* has since been greatly extended, but most, including many plastic materials and synthetic fibres, are dependent on the primary synthesis of calcium carbide.

In the Mulde valley, to the north-east of Halle, lie two more giant chemical works. The *Elektrochemische Kombinat Bitterfeld* concentrates on the production by electrolysis of caustic soda and potash. Much of this is used directly in the manufacture of synthetic fibres, but part of the output goes into bleaching and cleansing preparations and into insecticides and fungicides. The second factory in this area lies at Wolfen, a mile or two to the north of Bitterfeld. The production of the *Filmfabrik Agfa Wolfen* is more specialised, and, as its name suggests, its basic manufacture is that of photographic chemicals and film, but the range of manufactures has been extended to include sulphuric acid from local anhydrite, and synthetic fibres.

The last of the five major chemical works lies in the Elbe valley to the north. The *Stickstoffwerk Piesteritz* lies in the western suburbs of Wittenberg. Like the Bitterfeld works, it concentrates on electrochemical processes for the fixation of nitrogen and the manufacture of nitrogenous and phosphorous fertilisers, but like all other large plants, it has also developed the production of plastic materials.

These five very large works by no means exhaust the list of chemical factories in the vicinity of Halle. The *Chemiekombinat Coswig* produces sulphuric acid and super-phosphates; at Bernburg soda is made, and brown coal is used as a base for the extraction and distillation of tar, oil, paraffin and petroleum at Zeitz, Webau, Amsdorf, Rodleben and elsewhere.

Almost a half of the total East German chemical production is concentrated in *Bz.* Halle, but important elements extend into *Bz.* Leipzig to the south-east and into Magdeburg to the north, and a very large new complex is developing on the heathlands of Cottbus, where the richest reserves of brown coal are now to be found. This region of the Lausitz brown coal basin is not only becoming a major source of electric power, essential for the chemical industry of the Halle region, but at Lauchhammer a metallurgical coke is being produced from brown coal. By-product gases are piped to other industrial works of the region, and tar and related derivatives from the coal are distilled for their by-products. A second plant for the production of *Hochtemperaturkoks* from brown coal and for the treatment of the gases, tars and oils that are generated in the process, has recently been built at Schwarze Pumpe. A Fischer-Tropsch plant for the hydrogenation of brown coal and manufacture of fuel oil and petroleum has also been built at Lauchhammer.

The pharmaceutical and drug industry found itself heavily concentrated in West Germany at the end of the Second World War, and East Germany was obliged to develop a new branch of the chemical industry. This it has done in factories at Jena, the chief centre of the industry, and at Dresden-Radebeul, Magdeburg and Berlin.

Cellulose and synthetic fibres have become of great importance in East Germany because the highly developed textile industry had relied upon imported cotton and wool. In the absence of foreign exchange to purchase these raw materials, the industry has been obliged to use increasing quantities of synthetic fibres. The large chemical factories of *Bz.* Halle are a major source of the raw materials of the textile industries, but polymers and also cellulose, made from pulp and organic waste, are produced at a number of smaller centres. Many of these, such as Dresden, Pirna and Schwarza, lie in the traditional cloth-working areas of the Erzgebirge.

The petrochemical industries had already been developed at Leuna on the basis of the oils derived from brown coal, when the petroleum refinery at Schwedt on the Oder was built. Its purpose is to refine Soviet crude oil and to use the by-products as the basis of a complex petro-chemical industry.

The chemical industry of East Germany is basic to almost every other, and none can operate without some reference to this many-sided giant. The obligation to reduce imports as far as possible from the non-Communist world has led to the maximum use of local resources. The East German chemical industry is thus dependent as in no other country on local salts and brown coal. A very large part of the total production of the latter is fed into the chemical industry either as industrial power or as raw material. The chemical industry is said to consume no less than 4 per cent of the power generated. A significant part of the metallurgical and mechanical engineering industries is geared to the supply of tools and equipment for the chemical and its ancillary industries. The textile industries, agriculture and the export trade are all dependent in large though varying degree on the chemical industries, and their expansion is one of the chief preoccupations of the planning authorities.

Building materials industry. The progress of this branch of industry is often a measure of industrial progress as a whole, because factory development is overwhelmingly dependent on cement. Cement production had by 1966 increased nearly 500 per cent above the level of 1950. Crushed stone for concrete and road construction increased almost as rapidly and the expansion of brick production has risen by nearly 3,000 per cent in the same period. To some extent this expansion of the building materials industries reflects the need to make good the ravages of war, but in more recent years it indicates the extent of new building.

Cement manufacture is located as close as possible to its raw materials, lime-stone and clay. The outcrop of the Triassic and Jurassic rocks around the Harz Mountains offers the best conditions, and here, at Bernburg, Rudersdorf-Herzfelde, Karsdorf and Nienburg, are the largest cement works. The only other important centres of cement manufacture are East Berlin and the iron-smelting centres of Eisenhüttenstadt and Unterwellenborn, where cement is made from furnace slag.

Quarrying for building stone, road-metal and concrete aggregate is carried on, of necessity, mainly in the south-western part of the country. Brick-manufacture is, however, very much more widespread. Very large brick-making works have been established at Hoyerswerda, in the developing Cottbus industrial region, and in Rostock. Smaller brick and tile works are widely scattered where the clay is available.

Textile industries

Eastern Germany has long been noted for its textile and clothing industries. Before the Second World War 60 per cent of the woollen industry was in the area of East Germany, but only about 14 per cent of the cotton textiles and even less of the silk. Although it remains third in importance in East Germany after the mechanical and chemical industries, the textile industry has made very much less progress than either. The woollen cloth industry has by no means regained its prewar level and the manufacture of cottons reached this level only in the middle 1950s. Apart from a certain neglect of the consumer goods industries by the government, there are two reasons for this relative failure of the textile industries to regain their earlier level of importance. The first is that capacity had been overextended, especially in the woollen industry, and that the potential output was far larger than East Germany needed. The other reason is that economic circumstances have obliged the East German government to reduce imports of wool and cotton and to turn to synthetic fibres which can be produced domestically. There was, furthermore, a lack of balance within each branch of the textile industry. The East German cotton industry found itself with only a very small proportion of the fine-spinning and a relatively large proportion of the total cotton weaving. Most of the glove, hosiery and knitwear industries were in East Germany, and relied upon thread brought in from West Germany.

The textile industries are heavily concentrated in the foothills of the Erzgebirge of Saxony, where the original factories were powered by the mountain streams. The focal points of the industry are Plauen, Zwickau and Karl-Marx-Stadt, but the greater part of the industry is scattered through the small towns which line the Weisse Elster, the Mulde and the Zschopau. Another cluster of textile factories is found in the Lausitzer Bergland, where Zittau is the largest manufacturing centre.

Other light industries. This broad and varied group of manufactures includes leather and footwear, furniture, pottery and glass, printing, musical instruments and toys. The chief centres of the leather and footwear industry have long been Erfurt, Weissenfels (*Bz.* Halle) and Burg (*Bz.* Magdeburg), although at many other places one finds tanning, the preparation of skins and the fabrication of various leather goods.

Printing has long been associated with Leipzig and Dresden, and the printing of maps with Gotha. The manufacture of musical instruments developed early in the Vogtland, where it took over part of the labour-force which became available with the decline of mining. Glass manufacture is associated particularly with Cottbus and Suhl, in both of which quartz-sands are available. At the head of the pottery industry stands the porcelain factory of Meissen, whose products, marketed as Dresden china, are world-famous. On a lower plane of artistic production are the numerous pottery and ceramic factories in *Bze.* Suhl, Gera, Karl-Marx-Stadt and Dresden. Ilmenau, in *Bz.* Suhl, is dominated by the pottery industry, which is here carried on in an immense number of small factories and workshops.

Food industries. These are, almost of necessity, widely scattered through East Germany. Some food-stuffs must be processed where they are produced; others near the place of consumption. The result is that no branch of industry is so evenly distributed as this. On the north

Table 27. Distribution of undertakings, employment according to branch of industry, 1966

Branch of industry	Number of works, mines, etc.	Total employment	Total value of goods produced (1,000 DM)
Mining	107	189,838	2,587,654
Power generation	25	70,390	1,658,461
Smelting	31	114,079	4,510,837
Chemical industries	1,002	282,038	16,366,318
Building materials	656	88,259	1,988,628
Metal-working	3,509	1,053,277	35,614,872
Light industries	6,230	739,870	19,471,152
Food industries	1,891	199,704	12,365,899

Source: *Statistisches Jahrbuch der DDR, 1967.*

10*

coast one finds fish-processing, especially in the port of Rostock, as well as the preparation of imported foods. Sugar-refining is carried on throughout the broad area characterised by loess soils and the cultivation of sugar-beet, which covers much of *Bze.* Magdeburg and Halle. The manufacture of edible oils and fats, the milling of grain, the preparation of tobacco and making of cigarettes, brewing and the distillation of *Brantwein* are very widely dispersed in both the thinly populated north, where much of the agricultural production takes place, and in the densely populated south-west, where the largest market is found.

Table 28. Distribution of industrial workers by administrative divisions

Bezirk	No. of industrial works	Total population	Percentage industrially employed	Value of industrial production per head
Lightly industralised:				
Rostock	306	848,991	8·1	3,064
Schwerin	248	622,968	5·8	2,117
Neubrandenburg	231	652,624	3·9	1,324
Potsdam	571	1,152,741	10·1	3,620
Frankfurt	227	666,924	7·3	3,318
Heavily industrialised:				
Cottbus	508	823,021	16·7	4,167
Magdeburg	725	1,374,373	12·0	4,415
Halle	1,110	1,965,383	18·7	7,497
Erfurt	1,186	1,249,186	15·9	4,412
Gera	682	728,774	20·3	5,835
Suhl	897	546,677	20·2	4,954
Dresden	2,303	1,880,011	20·7	5,785
Leipzig	1,628	1,512,847	19·0	5,554
Karl-Marx-Stadt	3,481	2,091,267	24·2	6,131
Berlin (East)	755	1,065,296	16·1	5,110
	14,858			

Source: *Statistisches Jahrbuch der DDR, 1965.*

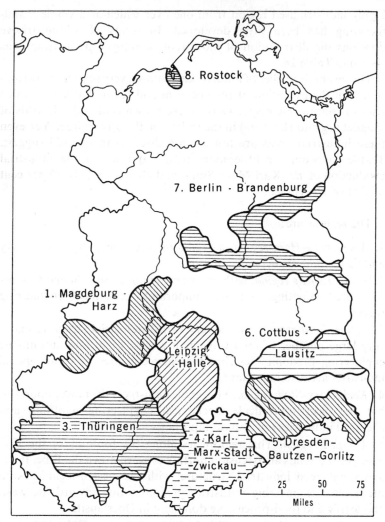

Fig. 7.15. Industrial regions in East Germany.

Industrial regions

It is implicit in the previous pages that, with the exception of the industrial complex of Greater Berlin, the larger part of the manufacturing industry of East Germany lies in the south-western half of the country. A line drawn approximately from the point where the Mittelland Canal crosses the zonal boundary to Cottbus separates a

highly industrialised region from one over which as a whole manufacturing has been little developed. In terms of administrative
divisions the distribution of industrially employed population is as
shown in Table 28.

The several branches of industry each show a very scattered distribution with the exception of the chemical and textile industries which
tend to concentrate respectively on the brown coal and salt fields of
Magdeburg and Halle and in the valleys of the Erzgebirge. Yet even
these industrial areas are not as specialised as this would suggest.
Textiles account for little more than a quarter of the industrial
production of *Bz.* Karl-Marx-Stadt, and chemicals only 40 per cent
of that of *Bz.* Halle.

The regions are:

1. *Magdeburg-Harz region*, a region of mixed industry, with heavy
and light engineering predominating.
2. *Halle–Leipzig region*, with brown coal mining and chemical industries predominating, but also important mechanical engineering
works.
3. *Erfurt–Gera region*, with a very varied industrial structure and a
very large number of relatively small works. Light and automobile
engineering predominates, but the chemical, precision and optical
industries are also important.
4. *Karl-Marx-Stadt region*. The textile industry is the most important,
but the electro-technical, mechanical engineering, clothing and
chemical industries are also of importance.
5. *Dresden region*. This region lies along the foothills of the Erzgebirge, and sends an extension north-westward down the Elbe. It has
a well-balanced industrial structure, with the electro-technical and
mechanical engineering industries predominating toward the west,
and textile and food-processing dominant in Oberlausitz.
6. *Cottbus–Lausitz region*. This is the most recent of the industrial
regions of East Germany and still the most specialised. Its basis is the
brown coal deposits of Lausitz, and the branches of industry developed hitherto consist largely of mining, power-generation and the
manufacture of coke, fuel oil and related by-products from the brown
coal.
7. *Greater Berlin*. As defined on the map this region consists of the
city of Berlin, together with the very varied industries which have

grown up along the waterways—the Elbe-Havel, Oder-Havel and Oder-Spree Canals—which radiate from the city. It is less intensively industrialised, except in Berlin itself, than the regions already defined; it is also very diversified in its industrial structure. Electro-technical and mechanical industries predominate in Berlin itself, though there is hardly a branch of light or consumer-goods industry that is not found here. The region includes the old centres of steel-finishing along the Oder-Havel Canal, at Eberswalde and Finow, and, by contrast, the new *Eisenhüttenkombinat Ost*, on the Oder above Frankfurt; the new petro-chemical works at Schwedt and the building of agricultural machinery at Brandenburg.

8. *Rostock*. The last industrial region is almost too small to be counted with those already listed. It has only one large and important industry, shipbuilding, and in this is foremost in East Germany.

TRANSPORT AND TRADE

East Germany inherited a developed railway system from the Third Reich, a road network which was adequate in its extent if not also in its quality, and a system of inland waterways which was among the best in Europe. The damage of war has been repaired, but little else has been done to extend or modify this system. Before the Second World War, the most intensively used routes were those from west to east, from the industrialised Rhineland to Berlin, Central Germany and Silesia. The Oder-Neisse and the zonal boundaries have changed this. Relatively little traffic except that between West Germany and West Berlin, moves across the latter, and the volume crossing the Oder-Neisse line is not great.

Transport network

Within East Germany the most used routes tend to be aligned in a south to north direction. The chief port is Rostock, on the Baltic coast; the largest industrial cities are Berlin, Halle, Leipzig, Karl-Marx-Stadt and Dresden, and movement between them demands north–south, not east–west, arteries of communication. The *Autobahn*, which crosses the Republic from Marienborn to Frankfurt-on-Oder and skirts Berlin, is almost deserted except for the traffic of West Berlin itself. The north–south *Autobahn* from Berlin to Karl-Marx-Stadt is well used. This new orientation of the main lines of traffic flow has somewhat restricted the usefulness of inland waterways. The only important navigable river, the Elbe, flows from south-east to north-west and discharges to the sea through West German territory. As long as most of East Germany lay within the hinterland of Hamburg the Elbe and its related waterways were vital avenues of communication. They do not significantly assist freight to reach Rostock. The more important canals were designed as parts of a chain of waterways which linked the Rhineland with the east. The ends of the system are now for practical purposes cut off. They are much used around Berlin itself, but elsewhere much of their traffic is due to the fact that some of the recently developed industrial sites have been chosen with reference to them.

The railways remain by far the most used means of transport both for freight and passenger movement. Freight, as measured in tons per mile, was transported by:

Railways	82·4 per cent
Inland waterways	5·3 per cent
Road vehicles	12·3 per cent

Passenger traffic is divided between railways and road vehicles in the ratio of about two to one.

Railway network. With a total mileage of about 10,000 miles East Germany has not only the longest railway system of any of the countries covered by this book, but also the densest network. As is to be expected the mileage of track is greatest in the most densely settled and highly industrialised *Bezirke*, such as Berlin, Karl-Marx-Stadt, Leipzig; and least in the predominantly agricultural northern *Bezirke*.

The chief railway centre is Berlin, from which some eleven trunk lines radiate. Notwithstanding the difficulties which still remain in the way of transit traffic across East Germany, Berlin is again becoming a focus of international routes. In particular, it lies on the shortest route from Western Europe to the Soviet Union and from Scandinavia to the Mediterranean. Rail-ferries run from Warnemünde to the port of Gedser on the Danish island of Falster, and from Sassnitz, on Rügen, to Trälleborg in southern Sweden.

Other important focal points of the railway system are Magdeburg, Halle and Leipzig, and the volume of traffic passing through Halle and Leipzig is in fact greater than through East Berlin. In terms of the volume of traffic handled, Leipzig is foremost in the eight countries covered by this book.[1]

[1] See *Die Volkswirtschaft der Deutschen Demokratischen Republic*, Berlin, 1960, pp. 207–13.

Steam traction still dominates the railways of East Germany, but is slowly yielding to diesel and electric traction. East Germany lacks the bituminous coal necessary for steam locomotives, and brown coal, burned under the locomotive boiler, is highly inefficient. The main north–south trunk lines in the Magdeburg–Halle–Leipzig industrial region have been electrified, and further electrification is projected in the brown coal region itself and southward to Karl-Marx-Stadt. This is, however, clearly dependent upon a considerable expansion of power generation, but recent plans called for the electrification of 5 per cent of the main line track by 1965.

Inland waterways. East Germany has about 890 miles of navigable waterway, including 256 of canal. This system consists essentially of two axes, the Elbe, which is navigable throughout its course in East Germany, and the canal which extends with changing nomenclature from the zonal boundary to the Oder. The Saale is navigable below Halle, and a network of canals spreads through Berlin and is linked with the lower Oder by the Oder-Havel Canal. The capacity of the Elbe and of the canals west of Berlin is large and they can take barges of 1,000 tons. The Berlin network as well as the Saale and Oder are more restricted, and cannot in general take barges of more than 750 tons. In addition to these waterways there are several navigable rivers with connecting canals in the north of East Germany. These include the rivers Warnow and Peene, and the Müritz-Elde and Müritz-Havel waterways. These waterways are, however, narrow and shallow, and since they run through thinly peopled and mainly agricultural areas, they are little used.

It has been noted that, notwithstanding their technical excellence, the East German waterways suffer from their general east to west orientation. The Elbe, however, flows between the two largest brown coalfields, and is close enough to both to provide transport for their bulky products. Brown coal, briquettes, coke, ores, potash salts, crude chemicals and unfinished iron and steel constitute, in fact, the greater part of the cargoes of industrial origin that are carried on rivers and canals. Grain and raw cotton are also among the goods carried.

The focal point of river traffic is Magdeburg, the crossing of the east–west canal system and the Elbe, through which passes not only the domestic barge traffic between the south and Berlin and places to the east, but also the transit traffic between West Germany and West Berlin. Other important river and canal ports are East Berlin itself and the Elbe river ports of Dresden, Riesa, which is chiefly important for the shipment of briquettes and coke from the Lausitz basin, and Schönebeck, which serves as port for the Stassfurt potash mining region. The Elbe, which is navigable to Prague in Czechoslovakia, also carries a transit traffic from the latter country to the dock facilities in Hamburg.

The Oder is also a navigable waterway of East Germany, since it constitutes the boundary from near Eisenhüttenstadt to Gartz, a distance of about 110 miles. The principal Oder ports are Frankfurt and Eisenhüttenstadt, though Schwedt may become important as its petrochemical industry develops. Grain is imported at Frankfurt from the Polish port of Szczecin, but the chief cargo is at present coal which is shipped down the Oder from Upper Silesia for the supply of the metallurgical plant at Eisenhüttenstadt.

Road system. Road vehicles handle only about an eighth of the goods transported within East Germany and no more than a third of the passenger traffic. There is, however, a well-developed road system, which is not however always maintained in the best condition. Its core is a net of *Autobahnen*, most of which was inherited from Hitler's *Reich*. Two trunk roads run from west to east, one in the latitude of Berlin, the other from Eisenach to near Görlitz. These are linked by two north–south roads, one from west of Berlin, through the Halle–Leipzig region to the zonal boundary and Nürnberg; the other from Berlin to Dresden. There are a number of spur roads, all unfinished, and an incomplete ring road around Berlin.

The number of private cars remains very small, but the total is not published. On the other hand the number of buses and heavy lorries has increased greatly in recent years. It is primarily publicly owned goods vehicles that one meets on the roads.

Coastal shipping. East Germany has too short a coastline and too few coastal ports for coastwise shipping to be of great importance. Small vessels are however used to transport freight, much of it bulky goods of agricultural origin, like potatoes, between the northern ports.

Airlines. The East German airline, *Deutsche Lufthansa*, was established in 1955, and limited its activities at first to international air routes mainly within the Communist sphere. In 1957, however, domestic flights were initiated. Today the airport of East Berlin, Berlin-Schönefeld, is linked by regular flights with Barth, on the Baltic coast between Rostock and Stralsund, and with the larger cities to the south.

Foreign trade

East Germany is, after the Soviet Union itself, one of the most important trading countries in the Communist bloc, with a total foreign trade valued (1965) at about 4,346 million US dollars. Most of this commerce is with other countries of the bloc, and is carried on across the land boundaries of East Germany.

Ports and seaborne commerce. The total commerce passing through East Germany's northern ports is, in terms of value, only a relatively small fraction of the whole. It does, however, include much of the bulky, low value materials and most of the commerce with countries outside Europe and the Soviet Union.

These ports are Wismar, Rostock-Warnemünde and Stralsund. Until recently Wismar handled almost half this trade, but current plans are to develop Rostock as the major port of East Germany. Why, it has been asked, should East Germany make this very great expenditure, when Szczecin is not only already developed, but linked with East Germany by water communications as well as by rail and road? The answer probably lies in the desire of East Germany, like that of other 'satellites', for as full a measure of economic independence as is permissible within the bloc.

The old city of Rostock lies 9 miles from the sea, where the river Warnow widens into its estuary. Its original docks, now old and small, lay close to the walled city. New docks have been constructed close to the sea, a fishing port established on the west shore of the estuary, and manufacturing districts and shipyards laid out along its banks. The choice of Rostock over Wismar or Stralsund as the major port of the Republic probably lies in the superiority of its estaury for the development of the range of those industries which are commonly associated with docks.

Direction of trade. A small part of the commerce with East Germany's neighbours is waterborne. Polish coal is brought by barge down the Oder; some trade between East Germany and Czechoslovakia uses the Elbe, and much of the small volume of generally bulky goods supplied to West Berlin makes it way into the city by barge. The rest of East Germany's foreign trade is carried on by rail or road. Even that with the Soviet Union, the most important trading partner, is by the railway routes across Poland. One significant import from this source, petroleum, has now been removed from the railways, and made to travel by pipeline to its western destination, Schwedt on the Oder.

The volume of East Germany's foreign trade has increased steadily during the past 15 years. Since it has been conducted by a system of barter, there is an approximate equality between the value of exports and imports. Approximately 80 per cent of both exports and imports continue to be with other members of the Communist bloc, and of the rest nearly half is with West Germany and West Berlin, principally the latter.

Table 29. Foreign Trade of the DDR (East Germany) in 1965

	Exports to	Imports from	Total	Percentage of total trade
Soviet Union	1,310·8	1,205·8	2,516·6	42.9
Eastern Europe:				
Poland	269·4	140·2	409·6	6·9
Czechoslovakia	291·9	262·7	554·6	9·4
Hungary	126·6	124·0	250·6	4·2
Romania	67·2	72·7	139·9	2·4
Yugoslavia	60·9	78·3	139·2	2·4
Bulgaria	97·3	93·7	191·0	3·2
Albania	5·2	6·0	11·2	—
Other Communist countries	67·7	63·7	131·4	2·3
Western Europe	529·7	524·6	1,054·3	17·9
Rest of the world	240·0	230·4	470·4	8·0
Total	3,066·7	2,802·1	5,868·8	100

Sources: *Foreign Trade of the European Satellites, in 1965*, Central Intelligence Agency, Washington, DC, 1966.

Among the non-bloc countries, the most important trading partner is Yugoslavia, followed by the Netherlands and Great Britain.

It is difficult to evaluate the relative importance of commodities which enter into this trade, because published statistics are for the weight, volume or even the number of articles. For example, exports in 1963 included 22,432 separate pieces of heavy mechanical equipment (*Schwermaschinenbauerzeugnisse*) and about 1·6 million tons of certain chemical products, but the values of these goods are not published. Although the categories are enumerated, the task of estimating their value would be difficult and perhaps none too accurate. It is evident, however, that the export trade is dominated by machinery and chemicals; that automobiles, electro-technical goods, precision and optical goods and textiles are important, and that fuel, building materials, and electrical energy are of only minor significance and enter principally into trade with West Berlin.

Imports, as might be expected, are dominated by fuel, industrial raw materials and food-stuffs. They include some 12 million tons of coal and coke, mainly from Poland and Czechoslovakia; over a million tons of iron-ore, as well as considerable quantities of the ores of non-ferrous metals. Over 3 million tons of crude petroleum were imported together with smaller quantities of other raw materials of the chemical industries. Raw cotton and wool, leather, pulpwood and lumber, and iron and steel 'semis' made up most of the remaining industrial imports.

Food imports included wheat and other grains, animal and vegetable fats, some fruit and vegetables, tobacco and coffee and cocoa. Purchases have been very sparing of these commodities, such as cotton, coffee and tropical fats and oils, which cannot be obtained easily within the bloc. Industrial technology within East Germany has been adapted to make the maximum use of those raw materials which can be obtained locally, and to cut to a minimum the use of those commodities which must be obtained from hard-currency countries.

CONCLUSION

Comparison between the resources and their development in the two Germany's is inevitable, and in this comparison East Germany always suffers. It is smaller in area; it inherited only about 37 per cent[1] of the industrial capacity of the prewar *Reich*, was subjected to extensive spoilation until 1953, and its population has for two decades been diminishing. West Germany, by contrast, has had a large influx of population of working age and a massive injection of capital and economic aid. Its commercial orientation has not been changed, and it continues to trade on a large scale with those countries which have long been commercial partners of Germany. It would, indeed, have been very surprising if West Germany did not make faster progress

[1] See *Die Volkswirtschaft der DDR*, p. 104, which gives 36·6 per cent. Other sources suggest a somewhat higher figure.

than East. Whether East Germany would have fared better under a different economic and social system is an academic question. The continued existence of East Germany is predicated upon the system which we now find there.

West Germany had regained its prewar level of production before 1950, whereas East Germany did not reach this level until about 1953. By 1957, West Germany had twice the productivity of the same area in 1936; East Germany had increased by only 27 per cent. In only one sector, mining, did the rate of progress in East Germany greatly exceed that in West. This is indicative of the East German position. Given the fact that the political situation made it impossible to draw raw materials from the West, East Germany has had to adapt its industrial structure to a wide use of substitutes: coke from brown coal, very low-grade iron ores, synthetic fibres, synthetic oils and petroleum fuels. These alternatives have required costly installations for their manufacture, and have not always been the most satisfactory substitutes. East Germany has furthermore chosen to establish industries and installations—of which the port of Rostock might serve as an example—which more friendly cooperation with its neighbours would have rendered unnecessary.

And yet East Germany is a great deal more than the rather shabby sister of West Germany. By any measure, other than that of West Germany itself, its capital investment would be creditable, if not impressive. One can only judge its performance within the limits set by its political system and orientation, and here it has had the fastest growing economy within the group of East European nations.

WEST BERLIN

The Western sectors of the city of Berlin cover an area of 157 square miles. They still constitute, as they did in the summer of 1945, the areas of the city allocated respectively to the American, British and French forces for occupation. The establishment of a city government for West Berlin, and the growing integration of its economy with that of West Germany does not alter this situation. West Berlin may be for practical purposes an outlier of the Federal Republic, but it lies deep in the Soviet Zone, is not in all respects a part of West Germany, and must therefore be examined in this chapter.

The location of Berlin has already been discussed. The old city (*Altstadt*) lies wholly within East Berlin, and West Berlin is made up of the western 'districts' of Reinickendorf Wedding, Tiergarten, Charlottenburg, Spandau, Wilmersdorf, Zehlendorf, Steglitz, Schöneberg, Kreuzberg, Templehof and Neukölln. Its population has remained fairly constant at about 2,200,000 (see Fig. 7.9), but it is an ageing population, its younger members tending to leave for West Germany, and it is one in which women outnumber men by 1·34 to one.

The territory of West Berlin is almost without natural resources which might support or employ its population. Areas which are not built up, such as Grunewald Forest, have little agricultural value and serve, in fact, as recreational areas for the West Berlin population. The very small area in which vegetables are grown contributes little to the food supply. Nor does the area contribute industrial raw materials except water and sand which can be used in concrete. The industrially employed population must therefore use materials that are imported into the city. Most come from the Federal Republic, and goods produced in West Berlin must be marketed in West Germany.

This of course places a very heavy strain on the transport facilities and adds appreciably to the overall cost of manufacture. The high cost of the products of West Berlin is part of the price which West Germany pays—on the whole willingly—to maintain the present status of the

Table 30. *Goods to and from West Berlin in 1962*
(in millions of D Marks)

	Imports from West Berlin	Exports to West Berlin
West Germany	6,817	7,741
Foreign countries	1,106	904
East Germany	64	165
	7,987	8,810

Source: K. H. Meyer, in *Geogr. Rdsch.*, **16** (1964), 133.

city. West Berlin has always had an adverse balance of trade. In 1962 the value of goods moving to and leaving West Berlin can be seen in Table 30. Trade with the Zone in which it lies thus accounts for only about 1 per cent of the total trade of West Berlin.

Over 40 per cent of the population of West Berlin was employed in the summer of 1963. The small number of unemployed were said to have been greatly outnumbered by that of unfilled positions. Of the total number of employed persons, about 897,000, slightly more than half, were engaged in handicrafts, manufacturing, or the provision of public services. Of these the industrially employed constituted by far the largest category. Some 13 per cent were engaged in commerce, and nearly 20 per cent in public service, such as teaching, and in public administration. The remainder worked in the transport services, banks, insurance and shops.

The obligation to import all industrial raw materials from the West has placed severe limitations on the range of industry that can be established. West Berlin's industries are therefore 'light', and in general the labour input is very high in relation to the value of the raw material used. Electrical engineering, long a speciality of Berlin, still leads among the industries of West Berlin.

Bibliography

General

Atlas Östliches Mitteleuropa, Bielefeld, 1959.

CASTELLAN, GEORGES, *La République Démocratique Allemande*. Paris, Presses Universitaires de France, 1961.

Das Ostliches Deutschland, Göttinger Arbeitskrein, Würzburg, 1959.

DICKINSON, ROBERT E. *Germany: A General and Regional Geography*, London, Methuen, 1953.

— *The Regions of Germany*, London, 1945; Kegan Paul, Trench, Trubner.

— *The German Lebensraum*, Harmondsworth, Penguin Books, 1943.

ELKINS, T. H. *Germany*. London, Chatto & Windus, 1960.

MCINNIS, EDGAR, RICHARD HISCOCKS, ROBERT SPENCER. *Shaping of Postwar Germany*. London, Dent, 1960.

POUNDS, NORMAN J. G. *Divided Germany and Berlin*. London, Van Nostrand, 1962.

PRITTIE, TERENCE, *Germany Divided*, Boston, Little, Brown and Co., 1960.

ROBSON, CHARLES B. *Berlin, Pivot of German Destiny*. University of North Carolina Press, 1960.

Statistisches Jahrbuch der Deutschen Demokratischen Republik. Berlin, published annually.

U.S. Army Area Handbook for Germany, 2nd edn. Washington, D.C. US Department of the Army, 1960.

Physical Geography

BRAUN, GUSTAV, *Deutschland*, Berlin, 1936.

GELLERT, JOHANNES F. 'Études récentes de morphologie glaciaire dans la plaine de l'Allemagne du Nord entre Elbe et Oder', *Annls Géogr.* **72**, 1963, 410–25.

GELLERT, JOHANNES F. *Grundzüge der Physischen Geographie von Deutschland*, Deutsch. Verlag d. Wissen., Berlin, 1958, **1.** Geologische Struktur und Oberflachen-gestaltung.

HAEFKE, FRITZ, *Physische Geographie Deutschlands.* Deutsch. Verlag d. Wissen. Berlin 1959.

HURTIG, THEODOR, *Physische Geographie von Mecklenburg*, Deutsch. Verlag d. Wissen. Berlin, 1957.

HELLMANN, G. *Klima-Atlas von Deutschland*, Berlin, 1921.

Klima-Atlas für das Gebeit der Deutschen Demokratischen Republik, Akademie-Verlag, Berlin, 1953.

SCHULTZE, JOACHIM H. *Die Naturbedingten Landschaften der Deutschen Demokratischen Republik*, Geographisch-Kartographische Anstalt, Gotha, 1955.

— Die Bodenerosion in Thüringen, *Petermanns Geogr. Mitt.*, Erganzungsheft 247, Gotha, 1952.

WALDBAUR, H. *Landformen in Mittleren Europa, Wissenschaftlischen Veröffentlichungen des Deutschen Instituts für Länderkunde*, N.F. Band 15/16, Beilage 1.

Economic Geography

Agrar-Atlas über das Gebiet der Deutschen Demokratischen Republik. Deutsche Akademie der Landwirtschaftswissenschaften zu Berlin, Gotha, 1956.

BARTHEL, HELLMUTH, Braunkohlenbergbau and Landschaftdynamik, *Petermanns Geogr. Mitt.*, Erganzungsheft 270, Gotha, 1962.

BURGER, KLAUS, 'Die Entwicklung der Bevolkerung von Gera', *Geogr. Ber.* **5** (1960), 228–45.

BLECKERT, HEINZ, 'Daten zur Fischwirtschaft der Deutschen Demokratischen Republik', *Geogr. Ber.* (1959), 112–19.

CASTELLAN, GEORGES, *La République Democratique Allemande.* Paris, Presses Universitaires de France (1961).

292   *East Germany*

CLOZIER, RENÉ, *L'Economie de l'Europe Centrale Germanique*, Paris Presses Universitaires de France (1947).

ELKINS, T. H. 'East Germany's Changing Brown Coal Industry', *Geography* 41 (1956), 192–5.

— 'The Brown Coal Industry of Germany', *Geography*, 38 (1953).

— 'The Central German Chemical Industry', *Geography*, 42 (1957), 183.

— 'East Germany's New Industrial Plan', *Geography*, 45 (1960), 217–20.

HARTSCH, ERWIN, 'Die Stadt Dresden seit 1945', *Geogr. Ber.*, 7 (1962), 270–8.

VON KANEL, ALFRED, 'Arbeiterpendelwanderungen im östlichen Bezirk Rostock', *Geogr. Ber.* 8 (1963), 10–25.

KOHL, HORST, 'Standortprobleme der Kaliindustrie der Deutschen Demokratischen Republik', *Petermanns Mitt.*, 108 (1964), 85–90.

— *Okonomische Geographie der Montanindustrie in der Deutschen Demokratischen Republik*, Gotha, 1966.

KRAMER, MATTHIAS, *Die Landwirtschaft in der Sowjetischen Besatzungszone*, Bonner Berichte aus Mittel - und Ostdeutschland, Bonn 1957.

MAY, JACQUES M. *The Ecology of Malnutrition in Five Countries of Eastern and Central Europe*, New York and London, Hafner, 1964.

MENDERSHAUSEN, HORST, *Agriculture in Communist Germany*, The Rand Corporation, Santa Monica, Calif., Rand Corporation, 1958.

MERKEL, KONRAD and EDUARD SCHUHANS, *Die Agrarwirtschaft in Mitteldeutschland*, Bonner Berichte aus Mittel - und Ostdeutschland, Bonn, 1960.

MEYER, KARL-HEINZ, 'Die Entwicklung der Wirtschaft West-Berlins', *Geogr. Rdsch.*, 16 (1964), 331–6.

MOHS, GERHARD, *Die Industrie im Bezirk Frankfurt (Oder)*, Deutsch. Verlag d. Wissen. Berlin, 1962.

RAUS, OTTO and SIEGFRIED FREYTAG, *Deutsche Demokratische Republik: politisch-okonomisch-geographische Ubersicht*, Berlin (East), 1961.

'Rostock: Notes d'Excursion', *Annls Géogr.*, 69 (1960), 15–21.

ROUBITSCHEK, WALTER, 'Die regionale Struktur der pflanzlichen Bruttoproduktion in der Deutschen Demokratischen Republik 1955 und ihre Veränderung gegenüber 1935', *Petermanns Mitt.*, 108 (1964), 69–78.

— 'Die regionale Differenzierung der agraren Bodennutzung 1935 im heutigen Gebiet der Deutschen Demokratischen Republik', *Petermanns Mitt.*, **103** (1959), 190–7.

SCHMIDT-RENNER, GERHARD, ed., *Wirtschaftsterritorium Deutsche Demokratische Republik*, Berlin (East), 1962.

SCHOLZ, DIETER, 'Johanngeorgenstadt: Eine stadtgeographische Skizze', *Geogr. Ber.*, **5** (1960), 246–58.

— 'Kleinindustrie und Verkehr in Ilmenau', *Geogr. Ber.* **8** (1963), 284–98.

SINNHUBER, KARL A. 'Eisenhüttenstadt and Other New Industrial Locations in East Germany', *Festschrift Leopold G. Scheidl zum 60. Gerburtstag*, Vienna, 1965, 328–48.

Die Volkswirtschaft der Deutschen Demokratischen Republik, Berlin, 1960.

SMOTKINE, HENRI, 'Les caractères originaux de la sidérurgie en République Démocratique Allemande', *Annls Géogr.* **70** (1961), 126–36.

STOLPER, WOLFGANG F. *The Structure of the East German Economy*, Harvard University Press, 1960.

THALHEIM, KARL C. 'The Development of the East German Economy in the Framework of the Soviet Bloc', *Eastern Europe in Transition*, ed. Kurt London, Baltimore, Johns Hopkins Press, 1966, 145–71.

WEIGT, ERNST, ed., *Wirtschaftsgeographischer Wandel in Deutschland*, Nürnberg (1957).

— 'Un type de complexe industriel: le district de Karl-Marx-Stadt en République Démocratique Allemande', *Annls Géogr.*, **76** (1967), 152–67.

Berlin

BAYNE, E. A. *Berlin and the Wall*, American Universities Field Staff, West European Service, **2**, No. 1, 1963.

ELKINS, T. H. 'West and East Berlin in 1959', *Geography*, **44** (1959), 268–71.

— *Germany*, London, Christophers, 1960.

MEYER, KARL-HEINZ, 'Die Entwicklung der Wirtschaft West-Berlins', *Geogr. Rdsch.* **16** (1964), 331–6.

PATERSON, JOHN H. 'Berlin in 1955', *Geography*, **41** (1956), 59–61.

ROBINSON, G. W. S., 'West Berlin: the Geography of an Exclave', *Geogrl Rev.*, **43** (1953), 540–57.

ROBSON, CHARLES B., ed., *Berlin, Pivot of German Destiny,* University of North Carolina Press, 1960.

Statistisches Jahrbuch Berlin, 1966, West Berlin, 1967.

STEPHAN, H. 'Rebuilding Berlin', *The Town Planning Review,* 29 (1959), 207–26.

STRASZEWICZ, LUDWIK, 'Aglomeracja Berlina', *Przegl. Geogr.,* 38 (1966), 77–105.

ZIMM, ALFRED, 'Die Veranderungen des Standortes West Berlin nach der Spaltung von Gross-Berlin', *Geogr. Ber.,* 4 (1959), 196–206.

CHAPTER EIGHT

Poland

Poland presents a section across the largest of the landform regions into which Eastern Europe has been divided—the North European Plain. This plain, bordered on the north by the Baltic Sea and on the south by the Bohemian and Carpathian Mountains, broadens eastward from Germany until it merges into the great plains of Russia. Between these limits to north and south the fortunes of Poland have fluctuated. In the tenth century of our era the western border of Poland ran approximately along the lower course of the Oder, and the eastern followed an indeterminate course east of the Vistula through the forests, the swamps and the steppe, from the line of the Carpathian Mountains northward to the lands of the ancient Baltic peoples.

THE POLISH STATE

During the following centuries, Poland lost territory on the west, when German settlers and the sovereignty of the German states extended beyond the Oder. At the same time Poland gained more in the east than was lost in the west. The boundary of Poland was advanced first by conquest and then by the political union with Lithuania and by settlement in the forests of White Russia and the grasslands of the Ukraine. The territory ruled by the Polish kings was almost doubled when Jagiełło, Duke of Lithuania succeeded to the Polish crown. The union of Poland and Lithuania was from 1386 until 1568 a personal one only, the two states sharing the same ruler, but not also the same agencies of government. In the latter year the Union of Lublin, by merging their more important institutions of government created a more nearly unified state, the largest that Europe has known west of the Russian or Soviet border.

The partitions
The Polish state was unquestionably over-extended; its peoples were too diverse; its elected king, too weak to administer, least of all to

defend this vast, inchoate 'republic', *rzeczpospolita*, as the Poles described it. Indeed, Poland could hold this sprawling area only as long as Germany to the west was politically divided, Austria to the south was busy with her Turkish enemies in the Balkans, and the Russia of the Tsars, weak and backward. Toward the end of the seventeenth century this situation began to change. Prussian pressure intensified to the west and north-west, and the Tsars began to nibble at the vast, amorphous mass of Poland. During the eighteenth century, the internal political structure of Poland weakened still further while Poland's neighbours, Prussia, Russia and Austria, moved from strength to strength.

Between 1772 and 1796 Poland's neighbours gathered no less than three times to feed corporately on the body of Poland, until by 1796 nothing remained. As a political entity Poland disappeared from the European map, where it had held an honoured as well as conspicuous position for over eight hundred years.

A Polish state, known as the Grand Duchy of Warsaw, was re-created by Napoleon. It was never more than a puppet and served only as a gesture to the Poles whose help he hoped to enlist in his war with Russia. Territorially it was merely a fragment of the area which the Poles could justifiably regard as theirs. With Napoleon's defeat and the restoration of Europe's dynasties to their ancient territories and possessions, even this emaciated ghost of the earlier Poland disappeared into the empire of the Russian Tsars. It is true that its status was legally independent, that the Tsar was titular king of Poland, with a government in Warsaw separate from that of Moscow. It is true too that this government showed a remarkable independence of action, and for a few years planned ambitiously for an industrial future for Poland. But Russian oppression and Polish intransigence combined to frustrate these plans. The Polish Rising of November 1830 was suppressed by the Russians, and two years later the Polish constitution, and with it Poland's titular independence, was suspended. Poland again disappeared from the map of Europe, to be revived only by the military defeat of its neighbours in 1918.

Modern Poland

The circumstances under which the Polish state was re-established have already been discussed (see page 99). Its boundaries were defined, as far as this was possible, by the treaties of peace between the wartime Allies and the defeated German and Austrian empires. The allied statesmen attempted the impossible task of separating Poles from Germans by means of a linear boundary. The line which they drew may have been, as Morrow claimed, the best that human ingenuity could devise, but this neither satisfied the extreme claims of the Poles nor reconciled the Germans to the loss of their former territories.

The two peoples were inextricably mixed along the whole course of the boundary, but nowhere were their geographical relationships as involved as in Upper Silesia and the Danzig region. After a period of international occupation and two civil wars, separated by a plebiscite, the industrial region of Upper Silesia was partitioned in a manner that did the greatest violence to the economic structure of the region and paid but little regard to its ethnic composition. So drastic was the division of Upper Silesia, that the services of an International Mixed Commission were necessary to restore some functional unity to the area which had been divided politically.

The future of the Danzig region had been compromised in advance by the declaration of Woodrow Wilson, in January 1918, that the future Polish state should have a 'free and secure access to the sea'. This, coupled with the fact that the area lying to the south of Danzig was ethnically mixed and in some parts predominantly Polish, led to the creation of Poland's so-called 'corridor' to the sea. However well founded Poland's claim to the 'corridor' might be, her title to the port of Danzig which lay upon its northern coast could be based only on economic necessity.

The city of Danzig at this time had a population over 95 per cent German. To hand about 250,000 Germans over to Polish rule because Poland needed their docks and the labour which they provided seemed to be a violation of the national rights which the Allied leaders were pledged to support. To deny to Poland the unrestricted use of a port which they regarded as necessary for her economic welfare was no less unreasonable. The solution was to convert the city of Danzig and its environs into a Free City with an area of 731 square miles. Its city government was to be conducted under the supervision of a High Commissioner nominated by the League of Nations. At the same time the Free City was to be in customs union with Poland, so that there might be no restrictions on Poland's use of the port for her foreign commerce.

It did not lie within the competence of the allies to delimit the boundary between the new Polish state and the Soviet Union, which at the time was in the throes of its own internal revolution. The Allies might only suggest and advise; the Poles decided the question by the arbitrament of war. A line which approximated the ethnic boundary between the Poles and the Byelorussians and Ukrainians was proposed, and has ever since been known as the 'Curzon Line'. It was rejected by the Russians and never accepted by the Poles, who succeeded in rolling back the Red Army and establishing their boundary almost 150 miles farther to the east.

The Fourth Partition. For almost 20 years these territorial problems continued to rankle. In the west the Germans resented Polish occupation of the 'corridor' and of much of the Upper Silesian industrial region; in the east, the Poles had to contend with a disaffected Ukrainian and Byelorussian minority and with a hostile Lithuania. The Ribbentrop–Molotov Agreement of August 1939 proposed to divide Poland into a German and a Soviet sphere along a line that accorded roughly with the eastern boundary of Polish settlement. A Polish minority of over four million was left in the Soviet Union, and a very much smaller Byelorussian and Ukrainian minority remained to the west of the line. This new boundary was established after the conclusion of the military campaign of September 1939, and with only small modifications, continues to serve as the Polish–Soviet boundary. All Polish territory lying west of this newly established boundary was either absorbed into the German Reich or erected into the puppet *General Gouvernement* of Poland.

Many of the discussions at the inter-allied wartime conferences were dominated by the Polish question. It soon became apparent that the Soviet Union had no intention of voluntarily relinquishing any of the territories which it had acquired in 1939, nor was it possible to advance any compelling reasons why the Soviet Union should be asked to restore to Poland the predominantly non-Polish territories which it had gained.

The Oder–Neisse Line. Churchill claimed credit for suggesting that Poland might be compensated at Germany's expense for her losses in the east. This was at the Teheran Conference (November 1943). 'Personally,' he wrote, 'I thought Poland might move westward, like soldiers taking two steps "left close". If Poland trod on some German toes that could not be helped, but there must be a strong Poland.'[1] It may not have been anticipated that Poland would step on six million toes, nor that the 'strong Poland' would add its strength to that of the Soviet bloc.

[1] Winston S. Churchill, *The Second World War*, Cassell, 1952, vol. 5, p. 319.

The line of the lower river Oder (Odra), continued by that of the Neisse (Nysa), was proposed as the future western boundary of the Polish state. The argument that it had been approximately the boundary of tenth-century Poland probably had no significance, although it has since been much used in justification of Polish occupation of her 'recovered territories'. More important probably was the fact that these rivers were conspicuous features of the map and seemed to delimit a suitable area to be given to Poland as compensation for her losses to the Soviet Union. Churchill pointed out that 'the value of the German land was much greater than the Pripet Marshes. It was industrial and it would make a much better Poland. We should like to be able to say to the Poles that the Russians were right, and to tell the Poles that they must agree that they had had a fair deal'.[1] Despite Churchill's geographical errors and misconceptions, his argument was substantially correct. Poland lost about a quarter of her forest and wheat acreage and small proportions of her rye and potato lands, but gained about three times as much capital investment as she lost.[2] Ties of sentiment aside, in terms of resources and land values, the Poles would profit greatly in terms of industrial resources, but lose considerably in agricultural.

The Yalta Conference (January–February 1945) clarified the issue. The protocol of the conference declared its agreement 'that the Eastern frontier (i.e. boundary) of Poland should follow the Curzon Line with digressions from it in some regions of five to eight kilometres in favour of Poland. They recognise that Poland must receive substantial accessions of territory in the North and West',[3] but they agreed also that the precise extent of this territory should be determined later. This was done at the Potsdam Conference (August 1945). Not without some misgivings on the part of the western representatives, it was decided that

> pending the final determination of Poland's western frontier, the former German territories east of a line running from the Baltic Sea immediately to the west of Swinemunde, and thence along the Oder River to the confluence of the western Neisse River and along the western Neisse to the Czechoslovak frontier, including that portion of East Prussia not placed under the administration of the

[1] *Ibid.*, 350.
[2] Stanisław Leszczycki, 'The Geographical Bases of Contemporary Poland', *Journal of Central European Affairs*, 7 (1948), 357–73.
[3] Herbert Feis, *Between War and Peace: The Potsdam Conference*, Princeton University Press, 1960, p. 32.

Union of Soviet Socialist Republics in accordance with the understanding reached at this conference and including the area of the former Free City of Danzig, shall be under the administration of the Polish State.[1]

The boundary thus delimited has continued to separate Poland from East Germany, excepting only in the Szczecin (Stettin) area, where the city, which lies on the west bank of the river, together with its immediate environs, also passed under Polish occupation.

By the terms of the Potsdam Agreement, these former German territories are only under Polish administration, which could be terminated or modified by a treaty of peace between the Allies and a united Germany. The Soviet bloc countries have recognised Polish sovereignty over this territory, thus denying, in effect, that it is susceptible to review at any future peace conference. The Western Powers have given no formal recognition, though all must recognise that no change in the administrative boundaries of Poland is likely, and both France and Great Britain have informally recognised this fact.

LANDFORM REGIONS

Almost the whole of the present territory of Poland was glaciated during the Quaternary Ice Age, either by the ice sheets which moved southward from Scandinavia or by the valley glaciers which extended from the Tatra Mountains in the south. A long period of time separated the earlier from the later advances of the ice, during which the forces of denudation were active. The earlier advances of the ice covered most of the country, advancing during the Mindel phase as far as the foot-hills of the Sudety and the Carpathian Mountains. The later advances extended less far. The Middle Polish or Riss glaciation covered almost three-quarters of the country, reaching roughly to Upper Silesia, Kielce and Lublin. The last major advance—the Würm or Weichsel—was less extensive, and the most recent evidences of glaciation—the great moraine belts of northern Poland—were produced during temporary halts in the final retreat and disappearance of the ice. The map, Fig. 8.1, and the diagram, Fig. 8.2, illustrate both the extent of the several advances of the ice and the accumulation of end-moraine during pauses in its retreat.

[1] Cmnd 1552. *Select Documents on Germany and the Question of Berlin*, H.M.S.O., 1961, 57.

Warsaw, as seen from the summit of the Palace of Culture. The Old City lies on rising ground to the right of centre; beyond it is the Vistula

POLAND

Warsaw: The rebuilt Płac Zamky (Castle Square). In the background is the roofline of the cathedral of Warsaw, and in the middle distance, the column of King Zygmunt III, who in 1596 removed the capital from Kraków to Warsaw

A small town market, Piaseczno, to the south of Warsaw. Note that old car wheels and tyres are commonly used on peasant carts

Village in Central Poland, between Częstochowa and Kielce

The Swiętokrzyskie Góry (Holy Cross Mountains) to the west of Kielce. The ridge consists generally of hard quartzite and intrusive rocks; the surrounding lower country of softer Palaeozoic beds

A textile factory in Łódż Poland. Most of the factorie were built in the late nine teenth century

The earliest advance of the ice took place approximately a million years ago, and for almost as long a period of time, the boulder clay and the terminal moraine which it deposited have been exposed to weathering and denudation. In much of southern Poland, which was affected by this glaciation alone, the cover of glacial deposits has been reduced

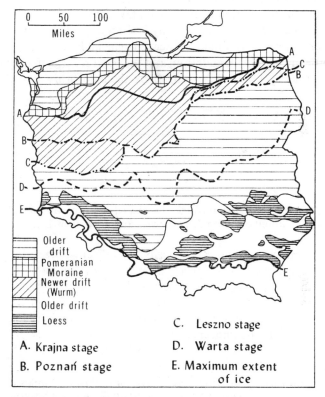

Fig. 8.1. Stages in the glaciation of Poland. After S. Lencewicz *Geografia Fiziczna Polski*, Warsaw, 1955.

to a few patches of boulder clay and a handful of erratics, too large to be decomposed and removed in this period of time. Farther to the north, the accumulation of glacial deposits was thicker, and since they were laid down more recently, there has been less time for their denudation. In consequence, the spread of boulder clay is more continuous, and its surface is still marked by traces of terminal moraine, which generally constitute the most significant elevations in

11

this plain, and by drumlins, lakes and patches of sand and gravel, spread by the melt-water as it escaped from the ice.

In the extreme north, the moraines, the drumlins, the aprons of outwash and the hundreds of small lakes look so fresh and new, that it appears as if the ice melted away from this region only yesterday. The phases of the glaciation of Poland and the consequent degree of freshness or denudation of the glacial landforms provide a basis for dividing the region into major physical regions. These are three in number: (1) northern Poland, where the glacial landforms have been but little affected by denudation, and the local relief is in many areas quite strong; (2) central Poland, where the landforms, though made

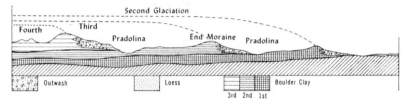

Fig. 8.2. A cross-section through the glacial deposits of Poland, highly simplified. After J. Lencewicz and J. Kostrowicki.

up predominantly of glacial deposits, have been subjected to a very much longer period of erosion and have in consequence a more mature appearance, and lastly (3) southern Poland, where a more complex relief has resulted from the almost complete stripping of the glacial deposits and the exposure of underlying rocks, ranging in age from the Cambrian to the Pliocene.

Northern Poland
This region forms a curving belt of territory, about 80 miles in width, lying more or less parallel with the Baltic Sea, with which it is genetically connected. Its dominant feature is the great end-moraine, commonly known as the Great Baltic or Pomeranian moraine, which marked a prolonged pause in the retreat of the ice from its last significant advance during the Quaternary period. On its southern, or outer face, the moraine drops—locally quite steeply—toward the lowland traced out by the rivers Narew, Vistula (Wisła), Noteć and Warta. To the north, it slopes more gently to a flat coastal plain.

Coastal plain. This is a narrow, low-lying region, created—or at least greatly modified—since the disappearance of the ice from the clays and sands borne northward from the moraine by the many small streams which discharge into the Baltic Sea. Its almost level surface is occasionally interrupted by fragments of moraine and by less frequent outcroppings of the underlying Cretaceous and Tertiary beds. The coast has been smoothed by the eastward flow of the Baltic current. Former bays and estuaries have been closed, and a series of lakes and lagoons has been formed. The largest of these, Lake Łebsko, has an area of 29 square miles, and Jamno, Bukowo and Gardno are each of over 7 square miles. In a few places the coast is formed by low cliffs, cut into the boulder clay or into the underlying 'solid' rock. More often it is backed by towering sand dunes, formed where the wind has piled up the sand washed from the boulder clay by the action of the sea. Marshes lie behind the coast for much of its length, perpetuated, despite attempts to reclaim and settle them, by the tendency of the whole of this coastal region to sink very slowly in relation to the sea.

The coastal plain is distinguished by the mildest winters and the coolest summers experienced in the Polish Plain (Figs. 8.5a and 8.5b). It also receives the heaviest rainfall known outside the mountain region in the south of the country. It is a region noted more for its meadows and its dairy farming than for its crops; for small and thinly scattered hamlets, than for large agricultural villages. Its soils are poor. Large areas are sandy and infertile; others are made up of clay, heavy and difficult to cultivate, or of peat deposits, potentially fertile if only they can be drained. It is a thinly peopled region, with no large cities, except Szczecin and the Gdańsk-Gdynia complex, which are, in fact, marginal to it, and but few small towns. Largest of these are Koszalin (*G.* Koslin) and Słupsk (*G.* Stolp), each lying from 10 to 15 miles inland from the straight and inhospitable coast. Few settlements lie on the shore of the Baltic where their chances of developing a port or even a small fishing industry would seem to be small. Indeed, in the 180 miles which separate the mouth of the Odra from the Bay of Gdańsk, there are only three small harbours—Kołobrzeg (*G.* Kolberg), Darłowo and Ustka, each with a small sea-fishery and a quite negligible coasting trade. Kołobrzeg is being developed as a seaside resort.

The regularity and monotony of Poland's Baltic coast is interrupted at its western and eastern extremities by the mouths of the Odra and Vistula. Both rivers have cut wide, flat-floored valleys across the end-moraine, and as they enter the coastal plain, they divide into distributaries and make their way to the sea. The Odra never forms a distinct delta. Instead, the many channels which make up its lower course discharge into the Bay of Szczecin or Zalew Szczeciński. This is, in fact, an incipient delta, and is cut off from the sea by the irregularly shaped islands of Uznam (Usedom) and Wolin (Wollin), separated from one another by a narrow channel, the Swina, which ranks as the main outlet of the Odra. Wolin lies within Poland, together with enough of Uznam to place the Swina Channel securely under Polish

Fig. 8.3. Landform regions of Poland. Adapted from J. Lencewicz, J. Kostrowicki and S. Jarosz (see bibliography).

control. The Bay of Szczecin is extremely shallow, and the ship channel through it to the port of Szczecin has to be kept clear by dredging.

About 200 miles to the east is the Bay of Gdańsk or Zatoka Gdańska, which remains from a former extension of the sea up the valley of the lower Vistula. This river, the longest in Poland and the largest in its volume of discharge, has created a true delta, which extends 35 miles from the point where the river divides, to the sea, and considerably more along the coast from the most easterly to the most westerly branch of the river. The margin of the delta is formed by the low, but steep bluffs which lie behind Tczew and Gdańsk on the west, and Malbork and Elbląg on the east. The whole region is flat, low-lying and liable to flooding. The dykes and drainage works which protect its low-lying meadows were severely damaged during the German retreat in 1944, and it was many years before the area was

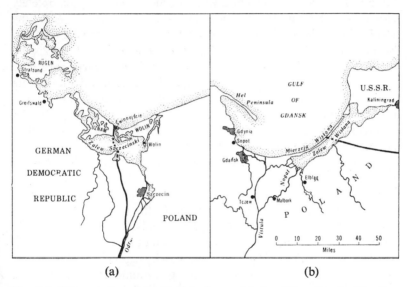

(a)   (b)

Fig. 8.4. The mouths of the Polish rivers: (a) the Odra, (b) the Vistula.

again reclaimed for agricultural use. Today its extensive fields are cut up by drainage ditches and grazed by cattle and sheep. There are few settlements in the area, and those who farm this area live mostly in villages on the higher ground which borders it to east and west.

There have been conspicuous changes in the coastline of the Vistula within the historical period, and even within the last century. The chief branches are the Vistula itself and the more easterly branch, the Nogat, on the banks of which the Teutonic Knights built their enormous fortress of Marienburg or Malbork. The Vistula channel divides about 35 miles from the sea into the more easterly Elbląg

Vistula (Wisła Elbląska) and the more westerly channel, partly artificial, on which the medieval port of Gdańsk was built. During the nineteenth century this more westerly branch abandoned much of its course, opening up shorter cuts to the sea (Fig. 8.4). The city of Gdańsk now stands beside the still waters of the Motława, a branch of the Martwa Wisła—the 'Dead Vistula'.

The eastward run of the surface currents of the Baltic Sea has not only smoothed the coastline, but drawn out spits of sand and shingle across each embayment of the coast. The Bay of Gdańsk itself is too large to have been either filled with deltaic deposits or completely closed by such a spit. Its entrance is, however, partially barred by the Hel Peninsula, built of materials eroded from the coast to the west and borne eastward by wave action. On the eastern margin of the Vistula delta, another spit, the Mierzeja Wiślana (Frische Nehrung) reaches north-eastward for 40 miles from the delta, cutting off the Vistula Lagoon (*P*. Zalew Wiślany; *G*. Frisches Haff) from the sea and extending deeply into Soviet territory. Indeed, the spit and the Soviet border together cut off the small port of Elbląg from access to the sea and its commerce is now of negligible importance.

Great Baltic end-moraine. Immediately to the south of the coastal plain lies the belt of moraines which extends westward through Mecklenburg and into Denmark, and north-eastward across Lithuania. The Great Baltic end-moraine marks the Pomeranian phase in the retreat of the ice after its last (Würm) advance. It is made up in reality of a large number of small, discontinuous belts of moraine, set one behind the other and giving a hummocky aspect to the landscape. Along the southern face of most of these morainic ridges lie banks of sand and gravel outwash. Between them lie lakes, some large and irregular in shape, where natural drainage has been impeded by the morainic ridges; others narrow and elongated, where channels have been gouged out by the rush of melt-water, and yet others small and shallow, mere dimples, produced by the slow melting of masses of dead ice left buried in the moraine. By and large, the landforms of the moraine belt are as they were shaped by the ice. Too short a time has elapsed for them to have been greatly modified by erosion. Very slowly the lakes are being filled with peat and clay. Many have been transformed into marshy hollows or small peat-bogs.

To the north, on the inner side of the moraines, is a region of boulder clay, strewn with small hills, the relics of drumlins and eskers, and with morainic fragments, representing momentary pauses in the glacial retreat. To the south, the aprons of outwash reach down to the great valleys which bordered each of the major pauses in the glacial retreat. Toward the north the coarser materials, the gravel and sand, were laid down by the escaping meltwater, but toward the south these deposits become progressively finer until they merge into the clays of the great river valleys.

This is a poor and beautiful region. Its soils are either heavy, ill-drained clays or light and sterile sands, the one difficult to cultivate and the other not worth the trouble of ploughing. Meadow and grazing land alternates with forest and woodland. Water is rarely out of sight, either large, irregular lakes, with wooded peninsulas and islands, which make the Masurian and Pomeranian lake regions one of the most frequented resort areas in Poland, or small ponds which reflect the dark pine trees and the lighter green of the beeches.

The end-moraine country is divided into segments by the valleys of the Odra, the Vistula and the Niemen, which all rise to the south of it and flow across it to the sea. These rivers, at least in those parts of their courses which lie across the end-moraines, were formed after the retreat of the ice. They represent the enlargement of rivers which formerly originated in the moraines, but which cut back to the south to tap the great river valleys which lay beyond. This explains the youthful appearance of the Vistula valley between Bydgoszcz and the delta, and of the Odra valley below Kostrzyn.

The Niemen is no longer a Polish river. Today only a few of its minor tributaries rise within the borders of Poland, and are linked by way of the Narew *pradolina* with the Vistula. The Polish end-moraine region is divided into two almost equal parts by the valley of the Vistula. To the west is Pomerania (*P.* Pomorze; *G.* Pommern), extending to the Odra; to the east is Masuria (*P.* Mazury; *G.* Masurien). It is indicative of the dominant features of this landscape that the Polish nomenclature emphasises, not the moraine, but the intervening lakes. The regions lying west and east of the Vistula are known respectively as Pojezierze Pomorskie and Pojezierze Mazurskie—the Pomeranian and Masurian *Lake* Country. It has been estimated that in the Pomeranian Lake Country there are no less than 4,129 lakes, each of over 1 hectare (about 2·5 acres) in area, and in the Masurian region over 2,700. The largest of the Masurian Lakes, Mamry and Śniardwy, are each over 38·6 square miles (over 100 square kilometres) in area. Most of the lakes are drained southward to the line of the Narew, Vistula and Noteć. Some are interconnected by small rivers much frequented in summer by those who spend their vacations canoeing and camping. In a few instances the drainage is indeterminate, with the north-flowing rivers slowly gaining the ascendancy over those discharging to the south.

The summits of the morainic ridges generally approach and often surpass heights of 650 feet. In a few areas they exceed 980 feet. The highest point in the whole region is Wieżyca, 1,079 feet, lying 22 miles to the south-west of Gdańsk. In the Masurian region, Dylewska Góra, 27 miles south-west of Olsztyn, reaches 1,023 feet, and the Szeskie Góry, near Gołdap, in the extreme north-east of the state, 1,014 feet.

The end-moraine region is one of the most thickly wooded and least populous regions of Poland. No part of the country, except the marshes and forests along the Soviet border has so few and such small towns. No area is as lightly industrialised, or as heavily dependent upon the lumber and woodworking industries. Settlements are few, small and widely scattered, each merely a string of cottages along a road, set in a clearing in the woodland.

Great Poland. The conspicuous moraines of Pomerania and Masuria belong to phases or prolonged pauses in the retreat of the ice sheet from its maximum extent during the last, or Würm glaciation. As the ice withdrew, its speed of regression became faster in north-western than in north-eastern Poland. The end-moraine which marked the limit of the ice during the Würm extended from near Suwałki, in north-eastern Poland down to the Vistula near Płock, and from here in a generally westerly direction through Konin, Leszno and Zielona Góra, to the Odra (Fig. 8.1). West of Płock the ice withdrew quickly. It built up fragmentary end-moraines, like the hills to the north of Poznań or the ridge which gave its name to Zielona Góra, but did not halt sufficiently long for vast spreads of sand and gravel to accumulate. Not until the Pomeranian phase did the ice sheet again pause sufficiently to build up a vast, wall-like moraine, with an even more extensive *glacis* of outwash gravels banked up against it. The consequence is that the region bounded on the north by the great valley from Toruń, through Bydgoszcz to Kostrzyn on the Odra, and on the south by the Würm end-moraine, is a fresh boulder clay plain, pitted by small depressions, mostly occupied by lakes, and interrupted by fragments of end-moraine.

This region, furthermore, is traversed and bounded by great valleys excavated by the flood waters which accompanied the glacial retreat. Three such valleys stand out in this region: the Barycz-Odra valley in the south; the Warta-Obra-Odra Valley in the middle, and Vistula–Noteć–Warta valley in the north. Their valleys are flat-floored and covered with alternating peat-bog and loose sand, with misfit streams, incised into the low plateau of which this region is largely composed. The valley sides are usually conspicuous and sometimes quite steep, and the region as a whole is dissected by these valleys into a series of tabular masses.

This region is commonly included, along with Pomerania, as part of the lake and moraine region of northern Poland,[1] because its landforms were shaped by the events of the last or Würm advance of the ice sheet. It differs, however, from the area lying to the north of the Noteć and Warta in its gentler landforms, in its smaller area of sand and gravel and in the greater fertility of its soils. Above all, it differs from the areas lying to the north in the greater density of its population, the larger size and importance of its towns, and the greater antiquity of human settlement.

It was in this region that the Polish state emerged during the tenth century (see page 81). There was sufficient agricultural wealth to provide it with an economic base. Amid its lakes were easily fortified sites for the earliest cities, and the marshes and the line of intractable valleys that enclosed it

> . . . serves it in the office of a wall
> Or as a moat defensive to a house . . .

This was Wielkopolska or Great Poland. Gniezno, the earliest capital, lay in its midst, between the Warta and the Vistula, and Poznań, the second capital, lay at the crossing of the Warta, which divided the region into two almost equal parts. Toward the east, a series of elongated glacial lakes, of which Lake Gopło is the largest, formerly provided a means of waterborne transport on the route between the upper Warta valley and the great bend of the Vistula near Bydgoszcz. Even today this waterway, supplemented by a small canal, is still available for small barges, but is now very little used.

The political focus of Poland has moved eastward from Wielkopolska to Warsaw, and the economic focus southward to Silesia, but this region retains from its early primacy a close net of rural and urban

---

[1] See for example Jerzy Kondracki, 'W sprawie terminologii i taksonomii jednostek regionalnych w geografii fizycznej Polski', *Przegląd Geograficzny*, **33**, 1961, 23–38.

11*

settlement, a denser population, a more developed agriculture, and a more broadly based industrial structure than the regions lying north of it.

The Middle Polish Plain

The Polish Plain *par excellence* is the region of older drift, left by the third or Riss glaciation. It extends southward from the end-moraine of the Würm to the older, more fragmented and less conspicuous end-moraine left by the Riss. The southern margin of the plain is somewhat indeterminate. It extends as far as the foothills of the Bohemian Massif and to the uplands near Częstochowa and Kielce. Over much of this area the glacial deposits have been thinned by erosion, and survive only as discontinuous patches of boulder clay. Although the map may show the southern limit of the Riss glaciation, this is far from conspicuous in the field, and it needs an eye of faith to recognise the traces of end-moraine. On the other hand, the Warta phase in the retreat from the maximum of the Riss glaciation is conspicuously represented in the landscape. Its end-moraine gives rise in part to the Trzebnica Hills (*P.* Wzgórza Trzebnickie) which stretch across Lower Silesia to the north of Wrocław (*G.* Breslau), and the hilly ridge, the Wyzyna Łódźka, on whose western flank the city of Łódź has grown up. But east of the Vistula these depositional landforms are more eroded and less conspicuous, and the districts of Mazowsze, around Warsaw, and of Podlasie, extending eastward to the Soviet border, have an extremely gentle relief.

River valleys are more open and less deeply entrenched than in Wielkopolska, and, although the streams are generally bordered by a flood plain, the valley floors do not present so great a barrier to movement as do those to the north, although parts of the Narew valley are ill-drained and difficult to cross. In all respects the landscape is more mature. Lakes are few, and over large areas they are not to be found, since here these inevitable features of glaciation have been filled up, drained or simply destroyed by the processes of denudation.

The western part of the region is drained toward the north by the Odra and its tributary, the Warta, and the eastern by the Vistula with the Pilica, Narew, Bug and Wieprz. Divides between their basins are distinct, and there is no question here of the indefinite drainage, such as occurs in the immature landscape of northern Poland. At the same time the lines of the *pradoliny* are less conspicuous and less easy to trace across the map from one river basin to the next. The eastward extension of the Toruń-Kostrzyn trench into the middle Vistula, and beyond it to the Narew and Bug is clear enough, as is the line of the Warta and Bzura, but the line of an ancient river from the Pilica to the upper Warta and thence to the Odra and the Spree valley in East Germany is far less apparent.

In many parts of Poland, particularly along the *pradoliny*, there are areas of wind-blown sand, arranged in dunes and sometimes fixed by means of a cover of xerophytic grasses and conifers. The sand derives from the boulder clay and has been re-sorted by water and wind. Nowhere are sand dunes more extensive than in this region, where they make large areas infertile. The Puszcza Kampinoska, lying in the Vistula valley to the north-west of Warsaw, consists of about 200 square miles of dunes resting upon the undrained clays of the valley floor. Along the valley-terraces which border the larger valleys are sand dunes, and scattered over the plain are patches of sand, large and small, generally held in place by the roots of a few pines, but always liable to blow again and injure the surrounding cropland.

Another wind-blown deposit, though one of incomparably greater value than the sands, is the loess which appears to have accumulated over southern Poland during the cold, dry interglacial periods. Over the plains of Middle Poland the deposits of loess are far from extensive; they were laid down more thickly in southern Poland, but in Middle Poland there are a few small deposits and an extensive area of loess-like deposits in the Odra valley in Silesia.

Despite the variations in the quality of the soil, from the black earths developed on the peaty soils of Silesia to the sterile sands of the Białowieża region in the east, this is one of the more productive agricultural regions of Poland. Over most of its area at least 70 per cent of the surface is cultivated. Forest is extensive only on the morainic hills in the west of the region and over the very extensive sandy areas in the valleys of the Narew and Bug. The Białowieża Forest, the only certain example of primeval forest remaining in Poland, spreads over the sandy and uninviting soils to the east and south-east of Białystok, and extends across the boundary into the Soviet Union.

Middle Poland is a region of closely spaced villages, each surrounded by its open fields of intermixed peasant strips. The villages are most often long, straggling street villages, the cottages well separated from one another and each surrounded by its small garden and few fruit trees. Isolated cottages generally mark the beginning of a newer and more dispersed pattern of settlement, where the villagers have moved out from the loose village agglomeration in order to be nearer their fields, though a few such settlements may in fact be older than the street villages. Meadow usually lies along the shallow valleys and covers the poorly drained soils which probably are all that remain of glacial lakes. Small woods are numerous, not only because the patches of sandy and inferior soil are frequent, but also because this peasant society needs the lumber for its building and fencing needs.

With the exception only of the industrial region of Upper Silesia, this is the most urbanised region of Poland. The towns form a distinct hierarchy. The smallest, with only a few thousand inhabitants, serve primarily as market centres for the surrounding rural communities, and their frequency depends on the richness of the agricultural region which they serve. The small towns in Middle Poland may have a saw-mill, a brickworks or some small engineering works, but their predominant character today is not industrial; their network of communications is undeveloped; they lack a technically trained labour force, and they cannot attract new industries to their area.

The medium sized towns, of up to about 50,000 inhabitants, are much less numerous but also a great deal more prosperous. They are a category almost entirely lacking in northern Poland. They serve as market centres for the surrounding countryside, but they are also well served by rail and road transport. They have usually a dominant manufacturing industry as well as a number of subsidiary industries. Typical among such cities is Kalisz, with its clothing manufactures; Wrocławek, with chemical, paper and rubber; Zgierz, Pabianice, Tomaszów and Białystok with textiles, and Radom, with engineering and machine construction.

Lastly, Middle Poland contains a small group of cities of large size and national—if not also international—importance. These include Warsaw, the capital, Łódź and Wrocław, and, if we may revert here to the region of Wielkopolska, which in terms of landscape and resources, belongs to Middle Poland rather than to northern, also Poznań, Bydgoszcz and Toruń. Each has a broad-based industrial structure, and well-developed network of transport services, and serves as commercial focus for a large area.

Hills and plains of southern Poland

The 'solid' begins to appear from beneath the drift long before the southern limit of Middle Poland is reached, but only beyond the end-moraines of the Riss glaciation does it rise into commanding hills. It is as if the hills of southern Poland had permitted the ice sheet to approach their northern fringe, to advance southward wherever they were embayed to receive it, but never to climb over their flanks. The transition from the glaciated plain of Middle Poland to the hills of southern is abrupt to the east of the Vistula, but more gradual elsewhere, and the contrast between the landscapes and the human geography north and south of the line is generally strongly marked.

The geological structures which are thus revealed are oriented in a north-west to south-east direction, and consist broadly of two complex anticlines, which bring Palaeozoic rocks to the surface, separated by a syncline, in which the Cretaceous is preserved, and bordered on the south-west by the Silesian Basin, and on the north-east by the deeply buried syncline which underlies Mazowsze. The Silesian Basin, whose axis is very approximately traced by the Odra river, is filled in with Permian, Mesozoic and Tertiary beds and, over much of its area, these are sealed in as it were by glacial drift, diluvial deposits and loess.

To the north-east, however, the uplift of the first of the two anticlines has brought Palaeozoic rocks to the surface over a small area in Upper Silesia. These are Carboniferous in age and coal-bearing and, in terms of economic geography, have given rise to the Upper Silesian industrial region.

To the north-east is the syncline, sometimes known as the Nida Basin, from the small Nida river which drains approximately along its axis to the Vistula. The Triassic and Cretaceous beds which fill the syncline outcrop along its wings, forming outward facing escarpments. Between, Cretaceous beds fill the middle of the syncline. The most conspicuous escarpments are along its south-western margin. These consist of a low cuesta formed by the outcrop of the *Muschelkalk*, the relatively hard Middle Triassic limestone, and the higher and more impressive scarp of the Kraków Jura (*P.* Jura Krakowska), formed of Jurassic limestone. In the former, occupying solution cavities in the limestone, are the ores of lead (galena) and zinc (calamine and blende), together with small quantities of the ores of cadmium, copper and silver. The Jurassic limestone includes bedded iron ores, similar in mineralogical content to those of Lorraine, but far smaller in quantity and geographical extent.

The north-eastern anticline is more completely revealed, and indeed presents the area of strongest relief in all Poland north of the Carpathian system. Its core is made up of older Palaeozoic beds, with younger beds on its flanks, strongly folded and metamorphosed and weakly mineralised, which give rise to a series of straight, steep ridges, according roughly with the outcrop of beds of very hard quartzite. These hills, the so-called Holy Cross Mountains (*P.* Góry Swięto-krzyskie), are set in a frame built of younger and softer Jurassic beds. The latter form a series of denuded scarps which look inwards toward the Palaozoic core. The limestone beds, however, generally dip rather steeply; the areas over which they outcrop are narrow, and the beds themselves are so eroded that it is impossible to trace a continuous escarpment in any way comparable to the Kraków Jura. But, like the opposite wing of the Nida syncline, this one also contains deposits of iron-ore. They are smaller in quantity and more widely scattered than those in the Kraków Jura. They were important during the nineteenth century, when they gave rise to an iron-smelting industry. A languishing iron industry survives in these hills, and a little iron-ore is still worked, but by itself is insufficient to supply and maintain a modern smelting plant.

To the north-east of the Holy Cross Mountains the Palaeozoic beds continue, beneath the plains of Eastern Poland, into the Soviet Union. But they cease to influence the surface relief. The boundary of the Holy Cross Mountains on this side is set by a fault-line, along which the ancient rocks are let down many thousands of feet. Beyond this line they form a stable substratum to the plains of Russia, but they are thickly covered with Cretaceous and later deposits, invisible and almost unknown. Beyond the line of the Holy Cross fault the Cretaceous beds—mainly a very porous limestone—form a rolling tableland, the Lublin Uplands (*P.* Wyżyna Lubelska), which broadens eastward to the Soviet border and into the Ukraine.

Silesian Plain. The Silesian Plain forms an elongated region which extends from the low divide which separates the Odra Basin from that of the Vistula north-westwards to the East German border in the Lausitz region, a distance of about 200 miles. It is a low-lying and generally flat region, bordered on the south-west by the foothills of the Sudety and on the north-east by the limestone plateau of Upper Silesia and its extension toward the west, the Góry Kocie. At most the plain is about 40 miles wide, and it narrows to the west to less than 20. The river Odra forms an axis to the region for about two-thirds of the length of the latter, but about 30 miles below Wrocław, the river turns sharply to the right and crosses the Góry Kocie before resuming its north-westerly course. The plain however continues, somewhat narrower and crossed in turn by the Bóbr, Kwisa and the western Nysa, (Nysa Łużycka) into Germany. It is the most southerly and the oldest of the *pradoliny*, and has long since lost the physical character-istics which still distinguish the great valleys which lie to the north.

The plain, as has been noted, is essentially a syncline, filled in with Secondary and Tertiary beds and covered with Quaternary deposits, of which the alluvium laid down by the rivers and the loess spread by the winds of the interglacial periods are the most extensive and today the most important. The prevailingly gentle relief of the plain is broken by small inliers of the harder rocks which underlie it. Most conspicuous of these is the isolated hill of Ślęza (*G.* Zobten), which rises steeply to a height of 2,355 feet to the south-west of Wrocław, and is said to have given its name to the province of Silesia or Śląsk.

Along the Odra lies a broad belt of alluvium. To the north-east the soils are developed on diluvial deposits and are of indifferent quality, but to the south-west, between the river-terraces and the Sudeten Mountains, the low plateau has been covered with loess. A rich, dark soil of chernozem type has developed, and this region is agriculturally one of the most productive in Poland (Fig. 8.7).

Throughout its history population has been relatively dense. The growth of towns during the Middle Ages was more rapid here than in most other parts of Poland, and it is today one of the most highly urbanised areas of Poland. In the centre of the region lies Wrocław (*G.* Breslau) itself, not only the regional capital since the Middle Ages, but also one of the major industrial and transport centres of the country. German peasants and entrepreneurs moved into Silesia in greater numbers than into other regions of Poland, with the result that large areas of it were left void of people at the end of the Second World War.

Upper Silesian plateau and Kraków Jura. The Upper Silesian plateau is a region of gentle relief where the tributaries of both the Odra and the Vistula interpenetrate, separated by no conspicuous features of the landscape. The Palaeozoic beds, here made up of the coal measures, outcrop over only a relatively small area, and are else-where hidden by Triassic and diluvial deposits. The known coal-field, however, covers a triangular area of over 2,000 square miles, which in the south-west extends into Czechoslovakia, and along its southern margin spreads beneath the folds of the Carpathian Mountains.

The Triassic beds include the Bunter Sandstone and the economic-ally more important and scenically more conspicuous shelly limestone or *Muschelkalk*. The latter, as has already been noted, contains the ores of lead and zinc as well as of other ferrous and non-ferrous minerals. It gives rise to an open, rolling country, markedly deficient in surface drainage, and of only limited fertility. Toward the north-east this is hidden by clays and marls of the Keuper and Lower Jurassic series. These constitute a typical 'clay vale', damp and poorly drained, with a considerable area under forest. Beyond this to the north-east, the Upper Jurassic limestones give rise to the Kraków Jura, whose strongly scarped west-facing edge is continuous from near Kraków itself to Częstochowa, 60 miles away to the north-west.

The Kraków Jura shows well-developed karst features. Its surface is undulating, with solution hollows and gorges, of which that at Ojców, with its limestone crags and touristic amenities, is the best known. The limestone plateau is drained mainly to the north-east, toward the Nida depression, where the rivers are gathered together and delivered to the Warta, Pilica or Vistula. Its surface slopes gently in this direction, until its dry limestone is lost beneath the Cretaceous, glacial and alluvial clays of the adjoining region. The Riss glaciation never covered this region, and the evidences of the earlier, or Mindel, glaciation are here too fragmentary to have any direct influence on the landscape.

Human settlement is here a response to simple and well-known physical phenomena. Villages gather along the spring lines at the foot of the limestone escarpments, avoiding as far as possible both the drier areas of limestone and the damp claylands. Areas of most intensive cultivation lie between these two physical extremes. In general, the limestone, whether Triassic or Jurassic, supports cultivation with subsidiary grazing, and the moister clay lands provide meadow or are left under forest.

An exception to this is provided by the Upper Silesian industrial region. Here coal-mining and metallurgical industries (see page 355) have combined to drive agriculture from an area of about 150 square miles. About a dozen large towns, together with several of intermediate size have grown together to form a vast urban and industrial complex, which is examined more fully later in this chapter. At the north-western and south-eastern extremities of this region lie the cities of Częstochowa and Kraków. Both are route centres of some importance, and transport facilities have combined with their proximity to the Upper Silesian coal-field to bring into being a number of heavy manufacturing industries. Around, and especially to the north of Kraków is an area of high agricultural fertility, which formed the nucleus of the early medieval state of 'Little' Poland.

The Nida depression. The ice sheets of the Riss glaciation, which had failed even to mount the flanks of the Kraków Jura, nevertheless invaded the Nida depression and left extensive deposits of boulder clay over at least its northern half. The southern half of the depression must have constituted a broad channel through which the melt-water was delivered to the Upper Vistula, and thence to the Dnestr and Black Sea. The present drainage pattern, with its great number of small rivers which discharge south-eastward to the Vistula survives from this time.

The Nida depression has a gentle relief, its inequalities smoothed by Quaternary and later deposits. It is not a heavily wooded region; the lowlands along the Nida and other rivers are used as meadow and pasture, and much of the better drained soil is under cultivation. Towns are neither numerous nor large, and this region is in fact less densely peopled than the agriculturally unattractive Holy Cross Mountains.

The Holy Cross Mountains. The Palaeozoic core of the second anticline gives rise to the Holy Cross Mountains (Góry Swiętokrzyskie). They derive their curious name from the monastery of the Holy Cross, which still today raises its simple tower above the south-eastern extremity of the highest and most impressive ridge in the region—the Łysa Góra, or Bald Mountain. In many ways the Holy Cross Mountains constitute one of the most interesting and attractive regions in Poland. Their complex relief, consisting of a series of parallel overlapping ridges, steep-sided with sometimes narrow arête-like crests, is more than matched by its complex geology. The core of the range is an interrupted ridge, stretching altogether 60 miles from north of Kielce almost to Sandomierz, where it ends in high bluffs overlooking the Vistula. It is composed of hard sandstones and even harder quartzites. The Łysa Góra itself is about 12 miles in length, rising to an almost level crestline which at its north-western end reaches 2,004 feet and at its eastern, 1,942 feet. Its summit is covered with a kind of natural scree, the Gołoborze, composed of huge fractured masses of quartzite.

Hills of Central Poland. Ridges to north and south consist most often of Devonian dolomite, and the valleys which separate them have been excavated in softer sandstones and shales. The slopes are wooded; the summits are covered with short grass or bare rock, and only the valleys are settled and cultivated.

The anticline pitches toward the north-west, dipping beneath the Triassic and Jurassic beds, which form a narrow 'frame' to south-west and north-east, and a very much broader one to the north-west. The harder limestone beds, dipping steeply away from the core of the anticline, produce a pattern of short, steep ridges, separated by broad valleys, which reproduces in somewhat subdued form the relief features of the Holy Cross Mountains themselves.

The whole region, with forested ridge rising behind forested ridge, and cultivated lowlands lying between, is one of great natural beauty. It is, however, a wetter region with more severe winters than those met with in the plains of Middle Poland. Over much of its surface, the soils are strongly podzolised, infertile and shallow, and over many of the summits there is virtually no soil at all. Only on the enclosing belt of Triassic and Jurassic rocks have soils of better than average quality been developed.

The antiquity of settlement and the density of population stand in sharp contrast with the agricultural poverty of this region. The paradox can be explained only in terms of early industrial development. The region provided, in close juxtaposition, two industrial resources, iron-ore and timber for making charcoal. A prehistoric iron-smelting works has been excavated at Stara Słupia, on the northern flank of the Łysa Góra. During the Middle Ages and early modern times this became one of the more important centres of iron-smelting of Poland and, in fact, of Central Europe. Early in the nineteenth century an attempt was made to emulate in this region the achievements of the Industrial Revolution in Western Europe. It failed, more for political than economic reasons, but it served to reinforce the ancient legacy of iron-working. Indeed, the old iron industry disappeared over much of this area only when it ceased to be practicable to smelt iron with charcoal. Nevertheless, an iron-smelting industry has survived at Starachowice and Ostrowiec, and small iron-working and iron-using industries are widely distributed (see page 372).

Most of these industries are, from the nature of their origin and their early dependence on charcoal, widely scattered throughout the region. There are many small industrial towns, with specialised mechanical and metallurgical industries. The local capital for these industrial centres, as well as for the agricultural communities of the region, is Kielce, located to the west of the Łysa Góra, close to the boundary between the Palaeozoic core of the region and the agriculturally richer and more attractive Triassic area.

The Lublin Uplands. To the north-east and east of the Holy Cross Mountains is the undulating plateau of the Lublin Uplands (*P.* Wyżyna Lubelska). It is an undulating, loess-covered region, which culminates along its southern margin in the steep scarp of the Roztocze. Aside from the few rivers which have cut deep valleys into its surface, it is a dry and almost waterless region. The rainfall is quickly absorbed by the porous loess and yet more porous chalk beneath. There is very little forest, and the villages of the elongated 'street' pattern wind along the valley bottoms, where springs may break out and water can be reached more easily by means of wells. The Vistula, after its junction with the San, crosses this region by a narrow valley, contained between loess-covered bluffs. This is a region of fertile soil, long settled and intensively cultivated. It was once a region of wheat surplus, much of which was once shipped down the Vistula for export from the port of Gdańsk.

Despite its fertility, this is not a densely settled region. Its economy formerly was dominated by great estates; its food surplus was exported rather than used to support a local industry. Its towns are few and small, and their industries consist of little more than the processing of locally produced food-stuffs. At the same time, however, they bear witness to the great wealth of the local landowners and of the merchants who served as middle men in their wheat trade. The small town of Kazimierz Dolny, once a shipping point on the Vistula for the wheat of this region, is a museum of sixteenth-century architecture. The town hall of Zamość and the old houses of Lublin are evidence of the wealth which the rich loess soil has provided. To the generalisation—that this agriculturally fruitful land has never come to support modern manufacturing—the city of Lublin, its regional capital, is an exception. To food processing it has added engineering and chemical industries.

The Upper Vistula–San Basin. South of the hills and plateaus of southern Poland is a triangular region, drained by the upper Vistula and the San, which unite at its northern apex, close to the city of Sandomierz. The region is sometimes known as the Sandomierz Basin (*P.* Kotlina Sandomierska) or as the Subcarpathian Basin. In reality it is a tectonic depression, bounded in part by faults, between the hills of southern Poland on the one side and the younger Carpathian fold mountains on the other. It became the site of a shallow sea during the Tertiary period, and thick beds of sand and clay were laid down on top of the older structures. Though covered by the earliest advances of the Scandinavian ice, glacial deposits have been almost entirely removed.

The present surface of the region is made up of clays and sands spread by the melt-water from both the Scandinavian and the Carpathian ice sheets. It is a region of low relief, where interfluves, built of sand and clay, are separated by the broad belts of alluvium which extend up the valleys of the Vistula and San and their tributaries, the Dunajec, Wisłoka and Wisłok, into the mountains.

Much of the area is damp and poorly drained. Its valleys are lined with meadow and pasture, and the sandy areas, which are extensive between the confluence of the Vistula and the San, are forested. Here and there is a patch of loess, crowning a low eminence above the clay-lands, but mostly it is a poor region, but one of the more densely populated in Poland in relation to its resources. Its cities are marginal to it. Sandomierz crowns the bluffs in which the Holy Cross Mountains terminate along the banks of the Vistula. Only a few very small towns are to be found in the centre of the region. Yet it was in this wilderness of forest and sand that the iron and steel town of Stalowa Wola was founded before the Second World War, as part of the planned development of what was then called the Central Industrial Region. But Stalowa Wola remains alone, and more recent industrial growth in the region has been located along its southern margin.

Here a narrow strip of country, widening towards the east and at most some 10 miles wide, provides a kind of transition from the lowlands of the Sandomierz Basin to the Beskid Mountains which overlook it. This is well-drained country. A belt of loess soil stretches, almost without interruption, from Kraków in the west to the Soviet border. This was never more than lightly wooded, and since prehistoric times has provided an avenue for human movement between the forests and swamps which lie to the north and the mountains to the south. Eastward it continued out of the San valley and through the so-called Przemyśl Gap into the Dnestr valley and the Ukraine.

To the advantages of a light and fertile soil and a relative absence of dense forest must be added the minerals of the subsoil. Two have long been of great importance: salt and petroleum. The earliest to be exploited were the deposits of rock-salt which occur at many points along this foothill zone, and in very large quantities at Wieliczka, near Kraków, and at Bochnia, 8 miles to the south-east. They have been worked continuously at Wieliczka since the Middle Ages. Salt continues to be worked here today though no longer on an important scale. The petroleum reserves along the Carpathian border of this region were developed very much later, but they have for practical purposes been exhausted, except towards the east, in the vicinity of Przemyśl and Jarosław. Natural gas has been gaining in importance in recent years. To these must be added the sulphur deposits, recently discovered and now being worked at Tarnobrzeg, near Sandomierz.

This narrow belt of loess soil, rich and easily traversed, has long been one of the most highly urbanised regions in Poland, and today it attracts more than its share of new industries. Evenly spaced along it, from Kraków to the Soviet border, are Tarnów, Rzeszów and Jarosław, and the new steel town of Nowa Huta, administratively part of greater Kraków.

The mountain borderland
The whole of the south-western and southern border of Poland is made up of mountains; the Sudety to the west, the Carpathians to the east. Their continuity is interrupted only by the small plain which constitutes the northern approach to the Moravian Gate in Czechoslovakia. The 'Gate' itself, at the height of 1,018 feet, is the lowest pass across the mountains between the western Nysa in the west and the Bieszczady on the Soviet border. The Moravian Gate in fact coincides with an abrupt change in geological structure. To the west, the hills are part of the Bohemian Massif; mainly they are Palaeozoic, much folded, metamorphosed and intruded by igneous rocks. To the east, the Carpathian Mountains, at least as they occur within the boundary of Poland, are built of younger rocks, Cretaceous and early Tertiary in age, intensely folded during the Alpine mountain-building process which accompanied and followed their deposition.

This sharp contrast in their geological age and origin is not wholly reflected in differences in landscape. On the contrary, there is a certain similarity between the forested ridges of the Sudety, with their often rounded summits and level skyline, and the short segments of similarly rounded and forested mountains which comprise the Beskidy, the outermost ranges of the Carpathian arc. Although the northern ice sheet, at its most extensive advance—the Mindel—reached almost to the foot of these mountains, they were themselves not heavily glaciated. Only over their highest surface were there ice-fields, and these were relatively small. In consequence the landforms, even in the higher mountains are predominantly those produced by erosion in a humid, temperate climate. Erosional landforms of glacial origin—sharp peaks, arêtes and cirques are really discernible only in the Tatry (Tatra) Mountains.

The Sudety. The Sudety, as this system of short overlapping mountain ranges is sometimes called, extends from the valley of the western Nysa (*G.* Neisse; *P.* Nysa Łużycka) to the Moravian Gate, a distance of about 155 miles. The mountains constitute a broad belt, at least 20 miles across, and more often 30. Geologically it is composed of beds ranging in age from the pre-Cambrian to the Cretaceous and even Tertiary, strongly metamorphosed in many areas, and intruded by igneous rocks and volcanics. On its north-eastern side a fault-line provides an abrupt boundary to the region; beyond lies the lowland plain of Silesia, whose gentle relief is interrupted only by a few igneous outliers of the Bohemian Massif. Folding and the intrusion of igneous rocks, followed by a long period of denudation, have produced the present pattern of mountains and valleys. There is no continuous range. Instead, a series of short ranges, none of them more than about 30 miles in length, overlap in a kind of echelon pattern. There are many circuitous routes by which the range can be circumvented without the obligation of ascending their steep flanks. The Sudety as a whole constitute a mass of difficult mountain country, but they never constituted any real barrier to human movement. The medieval kingdom of Bohemia experienced no difficulty in linking the plains of Silesia with those of Bohemia in one state.

The boundary between Poland and Czechoslovakia takes a highly irregular course through these mountains. It follows consistently neither the mountain ridges nor the divide between the Odra and Elbe (*Cz.* Labe) basins. Instead it leaps from ridge to ridge, following none to its termination. It curves into Bohemia in order to enclose the Kłodzko (*G.* Glatz) basin (*P.* Kotlina Kłodzka); then doubles back in order to give to Czechoslovakia a finger of territory lying on the Silesian side of the great Sudeten boundary fault. It then follows, though with many detours and indentations, the eastern flanks of the mountains, until it reaches the northern approach to the Moravian Gate.

The Sudety can be divided into two contrasting sectors. In the north-west the dominant form is that of short overlapping ranges. The longest and highest is the Karkonosze (*Cz.* Krkonoše; *G.* Riesengebirge), which carries the international boundary for about 20 miles along its crest, and rises in Śnieżka (*Cz.* Šnezka; *G.* Schneekoppe) to 5,260 feet, the highest point of the whole Sudeten range. The Karkonosze are built of granite and the metamorphic rocks which have been formed in contact with it. Its summit at between 4,500 and 4,750 feet is the relic of a Tertiary peneplain, and into its steep northern face corries have been eroded by small ice sheets which formed here during the Quaternary glaciation. Parallel to the Karkonosze, and 15 miles to the north-east, are the Góry Kaczawskie, a lower range built of folded and metamorphosed sedimentaries of Cambrian and even greater age. Between lies a mountain valley, noted for its beauty, in which lies the resort of Jelenia Góra (*G.* Hirschberg).

South-east of Jelenia Góra faulting has brought Carboniferous rocks to the surface. Igneous and hard metamorphic rocks occur less frequently, and the landscape becomes one of rounded hills, without the regular alignment which characterises the area to the north-west. The Carboniferous beds are nevertheless strongly folded, and the mining of their small reserves of coal presents serious technical problems. The city of Wałbrzych (*G.* Waldenburg) lies within these hills, and is the commercial and industrial focus of the small Lower Silesian coal-field.

South-east of Wałbrzych the older and harder granites and gneisses reappear, and the pattern of elongated ridges and intervening depressions reasserts itself. The Góry Sowie (*G.* Eulengebirge), built of Archaean gneiss, rise abruptly from the Silesian plain, and sink equally abruptly to the Kłodzko Basin. South-east of the narrow gap cut by the eastern Nysa (*P.* Nysa Kłodzka), the Złote Góry (*G.* Reichensteiner Gebirge) merge into the broad mountain mass, the Jesioniki, (*Cz.* Ješenik; *G.* Altvatergebirge) which comprises the south-eastern sector of the Sudety.

Parallel with the Góry Sowie, and about 20 miles to the south-west, are the steep and rugged Góry Bystrzyckie and Orlickie, built like the Góry Sowie of Archaean and Palaeozoic quartzite and gneiss. Between lies the Kłodzko Basin, where younger rocks—Triassic and Cretaceous—have been preserved, producing a gentler relief and a deeper and richer soil.

The Sudety were never, as has been seen, the barrier to movement and communication that they are sometimes reputed to have been. Their innermost valleys have centuries ago been opened up for settlement, and throughout the length of these mountains, the small, swift streams were used to power mills. Thus the area became an important centre for the manufacture of woollen textiles. Small mills, standing isolated and often enough in ruins beside the streams which once provided them with power, are often met with amid the hills. But during the last century, when steam power began gradually to replace water, the industry itself concentrated at a number of more accessible sites. Today small mill-towns like Nowa Ruda, Świdnica and Kamienna Góra are scattered through the mountain valleys, or lie against their steep north-eastern flanks.

South of the Kłodzko Basin this changes. The south-eastern third of the Sudeten range is made up, not of ridges eroded from alternating hard and less hard rocks, but of a broad mass of Devonian and Carboniferous rock, intruded here and there with igneous. Though it rises at its greatest elevation to 4,894 feet, its relief is more gentle than that of the north-western Sudety, and forms a broad and almost level peneplain. Only its northern slopes lie within Poland, and a more detailed examination of this sector of the Sudeten mountains is postponed to the next chapter. Throughout the Sudeten region are found springs of hot and mineralised water; some of which have given rise to small, sad-looking spas.

The Beskidy and Carpathian Mountains. The Moravian Gate lies 35 miles within the territory of Czechoslovakia. In front of it to the north is a wedge-shaped area of lowland, driven in between the eastern spurs of the Sudety on the one side and the steep rise of the Beskidy on the other. This area of lowland, at most 30 miles across, and now thickly settled and heavily industrialised, masks the transition from the Palaeozoic and even older rocks of the Sudety to the young rocks, Cretaceous and early Tertiary for the greater part, which were folded to make the Polish Carpathians.

The mountain range which thus extends from the plains of Moravia in the west into the Soviet Union and Romania in the east, is the most formidable in Eastern Europe. Its general features have already been discussed (pages 13–14), and a more detailed consideration of its more spectacular features must be deferred until later. Although the Polish boundary just reaches into the Tatra Mountains (*P.* Tatry) the higher and more impressive regions of the Carpathians lie within Czechoslovakia.

Despite their apparent complexity the Polish Carpathians are, in reality, a comparatively simple region. They consist geologically of a core of igneous and metamorphic rock, which gives rise to the strongest relief, flanked by folded sedimentary rocks, mostly of Cretaceous and Lower Tertiary age. In terms of relief, the Polish Carpathians are made up of two distinct ranges, corresponding with this geological division. The more northerly of the two, commonly known as the Beskidy, is made up of a large number of relatively short ranges, which collectively assume the pattern of a curve open toward the south. The more southerly is a region of stronger relief, the High Tatra, only a very small part of which lies within the Polish region of Podhale in the extreme south. Here, in the peak known as Rysy, it rises to a height of 8,185 feet.

The region as a whole is drained northward to the Vistula, and for part of its distance the international boundary follows the watershed which separates the Vistula Basin from that of the Danube. The north-flowing rivers are made up of alternating longitudinal courses, where they have excavated valleys, frequently wide and open, between the ridges, and transverse sections, where they have cut deep transverse valleys across the mountains. Apart from the Vistula itself, which has only a very short course within the Beskidy, the most important rivers are the Sola, Skawa, Raba, Dunajec, Wisłoka, Wisłok, and San. The Dunajec, after rising in the Tatry, has a longitudinal course through the vale of Podhale, between the latter and the High Beskidy (*P*. Beskid Wysoki). Cutting across the more southerly chain of the Beskidy, here formed by the highly scenic Pieniny Mountains, it emerges into another longitudinal valley, in which lies the town of Nowy Sącz; then, after cutting across the Beskid Wyspowy, it reaches the last longitudinal trench, before flowing across the foot-hills—Pogórze—to the plains. The Wisłoka and Wisłok have broadly similar but yet more angular courses. Both rise in the low or eastern Beskidy (*P*. Beskid Niski), almost unite their waters in the broad longitudinal valley which they have jointly eroded, but then take their separate routes across the Pogórze to the plains and their confluence respectively with the Vistula and the San. Several of these rivers have now been dammed for the generation of hydro-electric power.

Toward the east the longitudinal Wisłoka–Wisłok valley narrows. East of Sanok the ranges increase in number, and from the valley of the San eastward to the Soviet border is a maze of forested, trackless hills, separated by narrow and frequently uninhabited valleys. This is the Bieszczady, the most remote, the least settled and least developed part of Poland.

The nomenclature used to describe and define the Polish Carpathians is unusually confusing. Two words predominate: Pogórze (plural Pogórza) and Beskid (plural Beskidy). The former is literally 'the Foothills', and is used to denote a line of hills, extending from the Czechoslovak border near Třinec to the Soviet border at Przemyśl. Its continuity is, however, broken by the rivers which cross it from the south, thus dividing it into a series of at least ten segments. These are grouped, each group being known as *Pogórze*, followed by a descriptive adjective. We thus have the Pogórze Śląskie (Silesian Foot-hills) in the west, followed in turn by Pogórze Wielickie, Pogórze Cieżkowickie and Pogórze Dynowskie.

The Pogórza rarely exceed 1,500 feet in altitude. The Beskidy are higher and more complex. They constitute a series of sub-parallel ranges which face the Pogórza across the discontinuous valley which separates them. The individual hill masses, which make up the Beskidy, are separated by transverse and often gorge-like valleys. They are grouped into the Western or High Beskid (*P.* Beskid Zachodni or Wysoki) and the Eastern or Low Beskid (*P.* Beskid Wschodni or Niski). In the western group are the Beskid Śląski, Beskid Średni, Beskid Wyspowy and others. Most of these ranges rise to heights of considerably over 3,000 feet. The Barania Góra, in the Beskid Śląski, rises to 3,982 feet; Pilsko and Babia Góra in the Beskid Żywiecki reach respectively 5,107 and 5,658 feet.

The international boundary in the western Beskidy lies at right angles to the line of folding. Only in the Beskid Żywiecki and the Tatry themselves, does it follow for any considerable distance the crest of one of the mountain ranges. For the rest, there is in no sense a 'natural' boundary between Poland and Czechoslovakia, and movement across the line of the boundary has never presented any great difficulty. The result has been the interpenetration of Poles and Slovaks along this line. The Spiš region of Slovakia had long been considered part of Poland before it was occupied by the Habsburgs in 1769, and in 1920–21 the Orawa (*Cz.* Orava) and Spisz (*Cz.* Spiš) regions, in dispute between Poland and Czechoslovakia, were partitioned between them, with Czechoslovakia taking the lion's share.

East of the valley of the Poprad, a right bank tributary of the Dunajec, lies the Low Beskid. Its summit levels are appreciably lower than those of the High Beskid, and are in general not above 2,500 feet. Indeed their summits have the appearance of a dissected peneplain. At the same time, the principal range of the Beskidy becomes more continuous, and coincides for no less than 100 miles both with the international boundary and the divide between the drainage basins of the Vistula and the Tisza. It is, however, crossed by a number of passes between the valleys tributary to the Wisłoka and San and those opening to the Tisza. The Poprad itself, which rises on the south-eastern flanks of the Tatry, has cut a broad valley across the western end of the

Low Beskid. To the east are the Tylicka, Dukielska and Lupkowska Passes, in addition to several others more difficult and historically less important. The Dukielska Pass crosses the main range at a height of only 1,647 feet.

Around the headwaters of the San the Low Beskidy merges into the Bieszczady, the thinly populated wilderness that makes up the south-eastern corner of Poland. Almost on the Soviet border lies Halicz, which at 4,379 feet, is the highest mountain in south-eastern Poland.

There is a superficial similarity between the short, truncated mountain ranges of the Sudety and the Beskidy and Pogórze. But in their human geography, as well as in their geological age and structure, they are widely different.

The Carpathian region is too large and complex for generalisation. There are within the limits of the mountains fertile and populous regions like Podhale and Doły Jasielsko-Sanockie, as the broad vale from Biecz to Sanok is called. But the region as a whole is only slightly urbanised and it is economically underdeveloped. This is not to say, however, that it is thinly peopled; indeed, as a whole its average population density is very high in relation to its resources, but it is heavily rural. Most of the population lives in villages and engages in agriculture. Given the infertility and strong relief of most of the region, it follows that farm holdings are generally small and the level of subsistence lower than in most other parts of the country. Subsistence agriculture is more widely practised than elsewhere. In the higher mountains, the custom of transhumance, which has disappeared from most other mountainous areas, is still of some importance. Traditional folk-ways have not merely survived, but in much of the Carpathian region remain dominant. Costume and custom, architectural style and agricultural practice survive not as quaint local practices, but as a way of life on which the outer world has hitherto made only a limited impact. Ukrainians, or Ruthenes, were formerly important in this region, but have now largely migrated to the Soviet Union.

Villages are often large within the mountains; many are long, irregular street or forest villages, straggling for miles along the narrow valley bottoms. Except in the broader lowlands, like Podhale and the valleys around Krosno, there are no extensive areas of cropland, and the peasants of necessity combine animal husbandry on the mountains with cultivation in the valleys. The severity of the winters makes a form of transhumance necessary in some areas, and farm animals regularly make their pilgrimage to the higher slopes in spring, returning to the valleys in winter. Lumbering remains, as it has always been, an important industry. Almost half the area of the Beskidy is forested, primarily with beech on the lower slopes and spruce and fir on the higher. But into this region has come in recent years a new source of wealth—tourism. It is still not highly developed, and very few of the tourists are able to pay for the kinds of service that would employ large numbers of the local people. In such areas as the Bieszczady the visitor is primarily a hunter and camper, and contributes relatively little to the local economy. Nevertheless some small towns, like Wisła, Zakopane and Krynica, have grown up to serve almost exclusively the needs of the holiday-makers, and as the wealth of Poland increases, and as its scenic attractions become more widely known, so are the Carpathians likely to rival the Austrian Alps, as the latter have the Swiss. Other small towns like Nowy Sącz and Myślenice, grew up on the trade routes which formerly threaded the mountain valleys to link Poland with Hungary.

CLIMATE

Poland, like all of Central and Eastern Europe, is climatically inter-mediate between the mild, moist, marine climate of north-western Europe and the climate of greater extremes which characterises most of European Russia. There is a slow transition across the great plain of Northern Europe, and even within the limits of Poland itself a distinct contrast occurs between the west and the east. The dominant climatic influences are the 'lows' which move along fairly well defined tracks from the Atlantic, and the 'highs' which build up, especially in winter, over the Russian land-mass, and at intervals push out across Central Europe. These general influences are everywhere modified by altitude and slope, which produce, even within an area as relatively uniform as Poland, a great variety of local climatic conditions. These microclimatic features are so significant and, on the other hand, the regional changes so gradual that it is very difficult indeed to divide Poland into climatic regions. Indeed, only one such region, the belt of mountains in the south-west and south can be said to be climatically distinct and sharply differentiated from other regions of the country.

Temperature. This transitional character is most conspicuous in winter, when, on average, the eastern third of the country is up to 4°C (7°F) colder than the western (Fig, 8.5a). The Baltic Sea modifies the temperature of a narrow coastal strip, and a belt of relative warmth extends up the Odra valley, as far even as Upper Silesia. Across the plain of Poland temperatures fall off slowly and evenly, running a degree or two lower in the hilly areas: the Pomeranian end-moraine, the Kraków Jura and the Holy Cross Mountains. East of the Vistula the decline in temperature becomes somewhat sharper. Mountains make their own climate, and both the Tatry and the higher ranges of the Sudety have average January temperatures below −6°C (21°F).

The summer isotherms tend, in contrast with those of winter, to run from west to east. Apart from the mountains, the lowest temperatures are met with along the Baltic coast and in the moraine regions of

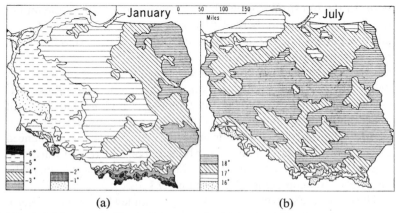

(a)   (b)

Fig. 8.5. Mean monthly temperatures in degrees centigrade in (a) January, (b) July. After *Atlas Polski*, Zeszyt III, Warsaw, 1954.

Pomerania and Masuria. The great river valleys, notably the middle Vistula, the Warta and the Odra, are significantly warmer, though here the Kraków Jura and the Holy Cross Mountains provide cool islands amid the frequent heat of the plains.

The duration of winter and the length of the growing season are no less important than the temperature extremes in their influence upon agriculture. The duration of frost increases eastward. In the Odra valley the number of days when the temperature never rises above freezing is usually less than 30. In a broad belt which traverses central Poland from north to south there are on average from 30 to 40 days with temperatures continuously below freezing, and east of the Vistula, this number rises to over 50. In the Odra valley there are less than 100 days experiencing frost, but this number rises near the eastern boundary to over 130 days. But there are numerous local exceptions. Frost is experienced least along the Baltic coast; the mountains of southern Poland experience more frequent frost than either the plains to the north or the Silesian and Sandomierz Basins, but such highland areas as the Kraków Jura and Holy Cross Mountains are not conspicuously more frosty than the surrounding regions because of the tendency for cold air to 'drain' away from their flanks. The Silesian Plain and Sandomierz Basin have considerably shorter periods of frost and the extreme south-east of Poland experiences the mildest climate of any part of Poland.

The length of the growing season is closely related to the duration of frost. In Poland spring comes first in the plain of lower Silesia and in the Sandomierz Basin, between Kraków and Rzeszów. From here it advances slowly into the mountains and more quickly across the plains toward the north-east. Despite the relative mildness of winters along the Baltic coast, spring comes slowly here. The onset of spring, as defined by the earliest day with an average temperature above 5°C (41°F), comes before March 25 in the mildest regions, but does not reach the Pomeranian and Masurian end-moraine country until after April 10. The north-eastward progress of spring is not only influenced by relief, but also by soil and water bodies. The lake region warms up slowly, but retains its warmth longer into the autumn; everywhere the heavy clays remain colder than the lighter sands.

The end of the season of growth reveals a somewhat similar pattern. Autumn ebbs back toward the south-west, lingering longest in the Odra valley and in the Sandomierz Basin. Winter comes earliest in north-eastern Poland, but along the Baltic coast and around the lakes of Pomerania and Masuria, where the water bodies give up their warmth only slowly, the colder weather comes only haltingly and reluctantly.

Precipitation. The rainfall map of Poland shows sharper and more sudden variations than those for temperature. Rainfall is associated as in all of north-western Europe, mainly with 'lows' which move in from the Atlantic. It is, in Poland, characteristically a summer rainfall, since in winter Poland falls to greater or lesser degree under the influence of high pressure systems which form over Russia. Altitude and consequent variations in exposure to the rain-bearing winds, is the chief factor within Poland influencing the volume of rainfall, and the rainfall map (Fig. 8.6) bears a certain resemblance to that of relief. The greatest precipitation is experienced in the Sudety and Beskidy, where it is over 900 millimetres (35 inches) on the higher ground. This drops off to 650 millimetres (26 inches) or less in the adjacent plains to the north. A broader belt of relatively high rainfall—from 650 to 800 millimetres (26 to 32 inches)—lies out in front of the Beskidy from Upper Silesia eastward to the Soviet border. Apart from small areas of relatively high rainfall, such as the western face of the Kraków Jura,

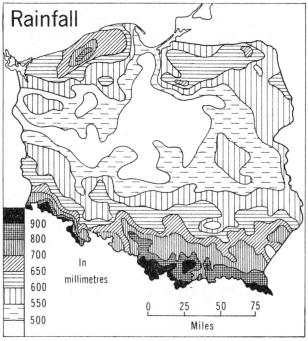

Fig. 8.6. Average annual rainfall. After *Atlas Geograficzny Polski*, Warsaw, 1956.

the Holy Cross Mountains and the Lublin Uplands, the whole of Central Poland is relatively dry. Much of the valley of the Warta and the whole middle Vistula basin have an average annual rainfall of under 550 millimetres (22 inches). This increases toward the north and culminates in the heavy rainfall, by Polish standards, of Pomerania and Masuria, where the effects of altitude are reinforced by a greater degree of exposure to the westerly winds. Over the higher ground in Pomerania rainfall exceeds 700 millimetres (28 inches), and in most of Masuria it is over 600 millimetres (24 inches).

Poland would be faced with problems of water supply even more acute than those which actually exist if the rainfall were evenly distributed through the year. As it happens, the rainfall of Poland is very conspicuously a summer rainfall. Everywhere the maximum comes between May and September. On the Baltic coast this summer maximum is least marked, but over most of the country the months of June, July and August have almost three times the rainfall of the three winter months. This disparity becomes most marked in the mountains, where Zakopane receives within the summer period no less than 457 millimetres (18 inches), and in winter only about 114 millimetres (4·5 inches).

Much of the winter precipitation is in the form of snow over all Poland. In the milder west, the snow lies for only short periods, melting away before the next snowfall. Toward the east the duration of snow cover is longer, increasing from less than 40 days in the Odra valley to 60 and even more in the east (Fig. 1.9 b). There are no permanent snowfields, not even in the Tatry, where, however, snow patches linger until mid-summer and may last even through the year. Nevertheless the Sudety are very snowy, as the names of some of the summits—Śnieżka and Śnieżnik for example—suggest. Here snow lies for over 150 days, and in the Beskidy and Tatry it may last for 200 days in the year on the higher ground.

The climate of Poland is not distinguished by its abundance of sunshine. It is cloudy much of the time, and, despite the relatively low rainfall, the humidity is high. Very few areas have more than fifty really fine days in a year, and these occur along the Baltic coast, in western Poland, and in Lower Silesia. Eastern Poland and the mountains are notable for the heavy cloud-cover which may occur on as many as half the days in the year.

Rivers and run-off. The pattern which the rivers of Poland make on the map has been mentioned several times in the discussion of regional geography. Most of the country lies within the drainage basins of the Odra and the Vistula (Fig. 1.4), and both rivers also drain very small areas outside Poland, the Odra in East Germany and Czechoslovakia, and the Vistula in Czechoslovakia and the Soviet Union, but they are predominantly Polish rivers, and their regime derives almost exclusively from the climatic conditions of Poland. Only in Pomerania and Masuria are there extensive areas drained by rivers which flow to neither the Odra nor the Vistula. There are furthermore minute areas, totalling only a few square miles, which are drained to the Elbe, the Danube, the Dniestr and the Niemen.

The regime of the Odra and Vistula is that described by Pardé as 'pluvio-nival'.[1] It derives primarily from the incidence of rainfall, but is modified by the seasonal melting of snow both in the mountains and on the plains. The graph (Fig. 1.5) showing the coefficient of discharge, by months, of the Odra and of its tributary, the Nysa Kłodzka, appears to be in conflict with the seasonal distribution of rainfall. This is because the winter rainfall, though relatively small, loses little

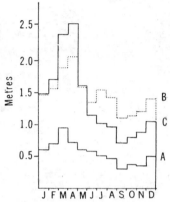

Fig. 8.7. Average monthly level
of the Vistula at: (A) Kraków,
(B) Zawichost, (C) Toruń.
After J. Lencewicz.

by evaporation and is, in part at least, stored up as snow until it is suddenly released by the melting in early spring. The summer discharge is reduced by the high rate of evaporation. Though liable to be distorted by summer storms of great violence, the graph of the rivers' discharge in summer and early autumn suggests a low rate of run-off. Fig. 8.7 shows the level of the Vistula through the year at three points along its course. The late winter maximum is apparent, but superimposed upon it is a secondary maximum, particularly apparent at Zawichost, in July and August, deriving from the summer storms of the plains.

For much of their courses, the more important Polish rivers occupy broad flood-plains, over which they formerly meandered in a dangerous and undisciplined fashion. Today their courses are trained between levées which assume impressive dimensions along parts of the middle Vistula and Odra valleys. The danger of flood during both

[1] Maurice Pardé. *Fleuves et Rivières*, Paris, 1933, pp. 101–7.

the spring melting of the snow and the period of summer storms has been reduced but not eliminated. Occasionally the floods are disastrous, and their frequency lends point to the siting of older river towns, like Płock, Toruń, Fordon and Warsaw itself, on the low bluffs which sometimes border the river.

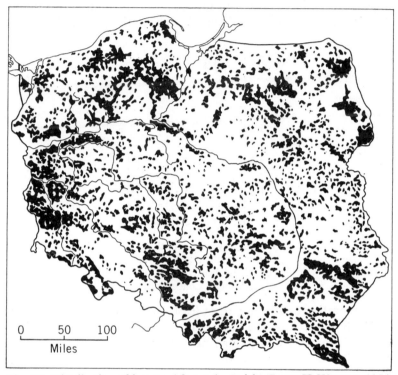

Fig. 8.8. Distribution of forests. After *Atlas Polski*, Zeszyt II, Warsaw, 1954.

VEGETATION AND SOILS

In contrast with most other countries of Eastern Europe, Poland is relatively homogeneous. Except in the mountains of southern Poland, the landforms are relatively simple; there are no marked contrasts in climate; soils belong mainly to a few closely related categories, and vegetation is fairly uniform over the whole country.

Vegetation
Only in the north-east of Poland, in the Białowieża Forest, does any considerable extent of the country's primeval vegetation cover survive.

It is mixed forest, with oak, hornbeam, pine and spruce the predominant species. Similar forests had formerly extended over the
whole region of the older drift. In general conifers tended to occur on
the sandy soils, and oak on the clay. In the damp flood-plains alder
and willow, with stands of elm, predominated, as in some areas they
still do (Fig. 8.8). The areas of newer drift in Pomerania and Masuria
show beech and oak, with fir on the lighter soils, as the predominant
forest types. Only in the mountain regions of southern Poland does
one meet with extensive areas of predominantly coniferous forest.
The loess areas of Silesia and southern Poland were formerly only
lightly wooded, but it is probable that forest covered the whole country
at the beginning of the historical period.

Today, about 26 per cent of the area remains under forest and most
of the remainder is under some form of agricultural land-use. Except
in the Białystok region, the present forest cover bears evidence of the
hand of man. Much of it has been planted, and this has tipped the
balance in favour of the faster maturing conifers. Elsewhere the woodlands have been maintained by the peasantry which depended upon
them for firing and building materials, and this has in turn tended to
eliminate the less useful species.

Soils

The pattern of soils in Poland is, in its broad lines, a relatively simple
one. Over much of the country there is a clay, most of it of glacial
origin and more or less strongly podzolised (Fig. 8.9). In northern and
western Poland are areas of sand, derived in the main from the outwash deposits of the glacial period. These vary in size from a fraction
of an acre to many square miles. They have no agricultural value, and
the most that can be done is to prevent them from blowing and injuring
other land than that which they already cover.

Along the valleys lie broad belts of alluvium, potentially fertile but
in general poorly drained and still exposed to the danger of severe
flooding. Peaty soils have formed along the *pradoliny* and in many of
the depressions left in the cover of boulder clay. Most are small, and
originated in kettleholes in the moraine, but in a few areas of northern
Poland black, peat soils cover extensive areas. But in general, podzolised clays, sands and peat form a mosaic, far too complex to represent
on a small-scale map.

The loess soils, which have been formed beyond the extent of all
except the earliest glaciation, are the best in Poland. They cover part

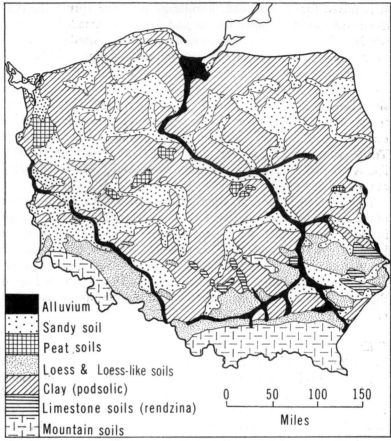

Fig. 8.9. Distribution of the principal soil types. After *Atlas Polski*, Zeszyt
I, Warsaw (1953) and J. Lencewicz.

of Silesia; they occur around Kraków; extend in a narrow belt
along the north of the Beskidy, and are found around Sandomierz and
over the Lublin plateau in south-eastern Poland. Limestone soils,
lastly, cover parts of the hilly regions of southern Poland where
Secondary limestone outcrops, notably in the Kraków Jura and in the
higher parts of the Lublin Plateau.

POPULATION AND SETTLEMENT

Poland is today, as it has been for most of its history, one of the most
populous states in Europe. According to the census of 1960, the total

population was 29,731,000, and given the very high birthrate, this
must now, in 1967, be about 32 million. At the time of the 1931 census,
the population within an area almost 25 per cent larger was 32,107,000,
and by the time of the outbreak of the Second World War, this had
probably risen to about 34,500,000. What fraction of this population
died or was killed during the war can never be known with certainty.[1]
Most of the Jewish population, which had exceeded three millions,
was exterminated; a large number of Poles were killed on battlefields

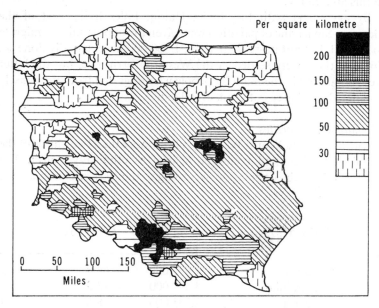

Fig. 8.10. Distribution of population. After J. Loth and Z. Petrazycja,
Geografia Gospodarcza Polski, Warsaw, 1960.

of Europe and North Africa, in concentration camps, or in the savage
suppression of 'risings' within Poland itself.

The postwar changes in Poland's boundaries might have been
expected to bring about a reduction in population. The 'lost' territories in the east had contained over 10 million people before the
Second World War, whereas the 'recovered' territories in the west had

[1] Polish estimates put this total at about 6 million. H. Zielinski, *Population
Changes in Poland*, New York, 1954, gives 4·9 million, and the *Economic Bulletin
for Europe*, United Nations, **1**, no. 1 (1949), at 4·3 million.

a population of about 8,855,000 at the outbreak of the war. In reality, however, most of the Germans, who made up the greater part of the population in the latter, either fled or were expelled as the war neared its close. The population of the Western Territories, it is claimed, included about 1,260,000 ethnic Poles, who remained after the transfer of sovereignty. Some four million Germans must have left by 1946, and a further two million have departed less precipitately in the years following. It is very unlikely that more than 150,000 Germans remain in this area today.

By agreement with the Soviet Union, Poles living east of the German–Soviet line of partition were given the opportunity to migrate to Poland, but not more than about 1,500,000 have actually done so. Some of these were settled in the Western Territories, but the latter were populated in the main by people who migrated from the densely populated rural areas of Central Poland.

The national minorities
Before the Second World War only a little more than two-thirds of the population of Poland could be defined as ethnically Polish. The composition of the population according to the 1931 census, is shown in Table 31.[1]

Table 31. National groups in Poland—1931 census

Polish	21,993,000	68·9
Ukrainian	4,442,000	13·9
Jewish	2,733,000	8·6
Byelorussian	1,697,000	5·4
German	741,000	2·3
Russian	139,000	0·4
Others	172,000	0·5

As a result of changes of boundary and migration of peoples, a far more homogenous population has been created. In 1963 the national minorities were estimated as Table 32 shows.

As a result of wartime losses, territorial changes, and the resulting movement of people, the population of Poland was reduced in 1946 to

[1] Based on language; it underestimates the number of Jews.

Table 32. National minority groups—1963 estimates

Ukrainian	180,000
Byelorussian	165,000
Jewish	31,000
Slovaks	21,000
Russian	19,000
Gypsies	12,000
Lithuanians	10,000
German	3,000
Czechs	2,000
Others	10,000
	453,000

about 23,930,000, but, despite a continued loss by migration from the Western Territories it rose by 1950 to 25,008,000, and in 1960 to 29,731,000. The Polish birth-rate, which had previously been one of the highest in Europe, has dropped sharply in recent years to the relatively low level of 17·3 per thousand in 1965. It is predominantly a young population (Fig. 8.11); a third of it is under 16, and the older age groups are relatively small with a marked predominance of women. This is a factor of great importance in assessing the industrial resources of Poland during the coming years.

Another feature of the growth of Poland's population in recent years has been the sharp increase in the number of those living in towns. In 1931, only 27·4 per cent of the population was described as urban. By 1946 this had risen to 31·8, and by 1950 to 39 per cent. At the time of the 1960 census only 51·9 per cent was still rural, the rest of the population being classed as urban. The latest estimates show that a majority of the population is now urban, and it must be assumed that most of the future increase in population will have to be absorbed into the towns.

Rural settlement

Nevertheless, Poland must still be considered in many respects an agricultural and peasant country. Every small town is partly rural in its function, and like medieval cities in western Europe, still contains a proportion of farmers who journey daily to the fields. The converse practice, so common in western Europe and North America, whereby city-workers live in rural areas and commute daily to the city, is only now developing significantly. In consequence a rather larger fraction of the total population is engaged in rural pursuits than is apparent from the simple division into those who dwell in town and country.

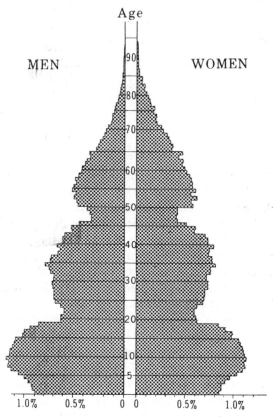

Fig. 8.11. Structure of the population of Poland, 1964. After *Rocznik Statystyczny, 1966.*

The rural population lives mainly in villages surrounded still, except in the few areas of state or collective farms, by open-fields across which lie scattered the peasants' strips of farmland. Most of the villages have been occupied continuously since their first establishment, generally in the Middle Ages. But the individual houses of which they are composed have no such longevity. To the natural tendency of wooden huts to rot and decompose in a damp climate must be added their liability to catch fire and to be destroyed in wartime. Every village, except the newest, must have been rebuilt many times, and with each rebuilding its shape must have become to some extent distorted. The earlier villages tended to be relatively compact, as this gave the villages some degree of protection from enemies, both natural and human. In recent years settlement has tended to become more dispersed. A very slow movement toward the concentration of previously scattered farm strips has led to the building of cottages at a distance from the main village and within the limits of a compact farm holding. A scattered settlement pattern dates, in a few areas such as the mountains, from the earliest period of human settlement in the area. The same is true of the lake-country of northern Poland, where isolated settlements also tended to develop in this much dissected country. But over much of the Polish Plain scattered cottages and houses are of relatively recent origin.

Villages in Poland tend to conform to a small number of distinct types. Most belong to some variant of the street-village, in which the houses lie on each side of the road along which the settlement grew up. Sometimes the houses are irregularly spaced on each side of a winding street—the *ulicówka* (*G. Strassendorf*). Sometimes their spacing is more regular, and the streets may look as if they had been planned—the *szeregowka* (*G. Reihendorf*). Or the settlement may have originated in cottages located along a trackway through the forest, and the cultivated land of each, instead of being scattered through the open-fields, consists of a narrow strip extending from its narrow frontage on the road back to the distant forest margin. This is the forest-village, *Lancuchowka* (*G. Waldhufendorf*).

The great majority of Polish villages belong to one or other of these types, but three more highly nucleated forms also occur, especially in western Poland. These include the round-village, which Meitzen called the *Runddorf* and regarded as a typically Slav form of settlement. In Poland it is known as *wies okrągła* or *okolnica*, but it is very far from widespread, and is typical of East Germany rather than of Poland. The oblong-village, *owalnica* (*G. Angerdorf* or *Langdorf*) is more common. Its English name is something of a misnomer; it is oval or spindle-shaped rather than oblong, and is made up of a street which divides to enclose an elongated 'green' before reuniting. In form and function, if not also in origin, it appears to have affinities with the round-village, and, like the latter, occurs most frequently in western Poland.

12*

We have lastly the infrequent compact or nucleated village, *wielo-drożnica* (*G. Haufendorf*), consisting of a tight, confused pattern of streets, houses and farmyards, and sharply distinguishable from the fields. It is commonly regarded as typically German, and its existence in Poland may represent the cultural influence of German settlers. It is, however, most common in the loess areas, where the soil is fertile, the former woodland cover was light, and there was no impediment in the form of marshes, patches of sand and of low quality soil to the extension of cropland in all directions from the village nucleus.

None of these village patterns was ever absolutely distinct, and re-building through the centuries has tended to blur their original out-lines. Nor were they ever clearly differentiated from one another geo-graphically. In most parts of Poland *scattered* settlements are spread among the larger and more nucleated; in western Poland the spindle-shaped and forest-villages are diffused among the street villages. Nevertheless, it is possible to represent on a map, if only approxi-mately, the dominant village types in Poland. (Fig. 5.4.)

The traditional building materials in the villages and to some extent also in the towns is wood, though brick is now replacing timber in the construction of cottages and farm buildings, especially in western Poland. The traditional Polish farmhouse is usually rectangular and built of logs set horizontally and morticed at the corners. It is usually set at right angles to the road, and its entrance may be towards the street or into the small yard which lies to one side. Inside it is divided into two rooms, with a central fire-place, and brick-built chimney. The roof design varies greatly, but its covering in the plains is usually thatch, and in the mountains, wooden shingles. In some areas there is an ornate gable end and a porch facing the street. All too often the traditional roof of thatch comes to be replaced by a covering of corrugated iron or of tar-paper spread over wooden boards, while the picturesque wood construction is now being abandoned in favour of the more hygienic brick and concrete.

The cottage usually lies on one side of a small yard. Along another there may be a similar building in which one or two cows and horses may be kept, and sometimes a third serves as storage for crops, seed and implements. The small group of buildings is sometimes almost enveloped in fruit and shade trees, so that in summer it is almost im-possible to gain a view of a village as a whole owing to the masses of greenery which envelop it. In some parts of western and north-western Poland, the settlement derives from the manor-house (*dwór*), farm buildings and workers' housing of the feudal estates. Land reform has broken up the estates, but has not always altered significantly the pattern of the settlement.

Urban settlement

There is a small number of large cities; a greater number of towns of

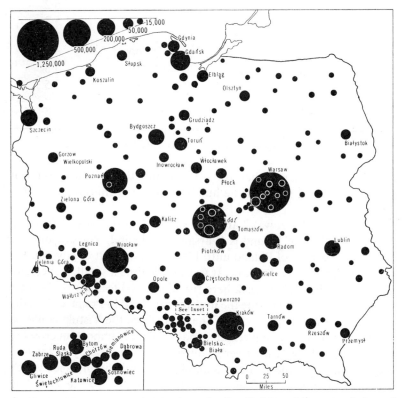

Fig. 8.12. Distribution of cities in Poland; all cities with a population of more than 10,000 are shown, and those with over 50,000 are named. Data from *Rocznik Statystyczny, 1965.*

intermediate size, with a population between 20,000 and 100,000, and a large number of small towns which present the greatest problem in the urban geography of Poland. As Table 33 shows in 1964 there were no less than 891 towns (*miasta*).

It is possible in the following pages to describe the location and

Table 33. Size and number of towns and urban population, 1966

Size in thousands	Number of towns	Urban population (thousands)	Percentage of population
Over 200	10	4,840	15·3
100–200	13	1,970	6·2
50–100	26	1,699	5·3
20–50	79	2,336	7·4
10–20	151	2,090	6·6
5–10	246	1,749	5·5
Under 5	366	1,115	3·5
	891	15,799	49·8

Based on *Rocznik Statystyczny, 1967*.

function of those larger than 100,000 and only the more important of the cities of lesser size. For the hundreds of small cities one can only generalise.

Warsaw (*P.* Warszawa). Largest in size and most varied in function among the cities of Poland is Warsaw, the capital. Warsaw did not become the capital of Poland until 1596 when the seat of government was transferred from Kraków. It was at this time a small, walled city sitting atop the bluffs, which here rise about 100 feet above the west bank of the Vistula. Despite the low, marshy land in Praga, across the river to the east, this was one of the sites where the Vistula could be most easily crossed, and it remains today the most important crossing point in the whole of the river's course from the Beskidy to the sea. To the north lies the Puszcza Kampinoska and the marshes which surround the junction of the Bug and the Vistula. To the south the damp flood plain of the Vistula, protected by levées, becomes wider. Medieval Warsaw had been a small and relatively unimportant town. During the seventeenth century its growth was inhibited by the 'deluge'[1] of foreign invaders who ravaged the country at intervals during the second half of the century. During the uneasy peace which marked much of the eighteenth century it expanded rapidly. Adjoining

[1] The 'Deluge' is the name sometimes given to the period from 1655–67 when Poland was invaded by the Swedes, Russians, Turks and Tatars and others. It is the title (*Polish:* Potop) of one of the novels in the *Trilogy* of H. Sienkiewicz.

the Old City (*Stare Miasto*), to west and south there grew up the city of the aristocracy, who were attracted to the city, as the French aristocracy was to Paris. Here they built their baroque or Palladian-style palaces, many of which survive, some still set in their parks and gardens, to provide homes today for government departments and cultural institutions. The Partitions, wars and risings prevented any significant expansion of Warsaw until well into the nineteenth century. In 1848 the standard gauge railway was completed from Vienna to Warsaw, and the city was at once put into closer contact with western Europe. Factories and small industrial cities burgeoned along the railway to the south-west of Warsaw: Włochy, Ursus, Piastów, Pruszków, Grodzisk Mazowiecki, Żyrardów. Nineteenth century expansion was, however, restricted by the fact that, after the suppression of the 1830 rising, the Russians built a citadel to the north-west of the city, together with a number of forts. Building was permitted in the vicinity of these establishments only on the condition that it could be torn down if considered necessary by the military authorities. In consequence, the city-centre was very densely built, while many peripheral areas had poor quality building or none at all. It was not until the present century that permanent buildings were erected in some of these areas. The spread of the city has now moved westward to incorporate the suburbs of Muranów, Mirów and Młynów, and north-westward to the predominantly residential suburbs of Żoliborz and Marymont. Muranów became the unofficial ghetto, and as such was sealed off by the Nazis and, in 1943, utterly destroyed. South of the old city and its nineteenth-century suburbs, a belt of low-lying and marshy land, much of it now laid out in parks, separates the low bluffs from the river. Over the higher ground, well to the west of the Vistula, spread the late nineteenth-century suburbs of Mokotów, Sielce and Rakowiec.

The population of the city grew rapidly from about 250,000 in the 1870's to 700,000 at the end of the nineteenth century. Even under Russian rule, Warsaw was an administrative centre of considerable importance. The building of a network of railways radiating from the city and the subsequent rise of factory industries attracted labour from the surrounding districts. When Poland regained her independence in 1918, the population of the city was about 760,000. Further economic growth and the expansion of administrative services raised the population to about 1,289,000 on the eve of the Second World War. Warsaw suffered more severely than any other city in Eastern Europe in the course of the fighting. Destruction began with the German assault in September 1939; continued during the period of German occupation with sporadic destruction, which included the obliteration of the Muranów suburb, and culminated in the 'Rising' of the summer of 1944. When it was over the city was about 80 per cent destroyed, and its population in January 1945 was reduced to about 162,000. The rebuilding of the centre of Warsaw was unlike that of any other devastated city. It was backward-looking, aiming not so much to create something new as to revive the glories of the past. This it has done by the use of drawings and sketches, especially those of the eighteenth-century painter, Bellotto (Canaletto), who was for a time court painter to Stanisław Poniatowski, the last king of Poland, in order to revive the pristine beauty of baroque and Palladian Warsaw. This work seized the imagination of a uniquely romantic people, and despite the high cost, which Poland was in no condition to afford, the rebuilding of the Old City and the Kraków suburb (Krakowskie Przedmiescie) is now complete, and Warsaw has become even more than it was before the destruction of the Second World War, a museum of the nation's history and a focus of its loyalty.

But the congestion of Muranów and the slums of the industrial quarters have not been revived. Instead their sites have been largely cleared of the debris of war, and apartment blocks built. In the heart of the older commercial city, on the Marszalkowska, once the foremost shopping street, the over-elaborate Palace of Culture (*P. Palac Kultury*), has been built by the Soviet Union, in accord more with the modern architectural style of Moscow than of Warsaw.

The nineteenth-century industries of Warsaw included wood- and metal-working, paper-making and printing, food-processing and the fabrication of textiles and the manufacture of clothing. They were oriented primarily toward the consumer. These industries remain, though somewhat depressed in their relative importance by the establishment of heavy industries. The latter include the building on the north-western margin of the city of a steelworks, designed to produce high-quality steel; the erection of a large power station at Żeran, on the right bank of the Vistula, and the establishment nearby of one of Poland's automobile factories. The population of the city recovered rapidly with its rebuilding, and by 1966 had, with 1,261,300, almost regained its prewar size.

Warsaw became during the nineteenth century the foremost transport centre in Poland, and it has during the ensuing years further developed this role. It lies at the convergence of the main roads and railways. Only the use of the river has failed to keep pace with the city's commercial expansion. A small river dock lies on the east bank of the Vistula, in the Praga suburb, but the volume of traffic downstream from the city is small, and upstream it is almost non-existent.

The plain of Middle Poland is relatively highly urbanised, and four of the five largest cities are found here.

Łódź, the second largest city of Poland, with 745,400 (1966) inhabitants, lies 80 miles to the west-south-west of Warsaw. In every way it contrasts with the capital. It is the creation of the nineteenth century, whereas Warsaw derives from a medieval settlement. Its range of industry is probably narrower than that of any other great city, and it is as ugly as Warsaw is beautiful. The district of Łódź was chosen in the 1820s by the government of the autonomous 'Kingdom' of Poland as the site of a textile industry. The advantages which the area offered were an abundance of labour, proximity to the boundary of Prussia which was destined to supply much of the capital and skill, and numerous streams, individually very small, but each capable of providing power for a succession of textile machines. So the manufacture of woollens, later supplemented by that of cottons and linen, grew up as a domestic industry. The completion of the branch railway from Koluszki, on the Warsaw–Vienna line, coupled with the introduction of the steam-engine, provided the technical basis for the industry's spectacular growth in the late nineteenth century. The liberation of the serfs in 1864 provided the numbers of unskilled labourers which the industrial expansion required, while the skilled came largely from the older textile centres of Lower Silesia and Saxony.

Łódź grew up along a north–south axis, the seven-mile long Piotrkowska street, which remains today the city's principal thoroughfare. Factories large and small, manufacturing cottons, woollens, linen and even silk, grew up behind the dingy facades of Piotrkowska. Their biggest concentrations were at its extremities where a few, large, fortress-like factories, built of red brick, powered by steam-engines and quickly blackened by the grime of Łódź, dominated the landscape. But the textile mills of Łódź ran to hundreds; most were small, and some, occupied only a single floor in a huge, sunless block of flats. The expanding city of Łódź of about 1900, with its filth and misery, its grasping *entrepreneurs* and landless peasants who were attracted to it, are all depicted by Władysław Reymont, in his novel *The Promised Land* (*P. Ziemia Obiecana*) with bitterness but also with an

attention to detail that allows one to recognise in the present landscape the sights and scenes which he depicted.[1]

The industries of Łódź developed with the whole vast market of the
Russian Empire before them. This eastern market was cut off in 1917,
and Łódź has not really been able to expand sales elsewhere to compensate for this. Nevertheless, sales are today increasing within the
Socialist bloc. Rationalisation of production, made possible by the
nationalisation of the whole industry, is eliminating the smaller mills,
reducing costs of production, and improving Łódź's competitive position. The city is, however, fundamentally unsuited for the industry it
supports. It produces locally none of the raw materials which it uses,
and the local water-supply, once thought adequate to provide power
for the industries, no longer suffices for the textile-finishing processes.
Attempts are being made to diversify the industry, by bringing in
other manufactures, including chemicals and synthetic fibres.

Łódź is the focus of an industrial region, in which the various
branches of the textile industry predominate. It was merely the
textile-fabricating village which grew as a result of the coming of the
railway. The others, left behind by Łódź, remain today only medium-
sized or small towns, engaged overwhelmingly in the textile industries,
and disposed in an arc to the west of Łódź itself. Foremost among these
satellite cities are Pabianice, Konstantynów Łódzki, Aleksandrów
Łódzki, Zgierz, and Ozorków, but various branches of the textile
industry are spread out through the small towns north to Łęczyca;
east to Tomaszów Mazowiecki, south to Piotrków, and west to Kalisz.

Wrocław. A little more than a hundred miles across the plain to the
west-south-west of Łódź is Wrocław (*G. Breslau*). The city passed into
Polish possession in 1945, and had not previously been Polish since
the fourteenth century when Kazimierz the Great of Poland formally
ceded Silesia, which had in effect long been lost, to the Bohemian king.
Its nucleus was a group of islands in the Odra, where the medieval
cathedral now marks the site of the early medieval settlement. The
commercial city, planned in the rectilinear fashion common among
medieval cities in Central Europe, spread over the left bank of the
Odra. In the mid-nineteenth century the city had still not spread far
beyond its medieval walls. It was the railway which contributed most
to the developmenent of Wrocław as an industrial city in the second
half of the nineteenth century. It lay between Upper Silesia with its
mining and smelting industries, and the great consuming centres of

[1] Władysław Reymont, *The Promised Land*, New York, Knopf, 2 vols. 1927.

Berlin and Saxony. It fabricated the products of the one and sold them in the markets of the other. Engineering became its principal industry, but to this it added chemical and textile industries as well as the processing of the food products of the Silesian Plain. The Odra was a navigable river of uncertain value. Many attempts had been made to adapt it to the needs of nineteenth-century shipping, but the volume of riverborne commerce remained small and has contributed little—beyond the downstream transport of Upper Silesian coal—to the growth of Wrocław.

Wrocław suffered more severely than almost any other Polish city, except Warsaw, during the Second World War, primarily when it was defended by the Germans against the attacks of the Red Army. Rebuilding is still very far from complete, and its population—477,300 in 1966—remains far short of its prewar level of 621,000 (1939).

Poznań. The city of Poznań (*G. Posen*) shares in some ways the characteristics of both Kraków (see page 358) and Wrocław. It is one of the oldest of Polish cities, and was for a short time the capital of the Polish kings before they transferred their seat to Kraków. Like Wrocław, it grew up within the protection afforded by the braided course of a river, the Warta. The cathedral remains to the east of the present course of the Warta, in the suburb of Ostrów Tumski, while the medieval, commercial city and its modern successor lie to the west. While under German rule, from 1793 to 1918, Poznań grew into a large industrial city, with a population in 1966 of about 440,700, without ever losing its commercial function. Mechanical engineering continues to be dominant, but the annual international fair is evidence that Poznań remains an important centre of trade and commerce.

Bydgoszcz. (*G. Bromberg*), a city of about 258,300 (1966), lies in the marshy *pradolina* which links the valley of the Vistula with that of the Noteć and formerly carried the melt-water of the retreating ice-sheet westward to the sea. It was founded during the fourteenth century, but has none of the charm of most other ancient cities of Poland. It was destroyed in the course of the Swedish wars, and in its rebuilding has become a rather characterless nineteenth-century industrial city. It lies 4 miles to the west of the Vistula, on a small tributary, the Brda. In the eighteenth century a canal was cut from the Brda to the Noteć along the floor of the *pradolina*. This was enlarged in the nineteenth, and has since been of some importance in the waterborne commerce of Bydgoszcz. Among the industries of Bydgoszcz those based upon local agricultural and forest resources are still important. The city is a centre of wood-working, tanning and leather and paper manufacture. But to these have been added mechanical and engineering industries, notably the building of agricultural machines and bicycles, and the manufacture of electrical goods and glass.

Cities of Central Poland. Other cities in Middle Poland are considerably smaller. They include Toruń (115,300) (*G. Thorn*), an ancient city established in the twelfth century by the Teutonic Knights, and still today retaining some of its medieval fortifications and architecture. It is today a university town of great charm, but outside its ancient walls engineering, chemical and printing industries have been established. Toruń was once a river port of importance. The quays along the river, between the latter and the city walls, are still used, though the volume of shipping is today very small.

Upstream from Toruń is Włocławek (68,700), with its manufacture of cellulose and paper, and Płock, now a major oil-refining and petrochemical centre situated on the Friendship Pipeline from the Soviet Union. Scattered through the plains of Wielkopolska is a network of small towns, some little different except in status from villages, most of them having small local industry based upon local agricultural produce or catering for the local demand for machines, fertilisers or bricks. The density of these towns varies roughly with the fertility of the soil and the wealth of the local communities. Towns are fewer in the *województwo* of Zielona Góra (*G. Grunberg*) (63,600) and in the northern part of that of Wrocław, where poor, sandy, forested soils are more extensive.

East of the Vistula cities are fewer and Biayłsłok is the only city of more than local importance in the plains of eastern Poland. Białysłok (142,100), is, like Łódź, a textile manufacturing city, though there can be few as unfavourably placed. The industry was established here for political reasons. It was throughout the nineteenth century part of Tsarist Russia, not of the 'Congress' Kingdom. Whereas the industries of Łódź, lying in 'Congress' Poland, never basked continuously in the light of Tsarist favour, Białystok was always within the Russian customs barrier, and the freedom of the Russian market enjoyed by its manufacturers had no fiscal restriction. But this very advantage of a location close to the Soviet border has now become a hindrance. It is far from both the source of its raw materials and the Polish market for its manufactures, and after the First World War underwent a severe decline, from which it is only now beginning to recover.

Central Poland is the classic region of the Polish small town which has, with improvements in transport, outlived its earlier function of local market and business centre, without at the same time developing other functions.

Cities of northern Poland. The cities of northern Poland are fewer and more widely scattered than those of central. Apart from the port cities, only Koszalin (*G.* Koslin) (54,000) and Słupsk (*G.* Stolp) (59,900) in Pomerania, and Olsztyn (*G.* Allenstein) (78,000) in Masuria have achieved more than a local importance. The port cities, are, however, among the largest and most varied in Poland. They are Szczecin and the Gdynia-Gdansk complex, to which should be added the small town of Elbląg.

Szczecin. The Odra breaks up into a complex system of channels, separated by marshy islands, some 20 miles before it enters the Bay of Szczecin. The city of Szczecin (*G.* Stettin) (314,700) grew up on the left or western bank, where the river was overlooked by a low bluff. The medieval city spread along the bluff, and its docks were established on the river's bank below. Only in recent years have docks and warehouses spread over the islands of the Odra and along the river's banks to the north. Szczecin has from its earliest days been the port of the Odra Basin. The river was much used for transport during the Middle Ages. It then declined in importance, and Szczecin became a railway port, serving the needs of much of eastern Germany. It was the nearest seaport to Berlin, and was Hamburg's rival in handling the seaborne commerce of areas east of the Elbe.

The advance of the Soviet army combined with wartime bombing to reduce Szczecin to ruins. Nevertheless, its earlier role as port of the Odra Basin led to its inclusion within Poland in spite of its location west of the river. The docks were quickly cleared and trade re-opened, but the city itself was rebuilt more slowly. The industries of Szczecin have been redeveloped. In part they are the industries commonly associated with a great port: milling, the preparation of fats and soap, the roasting and grinding of coffee, but Szczecin has also an iron-smelting plant, located on the waterfront to the north of the city, shipbuilding yards, and engineering and chemical works.

Gdańsk and Gdynia. The ancient port city of Danzig, the most illustrious on the whole Baltic coast after Lübeck, lies beside the sluggish Motława, near the point where it joins the yet more stagnant 'Dead' Vistula. The medieval city of brick gothic churches and renaissance merchants' houses, of granaries and warehouses along the waterfront, grew up within the protection of strong walls and was sustained by the commerce of the Vistula Basin. Gdańsk did not suffer the abrupt decline in its fortunes that characterised many European cities after the Great Discoveries had reoriented the trade of the continent. From the time of the Partitions the political boundary of Russia and Prussia divided the basin of the Vistula, stunting the growth of the port which lay at its mouth, but Gdańsk continued to be the chief outlet of the grain of Eastern Europe and even in the nineteenth century the Danzig market powerfully influenced wheat prices throughout Europe.

Navigation on the Vistula had by this date sunk to negligible importance, but still Gdańsk was regarded as the natural port of the river basin, economically inseparable from it. In 1918 the Polish state was recreated, and the functional unity of Gdańsk with its hinterland became, as has been seen (page 297), a matter of political urgency. The compromise, whereby Danzig, with its predominantly German population, became a 'free city', in customs union with Poland, has been discussed. The failure of the Danzigers to cooperate with the Poles—at least to the satisfaction of the latter—led to the decision to found the neighbouring port of Gdynia and thus to inaugurate the period of bitter rivalry which led directly to the Second World War. Gdańsk has, however, continued to develop its manufacturing industries, among which mechanical engineering and shipbuilding are foremost, and in 1966 had a population of 324,300.

In all fairness it should be said that the docking facilities of the port of Gdańsk were inadequate for the needs of the new Poland, and that it would not have been easy to extend them along the banks of the narrow, winding Motława. The new port was established on the open coast 12 miles to the north-north-west. There was a fishing port on the site, but no natural harbour, and only the Hel peninsula provided a natural protection for the port. Nevertheless, for reasons partly economic, but primarily political, the Polish state in 1925 began the construction of the port of Gdynia. The port is entirely artificial. Its basins were created in part by excavating sand and peat behind the coastline, in part by building jetties and breakwaters into the shallow Gulf of Gdańsk (see Fig. 8.4). The port was equipped for handling bulk cargoes, especially coal and iron-ore, and its industries were established to process imported raw materials and food-stuffs.

The population of Gdynia has risen from a few hundreds in the early 1920s to 167,700 in 1966. It has been the fastest growing city in

Poland, but the city itself is entirely subordinated to the port. It lacks charm and interest, and despite the parks and open spaces that have been laid out in it, it remains unattractive in comparison with the rich beauty of its neighbour, Gdańsk.

Gdynia and Gdańsk, separated by 12 miles of straight sandy beach and sand dunes—on which has grown up the seaside resort of Sopot—are administered as separate cities, but their ports are subject to a single authority. They are, however, tending to develop their own different specialities, Gdynia handling bulk cargoes, especially coal and iron-ore, and Gdańsk, the lighter and more varied goods. The commerce of both has in the past been dominated by the export of coal, and indeed the structure of their trade differs from that of Szczecin only in the greater relative importance of iron-ore in the latter. Over the past decade there has been a small decline in the total turnover of all these ports. The rise in the volume of iron-ore, grain and other commodities handled has been insufficient to offset the almost catastrophic fall in the export of coal.

Elbląg (*G.* Elbing) (85,100) is a decayed port. It was once one of the the bases for the invasion of Prussia by the German Knights; it became a member of the Hanseatic League and was prominent in Baltic trade. But its location on a small Masurian river discharging into the landlocked Zalew Wiślany, and linked with the Vistula only by a tortuous waterway, offered it little opportunity to expand. It has faced the competition of Gdańsk and Gdynia, and its seaborne commerce has now come to an end.

Southern Poland. The hills of southern Poland are also less urbanised than the plains of central, for here too agricultural land, on which the prosperity of the small town is based, is less extensive and less fertile. The Lublin Upland, with its loess soil, is an exception, but here the growth of towns with their attendant crafts and industries was discouraged both by greater exposure to invasion and also by the great feudal estates of the East, which themselves constituted the focus of economic life. The cities of this region, then, owed their growth to something other than the agricultural wealth of the surrounding country.

Częstochowa, (176,400) lying near the north-western extremity of the Kraków Jura, grew up on the edge of the central Polish plain, on a small outlier of the Jurassic hills, the so-called Jasna Góra. On its summit was founded in the fourteenth century a monastery of the Paulist Fathers, around which the city grew. The monastery itself was defended in 1655 against the Swedes. The defence may have been less spectacular than subsequent legend has represented it,[1] but it was a turning point in the Swedish campaign, and subsequent generations have seen in this event the direct intervention of the 'Virgin of Częstochowa', whose blackened painting still hangs in the monastery.

Częstochowa became, as it still remains, by far the most important place of pilgrimage in all Poland. Today the city consists of a wide street which ascends the gentle slope of the Jasna Góra from the railway station at the bottom to the baroque towers which rise from its summit. Beyond the railway is the other Częstochowa. Here in the nineteenth century an iron-smelting works—the Raków works—was established to smelt the bedded ores of the Jura, and at a greater distance from the old city lies the far larger Bierut works, a fully integrated iron and steel plant, that was built in the 1950s. The industrial importance of Częstochowa begins to take precedence over its emotional and religious significance, a result that was not unintended by the Polish planners.

Kielce (109,100) lies 60 miles to the east and on the margin of the Holy Cross Mountains. It is an older city which grew up in response to an older mining and metallurgical industry. In the surrounding hills are the remains of a decayed industry, and the city itself was of declining importance until revived in recent years by the redevelopment of its mechanical and engineering industries.

The three nearby cities of Skarzysko-Kamienna (37,100), Starachowice (39,600) and Ostrowiec Swiętokrzyskie (44,200), lying along the valley of the small river Kamienna, which discharges eastwards to the Vistula, all derive their importance from the mineral, rather than the agricultural wealth of the region. The ancient iron-smelting industry of the Holy Cross Mountains survives in Starachowice and Ostrowiec, and in all three are mechanical and engineering industries. In Starachowice are made the 'Star' lorries, now so familiar a feature of the Polish transport services.

Lublin (206,000) is the regional capital of the Lublin Uplands and Podlasie Plain. It lies on rising ground, almost surrounded by the branches of the small river Bystrzyca. It was a walled city, with narrow streets along which lay the handsome town houses of many of the great landowners of south-eastern Poland. It became an economic as well as social centre, handling the export by way of the Vistula of part

---

[1] See particularly the account of the siege given in the second part of Henryk Sienkiewicz's Trilogy, *Potop* (*The Deluge*).

of the agricultural surplus of this rich region. In recent years Lublin has added engineering, particularly the manufacture of lorries, to its traditional industries of food processing. Apart from Lublin, the only important towns of the Lublin Uplands are Zamość and Chełm, both of them small, but with long histories, dominated until recently by the aristocratic families whose great estates once covered much of the region.

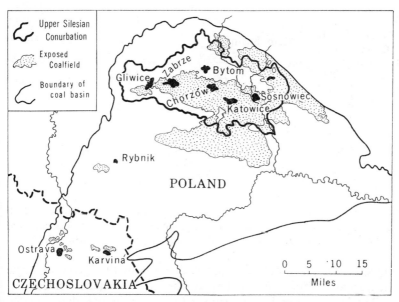

Fig. 8.13. The Upper Silesian coal-field and industrial region. After N. J. G. Pounds, *The Upper Silesian Industrial Region.*

Upper Silesia. South of the Uplands, from Silesia eastward to the Soviet border, lies the most densely settled and most highly urbanised region of Poland. This derives in part from the fertility of the loess belt which extends across the region, and from the commercial highways between Central Europe and the East which traversed it, but, above all, from the coal and metalliferous deposits of Upper Silesia. This latter area had little to recommend it until the eighteenth century. There were a few small towns of medieval origin; lead and silver and later zinc were mined, and a few small charcoal iron works, scattered through the forests, made agricultural implements. But its agricultural wealth was negligible. Only when, in the later years of the eighteenth century, the Prussian government encouraged the coal-mining and iron-smelting industries, did the region begin to change. A cluster of towns lying on or close to the exposed area of the coal-field grew from either villages or small walled towns into large industrial cities, sending out long tentacles of ribbon-development, which met and intertwined. The areas of open country which they enclosed grew smaller, as the land became covered with factories and huge, ugly blocks of.

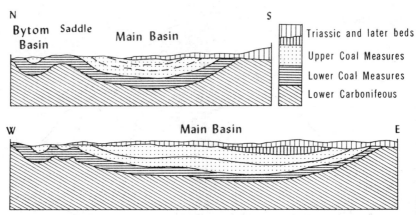

Fig. 8.14. Geological cross-sections through the Upper Silesian coal basin. After N. J. G. Pounds, *The Upper Silesian Industrial Region.*

flats, or was taken out of all productive use by the spreading waste heaps and 'flashes' of stagnant water where the land had subsided.

The industrial region, as defined by its planning authority, (Fig. 8.13) is an area of 154 square miles with a population in 1964, of about 1,500,000. Formally it consists of about a dozen cities, among which the largest are shown in Table 34. Around and between these are grouped a number of smaller towns, most of them primarily industrial, some serving as dormitories for the factory workers. In the whole area only two towns, Gliwice and Bytom, are older than the nineteenth century. The rest have mushroomed with the growth of industry: unplanned, ugly, insanitary. Coal workings burrow beneath them, and the spoil heaps from mines and smelters encroach on them. Wherever there are no buildings, it is usually because the danger of subsidence makes it unsafe to construct them.

The industrial plans of Poland make it necessary that these towns should grow; the supply of water and of other services and utilities

Population and Settlement

Table 34. Cities of the Upper Silesian industrial region (1966)

Katowice (*G.* Kattowitz)	286,800
Zabrze (*G.* Hindenburg)	197,500
Bytom (*G.* Beuthen)	190,900
Gliwice (*G.* Gleiwitz)	163,900
Chorzów (*G.* Konigshütte)	154,000
Ruda Sląska	141,800
Sosnowiec (*G.* Sosnowitz)	140,700
Siemianowice Sląskie	66,400
Tychy	64,400
Dąbrowa Górnicza	60,500
Swiętochlowice	58,400

Source: *Rocznik Statystyczny, 1967.*

makes it difficult for them to do so, and the shortage of land makes it almost impossible. The planning of the Upper Silesian industrial region has faced greater problems than that of most other industrial areas in Europe, and it was obliged to resort to more drastic means. The urbanised area must expand its industries, many of which are tied to particular sites, but more and more of the workers are obliged to live outside the area. Satellite or dormitory towns are being built, each made up of huge apartment blocks for industrial workers who travel daily by train, bus and bicycle to the factories and mines within the urban-industrial complex. Nowy Tychy, with a population of over 50,000, is the largest of such proletarian towns.

The water needs of this region are immense and are growing daily, with the expansion of branches of industries, such as steel-making, which are heavy consumers of water. Local sources have long since been exhausted; the Vistula itself, 25 miles from the industrial region has been dammed at Goczałkowice to supply it; the Beskidy have been tapped, and now attention is turning to more distant sources in the Tatry.

Outside the industrial area and beyond its ring of satellite towns, lie smaller industrial towns, such as Tarnowskie Góry (*G.* Tarnowitz) and Racibórz (*G.* Ratibor), the chemical-manufacturing centres of Kędzierzyn and Oswięcim (*G.* Auschwitz), and the cement centre of Opole (*G.* Oppeln) (76,500). Others, like Pszczyna (*G.* Pless) and Rybnik, are small country towns in which manufacturing and mining are only now beginning to develop.

In the rest of this southern region of Poland, the basis of its wealth and urbanisation has been agriculture and trade. Its cities are old—almost all are medieval. Most were once walled and still retain some fragments of the gateways and fortifications, as well as medieval and baroque churches and a Renaissance town hall and merchants' houses. Such are Tarnów (78,700), Rzeszów (70,000), Przemyśl and Sandomierz, but the largest, richest and most beautiful is Kraków.

Kraków. The expansion of the city limits to include the new industrial township of Nowa Huta, 5 miles to the east, has brought Kraków into third place among the cities of Poland, with a population of about 525,000. Kraków grew up during the early Middle Ages on the north bank of the Vistula, here quite a small river and navigable only by the smallest river craft. Its nucleus was the limestone bluff, on which the Wawel fortress was built. In 1305 this became the seat of the Polish kings and the capital of Poland. Within its walls was built the gothic cathedral of the bishops of Kraków, and in the sixteenth century much of the fortress was rebuilt in the Renaissance style which we see today. The medieval city—its walls now replaced by parks and gardens, known as the *Planty*—grew up to the north of the Wawel in two stages, first the Slav city close to the fortress, and then the planned German city beyond. At the centre of the latter lies the Town Square —*Rynek Główny*, in which during the sixteenth century the city merchants built the Cloth Hall, or *Sukiennice*. Kraków was for much of its history more a commercial than an industrial city. It lay where the ancient trade routes from Silesia and Moravia converged and then continued eastward along the loess belt to L'vov (*P.* Lwów) and the Ukraine. At the time of the Partitions it had passed into the possession of Austria. From 1815 until 1846 it was a penurious 'free city', but was thereafter again placed under the foolishly ineffective rule of Austria. Its economic growth was discouraged in consequence, and Kraków remained merely a small town with a great past, until in 1918 it again became part of an independent Poland. At the beginning of the century its population was only 85,000. It was the finest historical monument in Poland, but it contributed little to the country's industrial future. Its industrial undertakings were small, and had grown up in spite rather than because of the policy of the Austrian government. They included a few metallurgical and engineering works and some textile, food-stuffs and other consumer goods industries; even in 1945 Kraków remained one of the least industrialised and most bourgeois of Polish cities.

This was one of the reasons among many which led to the location on the eastern outskirts of the city of the integrated 'Lenin' iron and steel works of Nowa Huta, and the extension of the city's boundaries to enclose this working-class suburb of at least 100,000. The character of Kraków has been changed. About half its industrial employment is now in iron and steel, and the old Kraków residents lament the changed character of this once conservative and middle-class city.

Nowa Huta was begun in 1949 on a river terrace almost a mile to the north of the Vistula and five miles east of Kraków. A new town of immense characterless apartment blocks was built nearby, and quickly filled with workers drawn in from the overcrowded farms of Galicia. Coal comes from Upper Silesia and Moravia; iron-ore from the Soviet Union, and the limestone flux from the nearby Jura. The possibility of river navigation, undoubtedly a factor in choosing this site, has not been realised. The Vistula remains a river of uncertain value (see below, page 384), and dock basins at the works and a canal linking them to the river have yet to be constructed. The reasons for locating the plant here appear to have been overwhelmingly political —to proletarianise the city of Kraków—and social, to provide employment in a heavily overpopulated part of the country.

The other towns of southern Poland are very much smaller, but several have grown rapidly in recent years. Tarnów has risen from 37,400 people in 1950 to 78,700 in 1966; Rzeszów, from 28,100 to 70,000. It has been the policy of the Polish government to locate new industries in these towns of overpopulated south-eastern Poland. Tarnów has become a very important centre for the manufacture of basic chemicals and fertilisers, and Rzeszów, of engineering and the building materials industries. In this area the Polish government planned in the 1930s to establish its Central Industrial Region. Although the project was unfinished when the Second World War began, one of its achievements was the building of the small city of Stalowa Wola and its accompanying steel-works.

In terms of urban growth, there is a sharp contrast between the Sudety and the Beskidy. In the former lies the small Lower Silesian coal-field which has been worked since the eighteenth century, and there are many small rivers which were formerly used to power textile factories. Scattered through the mountains today is a large number of small towns, in most of which the woollen textile industry provides the most important branch of industry, as in Dzierżoniów, Świdnica and Jelenia Góra. Towns are fewer in the Beskidy, where the local crafts have rarely been developed into important factory industries. The exceptions are the towns of Bielsko-Biała and Andrychów, both in the western Beskidy, where the cotton industry has become important, and Nowy Targ and Nowy Sącz, which have developed footwear and engineering works. Zakopane is a mountain resort of growing importance. For the rest, only a few small towns are found in the mountain valleys.

AGRICULTURE

Until very recently Poland has been a predominantly agricultural country, and the peasantry have constituted the majority of its population. This situation is now changing. Already, as we have seen, urban

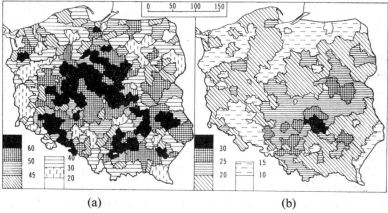

(a)   (b)

Fig. 8.15. (a) Distribution of cropland, as percentage of total area, (b) distribution of land under potatoes, as percentage of total cropland. Both maps after J. Loth and Z. Petrażycka.

dwellers outnumber rural, and the contribution of agriculture to the national economy is in relative though not in absolute decline. In 1950 it had contributed about 47 per cent of the gross national product; by 1960 this had fallen to 23·6, and the latest figures (1966) show that only 19·9 per cent was derived from agriculture.

Poland is by no means well endowed with the resources for agriculture. The climate is nor particularly favourable, and the soils, developed mostly on ground moraine, tend to be either heavy and poorly drained or light, sandy and infertile. The areas of sand and gravel are almost valueless for cultivation, and the extensive areas of damp valley bottom can at their best be used only as meadow and pasture. Sharp variations in soil quality occur over very short distances, and it is difficult to generalise even for the physical regions as delimited earlier in this chapter. The only areas of outstandingly good soils are in southern Poland, where, during a long, dry interglacial period vast quantities of loess were deposited. Patches of loess occur in Silesia south of the Odra river, in the Kraków region, along the edge of the Beskidy and, most extensively of all, over the Lublin Uplands. In some parts of these areas a chernozem has begun to form on the loess, and everywhere the soil is rich, light and easy to till, and crop yields are high in these areas. At the opposite extreme the thin, leached mountain soils of the Sudety and Beskidy are among the poorest in Poland. The pattern of cropping is related to soils, but it must be remembered in discussing the distribution of the more important crops that social and economic factors are often more important than edaphic.

Structure of agriculture
When the Polish state was re-established in 1918, its agriculture was dominated by large estates. Almost half the farm land was in estates of over 50 hectares (123·5 acres), while almost two-thirds of the farms themselves had less than 5 hectares (12·35 acres). Some of the estates of the leading Polish families such as Zamoyski and Radziwiłł, exceeded 20,250 hectares (50,000 acres). Between 1921 and 1939 the Polish government carried through a land reform which reduced somewhat the size and number of the great estates, and used the land taken from them to create or enlarge peasant holdings. It must be noted, however, that this kind of land reform could not touch the peasant problem where it was most serious, that is in overcrowded areas like Galicia, where there were very few great estates to be broken up. In such areas, however, the programme of consolidating the scattered parcels of land at least made peasant farms more workable if it did not increase their size. When the Second World War ended in 1945, further reform was seen to be necessary in Poland proper, whereas in the territory recovered from Germany there had never been any real land reform, and land-holding was still characterised by large farms and estates, Two-thirds of the land confiscated was allocated to landless peasants and to families which had hitherto supplied only labourers on the estates and large farms. The rest was used to supplement very small farms.

At the same time the government established state farms (*gospodarstwa państwowe*) and collectives (*spółdzielnie produkcyjne*) and also instituted co-operatives as a kind of compromise between individual holdings and a fully socialised system of land tenure. The Polish peasant entered the socialised sector unwillingly and at the first opportunity, which occurred in 1956, many withdrew. The socialisation of agriculture remains the declared policy of the government, but little had been done to implement it, and Poland remains the least collectivised of all the countries of Eastern Europe.

The area in each of the three sectors—private, collective and state—in the period 1955–65 is shown in Table 35.

Table 35. Area of private, collective and state farm sectors, 1955–65 (area in thousands of hectares)

	Total farmland	Private	Per- centage	Collective farms	Per- centage	State farms	Per- centage
1955	20,402·8	15,767·9	77·3	1,875·0	9·2	2,759·9	13·5
1958	20,402·8	17,585·1	86·2	205·5	1·0	2,612·2	12·8
1960	20,402·8	17,726·6	86·8	251·3	1·2	2,424·9	11·9
1964	20,130·2	17,189·6	85·4	208·6	1·3	2,609·4	13·3
1966	19,946·8	16,930·6	84·9	337·9[1]	1·7	2,678·3	13·4

[1] Includes land in agricultural 'circles' or cooperatives.

Source: *Rocznik Statystyczny*, various years.

It is evident that peasants withdrew in 1956 on a massive scale from the collectives, but only on a very small scale from the state-farms. In part this was because socialisation tends to be a one-way process, and the changes associated with it are often irreversible. But a reason is to be found also in the distribution of the state-farms themselves. In 1958 the three categories of land tenure were divided between

Table 36. Divisions of land tenure in 1958 between Former Lands and Western Lands (area in thousands of hectares)

	Private	Percentage	Collective farms	Percentage	State farms	Percentage
Former lands	14,126·7	92·8	170·8	1·2	850·4	6·0
Western lands	6,276·1	71·4	34·7	0·5	1,761·8	28·1

the Western or Recovered Lands and the 'Former Lands' (*Ziemie Dawne*) as Table 36 shows. Over a quarter of the farmland in the newly recovered territories was thus in the socialised sector, largely because the peasants, many of whom were new to the area after 1945, had never possessed rights in the land before collectivisation, and, partly because labour was scarcer here than elsewhere and farming methods had to be employed that made the greatest possible use of the labour force. The pattern of cropping differs little between the private and the socialised sectors, though there is a tendency for the former to grow rather more potatoes and the latter more cereals and sugar beet and also to rear larger numbers of cattle.

As a result of the land reforms following both World Wars, the average size of farm holdings is lower than at any previous time. Only about 10 per cent of the farms have over 10 hectares (24·7 acres), and over 70 per cent of the farmland is in farms of less than this size. In 1958 the distribution of private farms was as shown in Table 37.

Table 37. Distribution of private farms—1960

	Thousand hectares							
	0·5–2	*2–3*	*3–5*	*5–7*	*7–10*	*10–14*	*14–20*	*Over 20*	*Total*
Number of farms	829·9	427·0	664·9	475·7	462·0	283·6	66·6	34·5	3,591·9
Percentage of total farms	32·8	11·9	18·5	13·2	12·9	7·9	1·8	1·0	100·0
Percentage of farmland	6·3	6·2	15·5	16·7	22·8	20·1	6·7	5·7	100·0

Source: *Rocznik Statystyczny*, 1967.

Land use

Almost two-thirds of the entire area of Poland is farmland, and almost a quarter is under forest. Table 38 illustrates the main categories of land use in 1966.

Forest is most extensive, as might be expected, over the sandy and outwash areas, especially in the *Województwo* of Zielona Góra, in the regions of terminal moraine in the north, and in the mountains. Meadow is more widely and also more evenly distributed. It forms broad belts along the great river valleys, and lies in small and scattered patches over the ground-moraine, wherever the natural drainage is

Table 38. Land use in Poland in 1966

Land use	Area (in thousands of hectares)	Percentage
Agricultural land:	19,946·8	64·0
of which: Field crops	15,434·6	49·5
Orchards	247·7	0·8
Meadow	2,430·5	7·8
Pasture	1,834·0	5·9
Forest	8,140·3	26·1
Land not used agriculturally	3,085·9	9·9
Total	31,173·0	100·0

Source: *Rocznik Statystyczny, 1967.*

impeded, and especially in the north-eastern third of the country. Pasture is less extensive; it occurs on upland areas, where the soil is adequately drained but too poor and shallow to be worth cultivating. All the rest, except the 10 per cent that is built on, covered with spoil heaps, quarries or roads, is cropland.

Cropland forms the largest proportion—over 50 per cent—of the total land surface in a broad belt of Middle Poland, between Warsaw in the east and Poznań in the west. It embraces Wielkopolska and neighbouring Kujawy and Mazowsze, and its existence helps in retrospect to explain why this was the heart of the earliest Polish state. Other, though less extensive areas where over half, or even more than 60 per cent of the land is cultivated, are the loess plains of Silesia, the Lublin Uplands, and the narrow strip of rich soil which borders the Beskidy. The areas where cultivation is least extensive are the end-moraine regions of Pomerania and Masuria, the outwash sands which cover much of the Zielona Góra *województwo*, and the hills and mountains of southern Poland.

Crop patterns. In 1966, the sown area was about 5,960 square miles (15,435 square kilometres), almost exactly half the total area of Poland. The peasant communities remain to a large degree self-supporting; their chief crops are those required by themselves and

their farm animals, and cash and industrial crops are relatively unimportant, even on the collective farms. The food shortages that have
arisen in Poland in recent years have sprung from the failure of the
peasants to increase their supply of food-stuffs to the growing population of the towns.

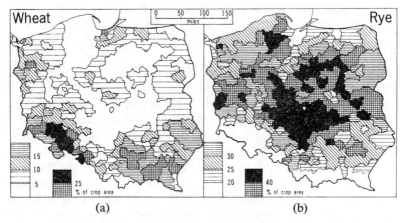

(a) (b)

Fig. 8.16. (a) Distribution of land under wheat, as percentage of total
cropland, (b) distribution of land under rye, as percentage of total cropland.
Both maps after J. Loth and Z. Petrażycka.

Table 39. Cropland in 1966

	Thousand hectares	Percentage of cropland
Grain crops:	8,546·0	55·6
of which: wheat	1,699·0	11·0
rye	4,376·0	28·5
barley	688·0	4·5
legumes	435·0	2·8
Potatoes	2,766·0	18·0
Industrial crops:	952·0	6·2
of which: sugar beet	435·0	2·8
oil seeds	306·0	2·0
flax and hemp	138·0	0·9
Fodder crops	2,204·0	14·3

Source: *Rocznik Statystyczny, 1967.*

13

There are certain regional variations in the cultivation of the principal crops. Rye dominates throughout the plains of Middle Poland, where it occupies over 40 per cent of the cropland over large areas (Fig. 8.16 b), and is the most important single crop in much of Pomerania and Masuria. On the other hand it occupies only a relatively small area—under 25 per cent of the cropland—in most of southern Poland. Here the gentler climate and more rewarding soil favour wheat (Fig. 8.16 a), which is the most important crop in most of the area except Upper Silesia.

Potatoes, which serve as fodder and industrial crop and as a staple in the peasant's diet, are the most widely and uniformly cultivated of all the more important crops (Fig. 8.15 b). Over almost the whole country they occupy from 10 to 30 per cent of the cultivated area. Sugar beet is extensively grown only in a belt of territory extending from Gdańsk south-westward through Bydgoszcz to Poznań and Wrocław, and here its cultivation tends to be fixed by the presence of the factories which process the beet. Among the less widely cultivated crops are oats, preeminently a crop of the poor and acid soils of the northern lake-country and southern mountains; barley, grown mainly for brewing and suited to the good soils of Middle Poland and the southeast; rape-seed and flax, found mainly in the west and north; hemp and tobacco, most common in the east and south-east; and maize important in southern Poland where alone it is warm and sunny enough for it to grow well.

There has been little change in recent years in the total cultivated area, and the acreages of the more important crops have not varied significantly. Production however has increased sharply, despite a

Table 40. Crop yields, 1934–63 (in quintals per hectare)

	Wheat	Rye	Barley	Oats	Potatoes	Sugar-beet
1934–38 average[1]	14·6	12·8	15·7	14·5	138	265
1946–49 average	10·8	11·2	11·1	12·1	119	179
1955	14·9	14·1	15·1	13·9	100	186
1960	16·9	15·4	17·4	16·9	131	256
1963	19·9	16·3	19·8	16·8	150	287
1966	21·5	17·8	20·8	18·8	169	313

[1] Within present boundaries.

Source: *Rocznik Statystyczny, 1967.*

decline in grain yields during the years of enforced collectivisation. Table 40 illustrates the improvement in yields.

Output per hectare for all the grain crops was somewhat higher on cooperatives than on individual farms, and lowest on state farms. Yields of potatoes and sugar-beet were also highest on private farms and lowest on state farms. The amount of agricultural machinery in use has increased in recent years, though less rapidly than in Czechoslovakia and in most West European countries. In 1960 there were still only 62,450 farm tractors, of which over two-thirds were state-owned and operated. Fields on the farms in the private sector are in general ill-suited to the use of machines, and the farm labour force is still so large that there is little inducement to save labour. The greatest increase in farm equipment has been in the lighter, horse-drawn machines, such as mowers.

On the other hand efforts to improve the quality of the land have met with considerable success. Large areas of farmland—5,713 square miles in 1960 alone—have been improved by drainage or other means, and the increased use of fertiliser and lime has been striking. The land is now receiving on average 48·6 kilogrammes of fertiliser per hectare as against 38·2 within the same boundaries in 1937–38. The use of lime, particularly necessary on the heavy clay soils which cover much of Central Poland, has risen to 25·3 kilogrammes per hectare. The improved crop yields are to a large degree, to be explained in terms of a greater use of fertiliser and a general improvement in soil quality.

Farm animals

Almost every farm in Poland has a few animals. A horse is essential to pull the plough or draw the farm wagon to the neighbouring market. One or two cows will supply the farm family with milk and perhaps a small surplus for sale; a couple of pigs may grow fat on the farm waste, and a few hens, ducks and geese may pick a living around the yard and along the nearby street. Most farmers do not have grazing land, and they may only share a small patch of meadow with others. Any extensive animal husbandry is impossible, and the feeding of the two or three essential animals stretches to the utmost the resources of the smaller farms. Indeed, the tethered goat grazing by the roadside is an all too common sight both here and in many other parts of Eastern Europe. Only in western Poland is the rearing of animals for the market practised on any considerable scale.

Pigs are the most numerous, and horses the most necessary farm animals, because the horse, rather than the ox, is the conventional draft animal. The total number of farm animals in 1966 was:

Cattle:	10,387·3
of which: cows	6,010·1
Pigs	14,251·1
Sheep	3,164·2
Horses	2,589·7
(In thousands)	

These animals are essential to peasant farming, and for this reason, their distribution shows little regional variation and concentration. Pigs, being mainly scavengers, are most numerous where the cultivated land makes up the greatest proportion of the whole, that is, in the plains of Central Poland and the loess regions of the south. The pattern of sheep-rearing is the opposite; sheep are most numerous in those regions—the northern lake-country and the hills and mountains of the south—where cultivation is least extensive. Horses are most numerous where cropland is most extensive, and the distribution of cattle forms a similar pattern, with the southern half of the country having greater numbers than the north.

It is difficult to summarise in a few pages the peasant agriculture of Poland, which is, apart from Yugoslavia, the only Central or East European country to retain with little alteration its peasant agriculture. Chapter 6 has described the main features of this system of agriculture which is also a way of life for those who practise it. That it is wasteful of time and energy is apparent; that it duplicates labour can readily be seen from the dozens of half-empty wagons which set out in the morning from each village and move, as if in convoy, to the market of the nearest town, and return even less heavily laden in the afternoon. It may not get the most out of the soil, but recent events have shown that the only real alternative, collectivisation, is likely to obtain even poorer returns per unit area. The government has put on record its opposition to the system of peasant agriculture and its desire to see it incorporated into the socialised sector, but it has also made it clear that it is wise enough not to try to make the change by forceful means. At present peasant cooperatives, or 'circles', are gaining in importance, and may provide an alternative to collectivisation.

MANUFACTURING INDUSTRY

Poland is made up of territory which during the nineteenth century, the period when the industrial pattern of most of Western Europe was established, was divided between the empires of Prussia, Russia and Austria. In each of these divisions of its territory industrial growth was encouraged or restricted according to the vagaries of domestic policy, so that the Polish republic after 1918 was obliged to draw together and harmonise the industrial growth in the three disparate sectors of the country. The situation was aggravated after 1945 with the addition to Poland of those parts of Germany lying east of the Odra and Nysa.

During the nineteenth century the chief centres of industrial growth were the coal-field area of Upper Silesia and its adjacent areas of non-ferrous mining, the Łódź region, and the hilly region around Kielce. The first of these (see above, page 355, and below, page 377) grew into one of the major industrial regions of Europe; Łódź became the most important centre of the textile industries east of Saxony, but the industrial revolution in the Holy Cross Mountains, the most carefully planned of them all, failed in most of its branches and met with only very limited success in others. Its legacy today is an almost moribund iron industry.

After 1918 the Polish government tried to knit these elements together. Extension of industry in Upper Silesia seemed unwise in view of the political division of the area and proximity to the German boundary, and instead, the Polish government planned to establish a Central Industrial Region between the valleys of the Upper Vistula and the San. The iron and steel works of Stalowa Wola were part of this plan, as also was the extension of the Starachowice works and a few engineering and chemical works. But the plan was barely started when the Second World War made all progress impossible. The boundary changes of 1945 united the Upper Silesian industrial complex under Polish control, and added the centres of heavy industry in Lower Silesia and Szczecin as well as the older textile industries of the Sudety. Within these new limits the government planning authorities have developed a new industrial pattern on a broader resource base than they had ever possessed before.

Fuel and power
Poland is more richly endowed than any Central or East European country, except perhaps West Germany, in the essential basis of its

industry, fuel. Poland contains two bituminous coal-fields, those of Upper and Lower Silesia, as well as several extensive deposits of brown coal and lignite, and small and now rapidly diminishing reserves of petroleum. The natural gas resources, however, have recently been greatly extended by discoveries in the Carpathian foot-hills of south-eastern Poland. The hydro-electric potential of the mountain streams is considerable, but hitherto little developed, and existing dams have been built more for water conservation than power generation.

Bituminous coal. The Upper Silesian coal-field forms a triangular area of over 2,000 square miles (5,180 square kilometres), of which about a fifth extends across the boundary into Czechoslovakia. Structurally the coal-field is a basin with a clearly defined rim. The whole coal series is preserved in its central portions, but around the upturned margins, only the middle and lower coal measures remain. (See Fig. 8.14.) Several small anticlines within the limits of the coal basin bring the lower parts of the coal series close to the surface and within the range of contemporary mining techniques. Most important of these is the 'main saddle' (*siodło główne*), which extends from west to east across the north of the basin, but a similar saddle at Rybnik, near the western edge of the basin is now being exploited. The significance of these 'saddles' is that they bring the economically more valuable middle and lower coal measures within reach of current mining techniques and supply, in particular, coking coal, which is now in great and increasing demand. The central portions of the coal-field have never been opened up or indeed really explored. The obstacles to their development are the great depth at which the coal seams lie and the relatively low quality of the uppermost seams in the series. Mining is likely to spread around the margins of the basin and to attack the 'saddles' before it faces the tasks of extracting coal from much of the central areas of the field.

The reserves are immense, and, among European coal-fields, are exceeded only by those of the Ruhr. The seams are unusually numerous, numbering over 200, many of which, however, are thin and discontinuous. On the other hand some of the seams are among the largest known and in exceptional cases are as much as 30 feet thick. Seams of this thickness constitute an *embarras de richesse*; the workings are difficult to support, and the subsidence which follows the extraction of the coal has, in the past, wrought great damage to the ground surface. This difficulty is now being overcome by a process of forcing sand into the workings as the coal is removed. Output has risen steadily since the end of the Second World War, in response both to increasing demand and also to the political unification of most of the coal basin. Output from the same area in 1938 was 64,100,000 tons. In 1946 it dropped to 44,300,000, but from that date rose steadily to 91,600,000 in 1956 and to about 118.8 million tons in 1966.

The Lower Silesian coal-field is all that remains of the once extensive coal measures that were caught up in the earth movements which built the Sudety. The seams occur in a narrow belt only locally more than two miles wide, which forms a horseshoe pattern, part in Poland, part in Czechoslovakia. Reserves are very small—currently put at about 3,000 million tons—and the seams are much folded and faulted, and are difficult to work. On the other hand, the coal-field produces a high proportion of coking coal, and its small contribution of no more than 3,200,000 tons in 1966, is more valuable than its small volume would suggest. The mines—only three are now active—are today concentrated in the neighbourhood of Wałbrzych (*G.* Waldenburg), where the width of the coal series broadens to about four miles.

Brown coal, lignite and peat. Among the more valuable assets of Poland's Western Territories are the immense reserves of brown coal. These had been little exploited, as German industry had largely confined itself to reserves lying west of the Odra. Brown coal underlies much of the Zielona Góra *województwo*, and scattered deposits extend up the Odra valley in the direction of Wrocław and eastward into Wielkopolska. Brown coal is now being extracted mainly by opencast methods at some eight sites close to the western boundary, and also at Konin, east of Poznań, which is the most important site. Production had increased from 20,000 tons within present boundaries in 1937 to 9,300,000 tons in 1960 and to about 24,508,000 in 1966. Much of the fuel is used directly in thermal power stations, as at Turoszów, very close to the East German border in Lower Silesia, and the potential power development of Central Poland is great enough to justify plans for a more intensive industrialisation of this region.

Peat deposits are more widely distributed even than those of lignite. They are particularly extensive over the most recently glaciated areas and in north-east Poland in particular are capable of supplying thermal-electric generators, though their calorific value is low. They are, however, at present used only by the local peasantry for their own domestic purposes.

Petroleum. Poland is now one of the least important of the world's producers of petroleum and natural gas. In 1965 output of petroleum amounted to only 340,000 tons, a quite negligible quantity in terms of world production, and it had in fact been increasing very slowly, despite efforts to stimulate production, for many years. Natural gas production, despite a sharp increase in recent years, is also produced in only small quantity, which in 1965 amounted to 1,312 million cubic metres. The whole of the petroleum and natural gas production comes from the Eastern Beskidy, from an area extending from Nowy Sącz to the Soviet border, where the deposits are a continuation of those of Romanian Moldavia.

Poland today relies heavily on imported petroleum and petroleum products. The Soviet Union supplies the greater part, and an oil pipeline has been completed from the Soviet border to East Germany, by way of Płock, on the Vistula, where a refinery has been built to the north of the city. Much of Poland's needs in petroleum and petroleum products will in the future be satisfied from this source. The output of natural gas is however expanding rapidly, especially from wells at Lubaczów, near Przemyśl, in south-eastern Poland.

Electric power. Industrial power is derived almost wholly from bituminous coal. Of 9,672,000 kw. of installed capacity in 1965, over 96 per cent was generated in steam turbines, using bituminous or brown coal. Only 4 per cent of total capacity, was based on water power, and most of the remainder used coal-burning equipment. The present trend is toward a vigorous increase in the generation and consumption of thermal-electric power. While bituminous coal remains the most important fuel used, it may be expected that brown coal will make a relatively larger contribution in the future, and that further generating stations on the scale of those of Konin and Turoszów will be built.

Metals and minerals

Poland's inadequate reserves of iron-ore stand in marked contrast with the importance of its iron-smelting industry. There are numerous deposits, many of them low-grade and most too small to be worth mining under modern technological conditions. The iron-ores of Upper Silesia, once important in locating the smelting industry here, have been for practical purposes exhausted, and the most important sources are now the bedded Jurassic ores of the Częstochowa region and the older and more fragmentary reserves of the Holy Cross

Mountains. The search for more reserves has been carried on assiduously in recent years, and a number of finds have been made in central and eastern Poland, but these hold out little hope of satisfying Poland's needs. In recent years production of iron-ore has increased, and in 1966 amounted to 3,054,000 tons of ore. The sharp increase in recent years has been achieved at the price of extracting ores of steadily diminishing metal content. The iron content of the ores extracted in 1966 was only 768,000 tons, or 26 per cent about an eighth of the needs of the smelting industry. The rest was imported, mainly from the Soviet Union.

Several non-ferrous minerals are obtained but for practical purposes only lead, zinc and copper are significant. The lead and zinc ores, closely associated with one another, occur in the Triassic shelly limestone, which overlies the northern margin of the Upper Silesian coal-field and extends a short distance north and east of it. The ores have filled solution cavities in the limestone, and were formerly extracted in open pits, but are now worked in half a dozen deep mines, most of them lying to the north of Bytom and near Olkusz, to the east of the Upper Silesian industrial region. Smelting has always been carried on close to the coal mines owing to its very heavy fuel demands. By-products of the lead-zinc smelters are small quantities of cadmium, copper and silver. Copper has recently been discovered in Lower Silesia; mines have been opened near Lubin, and copper smelters built at Legnica and Polkowiec. Table 41 shows the output of non-ferrous metals in recent years.

Table 41. Output of non-ferrous metals (in thousands of tons)

	1937	1950	1955	1960	1964	1966
Crude lead-zinc ores	792	1,284	2,378	2,461	2,597	2,534
Refined zinc	107	114	156	176	187	193
Refined lead	20·5	22·2	34·2	39·7	41·5	43·5
Refined copper	—	10·5	15·7	21·7	36·6	39·8

Source: *Rocznik Statystyczny, 1967.*

The rock-salt deposits at Wieliczka and Bochnia in southern Poland have been known and exploited even longer than the ores of lead and zinc. Trade in rock-salt was well developed during the Middle Ages, and the reserves continue to be worked. But deeper beds of salt which

13*

lie in a narrow belt under central Poland from near Łódź to Inowrocław, are now more important. They are exploited by the now accepted method of dissolving the salt and pumping brine to the surface rather than by underground mining.

Sulphur occurs along the upper Vistula valley to the south of the Holy Cross Mountains, and is now being extracted by the same solution process near Tarnobrzeg, where a chemical industry based on it has been established. Mention should also be made of the gypsum, also Tertiary in date and occurring in close association with the salt deposits of Central Poland; of the granite and other ornamental building stones found in the Sudety; of the sand for glass manufacture; the limestone and marl for cement, especially near Opole, and the omnipresent clay, ranging in quality from that suited for ceramic manufacture to that fit only for common bricks.

Manufacturing industries
In contrast with the small increase in total agricultural output, industrial production increased by 545 per cent between 1950 and 1966. This result was achieved only by a very heavy capital investment in manufacturing, which is almost entirely state-owned and operated as shown in Table 42. The nature of the investment was provided for in

Table 42. Industrial production, 1955–64 (value in milliards of złoty)

	1955	1957	1959	1960	1964	1966
Total industrial production:	241·1	288·8	346·5	487·5	672·0	786·9
of which:						
(1) state-owned	216·4	248·9	298·9	434·7	600·3	784·0
(2) cooperative	23·3	37·5	44·4	48·6	66·9	81·0
(3) private	1·4	2·4	3·2	3·0	2·4	2·9

Source: *Rocznik Statystyczny, 1967.*

the sequence of plans, which have operated since the end of the Second World War. The greater part of the new investment has been in heavy or capital goods industries, and the expansion of consumer goods industries has been relatively small.

The map of manufacturing industries has not been significantly changed as a result of this industrial expansion. The older industries have tended to attract new industries, owing to the locational advantages which they already possessed, and there have been few instances of the deliberate establishment of new industries in hitherto nonindustrialised areas. The most conspicuous example of the latter was the founding of Nowa Huta, for reasons already given, a few miles to

Fig. 8.17. Industrial regions of Poland. Based on K. Dziewoński and St. Leszczycki, in *City and Regional Planning in Poland*, Cornell Univ. Press, 1966.

the east of Kraków. Some new industries, notably chemical and mechanical, have been established in and near Tarnów and Rzeszów, apparently because it was thought to be socially desirable to locate industry in this densely peopled and predominantly agricultural region. There has been a good deal of rearrangement of industry within existing industrial regions, but few new industrial complexes—

except Nowa Huta and the petrochemical combine near Płock—have been created.

The map (Fig. 8.17) shows the industrial regions of Poland. Three levels of industrialisation are distinguished. First are industrial districts, consisting, apart from the larger cities, of regions in which industrial production is far above the national average. These include the Warsaw region, the Łódź region and Upper and Lower Silesia. In the second category, industrialised areas, manufacturing is dominant, but not overwhelmingly so. Such areas are the Gdańsk-Gdynia regions, Bydgoszcz–Toruń, the Kielce-Holy Cross Mountains region, and the rest of Silesia and the Sudety. In the last category, industrialised areas, manufacturing is important, but over the area as a whole, is not the dominant occupation. Such areas are Wielkopolska, the Zielona Góra-Zgorzelec area and much of south-eastern Poland.

The types of industrial specialization in each of these industrial districts and areas have already been mentioned in the course of the examination of the regional geography of Poland. It remains to discuss briefly the more important branches of industry and their distribution in Poland today.

In 1966 the capital goods industries accounted for well over half of total industrial production, and consumer goods industries for the remainder. Table 43 shows the most important groups of manufacturing industries in that year.

The fastest growth has in recent years been in the chemical, metallurgical, and metal fabricating industries, and the slowest, as might have been expected from the general nature of national policy, has

Table 43. *Major groups of manufacturing industries*

	Percentage of total industrial output
Ferrous and non-ferrous metallurgy, machine construction	35·9
Textile, clothing, footwear	13·2
Fuel and power	10·2
Building materials	3·2
Food industries	19·4
Chemicals and rubber	9·8

been in the textile, food-processing and other consumer goods industries. In the following paragraphs the distribution of the more important branches of the manufacturing industries is reviewed.

Iron and steel industry. In 1966 Poland smelted 5,856,000 tons of pig iron and refined 9,850,000 tons of steel. Both the smelting and

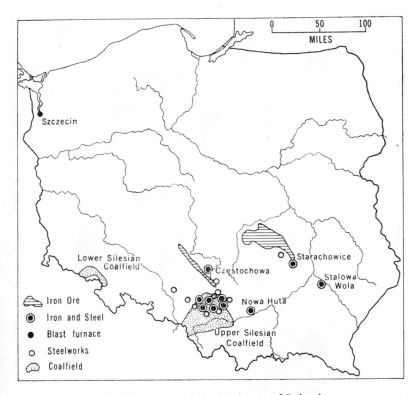

Fig. 8.18. Iron and steel industry of Poland.

refining branches are concentrated on or near the coal-field area of Upper Silesia, and over half the industrial capacity is located within the Upper Silesian Industrial Region (Fig. 8.13). The individual works are old, though modernised in some degree, and most are small. The largest, the Kościuszko Huta in Chorzów derives from the works established here by the Prussian government in 1802. This location still has the advantage of a local fuel supply, but the coal is at best of only a poor coking quality, and needs to be blended with coal from

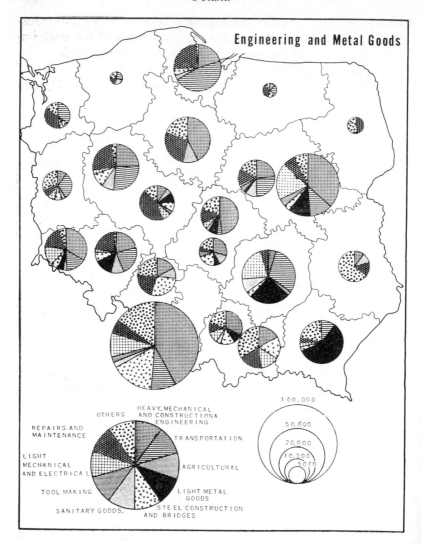

Fig. 8.19. Distribution of the engineering and metal goods industries.
Reproduced from *Econ. Geogr.*, **36** (1960), 247.

other sources, such as Moravia or Lower Silesia. The disadvantages
of the Upper Silesian Industrial Region are considerable, and include
the domestic crowding and lack of space for a modern works, the
danger of subsidence and the exhaustion of local ore-supplies. No

new works have been built here since the end of the nineteenth century. The most ambitious and important post-war developments have been at Częstochowa (Bierut Works), close to the Jurassic ores; at Nowa Huta (Lenin Works), and at Warsaw itself where a plant has been established in the northern suburb of Bielany for making high-grade steel. In addition, there are small and rather old works at Szczecin, Starachowice, Ostrowiec, and a somewhat newer plant at Stalowa Wola.

The mechanical engineering industries are developed in all except the northern tier of *województwa*, and in the latter the shipbuilding industry is important at Gdańsk and Szczecin. The map (Fig. 8.19), based on a census of industrial employment of 1958, shows the distribution by major administrative units of the varieties of engineering and metal goods industries. It is not difficult to see represented on this map, the heavy metal construction industries of Upper Silesia, Warsaw and Bydgoszcz; the shipbuilding of Gdańsk; the railway equipment manufacture of Poznań; the construction of lorries at Starachowice, and the aluminium industry near Rzeszów.

Textiles and clothing. This branch of industry is dominated by the city of Łódź (see above, page 347) and its satellites, which together account for about 63 per cent of the cotton goods, 60 per cent of the woollen, and 64 per cent of the silk and synthetic fibres. The series of accidents by which the textile industry came to be located here has already been traced. A not dissimilar chain of events led to the choice of Białystok as the second manufacturing centre, but after 1918 the conspicuous disadvantages of the latter location led to a decline in importance which has been halted only recently. Outside Łódź and its peripheral cities and Białystok, the cotton industry is important only in Bielsko-Biała, Andrychów and some of the small towns of Silesia. The woollen industry is more widespread. It is carried on in a chain of little mill-towns strung out through the Sudety, in Zielona Góra and Bielsko-Biała, in Warsaw and its environs, notably in Żyrardów, and in many centres, individually quite small, in central Poland. The clothing industries are yet more widespread, and it might be said that they are carried on wherever enough people are gathered together to constitute a market. The leather and footwear industries are also widespread, but are particularly well developed in Silesia and the little Beskidy towns of Bielsko-Biała and Andrychów.

Chemical industries. The chemical industry is of very much more recent origin, and for this reason is more strongly concentrated in a few large units of production. With few exceptions, the chemical industries concentrate on the less sophisticated types of chemicals. Production of the common acids, and of fertilisers, paints and varnishes is relatively important, and, given the immense importance of agriculture, a good deal of recent investment capital has gone into

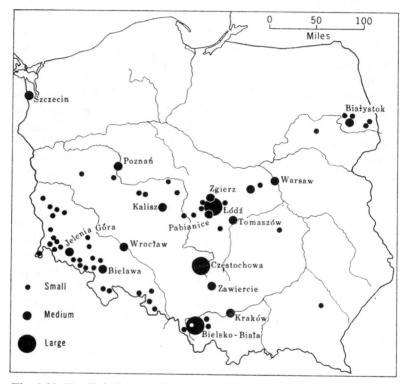

Fig. 8.20. Textile industry of Poland; no distinction is made here between cotton and woollen textiles, nor between spinning and weaving factories. Based on *Atlas Polski*.

fertiliser plants. The largest are on or relatively close to the Upper Silesian coal-field, at Kędzierzyn, Chorzów, Puławy, and Tarnów. The manufacture of pharmaceutical goods is most important in Warsaw and Lublin, that of paint and varnish in Bydgoszcz, and of petrochemicals at Płock.

Building materials. The materials of the building and construction industries are very widely produced. No part of the country is without its small brickworks, using whatever local bed of clay may be available. Lime-burning and cement manufacture are necessarily more narrowly located, and for geological reasons are restricted to southern Poland. The focus of the cement industry is the Opole region of Silesia, where the raw materials occur in fairly close proximity to the coal of Upper Silesia. By far the larger part of Poland's cement capacity is to be found in this region.

Food industries. It is impossible to describe in a few words the distribution of a group of industries as complex as those which prepare food-stuffs for human consumption. Imported materials are processed, oil seeds crushed and margarine made at the ports. Throughout the agricultural regions there are flour mills, sugar-beet factories, distilleries, dairies, and oil-seed crushing plants. In every town there are bakeries and slaughter houses, and in the larger cities these are important and essential industries.

TRANSPORT AND COMMUNICATIONS

The specialised industry described in the previous pages could not have been created without a developed network of transport and communications. Poland is physically well adapted to the creation of such a net, but the developments of the nineteenth century still left many parts of the country poorly served with railways and roads, and little has in fact been done to use the great natural facilities for canal construction.

Railway system. The first railway to be built within the present territorial limits of Poland was a short, suburban line, near Wrocław, opened in 1842. This was followed by short lines near Warsaw and in the Upper Silesian industrial region. These were later linked together to form the rudiments of a railway system. But all attempts to build a unified railways system over the plains of east-central Europe were frustrated by the threefold political division of the country, by the conflicting economic and political policies, of their governments and by the difference in railway gauge between lines constructed within and without the Tsarist empire. In fact, only the Warsaw–Katowice line, built on the standard or western gauge, offered a through connection between Russian Poland and the rest of Eastern and Central Europe.

By the time when the First World War broke out, an adequate and in some areas a fairly dense railway net had been constructed in those parts which lay within the German Empire. In Silesia, it was fully adequate for local needs, and all parts of the German Empire lying east of Berlin were linked by a frequent and efficient railway service with the capital.

Strategic needs undoubtedly contributed to the excellence of this railway system, but no comparable system evolved on the Russian side of the boundary. It was the Russian practice to lay the tracks as straight as possible, to link up the major centres of population and almost to ignore the less important, as the primary function of the railway was conceived to be the transport of troops and military supplies. Frequently the railway station was located a mile or more from the city it was intended to serve, as if in fear of hostile actions of the populace, and communications were always poorly developed in frontier regions. Thus the railway net in Russian Poland contributed little to the country's economic development, and only the standard-gauge line south-west from Warsaw ever attracted much industry to it.

The railway system in the Austrian sector, or Galicia, was little better. It was the deliberate policy of the Austrian government to limit the economic development of Galicia in favour of that of Bohemia and Moravia, areas which it felt in a better position to control.

Thus in 1918 the Polish state had the task of linking together three railway systems, with two different gauges, created for different purposes and, for political reasons, provided with as few links between them as possible. By 1939 the task was still incomplete, and in 1945 was immensely increased by the addition of the Western Territories and the destruction of much of the existing railway equipment. A new railway system, that of Germany east of the Odra, had now to be re-built and integrated with the other systems which had themselves never been wholly fused.

The Polish railway system today, as is apparent from the map, is made up of two separate systems. The first focuses on Warsaw, the most important railway centre of the country. From its five stations the main arteries of the country radiate to Katowice and Łódź, to Poznań, to Bydgoszcz and Gdańsk, and to eastern points, such as Białystok, Brześć (for Moscow) and Lublin. The second system, German and Austrian in origin, is made up of a series of smaller nets, radiating from the cities of western and northern Poland, expecially from Gdańsk, Bydgoszcz, Szczecin, Poznań, Wrocław and the cities of Upper Silesia.

The western lines are not only far more extensive in terms of miles of track per square mile, but are also more intensively used, because built more for economic than political purposes. A few, however, whose purpose was more strategic than economic, have in fact been abandoned. The only major addition to the railway net made in the inter-war years was the construction of a line, specifically for the transport of coal, from Upper Silesia to Gdańsk-Gdynia.

The current plans have not extended the mileage of railway. Much attention has however been given to improving its quality. The greatest reliance is still placed upon steam traction, but the mileage of electrified track has been increased in recent years from 97 miles to 1,592 miles out of a total of 16,767. The main line from Warsaw to Katowice is now electrified, and progress is being made with the electrification of other important routes.

Road system. The pattern of roads and of road transport is not dissimilar. Poland inherited from Germany an adequate and, locally at least, a good road net in the western parts of the country, where main roads at least are wide and well built. The parts of Poland formerly under Russian and Austrian rule are still much less adequately provided with modern roads. Good roads radiate from Warsaw, generally following fairly closely the pattern of the railways. But cross-country routes are few, and the net of secondary roads is quite inadequate in many areas.

Throughout Poland rail transport is far more important than road for the movement of freight. On the basis of tons per mile, the roads carry only about a fiftieth of that carried by the railways, but in the field of passenger transport the roads are far more important and, measured on a similar basis, carry a quarter of the number of persons conveyed by rail. Despite the thinner road net and the frequently poorer quality at least of the secondary roads in former Russian Poland, the latter's are relatively more important in the transport pattern. Every town of more than average size is the focus of bus routes, whose direction and extent delimit approximately the service area of the town itself. In this respect the road transport system of the eastern half of the country is well developed. In the western half, a far greater reliance is placed on the railway system in local and inter-city transport.

Internal navigation. Water transport is relatively little developed despite the suitability of much of the country for it. Of negligible importance for the carriage of passengers, the existing internal waterways carry a great deal less freight per mile than the roads, and in the aggregate are used for only about a sixteenth of that conveyed by lorries, and only about 1 per cent of that by the railways.

Poland has two river systems, which together drain almost the whole country. Both the Odra and Vistula are considered navigable for most of their courses, the former to Koźle and the latter to the junction of the San. In addition, the Noteć, the Warta below Poznań, and the Bug as far as the Soviet border are also navigable. Of these only the Odra is much used. It is linked by the Gliwice Canal (*P.* Kanał Gliwicki) with the Upper Silesian Industrial Region, and the combined waterway is capable of taking barges of over 500 tons. It is used principally for the downstream movement of coal to Lower Silesia, East Germany and the port of Szczecin and the upstream movement of iron-ore. Other bulk materials—lumber, grain, metallurgical products, and building materials—are also carried.

The Warta and Noteć are very much less used, though there is a traffic by small barges between Poznań and the Odra. The Vistula presents the greatest problems and also the greatest opportunity. Though technically navigable to above Kraków, it is used by large barges only up to Toruń, and above Warsaw is scarcely used at all. The difficulty lies largely in the nature of the river: its fluctuations of level, its swift current in summer, and the great quantity of sand which it carries and builds into shifting banks along its course. The lower and more navigable course of the Vistula is linked by the Bydgoszcz Canal with the canalised Noteć. The effect of this is to make Bydgoszcz a Vistula river and canal port of some importance but the Noteć itself is not much used. The only other link between the two most important river basins is by way of the upper Noteć, Lake Gopło, and the Gopło Canal to the upper Warta. This waterway has only a small capacity and is little used.

In north-eastern Poland there are a few short waterways of slight importance. The Narew is navigable near Łomża, and is linked by the minute Augustow Canal (*P.* Kanał Augustowski), built in the eighteenth century and scarcely used since then, with the Niemen valley. The Elbląg Canal joins up a series of lakes and gives Elbląg a little used connection with the Olsztyn area.

Recent plans have called for the improvement of the Vistula at least as far upstream as Kraków and at the same time for the canalisation of the Bug to the Soviet border, where an existing canal will be im-improved to link it with the Prypeć and so with the Dnepr. A short canal to the north of Warsaw would give the city a more direct connection with the Bug than the circuitous route by way of Modlin. These improvements have barely been begun, and it will be many years before barges bring iron-ore from the Ukraine directly to the furnaces of Nowa Huta.

Most ambitious of all Poland's plans for internal waterways is that to join the upper waters of the Odra, Vistula and Morava, and thus to forge a link with the Danube. Surveys have been made and plans prepared, but construction is probably even more distant than the improvement of the Vistula and the Bug.

Polish Airlines. Polish internal airlines are controlled by the state-operated 'LOT'. The focus of all airlines serving Poland is Warsaw, where the Okecie airport, lying about 4 miles to the south of the city, is able to handle all except the largest of modern aircraft. Foreign airlines use only the airport of Okęcie, but Warsaw is now connected by regular flights with most of the larger and more distant cities. Flights between Warsaw and such relatively close cities as Łódź have been discontinued as the saving in time over that taken by the railway has proved to be small.

Merchant marine. Poland has a stronger maritime tradition than any other East European country, with the possible exception of Yugoslavia, and it was with justifiable pride that Poland developed its own port of Gdynia and laid the foundations of a merchant marine in the 1920s. Poland, with over a million tons of shipping (1965 figures), now has a larger merchant fleet than any other East European country and also three large and well-equipped ports in Gdańsk, Gdynia and Szczecin. Most ships in the present fleet were built in Polish yards, chiefly at Gdańsk, and there is now an important shipbuilding industry for other countries.

FOREIGN TRADE

The total volume of Poland's foreign trade has increased steadily since the postwar years, and has approximately doubled in a period of ten years. Throughout this postwar period there has consistently been a small excess of imports over exports.

Throughout most of this period about two-thirds of Poland's foreign trade has been with the countries of the socialist bloc, and about a third of it with the Soviet Union. After the USSR came East

Germany and Czechoslovakia. Among the more important non-Communist trading partners of Poland are the United States, whose exports to Poland have tended to increase in recent years, and the United Kingdom which has in recent years been of declining importance in Poland's commerce.

Table 44. Poland's foreign trade—by countries (in millions of US dollars)
(1965)

	Exports to	Imports from
Other European socialist countries:	587·3	775·0
of which: East Germany	153·1	271·3
Czechoslovakia	208·4	244·1
Hungary	85·9	105·7
Romania	35·8	44·7
Yugoslavia	54·1	63·1
Bulgaria	44·9	39·8
Albania	5·1	6·3
Soviet Union	781·4	728·4
Industrial West (incl. USA)	520·8	464·8
Other	253·0	291·7

Source: *Foreign Trade of the European Satellites in 1965: A Statistical Summary*, CIA., Washington, 1966.

Table 45. Poland's foreign trade—by commodity (in millions of zloty)

	Imports	Exports
Live animals	2·4	45·6
Food-stuffs	388·7	1,306·3
Raw materials for the food industry	845·2	264·7
Other raw materials of vegetable and animal origin	1,329·4	449·3
Fuels, minerals and metals	2,290·4	2,237·1
Chemicals, fertilisers and rubber	747·8	339·0
Building materials	60·2	103·9
Machinery and equipment	3,066·8	3,069·1
Consumer goods of industrial origin	630·1	1,096·4

Source: *UN Yearbook of International Trade Statistics, 1965*.

The composition of Poland's trade is such as one would expect from an agricultural country in process of building up its manufacturing industries. Over half the imports by value are fuel and raw materials, and over a quarter is made up of machinery and equipment which may be classified as capital goods. Food-stuffs, in part those of tropical origin, but also wheat and other bread crops to supplement Poland's production, have made up a proportion which in recent years has been increasing, and now amounts to about 16 per cent of the total.

Bibliography
General
Atlas Geograficzny Polski, Warsaw, 1956.
Atlas Polski, parts 1–4, Warsaw, 1953–56.
Atlas Ziem Odzyskanych, Warsaw, 1947.
BARNETT, CLIFFORD R. *et al. Poland: its People, its Society, its Culture*, London, Evergreen Books, 1958.
GEORGE, PIERRE and JEAN TRICART, *L'Europe Centrale*, 2, *Les Etats*, Paris, 1954.
HALECKI, OSCAR, *Poland*, Mid-European Studies Center, New York, 1957; London, Stevens, 1957.
KOSTROWICKI, JERZY, 'Geography in Poland since the War', *Geogrl J.*, **122** (1956), 441–50.
LESZCZYCKI, STANISŁAW, 'The Geographical Bases of Contemporary Poland', *Journal of Central European Affairs*, 7 (1948), 357–73.
Livret-Guide du II Congrès de Géographes et Ethnographes Slaves en Pologne, 1927, Kraków, 1927.
Mały Atlas Polski, Warsaw, 1947.
MARKERT, WERNER, *Polen*, Osteuropa Handbuch, Köln-Graz, 1959.
Polish Encyclopaedia, Geneva, 1922.
REDDAWAY, W. F. *The Cambridge History of Poland*, 2 vols, Cambridge University Press, 1950–51.
SCHMITT, BERNADOTTE E. ed., *Poland*, Cambridge University Press, 1945.
WOJCIECHOWSKI, Z. ed. *Poland's Place in Europe*, Instytut Zachodni, Poznań, 1947.

Historical and Political Geography
BAGIŃSKI, H. *Poland and the Baltic*, London, Oliver & Boyd, 1942.
BUJAK, FRANCISZEK, *Studja Geograficzno-Historyczne*, Warsaw, 1925.
The Cambridge History of Poland, Cambridge University Press, 2 vols, 1950.

CONZEN, G. 'East Prussia', *Geography*, vol. 31, 1946, 1–10.

DUROSELLE, JEAN-BAPTISTE, *Les Frontières Européennes de l'URSS*, 1917–1941, Paris, 1957.

HALECKI, O. *A History of Poland*, New York rev. edn, 1956; London, Dent, 1956.

HARTSHORNE, RICHARD, 'The Polish Corridor', *J. Geogr.*, **36** (1937), 161–76.

HELMOLD, *The Chronicle of the Slavs*, ed. F. J. Tschan, Columbia University Press, 1935.

JAŻDŻEWSKI, KONRAD, *Atlas do Pradziejów Słowian*, Lodz, 1948.

KOSTRZEWSKI, JOSEF, *Les Origines de la Civilisation Polonaise*, Paris, Presses Universitaires, 1949.

LESLIE, R. F. *The Polish Question—Poland's Place in Modern History*. London, The Historical Association, 1964.

Les Origines des Villes Polonaises, École Pratique des Hautes Études, Paris, 1955.

MORROW, IAN F. D. *The Peace Settlement in the German–Polish Border-land*, Oxford University Press, 1936.

POUNDS, N. J. G. *Poland between East and West*, London, Van Nostrand Searchlight Books, 1964.

SLOMKA, JAN, *From Serfdom to Self-Government*, London, Minerva Publishing Co., 1941.

WANDYCZ, PIOTR S. *France and Her Eastern Allies 1919–1925*, Oxford University Press, 1962.

WISKEMANN, ELIZABETH, *Germany's Eastern Neighbours*, Oxford University Press, 1956.

Physical Geography

BOYD, LOUISE A. 'The Marshes of Pinsk', *Geogrl Rev.*, **26** (1936), 376–95.

Polish Countrysides, American Geographical Society, New York, 1937.

BROWN, E. H. 'Glacial and Periglacial Lansdcapes in Poland', *Geography*, **50** (1965), 31–44.

GALON, RAJMUND, *Morphology of the Noteć-Warta (or Toruń-Eberswalde) Ice Marginal Streamway*, Polish Academy of Sciences, 1961.

JAHN, ALFRED, *Wyżyna Lubelska*, Polska Akademia Nauk, 1956.

KLIMEK, KAZIMIERZ, 'Deglacja północnej części Wyżyny Śląsko-Krakowskiej w okresie zlodowacenia środkowopolskiego', *Pr. Geogr.*, No. 53, Institut Geograficzny, Warsaw, 1966.

KONDRACKI, JERZY, 'Types of Natural Landscape in Poland', *Przegl. Geogr.*, **32** (1960), Supplement, 29–39.

KOSTROWICKI, JERZY, *Środowisko Geograficzne Polski*, Warsaw, 1961.

KSIAŻKIEWICZ, M. and J. SAMSONOWICZ, *Zarys Geologii Polski*, Warsaw, 1953.

LENCEWICZ, STANISLAW, *Geografia Fizyczna Polski*, Warsaw, 1955.

— 'Le massif hercynien des Łysogóry et ses enveloppes', *Congrès International de Géographie*, Warsaw, 1934.

PAWŁOWSKI, STANISŁAW, 'La Pomeranie et le littoral de la Mer Baltique', *Congrès International de Géographie*, Warsaw, 1934.

SMOLEŃSKI, JERZY, 'Cracowie, vallée du Dunajec, Haute Tatra', *Congrès International de Géographie*, Warsaw, 1934.

SZAFER, WTADISTAW, ed., *The Vegetation of Poland*, PWN, Warsaw, 1966.

ZABORSKI, BOGDAN, 'La partie nord-ouest du plateau de Lublin', *Congrès International de Géographie*, Warsaw, 1934.

Population and Settlement

DAVIES, A. 'A Study of City Morphology and Historical Geography', *Geography*, **18** (1933), 25–37.

DERÉPARAZ, G. A. 'Notes sur les Campagnes et la vie rurale du Nord-Est Polonais', *Revue Géographique de l'Est*, **5** (1965), 41–75.

DOBROWOLSKA, MARIA, 'The Morphogenesis of the Agrarian Landscape of Southern Poland', *Geogr. Annls*, **43** (1961), 26–45.

DZIEWOŃSKI, KAZIMIERZ, 'Changes in the Urban Network of Poland', *Festschrift Leopold G. Scheidl zum 70. Geburtstag*, Vienna, 1965, 218–26.

European Population Transfers 1939–1945, Oxford University Press, 1946.

FRUMKIN, GRZEGORZ, 'Pologne: dix années d'historie démographique', *Population*, **4** (1949), 695–712.

GEORGE, PIERRE, 'Varsovie 1949: reconstruction ou naissance d'une nouvelle ville', *Population*, **4** (1949), 713–726.

KIEŁCZEWSKA-ZALESKA, MARIA, 'Various Trends of Transformation of Polish Rural Settlements', *Geogr. Annls*, **43** (1961), 321–8.

KOSIŃSKI, LESZEK, 'Demographic Problems of the Polish Western and Northern Territories', *Geographical Essays on Eastern Europe*, ed. N. J. G. Pounds, Indiana University Press, 1961, 28–53.

KOSIŃSKI, LESZEK, 'Migrations of Population in East-Central Europe from 1939–1955', *Geographia Polonica*, 2 (1964), 123–31.

— 'Warschau', *Geogr. Rdsch.* 17 (1965), 259–69.

— 'Les problèmes démographiques dans les territories occidentaux de la Pologne et les régions frontières de la Tchécoslovaquie', *Annls Géogr.*, 71 (1962), 79–98.

Les Origines des Villes Polonaises, Paris, 1960.

LESZCZYCKI, STANISŁAW, 'Die räumliche Struktur der Volkswirtschaft in der Polnischen Volksrepublik', *Petermanns Mitt.*, 110 (1966), 273–83.

MAAS, WALTER, 'The "Dutch" Villages in Poland', *Geography*, 36 (1951), 263–8.

NORTH, GEOFFREY, 'Poland's Population and Changing Economy', *Geogrl J.* 124 (1958), 517–27.

SCHECHTMAN, JOSEPH B. 'The Polish–Soviet Exchange of Population', *Journal of Central European Affairs*, 9 (1949), 289–314.

The Population of Poland, Washington, DC, US Department of Commerce, 1954.

WANKLYN, H. G. 'Geographical Aspects of Jewish Settlement East of Germany', *Geogrl J.*, 95 (1940), 175–90.

WRZOSEK, ANTONI and BRONISTAW KORTUS, 'Krakau', *Geogr. Rdsch.*, 17 (1965), 270–7.

ZABORSKI, BOGDAN, *O Ksztaltach Wsi w Polsce i ich Rozmieszczeniu*, Kraków, 1926.

ZIELINSKI, H. *Population Changes in Poland*, New York, Free Europe Committee, 1954.

Economic Geography

ALTON, THAD P. *Polish Postwar Economy*, Oxford University Press, 1956.

BARCIŃSKI, FLORIAN, B. KRYGOWSKI, S. ZAJCHOWSKI, *Województwo Zielonogórskie*, Poznań, 1961.

BEREZOWSKI, STANISŁAW, 'Die Binnenregionalisierung der War-schauer Wirtschaftsregion', *Festschrift Leopold G. Scheidl zum 60. Geburtstag*, Vienna, 1965, 194–206.

— 'Problèmes économiques des Karpates polonaises,' *Revue de Géographie Alpine*, 51 (1963), 515–44.

Carte économique de la Pologne, Paris, Ministère des Finances et des Affaires Economiques, Carte No. 34.

GEISTER, WALTER, *Wirtschafts- und verkehrsgeographischer Atlas von Schlesien*, Breslau, 1932.

HAMILTON, F. E. I. 'Geological Research, Planning and Economic Development in Poland', *Tijdschr. Econ. Soc. Geogr.*, **55** (1964), 252–3.

HARTSHORNE, R. 'The Upper Silesian Industrial District', *Geogrl Rev.*, **24** (1934), 432–38.

KOPCZYŃSKA-JAWORSKA, BRONISŁAWA, 'Das Hirtenwesen in den Polnischen Karpaten', *Viehzucht und Hirtenleben in Ostmitteleuropa*, Budapest, Academy of Sciences, 1961, 389–438.

KOSTROWICKI, JERZY, 'Land Utilization Survey as a Basis for Geographical Typology of Agriculture', *Przegl. Geogr.*, **32** (1960), Supplement, 169–83.

La Pologne: mémento économique, Institut National de la Statistique et des Études Économiques, Paris, 1954.

Land Utilization, Geographical Studies, No. 31, Polish Academy of Sciences, Warsaw, 1962.

Land Utilization in East-Central Europe: Case Studies, Geographia Polonica, **5** (1965).

LESZCZYCKI, STANISŁAW, A. KUKLIŃSKI, M. NAJGRAKOWSKI, J. GRZESZCZAK, 'Spatial Structure of Polish Industry in 1956', *Przegl. Geogr.*, **32** (1960), Supplement, 139–47.

LOTH, J. and Z. PETRAŻYCKA, *Geografia Gospodarcza Polski*, Warsaw, 1960.

MONTIAS, JOHN MICHAEL, 'The Polish Iron and Steel Industry', *The American Slavic and East European Review*, **16** (1957), 301–22.

The Polish Countryside in Figures, Polonia, Warsaw, 1954.

POUNDS, N. J. G. 'The Industrial Geography of Modern Poland', *Econ. Geogr.*, **36** (1960), 231–53.

— 'Planning in the Upper Silesian Industrial Region', *Journal of Central European Affairs*, **18** (1959), 409–22.

— 'The Spread of Mining in the Coal Basin of Upper Silesia and Moravia,' *Annals, Association of American Geographers*, **48** (1958), 149–63.

— *The Upper Silesian Industrial Region*, Indiana University Press, 1958.

Problems of Applied Geography, Polish Academy of Sciences, Geographical Studies No. 25, Warsaw, 1961.

Problems of Economic Region, Polish Academy of Sciences, Warsaw, 1961.

RUDZKI, ADAM, *Polish Transport: Organization and Economics*, New York, Mid-European Studies Center, 1955.

SERAPHIM, P. H. *Industrie-Kombinat Oberschlesien*, Koln-Braunsfeld, 1953.

STRASZEWICZ, L. *Opole Silesia*, Warsaw, 1965.

Studia Geograficzne nad Aktywizacja Małych Miast, Instytut Geografii, Warsaw, 1957.

VAN CLEEF, EUGENE, 'Danzig and Gdynia', *Geogrl Rev.* 23 (1933), 101–107.

WRÓBEL, ANDRZEJ, 'Study of Economic Regional Structure', *Przegl. Geogr.*, 32 (1960), Supplement, 127–32.

WRZOSEK, ANTONI, 'Veranderungen der raumlichen Struktur der Industrie Polens im Zeitraum 1946–1962', *Festschrift Leopold G. Scheidl zum 70. Geburtstag*, Vienna, 1965, 382–93.

ZAUBERMAN, ALFRED, *Industrial Progress in Poland, Czechoslovakia and East Germany*, Oxford University Press 1962.

ZWEIG, FERDYNAND, *Poland Between Two Wars*, London, Secker & Warburg, 1944.

CHAPTER NINE

Czechoslovakia

The Republic of Czechoslovakia came into being in October 1918. This event had been preceded not only by the careful preparations made by the Czech leaders in exile but also by an agreement between the Czechs and Slovaks to join together in a single state. The Austro-Hungarian state was at this time defeated and on the verge of collapse, and the Western Powers had already approved in principle the creation of the new state.

CZECHS AND SLOVAKS

The creation of a joint state of the Czechs and Slovaks had much to recommend it. Both peoples were relatively small in number. The Czechs at this time were about 6,800,000, and the Slovaks only 2,000,000. Their languages were so similar that they were mutually understandable, and the two peoples held in common certain elements of their cultural traditions. Yet beneath these similarities were profound differences. Though subjects of the Habsburg King-Emperor, they had in fact been members of two different states, the Czechs of the Austrian Empire and the Slovaks of the Hungarian Kingdom. The former had been oriented politically toward Vienna, the latter toward Budapest. Except for the period from the Austrian reconquest of Hungary from the Turks at the beginning of the eighteenth century until the *Ausgleich* of 1867, they had been subjected to different political systems and traditions.

The Czechs were the more experienced politically, and had in fact played a prominent role in the government and councils of Austria. The Slovaks had enjoyed no such privileges under Hungarian rule, which had always tended to be more despotic and more feudal than that of Austria. For these reasons, if for no other, political leadership and power in the new state tended to fall into the hands of the Czechs.

The Czech lands, furthermore, were more fertile and productive, more richly endowed with minerals, and had been more intensively developed during the nineteenth century. Indeed, the Austrians, as a matter of policy, had tended to establish industries in the Czech lands rather than in other parts of their Empire. With their greater political awareness the Czechs were thus able to combine a business acumen and experience which the Slovaks entirely lacked.

The traditions of the Czechs and Slovaks were far from comparable. A Czech state had emerged in the tenth century, with its focus near Prague. It had flourished during the Middle Ages, and during the fourteenth century had provided a Holy Roman Emperor. Prague at this time was one of the largest and most distinguished cities in Europe. The battle of Mohács in 1526, which saw the defeat of Hungary by the Turks, also witnessed the end of Bohemia's line of kings. The crown was claimed by the Austrian Habsburgs by inheritance, and retained by them, despite Czech revolts, of which that of 1618 was the most momentous, until the defeat of Austria in 1918.

The Slovaks, on the other hand, passed under Hungarian rule soon after the Hungarian conquest of the plains at the beginning of the tenth century. The plains of southern Slovakia were settled by Hungarians and their inhabitants were Magyarised, and, if the Slovaks did retain some trace of independence in the mountains, this was at the price of isolation and cultural stagnation. The Czechs had, during the period of Austrian rule, the traditions of the Bohemian Kingdom to inspire them and, after independence, to give an historical depth to their state. The Slovaks had none of this. Their traditions were cast in a less heroic mould. They could point to the times when they followed their Hungarian masters—the Rákoczy, for example—against the Austrians, but for the greater part they were a peasant people.

Such were the two unevenly matched peoples whose destinies were brought together when their leaders and representatives in exile agreed at a meeting held on foreign soil to create a Czechoslovak state.

The boundaries of Czechoslovakia
The boundaries of Czechoslovakia were determined at the Paris Conference of 1918–20. It was decided early in the meeting that the new state should include the Sudeten territory, with its predominantly German population, and that Czechoslovakia should incorporate most of the small towns which lay along the northern border of the Hungarian Plain. It transpired that the Czechs and their Western Allies had misjudged the temper of the times and had underrated the strength of German and Hungarian nationalism, but at the time and in

the light of history these decisions seemed wise. So also, it appeared, was that to add the Ruthenes, less developed even than the Slovak and, furthermore, speaking a distinct Slavic language, to the already complex ethnic pattern of the Czechoslovak state.

Bohemia. The boundaries of Bohemia had been hallowed for centuries, and in 1919 differed little from those that had enclosed the kingdom of Charles IV or George of Poděbrady in the later Middle Ages. They were, furthermore, reinforced by the hilly or mountainous terrain through which they ran and were conceived to be a military advantage. Not surprisingly the Czechoslovak leaders chose to retain the ancient boundaries. This, however, necessitated the inclusion of a German-speaking minority of, in 1919, more than two millions in the Sudeten territory alone. Masaryk was aware of the problems which a minority of this size could create, but considered that a Bohemia without the predominantly German *Randgebiet* would be economically weak and militarily indefensible. The Sudeten Germans, it was noted, had never been subjects of the German state, and their territory had never at any time in its history been part of the German Reich; it had been only Bohemian and Austrian, and there seemed little reason to suppose that they were strongly opposed to membership in a Czechoslovak state. Masaryk was confident that any hostility which they might show could with patience, tolerance and understanding have been overcome. Events would very likely have proved him right if a decade later a psychopathic nationalism had not developed in Germany itself.

Hlučín. The only area which Czechoslovakia in fact acquired from Germany was Hlučín, a small region of poorly developed farmland on the north-western margin of the Moravian coal basin. Its population was overwhelmingly Slav, and spoke a dialect of Czech. They had, however, long been accustomed to seek employment in German Upper Silesia, and continued in fact to do so long after they had become citizens of Czechoslovakia.

Těšín, Orava and Spiš. These small, but in some respects valuable territories were in dispute with Poland (see page 103). Orava and Spiš were partitioned by the Council of Ambassadors, the body which existed to complete the unfinished business of the Paris Conference after the latter had broken up, and Czechoslovakia received the lion's share of this territory. Těšín presented a more critical problem because its economic resources—chiefly coking-coal—and its industries—primarily iron and steel—were attractive to both parties. A plebiscite was ordered, then cancelled, and the matter settled for a time by partitioning the territory. Czechoslovakia acquired somewhat the larger share, together with the more valuable part of the coal-field and also the Třinec iron and steel works.

Hungarian Boundary. On its southern border Czechoslovakia was allowed to extend into the Pannonian Plain and to include significant areas of lowland along the Danube and its tributary, the Ipel, and around the headwaters of the Tisza. These were inhabited mainly by Hungarians, and the chief reason for compelling their cession to Czechoslovakia was that their small market towns served the mountainous Slovak hinterland and controlled the chief means of transport and communication in the area. Czechoslovakia thus came to have a Hungarian minority of about 750,000. It should be added, however, that not all the minority peoples were on the Slovak side of the boundary. There remained a number of Slovaks in Hungary, whose repatriation to Czechoslovakia was the subject of an agreement which has never been carried out.

Ruthenia. The addition of Ruthenia to the Czechoslovak state was a matter in which the Western Allies played no part. Around the Tisza headwaters the low passes across the Carpathian Mountains had facilitated the movement of Ukrainians toward the Hungarian Plain. There they had lived under Hungarian rule and in isolation from the rest of the Ukrainian nation. They were among the most underprivileged and backward of all the subjects of the Hungarian crown, and in their desperate conditions had furnished a disproportionately large number of immigrants to the New World. It was the latter who in 1918 took the initiative of calling for union with Czechoslovakia. This was confirmed by the Ruthenes at home who in 1919 became citizens of Czechoslovakia, with 'the widest autonomy compatible with the unity of the Republic'. This arrangement was confirmed in the treaties of peace.

Partition of Czechoslovakia

In Eastern Europe only Yugoslavia faced ethnic conditions more divisive than those of Czechoslovakia, and Yugoslavia did not have a neighbour as consistently hostile and as determined to exploit every division in the state as was Germany. The record of German intrigue is well known. The Sudeten minority was consolidated and its policy and actions determined by Germany. And the actions of Germany served only to encourage the Hungarians and Poles to exact territorial concessions, and the clerical Slovak leaders to demand autonomy and then independence. The tragedy is that of all the East European countries, the one which held the greatest promise of becoming a liberal democracy contained in fact the most obdurate problems, which in the end made the realisation of its hopes impossible. It does not belong to this chapter to examine the role of the Western Powers. One cannot be sure that if their ignorance and their apathy had been less pronounced the course of events would have been in the long run markedly different.

Sudetenland Crisis. German pressure on Czechoslovakia built up during the 1930s. The Czechoslovak government was given no outside help in resisting them, and in the end was forced to yield in the Munich Crisis of September 1939. The Sudetenland was annexed by Germany —some 11,236 square miles, with an estimated population of 3,396,000. Bohemia was reduced to the condition which had in 1919 been described as unviable and indefensible. Czechoslovakia had not long to wait. While the western leaders were still congratulating themselves on their statesmanship at Munich, and the British Foreign Secretary was ushering in a new Golden Age, German troops occupied Prague. Bohemia and Moravia were absorbed as 'Protectorates' into the German Reich.

Těšín. The Těšín question had been settled amicably in 1920. This, however, did not prevent the Polish Foreign Minister, Beck, from profiting from Czechoslovakia's humiliation by demanding peremptorily the cession of the western part of Těšín. In October 1938, Polish troops occupied the whole of it. It is difficult to understand Polish infatuation with the Těšín-Cieszyn territory, but there can be no doubt that Beck's action was popular in Poland. The annexation had no great ethnic justification. The Poles undoubtedly wanted the economic resources of western Těšín, but their motivation seems to have gone beyond this to the strange illusion that they were asserting an historic claim and with it reviving Poland's earlier role as a great European Power.

Slovakia. During the 20 years of their association with the Czechs, the Slovaks had made great material progress, but could not overcome in so short a period the neglect of centuries. There was resentment that the national government was still dominated by Czechs, and some feeling also among the Catholic peasantry that the Czechoslovak state was becoming too secular. As happens so often among a backward people, political leadership of a Slovak nationalist movement fell into

14

the hands of the priesthood. While the Germans were occupying the Sudetenland the Slovak leaders were demanding autonomy within Czechoslovakia. This they obtained, and in the following March declared their independence, subject only to the 'protection' of the German Reich.

Pannonian Plain. The Hungarians took this opportunity to press their claims to the plains of southern Slovakia. The new Slovak government showed no desire to honour them, and an unequal war between them was averted only by a decision to ask the Axis powers to arbitrate. The Vienna Award of November 1938, tipped the scales heavily in favour of Hungary. The Magyars got much, except the cities of Bratislava and Nitra, of what they had asked. Slovakia was reduced to its mountain core, and communication between one part and another could in certain places be maintained only by way of Hungarian territory.

Ruthenia, meanwhile, whose promised autonomy had never been fully granted, seized the opportunity in October 1938, to set up a government of its own. The Vienna Award of the following month extended to the plains of southern Ruthenia as much as to those of Slovakia, and Carpathian Ruthenia, as it called itself, found its capital, Užhorod(*Rus*. Uzhgorod), and the few remaining urban centres transferred to Hungary. Its plight was worse than that of Slovakia. It continued in unhappy independence until the final break-up of the Czechoslovak state in 1939, when it was transferred to Hungary.

Czechoslovakia after 1945

The territory of Czechoslovakia remained partitioned and exploited until the defeat of the German armies. Decisions affecting it since September 1938 were reversed and the state regained the shape which it acquired after the First World War. In one respect, however it was territorially different. The territory of Subcarpathian Ruthenia was in July 1945 ceded to the Soviet Union by the Czechoslovak government in exile. The Soviet Union came thus to intrude into the Pannonian Plain, a fact not without significance in the postwar history of Hungary, and Czechoslovakia lost her direct contact, which had been in fact of negligible strategic and economic importance, with Romania.

Minorities question. The ethnic minorities had been the downfall of the first Czechoslovakia. The government was determined that they should not continue to disturb the peace of the country. The most troublesome, the German, was to be eliminated, and the Magyars exchanged. Many of the Germans had in fact fled from the Sudeten-land, and most of those who sought to stay were forced to leave. In all about 3 million German-speaking people from Czechoslovakia became refugees in Germany. Not all were forced to leave, however, and it is estimated that about 165,000 of the former German-speaking population remain.

The Ruthene question was eliminated by the cession to the Soviet Union of Subcarpathian Ruthenia. The Hungarian question remains. An agreement was reached in 1945 between the Czechoslovak and Hungarian governments to exchange their respective minorities. This agreement was imperfectly implemented, and it is said that only about 92,000 Magyars from Slovakia were actually repatriated in exchange for a much smaller number of Slovaks. There remains a Hungarian minority of about 420,000, distributed mainly through the lowland regions which border the Pannonian Plain.

LANDFORM REGIONS

Czechoslovakia stands in sharp contrast with both Poland and East Germany. These countries are relatively compact and their relief features have never hindered movement or presented any obstacle to unity. Czechoslovakia, on the other hand, is elongated and highly irregular in plan. Relative to the area, its boundary is the longest of any East European state, and it is almost 600 miles by road from the western extremity to the eastern, and 500 as the crow flies. Its internal relief has divided it into a series of compartments and at the same time presented barriers to communication between them. Whereas both Poland and East Germany belong to the northern plain and are drained throughout their extent northwards to the Baltic Sea, Czechoslovakia lies astride the European divide. Most of Bohemia and the most northerly part of Moravia are drained northwards by the Elbe, Odra and Vistula, but the rest of the country, except only the Poprad valley in the Western Tatra, lies in the drainage area of the Danube. The drainage system does not explain, though it may have assisted, the German penetration of the western and the Hungarian domination of the eastern parts of the country. Poland and East Germany lie in the glaciated North European plain, and were to a not inconsiderable degree shaped by it. Czechoslovakia lies across the areas of Hercynian and Alpine folding, and, though far more mountainous than either, was glaciated only over the higher summits of the Tatra mountains.

It is customary to divide Czechoslovakia into three contrasting physical regions, the predominantly Hercynian Massif of Bohemia; the plain of Moravia, floored with younger and softer beds, and the mountainous region of Slovakia, formed for the greater part during the Alpine mountain building. Each of these regions has a certain unity, despite the complexities of its geological and structural detail. The physical contrasts between them have done much to intensify the divisions inherent in the ethnic pattern of Czechoslovakia.

Bohemia
The province of Bohemia covers an area of about 20,368 square miles, or 43 per cent of the whole country. It is a compact region, and is often described as diamond-shaped. Very broadly, it is a plateau of Palaeozoic rock, within the northern part of which erosion has created an extensive area of lowland, since partially filled with later deposits. A superficial examination suggests that it is ringed by a mountain barrier, which cuts it off from Germany and Poland. 'Hardly any other country in the interior of our continent,' wrote Joseph Partsch[1] at the beginning of the present century, 'has so clear and self-centred an individuality as Bohemia . . . the radial convergence of the water courses toward the middle of the country, tends to give it an unusual inner solidity and unity.' Bohemia, with its pronounced physical individuality and its central location, appears to occupy a commanding position in Central Europe. 'Whoever controls Bohemia' Bismarck is alleged to have said, 'controls Europe.'

Such has been the popular estimate of Bohemia's role in history, and, however fallacious it may be, it has influenced political judgment and political action for generations. The relief of Bohemia is less simple than has been supposed, and the role of the mountain girdle in protecting the individuality of the regions which it encloses is more than suspect.

Bohemia is, as has been shown in Chapter 1, part of a series of Palaeozoic masses which extends from France eastward into Poland. In general they tend to be steep-sided, and to have level or rolling summits which rise commonly to from 2,000 to 4,000 feet. The Bohemian Massif is one of the most extensive of these, and is considerably larger than either the historical province of Bohemia or the present boundaries in the west of the Czechoslovakian state. On the south-west, its Palaeozoic and pre-Cambrian rocks reach to the

[1] Joseph Partsch, *Central Europe*, Heinemann, 1903, p. 214.

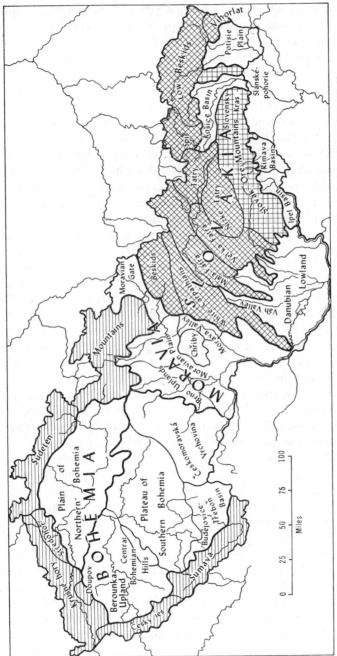

Fig. 9.1. Landform regions of Czechoslovakia. Adapted from V. Häufler, J. Korčák and V. Král.

Danube river, where they form a series of towering bluffs. North-eastwards they reach far into the plain of Silesia, and to the north-west they form the hills which border the Saxon and Thuringian basins. In this direction the mountains which border Bohemia, culminate in the steep-sided massif of the Fichtelgebirge, which lies entirely within West Germany. From the Fichtelgebirge the Thüringerwald extends finger-like to the north-west, until it terminates close to the German zonal boundary, to the south-east of Kassel. To the south-east the margin of the Bohemian Massif is less distinct than elsewhere. Here the surface of the plateau slopes gently down to the plain of Moravia, whose Secondary and later deposits overlie it along a line from the Moravian Gate through Brno to the Danube at Krems. The Bohemian Massif thus covers an area considerably larger than the area of the historic province whose name it bears.

Over most of its extent the massif is made up of granite and gneiss of lower Palaeozoic or pre-Cambrian age. The upper Palaeozoic rocks which once covered this, as they do parts of other Hercynian massifs, have been stripped away, leaving only a series of scattered basins. Among these are the Plzeň and Kladno coal basins, in each of which the coal measures have been preserved over a small area; the Brdy Forest region of Central Bohemia, where Silurian and Dvenonian formations have given rise to especially rugged relief, and also the Carboniferous rocks which border the massif on the east, and give rise to the coal basins of Northern Moravia and Brno.

The present relief of the Bohemian Massif is the product not only of a long period of denudation, but also of extensive faulting and wide-spread volcanic action. The denudation of much of the cover from the foundation of granite and gneiss must have been completed before the end of the Palaeozoic period, for beds ranging from the Permian to the Cretaceous and Tertiary in some areas lie directly on the pre-Cambrian. The shattering of the massif by faulting began early, and reached a climax probably in the Tertiary. In this way series of faults were formed along the south-western, the north-western and north-eastern borders of the massif.

It is these lines of faulting, and the differential erosion to which they have given rise, that in large measure determine the character of the diamond-shaped pattern of mountains which enclose Bohemia. Among the more conspicuous of the fault-lines are those which today are represented in the steep south-western face of the Bavarian Forest, where it is bordered by the course of the Danube, and in the parallel face of the Šumava. Both these fault-lines lie well within West Germany, and are continued to the north-west by the steep face of the Fichtelgebirge and Thüringerwald.

The downthrown side in this series of faults lies to the south-west, and here the plains of Bavaria and Franconia are brought sharply up against the crystalline Bohemian Massif. To the north-west the line of faulting is even more continuous, and its influence in the landscape is yet more pronounced. Here the downthrown side is to the south-east, toward the centre of the massif. The mountains of north-western Bohemia, the Krušné hory, present a steep and regular scarp toward the interior of Bohemia, while a more gentle slope dips north-westward, beyond the boundary of East Germany, into Saxony.

In front of this north-western fault is a depression, partially filled in with Tertiary and recent deposits, among which are to be found most of Czechoslovakia's extensive deposits of brown coal. Facing this fault-line, to the south-east, is an opposing series of faults, partially hidden by the products of Tertiary vulcanicity, and showing up in the landscape only in the steep slopes of the Slavkovský les, between Mariánské Lázně and Karlovy Vary.

The fault-lines which bound the massif on the north-east are less regular and continuous than those on the other sides. The rocks, here intruded extensively with granitic masses, have been shattered by many short faults, and erosion has since etched them into a series of short mountain ridges. The downthrown side is, in general, toward the north-east, and the faulted zone lies mainly in the Polish province of Silesia rather than in Czechoslovakia. On the Czech side the surface of the massif tends to drop more gradually toward the centre of the Bohemian Basin.

The relief of this region, however, is immensely complicated by the deposition and subsequent tilting and partial erosion, of beds of Cretaceous sandstone and marl. The sandstone today forms a belt of rough and generally hilly terrain, extending from the extreme north of Czechoslovakia south-eastward and roughly parallel with the boundary, to Hradec-Králové. To the north-west, erosion has produced in the sandstone the bizarre landforms which form the 'Saxon Switzerland' inside East Germany and the Český Raj within Bohemia. To the south-east the sandstone, tilted downward toward the middle of the basin, presents a minor escarpment towards the north-east.

The geological history of the massif is thus one of denudation and faulting; of the gradual sinking of the northern part of the Bohemian

Basin and of its infilling with Cretaceous deposits; of widespread Tertiary volcanic activity, especially along the north-eastern lines of faulting, and of peneplanation during the Oligocene. The history of the formation of the Bohemian peneplains, is a complex one. Not infrequently even the highest parts of a mountain chain consist of flat-topped ridges.[1] As the base-level of erosion fell, the massif was planated at lower levels, thus forming a series of giant steps. During the later Oligocene and the Miocene, lakes formed in which Tertiary sands and clays and, above all, brown coal accumulated. The most extensive of these later Tertiary deposits today occupy the depression which lies along the south-eastern foot of the Krušné hory; they lie scattered over the northern plain of Bohemia, or occupy depressions in the plateau-like southern part of the massif, especially near Tabor and České Budějovice.

The final stage in the evolution of the Bohemian Massif has been the lowering of the base-level of erosion, accompanied by the incision of rivers, many of which—notably the middle course of the Vltava and its tributaries, the Berounka and Sázava—have etched deep, narrow valleys into the plateau.

Drainage. Partsch commented on the hydrographic unity of Bohemia. Thanks to the down-faulting of much of its interior, drainage is drawn toward the northern plain of Bohemia, there to form the river Labe, or Elbe. The Labe itself rises in the Krkonoše, the highest part of the Sudeten mountains. It flows southward and then eastward across the northern plain—the Polabí—of Czechoslovakia; turning to the north-east, it crosses both the volcanic Středohoří and the Krušné hory by a deeply incised valley and enters Germany. The depression which it follows across the latter mountains is one of great geological age. It must have been formed by erosion during the late Palaeozoic, and was later partially filled with Cretaceous sandstone. It is through these picturesque sandstones (See above page 216) that the Labe has cut its present course.

A number of minor tributaries rise in the Sudeten Mountains and join the Labe from the north, but the most important, the Vltava, rises near the southern margin of the massif and flows northward to join the Labe at Mělník, 20 miles below the city of Prague. A complex network of rivers is gathered to the Vltava, before it escapes from the plateau and enters the northern plain. From the Moravian Hills to the

---

[1] Julie Moscheles, 'Natural Regions of Czechoslovakia', *Geogrl Rev.*, **14**, (1924) 561–75.

east it is joined by the Sázava and Lužnice; from the west by the Berounka. The superficial evidence of the map suggests that there must have been extensive river-capture in the course of the rapid down-cutting which produced the present over-deepened valleys. Just before the Labe enters the gorge which it has cut through the Středohoří, it receives the Ohře, which drains the Tertiary basins along the foot of the Krušné Hory.

Only rarely does the present political boundary, which coincides closely with that of the historic province of Bohemia, follow the divide between the Labe drainage and that of neighbouring basins, though at no point does it diverge greatly from it. At only two points have the rivers eroded significant gaps through the encircling hills. One of these, as we have already seen, is occupied by the Labe as it flows from Czechoslovakia to Germany. The other, at the most westerly point of Czechoslovakia, has been cut by the Ohře river, in its course eastwards from the Fichtelgebirge into Bohemia. This is one of the most distinct and historically one of the most important gaps through the hills which encircle Bohemia. It has long been an important routeway, and in it, four miles from the German border lies the Czech city of Cheb (*G.* Eger).

Bohemia can itself be divided, on the basis of relief, into three major regions, the mountain framework, the southern plateau and the northern plains. All except the last are further subdivided.[1]

Šumava. This is the most massive of all the segments of mountain which enclose the Bohemian Basin. For about 100 miles, from the Novohradské Hory in the south-east almost to the neighbourhood of Domažlice, the Šumava presents a series of high, rounded summits, very many of which exceed 4,000 feet and Arber (*Cz.* Javor), the highest, reaches 4,779. The higher surfaces of the Šumava form part of the Oligocene peneplain, noted earlier. On the Czech side they have been dissected by the upper Vltava and its tributaries. The massif is built mainly of granite and metamorphic rocks. It is notably lacking in easy crossing points, and is the most densely forested and the least populous region of Bohemia.

Český les. A depression, cut in part by the headwaters of the Berounka, in part by those of the westward-flowing Regen, separates the Šumava from the Český les, or Bohemian Forest. The latter, like

---

[1] The regional classification fcllows with minor adaptations that adopted by V. Haufler, J. Korčák and V. Král, *Zeměpis Československa*, p. 58, and by A. Wrzosek, *Czechosłowacja*, p. 26.

14*

the Šumava, is built of granite and altered pre-Cambrian rocks, but is lower, narrower, more dissected, and is a less significant barrier to communications. At its north-western extremity, the Český les terminates in one of its highest points, Dylen (3,086 feet) from which the hills drop steeply to the Ohře valley and the Cheb gap.

Krušné hory (*G.* Erzgebirge, Ore Mountains). The Krušné hory is one of the most strongly marked and continuous topographical features in the whole of Czechoslovakia. It consists of a ridge of crystalline materials, in general more complex than the Šumava and Český les, which stretches with no interruption from the Fichtelgebirge to the defile cut by the Labe river, a distance of about 100 miles. This mass has been strongly faulted, and the straight, abrupt south-eastern face of the mountains follows the line of the major faulting. The plateau surface of the Krušné hory lies generally at over 2,500 feet but the highest points (Klínovec 4,080 feet) rise very considerably above this level.

Though the range is interrupted by no conspicuous gaps, it is crossed without great difficulty, and the undulating surface of its summit platform and the gentle slope downward toward the north make for relatively easy movement. The mineral wealth of this region led to its penetration and settlement in the Middle Ages and even earlier. During the Middle Ages it became one of the most important European centres of non-ferrous mining. Minerals obtained included silver, lead, zinc and copper, but in recent years the Czechoslovak area of the Krušné hory has been especially noted as the chief European source of pitchblende, which continues to be mined near Jáchymov. The mining of other metals has now been abandoned or is of very slight importance.

The trench which lies in front of the Krušné hory is, in fact, a miniature rift valley, and the Krušné hory itself the tilted north-western edge. The parallel fault line to the south-east is obscured for much of its length either by outpourings of Tertiary lavas or by Cretaceous and later deposits. Nevertheless, the steep-sided, plateau-like massifs of the Slavkovský les and Tepelská hora mirror on the south-east side of the trench the structure and forms of the Krušné hory beyond it. The Doupovské hory, lying to the east, represents a basaltic outpouring, presumably from the line of faults, which has almost closed the rift valley, forced the Ohře river northward and obliged it to cut into the foothills of the Krušné hory.

East of the Doupovské hory lie the České středohoří, a highly picturesque line of volcanic hills, which stretch north-eastward beyond the Labe valley until they merge into the hills of north-eastern Bohemia. Throughout their length, the double fault-lines are associated with hot springs, which have given rise to the well-known resorts of Mariánské Lázně and Karlovy Vary (Carlsbad), as well as to lesser resorts, such as Teplice.

As a relief feature this trench is narrow everywhere, and between the Doupovské hory and the Krušné hory is almost completely closed by lava flows. It has, however, constituted a lake-basin for much of its geological history, and in it accumulated most of the extensive brown coal and lignite deposits of Czechoslovakia.

Sudeten Mountains. The mountains which border Bohemia on the north-east are in both structure and relief more complex than those which fringe the other parts of the massif. The region is made up of a series of faulted blocks, each of which gives rise to a separate segment of mountain range. Palaeozoic rocks, generally highly folded and faulted, are preserved here more completely than in the other regions examined so far, and they include in the Western Sudety a small area of exploitable coal measures. During the Cretaceous period the whole region appears to have been covered with sandstones and marls. These survive within the mountains in the mesa-like sandstone beds of the Polish Góra Stołowa and the neighbouring areas of Czechoslovakia. Along the south-western margin of the Western Sudety these sandstone beds form a continuous belt dipping slightly toward the centre of the Bohemian Basin and presenting in the Lužické hory and the Krkonošske Podhoří a scarped edge toward the mountains.

The Western Sudety are dominated by the Jizerské hory and the Krkonoše. The greatest altitudes are developed in the granitic core of these ranges, and reach in Sněžka a height of 5,258 feet. At the eastern end of this range the coal series, which appears in the Lower Silesian coal-field, extends into Czechoslovakia. Mining has, however, never been important and has now been abandoned.

In the middle section of the Sudety the Polish boundary intrudes more deeply into the mountains and includes the Kłodzko Basin within Poland. This basin is bordered by masses of schist and gneiss which give rise to the Orlické hory. These mountains extend southward until, near Svitavy, they merge into the Českomoravská vrchovina.

In the Eastern Sudety the mountains broaden into a rounded upland region whose summits exceed 4,000 feet and even reach 4,593 feet. This region is developed toward the west in gneiss and schist and to the east in sedimentaries of the lower Carboniferous series. This latter massif sinks gently toward the Moravian Gate, but more steeply toward the south-west and south to the valley of the Morava river and the plains of Moravia.

Plateau of southern Bohemia. Within the curving line of the Šumava, the Krušné hory and the Sudety lie the two contrasted regions of southern and northern Bohemia. The former is built like the enclosing mountains of Palaeozoic and pre-Cambrian rocks, intensely folded, eroded through a long period of geological time, and finally planated during the Oligocene and Pliocene. The latter, in its main features a faulted depression, has been filled with Cretaceous and Tertiary deposits. The former is a rolling and, in some parts, distinctly hilly plateau; the latter, a lowland region of gentle relief; the one a region of generally poor soil, extensive forest and relatively small rural population; the other is amongst the richest, most densely settled and intensively cultivated regions in Czechoslovakia.

The Berounka Uplands (vrchovina Berounka). The southern uplands are divisible, according to their structure and relief, into four regions. The vrchovina Berounka lie within the angle formed by the Český les and the Krušné hory. In contrast with the rest of southern Bohemia, it is built of Palaeozoic sedimentaries, which form roughly a syncline lying from south-west to north-east. The outcrop of alternating hard and relatively soft beds has produced a series of ridges, so that this region is sometimes described as having an 'Appalachian' type of relief. The strongest relief feature within the region is the Brdy, a long, narrow ridge of schist which reaches at its highest point 2,831 feet. Locally the region has been intruded by igneous rock and in some areas deposits of non-ferrous metals were formed. The once important silver–lead resources of Příbram occur in the south-eastern flanks of the Brdy. In the midst of the region, and forming the trough of the syncline, are small deposits of coal measures. These are of no great size and are of only local importance, but have long been worked near Plzeň and Kladno.

The river Berounka forms, as it were, the axis of this region. Its headwaters rise in the Český les and converge on the undulating plain in the midst of which lies the city of Plzeň. It receives tributaries from both the Doupovské hory and the Brdy. Its lower course is deeply incised, and its valley assumes almost gorge-like proportions where it cuts across the northern extremity of the Brdy ridge, before joining the Vltava.

This is a region of better soil, of denser rural population and of more intensive agricultural land use than any of the regions of Bohemia examined hitherto. It contains, in addition to the industrial city of Plzeň and the mining city of Kladno, a number of small market towns, like Rakovník, Rokycany and Klatovy, and a close scatter of villages, many of them large and compact.

Central Bohemian Hills. South-east of the Brdy is a dissected and hilly region known as the Středočeská vrchovina. Structurally it is a massif of granite and other intrusive rocks, similar to that which composes the higher parts of the Šumava. It is a hilly region, with poor soil and only a scanty rural population. It is drained by the Vltava, which follows a deeply incised valley and has been damned at several points to make an almost continuous lake. There are no important industries in the region, nor indeed are there towns apart from Tabor and Písek, which are in fact marginal to it.

Budjěovice–Třeboň Basin. During the Miocene shallow lakes were formed on the surface of the plateau of southern Bohemia, and extensive deposits of clay and sand were laid down. These depressions are now drained by the Vltava and its important tributary, the Lužnice. The entrenchment of the river in the narrow valley, which distinguishes its middle course, has not reached back to these old lake basins. In consequence their relief is gentle; there are many surviving lakes, and the rivers meander across this undulating region. There are, in fact, two such basins; that of České Budějovice, drained by the Vltava, and that of Třeboň, drained by the Lužnice. Between them is a ridge of low hills, where the underlying pre-Cambrian massif comes to the surface. The Tertiary deposits of the lake basins yield a heavy soil, difficult to drain. In some areas there are peat deposits, and a few of the lakes are artificially maintained for the sake of their fisheries which are an important source of carp. Nevertheless, the soil, when drained and brought under cultivation, yields better than most other areas of the Bohemian Uplands. The region supports not only a denser rural population than its neighbouring regions, but has in České Budějovice one of the more important industrial cities of Bohemia.

Českomoravská vrchovina. The Bohemian–Moravian Uplands form the most extensive of all the physical regions of Bohemia. It is a rolling upland, rising gently on the south-east from the Moravian Plain and dropping equally gently on the north toward the plain of northern Bohemia. Geologically, it is made up of the crystalline rocks which compose the foundation of the Bohemian Massif, overlain in a few small areas, by patches of Tertiary lacustrine deposits. The region is drained both north-westward toward the Labe and Vltava and also south-eastward toward the Morava. In their lower courses the rivers are deeply incised in the flanks of the massif, but over the summit they occupy broad, shallow valleys. The rounded and often forested summits rise to heights of from 2,000 to 2,600 feet, but only in the highest parts of the whole region, the Žďárksé vrchy, or Žďár Upland, in the east, and the Jihlavské vrchy (Jihlava Upland) in the south, do they rise significantly above 2,500 feet. On this side the Bohemian Massif is not bounded by clear and distinct mountain ranges; only by this moderately dissected hill country.

Heights are somewhat greater here than in the Central Bohemian region and climates are proportionately more severe. The difference of a degree or two in the temperature throughout the year; an inch or two more of rainfall, and the somewhat greater duration of snow-cover and cloud have brought about a change in the quality of soil and the nature of the land use. The area of poor skeletal, mountain soil is greater. More land is under forest and rough grazing; fodder crops and potatoes are more important than cereals, and rural population is less dense than in most other ports of the South Bohemian plateau, with the exception of the Brdy.

Nevertheless, there are many small industrial towns scattered through these uplands. They generally have less than about 25,000, and are characterised by small factories engaged mostly in some branch of the textile, woodworking or metal using industries. In general these branches of industry derive from the local raw materials —timber and wool—or satisfy the needs of this poor, upland region. The largest amongst the towns are Jihlava, with a number of factories engaged in the metal, textile and wood-working industries; Pelhřimov and Žďár nad Sázavou, where engineering industries are the most important.

Plain of northern Bohemia. This region, known in Czech as the Česká křídová tabule, or Bohemian Cretaceous Plain, is a roughly triangular region, framed by the older and more rugged terrain that has already been described. It is agriculturally by far the most important region of Bohemia, and also the most densely settled. It owes this distinction to its lower altitude, gentler relief, milder climate, and, above all, to its deeper and richer soil. It covers an area of approximately 2,400 square miles (6,220 square kilometres), and occupies a basin which must have been eroded in the Bohemian Massif very early in its geological history. This basin was subsequently filled with Cretaceous and Tertiary deposits, eroded to its present form of an undulating lowland, and then largely covered with recent diluvial deposits of silt and sand.

The whole region is drained by the Labe, which rises in the Krkonoše hory and takes a winding course, first southward and then westward, before turning to the north and crossing the Krušné hory by its deeply incised valley. It receives tributaries from the Sudeten Mountains and the Bohemian–Moravian Uplands, but none of these is as important as the Vltava, which joins the Labe at Mělník, and could rightly claim to be the principal headstream of the river. The Vltava is a navigable river and is regularly used as far upstream as the northern edge of the city of Prague. The Labe itself is little used above Mělník, but below this point forms an important means of communication between Czechoslovakia and East Germany.

Along the Labe, from Pardubice down to Mělník, the plain—Polabí, as it is called—is level, rich and intensively cultivated. Toward the north its level rises and it becomes more undulating. Volcanic outliers of the Středohoří break the surface and give a bizarre quality to the landscape of this region, which is transitional from the plain to the Krkonoše.

The North Bohemian Plain has a milder climate and smaller rainfall than all other regions of Bohemia, and its growing period may be over 50 days longer than on the Bohemian–Moravian uplands. It is a wheat-growing region, with subsidiary sugar-beet and potatoes. Vegetables are grown for the nearby urban markets; hops are important, and locally, as at Mělník, the grape vine is grown and wine is made.

Despite its agricultural wealth and prosperity, there are no large towns within this region. Prague and Kladno lie beyond its border to the south. Within its limits the largest settlements are Hradec-Králové, Pardubice and Mladá Boleslav. There is in addition a considerable number of smaller towns, each with its specialised branches of industry. These include food processing, which is more important in this good farming country than in any other region of Bohemia, or even of Czechoslovakia, mechanical engineering, chemicals, paper and rubber manufacturing.

Moravia
This, the second of the three major landform regions of Czechoslovakia, is the depression which has been eroded along the line of junction

of the Hercynian Massif of Bohemia with the region of young, folded mountains. Its importance in both the history and economy of Europe arises from the fact that it was further deepened and converted into a through route, joining the northern plains with the Danube Basin, by the waters which escaped from the Polish ice sheet. The Moravian Gate, which was thus formed, now constitutes the lowest and most easily used break in the continuity of the central European watershed between the Baltic and the Danubian drainage. Trackways through it have been used since prehistoric times; it constituted an important medieval routeway; a railway was built through the Gate in 1847 as part of the direct line from Vienna to Warsaw and the Russian Empire, and there are at present plans to cut a canal to join the Odra with the Danube by way of the River Morava.

Brno Uplands. The Moravian Plain is bordered on the west by the Brněnska vrchovina, which separates it from the rolling Bohemian–Moravian plateau. It is more hilly than the plain, and lower and more dissected than the plateau. The rocks of which it is composed are intermediate in both hardness and geological age, just as the region itself is intermediate in the quality of its soil and in the level of its agriculture. The region belongs essentially to the Bohemian Massif, but the older rocks are masked beneath younger, showing through in small inliers. One of these is the Rosice coal-field, some 10 miles to the west of Brno. The region is sheltered on the west by the Moravian plateau, and is drier and more sunny than the latter. Crop-farming predominates, rather than animal husbandry, and, except over the forested higher ground, the land is mainly under grain, fodder and root-crops.

Brno, the regional capital and largest city of Moravia, lies within these rolling hills where several rivers from the Moravian plateau unite to form the Svratka which in turn makes its way to the Morava.

Moravian Plain. The plain itself is narrowed almost to an hour-glass shape by the Moravian Gate. It is in fact made up of the small triangular Ostrava Plain to the north of the Gate, and, to the south, of the valley of the Morava river and of its west bank tributary, the Dyje. The Ostrava Basin is sharply bounded by the steep, abrupt slopes of the Bohemian Massif, here called the Oderské vrchy, on the west, and by the somewhat gentler slopes of the higher Carpathians to the south-east. The plain is here overlain by the diluvial deposits left by the great floods of the Ice Age, as they were funnelled south-westwards toward the lowest gap through the encircling mountains.

The Odra river rises in the hills to the north-west of the Moravian Gate, and flows north-eastward to enter Poland at the border town of Bohumín. The direction of drainage has been reversed since the end of the Ice Age, and the Ostrava Basin would today be a region of damp meadowland, rough grazing and forest, if the coal measures did not occur at a shallow depth beneath the Tertiary and later deposits. Approximately the north-eastern half of the coal-field has been transformed into the sprawling, loosely built, industrial and mining region of Ostrava. The landscape has the untidy appearance that is normal in coal-fields developed during the nineteenth century. Such land as has not been absorbed by the urban sprawl, covered with mine and furnace waste, or ruined by subsidence, is cultivated more intensively than its natural fertility would warrant in order to satisfy the needs of the nearby urban population.

Moravian Gate. The Gate itself is a narrow depression, cut by the escaping melt-water from the Polish ice sheets along a depression which had from late Tertiary times separated the most easterly bastions of the Bohemian Massif from the outermost ranges of the Carpathian system. The Gate, where the railway passes through it, lies at 991 feet, and has in no sense the appearance of a pass. The land rises gently on each side, notched by terraces of late Tertiary age. Although the railway and the projected course of the Odra-Danube canal lie through the Gate in its narrow sense, roads have never been so confined, and they seem always to have followed the terraces above the damp valley floor. The Moravian Gate was thus never traversed only by a single road. Instead, a number of routes crossed the low divide between the Odra river and the Bečva, a small tributary of the Morava, in a broad belt up to ten miles wide.

Morava valley. The Morava river rises in the Eastern Sudety, very close to the Polish border, and takes a southerly course for some 60 miles before it is joined by the Bečva. Then, near Kroměříž, its valley narrows between the Carpathian foot-hills to the east and the isolated hilly region of Chřiby to the west. Thus far the Morava flows across a broad, undulating lowland, floored over much of its area by the diluvium laid down during the glacial period. This is distinguished as the Hornomoravsky úval—the upper Moravian valley, and its fertile plains around the junction of the Bečva with the Morava, known as the Haná, are one of the richest agricultural regions in all Czechoslovakia.

Below Kroměříž the valley narrows and its flood plain almost disappears. From here almost to the Austrian border the valley of the Morava remains a narrow belt of alluvium bordered by the low hills of southern Moravia. The latter constitute an undulating terrain, forested over the higher ground; the lower ground is commonly under meadow, and the rest cultivated. This region is by and large good farming country, and has always supported a dense rural population. The climate is drier and more sunny; the growing period longer, and the soil generally superior to that of the Labe valley of Bohemia. This superiority is reflected in the cluster of towns in the upper Morava valley and along the lower course of the river. Largest of these is Olomouc, the focal point of the upper Moravian Plain. Others are Prostějov, Přerov and Kroměříž, and along the lower Morava lie Uherské Hradiště and Hodonín. Although developed to satisfy the needs of a rich farming region, and reflecting the local wealth in their architectural styles, they have all become the scene of specialised industries. The food industries, tanning and leather-working are widespread. The textile industry has overflowed from the Sudeten region, and in the foot-hills, a mile or two to the east of the river, is Gottwaldov (Zlin), where in the late nineteenth century, Tomaš Bată established his boot and shoe industry.

Chřiby. The Chřiby is in reality an outlier of the Carpathian Mountains, from which it is separated only by the Morava valley, here reduced to a narrow trench. It is a hilly region, whose flattened summits reach to 1,500 feet. It is well-wooded, but the valleys that have been cut into its relatively soft sediments are well settled and cultivated.

Moravia is as conspicuous on the population map as it is on the relief map of Czechoslovakia. It is a region of relatively dense population, bordered by thinly-peopled uplands. This it owes in part to its superior soil, but it is also, in the Ostrava district, endowed with the most significant fuel resources to be found in the whole country. But it also owes its denser population and higher level of economic development to its historic role as a routeway between the Danube Basin and the northern plains, between Vienna and Kraków. The larger cities, Brno and Olomouc, and the many small towns, with their arcaded market places and baroque churches, are witnesses to former wealth and prosperity which did not come wholly from local agriculture.

SLOVAKIA

To the east of the Ostrava Plain and of the Bečva and Morava valleys rise the foot-hills of the Carpathian Mountains, at first gently in low and rounded hills; then increasingly steeply until they merge into the high, glaciated Tatry, with their permanent cap of snow. The orientation of the mountains—a series of concentric arcs, extending at each end into the Pannonian Plain, tends to isolate them from the Moravian lowlands. Their interior valleys and basins are most easily reached up the valleys of the Váh, the Nitra, the Hron and the Hornád, and these all flow toward Hungary rather than Moravia. Slovakia has traditionally focused on the plains of the Middle Danube, and for much of its history was divorced from the Czech lands to the west. Of the twin poles of attraction, Prague and Budapest, the Slovaks under military pressure and economic necessity chose the latter.

In terms of physiography Slovakia consists of the Western Carpathians with their bordering plains to the south. The region, however, is a complex one, and can be divided into four distinctive mountain regions and at least five separate areas of lowland which together form extensions of the great Pannonian Plain.

Western Carpathians and Beskidy
This region of forested hills and low mountains extends across the north-western border of Slovakia from Poland to the Danube and forms a significant though by no means insuperable barrier to communication and movement. Toward the south-west it narrows until it becomes a single ridge, the Malé Karpaty or Little Carpathians, which terminates in the castle-crowned bluffs of Bratislava. Toward the north-east, however, the region expands to a width of some 40 miles, made up of steep, forested ridges rising one behind the other. These are the Beskidy, which are continued into southern Poland. Structurally the whole region consists of a core of Secondary beds— Triassic and Jurassic in age—which are overlain by Cretaceous and largely covered by *Flysch* and other Tertiary beds. The older beds appear mainly in the Little Carpathians in the south and in the Moravian and Silesian Beskidy, near the Polish border. Between these extremes the Tertiary sands and clays have been dissected to produce an extremely rough terrain.

Little Carpathians. The Malé Karpaty reaches the Danube, like a finger pointing to Austria. It is only a few miles in breadth, but rises steeply on each side to a summit level at over 2,000 feet. Its craggy extremity is formed in diorite, a few outliers of which lie beyond the Danube, producing the steep, isolated hills of Hainburg, in Austria.

White Carpathians and Javorníky. About 55 miles to the north-east of Bratislava, the narrow ridge of the Little Carpathians merges into the broader mass of the Bílé Karpaty or White Carpathians which are almost continuous with the Javorníky. Along the south-eastern margin of the region the harder Secondary rocks, which underlie the region as a whole, come to the surface in a series of summits which exceed 3,000 feet at many points. They drop steeply to the Váh valley, but on the north-west they merge into a plateau which sinks more gently toward the Moravian Plain. This plateau has been cut up into a series of ridges, which trend from west to east, and lie, as it were, *en echelon* to the principal trend of the range. The valleys tend to be deep and narrow, their sides steep and forested, and the roads across the region necessarily indirect. The traveller who has made the journey across this region, even by the good roads which the Czechoslovak government has built, does not find it hard to visualise how effective a barrier this region was between Slovak and Czech.

Beskidy. The summit levels of the Western Carpathians become higher toward the north, and the Moravian, Silesian and Slovak Beskidy reach heights of over 3,500 feet. Though higher than the Javorníky, this region is somewhat more accessible because it is more completely dissected by the headwaters of the Odra. One of the latter, the Olše, has cut back into the mountains and, together with the Kysuca tributary of the Váh, has formed the Jablunkov Pass, which, at 1,814 feet, is the easiest and one of the lowest crossings of the whole Carpathian range.

The Jablunkov Pass constitutes the most important route into northern Slovakia, and is now followed by the railway from Ostrava to Uzghorod in Ruthenia, along which Soviet iron-ore is accustomed to travel. Industry has penetrated the valleys of the Beskidy from the Ostrava plain. Market towns, now with modern industry grafted on to their older functions, have grown up at the junction of mountain and plain, like Nový Jičín, Frýdek-Místek and Český Těšín. At Třinec on the Olše just within the mountains is one of Czechoslovakia's largest metallurgical complexes.

Eastern Carpathians and Low Beskidy

The Beskidy Mountains of Moravia are continued beyond the projecting lobe of Poland, the Podhale, in the Low or Eastern Beskids, the

Nízké Beskidy. The geological structures are closely similar to those of the Western Beskidy, a Palaeozoic core overlain by Secondary and Tertiary beds. The latter cover almost the whole region, and the older rocks appear only as a few inliers, conspicuous by reason of their stronger relief. The Tertiary beds—mainly sandstone and a marly limestone—are soft, and the region as a whole forms a plateau at about 4,000 feet in the west, but only about 2,000 in the east. It is well dissected by an intricate pattern of rivers, which flow either to the Vistula or the Tisza. It is an undulating region within which movement has never been particularly difficult, and it has historically provided one of the main routes into the Pannonian Plain, between the Tatry to the west and the higher mountains of northern Romania to the south-east.

Spiš Hills. Erosion has divided this region into a number of distinctive areas of hill, the Spišská Magura, which adjoins the Tatry, the Levoča, the Čerchov, the Branisko and the Šariš hills. These are forested mainly over their higher ground, but between them are broad upland valleys, drained by the Poprad, Hornád and Torysa. Though damp and cool, they provide good cropland, and have long been areas of relatively dense population.

This region is one of contrasts, between the abrupt hill masses and the flat and sometimes extensive lowlands and basins; between the poverty and backwardness which still have not vanished from the upland villages, and the relative wealth and prosperity and the very considerable artistic achievement of many of the small towns. Prominent among the latter are those of the Spiš Basin, lying between the Levoča Hills and the Low Tatry, and drained by the Hornád. Its agricultural wealth is tempered by its altitude, but the mineral wealth of the mountains bordering it attracted settlers from Central Europe at an early date and yielded the wealth with which to build its cities. The 'twelve' cities of Spiš are little architectural gems set amid this poor, mountainous country. The more prominent of them, such as Poprad, Kežmarok, Levoča and Prešov, are distinguished by their late medieval gothic architecture and their Renaissance domestic architecture which derives from the sixteenth-century period of mining prosperity.

Low Beskidy. East of the Spiš hills this dissected plateau becomes lower and its valleys more open. The political boundary with Poland here follows the hydrographic divide, which rarely climbs higher than 3,000 feet. The mountains could be crossed at numerous points by passes at less than 2,000 feet if roads had been built.

Slanské Pohorie–Vihorlat. This region of rolling, forested hills and of broad, well-cultivated valleys is interrupted by two small areas of higher and stronger relief. Both represent the older rocks of the region protruding through the otherwise continuous cover of soft Tertiary beds. First is the Slanské range, extending from north to south between the Hornád and the Ondava, and continued into Hungary in the Zempléni Hegység (see page 482). It is built mainly of basalts, similar to those which make up the Slovak Ore Mountains (see page 421). The Vihorlat and its eastward continuation, the Poprichý, lie close to the eastern boundary of Slovakia, and the latter extends into the Soviet Union. Together they represent yet another area of basalt flows. They rise steeply from the plain to considerably more than 3,000 feet; their summits are forested, but their slopes, especially those facing south, are under cultivation.

Central Carpathians

The central parts of the Slovak Carpathians are in marked contrast with the western and eastern parts of the range. Not only are they higher and incomparably more rugged, but they are built almost entirely of the older and harder rocks, amongst which intrusive igneous rocks and basaltic flows are particularly conspicuous. The older rocks are partially covered by beds of Mesozoic age, but the Tertiaries, which make up most of the Beskids occur here in only a few mountain basins and are of no great extent. The landforms into which these formations have been eroded show the same general orientation as the Beskidy. They are elongated from west to east; slightly curved, and embayed toward the south. Ignoring the lesser complexities of their relief, these mountains form three distinct ranges, separated from one another by depressions which are floored with younger and softer rocks. In general, granite forms the core of the ranges and outcrops along their rugged and serrated crests. Together they make up the highest mountain mass in the whole Carpathian system.

The rivers of Slovakia flow as a general rule between the roughly parallel ranges which make up the Central Carpathians. This is particularly apparent at their extremities, where the ranges fan out like the fingers of a hand pointing south toward the Hungarian Plain. In the central parts of the range this adjustment of drainage to structure is far less clear. The Váh, the principal river of the region, rises on the southern flanks of the Tatry and flows westward, rather than south-westward, crossing the Vel'ká Fatra and then the Malá Fatra, before reaching the longitudinal valley which it then follows until it enters the Danubian Plain. In each instance its valley is narrow and deeply incised as it crosses the ranges.

Malá Fatra. The outermost of the three mountain ranges which together make up the Central Carpathians is the Malá Fatra. It is a granitic massif extending for about 30 miles and rising to 5,615 feet at its highest point. Above Strečno where the ruins of one of the most spectacular of the many castles of Slovakia crown the cliffs, the range is crossed by the Váh, which, in the fashion of superimposed rivers, has cut its gorge across an outcrop of the most resistant rocks in the Carpathians. The mountains taper away to the south-west, and their summit levels diminish until the hills die away in the undulations of the Danubian Plain between Trnava and Nitra.

Tatry and Vel'ká Fatra. The High Tatry are not only the highest but the most rugged and intensely glaciated part of the whole Carpathian system. Yet the range covers only a very small area. It extends only about 40 miles from the Orava valley in the west to the Poprad in the east, and only 26 miles separate its most westerly peak, Sivý Vrch, from Lomnický štít, the most easterly. Within this short distance a succession of peaks rise to 7,000 feet, and the highest, Gerlachovský štít, reaches 8,735 feet. This crest is followed for about 20 miles by the boundary with Poland. The range is characterised by its large number of corrie lakes, biggest and most numerous on the northern or Polish side of the range. The southern or Slovak face of the mountains rises very steeply from the Liptov Basin, which separates it from the parallel range of the Low Tatry.

The High Tatry end abruptly on the east, when the Poprad curves around their eastern end, beneath the towering summit of Gerlachovský štít and Lomnicky štít. The western extremity is less abrupt, but here too the level drops abruptly to the west of Sivý Vrch, and the direction of the mountains is continued in the very much lower Chočské pohorie. This change in level marks the transition from the granite of the High Tatry to Secondary and Tertiary sedimentaries. This ridge is here, at Ružomberok, crossed by the Váh, but south of the river the summits rise to the granitic heights of the Vel'ká Fatra, which extend south-westward until this range too becomes a series of rocky fingers reaching into the Danubian Plain.

The whole region represented by the High Tatry and Vel'ká Fatra is one of negligible agricultural value. The higher slopes have at best only skeletal soils. Most of the surface is forested; there is rough grazing and 'alpine' meadow over some of the higher ground, but crop-farming—mainly rye, potatoes, fodder crops and vegetables—occurs only along the valley floors.

Low Tatry. The third of the mountain ranges which make up the Central Carpathians is the Nízke Tatry. It is a mountain range about 50 miles from west to east, rising to a smoothed or peneplaned summit at over 5,000 feet for most of its length. At its western extremity a col, which carries the road from Ružomberok to Banska Bystrica, separates it from the southward sweeping Vel'ká Fatra. At the eastern end a similar gap divides it from the Slovakian Ore Mountains.

The Low Tatry, like the High, have a core of granite and gneiss, partially covered by younger sedimentary rocks. Limestone and dolomite are prominent among the latter, and give rise, like the granite itself, to surfaces that are extremely rugged. Over parts of the Low Tatry karstic landforms have developed. The drainage of the Low Tatry is simple; a series of short rivers flow either north to the Váh or south to the Hron. Except over its higher summits the Low Tatry are forested, and lumbering is today a major industry of the region.

Váh valley. The Váh, the longest river of Slovakia, rises in the High Tatry. Its upper course is across the Liptov Basin, the depression, partially filled with Tertiary deposits, which separates the Low from the High Tatry. This basin lies at a height of about 2,000 feet and is ringed by mountains. It is a region of stock-rearing and the cultivation of hardy crops like rye, potatoes and fodder crops. The Váh leaves the Liptov Basin at Ružomberok, the largest city of the central region of the Slovakian Carpathians, and crosses in turn the Vel'ká Fatra and the Malá Fatra by the narrow and gorge-like valleys already mentioned. Between these defiles lies another upland basin, that of the Turiec, a little lower in altitude than the Liptov Basin, but practising the same kind of cool temperate mixed farming. At Strečno the Váh escapes from the Malá Fatra. From here down to Piešťany, a distance of 80 miles, it traverses the gradually widening valley which separates the White Carpathians from the Malá Fatra and its southward continuation into the plains.

This is one of the most industrialised parts of Slovakia. Dams, built at intervals along the Váh, are used to generate power. Industries, not only those traditional in the mountains like wood-working and textile manufacture, but also mechanical engineering and chemicals have been established. To the older urban centres, like Žilina and Trenčín, have been added small towns which have grown up around the new factories, established here fully as much to diversify the economy of this formerly backward region as to use its local resources.

Slovakian Ore Mountains. These mountains lie to the south and south-east of the Low Tatry. They are lower than the latter, and their rounded hills rise in general to between 4,000 and 5,000 feet. The conformity of their summit levels and their flattened or rounded crests are eloquent testimony to the peneplain from which they have been carved. Toward the east, the Ore Mountains are built, like much of the Low Tatry, of gneiss, over which have survived patches of later sedimentary rocks. This region has been extensively intruded by igneous rocks, which, outcropping as they do over only very small areas, have given the landscape a bizarre quality with the resulting steep and isolated hills. Toward the west these outcrops become more extensive, and the western part of the region is made up of one of the most extensive basalt flows in Europe. To the south-east, where the Ore Mountains sink toward the Pannonian Plain, the gneisses are masked by limestones which have produced the karst phenomena of the Slovenský kras.

This region lacks the ruggedness which characterises both the High and the Low Tatry. The mountain slopes are more gentle, and rise to undulating upland surfaces, which rarely exceed 4,000 feet. Altitudes are greatest in the north of the region, where it has been dissected by the Hron and its tributaries into a series of distinct massifs.

This region, like most others in Slovakia, is extensively forested, but altitudes are lower than in regions considered hitherto; the valleys are wider and their slopes gentler, and crop-farming is more widely practised. Most of this is rye, potatoes, and fodder country, but as the valleys open toward the plain, the cropping becomes more diversified. Wheat appears; fruit orchards are established; here and there one sees a vineyard, or a patch of maize, or a field of sunflower.

Forestry remains important, despite the growing competition of crop-farming. Indeed, it is made more important by the proximity of large rivers down which to float the lumber, as well as of factories and markets. One most not forget, however, that this is the Slovenské rudohorie, the 'Ore Mountains', and that this title was not conferred on them without reason. Toward the east the most important mineral mined today is iron-ore. In the west of the region mining has been dominated by gold and silver, lead and copper.

In this area the mines, most of them in the Kremnica and Štiavnica Mountains, were opened up in the later Middle Ages. Before the Turkish invasions a controlling interest in these sources of precious metals had been acquired by the Függer, the merchant bankers of Augsburg. This control was relinquished while the plains remained under Turkish control, and mining stagnated only to be revived after their expulsion and the annexation of this area to Austria.

The ores occur in veins in the gneiss which underlies the basalt and is exposed in the valleys. The profits of mining largely went to endow German families and to finance the adventures of the Habsburgs. Some, however, remained where it was won, and was used to adorn the miners' towns of Banská Bystrica, Kremnica, and Banská Štiavnica. These are gems of baroque architecture, like the Spiš towns farther east, with just a little gothic surviving from an earlier age to show that this region had its economic roots far back in the Middle Ages. Little remains of this ancient mining industry, though the traveller still sees a few inconspicuous workings in the mountains near Kremnica.

The valleys of the Hron and of its tributaries are less developed industrially than that of the Váh. Traditional industries—wood- and leather-working—are relatively more important, and the hydro-electric power potential has not yet been fully realised. Lignite is obtained in small quantities from small Tertiary basins within the mountains and used in power generation. Of the branches of the mining industry that formerly gave this region its importance in Europe, only iron-mining today remains significant. Iron-ore occurs as veins in the gneiss of much of the eastern Ore Mountains. It has been worked on a small scale for a very long time, and has been used to supply charcoal-burning furnaces both here and beyond the Hungarian border (see page 517). In recent years ore from this area has been sent west to the furnaces of Moravia, but a new iron and steel works, the Vychodo-slovenské železiarne (East Slovak Ironworks), commonly referred to as VSŽ, has been built four miles from Košice, for the purpose of smelting the local ore with fuel imported from the Soviet Union.

Plains of southern Slovakia
The southern boundary of Slovakia was established in 1920 by the Treaty of Trianon. It was then modified by the Hungarian annexations of 1938, but restored to its earlier position in 1945. The areas which were thus in dispute are topographically part of the Pannonian Plain.

Their population, particularly in the cities, was more Magyar than Slovak, and Czechoslovakia acquired these areas at the peace conference because the fortunes of their towns were held to be more intimately bound up with those of the mountains to the north than with the rest of the plain. These lowland regions form five separate units, separated one from the other by extensions of the hilly region to the north.

Danubian Lowland. The Podunajská nížina is the largest and by far the most important of these areas of lowland. It is bounded on the south by the main channel of the Danube from Bratislava down to the junction of the Ipel' river. To the west is the steep rise of the Malé Karpaty; to the north the last, low ridges of the Malá and Vel'ká Fatra fade into the plain, while fingers of plain extend northward until they narrow and disappear between the mountain ranges.

This region is further divisible into a low-lying and more southerly area, laced by the branches of the Danube and by the lower courses of its Carpathian tributaries, and a somewhat higher and more undulating region to the north of it. The Danube is here a braided, marsh-fringed river, along which there are no settlements of importance between Bratislava and Komárno. To the north is its secondary branch the Malý Dunaj, or Little Danube, which leaves the main stream below Bratislava to rejoin it at Komárno. Between lies the damp, fertile, alluvial Žitný Ostrov, or Ryc Island, cultivated whereever it is dry enough and under grass or woodland where the soil is too poorly drained for crops.

North of the Little Danube a slight rise in the land surface lifts it a few feet above the level of the marshes which border the river and creates one of the richest and most intensively cultivated areas in Czechoslovakia. Back from the rivers the land rises in gentle undulations toward the hills which are never far distant. A line of small towns, like Trnava and Nitra, lies along the edge of the higher ground, which sends low, flattened ridges southward to the Danube, where they end in low bluffs.

Ipel' Basin. This is a small area of lowland lying along the valley of the Ipel' river, which for much of its length constitutes the boundary with Hungary. Only low hills separate it from the Danubian Plain to the west and from the plains which lie to the east.

Rimava Basin. This is a more extensive lowland formed by the headwaters of the Hungarian Sajo. It is a rolling and in parts a hilly region. Most of it is good cropland. To the north rise the Slovakian Ore

Mountains, whose ore deposits formerly supplied countless charcoal iron furnaces in the plain and its surrounding hills.

Košice Basin. The Košice Plain is larger than those just considered. Its floor is more level and its soils are better. It is a triangular region lying along the valley of the Hornád and its tributaries, the Torysa and Olšava, and widening from its apex amid the hills at Prešov southward to the Hungarian border. In its midst lies Košice, the largest city in Slovakia after Bratislava, the market centre of a productive agricultural region, and now, under the fostering hand of the Czechoslovak government, an industrial city of growing importance.

Potisie Plain. This, the last of the areas of lowland which lie along the southern border of Slovakia, is essentially the upper basin of the Bodrog, a branch of the Tisza, and its tributaries. It is larger than any except the Danube lowland, but is divided by the boundary, established in 1945, between the Soviet Union and Czechoslovakia. About one-third of its total extent lies within Slovakia, an almost level, but well-drained lowland, from which the Slanské pohorie and the Vihorlat rise steeply on respectively the west and north. Its soils are mainly alluvial and fertile, and its surface, except in a small hilly area in the south, is under cultivation.

It is, however, a region of villages rather than of towns. The regional capitals, which formerly focused its economic activities, Uzghorod and Mukachevo now lie within the Soviet Union, and their regional role in eastern Slovakia has been taken over by Košice.

REGIONAL CONTRASTS

In most of the countries of Eastern Europe there are sharp internal contrasts in the levels of economic development and human welfare, but in few are they more conspicuous than in Czechoslovakia. To some extent these cultural distinctions are implicit in the physical geography. Given the technology of recent centuries, one would have expected a greater economic advance in Bohemia than in Slovakia. But the latter was not without resources; the Fuggers and Thurzos removed a very considerable wealth from Slovakia in the sixteenth century. The development of the Spiš region is a small example of what might under different circumstances have been done over much of Slovakia. Why, one may ask, has it always been poorer than the analogous region of, say, Slovenia in north-western Yugoslavia?

Slovakia's misfortunes reduce themselves to two. Throughout the Middle Ages and again after the defeat and withdrawal of the Turks, the country lay under Hungarian rule. Much may be said against the Austrian Habsburgs and the clumsy bureaucracy which they helped to create, but their rule over Bohemia was in all respects more enlightened than that of the Hungarians over Slovakia. The Austrians invested in Bohemia and Moravia, and encouraged the improvement of agriculture and the development of industry. In the Carpathians the Hungarians did neither. Instead they inhibited economic growth, repressed the peasantry and developed only the resources which they needed to supplement those of the Hungarian Plain.

On the other side of the picture it must be admitted that the Hungarians were faced in the eighteenth century with the re-colonisation of much of their own plains (see page 56) which had suffered disastrously from nearly two centuries of Turkish rule and the wars that were necessary to bring that rule to an end. They had little reserve to develop their mountain regions, inhabited by non-Magyar peoples. Slovakia suffered all through the sixteenth and seventeenth centuries from war, invasion and neglect. Turkish inroads wrecked the Függer mines at Banská Bystrica and led the family to withdraw from the area. And when Slovaks were not resisting Turks, Slovakia was all too often the scene of conflict between the Austrians and the Szekély-dominated peoples of Transylvania.

Thus, when the Czechoslovak state was formed in 1918, the White and Little Carpathians constituted, not merely a provincial boundary but a cultural divide. The difference in cultural level between the two principal divisions of the country presented political problems. The Slovaks were unable, because of their lower level of education, to play as significant a role in public life as the Czechs. They were unable to command their share of posts of responsibility, and complained that they were neglected and ignored by the politically dominant Czechs. During the 20 years of political democracy, from the formation of the state in 1918 until its dismemberment at Munich 20 years later, the Czechs attempted to level up the standards of living and of education, within their country, but always they faced a strange, misguided opposition from many of the Slovaks. Czech leadership was radical and progressive; their geographical isolation, with the centuries of Hungarian rule, had made the Slovaks conservative, obscurantist and clerical, and it was hard for them to realise that it was in part their own traditionalism which made it difficult for them to play a larger role in

Czechoslovak national life. It was no accident that the two leaders of the Slovak autonomous movement were both priests.

CLIMATE

The whole of Czechoslovakia has a continental climate, with warm summers and cold winters. In no country of Eastern Europe, except parts of Hungary, are maritime influences less marked than in Czechoslovakia. In winter, the weather tends to be dominated for long periods by the high pressure system which forms over Asia and intermittently extends westwards to Central Europe. Contrasted pressure conditions form in summer, and air masses are drawn toward the Eurasian land mass from the west. Only at this season do oceanic influences become marked, but even then they are often interrupted by the northward extension of high pressure systems, with their accompanying hot and dry conditions.

Temperature. Temperatures are strongly influenced by altitude and by local relief, with resulting frost-drainage on still winter days and intense local heating in summer. In January the whole country has an average temperature below freezing, mildest in the North Bohemian, Moravian and Danubian plains, but relatively severe in the mountains. In the plateau region of Bohemia temperatures range from −6° to −2°C (21° to 29°F), with very much lower temperatures in the many frost pockets of the plateau. In the mountains of Slovakia temperatures are a degree or two lower.

The influence of relief is no less marked in summer. In July the plains of Slovakia, have averages in excess of 21°C (70°F), and the lowlands along the Labe and Morava may have averages of over 20°C (68°F). Elsewhere the extremes are modified by altitude. Temperatures over the Bohemian plateau average as much as 6 degrees below those of the Labe Plain, and in Central Slovakia temperatures in the valleys and basins rarely exceed 15°C (59°F) on average, and on the mountain slopes are very much lower.

The severity of winter results in ice-formation on the rivers, the cessation of navigation for varying periods on the Danube, Vltava and Labe, and a low rate of discharge on those rivers which are used for power generation. No visitor to Prague can have failed to notice the wooden cutwaters on the Charles Bridge, designed to protect its ancient masonry from the drifting ice on the Vltava.

Rainfall. No place in Czechoslovakia has much less than 610 millimetres (24 inches) of rainfall a year, and over most of the country the
average exceeds 711 millimetres (28 inches). In most parts of the
country the heaviest rainfall comes in early summer, and June tends
to be the wettest month. There is generally a secondary maximum
about October, but late summer, winter and spring are generally fairly
dry.

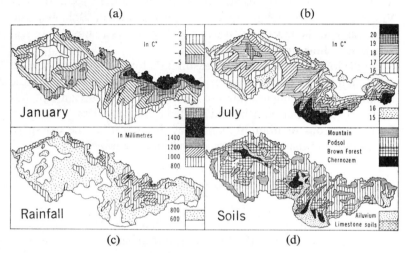

Fig. 9.2. Mean monthly temperature in (a) January, (b) July, (c) Average
annual rainfall, (d) principal soil types. All maps after *Československá
Republika*, Súbor Politických Máp.

River regimes. With the exception of the Danube, the rivers of
Czechoslovakia rise within its borders and are subject only to its
relatively simple climatic regime. High water and an acute danger of
flood accompany the melting of the snows in spring and occur again
at the time of the early summer rains. The autumn rains, smaller in
amount, and coming after the late summer drought has parched the
land, contribute very much less to the run-off. The regime of all the
Czechoslovak rivers is, then, characterised by high water in spring and
early summer, and a secondary and very much less marked high level
in autumn. The Danube, where it forms part of the southern boundary
of Czechoslovakia, already reflects more than one climatic regime: the
winter rains of western Europe, the melting snows of spring and, in the
Alps the prolonged melting of the summer months. Its high level at

Bratislava is a resultant of all these factors. The river level rises in late winter, remains high through the spring and reaches its flood stage in June. It then sinks gradually through the summer and more suddenly about September when melt-waters cease to come down from the Alpine tributaries.

Growing season. Spring comes to Czechoslovakia first in the Danubian Plain. It spreads to the lowlands of eastern Slovakia and of Moravia; then leaves break out on the trees along the Labe and lower Vltava. It spreads slowly up on to the plateaus of Bohemia and Moravia, and the forests of Slovakia, where the last snows may still be falling in June, are last to be reached.

On the lowlands the growing season lasts for half the year or even more, and on the plateaus for from four to five months, but in the mountains and the highest parts of the Bohemian–Moravian Uplands it rarely exceeds four months and is often a great deal less. This, apart from conditions of humidity and cloudiness restrict the extent of agriculture and the variety of crops that may be grown.

SOILS

The damp climate has tended to produce soils which are in general somewhat podzolised, although the forest cover, which must once have been almost continuous over the whole country, has contributed to its humus content. The higher mountain areas have skeletal soils of no agricultural value. Over the lowlands there are extensive areas of alluvial soil, generally rich in mineral content, but sometimes poorly drained and with no clearly marked vertical structure. They are, however, amongst the most productive in the country. At somewhat higher levels, and primarily on the terraces which border the alluvial deposits, are well-developed brown-forest soils and even areas which approximate the chernozems of parts of southern Poland. The latter occur only where the rainfall is relatively low, and this, in effect, limits them to the lowland areas of Bohemia, Moravia and southern Slovakia. They are in part developed on loess, which gives them a light texture, easy to cultivate, and they have generally a high lime content (Fig. 9.2d).

Over the rest of the country the soils are in some degree podzolised. They are poor in lime and in general need heavy fertilising. The black and brown soils are the wheat and sugar-beet country; the podzol produces rye, potatoes and fodder crops.

Brown-coal working, near Most. In the distance is the Krušné hory

CZECHOSLOVAKIA

Sawmill in the Hron valley, near Banská Bystrica

Prague: the Old Town Square in the right-bank section (Staré Mésto) of the city, overlooked by the Týn Church, the chief church of the citizens of medieval Prague

Prague: the Václavské náměsti (Wenceslas Square) in the area of nineteenth century growth. In the distance is the National Museum

VEGETATION

Czechoslovakia must have lain within the area which the ancients called the Hercynian Forest. At the beginning of historical time it was still densely forested, much of it with broadleaved trees, but with coniferous trees on the higher ground in both the Czech and the Slovak lands. Place-name evidence, indeed, shows that the conifers were by no means restricted to the mountains or even to higher ground.

The earliest human settlements were on the areas of black earth and brown-forest soil in northern Bohemia, Moravia and southern Slovakia. Woodland here was probably thin and easily cleared; the soils were good, and these became the core areas of the earliest political units in Czechoslovakia. Their vegetation today has been almost entirely shaped by man. Only in the mountains does one find a vegetation that can be termed 'natural', but even here there has been extensive forest clearance and replanting often with different species from those originally found. Large areas in the hills of eastern Slovakia have been reduced by deforestation and grazing to poor grassland in which soil erosion, locally at least, has reached alarming proportions.

POPULATION AND SETTLEMENT

The population of Czechoslovakia was in 1938 estimated to have been about 14·6 million. When the census of 1947 was taken there were only 12·3 million. Czechoslovakia had lost proportionately more people as a result of the war and of the events that preceded it than any other country of Eastern Europe. The prewar level of population has not in fact been regained. The losses were due primarily to the loss or flight of the Sudeten Germans from the border regions of Bohemia, but about 800,000 went with Ruthenia to the Soviet Union, and a very much smaller number of Hungarian-speakers was expelled. Though these losses were to a small degree offset by the return of Czechs and Slovaks from abroad, Czechoslovakia nevertheless found her population smaller by about 16 per cent than before the Munich crisis.

Migration and growth

The years following the Second World War were marked by an extreme mobility of population. Lands formerly inhabited by Germans had to be resettled; new industrial settlements were established,

15

and people left the overpopulated mountain valleys of Slovakia to settle in the plains of Moravia and Bohemia. Some two million people ultimately moved into the former German-settled areas, and a substantial number of these were from Slovakia. Slovaks also migrated in large numbers to industrial centres in Moravia and Bohemia. Another feature of these years was the sharp difference between the birth-rates of the Czechs and Slovaks. The birth-rates of the Czechs had been higher than among the Slovaks since the foundation of the Republic. It declined sharply in both groups during the 1930s and the war years, but the drop was more serious among the Czechs. Until very recently the Slovak birth-rate remained of the order of four per thousand higher than that of the Czechs. One would expect the Slovak birth-rate to drop as the population becomes more urbanised, and current statistics suggest that this is in fact the case. It nevertheless remains true that, without the fecundity of the Slovaks, the Czechoslovak government would have had a much more severe labour shortage than in fact it had.

The migration of recent years has been mainly one from the country districts to the towns.[1] In 1947 the state was defined as 51·1 per cent rural. The movements of the last few years have made Czechoslovakia the most urban of all the East European countries, with the exception, of course, of East Germany, and in 1964 no less than 60 per cent of its population was regarded as urban.

The population growth of recent years has not been primarily in the larger towns, a number of which even showed some loss in the 1950s, but in the small and medium-sized towns. Most towns in the former German settled territory belonged to this category. The government adopted the policy of decentralising industry as far as practicable, and it also founded a number of new industrial towns, none of which has been allowed to grow to more than 75,000.

In 1966 the total population of Czechoslovakia was estimated to have been 14,240,000. Of this 4,414,300, or 31 per cent, lived in the Slovak *Kraje*. At the same time the Slovaks made up 28·9 per cent of the total population and 85·6 per cent of that of Slovakia. In the predominantly Czech lands of Bohemia and Moravia, 3·5 per cent of the population was Slovak. The minority peoples made up only a very small proportion of the total population. Hungarians constituted the largest group, with about 555,000, and the Germans the second largest with 130,000. The Poles of northern Moravia numbered about 69,000,

[1] Defined as settlements of over 2,000.

and there was a small number of Ukrainians, Russians and others. The Jewish community is not listed separately in current Czechoslovaks but is unofficially put at about 50,000. In all, the non-Czech–Slovak minorities amount to 858,000, only 6·1 per cent of the total, as against 35 per cent in 1921.

Population structure. The population of Czechoslovakia is made up, as was noted earlier, of two distinct groups. Both groups show small age groups corresponding with the lowered birth-rate during the First and Second World Wars. Since the end of the latter, however, the Slovaks have maintained a high birth-rate, whereas the Czechs have had a reproduction rate that is decidedly low for Eastern Europe and

Bohemia and Moravia   Slovakia

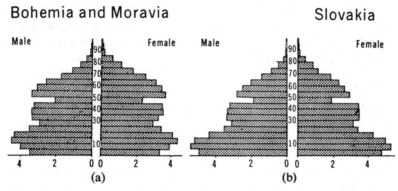

Fig. 9.3. Structure of population in (a) Bohemia and Moravia, (b) Slovakia. After *Statistická Ročenka ČSSR, 1965.*

much closer to levels in Western Europe. So distinct are the two groups that separate pyramids have been constructed (Fig. 9.3a, b). The implications of this difference for economic growth will be touched on later. An expanding work-force in the Czech lands can be maintained only by immigration from Slovakia, and the greater availability of labour constitutes a powerful reason for the establishment of industry in the latter.

Rural settlement
Czechoslovakia has long since ceased to be a predominantly agricultural country, and in 1961 only 19·3 per cent of the total population— 15·9 in the Czech lands, 27·0 per cent in the Slovak—was engaged in agriculture. Nevertheless, about 40 per cent of the total population

still lives in settlements of less than 2,000 inhabitants, and 27 per cent in settlements that can only be called villages or hamlets.

Village patterns. The broad distinctions between village types conform very roughly with the landform divisions of the country. The girdle of mountains which encloses Bohemia is characterised in the main by forest-villages (Fig. 5.4), with hamlets and isolated farmsteads here and there. Within Bohemia a distinction can be drawn between the northern lowlands, which are characterised by irregular but compact villages (*Haufendorf*), similar to those of much of central and southern Germany, and the plateau region of southern Bohemia, together with most of Moravia, which are characterised by street-villages, similar to those of East Germany and Poland. Settlement types are not absolutely uniform within each of these areas, and there is an area with predominantly compact villages in southern Bohemia. There does, however, appear to be some correlation between the nucleated village and the superior soils.

In Slovakia, the nucleated village makes its appearance only on the plains of the south. Over much of the Carpathian valleys and foothills the street village again predominates, while on the higher ground of the mountains, settlements are either scattered or form very loose clusters.

House-types. The styles of the village house, no less than the plan of the village itself, display a certain regional pattern. They are, in some degree, responses to physical—especially climatic—and economic conditions, but they also have characteristics for which there is no such simple explanation.

Bohemia and Moravia and parts even of Slovakia are characterised by a house-type not unlike that found in much of central Germany. House and farm-buildings are traditionally grouped around a small yard, entered in many instances by way of a high, arched gateway. The house, frequently of wood on a stone foundation but occasionally stone-built, may be of two storeys or even more, has a steeply pitched roof, and is often colour-washed. Although the scale and degree of elaboration of such buildings varies greatly, they usually suggest, by peasant standards, a certain degree of affluence.

In southern Moravia the Danubian house makes its appearance. It is a long house, and in the detail of its design it is adjusted more to bright hot, summers than to the snows of northern Europe. A shaded porch extends along at least part of one of its longer sides. Such houses extend far up the Carpathian valleys, but in the mountains, the housing is simpler in its design, but frequently more complex in its ornamentation. The mountain house is more compact; its roof is steeper to shed the snow; it is built almost wholly of wood, which has often been elaborately carved during the long winters; the yard is less well appointed, and the whole is simple, if not primitive.

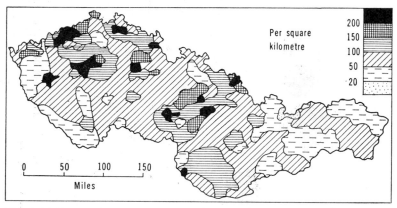

Fig. 9.4. Distribution of population in Czechoslovakia. After *Československá Republika*, Súbor Politických Máp.

Urban settlement

Czechoslovakia is essentially a land of small towns. Its urban pattern has in general been inherited from the period of medieval settlement and growth, and the distribution of towns accords fairly closely with that of agricultural wealth. This pattern has, of course, been distorted by the rise of mining settlements and of modern industry, but the

Table 46. Classification of towns according to size

	Number	Total population
Over 100,000	5	2,011,000
50,000–99,999	13	864,000
20,000–49,999	36	1,027,000
10,000–19,999	76	1,045,000
5,000–9,999	167	1,188,000
	297	6,135,000

Source: *Statistická Ročenka ČSSR, 1965.*

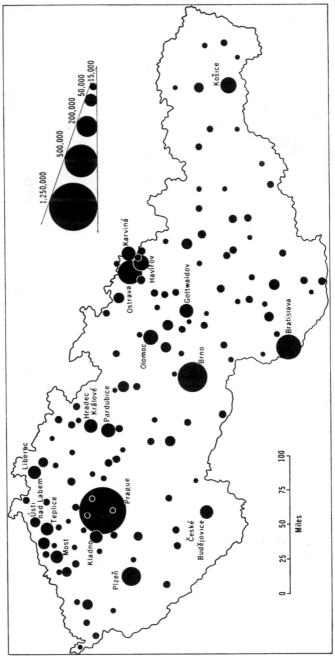

Fig. 9.5. Distribution of cities in Czechoslovakia. All cities of over 10,000 are shown, and those of more than 50,000 are named. Data from *Statistická Ročenka ČSSR, 1965.*

distribution of urban settlement remained little changed until the creation of 'socialist' towns in the recent period of planned development.

Population estimates of December 1964 indicate 297 towns of 5,000 population or more, and a further 775, sometimes classed as urban, having from 2,000 to 4,999. The functions of the latter, as also of many with more than 5,000 inhabitants, remain strongly rural and agricultural.

Towns of Bohemia. Fig. 9.5 shows the distribution and relative size of all settlements of more than 5,000 inhabitants. Two areas are outstanding: the plain of northern Bohemia, together with the foot-hill zone of the Ore Mountains and Sudety, and the Moravian Plain, including the Ostrava industrial region. In the plateau regions which make up southern Bohemia, towns are in general smaller, and less closely spaced, and in Slovakia, despite their growth in recent years, towns remain few and small.

The most intensive urban growth has taken place in and around Prague; in the lignite-mining region of northern Bohemia, and on the Moravian coal-field. Elsewhere, the towns, even the largest of them, tend to exist in isolation. Brno, Bratislava and Plzeň, all of them among the five largest cities, have very few satellite towns about them.

In northern Bohemia, the towns tend to be grouped either along the rivers or at the foot of the encircling hills. The former are still essentially market centres for the surrounding plains; the latter are more often mining and industrial centres. Among the former are not only Hradec Králové, Pardubice and Kolín, all of them on the Labe and important regional centres from the Middle Ages, but also such smaller towns as Litomyšl, Poděbrady and Mělník, whose functions have always been more local and proportionately more agricultural.

Apart from Prague itself, which will be examined below, the foothill towns include the textile and glass-making centres of Liberec, Jablonec and Trutnov, to mention only the largest of the towns of the Krkonoše; the lignite-mining centres of Sokolov, Most and Duchcov, and the chemical and mixed industrial towns of Ústí nad Labem, Teplice and Litoměřice. To these should be added Kladno, 12 miles west of Prague, which has become an important centre of coal-mining and of smelting and other industries based upon the local fuel resources. In the plateau region of southern Bohemia towns are fewer, and most, like České-Budějovice, Písek, Tábor and Jihlava, lie in small, sheltered and relatively fertile depressions in the table-land. The largest of them is Plzeň (142,700), originally a small, agricultural town like the others, but from the mid-nineteenth century the seat of an iron-smelting industry, and now a major centre of the mechanical engineering industries. Near the western limit of this region is Karlovy Vary, at one time the leading inland resort of the Austrian Empire and the meeting place of the *élite* of Europe, now a small manufacturing town, its vast hotels almost empty and its casino closed.

Prague (Praha). The city of Prague lies on the Vltava, just where its valley begins to broaden, and the plateau in which it has been incised to sink towards the plain of the Labe. It lies close to the junction of two physical environments, and must, like so many foot-hill towns in Eastern Europe, have derived some importance from this fact. There had been an important settlement here since the earliest historical times. A number of low hills rise steeply from the river, affording protection, without losing command of the valley. The first to be occupied was Vyšehrad, on the right bank of the Vltava, about 2 miles upstream from the present city centre. The combination of fortress and settlement which had grown up here, was then moved to the higher hill on the left bank, in reality a narrow spur of the South Bohemian Plateau. Here was built the castle of the Bohemian kings and the cathedral of the bishop of Prague. Modified, extended and rebuilt, it is now the Hradčany, probably the most impressive group of governmental and public buildings to be found in the capital city of any European country.

Opposite the Hradčany, on the lower and flatter bank of the Vltava, there grew up the merchants' city, the Staré Mešto, within a great bend of the Vltava. Here is the old town square, dominated by the late medieval Týn church; here, too, lay the Jewish quarter, the Josefov, and here successive lines of fortification were built to enclose the expanding commercial city. The Staré Město was joined with the Malá Strana on the left bank by the Karlův Most, or Charles Bridge in the fourteenth century, and the two complementary settlements, the one popular and commercial, the other governmental and aristocratic grew together to make the city of Prague.

Prague was the seat of the Bohemian kings from the eleventh century until the extinction of their line in the sixteenth. It then became the seat of the Austrian governor, and again assumed the role of national capital in 1918, with the Hradčany once more the seat of the government. Until the mid-nineteenth century Prague remained an administrative and commercial city and an important cultural and educational centre. Then, encouraged by good communications, a local market and the commercial prestige which the city had long enjoyed, modern industries began to develop. Iron from Kladno and Beroun supplied the metal industries. Coal was brought in from the fields of western Bohemia and lignite up-river from the pits along the foot of the Krušné hory. The manufacture of all kinds of machinery developed; the chemical and especially the pharmaceutical industry was established, and the clothing, furniture, food and other consumer goods industries were founded both to meet the growing local demand and to take advantage of the local communications network and consequent ease of distribution over all Bohemia and much of the Austro-Hungarian Empire.

The Vltava becomes navigable at Prague, and in the nineteenth century a river port was established about two miles downstream from the old city. Here, in the suburbs of Karlín and Holešovice many of the new factories were established. They have since spread out to the north-east and north of the city, and housing, much of it made up of large blocks of flats, stretched out toward the west, over the hills and plateaus behind the Hradčany, and eastward over the gentler slopes of Žižkov and Vršovice. The population of Prague grew steadily during the later years of the nineteenth and the twentieth centuries. In 1938 it reached about 900,000; it declined a little after the Second World War, but has again increased and in 1966 was estimated to have been about 1,030,330.

Towns of Moravia. The historic province of Moravia is smaller than Bohemia, though more densely populated. North of the Moravian Gate is the Ostrava conurbation, a group of industrial and mining towns among which Ostrava, Havířov and Karviná are the largest. Most are the product of the nineteenth century, and witness to the urban sprawl, ugly and uncontrolled, of the period of rapid industrial growth. Havířov was founded after 1950 and consists mainly of large blocks of workers' flats.

South of the Gate, the largest urban centres are Olomouc and Brno. Olomouc lies on the Morava, and in the midst of the wide, fertile Upper Moravian Plain. Its early wealth and importance are indicated by its medieval cathedral and Renaissance town hall. In the eighteenth century, it became one of the fortress cities guarding the approaches to Vienna. It is today the focal city of its region, the centre of a transport net and the site of a number of food and clothing industries.

15*

Brno is the regional capital of southern Moravia. It lies at the junction of the river Svratka and Svitava, in an embayment of the Moravian hills. The site was determined by two low hills between the rivers, on one of which the medieval castle was built, and on the other the cathedral. The town grew up on the slopes of the hills, and has in recent times spread out over the surrounding lowlands. With about 333,000 inhabitants, Brno is now second only to Prague in size, and is one of Czechoslovakia's foremost industrial towns. Its chief industries are mechanical, and Brno is particularly important for its manufacture of tractors, as well as of textiles, clothing and food-stuffs.

Along the valleys of the Bečva and of the Morava lies a succession of small towns, from Hranice, close against the Moravian Gate, through Přerov and Kroměříž to Hodonín on the lower Morava. Each was originally a market centre, but to their local functions they have added manufacturing industries, most of them light, and often related to the local agricultural production. The largest of these towns, however, did not originate in this way. The village of Zlín was selected by Tomáš Baťa to be the site of his leather and footwear industry; now, as the town of Gottwaldov, nestling against the Slovakian hills, from which it draws its labour, it is a large 'socialist' town with very extensive leather and rubber industries.

Urban growth in Slovakia. With the exception of Bratislava, the towns of Slovakia were few and small before the economic plans began to bring industry to the mountain valleys. Hydro-electric power along the Váh; brown coal in the Nitra valley; iron-ore in the Rudohorie; a more abundant labour supply than elsewhere, and the government's decision to develop Slovakia have all contributed. The little towns along the Váh from Liptov down to Trnava, which formerly had little to recommend them beyond a peasant market and a saw-mill, now have mechanical, chemical and textile industries. Along the Hron a new life has been given to towns like Banská Bystrica and Zvolen, and new towns built like Žiar nad Hronom, with its aluminium smelter.

Growth has been slowest in eastern Slovakia, which remains the least urbanised part of the whole country, but here too woodworking, paper and, above all, smelting industries have been either established or expanded.

The towns of Slovakia lie either along the larger valleys or at the junction of the Carpathian Mountains with the Hungarian Plain. Largest of these, and the capital of Slovakia, is Bratislava (276,500). It was founded in the early Middle Ages, where spurs of the Malé

Karpaty run down to the Danube, forming a divide between the Little Alföld and the plain of Vienna. Bratislava became an important commercial city during the Middle Ages, and later one of the major defences of Europe against the Turks. With the Austrian reconquest of the Pannonian Plain its defensive role vanished, and Bratislava sank to a position of little importance between the major cities of Vienna and Budapest. From this position it was rescued when it passed to Czechoslovakia. It has a large riverborne commerce; its docks line the banks of the river, and its industrial quarters spread out over the Danubian Plain to the east.

A line of towns curves to the north-east and east from Bratislava, in origin market centres where the hill people came down to sell and buy at the margin of the plain. They include Trnava and the ancient city of Nitra. Small towns border the Ore Mountains, but the hills here reach into Hungary, and it is the Hungarian cities of Gyöngyös, Eger and Miskolc which in the past served as intermediaries between hill and plain. A few small towns grew up during the Middle Ages as centres of the silver mines; among them Kremnica and Banská Štiavnica, though small, have preserved their urban functions and also something of their old world architecture and charm.

In the Hornád valley of eastern Slovakia, where an undulating lowland reaches north between the mountains, is Košice (112,400), the largest and most important city in eastern Slovakia. It was founded in the thirteenth century as a trading town on the route across the mountains to Poland. The old city still clusters around the late medieval Gothic cathedral, but modern industries have spread around it, among them the new East Slovakian iron and steel works.

AGRICULTURE

The fact that in Czechoslovakia a far greater proportion of the labour force is engaged in manufacturing than in agriculture, and that the latter contributes only 14 per cent of the gross national product should not hide the fact that Czechoslovak agriculture has long been one of the most developed and efficient in Eastern Europe. Although one of the most mountainous of the countries of Eastern Europe, it has extensive areas of high quality agricultural land, notably in northern Bohemia, the Morava valley and southern Slovakia, and these areas have been long and efficiently cultivated.

Land reform

Under Austro-Hungarian rule most of the land had been held in large estates, mainly by German-speaking or Hungarian owners. A law of 1919 provided for the break-up of these holdings and their distribution amongst the less affluent peasantry. The reform was one of the more thorough and effective in Eastern Europe, and provided most of the peasantry with adequate farm-holdings. As a result, nearly three-quarters of the agricultural land was held in units of not more than 20 hectares (49·4 acres).

After 1945 a second measure of land reform was necessary. Not only was it thought desirable to break up the few remaining estates, but the German-speaking population had very largely left, and their lands fell into the possession of the Czechoslovak state. Large areas were made available to Czech immigrants into the area, and conditions had to be made attractive for them. An upper limit of 50 hectares (123·5 acres) was set on farms, and it is estimated that 1·7 million hectares (4·2 million acres) were distributed between 1945 and 1948. A much larger area was held and operated by the government. At the time of the census of May 1949 there were over 1·5 million farm units, of which almost 97 per cent were each of less than 20 hectares (49·4 acres). Despite the land reforms, no less than 32 per cent of all holdings were of less than 1 hectare (2·47 acres).

Table 47. Size and number of holdings

Size of holding	Number of holdings	Percentage of holdings	Percentage of Agricultural land
Under 0·5 hectares	267,046	19·7	0·7
0·5–1·0	191,696	12·7	1·3
1–2	206,636	13·7	2·7
2–5	350,904	23·3	10·6
5–10	255,293	16·9	16·0
10–20	158,874	10·6	18·9
20–50	35,159	2·3	8·8
Over 50	11,489	0·8	41·0
Total	1,484,794	100·0	100·0

Source: *Statistický Zpravodaj*, **13**, no. 2, 1950, quoted in *Czechoslovakia*, ed. V. Bušek and N. Spulber, p. 251.

The very considerable area that remained in units of more than 50 hectares (123·5 acres) was, of course, in the possession of the state, and had not been distributed in part because of the shortage of agricultural manpower. The number of persons active in agriculture—about 2·2 millions at this time—was some 600,000 fewer than before the Second World War, and this was a major factor in hastening the collectivisation and mechanisation of Czechoslovak agriculture.

Collectivisation. The formation of collective farms was begun in 1949. By 1953 about 46 per cent of the agricultural land was collectivised. During the period of relaxation which followed, many collectives were broken up, and progress was not really resumed until 1958. By 1964, 89·4 per cent of agricultural land had been socialised, and most of the remainder was in the small personal plots which members of collectives were permitted to retain.

Land use
There has been little change in the general pattern of land use since the period before the Second World War. A small amount of farmland has been lost to other uses, particularly urban and industrial development, and there has been some change in the types of crop grown, but the interrelationship of the broad categories has remained almost constant, as Table 48 shows.

Some of the changes shown, such as the increase and diminution of the area of pasture, are to be related to the acute shortage of agricultural labour.

Table 48. Land use in Czechoslovakia, 1934–64 (in hectares)

	Average[1] 1934–38	1948	1960	1966
Total area:	12,781	12,786	12,787	12,787
Farm land:	7,756	7,561	7,362	7,144
of which: arable	5,602	5,279	5,143	5,054
meadow	1,124	1,100	1,091	984
pasture	895	927	833	788
vineyards	20	20	24	29
hopfields	12	7	8	10
Non-farm land:	4,926	5,127	5,425	5,643
of which: forests	3,999	4,066	4,359	4,450
other	145	151	52	54

Source: *Statistická Ročenka ČSSR, 1967.*
[1] Excluding Ruthenia.

The increase in agricultural production has been less marked in Czechoslovakia than in other East European countries, as a result in part of labour shortage, in part, also, of the fact that Czechoslovakia began its planned growth from a relatively high level of efficiency. The overall increase above the level of 1936, corrected for changes in

(a)

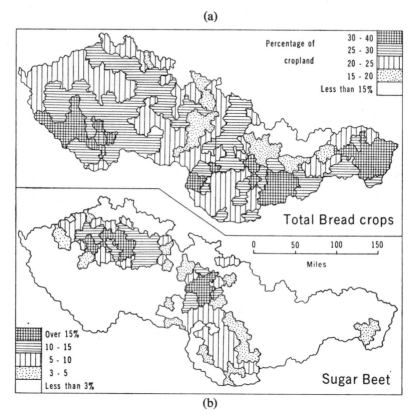

Fig. 9.6. Agriculture: Distribution of (a) bread crops (wheat and rye), (b) sugar-beet. After M. Blažek.

area, has been 14·0 per cent, and the breakdown of the statistics between the Czech and Slovak regions shows a growth of only 6·6 per cent in the Czech lands as against 41·4 in the previously much more backward Slovakia. On the other hand, the output per unit of labour has shown a remarkable increase, and in 1963 stood at about 262 per cent of the prewar level. This remarkable expansion has been achieved by a more complete mechanisation of farming than in any other East European country, and has been accompanied by a diminution of the number engaged in agriculture to 1·25 millions in 1966—less than half the number so employed before 1939. The increase in the use of farm machinery has been striking. The number of tractors—counted in 15-h.p. units—has increased from about 26,000 in 1951 to about 186,000 in 1966, and much of this increase had taken place in the previous four years. The growth in the number of combine-harvesters has been even greater, though beginning from a very low level. In 1951 there were 392; in 1960, 6,326, and in 1966 12,778. The increase in other forms of mechanisation—including sowing machines, disc ploughs, and sugar-beet and flax harvesters—has been significant, though less striking.

About half the cultivated land is, as it has long been, under grain crops, of which wheat, barley and rye are the most important. Much of the remainder is planted with potatoes and fodder crops, with locally an important cultivation of such industrial crops as sugar-beet and flax.

Grain crops. The planned increase in the production of bread-grains has not been achieved, and Czechoslovakia is today a net importer of wheat on a considerable scale—in 1966, 1,032,000 tons, as against a domestic production of 2,247,000. There were in addition small imports of other grains which seem to have been used primarily as fodder. The bread-grains are cultivated primarily in the areas of good and intermediate soil, though in the former they commonly share the land with maize or specialised industrial crops, such as sugar-beet and flax, and in the latter, with root and fodder crops.

Table 49. Area cultivated and yield of chief grain crops in 1966

	Area (hectares)	Yield (thousand tons)
Wheat	892,327	2,247
Rye and mixed rye-wheat	395,065	790
Barley	690,042	1,608
Oats and mixed oats-barley	388,988	746

Source: *Statistická Ročenka ČSSR, 1967.*

The area cultivated and the volume of production of the chief grain crops in 1964 are shown in Table 49. The trend in recent years has been for the area under wheat to increase at the expense of most other grains, but particularly of rye.

Maize is grown chiefly in southern Moravia and in the Danubian Plain of Slovakia where the hot summers and deep soil suit it. It is used primarily as fodder. The area under maize has fluctuated greatly, but has tended on the whole to increase.

Fodder crops. These include many of the grain crops; maize and oats are in the main fed to the animals. Green fodder such as lucerne and clover is widely cultivated in the upland areas, where wheat and barley do less well.

Potatoes. These enter prominently into the human diet, and are also fed to the animals. They are grown most extensively on the areas of intermediate and poor soil, and are not often seen in the areas of good cropland. Both the production of potatoes and the yield per hectare have tended in recent years to diminish, evidence both that their cultivation is being relegated to the poorer soil and that their importance in the diet is declining. In 1966 potatoes were grown on 437,140 hectares (1,079,736 acres), only a little more than that under rye.

Industrial crops. The cultivation of industrial crops—sugar-beet, flax, hemp and oil-seeds—has been increasingly important in recent years, and in Europe Czechoslovakia now ranks next after France, West Germany and Poland in the production of beet-sugar. Beet cultivation demands a good quality soil, and an abundant labour force for hoeing and harvesting. The provision of the latter has been difficult, and for this reason attempts are being made to mechanise beet production. The areas of intensive beet growing are the North Bohemian Plain, where Kolín and Poděbrady are surrounded by beet fields, and the Haná region of Moravia. Less intensive cultivation (see Fig. 9.6 b) is found over much of northern Bohemia, southern Moravia and south-western Slovakia. The existence of sugar-beet processing plant—apart from considerations of soil and climate—is likely to prevent any great change in the geographical pattern of sugar-beet cultivation.

At present about 235,700 hectares (582,179 acres) are under beet. Production fluctuates greatly with the seasons, and in 1963 reached over eight million tons of beet.

Flax has long been grown for textile purposes in the hilly districts of northern Bohemia and of the Šumava and plateau region of South Bohemia, and the linen industry is well established in these regions. The production of flax has been greatly increased in recent years, with the concurrent growth of linen-weaving, and there has also been some growth in hemp production.

Oil-bearing plants are widely grown, rape-seed in northern Bohemia; poppy and mustard further south, and sunflower in the hotter and more sunny plains of southern Slovakia. The domestic production of vegetable oils has, however, to be supplemented by a large-scale import.

Tobacco is important only in areas bordering the Pannonian Plain, especially near Komárno. Over 90 per cent of the tobacco produced is grown in Slovakia. It is, however, insufficient for domestic needs and there is an import mainly from the Danubian and Balkan countries.

Fruit-growing. Temperate fruits, especially the apple, plum and cherry, are grown intensively in northern Bohemia and to a lesser degree in most other parts of the country. Viticulture is relatively unimportant. Czechoslovakia lies near the climatic limit of the vine, and vineyards cover only 26,000 hectares (63,000 acres). Although small areas of vineyard are found in Bohemia, notably at Mělník, most are to be found where the Carpathian foot-hills give place to the Pannonian Plain, and summers are hotter and brighter than in the Czech lands.

Hop cultivation, in a sense, takes the place of viticulture in Bohemia, where hop gardens cover large areas between Kladno and Karlovy Vary, and have contributed to the rise of the brewing industries of Plzeň (Pilsen) and České-Budějovice (Budweiss).

Animal farming
Grazing land makes up about 14 per cent of the total area of Czechoslovakia and about a quarter of the farm land. Animal rearing is encouraged by the considerable extent of land that cannot profitably be cultivated, but it is also practised on much of the best cropland. Here fodder crops are grown in rotation with bread-grains and industrial crops, and animal products figure more prominently in the diet than in most other countries of Eastern Europe. The availability of milk and meat has increased though in no spectacular fashion since the Second World War, and has only recently begun to exceed the level of production in 1938.

Cattle. The rearing of cattle for both meat and dairy produce is carried on principally in southern and eastern Bohemia and in Moravia, and only about 30 per cent of all cattle are found in Slovakia.

Sheep. On the other hand, sheep are met with almost exclusively in the mountainous and hilly regions, both those which enclose Bohemia

(a)

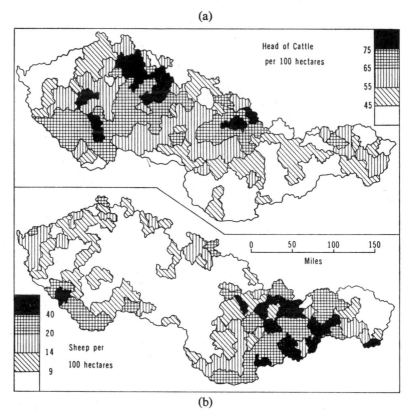

(b)

Fig. 9.7. Agriculture: Distribution of (a) cattle, (b) sheep. After M. Blažek.

and also those which make up the greater part of Slovakia. Almost 80 per cent of the sheep are, in fact, found in Slovakia, where they contribute not only wool and meat, but also milk for the manufacture of local cheese.

Pigs. The branch of animal husbandry that has increased the most rapidly has been pig-rearing. Numbers have risen by about 140 per cent since 1948. Pigs are reared in every part of the country. They are most numerous in the crop-farming regions such as northern Bohemia, Moravia and the Danubian Plains, where they consume fodder crops and a variety of plant waste.

Agricultural regions

The map of agricultural regions (Fig. 9.8) shows a close correspondence with that of landform regions. Three regions of high agricultural potential stand out: North Bohemia, the Moravian Plain and the

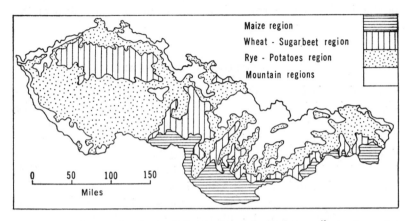

Maize region

Wheat - Sugarbeet region

Rye - Potatoes region

Mountain regions

0   50   100   150
Miles

Fig. 9.8. Agricultural regions of Czechoslovakia. Based on *Československo, Poznáváme Svět.*

Danubian Plain, with smaller regions of secondary importance in the Ostrava, Rimava and Košice regions. The dominant crops differ between them. In North Bohemia and in the Olomouc region of the Moravian Plain they are wheat, barley and sugar-beet. In the lower Morava and Danubian plains, maize and fodder grains are important and locally predominant.

A region dominated by rye, oats and potatoes, with important cattle and pig-rearing extends over the whole of the Bohemian plateau and into northern Moravia, and a similar association with sheep tending to replace the cattle, is found in parts of Slovakia.

The mountains which enclose Bohemia are characterised by the cultivation of hardy cereals and potatoes and by grazing. In the mountains of Slovakia, grazing is more important and grain cultivation less extensive.

Forestry

About 35 per cent of the total area of Czechoslovakia is forested. The forests are government owned, and have in recent years been extended by a policy of re-afforestation. They are regularly cut and replanted, and supply raw materials not only for building, but for furniture, plywood and veneer manufacture, and for cellulose and paper. The forests are very extensive in the mountains which partially enclose Bohemia and in Slovakia, where much of the province is more than 40 per cent forested. The cut is predominantly of softwood, spruce predominating, and hardwoods make up only about a fifth of the total.

MANUFACTURING INDUSTRIES

Czechoslovakia is, with the exception of East Germany, the most highly industrialised country of Eastern Europe. Even before the Second World War, almost a third of its gross national product came from manufacturing, and this fraction has now increased to over two-thirds. The industrial ascendancy of Czechoslovakia derives from a long period of industrial growth in the nineteenth and early twentieth centuries, when Bohemia and Moravia were the favoured provinces of the Austrian Empire. Aside from the small industrial region of Upper Silesia, these were the only parts of Eastern Europe upon which the Industrial Revolution made any significant impact.

The natural endowment of Bohemia and Moravia was considerable. Coal was abundant; iron-ore was adequate for the nineteenth-century scale of growth; there was water power, and an industrious, technically able and relatively dense population, as well as developed lines of communication both with the Habsburg Empire and with all Western Europe. On the eve of the First World War about 85 per cent of all the coal mined within the Austro-Hungarian Empire came from the Czech lands, as well as 60 per cent of the metal goods and 75 per cent of the chemicals.

Such was the developed industry which passed to the Czechoslovak state in 1918. Its market was at once contracted not only by diminished purchasing power but also by the political and tariff barriers that now cut off its former customers. The light industries, more easily duplicated in each of the other succession states, suffered acutely. The heavy industries, which could command a market more easily, continued to grow. Partly for political reasons French capital was invested heavily in the iron, steel and mechanical industries which became technically among the most advanced in Europe.

There was little significant change in the location of manufacturing. It was predominantly in western Bohemia and northern Moravia. There was no important development in Slovakia, whose contribution to a slowly expanding industrial production tended relatively to decline.

Planned development

Despite the bombing of a few key industrial undertakings, Czechoslovak industry suffered comparatively little material damage during the war. Immediately after the war all the larger and many of the smaller industrial undertakings were nationalised; in the case of those formerly in German possession the government had no alternative but to take them over. A Two-Year Plan aimed to restore the prewar level of production, and in 1949, the first of the Five-Year Plans aimed to increase greatly the capital investment of the country. Heavy industry, which one might have thought to be well-developed already, received the lion's share of the investment. Iron and steel capacity was increased and work was begun on a large new plant in eastern Slovakia; a number of electric generators was built, and there was a big expansion in most branches of mechanical engineering.

Plans, however, were not well coordinated; targets were not achieved, and work had even to be abandoned on the East Slovakian steel combine. Successive plans, even after Stalin's death, showed no change in objective, but somewhat greater skill in carrying them out. Light and consumer goods industries received a much smaller share

Table 50. Industrial growth, 1937–65 (in thousands of tons)

	1937	1948	1956	1960	1965
Coal, bituminous	16,951	16,683	21,788	26,214	27,731
Coal, lignite	18,042	23,588	46,299	58,403	73,216
Pig-iron	1,675	1,648	3,308	4,739	5,927
Steel	2,315	2,621	4,882	6,768	8,598
Cement	1,350	1,658	3,148	5,051	5,713
Sulphuric acid	n.d.	215	422	553	933

Source: *UN Statistical Yearbook, 1965; Annuaire Statistique de la Société des Nations, 1940–41; UN Statistical Yearbook, 1966.*

of total investment, but were, in fact, far from neglected. The social
aspects of economic growth received considerable attention; new
industrial cities were built, and the industrial development of Slovakia,
at whatever cost, became a prime objective. Table 50 illustrates the
rate of industrial growth during the last two decades.

Table 51 of production of selected consumer goods shows a much
slower rate of growth.

Table 51. Production of selected consumer goods, 1948–65

	1948	1956	1960	1965
Cotton yarn[1]	68·1	81·7	102·2	108·1
Cotton fabrics[2]	280	366	464	496
Flax and hemp yarn[1]	n.d.	n.d.	29·2	22·3
Wool yarn[1]	32	31·8	39·3	41·7
Wool fabrics[2]	42	37	46	44

[1] In thousands of tons.   [2] In thousands of metres.

Fuel and minerals

It was the rich reserves of fuel and a long history of mining that perhaps did most to attract industry to Bohemia and Moravia in the
nineteenth century. Non-ferrous mining has now almost ceased; iron-
ore reserves are not large; there is little petroleum or natural gas, but
the reserves of solid fuel are still amongst the largest in Europe.

Bituminous coalfields. It appears that the bituminous and sub-
bituminous coal resources are roughly comparable in size. The former
are associated exclusively with the Bohemian Massif, and occur in
basins that have been preserved on its surface by folding. Only five of
these are today of economic significance, and some of these are very
small in reserves and in output. The Kladno and Plzeň fields lie to the
west of Prague, and together form a curving belt of coal measures from
near the Labe to a point west of Plzeň (Fig. 9.9). Coal is good quality,
but reserves are relatively small, and these two fields have in recent
years contributed approximately 10 and 5 per cent respectively to the
total Czechoslovak production.

The Trutnov Basin lies at the eastern end of the Krkonoše, and
is in fact an extension of the Wałbrzych field of Lower Silesia. Its output is very small, and is probably no more than 2 per cent of the total.

Ten miles west of Brno, on the flanks of the Moravian Uplands, is the Rosice coal-field, which appears to be no larger in reserves or output than that of Trutnov.

The Moravian coal-field yields over 80 per cent of the bituminous coal, and its relative importance is likely to increase. It is the south-western extremity of the Upper Silesian coal-field, and is distinguished from the rest of the field by the generally better quality of its coal and the higher proportion of coking coal in the total reserves. The mines are grouped around Ostrava and Karviná, many of them in the

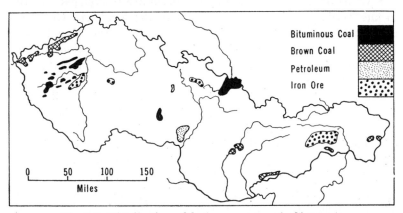

Fig. 9.9. Distribution of fuel resources and of iron-ore.

Těšín area claimed by Poland. The coal seams are more numerous, thicker and less folded than in the other coal basins, but are buried beneath the later deposits of the Ostrava and Silesian plain, which here overlap the flanks of the Palaeozoic Massif. There is said to be a total of 173 workable seams, with an aggregate thickness of 497·1 feet (152·5 metres) of coal. The significance of this resource, not merely for Czechoslovakia, but potentially for the whole of Danubian Europe has already been indicated (page 177).

Brown coal and lignite. Czechoslovakia's reserves of brown coal are amongst the most extensive in Europe. The greater part by far are found in the sequence of basins and depressions (see page 407) which lie in front of the Krušné hory fault, from Cheb to Teplice. The most important are the Sokolov-Loket and the Most-Teplice basins. Other deposits are worked near Cheb and Chomutov. The coal beds vary in number, thickness and quality. The latter commonly changes downwards from lignite into brown coal. Over most of the area there is a single workable bed, which is locally of immense thickness. The coal is sometimes worked underground by shafts, but mostly opencast, as in East Germany and Poland (see page 261). The fuel is mostly briquetted and used directly as fuel. Some becomes a raw material of the chemical industry of northern Bohemia. Over 90 per cent of the sub-bituminous coal mined is from these fields. There is also a small production from lignite fields, preserved in Tertiary basins near Hodonín in southern Moravia and near České Budějovice.

Several rather similar lignite deposits occur in Slovakia, particularly in late Tertiary basins on the margins of the Rudhorie. Only one appears to have industrial significance today, the Handlová— Nováky basin in the upper Nitra valley. It is used for power generation, and is thus a factor in the founding of a large aluminium smelter at Žiar nad Hronom.

Petroleum. Resources of natural gas and petroleum are small and of slight importance. They occur along the lower Morava valley, close to the Austrian border, and are, in fact, a continuation of the Marchfeld oilfield. Despite continued prospecting the production of both oil and natural gas has increased by only about 50 per cent, and in 1965 domestic production of crude oil amounted to only 192,000 tons.

Non-ferrous mining. Although the mines of Příbram and of Kremnica and Banská Bystrica were once one of Europe's most abundant sources of the precious metals, non-ferrous mining is now of negligible importance. The deposits of lead, zinc, copper and tin have been depleted, and such mining as has taken place in recent years has been at a high cost and designed to avoid dependence on imports. The only metals, apart from iron, to have any great importance in recent years have been manganese, antimony and uranium.

Manganese is obtained from several deposits in the Bohemian Massif, but production has now been declining steadily for many years. Antimony, also apparently in diminishing quantities, is obtained from the Slovak Rudohorie. Uranium has continued to be mined at Jáchymov, which before the Second World War, had been one of the largest sources of supply. In 1945 control of the mines was taken over by the Soviet Union; their exploitation was clothed in the greatest secrecy, and it is not known how significant ore production remains today.

Ferrous mining. Iron mining is today the most important extractive industry after coal. Deposits of iron-ore are widespread, but most are too small to justify the use of modern mining techniques. Almost all the present production is from two groups of deposits. A series of ore bodies extends from Nučice, near Prague, to Zdice. They have long supplied iron work in the Kladno and Beroun areas, and their reserves are still said to be large and of high quality. Nevertheless, the current developments in the Czechoslovak iron-smelting industry are stressing the ore deposits of eastern Slovakia. These occur in the Rudohorie and are at present mined near Rožnava and Jelšava, and it is these ores which are now being used to supply the new Košice iron works. Many new mines have been opened, and ore production has increased. Production remains inadequate for current needs. Table 52 shows the amount of ore mined and imported.

Table 52. Iron-ore mined and imported, 1937–65 (in thousands of tons)

	1937	1948	1956	1960	1965
Ore mined (Fe content)	600	430	771	948	723
Ore imported (gross)	n.d.	n.d.	3,909	7,211	9,553
Pig iron produced	1,675	1,648	3,308	4,739	5,927
Ore from domestic sources (estimated)	n.d.	n.d.	c. 33%	c. 24%	14%

Source: *UN Statistical Yearbook, 1966*, and *UN Yearbook of International Trade Statistics, 1965*.

Industrial energy

The rapid expansion of electric energy was a prerequisite of the industrial expansion of recent years, and the construction of generating stations, both thermal and electric, has been prominent in all the industrial plans. The abundance of lignite has ensured the continued predominance of thermally produced power, which now accounts for about 90 per cent of power production. Hydro-electric installations represent about 20 per cent of installed capacity, but for climatic reasons they are obliged to operate at reduced capacity for part of the year. The expansion of generating capacity has been rapid since 1948, as Table 53 shows.

Thermal electric stations are situated very close to the coalfields of northern Bohemia and the Ostrava region, with a smaller capacity on the fields of Rosice and Handlová. Hydro-electric capacity has been

Table 53. Generating capacity, including hydro-electricity, 1948-65

	Production (million KWh)	of which Hydro-electric	Capacity thousand KW	of which Hydro-electric
1948	7,515	909	2,624·5	300·2
1950	9,280	875	2,800·8	319·8
1956	16,591	1,899	4,209·6	644·4
1960	24,450	2,495	5,662·4	928·9
1965	34,190	4,456	8,186	1,540

Source: *Statistická Ročenka ČSSR, 1965*, Prague.

most developed on the rivers of Slovakia, where a succession of dams has been built along the Váh and its tributary, the Orava. The only major installations in the Czech lands are on the Vltava river above Prague, especially at Slapy. There is considerable scope for the further extension of generating capacity in Slovakia, and one may assume that, with the further expansion of industry in Slovakia, the potential of the Nitra, Hron and Hornád will be used.

Iron and steel industries
The iron-smelting, steel-making and mechanical engineering industries were developed in the Czech lands during the nineteenth century. They had there an abundance of fuel which was scarce in Austria itself, together with an adequate supply of ore. The chief areas of manufacture were two: the coal-field to the west of Prague, where the chief centres were Kladno and Králův Dvůr, and the Ostrava region, with the major works of the country, Vítkovice and Třinec.

This pattern has been changed only in detail. The Bohemian works, which have not been greatly expanded, now concentrate mainly on the production of quality steel. On the other hand, a third large and fully integrated works has been built at Kunčice, near Ostrava, and steel-making and rolling mills in the vicinity at Bohumín and Lískovec. The Ostrava region has recently been producing about 80 per cent of the pig-iron, and 70 per cent of the steel made in Czechoslovakia.

The ancient iron industry of Slovakia declined in competition with the larger and more efficient works of Moravia and Bohemia, but was never allowed wholly to lapse. It had the advantage of good quality ores in the Rudohorie, which have for many years been smelted at Podbrezová in the upper Hron valley, and at Tisovec, in the heart of the Rudohorie, with fuel brought in by rail from Moravia. To these very small works is now added the large and fully integrated East Slovakian iron- and steel-works, near Košice, begun under the First Five-Year Plan, but subsequently abandoned and not completed until

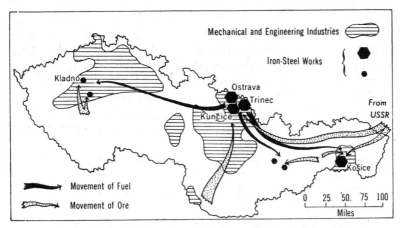

Fig. 9.10. The iron and steel industry of Czechoslovakia.

the middle sixties. It is planned to smelt the local ore with fuel from Moravia. Available estimates of the ore reserves suggest that these may soon be exhausted, and are being replaced by Soviet ore. Certain site advantages would clearly be lost, though fuel could

Table 54. Iron and steel production, 1948–64 (in thousands of tons)

	Pig-iron	Crude steel	Rolled goods
1948	1,645	2,621	n.d.
1956	3,282	4,882	n.d.
1960	4,696	6,768	4,487
1966	6,296	9,128	6,094

Source: *Statistická Ročenka ČSSR, 1967.*

continue to be brought in as return freight by the railway wagons taking Soviet ore to Ostrava.

The expansion of iron and steel production is illustrated by Table 54. These figures may be expected to increase as the East Slovakian works come into full production and others are expanded. About 85 per cent of the steel is produced by the open hearth method, and most of the remainder in electric furnaces.

Mechanical engineering. The mechanical industries are almost as old in Czechoslovakia as iron-smelting, and are said now to employ some 30 per cent of all who work in manufacturing industries. They were formerly concentrated in the cities of Bohemia and Moravia, especially in greater Prague, Plzeň, Brno and the Ostrava region. In recent years the rate of growth of these industries in Slovakia has been about twice that in the Czech lands, and a number of major centres have emerged, notably at Bratislava and along the Váh. Steel production in Slovakia may be expected to give rise to a number of processing and fabricating industries in eastern Slovakia.

By far the biggest centre of the mechanical and engineering industries is greater Prague, with its manufacture of heavy equipment, such as turbines, generators, precision machines and transport equipment, for which the Kladno region supplies much of the raw material. The Plzeň region produces a similar, but somewhat more restricted range of goods, among which armaments have traditionally formed a conspicuous part. Brno is the third major centre of the metal-using industries, which are carried on not only in the city itself, but also in a number of smaller towns of the region. Among the specialised products are boilers, heating and power equipment, electrotechnical goods, and tractors and other forms of heavy farm equipment.

Other industrial centres of Bohemia and Moravia are smaller and more specialised. Mladá Boleslav produces transport equipment, including the Škoda car; Kolín, light machinery; Děčín, electrical equipment; Hradec Králové, heavy machinery. Scarcely a town has not got some branch, however small, of the metal industries.

Chemical industries

The chemical industries, by contrast with the smelting and metal-using industries, were relatively undeveloped in the Czech lands before the First World War, and the former Austro-Hungarian Empire satisfied its needs for chemical products very largely in Germany. Even between the two world wars this branch of industry was not strongly developed, and it was not until after 1949 that it received any great impetus. Recent developments have tended to follow the pattern of growth in East Germany, and are similarly based upon the reserves of brown coal. There tends to be a marked concentration of chemical works in northern Bohemia, especially in close proximity to the brown coal deposits. Here, especially at Most, Lovosice and Ustí nad Labem, and at Neratovice, to the north of Prague, are the most important factories for the manufacture of the basic acids and alkalis, fertilisers and synthetic fibres. Most of the factories lie along the river Labe which satisfies their very heavy demand for water. A more restricted range of chemical industries is found in association with the coke-oven industries of Ostrava, and the manufacture of cellulose and paper is mostly carried on in the mountainous regions, whose forests supply the basic raw materials. The latter is relatively more important in Slovakia than in the Czech lands. The brown coal deposits of the Nitra valley have given rise to the manufacture of synthetic fibres at Nováky.

The manufacture of rubber has been attracted to Gottwaldov, where the footwear industry was already consuming large quantities. It is also carried on at Náchod, close to the Trutnov coal-field, and at Puchov in the Váh valley.

Petroleum production is very small, and Czechoslovakia has never found it necessary to develop the refining and related petrochemical industries. There is a small refinery near Bratislava, which processes oil from the south Moravian field, as well as imports brought by barge up the Danube. Crude oil, imported by pipeline, is refined at Pardubice and Kolín.

Cement industry. The Prague region, particularly Kralův Dvůr, remains the chief centre of cement manufacture, though several new factories have been established in Moravia and Slovakia. Cement production has been increased from about 1·6 million tons in 1948 to 6·1 in 1966.

Brick and tile manufacture has long been widespread in Bohemia and Moravia, and has been recently much expanded in Slovakia, where demand has risen most sharply.

Light industries
The fortunes of light industries in Czechoslovakia have been particularly chequered. Vigorously developed under Austrian rule, they were necessarily cut back as the market contracted after the First World

War. They suffered yet further from neglect during the period of the Second World War and then from the migration of much of the German-speaking population, in whose settlement area the light industries were largely concentrated. Since 1949 investment capital has gone largely to investment industries, and the light industries have been expanded to only a relatively small degree. In some instances, it is alleged, plant and equipment have barely been maintained at the prewar level of efficiency.

Textile industries. These formed before the Second World War the largest branch of Czechoslovak industry and employed 29 per cent of the industrial labour force. Though it has since increased absolutely, it has sunk greatly in the scale of Czechoslovak industries. The difficulties which faced light industries in general have been particularly acute in the textile industries, and have furthermore been accentuated by a grave shortage of materials.

The industry was established mainly in the nineteenth century and to a considerable extent by German *entrepreneurs*. Its early dependence on water power tended to restrict it to the hills, and it is still found today very largely within the mountains which border the North Bohemian Plain. It was made up of a very large number of small factories. Many failed financially during the 1930s, and many more have been merged to make larger and more economic units. Yet others have been closed, and their equipment moved to Slovakia, where the textile industries have been very greatly expanded since the beginning of the industrial plans.

The cotton industry is by far the most important branch of textile manufacture. It is chiefly located in the small towns which border the Krkonoše, and is geographically almost continuous with the similar industries in the East German Erzgebirge and Polish Lower Silesia. It has, however, been established in Slovakia, where Ružomberok is its most important centre. It was formerly dependent on cotton imported chiefly from America by way of Hamburg; chief reliance is now placed on Soviet and Egyptian cotton for the import of which the manufacturing centres are less well placed.

The woollen industry is older and tends to preserve its original geographical division between the spinning and weaving branches. The largest centre of the industry, Brno in Moravia, emphasises spinning and supplies part of the yarn used in the more numerous weaving centres. Second in importance to Brno is northern Bohemia, where the woollen weaving and, to, a lesser extent, spinning are strongly developed in and around Liberec, Nejdek and Aš. In Slovakia the woollen industry, either newly introduced or greatly expanded, is found along the valley of the Váh, particularly at Trenčín and Žilina. The linen industry, particularly the manufacture of part linen fabrics, is more strongly developed than that of woollens. The domestic flax production is supplemented by imports, which are prepared and woven chiefly in the towns of the North Bohemian foothills, where the linen industry is found alongside the cotton, in such towns as Trutnov, Dvůr Králové and Jaroměř.

There is a small production of hemp and jute fabrics and of carpets, largely in the areas where cotton and linen weaving are mainly found. Natural silk is of small and diminishing importance, but synthetic silk fabrics are being produced in steadily increasing volume, chiefly in the small mill-towns of the Bohemian–Moravian Uplands: Svitavy, Šumperk, Moravská Třebová.

Table 55 shows not only the relative importance of the chief branches of the textile industry, but also their slow rate of growth relative to other branches of industry.

Table 55. Textile production, 1948–66

	Cotton yarn (tons)	Cotton fabrics (thous. metres)	Woollen yarn (tons)	Woollen fabrics (thous. metres)	Linen yarn (tons)	Linen and part linen fabrics (thous. metres)	Rayon and acetate yarn (tons)
1948	68,100	280,000	32,000	42,000	—	—	22·4
1955	76,215	342,025	32,163	39,454	11,901	55,317	50·3
1960	102,210	446,231	39,262	46,230	18,071	66,945	58·9
1966	112,195	493,580	42,928	44,928	17,782	68,944	69·2*

*1965

Source: *Statistická Ročenka ČSSR, 1967.*

Clothing industry. The factory manufacture of clothing has made less progress in Czechoslovakia than in many West European countries. It is carried on principally in the larger towns: Prague and Brno, but has been established also in a number of smaller towns, such as Prostějov, near Brno, and Trenčín and Púchov in the Váh valley, and at Prešov in eastern Slovakia.

Leather industry. The very large and important leather industry was developed at the time when the Czech lands supplied much of the consumer goods needed by the Austro-Hungarian Empire. Both tanning and leather-working were formerly widely distributed, but many of the smaller works, especially in Bohemia, have become obsolete and have now closed. The industry is now concentrated in a few large centres of production, of which the most important are Gottwaldov, Partizanské in the Nitra Valley, and Zruč nad Sázavou. Gottwaldov, the former Zlín, has one of the world's largest boot and shoe factories. It was developed by Tomáš Bata from a small workshop which he inherited in 1894, to provide cheap durable footwear for the East European peasantry, whose purchasing power was at this time beginning to rise. In this he succeeded only too well, and built up an industry that became far too large for the restricted Czechoslovak market after 1918. Footwear became and still remains an important branch of the Czechoslovak export trade.

Glass and ceramic industries. The light industry that has probably suffered the most in recent years is the manufacture of quality glass and porcelain, once traditional industries in Bohemia. It had declined in importance with the loss of markets between the two world wars, and was virtually brought to a standstill by the removal of the German-speaking population, which had provided the greater part of the skilled labour. Although it is claimed that Czechs have been trained to take their place, it is clear that the glass which they produce is more utilitarian, and that the porcelain is chiefly for insulators and scientific equipment.

The total production of glass, mainly from the old centres of production, near Karlovy Vary, and at Bílina, Jablonec and Turnov, has increased, but consists mainly of window glass and table glass and other forms of low-quality hollow glassware.

Porcelain and chinaware continue to be made in the towns of Western Bohemia that have long been famous for their manufacture: Karlovy Vary; Skalná, near Cheb, and Stará Role. New types of ceramic, made basically from fused igneous rock, are now being produced primarily for industrial and chemical purposes.

Wood industries. The fabrication of wood has long been carried on in Czechoslovakia, and remains, especially in Slovakia, an industry of very considerable importance. It has been aided by the abundance of both hardwood and softwood forests, though great care has now become necessary in the exploitation and replanting of the woodlands.

A *tanya* in the Plain of Hungary

Budapest: looking across the Danube from the Hill of Buda to the flat land of Pest. The highly decorative building with a dome is the Parliament building

A street in the little baroque town of Sopron (Ödenburg)

Veszprém, western Hungary; the town lies on low hills bordering the Bakony

The sawmill industries are most common in the mountain regions, and one finds countless mills along the valleys of the larger Slovakian rivers. Many of the smaller sawmills have been closed, and a number of large factories making plywood, veneer and pulpwood have been established, particularly near Banská Bystrica and in the Liptov Basin.

The manufacture of furniture is carried on in Slovakia, but is in fact more important in the larger centres of population. It is found in Brno and Prague, and also in a number of smaller towns in Moravia and in the hills of northern Bohemia.

Food-processing industries. Many branches of the food-processing industries have long been important in Czechoslovakia, notably sugar-refining and brewing. In recent years the range of these industries has been broadened, and the dairy and meat and fruit-preserving industries developed. Those branches which are based upon domestic food production are strongly concentrated in three regions: the plains of North Bohemia, the Moravian lowlands and the Danube Plain, where is found the greater part of the total crop production. A few factories are found within the plateau region of southern Bohemia, notably the breweries of Plzeň and České Budějovice, but most of Slovakia is notably lacking in such industries.

Sugar refining is the largest and probably the most efficient branch of the food industries. The leading area of beet production (see page 444) is the plain of the Labe and Ohře, and here the sugar factories are most numerous. The Moravian and Danubian plains are less important.

The brewing industry remains where it has been for decades: Plzeň, České Budějovice and Prague, and on a somewhat smaller scale, Brno, though these are by no means the chief producing areas of either malt or hops. The former comes mainly from the upper Morava valley and the hops from western Bohemia.

The dairy and meat-processing industries tend to be situated near the larger towns, but the wider use of deep-freezing is allowing these branches of food preparation to be established in areas remote from the principal areas of consumption. The statistics show a steady, but by no means striking increase in most branches of the food-processing industries. Only sugar refining has shown a sharp increase, and the cultivation of sugar-beet, it might be added, is likely to benefit from the increasing scale of farm operations made possible by the collectives.

The processing of imported foods—chiefly vegetable fats, cocoa, and tobacco—is carried on in the larger towns and in the ports of entry, notably Bratislava, Děčín, Ustí nad Labem, Prague and Brno.

16

Industrial regions
In no country of Eastern Europe has the planned economic development of recent years brought about a more radical geographical
change than in Czechoslovakia. The planning authorities had from the
first the intention to develop and industrialise Slovakia. This province
received, relative to its population and previous level of industrialisation, a very liberal injection of capital; over the period 1950 to 1964
rather less than a third of all investment capital has gone to Slovakia.

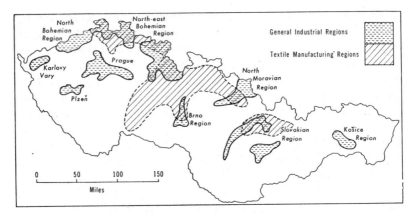

Fig. 9.11. Industrial regions of Czechoslovakia.

The number employed in manufacturing rose very sharply, and total
industrial production is estimated to have increased almost ten-fold
between 1948 and 1960.

   In 1960 the geography of the administrative divisions of Czechoslovakia underwent a considerable change, at the same time that
broader powers were delegated by the central planning authorities to
the regional. Ten regions, or *kraje*, were established with the city
of Prague constituting an eleventh. Each region was conceived
as a discrete economic whole, within which links between places and
industries were more important than links with sites outside the region.
Such a plan cannot, of course, be applied with any high degree of
completeness in an economy as sophisticated as that of Czechoslovakia; there was nevertheless an attempt to build an economic region
around each of the major industrial and commercial centres, as its
central place.

   The industrial regions, defined as those areas in which a very high proportion of the total population is engaged in manufacturing, show some degree of conformity, as is to be expected, with the *kraje*. The foremost industrial regions of Czechoslovakia are as they have been since the late nineteenth century, the Ostrava region; the Prague, or Central Bohemian region, and the North Bohemian region. To these should be added a number of highly important industrial centres: Sokolov-Karlovy Vary, Plzeň, Brno, Bratislava, and certain lightly industrialised areas, including the Morava valley, the Váh, upper Nitra and the Hron valleys and the Košice region.

Ostrava region. The North Moravian *kraj* has the highest proportion of industrially employed of any, and the great majority of these are in the Ostrava region and are employed in a relatively narrow group of heavy industries. The dominant industries of the region are coal-mining and related coke and by-product processing, and iron and steel manufacture. The steel-using industries are not strongly developed, and this region tends rather to supply steel to the steel fabricating industries of the country.

The chief city of the region is Ostrava within whose generous limits most of the iron and steel works, with the important exception of Třinec, are situated. Around it, and separated from it by open or semi-industrialised countryside, are Bohumín, the limit of navigation on the Odra, Karviná, the new town of Havířov, and Frýdek-Místek.

Central Bohemian region. This is essentially the Prague region, with extensions to the west to include Kladno, Rakovník and Beroun; to the east, to Kolín and Poděbrady, and north to the Labe. South of Beroun and the Prague suburb of Modřany the industrial region ends against the dissected plateau of southern Bohemia. This is the most varied and complex of the industrial regions. It benefits from well-developed means of transport, including river transport, and has a large local market of almost 2·5 millions. Its industrial structure ranges from the coal-mining, iron-smelting and high-grade steel manufacture of Kladno and Beroun and the chemical industries of Prague, Kralupy and Neratovice to the metal, furniture and food industries of greater Prague. The only branch of industry which is not important here is the textile, represented only by the clothing industry of Prague.

North Bohemian region. This region embraces the arc of industrial towns, many of them small, which extends from Chomutov in the west to Hradec Králové and Pardubice in the east. It is almost as varied in its industrial structure as the Prague region. To the west of the Labe valley, the industries are mostly based for their raw material or their power, on the brown coal and lignite of the Most–Teplice Basin. The chemical industries are especially important; there is a large steel works at Chomutov, and the glass and ceramic industries, long important in this region, continue to be practised.

East of the Labe there is a change in the general nature of manufacturing. Although there is a small coal production at Trutnov, water power in the Krkonoše and nearby ranges long furnished the chief motive power. The dominant industry is here textiles, which are manufactured in all their variety. Mechanical engineering and glass manufacture are here of secondary importance. Toward the east the industrial structure becomes more varied, with leather working at Dvůr Králové and chemicals manufacture at Hradec Králové and Pardubice.

Industrial centres. These are industrial cities which, with their suburbs and sometimes their satellites, exist in comparative isolation from other industrial centres. They include Karlovy Vary and Sokolov, with their brown coal, chemical and ceramic industries. Plzeň, with its highly important metal industries, Brno with its metal and textile industries, and Bratislava, where development has been on a somewhat broader front.

The Morava, Váh, Nitra and Hron valleys have been developed as industrial areas in recent years. Local resources are limited to lumber, water power and a little brown coal. Labour, on the other hand has been abundant, and was formerly considered cheap. Very many industrial undertakings, most of them small, grew up along the Morava valley, which is notable for the large number of small industrial towns, with only two—Ólomouc and Gottwaldov—of greater size. Along the Váh, Nitra and Hron the few small industrial undertakings of an earlier age have been completely overshadowed by the new. Martin, Žilina, and Trenčín on the Váh; Nováky and Partizanské on the Nitra, and Žiar nad Hronom, Zvolen and Banská Bystrica on the Hron are the scenes of varied but rapid industrial growth.

TRANSPORT, COMMUNICATIONS AND TRADE

The two peoples who came together in 1918 to make the Czechoslovak state not only had radically different standards of living and levels of industrial development; they were also differently oriented in their communications and trade. Slovakia had been part of Hungary, and was in all respects tributary to the Pannonian Plain. Its weak net of roads and railways focused upon Budapest; its small volume of commerce was handled in the towns which bordered the plain from Bratislava to Košice; its raw material production was monopolised by Hungarian industries. Bohemia had its own focus in Prague, from which its communications network radiated. It was linked directly with Germany and Austria. Moravia, more directly tributary to Vienna, nevertheless carried the main routes from Vienna to Kraków and Silesia.

The means of transport and communication were well developed in the Czech lands which had an important trade not only with other parts of the Austro-Hungarian Empire, which they supplied with metal goods, textiles and a number of other factory products, but also with much of Central Europe.

Communications

It became the task of the Czechoslovak Republic to knit together these two disparate segments and to retain as much as possible of the markets which both had formerly served. Czechoslovakia achieved a considerable measure of success in the former, and if much of the former Austro-Hungarian market was lost, it was in some degree replaced by markets in the west.

Railway system. By building cross-country routes the Bohemian, Moravian and Slovakian railways were interlinked and a west to east system replaced a series of railways whose traffic had been mainly between north and south. The railway system which resulted came to have a total length of 8,195 miles, of which only about a fifth is double-tracked. All, except a very few minor branches, is of standard gauge, and the main west to east route is electrified.

The railway system today consists essentially of a series of west to east lines, extending from Cheb and Sokolov in the west to Košice and the Soviet border of eastern Slovakia. These lines link the industrial cities of central and northern Bohemia; are continued by way of Olomouc and Brno with the Moravian industrial centres, and thence by three separate routes across the western Carpathians with the trunk lines which follow the Váh and Hron. The routes between Most, Prague, Olomouc and Ostrava and from Ostrava eastward by way of the Jablunkov Pass, the Liptov Basin and Košice to the Soviet border are very intensively used, especially for the transport of coal, coke and iron-ore. It is said that about 90 per cent of all freight, as measured in ton-miles, is by rail.

Road system. With over 45,000 miles of main road, Czechoslovakia has a denser road network than any other country in the region except East Germany. In the main it was created before the Second World War, it contains no less than six main roads across the Western Carpathians between Moravia and Slovakia, and is entirely adequate for current needs. Good, hard-surfaced roads follow most of the valleys of Slovakia and even the passes over the Nízke Tatry and Rudohorie are easily crossed. The physical barriers to communication have been overcome.

Inland navigation. Czechoslovakia lies on the watershed between the Danubian and northern drainage, and for that reason internal navigation is of negligible importance. The only rivers regularly used are the Labe, the lowermost section of the Vltava, and the Danube. They serve the needs of foreign trade rather than domestic, and the Danubian ports of Komárno and Bratislava are of great importance, especially for the import of petroleum and the export of some manufactured goods.

The Labe and Vltava are used commercially as far upstream as Kolín and Prague, though pleasure craft go even higher up the rivers. Their chief river ports are Prague and Děčín, whose importance has been diminished by the new orientation of Czechoslovak commerce away from the port of Hamburg and toward Eastern Europe.

The Odra is not navigable within Czechoslovakia, and begins to be used only near the Polish border at Bohumín. The Ostrava industrial complex is not accessible to waterborne traffic, as is at least the western part of the Silesian region. A canal has, however, long been projected from the Odra near Koźle in Poland, through the Ostrava region and the Moravian Gate to the river Morava and the Danube. The value of such a waterway would be immense, and the technical difficulties of constructing it by no means insuperable. It would permit the Ostrava region to import iron-ore by way of Szczecin and the Odra, and to export coal—including coking-coal—to iron-works and industries down the Danube as far as Romania. Although this project has long been in the planning stage, work has not yet begun on it.

Air Transport. The distances within Czechoslovakia are great enough for air transport to play a very significant role in internal transport and communications. Prague is linked by regular air service with the larger towns of Slovakia, and it is claimed that no less than 54 towns have some kind of air connections with at least the larger centres of population.

Foreign trade

Since its creation in 1918 Czechoslovakia has been essentially an importer of food-stuffs and industrial raw materials, which it has paid for by the export of manufactured goods. The industrial growth of recent years has had the effect of intensifying this pattern, and of increasing Czechoslovakia's dependence upon imported raw materials.

Total volume of foreign trade has increased steadily since 1948. According to official statistics, which have not been corrected for the diminishing value of the Czech crown, the value of imports increased from 4,906 million crowns a year when the development plans were initiated, to 19,699 in 1966, and imports from 5,422 to 19,764 in the same period.

The present breakdown of foreign trade by major categories in 1964 is shown in Table 56. Food imports included large quantities of tea

Table 56. Czechoslovakia's foreign trade—by commodity (in million Czech crowns)

1965	Imports	Exports
Live animals	24	34
Food-stuffs	1,679	573
Raw materials for the food industries	1,380	281
Other raw materials of vegetable and animal origin	2,398	930
Fuels, minerals and metals	5,297	3,937
Chemicals, fertilisers and rubber	1,462	732
Building materials	238	291
Machinery and equipment	5,758	9,385
Consumers' goods of industrial origin	1,006	3,194
	19,242	19,357

Source: *UN Yearbook of International Trade Statistics, 1965.*

and coffee, but Czechoslovakia achieved an approximate self-sufficiency in most other food-stuffs. The category of 'Fuels, minerals and metals' consisted mainly of 9·3 million tons of iron-ore and 5 million tons of coal. The ore may have represented about 5·5 million tons of metal, and thus have accounted for most of Czechoslovakia's pig-iron production. The coal included some coking-coal from the Soviet Union, but consisted mainly of non-coking coal from Poland for general uses, including power generation. In the category of 'Machinery and equipment' were considerable numbers of cars, lorries and tractors, presumably of sizes and types not produced in Czechoslovakia, as well as other types of mechanical equipment.

Exports were dominated by factory products, which accounted for no less than 64 per cent of the total, with 'Fuel, minerals and metals' accounting for a further 21 per cent. The latter category included 2·5 million tons of coal, most of it presumably of coking quality and sent mainly to Poland and Hungary, and 1·4 million tons of lignite.

About two million tons of steel pipes and rolled steel goods—nearly a quarter of the total Czechoslovak steel output—were exported. There was also a large export of electrical motors and diesel engines; tractors and cars, particularly the small 'Skoda'; motor cycles and bicycles; pumps, compressors and railway locomotives.

Export trade took also a significant share of the products of the textile industry, including almost a third of the output of linen and

Table 57. *Czechoslovakia's foreign trade by countries, in millions of US dollars*

1965	Exports to	Imports from
U.S.S.R.	1,022·8	954·7
Eastern Europe:	866·8	933·2
of which: East Germany	277·1	287·9
Poland	248·8	208·6
Hungary	132·2	171·4
Yugoslavia	69·2	71·8
Romania	68·9	94·3
Bulgaria	61·8	89·2
Albania	8·8	10·0
Other Communist countries	76·2	73·1
Industrial West (including Japan)	433·5	479·2
Total	2,399·3	2,440·2

Source: *Foreign Trade of the European Satellites in 1965: A Statistical Summary*, C.I.A. Washington, 1966.

part-linen fabrics, and an eighth of that of woollens. Such traditionally important exports as glass and ceramic goods do not figure conspicuously in the tables of exports, but—significant of the new trend in the industry—plate glass is now important.

Direction of trade. Foreign trade is directed overwhelmingly to the other members of the Soviet–East European bloc. No less than 41 per cent of total trade was in 1965 with the Soviet Union itself, and 30 per cent with the countries of Eastern Europe, excluding Yugoslavia and Albania. The greatest volume of trade within Eastern Europe is with East Germany, followed by Poland. Trade with other Communist countries, including China and Yugoslavia is very small, and amounts to only 5 per cent. The most important non-Communist trading partners are West Germany and the United Kingdom, followed by Austria, Italy and France.

Bibliography
General
Atlas Československé Socialistické Republiky, Prague, Ústřední Správa Geodezie a Kartografie, 1966.
Atlas Republiky Československé, Prague, 1935.
BUSEK, VRATISLAV and NICHOLAS SPULBER, eds., *Czechoslovakia,* Mid-European Studies Centre, London, Stevens, 1958.
Československo, Soubor Map 'Poznáváme Svet', Ústředni Správa Geodézie a Kartografie, Prague, 1965.
Československo v mapách, Prague, 1954.
HÄUFLER, VLASTISLAV, JOROMÍR KORČAK, VÁCLAV KRÁL, *Zeměpis Československa,* Prague, 1960.
KOLACEK, FRANTIŠEK, *Zeměpis Československa,* Prague, 1934.
Přírodni Poměry Československa, Statní Pedagogické Nakladatelství, Prague, 1956.
Statistická Ročenka ČSSR 1965, Prague, 1965.
WANKLYN, HARRIET, *Czechoslovakia,* London, G. Philip, 1954.

Historical and Political Geography
Atlas Československých Dějin, Prague, 1965.
LUŽA, R. *The Transfer of the Sudeten Germans: a Study of Czech-German Relations, 1933–1962,* London, Routledge & Kegan Paul 1964.
MACARTNEY, C. A. *Hungary and Her Successors,* Oxford University Press, 1937.

16*

PAULAT, VLAD J. *Czechoslovakia in East Mid-European Federation*, New York, Mid-European Studies Center, 1953.

SETON-WATSON, R. W. *A History of the Czechs and Slovaks*, London, Hutchinson, 1943.

SHUTE, JOHN, 'Czechoslovakia's Territorial and Population Changes', *Econ. Geogr.*, **24** (1948), 35–44.

THOMSON, S. HARRISON, *Czechoslovakia in European History*, Oxford University Press, 1953.

WISKEMANN, ELIZABETH, *Czechs and Germans*, Oxford University Press, 1938.

— *Germany's Eastern Neighbours*, Oxford University Press, 1956.

Physical Geography

BAECKEROOT, GEORGES, 'Le relief de la Bohême Centrale: essai de morphologie hercynienne comparée', *Annls Géogr*, **58** (1949), 289–94.

ENGELMANN, RICHARD, 'Der Elbedurchbruch', *Abh. der Geogr. Ges. in Wien*, **13**, Heft 2 (1938).

HASSINGER, HUGO, 'Die mährische Pforte und ihre benachbarten Landschaften', *Abh. der K.K. geogr. Ges. Wien*, **11**, Heft 2 (1914).

Lesnický a Myslivecký Atlas, Prague, 1955.

MOSCHELES, JULIE, 'Natural Regions of Czechoslovakia', *Geogrl Rev.*, **14** (1924), 561–75.

Přírodní Poměry Československa, Prague, 1956.

DE MARTONNE, EMMANUEL, 'Deux massifs hercyniens: le Boehmerwald et la Lysa Gora', *Annls de Géogr.*, **35** (1926), 27–50.

SEDLMEYER, KARL AL, 'Die natürlichen Landschaften der Sudetenländer', *Abh. geogr. Ges. Wien*, **14**, Heft 2 (1941).

Population and Settlement

BENEŠ, VÁCLAV L., "The Slovaks in the Habsburg Empire: A Struggle for Existence," *Austrian History Yearbook*, **3** (1967), 335–664.

BLANC, ANDRÉ, 'Le problème des régions frontières: le cas de Tachov', *Revue Géographique de l'Est*, **3** (1963), 155–65.

BLAŽEK, MIROSLAV, 'Esquisse des problèmes de géographie de la population en Tschécoslovaquie', *Annls Géogr.*, **69** (1950), 477–83.

DICKINSON, ROBERT E. *The German Lebensraum*, Harmondsworth, Penguin Books, 1943.

— *The West European City*, London, Routledge & Kegan Paul, 1951.

HÄUFLER, VLASTISLAV, 'Mniejszości narodowe w Czechosłowacji ze szczególnym uwzględnieniem Polaków', *Przegl. Geogr.*, **38** (1966), 191–8.

KOSIŃSKI, L., 'Les Problèmes démographiques dans les territoires occidentaux de la Pologne et les régions frontières de la Tschécoslovaquie', *Annls Géogr.*, **71** (1962), 79–98.

MEYER, PETER, *et al.*, *The Jews in the Soviet Satellites*, Syracuse University Press, 1953.

MOSCHELES, JULIE, 'Demographic, Social and Economic Regions of Greater Prague', *Geogrl Rev.*, **27** (1937), 414–29

STŘIDA, MIROSLAV, 'Probleme der Siedlungsstruktur der Tschechoslowakei', *Festschrift Leopold G. Scheidl zum 70. Geburtstag*, Vienna, 1965, 350–67.

STEERS, M. J. B. 'The Middle People, Resettlement in Czechoslovakia', *Geogrl J.*, **112** (1949), 28–42.

VOTRUBEC, CTIBOR, 'Matériaux pour l'étude des villes nouvelles en Tchécoslovaquie', *Revue Geographique de l'Est*, **3** (1963), 137–43.

— 'Der gegenwartige Stand und die weitere Entwicklung der Tschechoslowakischen Städte', *Geogr. Ber.*, **8** (1963), 32–50.

WYNNE, WALLER, *The Population of Czechoslovakia*, International Population Statistics Reports, Series P-90, No. 3, Washington, DC, 1953.

Economic Geography

BEHNKE, A., 'Die Slowakei', *Geogr. Rdsch.*, **14** (1962), 129–38.

BLAŽEK, MIROSLAV, *Hospodářský Zeměpis Československa*, Orbis, Prague, 1958.

— *Ökonomische Geographie der Tschechoslowakischen Republik*, Verlag die Wirtschaft, Berlin 1959. (An abridged translation of the above title.)

— 'Die Konzentration der Industrie im der Tschechoslowakei', *Festschrift Leopold G. Scheidl zum 70. Geburstag*, Vienna, 1965, 207–17.

DEFFONTAINES, PIERRE, *La Vie forestière en Slovaquie*, Travaux publiés par l'Institut d'Études Slaves, Paris, 1932.

GEORGE, PIERRE, 'L'industrialisation de la Slovaquie', *Revue Géographique de l'Est*, **3** (1963), 145–53.

HORBALY, WILLIAM, *Agricultural Conditions in Czechoslovakia*, 1950, University of Chicago, 1951.

472 *Czechoslovakia*

ISNARD, H., 'Notes sur l'agriculture tchécoslovaque', *Revue Géographique de l'Est*, 3, 1963, 117–30.

IVANIČKA, KOLOMAN, 'Geografia rajónu Vychodoslovenských Železiarní', *Acta Geologica et Geographica Universitatis Comenianae*, Bratislava, 1964.

— 'Geografia Přemyslu Hornej Nitry', *Acta Geologica et Geographica Universitatis Comenianae*, Geographica Nr 2, Bratislava, 1960.

KAHOUN, FRANTIŠEK, 'Geographische Aspekte des 3. Funfjahrplans der CSSR', *Geogr. Ber.*, 7 (1962), 170–93.

MICHAL, JAN M., *Central Planning in Czechoslovakia*, Stanford University Press, 1960.

PURŠ, JAROSLAV, 'The Industrial Revolution in Czech Lands', *Historica*, Czechoslovak Academy of Sciences, 2, (1960), 183–272.

SPERLING, WALTER, 'Das Gebiet der ostslawischen Eisenwerke', *Erdkunde*, 20 (1966), 60–2.

STAPAN, LADISLAV, *The Coal Industry in Czechoslovakia*, Monograph 32, New York, Mid-European Studies Center, 1954.

STŘIDA, MIROSLAV, 'Les méthodes de détermination des régions économiques en Tchécoslovaquie', *Annls Géogr.* 70 (1961), 137–44.

VEYRET, PAUL, 'Le tourisme en Tchécoslovaquie', *Revue Géographique de l'Est*, 3 (1963), 131–6.

WRZOSEK, ANTONI, *Czechoslowacja*, Warsaw, 1960.

— 'Szkic zagadnień energetyki w Czechosłowacji', *Przegl. Geogr.*, 30 (1958), 659–70.

CHAPTER TEN

Hungary

Hungary is in many respects the simplest country to be described in this book. Its population is homogeneous; its ethnic minorities small and relatively unimportant, and its relief is simple and easily comprehended. These facts are not unrelated. The plain of the middle Danube was invaded at the end of the ninth century by the Magyar tribes, which quickly spread over the lowland. It is impossible that the small Slavic population could have been either exterminated or driven out. They were suppressed and ultimately magyarised, not however without leaving a ghostly evidence of their presence in place-names and the physical appearance of many of the people today. But along the margin of the surrounding hills the Magyar conquest stopped, or was too ineffective to change radically the language and culture of the people. Only to the east, in the Transylvanian Basin was there any significant settlement of Magyars beyond the limits of the Pannonian Plain. Thus the Magyar people came to be identified with the plain, and the plain with them.

THE HUNGARIAN STATE

An earlier chapter has traced in broad outline the fortunes of the Hungarian state: its rise and splendour during the Middle Ages, its eclipse at the hands of the invading Turks early in the sixteenth century, and its revival as part of the empire of the Habsburgs. As the Turks fanned out over the Pannonian Plain after their capture of the fortress of Beograd in 1521, their main attack was northward. They defeated the Hungarian army at Mohács, close to the west bank of the Danube, and killed its young king, Lewis. Then driving northward, they occupied the fortified hill of Buda and pressed on toward Vienna. On their left flank rose the undulating ridge of Bakony; to the east lay the distant hills which cut off the Pannonian Plain from Transylvania. To the north rose the Carpathian Mountains of Slovakia, and, though their valleys opened invitingly toward the plain, these were guarded by fortresses wherever they narrowed, and the Turks rarely penetrated the mountain region.

West of Bakony also the Turks made no permanent conquest. This region came to be attached politically to Austria, through whose armies it was able to hold back the invader. Eastern Hungary, made up of Transylvania and its bordering mountains, similarly proved difficult for the Turks to invade, or at least to subdue. Here Hungarian princes continued to live, claimants to the Hungarian crown and foci for Hungarian patriotism. During the years of Turkish rule, from the

Fig. 10.1. The break-up of the Austro-Hungarian Empire in 1919–20.

1520s until the end of the seventeenth century, the Princes of Transylvania—prominent among them Bethlen Gabor and Rakoczy Ferenc—maintained their somewhat circumscribed independence.

By the end of the seventeenth century, Turkish power in the Danubian plains had spent its force. Repulsed from the walls of Vienna in 1683, not without, it must be admitted, the help of the Polish king, the Turkish tide receded. In 1686 Buda was recaptured. In 1717 Beograd was besieged, and when in 1718 peace was made at Passarowitz, the whole plain had been cleared of Turks, and peace reigned over the waste created by decades of fighting. The Hungarians of Transylvania were again united with their fellow countrymen in the west who had already been brought under Habsburg rule. The Habsburgs now controlled Hungary, and maintained their authority, at least in part, by playing off one ethnic group against another. This continued until the middle years of the nineteenth century, when Austria, weakened by her disastrous conflict in 1866 with Prussia, could maintain her position no longer. By the *Ausgleich*, or 'Compromise', of 1867 Hungary was separated from Austria and became again an independent state, with its own machinery of government, capital city and monarch. The latter, however, continued to be the person of the Austrian emperor, who thus added to his numerous titles that of King of Hungary.

The boundaries of the Magyar state were approximately those of the medieval state. They followed very roughly the Carpathian watershed, the Sava river and the Danube below Beograd. They excluded, however, Bosnia and the province of Dalmatia, which had acknowledged the overlordship of the Hungarian kings during the Middle Ages, but included numerous non-Magyar peoples who in general would have preferred the rule of the more distant Austrians to that of the nearby Magyars.

In 1910 the population of Hungary was about 18·25 million. Of this the Magyars themselves, together with the Székely of Transylvania, accounted for only about 9,945,000 or 54 per cent of the total. The other ethnic groups were:

Slovaks	1,946,357
Romanians	2,948,186
Germans (including Austrians)	1,903,357
Serbs and Croats	656,324
Ruthenes	464,270
Jews and others	401,412

The Trianon settlement

In his 'Fourteen Points' of January 1918, Woodrow Wilson had urged, as part of his prescription for a lasting peace: '(10): The peoples of Austria–Hungary, whose place among the nations we wish to see safeguarded and assured, should be accorded the freest opportunity of autonomous development.'

Most of these peoples had, as we have already seen in Chapter 2, made their desires known, and at the end of 1918 they broke away to become members of the Czechoslovak, Romanian and Southern Slav states. The boundaries of the new Hungary were delimited in the Treaty of Trianon (June 1920), and subsequently demarcated by boundary commissions.

The Treaty of Trianon has been vigorously criticised both within

Hungary and outside. Criticism focuses on two points: the interruption which it brought about in the functional unity of the Hungarian Plain, and the failure of the boundary itself to separate Magyar from non-Magyar. Hungarians and their apologists have repeatedly emphasised that they

> had established an elaborate reclamation service, begun fully a century ago. Since that time there have been built nearly 4,000 miles of dikes . . . and about 8,000 miles of canals, by which nearly 15,000,000 acres of land are protected from floods. . . . The cutting of pieces of this protective system by the new frontiers is now the greatest danger threatening our lowlands.[1]

A reciprocity, it is claimed, had been developed between the plain, with its abundant agricultural production, and the surrounding mountains with their minerals and their wealth of lumber. 'The co-operation of the different regions,' wrote Count Teleki, 'so widely diverging as to natural conditions of production, and of the products themselves, formed together the greater economic energy of old Hungary.'[2]

The other point of criticism concerned the detail of the new boundary. A line of towns encircled the plain, lying as a general rule a few miles in front of the mountains, and serving as markets for the exchange of the products of mountain and plain. They were characterised also by a mixed population, in which Magyars were prominent. Almost without exception, the cities of this 'market line' were allocated to the succession states. In some instances the boundary chosen flagrantly violated the ethnic principles on which it was supposed to be based. In the extreme west of Hungary, between the Hungarian town of Szentgotthard and the River Mura, the boundary

> cuts off from Hungary a band of purely Magyar villages which lie all along the frontier as far as the Mura. The inhabitants of these villages had for generations been accustomed to go down to the Hungarian plains as labourers at harvest-time and they received their pay largely in kind . . . the soil of the Prekmurje itself is poor and does not produce enough for the inhabitants. The wheat thus earned they brought back with them on their return. . . .[3]

[1] Paul Teleki, *The Evolution of Hungary and its Place in European History*, New York, 1923, pp. 95–96.
[2] *Ibid.* p. 109.
[3] D. Cree, 'Yugoslav–Hungarian Boundary Commission', *Geogrl J.*, **16**, 1925, 101.

Attempts to change the boundary met with the obdurate resistance of the Yugoslavs, and the incident, like many others, added only to the fires of Hungarian resentment.

Perhaps no aspect of the Trianon treaty did more to antagonise the Hungarians than the settlement along their western border. Throughout the Middle Ages the boundary between Hungary and Austria had been along the Leitha river. The linguistic boundary had, however, advanced to the east, enclosing within the area of Germanic speech the hilly province of Burgenland. By the terms of the Treaty, this province of about 1,530 square miles (3,960 square kilometres) and about 218,000 people, was transferred to Austria with the exception only of the city of Sopron which the Hungarians by protesting vigorously managed to retain. As Bowman pointed out, this was 'the only case in Europe where an enemy power was given additional territory'.[1] It was bad enough to lose territory to their victorious enemies, but Austria had been their friend and defeated ally.

Thus by 1920 Hungary was reduced from a state of about 110,000 square miles to one of only 35,164. Essentially Magyar areas alone were left, and as these were the lowland areas of the Pannonian Plain, Hungary became a country as simple in its relief as it was homogeneous in its population.

LANDFORM REGIONS OF HUNGARY

There is a superficial uniformity in the physical geography of Hungary. It is a small country; its relief is relatively simple and an inspection of the map suggests that there is little difference in physical geography between one part of the country and another. This is deceptive; there is far more variety in Hungary than contours and isotherms reveal.

The physical divisions of Hungary are at once clearly defined and well differentiated, and they make their influence felt in most aspects of the geography of Hungary. There are four major regions, three areas of lowland separated from one another by the Danube and by the fourth region, the line of the Bakony-Mátra-Bükk hills.

Central and northern mountains
The strongest relief in Hungary is provided by the chain of hills which extends from south-west to north-east for 235 miles across the country. They are not particularly high, and only in the Mátra do they exceed

[1] Isaiah Bowman, *The New World*, New York, 4th edn., 1928, pp. 311–12.

3,000 feet—Kékes reaches 3,329 feet—but they are strongly dissected
by rivers, and rise steeply from the nearby lowlands, thus giving an
impression of height and ruggedness which, in fact, they do not
possess.

Structurally they belong to the Alpine system, and consist of a complex, much faulted anticline, in which Tertiary beds cover a core of
Jurassic, Triassic and Permian deposits. Triassic limestone and
dolomite have been exposed along most of the crest of the anticline,

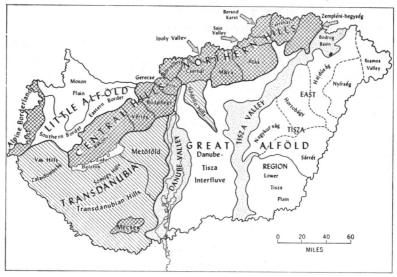

Fig. 10.2. Landforms of Hungary.

leaving the rather varied Tertiary rocks to form its flanks. The
folding of the mountains in the early Tertiary was accompanied by
igneous and particularly by volcanic activity. Extrusive rocks today
cover much of the northern part of this region, and give rise to the
strongest relief. The Mátra, the highest part of the Bükk and the
Visegrádi-hegy and Börzsöny, which confront one another across
the Danube from Esztergom down to Vác are of igneous rock.

Most of Hungary's extensive and important deposits of bauxite are
associated with the central mountain range, more especially with
Bakony and Vértes. The ore occurs as a product of the subaerial
weathering of limestone, and has been preserved along the northern
flanks of the range.

The frequent changes in rock facies and the erosion which has been continuous from late Tertiary times to the present have cut the range as a whole into a number of distinct units. Foremost is the division of the range made by the Danube itself into the more south-westerly Transdanubian Mountains (Dunántúli-középhegység) and the Northern Mountains (Eszaki-középhegység).[1] Each can be subdivided on the basis of structure, rock-type and relief. The significant divisions of the Transdanubian mountains are five in number (Fig. 10.1).

Bakony. About half the total extent of the Transdanubian Mountains is made up of the Bakony, the most extensive and widely known of all the hill masses of Hungary. It is made up essentially of a series of flat-topped ridges of limestone or dolomite, trending from south-west to north-east. The conformity of the summit levels of the higher ridges at about 2,000 feet witnesses to a late Tertiary peneplain, which has since been dissected by deep and steep-sided valleys. Among the results of this erosion cycle are a number of longitudinal depressions, of which that containing the towns of Veszprém and Tapolca is the widest and most densely settled.

The Bakony is characterised by its small depressions, many of them structural in origin, and now mantled with loess, giving them a greater agricultural value than the surrounding limestone hills. The latter, with steep flanks and relatively level summits, are built mainly of limestone, which has developed strongly marked karst features. In general they end abruptly, and their steep flanks overlook the lowland on each side. In the Tapolca district, in the extreme south, a number of basalt flows have survived forming the resistant caps to a number of steep-sided, isolated hills. Along its south-eastern margin, the Bakony is bordered by Lake Balaton.

Vértes. A small, transverse rift-valley separates the Bakony from the next segment of this chain of mountains, the Vértes. This is a similar plateau of limestone and dolomite, but it is narrower, shorter and much lower than the Bakony itself. Its surface is mainly forested, but its chief resource is the large deposits of bauxite which occur near Gánt, on its south-eastern flank. Along the north-western margin of the Vértes, and particularly near Tatabánya, is one of the more important sources of coal in Hungary, though the deposits are of lower Tertiary age and their quality is in general poor.

To the south-east, about ten miles away from the steep face of the Vértes, are the small, rounded hills of the Valencei-hegy. Their

[1] Literally Transdanubian and Northern *Central* Mountains.

interest lies in the fact that they are a small inlier of Hercynian Europe. They are the summits of a granitic bathylith, surrounded by the Carboniferous rocks into which it was intruded.

Gerecse. A series of faults separates the Vértes from the Gerecse, a triangular area of Tertiary limestone and dolomite, which on the north rises from the Danube and is dissected by the many streams which drop steeply to the river. On the margin of these hills, just as along the northern edge of the Vértes, are small but workable deposits of coal of lower Tertiary age.

Budai-hegy. Low hills separate the Gerecse from the Buda Hills, which reach down to the Danube and provide the site of the fortress-city of Buda. It is an undulating region of rolling limestone hills, their upper slopes wooded, their lower penetrated by the ever broadening suburbs of Budapest.

Pilis. The last of the divisions of the Transdanubian Mountains is the Pilis, the highest, steepest and most rugged part of the range. It is separated from the Buda Hills by the structural depression which cuts across the sharp bend of the Danube and today carries the main road from Vienna to Budapest. Unlike the rest of the region, in which volcanic rocks are inconspicuous, this is composed entirely of andesitic lava and turf. It was noted above that the lava flows extend to the north of the river, where the Börzsöny in most respects resembles the Pilis. The lava flows were weakened by faulting, and it was along a series of fault-lines that the Danube later cut its picturesque course.

The Transdanubian Mountains form one of the most attractive regions of Hungary. The oak and beech woods of Bakony; the resorts which fringe Lake Balaton; the rolling hills to the west of Budapest, and the towering hill of Visegrád, where the range ends abruptly against the Danube, combine to make the whole a recreational region for the capital city. It is also, with its coal and bauxite and its small quantities of manganese and other non-ferrous metals, one of the more important of Hungary's few mineralised areas. It serves in addition as a cultural divide. The Little Alföld to the north-west was never long under Turkish rule; Transdanubia and still more the Great Alföld were long subjected not only to Turkish invaders from the south but also to Tatars from the north-east. The ruined castles, such as Sumeg on its northern edge and Visegrád itself witness to the fact that this was an outer line of defence of Central Europe against peoples from the east.

The Northern Mountains differ from those of Transdanubia in their greater complexity of relief and the bigger role in their formation played by igneous and eruptive rocks. They are in some respects similar to the Rudohorie of Slovakia, from which they are separated by the valleys of the westward-flowing Ipoly (*Cz.* Ipel') and of the Sajó, a tributary of the Tisza. For a considerable distance from the Danube eastwards the northern boundary of Hungary follows the Ipoly river, and then takes a somewhat irregular course through the mountains, following generally the higher ground but cutting across the valleys of the Sajó, Hernád and Bodrog before reaching the Tisza. The Northern Mountains form an arc, convex toward the plain, extending some 140 miles from the Börzsöny in the west to the Zempléni-hegység. They are made up, like the Transdanubian Mountains, of five clearly distinguishable massifs, contrasted in relief and separated by the valleys of rivers which flow south to join the Tisza.

Börzsöny. This abrupt and steep-sided massif of lavas and tuffs faces the Pilis, forming with the latter one of the scenically most attractive parts of the whole course of the Danube. It is a thinly settled region; its steep slopes are little suited to agriculture, and much of it is forested.

Cserhát. To the east lies the gentler region of Cserhát. This also was the scene of Tertiary igneous activity, but on a smaller scale. The region is one of rolling hills, developed in soft Tertiary clays and sands. The strongest elements of the relief occur where andesitic lavas give rise to isolated hills. On the south this region slopes gently down to the Great Alföld, where it is continued by the low Gödöllő Hills (Gödöllői-dombság), extending like a finger pointing to the heart of the Plain.

Mátra. Viewed from the great plain the Mátra seems the most mountainous of all the rather unspectacular mountains of Hungary. On all sides except the north it rises steeply; its flattened crest lies at over 2,500 feet, and at its highest point, Kékes rises to 3,329 feet, the highest point in Hungary. The Mátra is composed entirely of volcanic rocks, similar to those met with farther to the west. Truly volcanic forms have long been obliterated by erosion, and along the foot of the mountain lies a belt of low hills, the Mátraalja, or Mátra Foreland, made up of materials worn from the higher ground. These lower slopes are fertile; their southerly aspect is sunny, and they are today clad with vineyards, amid which nestles the town of Gyöngyös. The higher slopes, by contrast, are among the coolest and wettest parts of Hungary, and constitute one of its most extensive areas of oak and beech forest.

Bükk. Beyond the Tarna valley, to the east, is the similar Bükk Massif. It is a rounded plateau lying at between 2,500 feet and 3,000 feet, and dropping steeply to the plain on the south and more gently northward to the Sajó valley. Unlike the Mátra, however, it is made up of Triassic limestone, 'the most extensive and the most attractive limestone plateau in the country'.[1] This plateau is ringed round by lower ground. Volcanic rocks are present here, as they are in every other section of the Northern Mountains, but here they are soft rhyolite tuffs, which give rise to the dissected southern foreland, or Bükkalja. To the west and north the central limestone is ringed by Tertiaries, like those of the Cserhát, with a few small areas of volcanics to give diversity to this landscape of rolling hills.

Zempléni-hegység. The last of these northern hills is made up, like the Mátra, almost wholly of volcanic rocks. It extends southward from Slovakia between the Hernád and Bodrog valleys, and terminates in a few small outliers, of which the vein-covered hills of Tokaj are the last. Its surface is still marked by partially eroded forms of volcanoes and craters, but loess has covered the lower and gentler slopes, producing, with the volcanic ash, a soil of high fertility, especially favoured by the grape vine and other fruit trees. This region of Hungary has the doubtful distinction of having the most extreme climate in the country, with winters of exceptional severity.

Northern valleys and basins. Only the last-named of these segments of the Northern Mountains extends beyond the boundary of Hungary into Czechoslovakia. The others are bordered on the north by the lowlands which lie along the Ipoly and Sajó valleys, to the west the Nógrád Basin; to the east, the Borsod Basin. Both are developed in soft Tertiary beds, amid which the occasional volcanic dykes and lava flows form a kind of hard and resistant skeleton. Hardwood forest still covers the hills, but most of the lowland has been cleared and cultivated. In both basins are deposits of lignite, and iron-working has long been carried on in the Borsod Basin, and remains significant today at Ózd and at Miskolc, near the southern margin of the region.

Borsod Karst and Cserehát. In the valleys of the Sajó, Bódva and Hernád, all of them tributaries of the Tisza, the boundary of Hungary curves northward to include the two southward extensions of the Slovak hills, known as the Borsod Karst (Észak-Borsodi karszt) and the Cserehát. The former, lying between the Sajó and the Bódva and

[1] Márton Pécsi and Béla Sárfalvi, *Die Geographie Ungarns*, Budapest, 1962, p. 194.

crossed by the international boundary, is an upland built of Triassic limestone and dolomite, in which karst forms are more strongly developed than at any other place in the country. Beyond the Bódva valley to the east lies the Cserehát, a rolling region of low hills, where the Tertiary beds are hidden beneath loess and glacial clays, spread outwards from the Slovakian mountains. This area, unlike the Borsod Karst is largely cleared and under cultivation. The wealth of the Karst region lies in part in its lumber, but mainly in its minerals. At Ruda-bánya are the most extensive iron-ore deposits of Hungary. They are carbonate ores, or siderite, which occur in the limestone, and formerly supplied the iron industry of northern Hungary. They continue to be worked, but for the modern iron industry of Hungary have been replaced by imported ores.

The Little Alföld

The Little Hungarian Plain, or Kisalföld, is framed by mountains, which are rarely out of sight. Along its south-eastern margin the land rises gently towards the long line of the Bakony and Vértes. In the south is a region of low hills formed by the erosion of the Tertiary sands and clays of which they are built. Toward the west is the more sudden rise to the Alps of Austrian Burgenland, which beckon from just beyond the boundary. To the north, the plain runs down to the Danube and, beyond it, continues in the plain of south-western Slovakia. In the far distance lie the jagged crests of the Carpathian ranges, their ruggedness accentuated by the way in which they fan out and present their steep slopes of their spurs to the viewer.

The plain has been in recent geological times a region of subsidence. The Danube and its Carpathian and Alpine tributaries continued through Tertiary and later times to deposit gravels, sands and clays to a very great thickness, of which the relict hills, such as the Kemenes Ridge, or Kemeneshát, give some indication. The pre-Pliocene Danube in all probability took a more southerly course toward the present Dráva valley, but the present course through the Visegrád gorge was established before the end of the Tertiary, and has since been deepened as the Danube eroded its bed downward into the Visegrád-Börzsöny Massif.

The lowering of the eastern outlet from the Little Alföld has permitted the Danube and its tributaries to strip away the Tertiary deposits from much of the basin. The progress of this denudation can be traced in the relics of valley terraces found here and there cut into the sides of the hills. The highest of them, Terrace VII in Pécsi's enumeration, lies at from 700 to 900 feet above the present river level, and has been ascribed to the Upper Pliocene.[1]

Moson Plain. The continuance of the very slow subsidence of the plain has brought about sedimentation along the Danube. The river (see page 479) divides, reunites and divides again, enclosing damp, unstable islands of alluvium. Largest of these is the Moson Island, or Szigetköz. Its fertile soil is mostly under cultivation, but meadows border the waterways, and a fringe of woodland—willow and poplar—lies along the river bank. An alluvial plain, coated with loess and highly fertile lies south of the Moson Danube. Across it, however, and forming, as it were, the west–east axis of the Little Alföld, lies the damp depression known as the Hanság. Here, between the Fertö lake,[2] or Neusiedler See, and Györ, is the area of greatest subsidence. The shallow Fertö is a relic of a once more extensive lake. To the east of it peat accumulated, and the Hanság marshes were formerly a serious barrier to communication. Even today the Hanság is famous for its wildlife, but most of its area was reclaimed during the nineteenth century, and is now under cultivation.

Györ is in many respects the capital of the Little Alföld. It lies on the Moson branch of the Danube where the Rába joins it, and also on the routeway which lies along the low ridge between the Danube marshes on the north and the Hanság to the south. The plain is almost wholly under some form of agricultural use; the loess-covered alluvium is cultivated; the damper areas provide pasture, and woodland is restricted to the fringe of trees along the river banks.

The Alpine borderland. Since 1920 Hungary has ceased to be an Alpine state. Until that date Hungary had contained the Burgenland, and with it the eastern foot-hills of the Styrian Alps. The boundary, as defined by the Treaty of Trianon, left within Hungary only two very small areas of mountain, neither of them as high as the Mátra: the Soproni-hegy which overlooks Sopron, and the Köszegi-hegy, which similarly dominates the small town of Köszeg. Between is a tumbled region of low hills, carved, like the southern and eastern margins of the Little Alföld, out of soft Tertiary deposits.

At the meeting place of mountain and plain have grown up a number of small towns, including Sopron, or Odenburg, a bilingual town

---

[1] Márton Pécsi, 'Morphogenesis of the Hungarian Section of the Danube Valley', *Studies in Hungarian Geographical Sciences*, ed. Gyula Miklós, Budapest, 1960, pp. 25–37.

[2] 'Tö' means *lake* in Hungarian, and the word 'lake' is actually redundant.

formerly disputed with Austria, Köszeg and Szombathely. Most of this mountain rim is under cultivation, and woodland covers only the highest ground. Vineyards cover a large part of the low hills around Sopron, which is well known for its wines.

The southern and eastern border. The alluvial plain of the Little Alföld passes southward and eastward into a region of low, rounded hills, across which flow the Rába and Marcal in wide, shallow and occasionally marshy valleys. No significant barrier separates the Alföld drainage from that of the Zala, which takes its twisting course southward to Lake Balaton. The most common pattern of land use in this region is one of pasture along the valleys, of forest on the hilltops, and cultivation over the rest of the land. It is one of compact villages and small towns. Pápa, near the foot of the Bakony, and Sárvár, in the Rába valley are the largest. Viticulture is important on the hillsides near Sumeg. Lignite is mined from the lower Tertiary beds near Ajka; bauxite is obtained nearby from the decomposition products that cover the Triassic limestone, and small quantities of petroleum are obtained near Zalaegerszeg.

Transdanubia. The name given to the region of Hungary lying west of the Danube, Danántül—Transdanubia—suggests the eastern orientation of the early Magyars. It connotes a region of varied relief: low and flat in the east, passing westward into an area of low hills, and culminating in the south in the Mecsek and related hills, with their core of primary rocks.

Mezöföld. This is the triangular area of plain, which, broad-based on the Danube, extends westward with its apex on Lake Balaton. In many respects it resembles the greater plain east of the Danube; it has little surface drainage; its late Tertiary deposits are unevenly covered with sand spread over the region during the Ice Age, and with deposits of loess, and form high bluffs above the Danube.

Its settlement pattern, dominated by large, compact villages, also resembles that of the Great Alföld. The Mezöföld differs from the greater plain to the east, however, in its higher altitude, its lower water table and the absence of the small alkaline lakes which characterise much of the Great Alföld. For the same reason one rarely sees the tall well-sweep, or *köz*, so typical of the plain, because the water lies beyond the reach of this simple but effective device. The Mezöföld is mostly under cultivation, and is, in fact, the most extensive area of cropland in the western half of the country. On its western edge is the town of Székesfehérvár, the capital of Hungary before Buda was chosen, and still one of the larger cities west of the Danube. It is a road junction, where the route south-west from Budapest crosses the route running south-east from Vienna and Györ, through the fault-bounded depression which separates the Bakony and the Vértes.

Transdanubian Hills. From the Mezöföld south-westward to the Yugoslav boundary stretches a unique region of low hills and wide shallow valleys. The traveller who takes the narrow, twisting roads across it to the south-west is conscious of a corrugated landscape, in which the rounded uplands lie parallel and separated by straight, evenly-spaced valleys, each with a small and often undersized stream. These valleys trend from north-north-west to south-south-east. Across them lie transverse valleys, especially the Kapos, and its tributary, the Koppány, which flow to the Mezöföld, and the Zala which, after a course alternately with and against the grain of the country, enters Lake Balaton.

The origin of this peculiar drainage pattern is far from clear. It is apparent, however, that the Transdanubian hill-country has not shared in the recent sinking of the Little and Great Alföld, and that the rivers have thus cut valleys into it, adjusted to their local base-level, which is the Danube. This does not, however, explain their rectilinear pattern which appears to be due to the underlying structures.

That part of the region lying to the south of Lake Balaton, the Somogy Hills (Somogyi-dombság), can be distinguished from that to the west, the Vas and Zala hills (Vasi-hegyhát, Zalai-dombság). The former has a drainage pattern even more conspicuously rectilinear than the latter. Its hills are deeply covered with loess, which is almost entirely absent from the more westerly Vas-Zala region. The latter has an appreciably higher rainfall, is more extensively forested, of lower fertility, and more thinly peopled. Towns are few and small in both parts of the region. The largest, Kaposvár on the southern margin of the Somogy hills, has only about 43,000 inhabitants. Nagykanisza has about 30,000, and Zalaegerseg, centre of Hungary's most important petroleum and natural gas field, has only 18,000.

Mecsek. Within the triangle formed by the Kapos river, the Danube and Dráva lies the small isolated Mecsek, a primary inlier which broke the surface of the Triassic Pannonian Sea. It is a ridge, with steep sides and a broad, rounded summit, built mainly of limestone and trending from south-west to north-east for about 25 miles. Its faulted southern face drops steeply to the small lowland which contains the city of Pécs. Its highest point, the Zengö (2,237 feet), accords closely with the higher levels of the Bakony, and is part of the same planation. An apron of lower land slopes downward on all sides except the south-west, built, like the Somogy to the north, of Tertiary and Pleistocene deposits, thickly buried under a covering of loess. South of the Mecsek itself, and only a few miles from the Dráva river the narrow Villany ridge (Villányi-hegy), a limestone hill with its sunny southern face covered with vineyards, is the most southerly outpost of the Hungarian hills. The Mecsek is a forested area, and forest extends outwards over the surrounding hills, but quickly dies away where the loess made the soil attractive to the early farmer. Along the northern and southern margins of the Mecsek lies the most extensive and, in geological terms, the oldest coal-field in Hungary. The coal is of Jurassic age; some is of coking quality, and it occurs in up to 200 seams, very many of which are too thin to be mined economically. It yields at present about four million tons a year, most of it from mines near Pécs on the southern side of the hills and near Komló on the northern.

The area lying south of the Mecsek, known as the Baranya, is almost wholly under cultivation. Forest has been reduced to a few small patches on the higher ground, and south-facing slopes have been terraced for the vine. Fields of maize, sunflower and wheat stretch down to the damp pasture and the lines of poplar and willow that border the Dráva and the Danube.

The Great Alföld

The Great Alföld makes up about half the total area of Hungary, and is, by common consent, the most characteristically Hungarian part of the whole country. It is a plain, level over much of its area, but rising to low and inconspicuous hills along parts of its western and eastern margins. Its altitude ranges from about 260 feet above sea-level along the lower Tisza to 597 feet in the Nyírség of the north-east. Local relief is everywhere slight, and the strongest relief is often presented by the sand-dunes that have formed (see page 489) in comparatively recent times. Despite the simplicity of its relief and drainage, the great plain is nevertheless capable of division into a number of contrasting 'landscapes', according to the surface materials, the level of the water table below the surface, and the nature of the drainage.

Over the whole of its surface the great plain is covered with loess, blown sand and alluvium. Beneath these comparatively thin deposits is a large though somewhat variable thickness of Tertiary beds. In recent years bores, put down primarily in search of oil, have yielded a great deal of information on the hidden structures of the Hungarian Plain. They have revealed a basin, floored generally with Palaeozoic rock, with ridges trending from south-west to north-east, rising from it. Two of these rise above the level of the Tertiaries to form the Mecsek and the Bakony. The basin, however, has been sinking throughout upper Tertiary and later times, and beds, generally of clays and sands, have formed to an ever increasing thickness within it. These beds are now from 3,000 to 6,500 feet thick over most of the basin. They were formerly thicker, but denudation over the plain kept pace with the lowering of the local base level at the Iron Gate, while continued subsidence of the region has led to further sedimentation on the rivers, slowing down and obstructing their flow.

Along the foot of the mountains to the north was spread an apron of detritus worn from the mountains. This tapers away until it is lost in the plain, and is chiefly important today for the vineyards which grow on its warm and dry soils. During the Ice Age the Danube and Tisza meandered over the plain, depositing their load of sand brought from the Alps and Carpathians. Much of the area at present lying between the two rivers thus came to be covered with coarse sand, which has since been redistributed by the wind and built into elongated dunes. The marshy lands along the Tisza trapped the blowing sand, so that little crossed the river to the Tiszántül, or region beyond the Tisza. East of the Tisza the only extensive area of sand is the Nyírség, in the north-east. Elsewhere the surface is made up of loess or alluvium, and its local peculiarities result by and large from the varying water level within it.

The Great Alföld can be subdivided into four major divisions, and each of these is capable of further subdivision. The Hungarians themselves distinguish the small differences in soil and water table and in the resulting land use and landscape by the use of regional names. It is not difficult, in fact, to divide the plain into small, distinctive *pays*.

Danube valley. Most westerly of the four major divisions of the plain is the north–south valley of the Danube itself. Its flood plain varies from about four to over 20 miles in width. It is floored with recent alluvium, and bordered by low and occasionally steep bluffs. On the west, the line of bluffs, composed mainly of loess, lie close to the river, withdrawing from it for a considerable distance only in the latitude of the Mecsek. Here a damp area of flood plain, laced by the abandoned meanders of the Danube, is known as the Sárköz. Damp meadowland lines the river bank. Away from it, where there is today no danger of flooding, the fertile alluvium is under cultivation. But there are few settlements in the flood plain, and almost none along the river. In the extreme north of the region Csepel Island (Csepel-sziget) is industrialised where it extends upstream into the Budapest suburbs. On the Danube terraces to the west, almost opposite the southern end of Csepel Island, is Dunaújváros, recently developed as the foremost metallurgical centre in Hungary. Other river settlements occur only where loess bluffs come close to the river: Paks and Mohács, scene of Hungary's defeat in 1526, on the west bank, and Kalocsa, one of the oldest cities in the Hungarian state, and Baja on the east.

Danube–Tisza Interfluve (*Duna–Tisza–köze*). This extensive region stretches southward from the Mátra and the Gödöllö Hills to the Yugoslav boundary and beyond it into Slavonia. On both west and east it is bounded by the inconspicuous terraces which lead down to the Danube and Tisza valleys. The region itself is almost level, and lies at between 300 and 500 feet. The appearance of relief has, however, been given to it by the sand dunes which have been formed over it in comparatively recent times. These derived from Pleistocene sand beds, laid down by the rivers and later reworked by the wind. Predominant north-westerly winds have elongated these dunes in a north-west to south-east direction. In the past they were quite inadequately stabilised by grass, and were in fact mobile into the nineteenth century. Since then, it has been found that not only does the sand provide a warm, dry soil for vines and fruit trees, but that the former even do well on the sands. Today, the most extensive areas of viticulture in Hungary are found on the sands near Kecskemét. The vegetation map nevertheless still shows elongated belts of woodland, indicative of the lines of sand dunes which they cover.

The drifting sands have in part covered the loess which was laid down over this area in glacial times. Toward the south, however, the sands are less extensive, and the loess yields a more productive soil, now intensively cultivated, especially in the Hungarian Bácska. Over the central parts of the region the drifting sand has obscured or obstructed the drainage. Shallow lakes have formed between the lines of dunes, their water often contaminated by the high alkali content of the subsoil. Large areas have been in some degree poisoned for agriculture, particularly to the south of Kecskemét, where the Bugac Steppe is an extensive area of poor grazing land, flecked with small, shallow, salty lakes.

The Kiskunság, as this sandy region is called, is important agriculturally only around its margins. Here is an open pattern of very large villages, urban in size but rural in function. Hamlets and scattered settlements are beginning to appear but the large villages, with the long journeys to the fields that these necessitate, still dominate the pattern of settlement. Kecskemét, with a population of about 67,000, is the largest and most centrally placed town of the region. To the north is the smaller town of Cegléd, on the main routeway east from Budapest to Transylvania; to the south, beyond the Bugac steppe, is Kiskunhalas.

Tisza valley. The peculiarities of the Tisza river will be described later: its steep gradient in its upper course, the sudden levelling off of its course as it enters the plain, its violent floods, and the rapid sedimentation and changes of course along its lower valley. The effective flood plain of the Tisza is, in fact, wider than that of the Danube, and the area marked by its abandoned meanders proportionately greater. Despite the work done during the nineteenth century to straighten and regulate the river's course, its meanders still remain conspicuous and also susceptible to sudden changes. A consequence of this is that for most of its course the Tisza is bordered by meadow and pasture, with levées to protect them from the ravages of the river's floods. The river has always presented obstacles to movement between east and west, and today the main roads cross only where the flood plain narrows and terraces approach the river on west and east. It is at these crossing points that the towns of the Tisza have grown up: in the north at Tokaj, where the hill of Tokaj on the west comes within a mile or two of the sands of the Hajdúság, and 60 miles downstream at Tiszafured, where the crossing is made despite a wide alluvial belt to the west of the river. Then at Szolnok, just south of the wide alluvium which extends up the Zagyva valley, lies the most important crossing of all. Here a low ridge extends south-eastwards from the Gödöllö Hills toward the river and is separated by only a narrow belt of alluvium from the loess-covered plain of the Nagykunság to the east. The next crossing point lies between Csongrad and Szentes, just to the south of the junction of the Körös river, and the last, on the road to the Banat, is at Szeged, similarly placed in relationship to the Maros.

Szeged, with a population of about 99,000, is the largest settlement of the Tisza valley, an industrial city, and the chief route centre of south-eastern Hungary. Szolnok has about 43,000, but the other river-crossing towns, including the famed Tokaj, are quite small.

East-Tisza region (Tiszántúl). This is the largest and, despite the uniformity of its relief and its superficial simplicity, it is one of the more complex regions. It can be divided, largely on the basis of soil and water level into distinct units most of which are not distinguishable from the contours of the ground. In the extreme north-east is a triangular region where the Tisza and Szamos receive a fan of small tributaries from the Ruthenian and Romanian hills. In Quaternary times coarse detritus from the mountains was spread over the area, lakes formed and have since filled with peat, but the Tisza is here a swifter river, with a steeper gradient, than to the south, and it has not been difficult to drain and improve the marshes—especially the Ecsed Moor (Ecsediláp)—in this area, though not all the reclaimed land is fit for cultivation.

Enclosed by the great northern bend of the Tisza is the Nyírség, a region of alluvial sands, resorted in some degree by the wind, that resembles the Kiskunság. It includes the highest ground east of the Tisza in the sands of Koportyok (597 feet). There is more woodland here than in any other area of Hungary east of the Tisza—the place-name element 'Nyir-' means birch-tree—and much of the sand area forms rough grazing land.

Toward the south-west, the Nyírség passes gradually and almost imperceptibly into the Hajdúság. This is also a region of Quaternary sands, but its altitude is a few feet lower, and a number of small shallow lakes occur. Its surface is partly covered by loess, and it is thus more intensively cultivated than the Nyírség. An irrigation canal, the Keleti föcsatorna, was completed in 1954 to take water from the Tisza near Tiszalök and to deliver southward to the Berettyó, a tributary of the Körös, whatever water goes unused along its course.

Debrecen, with 129,000 the biggest city of eastern Hungary, lies in the Hajdúság, at a distance from the nearest river, but serving as a route centre for north-eastern Hungary.

The Hajdúság passes beyond the Tisza-Berettyó canal into the *Hortobágy*, a region which has impressed its image more deeply on Hungary and the world than any other part of the country. Here only one finds today an extensive area of grassy, treeless steppe, and only here in recent years has it been possible to see herds of cattle and horses under half-wild conditions, tended by the *csikós* in traditional *szür*, or cloth cape. In summer these treeless, shadeless plains become one of the hottest areas of Hungary, and here once came visitors in the hope of seeing the Délibáb, the 'Noonday Witch', or mirage.

The Hortobágy is low-lying and flat, and rises only a few feet above the level of the Tisza. Across it wanders inconsequently the Hortobágy river, marking out what was once approximately the course of the Tisza. It flows southward into the Körös, but at its northern end it is still joined at several points with the Tisza, so indeterminate is the drainage. The plain is made up of alluvial sands and clays, which are in turn covered with loess, but the drainage is so poor and the water table so close to the surface that crop-farming has made little impression on this steppe. The underground water over large areas of the Great Plain is strongly impregnated with salt. Much of it is undrinkable and not fit for use in irrigation. Where the water table comes very close to the surface, as it does in the Hortobágy, shallow lakes form. In a dry summer these may dry out, leaving an encrustation of sodium salts. At one time this was scraped from the floors of these depressions and used, especially at Debrecen, in the manufacture of soap. The soil is in consequence highly alkaline, unsuited to most forms of woodland and of commercial crops, and so it remains under grass.

The Nagykunság, lying to the south of the Hortobágy between the Tisza and the Körös, is almost indistinguishable in relief from the Hortobágy. It is a level plain covered deeply by loess, but the water table lies somewhat lower, and a good chernozem soil has developed over parts of it. Most is under cultivation. There are scattered farms, usually sheltering from wind and sun beneath an acacia tree or behind a few poplars, and the well-sweep, symbolic of the Great Alföld, lifts its long arm above the roof of the low cottage.

East of the Nagkunság lie the Great and Little Sárrét (Nagy-Sárrét; Kis-Sárrét), where the Körös and its tributaries, after dropping steeply from the Bihor Mountains of Romania, have spread wide banks of sand and gravel. There is a complex pattern of small rivers which divide and reunite, enclosing islands of sand, between which are peat-filled hollows. This region is more wooded than most other parts of the Tiszántúl; the better soil is cultivated, but considerable areas remain under grass.

The Lower Tisza Plain. From the Körös south to the Romanian border stretches the largest of these divisions of eastern Hungary. It is a level plain, almost wholly covered with loess, and rising above, the Tisza just sufficiently to ensure good drainage, but with a water table high enough to meet the needs of agriculture. This region, with its extension southwards into the Banat of Romania and Yugoslavia, was the classic area of eighteenth-century settlement, where planned, rectilinear villages were laid out by Maria Theresa's settlers. This is also a region of giant villages, from which the peasants make their daily pilgrimage to their distant fields.

The city of Szeged, on the other side of the Tisza, serves in some measure the needs of this region, but the largest local towns are Hódmezövásárhely, with a population of 54,000, and Békéscsaba, with 50,000. But others are only a degree less conspicuous: Szentes, above the Tisza flood plain; Békés, in the Körös valley; Orosháza in the centre of the region, and Makó on its southern border.

CLIMATE AND DRAINAGE

Hungary is too small in area and too simple in relief to have any very great variations in climate. It belongs to the region of continental climate, with hot summers, cold winters and a rainfall maximum in summer. In winter the Hungarian Plain tends to be dominated for long periods by the subarctic high-pressure systems which form over Russia, and force low-pressure systems, as they move inland from the Atlantic, to pass out around them. Some cyclonic disturbances are able to move into the region even in winter, but during spring the high pressure system over Russia weakens, and the passage of lows becomes more frequent. In summer a low pressure system replaces the high which prevails in winter over Russia. The movement of lows from the Atlantic and Mediterranean is more often across Hungary, but not infrequently the planetary circulation is moved northwards sufficiently to bring the subtropical high over the Hungarian Plain. In such circumstances extremes of heat and aridity are experienced. During autumn, the sub-tropical high pressure system recedes as the continental high again asserts itself. Lows again follow one another across the Danube Basin until they again retreat to the Mediterranean basin, and cold, sub-arctic air spreads over the Hungarian Plain. Hungary is thus far enough south to experience sub-tropical heat in summer, and far enough north to know the sub-arctic high in winter, and sufficiently flat and exposed to feel to the full the asperities of both. Its climate is the most continental and extreme of any country west of the Soviet Union.

17

Temperature. In western Hungary, the continental character of its climate is tempered somewhat by oceanic influences. Toward the east these are less apparent. Temperatures fall off toward the north-east in summer. The temperature range in January is over 4°C (7°F) from the extreme south-west to the north-east (Fig. 10.3 ab). The summer range is about the same between the mountains of the north and the south-east (Fig. 10.3 ab). The lowest January average—less than -4°C (25°F)—is experienced in the upper Tisza valley; and the highest in July—over 22°C (72°F)—in the plains of the Banat. The absolute extremes are -34°C (29°F) at Baja and 41·3°C (106°F) at Pécs;

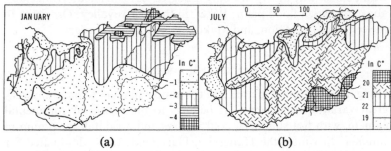

(a)   (b)

Fig. 10.3. Mean monthly temperature in (a) January, (b) July.

extremes only a little less severe than these are not infrequent. The dry heat of the Hungarian Plain in summer is notorious. Here the distortion of light rays reaches mirage proportions. By contrast, no European rivers are more obstructed by winter ice than those of the Hungarian Plain.

Rainfall. There is a gradual transition from west to east in the rainfall regime. Total precipitation reaches over 800 millimetres (31·5 inches) in the Alpine foothills and on the western flanks of the Bakony. It is generally over 700 millimetres (27·5 inches) in the hills of southern Transdanubia and in the Mátra, Bükk and other hills in the north. But it falls off to less than 600 millimetres (23·5 inches) in most areas east of the Danube and to less than 500 millimetres (20 inches) in some areas beyond the Tisza. It increases somewhat along the eastern and south-eastern border of the country, as the foothills of the Bihor and Carpathian Mountains are approached. Throughout the country the rainfall shows a pronounced summer maximum. Debrecen, for example, receives about a quarter of its total precipitation in the months of June and July and less than a third in the five months from December to April. Except in the mountains and on the plains where the winds cause heavy drifting, the depth of snow accumulation is comparatively small, and the protection to the soil given by the snow cover is proportionately small. Much of the summer rainfall comes in severe convectional storms, accompanied sometimes by violent hail. The value of this summer rainfall to agriculture is reduced by the rapid rate of evaporation, for the air, in general remains very dry. The duration of sunshine is very considerable, and averages over 2,000 hours a year over all the central and more southerly parts of the

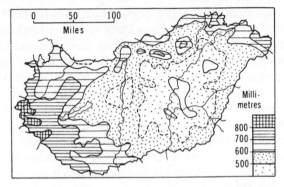

Fig. 10.4. Average annual rainfall. (After *Politkai és Gazdasági Világatlasz*, Budapest, 1961.

plain. Even in the hilly borderland to north and west there are generally over 1,700 hours of sunshine yearly. The duration of sunshine is greatest in summer, despite the heavier rainfall, and locally it approaches the theoretical maximum. Everywhere the months of November–February are very cloudy, though the actual precipitation is very much smaller.

River system

The whole of Hungary lies within the drainage basin of the Danube and its tributaries. The Danube itself enters Hungary in the extreme north-west and forms the boundary with Czechoslovakia, before turning abruptly near Vác, and flowing southward to the Yugoslav border.

The most important right bank tributary, the Dráva (*G.* Drau; *S-C.* Drava) forms for part of its distance the south-western boundary of Hungary, but its confluence with the Danube is within Yugoslavia.

Between the Danube and the Dráva is a complex pattern of small rivers. North of the Bakony most of these are gathered to the Rába, which joins the Danube below Györ, but south of the Bakony there is a peculiar pattern of small north–south river valleys, cut across by the Kapos, whose sharp turns bear witness to a complex history of river-capture (see page 486).

The Tisza. The pattern of drainage of the plains east of the Danube is in marked contrast with that to the west. Over much of the area there is no surface drainage, though the surface itself is studded with small lakes and the water table lies at most only a few feet below the surface. The only important river is the Tisza, which rises in the Ruthenian Carpathians, enters the Hungarian Plain in the extreme north-east, and then takes its meandering course south-westward and southward to the Danube, receiving as it goes the Szamos, Körös and Maros from the mountains of Romania. On the west a handful of small tributaries, among them the Bodrog, Hernád, and Sajó, join the Tisza from the mountains of northern Hungary and Slovakia. But from the plain, both west and east of the Tisza, the river receives very little surface drainage. In part this is because the rainfall is low and the rate of evaporation high; in part because much of the movement of ground water takes place through the sandy deposits which make up much of the Hungarian Plain.

Once it reaches the plain the Tisza is a river of very gentle gradient and of violent floods. After summer storms and the melting of spring snows the runoff is rapid, and the flood carries vast quantities of sand and silt down to the plain, blocking the channel, bringing about changes in the course of the river, and causing floods of exceptional severity. Before the work of regulating the Tisza was begun in the nineteenth century, the river was noteworthy for the number of its meanders and the frequency with which they changed. Attempts to straighten the river's course, and thereby to steepen its gradient, began in the seventeenth century, were renewed in the eighteenth, but were not really successful until the end of the nineteenth. Some measure of the task involved is shown by the changes effected in the length of the river. The shortest distance from source to mouth of the Tisza is 285 miles. Before regulation its length was 886 miles which by straightening its course and eliminating meanders was reduced to 607 miles.[1]

---

[1] Paul Vujević, 'Die Theiss: eine potamologische Studie', *Geographische Abhandlungen herausgegeben von Albrecht Penck in Wien*, Band VII, Heft 4, 1906, p. 10.

The Tisza—at least in its plain tract—is today only very slightly incised into a valley so broad and shallow that it is difficult to detect the slope. On the outer curve of its bends it may have cut into soft rock sufficiently to form a low bank, but for most of its course it is bordered by damp flood plain and a continuous line of levées. The land-use map shows an almost continuous strip of grazing land along both banks of the Tisza from the edge of the mountains to its confluence with the Danube. The flood season on the Tisza is from March to May or even June. The water derives primarily from the melting snows of Transylvania and the Carpathians, and is extended over a relatively long period of time because the area of highland from which it is fed has a large latitudinal extent. No less than 42 per cent of the river's total annual flow comes in the three spring months. The summer rainfall maximum in the Hungarian Plain is not reflected in an increased discharge of the river, as the runoff is reduced to a small fraction of the actual rainfall by the very high rate of evaporation.

Closely associated with the regulation of the river was the construction of canals. These were designed to serve several purposes, among which were the swifter evacuation of flood water in spring, the irrigation of dry areas in summer, and the transportation of agricultural produce to urban and transport centres. Some of these canals were begun in the eighteenth century, but most owed their origin to the reclamation works carried out in the nineteenth in part by the more enlightened of the landowners, in part by the Austro-Hungarian government.

The Danube. The Tisza is Hungary's river, but the Danube, only 16 per cent of whose course lies in Hungary, is in all respects the most important. The Danube enters the Hungarian Plain after crossing the Leithegebirge and Malé Karpaty ridge at Bratislava. Almost at once it divides into three branches, of which the most northerly, the Little Danube, encloses the Žitný Ostrov of Czechoslovakia (see page 423), and the most southerly, the Mosoni Duna (Moson Danube), the Szigetköz. The middle branch is the main stream of the river and carries most of its discharge and all of its shipping. The Moson Danube receives the Rába, the river of the Little Alföld, and the Little Danube, the Váh and Nitra, before both rejoin the main course of the river. Near Komárom, the Danube draws close both to the Bakony and to the Carpathian foothills. Toward the west, its course is braided, and fringed with cutoffs and marshes. Here, however, these are gathered into a single stream, which is notably narrower and swifter. Below

Esztergom the river enters the short and rather unspectacular gorge tract by which it crosses the Bakony–Börzsöny ridge and enters the Great Alföld. At this point the river is dominated by the mass of Pilis (2,483 feet), the most northerly bastion of the Bakony. Beyond the river to the north lies the higher but more distant summit of Csóványos (3,080 feet). On a high bluff above the south bank of the river are the ruins of the fortress of Visegrád, once a castle of the Hungarian kings. It is near this point that it is planned to build a dam to regulate the flow in this turbulent section of the river and also to generate power.

This section of the Danube valley ends at Vác, and at once the river divides into two channels to enclose St Andrew Island or Szentendreisziget. This extends to the northern suburbs of Budapest. At the southern margin of the city the river again divides to enclose the larger Csepel Island or Csepel-sziget. Below this point the river widens, and is up to a mile across, and even wider at flood stage. Below Paks its flood plain widens to a width of from 6 to 16 miles. The river is fringed by cut-offs and swamps, and its channel becomes shallow during much of the year and inconstant. Below Mohács, the Danube enters Yugoslavia, but the same physical conditions extend beyond the boundary to its junction with the Dráva.

These physical conditions along this tract of the Danube can be understood in terms of the slow subsidence, to which the plain, or at least its central parts, have been subject since the end of the Tertiary. As there was no commensurate lowering of the local base-level at the Iron Gate gorges, the speed of the current, both of the Danube and of the Tisza was reduced, with accompanying sedimentation and the formation of the present braided pattern of the river.

The Danube enters Hungary as a river with a marked maximum flow in late spring and summer, and low water in late autumn and winter. This regime is very little modified. The seasonal contrasts are sharpened somewhat by the greater severity of the Hungarian winter and the reduced discharge of the rivers at this season.

The period of freeze on the Hungarian rivers may last several weeks. It is longest in the north-east and on the slow-flowing rivers of the plain; shortest in the south-west and where the rivers flow more swiftly from the Alpine foothills. Commonly the surface of the rivers is covered with broken ice, sufficiently thick to prevent navigation without some form of ice-breaker, and at the same time not continuous enough to permit the river to be crossed on foot. The twin cities of Buda and Pest, separated by the Danube, were said to have been completely cut off from one another for a period of many weeks each year before the building of the first Danube bridge in 1848, because the small ferry boats were unable to negotiate the ice-covered river.

VEGETATION

The picture of the Hungarian Plain that has become traditional is one of rolling grasslands. Maurus Jókai thus described the Hortobágy, to the west of Debrecen:

> The puszta has no pathway, grass grows over hoof-print and cart track. Up to the endless horizon there is nothing but grass, not a tree, a well pole, or a hut to break the majestic green plain . . . soon the hills of Zám, the little acacia wood, and the three tall well poles began to peep above the horizon . . . a low line of bluish mist marked the course of the Hortobágy river . . . [which] wound silently along, between banks fringed with reeds and willows.[1]

Small patches of treeless, grassy Puszta remain today, especially east of the Tisza. They were once more extensive. The naturalist, Anton Kerner, described the changes that were going on here in the mid-nineteenth century:

> As yet the Pusztaland remains in places untouched in its primeval state. As yet one can see there a life and occupance which has continued essentially unchanged for hundreds of years. . . . Already dikes are being built to direct the streams and rivers in their courses, and to prepare the wide marshes for cultivation. Waving wheatfields spring up on the overturned prairie soil. Broad pastures are changed to arable. Present day culture has possessed the Alföld, to produce there such a landscape as we see in the far-off Italian lowlands. In another half century the romantic life of the Puszta will have vanished, along with the vegetation which originally clothed the steppe. . . .[2]

The assumption made here, and repeated by most writers on the subject, is that the Hungarian Plain, or at least the greater part of it, is natural steppe. 'The intrinsic character of the steppe', wrote Kerner,

---

[1] Maurus Jókai, *The Yellow Rose*, translated by Beatrice Danford, London, n.d., p. 13.
[2] Henry S. Conard, *The Background of Plant Ecology*, Iowa State College, 1951, p. 24. This is a translation of Anton Kerner, *Das Pflanzenleben der Donauländer*.

'is its primeval treelessness.'[1] And again Sir Halford Mackinder described the plains as 'a detached area of steppes',[2] and A. Austin Miller wrote that 'steppe conditions occur in the Hungarian basin some 500 miles west of the general boundary of the steppe'.[3]

The lack of logic in Kerner's claim is shown by his anticipation that a landscape resembling that of the Italian lowlands would be created here by human effort. This would be impossible in any region of natural steppe. The fact is, however, that, insofar as the Hungarian Plain had a steppe vegetation, this was a man-made steppe. The plain may never have been densely wooded, but all the historical evidence tends to show that wooded it originally was.[4] Many factors contributed to the destruction of woodland over much of the Great Alföld: warfare, grazing by the animals of the Magyar invaders, the need of lumber for building and burning, the military campaigns of the late seventeenth century, and the blowing sand which the destruction of the trees set in motion. To these must certainly be added the unexpected consequences of the attempts to reclaim the land for agricultural use that were begun in the eighteenth century and continued in the nineteenth. From 1722, when the Turks had at last been swept from the plain, there was great activity in land drainage, especially along the Tisza valley. The result was to lower the water table. The drying out of the soil in summer extended over an ever widening area and penetrated ever deeper into the subsoil. The effect was to restrict the natural growth of trees, and set loose the sands that were widespread in the central parts of the plain. Sand pusztas were actually formed in the eighteenth century. Between Cegléd and Kecskemét, it was claimed, blowing sand actually destroyed standing woodland, and a traveller in 1818 wrote that 'most of the lands that are not inundated, produce only heath and brambles, and have an aspect of extreme aridity. The plains of Kecskemét are covered with white and moveable sands, which the winds raise and transport like clouds to great distances'.[5]

During the eighteenth century the growing demand for wheat in the cities of Central Europe led to the cultivation of all areas capable of

[1] Henry S. Conard, *The Background of Plant Ecology*, p. 26.
[2] H. J. Mackinder, 'The Geographical Pivot of History', *Geographical Journal*, **23**, 1904, 421–437.
[3] A. Austin Miller, *Climatology*, London, 1944, p. 213.
[4] Norman J. G. Pounds, 'Land Use on the Hungarian Plain', *Geographical Essays on Eastern Europe*, Russian and East European Series, Indiana University, vol. 24, pp. 54–74.
[5] F. S. Beudant, *Travels in Hungary in 1818*, London, 1923, p. 116.

bearing a crop. At the same time the regulation of the Tisza quickened the run-off and lowered the water table. The sandy areas presented a serious problem until these were either afforested or planted with the grape-vine which possessed an unusual ability to fix the sand and even to thrive in this unpromising soil. Thus settlement encroached upon the puszta, which came to be broken up into fragments of even smaller size. Today it is no longer possible to see the apparently endless grass-lands which appealed so much to the romantic imagination of earlier travellers. Trees grow well on the Great Alföld, which is now dotted with farm settlements, few of which do not have a windbreak of poplars or an acacia grown for shade in the hot summer.

The Bakony and the hilly masses of northern Hungary are today forested, as they have been for several thousand years, predominantly with oak, and beech, with the yew especially in the Bakony. Large stands of timber are very rare east of the Danube, except in the north-ern hills, but are quite common in Transdanubia, even on the lower ground.

POPULATION AND SETTLEMENT

The population of Hungary was estimated in 1965 to have been about 10,135,500. Of this more than 95 per cent were regarded as Magyars; most of the remainder were German, with small numbers of Slovaks, Romanians, Southern Slavs and Gypsies. Hungary ethnically is one of the most homogeneous countries in Europe today, thanks to the drastic pruning which her boundaries underwent in 1920, and to the small-scale population exchange that has taken place since.

The balance of age and sex in Hungary has not been as gravely disturbed as it has in Poland, by war and the virtual extinction of certain segments of the population. Life expectancy compares favour-ably with that of Western Europe; there has been no sharp increase in the birth-rate in recent years, and the population has during the present century been growing relatively slowly. The population pyramid is tall and narrow, and much more like that of a Scandinavian country than one in Eastern Europe. Indeed, it shows only two abnormalities: the small size of the age-groups born during the First World War, and the large size of those born during the decade following the Second.

The distribution of population in Hungary is the result of a long and complex history. Before the Turkish invasions, Transdanubia was by far the most densely settled part of the country. There was a moderate

17*

density of population in the northern hills, but the Great Alföld was itself only thinly peopled. The Turkish invasions and conquest intensified this contrast. When it was reconquered by the armies of Austria at the end of the seventeenth century, the Great Plain was almost depopulated, and the only areas of Hungary where the population was

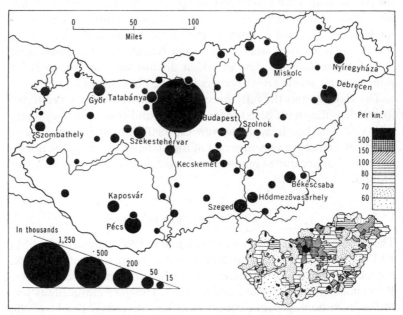

Fig. 10.5. Distribution of population and of towns. All towns of more than 10,000 are shown; those having over 50,000 are named, based on *Statisztikai Évkönyv* and *Politikai és Gazdasági Világatlasz*.

adequate were the northern hills and the western margin of the Little Alföld where respectively the terrain and the proximity of Austria deterred the ravages of the Turks.

During the eighteenth century the Great Alföld was repeopled. It 'consisted for the most part of unpeopled marshland or forest-covered country. The main source of income was cattle breeding.'[1] This changed but slowly. Much of the land in the Great Alföld was taken over from the Turks by the Austrian State and distributed among the Austrian and to a small extent the Hungariar. nobility. The latter thereupon developed the estates they acquired either by establishing

[1] Henry Marczali, *Hungary in the Eighteenth Century*, Cambridge University Press, 1910, p. 25.

farms where cattle could be reared and then driven, in a manner that resembled the early cattle drives of the American West, to Vienna for sale, or by founding agricultural colonies. The former type of land-development was the easier, because it called for little capital, other than that represented by the animals themselves, and made small demands on labour. Later in the eighteenth century it was supplemented and then replaced by the agricultural settlements. Colonies of peasants, conscripted from all parts of the Austro-Hungarian Empire and even from areas beyond its borders, were settled on the Alföld. The Austrian government, always distrustful of the loyalty of its Hungarian subjects, tried to establish more reliable settlers close to the exposed southern frontier. Large, compact and well-planned villages were established for them. In general members of each village community belonged to a single ethnic group, but parts of the plain became a patchwork quilt of nationalities, a pattern which with some modification has survived until the present.

Agricultural settlements moved first to the loess areas, especially those of the Banat and Slavonia. Here the government of Maria Theresa encouraged a dense settlement in order to strengthen her hold on the country and to discourage renewed Turkish invasion. Sandy areas, especially those of the Kiskunság, and areas where the water table and alkali content of the soil made cultivation difficult, remained longest as rough grazing land.

Some areas west of the Danube, notably the Mezöfold and parts of the Somogy region partake, insofar as their resettlement is concerned, of the character of the great plain. With this exception, however, there is a sharp contrast between the settlement history and present-day settlement pattern between the Great Alföld and the rest of the country.

Rural settlement
Transdanubia and the Little Alföld are regions of villages and scattered farms. The styles of domestic architecture and the ways of arranging farm buildings around their farmyard are characteristically those of the Pannonian Plain, but the pattern of the settlements themselves resembles that of Austria and Moravia more closely than it does those of the Great Alföld. Villages are most often elongated along the road. The houses, single-storied, long and narrow, are usually set at right angles to the road. Windows and a porch for shade occupy the wall that faces most nearly south, while the opposite wall, which often

serves as the boundary of the adjoining farmyard, has no windows at all. Sometimes the village street divides to form a rather crude spindle-shaped village, often dominated by the baroque tower of its church. Beyond the periphery of the village are isolated farms, similar in style and as substantially built as those in the village. The appearance both of the villages and of the individual houses is indicative of an older and more mature society than that met with in the great plain to the east.

We do not know precisely how the great plain was settled before the period of the Turkish invasions. It is believed that pastoralism dominated, and that village settlements were adjusted to this way of life. A cluster of houses was surrounded by so-called 'gardens', fenced enclosures where animals could be kept under the supervision of a cowherd. Beyond lay the open grazing lands.

A broadly similar type of settlement developed after the expulsion of the Turks. Times were unsettled and the large village gave security. Much of the open grazing land was held in common, so that no individual plots were available for building scattered farms. Thus the Hungarian Plain acquired its familiar pattern of huge villages, urban in size but rural in function, with their confused pattern of twisting streets which give access to the farms of which they are largely composed. But towards the end of the eighteenth century and during the nineteenth a change took place. Crop-farming spread over the drier areas and the better soil; land passed into private ownership; brigandage was gradually suppressed, and life became more secure. This encouraged the formation of small scattered settlements in the *puszta*. At first these were temporary, inhabited only during the summer months. Then, as population became more dense and land use more intensive, they came to be inhabited throughout the year. Their earliest inhabitants were the men, sent out from the over-sized villages to tend the fields or watch the cattle; when they married, they sometimes stayed out on the *tanya*, retaining a town residence for winters and for retirement. In the end even this was given up, and the *tanya* became a permanent family home.

The settlement in the village or town, the *kert*, ceased gradually to be the focus of farming activities; its 'enclosures', modified or rebuilt, became simple houses, like those at the centre of the spreading agglomeration, and more and more of the actual farming activities were transferred to the *tanyák*. The latter are the newest features of the landscape of the great plain, and they are still in most cases simple and sometimes primitive, consisting of the Hungarian 'long house', a few small farm buildings, a shade tree and the inevitable well-sweep. The *tanya* movement is not old enough to have made any great difference to the over-sized villages and rural towns of the plain. The journey to the fields each morning, and the return in the evening still consume much of the peasants' time and obstruct the roads with slow-moving traffic. And now the regime has set its face against the *tanyák*, too individualistic for a Communist state, too scattered to be absorbed into a collective. The present policy is to establish new villages in the *tanya* areas, each socially organised and centred in the work of a collective. There is no evidence yet that the *tanyák* are being compulsorily abandoned, but large villages are again being established, though for quite different social reasons.

Urban settlement
At first appearance Hungary appears to be highly urbanised, but this is deceptive, as many of the larger agglomerations of settlement are rural in character. A dozen Hungarian towns have each a population of over 50,000, and there are no less than 35 with between 20,000 and 50,000. Several of the latter, together with many of those of yet smaller size, must be regarded as functionally little more than over-grown villages. The towns of Hungary fall into three groups on the basis of their morphology and function. First the city of Budapest, by reason of its size and its governmental and industrial functions, stands in a class by itself. The towns west of the Danube and along the border of the northern mountains have had a longer and less interrupted history than those of the great plain. In appearance and plan they resemble those of Austria, and their functions are, and long have been predominantly urban. By contrast those of the Great Alföld remain today more rural in function than those of western Hungary, and their morphology, despite the changes of recent years, still derives largely from their former agricultural pursuits.

Budapest. The twin cities of Buda and Pest grew up on opposite banks of the Danube under different conditions and to perform different functions. West of the river the low, but steep and isolated hill of Buda is an outlier of the central hill system. To the east the undulations of Gödöllö hills reach into the suburbs of Pest. To the north the Danube valley narrows between the Pilis and the Börzsöny, and southward the river's flood plain widens into a wet and at times impassable lowland. The site of Budapest is thus the easiest crossing point in the whole of the north–south tract of the river. A little to the north of Buda the Romans had established their frontier city of Aquincum. On the hill of Buda the Hungarian kings established their residence after the Tatar invasion of 1241 had demonstrated the necessity for strong fortifications, and the fortress which they built there resisted—though not for long—the assaults of the Turks in 1541, and of the Austrians in 1686. Thereafter its military significance diminished, and the area within the walls of Buda came to be used more and more for the purposes of government. The commercial suburbs of Óbuda grew up immediately to the north of the hill of Buda, and across the river lay the sprawling city of Pest. It was not until 1848 that the first bridge was built across the Danube at the site of Budapest. Before this date communication was maintained between Buda and Pest by means of ferryboats, except in winter, where ice on the river obstructed them and held the twin cities apart. The construction of bridges made possible a closer liaison between them, and in 1873, the three cities—Buda, Óbuda and Pest—were merged to form the city of Budapest. Buda remains a quaint, baroque city, with the restored gothic church of St Matthias raising its ornate spire from the summit of the hill. Pest, however, is very largely the creation of the nineteenth century. Its concentric boulevards enclose a semi-circular area of wide streets, ornate buildings with stuccoed fronts, and the shops, banks and museums of a large capital city. Government functions have now overflowed the restricted space on the hill of Buda. The ornate Parliament building, one of the most familiar in Budapest, rises from the left bank of the river, and government offices are now scattered through the central areas of Pest.

During the present century Buda has extended up over the low hills which enclose it on the west, and Pest has spread yet farther out over the plain. Railways radiate from Pest over the Alföld, and manufacturing industries have developed along the main routes. Much of the varied industrial development of Budapest is related to the agricultural production of Hungary: flour-milling, sugar-refining, tanning and the manufacture of fertilisers and agricultural machinery. To these have been added the preparation of food, and textile, chemical and engineering—especially electrical engineering—industries.

Several of the industrial districts lie along the river, where they are served by the quite intensive barge traffic. Most important of these is the northern part of Csepel Island, where, framed by the branches of the Danube, and bordered by docks is the chief centre of the smelting and metallurgical industries.

The population of Budapest is today (1966) about 1,951,000 within the administrative area—about 203 square miles—of the city. Thsi has grown rapidly from about 50,000 for the three cities at the beginning of the nineteenth century, and has doubled in size within the last half century. At present the industry of the city is expanding, and large blocks of flats, of the kind that are becoming familiar in all the large cities of the Peoples' Republics, are growing up around the outer fringe of Pest.

Towns of western and northern Hungary. West of the Danube and in the northern hills most of today's towns are of medieval if not earlier origin. They grew up as market towns; they attracted crafts and later industries, and became the centres of long distance commerce. Some bear witness in their architecture to their earlier prosperity, though few buildings antedate the Turkish invasions, and some cities, Györ (78,400) and Székesfehérvár (65,100), for example, were completely rebuilt after the wars. These western cities include Sopron (42,250), the attractive baroque city that lies within three miles of the Austrian boundary; Györ, the Danube river port; Szombathely (60,000) and Köszeg, in the Alpine foot-hills; Veszprém (31,400), in the Bakony, and Székesfehérvár (65,100), onetime capital of Hungary and now the chief city of the fertile Mezöföld. To these cities, all of them of medieval origin, have been added in recent years the industrial city of Mosonmagyaróvár, with its aluminium-smelting plant and the mining cities of Tatabanya (61,250) with its coal and Ajka with its bauxite mines, and the new iron-smelting and steel-making centre on the Danube, Dunaújváros (41,700).

The largest town west of the Danube is Pécs (135,000) situated below the steep southern slope of the Mecsek. It was a small town of medieval origin, until coal was discovered in its vicinity. It then grew into an important centre for engineering, leather, woodworking and alimentary industries.

There is a line of towns where the northern hills meet the plain: Vác (28,200), Hatvan, Gyöngyös (30,500), Eger, Miskolc, Tokaj. Most remain quite small. Some, like Gyöngyös, Eger (42,700) and Tokaj, have become centres of viticulture; only Miskolc (171,000) has grown to be a large city. Lying where the Sajó and Hernád valleys open on to the plain, Miskolc became a commercial centre at an early date, and later developed an iron and steel industry. Today Miskolc, now merged with Diosgyör to the west, focuses the iron-smelting and mechanical engineering industries of the hills of northern Hungary, and has in addition developed textile, woodworking and cement industries.

Towns of the Alföld. These differ from the towns of northern and western Hungary in being less developed industrially and more agricultural in form and function. In all there is an urban core, with market-place or square, church, public buildings and shops. In most, however, this covers only a small part of the urban area, and then merges into buildings more typical of the village; farms, and wide streets which were once drovers' roads linking them with the open *puszta*. This is the *kert*, functionally almost replaced by the *tanyák*, but retaining still the appearance and part at least of the functions of a farm.

Largest of the Alföld towns in Debrecen (148,000). Its location in the Hajduság, on the eastern margin of the plain, gave it some protection during the Turkish wars. Its economic life, though gravely hindered, was never interrupted; nor was the town ever destroyed. Cut off by the Alföld from Austria and the forces of the counter-reformation, it became and has since remained a centre of Protestant-ism in this predominantly Roman Catholic country. Its centre is probably the most impressive of any in the Alföld towns, but only a block or two away, the buildings diminish to two and then to one storey; farm buildings—not all used as such today—make their appearance and the character of Debrecen changes from a town to that of a large village.

The same is true of Szeged, (176,000) the largest town in south-eastern Hungary. It lies on the Tisza, which in 1879 almost obliterated the town with its floods. Its centre is not unimpressive, but it too soon passes into a maze of low buildings more representative of a village. Other town of the Great Alföld, notably Békéscsaba (52,500), Hód-mezovásárhely (52,600) and Orosháza (32,000) in the south-east, Kecskemét (72,800), Nagykörös and Cegléd (37,250) between the Danube and Tisza; Karcag and Nyiregyháza (62,000) in the north-east, have little of urban character; they are little more than oversized villages.

Until very recently these towns of the plain were almost devoid of manufacturing industries except the crafts essential to their agrarian population. In recent years, and especially since the implementation of the Five-Year Plan in 1950, factory industries have been established. Most bear some relationship to local agricultural resources: flour-milling, the preparation of food-stuffs and tobacco. But textile, woodworking, chemical—particularly fertiliser—industries and the manufacture of machinery—especially agricultural equipment—have been established in many of them.

AGRICULTURE

The time has passed when Hungary could be regarded as primarily an agricultural country. The population dependent on agriculture dropped from about 56 per cent of the total in 1910 and 52 in 1930 to 49 in 1949. It has since declined rapidly, and in 1965 was said to be only 31 per cent of the total. This rapid diminution of employment in agriculture was made possible first by the elimination of very small farms and then by the collectivisation of much of the country's agriculture. The socialised sector rose to over 40 per cent of the total agricultural land in 1953; declined during the period of relaxation following the death of Stalin, but then, as a result of an intensive drive by the government, quickly recovered the ground lost, increased to about half in 1959, and to over 97 per cent in 1965.

This diminution of agricultural employment has not been accompanied by any reduction in output. There has, in fact, been a very slight increase during the past decade, owing to the employment of more scientific farming methods. In the ten-year period from 1949–59 the use of artificial fertilisers increased sixfold, and within the same period the number of farm tractors trebled and that of other agricultural machines increased to a smaller degree. At the same time the quality of land has been improved. Drainage and soil improvement have made progress in the low-lying, alkaline areas of the Great Alföld. Paradoxically irrigation has been extended, and in 1960 nearly quarter of a million acres, mainly in the Tisza and Körös valleys, were under irrigation. The Keleti-föcsatorna, or Eastern Canal, which has been cut across the margin of the Hortobágy, is used to bring water from the upper Tisza to a wide belt of cropland which extends south from Tiszalök to Berettyóújfalu.

Land use
Hungary has a higher proportion of its area under agricultural land use than any other country in Eastern Europe, and the area actually under crops amounts to about 55 per cent of the whole. The present

Table 58. Land use in Hungary, 1965

	Thousand hectares	Percentage
Cropland	5,084	60·5
Meadow	419	5·0
Pasture	885	10·5
Orchards, Gardens	319	3·8
Vineyards	247	2·9
Forest	1,422	16·9
Marshland	—	0·4
	8404	100
Of no agricultural value	899	—
	9,303	—

Source: *Magyar statisztikai zsebkönyv*, 1966

land use of the country as a whole can be seen in Table 58. Land improvement is having the effect of increasing cropland at the expense of meadow and pasture, which, as has been seen, were extensive only on damp and alkaline land. Forest is considerable only on the Transdanubian and northern mountains. Most is deciduous forest, mainly beech and oak. Conifers have been established over some of the sandy areas of the plain, and shade trees, chiefly acacia, have been planted along many village streets and around isolated farms. Little extension of forest can be expected, and since the forests cover land of negligible agricultural value, it is not expected that they will be reduced significantly in area.

Almost two-thirds of the agricultural land in Hungary is under crops; this fraction rises to three-quarters in parts of the great plain, but sinks to a great deal less than a half in much of Transdanubia. Meadow and pasture form strips of varying width along almost all the river valleys, where the high water table and the liability to flooding have restricted crop husbandry. Around all the larger towns and many of the smaller is a belt of land given over mainly to the cultivation of market vegetables and fruit. But away from the towns, fruit cultivation is important in two kinds of environment: the sands between the

Danube and Tisza and the steep, south-facing hill slopes, particularly of the Mátra, Bakony, Mecsek and Villányi. The distribution of cropland accords very closely with that of the better soils. The latter occurs in parts of the Little Alföld, but primarily in the Danube valley south of Budapest, in parts of the Tisza valley and over most of the Tiszantúl, where, however, arable farming has been restricted by excessive waterlogging of the soil. The poorest quality

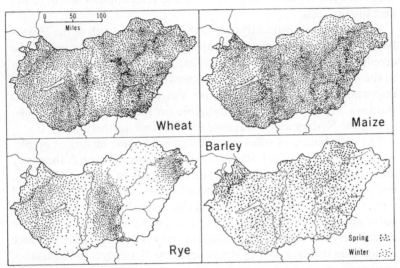

Fig. 10.6. Distribution of the principal crops of Hungary. After M. Pécsi and B. Sárfalvi.

soils are found in the hills and in the sandy regions of the Nyírség and between the Danube and Tisza. Cropland forms over 80 per cent of the total area in much of the Békés area of the south-east and of the Szabolcs-Szatmar areas in the north-east, and in parts of the Little Alföld, Somogy and Mezöföld.

Crop-farming. Hungary has traditionally been the granary for central Europe. It was the demand for bread-crops in Germany and Austria during the nineteenth century that drove animal husbandry from much of the plain, and led to the ploughing up of all land that was not too sterile or too damp. The bread-crops, easily stored and transported and always in steady demand, dominated the agriculture of most of Hungary. In 1938 the five crops: wheat, rye, barley, oats and maize, covered no less than 73·4 per cent of the total cropland.

The area has since diminished. In 1957, it was 68·2 per cent and in 1965, 61·2. The reduction has been almost entirely in the bread-crops, wheat and rye, compensated in part by an increase in acreage under maize. The yield of rye has fallen off sharply during this period, suggesting that it is cultivated today very largely on soils of the poorest quality. Total wheat production, however, is little reduced—2·35 million tons in 1965 as against an average of 2·19 in the 1930s, which suggests both better farming methods and restriction of wheat to the best quality soils.

Wheat is grown primarily east of the Tisza and south of the Hortobágy and Nyírség, where it generally occupies over 40 per cent of the cropland. This wheat-growing area extends west of the middle Tisza in the region of loess and alluvium known as the Jászság. It is locally important in the Little Alföld, the Vas and Zala regions and the Baranya and Bácska, but is negligible on the Danube-Tisza sands, and in the Nyírség and the Transdanubian and northern hills.

The distribution of other grain crops is in some measure complementary to that of wheat. Rye is overwhelmingly the crop of the sandy areas of the Great Alföld and of the hilly areas of western Hungary, and oats are most grown in the mountainous areas of the north and west. Only along the Dráva valley in the south does the cultivation of oats appear to have usurped land that might have been used for more valuable crops. The reason lies almost certainly in the great importance of horses in this area. Barley is nowhere a particularly important crop, but where grown tends to occupy the areas of heavier soil along the river valleys. Autumn-sown barley dominates in the south, spring-sown in the north.

Both maize and rice have come to be important only in recent years, though both have long been known and cultivated. Maize now covers over a quarter of the cropland, and is today so conspicuous in the Hungarian landscape that parts of the country have come to resemble the plains of the American Midwest. It is mainly a crop of the Great Alföld, where it is grown both on the poorly drained soils of the Hortobágy and on the dry soils between the Danube and Tisza. It occupies over a third of the cropland in large parts of Békés and Bácska, and is very important in the Mezőföld and all parts of the Tiszántúl except the extreme north.

Rice is grown only with irrigation, and is confined at present to the valleys of the Tisza, Körös and their tributaries, where the summer heat is greatest, and the lowlands most easily inundated. In 1964 the area under rice amounted to less than a half of 1 per cent of the cropland, and is not likely to increase greatly.

Root crops—potatoes, mangolds, and sugar-beet—together cover about 8 per cent of the total area, a proportion that has changed little for many years. The present tendency is for the acreage under potatoes and mangolds to decline and for that under sugar-beet to increase. The areas in which these crops are grown differ so sharply that there is no question of the one actually replacing the other. Sugar beet, its distribution controlled and fixed by that of sugar factories, is most important near Sopron, in the north-west, and near Békés in the east and in the upper Tisza valley. Potatoes are most grown in areas of light soil, unsuitable for most other crops. The Nyírség is an intensive potato-growing area, and the crop is important in the sands between the Danube and Tisza as well as in the Transdanubian and northern hills. Mangolds are cultivated most widely in the sands around Kecskemét and in the Little Alföld, where the demand for fodder crops is greater than in most other parts of the country.

The cultivation of fodder crops forms a pattern which is largely complementary with that of field grains. They are particularly important in the Little Alföld and Transdanubia, and of little significance over most of the Great Alföld. Clover is the most important fodder crop in the west and north; lucerne in the south and east.

Among the less important field crops is the sunflower. Its blaze of colour at midsummer gives the impression that it covers a wider area than in fact it does—a little over 1 per cent of all cropland, most of it in the north-eastern part of the Alföld. Flax is grown for linseed oil in some of the moister areas, especially the Sárret, Mezöföld and Hanság. Rape makes its appearance in the Tisza valley and in parts of Transdanubia and the Little Alföld, and tobacco cultivation is highly concentrated in the Nyírség and upper Tisza valley.

The grape-vine, most widely cultivated of all the fruit crops, is intensively grown on the sandy areas between the Danube and Tisza, where is to be found over half the area of vineyard, and on the sunny hillsides, especially of the Bakony, Mátra, Bükk, Zemplén and Villányi. In general, the sandy regions yield a *vin ordinaire*, and the hills, especially those which overlook Gyöngyös, Eger and, above all, Tokaj, yield a quality wine which is exported.

Animal husbandry. Animal rearing, formerly the dominant occupation of the Hungarian Plain, has given place to crop-farming over most of the area. Pasture covers only about 10 per cent of the total area, but

the extensive grazing of the Bugac, Hortobágy and Hajdúság is considered to be of poor quality. Good quality meadowland is extensive
only along the Danube and Tisza valleys.

Unlike Poland, Hungary did not lose a large part of its farm stock
during the Second World War, and the total number of farm animals
in 1964 was little different from the prewar totals. The number of
horses is reduced; that of pigs has increased considerably, and that of
sheep has almost doubled. The density of farm animals is far greater
west of the Danube and in the northern hills than over the great plain.
Cattle, both dairy and beef, are relatively numerous in the Little
Alföld, the Vas-Zala hills and the Mecsek. The long-horned, white
Hungarian cattle are scarce over most of the country, and can be
found in considerable numbers only in the north-east, where the traditions of animal rearing have survived most strongly. Pigs show a
similar predominance in the west, and are kept in immense numbers
near Budapest, where swill from the city is used to feed them. Sheep,
on the hand, show a more intensive distribution in the Great Alföld
than in western Hungary, and are more numerous on the poor
grazing land which is relatively extensive east of the Danube.

It is apparent that crop-farming contributes most to the total value
of agricultural production—about 60 per cent. The share of animal
husbandry has been declining steadily for the last ten years, and in
1960 was 38·2 per cent.

MANUFACTURING INDUSTRIES

Hungary has usually been thought of as a predominantly agricultural
country. Until the later years of the nineteenth century manufacturing
was, in effect, limited to the processing of the country's agricultural
products, and when factory industries were introduced, these were
commonly located in the mountainous borderland, in areas which are
no longer within the Hungarian state. Industrial development within
the reduced boundaries of Hungary was made difficult by the lack of
raw materials and for this reason tended to concentrate on light manufactures. On the eve of the Second World War, the total employment
in manufacturing industries, including those working in small crafts,
was only 721,000.

Since the establishment of the present regime and the introduction
of industrial plans, a sharp change has taken place. The number employed in manufacturing industries has approximately doubled since

1949, and since those engaged in crafts are now less numerous, employment in large factories has, in fact, increased almost threefold. A second change has been in the nature of the industries carried on. Light industry, which before the war was the dominant branch, now employs no more than a quarter of the industrially employed population. The food industries have declined sharply in relative importance, and heavy industry now accounts for two-thirds or more of both industrial production and employment. By 1956 over half the industrial workers were engaged in factories of over 1,000 employees, as against less than 2 per cent in 1938, and the importance of large factories becomes greater each year.

Fuel and energy

Hungary is not well placed to provide the power resources necessary for such an industrial development. Despite the developments now about to take place near Vác, on the Danube, the country's rivers have too flat a gradient and their flow is too variable for them to become an important source of hydro-electric power. In fact, at the present time there is only one hydro-electric station in the whole country, on the upper Tisza near Tokaj.

Coal mining. The coal resources of Hungary are relatively small; reserves have been put at about 113 million tons.[1] The only bituminous coal basin is in the Mecsek region, near Pécs and Komló, and in terms of total reserves it is by far the smallest in the country. The coal is of high calorific value, but occurs at a relatively great depth (2,000 to 2,500 feet) in seams which are thin and much folded. Despite the very great demand in recent years for coal of this quality, production has risen quite slowly. In 1954 it was 2·44 million tons; in 1964, only 4,125,400.

All other coal-fields yield at best a good quality brown coal; at worst, a low grade lignite. These come from beds of Tertiary age, and occur generally at depths shallow enough to permit open-cast mining. The best of the Tertiary coal is obtained from deposits—Eocene in age—along the northern margin of the Bakony, where the chief centres of mining are at Dorog and Tatabánya. Considerably more than half the total solid fuel reserves are in or close to the northern mountains. Most extensive of these reserves occur in the Sajó and adjoining

[1] A Hungarian source gives 2,400 million; this must include sub-bituminous coal and lignite.

valleys to the north of Miskolc; somewhat less abundant are the low grade upper Tertiary deposits which border the Mátra.

In contrast with the production of bituminous coal, that of brown coal and lignite has increased very sharply in recent years. From an output of 8·32 million tons in 1938, production rose to only 10·46 in 1949, but then expanded more rapidly, and in 1964 was about 27·5.

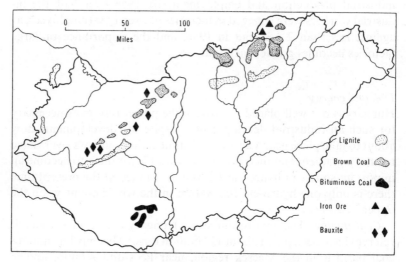

Fig. 10.7. Distribution of the principal mineral resources in Hungary. Based on *Politikai és Gazdasági Világatlasz*, Budapest, 1961.

Tatabánya has become by far the most productive of Hungarian coal-fields. A large part of the brown coal and lignite is used in electric generators close to the mines, and this has been a factor in the recent dispersion of manufacturing industry in Hungary.

Petroleum and natural gas. In recent years the middle part of the Danube valley has become important as a source of petroleum, but gives no indication that it will ever rival the resources and production of the lower valley. The largest reserves and most of the current output is from the Zala district, to the west of Lake Balaton. There is also a very small production from wells in the great plain near Szolnok, and from its northern margin at Eger.

The petroleum resources of the Hungarian Plain were not discovered until shortly before the Second World War, and production began only in 1938. Wells were exploited during the war which followed. Production recovered from its depressed postwar level, and reached its peak in 1955. This level has not been attained since, though output has again risen, and in 1964 was 1·8 million tons. In only one year, 1955, was Hungary able to cover more than half its petroleum needs from domestic sources. Imports, now mainly from the Soviet Union, but supplemented by a small import from Romania, considerably exceed domestic production. The 'Friendship' Pipeline, which enters Hungary from Slovakia to the north of Budapest, is beginning to replace the river tanker in the import of oil. Hungary's refineries, except that at Zala, are located on the river, and the new pipeline supplies crude oil to the refinery at Budapest.

Natural gas fields occur near the Zala oilfield and also more widely east of the Tisza. The production of natural gas has however been declining for several years. In 1964 it amounted to 784 million cubic feet, and was supplemented by an import of natural gas by pipeline from Romania.

Electric power production has been greatly expanded since the Second World War, and has been, in fact, the key to the country's industrial growth. From 2,625 million kilowatts in 1948 production has risen to 11,176 in 1965, but less than 1 per cent of this is generated at hydro-electric plants, and, unless the projected dam on the Danube at Vác is built, there is little chance of this being greatly expanded.

Metalliferous mining. The mines of Hungary were an important source of wealth for German bankers and merchants of the Renaissance, but the metalliferous areas of the country lay, with only minor exceptions, in the surrounding mountains, and were cut off from modern Hungary by the Treaty of Trianon. Today Hungary produces only one metalliferous mineral in significant quantities, bauxite; all others, including iron-ore, are very small in both total reserves and also in annual production.

Hungary's resources in bauxite, however, are among the largest in the world, and probably the most extensive in Europe. The deposits are closely related to the Bakony-Vértes hills, and occur in downfaulted basins along their north-western edge. The ore, aluminium hydroxide, was formed subaerially on the surface of Mesozoic limestone and dolomite, and was covered by the lower Tertiary before it could be denuded and lost. The ore occurs in thick beds, slightly faulted, and in general near enough to the surface to be extracted from open pits. The chief centres of production are today the Gánt field in the Vértes, and Iszkaszentgyörgy, Halimba and Nyirád, in the Bakony.

The only significant iron-ore deposits that were left to Hungary after 1920 are those of Rudabánya, in the Sajó valley, close to the Czechoslovak boundary. The ores occur as infillings in the limestones of the Borsód Karst. Total reserves are small, and production in 1964—the most productive year since the war—was only 188,000 tons, smaller than that of any other East European country with the exception only of Albania.

Other metals occur in Hungary, but in minute quantities: manganese, in association with the bauxite deposits; copper, lead and zinc, in association with the volcanic rocks of northern Hungary, and uranium. Of these, only manganese has any importance for modern Hungary.

The aluminium industry
The refining and smelting of bauxite is not only the most important metallurgical industry in Hungary, but the only one for which the country can be said to be naturally suited. It was not until the late 1920s that bauxite mining became important. Until 1935 the ore was exported, mainly to Germany, for refining. Since then, a domestic refining and smelting industry has been developed, and now handles about 60 per cent of a greatly increased ore production.

The aluminium industry consists of three distinct and often geographically separate processes: the preparation of alumina from the ore, the actual smelting by an electrolytic process, and the rolling of ingot aluminium into sheet. Oldest of the Hungarian processing works is the alumina works at Mosonmagyaróvár. During the Second World War a similar plant was built at Almásfüzitö. The very large demands on electric power made by the smelting industry delayed the building of smelters until after the war, when the Inota works, with a generator powered by local brown coal was put into operation. Smaller smelting works have been built at Ajka and Tatabánya. The aluminium rolling industry, lastly, is located at a distance from the smelters in Székesfehérvár and Budapest. The production of refined aluminium had risen by 1965 to 58,099 tons, and was still being expanded. The production of alumina was 267,000 tons in 1965, of which over half was exported to be smelted chiefly in East Germany and Czechoslovakia.

The iron and steel industry
The iron industry, formerly widely scattered through the northern hills, was important in nineteenth-century Hungary. The exhaustion

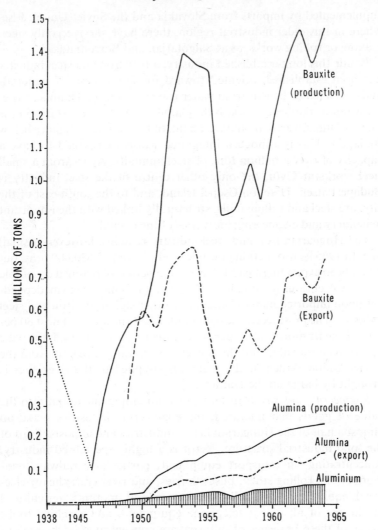

Fig. 10.8. Production and use of bauxite in Hungary, 1938–64.

of the iron-ore deposits and the replacement of charcoal with coal as fuel led to the abandonment of many of the small works, and the industry came to be concentrated at only a very small number of sites. In the northern mountains these have been reduced to only two integrated works—at Diósgyőr and Ózd respectively, which use local ore, supplemented by imports from Slovakia and the Soviet Union. Elsewhere in this older industrial region, there have survived only steel-making or rolling works, as at Salgótarján and Borsodnádasd.

Beside this long-established industry, a new iron and steel industry has been established, oriented toward foreign sources of materials and well sited to benefit from water transport on the Danube. Foremost among the newer works is the plant built under the first Five-Year Plan at Dunaújváros, on the west bank of the Danube, 40 miles below Budapest. This is a modern integrated works and is said to have a capacity of over a million tons of steel annually. Apart from a small steel works at Györ, the only other centre of the steel industry is Budapest itself. Here, on Csepel Island, and to the south-east of the city, are steel and rolling mills, structurally linked with the important machinery and engineering industries of the capital.

The Hungarian iron and steel industry remains, however, a small one. In 1965 its production of crude steel was only 2,520,000 tons, but it had been expanding steadily during the period of planned economic growth. A curious feature, however, is that it is more heavily dependent upon imported materials than any other significant iron and steel industry. The most recent statistics published show that almost 80 per cent of the iron-ore and 75 per cent of the fuel are imported, the coke from Czechoslovakia and the Soviet Union, the ore mainly from the Soviet Union. Much of the materials supplied to the river sites is brought by barge up the Danube.

Engineering industries. In terms of both employment and also the value of goods manufactured, the engineering industries make up almost a half of the Hungarian heavy industries and almost a third of the total industrial structure. Yet it is a highly specialised industry, concentrating on transport equipment, particularly railway locomotives and rolling stock, buses, lorries, and river craft; heavy electrical equipment, especially generators and motors; agricultural machinery of all kinds; telephone equipment, and machine tools. Many of these branches of industry are concentrated in the area of greater Budapest, where the northern part of Csepel Island has the most important concentration of heavy industry in the whole country. But metal-using industries are also found in the older industrial areas of northern Hungary, at Miskolc, Eger and Gyöngyös, as well as at Györ and near the Austrian border. Recently there has been a wider dispersion of these industries, and most cities except the smallest today have a factory in one branch or other of the metal industries. Some of

the more important of these newer centres of the engineering industries are Kiskunfélegyháza (steel construction work), Békéscsaba
(machine tools), Mosonmagyaróvár and Szombathely (agricultural
machinery), Gödöllö, Pápa and Debrecen (electrical equipment), and
Székesfehérvár (telephone equipment).

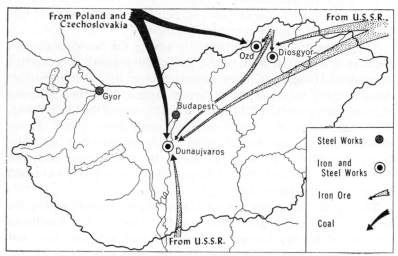

Fig. 10.9. The iron and steel industry, showing the source of raw materials.
Based on M. Pécsi and B. Sárfalvi.

Chemical industry
The Hungarian chemical industry was established between the world
wars and greatly expanded after the Second. It is located mainly in the
area of greater Budapest. Its most important branches are still the
processing of the by-products of the coke ovens and oil refineries. The
manufacture of agricultural fertilisers is being expanded, and new
factories have been built along the Danube south of the city and at
Szolnok, on the Tisza. The manufacture of rubber, dyestuffs and
pharmaceuticals is concentrated in Budapest. Cement manufacture
has been much expanded, as it has also in other East European
countries, but in 1965 had reached only 2,383,000 tons, much of it
from the neighbourhood of Tatabánya, where brown coal as well as
clay and limestone are available.

Light industries
The light industries play a comparatively small role in Hungary's
industrial structure, and contribute not more than a quarter of the

total industrial output. The industrial plans of recent years have given little emphasis to industries of this kind, and their relative importance has long been declining. The food industries form the most important group, and are also the oldest branch of manufacturing industry in modern Hungary. The flour-milling and sugar-refining industries, brewing and the preparation of meat and dairy products are carried on mainly in small factories widely scattered over the Great and Little Alföld and in the region of greater Budapest.

Textile manufacture is outstanding among the branches of light industry. It is also one of the oldest, and for this reason is concentrated in western Hungary. Cotton manufacture is the most important branch; about two-thirds of its factory capacity is in Budapest, and the remainder is scattered through the small towns of the Little Alföld. The manufacture of woollen and linen cloth shows a very similar distribution. The only branch of the textile industry that has really become established in the great plain is the manufacture of coarse fibres—hemp, flax and jute—at Szeged, where the industry was based originally on local materials.

The leather industries are carried on almost entirely within the Budapest industrial region. Industries based on wood and cellulose are obliged to rely heavily on imported materials and have not achieved any great importance. The furniture industry is located mainly in Budapest, with small establishments in the larger provincial cities. The cellulose and paper industries are also mostly in Budapest and along the upper Danube, where river transport is available for their bulky raw materials.

TRANSPORT AND TRADE

The modern transport pattern of Hungary was developed during the nineteenth century when much of Hungary was little more than a colonial dependency of Austria. Its purpose was primarily to link Hungary with Austria, but the arrangement of rivers and hills made it inevitable that the Hungarian part of the Austro-Hungarian transport system should focus on Budapest.

Internal transport
A feature of the transport system of Hungary is the relatively considerable use that is made of the roads. Well over half the goods transported are carried by lorries. It is evident, however, that road transport

predominates only in short hauls, and that for longer distances, the railway comes into its own. Table 59 illustrates the relative importance of the several means of transport.

Table 59. Means of transport

	Goods carried (*thousands of tons*)	Goods carried (*millions of ton-kilometres*)
Railways	114,658	17,036·7
Roads	197,711	2,608·2
Rivers and canals	7,558	1,759·0
Air	5	6·9
Pipelines	3,419	346·6
	323,351	21,757·4

Source: *Statisztikai Évkönyv, 1965*, Budapest.

Railway system. The 5,500 miles of the Hungarian railway system forms a pattern radiating from Budapest. The most important branches are the lines westward to Györ and thence to Bratislava and Vienna; south-west through Székesfehérvár to Ljubljana and Italy; eastward to Miskolc and, via Szolnok, to Debrecen, and south-eastward, through Békéscsaba, to Romania, and through Kecskemét and Szeged to Yugoslavia. There are comparatively few cross-country routes, and travel between west and east Hungary is hindered by the absence of bridges across the Danube below Budapest, except at Dunaföldvár and Baja.

Only the main lines are double tracked, and 88 per cent of the system still has only a single track. Most are operated with steam locomotives, but the line from Vienna to Budapest has been electrified, and that eastward to Miskolc is in process of being converted to electric operation; in 1964, only 310 miles had been electrified.

Road system. The network of main roads parallels very closely that of the railways, and consists basically of a pattern radiating from Budapest. The main roads are surfaced, but are sometimes rather narrow. The secondary roads, which constitute very roughly a series of concentric circles around Budapest, are often narrow and rough.

Navigable waterways. The course of the Danube through Hungary is navigable in its entirety, except when obstructed by ice. In addition the Tisza is regularly navigable from Dombrád, near the Slovak border, to the Yugoslav boundary, and at times also upstream to Vásárosnamény close to the Romanian. The Körös is navigable upstream as far as Békés. The Hortobágy, Ferenc, and Sió Canals are also sometimes navigable though little used,

The Danube in its course across the Hungarian Plain is one of the most intensively used of European rivers, and a very large part of Hungary's commerce with the Soviet Union and also with Bulgaria and Yugoslavia is by river barge. The most extensive docks are in Budapest itself, where they are located mainly on Csepel Island, close to the industrial suburbs. Other important river ports are Györ, Komárom, Dunaújváros, Baja, and Mohács. The Tisza has been made navigable for almost its entire course in Hungary by the building of the Tiszalök dam. It takes, however, a smaller barge than is usual on the Danube, and is very much less used. It is planned to make the Hortobágy canal navigable throughout its length, and this is likely to lead to a greater use of the Tisza, as agricultural products from the Hortobágy and Hajdúság will be able to take a water route to market.

Foreign trade

Until very recently Hungary was primarily an exporter of farm products and an importer of manufactured goods, fuel and industrial raw materials. Though domestic manufactures increased in importance between the two wars, this traditional Hungarian pattern of trade came to be modified only in detail. Hungary's commercial agreements with Germany in the 1930s tended, in fact, to stereotype the earlier trading pattern. This has changed radically since the Second World War. Manufacturing industries have come to be more important in the national economy than agriculture; the volume of total trade has grown more than four-fold, and the import in particular of fuel and industrial raw materials has increased. The import of manufactured goods has increased steadily, as the more complex industrial economy comes to require a wider range of factory made goods. At the same time, the export of manufactured goods increased; about 1940 it drew level with that of agricultural produce, and by 1965, the volume of export of factory-made goods was more than three times that of farm products.

The value and relative importance of the chief categories of exports and imports is shown in Table 60.

Table 60. Hungary's foreign trade 1965—by commodity (in millions of exchange forints)

	Imports	Exports
1. Live animals	5·0	38·4
2. Food-stuffs	909·7	2,966·6
3. Raw materials for food industries	806·0	909·8
4. Other raw materials of vegetable or animal origin	3,277·4	896·2
5. Fuel, minerals, metals	4,904·0	2,570·4
6. Chemicals, fertilisers, rubber	1,783·7	612·5
7. Building materials	203·8	150
8. Machinery and equipment	5,014·5	5,800·5
9. Manufactured consumer goods	944·4	3,776·9
	17,848·5	17,721·3

Source: *UN International Yearbook of International Trade Statistics, 1965.*

Hungary's trade is strongly oriented toward other members of the Communist bloc, though trade with non-bloc countries has tended to increase in recent years. In most instances there is an approximate equality in the value of exports to and of imports from each trading partner, the result of the barter-agreements negotiated by the Hungarian government. The direction of Hungarian trade in 1965 was as shown in Table 61.

The volume of trade has increased very sharply in the fifteen years following the Second World War. There was a recession in 1956–57, the result of the Hungarian 'Rising' of October 1956, followed by an almost continuous growth.

18

Table 61. *Hungary's foreign trade—by countries* (*in millions of U.S. dollars*)

	Exports	Imports
USSR	525·4	553·3
Eastern Europe:	499·6	444·2
of which: East Germany	135·1	131·2
Poland	105·0	88·3
Czechoslovakia	179·3	131·5
Romania	28·7	38·8
Yugoslavia	29·2	27·3
Bulgaria	20·3	22·1
Albania	2·0	2·0
Other Communist countries	32·7	20·7
Industrial West (including Japan)	321·5	381·2

Source: *Foreign Trade of the European Satellites in 1965: A Statistical Summary*, CIA, Washington, 1966.

Bibliography
General
Földrajzi Atlasz, Budapest, 1958.
HELMREICH, ERNEST, ed., *Hungary, East-Central Europe under the Communists*, London, Stevens, 1957.
PÉCSI, MARTON and BÉLA SÁRFALVI, *The Geography of Hungary*, London Collets, 1964.
Politikai és Gazdasági Világatlasz, Budapest, 1961.
Ungarn: das Antlitz einer Nation, Budapest, 1940.

Historical and Political Geography
BURGHARDT, ANDREW F. *Borderland*, University of Wisconsin Press, 1962.
KAAN, KAROLY, *A magyar Alföld*, Budapest, 1927.
LENTACKER, FIRMIR, 'L'installation humaine dans la grande plaine hongroise', *Annls Géogr*. **59** (1950), 51–3.
MACARTNEY, C. A., *Hungary and Her Successors*, Oxford University Press, 1937.
— *Hungary, A Short History*, Edinburgh University Press, 1962.

MACARTNEY, C. A., *October Fifteenth: A History of Modern Hungary*, Edinburgh University Press, 1947.

MARCZALI, HENRY, *Hungary in the Eighteenth Century*, Cambridge University Press, 1910.

SINOR, DENIS, *History of Hungary*, London, Allen & Unwin, 1959.

TELEKI, COUNT PAUL, *The Evolution of Hungary and its Place in European History*, New York, Macmillan, 1923.

VON SOO, RUDOLF, 'Die Entstehung der ungarischen Puszta', *Ungarischer Jahrbucher*, **6** (1927), 258–76.

WANKLYN, HARRIET, 'The Role of Peasant Hungary in Europe', *Geogr. J.*, **97** (1941), 18–35.

Physical Geography

CONARD, HENRY S. 'The Background of Plant Ecology', Iowa State College Press, 1951 (essentially a translation of Anton Kerner, *Das Pflanzenleben der Donaulander*).

MIKLOS, GYULA, ed. *Studies in Hungarian Geographical Sciences*, Hungarian Academy of Sciences, Budapest, 1960.

NEMETH, KALMAN, 'Die genetische Gliederung der Boden Ungarns', *Giessener Abhandlungen zur Agrar- und Wirtschaftsforschung des Europaischen Ostens*, Giessen, 1962.

PECSI, MARTON, ed. *Ten Years of Physico-Geographic Research in Hungary*, Budapest, Hungarian Academy of Sciences, 1964.

RUNGALDIER, RANDOLF, 'Natur- und Kulturlandschaft zwischen Donau und Theiss', *Abhandlungen der Geographischen Gesellschaft in Wien*, **14**, Heft 4 (1943).

SÁRFALVI, B., ed. *Applied Geography in Hungary*, Budapest, Hungarian Academy of Sciences, 1964.

Population and Settlement

BEYNON, ERDMANN D. 'Budapest: an Ecological Study', *Geogrl Rev.* **33** (1943), 256–75.

COMPTON, P. A. 'The New Socialist Town of Dunaujvaros', *Geography*, **50** (1965), 288–91.

DEN HOLLANDER, A. N. J. *Nederzettingsvormen -problemen in de Groote Hongaarsche Laagvlakte*, Amsterdam, 1947.

— 'The Great Hungarian Plain: a European Frontier Area', *Comparative Studies in Society and History*, vol. 3, 1960–61, 74–88; 155–69.

ENYEDI, GEORGE, 'Le village hongrois et la grande exploitation agricole', *Annls Géogr.*, **73** (1964), 687–700.

DE LACGER, L. 'La Plaine hongroise: Alfold et Puszta', *Annls Géogr.*, **10** (1901), 438–44.

LEWIS, W. STANLEY, 'Some Aspects of *Tanya* Settlement in Hungary', *Scott. geogr. Mag.*, **54** (1938), 358–66.

MAYER, ROBERT, 'Die Alföldstädte', *Abhandlungen der Geographischen Gesellschaft in Wien*, **14** (1943).

MEYER, PETER, *et al. The Jews in the Soviet Satellites*, Syracuse University Press, 1953.

PRINZ, GYULA, 'Die Siedlungsformen Ungarns', *Ungarischen Jahrbucher*, **4** (1924), pp. 127–42; 335–52.

SIEGEL, JACOB S. 'The Population of Hungary'. Washington, DC, US Department of Commerce, Bureau of the Census, 1958.

RUNGALDIER, R. 'Kecskemet, Landschaft und Wirtschaft im Mittelpunkt der ungarischen Flugsandkultur', *Mitt. geogr. Ges. Wien*, **74** (1931), 113–34.

— 'Szegedin: Landeskundliche Skizze einer sudungarischen Stadt', *Geogr. Anz.*, **32** (1931), 65–74.

ZOLTAI, LOUIS, 'Debrecen and the Hortobagy Puszta', *Sociological Review*, **16** (1924), 336–43.

Economic Geography

ALBITRECCIA, ANTOINE, 'La région vinicole de Tokaj', *Annls Géogr.*, **45** (1936), 190–92.

ENYEDI, I. 'The "Kossuth" Collective Farm of Bekescsaba in the Southern Part of the Great Hungarian Plain', *Geographica Polonica*, **5** (1965), 407–20.

GEORGE, PIERRE, 'Les transformations des campagnes Hongroises', *Annls Géogr.*, **60** (1951), 199–209.

Magyar statisztikai zsebkönyv 1966, Budapest.

MIKLÓS, GYULA, ed. *Studies in Hungarian Geographical Sciences*, Hungarian Academy of Sciences, Budapest, 1960.

'The Party and the Peasant', *East Europe*, **6** (1957), No. 11, 14–24.

SÁRFALVI, B. 'The Village of Csepreg in Western Hungary', *Geographica Polonica*, **5** (1965), 437–52.

— ed. *Geographical Types of Hungarian Agriculture*, Budapest, Hungarian Academy of Sciences, 1966.

SIMON, L. 'Nyiradony-Village in North East of the Great Hungarian Plain', *Geographica Polonica*, **5** (1965), 421–36.

Statistical Yearbook, annually, Budapest (English and Russian translation).

VON TAUBINGER, LASZLO M. 'Die Industrialisierung Ungarns', *Ost-Probleme*, 7 (1955), 712–17.

WINKLER, ARNO, 'Ungarns landwirtschaftsgeographische Gestaltung', *Ungarische Bibliotek*, 2er Reihe, Bd 8, Berlin 1938.

ZAGOROFF, S. D. *The Agricultural Economy of the Danubian Countries 1935–45*, Oxford University Press, 1956.

CHAPTER ELEVEN

Romania

The nucleus around which modern Romania has been built, as Yugoslavia was around the Kingdom of Serbia, consisted of the two principalities of Walachia and Moldavia. They lie against the outer curve of the Carpathian Mountains-Transylvanian Alps, and extend respectively to the Danube and to the Prut. These provinces were subject to the Turks, but distance spared them the worst excesses of Turkish rule. Here the Turks did not settle; they created no feudally-owned estates and they established no *čiflik* villages. Their exploitation of the country consisted rather in drawing off its agricultural surplus to feed Constantinople. The provinces were for centuries ruled by *hospodars*, sometimes chosen from among the native aristocracy, but more often Greeks from the Phanar quarter of Constantinople.

THE MAKING OF THE ROMANIAN STATE

During the eighteenth century, as Turkish power and authority waned in the Balkan peninsula that of Russia increased (see Chapter 4). The Russian Tsars became by the Treaty of Kuchuk Kainarji (1774) the protectors of the Christianity within the Turkish Empire and thus acquired in effect a vague right to interfere whenever and wherever they desired in the affairs of the Turkish Empire in Europe. Russia's interests lay primarily in securing a foothold near the Turkish Straits, or at least in preventing anyone else from doing so, and Romania lay directly in her path towards that goal. Russian influence with the *hospodars* and among the boyars of Romania was steadily increasing. For much of the first half of the nineteenth century the two principalities constituted a sort of dual monarchy in which legal power was vested in the Turkish Sultan and effective control in the Russian Tsar.

Romanian independence
From 1821 the hospodars ceased to be Phanariote Greeks, brought up in the civil service of the Sultans, and henceforward were native

Romanians, co-religionists of the Tsar and more susceptible to Russian influence, but at the same time more distrustful of the Tsars. At the same time a sense of Romanian nationhood was growing. In the past the dominant cultural influences had been Slav; more recently Greek influences had become important with Ottoman control of the country exercised through Phanariote officials. Only in the ninteenth century did a truly Romanian feeling begin to show itself. It owed much to French encouragement and was limited for a time to young intellectuals who had been strongly influenced by the writings of the French enlightenment and had come to think of their country as an eastern outpost of Romance culture. Then came the realisation that Romania, like France, had been part of the Roman Empire, whose language and culture they fondly thought had survived in the mountains of Transylvania, while Slav and Magyar barbarism swirled around this region of refuge. Nations are built upon illusions regarding their past, and not least the Romanian. Trajan's column in the Roman forum, with its portrayal in *bas-relief* of the Roman conquest of Dacia, became almost a symbol of Romanian nationalism.

An unsuccessful insurrection took place in 1848. Its leaders were weak and divided; they had failed to enlist the support of the peasants, whose lot was amongst the heaviest of any in Eastern Europe; above all, the military power of Russia lay beyond the Prut, able and ready to intervene to suppress any movement that seemed to threaten the interests of the Tsars.

It was the Crimean War (1853–56) that in the end brought about the union of the two Principalities and the creation of the modern Kingdom of Romania. The British and French aimed to protect what remained of the Turkish Empire from the Russians, and to free the Principalities from subservience to the Tsar. At the same time they were becoming increasingly aware of Romania as a source of food for their growing urban populations, and aimed to improve Danube navigation so that it might reach their markets more cheaply. It was easier at the end of the Crimean War to exclude Russian influence from the Principalities than it was to secure agreement on what to do with them. France, in line with her 'romance' policy towards them, hoped to unite the Principalities into a Romanian state. Great Britain, opportunist as always, hoped to preserve the authority of the Sultan, whose cause they vigorously supported, over two weak Principalities. The result was a compromise which had nothing to recommend it except that none of the Powers was prepared to reject it. The Principalities, it was decided, primarily by Great Britain and France in 1858, were to remain politically separate, to elect each its own parliament and prince, but to entrust to a joint commission matters which concerned them jointly.

The Romanian Principalities. This settlement, 'intrinsically clumsy and grossly insulting to the national sentiment of the Romanians',[1] was quickly nullified. The two Principalities elected the same prince, Alexander Cuza, an act which the Western politicians had not the wit to foresee, and two years later Cuza proclaimed the union of the two principalities. Thus, on 23 December 1861, Romania was born, and Walachian Bucharest was chosen as its capital, in preference to Iaşi, the rival capital of Moldavia.

In 1866 those whose interests had been threatened by Cuza's attempts at reform brought about his deposition. The throne was then offered to Prince Charles of Hohenzollern-Sigmaringen, a member of a branch of the Hohenzollerns of Prussia. Bismarck, his eyes on the strategic advantages of a dynastic ally in the lower Danube, urged Charles to accept, and the latter, travelling in disguise by Danube steamer, reached Orşova, was acclaimed, accepted, and ruled until his death in 1914.

Rounding out the state

The reign of Charles, or Carol, as he was known in Romania, was one of relative stability politically and of economic growth. A railway system was built; the grain export reached substantial proportions; petroleum was discovered and its exploitation brought Romania to the forefront as an oil producer. At the same time the lot of the peasantry was improved, though Charles, unlike his predecessor, undertook no far-reaching schemes for land reform, and a sense of Romanian nationhood spread downwards from the small intelligentsia to the masses. The Romanians of the two Principalities began to view with increasing concern the fate of their fellow Romanians in Hungary, Russia and Bulgaria and even in the remote Píndhos Mountains of Greece. There was thus a *Romania Irredenta* upon which Romanian nationalists began to focus their ambitions.

The Bessarabian question. In this respect the history of Romania began inauspiciously. The Turkish Empire had at its greatest extent reached far into the Ukraine (see page 83). The Tsar had in 1791 stripped away the lands beyond the Dnestr, and in 1812 took from

[1] J. A. R. Marriott, *The Eastern Question*, Oxford, 1924, pp. 299–300.

the Sultan the whole of Bessarabia (Basarabia). This province lay between the Dniestr and the Prut, and extended south to the lower Danube and to the most northerly of the channels, the Chilia (Kilia) branch, in its delta. Its population was mixed, but Moldavians formed a large minority and locally a majority of the population, and Moldavian boyars were the leading landowners and had played an important role in the administration of the province. It was not without reason that Romanian nationalists look covetously at Bessarabia.

In 1856 they reaped a partial reward, when, by the Treaty of Paris which ended the Crimean War, the Western Powers forced Russia to give up the three most southerly districts of Bessarabia, and to allow them to be added to Moldavia. By this means Romania acquired a curving tract of land, almost 40 miles wide, extending from the middle Prut valley to the Dniestr estuary near Cetatea Albă (Akkerman).

In 1877 Russia was again at war with the Turkish Empire (see page 91), and in return for the privilege of sending troops across Romania to the borders of the Turkish Empire, the Tsar undertook to 'maintain and defend the integrity of Romania'. In the next year he annexed southern Bessarabia. The loss was keenly felt in Romania, and during the First World War the Central Powers held out the possibility of its restoration if Romania would only side with them against Russia. The Moldavian national movement meanwhile had made progress within Bessarabia, and seized control of its organs of government at the time of the Menshevik revolution. Attempts by the Bolshevik army to quell this movement served only to intensify it and bring Romanian forces to its aid. The provisional government early in 1918 declared the complete independence of Bessarabia, and a couple of months later voted for union with Romania. Most of the Western Allies recognised the change, but the Soviet Union never acquiesced in the loss. The boundary along the Dniestr remained closed for most of the years between the two world wars, and for much of this period diplomatic relations were severed between Romania and the Soviet Union.

With the outbreak of the Second World War the Soviet Union renewed its claims on Bessarabia, and in June, of 1940, when most of Romania's allies were deeply committed to the war in the west, the Soviet Union issued an ultimatum, demanding the session not only of Bessarabia but also of the northern part of Bucovina, a province which Romania had acquired from Austria at the end of the First

18*

World War (see below, page 537). Romania had no recourse, and by the end of the month Soviet troops had taken possession of the territory in question. Romania, it is true, reoccupied both Bessarabia and Bucovina for a short period, when the German armies had driven deep into Russia, but in the course of 1944 the Soviet forces returned, and the peace treaty of 1947 between Romania and the allies confirmed the cession of Bessarabia, most of which was absorbed into the Moldavian SSR, and of northern Bucovina, which was added to the Ukrainian SSR.

The Bessarabian question may again become a political issue. The Moldavian SSR has still a large Romanian population, and Romanian authorities have been emboldened in recent years to suggest its return. The Soviet Union is now, in virtue of its annexation of Bessarabia, a Danubian Power, occupying the left bank of the lower river, below the junction of the Prut, and of its Chilia Channel.

Dobrogea. When the Russians occupied Southern Bessarabia in 1877–78 they allowed Romania to seek compensation at the expense of the Turkish territory south of the Danube. Dobrogea is a low plateau, bounded on the west and north by the Danube. To the east is the Black Sea, and towards the south the plateau merges into the platform of northern Bulgaria. Its population was almost as diverse as that of Bessarabia. Toward the north Romanians were numerous, but over much of the area Bulgars constituted the largest single ethnic group, and Turks a large minority (see page 565). In 1878 the province of Dobrogea, as far south approximately as a line from Silistra on the Danube to Mangalia on the Black Sea, was ceded to Romania. During the First Balkan War (1912–13) Romania began to demand changes in the Dobrogea boundary. In the following year Bulgaria, defeated in the Second Balkan War, was obliged to cede Southern Dobrogea to Romania, though its population was made up overwhelmingly of Bulgars and Turks.

By the Treaty of Bucharest of May 1918, the Germans forced Romania to cede to Bulgaria not only Southern Dobrogea, but also Northern, which had been in Romanian possession since 1878. This treaty was, however, never ratified, and was in fact renounced as a condition of the German armistice six months later. The Treaty of Neuilly made no further change: Romania already held more territory in Dobrogea than was justified by any ethnic consideration. Possession of Dobrogea was, however, of great importance. It gave Romania control of the Danube mouths, possession of the port of

Constanţa, and the opportunity to develop resorts along the Black Sea coast.

In September 1940, the Treaty of Craiova was imposed upon Romania by the Germans. Though it was concerned primarily with Hungarian claims, the Romanians were compelled to retrocede Southern Dobrogea to Bulgaria. The treaty did, however, make provision for an exchange of the Romanian population living in the area for Bulgars living in Northern Dobrogea. In this way, it is said, about 50,000 left Romania, and about twice as many Romanians from Southern Dobrogea moved north. The loss of this essentially non-Romanian territory seemed to cause little criticism within Romania.

The peace treaty of 1947, in this respect at least, confirmed the Craiova agreement, and the Romanian boundary in Dobrogea was thus restored to the line established by the Russians in 1878.

Transylvania and the Banat. Throughout the period of its existence as an independent state Romanian irredentism was focused on the lands beyond the Carpathian Mountains and Transylvanian Alps. Here, they liked to think, lay the homeland of the Romanian people, and here, during the later years of the nineteenth century and early years of the twentieth lived no less than 2,800,000 Romanians under the unenlightened and unsympathetic rule of the Hungarians. It was to secure the return of these peoples to the Romanian fold that Ion Brătianu, the prime minister, sided with the Allies and in August 1916 attacked the Central Powers. The war which followed was short and disastrous. The country was quickly overrun by German, Bulgarian and Turkish forces, and by the Treaty of Bucharest of May 1918, Romania ceded, not only much of Dobrogea, as has been noted, but also a tract in northern Moldavia and a narrow strip of territory, on average about five miles wide, which followed the Transylvanian Alps and Carpathian Mountains for most of the distance from the Iron Gate to Bucovina. The purpose was thus to establish Germany or her allies on the outer face of the mountain range and to deprive the Romanians of any tactical advantage which possession of the crest might have conferred. A year later Romania reaped an abundant revenge. The price of her intervention in the war was paid, though not in quite as full a measure as Brătianu had hoped. Romania secured Transylvania, the Banat and Bucovina.

These are, we have seen (page 58), regions of extreme ethnic diversity. Romanians, or Walachs, were a kind of substratum, but over the area as a whole formed only about 58 per cent of the population of these provinces.[1] The rest was made up of Magyars, Germans, Jews, Slovaks, Ruthenes or Ukrainians, Gypsies and even Bulgars. The Jewish population was predominantly urban. The German minority lived mainly in the Transylvanian Basin, between Braşov in the east and Alba Iulia, and in the plains of the Banat. The Hungarian-speaking peoples, here known as the Szeklers, or Szekély, constituted the largest minority, at least a quarter of the total population at this time. They inhabited (see below) the margin of the Pannonian Plain from the region of Timişoara in the south to the Slovakian hills in the north. Very few had settled in the Bihor region, but they were scattered through the hills between the Cara (Körös) and Someş, without however constituting a majority. To the east, however, they were more numerous. Cluj was predominantly a Szekler town; many of the surrounding villages were inhabited mainly by Szekély, and eastern Transylvania, from Targu Mureş south-east to Braşov and eastward to the Carpathian ranges was, with few interruptions, solidly Szekler.

The pattern of ethnic minorities greatly complicated the drawing of boundaries. In order to include the numerous Romanians of Bihor and of the hills lying to the north, Romania was obliged to incorporate the Transylvanian Germans and Szeklers. And these Romanians of the north-western hill-country were themselves dependent upon a line of cities and market-centres which bordered the Hungarian Plain and were predominantly Magyar. Furthermore, these cities, from Satu Mare to Timişoara, were linked by a railway which skirted the hills and ran through some rural areas which were heavily Hungarian. Efficiency, as understood by Romania and her allies, required that the hillpeople should not be cut off from their markets, and that the latter continue to be interconnected by rail. Thus, Romanian claims extended well into the Hungarian Plain in the north-west, and to the west aimed to include the Banat. The Western Powers recognised these claims, though not without some misgiving. The boundary which they delimited was recognised as discriminating against Hungary, but the alternative was felt to be unduly harsh towards Romania.

In the Banat, however, they encountered the claims, no less strongly pressed, and supported by western opinion, of Yugoslavia. The Banat was partitioned, and approximately the north-eastern half was incorporated in Romania. Even here, though the Romanians constituted

[1] This is based on postwar Romanian statistics and probably does less than justice to the minorities.

the largest ethnic group, they probably formed at this time something less than a majority.

Bucovina. The case of Bucovina differed from that of Transylvania and the Banat in so far as it was taken from Austria, not Hungary, and that its non-Romanian population was Ruthene rather than Magyar. In terms of physical geography it represented an extension of the plains and plateaus of northern Moldavia. It extended from the high Carpathians to the Dniestr, and was historically a passage way from Podolia into the Ukraine. In 1776 it was acquired by the Austrian Empire from the Turks, and during the nineteenth century the area, which had not previously had any separate administration, became a distinct governmental unit within the Habsburg Empire. It had always been a borderland between Romanian and Slav. The northern, or lowland area of Bucovina was predominantly Ruthene; the more southerly and mountainous, Romanian. In Cernăuţi, the capital and in the market towns was a large Jewish population, and there was also a scattering of Germans in the southern parts of the province. During the nineteenth century the Ruthene and Jewish population increased relative to the Romanian, and the Romanian government expressed fears for the survival of Romanian culture. The addition of Bucovina to the Romanian state was desired as ardently as that of Transylvania, and when, at the end of the First World War, the Ruthenes in Bucovina attempted to have their province incorporated in the Soviet Ukraine, Romanian armies marched in. Shortly afterwards the other ethnic groups of Bucovina voted for incorporation into Romania. By the Treaty of St. Germain (September 1919) Austria was obliged to cede Bucovina to Romania, with the exception only of a minute area in the north. This went to Poland solely on account of the minor railway centre of Zaleszczycki, which was necessary for the maintenance of communications in south-eastern Poland.

Thus were established the boundaries of the Romanian state. Romania reaped generously the reward for her participation in the war and of the military defeat of all her neighbours, to which she had contributed so little. Romanians made up less than 72 per cent of the population of the state, and with most of the half dozen significant minority groups the Romanians felt that they had little in common. The ethnic problems which resulted are, however, discussed later.

The Second World War and after

The hostility of Hungary, Bulgaria and the Soviet Union towards

Romania lasted throughout the inter-war years. As the danger of hostilities grew closer, the Romanian government attempted to protect itself, on the one hand, by increased dependence upon Hitler, and, on the other, by building defences against Hungary. Neither succeeded. Hitler did not protect Romania from Hungarian irredentism, and when the two countries failed to agree on redrawing the boundaries in Transylvania, Germany and Italy intervened and did the job for them. The Vienna Award of the end of August 1940, gave to Hungary a broad tongue of land, about 16,000 square miles in area which extended, north of the Bihor massif, eastward and southeastward almost to Braşov. It included most of the Magyar and Szekler minorities and about a million Romanians as well.

Romania declared war on the Soviet Union in June 1941, at the same time as Germany, and Romanian armies fought alongside German in the invasion of the Ukraine. As if to compensate for the loss of much of Transylvania, Hitler allowed the Romanians to annex and administer the area lying east of the Dniestr, much of which made up the Moldavian SSR. But the Romanians became restless when Hitler's advance was stopped, and actually rebellious as his armies began to retreat. In the spring of 1944 Romania agreed to Allied terms; acquiesced in the Soviet occupation of Bessarabia, but secured the return of northern Transylvania from Hungary. In August the Romanians, their country invaded by the Russian armies, turned on their former allies, the Germans and Hungarians, and recovered Transylvania by their own efforts. The old boundaries were reconfirmed by the treaty of peace of February 1947 between the Allied Powers and Germany's former satellites.

Romania emerged from the Second World War, shorn of some 19 per cent of its territory. Its population was reduced by about 3 million. but the size of its minorities was reduced more than proportionately. It is this Romania which is described in the following pages.

LANDFORM REGIONS

Despite the complexity of its structure and relief, Romania presents a relatively simple pattern of landforms: a sharply curving line of folded mountains, with, along its outer margin, foothills and plains, and, within it the isolated Bihor massif and the upland basin of Transylvania.

Carpathian Mountains

A distance of 50 miles separates Slovakia from the north-western boundary of Romania. Between lies the Podkarpatska Rus, that region of Czechoslovakia which was ceded to the Soviet Union in 1945. In this way Romania lost direct contact with its former ally, and the Soviet Union came to extend its direct control into the Pannonian Plain itself.

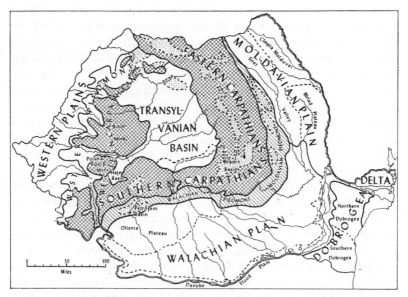

Fig. 11.1. Landform regions of Romania; based mainly on *Monografia Geografica a Republicii Populare Romîne*, Vol. I, Bucharest, 1960.

The structure and relief of the Carpathian Mountains of northern Romania resemble, despite the interruption, those of eastern Slovakia. They consist of ranges lying roughly parallel to one another, built of Secondary and Tertiary sediments around a crystalline core, intruded by volcanics and separated by upland basins of widely varying size and economic importance. These mountains extend south-eastward from the Soviet border for about 160 miles. Then the ranges appear to make an abrupt turn, as they continue to the west for another 140 miles. A more gentle curve towards the south-west then brings them down to the gorges of the Danube and the boundary with Yugoslavia.

The changes of direction delimit the three major segments of the range, which are here called the Eastern, the Southern and the Western Carpathians. Though differing somewhat in structure, they have all experienced a similar history. After they were folded early in the Tertiary period, the whole region was planated, and reduced to a platform. This is now represented by an undulating summit level at about 6,000 feet, called by de Martonne the Boresco surface. This surface is conspicuous in the Rodna Mountains in the Eastern Carpathians and over a more extensive area in the Southern and Western. Below the level of this highest surface is another, called the Rîu Şes, which has, as it were been cut into its flanks. It lies at an altitude of about 4,500 feet, and occurs as a broad shelf around the higher platform in the Southern and Western Carpathians, but is very much less extensive in the northern. The lowest surface, the Gornovitză is the most extensive. Not only does it appear as a shelf or terrace at about 3,300 feet around all the higher mountain masses, but it extends over much of the Eastern Carpathians.

Much work remains to be done in identifying these erosion surfaces, and determining more precisely their altitudes and relationship to earth-movements. Their extent and importance are clear. Much of the Carpathian system in Romania is in fact a plateau which rises, at least in the case of the two higher platforms, above the tree-line. It provides rolling, grassy surfaces, known in Romanian as *plaiuri*, dissected by the deep, narrow, incised valleys of the rivers. '. . . you can walk all day long,' wrote de Martonne of the Boresco surface, 'in the fog on the slightly undulating plateau and cross swampy grounds with peat bogs, without knowing where you are, until the wind suddenly shifts, the fog is dispelled, and you find yourself on the verge of a valley a thousand meters deep.'[1] It is on these upland surfaces, broken only by the valleys and the relict hills which erosion had spared, that the Romanian shepherds have for centuries been accustomed to passing their summer months.

Eastern Carpathians. Within Sub-Carpathian Russia the mountains are low, and consist of short segments around which the headwaters of the Iza (Tisza), the San and the Dnestr have opened up easy lines of movement. They have never constituted a significant barrier to the movement either of man or of other biological species. As the Iza river itself is approached, the mountain ridges become higher and

[1] Emmanuel de Martonne, 'The Carpathians: Physiographic Features Controlling Human Geography', *Geogrl Rev.*, **3** (1917), 423.

more continuous, reaching 6,000 feet and assuming once again the barrier nature which characterises the Tatra. This change in the general character of the range results from the reappearance at the surface of its crystalline core. A large part of the Romanian Carpathians is in fact built of Palaeozoic schists and intrusive igneous rocks.

The Eastern Carpathians themselves consist of three longitudinal zones of contrasting structure and rock type. In the centre lies the core of older and harder rocks. The river Bistriţa and its tributaries, which drain most of the area, form a rectilinear pattern, cutting the mountain ranges into segments with their transverse valleys. The individual ranges, the Maramureş and Rodna Mountains in the north, followed by the Bistriţa and Tarcău Mountains, are all high, rugged massifs, whose thickly forested flanks rise to a grassy plantation surface—Boresco or Rîu Şes—at from 5,000 to 6,500 feet.

This crystalline core extends over little more than the northern half of the region. On the east it is bordered by a zone of intensely folded beds of Secondary age and by somewhat less disturbed *Flysch*. Towards the south the width of this latter zone increases, and these young, folded beds completely overlie and obscure the Primary core. The relief of this zone is more gentle, and, although the Tarcău Mountains reach more than 5,000 feet, most of the ranges rarely exceed 4,000. Their slopes are gentler, and their valleys more open. To the east the mountains break up into a series of low, short segments of hill, which merge with the undulations of the Moldavian Piedmont.

To the west, however, the central core of the range is bounded by a region of entirely different character. It is a line of volcanics which extend, with interruptions, from the Soviet border to the valley of the Olt. It is made up of a number—at least ten—of rounded massifs, each with a radial drainage pattern and, in most instances, the still fresh forms of the volcanic craters at their summits. The highest, the Călimani mountains, reach 6,895 feet, but towards the south they become lower and less extensive. Each is surrounded by a zone where the clastic products of vulcanism have been laid down and subsequently eroded to a gentle slope.

Within the Eastern Carpathians these upland surfaces are in general too high for settlement, and the valley sides too steep. The population is therefore spread out along the valleys or gathered into the basins which are a feature of this, as of most other mountain ranges in Eastern Europe. No less than nine such basins can be distinguished within the Eastern Carpathians, most of them between the volcanic hills and the central crystalline massifs. Some, such as the extensive Braşov basin (Depresiunea, Birsei), the Ciuc Basin which lies along the upper Olt, or the Giurgeu Basin on the upper Mureş, are broad expanses of late Tertiary deposits, loess and alluvium, intensively cultivated and densely settled, with the mountains rising steeply on all sides, broken only by the narrow gaps where the river enters and leaves. Others, such as the Maramureş Basin along the upper Ixa and several small basins in the northern part of the region: Cîmpulung, Vatra-Dornei, Borsec, lie at a greater altitude; their relief is more dissected, and they lack the high agricultural potential of the lower and more extensive basins.

Despite their altitude the northern Carpathians do not by any means constitute a formidable barrier between the plains of Moldavia and the Transylvanian Basin. A great many transverse valleys have been eroded across both the crystalline core and the more easterly zone of fold-mountains, and a fan-shaped pattern of valley routeways radiates from the Braşov Basin. Although only three railways have been built across the mountains, the number of main roads is considerable, and the region is relatively well provided with communications. It is, however, except in its basin areas, a region of low population density relative to the rest of the country (Fig. 11.4).

Southern Carpathians. South of Braşov is the most used routeway across the mountains, that which links Braşov with Ploieşti and Bucharest by way of the Predeal Pass. To the east the mountains have been broken by erosion into many short segments, easy to circumvent. To the west they are by contrast higher and more continuous than in any other part of the range. This is in large measure the consequence of the reappearance at the surface of the crystalline core of the mountains, here greatly expanded and made up of Palaeozoic beds, in general highly metamorphosed and widely intruded by granite and diorite.

This east to west sector of the Carpathian Mountains is commonly distinguished as the Transylvanian Alps. In general it deserves this appellation. Above its high peneplaned surface rise residual masses which were glaciated during the Quaternary period. Above about 7,500 feet in the Făgăraş, Parîng, Retezat and Godeanu Mountains one finds extensive series of cirques, most of them oriented towards the north and often separated by arêtes. Across many of the higher valleys are fragmentary terminal moraines.

The Southern Carpathians—or Transylvanian Alps, as it will be more convenient to call them, fall naturally into three sectors, each bounded by a transverse valley. From the Predeal Pass to the Olt the region is dominated by the Făgăraş Mountains, which rise continuously for 30 miles to heights of over 6,000 feet. Their northern flank is steep and straight, where they look down on the Olt valley. Their southern slope, furrowed by the countless rivers that flow down to the Danube, is more gentle and merges into the Carpathian foothills.

The Olt rises in the Eastern Carpathians, where it links basin with mountain basin, crosses the volcanic hills and then flows along the foot of the Făgăraş Mountains as if seeking a way through. It crosses the mountains to the south of Sibiu by a spectacular gorge to reach the Walachian Plain.

West of the Olt the mountains become more complex. Their summit peneplain spreads over a number of ranges which are linked together in the knot formed by the Parîng Mountains. Together they constitute a formidable massif into which movement is possible only by mountain track.

To the west of the Parîng Mountains is another gap, cut by the south-flowing Jiu and by the Strei which flows northwards to join the Mureş. For much of their courses across the mountains the two rivers are deeply entrenched, and the gorge of the Jiu is even more spectacular than that of the Olt. Near the source of the two rivers, however, is another basin, of the kind that has become familiar amid these mountains. It is completely ringed by the high bare summits of the mountains, and was formed by the down-faulting of a fragment of the massif. A Tertiary lake formed here, and its soft deposits, augmented by more recent alluvium, give rise to a small region of gentle relief and good soil. This is the Petroşeni Basin, the only area within this central region of the Transylvanian Alps to have even a moderately dense population.

The third sector of the Transylvanian Alps extends from the Jiu-Strei valley to that occupied by the Timiş and Cerna. Its structure is more complex. The igneous and metamorphic core has been much faulted, secondary rocks have been caught up in its movements, and are now preserved in narrow zones, which follow the trend of the range as a whole. The forces of erosion, operating in rocks of such varied degrees of hardness, have produced a series of roughly parallel ranges, which here curve towards the south-west in the direction of the Danube. The highest of them—the Tarcu, Godeanu, Retezat and

Vîlcan Mountains—are comparable in altitude with the Făgăraş Mountains; they embody extensive areas of the Boresco peneplain, and have been widely glaciated. On the other hand the valleys are more open, and the mountains are more easily penetrated than those which lie to the east.

Western Carpathians. Romanian geographers commonly use this term to denote the mountains which lie to the west of the Transylvanian and extend like a chord across the arc made by the Eastern and Southern Carpathians. This practice is being followed here, though it must be noted that in both structure and relief these mountains are far more complex than the relatively simple ranges dealt with so far. The Western Carpathians divide themselves into three separate masses, together with foothills regions which separate them from the Pannonian Plain.

First of these is the region to the west of the Timiş-Cerna valley. Its southern boundary is clearly the gorge tract of the Danube from Moldova Nouă down to Turnu-Severin; to the west lie the plains of the Banat. The region is structurally similar to the more westerly parts of the Transylvanian Alps, but it has been more deeply dissected and the peneplain which extends over much of its area belongs to the lower Rîu Şes surface. Though decidedly mountainous, it is as open and as accessible as any part of the Eastern Carpathians, and has in fact a fair network of roads.

The second division of the Western Carpathians is the Poiana Ruscăi Massif. It is made up mainly of Palaeozoic schists similar to those which comprise the central parts of the Transylvanian Alps, from which it is in fact separated only by the Haţeg Basin. Its extensive plateau surface is, however, much lower and closely comparable with that of the first division of the Western Carpathians.

The Haţeg Basin can be viewed either as an intramontane basin, similar to that of Petroşeni, or as an extension of the Transylvanian, with which it is joined by an alluvial lowland along the Mureş valley. It is a basin, floored with Tertiary and alluvial deposits, and drained by the Mureş and its tributary. the Strei.

The Poiana Ruscăi Mountains drop steeply to the Mureş valley, beyond which rises no less steeply an incomparably larger and more complex massif. This rounded area of highland, with a diameter of about 80 miles, is commonly known in Western literature as the Bihor Mountains. This name—Muntii Bihorului—belongs correctly only to one of its more westerly ranges. There is no name, other than Western

Carpathians (Carpaţii Occidentali), which can correctly be used to embrace the whole. The term Muntii Apuseni is sometimes used, but the familiar name of Bihor will continue to be employed in this book. On the south it is bounded by the Mureş valley, on the north by that of the Criş and the headwaters of the Someş. Between lies a plateau which exceeds 4,000 feet in altitude over most of its extent and rises in parts to considerably above 5,000. Secondary beds, much folded and even metamorphosed, overlie the crystalline to the south-east, where their sharp variations in hardness have produced a more accidented relief. In the southwest of the massif are volcanics, similar in age to those of the Eastern Carpathians. They give rise today to the aptly named Munţii Metalici, where until quite recently the Gypsies used to pan gold along the streams. It has been dissected mainly by rivers which flow eastwards to the Transylvanian Basin and there join the Mureş or Someş. The valleys are deep and narrow; in their lower courses their sides are steep and forested. There is little room for settlement along the valleys, but in the interior of the massif these valleys are broader and more shallow, and here are found the villages of the mountain people. The population of the region is small and tends to live in the interior, cut off from the lowlands by forests, the steep slopes of the mountains and the narrow gorges through which the rivers issue. It has long been among the most isolated parts of Romania. Germans and Magyars moved up the Mureş and Someş, but never really penetrated these mountains which have remained essentially Romanian. The Bihor has provided, more than any other mountain area, as de Martonne expressed it, a 'refuge for the Romanian people', where they have tended to remain largely pastoral and primitive, in the sense that folkways, abandoned elsewhere, are here preserved.

The Bihor Massif ends abruptly on the north along the line of the Criş, but lower spurs from it stretch out to the north-west and north-east. They consist essentially of the same Palaeozoic complex that has been met with throughout the Southern and Western Carpathians, but here much worn down and almost wholly covered by younger sediments. The Mezeş Mountains rise little above 2,000 feet, and, in fact, terminate at the valley of the Someş. Their direction is continued in the line of broken hills which continues north-eastwards until it merges with the foothills of the Northern Carpathians.

The circuit is complete, and the ring of mountains is broken only by the narrow gaps, no more than a half-dozen of them, by which the rivers rising within this ring of mountains break through to reach the plains beyond. In reality we have something more closely resembling a dish with upturned rim, built of crystalline rocks of great age and hardness. Around most of this rim the material of which the dish is made shows through, but in some parts, particularly the south-east and north-west, it is covered by the softer deposits of a later geological age. Such deposits also fill the whole central portion of the dish; this is the Transylvanian Basin.

Transylvanian Basin

The Basin of Transylvania resembles the small basins already met with in the Carpathian range, such as the Braşov and Petroşeni Basins. It differs from them in its incomparably larger size and its greater historical importance. It is one of the most distinctive of the landform regions of Eastern Europe. It is compact in form, extends about 90 miles from west to east, and 120 from north to south, and on all sides, with the exception of the north-west, is clearly differentiated from the regions which enclose it. In altitude it is lower, ranging from a little below 1,000 feet along some of its valleys to over 2,000 in its highest hills; in relief it is gentler, and in terms of soil-fertility, population density and settlement it also presents the strongest contrast with its surrounding mountains.

The basin was formed during the early Tertiary. Through the later Tertiary it contained a lake in which deposits—sands, marls and clays —accumulated from the destruction of the surrounding mountains. These beds were slightly warped, but remain today substantially level and extend to a depth of from 9,000 to 12,000 feet in the central parts of the basin.

Erosion of the almost level strata and the deposition of loess and alluvium have brought the landforms of Transylvania to their present form. The only other factor which has greatly modified the landforms of the basin has been the later Tertiary volcanic hills along the western border of the Northern Carpathians. These belong to the mountain region, but their lava flows and ash deposits have spread out over the Tertiary deposits, and along the eastern margin of the Basin the latter extend for distances of up to 20 miles beneath the volcanic deposits.

The drainage pattern of Transylvania is complex. The basin is drained mainly to the Pannonian Basin; only a small area in the south lies within the Olt drainage, and none is drained across the Northern Carpathians to the Siret and the Moldavian Plain. Two rivers take most of the drainage, the Mureş and Someş. The former is joined by a fan-shaped pattern of tributaries from the southern two-thirds of the basin. These include the east-flowing Arieş which drains much of the Bihor Massif. The Mureş then flows between the Transylvanian Alps and the Bihor Massif to join the Tisza at Szeged. The Someş also rises within the Northern Carpathians, and takes a somewhat irregular course westwards between the most northerly extensions of the Bihor Massif and the Carpathians also to reach the Tisza. In the north of the Transylvanian Basin it picks up the Someş Mic, or the 'Little' Someş, which, with its tributaries, has flowed east from the high Bihor peneplain.

The history of Transylvanian drainage is very far from being understood. It is possible that much of it was originally eastward, and that this direction is preserved in the incised valleys of the Bihor. Rivers then headed back from the Pannonian Plain, capturing the rivers which had already developed within the Basin and thus producing the present pattern.

Regional variations within the Transylvanian Basin are not pronounced. It is a region of rolling hills and broad, shallow valleys. The soft rock of which the basin is composed and the widespread covering of loess have produced both gentle contours and a deep and fertile soil. Woodland now covers only a very small part of the area and probably was never dense or extensive. Patches remain over the higher ridges, especially those which separate the Olt drainage from that of the Mureş, but most of the Basin is under cultivation and is dotted with the large villages and the market towns of the German and Hungarian settlers. The only distinctive areas within the basin— and these are distinguished only by their relative isolation from the rest of the region—are the Făgăraş and Haţeg basins. The former occupies the Olt valley, cut off by the high ground which separates it from the Mureş Basin, and the latter, joined to the Transylvanian Basin only by the narrow valley of the Mureş, is for practical purposes a distinct and separate region.

Transylvania is the most distinctive region in Romania, perhaps also in Eastern Europe. The physical qualities which differentiate it from surrounding regions have been reinforced by those which have resulted from the hand of man. It has been occupied, at least in part, by a sedentary and agricultural population from Neolithic times; it has had a sequence of distinctive and generally advanced cultures; the Romans established towns here, and during the Middle Ages German and Hungarian peasants settled here. Their techniques, advanced by the standards of Eastern Europe, made Transylvania one of the more prosperous regions of the continent.

The Carpathian Piedmont

The mountains rise gently, in some places almost imperceptibly from the plains which surround them. Nowhere do they present to the outer world so steep and formidable a face as, for example, the Făgăraş Mountains do to the Transylvanian Basin. There is a transitional zone between mountain and plain, wide as in western Walachia and northern Moldavia, or narrow, as between the Bihor Massif and the Pannonian Plain.

The Western Piedmont. From the Danube above the Iron Gate almost to the Soviet border there extends a zone of hills. It varies in width from 5 to 30 miles, but is generally nearer the lower limit and occasionally, where the mountains rise directly from the plain, it almost disappears. Spurs from the Western Carpathians protrude into it; from the other side, embayments of the Pannonian Plain extend up the valleys of the major rivers which cross it.

Both the geological structures and the contours of the land itself resemble those of the Transylvanian Basin. It is a region where Tertiary beds overlie Secondary, and are themselves partially buried beneath variable but generally shallow deposits of loess and alluvium. These wrap around the spurs of the Western Carpathians, producing a region of gentle but by no means uniform relief.

The Walachian Piedmont. Like the Western Foreland, this is a relatively narrow belt of hilly country which borders the Carpathians. It extends from the Danube at the Iron Gate north-eastwards and then eastwards along the southern margin of the Translyvanian Alps. It is built essentially of upper Tertiary beds, mainly sandstones and clays. They have been gently folded, and erosion has produced relatively simple landforms, basically a pattern of asymmetrical ridges and valleys. The countryside is hilly, but well settled. Much of it is cultivated, but broad-leaved forest still covers the hilly ridges. Within this region the valleys sometimes widen into more extensive lowlands, similar to the basins within the Carpathian Mountains, except that here the contrasts are less pronounced. Such are the lowlands along the Olt after it has left the mountains, and around Cîmpulung.

The Moldavian Piedmont. Along the Dîmboviţa valley the Foreland terminates against a southward extension of the main Carpathian range, only to resume some 15 miles to the south as the Foreland of the Eastern Carpathians. The structures and landforms are similar, although the Tertiary beds are here more strongly folded, and the terrain somewhat more hilly. A series of ridges, some of them rising to heights of more than 2,000 feet, lie parallel to the sharp curve of the Carpathians themselves, and are cut into short segments by the rivers which radiate from the mountains towards the Danube and the Siret. It is amid the folded Tertiary beds of this region that much of the petroleum deposits of Ploieşti are found.

The Foreland, conforming with the trend of the mountains, continues to the north-west. The general direction of drainage, from north or north-west to south or south-east, conforms with the strike of the rocks. The relief of the regions thus tends to be made up of broad, flat-topped ridges, separated by wide shallow valleys, lying roughly parallel with the main ranges. These valleys sometimes expand into basins similar to those met with in the Moldavian Foreland. Those along the Tazlău, Bistriţa and Cracău rivers are large and distinctive enough to constitute minor regions in their own right. Each has one or more market towns to focus its economic life, and these regions are among the most densely peopled parts of Moldavia.

The Plains

Beyond the foot-hills of the Carpathian Forcland lie the Plains. They form only a relatively narrow belt of country on the west, between the Foreland and the Hungarian border. On the south, however, between the mountain foot-hills and the Danube, they constitute the largest and economically the most important region of Romania. In Moldavia the lowlands extend northward around the outer perimeter of the mountains, but here, between the Siret and the Prut, the land ceases to be either level or low-lying, but merges into the rolling Moldavian plateau.

Western Plains. There is little variation in the level of the Western Plains, and the whole region lies only a few feet above or below 300 feet. Along the major rivers, the Someş in the north, the two branches of the Criş, the Mureş and the Timiş, lie very wide belts of alluvium. Farther back from the rivers and above the level of recent floods, lie the terrace deposits formed at a somewhat earlier phase in the development of this region, and partially covering these and spreading out over the flattened interfluves is loess. In the north-west is an area of sand-dunes, an extension of the sandy region of north-eastern

Hungary (page 491). The Western Plains form a well-farmed region. Crop-growing predominates, with areas of more varied and more intensive cultivation around the towns.

Walachian Plain. This plain borders the Danube from the Iron Gate to the head of the delta, a distance of over 200 miles, and varies in width from 60 to 100 miles. It is known in the west as Oltenia, and in the east as Muntenia. It is essentially the northern arm of a syncline, formed in the course of the Tertiary mountain-building, and subsequently filled in with later sediments. The whole region is now floored with Pliocene deposits, masked over much of their extent by terrace deposits, alluvium and loess. The relief is simple; the land slopes south-eastward from a plateau, often known as the Getic Plateau, towards the Danube. Along its northern margin the region lies at about 1,000 feet above sea-level; the marshes which border the Danube are at about 100 feet in the west and 30 at the head of the delta. The slope is gentle and almost uniform. The rivers flow by way of almost parallel valleys from the mountains across the northern half of the region; then converge to give a small number of major rivers: the Jiu, Olt, Argeş, Ialomiţa and Buza, which join the Danube. Towards the north the valleys are cut into the soft Pliocene deposits, and the landscape has a corrugated aspect. To the south the surface is both lower and flatter, and the valleys wider and more shallow, and floored with broad tracts of alluvium.

The tributaries which flow from the Southern Carpathians to the Danube are not only more numerous than those which descend from the Bulgarian Platform, but their discharge is incomparably greater. The Danube has itself been forced towards the south; it has cut into its southern bank, producing the bluffs which characterise the Bulgarian side of the river, and leaving a wide belt of marshy alluvium along the northern bank. In recent geological times a rise in the level of the Black Sea has led to sedimentation upstream almost to the Iron Gate. For much of this distance, the Danube is itself a braided stream. It is dotted with islands, fringed with lakes, marshes and damp meadowland, and, below the Bulgarian town of Silistra, the main stream of the Danube divides to enclose two large marshy islands, Balta Ialomiţei and Balta Brăilei.

The breadth of this tract varies from less than a mile to as much as twenty. Though bordered by roads and paths, it can still be crossed only at two points. One of these is between Giurgiu and Ruse in Bulgaria, where the low plain of Walachia extends between the marshes almost to the river. The other crossing is at Cernavodă, where an embankment has been built across Balta Ialomiţei and bridges across the branches of the Danube. Elsewhere, small river towns have grown up only where permanently dry land approaches the river. On such sites are Calafat and the important river port of Brăila. Nowhere in Europe does a river form so formidable a natural barrier as the Danube below the Iron Gate. Similar physical conditions extend for short distances up the tributaries of the Danube, many of which are fringed along their lower courses by marshes and lakes.

The Walachian Plain is very much drier than the Western Plains. Its average rainfall is less than 609·5 millimetres (24 inches) over the region as a whole, and near the river and towards the east this drops to less than 508 millimetres (20 inches). This prevailing dryness, accentuated locally by the permeable sandy soil, is reflected in the vegetation. The former consists of broad-leaved vegetation in the north-west, passing southwards and eastwards into wooded steppe. In the extreme east lies the Bărăgan Steppe, an area of true prairie. In all the drier areas of the plain a salty efflorescence may form at the surface, similar to the *szik* of Hungary (page 492).

Moldavian Plain. There is a superficial similarity between the Walachian and Moldavian Plains. Both are lowland regions built of soft upper Tertiary and Recent deposits and furrowed by a fairly simple pattern of rivers which flow to the Danube. But in Moldavia the relationship of these elements is different. The plain extends from north to south for about 200 miles, and varies in breadth from 45 miles to 70. Whereas the Walachian Plain is bordered throughout its length by the Danube, the Moldavian reaches the river only at its south-eastern extremity. Most of the latter lies more distant from its base-level, and it is very much less maturely eroded.

On the east the plain is bounded by the Prut, which at present forms the boundary with the Soviet Union, and to the west it includes the valley of the Siret. The latter is fed by tributaries from the Eastern Carpathians, but the Prut derives its flow entirely from the multitude of small and in many instances seasonal rivers of the Moldavian and Bessarabian Plains. These have eroded straight, deep and generally short valleys, lying roughly parallel to one another, so that the land has the same corrugated form that was met in Oltenia.

In the extreme south of the region the valley of the Siret is low lying and marshy and has the same general character as that of the Danube which it joins above Galaţi. Similar damp lowlands extend up the lower Prut, which has a marked deltaic character. But between the two rivers the low Bîrlad plateau rises—locally to over 1,500 feet— and extends as far north as Iaşi. It slopes gently towards the south, trenched by the river Bîrlad and its many tributaries. This part of the region is analogous, except in its stronger relief, with Oltenia. Near Iaşi the plateau ends abruptly, and an escarpment overlooks the Iaşi Basin. The latter, known in Romania as the Cîmpia Moldovei, is an undulating lowland, drained by the most extensive of the tributaries that feed the Prut. Much of its surface is made up of either loess or alluvium, and it is one of the richest farming areas in Romania. Along its western margin the Bîrlad plateau merges into the Suceava plateau. The latter, a less dissected version of the Bîrlad, extends beyond the Siret to the Carpathian foot-hills.

The Moldavian Plain is even drier than the Walachian. Woodland is still extensive over the high rim which encloses the Iaşi Basin, but elsewhere both woodland and steppe have largely given place to cultivation. Moldavia has become almost a byword for extreme poverty amid immense potential wealth. The chernozem and forest soils which cover much of the region and the alluvial soil of the Siret and Prut are naturally amongst the most fertile in Eastern Europe. Yet it was along this 'famous strip of dark black soil . . . that Tatars and Turks rode northward against the Poles. . . . On this familiar fighting ground, still strewn with castles ruined in the Tatar Wars of the seventeenth century'[1] the Poles defended Central Europe from invaders from the east. The periodic destruction by war and invasion, accompanied by the endemic evils of a bad system of land-tenure, by poorly developed means of transport and communication, and by neglect on the part of whatever governments were charged with its administration, made this one of the poorest and most backward regions.

The Delta. The delta of the Danube is one of the smallest, but most distinctive of the physiographic regions of Romania. The Danube itself, after meandering, dividing and redividing into countless branches, unites above Galaţi into a single stream. At this point, a low spur from the Moldavian plateau reaches to within ten miles of a similar low extension of the Dobrogea plateau. Through this incon-spicuous gap flows the Danube. Almost immediately the alluvial

[1] H. A. L. Fisher, *A History of Europe*, Eyre and Spottiswoode, 1938, vol. 2, p. 732.

lowland widens; the river swings to the east and the belt of fringing marshes grows wider. For 25 miles approximately as far as Tulcea, the river flows as a single stream. Then it divides, first into two and then into three major branches, which constitute the major arteries of the delta.

The most northerly—the Braţul Chilia, or Chilia Channel, as it is more often known in Western literature, is tortuous and has a great many branches. Though navigable for small craft, it is difficult to enter and is really very little used. It reaches the sea through a fan shaped pattern of distributaries which constitute in fact, a separate and subsidiary delta, a reflection of the fact that is takes about two-thirds of the total discharge of the Danube. The Chilia Channel, furthermore, constitutes the boundary with the Soviet Moldavian Republic, in which most of its mouths lie.

The Sulina Channel—Braţul Sulina—diverges from the Chilia Channel about four miles to the north-west of Tulcea. It normally takes only about a tenth of the total discharge of the river, and an embankment has been built out into the river to divert sufficient water into it to insure an adequate scouring action in the Channel itself. The latter, artificially straightened and dredged, now constitutes the main shipping channel. It normally has a depth of over 20 feet, and a width of at least 300 feet. Levées border the channel, and are above flood level.

The most southerly and also the largest and least useful of the Danube's distributaries is Braţul Sf. Gheorghe, or St. George's Channel. No attempt has been made to straighten its meanders or to dredge the shallow sandbars which partially close its entrance. It is however linked by artificial cuts with the lakes which lie south of the delta in the direction of Constanţa, and small craft can use this route to reach the head of the delta and the river.

Between the distributaries lie large expanses of marsh, important mainly for their fisheries and the sedge, which is harvested every winter when the water level is low, to provide a raw material for cellulose manufacture. The marsh is interrupted by numerous lakes and sandy islands, some of which, originating as offshore bars, cut off the marshes from the sea. Most of the area is, however, inundated during the period of maximum discharge in late spring and early summer. Apart from the annual harvest of marsh grasses, the delta is important only for its fisheries, and most of its scanty population lives in small, simple fishing villages built on its sandy islands.

Dobrogea

The last region to be examined is that which lies between the lower Danube, its delta and the sea. It constitutes a peninsula extending about 100 miles northwards from the platform of eastern Bulgaria. Except in the south, it is little more than 45 miles across. Its relief is simple; it is a low plateau rising to about 700 feet in the north; dropping in the latitude of Constanţa to a depression along which the Romanians planned at one time to cut a canal from the Danube to the sea, and rising again to the Dobrogea plateau which again reaches over 500 feet along the Bulgarian border.

The geological structure of this small region is in marked contrast to the rest of the lowlands. It consists of Palaeozoic beds, ranging from Silurian to Permian in age, overlain by Triassic and Cretaceous, and the whole partially hidden by Tertiary beds and loess. The Palaeozoic beds outcrop in the plateau of northern Dobrogea, where relief and drainage have come to be closely adjusted to the structures. To the south the older beds are exposed only where the rivers have incised their beds through the superficial deposits of more recent age. The hills which rise within the sharp bend of the Danube near Galaţi are in fact a planated granitic massif. To the south, in both the northern and the southern sectors of the Dobrogea plateau, extensive beds of limestone have given rise to a karstic land surface.

The Dobrogea and delta regions are the driest in Romania, and their natural fertility is qualified by the prevailing lack of rainfall. Cereal cultivation predominates, and the density of sheep is greater here than in any other region of Romania, an indication of the relatively great extent of the dry grazing lands.

Dobrogea has almost as thin a population density as the Carpathians themselves. Along its coast, however, where a low promontory gives some shelter from northerly winds, is the city and port of Constanţa. To the west, the depression extending to the Danube, is followed by both road and railway to Cernavodă, and was the line of the projected Danube-Black Sea canal. North and South of Constanţa, coastal resorts, of which the most noteworthy are Mamaia and Mangalia, have sprung up to capitalise on the chief asset of this otherwise flat and unattractive coast: its sunshine.

CLIMATE

Relief is by far the most important factor in climatic variations within Romania. The whole country, with the exception only of a narrow belt along the Black Sea coast, has a continental climate, more extreme than that of Hungary; less so than that of the Ukraine. In this sense the climate is transitional, but everywhere the summers, unless moderated by altitude, are warm, and winters are cold. Rainfall is everywhere light except in the mountains, and its distribution shows the early summer maximum, typical of continental climates.

Temperature
The dominant influence in the winter months is the high pressure system which develops over Russia. Predominant winds are from a northerly to easterly quarter—the Crivăl—and reduce the temperature in Moldavia two or three degrees below that in Walachia or the Western Plains. The whole country has a January average below freezing, with the exception only of a very small area on the Black Sea coast near the Bulgarian border. In Transylvania and northern Moldavia the temperature drops to $-3.5°C$ (25°F), and absolute minima throughout the plains have been known to fall to below $-28.9°C$ ($-20°F$). The rivers freeze over, and navigation on the Danube may be interrupted for as long as three months. In extreme years the still waters of the delta may freeze and ice has been known in the harbour of Constanţa.

The transition from winter to summer is abrupt. Summers are hot, especially in the Pannonian Plain and along the valleys of the Danube and the Prut. There the July average is $22.8°C$ (73°F) or above, with absolute maxima of $43.3°C$ (110°F). At all seasons temperatures fall off rapidly in the Carpathian foot-hills, but the gradient in summer is appreciably steeper than that of winter, when temperature inversions may modify the normal pattern of temperature. The absolute minima at mountain stations are in fact very little lower than those met with in the plains.

Rainfall
The distribution of rainfall reflects the pattern of relief with remarkable faithfulness. The higher land in the Carpathians receives normally more than 1,150 millimetres (47 inches) a year, and in the foot-hills precipitation rises to over 700 millimetres (28 inches) except in Moldavia which lies within the rain-shadow of the Northern Carpathians. The lowlands are everywhere relatively dry. Over most of the Western Plains, the fall is less than 600 millimetres (24 inches), and in Walachia and Moldavia the total sinks to less than 500 millimetres (20 inches).

(a)

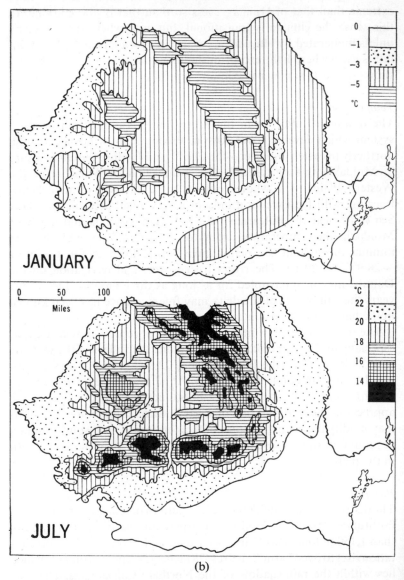

(b)

Fig. 11.2. Mean monthly temperatures in (a) January, (b) July. After *Atlas Geografic Republica Socialista România*, Bucharest, 1965.

The lowest stretch of the Danube valley, the delta and Dobrogea have less than 400 millimetres (16 inches). The Transylvanian Basin has a somewhat heavier rainfall than the plains which lie outside the arc of the Carpathian Mountains. Over much of its surface totals are more than 600 millimetres (24 inches), and drop below this level only in the Braşov and Haţeg Basins and in the rain-shadow of the Bihor Mountains.

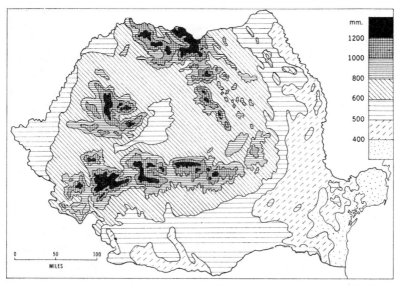

Fig. 11.3. Mean annual rainfall. After *Atlas Geografic Republica Socialista România*, Bucharest, 1965.

The seasonal distribution of rainfall varies but little. In all parts of Romania the heaviest falls are in late spring and early summer and the smallest in late autumn and winter. The difference between the total precipitation in the summer half-year and that in the winter half is least near the Black Sea coast, and greatest in the interior. At Tulcea, at the head of the delta, summer rainfall barely exceeds that of winter, while in Sibiu nearly half occurs in the three summer months and more than two-thirds in the summer half-year. Late summer is commonly dry, and occasionally so dry that crops which have not fully ripened are threatened. Irrigation is important in all the lowland regions of Romania, and is especially necessary if cropping is to be

19

extended in the more easterly regions. The Bărăgan Steppe of eastern Walachia and the Dobrogea, in both of which the natural dryness is intensified by the highly porous subsoil, are both particularly liable to prolonged drought. The area under irrigation has been greatly extended in recent years, especially along the Hungarian border and in the larger river valleys of Walachia and Moldavia. In 1960, it is said that about 200,000 hectares (494,000 acres) were regularly irrigated, but it is planned to increase this area fourfold during the 1960s.

Snow occurs in all parts of Romania, and snow-cover is prolonged over much of the country. Bucharest, in the midst of the dry Walachian Plain, has total snowfall on average of 101·6 millimetres (4 inches), and on the Predeal Pass, which carries the main road from Bucharest across the mountains to Braşov, the accumulation rises to over 254 millimetres (10 inches). Over the plains the snow-cover protects the autumn-sown crops from the full severity of the cold, and in spring its melt-water provides much needed soil moisture. The severe winter winds from the Russian Steppe, however, are apt in exposed places to produce blizzard conditions and to blow away the snow, thus exposing the soil to the intense cold.

Climatic regions
Climatic regions in Romania are largely a function of altitude; the lowland regions all have closely similar climatic conditions. Romanian geographers none the less distinguish five climatic divisions of the country.

1. *Transylvania and the Western Plains*. This region is distinguished by cold winters and warm summers, and a light rainfall concentrated heavily in the summer half-year.

2. *Walachian-Moldavian Plains*. Here the range of temperature is somewhat greater than in the Western Plains. Summers are much hotter along the Danube valley, and winters appreciably colder throughout these areas. Rainfall is lower than on the other side of the mountain ranges, and its seasonal pattern is a little less marked as the Black Sea is approached. There is a marked Föhn effect as westerly winds drop down from the Carpathian Mountains to the plains, and this in turn raises the temperature in the foothill zone, so that it becomes—relatively at least—a zone of warmth between the cold of the plains and the greater cold of the mountains.

3. *The Carpathian Mountains*. The mountains make their own

climates, and conditions are so variable that generalisation is difficult. They are, of course, colder in winter, very much cooler in summer, and wetter at all seasons than the plains which surround them. Precipitation is very heavy on west-facing slopes; over 1,400 millimetres (55 inches), for example, on the summits and windward flanks of the Western Carpathians. Frost drainage significantly modifies the temperature conditions in mountain valleys and basins, especially during the winter. Snow lies on the higher ground sometimes until late summer, but, despite the abundant evidence of glacial erosion on their higher surfaces, not even the summits of the Făgăraş and Retezat Mountains have today permanent snowfields.

4. *Banat and Western Walachia.* The continental conditions which prevail over most of Romania yield somewhat in the extreme south-west and south-east of the country. In the former, Romanian geographers are apt to recognise a Mediterranean influence, difficult though it may be for us to detect it. In reality the area bordering Yugoslavia has slightly milder winters than the rest of the country, and a greater tendency for winter storms to break through from the Mediterranean. At Turnu-Severin, for example, the wettest months are still May and June, but autumn and early winter have scarcely less rainfall, and show a secondary and Mediterranean-type maximum.

5. *Black Sea Coast.* Continental conditions are also moderated somewhat over a narrow belt of territory which borders the Black Sea from the Soviet border to the Bulgarian. Temperatures are moderated, especially in winter, and Mangalia, in the southern part of the region, is the only place in Romania where the average temperature in January is above freezing. Rainfall, however, is very low, and in the delta drops to about 355 millimetres (14 inches). Constanţa itself has only 360 millimetres (14·6 inches) on average, and an absolute minimum of less than 203 millimetres (8 inches), making it probably the driest place in the whole of Europe. It is at the same time one of the sunniest, a fact to which the Romanian government gives the fullest publicity in developing its tourist resorts along this coast.

VEGETATION AND SOIL

If the climatic regime differs little from one part of the country to another, this cannot also be said of the vegetation and soil. Romania, intermediate between the chernozem and the steppe on one side and the broadleaved forests and their forest soils on the other, shows great range and variation in both.

Vegetation

There is a marked contrast in their natural vegetation between the plains and the mountain regions. In general the former were at one time wooded steppe, passing into true steppe in the Bărăgan region of Walachia, in parts of Moldavia and in the Dobrogea, and into broadleaved woodland, predominantly oak and beechwoods, as the foothills are approached. Light woodland covers the higher parts of Dobrogea plateau, and marsh vegetation extends along much of the Danube.

The Transylvanian Basin together with the Braşov, Hațeg and other basins within the Carpathian Mountains had in general a vegetation of broadleaved forest trees, intermixed with conifers on the higher ground and poorer soils. Encircling the Transylvanian Basin is a belt of mixed forest, which passes upwards in the Bihor Mountains and in the Eastern and Southern Carpathians into pinewoods. At the highest levels, roughly from 5,000 to 6,000 feet, are alpine pastures, used in summer by transhumant sheep, and the tundra vegetation of the former ice-fields at even greater altitudes.

In the Banat and Oltenia, where the prevailing continental climate is modified by influences from the Mediterranean, plant species of southern origin make their appearance. The increasing severity of winter has prevented their deeper penetration of the country. In the same way species associated with the Russian Steppe are found in the plains of the east.

Soils

Soils range from the stony, skeletal soils of the mountains to the true chernozem of the Moldavian Plain, lying in roughly concentric zones around the central mountainous regions of the country. At their centre, in Transylvania, is an area of degraded chernozem, which passes outwards and upwards into the brown forest soils of the area of broadleaved and mixed forests. These in turn pass in the hills into podzols of varying quality, and these in turn into skeletal soils and bare rock.

On the outer margin of the mountains the podzols merge into a continuous zone of brown forest soils, which is most extensive in Walachia, where the broadleaved forest formerly covered the largest areas. As the trees thin away towards the south-east and east and conditions become drier, the forest soils pass into degraded or modified chernozem, and this into restricted areas of true chernozem in eastern Walachia and Dobrogea. Along the valleys of the Danube and of most of the larger rivers lie belts of alluvial soil, highly fertile where it is dry enough for regular cultivation, elsewhere bearing meadow or marsh vegetation.

Loess was laid down very extensively over the lowland regions of Romania. It yields a fertile but dry soil, and tends to become severely eroded by the heavy summer storms. Soil erosion is a serious problem in the foothill regions, and here one sometimes comes across areas which have been acutely gullied. Near the Hungarian border and in the Danubian Plain, especially its drier and more easterly parts, are extensive sandy areas. The sand derives mainly from old terrace deposits, but has been accumulated by the wind to form large areas of mobile dunes.

POPULATION AND SETTLEMENT

In the composition of its population Romania lacks the simplicity found in Hungary, and resembles rather the ethnic complexity of Yugoslavia. This is due in part to the fact that Romania was treated generously at the Paris Conference in 1919. On more than one occasion ethnic realities were secondary to strategic and economic considerations. Even after the loss to the Soviet Union of the province of Bessarabia and the flight or emigration of many of the minority peoples, about 15 per cent of the total population at the time of the last census in 1956 belonged to ethnic minorities.

Ethnic composition
In its composition the population of Romania shows better perhaps than that of any other East European country the ethnic history of the region. In Hungary an incoming people was able to destroy all except the genetic inheritance of that which had previously occupied the region. In Romania, by contrast, the shattered remains of defeated tribes could always find refuge in the mountains. In a sense the contrast between Romania and Hungary is that depicted by Sir Cyril Fox in his classic study[1] of the Highland and Lowland Zones of the British Isles.

[1] Sir Cyril Fox, *The Personality of Britain*, Cardiff, National Museum of Wales.

Romanians. Exactly how the present mélange of peoples developed is, as has been explained in Chapter 2, a matter of controversy. Do the Romanians derive from the Romanised Dacians of the second century A.D., or are they descended from migratory groups akin to the Vlachs who came from across the Danube? In either case they can be regarded as part of that Indo-European substratum of the continent which is variously known as Illyrian, Thracian and Dacian. The cultural inheritance from this early phase in Romania's ethnic history has largely vanished, but the Latin acquired during the period of the Roman Empire has survived.

The Romanian language is today classed as 'romance', and the Romanians themselves, not altogether unconsciously, have tended to strengthen its similarities with the cognate languages of Italy and France. This is, however, to exaggerate the classical inheritance in modern Romanian. Although the morpho-syntactic similarities with Latin are apparent, Romanian has borrowed from Slavic, Hungarian and even Turkish. Modern Romanian as a literary language was developed in the eighteenth century from the romance dialect spoken by the peasants of Walachia, but it was not until the nineteenth that a considerable literature developed and a national tradition took shape.

From the earliest periods for which we have records we find the Romanians inhabiting mainly the hilly and mountainous areas. They claim to have been displaced from the Transylvanian Basin by Germans and Szeklers, but in the Eastern and Southern Carpathians and in the Bihor Massif the antiquity of their settlement is not in doubt. The earliest travellers' accounts, such as those of Peter Mundy, William Lithgow and Fynes Morison, show a simple and predominantly pastoral people inhabiting these regions, and Austrian census data from the mid-nineteenth century allow a distinction to be drawn between the basin of Transylvania, with its heavily German and Szekler population, and the surrounding mountain rim which was in places almost exclusively Romanian.

Today the Romanians are reckoned to make up about 85 per cent of the total of about 18,927,000. At the time of the 1956 census they were still, relative to their numbers, somewhat more rural than either Szeklers or Germans, and although more widely distributed than formerly, still make up only 20 per cent of the population in the Magyar Autonomous Region, and constitute over 90 per cent only in Walachia and Moldavia.

Magyars and Szeklers. The Romanian statistical sources do not differentiate between these two peoples, and any distinction between them is historical. The Magyars lived in the Pannonian Plain, and their settlement area was continuous with that of the Hungarians themselves. The Szeklers, or Szekély, lived beyond the forests and mountains, in Transylvania, cut off from the main body of the Hungarian people by an area inhabited mainly by Romanians. How they came to be there is a matter of folklore rather than of history. Transylvania does not appear to have been part of the original Hungarian settlement area, and it is possible that the Szeklers moved eastwards into this area along with the 'Saxons' in the thirteenth century.

During the period of Transylvanian independence, the Szekler nobility assumed a role of leadership and were active in their resistance to the Turks. After Hungary had been reconquered by the armies of Austria, the Szeklers became reluctant and turbulent subjects of the Habsburgs, and when a Hungarian kingdom was again established in 1867 they continued to enjoy a privileged position within the Dual Monarchy. The inclusion of the Szeklers proper within the Romanian state in 1919 was necessary if all the Romanian people were to come within its borders. The western leaders had misgivings and, as a sop to the Hungarians, the Romanian government was called upon to sign the Minorities Treaty. It was not necessary, however, for Romania to embrace all the Magyars. Most of them lived along the border of the plain and were transferred to Romania primarily to give the latter possession of the piedmont belt with its towns and means of communication (see page 536). Even today the Romanians make up no more than two-thirds of the population of this region.

During the period between the two world wars both Magyars and Szeklers formed a discontented minority, but there was no change in their status, and they resisted on the whole successfully Romanian attempts to weaken their cultural integrity. In 1952 a Magyar Autonomous Region was created, embracing those areas of northeastern Transylvania in which the majority of the Szeklers are concentrated. The population of the Region is now more than three-quarters Szekler, and Romanians make up only a fifth. It nevertheless excludes a not inconsiderable Szekler minority in the neighbouring provinces of Cluj and Braşov, and the degree of autonomy is small.

Transylvanian Germans. The second largest minority is the German. It is found, like the Magyar, in two distinct areas. The older and historically the most important is that which settled in southern Transylvania in the twelfth century and which is now found mainly in the districts of Braşov and Sibiu. Though often described as Saxon, this community came mainly from the Rhineland and Luxembourg and succeeded in its new home in maintaining its language and culture with quite remarkable success. Today the 'German' villages of Transylvania differ sharply in their architecture and plan from the Romanian, and their inhabitants are said to speak still with the accents of the Mosel valley.

The second German community, sometimes known, in order to distinguish them from the 'Saxons', as the 'Swabians', lives in the plains of Timişoara, in the area once known as the Banat. They are the descendants of the Maria-Theresa Germans, established here in the eighteenth century on lands recently abandoned by the Turks. Both groups have greatly diminished in numbers since the Second World War, and the total German community had been reduced by flight and migration from over 700,000 in 1930 to 384,708 at the time of the 1956 census.

The Transylvanian Germans—or *Siebenbürger Deutsche*—enjoyed a privileged status in the medieval Hungarian state. Their cities were defended by walls, and even in the villages the churches and church-yards were fortified; they adopted Lutheranism in the sixteenth century, and were allowed to make their settlement area of Szeben an autonomous region within the Hungarian and later the Transylvanian state. Like the Szeklers, they resisted the centralising policies of the Habsburgs and later the ethnic policies of the Romanians. In recent years they appear to have been victimised by the Romanians, and they have seized every opportunity to migrate to Germany.

Jews. The Jewish community of Romania amounted before the Second World War to about three-quarters of a million. They derived from two sources. The older Jewish communities were of Spanish origin, and had come by way of the Turkish Empire. The newer and larger had spread, principally in the nineteenth century, from Russia. This was reflected in their distribution. The largest Jewish communities were in the east and north. In Bucovina they comprised over 10 per cent of the population and in Bessarabia, over 7 per cent. The Jewish communities were smallest—at least relatively—in Walachia, Dobrogea and Banat. The Jewish population has generally been pre-dominantly urban, and tended until recently to live in the ghetto areas of the towns. In Walachia and Moldavia it was well on the way towards assimilation by the predominant Romanian population, but this was very far from being the case in the heavily Jewish areas in the north and north-east, where the great majority of them spoke Yiddish rather than Romanian.

The Jewish population suffered during the Second World War, though less so than in the countries examined hitherto. In the territories ceded to Hungary and the Soviet Union, which included both Bessarabia and Bucovina, it was reduced from about 450,000 to about 100,000. In the rest of Romania losses were relatively small, and when the war ended Romanian Jewry was reduced to about 425,000. Thereafter it diminished rapidly as opportunities arose to migrate to Israel. An unofficial estimate put the total at 256,000 in 1949 and at 175,000 by the end of 1955. The Romanian census recorded 146,264 in 1956, of whom only about 40,000 spoke Yiddish. Migration has since reduced the Jewish community yet more.

Serbo-Croats. The acquisition of the Banat gave Romania not only the 'Swabian' Germans already mentioned, but also a Serbo-Croat minority of about 46,500.

Gypsies. Despite wartime losses Romania has still one of the largest communities of Gypsies in Eastern Europe. They numbered about 53,000 in 1948, and, although met with throughout the country, were most numerous in the north-eastern provinces of Iaşi and Suceava. They remain partly itinerant, though increasing numbers are now being settled in small and insanitary Gypsy ghettos on the outskirts of the towns, where they are employed mainly in menial and unskilled occupations.

Russians. This somewhat diverse group includes the Ruthenes of Bucovina, the Ukrainians of the northern provinces, and of Dobrogea, and the Russians proper, who form small and widely scattered groups, and are numerous only in Dobrogea. The Russians themselves originated as refugee groups; the Ruthenes and Ukrainians were caught within Romania when the present boundaries were established.

Tatars and Turks. These are also relict peoples, descendants of groups who had immigrated and settled at a time when boundaries were more fluid or even non-existent. They numbered about 55,000 in 1956, and were to be found almost exclusively in the Dobrogea. Bulgaria, it might be noted here, has a similar minority living in its own Dobrudža.

Bulgarians. In Dobrogea there was formerly a Bulgarian minority,

19*

about 360,000 in 1930, which constituted the basis for the Bulgarian claim to this area. This has been reduced by flight and expulsion to about 12,000.

The other ethnic minorities in Romania are very small. A handful of Slovaks is to be found in the north-west. Small Greek and Armenian communities are all that remain of the more numerous groups who carried on much of the commerce and administration under Turkish rule. Almost all these groups have tended to diminish as a result of flight and repatriation during and after the Second World War.

Religious affiliation. The ethnic division of the population is matched by its religious differences. The Romanians are traditionally members of the Romanian Orthodox Church, an autocephalous branch of the Eastern Church. The Transylvanian Germans are mainly Lutheran, and the 'Swabians' of the Banat, Roman Catholic. A majority of the Hungarian-Szekler community is also Roman Catholic, but among the Szeklers of Transylvania is a considerable Calvinist group (see page 508). The Ukrainians and Ruthenes have always been Orthodox, and the small Turkish group, Moslem.

Structure of the population

The population of Romania is estimated to have been about 19,105,000 in 1966. The urban share of the total population has been increasing slowly. In 1930 it was 21·4 per cent; in 1948, when the first Five-Year Plan was introduced, 23·4, and in 1966, 37·6 per cent. This diminution in the rural sector has been accompanied by a parallel change in employment. Those employed in agriculture have dropped from 74·1 per cent of the total in 1950 to 55 per cent in 1966, and employment in industry and building construction has increased respectively from 12·0 and 2·2 per cent to 19·7 and 6·7 per cent.

Age structure. A feature of the Romanian population for a number of years has been its low and diminishing birth-rate, which is now one of the lowest in the East European group of countries. From 26·2 per thousand in 1950 it has fallen almost without interruption to 14·6 in 1965. The population total continues to grow, though at a diminishing rate. A consequence is that the population pyramid shows marked constrictions, which represent the fewer births of the years of the First and Second World Wars and of the period from approximately 1956 onwards. Within ten years this diminished birth-rate will begin to show itself in a reduced labour force.

Rural settlement

About two-thirds of the population of Romania lives in the villages and hamlets, and most of them are engaged in agriculture. The characteristic rural settlement of Romania is quite distinct from that of the countries and regions discussed hitherto, and resembles in origin and morphology those to be discussed later in Yugoslavia and Bulgaria.

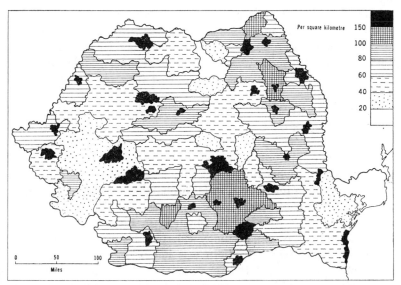

Fig. 11.4. Distribution of population in Romania. After *Atlas Geografic Republica Socialista România*, Bucharest, 1965.

Village morphology. Although the rural settlements of Romania range from the isolated farmstead to the tightly nucleated and regularly planned village, the typical settlement is intermediate between these extremes. It is a hamlet made up of houses, each standing in its own courtyard, with its farm buildings nearby, and each separated from the others by as much in some cases as several hundred yards. There can be little doubt that this is the oldest form of settlement in this region, and that it antedated the Roman conquest of Dacia. It was situated on the hillsides; around it lay cultivated lands though most of the cropland was in the valley below; above it was forest and rough grazing. Such settlements are still typical of the hilly regions of Romania.

The increase in population and the subdivision of farms led to a thickening of the settlement as the housing plots, initially large, came to be divided and subdivided. The open hamlet gradually became an irregularly nucleated village. At the same time, however, the same forces led to migration from the village and the formation of isolated settlements, surrounded by their own fields. The hillside situation may have been chosen for easier defence or to avoid the dampness and the long shadows of the valley. In time many of the communities gravitated towards the lower ground where lay much of the cropland.

Thus was evolved, in a manner which seems to have been typical of south-eastern Europe, the typical Romanian village. But other types of rural settlement were introduced by other peoples, notably the Germans and the Turks, who moved into and settled in the Romanian region. Their settlements are characterised by a more orderly if not by a completely planned settlement pattern. There came the street-village of the German and Hungarian settler in the Transylvanian Basin, made up generally of 'long houses', fairly regularly spaced and lying at right angles to the road. The roads themselves are wide, as is usual when the flocks and herds are expected to pass regularly. Though introduced in all probability by settlers from the west, this pattern of village must have ceased quite early to be a monopoly of those who had first built it. It was taken over by the Romanians themselves and is today widespread in northern Romania.

An even more regular pattern was imposed by the Turks who settled parts of south-eastern Romania. It was the extreme form of the feudal village, in which the houses of the peasantry were grouped around an open square for the greater ease of supervision. Similarly planned are the 'gridiron' villages of the Banat which were laid out in the eighteenth century on lands recently conquered from the Turks. They remain very largely the homes of the 'Swabians', the descendants of the settlers who were brought in at this date. Such compact and authoritarian villages are found also in the Walachian Plain, where they were laid out by the boyars during the nineteenth century, in the course of its settlement and development as a great wheat-growing region.

Village architecture. On the northern outskirts of Bucharest is an outdoor museum made up of cottages, farm-buildings and even of churches, which have been assembled from all parts of Romania. They range from the elaborately carved wooden house of the Carpathians to the dwelling of the Bărăgan Steppe, which is sunk into the

ground and roofed with turf. This collection shows the extreme richness of peasant art. Most of the cottages are of wood, and almost all
have a wealth of carved decoration. A log construction on masonry
foundations, with a steeply pitched roof of shingles characterises the
mountain villages. In the Transylvanian Basin masonry and plaster
are used more often. In the German villages the cottages are often
plastered and colour-washed. In the plains, especially those of Walachia
where the summer sun is brighter and hotter, the cottage is set to
catch the breeze and has a porch supported by wooden posts, sometimes elaborately carved, along at least its south-facing wall.

In the street-villages, the cottages, elongated and closely spaced,
have small courtyards behind them, in which tools and produce are
stored, a few vegetables grown and poultry and an animal or two kept.
In the more loosely arranged hamlets and villages, these courts are
larger, often enclosed by a stout wooden fence and entered by a gate
with a highly ornamented arch.

Such cottages have a short life. The timbers decay; the plaster
cracks and falls off, and they have to be rebuilt. Very rarely are the
old styles retained. The modern cottage in all the more accessible
parts of the country is built of brick, with a generous use of reinforced
concrete—a more durable, more sanitary and more comfortable house,
even if its aesthetic appeal is non-existent.

Urban settlement

Romania and the Balkans have been in modern times among the
least urbanised parts of Europe. In 1930 Romania had 142 towns and
cities, which together contained only 21·4 per cent of the country's
population. Since the Second World War older cities have been
expanded and many new towns, mostly based upon a single newly
developed manufacturing industry, have been established. The
census of 1956 recorded 172 towns and an urban population which
amounted to 31·3 per cent of the total. It is now 37·6 per cent. There is
still only one really large city, Bucharest, with an estimated population
in 1966 of about 1,365,900, and of 1,511,400 in its conubation.
There were, however, no less than 13 cities each having more than
100,000, and most of these had grown rapidly during the previous
two decades. Below this level was a very large number of small
towns, each having from 20,000 to 50,000 inhabitants, and an even
larger number of towns of even smaller size. At this level it is difficult

to distinguish in size and function between the smaller towns and the larger villages; in both respects they overlap.

In 1963 there were said to be no less than 353 towns and other settlements having urban functions. Their estimated population is shown in Table 62.

Table 62. Size and population of towns

Population	Number of towns	Total population	Percentage of urban population
Over 1,000,000	1	1,236,065	19·8
100,000–200,000	12	1,502,838	24·1
50,000–99,999	5	311,404	5·0
25,000–49,999	22	756,348	12·1
10,000–24,999	86	1,344,905	21·6
5,000–9,999	90	631,303	10·1
3,000–4,999	86	345,325	5·6
Less than 3,000	51	106,029	1·7
	353	6,234,217	100·0

Source: *Dezvoltarea Industriei Republicii Populare Romîne*, Directia Centrală de Statistică, Bucharest, 1964.

The urban pattern. The Romanian town is the product of two diverse traditions. The western tradition of the walled city, inhabited by a bourgeoisie which practised commerce and carried on crafts, was brought by the Germans, and is exemplified in the cities which they founded, such as Cluj and Braşov. The other is represented by the sprawling agricultural town, in which craftsmen catered only for local needs, and the town, more agricultural than urban in its functions, serves principally as market centre for the surrounding villages.

Although this contrast remains apparent in the physical appearance of the towns, their functions are undergoing change. New industries are being grafted on to the older urban centres; many towns are broadening their industrial base and incorporating the surrounding villages, and a number of new and generally single-industry towns has been founded.

The geographical pattern of Romanian towns is also changing. The expansion of the old and the founding of new towns is intensifying the urbanisation of certain areas, while some parts of the country are little touched by recent urban growth. In the past one would have described the geographical pattern of Romanian towns as made up of two concentric rings, the inner enclosing the Transylvanian Basin and

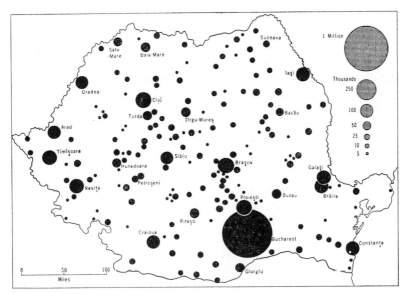

Fig. 11.5. Distribution of cities in Romania. Based on *Anuarul Statistic al RPR, 1964.*

including Braşov, Sibiu, Cluj and Tîrgu Mureş, and the outer encircling the whole Carpathian system from Baia Mare in the northwest round to Suceava in the north-east. The towns themselves lay, as was common in much of eastern Europe, in areas of good farmland, but within sight of the mountains. Such locations suited well the needs of the local peasantry and their relatively small volume of long distance traffic. This urban pattern is now being overlaid by another which conforms to the needs of modern industry and the distribution of fuel and power.

Foremost among the latter are ease of long-distance transport and the access to fuel and raw materials. Towns which have grown most in the past two decades have been the port towns, Bucharest, Ploieşti and other towns near the petroleum field of eastern Walachia, the coal-mining and heavy industrial centres of Petroşeni and Hunedoara, and, above all, those which lie along what is rapidly becoming the main axial belt of Romania, the route from Oradea, through Cluj to Braşov and Bucharest. There are, of course, towns whose recent expansion is not susceptible of such ready explanation: peripheral towns like Iaşi, the regional capital of Moldavia, and Timişoara, and Craiova, the capitals respectively of the Banat and Oltenia.

For social reasons the Romanian government attempts to disperse new industries as widely as possible over the country. But there are regions where the social benefit can be obtained only at too high a cost. Urbanisation and industrialisation have made comparatively little progress in Dobrogea and Oltenia, and it is interesting to note, in this context, that the corresponding regions of Bulgaria have also been little developed. The northern provinces of Maramureş and Suceava have also shown little urban and industrial growth.

A classification of Romanian towns on the basis of 1956 census data showed 42 out of a total of 171 as 'agricultural towns', in which the major part of the active population was actually engaged in farming or in ministering to the needs of the local farming community.[1] At the same time 88 were defined as industrial towns, and 26 as towns in which transport and other tertiary occupations predominated. Most of the industrial towns have, as is inevitable, a large 'service' component, but no less than 12 are classed as 'specialised industrial towns', in which the dominant—usually the only—local industry employed 60 per cent or more of the active population. Such intensive industrial centres were not amongst the largest towns but they did include the metallurgical centres of Reşiţa and Hunedoara and the newly founded chemicals centre of Victoria.

Bucharest. The countries of Eastern Europe are notable for the very large relative size of their largest city, and in Romania and the Balkans, this 'primate' settlement is particularly exaggerated. With an estimated population (1966) of about 1,365,900, Bucharest has more than seven times the population of Cluj, the second largest. The rapid growth of Bucharest in the past century is to be attributed to its selection as capital of the Romanian state, to the construction of modern means of transport and communication radially from it,

[1] Ion Sandru *et al.*, 'Contribution géographique à la classification des villes de la République populaire roumaine', *Annls Géogr.*, **72** (1963), 162–85.

and to the exploitation of nearby petroleum and lignite. For the rest, it owes its size to the cumulative effects of its initial advantages.

The medieval town grew upon a low hill which rose above the right bank of the Dîmbovița River, where are today a number of churches of the sixteenth and seventeenth centuries together with a group of government buildings of more recent date. The whole complex cannot rival the corresponding hills in Prague and Budapest in grandeur and beauty, but it nevertheless has its charm and deep historical interest. The modern town has spread over both banks of the diminutive river, and towards the north is limited for practical purposes by the Colentina River, which here forms a chain of lakes. The centre of the modern city lies to the north of the Dîmbovița, and is marked by wide streets and by impressive if not beautiful modern buildings. The well-built centre quickly degenerates into a broad area of poor housing, much of it nineteenth century in date and incorporating some which derives from the suburban villages. Amid these squalid suburbs lie the modern factories and the tall blocks of flats, ugly and utilitarian, but nevertheless incomparably better than the decaying cottages which they are gradually replacing.

Bucharest is the foremost industrial city of Romania. Every significant branch of industry is carried on here, except iron and steel manufacture and oil refining. The chemical and metal-working industries may be regarded as basic, but a very wide range of alimentary and consumer goods industries has been established to supply not only the expanding local market but also industrial regions such as Ploiești and Brașov.

The chief source of industrial power is the thermal-electric generators, which burn lignite from the Carpathian foot-hills, oil and natural gas. The city has no navigable waterway, and its nearest port is Giurgiu, on the Danube 40 miles away. Bucharest is, however, surrounded by farmland, which includes the irrigated vegetable-growing areas along the Ialomița River. The source of much of the city's food supply thus lies within easy reach.

The Transylvanian towns. These towns, among which the most prominent are Brașov, Sibiu and Cluj, are of Western origin, founded by German or Hungarian settlers, and conforming with the urban plans met with in western Hungary and Czechoslovakia. They are typically compact; their plan is sometimes rectilinear; they were walled during the Middle Ages, and they have large market places, dominated by a Gothic church of late medieval date. They suggest in their layout and architecture that commerce and the crafts were more important than agriculture.

Cluj is today the largest of these cities with an estimated (1966) population of about 185,800. It was formerly a predominantly Hungarian city, lying on the main routeway around the northern flanks of the Bihor Mountains from the Hungarian Plain to the Transylvanian Basin. It lies on the Someş Mic (Little Someş), here little more than a torrent after emerging from the mountains, and is overlooked by forested hills. To the east stretches the plateau of northern Transylvania. the chief area of Szekler settlement in which the chief urban centre is Tîrgu Mureş (86,500). Cluj has long been the chief cultural centre of the Szekler region. It has in recent years become also the economic focus of the industrial development of the northern part of the Transylvanian Basin, and to its own textile, food and engineering industries it adds the chemical and cement industries of Turda, the steel works of Cîmpia-Turzii and the chemical industries associated with the Transylvanian natural gas field.

Sibiu, with about 109,500 inhabitants, is a somewhat smaller city. It nestles against the Făgăraş Mountains; to the north stretches the fertile Transylvanian plateau, to the east the upper Olt valley and to the west, the twisting road into the Mureş valley and so down to the Pannonian Plain. Sibiu was founded by the German settlers, and, as the city of Hermannstadt, was long the capital of the German 'nation'. To this role it bears witness today in its walls, towers and churches. But like Cluj it has become not only an industrial city, but the focus of a ring of smaller industrial centres, in which textile manufacture and mechanical engineering are the most important.

Braşov (163,350) is overlooked by the frowning and forested Southern Carpathians, through which the Predeal Pass leads to Bucharest. To the north stretches the fertile and sheltered Braşov Basin (Depresiunea Bîrsei). Braşov was founded by the Germans, traditionally by the Teutonic knights before their energies were diverted to the Baltic region. Their castle stood on the heights, below which the compact and well-fortified town was built. Braşov became an important commercial centre from which merchants could cross the passes into the more exposed and more dangerous provinces of Muntenia and Moldavia. Braşov retains, more than any of the Transylvanian towns, its earlier and picturesque aspect. But it has also become one of the major industrial centres of the country. The manufacture of railway equipment and of aircraft was established here before the Second World War. The town has since been greatly expanded, and Braşov is today the foremost centre for the manufacture of tractors and lorries. It also produces chemicals, synthetic rubber, cotton textiles and furniture. For transport it relies overwhelmingly on the railway, but derives natural gas by pipeline from the northern part of the Transylvanian Basin.

The Western towns. At the junction of the Western Carpathians and the Pannonian Plain is a line of towns from Satu-Mare (68,300) in the north, through Oradea (122,500) and Arad (126,000), to Timişoara (174,400) in the south. They are part of that ring of towns which encircles the plain and has for centuries served as outlets for the products of the mountains. It was primarily in virtue of this economic function that they were included in 1919 within the Romanian state. The cities themselves were mainly Hungarian in population, with a large Jewish minority in most, before the First World War. The Jewish population has since been reduced to very small proportions and the Romanians—mainly immigrants from the mountains—are now the most numerous group. Their market role, their service industries, and their administrative functions—Timişoara had been the capital of the Hungarian Banat—ensured a considerable growth during the nineteenth century. This growth has been continued. All have important food, engineering and textile industries, and Oradea and Timişoara are also centres of the chemical industries.

The Port towns. The chief ports of Romania are Constanţa, Galaţi and Brăila. They are closely comparable in size and function. Constanţa, which handles the greatest volume of shipping, lies on the flat Dobrogea coast, where a low headland, Cape Constanţa, affords some protection from the north. Both Galaţi (151,300), and Brăila (138,600) lie on the west bank of the Danube, the latter where the river had cut into the low platform, covered with terrace deposits, which forms the eastward extension of the Bărăgan Steppe; the former where the hills which separate the Siret from the Prut similarly terminate in very low bluffs against the river banks. Not until one reaches Giurgiu (39,200) is there a comparable dry site so close to the river's bank. The towns have spread both along the waterfront, where their docks line the river, and back over the low platform to the west, where the modern industries have grown up.

The only other town which deserves separate discussion is Iaşi (160,900), capital of Moldavia, and for a short period also of Romania. It lies amid rolling hills some 10 miles west of the Prut. To the south is the high forested plateau of central Moldavia, but around the town and stretching north-eatwards into Bessarabia the loess deposits have produced gentle contours and have developed a rich chernozem soil. The town itself developed in the Middle Ages, and may in fact derive its name from the Tatar Jazges. It became the seat of the Moldavian princes in the sixteenth century, and at the same time an important religious centre. The town today is noted for the splendid Byzantine churches which survive from this most illustrious period in Moldavia's history.

Like many other cities of the 'Old Kingdom', Iaşi today is architecturally a combination of Moldavian village, late nineteenth-century stucco and mid-twentieth proletarian architecture. It is now a centre of textile, light chemical and food industries, but its peripheral location in one of the least developed areas of Romania has hindered its industrial and urban growth.

AGRICULTURE

Feudalism came late to Romania, and it was not until the sixteenth century that serfdom was widely established on the lands of the boyars. Increasing profits were to be gained from the export of grain, and large landed estates were formed in Moldavia and Walachia. The peasants suffered severely in the process. Early in the nineteenth century attempts were made to ensure that they had sufficient land for their own needs, but the laws were both made and enforced by the landowners, and the peasants benefited little. In the first half of the nineteenth century agriculture was being extended rapidly at the expense of the forest and the steppe; there was a premium on serf labour, and it was not until the more liberal Alexander Cuza was elected Prince of Romania that any measure of reform was possible.

The serfs were then liberated and were given the right to acquire on payment to the government full title to their own plots of land. The law of 1864 was, in Evans' words, 'hastily conceived, imperfectly prepared and frequently badly applied'.[1] The peasants were, in fact, badly treated; they received the poorer land which was soon reduced by the customary division between heirs to holdings that were uneconomically small. Early in the twentieth century the condition of the Romanian peasantry was as unhappy as that of any in Eastern Europe.

[1] Ifor L. Evans, *The Agrarian Revolution in Romania*, Cambridge University Press, 1924, p. 41.

Conditions were somewhat better in Transylvania and the Western Plains, because these were under Austrian rule and benefited from the modest reforms introduced by the Habsburgs. Serfdom was abolished here by Joseph II, but even in these more favoured lands division and subdivision of holdings had reduced the peasants to desperate straits. Despite the hesitant reforms of the nineteenth century, Romania in 1918 was predominantly a land of great estates. Indeed, the popular assemblies of some parts of the future state had made land reform a condition of their incorporation.

Land reform
Hostilities had barely ended when the Romanians began to tear to pieces many of their overlarge estates. They were reduced to areas of from 100 to 500 hectares (247 to 1,235·5 acres), and no less than about 6 million hectares (14·8 million acres) were appropriated, and most of it distributed among the peasantry. The object was to secure to every peasant family a farm of about 5 hectares (12 acres). The reform was described as 'the most sweeping and equitable land reform in south-eastern Europe',[1] but Table 63 shows that it did not even secure an approximate equality:

Table 63. Size and number of holdings

Size of holdings (in hectares)	Number	Per cent of total holdings	Per cent of cultivated area
0–1	610,000	18·6	2·1
1–3	1,100,000	35·5	14·4
3–5	750,000	22·8	19·3
5–10	560,000	17·1	24·2
10–20	180,000	5·5	13·3
20–50	55,000	1·7	7·9
Over 50	25,000	0·8	18·8
	3,280,000	100·0	100·0

Source: S. Fischer-Galati, 197, based on *Anuarul Statistic al României, 1939–40*.

[1] *Romania*, ed. Stephen Fischer-Galati, London, 1957, p. 196.

There was no commensurate provision of agricultural capital. If the standard of farming on the estates had been poor, that on the newly established peasant holdings, with little by way of tools, equipment, seed and even livestock, was even lower. And this situation the Romanian government took no steps to remedy. The price of farm produce in the world market fell, the rural population increased rapidly, and slowly developing industry proved quite incapable of absorbing it. Holdings were further divided and fragmented, so that at the time of the 1930 census, over half were of less than 3 hectares (7 acres), and could fairly be called micro-holdings. The marketing of farm produce was unorganised, agricultural credits were in general not available, and the peasants would in any case have lacked the technical knowledge to use them wisely. Such was Romanian agriculture in the 1930s; land reform was needed as desperately as it had been on the eve of the First World War.

Collectivisation. In Romania, as in most other countries of Eastern Europe, a further measure of land reform was a prelude to the collectivisation drive. All estates in excess of 50 hectares (123·5 acres), together with lands belonging to the churches and certain other bodies, were confiscated, and distributed among the poorer peasantry. The rich peasants, as well as what had survived of the previous land-owning class, were eliminated. Compulsory quotas of farm produce were levied on the peasants, and the services, such as mills and presses, which they required to use were nationalised.

In 1949 the actual collectivisation of the land was begun. It made slow progress until about 1956, when it was stepped up, and it was allegedly completed in 1962.

At the end of 1964 there were 4,716 collective farms of an average size of about 1,570 hectares, together with 683 state farms with an average size about twice that of collectives. In all 95·6 per cent of the cropland had been collectivised.

Collectivisation has been accompanied by technical improvements which were long overdue and still not as effective as they should be. Horse and ox have been replaced in the fields by tractors. In 1964 there were 151,122 tractors,[1] with a comparable number of sowing-machines and reapers. The number of scientifically trained agronomists has been greatly increased and the cropping pattern has been diversified by the introduction or the extension of the acreage under industrial and fodder crops. The area under irrigation has been

[1] In 15-h.p. units.

extended, and the output of animal products greatly increased. Despite the very numerous shortcomings of the Romanian collectivisation programme, farm production has in fact increased notably during the past 15 years.

Table 64. Crop output in Romania, 1948–64
(in thousands of tons)

	1948–52	1958	1961	1966
Maize	2,369	3,657	5,740	8,022
Wheat	2,486	2,914	3,990	5,065
Potatoes	1,561	2,777	2,875	3,352
Sugar-beet	888	1,732	2,911	4,368

Sources: *UN Statistical Yearbook: FAO Production Yearbook: Anuarul Statistic al Republicii Socialiste România, 1967.*

Land use

Romania has always been a predominantly agricultural country. Agriculture continues to employ, despite the industrial growth of recent years, no less than 59 per cent (1963) of the working population, and almost two-thirds of its area is used agriculturally. Cropland, as a percentage of the total, has in fact tended to increase as, with mounting population pressure, marginal land has been brought under the plough. The proportions of the total area under the chief categories of land use in recent decades are shown in Table 65.

Table 65. Land use in Romania

	1921[1]	1938[1]	1948[2]	1952[2]	1963	
Crops	35·3	47·1	37·1	40·2	10,475*	44·2
Meadow and grazing	12·6	17·1	18·8	20·4	4,316	18·2
Vineyards and fruit	1·7	2·3	1·0	1·0	—[3]	—
Forests	24·5	22·3	43·1	38·4	6,378	26·8
Unproductive	25·9	11·2			2,581	10·8
	100·0	100·0	100·0	100·0	23,750	100·0

[1] Inclusive of Bessarabia.   [2] Without Bessarabia and northern Bucovina.
[3] Included with crops.   * in thousands of hectares
Sources: *Romania*, ed. S. Fischer-Galati, p. 219; *Production Yearbook*, FAO, 1965.

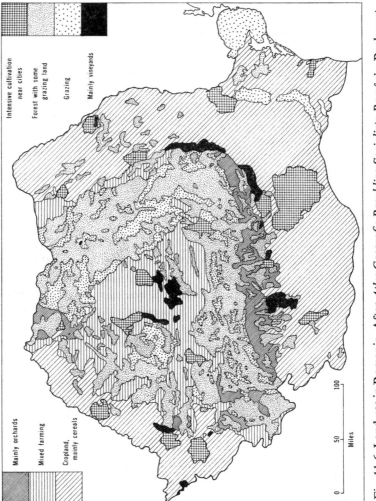

Fig. 11.6. Land use in Romania. After *Atlas Geografic Republica Socialista România*, Bucharest, 1965.

These figures show a gradual expansion of farmland at the expense of forest and waste. Romania lay until quite recently on the agricultural frontier, where the cropland gave way to the steppe. Large areas of Walachia were brought under the plough for the first time in the nineteenth century, and some farmland in Muntenia was first ploughed only after collectivisation. Cereals, though diminishing in importance relative to other crops, continued to dominate Romanian farming, and are grown on nearly three-quarters of all cropland. Industrial crops—primarily sunflower, sugar-beet, flax and hemp— are increasing in importance, but still are grown on only about three per cent of the land. The area under potatoes, vegetables, vineyards and orchards has always been small, though locally very important. Acreage and production have fluctuated, but at present production is being expanded.

An increased emphasis on animal rearing and on dairy farming has necessitated an increase in the area of meadow and grazing. In general, however, the population pressure has prevented the use of anything other than marginal land for grazing. Much of the grazing land is in fact seasonal. It lies in the Carpathian Mountains above the tree-line, and is visited in summer by the transhumant flocks which winter in the valleys and lowlands.

Cereal crops. Almost everywhere in Romania the pattern of cropping is dominated by cereals, and primarily by maize and wheat. Before the middle years of the nineteenth century, wheat, barley, oats and rye had all been grown for local consumption, and in the eighteenth century maize had been introduced. In 1829, by the Treaty of Adrianople, the Romanians were first permitted by their Turkish masters to export farm products to Central and Western Europe. The greatest demand from the first was for wheat, and it was in response to this that farming spread across the plains of Walachia and Moldavia. Between 1837 and the First World War the area under cultivation is said to have expanded from 1 to 6 million hectares (2·5 to 14·8 million acres), and most of this increase was under wheat.[1] Immense quantities were shipped to Central Europe.

Wheat has since continued to be grown in all the lowland regions. It does well on the chernozem, and is tolerant of the low rainfall commonly experienced. It is almost exclusively winter sown, and is rarely grown at altitudes of more than 1,300 feet.

The area under maize has increased rapidly during the present

[1] Mihail Haşeganu, *Geografia Economică a RPR.*, Bucharest, 1957, p. 201.

(a)

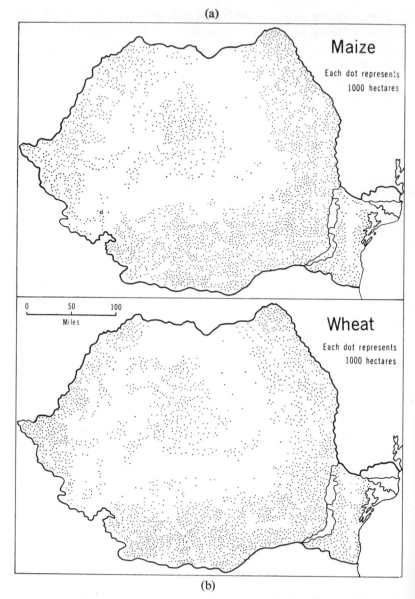

Maize

Each dot represents
1000 hectares

0   50   100
Miles

Wheat

Each dot represents
1000 hectares

(b)

Fig. 11.7. Agriculture: distribution of (a) maize, (b) wheat. After *Atlas Geografic Republica Socialista România*, Bucharest, 1965.

century. It is grown both as fodder and as human food. Its area of cultivation is almost identical with that under wheat, with the Walachian Plain particularly prominent. In 1965 no less than a third per cent of the cropland was under maize.

Other cereal crops are of minor importance and occupy less than 2 per cent of the cultivated land. Barley is the most important of them, and is found in much the same areas as wheat. Oats and rye, by contrast are crops of the mountain regions, and are very little grown in the lowlands. Rice, on the other hand, is locally important in Walachia and parts of the Western Plains. Though introduced by the Turks, it was not much grown until recently, when the Plans provided for its cultivation along the lower Danube and the lower courses of some of its tributaries, where it is not difficult to use the naturally flooded bottom-lands.

Table 66. Crop production and yield in 1966

	Area (1,000 hectares)	Production (1,000 tons)	Yield (in 100 kg per hectare)
Maize	3,288	8,022	24·4
Wheat	3,035	5,065	16·7
Barley	196	483	19·6
Oats	138	170	12·3
Rye	91	100	10·9
Rice	20	56	27·1

Sources: *FAO Production Yearbook, 1965: Anuarul Statistic al Republicii Socialiste România, 1967.*

Industrial crops. The sunflower stands first amongst the crops which are grown for oil. The area cultivated rose sharply during the years between the two world wars, and this trend has since been maintained. It is grown primarily in the plains of Walachia and Moldavia, and in 1965 it was planted on 467,000 hectares.

The sugar-beet was introduced more than a century ago, but it was not until after the Second World War that its cultivation achieved any great importance. Production has already increased tenfold, and much greater increases are anticipated. The chief areas of sugar-beet cultivation are the lowlands in Oltenia, parts of northern Moldavia and the Western Plains, and Transylvania.

Tobacco is widely though nowhere intensively grown in Walachia and southern Moldavia, and is of much smaller importance in Transylvania and the Western Plains.

The raw materials of the textile industries are grown, but only on a very restricted scale. Hemp is produced in the Western Plains and also in the hilly regions of northern Transylvania and Maramureş. Flax which needs moisture and can tolerate a poor soil, is important only in Transylvania and the hills of western Moldavia. Cotton, which assumes considerable importance in Bulgaria, is grown in Romania only in small areas along the Danube valley in Muntenia.

Table 67. Output of industrial crops in 1966

	Area (1,000 hectares)	Production (1,000 tons)
Sugar-beet	194	4,368
Sunflower	468	671
Tobacco	38	40
Hemp	26	91
Flax	25	77

Source: *Anuarul Statistic al Republicii Socialiste România, 1967.*

Vegetables and fruit. The cultivation of garden vegetables has also expanded greatly in recent years. It is practised intensively around all the larger towns, and tomatoes, paprika, onions and certain others are grown as field crops on the damp alluvium of some of the Walachian rivers.

Potatoes are increasingly important, not only as a food, but also for industrial purposes. Though found on the plains, they are primarily a crop of northern Romania, of Transylvania and of the mountains.

Fruit orchards are widespread, and the acreage under peaches, apricots, apples, pears and cherries amounts to about 378,700 hectares (936,000 acres). In general, peaches are the most extensively grown in Walachia, and apples and other 'hard' fruits in Transylvania and Maramureş. The increasing severity of winters in Moldavia greatly reduces the area under orchards.

Viticulture, it is claimed, has been practised since it was introduced by the Romans, but not until the nineteenth century did vineyards begin to cover an extensive area and wine to enter seriously into the export trade of Romania. The grape vine is grown in most parts of the country except the mountains, but commercial vineyards are more restricted in their distribution. The best wines, it is claimed in Romania, are from the climatically marginal province of Moldavia. Vineyards are extensive around Iaşi and in the Carpathian foot-hills of southern Moldavia. They are also developed throughout much of the Walachian foot-hill zone from Buzău to the Olt valley, in Transylvania, and in the Western Plains and their bordering hills. In 1964 the area under vineyards was about 326,000 hectares (805,000 acres). This is slowly being extended as Romania develops its export trade—primarily to the Soviet Union and the more northerly countries of the Eastern bloc—in wine and dessert grapes.

Animal husbandry
In this discussion of the distribution of the more important cultivated crops, it has been repeatedly emphasised that they are found in the Transylvanian Basin and in the ring of lowlands which encircles the Carpathians. Between these two regions of considerable though diverse agricultural potential lie the mountains in which arable farming can be practised only over small areas in the valleys. In the mountain regions, the most important agricultural pursuit is of necessity pastoral. We first meet the Romanian people as pastoralists, engaged mainly in raising sheep within the mountains. Their advance on to the plains in modern times brought with it the abandonment of animal in favour of crop-husbandry, but the change was nowhere complete. Transhumant pastoralism continued to be practised, and the drier parts of the plains, such as the Bărăgan Steppe and Dobrogea have remained in part as ranching rather than farming country.

Transhumance continues to be practised throughout the mountain belt. Industrialisation in the mountain valleys, however, and the extension of crop-farming over the lowlands which had formerly provided winter grazing, are today reducing the scope of the ancient practice. Much of this seasonal movement is today over only short distances, from the mountain villages, where the animals pass the winter, to the nearby summer grazing above the tree line in the Carpathian Mountains. Long-distance transhumance between, for example, the Carpathians near Braşov and winter grazing on the flood plain of the lower Danube has not been abandoned, in part, perhaps, because no alternative use has yet been found for these low-lands, liable to inundation for much of the summer half-year.[1]

With the building of collective farms, the improvement of meadows, and the increased production of fodder crops, cattle now rarely make the journey into the mountains in summer. The size of the herds has been increasing slowly, but, at least relative to the population, they are most numerous in the damper and cooler north. Sheep, on the other hand, remain very numerous, and Romania has one of the largest flocks in Europe. The distribution of sheep tends to be the converse of that of cattle, more numerous in the drier south and south-east of the country. They are important not only for the wool clip, most of which is of poor to medium quality, but also as a source of milk and cheese. Pigs are reared in most parts of the country, but are most numerous and important in the Transylvanian Basin and in the hills which encircle it. Though the horse is still prominent on the roads and at the small town markets, it has almost disappeared from the fields, where mechanical traction has now become general. The total number of horses has diminished sharply in the past decade.

Agricultural regions

The ring of the Carpathian Mountains divides Romania into contrasted agricultural no less than physical regions. Transylvania, the mountains, and the encircling plains have each a great deal in common in their patterns of land-use.

Moldavia-Walachia-Dobrogea. These three historic and physio-graphic provinces, which together make up more than two-thirds of Romania, constitute by far the most important of its agricultural regions. Over most of its extent it is cropland. Wheat is grown in every part of it, and is dominant in much of Walachia. Maize, on the other hand, is more widely grown in Moldavia. The damp lands along the lower Danube provide winter grazing, and the dry lands of parts of Bărăgan and Dobrogea are grazed by sheep at all seasons. Irrigated vegetables are cultivated along the valleys near Bucharest, vineyards clothe many of the hills, rice is grown along the lower valley of the Ialomița, and around the towns are broad belts of intensive market gardening. Forest covers the hills in Oltenia, northern Moldavia, and

---

[1] See particularly Ion Vladutiu, 'Almenwirtschaftliche Viehhaltung und Transhumance im Brangebiet', *Viehzucht und Hirtenleben in Ostmitteleuropa*, Budapest, 1961, pp. 197–241.

the Dobrogea, but this is today for the greater part a rolling, treeless region, with a low rainfall, intensely hot summers and cold winters.

Though carried on in almost every part of the region, farming is intensive only in the vicinity of the towns. Yields are low and the consumption of fertiliser is small. This is a region in which crop-growing could be intensified even though it could not be greatly extended.

Western Plains. The narrow belt of country which lies between the Western Carpathians and the Hungarian border resembles the previous region in its pattern of cropping. It is in the main wheat-growing country, with maize of secondary importance. Flax, sugar-beet and tobacco are relatively important; vines are grown on the hilly margin of the plain, and intensive vegetable cultivation is carried on with irrigation near the towns.

Transylvania. This constitutes the third agricultural region, but its more hilly terrain greatly reduces the area under crops. Its summers are cooler and moister than those of the plains, and this in turn in-fluences the pattern of land use. Wheat predominates, with maize as the second field crop; barley and oats are also grown; potatoes are more widespread than in any other part of Romania, and much of the country's flax is grown here. Vineyards and orchards are common, but the bright sunflower is rarely seen in the fields.

The mountains. The whole Carpathian region can for convenience be regarded as a single agricultural region. Over most of its extent it is forested. Its higher surfaces provide summer grazing. Cultivated land, interspersed with meadow, lies along its valleys, and in the small upland basins which occur within the mountains, wheat and maize are grown. But these crops are of very little importance in the region as a whole. It is oats and rye, potatoes and vegetables that are grown as human food, and meadow grass, fodder crops and the abundant rough grazing which support the animals. Animal rearing—both cattle and sheep—is relatively more important than elsewhere in Romania. Work in the fields and on the grazing lands is restricted in winter, and at this time of the year lumbering provides a secondary employment in much of the region.

Fisheries

Romania's fishing grounds are the channels and lakes of the Danube delta. The abundant plant life contributes to a very rich fauna, and the annual catch is said to amount to over quarter of a million tons. The fishermen live in small hamlets on the sandy islands of the delta, and make use of elaborate fish nets and traps in the smaller waterways and small fishing boats in the larger. The fish caught are mainly carp, pike, perch, and, above all the sturgeon, which makes its way in from the Black Sea and is caught primarily for its caviar. A fish canning and preserving factory has been established at Tulcea, near the head of the delta. Though other Romanian rivers make a small contribution to the total catch, the Black Sea fisheries are themselves of no great importance.

INDUSTRIAL DEVELOPMENT

Modern industry came late to Romania, later in fact than to any other country of Eastern Europe except Bulgaria and Albania. The industrial development, begun before the First World War, was intensified between the First and Second. But Romania suffered from a severe lack of investment capital, a small domestic purchasing power, and a certain reluctance on the part of West European countries to see it develop manufacturing industries of its own. Only those branches of industry, such as the exploitation and refining of petroleum, which satisfied Western needs were able to attract adequate investment capital.

When the Second World War began some 80 per cent of the employed population was still engaged in agriculture, which in turn supplied about half the gross national product. Nor was there much change until 1948. Then most mining and industrial enterprises were nationalised, and two consecutive One-Year Plans were introduced. Their object was to restore the prewar level of production, after which a series of Five-Year Plans aimed to transform Romania into an industrial country. Mining and heavy industry were stressed in the investment programme, and consumer goods industries neglected. Old factories were modernised and re-equipped, and a great number of new factories built. By 1961, it is claimed, gross industrial output was more than five times that of 1938. The manufacture of such items as tractors and lorries, which had not existed before the war, was introduced and greatly expanded. The increase in the power-generating capacity and in the manufacture of cement, iron and steel, all of which were basic to other forms of industrial growth, was much greater than the index already mentioned.

ROMANIA

The Predeal Pass across the Carpathian Mountains

The Transylvanian Basin to the north-west of Braşov; in the distance are the Eastern Carpathian Mountains

ae Gorge of Kazan, formed aere the Danube cuts across e Carpathian Mountains. e river here forms the ernational boundary, with mania to the right and goslavia to the left

Bucharest: an old Orthodox church, surrounded by modern office and apartment blocks

Ploieşti: the town centre, entirely rebuilt after its wartime destruction

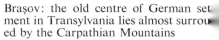

Bucharest: the Street of the Republ

Braşov: the old centre of German set ment in Transylvania lies almost surrou ed by the Carpathian Mountains

Table 68. *Production of basic fuels, iron and steel and cement*

	1938	1950	1960	1966
Electric power (million kwh.)	1,130	2,113	7,650	20,806
Coal (1,000 tons)	2,826	3,893	4,481	6,310
Lignite (1,000 tons)	273	811	3,682	6,503
Pig iron (1,000 tons)	133	320	1,014	2,198
Steel (1,000 tons)	284	555	1,806	3,670
Cement (1,000 tons)	510	1,028	3,054	5,886

Source: M. Haşeganu, *Wirtschaftsgeographie der Rumänischen Volksrepublik*, Berlin, 1962, p. 64; *Anuarul Statistic al Republicii Socialiste România, 1967.*

Fuel and power

The natural endowment of Romania is greater than that of any other Danubian or Balkan power. In addition to the reserves of petroleum and natural gas, which are the largest west of the Soviet Union, Romania has extensive deposits of low-grade coal and a large hydro-electric potential which has hitherto been little developed. The energy consumption has increased very greatly during the period of about 20 years since the initiation of the Plans; electric power capacity had risen almost tenfold by 1966. At the same time the contribution of petroleum and oil has declined somewhat, and is now about a half, while that of natural gas has increased to more than a third. Both direct water-power and wood-fuel, which was formerly important, contribute very little to the total available power.

Coal. As in most other countries of south-eastern Europe, the coal reserves, though extensive, are mostly of poor quality. Brown coal and lignite predominate, and there is little bituminous or coking coal. Almost a third of the total reserves occur in the Petroşeni Basin, in the Southern Carpathians. They are Cretaceous and Tertiary in age, sub-bituminous in quality and are found over an area some 30 miles from west to east and up to 5 miles in breadth. A depth of over 2,000 feet of deposits are said to contain some 25 seams. Means have been found of making a metallurgical coke from the Petroşeni coal, which now supplies much of the needs of the Hunedoara iron works.

Second in importance is the Banat coal field. The coal is superior in

20

(a)

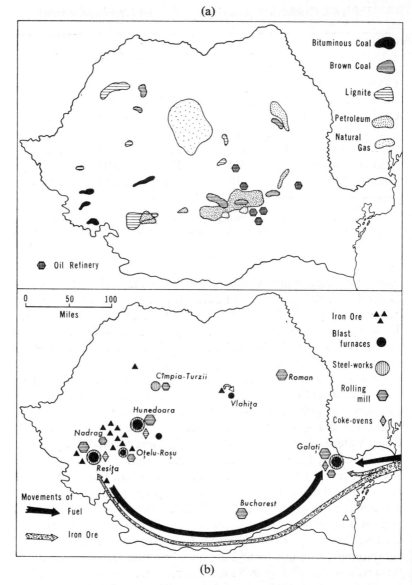

(b)

Fig. 11.8. (a) Fuel resources of Romania. Based on *Atlas Geografic Republica Socialista România*, Bucharest, 1965, and (b) Distribution of the iron and steel industry in Romania. Based on M. Haşeganu and *Atlas Geografic Republica Socialista România*, Bucharest, 1965.

quality to that of Petroşeni, though much less abundant, and it is said to yield a good quality coking coal. The mines lie south of Reşiţa, within the hills which reach down to the Danube. One mine is, in fact, situated within the gorge of the Danube, and loads its output directly on to river barges.

The remaining deposits are of brown coal and lignite. Most valuable are the brown coal fields in the Eastern Carpathians to the west of Bacău and in the Western Carpathians near Cluj. The most extensive deposits of lignite are found in the Southern Carpathians and in the north-western provinces of Crişana and Maramureş. In some areas, notably near Oradea and Cluj and in the foot-hills to north-west of Bucharest, the brown coal or lignite is extracted, briquetted and fed to large thermal-electric generators.

The coal production of Romania has increased sharply since 1948. Over half now comes from the Petroşeni field; about a sixth from the Banat field, with Oradea, Cluj and Southern Carpathians each making smaller contributions. Production, which was less than 2 million tons in 1921, and only 2·8 million in 1938, rose to 3·3 in 1955, to 4·5 in 1960, and to 6·3 in 1966.

Petroleum. Oil and natural gas are, and are likely long to remain the most important sources of energy in Romania. The proven reserves are the largest west of the Soviet Union, and Romanian geologists estimate that large areas of potential oil bearing land remain to be prospected. Oil occurs in a belt of land some 20 to 40 miles in width, extending around the outer margin of the great curve of the Carpathians, from Oltenia into northern Moldavia, from which it is continued through the Ukraine and into southern Poland (see page 372). The geological structures are strongly folded and made up of *Flysch* and of bedded deposits which range from Oligocene to Pliocene.

The presence of oil in parts of this region had long been known, and was mentioned in travellers' narratives of the seventeenth and early eighteenth century. It was not until the construction of a small refinery at Ploieşti in 1856 that the oil really began to be exploited. Oil production increased steadily during the later nineteenth and early twentieth centuries. The capital and equipment were primarily German, and it was to central Europe that much of the oil products was exported. After the First World War the technical and commercial control of the industry passed into West European and American hands; production continued to increase, and in 1932 accounted for a little over 4 per cent of the world production.

Until the Second World War production was almost entirely from the Ploieşti region, and fears began to be expressed that Romanian reserves were approaching exhaustion.[1] The diminution of production during the war years appeared to justify this opinion. After the war exploratory drilling was resumed, using modern Soviet equipment, and the re-development and expansion of the industry had a high priority in the earlier Five-Year Plans.

The early development had centred in the Prahova and Dîmboviţa valleys. New exploratory work took the drilling westwards into the Argeş valley, where important discoveries were made on the edge of the foot-hills, around the town of Piteşti. Oil was then found yet farther to the west, and the Oltenian field, near the town of Tîrgu-Jiu was opened up. In the opposite direction the Bacău field, long known to exist but hitherto supposed to have been small, was explored and developed. In 1961 these four fields: Ploieşti, Argeş, Oltenia and Bacău produced respectively 34, 24, 21 and 18 per cent of the total Romanian production.

The original refining centre was Ploieşti, and this remains the most important. Refineries have also been built on the Bacău oilfield, and at Braşov and Rîmnicu-Sărat. About half the crude oil obtained is refined and used within Romania; the rest is exported through the ports of Giurgiu, Galaţi and Constanţa, each of which is linked by pipeline with the oilfields and domestic refineries. Total production of crude oil has increased steadily since the implementation of the Plans. Present plans are to allow output to flatten off at about 13·2 million tons.

Natural gas. Petroleum deposits hitherto prospected and exploited have been around the outside of the arc of the Carpathian folds. Within the arc the comparable deposits are of natural gas rather than of oil, and in the Transylvanian Basin these are of very great extent and also of very high quality. Their existence had long been known, but their commercial exploitation dates only from 1908 when the gas was used locally for street lighting. For many years the natural gas was neglected in favour of petroleum, and it was only during the fuel shortage after the Second World War that attempts were made to use the Transylvanian gas more extensively.

Bores, mainly around Tîrgu-Mureş in the Magyar Autonomous Region, yielded immense quantities, which were piped not only to the

---

[1] See particularly *Report on Economic and Commercial Conditions in Roumania*, Department of Overseas Trade, H.M.S.O., 1937, pp. 31–3.

larger towns of the Transylvanian Basin, but also across the mountains to Bacău and Iași in Moldavia, to Bucharest, and to towns along the Hungarian border. An agreement between the Romanian and Hungarian governments provided for the construction of a pipeline to Budapest, where segments of Hungarian industry are powered with Transylvanian natural gas. Total gas production has increased from less than a thousand million cubic metres in 1947 to 15 thousand million cubic metres in 1965, and plans are to increase output to 18·5 thousand million cubic metres by 1970.

Not only does the gas, which in Transylvania is a very pure methane, serve directly as a raw material in certain branches of the chemical industry, it is also liquified to produce 'bottle' gas for domestic use and, above all, it is burned in industrial plants, such as cement works, which make heavy heating demands.

Electric power. Before 1952 the electricity supply was generated in a large number of very small urban units. In that year the Doicești thermal-electric station was opened. It lay to the north-west of Bucharest where it could be fed with lignite from a nearby field, and was designed to supply a large part of the needs of the capital. This was quickly followed by the building of many others, fuelled mostly with natural gas or brown coal. The installed generating capacity increased from 730,000 kilowatts in 1948 to 3,258,000 kilowatts in 1965, and it is expected to rise to 3,300 thousand kilowatts by 1970. The types of fuel used made it almost inevitable that the greater part of the new capacity would be located between Bucharest and Cluj, in that belt of territory in which most of the natural gas and much of the petroleum, brown coal and lignite are found. As was pointed out earlier it is in this belt that much of the urban and industrial expansion is now taking place.

Hydro-electric power capacity is in general more expensive to construct than thermal, and, with its abundance of fuel, Romania has shown an understandable reluctance to rely heavily on water power. Nevertheless, a number of small hydro-electric stations has been built, and in 1960 a station of major importance—Hidrocentrala V. I. Lenin—was opened on the Bistriţa river in the Eastern Carpathians, an area not particularly well provided with other sources of power. By 1970 the Iron Gate project is expected to be completed, and Romania's share of the total power generated will be about 5,000 million kilowatts per hour, perhaps a third of the national power production by that date. All the new and larger generating stations

are interlinked by a grid system, which is particularly well developed
in the Bucharest-Cluj axial belt.

Metalliferous mining and metallurgy
The metallurgical industries have enjoyed a very high priority in all
the economic plans of the Romanian government, and have, in this
post-Stalinist period, been intensified rather than the reverse. Romania
is attempting—and not without some success—to make itself an iron
and steel producer of at least secondary rank.

Iron-ore. For such a programme Romania is by no means well
equipped. Domestic reserves of iron-ore are small and of no high
quality, and the erection of the newest iron and steel works on the
navigable Danube at Galaţi is a concession to the fact that imported
ores must be used. Domestic ores are found almost exclusively in the
hills of the Banat and of the neighbouring province of Hunedoara.
In the latter they are mainly siderite, which chemical weathering has
in part enriched and converted to limonite. In the Banat, the very
much smaller reserves are partly of magnetite. Ten years ago total
reserves were put at only 14·4 million tons of iron content. This
estimate was unquestionably low, and a deposit, perhaps large, has
since been discovered in the Dobrogea. Nevertheless, Romania cannot
expect to build a large industry on a resource base as small as this
without drawing heavily on mines in other countries.

One metallic raw material of the steel industry does, however, exist
in abundance—manganese. There are extensive deposits of a low-
grade manganese ore in the former Bucovina, now the province of
Suceava, particularly in the mountains around the upper Bistriţa
river. A very much smaller reserve is found in the Banat. Manganese
mining for export was developed in the later 1930s, and, after a postwar collapse, received a new impetus from the Five-Year Plans.
Production was increased from 50,000 tons in 1950 to 370,000 in 1955,
and in 1963 reached 59,700. At Tîrnăveni, in Transylvania, is a plant
for the manufacture of ferromanganese for steel-making. The only
other metal of significance in the steel industry is chrome, which is
worked in the hills of the Banat, very close to the Iron Gate.

Metallurgical fuel. Only the Banat coal-field is capable of producing
a bituminous coal of coking quality, comparable with that used in
Western Europe. Before the Second World War a small battery of coke-
ovens at Resiţa used this fuel, but was unable to satisfy even the needs
of the small iron industry of this period. In 1952 the Reşiţa coke-ovens

were modernised and enlarged, and shortly afterwards two new batteries were built with Soviet aid at Hunedoara and nearby Călan. The former uses the sub-bituminous coal from the Petroşeni basin, with the addition of imported coking coal. The Călan ovens produce a soft 'Schwelkoks' from brown coal.

Production of metallurgical coke has risen from 80,000 tons in 1948 to 940,000 in 1961 and 1,135,000 in 1965. There appear, however, to be no plans for increasing the coking industry much beyond this point, and it appears that further increases in the smelting and steel-making capacity will be dependent on imported materials.

Iron and steel making. The modern steel industry of Romania grew out of the charcoal-iron industry formerly carried on in the Western Carpathians. A small but modern smelting industry was established in the Banat while the area was still under Hungarian rule, and was expanded after the incorporation of the area into Romania.

The first, and until recently the only integrated plant was at Reşiţa. It was established before the First World War, greatly extended between the First and Second, and further enlarged after the Second. It was established to use the ore and fuel of the Banat and Hunedoara provinces, but these have long proved inadequate even for this small installation, and both are now supplemented by imports. Until recently, Reşiţa was the largest in Romania, producing nearly half the crude steel output. It has now been overtaken by that at Hunedoara, in the Haţeg Basin, and will soon be exceeded also by the new works at Galaţi. The former is a newer and more specialised plant, designed in part at least to produce the steel tubes and other requirements of the petroleum industry. The local ores have to be supplemented by imports, but a satisfactory coke is, as has been noted, being made from the sub-bituminous coal of Petroşeni.

Five miles to the east of Hunedoara lies the very small and old Călan plant, which produces foundry iron, and to the north-east, at Vlăhiţa, in the volcanic mountains which border the Transylvanian Basin lies the only surviving charcoal ironworks. It uses ore from the small deposit at Lueta nearby and charcoal from the surrounding forests.

At present (1966) a large and fully integrated works is nearing completion at Galaţi, and it is planned to have a steel capacity of 4 million tons by 1970. There had previously been a small steel and rolling mill at the site. The decision to expand this undertaking was strongly criticised by the Soviet Union, which had not expected

Romania to advance as rapidly as an industrial power. The new works must inevitably rely on imported ore and fuel, though undoubtedly oil and natural gas will make a large contribution to total energy requirements.

Output of both pig-iron and steel have increased sharply in the past two decades, and current plans anticipate a further increase of steel production to 6·36 million tons by 1970. The steel made is mostly open-hearth, though the production of electric steel has increased recently from almost nil to about a tenth of the total.

Table 69. Output of pig-iron, steel and rolled goods

	Pig-iron	Steel	Rolled goods
1938	133	284	319
1948	186	353	274
1950	320	555	402
1956	583	779	522
1960	1,014	1,806	1,254
1962	1,511	2,451	1,665
1964	1,924	3,039	2,057
1966	2,198	3,670	2,585
1968 planned	—	4,760	—
1970 planned	—	6,360	—

Sources: *Dezvoltarea Industriei Republicii Populare Romîne*, Bucharest, 1964; *Anuarul Statistic al Republicii Socialiste România, 1967*.

The Reşiţa, Hunedoara and Galaţi works are fully integrated. There is a small semi-integrated works at Oţelu Roşu, between Hunedoara and Resiţa, and another at Cîmpia Turzii, near Cluj, which specialises in wire, nails and other drawn steel goods. Rolling mills, without accompanying steelworks, are found at Nădrag, in the Poiana Ruscăi Mountains of the Banat, at Roman in Moldavia, where it specialises in tubes, at Brăila, at Galaţi, where it is being absorbed into a new and fully integrated plant, and at Bucharest itself.

Before turning to the metal-using industries, it is necessary to complete this review of the metallurgical industries by examining the non-ferrous mining and smelting.

Non-ferrous metal industries. The non-ferrous metals have long been worked, without, however, achieving any great importance. They occur primarily in association with the volcanic rocks of northern Transylvania and the Apuşeni Mountains. In the former region the production is principally of lead, copper and manganese, though amounts are very small. These metals are smelted at Baia-Mare in Maramureş province. The Apuseni region has long been noted for its gold production, now the largest in Europe. Gold-working was formerly a monopoly of the Gypsies, who worked the small placer deposits of the Bihor region. It now comes from mines within the so-called Munţii Metalici, to the north of the Mureş River. A number of other minerals, including silver, cinnabar and lead, are found in association with the gold. A deposit of copper pyrites is worked in the hills of the northern Dobrogea, but far more important than any of these metalliferous deposits are the bauxite reserves of Crişana province on the margin of the Pannonian Plain. A plant at Oradea reduces the ore to alumina, and a smelter has been built at Slatina, on the Olt in Oltenia, with the intention presumably of using power from the Iron Gate hydro-electric project.

Table 70. Non-ferrous metal production
(thousand tons)

	1948	1956	1960	1965
Lead	4·0	12·0	12·0	15·0
Bauxite	n.d.	52·0	88·0	12·0

Source: *UN Statistical Yearbook 1965.*

The volume of non-ferrous metal production is relatively small, and, with the exception of the output of aluminium, it is not likely to expand greatly.

Metal-using industries
Before the Second World War the mechanical and engineering industries were well developed in only a narrow range of products, and at least a third of Romania's needs were satisfied by imports. Since 1948 they have been expanded more sharply than any other branch of manufacturing industry, and the indices published by the Romanian government indicated a production in 1966 more than

20*

fifteen times that of 1938. Even when allowance is made for the low base from which this growth began, it is nevertheless a remarkable achievement, and provides justification for the current expansion of the iron and steel industries.

There has been a great expansion in those branches of the metal industries for which Romania itself constitutes a large market, notably the manufacture of pipes and of drilling and oil-refining equipment. The manufacture of railway equipment, which had long been carried on in Bucharest, has been expanded. The construction of farm equipment, particularly of tractors, of lorries, of machine tools, and of electrical motors and equipment have all been developed. At the river and sea ports the building of small craft—barges, fishing boats and tankers—has been established.

The engineering and mechanical industries show a pattern of concentration which is, perhaps, to be expected. Bucharest is the largest and most varied centre, and employs about a quarter of the labour force. North of the city, in the province of Braşov is a large number of manufacturing centres, most of them with the exception of Ploieşti itself, relatively small. Sinaia, on the Predeal road across the Carpathians, has a large tractor factory, and beyond the mountains Braşov is second in size and range of production only to Bucharest. Braşov is particularly noteworthy for its manufacture of lorries, tractors and other types of farm equipment. Sibiu, Tîrgu-Mureş and Cluj are small manufacturing centres. The only important centres of this industry remote from the Cluj-Bucharest axis are those of the Banat: Arad, Timişoara and Reşiţa, of Craiova, of the port towns, and of Moldavia, where the government has located factories in an attempt to industrialise a province which had hitherto been very largely agricultural. The Moldavian industries are predominantly light. They include, in addition to the large ball-bearing factory at Birlad, a number of factories engaged primarily in the repair and maintenance of equipment. The development of the Bacău oilfield has encouraged the manufacture there of drilling and oil-refining equipment.

The engineering industries are strongly oriented towards the consumer. The iron and steel producing regions, with the exception of Galaţi, scarcely figure as centres of the metal-using industries. The fact that in 1966 nearly 50 per cent of the labour force engaged in this branch of industry was employed in the city of Bucharest and the provinces of Ploieşti and Braşov shows how strongly industries have been attracted to the Bucharest-Cluj axis.

Chemical industries

Romania is unusually well endowed with the raw materials of the chemical industry. Crude oil is refined within Romania, yielding a number of products which are themselves the basis of petro-chemical industries. The processing of natural gas is the source of another range of products; the salt, pyrites and by-products of the non-ferrous smelting industry are used in the manufacture of the basic chemicals, and the sedge which grows over much of the Danube delta has proved to be an excellent base for the cellulose industry.

The manufacture of the basic acids and alkalis is closely associated with the smelting of metalliferous ores, with the extensive pyrites deposits and with the very large and pure deposits of the Ploieşti region. The common acids are the basis of the manufacture of fertiliser, now widely manufactured in the principal agricultural areas. Rubber is made at Bucharest and near Ploieşti and Braşov, cellulose in a large new factory at Braila, and paper at a number of factories in or near the Carpathians, which produce its basic raw material, softwood timber.

The chemical industry shows to an even more marked degree than engineering that concentration, already mentioned, along the Bucharest-Cluj axis. Almost two-thirds of the employment in the chemical industries is in the provinces of Bucharest, Ploieşti, Braşov and Cluj.

Production has risen sharply in most branches, as Table 71 shows.

Table 71. Production of the chemical industry (thousand tons)

	1948	1956	1960	1966
Sulphuric acid	28	95	226	619
Hydrochloric acid	1	2·4	5·5	15·8[1]
Caustic soda	14·3	23·8	74·3	252
Superphosphates	1	55	326	790[1]
Nitrogenous fertiliser	—	6·3	18·9	166·3[1]

[1] 1965.

Sources: *UN Statistical Yearbook 1966: Anuarul Statistic al Republicii Socialiste România, 1967.*

Building materials. The manufacture of building materials is oriented strongly towards the source of its raw materials. Cement manufacture has greatly increased, but remains concentrated between

Bucharest and Braşov, where its raw materials are available and can be calcined with natural gas. Large cement works have also been built in the Dobrogea and in the small but growing industrial region in the Bistriţa valley of Moldavia. The output of cement has grown from about a million tons a year in 1950 to 5·9 million in 1966. The planned production for 1970 is 7·5 million, and it appears that the rapidly rising graph of production will flatten off at about this level.

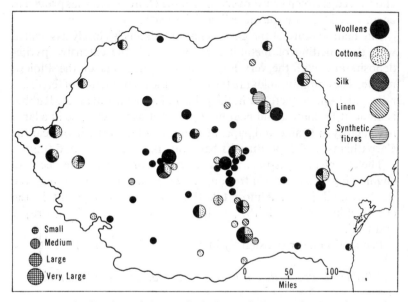

Fig. 11.9. Distribution of the textile industry in Romania. Based on *Atlas Geografic Republica Socialista România*, Bucharest, 1965.

The manufacture of other building materials—bricks and tiles, drain-pipes and plaster—is more widespread and, since these goods are oriented more towards the consumer than towards the capital goods industries, their expansion has been a great deal less rapid.

Light industries
Before 1948 Romanian manufacturing industry consisted largely of the light and consumer goods industries. With the exceptions of a few specialised branches, the heavy and capital goods industries were little developed. Since 1948 this situation has been reversed. After 1950 the heavy industries received nearly a half of the total investment,

and the consumers' goods industries less than 10 per cent. The result has been serious shortages of such goods as clothing, footwear, household furnishings and equipment, and certain foodstuffs. The government has always encouraged the hope that more capital would be diverted to these branches of industry, but always the demands of heavy industry have triumphed. The result is that, although a few works have been modernised and a very few new ones established, the geography of the light and consumer goods industries is still substantially as it was in 1938.

Textile industries. The manufacture of textiles, carried on as a domestic craft since the earliest times, was first carried into factories in the later years of the nineteenth century. The earliest mills were very small, and located mainly within the mountains, where they had the advantage of water-power, or in the region of Bucharest, where lay the greater part of their market. All branches of the textile industry showed between the two world wars a greater rate of expansion than they have since displayed. Since 1948, a few large mills have been built, some older mills expanded, and many small ones closed. The average size of the mills has greatly increased, and one assumes that their efficiency has increased proportionately. Nevertheless, the overall increase in some of the textile products has been small compared with that in capital goods industries.

Table 72. Textile production (thousand tons)

	1940	1956	1960	1965
Cotton yarn	21·4	43·0	51·6	78·3
Other vegetable fibre	—	—	12·7	19·3
Woollen yarn	8·2	17·3	19·4	24·8
Synthetic fibre	1·3	26	2·8	4·7

Source: UN Statistical Yearbook, 1966.

The cotton textile industry is the largest and most modern. It employs about 43 per cent of all the labour in the textile industries, and two-thirds of its total production is from factories which each employ more than 2,000 workers. The woollen industry had in 1963 no factories of this size. Cotton manufacturing is much more an urban industry than woollen. Its chief centres are Bucharest, Galaţi, Iaşi,

Arad and Timişoara. Large new factories have been built at Lugoj in the Banat, and Botoşani in northern Moldavia.

The woollen industry is the oldest and now the second most important branch of the textile industry, with about a fifth of the labour force. It continues to be carried on as a domestic industry, and it is far from uncommon to see a peasant woman guiding her cow along the road, distaff tucked under her arm and spindle in hand. The branch of the woollen industry for which there are statistical data is now carried on in very many small factories, chiefly in Transylvania, but also in northern Moldavia and in Bucharest. The domestic wool clip is in general of a very coarse quality and, though spun and woven by the peasants, little of it is used in the mills. The better domestic wool—chiefly merino—has to be supplemented by imported wool.

Flax and hemp have long been cultivated, especially in Transylvania, and employed in peasant industries. They are now woven in a few small factories in Bucharest and the hills to the north, but flax and the coarse fibres together do not employ more than 6 per cent of the whole labour force in the textile industries.

The silk industry is also little developed. Raw silk is produced by the peasants in the Banat, and reeled and woven locally. There are also silk-weaving mills in Bucharest and Transylvania, which use synthetic fibres, but the industry is small and its employment no larger than that of the flax and hemp industry.

Leather industry. The leather, like the woollen industry, began as a domestic craft and moved then to many small factories, most of them in Transylvania. Apart from a degree of rationalisation—the closing of small tanneries and the extension of the larger—there has been little change in the geography and structure of the industry.

Clothing industry. The factory manufacture of clothing was but little developed before the Second World War, the clothing worn by the peasantry being made at home. Increasing urbanisation has brought with it a demand for more fashionable clothing, and the manufacture of both clothing and hosiery has increased sharply in recent years. Most of the new factories are in the larger towns, especially Bucharest, Braşov, Sibiu, Timişoara, Arad, and Iaşi.

Food industries. Flour-milling and the baking of bread are the most widespread of the alimentary industries. Apart from a few large, up-to-date flour mills in the Western and Walachian Plains, these industries continue to be carried in very small units.

The cultivation of sugar-beet, greatly expanded in recent years, has necessitated the building of sugar-processing factories in all the more important agricultural regions.

Most of the fats in the Romanian diet are of vegetable origin, and come chiefly from the sunflower. The majority of the factories which crush the sunflower seed and process its oil are in Walachia and Moldavia, where physical conditions are most suited for the cultivation of the sunflower.

Other food-processing industries, particularly the manufacture of conserves, the tinning of vegetables and fruit juices, the commercial manufacture of butter and cheese, and the preparation of meat for the market, are particularly widespread. There are concentrations of these branches of industry in all the larger towns of the plains, and smaller and more specialised branches in Transylvania and its mountain fringe. Tobacco is processed in a number of towns, notably Bucharest, Craiova, Timişoara and Iaşi.

Woodworking industries. No less than 27 per cent of Romania is forested, about three-quarters of this with broadleaved trees. Lumbering and woodworking are long-established and important industries. Peasant art has for centuries taken the form of elaborate carving in the mountainous regions, and houses and farmyards are often elaborately decorated in wood. Wood is used as fuel in the villages; is burned to make charcoal, cut for pit-props, sawn into building timber, and made into panelling and veneer. Many of these branches of industry are carried on within the mountains, where the forests occur and water-power is available. The actual manufacture of furniture, office equipment and other carpenters' products is carried on in a very large number of factories in the plains and particularly in the larger towns which provide much of the market.

Industrial regions

This account of Romania's manufacturing industries will have shown that there are within its boundaries three types of industrial distribution. There are, first, those branches of industry whose location is determined by the nature of their materials. These include the extractive and smelting industries and also the manufacture of cement, bricks and tiles, and of some of the basic and petro-chemicals. Secondly, we have a small group of industries which grew up mainly in Transylvania and its surrounding mountains largely because these were at the time the most densely settled and developed parts of the country; they include the woollen, linen and leather industries, as well as many branches of woodworking. Lastly we have the great volume and range of industrial production which has resulted from the planned economic growth of the past 20 years and from a short period of generally uncoordinated development before the Second World War.

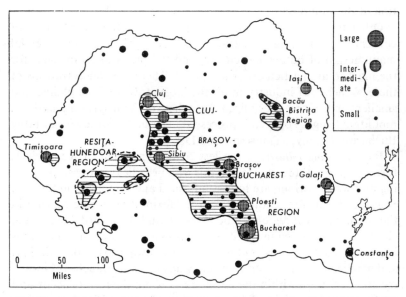

Fig. 11.10. Distribution of manufacturing in Romania; the nature of the industry is not distinguished. Based on M. Haseganu and *Atlas Geografic Republica Socialista România*, Bucharest, 1965.

The Bucharest-Cluj axis. Many of the industries in this latter group could have been located at any place that had adequate means of transport. In fact most were established between Bucharest and Cluj, with heavy concentrations around Ploieşti and Braşov, and, to a somewhat smaller degree, around Sibiu, Tirgu-Mureş and Cluj. Here they form an industrialised region, lying obliquely across the country, and resembling in some degree the industralised 'axial belt' of England.

This industrial region had unique advantages. It included Bucharest, chosen in 1859 to be the national capital, and the chief centres of Szekler and Saxon settlement; it had an adequate agricultural base, and it contained the earliest petroleum deposits to be prospected and exploited. To these it added certain of the raw materials of the chemical industry and almost unlimited reserves of natural gas. Lastly, through it ran the routeway—both road and rail—which linked Bucharest with the West.

Most branches of Romania's industry are represented in this region. We have the immense variety of the industrial structure of Bucharest, the more specialised manufactures of Ploieşti and Braşov, and the lighter industries of the Transylvanian Basin.

Hunedoara and Banat. The mountains which extend southwards from the Mureş valley to the Iron Gate contain the most extensive reserves of coal and iron-ore in Romania. The coal mines and power stations of the Petroşeni Basin, the iron and steel works of Hunedoara and Reşiţa, the smaller works at Nădrag, Oţelu-Roşu and Călan, and the mines of the Banat together make up a highly specialised industrial region.

The Bacău region. The only industrial region which is entirely the creation of the recent economic plans is that which lies along the eastern flanks of the Carpathians, in province of Bacău. Its basis—apart from the desire to bring industry to a hitherto backward and neglected region—lies in its lignite, its petroleum and its water-power. The Bistriţa is the only Romanian river whose potential can be said to have been developed. The large 'V. I. Lenin' Dam, within the mountains at Bicaz, is supplemented by a number of smaller dams which extend down to the junction of the Bistriţa with the Siret. In addition to industries based on the local timber supply and on the agricultural products of Moldavia, petroleum refining and petro-chemical industries have been established; chemical factories, producing particularly the basic acids and alkalis, rubber and fertiliser have been built, and at Roman a tube-mill has been established.

The port towns. The three major ports, Constanţa, Galaţi and Brăila, have a varied industrial structure. The food-processing industries are based on the products of their own agricultural hinterlands; the cellulose manufacture at Brăila, on the growth of sedge in the delta, but most others, including the cotton textile and the rapidly growing iron and steel industry, on imported raw materials.

Industrial centres. These four industrial regions employ about two-thirds of the labour force in Romanian industry. No other measure of their relative importance is possible. Other centres are engaged in a great variety of industrial undertakings distributed throughout the country. It has been the government's policy, for both political and economic reasons, to bring factory industry to the poorer and more backward parts of the country. To some extent the economics of plant location have been over-ridden by the social necessity of drawing such areas into the mainstream of Romanian life. Only thus can one explain the Roman tube-mill, the Bîrlad ball-bearing factory and the electrical engineering works at Craiova. The industrial map of Romania, especially the peripheral plain regions, is dotted with industrial centres, existing in seeming isolation. The fact that many are found in the best agricultural land is evidence that here was excess farm labour—the product of both rural overpopulation and of collectivisation—waiting to be absorbed into factory employment.

To this category belong the towns of the Western Plains, with varied but generally light industries; Baia-Mare, with its non-ferrous metal industries; Botoşani, with its new textile mills; Suceava with its cellulose plant, and Iaşi, with its chemicals and textiles. These centres stand out against a background of small factories and workshops, engaged primarily in the food and wood-working industries, which are found in almost every large village and small town of Romania.

COMMUNICATIONS AND TRADE

In both Poland and Czechoslovakia the transport networks were originally focused on places which now lie beyond the boundaries of the state. The same situation existed in Romania. The system developed in the Old Kingdom had few points of contact with that of Transylvania. Parts of Bucovina, until recently, could be reached by rail only from the Ukraine.

Transport system
The Romanian government after the First World War was faced with a heavy problem in unifying its transport system, and it cannot be said to have completed it when the Second World War began.

Road system. Romania had in 1964 only about 4,000 miles of modern road, roughly 1 mile for each 28 square miles and one of the lowest ratios in Eastern Europe. This means that, although the major cities are interlinked by motor roads, many of the small towns and most of the villages remain accessible by roads which are sometimes steep and narrow, and occasionally unusable by modern transport. Romania stands in as great a need as Yugoslavia of a system of modern all-weather motor-roads.

Railway system. This was pieced together after the First World War from a number of disparate segments. It is now longer by more than 50 per cent than the system of modern roads, a circumstance that is a little unusual. A few short lines have been built since 1948, including one into the Maramureş Basin, which had hitherto been accessible only from Soviet territory. A line has also been completed up the Jiu valley, thus linking the Petroşeni coal basin with Oltenia, but the most important link to be completed in the rail net is that which runs westward from Bucharest through the Walachian Plain to Craiova. A line which was planned from Braşov across the Eastern Carpathians to the Moldavian Plain remains unfinished. The Danube is now crossed at Giurgiu by the new 'Friendship' road and rail bridge, as well as by the older crossing at Cernavodă, on the Bucharest to Constanţa line.

The railway net is a very open one, even in the industrially developed regions of Bucharest and Ploieşti. It is most dense in the Western Plains, particularly in Timişoara, where it was inherited from Hungary. Most of the track is of standard gauge, and narrow-gauge lines are in fact mostly found in mountainous areas where a wider track might be difficult to install for technical reasons. The line is mostly single-tracked, and the only important sections that have been double tracked are those along the middle Mureş, between Bucharest and Braşov, and from Ploieşti eastwards through the oilfield region to the Siret.

The system appears to be inadequate to carry the burden that is put upon it. There are, for example, only six crossings of the Carpathian chain between the Soviet border in Bucovina and the Iron Gate—a distance of some 325 miles. A large proportion of the area of Romania lies more than ten miles from the nearest railway.

River navigation. Only the Danube is regularly used for navigation, but its usefulness to Romania is greatly reduced by the fact that for much of its course it borders one of the less developed parts of the country, and is, furthermore, rendered inaccessible for part of this distance by river marshes. It is noteworthy that none of the river towns between Turnu-Severin and Brăila, a distance of some 460 miles, had more than 20,000 inhabitants, except Giurgiu and Călăraşi, and that no industrial undertaking of national importance has been located along the river except the chemical works of Călăraşi and Turnu-Măgurele.

There are, however, a number of small river ports, which are indicated in Fig. 11.5. Data are not available on the volume of shipping handled, but it is unquestionably very small. Indeed, the most important domestic traffic carried by the Danube is the coal from the Banat mines which is shipped from Orşova, within the Iron Gate gorges, to Cernavodă to supply power stations in the Dobrogea. The use of the Danube in Romania's international trade is discussed below.

The Danube can only be used by boats drawing less than 6·5 feet (2 metres), and navigation is seriously hindered in summer by the low water-level, and in winter by ice, especially that which forms over the still waters of the delta.

Other Romanian rivers are of little use for navigation. The Prut is navigable upstream to the neighbourhood of Iaşi for small craft, but is in fact very little used. The same can be said of the lower Siret. A few rivers, notably the Mureş, are used for floating lumber, but none of these is considered navigable. The only navigation canal, other than regulated branches of the Danube delta, is the Bega Canal in the Banat province. It was cut when the area was under Hungarian rule from the city of Timişoara to join the Bega river inside present-day Hungary. Its purpose was primarily to provide irrigation water, but was intended also to serve for navigation, and it is of local importance in the western Banat.

Other means of transport. Great use is made of pipelines to transport Romania's most valuable mineral products, petroleum and natural gas. Not only are oilfields and refineries linked in this way, but pipelines also convey petroleum to the river ports of Giurgiu, Brăila and Galaţi, and the seaport of Constanţa which together handle most of the exports. Natural gas is generally moved by pipeline, and the gasfield of Transylvania is linked in this way with many of the towns and a number of the power generators and industrial works of central Romania. A pipeline to Budapest supplies gas to a number of Hungarian industries.

Air transport is entirely state-owned and is operated by TAROM. The domestic system is focused on Bucharest, and links the capital with most of the more important centres of population.

Ports and ocean shipping. Much of Romania's foreign trade is carried on by sea. The greatest volume passes through Constanţa, but ships of up to 6,000 tons are able to use the Sulina Channel and the lower Danube to reach the river ports of Galaţi and Brăila. Ocean shipping does not normally ascend the river beyond the latter, and goods are transshipped to barges in these ports. Giurgiu is the most important upstream river port. It is the port for the capital; it exports part of the petroleum products of the Ploieşti region, and is the port of import for a large part of Romania's imports from Czechoslovakia and Hungary, which are brought by barge down the Danube. In addition to their role in trans-shipping goods from river-barge to sea-going ship and vice versa, the ports of Brăila and Galaţi handle much of the grain export from Walachia and the shipments of Carpathian lumber. Amongst the most bulky of imports are iron-ore and metallurgical fuel which are transshipped to barges for the upstream journey to the river port of Orşova and the smelting centres of the Banat and Hunedoara. With the completion of the Galaţi iron and steel works Galaţi is itself becoming the major import point for iron-ore and coking coal.

Constanţa is the leading port, and handles a great deal of the petroleum export and general cargo, as well as transit traffic with Hungary and Czechoslovakia. It lies on the sheltered southern side of a low headland, and is far enough from the Delta to be free of silting. It is not a natural harbour, but is protected by jetties and has a depth of at least 28 feet. Constanţa has been linked with the Danube valley since 1860 by the railway across the Dobrogea and the Cerna-vodă bridge over the Danube. The proposal to link the port with the Danube also by canal had already been discussed intermittently for over a century, when it was proposed anew by the Romanian government in 1949. Such a canal would shorten the journey from up-river ports to the sea by about 150 miles. It would furthermore avoid the considerable difficulties of navigating the delta, and would link growing industrial centres within the Dobrogea with both the river and the sea. Work was begun on the project in the same year, but from the start it appears to have been badly organised and poorly equipped, and had made relatively little progress when in 1953 work was stopped. It has not since been resumed.

Foreign trade

Until recently the trading pattern of Romania was essentially that of an underdeveloped country. Exports were dominated by primary agricultural and mineral products, and imports by manufactured goods. Trade was oriented towards Western Europe, and Germany succeeded for a period in integrating Romania into its economy as a major source of agricultural and mineral raw materials. This situation has been changed by the industrial growth of the past two decades and by the country's new political orientation. The export of primary goods continues, but has declined both relatively and absolutely, while that of manufactured or processed goods has increased from almost nothing to a large part of the total. It is unfortunate that Romanian statistics give the value of exports and imports only by very broad categories, which do not coincide with those normally used in trade statistics. The more detailed figures are given by weight, volume or the number of items.

Table 73 shows how sharp has been the increase in the volume of trade since Romania began again to make data available.

Table 73. Romania's imports and exports, 1958–66
(in millions of Lei)

	Imports	Exports
1958	2,890	2,810
1959	3,012	3,135
1960	3,887	4,302
1961	4,888	4,755
1962	5,647	4,908
1963	6,132	5,490
1964	7,009	6,000
1965	6,463	6,609

Source: *Yearbook of International Trade Statistics, 1965.*

Exports. The export trade of Romania continues to be dominated by raw materials, both agricultural and mineral. In 1965, no less than 25 per cent of exports by value consisted of 'fuel, minerals and metals', and it is apparent from the detailed tables that most of this consisted of petroleum and petroleum products. At the same time 35 per cent was made up of raw materials of vegetable origin, and it is no less clear that this consisted largely of wheat—882,200 tons of it—and lumber—2,683,100 cubic metres. At the same time, however, manufactured goods were not unimportant. Machinery and mechanical equipment made up 18 per cent, and this proportion had been growing both absolutely and relatively.

The value of goods entering into Romanian foreign trade, by the broad categories employed by the statistical authorities, is shown, for 1965, in Table 74.

Table 74. Romania's foreign trade—by commodity (in millions of Lei)
1965

	Imports	Exports
Live animals	0·8	1·5
Foodstuffs	155·4	918·7
Raw material for the food industries	45·5	485·2
Other raw material of vegetable and animal origin	716·4	934·8
Fuels, minerals, metals	2,089·9	1,667·4
Chemicals, fertilisers, rubber	407·3	425·2
Building materials	92·3	224·5
Machinery and equipment	2,521·4	1,223·4
Consumer goods of industrial origin	433·7	728·5
	6,462·7	6,609·2

Source: *Yearbook of International Trade Statistics, 1965.*

Imports. The nature of Romania's economic development in recent years has dictated the nature of its import trade. Capital equipment, much of it machinery, made up 39 per cent of the total by value in 1964, and the record of previous years suggests that this proportion may be increasing. On the other hand, the import is growing of raw materials for industries already established. About 33 per cent is now made up of 'fuels, minerals and metals', a category which in this case consists almost entirely of coking coal, metallurgical coke and iron-ore. In other words, almost a third of the current volume of trade is a direct consequence of the Romanian decision to expand the iron-smelting and steel industries. As the Galați works are expanded to their planned limit, iron-ore and metallurigical fuel must assume an increasingly important role in Romania's trade.

In 1965 the gross tonnage of iron-ore imported was 2,623,200. On the assumption that most of this was from Krivoi Rog, it must have had an iron content of about 1,500,000 tons, and thus have contributed about three-quarters of the total blast furnace output. The 717,800 tons of coking coal produced and 945,600 tons of metallurgical coke imported would, on a normal ratio of fuel used to pig-iron produced, have covered the greater part of Romania's needs. Few countries in the modern world have embarked on so ambitious an industrial programme with so inadequate a domestic resource base. On the other hand, Table 75 shows the imports in the same year of finished or part-finished steel goods.

Table 75. Imports of steel tubes, rolled metal goods and ferro-alloys (thousand tons)

Steel tubes	81·3
Rolled metal goods	1,117·0
Ferro-alloys	52·6
	1,250·9

Source: *UN Yearbook of International Trade Statistics, 1965.*

If steel consumption could be expected to continue at the present level, then Romania is clearly justified in her policy. The raw materials of the smelting industry are no more difficult to acquire than half-finished steel goods, and the purchase of ore and fuel would present a smaller problem in Romania's balance of payments.

Direction of trade. Romania's trade is strongly oriented towards the other countries of the Communist block which in 1965 accounted for no less than 68 per cent. Trade with the Communist countries in Asia and with Albania was very small—2·2 per cent of the total. The rest was with the Soviet Union—39 per cent, and with the East European members of the bloc—22·5 per cent. The heavy volume of trade with the Soviet Union is due largely to the need to import substantial amounts of iron-ore and metallurgical fuel, which come mainly from the Ukraine.

Trade with the non-Communist world is tending to increase, especially that with West Germany, Italy, France and Great Britain. This trade, furthermore, tends to show a negative balance, and is very largely responsible for the fact that imports have generally exceeded exports in value. Romania's trade with other bloc countries is carried on more nearly on a barter basis, and shows only a very small balance in favour of one side or the other. Table 76 shows the volume of trade with the Soviet Union, other East European countries and with the rest of the world in 1964.

Table 76. Romania's foreign trade—by countries (in millions of Lei)

	Imports from Value	Exports to Value
Soviet Union	2,436·9	2,630·6
Eastern Europe:		
Bulgaria	78·4	55·3
Czechoslovakia	417·5	571·5
East Germany	375·0	430·4
Hungary	168·6	230·7
Poland	222·4	269·7
Yugoslavia	74·5	98·6
Albania	15·1	18·5
Other Communist countries:		
China, North Korea, North Viet Nam, Cuba	164·8	224·8
West Germany	662·8	379·4
Italy	311·6	395·7
France	295·3	131·2
United Kingdom	263·4	183·2
Other Western Europe	425·5	389·1
Rest of the world		
	6,462·7	6,609·2

Source: *UN Yearbook of International Trade Statistics, 1965.*

Bibliography
General
Atlas Geografic, Republica Socialistă România, Bucharest, 1965.
FISCHER-GALATI, STEPHEN, ed., *Romania,* Mid-European Studies Centre, London, Stevens, 1957.

KORMOS, C., *Rumania*, British Survey Handbooks, No. 2, Cambridge University Press, 1944.

MORARU, TIBERIU, VASILE CUCU, ION VELCEA, *The Geography of Romania*, Bucharest, 1966.

Republica Populară Romînă: Noua Geografie a Patriei, Bucharest, Editura Stiintifică, 1964.

SITWELL, SACHEVERELL, *Roumanian Journey*, London, Batsford 1938.

Historical and Political Geography

MARRIOTT, J. A. R. The Eastern Question, Oxford University Press, 1924.

ROBERTS, HENRY L., *Rumania: Political Problems of an Agrarian State*, Yale University Press, 1951.

SETON-WATSON, R. W. *A History of the Roumanians*, Cambridge University Press, 1934.

— 'Roumanian Origins', *History*, **7** (1922–3), 241–55.

Physical Geography

BAUER, LUDWIG, 'Landeskulturelle und ökonomisch-geographische Probleme des Donaudeltas', *Geogr. Ber.*, **7** (1962), 1–15.

GÜTHLER, WOLFGANG, 'Das Donaudelta und seine wirtschaftliche Bedeutung für die Volksrepublik Rumanien', *Petermanns Mitt.*, **102** (1958), 270–73.

IONESCU, G. *Communism in Rumania, 1944–1962*, Oxford University Press, 1964.

DE MARGERIE, EMMANUEL, 'L'évolution morphologique des Alpes de Transylvanie', *Annls Géogr.*, **17** (1908), 404–12.

DE MARTONNE, EMMANUEL, 'The Carpathians: Physiogeographic Features Controlling Human Geography', *Geographical Review*, **3** (1917), 417–37.

— 'Le Massif de Bihar', *Annls Géogr.*, **31** (1922), 313–40.

— 'Roumanie', in *Géographie Universelle*, **4** (Paris, Colin, 1931), 699–810.

NICULESCU, GH. *et al.*, 'Nouvelle contribution à l'étude de la morphologie glaciaire des Carpates roumaines', *Recueil d'Études Géographiques*, Bucharest, 1960, 29–43.

Population and Settlement

BĂCĂNARU, I. 'Contribution à l'étude géographique des établissements ruraux du Delta du Danube', *Revue Roumaine de Géologie, Geophysique et Géographie* **8** (1964), 27–32.

BONER, CHARLES, *Transylvania: its Products and its People*, London, Longmans, 1865.

BUGĂ, DRAGOŞ and CONSTANŢA RUŞENESCU, 'Territorial distribution and growth of population in the Rumanian plain in the 20th century', *Revue Roumaine de Géologie, Géophysique, et Géographie*, **8** (1964), 216.

CONEA, ION, 'Sur les types d'habitat de la population autochtone de la Dacie', *Revue Roumaine de Géologie, Géophysique et Géographie, Serie de Géographie*, **8** (1964), 203–11.

DEER, JOSEPH, and BELA PUKANSZKY, 'Saxons', in Louis C. Cornish, *Transylvania*, Philadelphia, Dorronce, 1947, 208–19.

HERBST, C., I. BACANARU and N. CALOIANU, 'Types de concentration territoriale de l'industrie en Roumanie', *Revue Roumaine de Géologie, Géophysique et Géographie*, **8** (1964), 39–44.

MIHĂILESCU, VINTILA, 'Une carte de l'habitat rural en Roumanie', *C. Congr. Int. Géogr., Paris, 1931* (Paris, Colin, 1934) **3**, 33–5.

— 'L'évolution de l'habitat rural dans les collines de la Valachie entre 1790–1900', *C. Congr. Int. Geogr., Varsovie, 1934*, (Paris, 1937), **3**, 474–81.

Roumania: Eastern Carpathian Studies, London, Le Play Society, 1936.

Roumania: South Carpathian Studies, London, Le Play Society, 1939.

SANDRU, ION, 'Les établissements humains de la dépression sub-carpathique de Oneşti', *Annls Géogr.*, **74**, 1965, 160–74.

— 'Vergleichende Betrachtung der rumänischen Stadte', *Geogr. Ber.*, **5** (1960), 29–41.

SANDRU, I. and V. CUCU, 'Classification of towns in Rumania', *Revue Roumaine de Géologie, Géophysique et Géographie*, **8** (1964), 13–20.

SANDRU, ION, V. CUCU and P. POGHIRC, 'Contribution géographique à la classification des villes de la République populaire roumaine', *Annls Géogr.*, **72** (1963), 162–85.

SYLVAIN, NICOLAS, 'Rumania', in *The Jews in the Soviet Satellites*, ed. Peter Meyer, Syracuse University Press, 1953, 491–556.

TUFESCU, V. *et al.*, 'Géographie de la population de la R.P. Roumaine', *Recueil d'Études Géographiques*, Bucharest, 1960, 129–41.

Economic Geography
BAUER, LUDWIG, 'Landeskulturelle und ökonomisch-geographische Probleme des Donaudeltas', *Geogr. Ber.*, (1962), 1–15.

EVANS, IGOR L. *The Agrarian Revolution in Roumania*, Cambridge University Press, 1924.

GEORGE, PIERRE, 'Études Roumaines', *Annls Géogr.*, **70** (1961), 71–8.

HOFFMAN, GEORGE W., 'The Problem of the Underdeveloped Regions in Southeast Europe: A Comparative Analysis of Romania, Yugoslavia, and Greece,' AAAG, **57** (1967), 637–666.

JORDAN, CONSTANTIN N., *The Romanian Oil Industry*, New York University Press, 1955.

PONCET, JEAN, 'Les transformations de l'agriculture roumaine', *Annls Géogr.*, **73** (1964), 540–67.

ROUBITSCHEK, WALTER, 'Zur Bevölkerungs- und Agrarstruktur Rumäniens', *Petermanns Mitt.*, **104** (1960), 23–32.

SPULBER, NICOLAS, 'The Danube-Black Sea Canal and the Russian Control over the Danube', *Econ. Geogr.*, **30** (1954), 236–45.

STAMS, WERNER, 'Agrargeographische Studien im Donautiefland südlich Bukarest', *Geogr. Ber.*, **3** (1958), 163–86.

ŠTEFĂNESCU. IOANA and NICULINA BARANOVSKY, 'Formes de l'exploitation agricole dans les Subcarpates de la Prahova et les changements survenus ces derniers cent ans', *Revue Roumaine de Géologie, Géophysique et Géographie*, **8** (1964), 51–6.

SURET-CANALE, J. 'L'évolution récente de l'industre roumaine', *Annls Géogr.*, **64** (1955), 396–400.

VELCEA, I. and GH. IACOB, 'Types of Land-use in the Danube Delta', *Revue Roumaine de Géologie, Géophysique et Géographie*, **8** (1964), 239–44.

Viehzucht und Hirtenleben in Ostmitteleuropa: Ethnographische Studien, Budapest-Academy of Sciences, 1961.

ZAGOROFF, S. D. *et al.*, *The Agricultural Economy of the Danubian Countries, 1935–45*, Oxford University Press, 1956, 229–88.

CHAPTER TWELVE

Yugoslavia

The People's Republic of Yugoslavia is the largest and geographically the most complex of the countries studied in this book. In terms of relief, climate and vegetation, and also of the cultures and ethnic composition of its peoples it is by far the most varied. The creation of a unified state has faced greater difficulties in Yugoslavia than in any other country in Eastern Europe, and the establishment of a federal constitution—the only one in the area—is a recognition of the exceptional diversities which characterise Yugoslavia.

Yugoslavia extends from the Austrian and Italian Alps in the north-west to the plains of Macedonia, and from those of the Pannonian Basin in the north-east to the rugged Dalmatian coast. It contains in the Julian Alps the highest mountain in Eastern Europe and in the Dinaric system one of the world's most extensive areas of karst. Its climate ranges from the Mediterranean of the Dalmatian coast to the continental extremes of the Danube valley. Ethnic and cultural diversity is no less great. Yugoslavia spans that division of Europe, described in the second chapter, between the westward- and the eastward-orientated countries of Eastern Europe. Though the whole country is predominantly Slav, its western provinces bear the imprint of Austria and Italy; its eastern bears the legacy of Byzantine rule and the marks of Turkish conquest and occupation.

THE MAKING OF THE STATE

The Yugoslav state was itself the fruit of expediency. A pan-Slav state had long been discussed, but it was not until 1915 that the first clear steps were taken in this direction. In that year a committee composed of Slav refugees from the territories of the Austro-Hungarian Empire was formed, and succeeded in enlisting some support among the allied leaders for the creation of a state for the southern Slavs. In the meanwhile, Serbia was overrun by the Austrians, and its government driven into exile. It was inevitable that the Serb leaders should make common cause with the Yugoslav Committee, with whose members they shared a common enemy. In July 1917 the representatives of both met on the Greek island of Corfu, pledged co-operation during the remainder of the War and throughout the years of peace that were expected to follow. They agreed to form a united state of the Serbs, Croats and Slovenes, and on 1 December 1918, shortly after the final collapse of the Dual Monarchy, the new state was proclaimed.

Fig. 12.1. Internal administrative boundaries, (a) 1918–29, (b) 1929–39. After G. W. Hoffman and F. W. Neal.

King Nicholas, the last king of Montenegro, had played a somewhat equivocal role during the world war that had just ended. His government in exile accepted the Declaration of Corfu, and a popular assembly, meeting at Podgorica (now Titograd) soon after the last of the Austro-Hungarian army had left, voted to merge its territory with that of Serbia.

The nucleus of the new state was thus defined: Serbia and Montenegro, which had previously been independent states, the former Hungarian province of Croatia, and the former Austrian provinces of Slovenia, Dalmatia, and the jointly administered province of Bosnia and Hercegovina. The boundaries of the new state, however, had yet to be defined, and since on most sides it was bordered by countries which had been defeated in the war just ended, this was essentially a matter for the peace conference.

Boundary questions
The Paris Conference did well by Yugoslavia. Woodrow Wilson, in the tenth of his 'Fourteen Points', had called for 'the freest opportunity

of autonomous development' for the peoples of Austria-Hungary, but in the territorial settlement that emerged the scales were tipped perhaps more than was necessary in their favour. Ethnic boundaries in Eastern Europe were nowhere precise and unambiguous. There was along every boundary a transition zone from the area predominantly of one ethnic group to the area within which another ethnic group prevailed. In some frontier regions, notably the more southerly extensions of the Pannonian Plain, the situation was complicated by the existence of ethnic groups—German, Romanian and Slovak—which were quite unrelated to the major peoples whom the boundary was to separate. A fair and equitable settlement in these circumstances would inevitably be a compromise, and compromise was an ideal to which the Balkan peoples had never accustomed themselves. In general the Yugoslavs were content with the settlement, a fact which in itself suggested that the boundaries were in some measure unfair to their neighbours. Only in the north-west, towards Italy and Austria, did the Yugoslavs obtain less than they hoped and expected.

The Pannonian Plain. The boundary with Hungary was made in part to follow the Drava, an ancient line of division, and then, before its junction with the Danube, to cut eastwards across the plains to meet the Romanian border. The Vojvodina, as the plains of Yugoslavia lying north of the Danube are called, was a region of great ethnic confusion in which the Serbs themselves, locally at least, formed a minority. The ethnic situation along the boundary with Bulgaria was no simpler and was furthermore complicated by considerations of military strategy. Projecting salients of Bulgarian territory, particularly that drained by the Strumitsa, a small tributary of the Struma, were thought to extend too far to the west and to threaten the safety of the north–south railway link of Yugoslavia. The Strumitsa salient came in fact to within five miles of the Morava-Vardar railway, and the Bosilegrad salient to within ten miles. Neither had any significant Serb population, but both, together with the Tsaribrod and Timok regions, were transferred from Bulgaria to Yugoslavia. The boundary with Albania had been delimited by the Treaty of London of July 1913. It was unchanged by the incorporation of Montenegro in Serbia, but had not been surveyed and marked on the ground. This operation, fraught with not inconsiderable danger and difficulty, was accomplished in the postwar years. It too was generous to Yugoslavia, including within the latter the Kosmet region which, despite its close associations with the early Serb state, had come to be predominantly a region of Albanian settlement.

The Julian region. The problems of Yugoslavia's north-western boundary proved to be the most difficult, because here the ambitions of Yugoslavia ran counter to the aims of the western allies. The nature of the difficulty has already been discussed (Chapter 4). Yugoslavia demanded, and, in fact, needed, a port near the head of the Adriatic Sea. This coastline had been promised to Italy by the Treaty of London of 1915. A compromise was reached, whereby Trieste, indubitably Italian in language and sympathy, was to go to Italy, while Fiume (Rijeka) in which the Italian population barely amounted to a majority, was to serve as the Adriatic port of Yugoslavia. We have seen (page 112) how an Italian *coup d'état* wrested Fiume itself from the Yugoslavs and left them with its small and inadequate suburb of Sušak. Of the rest of the Dalmatian littoral which Italy claimed, and had, in fact, been promised, she acquired only the small enclave of Zara (Zadar) together with a few islands.

Karavanke. The narrow, steep-sided range of the Karavanke (Karawanken Alps) appeared to be the most suitable line of division between Yugoslavia and Austria. It was the traditional boundary between Kranj or Carniola and Carinthia (Kärnten) but had never been an ethnic divide. A considerable, but at this time diminishing number of Slovenes lived in the Klagenfurth Basin to the north, a relic of a once large Slav population which had inhabited the Drau (Drava) valley. Yugoslav pressure for the cession of this small area was strong, but on this question the allies yielded only to the extent of authorising a plebiscite. The voting in October 1920, went convincingly in Austria's favour, and, as had been anticipated, the boundary was established along the line of the Karavanke.

Second World War

The next territorial changes in the Yugoslav state occurred during and after the Second World War. Yugoslavia was invaded in April 1941, occupied and partitioned. The north-west was attached to the German *Ostmark* (Austria). Part of Croatia and the Dalmatian coast were given to Italy, which thus obtained from the Germans themselves the territories she had been promised nearly 30 years earlier as a reward for making war on Germany. Hungary took part of the Vojvodina, and Albania and Bulgaria not only partitioned Yugoslav Macedonia between them, but encroached upon Serbia itself. The rump of

A *polje* in the Karst of Montenegro, near Cetinje.

YUGOSLAVIA

The Morava valley, above (south of) the Grdelica gorges

The Konavli, a small, elongated *polje*, lying close to the Dalmatian coast, between Cavtat and Herceg Novi

YUGOSLAVIA

Vranje, a small town in one of the Tertiary basins of the Morava valley in southern Serbia. The scene is taken looking west towards the Kopaonik region

Yugoslavia was split into three small protectorates: Croatia, Serbia and Montenegro.

The end of the war brought about the withdrawal of occupying forces and the termination of partition. It also brought a revival of Yugoslavia's territorial claims in the north-west. The claims against Austria for the Klagenfurth Basin were again pressed vigorously but unsuccessfully. The number of Slovene speakers in this region was unquestionably smaller in 1945 than it had been in 1920, though their precise number was still as difficult to determine. The case for Yugoslavia was weaker than it had been a generation earlier, and the western allies whose forces were in occupation of southern Austria, were in no mood to make concessions to a Yugoslavia whose leadership they disliked and distrusted.

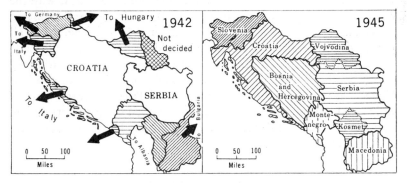

Fig. 12.2. Partition of Yugoslavia in 1942, and republics and autonomous areas of the People's Federal Republic of Yugoslavia, after 1945. After G. W. Hoffman and F. W. Neal.

The Yugoslav claim against Italy was stronger. Istria and the Julian Alps were far more Slav than they were Italian, Yugoslavia needed an Adriatic port, and could point clearly to the difficulty and hardship that had resulted from being deprived of Fiume. Yugoslavia considered herself entitled, furthermore, to some kind of compensation from Italy for the invasion and destruction she had suffered. But whether this all added up to a valid claim to Trieste and Gorizia was an open question.

Before the end of the fighting it had been agreed between Tito and the western allies that the former should occupy Fiume and the territory lying north of it to the Austrian border. The whole region,

21

however, had been the scene of Croat and Slovene partisan activities, and when British forces reached Trieste, they found the city and its Julian hinterland in the hands of the Yugoslavs. The latter were obliged to withdraw to a line, subsequently known as the Morgan Line, which very roughly followed the Isonzo to the north of Gorizia, and to the south of that city kept some ten miles from the coast until it ran down to the sea near Capodistria (Koper). Henceforward Tito's forces held the territory to the east of this line, and British forces that to the west.

In 1947 a treaty of peace was signed between the Allies and Italy. The territory in the north-east of Italy, lying roughly between the pre-1919 boundary and that established by the Treaties of 1920 and 1924, was taken from Italy. The question, however, was what to do with it. It continued to be divided into two zones: Zone A, with the city of Trieste, held by the British; Zone B, the Istrian peninsula and Julian Alps, held by Yugoslavia. In October 1954 it was agreed by all parties concerned that this divison should be recognised and made permanent. Zone B, with the addition of a minute piece of territory on the southern outskirts of Trieste, was formally incorporated into Yugoslavia; and Zone A, with the city of Trieste, became part of Italy. At the same time the zonal boundary, now an international boundary, became easier to cross and relations between Yugoslavia and Italy more normal.

LANDFORM REGIONS

The map suggests a simple division between a northern region of lowland, drained by the Danube and its tributaries, and the rest of the country, which is without exception mountainous. Although this division between mountain and plain is fundamental to the economic development of Yugoslavia, the physique of the country is far more complex than this suggests. Five major regions can be distinguished, each of which must be further divided.

In the north-west is an Alpine region, where mountain ranges, themselves extensions of the central alpine system of Switzerland and Austria, enclose small upland basins. From this area, the Dinaric region of high dissected limestone plateaus extends south-eastward. It parallels the Adriatic Sea, but broadens gradually until it terminates against the great trench which has been cut by the Vardar and Morava rivers.

The Dinaric region of high plateaus is bordered on each side by smaller regions made up of low hills and intervening lowlands. To the south-west this region is narrow and locally, where the Dinaric system approaches close to the Adriatic coast, is actually pinched out between the mountains and the sea. To the north-east, on the other hand, a belt

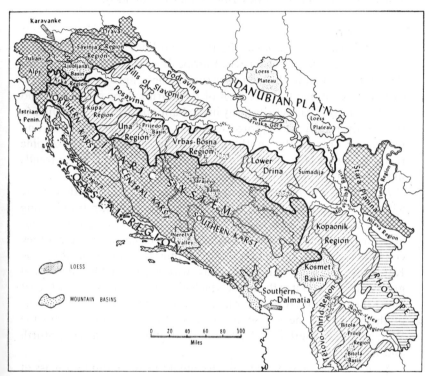

Fig. 12.3. Landform regions of Yugoslavia.

of rolling hills borders the higher plateaus, and extends from the Ljubljana Basin to the Morava, and then southwards into Macedonia.

The eastern boundary of Yugoslavia, like the north-western, runs through a zone of high and rugged mountains. Towards the north these constitute the link between the Transylvanian Alps of Romania and the Stara Planina of Bulgaria. To the south they form the most westerly extension of the ancient, crystalline massif known as the Rhodope.

The remainder of Yugoslavia, about a quarter of its total area, lies in the Pannonian Plain. It consists essentially of the valleys of the Sava and Drava, together with the ranges of hills—outliers as it were of the Alpine system—which lie between them, and the plains which lie around the junction of the Danube and Tisa (*Hung.*: Tisza). Fig. 12.3 shows these six regions, together with the lesser units into which for convenience of description they are divided.

The Alpine region

In north-eastern Yugoslavia the two trend-lines which characterise the mountain foldings of Eastern Europe diverge. To the east extends the Alpine system in the narrower sense. The ranges lie from west to east; they continue the direction of the Carnic Alps of Austria and northern Italy, and they die away in the Pannonian Plain. The Dinaric system diverges from the former; adopts a south-easterly trend and terminates only in the southern headlands of Greece. The Alpine region of Yugoslavia lies in the angle formed where these two trends in the folding of the Alpine system meet.

Karavanke. The Karavanke, or Karawanken, continue with scarcely a break the line of the Carnic Alps. They are not high, rarely exceeding 6,500 feet, but their steep-sided, serrated ridge makes them a formidable barrier. Viewed from the Klagenfurth basin on the north they constitute a truly impressive range along the southern sky. The Karavanke are built mainly of Trias, with a core of Palaeozoic and granitic rocks, and it is the latter which gives rise to the strongest relief along their rugged crest. The range is crossed by several passes, none of them well engineered or much used. The least difficult are the Würzen, to the south of Villach, and the Loibl, between Klagenfurth and Kranj.

Savinja Basin. The Karavanke terminate in the mountain mass of Saviniski, east of which the range is only continued in low, short, broken ranges, which become lower as they approach the Pannonian Plain. Of these the Pohorije, which looks out over Maribor and the Drava valley, is the highest and longest. The river Savinja takes a twisting course through this region from its source in the western Karavanke, before joining the Sava. Its valley, and those of its tributaries, are floored with upper Tertiary lake deposits and alluvium, through which rise the rounded hills of soft Triassic rocks interrupted here and there by small outcrops of igneous. The regional capital, Celje, lies on the Savinja. In the hills to the north is iron-ore, and this region of Kranj was once famous for its iron-smelting. Today only the ruins remain of the charcoal-iron works which were once active in the hills; the only legacy of the old industry is the small iron-works at Ravne and in Celje itself.

Ljubljana Basin. The Sava valley lies roughly parallel to the Kara-vanke, and is part of a depression which is continued into Italy, where it is drained by the Tagliamento. The Sava itself emerges almost on the Italian boundary from a marsh which covers the valley floor, and is itself an indication of the indeterminate nature of the drainage in this part of the trench. The Sava valley broadens as it continues eastward and then south-eastward into the Ljubljana Basin, where a fan of short rivers, discharging from the Julian Alps and the northern karst, converge upon it.

The basin itself is of no great size—its maximum extent is not much over 30 miles—and it is floored with quaternary deposits, from which a number of small steep hills rise. It was such a hill, rising steeply from the Ljubljanica, that served to locate the regional capital, Ljubljana.

Sava valley. The Ljubljana Basin is entirely surrounded by mount-ains and hills. Toward the east, between the Ljubljana Basin and that of Zagreb, lies a plateau made up mainly of Triassic limestone resting upon a foundation of Carboniferous. It rises to a fairly level summit plain at near 3,000 feet, but has been very deeply dissected by the Sava, Krka and their tributaries. The Sava itself crosses this region by a superimposed and gorge-like valley which until fairly recent times has not been followed by any route. The Zagreb *Autoput* crosses this very hilly plateau well to the south of the river. This region of green, rolling hills, scattered woodland and compact villages, Austrian-looking with their steep roofs, overhanging eaves and the belfries of their baroque churches, is one of great natural beauty.

Mura-Drava region. The Drava, or Drau, rises in the snow-fields of the Hohe Tauern, and flows eastward between the Karavanke and the massif of the Nieder Tauern. As it crosses the boundary from Austria into Yugoslavia its valley narrows and becomes incised in a plateau, the Pohorije, which extends northward into Austria. Just above Maribor (Marburg), this gorge tract of the valley ends, and a basin extends downstream to beyond Ptuj. To the north-east is the Mura (Mur), which rising in the Hohe Tauern in Austria, crosses the most northerly extension of Yugoslav territory, the so-called Prekomurje, and forms for some 25 miles the boundary with Hungary before joining the Drava. This is a region of gentle relief. It was covered by the Tertiary sea which spread over much of the Pannonian Plain. The low hills are made of soft upper Tertiary deposits; the valleys are wide belts of alluvium. This is a gentler region than that which surrounds the Savinja valley; there is little woodland, crop-farming is all important, and this region marks the transition from the mountains to the Pannonian Plain.

Julian Alps. South of the upper Sava lies the rounded mass of high mountains known as the Julijske Alpe, the Julian Alps. The trend of the individual ranges is somewhat uncertainly towards the south-east; their drainage mainly towards the south by the Soča, which becomes the Isonzo when, at Gorizia, it crosses the boundary into Italy. One range bears the present Italo-Yugoslav boundary southward from the Sava valley for some 25 miles. To the east, beyond the deep trench of the upper Soča valley lies a range shaped somewhat like a horseshoe opening towards the east. Within it lies the supremely beautiful Bohinjsko jezero (Lake Bohinj), drained by the Sava Bohinjska, which drops steeply down to the Sava itself. North of Lake Bohinj the majestic cone of Triglav rises from among the lesser peaks of the Julian Alps. At 9,394 feet it is the highest mountain in Eastern Europe, and is a lesser Matterhorn in appearance. This is primarily a pastoral region, where transhumant cattle, with all the picturesque ceremony of Switzerland and Austria, slowly eat their way into the high *planine* in summer and return to the deep, shaded valley settlements for winter.[1]

South of the mountainous Julian region the land assumes the form of a dissected plateau, the upper surfaces of which reach to over 3,000 feet. Short, steep-sided ridges rise from its surface, aligned with considerable regularity in a north-west to south-east direction; here the Dinaric trend becomes the dominant feature of the landscape. The prevailing rock is limestone; there is little surface drainage; the few rivers are discontinuous and quickly lose themselves underground, and karst features become conspicuous. This is the Julian Karst which forms a broad, uneven saddle, linking the Danube basin with the Adriatic, overlooked from the north by the Julian Alps, from the south by the terminal bastions of the Dinaric chain itself.

This saddle, which is locally dignified with the name of 'pass', has throughout human history carried the routeway between northern Italy and the Pannonian Plain. Across it came the Neolithic invaders

[1] So well described by L. Adamic, *The Native's Return*, New York, 1934, Harpers' Modern Classics, p. 89.

of Italy; it saw the amber traders make their journeys to the Baltic, and the Romans expand their empire into Pannonia by one of their most important roads. The Huns and the Goths came down into Italy across the Julian Karst, and if in later centuries the importance of the Karst route has appeared to decline, this is only because Italy's cultural and commercial relations came to be predominantly northward across the Alps.

The Julian Karst ends abruptly above the Gulf of Trieste, and then drops steeply to the narrow coastal plain on which the city and port of Trieste have grown up. Trieste and the inland city of Gorizia, 24 miles to the north-west, have since ancient times served as the Mediterranean termini of the Karst route. In recent times Trieste became the chief maritime port of Austria, and Fiume (Rijeka), less well placed and 50 miles to the south-east, of Hungary. We have already seen how Yugoslavia coveted, but failed to obtain Trieste, and had in the end to make do with a mere suburb of Fiume. Possession of a port on the seaward margin of the Julian Karst is, in the Yugoslav opinion, an absolute necessity, for there is no other easy or convenient route to the sea either around or across the Dinaric plateaus.

Dinaric region

Twenty miles north of Rijeka the summit of Snježnik rises to 5,891 feet, and towers 3,000 feet above the nearby Karst route. It marks the beginning of that system of mountain ranges, high, barren plateaus, and deeply incised valleys, which with no interruption at all, extends 350 miles to the Albanian border. Toward the south-east the range broadens and becomes increasingly significant as an obstacle to communication between the Pannonian Plain of the interior and the coast. For the whole of this distance the predominant rock is a massive limestone, which ranges in geological date from the Trias to the Cretaceous. Limestones of Cretaceous age predominate at the surface, but those lower in the geological series, together with sandstones and shales, occur prominently to the north-west, and in a narrow strip along the south Dalmatian coast, where the sinuous Gulf of Kotor owes its shape to the differential erosion of these rocks of varying hardness.

The Dinaric region is in fact the north-eastern limb of a highly complex anticline, whose axis formerly lay out over the Adriatic Sea. There is no question, however, of a gentle dip of the beds towards the Danube; rather of a complex, Jura-type folding, in which cuestas and steep, fault-bounded ridges are common. The region has been planated and further dissected. The harder beds give rise to ridges, which preserve the general north-west to south-east trend, but sometimes adopt a curving or transverse direction.

The principal rivers of the region rise close to its north-eastern margin and flow towards the Danube. They are, in fact, dip-slope rivers, though, as we see them today, their courses are frequently superimposed upon structures which underly the limestone. Much of the limestone region of the Dinaric mountains has no surface drainage, beyond the short streams which flow across the clay floor of a *polje* before disappearing underground. The surface of the karst is dry, even immediately after heavy rains. The water percolates downwards to be thrown out sometimes along the sides of the deeper valleys; sometimes along the Adriatic coast itself. The Dinaric region is notable for its spectacular waterfalls, of which those at Plitvice, in Croatia, and at Jajce in Bosnia have deservedly become tourist attractions.

But it is the limestone plateaus themselves that give character to the region. The limestone, for the greater part, is of exceptional purity and whiteness. Its solution by rainwater leaves very little by way of residue, so that over much of the region there is no mantle of *terra rossa* to provide a poor soil and nourishment for scrub. Extensive areas are in fact distinguished by *lapiez*, a surface of closely spaced, serrated ridges, left by the solution of the limestone along the intervening joint planes. The result is a surface useless for agriculture and exceptionally difficult to traverse. It is the larger solution features, however, which are in general the most conspicuous and important. These range from small 'swallow-holes' to giant *polja*.

Over most of its surface the limestone is pitted with *doliny*. These are small and generally circular depressions, ranging in diameter from a few yards to considerably more than a hundred. Usually they are like inverted cones, sometimes part-filled with limestone waste, like an abandoned quarry; sometimes having at their apex a small, rounded area of insoluble, residual clay. It often happens in the karst that these constitute the only patches of soil for miles, and are intensively cultivated. Seen from the air the *doliny* often form a close and fairly regular pattern. After rains they may give rise to small lakes, where the heavy residual clay holds up the drainage of the water.

It is generally held that the gorges and steep-sided, dry valleys of the karst have been produced as smaller and more rounded depressions merge into one another. Sometimes such valleys contain rivers, but usually they are as dry as the *doliny* from which they have been formed. Most rivers are in any event short and usually intermittent in their flow. Sooner or later they empty themselves into a shaft-like *ponore* or disappear less conspicuously through joints and crevices of the limestone, and continue their course underground. There is inevitably an immense, complex, and little known system of underground channels and caves. A few, such as those at Postojna (Postumia), in the Julian Karst, are accessible enough to have been developed as a tourist attraction; most are too remote and extensive ever to have been explored.

The most extensive of all the landforms produced by solution is the *polje*. It is larger than the *dolina*, though its origin is similar. It is a large, level area, usually elongated between the limestone ridges, and produced by the solution of the limestone itself. Small rocky outliers may rise from its surface, which is for the rest flat and composed of residual clay and alluvium. After rains water may accumulate on the *polje* floor, forming in extreme cases a seasonal lake. Water from the surrounding limestone plateaus may pass into the *polje* by way of underground channels and vigorous springs around the margin of the basin. In the dry season the water usually drains away, sometimes leaving a small area of marsh except in the height of summer. In general, the higher *polja* of the interior remain dry; those nearer the Adriatic coast, which lie at a lower level, may contain lakes for part of the year, and the Skadarsko Jezero (Lake Skadar), is a *polje* whose floor lies below sea-level and is in consequence permanently flooded. The limestone hills usually rise steeply from the floor of the *polje*, enclosing it completely and sometimes making access difficult. On the other hand the clay and alluvium of the *polje* floor often supports the only permanent settlements of the district.

The limestone karst makes up only part of the Dinaric region. Along its seaward margin the limestone is bordered by small, elongated bands of sandstone and shale. Towards the north-east the limestone thins away and becomes discontinuous; the karstic features become fewer, as the limestone, increasingly interrupted by beds of sandstone and shale, loses its massive character, and the underlying palaeozoic and crystalline rocks come to the surface. The relief features still maintain their Dinaric trend, but the mountain ranges are broader and more rounded; in scenic terms, they are greener and more forested. Drainage is very much more on the surface and

21*

underground streams are few. The drainage is in the main to a small number of rivers, the Una, Vrbas, Bosna and Drina, which cut across the grain of the mountains in deep, superimposed and sometimes spectacular gorges, separated by small areas of flatter and more easily cultivated land. The gorges, formed where the Drina has incised its valley across a mass of upper Palaeozoic rocks, are a well-known scenic feature.

For the greater part of its course, [in fact] the river Drina flows through narrow gorges between steep mountains or through deep ravines with precipitous banks. In a few places only the river banks spread out to form valleys with level or rolling stretches of fertile land suitable for cultivation and settlement on both sides. Such a place exists here at Višegrad, where the Drina breaks from the deep and narrow ravine formed by the Butkovo rocks and the Uzavnik Mountains.[1]

Here was built the bridge around whose story Ivo Andrić has woven a tapestry of Balkan history.

This region of karst and strong relief forms the 'mountain heartland' of Yugoslavia. It is the *dinarische Gebirgsfeste*, the mountain fastness, which has been in varying degrees impervious to outside influences. The Turks, for instance, gained no permanent foothold in the karst of Montenegro. It remains today a region of great isolation, not only from the rest of the country but also within itself. Life tends to focus upon individual valleys and *polja*, between which communication is made difficult by the terrain and hindered by the spirit of isolation which predominates among their inhabitants. This extensive region, which makes up no less than 20 per cent of the area of the country is broken down in the following pages into four sub-regions for the convenience of description.

Northern Karst. From the Snežnik there stretches south-eastward for 140 miles an extremely arid, karstic region. Its south-western face drops steeply to the sea without, for most of this distance, even an acre of coastal lowland. Rijeka lies at the north-western extremity of this coast, where the mountains draw back from the sea sufficiently to permit this very hilly city to develop. This inhospitable range is the Velebit, which rises at its highest point to 6,032 feet. Eastward beyond its summit the surface drops less precipitately to the Ličko *polje*, which, with a length of about 40 miles, is the largest in the northern

[1] Ivo Andrić *The Bridge on the Drina*, Allen & Unwin, 1959.

karst. This *polje* is bordered by others less extensive than itself, and shares with them a network of short, and in some cases intermittent streams, which flow across the floor of the basins, only to disappear into the surrounding limestone. East of these *polja* the land rises to the forested plateau of Plješevica and Velika Kapela, before dropping abruptly to the hills which border the Kupa, Dobra and Una.

Central Karst. In the central region the karstic features are developed more strongly than in the northern. The region itself extends from the valley of the Una to that of the Neretva. The mountain ranges are higher than in the north; the *polja* are larger and more deeply sunk in the karst. The mountain ranges are grouped into three elongated mountain masses, separated from one another by *polja*. Nearest the coast lies the Dinara, from which is derived the commonly accepted name of the whole system. It is straight, high and steep, like the Velebit, whose direction it continues. The Livanjsko *polje* separates the Dinara from the Vijenac-Staretine range. Then comes the valley of the upper Una and the Glamočko *polje*, beyond which rises the highest and most continuous range in the central region. This begins in the north-west with the arid limestone plateau of Grmeč, partially enclosed by the great bend of the Una; then come the Osječenica, Lunjevača, Cincar and Čvrsnica, individual names for segments of what is in fact one continuous mountain range of over 100 miles. These mountains rise to summit plains which lie with great consistency between 4,000 and 5,000 feet with the land rising in a few places to over 6,000 and in Cincer to 6,580 feet. There are no gaps and but few passes in these ranges which together raise one of the most formidable obstacles to movement and transport in Europe.

What little vegetation there is on the ridges, [wrote Adamic] is coarse, poor, hardly fit for goats; but over them graze also herds of sheep and *bushé*, a small, scrawny breed of cattle peculiar to Herzegovina and north-western Bosnia. Water is scarce. Karst-like, streams tumble out of one hole, run on the surface awhile, then vanish into another hole. Fertile *polja* are few, small, and far between, most of them suitable only for raising maize and tobacco. Beside each 'field' is a crude, primitive settlement, but one comes upon hamlets, utterly heart-breaking to see, even where no soil is available for cultivation, and people subsist mainly on sheep and goat cheese and meat.[1]

[1] L. Adamic, *op. cit.* pp. 206–7.

Southern Karst. East of the Neretva the character of the karst again changes. It becomes a high and continuous plateau rather than a series of parallel ranges. *Polja*, no longer as narrow and elongated as in the Central and Northern Karst, are sunk below its surface, and short limestone ranges and even rounded mountain massifs rise above its surface. On the south-west the high karst is bordered by a belt of lower plateaus, the heights of which do not exceed 4,000 feet. This latter area is notable for the Popovo Polje, which, unlike most others, is drained by a permanent river, the Trebišnjica. This stream traverses its whole length before disappearing under the encircling mountains and making its way either to the sea or to the Nevetva by underground channels. This *polje* is also known for the annual floods at the lower, north-western end of its plain, which have left a smooth cover of fertile alluvium.

To the east and north the plateau level rises abruptly. In the former direction lies the high, barren limestone plateau of Zeta, which looks down on the Gulf of Kotor from its summits of Orjen and Lovćen. This plateau is itself pitted with small *polja*, in one of which lies the old Montenegrin capital of Cetinje.

Towards the north the general level lies at least 1,000 feet higher than in the low karst and short, bare, rugged masses of limestone, such as Njegoš, Golija and Prekornica rise to heights considerably above 5,000 feet. Between lie *polja*, deeply sunk between the mountains, such as those of Nikšić, Gacko and Nevesinje. The whole of this region is almost completely without surface drainage. The *polja* have at most a mile or two of intermittent stream flow; all around is dry bare limestone with just enough soil in its joint-planes to support xerophytic scrub.

This region is the same today as it was twenty or even a hundred years ago. It is as poor as ever. Rocks, rocks, rocks. Sheep, goats and scrawny cattle snatch up every blade of coarse mountain grass as soon as it sticks its point above the stony bleakness, meantime nibbling at the leaves of scrub trees and bushes. In little gullies and ravines we came upon 'fields', tiny patches of more or less fertile soil, few larger than a city lot and most considerably smaller, hidden away among cliffs, as if they were something very precious, and therefore to be concealed. On such 'fields', growing corn, tobacco, cabbage, and potatoes, and often communally owned, subsist anywhere from one to ten families.[1]

[1] L. Adamic, *op. cit.* p. 140.

A few miles to the north-east of the Nikšić and Gacko *polja* the karst ends where the Cretaceous rocks are bordered by Jurassic and Triassic. Beyond this limit, as in the similar transition in the Central Karst, limestone occurs on a less massive scale and a developed drainage pattern appears. Drainage is here either northward to the Drina and upper Neretva or south-eastward by the Morača to Lake Skadar. These rivers have incised their valleys deep enough to expose lower Triassic beds and even in places the Carboniferous. This variety of geological structure has combined with a more abundant surface drainage to produce a highly dissected terrain. This area of extreme ruggedness extends approximately from the Zelen Gora, near the source of the Neretva, eastward, across the Piva, tributary of the upper Drina, to Durmitor and Sinjajevina; then, across the gorge of the Tara, which joins with the Piva to form the Drina, to the Bjelasica Massif, and, lastly, across the Lim to the Mokra Gora and the Prokletije mountains, which carry the Albanian boundary.

This area, which extends in a gentle curve, embayed towards the north, for some 110 miles, has probably the most rugged relief to be found in Eastern Europe. The mountain masses named all rise to considerably above 7,000 feet. Durmitor, the highest mountain in the Dinaric system, rises to 8,272 feet, and Daravica, which lies on the Albanian border, to 8,712. Durmitor and the Volujak massif which, at a distance of 17 miles, face one another across the gorge of the Piva, are both made up of residual masses of hard upper Jurassic limestone. The summits of Sinjajevina and Bjelasica consist of igneous intrusions, and the Prokletije and Mokra Gora are predominantly Carboniferous in geological age.

The contrast between this region of varied structure and strong relief and the karst which borders it is marked. The karst plateau is in many ways gentler, but human life is easier in this more rugged and mountainous region, where at least the valleys provide soil to support plant growth and water for man and beast. This latter region, by reason of its rugged relief, also provides shelter and protection. The karst could form no nucleus of a Slav state; its internal resources were too slight. The Serb state grew up in the valleys of the Ibar, Lim and upper Drina, and it was into these wild mountains that the early Serbs retreated before Bulgars and Byzantines and Turks.

Interior hills and plateaus. To the north of this region of high plateau and rugged mountain lies a somewhat lower region of more gentle aspect. It is nevertheless mountainous, and its ridges rise to heights of from 4,000 to 5,000 feet, but slopes are gentler, valleys are wider; settlement more dense, and in the broader basins within the region are towns like Sarajevo, Višegrad and Novi Pazar.

Geological structure is extremely varied. It consists essentially of palaeozoic rocks, predominantly of Carboniferous age, which have been widely intruded by igneous masses. The covering of Secondary rocks has been partially stripped from the area, exposing the older and harder rocks, which, as a general rule, give rise to the strongest relief. On the other hand, extensive areas of softer Triassic limestone give rise to the relatively gentle relief of the Stari Vlah area bordering the middle Drina. This minor region is in fact a small outlier of the greater karst region to the south. It is bordered on the north-east by a more rugged region, built predominantly of gabbro, across which the Drina has cut spectacular gorges.

From the Drina valley a confusing pattern of rounded hills and broad open valleys extends eastward until it is first interrupted by the Golija massif of hard primary rocks with a wealth of small igneous intrusions, and then terminated by the deep valley of the Ibar. In the opposite direction from the dissected plateau of Stari Vlah lie the rounded uplands which separate it from the Sarajevo Basin. Despite its hilly appearance, this latter is the most extensive of the basins which lie within the Dinaric system. In part it is of tectonic origin, and has been down-faulted against the Vranica-Bitovnja Massif which borders it on the south-west. The resulting depression became a shallow lake during mid-Tertiary times, and the resulting deposits extend from Sarajevo itself north-westward for over 40 miles to Zenica. This basin is not only the heart of Bosnia, but also the source of the Bosna river, which is formed from the numerous tributaries which flow down into it from the surrounding hills. The Bosna forms the axis of the basin, leaving it below Zenica to flow by way of narrow defiles, resembling those of the Drina, across the limestone ridges and igneous massifs of northern Bosnia.

The River Vrbas rises on the western slopes of Vranica. Its northward course takes it through the small Bugojno basin, which, with its Tertiary beds, is a miniature replica of the Sarajevo Basin. Then, like the Bosna, it plunges into a series of gorges and defiles from which it emerges only at Banja Luka.

This region is in many ways the heartland of Bosnia. More fertile and populous than the higher mountains and plateaus to the south-west, and protected from the plains to the north-east by the ranges through which the Vrbas, Bosna and Drina have cut their narrow valleys, it has served as the nucleus of both the Serb and of the short-lived Bosnian states.

This is also the most densely forested region in Yugoslavia, and the floating of lumber down its north-flowing rivers is a traditional occupation. The numerous igneous intrusions have brought with them deposits of metals, both ferrous and non-ferrous. Mining, especially of lead and silver, developed in Bosnia in classical times, and is still of importance today (see page 707). Iron-ore is also mined and supports the iron-smelting industries of Zenica and Sisak. The region from Sarajevo north-westward to Banja Luka today constitutes one of the major industrial regions of Yugoslavia.

Coastal region
The Karst region of Yugoslavia is nowhere far from the Adriatic shore. In the Velebit it plunges precipitously to the sea. Only in the Istrian peninsula and the Zagora, which extends in front of the southern Velebit and the Dinara, is it bordered by a coastal lowland. South-east of the latter the karst again approaches the coast, and, except for the marshes at the mouth of the Neretva, there is no extensive lowland between mountain and sea, until the alluvial plain of the Bojana, the outlet of Lake Skadar, is reached close to the Albanian border.

This coastal region of Yugoslavia may thus be said to consist of the low Istrian peninsula and the head of the Kvarner, or Gulf of Quarnero; the more extensive lowland which extends from the Velebit approximately to Split; the lower Neretva valley, and the fragmentary lowlands which border the southern Karst.

Istrian peninsula. The Julian Karst, itself a plateau of no great height, ends abruptly along a line from Trieste south-eastward to the Kvarner, and is bordered by the low platform of Istra (*It.* Istria). Its greatest heights, near the centre of the peninsula, seldom exceed 1,400 feet, and along its western margin and part of the eastern there is a belt of land lying below 500 feet. Low cliffs, broken by small drowned valleys, mark the coast, and offshore on the west is a fringe of very small islands, of which Brijuni (*It.* Brione), the retreat favoured by Marshall Tito, is the largest. The platform is built of limestone, covered in part by Tertiary deposits. The whole has been planated, and the few rivers are incised in the platform. Karst features are prominent, though the lower altitude, and consequently the higher water-table, have prevented the development of extreme karstic landforms, such as characterise the Dinaric mountain system. Much of the area is nevertheless covered only with a vegetation of dry scrub, with oak woods covering the residual Tertiary deposits.

An extension of the higher ground of the Julian Karst reaches southwards along the eastern coast of Istria, and drops steeply to the Gulf of Rijeka. The coastal region is pinched out, and Rijeka itself clings to a narrow shelf of rock between the towering limestone of Snježnik and Risnjak on the one side and the sea on the other.

The Zagora. It is not until one has passed to the south of the Velebit, that a lowland region again extends between the karst and the coast. As in the Istrian peninsula, the level of the limestone platform is lower than in the main karst region, and it is in part covered with Tertiary rocks. In general the former gives rise to low bare limestone ridges which in places rise as high as 1,000 feet above the sea. Between them are Tertiary deposits and alluvium, which are marked by narrow bands of cultivated land between the dry, white ridges of the limestone.

The coast is irregular, resulting from a geologically recent rise of sea-level, and the rivers, Zrmanja and Krka enter the sea by long branching estuaries. This region as a whole is known as the Zagora— literally 'Beyond the mountains'. It has always been the most densely settled and intensively developed part of the whole Dalmatian coast. The Romans had numerous settlements here, and on the site of Split the Emperior Diocletian built his palace. But a few miles to the east of Split, the mountains re-approach the coast, and along the coast near Makarska the high karst again drops precipitously to the water.

Lower Neretva valley. The coastal ranges are interrupted to allow the Neretva River to make its way across them to the sea. This is the only river of any considerable size to flow across the karst, and this it does because it derives a water supply from beyond the karst region to the north. The valley of the lower Neretva is in fact a succession of *polja*, their bounding ridges denuded to the point at which their level floors merge with one another. Only isolated hills and ridges remain of the once extensive karst. Tertiary deposits were laid down in the resulting basin, and its very low level, less than 200 feet above sea-level almost as far upstream as Mostar, has led to extensive aggradation. In the last twenty miles of its course the Neretva flows across a damp, alluvial plain, where irrigated agriculture is practised, before passing through its small delta to the sea.

Southern Dalmatia. To the south-east of the Neretva the coastal mountains are in general lower than those to the north, and small and generally isolated patches of lowland occur. Sometimes these are nothing more than terraces above the water, but they offer a slender foothold to a large number of coastal settlements. These include Dubrovnik, the small towns like Herceg Novi and Kotor, which cluster round the Gulf of Kotor, and the growing resorts of the extreme south. Beyond Ulcinj the hills come to an end and a low and rather marshy plain extends into Albania. This, like the lower Neretva valley, is essentially a series of low-lying and interrelated *polja*. The largest is occupied by Lake Skadar, to the north of which an alluvial plain of fairly recent geological origin extends up the valleys of the Zeta and the Morača. Lake Skadar discharges by way of the 25 mile long river Bojana, which serves also to carry part of the drainage of the Albanian Drin.

Hills of Croatia-Northern Bosnia

Between the mountains of the Dinaric system and the valley of the Sava lies a relatively narrow belt of hill country. It extends for no less than 325 miles from the margin of the Ljubljana Basin in the north-west to the Ibar valley in the south-east. At most it is 50 miles wide, and for much of its distance is substantially less than this. It is difficult to break it down into minor regions, because its physiographic make-up, though varied, presents common features over the whole of this distance. The contrasts between its five divisions are scenically quite small. All are characterised by short segments of hill or mountain range, aligned in a north-west to south-east direction, and crossed, sometimes by means of narrow defiles, by the Dinaric tributaries of the Sava. These are joined by a great number of short tributaries which mostly flow along the strike of the beds in valleys which are generally wide and open.

The structure of the whole region is one of Palaeozoic and igneous rocks, covered by Secondary, and these in turn by the Tertiary beds laid down by the sea which once filled the Pannonian Basin. The chief variations within the region arise from the differences in the extent to which the uppermost of these series has been stripped away to expose the older and generally harder rocks.

Krka region. In the extreme north-west is a small and hilly region in which both the Dinaric and the Alpine trends are found in close juxtaposition. The name given to this region is suggested by the small river Krka which drains much of it to the Sava. It is a highly dissected plateau, in which limestone predominates, but not sufficiently to give rise to a karst phenomenon. The conspicuous, and indeed the dominant relief feature of the region is the Žumberačka Gora, a massif of Jurassic limestone lying to the west of Zagreb. It rises to 3,874 feet, and its direction, from south-west to north-east conflicts conspicuously with the general direction of folding of the region.

Kupa Basin. The hills of the latter region drop suddenly to the basin of the Kupa. This river of the northern karst leaves the high plateaus west of Karlovac, takes a winding course eastward across an alluvial plain, and joins the Sava at Sisak. This is the Pokuplje, the lowest and least rugged of these divisions of the northern foot-hills region. A few hills rise from its rather damp and in places poorly drained surface, but in the main it is an agricultural region, centring on the town of Karlovac.

Una region. The region which borders the Una valley is, by contrast, higher and more dissected. Triassic and Palaeozoic rocks are extensively exposed, and the region terminates in the north in the Prosara, a massif with a granite core, which overlooks the Sava. To the south, along the valley of the Sana, a tributary of the Una, lies another of the longitudinal basins which once contained lakes and are now floored with Tertiary deposits and alluvium. In it is the small town of Prijedor.

Vrbas-Bosna region. From the Vrbas to the Drina extends a plateau, made up in the main of Tertiary deposits, with igneous rocks outcropping towards the south. Summit levels diminish gradually from over 2,500 feet in the south of the region to less than 1,250 as the Sava is approached. This is a region of rolling hills, forested over their summits and cultivated over the lower slopes and in the valleys, in whose pattern it is not easy to discern the Dinaric trend which is predominant in the structures of this region. The Spreča valley, however, flows north-westward to join the Bosna, following the line of another Tertiary basin, whose floor is today a level expanse of alluvium, ensconced between high rounded hills. Below the surface lie Tertiary lignite deposits which are among the best in the country, and small towns like Doboj, Gračanica, Lukavac and Tuzla, grew up as market centres serving this predominantly agricultural country, and are now becoming centres of industry based on the local reserves of coal.

Lower Drina. Towards the east the cover of Tertiary rocks thins away, revealing a region of Palaeozoic rocks into which granites and gabbros have been widely intruded. Hilly ridges, aligned approximately from north-west to south-east, and reaching in some instances heights of over 4,000 feet, make this an area of stronger relief than any other part of the foothills region. In relief and in structure it approximates more closely to the interior region of hills and plateaus from which it has here been separated it in a somewhat arbitrary fashion.

Serbia and Macedonia

The region which extends eastwards and south-eastwards from those already described towards the Bulgarian and Greek borders is structurally and topographically the most complex not only in Yugoslavia but in all Eastern Europe. It is a maze of hills which at first glance appear to have little order or system. It is channelled by valley routeways; interrupted by small basins in which Tertiary seas laid down their deposits of sand and clay, and drained by rivers which flow to every sea bordering the Balkan peninsula. And at the same time it bears, along the Morava, Ibar and Vardar valleys one of the most important routeways in Europe. Since the Neolithic this has been one of the two truly significant passage-ways between the Mediterranean and the Danubian basins, the other being the Julian Karst. Between them lies the whole of the trackless Dinaric system.

This Serbian-Macedonian region consists essentially of a platform made up of schists of Palaeozoic and even earlier date. It is an extension of the Rhodope of Bulgaria, and is sometimes known as the Rhodope or as the Pelagonian Massif. It has been extensively faulted; basins were formed in its surface; it was intruded by granite and gabbro, and volcanic activity has ejected igneous rocks on to its surface. Though largely covered by the seas which existed from Triassic through Cretaceous times, it was not greatly affected by the Alpine folding which followed. It seems rather to have been a relatively stable mass against which were folded the Balkan Mountains to the north-east and the Dinaric to the west.

It was covered by the sea in Cretaceous times, and at least some parts of it during the preceding Jurassic and Triassic. But the rocks—predominantly limestones—of these ages seem never to have been as thick as in the Dinaric system, and they have been stripped by erosion from most of the region. Secondary beds are extensive today only in the Šumadija, in the extreme north, and in the Kosovo and Metohija Basins. Elsewhere they outcrop over only very small areas as residual deposits, hitherto spared by the processes of denudation.

Much of the Secondary cover must have been stripped before seas again spread through this region, in middle and late Tertiary times, from the Aegean and Pannonian basins. At least the lower elevations were planated by the seas, and lakes formed in the many basins and depressions in the surface of the Rhodope schists. In some beds of lignite were formed. When the sea-level again sank most of the lakes drained away, gorge-like channels were cut connecting lake with lake, and the land began to assume its present form. Karst features developed in the few, restricted areas of limestone rock. But over much of the region the impervious schists shed their rainfall almost as quickly as it fell. With so quick a run-off stream erosion was vigorous. Valleys were deepened, and in some areas river-capture was active. In many of the lake-basins alluvium was spread over the Tertiary deposits, and on the higher slopes of the Osogovska and Šar Planina incipient glaciers developed during the Quaternary, fretting the summits into arêtes and corries.

Such is the region which, for the convenience of more detailed description, must be divided into regions. Such division is of necessity arbitrary, and in a region as dissected as this, with so many local facets which should be considered, no simple division can be wholly satisfactory.

Šumadija. The distinctive qualities of the Šumadija, however, are not in doubt. It is the region of rolling hills and broad valleys which extends northward from the mountains of Serbia between the Kolubara and the Morava valleys. On the south it is bounded by the depression which contains the Zapadna (Western) Morava, and in this direction it rises to heights in excess of 3,000 feet. But its summit levels decline towards the north, until they end in the bluffs which overlook the Danube and are now covered by the city of Beograd.

Over most of Šumadija the Palaeozoic foundation of the region is deeply buried, and it comes to the surface only in the south-east. Cretaceous limestone appears in the central area, and an inlier of basic igneous rocks to the north-west of Kragujevac gives rise not only to the strongest relief in the region but also to metalliferous mines. It is known, not inappropriately, as Rudnik. But over most of the Šumadija lie the soft beds laid down in Tertiary times when this region was covered beneath the Pannonian Sea. It is in these beds that the gentle relief and broad valleys of most of the region have been cut.

Medieval Serbia had developed amid the mountains and basins of

Raška, but the core of modern Serbia is formed by the hills of Šumadija. It was a forested country, with oak and beech predominating; its soils were fertile and good, and it lay on the margin of the Turkish Empire, looking across the Danube into the Habsburg lands, from which ultimately it derived both the incentive to revolt and the capital and skills needed by an independent state.

Morava valley. East and south of the Šumadija lies a wide valley, made up in fact of a series of rounded basins each of which became a lake as the level of the Pannonian Sea fell in late Tertiary times. The Serbian Morava rises to the south, and in its northward course has linked together, like beads on a string, a succession of small basins, each filled in with Tertiary and Recent deposits and surrounded by steep walls of Rhodope schist. At Grdelica the Morava, here called the Južna (Southern) Morava, leaves the gorge tract which it has cut across the andesites and schists of the Rhodope massif, and enters the Leskovac basin. Twenty-five miles to the north-west the steep valley walls again close in, and at Klisura, so descriptively named, a short gorge, with a castle above its crags, links the valley with the Niš Basin. This is longer and wider than the Leskovac Basin, but is also closed near Stalać by hills which rise 1,000 feet above the river. Below Stalać the Južna Morava is joined by the Zapadna Morava. The latter had risen to the west within a few miles of the Drina, and, like the Južna branch had drained in turn a succession of small Tertiary basins, interconnected by short defiles which, by reason of their steep walls and the turbulent river, made movement through the valley as a whole extremely difficult. In each basin is a small urban centre for the agricultural villages which are scattered over the floor of the basin. In this way one distinguishes along the course of the Zapadna Morava, the Požega, Čačak, Kraljevo and Kruševac basins.

Below the junction of the Morava rivers, the valley is wider and flatter, except only at Bagrdan, where it is partially closed by the last barrier of Rhodope schist. Below this point, however, for the last 45 miles of its course, the Morava meanders lazily across a flood-plain which increases in width to ten miles. The Morava is today a misfit stream, occupying the valley of a greater river of late Tertiary times, which drained the lakes, eroded the gorges which interconnect the lake basins, and cut the broad valley of the lower Morava.

The gradient of the lower Morava is very gentle, and the stream, like the Tisa, has in the past meandered and frequently changed course. Even today the valley floor is marshy, and it lacks the central-place, which is characteristic of all the basins along the upper and middle parts of its course.

The Morava region consists mainly of basins and valley floors, in which Tertiary deposits are partly hidden by more recent alluvium. It is a region of considerable agricultural value; it is well settled, and has its share of small towns. Its importance, however, lies partly in the role it has played as a routeway. Despite the defiles, which sometimes force the roads to climb up over the bordering hills to avoid them, this succession of basins has always provided the easiest routes southward from the Danube Basin to Greece and the Mediterranean. Both branches of the Morava are used. Above Grdelica, the gorges of the Morava lead southwards to the Vranje Basin, beyond which a dry valley, scoured like so many others in late Tertiary times, leads directly to a tributary valley of the Vardar. Until recent times, when a road and railway were built through them, the Grdelica gorges presented a serious difficulty, forcing travellers to take a difficult road over the high plateaus which border the gorge. An alternative was to leave the valley of the Južna Morava at Leskovac and to travel by way of its tributary, the Jablanica to the Kosovo Basin and so to the Vardar. It proved to be easier, however, to follow the Zapadna Morava as far as Kraljevo, and then the Ibar southward into the Kosovo region. This route, along a valley deeply incised between the Kopaonik Mountains and those around Novi Pazar, was far from easy, but road and more recently railway were here able to follow the course of the river.

Kopaonik region. This region, as defined here, is bounded by the Zapadna and Južna Morava on the north and east respectively; to the south lies the Skopje Basin. The western boundary is less definite. It is here taken as the lower Ibar, the Raška and the upper Ibar; the valley of the Sitnica, better known as Kosovo polje, which continues the direction of the middle Ibar, is included with Metohija (see below). This region is made up, except along its western margin and in the extreme south by the same basement complex of schists that appears sporadically at the surface in the Šumadija and Morava regions. In the west, however, is an extraordinarily varied group of igneous and metamorphic rocks—gabbro, andesite, granite and one of the most extensive areas of serpentine in Europe. These rocks of exceptional hardness give rise to the Kopaonik mountains and, across the deep Ibar valley to the west, the Rogozna Massif. The Kopaonik, a north–south range, rises in its rugged granite summits to over 6,000 feet.

The Ibar flows across this region, from Mitrovica to Kraljevo, in a deep and very rugged valley. This is now followed by road and rail, and, as has been noted above, has long been an important part of the routeway from the Danube to the Mediterranean. It was the nucleus of the Turkish Sanjak of Novi Pazar, although the town of Novi Pazar itself actually lies some ten miles up the tributary valley of the Raška to the west.

East of the Kopaonik the schists form a high dissected plateau which slopes from about 3,500 feet in the west to about 1,300 in the east, where it hangs above the valley of the Južna Morava. Igneous masses give rise to the areas of greatest altitude, notably the Veliki Justrebac in the north and the Radan and Goljak towards the south. In the extreme south of the region the Skopska Crna Gora (Skopje Black Mountain) rises to 5,092 feet and then drops steeply down to the Skopje Basin.

The Kopaonik region, like those already discussed, is characterised by its small tectonic basins, filled with Tertiary and recent deposits. Largest of these are the Prokuplje Basin, drained by the Toplica to the Južna Morava; the Gnjilane Basin, in which the Južna Morava rises, and the Malo or Little Kosovo Basin, with Podujevo as its central place.

Unlike the Šumadija, this remains a heavily wooded region. The Kopaonik planina rises above the tree line, but much of the plateau to the east is still covered with oak and beech woods. Most of the region offers at best only a thin, stony soil, but the Tertiary-filled basins, the gentler mountain slopes and the broader valleys are settled and crops are raised.

Kosovo-Metohija. This has become a political term for an autonomous region within Serbia, but is used here in a somewhat narrower sense to denote the two interlinked basins, or *polja* of Kosovo and Metohija. On three sides the region is very clearly delimited. To the south-west the Albanian border is traced through the line of rugged hills. On the north-west the Koprivnik planina and Žljeb and Mokra Gora rise steeply to heights greatly in excess of 6,000 feet, and on the south-east lies the Šar planina, one of the highest and least easily crossed of all the mountain ranges of the Balkans. These bounding mountain masses are, in fact, horsts, and their steep fronts follow lines of faulting. The down-faulted mass which separates them has been covered by Secondary deposits, and these in turn by Tertiary and Recent. Recent accumulations cover extensive areas in the north of the basin, near Peć, and in the south, around Prizren. Beyond them lie in order the Tertiary and Secondary beds. These give rise to a gentle terrain, with low rolling hills, and karst landforms on the Secondary limestone which covers much of the eastern half of the Metohija Basin.

The drainage of the Metohija Basin is mainly by the Bijeli (White) Drin. Its main stream flows southward across the basin, and then cuts across the hills along the Albanian border by a deeply incised valley, to join the Crni (Black) Drin, 10 miles within Albania.

Towards the north-east of the Metohija Basin Palaeozoic beds come to the surface. These rocks give rise to two roughly parallel hill ranges, the Crnoljeva and Čičavica planine. Neither rises to much over 3,000 feet, or poses any great difficulty to movement between the two neighbouring basins.

The Kosovo, or Priština Basin is smaller, narrower and more elongated, but like its neighbouring basin to the south-west, is floored with Tertiary and alluvial deposits. It is drained in the main by the northward flowing Sitnica, which joins the upper Ibar at Kosovo Mitrovica, where the basin in fact terminates. North of this point, as we have seen, the Ibar is incised between the Kopaonik and Rogozna massifs. Toward the south, however, near the town of Urševac, between the head of the Sitnica and that of the Nerodimka, a tributary of the Vardar, is a small area of indefinite drainage. This gap, which served in late Tertiary times to carry part of the Kosovo drainage south to the Vardar, is now an essential link in the valley routeway from the Skopje basin northward to the lower Ibar and Morava valleys. It was no accident that the battle which sealed the fate of the medieval kingdom of Serbia was fought against the invading Turks at Kosovo. Nor is it surprising that possession of the Sanjak of Novi Pazar, which included Kosovo, was fiercely disputed between Austrians and Turks.

South of Urševac the Nerodimka, picking up drainage from the Šar planina to the west, cuts across the line of the Šar planina-Skopska Crna Gora by the formidable gorges of Kačanik. Behind Mitrovica and Priština the mountains rise steeply, merging into the high, rugged tableland of the Kopaonik region.

Tetovo-Ohrid region. The Palaeozoic beds which made an inconspicuous appearance as the divide between the Metohija and Kosovo plains, continue southwards to the Grámmos and Píndhos mountains of Greece. They are harder than those which compose the Dinaric system; they rise high enough to have supported glaciers during the

Ice Age, and their summits are in many places fretted by the action of the ice. Their rocks are generally impervious, so that they shed their rainfall in a multitude of streams, but limestone comes to the surface in some areas—notably around lakes Ohrid and Prespa, and karstic landforms are developed here, though less conspicuously than in the great Karst of the Dinaric system. The rocks have, furthermore, been intensively faulted, and those down-thrown sections which have sunk between the lines of faulting, are now covered by lake deposits.

The Tetovo-Ohrid region is here defined as that part of western Macedonia which is characterised by north–south mountain ranges of the Píndhos system, separated by basin-like depressions. Most conspicuous is the Šar planina and its southward continuation, the Korab, Bistra and Karaorman ranges. These mountains rise to summits at over 8,000 feet, and for considerable distances their crest lies at a height of more than 6,000 feet. For almost 100 miles they constitute one of the most formidable barriers to movement within the Balkan peninsula.

The Karaorman planina ends a mile or two to the north of Lake Ohrid. To the west is the valley of the Crni Drin, following the line of one of the many tectonic basins which extend northward from the lake. The boundary with Albania, which farther to the north had followed in part the crest of the range, here drops into the Drin valley, and then climbs the steep flanks of the Jablanica range beyond. East of the Šar planina lies another and approximately parallel range, the Suva (Suha) Gora, which is continued southward into the Plakenska and Baba planine. Between these two dominant ranges lie the basins of Tetovo-Gostivar, Kičivo, Debar, Ohrid and Prespa. The Tetovo-Gostivar basin lies deeply sunk between the Šar and Suva planine, whose flanks rise almost precipitously from its borders. It is drained by the Upper Vardar, which leaves the basin at its northern end by a characteristically deep and narrow gorge. The Tetovo Basin remains difficult of access though a railway has now been built up the gorges of the Vardar. The Debar and Kičevo basins are smaller, the one in the Drin valley close to the Albanian border; the other, almost completely isolated between the Bistra and Suva planine.

The Ohrid and Prespa basins alone among those of western Macedonia, still contain lakes. The lakes appear to occupy the whole width of the valley floors which separate three of the north–south trending ranges, and the mountain slopes rise very steeply indeed from the shores of both lakes. Lake Ohrid is drained northward by the Crni Drin. It was formerly more extensive than at present, and an alluvial plain extends up the many small tributary valleys as well as down the Drin valley itself. The lake level has fallen in Recent geological times as the Drin has deepened its valley. There have however been fluctuations, and in modern times sedimentation of the Struško *polje*, as the alluvial plain to the north of the lake is called, has restricted the flow and led to the formation of seasonal marshes over parts of the valley floor.

Lake Prespa lies some 500 feet higher than Ohrid, from which it is separated by the high, rugged Galičica planina. It is more irregular in shape, and is fringed by small areas of alluvium. Its former outlet to the sea was clearly by way of the Malko (Little) Prespansko lake and the Devoli valley of Albania, but its surface has now sunk below the level of this outlet, and it has today no apparent discharge to the sea. It lies however at the junction of the folded Palaeozoic rocks of the Píndhos system and of the crystalline Rhodope Massif. Whereas the impervious rocks of the latter supply much of the inflow into the lake, the discharge is almost certainly through underground passages dissolved in the massive limestones which comprise much of the former. The more numerous lakes in northern Greece show somewhat similar features: marked fluctuations in level and lack of surface outlet.[1]

The Ohrid-Prespa region is one of great natural beauty, with the pastel-tinted mountains rising from the deep blue waters of the lakes. It is also one of immense historical interest and importance. Its alluvial basins became settlement areas of the South Slavs in the early stages of their penetration of the Balkans. The region was incorporated into the first Bulgarian Empire, and became one of its most important centres of political and religious power. This short period of greatness in the early Middle Ages has left a legacy of architecture, both ecclesiastical and military, which is among the most valuable in the whole Balkans.

Bitola-Prilep (Pelagonian) region. The region just described is bordered on the east by the Rhodope Massif. This is made up primarily of crystalline schists. The change in structure has little influence on the scenery. The same arrangement continues of predominantly north-south ranges, interrupted by down-faulted basins.

---

[1] Margaret Hasluck, 'Historical Sketch of the Fluctuations of Lake Ostrovo in West Macedonia', *Geogrl J.*, **87** (1936), 338–47, and 'The Archaeological History of Lake Ostrovo in West Macedonia', *ibid.*, 448–56.

In the north, partially enclosed by the curve of the Vardar, is the Jakupica Massif, which reaches a height of 8,331 feet, and sends out mountain ranges southward to enclose the Bitola Basin. These ranges build up to the Nidže and Kožuf mountains, which lie along the Greek border, and drop southward into the plain of Thessaloníke.

The Bitola-Prilep Basin is, like most others, elongated in a north to south direction, and extends for about 50 miles in Yugoslavia and for a further 12 miles within Greece. In general it is broader and more open than the basins of Ohrid and Tetovo; its surrounding slopes rise more gently to mountains that are lower and more rounded than those farther west, and it is in general a region of much easier access. Its drainage is entirely by the Crna Reka—the Black River—which rises towards the north of the basin, flows southward, receiving a great many tributaries from the surrounding mountains, then, turning abruptly to the north-east, cuts a deep valley through this mass of tangled mountains to the Vardar.

The Bitola-Prilep Basin is one of the larger, and has always been one of the most important of the Tertiary basins of the Balkans. Though it remains marshy in its more low-lying tracts, it is an important agricultural region, and has always had a relatively dense population. This is reflected in the presence here of two of the larger cities of southern Yugoslavia, Bitola (Bitolj) and Prilep.

Skopje-Veles Basin. The largest and in all respects the most important of the Tertiary basins of southern Yugoslavia is the valley of the Vardar itself. The basin is, in fact, divisible into two, the basin which centres in Skopje and the Titov Veles Basin, which lies down-river and is separated from it by encroaching mountains within the Rhodope Massif.

The Skopje Basin is triangular in plan. To the south-west lies the Jakupica Massif; to the east lies a high dissected plateau, which merges into the Osogovska planina on the Bulgarian border, and to the north the Skopska Crna Gora and the mountains which lie between Kosovo and the upper Morava. The basin is itself bounded by faults from beyond which the steep mountains which look down into the basin. Yet the Skopje Basin is no isolated cul-de-sac. It has three points of entry, and these have made it a focal point in southern Yugoslavia. To the north-east, between the Crna Gora and the mountains of eastern Macedonia lies the Morava valley and its southward continuation (see page 641). This widens into the Kumanovo Basin, which in turn merges into that of Skopje. The Vardar itself comes in from the north-west. Although its gorges lead upwards into only the Tetovo Basin, which has always been of minor importance as a routeway, the Lepenac, a left-bank tributary of the Vardar, opens a route northward between the Šar and the Crna Gora and by way of the Kačanik gorge, into Kosovo itself.

Skopje (Skoplje) is thus the meeting place of two of the most important routes across the Balkans from the Danube to the Aegean. The third point of entry is to the south, along the Vardar itself, which provides a generally easy route southward to the plains of Greece and the Mediterranean Sea.

Above Titov Veles the Vardar valley, as has been noted, has been incised across a barrier of harder rocks than those which make up the basin itself. Though the railway follows the river, the main road has been obliged to go out over the plateau to the east in its course from the Greek border to Skopje. To the north of Titov Veles, however, the valley begins to widen into the Veles Basin. This is in plan very much less regular than the Skopje Basin, and its surface is a great deal more hilly. It is formed very largely in older Tertiary rocks which have been hardened and folded sufficiently to produce a very accidented relief. This is a region of hills, often steep and rising at many points to 2,000 feet above the level of the river Vardar. These hills appear to have no pattern or regularity. They are generally bare of trees, though relics of their former forest-cover sometimes extend over their summits. Winter storms are often heavy and their bare slopes may sometimes be severely eroded. But in summer the smaller rivers dry out, and the land looks arid and burned up, and only along the valley is there the green of cultivation and the bright colours of human settlement.

Ridges run down to the Vardar, which cuts across them in a series of short gorges. The valley widens, only to narrow again, forcing the road away from its sometimes precipitous banks. This alternation of plain and gorge continues through the basin of Valandovo, to the Greek border which cuts the most southerly of these basins, that of Gevgelija, into two.

Rhodope. East of the Vardar lies the Rhodope in its narrower, topographical sense. Essentially this region is a high plateau of ancient schists, over which extensive beds of lava were spread in Tertiary times. The region has been dissected by the Pčinja, Kriva and Bregalnica, which flow to the Vardar, and by the Strumica, which drains the southern part of the region eastwards to the Bulgarian Struma. Summit levels of these mountains rise from less than 3,000 feet towards the west to heights of over 6,000 feet near the Bulgarian border. The mountain rangeswhich have resulted from the denudation of this region often have broad and almost level summits, in which it is possible to recognise remnants of the ancient plateau surface of the early Tertiary.

Down-faulted basins are less a feature of this region than those to the west. In fact the only Tertiary-filled basins that are large enough to be important are the Strumica valley; the Kočani Basin, which lies in the middle course of the Bregalnica, and the Berovo Basin near its headwaters. These are still not fully drained and reclaimed. In some parts their floors remain marshy in winter, and irrigation agriculture is widely practised in summer in the Strumica valley and near Kočani.

The Strumica valley has an importance out of all relationship to its size and agricultural potentialities. To the south and parallel with it lies the Belasica range, which is continuous with the hills of Chalcidike in Greece. To the west these hills run down to the Vardar. On the other hand, the Strumica valley presented no barrier to movement other than the seasonal marshes which bordered the river; and near Radoviš, at the head of the basin, a low gap offered an easy routeway into the Bregalnica valley and thus to the Vardar near Titov Veles. The Strumica valley thus provided the easiest route from the plains of Thrace and the Struma valley to the Skopje basin and the Danube valley. To the north the next practicable crossing of the mountains along the Bulgarian border lies along the Nišava valley, 120 miles away.

Mountains of north-east Serbia
The region last considered abuts along its northern margin against a section of the folded Carpathian mountain system. These mountains (see page 14), follow a sinuous course through Czechoslovakia and Romania, and in the south-west of the latter reach the Danube, which has breached them in the sequence of gorges that are sometimes known as the Iron Gate. South of the river the range pursues a curving course to the south-east and so into Bulgaria. The direction of folding, however, is only locally prominent in the relief of this region, because the structures of the Carpathian system have been either removed by erosion over large areas or obscured by more recent volcanic rocks. The geology of the region is in consequence very complex. Rocks of Secondary age, which participated in the actual folding of the mountain system, are present at the surface over

no more than half the area. Elsewhere the predominant rocks are the schists and igneous rocks of the Rhodope complex which underlies so much of the central Balkan region. In the north, close to the Danube, are north–south ridges of hard sandstone and limestone, and to the south are similar mountain ridges, here oriented from north-west to south-east. But between these extremes is a confusing pattern of small plateaus, ridges and deep valleys. Within this region as a whole it is possible to distinguish three separate divisions.

Nišava region. The river Nišava, the largest tributary of the Južna Morava, rises within Bulgaria. Its course from the international boundary to its junction with the Morava at Niš, is entirely within an area of folded secondary limestones. These rocks give rise to high, rugged and barren ranges, which flank the Nišava valley, to the south the Suva planina, to the north, the Vidlič and Svrlijiške planine. The course of the Nišava is inclined obliquely to the trend of the mountains. In consequence its valley tends to be made up of alternating basins and defiles, formed where the river cuts across the mountain ridges. The Pirot and Bela Palanka Basins are the largest of these, and are floored with late Tertiary deposits. Downstream from the latter the Nišava river cuts across the high limestone Suva planina by a gorge which is one of the most spectacular features of the region. The road formerly climbed over the spurs of the plateau which encloses the basin, but a modern road has recently been built through the gorge itself. The Nišava route has been throughout historical times the most important link between the Pannonian Plain and the Marica valley. The Romans built a road through it, which is followed approximately by the modern highway. This has only recently (1964–65) been rebuilt, with road tunnels to avoid some of the worst of the hills. To the Byzantines and Turks it was one of the most important of the strategic routes of their empires, and in modern times the approaches of the Nišava were guarded at each end by the fortresses of Niš and Sofia.

Stara Planina. This term is commonly used for the whole range which extends from the Danube gorges to the Black Sea. We are here concerned only with the relatively short section of this range which lies within Yugoslavia; it must be remembered that it is indistinguishable from that which lies beyond the international boundary, which, indeed, for about 45 miles, follows the crestline of its highest range. The structure and general features of the relief of the range have already been described. It culminates in the south in the high limestone plateaus of Ozren and Rtanj, each flanked by small Tertiary basins, in which are to be found most of the settlements and the majority of the population. North of the Rtanj a Palaeozoic inlier gives rise to the rolling, forested and almost uninhabited plateau of Kučaj. Limestones, with their mildly developed karstic features, recur to the north, but the ancient rocks again come to the surface, and it is in these that, for the greater part of their length, the gorges of the Danube have been cut.

The Iron Gate. The Danube gorges, commonly though incorrectly termed the 'Iron Gate', extend for over 90 miles, from Ram downstream to Turnu Severin. For the whole of this distance the river constitutes the boundary between Yugoslavia and Romania, sovereignty actually being divided along the middle of its main course.

In its gorge tract the river drops about 87 feet, from 205 feet at Ram at 118 feet at Turnu Severin at low water. This descent is actually accomplished in a series of rapids, each separated from the next by a stretch of calm water, where the river flows across one of the small basins which separate the individual gorge tracts.

For the first 20 miles the valley is wide, with gentle, vine-clad slopes. Here the speed of the stream is reduced by the rocky barriers which lie ahead; deposition is important, and many large, shifting islands have formed in the stream. At low water they dry out, and sand sometimes blows from the exposed deposits. Below Golubac is the first gorge, a tract of about 5 miles, cut through igneous rocks. Below this section, the valley widens, at least on its north bank, into the small Ljupkovska Basin, only to narrow again after about 11 miles. The Gospodjin Vir gorge, which follows for about 9 miles, is cut in varied limestones and schists. The latter predominate, producing steep cliffs, between which the river is narrowed to less than 300 yards at some points. But again it widens, as it makes a sharp bend to the north-east, to about 900 yards. This is the Donjo-Milanovac Basin, which is, in fact, one of the small Tertiary basins characteristic of the region.

At this bend the river enters the longest, deepest and most impressive of its gorges, that of Kazan. The river is narrowed to about 200 yards, and its speed increased proportionately. Its right bank consists of towering limestone cliffs. The left, or Romanian bank is less precipitous and more broken by short streams which drop steeply from the mountains beyond, for the river here follows the line of division between the Secondary beds and the underlying crystalline massif which comes to the surface to the north of the river. It is the latter which is the more deeply dissected because it alone has a considerable surface drainage.

The Kazanske *klisure* extends for 12 miles. For the whole of this distance there is neither road or settlement on the Yugoslav bank, though it is possible to travel along the Romanian bank through a succession of small villages. Again both the river and its valley widen as they turn more to the east and enter the Orşova Basin. Here the Danube is joined by the Cerna River, which has opened a routeway, northward across the Transylvanian Alps (see page 544). Below Orşova lies the last, shortest and most widely known of the gorges, the Iron Gate itself. The river here cuts across the rocks of varying hardness; it is wider than in gorges farther upstream, and the valley more open. This section of the river is, however notorious for the rocky bar, the *Prigrada*, which lies across the river, causing rapids at low water. This has always been the chief navigational hazard in the whole gorge tract of the Danube.

The obstacle presented by the gorges and their attendant rapids was recognised even in classical times, when different names even were used for the sections of the river above and below this barrier. The Romans made no attempt to use this section of the river. They built a road from the plain of northern Bulgaria (Moesia) across the hills of north-eastern Yugoslavia to Smederovo. Another road ran from Orşova up the Cerna valley and so to the Pannonian Plain. The gorges were thus by-passed by roads built to both north and south. The river itself, the shortest route and the most direct, seems to have been little used.[1]

In modern times traffic through the gorges increased, but could be carried on only with great difficulty, by using boats of shallow draught in certain sections of the river and even by portaging goods around such obstacles as the *Prigrada*. In 1832 improvements were made by blasting away some of the rocky bars and the creation in this way of deeper channels. By the end of the century masonry retaining walls had been built along the channel, and a railway track with locomotive was installed on the Yugoslav bank to pull ships upstream against the great speed of the current. In other gorge tracts a deep channel was blasted from the rock, and in some retaining walls were built to increase the speed and thus the scour of the current, and to prevent sand from filling the channel.

The degree to which the Danube is used for navigation has been discussed (see pages 177–178). Obstacles in recent years have been

[1] See W. Gordon East, 'The Danube Route-way', in *An Historical Geography of Europe*, Methuen, 1935, chapter 18.

The gorge of the Neretva, above Mostar. Two railway tunnels are visible to the left of the river; the higher carries the old narrow-gauge line, the lower, the new, standard gauge track

YUGOSLAVIA

The gorge of the Nišava, to the south-east of Niš. The recently constructed road uses a series of tunnels; the older followed a very difficult route over the mountains to the south

The Dalmatian coast of southern Yugoslavia. In the middle distance is the island-village, now a hotel, of Sveti Stefan; in the distance, the small coastal town of Budva

YUGOSLAVIA

The old, fortified bridge o
Mostar (the name mean
"old bridge") across th
Neretva in Hercegovina

more political than physiographic, and the significance of the latter is now being diminished by the construction of a dual purpose dam on the river below Orşova. This project was begun in 1964, and is expected to be completed by 1971 at the cost of 400 million dollars. Not only will the dam eliminate the Prigrada rapids, but it will also provide smoother water and easier navigation through the upstream gorges and narrows. It is also expected to yield from its turbo-generators about 10·7 billion kilowatts per hour which will be divided between Yugoslavia and Romania, which have jointly undertaken the project.

Timok region. The last physiographic division of north-eastern Yugoslavia to be considered is the valley of the Timok. This river rises far to the south, and in its northward course to join the Danube near Negotin, it flows through a series of linked basins, all of them containing Tertiary beds and alluvium, which combine to produce a gentler relief and more fertile soil than elsewhere in north-eastern Yugoslavia. The upper basins focus on Knjaževac and Zaječar. North of the latter town the Timok valley merges with that of the lower Danube to form the Negotin Basin, cut off only by low hills from the greater plain which, beginning at Vidin and Calafat extends eastwards to the Black Sea.

A section of the lower Timok valley, consisting essentially of the hilly tract which separates the Zaječar from the Negotin basins, was transferred from Bulgaria to Yugoslavia in 1919. This was necessary if the latter was to have access by other means than mountain tracks, to its own north-eastern salient, including the small towns of Negotin and Kladovo themselves.

Danubian plains

The hilly or mountainous regions of Yugoslavia considered so far make up about three-quarters of the country. The remainder is lowland, lying mostly below about 500 feet, and drained by the Danube and its principal tributaries, the Tisa and Sava. This region is, however, far from flat. A rather arbitrary line was drawn earlier in this chapter to cut the alpine region of north-western Yugoslavia off from the Danubian Plain. Two lines of low hills however, continue the direction of the hills of Slovenia into the plains. They consist in general of Tertiary beds which partially cover cores of Palaeozoic and crystalline rock.

These hills must at one time have been islands in the Tertiary sea

22

which filled the Pannonian basin. Around them rivers from the surrounding alpine system laid down sands and clays. The basin then drained away through the gorges which its waters had cut across the rising line of the Transylvanian Alps and Stara Planina. During the ensuing period the rivers of the plain cut their shallow valleys into these deposits. They were graded to the base-level established by the Iron Gate gorges, and there was an increasing sedimentation in this direction along the valleys. On the other hand, the light clay and sandy deposits became subject to widespread blowing by the wind. Patches of sand-dunes developed on the interfluves, and thick beds of loess were laid down.[1] The effect has been to produce wide flood-plains along the rivers, flanked by low river terraces, dry enough for cultivation, but only settled at their higher and drier level. Beyond lie loess-covered plateaus. It is on this basis that the following regional boundaries have been drawn.

Hills of Slavonia. The plain which lies to the south of the Drava forms the historic province of Slavonia. Through it from north-west to south-east lies a double line of hills, each composed of a crystalline or Palaeozoic core largely buried under Tertiary deposists. Both lines are broken up by areas of lowland which extend across Slavonia from the Sava to the Drava. The more southerly of these lines includes, to the west, the Medvednica, the steep, forested massif which rises above Zagreb to a height of 3,395 feet. To the south-east lies the granite upland of Moslavačka, and beyond it the Psunj which rises to an extensive platform at almost 3,000 feet. The lower hills to the east, the Požeška Gora and Dilj, are formed almost entirely in the more resistant of the Tertiary beds.

The northern line of hills begins in the Kalničko Gorje. It is continued to the south-east by a low, narrow ridge which rarely exceeds 800 feet. This expands into the Papuk and Ravna Gora. These are, in reality, a dissected plateau, lying at over 2,000 feet and formed in the ancient schists which must have stood out above the sea which once filled the Pannonian Basin. Only a narrow depression separates the Rana Gora from the Psunj, which is part of the more southerly line of hills. The Papuk narrows towards the east and disappears beneath the recent deposits of the plain. Some 70 miles to the east the ancient rocks, their nakedness partly covered by Tertiary beds, again break the surface of the Danubian Plain. This time they rise to

---

[1] See Borivoje Ž. Milojević, 'Les plateaux de loess et les régions de sable de Yougoslavie', *Mém. Soc. Serbe Géogr.* **6**, 1950.

form a long, narrow ridge, the Fruška Gora, which extends from west to east and rises in its sharp crest to over 1,500 feet. Its steep northern face, which looks out over the Danube, is forested. Its sunny southern slopes are dotted with villages and terraced for the vine. One last inlier of ancient rocks within the Danubian plain is the Vršačke *planina*, which forms a small but rugged upland close to the Romanian border.

A feature of all these short, steep segments of mountain is the contrast, exemplified above all in the Fruška Gora, between their northern and southern faces. The former, together with much of their summit areas, are forested. The lower slopes, where loess has been banked against them, are intensively cultivated. Large villages appear almost to follow the contour, a hundred feet or so above the plain, where the land begins to rise steeply towards the uplands. On the slopes, especially those facing southwards, are vineyards; on the flatter lands, cultivated fields.

Loess plateaus. The loess plateaus are peculiarly characteristic of the eastern half of the Danubian Plain. There they cover considerable areas lying between the main rivers, and rise to heights of two hundred or more feet above the flood-plain. In a few places, especially along the northern margin of the Fruška Gora, the Danube has cut into the loess and formed vertical cliffs. It is generally held that the deposits are of interglacial or immediate post-glacial date, and were laid down by winds from a generally north-easterly quarter. Presumably the wind-blown materials never reached the more westerly areas of the plain in sufficient quantities to give rise to such thick accumulations.

The surface of the loess plateaus is fairly level. There is little surface drainage, but the few valleys which dissect the loess plateaus are steep-sided and usually dry. The loess deposits sometimes survive as butte-like forms, where rivers have cut into and cliffed them. They are, of course, well-known for their natural fertility, and are under cultivation over almost all the whole of their extent. On the other hand, the shortage of water and the depths to which wells have often to be sunk restricts settlement. The extensive loess platform of the Bačka, for example, has very few settlements, but around its margin, which is very clearly marked, is a closely spaced line of villages. The same phenomenon is also apparent in the extensive loess platform to the south of Vukovar.

Podravina and Posavina. The plains which border the Sava and Drava had been deep gulfs in a Tertiary sea. Today the Tertiary sediments are partially overlain by recent alluvium. Sedimentation was

very active, especially during the glacial period, when the enlarged
Sava and Drava carried immense quantities of silt down from the
Alps of Slovenia and Austria. The present rivers are almost 'misfit'
streams. Their gradient is exceptionally gentle, and both rivers swing
across their plains in giant meanders. Cut-offs are numerous on both
rivers, and the Treaty of Trianon, in its boundary delimitation, made
special provision for changes that might occur along the Drava, which
was established as the international boundary.

The lower course of the Drava is strewn with islands, and the
Baranja, the triangular territory between the Drava and the Danube,
is studded with the lakes left from former meanders of the river,
separated from one another by wooded swamps. Both rivers have a
flood plain that may be as much as 5 miles across, bordered by
terraces which rise in steps to the level plains which are known as the
Posavina and Podravina. Settlements lie on the terraces, a mile or two
back from the river, with meadow extending to the river and cropland,
interspersed with forest on areas of poor, sandy soil, back over the
low plain of the valley floor.

Bačka. The Bačka is the name popularly given to the region between
the Danube and the Tisa. It rises towards the centre to a loess-
covered plateau, but between this latter and the rivers is a region,
some 25 miles wide, of low terraces and marshy flood plain. It is
crossed by canals, which in summer bring irrigation water to the dry
plain and in winter and spring help to rid it of surplus water. As
in the Sava and Drava valleys, settlements avoid the river, except
where, in the course of its meanders, it has cut into one of the valley
terraces.

Banat. This is the triangular area lying east of the Tisa and north of
the Danube. Like the Bačka, it is a flat and in some areas poorly
drained region. Towards the centre it rises to the loess platform
Deliblato, which lies up to 300 feet above the surrounding plain.
The same general pattern of settlement is found as in the plains
to the west, with villages and small towns avoiding the proximity of
both the flood plain of the rivers and also the dry loess platform of the
interior.

Across this region flow several of the rivers which have their source
in the mountains of Romania. These include the Tamiš, which joins
the Danube below Beograd, and the Zlatica. A number of other
streams, whose régimes were formerly as erratic as that of the
Tisa itself, were canalised during the nineteenth century, and the

plain is today criss-crossed by artificial waterways, designed to drain the Banat and to keep this particularly fertile region fit for agriculture.

CLIMATE

Yugoslavia belongs climatically, no less than physiographically, to both Central and Mediterranean Europe. The plains of north-eastern Yugoslavia, together with much of the mountain region of the interior, have a climate which, with their hot summers, moderated locally by altitude, and their cold winters, can only be described as continental. This grades through a region whose climatic affinities are somewhat indeterminate, into a coastal region which is uncompromisingly Mediterranean.

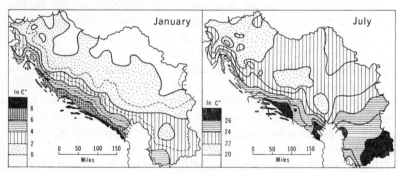

Fig. 12.4. Mean monthly temperatures in (a) January, (b) July. After *Geografiski Atlas Jugoslavije*, Zagreb, 1961.

The general features of these broad climatic regions have been described in chapter one. Here this detail is elaborated, and climatic regions delimited.

Temperature. Figures 12.4a and 4b show the average temperatures for January and July, corrected to sea-level. The patterns they present are essentially very simple. In winter we have severe cold covering the north-eastern plain, much of which has an average temperature in January below freezing. The mountain region is but a degree or two warmer when allowance is made for its greater altitude; in reality, the temperatures experienced are appreciably lower than those of the plains. Snowfall is not generally heavy, but is apt to lie for several weeks, especially on the higher ground. Only near the Adriatic coast is snow rarely or never seen. Temperatures increase rapidly towards the Adriatic coast, and less sharply towards the Greek border in Macedonia. Everywhere in the mountain region one is likely to find frost-pockets, resulting from cold-air drainage. Such pockets are the Slovene basin, around Ljubljana, and the Skopje basin.

The range of temperature in summer is very much smaller. When temperatures are corrected for altitude, the whole country is seen to be hot. In the mountainous regions the sensible temperatures are in reality considerably lower. Lowland areas along the Dalmatian coast, notably the Neretva valley, and in Macedonia are notoriously hot. The day-time temperatures are here intensified by the relative absence of vegetation cover, but nights cool off more sharply, so that averages give a somewhat imperfect picture of the heat of a summer's afternoon on the Montenegrin karst or in a Macedonian valley.

Rainfall. The amount of precipitation is related primarily to the relief, and its distribution through the year to the climatic régime. In terms of volume of rainfall, the north-eastern half of the country—the plains and the Morava-Vardar regions—have an annual rainfall of less than 762 millimetres (30 inches). The rest of the country, the mountainous west and south-west, has appreciably more than this. Much of it has over 1,143 millimetres (45 inches), and parts over 2,032 millimetres (80 inches). This general geographical distribution is what one would expect in a country in which most of the rainfall is borne by westerly winds.

The seasonal distribution of rainfall is strongly contrasted between the southern and south-western and the north-eastern divisions of the country. A division can be made (Fig. 12.6a) between the interior region with a maximum rainfall in summer, and the coastal region with a winter maximum. This however, simplifies the picture unduly. The coastal region has, it is true, a relatively dry summer, but autumn is usually quite wet, and there is, on average, a recurrence of rainy conditions in late spring. The Macedonian area, like the Adriatic coast, has the greater part of its rainfall in the winter half-year, but autumn and early spring are in fact the wettest seasons.

Within the area with a summer rainfall maximum there are also considerable variations. Situated between it and that described in the previous paragraph is an intermediate region in which the summer months of July and August are very little wetter than the winter months, and the rainfall maxima occur in fact in late spring (May–June) and early autumn (September–October). Even the regions

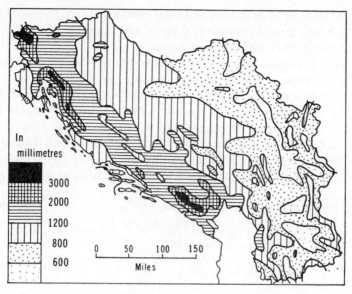

In millimetres

3000
2000
1200
800
600

0   50   100   150
Miles

Fig. 12.5. Annual average rainfall.

which display continental climatic characteristics in the most marked degree, the Danubian plains, is nevertheless relatively dry in July and August. Only in the small Alpine region of the north-west, can it be said that the contrast between the dry winter and wet summer is strongly marked.

No discussion of the climate of Yugoslavia would be complete without reference to its winds. Most well known are the bura (*It. bora*) and the *vardarac*, which are as notorious as the *mistral* and even more destructive. Like the mistral they are associated with a high pressure system over Central Europe or the Balkans, and a low pressure system moving eastward across the Adriatic or Mediterranean basins. The *bura* is experienced along the whole Adriatic coast. In winter it is a cold, dry wind of great violence. It drops off the steep scarp of the Dinaric mountains, gains in speed and dryness as it rushes down towards the sea, sears the vegetation and inhibits the growth of trees, until its energies are expended out over the sea. It is felt most violently at the foot of such precipitous ranges as the Velebit, especially opposite gaps and cols which open towards the sea. Through these the wind rushes and plunges down to the water at speeds which may even reach 100 miles an hour. The incidence of the *bura* is apt to be both sudden and local. Settlements tend to avoid the tracks which it most commonly follows, and ships are careful not to anchor where they may be overtaken by it.

The *bura* assumes several forms, depending on the relationship of the Mediterranean low to the high pressure system over the interior of the continent. Sometimes their relative positioning is such that bitterly cold winds from the eastern Alps are drawn down into the Mediterranean basin; at other times the source of the wind is the Central Balkans. As it descends from the high karst plateaus it acquires the characteristics of a katabatic wind, thus adding to its velocity. At the same time the wind gains in temperature from its descent, and

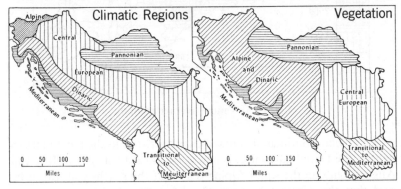

Fig. 12.6. (a) Climatic regions in Yugoslavia. (b) Principal vegetation types. After *British Naval Intelligence Handbooks*.

thus acquires its dry and searing qualities. The *bura* blows most frequently and violently in winter, which is when the Central European high-pressure system is most strongly developed. But it occurs also in summer, but never with the destructive violence which characterises its onslaught in winter.

The *vardarac*, by contrast, is a gentle wind. It is produced by pressure systems resembling those which generate the *bura*, but it blows down the Vardar valley, funnelled by the mountain masses, to the Aegean Sea. Like the *bura* it is a cold, dry wind, and blows most vigorously in winter. It is, in fact, an almost exact counterpart of the *mistral*.

Climatic regions. The delimitation of climatic regions is even more arbitrary than that of physiographical. One climate merges impercept-ibly into the next, and there are in general no sharp lines of division. Slovenia, with its more northerly latitude and higher relief, is more distinctive than others. Its winters are cold, snow-cover is prolonged, and its summers are cooler and wetter than in any other part of Yugoslavia (see Fig. 12.6a).

The karst region, extending from Slovenia to the Albanian border, separates the region of Mediterranean climate from that of modified continental. It is a region of considerable rainfall and cloudiness. Winters are sometimes snowy, and are usually cold. In an area of such strong relief, however, there are sharp climatic differences within small areas, and each valley or basin tends to have its own local variant of the general climatic type.

Between this last region and the sea lies the long, narrow coastal strip, characterised by Mediterranean climate. Its predominant features have already been described (pages 657 and 658). Its winters are mild and wet, though storms tend to be short-lived, and even in winter there are long periods of sunshine. Summers are hot and generally dry, though summer storms may occur in any part of the region. Autumn is usually marked by greater rainfall and more extensive cloudiness. The region is, as has been seen, exposed to the *bura* at all seasons.

The interior highlands have a more distinctively continental climate. The balance of rainfall is tipped towards the summers, and winters are relatively dry, but quite snowy. Winters are colder than in regions lying to the west, and summers are hotter, though temperatures are locally greatly modified by altitude.

Macedonia has a climate resembling that of the interior highlands, but its summers are hotter and its winters, cooled by the *vardarac*, which blows down from the Danubian plains, may be colder. It is also drier, lying as it does not only farther to the south, but also in the rain-shadow of the Albanian mountains. Much of it, in consequence is semi-arid, and agriculture has to make extensive use of irrigation in summer.

The most extreme form of continental climate is found in the Danubian plains. It is more uniform because less compartmentalised by relief. Winters are cold, and sub-freezing weather, brought by northerly or north-easterly winds, may last for weeks. Snow is prolonged and sometimes heavy; the small rivers are frozen over and the larger strewn with ice. Summers, by contrast, are very hot. Rainfall is fairly heavy, though much of it may occur in heavy thunderstorms. These are of relatively short duration, so that the period of sunshine is prolonged.

22*

VEGETATION AND SOILS

Yugoslavia is naturally a forested country, though its forest cover is interrupted on the dry karst, in the narrow coastal belt of Mediterranean climate, and on the loess platforms of the Danubian region. Today forest covers only 34 per cent of the total area, and over much of the country the former forests have been destroyed by man. Even in the karst and Mediterranean regions, the woodland cover would in all probability have been very much more extensive if man had not intervened.[1]

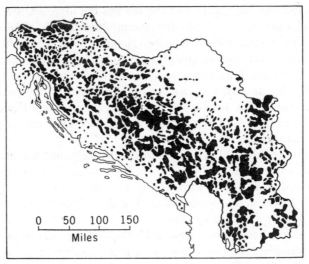

Fig. 12.7. Distribution of forest in Yugoslavia. After *Geografiski Atlas Jugoslavije*, Zagreb, 1961.

The region of Mediterranean climate is today characterised, where it is not under cultivation or some other form of improved land use, by *maquis*. This association of drought-resistant shrubs occupies a narrow belt, which tapers northwards between the mountains and the sea. It extends inland up the Neretva valley and into the Skadar basin, but, with the admixture of Central European species, loses its Mediterranean character along the north Dalmatian littoral. The *maquis* is interrupted by stands of Aleppo pine (*Pinus halepensis*), and at greater altitudes above the coast light deciduous woodland appears.

[1] Max Sorre, 'Les aspects de la végétation et des sols en Yougoslavie', *Annls Géogr.*, **39** (1930), 311–316.

The karst has its own peculiar plant-life. Over very considerable areas bare limestone appears, and vegetation is restricted to drought resistant species which can root in the joint planes where particles of residual soil are retained. Where sufficient soil has been retained, however, an open 'karst woodland' may appear, made up of those broadleaved trees, such as the hornbeam and certain of the oaks, which can stand the dry and highly calcareous conditions. Parts of the northern karst are, however, densely wooded, commonly with oak and beech (Fig. 12.7), which have established themselves on the residual clay which in some areas is deep and extensive enough to support such growth. The environs of the karstic lakes of Plitvice, for example, and the eastern flanks of the Velebit are noted for their dense woodland.

Macedonia may never have been a densely wooded province, and today woodland survives only on the mountains and higher plateaus. Much of the lowland bears the aspect of an arid steppe. The interior highlands, on the other hand, remain predominantly wooded, except in the valleys and basins where human settlement has been dense and prolonged. Forests are very extensive in Bosnia and Old Serbia. In general oaks, both sessile and Turkey, predominate, but at greater altitudes the beech may take over. These forests have long supported herds of swine, and the lonely swineherd is conspicuous in Yugoslavia's folklore and not unimportant in its history.

Towards the north the forest becomes broken into smaller units which are found usually on the summits of the mountains and hills. The destruction of the original deciduous forest cover has here been comparatively recent. The Šumadija was, as its name implies (*šuma* = woodland), originally a forested area; it is now very largely cleared and brought under cultivation. On the Danubian plains, forest has almost entirely disappeared with the exception only of the woodland which clothes the summits of such hills as the Fruška Gora, and of the willow and poplar woods which grow over the wet and unreclaimed land which borders the rivers. There can be little doubt that the plain was itself formerly wooded, though the woodland cover was probably thin on the loess and perhaps absent on the sands. Most of the area has now been brought under cultivation, though the reclaimed flood plains of the rivers are more important as meadowland than for their crops.

Soils. The soil is developed by biological processes within a matrix provided by the parent rock. Over considerably more than half the area of Yugoslavia the soils are classified as lithosols or skeletal soils. The material of the parent rock predominates; the soil is shallow, and there is little humus. Over much of the karst there is no soil at all, except the clay particles embedded in the joints in the limestone. Locally a residual clay covers the limestone, while alluvium, often poorly drained, is spread over the floors of the *polja*. Brown forest soils spread over much of the gentle hill country north of Bosnia and Serbia, and offer a far richer medium for agriculture. The northern plains are covered with sand, loess and alluvium of recent geological origin. Towards the west, where rainfall is heavier, a grey-brown podzolic soil has been developed; in the drier north-east, this passes through degraded chernozem into the true chernozem, which has formed in parts of Bačka and Vojvodina.

POPULATION

The distribution of population in Yugoslavia, and the types of settlement in which it is to be found must be seen against the background of the country's physical geography. The census of 31 March 1961 recorded a population of 18,549,291, and the total is currently (1968) estimated to be about 19,735,000. It remains predominantly a rural, agricultural and peasant population. Forestry and agriculture were said in 1961 to have occupied almost 57 per cent of the employed population, and industry and mining not more than 14 per cent. Employment in industry has been increasing in recent years, and at the time of the formation of the state, the population was about 75 per cent agricultural.

The urban population has always been relatively small. At present only seven towns have a population exceeding 100,000, and only 9 per cent of the population lives in towns of this size. Only 19 per cent are in towns of over 20,000, and 11 in those of over 50,000.

Ethnic composition

The name 'Yugoslav' itself suggests a Slavic population of somewhat mixed ethnic origin. Unfortunately, this term does less than justice to the variety of Yugoslavia's population. The state, when it was first established in 1918, adopted as its title the 'Kingdom of the Serbs, Croats and Slovenes'. The census of 1921, which did not err in favour of the minorities, could not find more than 83 per cent of the population which it could classify as 'Southern Slavs'. The rest was made up of no less than ten other linguistic groups, among which the Germans, Magyars and Albanians were the most numerous.

Germans. The Germans lived in compact communities, and had thus been able to preserve their language and culture from the eighteenth century when the ancestors of most of them first settled in the southern Slav lands. There were such communities in Slovenia, especially in and near Maribor. Another such group lived in the mountains to the west of Zagreb. But the majority were to be found in the Vojvodina, especially in the Banat, close to the Romanian border, and on the fertile river terraces of the Bačka and Baranja. A few were to be found in the Srem, between the Sava and the Danube, but south of the Sava German communities were few and small. These Germans of the north-eastern plains were for the greater part descended from the German and Austrian settlers brought here in the eighteenth century, especially by Maria Theresa, for the purpose of colonising and reclaiming the lands recently evacuated by the Turks, and of holding the military frontier against their return.

The German population diminished in all parts of Yugoslavia between the wars. Migration was of no great significance, but many Germans became assimilated especially to the Croats and Slovenes, with whom they shared the Roman Catholic religion. With the accession of Hitler to power in Germany, however, the *Volksdeutsche* in Yugoslavia became the object of a powerful propaganda. Many who had not been politically active responded to appeals first from Berlin and then from Vienna. The German minority was encouraged to maintain its identity and to demand political rights and privileges, and there can be no doubt that, as a disintegrating factor, it was increasingly potent.

The German minority suffered severely as a result of the war, just as it did in Poland and Czechoslavakia. For a time the German-settled parts of Slovenia were annexed to Austria; the Banat was placed under German administration, and elsewhere German *Volksgruppe* were encouraged to organise and to take control of their local areas. This, however, was short-lived. German defeat was followed by the flight of large numbers of Germans, most of whom reached West Germany. Yugoslav statistics show how the German minority has withered. The census of 1953 showed a total of 60,536 Germans. The German community at this time had an average age considerably above that of the Yugoslav nation as a whole; the number of women was greatly in excess of that of men, and the structure of the population was such that its numbers must inevitably continue to decline. Table 77 illustrates the diminution of the numbers of Germans within the territory of Yugoslavia.

Table 77. Numbers of Germans within Yugoslavia

Date and source	Number of Germans
1910 (Austro-Hungarian census)	579,000
1921 (Yugoslav census)	506,907
1931 (Croat Peasant Party estimate)	486,000
1953 (Yugoslav census)	60,536

Magyars. No other ethnic minority has declined as precipitately as the Germans. The Magyars have actually increased, though they constituted in 1953 a slightly smaller percentage of the total population than in 1921. They were always more concentrated geographically than the Germans, and the great majority have continued to live along the Mura valley in the extreme north, and in parts of the former Hungarian territories of Banat, Bačka and Baranja, close to the present Hungarian boundary. During the nineteenth century a few moved into Croatia and Slavonia, which after the *Ausgleich* of 1867, were again part of the revived Hungarian crown.

The Magyars were no favoured minority under Yugoslav rule; their language did not receive formal recognition, and, unlike Germany, Hungary was in no position to give them support and encouragement. The Second World War, however, reversed the position, and from 1941–45 the Bačka and Baranja, together with the small Prekomurje and Medjumurje territories, were restored to Hungary. In 1945 these territories were restored to Yugoslavia; there was no efflux of Magyar refugees, and the Magyar community is today larger than before the Second World War, as Table 78 shows.

Table 78. Numbers of Magyars within Yugoslavia

Date of source	Number of Magyars
1910 (Hungarian census and other sources)	c. 559,970
1921 (Yugoslav census)	467,658
1931 (Croat Peasant Party estimate)	c. 492,000
1953 (Yugoslav census)	502,175

Albanians. The Albanians, known in Serbo-Croat as Škiptari, today constitute the largest ethnic minority. They are found in many of the towns, where they perform a variety of menial tasks, but the great majority live in the Metohija and Kosovo basins and in nearby areas of eastern Montenegro. Their appearance in this region, which had been central to the medieval Serb state, resulted from the exodus of the Serbs in 1691 (see page 55). Today they are dominant in most of Metohija and around Mitrovica, and large communities are also found near Skopje, Ohrid, Bitola and elsewhere in Macedonia. Early estimates of their number are lacking. Between the First and Second World Wars the Yugoslav government attempted to establish Slav colonies among them, but frequently found it necessary to use the military to suppress unrest. Today the Kosmet Autonomous Region contains the great majority of the Albanians, and here they have the legal right to use their language and preserve their culture. The census of 1921 recorded 439,637 Albanians; that of 1953, a total of 754,245.

Turks. The Turkish minority, 150,322 in 1921 and 259,535 in 1953, lives mostly in Macedonia, especially in the area between the Vardar River the Bulgarian boundary.

Other minorities. Other minority groups are, according to current Yugoslav statistics, relatively small. Most numerous are the 'other Slav' groups, principally Slovaks and Czechs living in the Danube and Sava valleys, the former area of the military frontier. Then follow the Gypsies, mainly in the south; Bulgarians, chiefly along the eastern boundary from Timok south to the Strumica; Romanians, chiefly in the Timok district of the Stara Planina of the north-east, and in the Banat; Russians and Ukrainians, mainly 'White' Russian refugee groups, living in Beograd and other parts of the country, and Vlachs, Vlasi or Arumani, a romance-speaking group, formerly nomadic, but now mainly settled, found chiefly in Macedonia.

Italians are now more numerous in Yugoslavia than when the state was created. They formerly lived mainly along the Dalmatian coast and in the hinterland of Fiume, where the Yugoslav census of 1921 gave their numbers as 12,553. At the end of the Second World War Yugoslavia acquired Istria, with the predominantly Italian town of Pola (Pula). There was some degree of migration of Italians from Yugoslavia, but there were 41,800 Italians in 1948, and 18,142 at the time of the 1943 census. In 1961, there were 13,211.

It is clear that the great majority of the minority groups is to be found in the northern plains, particularly the Baranja, Bačka and Banat, and in southern Yugoslavia; Magyars, Germans and Romanians in the former; Turks, Albanians, Bulgars and Vlachs in the latter. The mixed population of the northern region results in large measure from the way in which it was resettled after the Austrian conquest of the region. That in Macedonia and Kosmet is due in large measure to the disturbed history of the region. The largest single group, the Albanians, entered only after the withdrawal under military pressure of a significant part of the Serb population.

The whole of the interior of the country is occupied by the southern Slavs themselves. They are grouped into four distinct ethnic communities: Slovenes, Croats, Serbs and Macedonians. The primary basis of differentiation between them is linguistic, but in fact the languages are very closely related, and they merge through dialects into one another. As a divisive force language is reinforced by religion, the use of different written and printed script, and by social custom.

Slovenes. Linguistically considered, the Slovenes are the most distinctive of all the southern Slavs. Their language is quite distinct from Croat, and the two are not mutually intelligible. The Slovenes inhabit the extreme north-west of Yugoslavia, where their cultural focus is the city of Ljubljana, and small groups of Slovenes are found beyond the Yugoslav border in the Klagenfurt Basin of Austria and in the Gorizia and Trieste districts of Italy. The Slovenes are, in the main, Roman Catholic, and their culture has been strongly influenced by that of Austria, of which Slovenia was for centuries a province. The towns in plan and architecture resemble the Austrian more than those of the rest of Yugoslavia. Manufacturing industry appeared here at a relatively early date; the local iron industry, for example, was an extension of that of Carinthia, and Slovenia remains today technically and educationally the most advanced of the republics of Yugoslavia.

Croats. The Croat language is linguistically the same as Serb, and important dialect differences within the Serbo–Croat language appear only near its geographical frontier where it passes into either Slovene or Bulgarian and Macedonian. The apparent difference between Croat and Serb results from the use by the former of the Latin alphabet, and by the latter of the Cyrillic. Beneath a simple difference in script lies a more profound cultural difference. In the ninth and tenth centuries Croatia was attached to the Church of Rome, and its resulting affiliation with the West brought it into the Italian and Austrian cultural sphere. From much of its history Croatia was attached to the

Hungarian crown, and though restless under Hungarian rule, the Croats derived great economic and cultural benefits from the connection.

Serbs. The most numerous people of Yugoslavia derived from the mountainous region of the southern Karst, of Metohija, Novi Pazar and Kopaonik. Their lands were overrun by the Turkish armies from the fourteenth century onwards and they remained subjects of the alien, unprogressive and unsympathetic rule of the Turks until the nineteenth (see above, page 51). During this long period the Serb people were enabled to maintain their identity primarily by two institutions: the Orthodox Church and the *Zadruga*. The Serbs had been converted to Christianity by missionaries from the Byzantine Empire which they bordered. In the twelfth and thirteenth centuries dualistic beliefs, probably of Middle Eastern origin, spread from Bulgaria into Serbia. These had a deep influence on Bosnia, where large numbers were converted to the Patarene or Bogomil beliefs and were in consequence persecuted by those who regarded them as heretics. The surviving Bogomil monuments, widely distributed through Bosnia. show how extensive was the movement. It was, however, weakened by the attacks of the Papacy and the King of Hungary; the area succumbed to Turkish conquest in the fifteenth century, and a great many of the Bogomils were converted to Islam.

The Islamic community of Bosnia has since remained numerous and important, and the mosque and minaret are as significant a feature of the cultural landscape of Sarajevo or Mostar as the baroque church is in the villages of Slovenia. The census of 1931 revealed about 1·5 million Moslems. Some, of course, were Turkish, but almost half the total was made up of Bosniaks, that is Serbs who had embraced Islam, and most of these continued to live in Bosnia.

For the rest, the Serbs are mainly members of the Orthodox church, whose priesthood played an important role in preserving the traditions of the Serbs through the years of Turkish rule.

A second factor in this preservation of Serb culture was the *zadruga*. This was a large, patriarchal family, often numbering more than a hundred persons, who lived together, cultivated the fields communally and, in fact, represented a primitive communism. It was found among the Croats, but was particularly common among the Serbs. Its close-knit social fabric, its self-sufficiency and its almost complete independence of outside influences were well calculated to preserve

Serb culture. The *zadruge*[1] declined in importance during the nineteenth century, when their social task had been accomplished. They split into smaller groups and most of these have since been merged into village communities and have lost their identity.

That the birth-rate was for centuries high and population growth rapid in the hills of Bosnia and Serbia was apparent. No less clear was the inability of this rough hill-country to support greatly increased numbers. Large villages and intensive cultivation, such as were possible on the Danubian plains, were inconceivable here. There was an exodus from the mountains and hills northward towards the Danube and Sava valleys. The chief centres of dispersion were Kosovo-Metohija and Raška, Stari Vlah and the Karst of Hercegovina and western Bosnia. Jovan Cvijić has traced the main lines of this movement, until the migrant families became lost in the farming communities of northern Serbia and Slavonia. It is apparent that these have been reinforced over a period of several centuries by Serb and Bosnian migrants from the south. Many have become assimilated to the local culture, but there remained considerable numbers in Croatia who called themselves Serbs and resisted complete assimilation by the Croats. Today over half a million Serbs, more than a tenth of all the Serbian people live in Croatia.

Centuries of Turkish rule kept the Serbs in a subordinate position. There was no economic development or social progress among the southern Slavs of the Turkish Empire, and the Serbs were ill-prepared for political independence when at last they regained it in the nineteenth century. Hungarian rule was, despite its oppressiveness, more enlightened than that of the Turks, and permitted the Croats to achieve a considerable economic and social progress. Thus the Serbs and Croats, when they were in 1918 brought together in a single state, were far from well matched. The rude vigour of the Serbs, combined with a century of rather primitive independence, allowed them to claim a political advantage over the Croats which they used to the full. The Croats, with no tradition of political independence, but culturally more sophisticated, resented the power and authority assumed by the Serbs. Their feuds, culminating in the murder both of Stjepan Radić, the Croat leader, and of the Serb King Alexander, pointed up the division between the chief peoples among the southern Slavs. Around this major rift were grouped the other animosities and

---

[1] It should be noted that the term *zadruga* has been used during the present century to indicate a peasant co-operative.

jealousies which characterised the relations with one another of most other ethnic groups of Yugoslavia. The political problem of the nationalities went unresolved until the end of the Second World War, and is discussed below.

Macedonians. The affinities of the Macedonians have always been indefinite. Not only is their territory inhabited by a number of ethnic groups unrelated to the southern Slavs, who have greatly influenced the local language, but the Slavic language of Macedonia was itself variously regarded as a dialect of Serbo–Croat and of Bulgarian. On this relationship a fierce political conflict hinged. While the territory was claimed by both Serbs and Bulgars, the Macedonians never ceased to assert their linguistic and cultural distinctiveness. Extremist elements among them allied themselves with dissident Croats, while much of their territory was claimed by Bulgaria and Albania. The proposals for a federal constitution, made in the late 1930s, made no provision for a separate Macedonia; the Serb opposition was too strong. And not until 1946 did Macedonia appear as a separate republic (see below, page 673). Since then the Macedonian dialect has been elevated to the status of a language comparable with Slovene and Serbo–Croat; its lack of dictionaries and grammars was quickly remedied, and the small educated community among the Macedonians is now creating a 'literature' which, it is hoped, will justify the inclusion of the Macedonians amongst the nations of Yugoslavia.

Administrative structure

These linguistic and cultural diversities presented a grave problem to the state which came into being on 1 December 1918. The Declaration of Corfu of a year and a half earlier had evaded the more difficult problems, and had called only for a union of Serbs, Croats and Slovenes, with a democratic constitution, and as the 'Kingdom of the Serbs, Croats and Slovenes' the new state was proclaimed. From the start there was disagreement between Serbs and Croats. The former demanded a centralised government with a strong executive, which their greater numbers would allow them to control. The Croats, together with the Slovenes, preferred a more nearly federal constitution, with as much governmental authority as possible delegated to the provinces.

The Vidovdan[1] constitution of 1921 reflected the political ambitions of the Serbs, and provided by a highly centralised monarchical form

---

[1] So called because it was adopted on Vidovdan (St Vitus's Day), 28 June.

of government. A system of administrative divisions was established which made few concessions to the fears and hopes of the minorities. The country was divided into 33 *oblasti* or provinces, approximately equal in population, if not in size. Administrative convenience was the chief criterion in drawing their boundaries, though the old boundaries of Austria and Hungary were in fact perpetuated. This territorial organisation lasted only until 1929, when it was replaced by nine *banovine*, together with a separate Prefecture for the city of Beograd. These new units were compact, and more equal in size than the *oblasti*. They bore little relationship to the ethnic situation, though the older boundaries of Austria and of Hungary, somewhat modified, were still apparent, and they were mostly named, like French *départements*, after their principal rivers (Fig. 12.1).

The object of this territorial organisation, like that established in France during the Revolution, was to break down the ancient provincial and local loyalties. In this it did not succeed. The rivalry of Croat and Serb was intensified, and to this was added the aspirations of Slovenes, Macedonians, Albanians and others. In the late 1930s the growing danger from Germany made some *rapprochement* between these groups essential. This was a chance to reorganise the administrative structure on the basis of nationalities; instead, however, the predominantly Serb government made concessions, the *Sporazum*, only to the Croats, and in 1939 formed the *banovine* of Savska and Primorska, together with small areas of Vrbaska and Drinska into the autonomous *banovina* of Croatia. For the short span of two years the Croats enjoyed their autonomy to the full. A Croatian parliament—the *Sabor*—met in Zagreb, and the Croats took delight in a radicalism which was by no means to the liking of the Serb authorities in Beograd. This was ended when, on 6 April 1941, German armies attacked Yugoslavia.

The territorial division of Yugoslavia during the period of German and Italian occupation represented in a crude and distorted way the distribution of the minority peoples. Whereas the *Sporazum* had recognised only the division between Serb and Croat, the wartime partition emphasised the claims of Germany, Italy, Hungary, Bulgaria and Albania. The state was broken into its primary elements: a diminutive Serbia, Montenegro and a grossly inflated Croatia. Albania took those parts of Montenegro, Serbia and Macedonia where there was any considerable number of Albanians. The rest of Macedonia, together with part of Old Serbia was occupied by Bulgaria. Italy took the Julian region and much of Dalmatia, and the rest of Slovenia was attached to the Austrian province of Germany. Hungary annexed the Baranja and Bačka and the two small areas of Prekomurje and Medjumurje in the Mura valley. The Banat was detached from Serbia and administered directly by the Germans, who evidently had not decided what they would do with it when the war ended.

For this partition of Yugoslavia there was a slender excuse in the existence of ethnic minorities, but the German government had gone even farther in the direction of recognising and encouraging them than the Yugoslav government of the inter-war years had in suppressing and ignoring them.

The Socialist Federal Republic. In November 1945, Yugoslavia was proclaimed a republic, and in the following January a new constitution was promulgated. Yugoslavia became a federal state, made up of six republics, together with two autonomous districts within the republic of Serbia. A new but closely similar constitution was adopted in 1963, but no change in the boundaries of the republics was introduced. The constitution of 1946 at the same time followed closely the example of the Soviet constitution of 1936 and also gave scope for cultural expression by the ethnic minorities. Care was taken, however, to prevent the republics from acquiring the power to secede from the federation.

The six republics, are formally listed in alphabetical order in Table 79.

Table 79. Size and population of six republics within Yugoslavia

	Area (square kilometres)	Population (1961)
Bosnia and Hercegovina	51,129	3,277,948
Crna Gora (Montenegro)	13,812	471,894
Croatia	56,538	4,159,696
Macedonia	25,713	1,406,003
Serbia	20,251	7,642,227
Slovenia	88,361	1,591,523
	255,804	18,549,291

The Republic of Serbia contains, Soviet-style, two autonomous regions, Kosmet and Vojvodina. Both are areas of mixed population in which the Serbs were at best in only a slight majority.

The political divisions of Yugoslavia bear a certain resemblance to the physical regions which have already been described. Slovenia corresponds approximately with the Alpine region; Croatia, with the Podravina, Posavina, northern Karst and north Dalmatian littoral, and Montenegro covers much of the southern Karst. The Republic of Bosnia and Hercegovina is made up of the remaining areas of the Karst, together with the greater part of the interior highlands and its bordering region of hills. Serbia, by far the most extensive republic, consists essentially of the Morava region, together with the Kosovo-Metohija region, which comprises the Kosmet Autonomous Region, and the Banat, Bačka and Srem, between the Danube and the Sava which make up Vojvodina. The Macedonian Republic is made up of the regions lying to the south of the Šar Planina, the Skopska Crna Gora and the mountainous divide between the Morava and Vardar drainage.

Such coincidence is by no means accidental. Relief features have greatly influenced the spread of the ethnic groups which today make up the Yugoslav nation. Certain physical barriers to communication have contributed to maintaining the individuality of Slovenia, as well as to setting limits to the expansion of Western Christianity, which has always been closely associated with Croat culture. The mountainous barriers which shut in the Albanian settlement area of Kosovo-Metohija and the Macedonian area linguistic and political regions are sharp and conspicuous.

SETTLEMENT

Despite the growth of towns and expansion of cities in recent years, Yugoslavia remains predominantly a country of rural settlement. No less than 57 per cent of the employed population was in 1961 engaged in agriculture. The proportion of the population resident in villages and scattered rural settlements was almost certainly a larger proportion of the whole.

Rural settlement

Rural settlement in Yugoslavia demonstrates a greater range of geographical forms than that of any other country of Eastern Europe. This springs in part from the great contrasts which are demonstrated in relief, soil quality and land use; in part from the range of cultural influences that have impinged upon Yugoslavia. Village patterns range from the widely scattered dwellings of a predominantly pastoral people to the tightly nucleated villages of peasant farmers, from the irregular plan that comes from spontaneous growth to the gridiron pattern that was imposed by the Austrian and Hungarian owners of estates in the Northern Plain.

These rather broad and generalised types of settlement have each their own particular pattern of distribution. In many instances it is not difficult to discern a relationship between the type of settlement and its physical environment. The primary division among the types of settlement is between the dispersed and the nucleated, the former in general characteristic of the mountains and plateaus, the latter of the valleys and plains.

Dispersed settlement. The whole of the mountainous interior of Yugoslavia is characterised in greater or lesser degree by a dispersed pattern of settlement, and over much of this area this is of the type named by J. Cvijić the *Stari Vlah*. It is characteristic of all of Bosnia and Hercegovina, and extends into Serbia, Croatia and even Slovenia. In this type of settlement the village is made up of a loose aggregation of hamlets, which are themselves only open groupings of a small number of houses. The hamlets sometimes have a rough alignment along a ridge or following a contour. They may be separated from one another by several hundred yards, but there is sometimes no clearly visible break between the houses of one village and those of the next. Such settlements clearly belong to an agricultural society, but to one in which the mutuality of the medieval village of Western Europe never appeared. The hamlet was, more often than not, the seat of a *zadruga* (see page 669). This did not, however, have the legal and political constraints of the medieval village; its members were free to break up, and in fact the *zadruga* normally divided if it became too large, giving rise to one or more additional settlements within the dispersed pattern of the neighbourhood.

This dispersed Stari Vlah pattern was formerly more widespread than it is today. In the Šumadija the growth in population and increasing size of settlements led to the appearance of loosely nucleated villages which came to be superimposed on the dispersed pattern. This Šumadija pattern is apparent also in the upper Sava valley, near Zagreb, but along the lower Sava and in Srem the process of nucleation went yet farther. Village houses came to be more closely spaced, sometimes aligned along straight roads—the Mačva type; sometimes grouped less regularly, as in the German *Haufendorf*. In the extreme case the houses are closely spaced along a road, with gardens extending behind each, and beyond these lie the strips of the communal open fields.

In Yugoslavia one can, in fact, trace the evolution of the scattered into the nucleated settlement pattern in all its variety. Cvijič has summarised the process:

> The Stari Vlah type is the original and primitive form. The Šumadija and Mačva types come later and are derived from it. They developed as a result of the growth in population in the lower-lying and more fertile areas, in imitation of the villages of Srem and Banat. They were at the same time under pressure from government authorities which preferred villages with more closely clustered houses, because they were easier to watch not only politically but also for police purposes.[1]

In both the Karst and the Raška region of crystalline massifs the primitive Stari Vlah pattern of settlement has been modified to accord more closely with conditions imposed by relief and water supply. In the *Karst* region the population is located almost wholly in the *polja*, where its number is directly related to the area of cultivable land. Settlements tend to be dispersed and houses to lie irregularly around the margin of the *polje*. Usually they are placed on the limestone outcrop, both to be above the danger of winter flooding and to avoid occupying precious cropland. The *Ibar* type of village is a further derivative of the Stari Vlah. It is divided into a number of small, tightly grouped hamlets, each of which tends to occupy a hill summit or the margin of a gorge. In this rugged countryside of ravines and steep mountain slopes the dispersed pattern of the true Stari Vlah type could not have developed, and an incipient nucleation was imposed by the nature of the terrain.

Nucleated settlement. The nucleated village is, locally at least, a derivative of the Stari Vlah. As such, it occurs along the Sava, Danube and lower Morava valleys. The east and the south of Yugoslavia are dominated by a pattern of nucleated settlement, which appears to have arisen independently of that in the northern plains. The eastern half of Serbia is characterised by the nucleated village of what Cvijić called the *Timok* type. It is irregularly laid out, with narrow, twisting lanes and closely built houses. It is normally a valley settlement, built commonly on a terrace above the flood-plain. Originally predominantly a pastoral settlement, it has now come to rely mainly on

[1] Jovan Cvijić, *La Péninsule Balkanique*, Paris, 1918, pp. 218–19.

crop-farming. Population has increased without any large-scale migration, leading to an increasingly dense settlement.

The *Čiflik* type of settlement owes its origin to centuries of Turkish rule, when the land was occupied by Turkish *beys* and the Slav peasants were reduced to the status of serf-like *rayas*. The settlements are estate-villages *par excellence*. They are built on the basis of one or more open squares. The miserable houses are contiguous and aligned along two or more sides, always under the close supervision of the *bey*, whose house and watch-tower commonly occupied one corner of the complex. Sometimes the compound was enclosed by a mud-built wall for greater security. The *Čiflik* village was characteristic of only very restricted areas, where the Turkish influence was particularly strong. These included the lower Vardar valley, the Skopje, Bitola, Kosovo and Metohija basins.

Over much of southern Yugoslavia Mediterranean cultural influences make themselves felt. The Mediterranean type of village is widespread in Macedonia, and extends into Metohija. It is a closely built cluster of houses, usually built of stone or mud brick, roofed with tile, and commonly clustered around a small market-place or square. Usually it lies above a steep slope, which gives it some degree of protection. Turkish villages are less widespread, and in fact really only occur in south-eastern Macedonia, where they are interspersed with villages of Mediterranean type. Like the latter, they are highly nucleated; sometimes they are enclosed by a wall for protection, but they differ chiefly in the style of the houses, which have a tendency to be surrounded by small gardens.

An even more highly nucleated pattern of settlement is met with in the plains to the north of the Sava. In general the villages are of more recent origin than those to be found in the south of Yugoslavia, and were established in the eighteenth century when this region was reconquered from the Turks. Villages are always compact, usually large and frequently laid out on a gridiron plan. For this there are two reasons. The insecurity of the region and the constant threat of Turkish raids from beyond the Sava and Danube led to a higher degree of nucleation than was in fact warranted by the economic circumstances. At the same time these were founded as estate villages, and in their planning one sees the controlling hand of the great landowner, eager to control and discipline his tenants who were for the greater part only half free.

Though many of these giant villages or agricultural towns are still to be found in the plains of the Bačka and Banat, there has long been a tendency for more dispersed settlements to develop in order to supplement the nucleated. As in Hungary (see page 504) *tanya*-like settlements, here called *salaši* or *pustara*, were founded first as summer residences, to be inhabited during harvest time; then as permanent homes. Here the process is the reverse of that found to the south; a dispersed pattern is being superimposed upon one of nucleated settlements.

In north-western Yugoslavia, northern influences on the pattern of settlement are no less marked, though they operated in very different ways. The nucleated peasant village, dominated by its church and surrounded by its cultivated fields helps to give a Central European aspect to the countryside. Such villages are commonly located on valley terraces, usually with a southerly outlook. Towards the east of Slovenia the average size of villages increases, and the excessive nucleation characteristic of the Hungarian Plain is apparent in the Mura valley. In the Podravina and Posavina the street or forest village is well developed, deriving less from the dispersed Stari Vlah type than from settlements along forest trackways.

Temporary settlements in the higher mountains are still a feature of rural life in Yugoslavia, though transhumance is no longer practised as vigorously or as widely as in the past. With the tendency for crop-farming to become more widespread at lower levels, pastoralism comes to be more and more confined to the higher, and, except at the very highest, the pastures now tend to be used for much of the year. Summer settlements are, however, still used in the Alpine region of Slovenia and in the high, crystalline regions of the centre of Yugoslavia. In Macedonia, where an inverse transhumance has long been practised, there still remain some of the large, compact, mountain villages of the Vlachs, from which a descent is made by some of the community into the valleys in winter.

Rural architecture. The styles of village housing show similar patterns of distribution to those of the village types themselves. Building styles are related both to the availability of materials and to culture and economy. Timber for building purposes is scarce both in parts of the northern plain and also in much of the Karst. In these regions other materials—bricks, often sun-dried, in the former; stone in the latter—are generally used. In Macedonia, also, where deforestation has been severe, stone is commonly used. But in the extensively wooded regions which make up the interior of the country, wood is the most readily available building material and is the most widely used. The nature of the material imposes certain conditions, as also do the weather hazards which the house has to withstand. The steep pitch of the roof in Slovenia and the mountains of Bosnia, first designed in all probability to shed the snow, contrasts with the low-pitched roofs of Macedonia which will be called upon to withstand nothing more than a Mediterranean storm.

The design of the house reveals primarily cultural influences. The long-house of much of Vojvodina and Slavonia, its gable-end toward the street and a shaded porch along the sunny side of the house, is similar to that found over much of the Hungarian Plain, and the style must have been brought in by settlers from the north. This contrasts with the more compact, log-built house, with steep, shingled roof, which, in many local forms, is found throughout the interior of Yugoslavia. Its walls may be plastered on the outside; planks may replace logs; a porch may be added on one side, with an overhanging roof, but the basic plan is the same and probably derives from the huts of the Neolithic settlers who brought agriculture to these regions. It is, in fact, a variant of a house type found throughout much of the Carpathian region and beyond it, in the Polish Plain. The house and its garden are commonly surrounded by a fence, with a gateway arch, which may sometimes be highly ornate.

The Alpine style of house was brought into Yugoslavia from Austria. It is large, with two or more storeys, the uppermost of which frequently overhangs the lower. The roof is steep and extends far out beyond the walls, thus providing a sheltered area for the storage of wood for winter fuel. Its style suggests an abundance of lumber for building; the inclusion under one roof of house and stables and storage for farm tools suggests that winters are severe and that outdoor work must be reduced to a minimum. Such a building style is normal in the Karavanke and Julian Alps. It has spread, however, into Croatia, where physical conditions would in themselves not have suggested such a style of building.

In the Karst and Mediterranean regions, timber could at most constitute a supplementary building material. Houses and farm buildings are of stone, usually only roughly trimmed and sometimes laid without mortar. Roofs tend to be low-pitched and are usually of stone slabs split thin. Houses are plain and simple, as the medium used permits few stylistic refinements. In some intermediate areas, as in the Vardar valley, only the first storey is of stone, and the upper level is of wood.

A feature of farms in some parts of Serbia, Montenegro and southern Bosnia is the *kula*. This is a stone-built tower of two or more storeys, with no window openings on the ground level and but few at the upper floor levels. The *kule* were built for defence as well as habitation by the wealthier members of the communities, and their function was not unlike that of the peel-towers of the Scottish border.

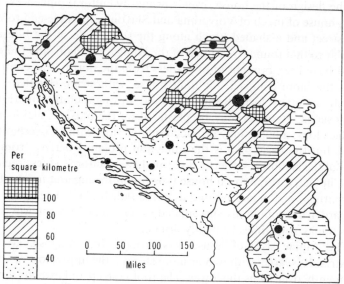

Fig. 12.8. Distribution of population in Yugoslavia; only cities of over 50,000 (1964) are marked, see also Fig. 12.9. After *Geografiski Atlas Jugoslavije*, Zagreb, 1961 and *Statistički Godišnjak SFRJ, 1965.*

They are particularly numerous near the Albanian border where the tradition of the blood-feud has died only very slowly.

More widespread and certainly more conspicuous is the so-called Turkish house. This is a feature of the large villages and towns, particularly of the southern parts of Yugoslavia. The Turkish *beys* commonly built large houses adjusted to the Islamic practice of the harem, in which their foremost object was to achieve as great a degree of privacy as possible. The ground floor is almost without window openings. The upper floors frequently overhang, and may command a wide view, without at the same time being exposed to the prying eyes of outsiders. The Moslem or Turkish house is conspicuous, if not also numerous.

Urban settlement

Yugoslavia is not a highly urbanised country. There were at the time of the 1961 census no less than 222 places each with a population of over 5,000, but of these only a half had more than 10,000, and as few as 13 had over 50,000. The map shows a marked concentration of settlements large enough to warrant the description of 'urban' in a certain number of restricted regions: the plains of the north-east; northern Serbia and Bosnia; the Sava and Drava valleys, and Macedonia. This distribution pattern is, in fact, so unusual as to deserve discussion. Most of the large cities—Beograd, Zagreb, Ljubljana, Sarajevo, Skopje—are the capitals of their respective provinces; Novi Sad is the economic centre of the Bačka; Niš of the upper Morava valley, and Rijeka and Split are coastal ports and industrial towns. Most of the remaining cities and towns are market centres; many have modern factory industries in addition to the crafts traditionally practised. The network of towns to be found along the Drava and Sava valleys, with an average distance of about 30 miles separating each from its nearest neighbour, may be regarded as normal for a predominantly agricultural region with a peasant economy (compare Poland, page 351).

The Bačka and Banat, however, present one of the densest urban patterns to be found anywhere in Eastern Europe. The distribution of these quasi-urban settlements is, however, very far from random. They lie along the Danube and Tisa valleys, usually on the river terraces back from the banks, and also along the margin of the loess which occupies the interior of these two provinces. Subotica itself, lying as it does in the midst of the Bačka loess and sand region, is the only conspicuous exception. These settlements are, of course, urban only in their size. In all other respects they are rural. They extend over a disproportionately large area for their population, they are made up predominantly of single-storied houses, which conform more to a rural than to an urban style of architecture. Each has a small garden and many have farm buildings. Public buildings are inconspicuous; there may be a square in the middle of the agglomeration, but few of them are market-towns, and in general cultural trappings are as lacking as they would be in any East European village. Functionally these towns of the Vojvodina are overgrown villages, from which a large part of the population makes its daily journey to the fields.

This settlement pattern is an inheritance from the eighteenth century, when security lay in numbers. The system is today breaking down here, as it is in Hungary, and a growing number of houses, generally isolated amid the fields, is beginning to draw off some of the

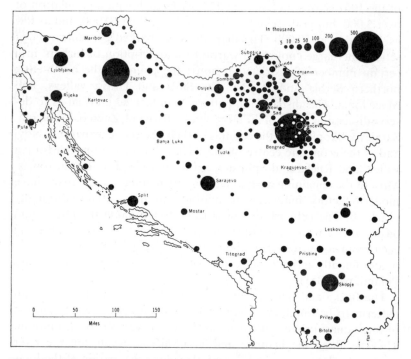

Fig. 12.9. Distribution of cities in Yugoslavia. All of over 10,000 are marked, and those of over 50,000 are named. Data from *Statistički Godišnjak SFRJ, 1965.*

urban population. As a general rule it might be suggested that settlements of less than 10,000 people remain predominantly rural; that urban functions, including market functions, become conspicuous only in settlements of greater size, and that rural pursuits are reduced to minor proportions only in towns of 20,000 to 25,000 or even more.

In the following pages the half dozen large cities are described. There are very few of intermediate size, and, as has been noted, an immense number of very small towns, which are shown on the map, but are too numerous to be described except in very general terms.

Beograd. The site of the 'white fortress' has always been an impressive one. The hills of Šumadija run down to the river where they form bluffs rising 200 to 250 feet above the junction of the Sava and Danube. The plateau above the bluffs rises very gently towards the south, but falls away more steeply to the Sava valley on the west and to the Danube plain on the east. It has been occupied since the earliest historic times. It was the site of a Roman and later of a Slavic city. It fell into the hands of the Hungarians, and in 1521 was captured by the Turks. Even after the Serbs had achieved independence, a Turkish garrison remained in Beograd, and was not withdrawn until 1867. The bluff above the rivers is crowned by the remains of the Kalemegdan, the so-called Turkish fort. The nucleus of this impressive but now largely ruinous work is medieval. The Turks added to it, but it achieved its present shape when Beograd was temporarily occupied by the Austrians after the Treaty of Passarowitz (1718). Below the bluff, between the Kalemegdan and the Danube lay the old Turkish town, inhabited until the Turks withdrew in the nineteenth century, and now represented only by a few striking ruins amid the greenery of a rather charming park.

The modern city extends southwards from the Kalemegdan over the narrow plateau. It has a nucleus of good nineteenth and twentieth century building, including the *Skupština*, or parliament, museums and university. The centre of the city was severely damaged by German air-raids in April 1941, but has been rebuilt. The old city can still show a Turkish house here and there, but most of the architectural evidence for its long and disturbed history has made place for the generally attractive modern rebuilding.

Beograd has always been a river port, and jetties are now found along the Sava and Danube. There is a good deal of barge traffic, though much of that which passes beneath the old iron cannon of Kalemegdan is, in fact, in transit between Hungary and the Lower Danube.

The growth of Beograd has been fairly recent. When it was under Turkish rule it probably had no more than 20,000 inhabitants. In the last decade of the nineteenth century it had little more than 50,000, and did not turn 100,000 until after it had become the capital of the new state. As capital of Yugoslavia Beograd grew more rapidly, and when the German bombs began to rain down upon the city its population was well in excess of quarter of a million. After the Second World War its growth was yet more rapid, a result in part of the expansion of the city's industrial and governmental functions, in part of the incorporation of surrounding areas, and in 1961 reached 598,350. Zemun on the Danube but beyond the junction of the Sava, was included within its boundaries, and between the old city and Zemun has grown up the residential and administrative suburb of Novi Beograd, with its forest of tall apartments and large government administrative buildings.

Beograd is the foremost centre of manufacturing industry in the country, with a remarkably broad range of production, which includes the metallurgical and engineering, textile and clothing and food processing industries, and the manufacture of a wide variety of consumer goods. The industrial quarters lie mainly to the south-west and south-east of the old city. The north bank of the Danube, opposite the city, remains undeveloped, owing to its poor drainage and liability to floods. The somewhat higher ground between the Danube and the the Sava, on the other hand, is becoming the scene of an intensive urban and industrial development which focuses on Zemun. Pančevo, beyond the Danube to the north-east, is also being developed industrially, and a large oil refinery and petro-chemical plant is planned for the north bank of the Danube at this point.

Beograd is the primary communication centre for at least the eastern half of the country. It is the railway focus for the southern part of the Hungarian Plain, and is the northern terminus of the all-important Morava valley route to Niš, which is continued to both Sofia and Thessaloníki. Beograd is also a focus of roads, and is the most important river port in the whole country.

Zagreb. About 240 miles to the west-north-west of Beograd is its rival city, Zagreb, the capital of Croatia. The two cities are strongly contrasted. Both grew up as frontier cities, but, whereas Beograd lay within the eastward-looking kingdom of Serbia and was later a boundary city of the Turkish Empire, Zagreb was never occupied by the Turks, though often threatened, and for much of its history was the capital of the Hungarian province of Croatia. The city grew up on the northern edge of the Sava valley, which provided a wide, marshy and protective tract along its southern margin. To the north, the land surface rises at first gently and then steeply to the isolated ridge, the Medvednica, which lifts its forested crest some 3,000 feet above the level of the Sava. At the site of Zagreb two small, low spurs extend

YUGOSLAVIA

Prizren, on the northern edge of the Šar Planina, Kosmet

Andrijevica, a village high up the valley of the Lim, a tributary of the Drina, on the western flank of the Mokra Gora, Montenegro

Dubrovnik: the town, still largely enclosed by its medieval walls, occupies a narrow shelf of land between the limestone mountains and the sea

YUGOSLAVIA

Dubrovnik: the Venetian style of Gothic architecture, which pervades the town

southward toward the plain. On the more westerly of these the Slav invaders of the seventh century established a small, fortified settlement. In the late eleventh century a church and small religious community was founded on the second spur, a quarter of a mile to the east. For many centuries they continued to exist as independent walled and fortified settlements, separated from one another by the narrow valley of a small stream which flows from the Medvednica down to the Sava.

This dual structure continued into the nineteenth century, when the civil and ecclesiastical settlements were at last merged to constitute the city of Zagreb. But already settlement had spread from the *Gornji Grad*—upper City—to the Sava Plain. The *Dojni Grad*, or Lower City grew up at the foot of the two spurs. Here was the *Novi Trg*, or New Market, now the *Trg Republike*, and streets, more or less regularly planned, were laid out around it. This development took on an east-to-west orientation, constructed between the foothills of the Medvednica and the marshes of the Sava. Further growth of the city was conditional on the coming of the railway. Zagreb became in the third quarter of the nineteenth century the crossing point of the Budapest-Fiume (Rijeka) and the Sava valley railways. At the same time, the political autonomy accorded to Hungary by the *Ausgleich* of 1867 allowed it greater scope in industrial development and commerce. Fiume became the chief port of the Hungarian Kingdom, and the commerce which moved between it and Budapest could not fail to influence the economic growth of Zagreb.

The main railway station was established well to the south even of the *Dojni Grad*, on the very edge of the Sava marshes. Here were laid out the railway yards, and as progress was made in draining the flood plain, factories were established here between the railway and the river. The east–west growth of the city was checked, and Zagreb began to expand southwards to the Sava. Better quality houses spread up the lower slopes of the Medvednica, but working-class housing—at first tenement blocks and more recently tall apartment buildings—was built out over the Sava Plain, despite the recurrent danger from the floods of this highly unpredictable river. The industrial quarter, which is today being expanded very rapidly, lies mainly between the railway and the river. Here are the metallurgical, chemical, woodworking and food-processing factories, and here in the near future it is planned to construct a river port on the Sava.

The population of Zagreb has grown even more sharply than that of

23

Beograd, and has not benefited, as has the latter, from the incorporation of nearby urban centres. In 1880, soon after the construction of its primary railway net, its population was only about 30,000, and on the eve of the First World War was only about 75,000. In 1921, the city's administrative area was increased and its population expanded to about 110,000. When the Second World War began this had reached over 185,000. By the time of the 1953 census the total was 250,000, and in 1961, the population of the city was 457,500, and that of the urbanised complex of which it is the centre, 822,000.

Though overlooked by the craggy Medvednica, Zagreb is in reality the urban focus of an extensive area of fertile lowland, the upper Sava basin, which formed the core-area of the early Croatian state. Zagreb dominates this basin to the exclusion of any significant rival. Only around the margin of the upper Sava basin does one find other towns of significance. The largest and most important of these are: Karlovac (40,180), a former Austro-Hungarian fortress town and now a centre of textile and engineering industries; and Sisak, once the Roman *Siscia*, the present limit of navigation on the Sava, a river port, and now one of the most important centres of heavy metallurgical industry in Yugoslavia.

Ljubljana. The Alpine ranges of Slovenia enclose the small Ljubljana Basin, in the midst of which the city of Ljubljana grew up. It lies beside the Ljubljanica River, a tributary of the Sava, where a steep rock rises some 600 feet above the plain. Here the Romans established their legionary fortress of *Emona*; the site was later occupied by the Slovenes. The surrounding region then became the German March of Carniola or Krain, and the precipitous rock of Ljubljana came to support the castle of a German margrave. The old city grew up in the shadow of this castle, within the sharp bend of the Ljubljanica River, but quickly spread across it to the more spacious area beyond.

Ljubljana is predominantly a baroque city, and with its city hall, its churches, and its old streets and footpaths along the Ljubljanica, resembles Salzburg more than any other city in Yugoslavia. It lies on the railway from Vienna to both Trieste and Rijeka, and has become the route centre as well as the commercial focus of the Ljubljana Basin. Its growth has been slower than that of Zagreb or Beograd. It must have been larger in the eighteenth century than either of these, but on the eve of the Second World War its population had barely reached 60,000, and in 1961 was only 157,412. Industrial expansion in Ljubljana has in recent years been a great deal less rapid than in most of the other large cities of Yugoslavia. This springs in part from the deliberate government policy of locating new industries in those parts of the country which have been economically less developed than Slovenia.

There are few large towns in the urbanised north-eastern region of Yugoslavia. The largest of them is Novi Sad (162,000), capital of the Vojvodina Autonomous Region. It lies on the north bank of the Danube. Facing it across the river is the huge Austrian fortress of Petrovardin, or Peterwardein, built as part of the Austrian Military Frontier, though on the site of an earlier Serb fortress. Novi Sad is an industrial town and river port, as well as commercial centre for the densely settled plains which surround it.

Second only to Novi Sad in the plains of the Vojvodina is Subotica (122,000), a centre of the Hungarian population of northern Yugoslavia. It is the chief urban focus of the northern Vojvodina, and has food-processing and engineering industries. It is the chief railway junction in the southern part of the Pannonian Plain, but does not lie on a navigable river. Other important towns of the northern plains are Osijek (118,500), agricultural and shipping centre on the Drava, and chief town of the Podravina; Sombor (96,500), in the Danube valley on the western margin of the Vojvodina; Zrenjanin (93,000), close to the Romanian border, and Pančevo (94,000), now becoming an industrial suburb of Beograd.

A number of towns in Slovenia and northern Croatia grew up under Austrian influence and in close association with the metallurgical industries of the Karavanke. Foremost amongst them are Maribor (153,000), a market and industrial town at the crossing of the Drava and close to the edge of the mountains, and Kranj (48,000), similarly situated in the Sava valley.

In the rest of Yugoslavia the small number of really large towns stands in sharp contrast with the prevailing lack of urban development. These towns lie either on important routeways through the mountains of the Dinaric system or along the Dalmatian coast. The former group includes Sarajevo, Niš and Skopje; the latter Rijeka and Split. Sarajevo (199,000), capital of Bosnia, lies in one of the more extensive basins, with gentler relief and more fertile soil, within the mountains (see page 634). The River Bosna opens a routeway northwards to the Danube, while to the south-west an easily negotiated col provides a routeway to the Neretva valley and the Dalmatian coast. At the same time Sarajevo lies on a routeway which follows the trend of the Dinaric folding from north-west to south-east. The city itself is a blend of the old and the new. It is a 'Turkish' town and a centre for the Muslim Bosniaks, and its multitude of mosques remain today its most conspicuous monuments. Its centrality has made it a commercial centre, and the mineral and fuel resources of Bosnia have contributed to the growth of manufacturing industries. It is, nevertheless, by far the most hilly of the larger towns of Yugoslavia. Flat land is at a premium, and the modern town climbs from the small valley of the Miljacka, a tributary of the Bosna, up and over the green rolling hills of Bosnia.

Within the hills of Bosnia are several smaller towns, market centres, some of them of great charm and beauty, which are slowly developing modern manufacturing industries. Amongst them are Banja Luka (132,000), on the Vrbas River, where it escapes from the hills; Tuzla (82,500), in a Tertiary basin of northern Bosnia; Travnik, Jajce, and the new steel town of Zenica.

Niš (145,000), is a smaller, but an older town. It lies in the Morava valley, at the junction of the Nišava. It has always been a route centre, perhaps the most important in all the Balkans. To the north lies Beograd and the Pannonian Plain; to the south, the Vardar valley and the Mediterranean. South-eastward runs the road up the Nišava valley to Sofia and Istanbul. From the west the routes from Bosnia and Croatia impinge on Niš by way of the Ibar and Western Morava. Niš was a town in Roman times; when the Crusaders crossed Serbia about 1098, they found Niš the most formidable city along their route. It became a Turkish fortress, and is today an important industrial centre and the second city of Serbia.

In the Morava valley and the hills of Šumadija are a number of smaller towns, formerly market and agricultural centres, but now developing factory industries. Foremost amongst them are Kragujevac (91,000) and Leskovac (68,000).

Skopje, or Skoplje (270,300) is the capital of the Macedonian Federal Republic, and the third largest city in Yugoslavia. It lies on the Vardar River, close to its exit from the gorges of the Šar. To the east and south-east is an extensive basin. Skopje lacks the centrality of Niš, but lies on the Morava-Vardar axis, and is linked by mountain roads not only with the basins of western Macedonia, but also with the Struma valley and Thrace. It grew to importance, as *Scupa*, in the classical and Byzantine period. It became a fortress town of the Turks, but only in recent years has it become an industrial city of major importance. The industrialisation of Skopje has been somewhat artificial and arbitrary, deriving more from the government's decision to develop the backward and politically sensitive province of Macedonia than from the resources and advantages offered by the region itself. In the summer of 1963 Skopje, not for the first time, was destroyed by an earthquake. Very little has survived of the nineteenth-century Turkish architecture which resembled that of Sarajevo. The city has now (1967) very largely been rebuilt as a Western city of tall, steel-and-concrete buildings.

Each of the basins in southern Serbia and Macedonia has its town. Most are small and picturesque, but in some ways primitive, and reminiscent more of the nineteenth than of the twentieth century. The largest of them are Priština (87,000), capital of the Kosmet; Bitola, or Bitolj (55,000), and Prilep (49,000).

The coastal towns are few and most of them are small. Their failure to grow with the expansion of Yugoslav commerce is a reflection of the barrier nature of the Dinaric Mountains (see below, page 725). The largest is Rijeka, the former Fiume (127,000), which has at present the best communications with the hinterland. The town lies at the head of the Kvarner, the Gulf of Quarnero, which here penetrates between Istria and the Velebit. It occupies only a narrow shelf between the mountains and the sea, and is severely pressed for space in which to expand its commercial activities.

Split, the Spalato of the Italians (133,000), occupies a similarly sheltered site, but has a greater expanse of lowland over which to expand. The earliest city was the classical *Salona* (*S–C.* Solin), a mile or two inland, near which the Emperor Diocletian built his palace. The latter lay on the water's edge, and became a place of refuge for the inhabitants of the former from the attacks of the Avars. The palace became the town; the mausoleum of Diocletian was used as a cathedral; the shops of the medieval and modern town gathered round the peristyle of the former Emperor's home, and Western artists sketched the detail of the classical architecture and thus initiated the Adam style. But modern Split has now spread far beyond the walls of Diocletian. Docks have spread along the waterfront, and modern industry, prominent amongst it the dusty cement manufacture, has grown up around it.

Most other towns of the Dalmatian coast have lost their former commercial importance, which was, in any case, linked with the Venetian domination of the Adriatic, but have retained their beauty unspoiled, and now yield some dividend to the Yugoslav government as tourist attractions. Prominent amongst them are Zadar, Šibenik, Trogir and that glorious fossil, Dubrovnik itself.

AGRICULTURE

Yugoslavia remains, despite the industrialisation of recent years, predominantly an agricultural and peasant state. The majority of its population lives on farms, in villages or in the large agrarian towns. The degree of collectivisation is at present small, and most of the peasantry remain in possession of their fields. A great many rural communities are still today remote from the main stream of national life, and their economy is largely self-sufficing.

Some account of the physical conditions under which agriculture is practised has already been given. Over much of the country winters are severe and the Adriatic coastal region is one of summer drought. Over large areas of the mountainous interior there are only skeletal soils, and in the karst region, rain water is lost so quickly by percolation that the region is biologically one of permanent drought. On the northern plains, where alluvium has been deposited in a broad belt

Table 80. Land use in Yugoslavia, 1938 and 1966

	1938	Percentage	1966	Percentage
Total area	(in thousands of hectares)			
Cropland	8,219	33·2	7,570	29·8
Orchards and vineyards			696	2·8
Meadow and pasture	6,219	25·1	6,450	25·4
Total agricultural land	14,438	58·3	14,716	58·0
Forest	10,316	41·7	8,831	34·8
Land not used agriculturally			1,826	7·2
Total	24,754	100·0	25,373	100·0

Sources: *International Yearbook of Agricultural Statistics: Statistički Godnišjak SFNJ, 1967.*

along all the river valleys, and loess over much of the intervening low plateaus, conditions for agriculture are better, but even here the valleys are liable to disastrous floods, and their floors are often poorly drained, while the loess lands, on the other hand, are sometimes excessively dry. The steep slopes which characterise much of the interior are unsuited to cultivation and are, in fact, extensively forested. Yugoslavia has the poorest conditions for agriculture of any country discussed in this book, with the exception only of Albania (see Table 97, page 845).

Structure of agriculture
There is very little scope for the extension of cropland, and the rural overpopulation has long been such that use was made of all land capable of cultivation within the limits of a peasant technology. Damp lands along the Sava, Drava and Danube are capable of reclamation; a fuller use could be made of some of the sandy areas of Bačka and Banat, but it is more likely that with improved living standards some of the marginal lands in the smaller *polja* will in fact be abandoned for cultivation.

Farm population. The past century has been a period of rapid population increase. Not all provinces are adequately documented, but in Serbia it grew from 829,000 in 1840 to about 3,020,000 when the First World War began. That of Croatia-Slavonia and Bosnia-Hercegovina grew somewhat less rapidly, the former from 1,605,000 in 1840 to about 2,700,000 in 1914, and the latter from 930,000 to 1,990,000.[1] This population was overwhelmingly agricultural. It became greater than the land could either employ or feed, and led to a large-scale migration both within the areas concerned and abroad. In particular, as has been noted, there was a movement of peasants from the hills of Serbia and Bosnia into the plains of the north. Croatia thus came to be heavily settled by Serbs, and only Slovenia, at this time a part of Austria, played little part in this population movement. So acute became the pressure on the land in the mountainous areas of southern Yugoslavia, that peasants sometimes formed work gangs which in winter-time went north in search of work. These 'pechalbars'[2] were traditionally masons, who played an important role in the building of the northern cities.

[1] Jozo Tomasevich, *Peasants, Politics and Economic Change in Yugoslavia,* Oxford Univ. Press, 1955, p. 152.
[2] From *pečalba*, the term used for seasonal migration.

Within the mountains crop-farming was expanded, and semi-nomadic pastoralism became increasingly restricted. Even so, the Serbian agricultural census of 1897 showed that 11 per cent of all rural families were without land, and that the average size of holdings was excessively small. The concomitant evil in much of Europe, the intense fragmentation of holdings, was less apparent in the Southern Slav lands, and was, in fact serious only in parts of the Slavonia and the Danube valley. Evidence for the size of farm-holdings on the eve of the creation of the Yugoslav state is uneven, and only very broad comparisons can be made between one part of the country and another.[1]

Feudalism and serfdom had officially ended throughout the area. The last of the Austro-Hungarian serfs had been liberated in 1848, and those of comparable status in the Ottoman Empire had been freed by the expulsion of the Turks themselves. This did not however, bring to an end over the area as a whole the institution of the great, feudally-owned estate. The large estates of Serbia had passed into the possession of the peasants who had worked them; there remained no large estates, and in 1897 nearly 97 per cent of all farm holdings were each of less than 20 hectares (49·4 acres). Even so, rural over-population was acute. In Croatia-Slavonia, by contrast, farms of this size occupied less than half the land, and almost a quarter of the land was held in estates of over 575 hectares (about 1,380 acres). A very similar pattern of land-holding was to be found in Bačka and Banat. In Bosnia and Hercegovina, however, which had been occupied by the Austrians as recently as 1878, the old Turkish type of feudalism survived. The *beys* in many cases remained in possession of their lands, and were, in fact, used as instruments of the Austro-Hungarian administration.

Land reform. The defeat of the Austro-Hungarian forces in 1918 was followed by some degree of expropriation of the larger estates by the peasants. There was a popular demand for land reform, and the Prince Regent Alexander publicly proclaimed that it was the government's policy to abolish the large estates and to distribute land among the poor and landless peasants. In the end, there was no change in Serbia and Montenegro.[2] In other provinces of the kingdom, an upper limit for agricultural holdings was set, varying from province to province. The limits ranged from 50 to 300 hectares (123·5 to 741 acres) of arable, and from 100 to 500 hectares (247 to 1,235 acres) of

---

[1] Summarised by Jozo Tomasevich, *op. cit.*, pp. 203–9.
[2] Rano M. Brashich, *Land Reform and Ownership in Yugoslavia, 1919–1953*, New York, 1954, pp. 24–7.

land of all varieties, figures which many regarded as far too high. Even so, exceptions were made in favour of estates which practised some specialised form of agriculture. In the end, over half a million hectares were expropriated, almost all of it in Croatia, Slavonia and Vojvodina, where the former German- and Hungarian-owned estates were broken up. Surviving feudal obligations were terminated in Bosnia and Hercegovina, but, although ownership passed from Turkish landowner to Serb peasant, relatively little change was made in the geographical pattern of farm holdings. In Macedonia, where Turkish-owned estates had been both large and numerous, there was a more extensive allocation of holdings to the Slav peasants.

In its declared object of reducing both the area of large estates and the number of landless peasants, the land reform conducted by the Royal Yugoslav government was undoubtedly successful. In all, it is claimed, about half a million peasant families benefited, at the expense of 10,000 to 12,000 landlords, whose estates were divided. The number of landless peasants was reduced, it has been estimated, to about 150,000, and the average size of the peasant holding was brought close to 5 hectares (12 acres). In 1931, before the land reform was completed, nearly 70 per cent of the holdings were in fact of less than 5 hectares (12 acres), and less than 12 per cent of 10 hectares (24 acres) or more, as Table 81 shows.

Table 81. Size and number of holdings in 1931

Size of holdings (hectares)	Number	Percentage of holdings	Area (hectares)	Percentage of farm area
Up to 2	671,865	33·8	693,544	6·5
2·1–5	676,284	34·1	2,287,571	21·5
5·1–10	407,237	20·5	2,873,155	27·0
10·1–20	174,068	8·8	2,380,825	22·4
20·1–50	49,314	2·5	1,388,570	13·0
Over 50	6,957	0·4	1,022,314	9·6
	1,985,725	100·0	10,645,979	100·0

Source: After Ranko M. Brashich, *op. cit.*, p. 37.

23*

The land reform has been criticised for increasing the number of uneconomically small farm units, and thus for bringing about an actual decline of crop-production in some areas. An opportunity was missed, it has been said, to create farms large enough to be efficient. Such is to misconstrue the spirit of the peasant movement. In face of the intense land hunger of the peasantry, it was essential to create as many individual holdings as possible, however marginal many of them might be.

Movement towards collectivisation. The land reform of the interwar years had clearly left many problems, which were intensified by invasion and civil war from 1941–45. Among these, as has already been indicated, were the small size of holdings and the number of landless peasants which was again beginning to grow. The remedy for these ills proposed by the postwar régime was the one which they had taken over from the Soviet Union: nationalisation, collectivisation and industrialisation. It was however pursued somewhat halfheartedly, and collectivisation was abandoned fairly early as an immediate goal of agricultural policy.

Legislation of 1945–46 provided for a drastic reduction in the maximum permitted size of an agricultural holding, which was reduced for peasant holdings, to 45 hectares (111 acres). A much lower limit was set for institutional holdings. The possessions of many Germans and of other 'enemies of the people' were confiscated. In these ways about a million and a half hectares (3,706,500 acres) passed into the possession of the state. About half of this was used to increase the size of existing holdings or to create new, while most of the remainder went to establish State Farms. As most of the sequestered land came from the former German population, it lay mainly in the plains of the north-east, and it is here that one finds today most of the socialised agriculture of Yugoslavia.

The government's attempts to collectivise agriculture have met with little success. At first it was content to set up agricultural cooperatives for the purchase of manufactured goods needed by the peasants and for the sale and distribution of farm produce. These were then supplemented by working cooperatives of the peasants (cf. East Germany, page 250). The Yugoslav peasant might have been expected to favour the institution of cooperatives. There was a long tradition of mutual help and even of communal cultivation in the *zadruga*, which had flourished in the recent past. In the years between the wars, the cooperative movement had been vigorous and on the whole successful.

But the government sponsored cooperatives of the postwar years proved unpopular.

Resistance was directed against the working cooperatives. In their first stage the peasant retained legal possession of his land, but allowed it, for purposes of cultivation, to be merged with the land of his neighbours. His remuneration may have been partly in the form of a rent, but was generally a proportion of the net income of the cooperative. The peasant under this system retained the right to withdraw his land from the cooperative. The government in the late 1940s and early 1950s, however, exerted pressure on peasants to relinquish their remaining rights in the land, and thus to create a genuine collective, in which all land was socially owned. The peasant was permitted to retain possession of a small garden plot and to keep a few animals for the supply of basic foodstuffs to the peasant family.

The number of working cooperatives remained small until, in 1949, the government brought more pressure to bear on the peasants. The working cooperatives reached their highest number in the following year, when their total fell little short of 7,000. At this time almost two and a half million hectares (6,177,600 acres) of agricultural land, about 18 per cent of the total, was worked by such cooperatives. Such socialised agriculture was far from evenly distributed. 'For the most part,' wrote Brašić, 'the peasant working cooperatives are located in the agriculturally richest regions of Vojvodina, eastern Slavonia, in the area of the Sava river in Bosnia, and in the relatively few plains in Macedonia.' This was to some extent due to the larger settlements to be found in these areas, capable of benefiting from the machines and equipment which the government made available for the cooperatives. But in part also it sprang from the fact that numerous Partisans, firmly indoctrinated with Communist ideology, were settled here, on lands which had in the main been confiscated from the Germans.

The government by a combination of threats and bribes, tried to convert the cooperatives to what its ideology regarded as their highest form, that in which all land was socially owned. Many peasants retaliated by withdrawing their land from the cooperative while they were still legally able to do so. Many cooperatives disintegrated over the next few years, and their number was reduced to about a third of the total in 1950. But the working cooperatives, or collectives as we may in fact call them, proved popular to some, and their break-up created problems for the peasants themselves. Many peasants could not easily do without the equipment which the cooperatives made available; they appreciated the credits that could be obtained from the government, and the marketing organisation which it provided. Furthermore, the cooperatives provided a regular employment for the large body of landless peasants, the *bezemljaši*. The breakdown of the working cooperative movement, it might be said, almost made necessary the agrarian law of 1953, which set at 10 hectares (24·7 acres) the maximum size of a privately owned farm holding. The land thus nationalised was used in part to provide holdings for the still landless peasantry.

In the later 1950s the government improved the conditions of membership of the cooperatives, and this, coupled with the very real disadvantages of non-membership, led to a renewed increase in their number. By 1960 the number of cooperatives had reached 4,634, with an average size of almost 200 hectares (494 acres). The number has since declined again. At the same time, with the very active encouragement of the government, there has been a much greater use of fertiliser and superior quality seed. The number of tractors increased more than six-fold between 1951 and 1966, and there was also a considerable expansion in the use of other types of farm machinery.

Agricultural production has fluctuated greatly. The peasant responds quickly to incentives, and can react as rapidly in the opposite direction if he considers that conditions are in any way adverse. Upon these fluctuations are imposed those which originate in the vagaries of the weather. There was a considerable increase in total production in the late 1950s, but a recession in the early 1960s. The government acted quickly to relieve peasants' grievances, and has, on the other hand, given itself the right to take over all land not properly cultivated. While in good years food production is adequate, imports of the basic foodstuffs are still sometimes necessary.

Land use. Despite these changes in the organisation of farming there has been little change in the pattern of land use. The area of farmland in 1966 was about 10,200,000 hectares (25,450,000 acres), 40 per cent of the total area of the country. To this should be added an area of 4,510,000 hectares (11,140,000 acres) of rough grazing. In 1966 the areas under the principal categories of land use were, as shown in Table 82. The area under each of these categories of land use, except that of meadow, was somewhat smaller twenty or thirty years earlier, but neither their relative proportions nor their distribution differed significantly from that of today.

The pattern of agriculture accords closely with that of landform

Table 82. Land use in Yugoslavia—1966

	Area 1964 (hectares)	Percentage of Farmland	Percentage of Total area
Cropland, including gardens	7,570,000	74·3	29·6
Orchards	437,000	4·2	1·4
Vineyards	259,000	2·5	1·0
Meadow	1,940,000	19·0	7·6
	10,206,000	100	39·6
Rough grazing	4,510,000	—	17·5
	14,716,000		57·1

Source: *Statistički Godišnjak FNRJ*, 1967, p. 148.

regions, which has already been presented. The plains of the north-east are predominantly under the plough and this region, which embraces only about a tenth of the area of the country, is said to produce about half the bread grains grown, 85 per cent of the sugar beet, 82 per cent of the oils of vegetable origin, 74 per cent of the vegetable fibres, and almost half the maize.[1]

The hill-country of Croatia, of northern Bosnia and of most of Serbia is wetter than the northern plains. Cropland is less extensive and animal husbandry is more widely practised. On the other hand this region is important for orchards and vineyards, and much of the *šljivovica*, or plum brandy, originates in the plum-orchards of Serbia.

The mountainous region, as a whole, has a high rainfall, a poor soil and a long and severe winter. On the other hand, the valleys and *polja* contain cropland and meadow, and there is extensive rough grazing over the high ground. This region has considerably less than a fifth of the country's cropland, but almost half of its grazing.

The same kinds of crops are grown and similar animals are reared over all three regions. The difference lies in the proportions in which these elements are combined. The other two regions differ radically from these. They are characterised by dry summers and scanty rainfall, and these conditions have dictated an entirely different pattern of

[1] Jacques May, *The Ecology of Malnutrition in Five Countries of Eastern and Central Europe*, New York, 1963, p. 135.

agriculture. In the Macedonian region, cropland covers only a small area, and almost a third of this is irrigated. The crops grown are those which demand heat and sunshine: rice, tobacco, and even cotton. Fodder crops are unimportant; cattle are scarce and the commonest livestock are the sheep and goats which graze the dry hillsides. The Mediterranean region is a narrow strip bordering the Adriatic Sea from the Italian to the Albanian boundaries. Rainfall is even more markedly seasonal than in Macedonia, and the winters milder. Only a very small proportion of its area can be ranked as cropland, and this is outranked in importance by vineyards and orchards. Livestock rearing is less important even than in Macedonia, and, as in the latter, is generally restricted to sheep and goats.

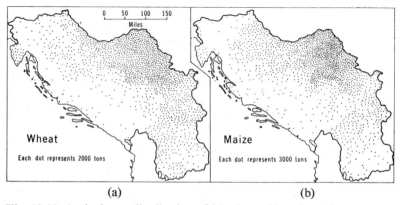

(a)   (b)

Fig. 12.10. Agriculture: distribution of (a) wheat, (b) maize. After *Geografiski Atlas Jugoslavije*, Zagreb, 1961.

Figs. 12.10 and 12.11 illustrate the area under crops. The units for which statistics are available are, of course, the political divisions of the country rather than its physiographic regions. The maps nevertheless emphasise some of the contrasts between the agricultural regions described above.

Of the area under crops in 1966, about 7,100,000 hectares (17,537,000 acres), almost three-quarters was sown with cereal crops. Most extensively cultivated was maize, which was grown on rather more than a third of the cropland. Next in importance was wheat, which covered a somewhat smaller area. The two show somewhat similar distribution patterns (Figs. 12.10a, b); they are most extensively grown in the plains of the north-east and are least important in the more mountainous areas of the south-west and south. Wheat, as is to be expected, makes a somewhat better showing than maize in the dry-summer regions.

Other grain crops are of only minor importance, and collectively occupy less than 1,000,000 hectares (2,470,000 acres). They are mostly grown in the more mountainous areas, rye in the hills of Serbia and Macedonia; barley in Bosnia and Croatia; oats in Serbia and Bosnia, and rice in the irrigated lowlands of the Vardar and Strumica valleys.

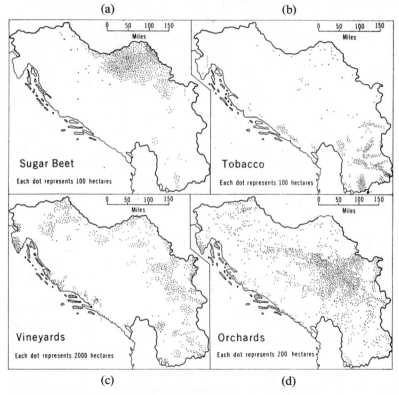

Fig. 12.11. Agriculture: distribution of (a) sugar beet, (b) tobacco, (c) viti-culture, (d) orchards (predominantly plum and cherry). After *Geografiski Atlas Jugoslavije*, Zagreb, 1961.

Potatoes are not widely grown, and have little importance except in Slovenia and parts of Croatia. Vegetables are grown chiefly in small garden plots attached to the rural cottages. Industrial crops are important only in the plains of the north-east, where industrial plant is located to process them. In terms of acreage the most important of these is suger-beet, almost all of which is grown in the Vojvodina. Sunflower and hemp and flax, which occupy a much smaller area, are also grown principally in the same area. At the same time, however, two industrial crops are grown, for climatic reasons, principally in the dry-summer regions of the south-west and south. These are tobacco most of which is grown in the plains of Macedonia, southern Serbia and Kosmet, and cotton, which is virtually a Macedonian monopoly.

Vineyards and orchards occupy a relatively large total area. Yugoslav wine has hitherto been somewhat underrated, but its growing popularity in Central and Western Europe is leading to a greater concentration on viticulture. The response to increased demand is in the case of vineyards a very slow one; nevertheless the area under vines has been increasing slowly. They are most important along the Dalmatian coast, where certain areas, notably that around Mostar, have become widely known for their vintage. Vineyards are also important over the hills of northern Croatia; on the south-facing slopes of the low hills of the Danubian plain, and in northern Serbia. The vine is grown in restricted areas in Macedonia and southern Serbia, but has not really developed in areas where the Muslim tradition was formerly strong.

Orchards are extensive and their area is increasing relatively fast. They are most abundant in Serbia and in the hill country of northern Bosnia. Over half their area is under plum trees (*šljiva*), the greater part of whose product goes to the making of plum-brandy, or *šljivovica*, the traditional Yugoslav drink.

Animal farming. Pig-rearing in the oak- and beech-woods of Serbia was formerly an important branch of agriculture, and provided one of the major exports of the state. Animal farming has, however, declined in importance. It has been forced from the lowlands by more intensive crop-farming, and it suffered severely from the effects of invasion and civil war. The expansion in the number of farm animals has been very slow, and though the land under fodder crops had increased recently, it still in 1960 amounted to only 6 per cent of the cropped area. Most numerous by far are sheep and pigs. They are in a sense complementary, with the former predominant in the dry-summer areas and in those with extensive poor mountain and hill grazing (Figs. 12.12 a, b), and the latter in the predominantly arable areas of the north-eastern plains. It is evident from the map that the pig is in Yugoslavia no longer a denizen of the forest, but a scavenger living on the waste and the surplus of the richest farming region in the country.

Cattle, on the other hand, are more widely and more evenly distributed, except in the karst region, along the Dalmatian coast, and in southern Macedonia. In these areas the lack of suitable summer fodder reduces the number of cattle that can be reared, and places very severe restrictions on dairy cattle. Dairy-farming is in fact of greatest importance in Slavonia and in the hills of northern Croatia, Bosnia

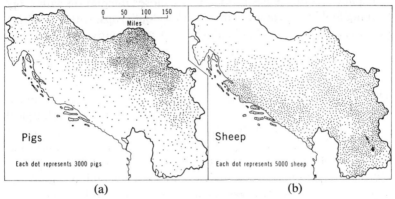

(a)   (b)

Fig. 12.12. Agriculture: distribution of (a) pig-rearing, (b) sheep. After *Geografiski Atlas Jugoslavije*, Zagreb, 1961.

and Serbia. It is of negligible importance in the karst and the Adriatic coastal regions, as well as in Montenegro, Kosmet and Macedonia.

Transhumance. The seasonal movement of flocks and herds between mountain and valley has been important since remote antiquity, and was formerly more widely practised than it is today. The normal pattern is for animals belonging to lowland settlements to be sent up into the hills in summer. This occurs notably in Slovenia, where cattle are sent up into the Karavanke and Julian Alps to graze the pastures which, during the remainder of the year, are under snow. In the coastal region the animals, here principally sheep, are led up into the higher mountains of the karst to escape the intense drought and the burning heat of the lowlands.

There are, however, many variants of this general pattern. In some areas intermediate pastures, grazed in spring and autumn, are found;

in others, particularly in Macedonia, the permanent villages are in the uplands, and the animals are sent down to the valleys in winter. This latter pattern of movement is particularly important among the Vlach population (see page 667) of the southern Balkans.

The practice of transhumance has long been declining in many parts of Yugoslavia. In Serbia, where it was formerly widely practised, the expansion of crop-farming has cut into the winter grazing land in the lowlands, and has even led to the conversion of some of the upland settlements to crop-farming. It is in this competition for land that we must look for the primary reason for the failure of livestock farming to expand. Its future lies probably in a closer integration with crop-farming and in a greater reliance upon fodder crops, with a resulting increase in the supply of animal manure for the cultivated land.

INDUSTRIAL DEVELOPMENT

The development of manufacturing industries is a recent phenomenon. Though there were a few manufactures, notably metallurgical and textile, in Slovenia in the early and middle years of the nineteenth century, factory industry came to Serbia only late in that century, and to the rest of Yugoslavia not until after the Turks had been expelled. During the period between the First and the Second World Wars, manufacturing industries were greatly expanded, and by 1939 Yugoslavia was able to produce most of the consumer goods required by its rather simple and predominantly peasant society. At the same time some progress had been made in building up capital-goods industries, especially iron, steel and cement. Most of the larger undertakings were established with foreign capital, and they tended to be established in the more developed regions of the north where there was a larger body of skilled labour and a greater volume of purchasing power.

In 1940 less than 12 per cent of the working population was officially classified as employed in mining and manufacturing. By 1966 this had risen to about 18 per cent. Despite the progress made, Yugoslavia remains one of the least industrialised of the East European countries. And yet the country's basic resources are considerable. Fuel resources are fairly large, though not of the highest quality. Although petroleum production is unlikely ever to be really important, there is scope for a considerable development of hydro-electric power, and its ferrous and non-ferrous metals put Yugoslavia among the richest countries in this none too generously endowed region of Eastern Europe.

That Yugoslavia has hitherto not made the most of its resources is apparent, and the reasons for this failure lie primarily in the long period of Turkish rule, which ended little more than a half century ago in some parts; in the political instability and insecurity which have characterised it for centuries, and in its lack of cohesion and its low purchasing power, which made it far from attractive to investment capital from without. It takes many decades for these evils to be entirely removed. The last twenty years, however, have been a period of greater stability than the region as a whole has known for a very long time. It has also been a period of more rapid economic growth than has ever occurred before.

Mineral and fuel resources

Yugoslavia is notable more for the great range and variety of its mineral and fuel resources than for their quantity. It is, like Spain, a country rich in small deposits, and poor in large ones. No less than 136 separate coal basins have been identified, though only 25 of these contain bituminous coal, and comparatively few have ever been seriously worked.[1] The coal resources of Yugoslavia contain every quality except anthracite, but their classification is far from satisfactory and estimates of total reserves available are far from reliable.[2] The best, that made by Mellen and Winston, puts their total at about 2,000 million tons. The coals range in geological age from the Carboniferous to the Pliocene, with a large proportion of it of Secondary and lower Tertiary age. Mellen and Winston, in the only thorough study yet made of Yugoslavia's fuel resources, classify all coal from Carboniferous to Eocene age as bituminous. It is evident, however, that some of these deposits, especially those of more recent geological age, have only a low heating power. The later coals are variously defined as brown coal and lignite, the latter being only a low-grade fuel with a calorific value but little higher than that of peat.

The best of the bituminous coal occurs in the mountains of north-eastern Serbia, where the series of small coal basins is an extension of the Romanian coal-field described on page 591. A little low-grade bituminous coal is worked in northern Bosnia, but most other mines

[1] M. Mellen and V. H. Winston, *The Coal Resources of Yugoslavia*, Mid-European Studies Center, New York, 1956, p. 33.
[2] A total of 40 million tons of bituminous coal in the basins of north-east Serbia was given in *European Steel Trends*, UN Economic Commission for Europe, Geneva (1949), p. 116. This is considerably less than the total for the whole country.

are in lignite or brown coal. These latter deposits occupy a great number of small basins, which were shallow lakes in early Tertiary times, when a sea occupied the Pannonian Plain. Most of the basins are elongated, in a west-to-east direction in Slovenia and northern Croatia, where they conform with the trend of the Alpine folding, and from north-west to south-east in most other parts of the country (see Fig. 12.13). In almost every instance the coal seams have been much

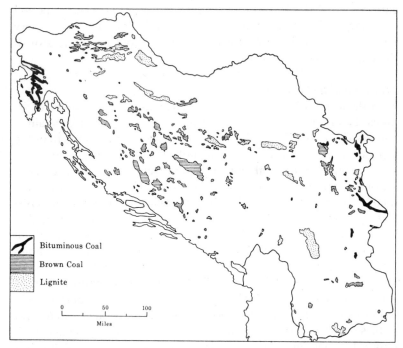

Fig. 12.13. Fuel resources of Yugoslavia. Based on M. Mellen and Victor H. Winston.

disturbed by subsequent earth-movements. Some are severely faulted; others are intruded by igneous rocks, and many cannot be regarded as workable under modern conditions. Less than two per cent of estimated reserves are of bituminous quality, and nearly 90 per cent is classified as lignite.

Most of the reserves lie in the Tertiary basins, already described, which occupy extensive areas of Bosnia and Hercegovina and northern Croatia and Slovenia. The beds as a general rule are too deep and too irregular for opencast mining, such as is practised, for example, in East Germany and Czechoslovakia. Drifts cut into the hillside or shallow shafts are generally used. The expansion of lignite production has been very rapid in recent years, though the output of bituminous coal has increased very little. Means have been devised to beneficiate the better Tertiary coals and to use them for coke production, and those of the Sarajevo-Zenica basins are today an important source of metallurgical fuel for the iron-smelting industry of Bosnia. The use of briquetting presses is increasing, and this in turn is permitting a wider distribution of lignite and brown coal. At the same time Yugoslavia is now beginning to adopt the German and Czech practice of building steam-powered generators close to the lignite fields and of transporting the energy by high-tension cable to consuming centres. The high degree of concentration of the lignite resources in Bosnia is not without its influence on the location of new industries in this area.

Yugoslavia shares to a small degree in the oilfield which underlies parts of the Pannonian basin. Before the Second World War there was a very small production along the Mura valley, in the extreme north of the state, from an oilfield which was in fact an extension of the Zala field of Hungary. Since the Second World War production, both here and in Vojvodina, has been greatly expanded, and in 1959 first exceeded 500,000 tons. Natural gas has been worked since before the Second World War along the middle Sava valley. In recent years, the number of wells has been increased, especially near Kutina, some 50 miles to the south-east of Zagreb. The volume yielded has fluctuated greatly. In 1955 it reached 34 million cubic metres, and in 1965 was 330 millions. Oil shales are said to be widespread, especially in Serbia, but are not yet worked commercially.

Metalliferous mining
Yugoslavia appears to have more abundant reserves of iron-ore than any other country in Eastern Europe, but they are distributed through a number of sometimes rather small deposits of uncertain quality. The largest and most important are those of Ljubija and Vareš, both in Bosnia. The Ljubija deposits lie near Prijedor, in the valley of the Sana, a right-bank tributary of the Una. They appear to have been worked during the Middle Ages, but their modern exploitation began only in 1916. The ore, a medium-grade limonite, occurring in Carboniferous rocks, is the primary source of supply for the blast furnaces at Sisak, about 40 miles to the north-west. Other deposits occur along the

Sana valley, and are being developed. The total reserves in this area have been put at 250 million tons of ore, and may well be higher.

The second important deposit lies around the town of Vareš, amid the hills of eastern Bosnia. The ores are haematite, and occur irregularly in the Triassic beds. Total reserves are smaller—about 50 million tons —than those of Ljubija, but they have been worked for an even longer period. Vareš, together with the Stanja valley in which it lies, has been the scene of a charcoal-iron industry for centuries, and smelting was continued here until quite recently, when the old Vareš furnaces were replaced by new iron-works at Ilijaš, near Sarajevo (see below, page 710).

Other deposits are small and little used. The Ljubija group of deposits extends westwards into Croatia, where they are mined at Bešlinac. The once important ores of Slovenia, which gave rise to the iron industry of Kranj, are virtually exhausted, and have now been abandoned for several decades. Ores of a somewhat intractable variety are obtained from mines at Majdanpek, in the mountains of north-east Serbia, and small deposits in western Macedonia are now being developed to supply the Skopje smelting industry.

Non-ferrous metals. Yugoslavia is unusually rich in its variety of non-ferrous ores, though not so fortunate in their quality and quantity. Most important are the ores of copper, lead and zinc. Others, including antimony, bauxite, mercury and bismuth, are worked, but production is relatively small.

Copper ores, principally chalcopyrite, are widely distributed in the regions of fold mountains. Foremost among these deposits are those of Majdanpek and Bor, in the Stara Planina, only a few miles to the south of the Iron Gate gorges. Those at Majdanpek were worked in classical and medieval times, but latterly have been exploited only for pyrites. Very recently, however, renewed prospecting has permitted new mines to be opened in the vicinity, and copper ore is again being produced. Bor, on the other hand, has one of the largest reserves of copper ore in Europe, and is said to have the largest single copper mine. It is an open-cast working developed in a low-grade ore. The ore is reduced to blister copper at the mine, and is then refined electrolytically, before shipment to copper-using factories in Yugoslavia.

Production from the Bor-Majdanpek mines regained its prewar level by 1950; it has since expanded steadily, and in 1964 it reached 62,100 tons of refined copper. Nevertheless, the planned output has not been achieved, and expansion has been at a diminishing rate. This reflects the difficulties encountered at the Bor mine. The higher grade ore has been exhausted, and ores now being mined are of a diminishing quality. There are a number of small deposits of copper in Bosnia and Croatia. None of these is at present mined, and it is doubtful whether any is large enough to support a large-scale, modern mining operation.

The second important centre of non-ferrous mining in Yugoslavia is the Kopaonik Mountains of Serbia. A number of mines have been active in recent times, but on the eve of the Second World War mining had been concentrated at the Trepča site, 6 miles north-east of Mitrovica and at the southern end of the Kopaonik range. The present mine at Trepča was opened up shortly before the Second World War. Its equipment is thus relatively modern, and has been further augmented and renewed after the war. The mine lies high in the mountains, and ore is transported to a smelting and refining plant in the valley below.

Trepča is primarily a lead mine, but produces also a considerable volume of zinc ore, which is intimately associated with that of lead. It is the largest but by no means the only lead–zinc mine now being worked. Second in importance is Mežica, in the highly mineralised eastern Karavanke range, where there is a mine and a small refinery. There are furthermore deposits near Srebrenica, in eastern Bosnia, once noted for its silver production, and at a number of sites in southern Serbia. These are not at present being exploited, though several have been worked in the past. It would be reasonable to assume that some four-fifths of the current production of lead–zinc ore is from the Trepča mines, where the ore is said to be of good quality and reserves abundant. There seems no reason why Yugoslavia should not maintain its position as the foremost European producer of lead, with a smaller but significant production of zinc.

Bauxite and aluminium. The bauxite deposits of Yugoslavia are extensive and occur generally as massive beds lying on the limestone in Istria and along the coast near Šibenik, in the hinterland of Split and west of Mostar.

These ores were first exploited during the First World War, but production remained small until the 1930s. In 1939, a bauxite refinery was established at Lozovac, on the Krka estuary inland from Šibenik. There is today a small alumina-refining mill at Moste, near Ljubljana, and a larger and more up-to-date mill at Strnišče, between Maribor and Ptuj, in Slovenia. The extraction of alumina from bauxite presents little difficulty, but reduction to metallic aluminium calls for quantities of electric power that are not readily available in Yugoslavia. Much of the alumina is exported, but with the increasing availability of electric-power, more and more is now being refined within Yugoslavia.

Yugoslavia is also rich in antimony and mercury. The former occurs widely, but is mined and smelted only at Zajača and Krupanj, in the mountains of north-western Serbia. Antimony is a metal of no great industrial significance, so that, though resources are large, the increase of production has been less marked than that of other metals. With an output of 3,969 tons of ore (metal content) in 1965, Yugoslavia is not only the largest producer in Europe, but the source of 10 per cent of the world's antimony.

The extensive reserves of cinnabar, the ore of mercury, were acquired as a result of boundary changes after the Second World War. They occur in Carboniferous beds at Idrija, near the northern margin of the Julian Karst, where they are mined and smelted by the relatively simple process of combining the sulphur with oxygen and so leaving the metallic mercury. Output of this far from essential substance has scarcely risen during the past ten years, and little investment has been made in expanding production.

This does not exhaust the production of metalliferous ores in Yugoslavia, though the output of all others is on a very small scale. Bismuth is obtained as a by-product of the Trepča mines; magnesite is mined in Serbia; pyrites at Majdanpek; asbestos in the hills of central Serbia; chrome in those of southern Serbia; manganese in northern Bosnia; silver along with the lead and zinc at Trepča, and gold at a number of sites from Slovenia to Serbia.

Non-metallic minerals

To these extractive industries must be added the not inconsiderable production of non-metallic minerals and earths. Barytes, graphite, gypsum and rock-salt are obtained, though, in general, in only small quantities. More important are the marls, or clayey limestone, which are used in the manufacture of Portland cement. Deposits are widespread, but are most abundant along parts of the Dalmatian coast and in Istria. A large cement industry has been established in the vicinity of Split and there are smaller centres of production at Pula and Omiš on the coast, and near the junction of the Northern Plain with its bordering hills, where the raw materials, clay and limestone, are sometimes found in close proximity. Cement has long been a significant export of Yugoslavia, and much of the output of the coastal works is destined for foreign markets. Production has increased steadily through the 1950s, and, with ambitious plans for building and industrial expansion both in Yugoslavia and other Mediterranean countries, the prospects for continued growth appear good (see page 166).

Building stone and clay for brick, tile and ceramic manufacture are widespread. Domestic building is now primarily with hollow, ceramic bricks, which are light and give good insulation. These are chiefly made in the plains of the north-east, where suitable clay is most abundant. Much of the pottery industry, which uses similar materials, is in the same area. Yugoslavia has an abundance of ornamental building stones, most of them igneous. They are too hard and intractable for general use, but serve well for monumental sculpture, and admirable use is made of them in the monument to the country's unity on the hill of Avala, near Beograd.

Metallurgical industries
The smelting and working of iron is one of the oldest industries in Yugoslavia, and was founded upon widespread ores and abundant charcoal. The reserves of iron ore remain considerable, and are the most extensive in Eastern Europe. Fuel, however, presents a problem. Yugoslavia has no reserves of good quality coking coal. The best available has a high ash content, and reliance has hitherto been placed on imported fuel. There has been no consistent source of supply, though over a period of some ten years the biggest supplier has been the Soviet Union, followed by the United States. Supply has been contingent on the political situation, and is clearly a source of grave concern to the government. Experiments are now in progress to produce a usable coke by blending Bosnian lignite with imported bituminous coal.

There has been a large but variable import of coke, but much of the fuel used is now coked in ovens, built in the early 1950s, at Lukavac and Zenica. These supply the smelting industries at Jesenice, in Slovenia; at Sisak, in Croatia, and at Zenica, in Bosnia. The separation of coke-ovens from steelworks means, however, that surplus gases are not available for the various heating processes in the steelworks and rolling-mills, and other and more expensive fuels must be used. To some extent these are being supplied by the natural gas field of

Slavonia. At the same time the shortage of mineral fuel is leading to an increasing use of electric power, in which Yugoslavia has large resources, for both the smelting and the steel-making branches of the industry.

Until recent years Slovenia was the most important centre of the iron and steel industries. This was due, in part, to the great antiquity of iron-working in this area, and in part to Austrian encouragement and initiative. In the 1930's a policy of dispersing the industry more widely was adopted. There were already old and very small plants at Vareš and Zenica. To these were added works at Sisak, on the Sava, 30 miles below Zagreb; at Smederovo, where a steelworks was built on the bank of the Danube downstream from Beograd, and at Zenica, in Bosnia.

Since 1946, when the iron and steel industry was taken over by the government, this policy of dispersing industry has been pursued further. The object of the government has been to establish works close to domestic sources of raw material and as near as possible to depressed or overpopulated areas (see page 715). Expansion in Slovenia in recent years has been small; Bosnia has become the most important centre of the industry, and plant has been built in Montenegro and Macedonia.

Slovenia remains, however, an important centre of production, despite its distance from fuel and ore and its location within a mile or two of the Austrian border. At Jesenice is a small integrated plant, spread out along the narrow valley of the Sava, and at Štore and Ravne, to the south-west and west respectively of Maribor, are steel-works which are coming to rely increasingly on electric power rather than on solid fuel.

At Sisak is a small but modern, integrated works, designed to use the Ljubija ores and coke from the ovens at Lukavac (near Tuzla). It is well placed for transport by river, road and rail, and uses natural gas from the Slavonian oilfield (see page 705) for its heating processes.

The Zenica-Ilijaš-Vareš region has come to be the most important in the Yugoslav iron and steel industry and now appears to have almost two-thirds of the total capacity. It has in the Vareš area adequate supplies of iron-ore, and the lignite of the Sarajevo Basin is among those best suited to metallurgical processes. Coke is obtained from Lukavac and limestone from Doboj. The old Vareš furnaces have been closed, and smelting is now concentrated at

Zenica, with a small, electric-smelting plant at Ilijaš. The only steel-works in the region is also at Zenica.

Social and political, rather than economic reasons have led to the establishment of steelworks at Nikšić, in Montenegro, and at Skopje, in Macedonia. An important objective was to establish heavy industry in areas where rural overpopulation was serious and political discontent had been a perennial threat to the government. The Nikšič plant obtains its pig-iron from Zenica and its fuel from the lignite basin near Mostar, and in turn supplies metal to fabricating industries at Titograd and elsewhere in Montenegro. The Skopje plant is more ambitious. It smelts low-grade Macedonian ore with coke made from Kosovo lignite, but technical difficulties are considerable, and Yugoslavia pays highly for this concession to political feelings in Macedonia.

Table 83. Iron and steel production

	Pig iron (*tons*)	Crude steel (*tons*)
1938	58,000	220,000
1948	183,000	368,000
1953	281,000	514,000
1961	1,055,000	1,532,000
1963	1,060,000	1,588,000
1966	1,143,000	1,867,000

Sources: *League of Nations and UN Statistical Yearbooks; Statistički Godrišnjak SFRJ, 1967.*

The expansion of the iron and steel industries has been remarkable, though less rapid than in Romania. Plans are nevertheless more ambitious than these figures would appear to justify. The planned production of 1,600,000 tons of pig iron and of 2,300,000 of steel in 1963 have not been realised, and it is unlikely that the objectives of 2,600,000 and 3,200,000 tons respectively in 1975 will be achieved.

Engineering and electrical industries. Despite the very rapid expansion of the past 15 to 20 years, Yugoslavia remains proportionately less industrialised than any of the countries discussed hitherto. Before the Second World War mechanical engineering was restricted to a few factories of moderate size and a large number of workshops. This has changed radically since 1950. By 1963 production of the metal industries as a whole was more than seven times that of 1939, and that of the electrical nearly forty times as great. So rapid a rate of increase could only be achieved if the starting level was very low. The expansion was spread across all branches of the metal industries, from foundry work to machine tools, from tractors to bicycles. It is of some significance that, in terms of weight, metal castings ranked far ahead of any other item, indicative of the technically rather simple nature of production.

The expansion of the electrical goods industry has been from a very much smaller base than the manufacture of machines. The production of generators, transformers, accumulators, telephone equipment and radio receivers was either negligible or non-existant in 1939. It is not large even today, but has shown, nevertheless, a very large percentage growth.

In 1939 these industries were heavily concentrated in the extreme north-west and north, in Slovenia, northern Croatia and Vojvodina, where they had been established primarily with foreign capital. The present pattern of distribution, despite the government's efforts to disperse industry, does not greatly differ. The chief centres remain: Ljubljana and Maribor; Zagreb and the small towns within its region; Slavonski Brod, Osijek and other towns of Slavonia; Subotica, Novi Sad and greater Beograd. The spread of the mechanical industries southward from the Sava and Danube valleys has been recent. Banja Luka, Doboj and Tuzla, in Bosnia; Kraljevo, Niš, Kruševac, Kragujevac and Smederevska Palanka, in northern Serbia, each became the centre of a branch of the metal-using industries. Some acquired several branches. But industry was slow in penetrating the hills of central Yugoslavia, and has done so in recent years largely as a result of government initiative. The Sarajevo-Zenica basin has proved the most attractive area. Skopje had no significant metal-using industries before the Second World War. It has now developed a number of engineering industries, and the establishment here of an iron and steel plant, can only serve to increase their number and variety.

Chemical industries. Expansion in the chemical industries has been even more rapid than in those already considered, but its scope continued to be restricted to a relatively narrow range of basic chemicals. The manufacture of sulphuric acid, for which the domestic reserves of pyrites serve as a base, may be considered fundamental for most other branches of the industry; it rose from 23,233 tons in 1939 to 435,000 in 1965. Other basic chemicals, such as caustic soda and nitric acid showed a not dissimilar rate of increase. There is a small but steadily increasing production of paint, enamel and varnish, of glue and ink, of bleaches and cleansers: all relatively simple chemical products requiring fairly unsophisticated processes. Yet it is for such simple products that the need is greatest, especially for fertilisers, of which the country has so long been starved. The manufacture of pharmaceutical goods remains inconsiderable, though certain vaccines and insecticides, commonly used in agriculture, are produced in small quantities.

Textile and clothing industries. The textile industry of Yugoslavia has been established on a strong base in the craft industries of the South Slav villages, and domestic spinning and weaving remains of considerable, though diminishing importance in remoter areas. Factories were established in large numbers during the inter-war years, and though most of these were very small and their technique was unsophisticated, Yugoslavia was able to produce most of the common textiles needed. Yugoslavia produces a small quantity of cotton in Macedonia, probably no more than 2 per cent of the needs of its industry, and a much larger proportion of the wool required, but the greater part of the raw materials of the textile industry must be imported.

Textiles have not constituted one of the faster growing branches of industry. The structure of the industry remains much as it was before the Second World War with the addition of a few large modern factories. A number of small and relatively unspecialised mills still remain. In 1965 there were no less than 404 separate units, and their average size appears to have been considerably smaller than that of factories in most other branches of industry. At least in the smaller mills there has been little effort to distinguish between the cotton and woollen branches, and none to specialise in spinning or weaving.

The older factories are situated mainly in the north-west—especially in Slovenia and the region of Zagreb—and in Serbia. The newer tend to be established for social reasons in areas of greater poverty and overpopulation. Vrapčiči (near Mostar), Sinj (inland from Split), Štip (in Macedonia), Priština and Novi Pazar now have factories which are amongst the largest in the country. Yugoslavia had in 1965 about 850,000 cotton spindles, as against 174,000 in 1950, most of the increase having been in the small number of new factories. The number of automatic looms increased in the same period from 6,107 to about 15,000, while there was a large decline in the number of ordinary looms. The number of woollen spindles and looms is not available, and it is possible that all were reported along with those used for cotton.

Flax and hemp have long been grown in the plains of north-eastern Yugoslavia, where they are used in the manufacture of linen, rope, coarse fabrics, and carpets in a number of factories in Vojvodina. The production of the Yugoslav textile industries as a whole has risen as shown in Table 84.

Table 84. Textile production

	1948	1956	1963	1966
Cotton yarn (*thousands of tons*)	27·8	38·9	74·9	95·5
Cotton fabrics (*millions of metres*)	161	183	348	416
Woollen yarn (*thousands of tons*)	13·0	12·2	26·4	35·2
Woollen fabrics (*millions of metres*)	29	28	48	56·5

Sources: *UN Statistical Yearbooks: Statistički Godnišnjak SFRJ, 1967.*

Wood-using industries. Yugoslavia remains one of the most densely wooded countries in Europe, and its lumber-based industries are proportionately important. Out of a total cut in 1966 of over 17,000,000 cubic metres of sawn lumber about three-quarters were hardwood, with beechwood making up nearly half the total lumber. The greater part of the production of hardwoods has long been from Croatia and Bosnia, and of softwoods from Slovenia. Sawmills are very numerous; the majority are small, and a great many are powered still by the mountain streams. Both sawmills and wood-processing factories are concentrated in Slovenia, Croatia and Bosnia, which contain about two-thirds of the total.

The timber-based industries include not only the manufacture of furniture, panelling, plywood and matches, but also of wood-pulp, cellulose and paper, chiefly near Ljubljana and Zagreb, with a single large plant at Drvar, in western Bosnia. There is also a small-scale chemical industry based on the dry distillation of wood.

Food-processing industries. This group of industries has always possessed an exceptional importance in a country as heavily dependent as Yugoslavia on agriculture. Flour milling is by far the most important, and is heavily concentrated in Vojvodina and Slavonia. Sugar-processing, closely connected with the cultivation of sugar beet, is predominantly in the same region. The dairy and meat-packing industries, the preservation of fruit and vegetables, and distilling are carried on to some extent in the northern plain, but are more important to the south, where the agricultural materials on which these industries are based, are produced in greater abundance. The tobacco-based industries are geographically complementary to those just mentioned. They are carried on chiefly in the southern half of the country, with the chief centres of production in Skopje, Prilep, Niš, Sarajevo, Mostar and other cities close to the tobacco-growing area.

Industrial regions
A feature of the manufacturing industry of Yugoslavia is its extremely scattered distribution. Though certain centres of manufacturing industry stand out, one cannot speak of industrial regions in the sense in which this term is used in East Germany, Czechoslovakia or Poland. To some extent this scattering is due to the fact that many manufacturing industries have still not advanced far beyond the craft stage, and, in a country of poorly developed transport facilities, have in the past catered predominantly for local markets. To some extent, too, this geographical pattern of production arises from the scattered nature of the local raw materials and resources. This pattern of manufacturing is, however, slowly changing. Manufacturing industries still cluster round Beograd, Zagreb and Ljubljana; new industries continue to be located in the relatively highly industrialised areas of Slovenia and northern Croatia, but there is a movement of industry to regions which until recently had little. There are several motives for the government's action. Among them are strategic considerations: the need that is felt to shift the centres of industry from places close to the boundary to areas of greater security in the heart of the country. Political considerations demanded that some attempt be made to develop industry and improve the level of income and standard of welfare in the most southerly and backward provinces, where, furthermore, rural over-population and unemployment had reached serious proportions. Thus we have the expansion of old and the establishment of new industries in the valleys of Bosnia and northern Serbia, in Montenegro and in Macedonia. A change is apparent within the last few years, with the growth of industry in Nikšić and Titograd (Montenegro),

in Skopje and Prizren, and above all in the Sarajevo–Zenica region of Bosnia.

Most conspicuous of the projects to industrialise the southern half of the country is the establishment there of iron, steel and metal using industries, which are expected to provide the local base for a more varied industrial growth.

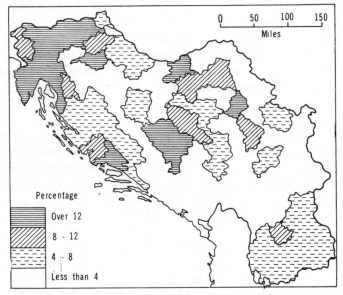

Fig. 12.14. Distribution of industry, as measured by percentage of the population engaged in manufacturing and mining. After *Geografiski Atlas Jugoslavije*, Zagreb, 1961.

Four industrial regions—*industrijski rajoni*—and six areas of smaller importance can be recognised. These are:

1. The North-western region, embracing much of Slovenia, together with northern Croatia, and including the city-regions of both Zagreb and Ljubljana.

2. The North-eastern region, including the Vojvodina, Banat, eastern Srem and northern Serbia. Its focus is Beograd, and its industrial structure somewhat less varied than that of the North-western region, with a somewhat greater emphasis on food and consumer industries.

3. The Central region, in which the current expansion appears most vigorous. Its somewhat excentric focus is Sarajevo, and it extends from

YUGOSLAVIA

Sarajevo, set amid the rolling
hills of Bosnia

Zagreb: the Trg Republike
(Square of the Republic); on a
low hill behind lies the cathedral

Skopje: the rebuilding of the
city after the earthquake of
1963. The mountains in the
distance are part of the Jakupica massif. In the middle
distance is the bridge over the
Vardar River

Split, the chief port of the central section of the Dalmatian coast

A thermal electric station, near Tuzla, Bosnia. It uses the resources of a brown-coal field, which formed here in a Tertiary basin

Grúž, the port which now serves the town of Dubrovnik. Mountains rise steeply behind it, so that its connections with its hinterland are difficult

here north-westward to include Banja Luka and Doboj. Its fuel resources are among the richest in Yugoslavia; it is already the most important centre of the iron and steel industries and several chemical and mechanical engineering factories have been established here.

4. The Eastern region, extending across central Serbia from Titovo Užice in the west to Niš and Leskovac in the east. This was the core of the former kingdom of Serbia, and as such underwent a small-scale industrial growth in the nineteenth century. Much of the investment capital of the Yugoslav state between the two world wars was, primarily for political reasons, also lavished on this area. It has today a number of engineering and some food-processing industries, but in general they are somewhat old and their average size is rather small.

The industrial areas are very much smaller both in the size and the range of their industrial activity. Six are distinguished:

1. The Koper-Pula-Rijeka industrial area, consisting essentially of the coastal strip of Istria. Its industries consist primarily of ship-building and port industries.

2. The Split-Sinj-Omiš area with a somewhat wider range of industries, including ship-building and the manufacture of cement and textiles.

3. The Bor-Zaječar-Prahovo area, important for its copper mine and for the reserves of the highest quality coal found in Yugoslavia.

4. The Kosovo-Mitrovica-Priština area in the eastern part of Kosmet, with a variety of relatively small industrial units, including textiles, chemicals and wood-based industries.

5. The Kumanovo-Skopje-Tetovo-Titov Veles area, in which industries have been based mainly on local agricultural products, but where metallurgical and chemical industries are now being developed.

6. The Bitola-Prilep area with mainly tobacco, leather and textile industries.

To these should be added a number of yet smaller centres of industrial activities, which stand alone and cannot be tied in with the industrial regions and areas. These include such places as Slavonski Brod, Mostar, Foča, and such rapidly developing industrial towns as Nikšič.

COMMUNICATIONS AND TRADE

It has been pointed out that much of Yugoslavia, until comparatively recently, was made up of rural communities which were in the main self-sufficing. While this is no longer true, there are still many areas in

24

which the volume of commerce with the outside is small and restricted to a narrow group of essential goods. In Kosmet, in parts of
the Karst region and of southern Serbia and Macedonia, the local
commercial turnover is not only small in absolute terms, but also in
relation to the population. There remains a sharp contrast between
the developed market economy of the north and north-west and the
basic self-sufficiency of much of the south and south-east.

Internal communications

Yugoslavia has never been an easy country in which to travel. Nature
itself presents formidable obstacles. The Alpine ranges of the north-
west, the Dinaric ranges which parallel the Adriatic littoral, and the
massifs of Serbia and Macedonia set barriers to human movement
which have locally at least still not been overcome. The mountains not
only constitute a large region within which movement is difficult, but
they also interpose a formidable barrier between the interior regions of
Yugoslavia and the coast. This is perhaps the most important physical
determinant of the country's economic development.

It must not be forgotten too that Yugoslavia was pieced together
less than a half century ago with fragments derived from five separate
political units: Austria, Hungary and the Ottoman Empire, together
with the Kingdoms of Serbia and Montenegro. Each had its own system
of transport and communication, ranging from the well-developed
networks of Austrian Slovenia and of parts of Hungarian Croatia, to
the virtual lack of a system in Montenegro and Turkish Macedonia.
These systems had to be knit together, a task of far greater difficulty
than those with which Poland and Czechoslovakia were faced. The
task was far from complete when the Second World War began, and
it cannot be said even now to be nearing completion.

Road system. In road construction Yugoslavia has always lagged
far behind Western Europe, and even behind much of Eastern. The
best of the roads were built as often as not, more for military than
economic needs. The network has always been most developed in
Slovenia and north-western Croatia, where the greater part of it was
built by the Austrians. Beograd became the focus of an open network
of roads before the Second World War, but in the mountains and in
Macedonia the roads were conceived in terms of animal-drawn
traffic rather than motorised.

Conditions have greatly improved in recent years. An *autoput*, or
motor road, was built from Zagreb to Beograd, replacing the poor

quality, circuitous road which formerly linked the leading cities of the country. This road has now been extended westward to Ljubljana and southward to the Greek border at Gevgelija. No less important has been a network of motor roads across the mountains to the Adriatic Sea and along the coast of the latter from Rijeka to the Albanian border. The latter has now been completed, and roads are now being improved *across* the mountains by way of the Vrbas, Bosna and Drina valleys. A motor road is also planned from Skopje, across Kosmet and the mountains of eastern Montenegro to the coast, where the present roads must rank amongst the worst in the continent of Europe. Much of Yugoslavia will remain inaccessible by automobile, but the country has recently been opened up by roads as never before.

The improvement in the roads has been paralleled by the increase in numbers of road vehicles. The number of passenger vehicles has increased about five-fold between 1946 and 1959, but that of commercial vehicles has grown somewhat more slowly.

Table 85. Numbers of road vehicles

	1938	1946	1956	1966
Motorcycles	7,661	9,992	15,586	112,318
Passenger cars	13,561	6,238	14,664	253,344
Buses	943	589	2,701	9,836
Lorries	4,286	11,385	21,112	70,111

Source: *Statistički Godišnjak FNRJ*, various years.

Railway system. The railway system of Yugoslavia was from its inception in the middle of the nineteenth century, subservient to the needs of other countries, and it was constructed in the main with outside capital. The earliest lines were built across Slovenia and north-western Croatia for the purpose of linking Vienna and Budapest with the ports at the head of the Adriatic Sea. The subsequent development of railways was in two directions: In the first place, what is now the northern plain region of Yugoslavia was in the late nineteenth century linked with the Hungarian railway system, so that its agricultural surplus could be funnelled north-westwards towards Central Europe. The second development consisted in linking Central Europe with the territory of the Ottoman Empire. There were two aspects of this development. The first, planned and initiated by the Serbs, was to link Beograd with the Aegean Sea, and then to build a line across northern Albania linking the Morava-Vardar route with the Adriatic coast. This latter line was never built. The other proposal sprang from Austrian and Turkish initiative. It consisted essentially of a plan to build a railway from Croatia, south-eastward across Bosnia to meet the Turkish boundary in the Sanjak of Novi Pazar. Thus, without

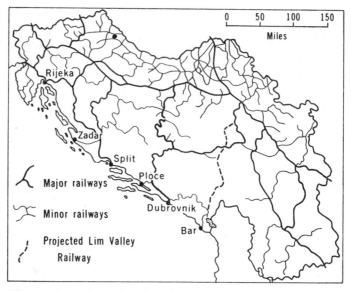

Fig. 12.15. Railways in Yugoslavia. Based on *Geografiski Atlas Jugolsavije*, Zagreb, 1961, and updated.

touching Serbian territory, it could reach the Kosovo Basin and thus Skopje, which was then in Turkish hands. The Turks built a line from Thessaloníki up the Vardar valley to Skopje, and thence to Kosovska Mitrovica, while the Austrian line reached Višegrad in the Drina valley. They were never linked together, and it is only in very recent years that the Višegrad line has been continued into Serbia. It still does not link with the Kosovo line.

The inadequacy of its railway net was felt acutely by Yugoslavia, and much effort was devoted to rebuilding some sections of the system and to constructing new links with parts of the Adriatic coast. Only the north Adriatic ports of Trieste and Fiume had adequate connections with their Yugoslav hinterland, and these were now in Italian hands. A standard gauge line—the 'Lika' railway —was built to link Zagreb and the Sava valley with the port of Split, and extensions and improvements were made to the narrow-gauge railways of the Bosnian hinterland. At the same time, improvements were made in the main line from Ljubljana to Zagreb and Beograd, and from Beograd south-eastwards towards Sofia and Istanbul, and southwards to Macedonia and Greece. In 1919 these lines began to be used by the Paris-Orient Express to Istanbul, and subsequently by its branches to Bucharest and Athens, and the improvements made in its track first put Turkey within a couple of days' travel of the western capitals.

At three points, it is true, railways from the interior did reach the Adriatic littoral. A standard-gauge but single-track line ran from Zagreb across the northern Karst to the port of Sušak, and carried most of the Yugoslav commerce that flowed through that small port. A branch from this line ran by way of the Gospič *polje* to Šibenik and Split, while a third line ran southward from Slavonski Brod, on the Sava, by way of the Sarajevo basin and the Neretva valley, to the small port of Metkovič, with a branch to Dubrovnik and the Gulf of Kotor. All three, including the Sušak line, were difficult to operate. With the exception of the former and also the 'Lika' line to Split, they were narrow gauge, and all were single-tracked. The Neretva valley railway used a rack-and-pinion device to ascend the summit which separated it from the Bosna valley. Sharp bends, steep gradients and high summit levels combined to reduce the efficiency of the railway system.

Railway-building was revived after 1945, and a plan was developed to fill in the gaps left by previous generations, and to tie the branches into a system. Difficult sections of line have been rebuilt; the Una valley railway has been carried across the Karst to join the line to Split; there has been extensive building and rebuilding along the Bosna valley, in the Sarajevo-Zenica Basin, and between Banja Luka and Tuzla, and the Neretva valley line has recently been rebuilt at the standard gauge. Indeed, a large part of the recent railway construction has been in the Central Industrial Region, which has thus been linked westward with the Croatian railways and eastward with those of the middle Drina and Ibar valleys. A number of branches and linking lines have been built in Serbia and Macedonia, but the most important work now in progress is the extension of the existing railway along the middle Drina valley both northward to Valjevo and Beograd, and southward up the valley of the Lim tributary of the Drina, and across the mountains to the valley of the Morača and so to Titograd. There it will link with the line already built from Titograd southward across the north-western arm of Lake Skadar and the hills which separate the latter from the sea and so to the new port of Bar.

The increased use of the railways has been more than proportionate to the extension of its mileage. The total volume of goods carried has increased from about 21 million tons in 1939 to about 38 in 1952 and 71·6 million in 1966. Coal is the largest single item, as it has been throughout this period, and in 1966 20·2 million tons were transported. Coal is followed by building materials, ores and concentrates, lumber and grain. Coal, however, was in most instances conveyed over relatively short distances, and in terms of ton-miles leads amongst the freights carried by a much smaller margin.

Internal navigation. Only in the north-east does internal navigation play any role in the economic life of Yugoslavia, because only here are rivers large enough and sufficiently regular in their flow to be used by shipping. The Danube itself flows for 364 miles across Yugoslavia. It is navigable throughout this distance, and is regularly used. Navigation, however, is not without its hazards and its difficulties. Floods, especially in spring and autumn, sometimes present serious dangers to shipping. From December to February the movement of boats is likely to be obstructed by ice, and in the dry period of late summer and early autumn, low water may increase the difficulties of shipping.

The obstacles presented by the Iron Gate gorges, with their rocky bed and the greatly increased speed of the current, have already been discussed (pages 651 to 653). Work has now begun on a dam below Orşova, which is expected to eliminate most of these difficulties, and is likely to be completed by 1971.

The Danubian tributaries, the Sava, Drava and Tisa, add to its problems by contributing their own flood waters, which may hold back the flow of the Danube itself. It is difficult to think of any river basin in which an overall control of discharge is more desirable than on the Danube, nor to conceive of one in which such unified control would be more difficult to achieve.[1]

The Sava is navigable from Beograd upstream to Sisak, together

---

[1] For an analysis of the most recent of the severe floods, see M. Pardé, Sandor Lang, Frédéric Probald, 'Les crues du Danube el la grande inondation de juin 1965', *Annls Géogr.*, **76** (1967), 273–287.

with the lower courses of its tributaries, the Kupa, Una and Bosna. It is planned to canalise the Sava as far upstream as Zagreb, whose industrial suburbs are spreading along the river's banks. The Drava, a very much less useful river, is navigable upstream for only 86 miles, and is, in fact, very little used above Osijek. The Tisa, by contrast, is used for the whole of its course of 101 miles through Yugoslavia, in spite of the seasonal difficulties which it presents from both high water and low.

To these navigable rivers must be added the canals that have been cut across the Bačka and Banat. Their purpose, however, was never to facilitate navigation. The oldest of them, the *Veliki Kanal*, formerly known as *Kralja Petra* (King Peter) Canal, begins near the Danube, west of Sombor, but, in fact, derives its water supply from the springs and small streams of the Hungarian Plain. It flows south-eastward, along the margin of the loess plateau of Bačka, to enter the Tisa north of Novi Sad. A branch canal, the *Mali*, or Little, *Kanal*, links it with the Danube at Novi Sad. These canals serve to drain low-lying areas after heavy rains and when the snows melt in spring, but their primary purpose is to irrigate the flood plains of the rivers in summer. The same is true of the smaller canals which fan out from the Romanian border over the plains of Banat.

It is planned however to enlarge and link up some of these waterways to form the Dunav-Tisa-Dunav canal, which will extend from the Danube, near the Hungarian border to the Danube again at Palanka, on the Romanian. This will not only shorten the river journey but is also expected to provide a more easily navigated channel than the river itself could ever offer.

The Dalmatian and Macedonian rivers are not navigable, except the last few miles of the Neretva, from Metkovič to the sea, and the Krka, which is in fact a drowned river valley, for a short distance above Šibenik. Neither is of more than slight, local importance.

The northern rivers are very much more intensively used today than before the Second World War. Traffic on the Sava remains small, and consists mainly of the movement of goods between Sisak, Slavonski Brod, and Beograd. Osijek is a port of minor importance on the Drava, and traffic on the lower Tisa is of negligible importance. Almost half the traffic on the Danube is in transit between Hungary and the lower river, and consists overwhelmingly of ores and concentrates, coal and petroleum. It is a heavily unbalanced movement, and about 85 per cent of the tonnage moves upstream.

Most of the Yugoslav commerce—about three-quarters of it—is domestic, and a surprisingly small proportion of the country's total foreign trade is carried on by way of the Danube. This is due in large measure to Yugoslavia's break with the Soviet Union and the resulting small volume of trade with the Black Sea ports.

Ocean shipping

Yugoslavia has the longest coastline of any East European country, and is by far the most richly furnished with natural harbours. Yet its seaborne commerce is one of the smallest. The reason for this paradoxical situation has already been examined. The industrialised and productive parts of the country have throughout most of its history been those farthest removed from the sea and have been cut off from the ports by the wilderness of the Dinaric mountain system. The desire to control a practicable route to the sea had become almost an obsession with the Serb politicians. First was their attempt to secure control of the Drim valley routeway of northern Albania from the Metohija Basin to the coast near Shkodër. Then, with the creation of the Yugoslav state, came the competition for Trieste and Fiume, in which Yugoslavia was worsted and obliged to content itself with the indifferent facilities of Sušak. Some compensation for this loss was provided by arrangements with the Greek government, by which the Yugoslavs obtained a free zone in the port of Thessaloníki. In 1945, however, Fiume, or Rijeka, passed at last into Yugoslav possession. Communications with other Dalmatian ports, notably Split, Dubrovnik and Bar, are being improved and Yugoslavia is attempting to create for itself an important place in the seaborne commerce of the Mediterranean.

The Dalmatian ports. The seaborne commerce of Yugoslavia is dominated by Rijeka, which handles over a half, and Split, with rather less than a quarter. Šibenik, Ploče, Dubrovnik and Pula handle very much smaller quantities of merchandise and other ports have been hitherto of negligible importance.

Rijeka lies between the steeply rising karst, the Gorski Kotar, and the shore of the island-studded Kvarner, or Quarnero Gulf. The old city lay immediately to the west of the small river, the Riječina or Fiumara, which gave its name to the city. Its growth has been along the coast, and dock facilities are today spread over a distance of almost 3 miles. The railway, upon which the port relies for its inland communications, comes in by a very difficult and twisting route which has been built across the Karst between the Gorski Kotar and Velika Kapella massifs. The port itself is used to capacity, and has little scope to expand its dock facilities or to improve its communications with its hinterland. Neighbouring bays to the east, particularly the deep, narrow Bay of Bakar, are being developed to supplement Rijeka itself.

Split, the second maritime port of Yugoslavia, lies at the head of a shallow bay, the Splitska Luka, now partially closed by the building of a jetty. The city itself grew up within the huge palace built here by the emperor Diocletian, and, in fact, replaced the older city of Salona (Solin), whose inhabitants sought refuge within the mighty walls of Diocletian from the attacks of the Avars. The city continued to grow during the Middle Ages. Legally it was part of the Byzantine Empire; in fact, it was for much of the time a quasi-independent state in close alliance with Venice, before it became part of the Venetian empire in the fifteenth century. As such it remained until, in 1797, many of the assets of this moribund empire passed into the hands of Austria.

Split was thus cut off from its Bosnian hinterland, and it was not until the early years of the present century that a railway link was completed across the mountains to the Sava valley. Its commerce did not greatly expand until the 1920s, when it found itself, after the Italian seizure of Fiume, the chief port of Yugoslavia. Its commercial importance was greatly increased when cement works were built along the shore of the Kaštelanski Zaljcv, the bay to the north-west of the city, and cement became a major item of export.

Other Adriatic ports are of very much smaller importance. Šibenik is the least inconsiderable of them. It lies, well sheltered from the sea, on the shore of the drowned estuary of the Krka. Its inland communications are no better than those of Split, and its seaward approaches far more difficult. Metkovič, 12 miles up the Neretva from the sea, had been the chief port of Hercegovina, with some parts of which it was linked by the Neretva valley railway. It is being replaced by Ploče, a small port situated on the northern margin of the Neretva delta and linked by a short branch with the main railway.

Dubrovnik, despite its illustrious history, is no longer a port of importance. Its small harbour, on the eastern edge of the old city, sufficed for the galleys of Venice, but cannot take modern ships. The harbour of Gruž, which has been developed nearly 2 miles to the north-west, is linked with the interior of the country only by a narrow-gauge railway of small capacity.

24*

Among the lesser ports of the Dalmatian coast are Pula, Pag and Zadar, along the northern part of the coast; Dugi Rat and Omiš, near Split; Zelenika and Kotor, on the shore of the Gulf of Kotor, the former being the terminus of the narrow-gauge line which runs down from Mostar, and Bar. Yugoslavia is in need of expanded port facilities, and a major question is which of the existing minor ports to develop. This has become a political issue. Most of the maritime ports are in Croatia. Nearness to the industrialising hinterland and the availability of communications would suggest Split, Šibenik or Zadar. But these are Croatian, and other republics have demanded with some success that their own outlets to the sea be enlarged and developed. The result is that investments are being made at three of the least advantageous sites: Koper, Ploče and Bar.

Koper, the former Capodistria, is Slovenia's maritime outlet, though at present it has no railway and only a poor harbour. It is destined to be a port for the rapid handling of tropical and perishable goods, and it is hoped that it will console the Slovenes for their failure to gain possession of Trieste. With Italian Trieste and Croatian Pula nearby, it is not needed, and it is being built for political rather than economic reasons.

Ploče is in Croatia, but only a short distance inland lies the boundary of Hercegovina and beyond it is Bosnia, and its development as a port is calculated to benefit these latter rather than Croatia. Its present development as a major port for handling bulk cargoes, especially iron-ore and coal, with the complementary rebuilding of the Neretva valley railway to Sarajevo and the Sava valley, is essentially a Bosnian project. It has been argued that Split could have been developed at a much smaller cost; but that would be to the advantage of Croatia, rather than of Bosnia.

The third port to be developed, and by far the most costly, is Bar. This development is, in fact, a revived and revised version of the Metohija-Drim valley outlet to the sea which Serbia aspired to open up at the beginning of the present century. Bar is one of the most southerly settlements of Yugoslavia. It lies 15 miles from the Albania border, and is separated from Lake Skadar by the high, rugged limestone massif of Rumija. Bar is in Montenegro, and it is the nearest possible Adriatic port site to Serbia. A standard gauge railway has been built across the mountains from Titograd, and the Drina-Lim-Morača railway from the Sava valley (see above, page 722) is under construction with help from the World Bank. There are good political reasons for giving the Montenegrins their own port, and the Serbs would like to have access to a port without the obligation of crossing Croat territory. But the project is an expensive one and its estimated completion date has been postponed until 1970. It has even been suggested that Bar may in the end prove to be nothing more than a small port serving the Nikšić-Titograd industrial area.

Foreign trade
Only a relatively small part of Yugoslavia's foreign trade is through its maritime ports. A small part is handled by the river ports, but the greater part is transported by rail and road. The foreign trade of Yugoslavia is carried on with a greater range of trading partners than that of other countries of Eastern Europe. This results from the ambiguous political situation in which Yugoslavia has found itself since 1948, Communist in ideology, but divorced from the Communist bloc. The direction of her foreign trade has fluctuated greatly. Trade with the non-Communist world has predominated, but periods of rapprochement have punctuated the general hostility which has existed between Yugoslavia and the bloc. In recent years trade with Eastern Europe in general has tended to be small; in 1965 it was again increasing in volume, but one cannot predict that this new situation will have any greater permanence than similar changes have had in the past. Nevertheless, Europe, both East and West, has always accounted for by far the greater part

Table 86. Yugoslavia's foreign trade—by countries
(in millions of old dinars)

	Exports		Imports	
	1964	*1965*	*1964*	*1965*
Asia	11	9	8	8
Africa	6	6	5	5
East Europe	26	41	28	29
West Europe	46	35	44	40
North America	7	8	11	15
South America	4	1	4	3
	100	100	100	100

Source: *UN Yearbook of International Trade Statistics, 1965.*

of Yugoslavia's foreign trade. In 1965, it took 76 per cent of Yugoslavia's exports and provided 68 per cent of imports. Foremost in recent years among the European trading partners have been Italy, West Germany, the Soviet Union, the United Kingdom, East Germany, France and Czechoslovakia. Their role has been primarily that of supplier of manufactured goods and of capital goods for industrial development. The regional breakdown of Yugoslavia's trade in recent months has been as Table 86 shows.

Table 87 shows that the volume of trade has increased very sharply.

Table 87. Increases in volume of trade
(in millions of old dinars)

	Imports	Exports
1939	4,751	5,521
1950	11,790	7,930
1956	142,243	97,011
1963	316,985	237,103
1965	386,385	327,452

Source: *UN Yearbook of International Trade Statistics, 1965.*

Even when allowance is made for the devaluation of 1951, when the value of the dinar was cut to a sixth, and for continuing inflation, this nevertheless remains a quite spectacular rate of increase. Trade, as is inevitable in a developing country, is unbalanced, with imports exceeding exports by about a third. This is compensated for by loans which include the very considerable investment now being made by the World Bank in Yugoslav railways.

Yugoslavia is a net exporter of foodstuffs and tobacco, of lumber, non-ferrous ores and concentrates, and of light manufactured goods, such as furniture and footwear. Imports are dominated by machinery, transport equipment and other manufactured goods. Foodstuffs, primarily bread grains, are an important but fluctuating item of import trade, as also are fuels, particularly petroleum. The nature and volume of Yugoslavia's foreign trade in 1965, according to the United Nations classification is as shown in Table 88.

Table 88. Yugoslavia's foreign trade—by commodity
(*in millions of old dinars*)

	Imports	Exports
0 Food	56,840·4	69,404·5
1 Beverages, tobacco	165·7	14,670·8
2 Crude materials	65,103·4	33,100·3
3 Mineral fuels, lubricants	21,585·9	3,214·9
4 Animal and vegetable fats	4,013·5	148·1
5 Chemicals	35,504·2	17,882·9
6 Manufactured goods	83,254·1	74,293·8
7 Machinery and transport equipment	106,958·0	77,023·0
8 Miscellaneous manufactured goods	13,017·5	37,544·9
9 Other commodities and transactions	108·2	119·1
	386,550·9	327,402·3

Source: *UN Yearbook of International Trade Statistics*, 1965.

Certain changes can be anticipated in this pattern of trade. It is hoped, by improving agricultural production, to cut down on the imports of bread crops; the very considerable developments now taking place in the chemical industries should greatly reduce the chemical imports, among which agricultural fertilisers are very prominent. On the other hand, the import of machinery and of capital goods may increase rather than diminish. Among exports there is a strong tendency for the export of manufactured goods, especially light metal goods, footwear and wood products, to increase, as Yugoslavia's manufacturing industries expand and begin production for export.

Bibliography
General
BLANC, ANDRÉ, *La Croatie Occidentale*, Paris, 1957.

BROWN, ALEC, *Yugoslav Life and Landscape*, London, Elek Books, 1954.

BYRNES, ROBERT F. *Yugoslavia*, East Central Europe under the Communists, New York, Praeger 1957.

FISHER, JACK C. *Yugoslavia-A Multinational State: Regional Difference and Political Response*, San Francisco, Chandler Publishing Co., 1966.

HOFFMAN, GEORGE W. and FRED W. NEAL, *Yugoslavia and the New Communism*, New York, Twentieth Century Fund, 1962.

MARKERT, WERNER, *Jugoslavien*, Osteuropa-Handbuch, Koln, 1954.

MILOJEVIČ, B. Ž. La Yougoslavie: *Aperçu Géographique*, Beograd, 1956.

Literary works which give insights into geographical and social conditions in Yugoslavia are:

ADAMIC, LOUIS, *The Native's Return*, Gollancz, London, 1934.

ANDRIČ, IVO, *Bosnian Story*, London, Lincoln 1959.

— *The Bridge on the Drina*, London, Allen & Unwin, 1959.

WEST, REBECCA, *Black Lamb and Grey Falcon*, 2 vols., London, Macmillan, 1942.

Historical and Political Geography

ANCEL, JACQUES, *La Macédoine*, Paris, 1930.

— *Peuples et Nations des Balkans*, Paris, Colin, 1926.

AUTY, PHILLIS, *Yugoslavia*, London, Weidenfeld & Nicolson, 1962.

Croatia: Land, People, Culture, ed. F. H. Eterovich and C. Spalatin, 2 vols., Univ. Toronto P., 1964.

FRANKEL, J. 'Federation in Yugoslavia', *American Political Science Review*, **49** (1955), 416–30.

MACARTNEY, C. A. *Hungary and Her Successors*, Oxford University Press, 1937.

MOODIE, A. E. *The Italo-Yugoslav Boundary*, London, G. Philip, 1945.

STEWART, CECIL, *Serbian Legacy*, London, Allen & Unwin, 1959.

VUCINICH, WAYNE S. *Serbia Between East and West: The Events of 1903–1908*, Stanford University Press, 1954.

WILKINSON, H. R. *Maps and Politics: A Review of Ethnographic Cartography of Macedonia*, Liverpool University Press, 1951.

— 'Jugoslav Macedonia in Transition', *Geogrl J.*, **118** (1952), 389–405.

— 'Jugoslav Kosmet: the Evolution of a Frontier Province and its Landscape', *Trans. Inst. Br. Geogr.* No. 21 (1955), 171–93.

— 'Perspective on Some Fundamental Regional Divisions in Yugoslav Illyria, *Liverpool Essays in Geography*, ed. R. W. Steel and R. Lawton, London. 1967.

Physical Geography

ADAMOVIC, L. 'Die Verbreitung der Holzgewächse in den dinarischen Ländern', *Abh. K.K. geogr. Ges. Wien*, **10**, No. 3 (1913).

BAULIG, H, 'Le littoral Dalmate', *Annls Géogr.*, **39** (1930), 305–10.

CHOLLEY, A. and G. CHABOT, 'Notes de morphologie Karstique du polje de Lika au Popovo', *Annls Géogr.*, **39** (1930), 270–85.

Die Donau als Grossschiffahrtsstrasse, Wirtschaftskammer Wien, Vienna, 1941.

HASLUCK, MARGARET, 'A Historical Sketch of the Fluctuations of Lake Ostrovo in West Macedonia', *Geogrl J.*, **87** (1936), 338–47.

— 'The Archaeological History of Lake Ostrovo in West Macedonia', *Geogl J.*, **87** (1936), 448–56.

— 'Causes of the Fluctuations of Lake Ostrovo, West Macedonia', *Geogl J.*, **90** (1937), 446–57.

MILOJEVIČ, BORIVOJÉ Ž. 'Les types de relief exhumé en Yougoslavie', *Annls Géogr.*, **64** (1955), 170–6.

— 'Les plateaux de loess et les régions de sable de Yougoslavie', *Mem. Soc. Serbe de Geogr.*, **6**, 1950.

— *La Yougoslavie: Aperçu Géographique*, Beograd (1956).

SANDERS, E. M. 'The Cycle of Erosion in a Karst Region (after Cvijić)', *Geogrl Rev.*, **11** (1921), 593–604.

SORRE, MAX. 'Les aspects de la vegetation et des sols en Yougoslavie', *Annls Géogr.*, **39** (1930), 311–16.

OGILVIE, ALAN G. 'A Contribution to the Geography of Macedonia', *Geogrl J.*, **55** (1920), 1–34.

Population and Settlement

ARBOS, PHILIPPE, 'Skoplje', *Annls Géogr.*, **39** (1930), 324–8.

BLANC, ANDRÉ, 'Structure Sociale en Yougoslavie', *Annls Géogr.*, **60** (1951), 149–50.

— *La Croatie Occidentale: Étude de Géographie Humaine*, Paris, Institut d' Études Slaves, 1957.

CASTELLAN, G. 'Elements d'une Sociologie religieuse en Yougoslavie Socialiste, *Annales ESC.* **14** (1959) 694–709.

COMBS, JERRY W. 'Demographic Changes in Eastern Europe', in *Population Trends in Eastern Europe, the USSR and Mainland China*, New York, Milbank Remorial Fund, 1960.

CORNISH, VAUGHAN, 'Bosnia, the Borderland of Serb and Croat', *Geography*, **20** (1935), 260–70.

DURHAM, M. E. *Some Tribal Origins, Laws, and Customs of the Balkans*, London, Allen & Unwin, 1928.

FISHER, JACK C. 'Urban Analysis: A Case Study of Zagreb, Yugoslavia', *Ann. Ass. Am. Geogr.*, **53** (1963), 255–84.

HALPERN, JOEL MARTIN, *A Serbian Village*, Oxford University Press, 1958.

KARGER, ADOLF, 'Die Entwicklung der Siedlungen im westlichen Slawonien', *Kölner Geographische Arbeiten*, Heft 15, Wiesbaden, 1963.

LEBON, J. H. G. 'The Jezera: a Mountain Community in south-west Yugoslavia', *Geography*, **20** (1935), 271–82.

LODGE, OLIVE, *Peasant Life in Yugoslavia*, London, Seeley Service, 1942.

— 'Villages and Houses in Yugoslavia', *Geography*, **21** (1936), 94–106.

MILOJEVIČ, BORIVOJE, 'Types of Villages and Village-houses in Yugoslavia', *Prof. Geogr.*, **5** (1953), No. 6, 13–17.

LEFEVRE, M. A. 'La Zadruga: forme de propriété collective de type patriarcal,' *Annls Géogr.*, **39** (1930), 316–20.

LARNAUDE, MARCEL, 'Un village de colonisation en Serbie du Sud', *Annls Géogr.*, **39** (1930), 320–4.

'La population urbaine en Yougoslavie', *Annls Géogr.* **60** (1951), 148–9.

MOSELY, PHILIP E., 'The Distribution of the Zadruga within South-eastern Europe', *The Joshua Starr Memorial Volume, Jewish Social Science Studies*, Publication No. 5, New York, 1953, 219–30.

MÜLLER, JOSEF, *Syrmien: Slawonien-Bosnien*, Munich (1961).

SHOUP, P. 'Yugoslavia's National Minorities under Communism', *Slavic Review*, **22** (1963), 64–81.

Yugoslavia, European Conference on Rural Life, League of Nations, Geneva, 1939.

The Population of Yugoslavia, Washington, DC, US Department of Commerce, 1954.

SAVORY, H. J. 'Settlement in the Glamočko Polje', *Geogrl J.*, **124** (1958), 41–55.

TROUTON, RUTH, *Peasant Renaissance in Yugoslavia, 1900–1950*, Routledge & Kegan Paul, London, 1952.

WALLIS, B. C. 'The Slavs of Southern Hungary', *Geogrl Rev.*, **6** (1918), 341–53.

WILKINSON, H. R. 'Jugoslav Kosmet: the Evolution of a Frontier Province and its Landscape', *Trans. Inst. Br. Geogr.*, **21** (1955), 171–93.

— 'Yugoslav Macedonia in Transition', *Geogrl J.*, **118** (1952), 389–405.

WILKINSON, H. R. '*Maps and Politics: a Review of the Ethnogeographic Cartography of Macedonia*', Liverpool University Press, 1957.

Economic Geography

AVSENEK, IVAN, *The Iron and Steel Industry in Yugoslavia 1939–1953*, New York, Mid-European Studies Center, 1953.
— *Yugoslav Metallurgical Industries*, New York, Mid-European Studies Center, 1955.

BEAVER, S. H. 'Railways in the Balkan Peninsula', *Geogrl J.*, 97 (1941) 273–94.

BLAŠKOWIC, VLADIMIR, *Ekonomska Geografija Yugoslavije*, Zagreb, 1962.

BRASHICH, RANKO M. *Land Reform and Ownership in Yugoslavia, 1919–1953*, New York, Mid-European Studies Center, 1954.

CAESAR, A. A. L. 'Yugoslavia: Geography and Post-war Planning', *Trans. Inst. Br. Geogr.* No. 30 (1962), 33–43.

CVITANOVIČ, ALFONSO, *Na Dunavu*, Širom svijeta, Zagreb, 1961.

DEDIJER, J. 'La transhumance dans les pays dinariques', *Annls Géogr.*, 25 (1916), 347–65.

HAMILTON, F. E. I. 'Yugoslavia's Hydro-electric Power Industry', *Geography*, 48 (1963), 70–3.
— 'The Changing Pattern of Yugoslavia's Manufacturing Industry', *Tijdschr. econ. soc. Geogr.*, 54 (1963), 96–106.
— 'Location Factors in the Yugoslav Iron and Steel Industry', *Econ. Geogr.*, 40 (1964), 46–64.
— *Yugoslavia: Patterns of Economic Activity* (1968) London, Bell.

HOFFMAN, GEORGE W. 'Changes in the Agricultural Geography of Yugoslavia', *Geographical Essays on Eastern Europe*, ed. N. J. G. Pounds, Indiana University Press, 1961.
— 'Yugoslavia in Transition: Industrial Expansion and Resource Bases', *Econ. Geogr.*, 32 (1956), 294–315.
— 'Changing Character of Rural Life and Rural Economy', *American Slavic and East European Review*, 18 (1959), 555–78.
— 'The Problem of the Underdeveloped Regions in Southeast Europe: A Comparative Analysis of Romania, Yugoslavia and Greece', *AAAG*, 57 (1967), 637–66.

ILEŠIČ, SVETOZAR, 'Les problémes du paysage rural en Yougoslavie nord-occidentale, et spécialement en Slovénie', *Géographie et Histoire Agraire, Annales de l'Est*, Memoire 21, Nancy, 1959.

ISNARD, H., 'La culture de la vigne dans la Fruška Gora,' *Annls géogr.*, **67** (1958), 404–29.

Land Utilization in East-Central Europe: Case Studies, Geographia Polonica, **6** (1965).

MACESICH, GEORGE, *Yugoslavia: The Theory and Practice of Development Planning*, University of Virginia Press, 1965.

MELLEN, MELRAD and VICTOR H. WINSTON, *The Coal Resources of Yugoslavia*, New York, Mid-European Studies Center, 1956.

MALOVRH, CENE, 'Die Bodenfragmentation als betriebsformende Kraft der Kleinbauerlichen Betriebe. Beispiele aus dem slowenischen Alpenvorland', *Festschrift Leopold G. Scheidl zum* **60**. Geburtztag, Vienna, 1965, 257–67.

PETROVIČ, RUDE and RADE M. PEROVIĆ, *Ekonomska Geografija Jugoslavije*, Beograd, 1958.

Statistički Godišnjak SFRJ, annually, Beograd.

SUGAR, PETER F. *Industrialization of Bosnia-Hercegovina*, University of Washington Press, 1964.

TOMASEICH, JOZO, *Peasants, Politics, and Economic Change in Yugoslavia*, Oxford University Press, 1955.

TROUTON, RUTH, *Peasant Renaissance in Yugoslavia, 1900–1950*, London, Routledge & Kegan Paul, 1952.

ROGIĆ, VELJKO and STANKO ŽULJIĆ, *Geografija Jugoslavije*, Zagreb, 1961.

RUNGALDIER, RANDOLF, 'Der Fremdenverkehr in Jugoslavien', *Festschrift Leopold G. Scheidl zum* **70**. Geburtstag, Vienna 1965, 307–27.

RUSINOW, DENNISON I. 'Ports and Politics in Yugoslavia', *American Universities Field Staff Reports Service: South-East Europe Series*, **11**, No. 3 (1964).

WANK, SOLOMON, 'Aehrenthal and the Sanjak of Novibazar Railway Project,' *Slavic and East European Review*, **42** (1963), 353–69.

'Die wirtschaftliche Bedeutung und Entwicklung der Donauschiffahrt', *Monatsberichte des Osterreichischen Institutes fur Wirtschaftsferschung*, **35** (1962), Beilage No. 72.

CHAPTER THIRTEEN

Bulgaria

The fortunes of Bulgaria have been closely linked with those of Romania. Both countries lie to the east of the Balkan peninsula. Both became a battleground of Russian and Turk and were occupied for varying periods of time by the armies of both. But whereas Romania has been protected by distance from the worst excesses of Turkish rule, Bulgaria experienced very much more profoundly the oppressive and unenlightened rule of the Ottoman Turks, and tended to look upon Russia as its friend and saviour.

THE BULGARIAN STATE

An earlier chapter has reviewed the fortunes of the Bulgarian 'Empire' during the Middle Ages and its ultimate overthrow at the hands of the Ottoman Turks during the last years of the fourteenth century. For over 500 years the Bulgars lived under Turkish rule, made all the more oppressive by their close proximity to its centre in Constantinople. Every time the Ottoman government fought a military campaign in Europe the Bulgars suffered. They lived right in the path of the Turkish armies, which were rarely fastidious in distinguishing friend from foe. Throughout this period the Bulgars were exploited by Turkish landowners and tax-gatherers, and as Turkish authority declined, the latter became more cruel and capricious.

In the absence of a middle class the leaders in the modern development of nationalism in Eastern Europe had in general been the priests. But the Orthodox Bulgars were subject to the Patriarch of Constantinople who was a Greek. Most of the bishops and religious leaders were also Greek, and few Bulgars entered the Orthodox priesthood. A result was that the intelligentsia was in general Greek-speaking, despising the Bulgar *patois*, and doing nothing to advance national feeling among the Bulgars themselves. Furthermore the Orthodox priests were often as corrupt and callous as any Turkish *bey*.

The Bulgars thus had a double yoke to cast off, religious and political.

The Exarchate. In spite, however, of the attitudes of the Greek bishops who dominated the Patriarchate, it was among the few Bulgars in the Church's hierarchy that the national movement took root. In 1762 a Bulgarian monk, Paisi, wrote a history of the Bulgars, which, though not printed for nearly a century, came to be widely copied. It was naively and crudely written in a Bulgarian language which had not taken on its present literary forms. It was therefore all the more calculated to appeal to this uneducated and still primitive peasant people. Paisi's work was continued by other Bulgarian priests and in 1870, just over a century after Paisi's history was written, a Bulgarian exarchate was established by the Turkish government within the Orthodox Church.

This act of the Sultan, who was under pressure from the Russian Tsar, created a national leader of the Orthodox Church in Bulgaria and removed it from the direct jurisdiction of the Greek Patriarch. Furthermore, the Sultan empowered the exarch to extend his jurisdiction into any area where the population expressed their desire for it by a two-thirds majority. The Turks were tolerant in religious matters; what they did not recognise was that religious nationalism would stimulate political, and that the Greek Patriarch had in effect been a buttress of Turkish rule.

Great Bulgaria. It was, however, the ineptitude of the Turks themselves that led directly to the overthrow of their rule in Bulgaria. There had been sporadic risings against Turkish rule during the earlier years of the nineteenth century, but in 1876 risings were more widespread and more carefully organised than in previous years. The Turks replied with the 'Bulgarian Atrocities', on a scale so hideous that they aroused the indignation of the Western Powers, which were not easily stirred on such matters.

Russian arms, however, proved more effective than Gladstone's oratory. Despite the protests of the Great Powers, the Turkish government appeared willing to make only token reforms. Russia, where sympathy with the Bulgars was strongest, posed as the protector of all the southern Slavs and declared war on Turkey in April 1877. Russian armies crossed Romania and the Danube, seized the Šipka Pass, the chief crossing of the central Balkan Range, and, after a long siege, reduced the Turkish fortress of Plevna (Pleven), which lay between the Balkan Mountains and the Danube. They advanced almost to within sight of Constantinople, and there imposed upon the Ottoman government the Treaty of San Stefano. Along with other conditions which related to Bosnia, Hercegovina and Turkish Armenia (see page 93), were those which established a Bulgarian state. Dobrogea was ceded to Romania, but in other directions the Bulgars were treated generously (Fig. 4.1a). The Bulgarian state was to extend from the Danube southwards to the coast of Thrace and Macedonia, and from the Black Sea westwards to Lake Ohrid and the upper Drim. It cut Turkey-in-Europe off from the fragmentary remains of the Turkish Empire in Bosnia, Old Serbia, Albania and Greece. It lay in the way of Serbia's territorial aspirations; it violated agreements given by the Russians to Austria, and it brought the territory of what was confidently believed to be a Russian puppet to the shores of the Mediterranean Sea. There was precedent for 'San Stefano' Bulgaria in both the First and Second Bulgarian Empires of the Middle Ages, but there was no contemporary justification. If one admits that Bulgaria had a legitimate ethnic claim to some part of Macedonia, these claims could not fairly be made to extend into Albania and to the coast of Thrace. A British fleet sailed to the Sea of Marmara to protect, if necessary, the feeble and despotic rule of the Sultans, and Queen Victoria herself demanded that the Russians be given 'such a beating' that they would relinquish their plans. Fortunately, the Russians were ready to compromise; Bismarck offered his services as an 'honest broker', and at the Congress of Berlin (June–July 1878), the honour of all parties was satisfied, except that of the Turks, who were presumably expected to count themselves fortunate in being allowed to remain in Europe at all.

Bulgaria was cut down to a size that could offend neither Austria, nor Great Britain, nor even Serbia. It consisted of the platform between the Balkan Mountains and the Danube, extending from the Timok river in the west (see page 619) to the Black Sea. It excluded the Dobrogea, north of the Silistra–Mangalia line, to which the Bulgars had some ethnic claim, but in the west it extended south of the Balkan Mountains to include the Sofia basin, the headwaters of the Struma and the north-western extremity of the Rhodope Massif. The Marica valley, with its predominantly Bulgarian population and considerable agricultural wealth, was constituted the province of Eastern Rumelia within the Ottoman Empire, but it was to have a Christian governor, and some degree of autonomy, and was to enjoy the protection of the Powers.

The fiction of Turkish sovereignty over Bulgaria itself was maintained, but the sovereignty and independence of both Serbia and Montenegro was proclaimed. We have already seen (page 93) how Austria was allowed to occupy Bosnia and Hercegovina, and Serbia to extend her territory southward up the Morava valley.

The Bulgarian Kingdom. During the following years Russian influence remained strong in Bulgaria, while at the same time the Bulgarian people began to display an intense feeling of nationalism. This showed itself in a growing hostilty to the Russians, who were prominent in the Bulgarian army and had begun a kind of economic imperialism in the country. The Prince of Bulgaria, a German named Alexander of Battenberg, who had been the choice of the Russian Tsar for the position, had, after adopting a variety of political attitudes, come down on the side of the liberal nationalists, thus earning the displeasure of the illiberal Tsar.

It was at this moment (September 1885) that a revolution, inspired by Bulgarian nationalism, erupted in Eastern Rumelia. The nationalists formed a provisional government, which announced its adhesion to Bulgaria. The Russians did not object strongly to this extension of Bulgaria: they could hardly do so in view of their policy at San Stefano, only eight years earlier. But they opposed this increase in the extent and the power of Bulgaria as long as it was under the rule of Alexander, whose policies they disliked and distrusted. At this moment Bulgaria was attacked by the Serbs, fearful that any expansion of the territory of Bulgaria would prejudice their own plans for aggrandisement. Unexpectedly the Bulgarians were completely victorious, and the Serbs were thrown back. After this show of strength there could be no question of forcing Bulgaria to give up Eastern Rumelia. Instead, the Russians eliminated Alexander, who was kidnapped and forced to abdicate.

After a short interregnum Ferdinand of Saxe-Coburg was chosen to be prince of Bulgaria. His reign, which lasted from 1887 until 1918, was marked by stability and some small economic growth. The Bulgars were fearful of again falling under Russian control, and relations were strained for much of the period. It was perhaps to be expected that Bulgaria, alone among the Balkan states, would find itself at the outbreak of the First World War in alliance with the Central Powers and at war with Russia, but for this the Balkan Wars were to form a prelude and to set the scene.

The Balkan wars. The union of Bulgaria and Eastern Rumelia in

1885 had not exhausted the territorial ambitions of the Bulgarians. They were not unmindful of the extent of the medieval Bulgarian empires, and the abortive San Stefano Treaty had served only to whet their appetite for expansion. In particular, they had set their sights on Macedonia. In this region of ethnic confusion the largest group was at this time generally considered by western Europeans to be Bulgarian.[1] This opinion together with the claims of the Bulgarian government—appeared to be vindicated by the fact that the authority of the Bulgarian exarch was being extended into Macedonia with the consent of the Turks and a two-thirds majority of each of the local communities. Macedonia itself was in ferment. Turkish rule was corrupt, cruel and inefficient. Revolutionary Macedonian organisations, notably the notorious IMRO,[2] were formed and conducted a campaign of terror directed against not only the Turks, but also ethnic groups which did not share their views. Public opinion in Bulgaria clearly favoured the aspirations of the Macedonians, whom it regarded as 'separated' Bulgars. The Bulgarian government was of necessity rather more discreet, but it too clearly favoured the ends of the revolutionaries.

These activities, however, aroused the fears of the Greeks and Serbs. The former hoped to extend the boundaries of Greece to include southern Macedonia and the port-city of Thessaloníki. The Serbs, it has been seen (page 94) had their own plans for expansion toward the Aegean, and these were clearly incompatible with the ambitions of Bulgaria. The working out of this drama in Macedonia and Thrace was interlinked both with the rivalries and ambitions of the Great Powers and with the attempts at reform within the Turkish Empire. The Young Turk movement was particularly active among the army officers stationed in Macedonia, where they had abundant opportunity to witness the political weaknesses of Ottoman rule. The revolution of the Young Turks in 1908 brought about the deposition of Sultan Abdul Hamid and led to their seizure—at least temporarily—of the reins of power. These events provoked a powerful reaction in both Austria–Hungary and in the Balkan states. Austria later the same year assumed sovereignty over Bosnia and Hercegovina (see page 93); Serbia and Bulgaria, in the face of a threat from the

[1] H. R. Wilkinson, *Maps and Politics: A Review of the Ethnographic Cartography of Macedonia*, Liverpool, 1951.

[2] The *Internal Macedonian Revolutionary Organisation*, to be distinguished from the external.

Turks, prepared to forget their differences and to combine with other Balkan countries against the common enemy, the Turk.

The Balkan League was slow in taking shape, and it was not until 1912 that a series of agreements was concluded between Bulgaria, Serbia, Montenegro and Greece. The terms of the alliance called for a joint attack on the Turks and arranged, in the event of its being successful, for the division of spoils among the allies. The attack, which came in the autumn of 1912, achieved its objects; Turkish strong points were overrun and the Turkish armies driven back almost to the outskirts of Constantinople. But it was only an alliance of convenience, and quarrels over the division of the spoils, which many had confidently anticipated when the war began, very soon led to its breakup.

As was to be expected, the chief bone of contention was Macedonia. This disputed province had been largely occupied by the Serbs and Greeks, while the main Bulgarian army had borne the brunt of the fighting in the advance towards Constantinople. The Bulgarians felt that their territorial rewards bore little relation to their efforts in the war. Their obvious discontent in turn made the Serbs and Greeks more wary in their dealings with the Bulgars, until in the summer of 1913 war again broke out in Macedonia.

The Second Balkan War was short and humiliating for the Bulgars who had, not without some provocation, begun it. The Montenegrins joined in with the Serbs; the Turks again took up arms and regained part of the territory, including the city of Edirne (Adrianople) which they had lost the previous year, and the Romanians, who had not been involved in the First Balkan War, also joined for the purpose of gaining Southern Dobrogea (see page 95). The result was the complete defeat of the Bulgarian armies, and the conclusion of the Treaty of Bucharest (August 1913). Bulgaria lost, in addition to Southern Dobrogea, much of the territory which her armies had helped to subdue the previous year, but her territory remained nevertheless larger by about 29 per cent than it had been before the Balkan wars began.

The World Wars. Bulgaria had gained from the Ottoman Empire a small triangular area of land on the Black Sea coast to the south of Varna, and a much more extensive area along the northern shore of the Aegean Sea. This included Eastern Thrace, the southern flanks of the Rhodope Massif, the Pirin Mountains, the middle valley of the Struma, and the small Strumica 'salient'. Despite these gains, however, Bulgaria felt 'sore, injured and despoiled of what she believed belonged to her'. She awaited the opportunity to regain what had been taken from her, and was prepared to make any alliance to further this end. Her opportunity came soon afterwards in the First World War. Her choice of sides was never in doubt; unquestionably she was against Serbia and Greece, two of the countries which had humiliated her, and on the side of the Central Powers, and with the latter she again suffered defeat in 1918.

Again Bulgaria lost territory, and was reduced to an irreducible minimum of unquestionably Bulgarian territory. Bulgaria was as harshly dealt with as Hungary. She lost eastern Thrace, and with it both the small port of Alexandroupolis (Dedeagach) and her access to the Aegean Sea; a small area in the Rhodope, and along her western boundary the four projecting lobes of territory which were taken by Yugoslavia (see Fig. 12.1a). Bulgaria still remained appreciably larger than before the First Balkan War, and even more hostile to the neighbours who had again despoiled her.

The attempts of the Stambolijski government (1919–23) to achieve a *modus vivendi* with Bulgaria's neighbours failed, largely because Bulgarian extremists, including the terrorist IMRO, would not let it succeed. Stambolijski was murdered by the extremists, and Bulgarian policy, in the hands of the governments which succeeded him, became intransigent in the extreme. So awkward a neighbour did Bulgaria become that in 1934 her neighbours, Romania, Yugoslavia, Greece and Turkey joined in forming the Balkan Pact, whose avowed object was to help one another to resist the irredentist ambitions of Bulgaria. But no state could live for long in conditions of such open hostility with almost all its neighbours. A year or two later the Bulgarian government succeeded in suppressing the activities of the IMRO within its own borders and made some progress in improving relations with Yugoslavia.

The estrangement of Bulgaria from her neighbours was far from ended when the Second World War began. Her course in siding with Germany was, like that of Hungary, dictated by her overriding desire to regain her lost territories. Her role in the war was, however, a minor one. Her armies assisted the Germans in their invasion and occupation of Yugoslavia and Greece, and she was rewarded with much of Macedonia and Thrace. Bulgaria took no part, however, in the Russian campaigns, and it is doubtful, indeed, whether the Bulgars could have been induced to fight against their traditional friend and protector, Russia. The attempt was never made. Bulgaria remained at peace with the Soviet Union and was the least belligerent of the Axis allies; her fighting was largely against Tito's Partisans in the mountains of Macedonia.

The invasion of Romania by the Red Army was quickly followed by change in Bulgaria. A new government broke with Germany, and soon afterwards declared war on its former ally. The Yugoslav and Greek territories, which had been occupied, were evacuated, and in the Treaty of Paris of February 1947, the boundaries existing before the war were confirmed. Bulgaria lost no more territory as a result of her participation in the Second World War, but after it was over she was no nearer to realising her ambition to annex Macedonia and to establish her own outlet to the Aegean Sea.

LANDFORM REGIONS

Bulgaria, within the boundaries established by the Treaty of Neuilly, is comprised of four major landform regions, all of which are in some degree extensions of regions already met with in Romania or Yugoslavia. A fifth, the plain of eastern Thrace between the Rhodope Mountains and the Aegean Sea, was lost at the end of the First World War. The four that remain lie from west to east as narrow belts of strongly contrasted territory. In the north is the low Bulgarian or Danubian platform, paralleling the Walachian Plain of Romania, though differing from it sharply in the detail of its surface. To the south lie the Balkan Mountains (Stara Planina) and Middle Mountains (Sredna Gora), a complex range of young folded mountains which continues the sinuous course of the Carpathian Mountains and the ranges of north-eastern Serbia. South of the Balkan Mountains lies a series of basins and depressions. Towards the west, the Nišava valley of Yugoslavia is continued in the Sofia Basin. The hills of the Sredna Gora bound this latter, but are in fact dissected by the valleys of the Upper Marica and its tributaries and interpose no great barrier between the Sofia region and the plain of the middle Marica and Tundža rivers. This plain, interrupted only by low and generally isolated hill masses, extends to the Black Sea coast. The fourth region is the most mountainous, and consists of the high, planated surfaces of the Rhodope and related mountain massifs, built mainly of hard, crystalline or intrusive rocks.

This alignment of the major relief forms has had the effect of canalising movement along the belt of lowland between the **Balkan** Mountains and the Rhodope Massif. The latter has always presented a serious barrier to human movement, and the Balkan range, though by no means high, and broken by a large number of passes, has also greatly reduced movement between the northern and the central plains. From Roman times until the present the major axis of the Bulgarian region has followed the Marica valley, the Sofia Basin and the Nišava valley. Along it, from classical times to modern, have been found the

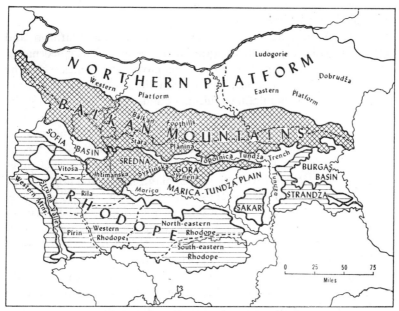

Fig. 13.1. Landform regions of Bulgaria.

largest and most prosperous cities: the ports of the Black Sea littoral; Adrianople, now the Turkish city of Edirne, Plovdiv (Philippopolis), Sofia and, beyond the Yugoslav boundary, Niš.

The other major lowland region, the Danubian platform, has always been more isolated from the civilising influences which emanated from the Aegean and Marmara regions, and has, at the same time been more exposed to those from the Russian steppe. It was here that the first Bulgar invaders settled in the seventh century. Here lay their earliest capital, Pliska, and the eastern part of this region formed the cradle of the Bulgarian nation. But the early Bulgars quickly merged with the Slavs, absorbed elements of Byzantine culture, and extended their culture and their authority far to the south and south-west. The centre of gravity of the Bulgarian nation and state was shifted to the Marica valley and Sofia Basin, and parts of the original Bulgarian core-area towards the east of the platform even came to be occupied by Romanians.

Each of the four main relief and structural regions of Bulgaria is now examined.

The Northern Platform

Variously known as the Bulgarian and Danubian Platform and Danubian Hilly Plains, this region has no generally accepted name, and even in Bulgarian its sub-divisions have local names while the region as a whole has none. Its individuality, however, is hardly in dispute. It is an undulating region, bounded on the north by the Danube and on the south by the foothills of the Balkan range. It extends a distance of 280 miles from the west, where the latter curve northwards to reach the Danube at the Iron Gate, to the Black Sea. It varies in width from a minimum of 15 miles in the west to over 60 miles in the east. In contrast with the Walachian Plain to the north of the Danube, it is an undulating region and, locally at least, is markedly hilly. Structurally, however, it resembles the former, and consists of the southern limb of the vast syncline which separates the Transylvanian Alps from the Balkan Mountains. This depression is floored with Jurassic and Cretaceous deposits. Tertiary beds, roughly contemporary with the folding of the mountains to the north and south, were laid down and have since been largely eroded from the southern part of the basin. Quaternary deposits—alluvium along the valley bottoms and loess over the plateau surfaces—complete the geological structure of the region.

The platform as a whole is divisible on the basis of relief into a lower and more dissected west and a higher and more continuous plateau towards the east.

Western Platform. This division of the Platform region extends some 140 miles from the Balkan foot-hills in the west approximately to the Jantra valley. The Cretaceous limestone, the dominant rock in the region as a whole, here outcrops only in the south. To the north are extensive and lithologically varied deposits of Tertiary age, made up in part of the débris (*Flysch*) of the Carpathian and Balkan systems, when in the early phases of their denudation. The region is traversed by a fan-shaped system of rivers, all of which rise within or even south of the Balkan chain and flow in directions which range from east-north-eastwards to northwards, to join the Danube. The largest of these are the Lom, Ogosta, Iskâr, Vit, Osam and Jantra (Fig. 13.1). Fed by the rain and melting snows of the higher and more westerly part of the Balkan range, they have proved active agents of erosion. They have cut deeply into the varied sediments of the platform, and along their lower courses, where their valleys broaden towards the Danube, there are extensive alluvial deposits.

The result has been to produce a series of corrugations, rounded uplands and broad, deep valleys, oriented roughly from south-west to north-east, extending from the mountains to the Danube. The interfluves commonly terminate in bluffs which overlook the marshes and islands of the Danube. Towards the south their surface climbs generally slowly and often with little interruption to the Balkan foot-hills, against which the plateau abuts at altitudes of from 1,000 to 2,000 feet.

The rolling plateau surface, formed of limestone and covered to varying depths with loess, is naturally dry but fertile. Little remains of its former woodland cover, and most of it is either cropland or, where the moisture content of the soil is too low for cultivation, rough grazing. Settlements are mostly situated in the valleys and hollows, where springs are thrown out by beds of less permeable rock. Patches of woodland occur on the slopes, but the valley floors, in sharp contrast with the plateau surfaces, are often moist and sometimes poorly drained.

The Danube is bordered, almost continuously along its Romanian bank but only intermittently on the south, by alluvial deposits. These are liable to flood in spring and summer, and during the rest of the year may form a narrow fringe of marshes, which, together with the Romanian marshes along the opposite shore, make this one of the most formidable of river boundaries in Europe. The international boundary follows the main stream of the river, and most of the Danube islands, unstable, uninhabited and covered usually with damp woodland and marsh vegetation, lie within Bulgaria.

Ludogorie and Dobrudža. To the east of the Jantra valley the Bulgarian platform is not only broader, but also less dissected. In contrast with the region lying to the west, it is built almost wholly of Cretaceous limestone, underlain by Jurassic, which occasionally outcrops over very small areas. Its surface lies higher, most being more than 600 feet above the sea and a large area lying at over 1,000 feet. East of the Jantra rainfall is smaller and river systems are less developed; none have cut valleys across the platform from the Balkan range to the Danube. Valleys are frequently dry and streams often intermittent. The two most considerable of the rivers rise within the plateau; the Lom flows to the Danube and the Provadijska to the Black Sea at Varna.

The platform is divided into the Ludogorie plateau and the less extensive Dobrudža plateau lying to the east and separated from it by the depression to the south of Tolbuhin. The latter merges into the dry steppeland of Romanian Dobrudja, and the northern parts of both the Ludogorie and the Bulgarian Dobrudža are in fact dry, and, except in the Deli Orman mountains, steppelike. Settlements are few and are found only in the valleys, and towns are absent. It was in this region that the Bulgarian immigrants first settled in the seventh century, finding here an environment not unlike that of their homeland on the south Russian steppe. From here they filtered southwards through the Balkan mountains, adopting an agricultural way of life as they merged with the Slavic population of the Balkan peninsula.

The Danubian platform as a whole is today the foremost agricultural region of Bulgaria (see page 785), and much of the dry east of the region has now been brought under cultivation. The whole region suffers from hot summers and long and severe winters. The rainfall, generally low and always somewhat unpredictable, imposes limitations on cropping, and is supplemented where possible by irrigation. The relief of the western platform restricts this to the valleys, while in the east there is an overall lack of water and methods akin to dry farming have to be employed.

The Balkan Mountains
The narrow and continuous mountain range which extends from the Iron Gate to Cape Emine—a distance of almost 400 miles—is known to the Bulgarians as the Stara Planina, the 'Old Mountain'. It is, however, only the dominant feature of a more complex region of mountain and upland basins, which consists of a northern zone of foot-hills, the Stara Planina, a longitudinal trench drained by the upper courses of the Strjama and Tundža, and, lastly, the Sredna Gora, or Middle Mountains.

Balkan foot-hills. It is not easy to draw a line separating the foot-hills from the Danubian platform; they merge gradually into one another.

The Jurassic and Cretaceous beds, which lie very nearly horizontally beneath the Danubian platform, are here upfolded towards the south. Their harder beds in consequence give rise to a series of narrow or scarp-like ridges. Since these are all crossed by the transverse rivers in their courses from the Stara Planina towards the Danube, the landscape has become one of short and generally asymmetrical ridges, truncated by the deep, steep-sided valleys of the rivers, and separated from one another by vales, floored with clays, of more gentle relief.

These ridges become higher as the main range of the Stara Planina is approached, reaching in several places heights of over 3,000 feet. In general their steeper and higher slopes—especially those which face towards the north—are forested, though clearings are numerous and extensive, and provide rough grazing for much of the year. The greater altitude causes a higher rainfall than occurs over the Danubian Platform, and this is naturally a region of forest and meadow rather than of steppe.

It is, however, less important for agriculture, though the vales which separate the ridges are both fertile and intensively cultivated. On the other hand, it is more urbanised than the platform, a consequence of the fact that the hills were a region of refuge for the Bulgarian people, and thus became relatively densely peopled. A succession of small towns lies within the belt of hills, opposite the passes across the Stara Planina and protected by the stronger relief from the open, steppelike platform to the north. Trnovo, capital of the Second Bulgarian Empire, is the largest of these towns; others, such as Gabrovo, Sevlievo, Botevgrad and Vraca, are market centres, lying, characteristically for eastern Europe, at the junction of mountain and plain.

This belt of foot-hills varies in width. West of the river Iskâr it is narrow, and tapers away as the Timok valley (see page 653) is approached. Between the Iskâr and the eastern margin of the Jantra basin, it is not only broader and its short mountain ranges more numerous, but it also embraces a number of basins, developed in the softer secondary beds. These productive basins are well populated and the larger amongst them have developed small market and industrial towns, such as Gabrovo and Botevgrad. East of the Jantra basin, however, the terrain changes. The short mountain ranges merge to form a plateau, rising to over 3,000 feet and consisting of Cretaceous beds less strongly folded than those which give rise to the more westerly foot-hills. This upland, known by a number of local names: Lisa, Kotlenska and Preslavska *planiny*, passes northwards into the

Ludogorie plateau and southwards into the more easterly ranges of the Stara Planina, and in neither case can a regional boundary be drawn with precision.

Stara Planina. The Balkan range, or Stara Planina, is, in the narrower sense of the term, a range of fold mountains extending from the Timok valley in the extreme north-west of Bulgaria, to Cape Emine on the Black Sea coast, a distance of 300 miles, with no interruptions other than the narrow transverse valleys of the Iskâr and Luda Kamezija rivers. It is, however, a range of extreme narrowness, and lacks the topographical complexities commonly associated with ranges of comparable extent and height. For much of its length it consists of a single high asymmetrical ridge, steep towards the south, where it conforms in part with a fault-line, but sloping more gently towards the foothill country to the north.

The Stara Planina is, as has been already noted, a part of the Alpine system, and a continuation beyond the Iron Gate of the Transylvanian Alps of Romania. It is made up of a core of Palaeozoic schists and intrusive igneous rocks, revealed by the erosion of its sedimentary cover in the western and central parts of the range. Over the greater part of the range, however, the older and harder rocks remain covered by strongly folded Jurassic and Cretaceous beds, among which limestones predominate, and by the *Flysch*, formed from material eroded from the mountains in the course of their formation. Its abrupt southern face is due in part at least to a line of faulting, which separates the Stara Planina itself from the basins and ranges lying to the south.

The narrowness and the topographical simplicity of the Stara Planina have made it a relatively easy range to cross. In addition to two transverse valleys, there are numerous passes with gentle ascents in many instances. There are at present no fewer than 15 north–south roads across the range, including those which follow the two water-gaps. Of these seven are paved—a quite remarkable achievement for south-eastern Europe.

The Stara Planina is usually divided on the basis of structure and relief into a western, a central and an eastern section. The western section of the range extends from the Timok valley to the Botevgrad pass, a distance of about 120 miles, for about half of which the mountain crest carries the boundary with Yugoslavia. The mountains rise steeply to rounded summits; much of their surface provides rough grazing, though there remain extensive areas of forest on the higher

BULGARIA

The Rila Monastery, high up in the Rila Massif of the Rhodope Mountains, which played an important rôle in preserving the historical traditions of the Bulgars. Note the medieval fortified tower within the monastery

The "Imperial Road" from Sofia to Istanbul, where it runs between the Sredna Gora and the Rhodope. In the distance is seen the Rila Massif

Hydro-electric power station on the Iskâr River to the south of Sofia

Bulgarian transport: one of the lorries and trailers which carry Bulgarian garden produce to Central Europe. This photograph was taken in Niš, Yugoslavia

slopes. The crestline ranges from 4,000 to 6,000 feet in the western and central parts of the range, with the highest but nonetheless inconspicuous summit of Botev rising to 7,793 feet. If transverse routes are poorly developed in this sector, this is because much of it lies close to or on the international boundary across which, in this sector at least, there is no official crossing point. The chief crossing points are the Iskâr valley and the Botevgrad pass. The Iskâr rises in the northern Rhodope, flows across the Sofia Basin, and about 20 miles north of the city of Sofia, enters the narrow gorge which takes it by a somewhat circuitous course across the mountains to the Bulgarian platform. The gorge itself is antecedent to the formation of the mountain range, and is in fact incised across its hard, granitic core. The valley today carries the main road northwards from Sofia to the Danube valley, as well as the only railway crossing of the western range.

The Botevgrad or Čureški pass, at 3,165 feet, is the easiest and most used crossing of the Stara Planina, and carries the main highway from Sofia to the central and western parts of the Danubian platform. The Central or High Stara Planina extends eastwards from the Botevgrad pass to the Vratnik pass, north-west of Sliven, a distance of 130 miles. Its crest, much of which is developed in igneous rocks, is several hundred feet higher than that of the western sector. Despite its continuously high crestline, the range is crossed by roads at several points. The most famous and also the most used of these is Šipka pass, which lies at 4,349 feet, and links the Trnovo and Gabrovo basins with the plains and valleys to the south of the Stara Planina.

The eastern section of the range, by contrast, is lower and broader, and is composed largely of secondary rocks and *Flysch*. East of the Vratnik pass, the range divides, and its two branches, becoming gradually lower and increasingly interrupted by gaps, extend to the Black Sea coast. This section of the Balkan range, in fact, resembles the northern foot-hills in its series of short ridges of no great height, lying approximately from west to east. Gaps are numerous; the more northerly range is crossed by the valley of the Luda Kamečija valley, which is followed by the main railway to Varna. The barrier nature of the mountains is in this sector of no real significance.

Sub-Balkan Trench
This awkward name is commonly used to denote the series of basins, tectonic in origin, which border the Stara Planina on the south. They are narrow and elongated between the Stara Planina itself and the

25

crystalline outliers of the Rhodope Massif, which extends over much of southern Bulgaria. Four interconnected basins are readily distinguishable.

Sofia Basin. The largest and by far the most important is the Sofia Basin itself. This region of plain, covering about 450 square miles (1,165 square kilometres), extends for some 50 miles in a north-west to south-east direction, and attains a maximum width of about 20 miles. Its surface appears level, though it rises gently towards the edge of the mountains which enclose it. Its surface, furthermore, is interrupted by a number of isolated hill masses, such as the Mala Planina, a few miles to the north of Sofia, and Čepân, which lies close to the Yugoslav boundary. These are inliers of the older rocks which enclose and underlie the basin. The Sofia Basin is floored with Tertiary limestones and clays, overlain in its central portions by more recent alluvium. It contained a lake during late Tertiary times, when lignitic deposits were laid down, but this would appear to have been drained first towards the north-west by the Nišava, and later northwards by the gorges of the Iskâr.

All except the north-west of the basin lies today within the drainage area of the Iskâr. This river rises within the Rila Mountains, flows by way of gorges across the eastern flanks of the Vitoša Massif, and enters the Sofia basin about 10 miles to the south-east of the city. Sofia itself avoids its marshy course, and has spread over the drier terraces to the west. Tributaries from most parts of the basin join it north of the city before the river, after cutting across a few outlying ridges of the Stara Planina, enters its gorge.

The boundaries of the basin occur where the crystalline rocks emerge from their soft Tertiary cover, and are in general steep. Towards the south-west this limit is formed by Vitoša, whose cone-shaped summit shuts in the southward view from the city. Vitoša is, in fact, an outlier of the Rila Mountains, and, although its summit rises in splendid isolation, the granitic rocks of which it is composed extend north-westward in the Viskjar hills towards the Yugoslav border, and south-eastwards to join the Rhodope Massif itself.

The floor of the Sofia Basin lies at an altitude of about 1,120 feet, high enough to sharpen the cold of winter and temper the heat of the Balkan summer. In calm weather there is a tendency for temperature inversions to develop, and the basin may be shrouded in mist or haze while the surrounding heights enjoy bright sunshine. The basin as a whole has a fertile soil, and its rainfall—about 635 millimetres (25 inches) a year near Sofia—is being supplemented by irrigation from the Iskâr system. But the climate restricts agriculture to the more hardy crops. The grapevine is not grown; maize and sunflower are less important than in more low-lying regions of Bulgaria, and cropping is dominated by wheat, barley and potatoes, although market-gardening and dairy-farming to supply the Sofia market are now of growing importance.

The Topolnica–Strjama–Tundža Trench. The Sofia Basin is shut in on the east by a mass of rounded hills, which form part of the Sredna Gora. Along their northern margin, where they abut against the Stara Planina, is a slight depression, followed today by the main road and railway to the east from Sofia. This depression then broadens to form to the Zlatica Basin. This is the smallest of the basins which separate the Stara Planina from the Sredna Gora. It is floored with Tertiary beds, and forms an agricultural oasis between the tumbled hills of the Sredna Gora and the steep, forested slopes of the Stara Planina. Its drainage is by the Topolnica river, which has cut a deep valley southwards across the mountains to the Marica.

East of the Zlatica Basin the longitudinal Balkan Trench becomes less conspicuous. The railway is obliged to tunnel through the schists to reach the Strjama valley, while the road climbs over a low pass. The Strjama Basin is larger and lower, but in many respects similar to that of Zlatica. It is bounded by faults and floored by Tertiary and Recent deposits. Its river, like the Topolnica, escapes southwards by a narrow valley across the Sredna Gora, and its economic activities focus upon its chief town of Levskigrad.

An area of hills, joining the Sredna Gora with the Stara Planina, separates the Strjama valley from the headwaters of the Tundža. The latter flows to the east for 80 miles before it too turns towards the south, crosses the Sredna Gora, here reduced to a few inconsiderable ridges, at Jambol, and flows to the Marica. Its basin, however, extends farther to the east, where it is drained by its tributary, the Močurica.

The Tundža basin is the largest, the lowest in altitude, and economically the most important of this series of elongated depressions. It is however divided by constrictions in the valley into no less than three smaller basins, in a way that has already been noted along the Morava and Vardar valleys and will be seen again in those of the Rhodope rivers.

Highest and most westerly of these basins is that of Kazanlâk, a wide area of Tertiary and Recent deposits. The Tundža has here been dammed to form the Georgi Dimitrov Lake, a source of power and of irrigation water for the whole Kazanlâk basin. This region is relatively open and accessible. To the north the Stara Planina, here called the Šipčenska Planina, is low and easily crossed by the Šipka Pass, and to the south-east a dry valley which, it is presumed, formerly carried the drainage of the basin, now provides a route for road and rail across the mountains to Stara Zagora. This is an agricultural region par excellence, and is known to the world for its cultivation of roses for the manufacture of scent.

The second division of the Tundža valley is less expansive and more interrupted by hills, and the younger and softer geological deposits are less extensive. This region is agriculturally less important, and it lacks, in fact, a developed central-place such as characterises the other basins and sub-basins of the region.

The last and largest of these divisions of the Tundža valley is that which extends eastwards from near Sliven to Karnobat. It is a level, alluvial plain, bordered on the south only by low hills which interpose no barrier to movement into and out of the basin. The importance of its agricultural development is reflected in the three towns of medium size which lie on the edges of the basin: Sliven, Jambol and Karnobat. The completion of the proposed dam on the Tundža, where it enters the basin from the west, will have the effect of increasing the already considerable area under irrigated agriculture.

Sredna Gora

The Sredna Gora, or Middle Mountains, make up the greater part of the belt of mountains which enclose the sub-Balkan Trench on the south. Towards the west they abut against the higher Rila and Vitoša massifs; to the east, their direction is continued in the Strandža hills. The whole complex is built of Palaeozoic schists and intrusive igneous rocks, and is thus structurally a part of the Rhodope Massif of southern Bulgaria, Greece and Macedonia. Unlike the latter, however, it was involved in the Alpine folding, and is today partially covered by *Flysch* and by folded Secondary rocks.

The hills rise along a broad front to the south-east of the Sofia Basin, but taper eastwards to disappear at the Tundža river, a distance of about 160 miles. Within this distance they are crossed by the deep valleys of the Topolnica and Strjama, which divide them into three contrasted sectors.

Ihtimanska Sredna Gora. The most westerly, the Ihtimanska Sredna

Gora, is a hilly but by no means mountainous region of infertile schists. It is thinly peopled, and much of it is forested, but it has never constituted a serious barrier to movement. Indeed, there are today several routes through the region from the Sofia Basin to the Marica valley. The most important has since classical times been that which follows the upper course of the Marica and links the small towns of Kostenec and Ihtiman. It was used by the Romans, and after serving as the main Turkish route into the Balkans, it was followed by the Orient Express railway.

Syštinska Sredna Gora. The deep and narrow Topolnica valley separates this from the middle section of the range, the Syštinska Sredna Gora. Instead of the irregular hills of Ihtiman, we here have a distinct and continuous mountain ridge, which rises at its highest point, Bogdan, to 5,261 feet. This change in the character of the mountains is due to the outcropping of a narrow spine of intrusive igneous rock, whose resistance to erosion gives rise to the dominant relief features of the range.

Syrnena Sredna Gora. The Strjama valley is wider than that of the Topolnica, and constitutes an easier route across the range. To the east, however, the mountains reappear in the Syrnena Sredna Gora. This range, tapering eastwards and diminishing in height, forms the southern boundary of the Tundža basins. The igneous rocks which form its core, come to the surface towards the west, where they give rise to the highest summit in this part of the range, Morozov (4,054 feet). To the east the granites sink beneath a cover of *Flysch* and of Secondary beds; the hills become lower, more gentle, and more frequently interrupted by gaps, and the last low hillocks look out over Jambol and the Tundža gap.

The southern face of the Sredna Gora drops steeply to the Marica Plain, but the disappearance of its hard rocks beneath the younger sediments is not final. They reappear to give rise to two small, isolated hill masses, both of them built, at least in part, of Palaeozoic schists. Only a few miles to the north of the Marica River and near the small town of Čirpan lie the Čirpanski hills. Farther to the east, between Stara Zagora and Jambol are the Sveti Ilijski hills. These small areas of hill country rise respectively to 2,135 and 1,364 feet above the level of the sea. Their presence amid the flat or gently rolling plains of the Marica serve to remind one that at a shallow depth below the Tertiary and Recent sediments lie the crystalline rocks of the Rhodope Massif, constituting an invisible link between the Sredna Gora and the abrupt mountain mass which straddles the whole of southern Bulgaria.

Marica–Tundža Plain

The Marica valley is both the geographical and the economic heart of Bulgaria. It is a triangular area of about 8,000 square miles (20,720 square kilometres) in area, bounded on the north and north-west by the Sredna Gora, and on the south by the Rhodope Massif. The eastern side of the triangle lies from north to south along the foot of the Sveti Ilijski, the Manastir and Sakar hills, but between these areas of hill, the plain extends eastward to include the valley of the middle Tundža from Jambol southwards to Elhovo. The plain narrows somewhat in the longitude of Čirpan, where the Čirpan hills from the north and the steep, granitic massif of the North-eastern Rhodope encroach upon the valley. This constriction divides the upper, or Plovdiv Basin from the middle of Dimitrovgrad Basin. The region as a whole will sometimes be referred to as the Central Lowlands of Bulgaria.

Marica valley. The river Marica constitutes the axis of these two divisions of the plain. It rises within the Ihtiman Sredna Gora, and draws tributaries from both the Rhodope and Sredna Gora in its course at first eastwards and then south-eastwards to the Turkish border. The Plovdiv Basin lies somewhat higher than the Dimitrovgrad Basin. Its surface is mostly level, and is mantled with alluvium, laid down by the Marica and its tributaries over almost the whole of its extent. It is a region of the highest agricultural wealth; dams constructed in the surrounding hills provide water for irrigation, and much of the area is given over to the intensive cultivation of fruit, tobacco and vegetables.

The edge of the mountains is abrupt, especially on the south, where the forested granitic slopes contrast with the intensive cultivation of the rich soils of the plain. Yet the older rocks lie at only a shallow depth. It is said that the total thickness of alluvial and Tertiary deposits does not exceed 600 feet, and is often very much less. Plovdiv, the regional capital is built over a number of hills—traditionally seven, all composed of Rhodope granite, which here forms an inlier of the main massif.

East of Čirpan, the plain is somewhat more dissected. Alluvium extends along the course of the Marica and up the valleys of many of its tributaries, but the plain is here covered with Tertiary deposits, clays and soft limestones and sandstones. Among these is an extensive lignite deposit to the east of Dimitrovgrad. These beds have been eroded into gentle undulations by the tributaries of the Marica. The soil is variable, despite the loess which has been scattered over much of it, and as a whole the region lacks the high fertility of the Plovdiv basin. It remains nevertheless an agricultural area of great importance, with less emphasis on fruit, viticulture and market gardening, and a greater emphasis on cotton-growing and animal husbandry.

No central place dominates the economy of this central section of the plain as Plovdiv does the western. The small industrial town of Dimitrovgrad lies at an important crossing of the Marica, but other towns: Čirpan, Stara Zagora, Haskovo and Harmanli, lie rather on its margin, at the junction of the plain with the surrounding hills.

Tundža valley. The Tundža region is even more hilly and less fertile. Alluvium extends along the banks of the Tundža, but outcrops of the crystalline foundation of the region are numerous and extensive, even if they do not give rise to areas of strong relief.

The Marica region has been as receptive to influences from Asia Minor as the Danubian Platform has been to those from the Russian Steppe. Turkish conquest of this region was completed by 1362, and Turkish settlement was denser here than in almost any other region of the Balkans. This was, *par excellence*, the area of the large Turkish estate, or *čiflik*, worked by the *raya* labour of the local peasantry. When the modern Bulgarian state was created in 1878, the Sofia Basin was included, but the whole of the Marica Plain remained within the Turkish Empire as part of the autonomous province of Eastern Rumelia. It was not until 1885 that it was incorporated into Bulgaria; the Turkish landowners left, and their estates were divided amongst the Bulgarian peasantry. Yet many evidences remain still of the long Turkish occupation of the region, not only in costume and diet, but in religious belief and architectural styles.

Burgas Basin

The lowlands which have just been described, extend eastwards, broken here and there by hills, until they reach the Black Sea. But east of the middle Tundža valley there is a change in both terrain and structure. The underlying granites come to the surface, and form, as it were, an amphitheatre facing eastward and encompassing the basin of Burgas. At its centre lie the Burgasko, Atanasovsko and Mandrensko lakes, cut off from the sea only by bars of sand and shingle. A fan-shaped pattern of rivers discharges into these lakes from the amphitheatre of hills. The plain behind them is made up of Tertiary and alluvial deposits, and is fertile but lamentably short of rainfall.

The coast is here deeply indented though its profile is gentle. The many low promontories formed the sites of classical settlements, which thus had easy contact with the sea and a maximum of protection on the landward side. Several of these, including Sozopol, Pomorie and Nesebâr, survive as ports from which sea-fishing and a small coastwise trade are carried on. The Bay of Burgas—Burgaski zaliv— is the dominant feature of the coast, a deep bay sheltered from the westerly winds and, despite its shallowness, providing a good anchorage for smaller craft.

Strandža and Sakar

The curving line of hills which encloses the Burgas Plain is an extension of the higher and broader hill mass, the Strandža, which lies along the Turkish border and extends far into European Turkey. This region is one of low, rounded hills, reaching at their highest summits little more than 1,500 feet above the sea. It is built mainly of Palaeozoic rocks, extensively intruded by igneous. Here and there are relict areas of *Flysch*, which yield a softer rock and deeper soil. But over this region as a whole soils are poor and rainfall is low; the crop maps show a low level of agricultural production, and the hills tend to be covered with rough grazing or thicket and stunted trees resembling somewhat the *maquis* of the Mediterranean. Similar landforms and landscape extend beyond the irregular ridge which forms the boundary with Turkey, becoming ever drier and more steppe-like.

The river Tundža flows entrenched across the western margin of this region. Beyond its narrow valley, between the Tundža and the Marica, lies the Sakar, an area similar in many respects to the Strandža. It is a rounded area of ancient schists, its flanks furrowed by its radial drainage pattern, and surrounded by the alluvium of the Tundža and Marica. Like the Strandža, it is an area of poor soil and low rainfall. Its agricultural potentialities are small, and it contains few settlements and only a small population.

The Rhodope

The Rhodope Massif is the dominant topographical feature of Bulgaria, and indeed of the whole Balkan peninsula. It is a massif of Palaeozoic schists and intrusive igneous rocks, eroded to a high, undulating plateau, and uplifted during the Tertiary earth movements. Its flanks are steep, and the renewed cycle of erosion has done no more than etch a series of deep, narrow and tortuous valleys into its resistant surface. Such is the Rhodope in the narrow sense of the term, a triangular region of some 33,750 square miles (87,400 square kilometres), constituting the most formidable and least accessible mountain region in the whole of Eastern Europe. But this is only a part of a very much more extensive geological complex. In a wider sense the Rhodope is the shield of ancient and resistant rocks against whose flanks both the Stara Planina and the Dinaric mountains were folded. It underlies the Marica Plain, revealing its presence by the occasional inlier, such as the Sakar and the granite hills of Plovdiv. It extends into Turkey and Greek Thrace, and in the opposite direction embraces Vitoša and the Viskjar hills. The Struma valley has been incised into its surface, and beyond the trench thus formed the massif is continued into Yugoslavia almost to the line of the Morava and Vardar rivers.

The western and southern parts of this larger Rhodope region are drained mainly to the Vardar, Struma and Mesta, which flow south to the Aegean Sea. The Iskâr drains the northern parts of the region to the Danube, and much of the east discharges to the Marica by way of many short torrents. The drainage pattern is young, and in parts of the high Rhodope plateau is still indeterminate. A feature of most of the valleys of the region is their tendency to expand into small basins where their courses lie across outcrops of less resistant rock, and to contract to gorges wherever the greater hardness of the rock has restricted the erosive power of the rivers. Some of these basins contained lakes in late Tertiary times, and in all there has accumulated a certain depth of alluvial deposits. The larger of these basins have considerable agricultural value, and in the most extensive, especially those along the Struma and Mesta rivers, centrally-placed towns of moderate size have grown up.

The river valleys, despite the grave difficulties presented by their narrower and more gorge-like tracks, constitute the only practicable routeways through the region. The Struma valley, the most important of them, fortunately communicates by easily traversed cols near its headwaters with both the Sofia basin and the Marica valley, and some of its right-bank tributary valleys have opened up routes across the more westerly ranges and into Yugoslavia. But in the central or High Rhodope there are no such routeways. The valleys are mostly narrow and difficult, and communicate with one another only by high cols which are closed by snow in winter. It is not surprising that this region, like the mountains of Raška and Montenegro, constituted a region of refuge, in which few Turks settled and where Slav folk traditions could survive the years of Turkish occupation.

25*

The High Rhodope. This term is here given to the area of high mountain and plateau lying between the Struma, the Marica and the Greek border, to distinguish it from the Rhodope region in the wider, geological sense. It is a compact region of about 5,500 square miles (14,250 square kilometres), a quarter of which lies in Greek Thrace. Its boundaries are straight and remarkably clearly defined. Along its western margin, where it borders the Struma, its flanks rise like a wall from the valley, and the northern margin from Stanke Dimitrov to Plovdiv marks a no less sudden transition from lowland to mountain. Only in the east is the boundary less decisive. Here the Palaeozoic and crystalline surface is overlapped by the Tertiaries of the Marica plain, and the High Rhodope plateau merges gradually into the lowland. Along its southern boundary, which lies entirely within Greece, the margin of the massif is no less clearly marked than in the north and west.

The massif itself is characterised by a series of high planation surfaces. The highest, which extends over the Rila and the Pirin, lies at about 7,000 feet. To the east the plateau surface lies at a height of less than 6,000 feet, and in the North-eastern and South-eastern Rhodope the levels sink gradually to less than 3,000 feet. Little geomorphological work has been done in the Rhodope, and it is impossible to define the extent and altitude of the plateau surfaces with any precision. There can be no doubt, however, that we have here a series of Tertiary planation surfaces, uplifted and dissected by the present river systems. The more important and more deeply incised of the latter divide the region into five quite distinct parts.

The Rila and the Pirin make up the high western part of the High Rhodope, and include the highest peaks not only in the Balkans but in all Eastern Europe. The *Rila* massif, like a huge rounded bastion, forms the north-western corner of the High Rhodope. It is built mainly of schists and intrusive igneous rocks, and its steep northern and western flanks follow in part lines of faulting. Drainage is by a radial pattern of rivers which flow deeply entrenched in narrow valleys. Within a few miles of one another are the sources of the Marica, the Iskâr, the Mesta, and the Rilska, a major tributary of the Struma. The Rila plateau rises at its highest point, Musala, known for a time as Stalin Peak, to 9,594 feet, and around it are several summits, including Dimitrov at 9,519 feet, which are only a little lower. The plateau has been intensively glaciated, and above about 7,500 feet there are numerous cirques and arêtes, evidence of the small glaciers and permanent snowfields which covered the Rila during the Quaternary. Even today snow covers the higher ground from September to May and there are areas on north-facing slopes from which it has not been known to melt.

The lower slopes are clothed with hardwood forests, which pass upwards into coniferous. Lumbering is today the chief economic activity. Agriculture, practised on the few scraps of available land along the valley floors, is of negligible importance, though the upper slopes continue to provide summer grazing for the flocks of the villages of the surrounding lowlands.

It was in the heart of this mountain mass, at an altitude of about 3,760 feet that the Rila Monastery—Rilski Monastir—was founded in the tenth century. Through the centuries of Turkish occupation it preserved Slav cultural traditions and helped to shape modern Bulgarian nationalism.

The *Pirin* Massif adjoins the Rila to the south, and is separated from it only by a tectonic depression. The Struma valley bounds the Pirin on the west, and the Mesta valley on the east; towards the south the plateau surface, diminishing in altitude and increasingly broken up by transverse gaps, is continued into Greece. Like the Rila, it is a fault-bounded massif of schists and igneous rocks, and its plateau surface lies at a closely similar height. Its highest point, Vihren, is 9,558 feet above sea-level. The surface of the higher and more northerly part of the Pirin has been glaciated, and displays Alpine landforms on a scale not found elsewhere east of the Alps themselves.

East of the Pirin lies the Mesta valley, remarkably wide and open for a valley of the High Rhodope. The Mesta itself rises within the Rila, but much of its drainage comes from the Pirin. The upper part of the valley forms the Razlog Basin, typical of the upland basins met within the mountains, though larger than most. It contained a lake in late Tertiary times, and its richer soils today make it an oasis of cultivation amid the wastes of the surrounding mountains. Below the Razlog basin the valley narrows, only to widen again to give the Goce Delčev Basin, and finally to narrow again at the Greek border.

The misnamed Western Rhodope[1] occupies the centre of the region, from the Mesta valley to the Vâča. It is lower by far than the Rila and Pirin, and its greatest heights barely exceed 6,000 feet. It

---

[1] It is apparent that in the local nomenclature the term Rhodope did not embrace the Rila and Pirin, whose distinctive character seemed to warrant separate names.

forms an undulating and mainly forested plateau, whose wealth lies in its lumber and in the irrigation water and hydro-electric power which it can supply to the nearby Marica valley. Settlements are few and population small except in the restricted areas of more gentle relief which lie along the rivers.

Only about 10 miles to the east of the source of the Vâča lie the head-waters of the Arda, the most developed river system within the High Rhodope. Its main course, eastwards to join the Marica near the Turkish city of Edirne, divides the eastern Rhodope into two contrasting regions. North of the Arda lies the so-called North-eastern Rhodope, an extension of the high plateau which dominates the central part of the region. Its higher surfaces are formed mainly in granite, but east of Assenovgrad Tertiary deposits begin to overlap the crystalline rock, and east of Kărdžali these extend over most of the North-eastern Rhodope. Altitudes diminish eastwards, and as the younger rocks gradually come to dominate in the surface structures, so the relief changes, and becomes one of hills lying from west to east and formed of the harder Tertiary beds.

South of the Arda river, the older rocks continue to dominate, and, except in the Momčilgrad Basin, south of Kârdžali, the region has a plateau character similar to that of the central parts of the High Rhodope. It is very broadly true that the plateau surfaces, formed in crystalline rocks, have a poor soil and are in general forested. The Tertiaries, which prevail in the Vârbica valley (Momčilgrad Basin), along the Arda valley and over much of the North-eastern Rhodope, give rise to an undulating and lower terrain and yield a very much better soil. They are in consequence more densely settled and intensively cultivated. The Arda itself offers a considerable water-power potential. Three large dams have already been built along its course and two more are either projected or under construction. They will serve to make the Arda valley an almost continuous lake for over 60 miles from near the Turkish boundary westwards almost to the border of Greek Thrace. The water thus conserved will not only serve to generate power for the growing industries of Bulgarian Thrace, but will also provide irrigation water for the dry, almost steppe-like plains which border the eastern Rhodope.

The High Rhodope has played an important role, both negative and positive, in the history of both Bulgaria and the Balkans. It has in turn been a negative area, avoided by invaders and conquerors, and a refuge in which ethnic groups and cultural traits have been preserved and given some degree of freedom to develop. Greek and Roman impact on the High Rhodope was slight; the road system of the Roman Empire encircled but never penetrated it. In the Byzantine period which followed, it served as a refuge for romance-speaking Vlach and Greek-speaking Karakačan communities which fled to its fastnesses, and there preserved or developed their pastoral way of life. The Turks, no less than the Romans, surrounded, neutralised and then ignored the High Rhodope, and again it became a refuge, this time for small groups of Orthodox Bulgarian Slavs, who there maintained their monastic institutions, such as Rila and Bačkovo, and helped to develop the Bulgarian literary and cultural tradition. At the same time, however, a number of the Bulgars, chiefly in the eastern Rhodope, were converted to Islam, and, as the 'Pomaks'—literally, the 'helpers'—they served the interests of the Turks.

Since 1885 most of the High Rhodope has been incorporated into modern Bulgaria. Bulgarian claims to the southern borderland of the massif were vigorously pursued in the Balkan Wars but finally defeated in the First World War. They were not however abandoned. They disturbed relations between Bulgaria and both Greece and Yugoslavia in the 1920s, were revived again during and after the Second World War, and do not seem yet to have been formally abandoned. The boundary now follows the crest, where there is one, of the South-eastern Rhodope, crosses the plateaux of the Western Rhodope and Pirin near their southern margins, and the Mesta and Struma valleys where these are reduced to defiles between the hills.

Only in recent years have the economic potentialities of the region begun to be exploited. Lead and zinc mining and forest industries have become important; the water resources are now being used by surrounding areas which stand in great need of them, and the recreational facilities of the High Rhodope are now being more fully exploited.

Vitoša. Vitoša is the high, symmetrical peak which rears its head above the Sofia Basin. It rises 7,511 feet above sea-level, and is thus comparable in height with the Rila and Pirin plateaus, of which it is in fact an outlier. It is built entirely of intrusive igneous rocks. Its flanks are steep and forested; its summit snow capped for much of the year. While suburban Sofia is now spreading over its foot-hills, its upper slopes have been converted into a national park and nature preserve.

Between Vitoša and Rila lies another of the upland basins which characterise the region. It is floored to a shallow depth with Tertiary deposits and is drained by the upper Iskâr, which escapes from it by way of spectacular gorges. This basin centres in the town of Samokov, and, despite the severity of winter, it is important for growing fruit and the production of food for the Sofia market.

Struma valley. Vitoša stands in splendid isolation. Over its western flanks lies the route to the head of the Struma valley, which lies only 14 miles from the centre of Sofia, and opens southwards to the Aegean. It consists in fact of a series of basins aligned along the line of faulting which bounds the High Rhodope on the west. To the west of the fault-line the crystalline Rhodope Massif is partially covered with Secondary and *Flysch* beds. The result is that around the upper Struma is an area consisting mainly of rolling hills, with gentle contours and soils which are above the average quality for the mountainous regions of Bulgaria. Along the Struma valley itself lies a series of no less than four basins each filled by Tertiary deposits which include large reserves of brown coal and lignite.

Near the source of the Struma lies the Dimitrovo or Pernik Basin, important for its good quality brown coal and for the industrial development which has recently been based on it. To the south, drained by tributaries of the Struma, lies the Stanke Dimitrov (Dupnitsa) Basin, with the town of the same name. Along the Struma itself, which here makes a large bend to the west, lies the Kjustendil basin, and farther downstream that of Blagoevgrad (Gorna Dzhumaya). Each of these is an extensive and fairly level area, with good soil, a dense agricultural population, and a small central town with developing industries based mainly on local timber and agricultural resources.

Below Blagoevgrad the river Struma drops more steeply and the valley itself narrows between the Pirin and the Maleševska Planina, which lies along the Yugoslav border. Above Simitli the river and its accompanying road and railway are forced through a defile. This opens out into the small Simitli Basin, only to narrow again above Gara Pirin, and again to expand into the Sandanski–Petrič Basin. The latter is the most extensive and agriculturally the most valuable of the Tertiary basins of the Struma region. It broadens southwards for over 30 miles until it is shut in by the Belasica range, across which the Struma has cut the narrow defile below the boundary station of Kulata. Opening westwards from it is the Strumešnica—the Yugoslav

Strumica—valley, also floored along its lower course with rich alluvial deposits (see page 649).

This, the lowermost of the basins along the Bulgarian Struma, is more Macedonian than Bulgarian. Its hot summers and its winters, more nearly Mediterranean than those of the rest of Bulgaria, have made it a centre of tobacco, fruit and vegetable cultivation. Cropping here makes intensive use of irrigation, and approximates more closely to gardening than to farming in the accepted sense.

The Western Mountains. The last region to be considered consists of the series of separate and in some instances isolated mountain ranges which lie to the west of the Struma valley and extend across the international boundary into Yugoslavia (see pages 648 to 649). It belongs essentially to the Rhodope massif, though the schists and intrusive rocks which characterise the latter have over at least the northern half of the region been covered by Secondary beds, through which here and there 'windows' have been eroded, revealing their underlying crystalline base.

The relief is more varied than in most other regions defined in this chapter, a result in part of the frequent alternation of outcrops of old, hard and of young and soft rocks. A series of massifs is aligned roughly parallel with the Struma from the Nišava–Sofia region in the north to the Belasica range, on whose summit of Tumba (6,166 feet) the boundaries of Bulgaria, Yugoslavia and Greece meet. The highest and most extensive of these are, from north to south, the Milevska Planina, the Osogovska Planina and the Vlahina and Maleševska Planiny. Their summits lie at about 5,000 feet, with the Osogovska Planina rising to over 6,000 feet. Their higher slopes are mostly rugged and bare of vegetation, and their lower are forested. The valleys which drop steeply to the Struma are narrow, steep, and but thinly settled. This is, in fact, one of the least populous and developed of the regions of Bulgaria, and its lack of resources would appear to restrict its usefulness to lumbering and summer grazing.

Between each of the ranges of which the region is mainly composed lies a tract of somewhat lower ground. Through these 'gaps' lie potential routeways from the Struma valley to the Morava and Vardar. None of these approach the ease and convenience of the Strumešnica routeway (see page 649) and the Sofia–Nišava route. Most are little more than tracks and at only two is the boundary open. One of these is the road which runs west from Kjustendil and crosses the Velbâždki Col (3,910 feet), to the north of the Osogovska

Planina, to reach the Kriva valley and Skopje. The other lies to the south of the same mountain range, and links Blagoevgrad with the Bregalnica valley and Štip. These mountains thus present so formidable a barrier to movement that it is surprising that such extensive transfers of territory should have taken place within them. In 1919, by the terms of the Treaty of Neuilly, Bulgaria relinquished three separate tracts of land.[1] Two of them, the Pirot region in the north and the Strumica 'salient' in the south, were equally accessible from Yugoslavia and Bulgaria, and constituted in fact avenues of communication between them. This, however, cannot be said of the Bosilegrad region. It is almost enclosed by high mountains, though drained to the Struma, and constitutes an upland basin, difficult of access and with few resources. Its significance lay in the fact that it approached to within a dozen miles the vital Morava route. Security seemed to the Yugoslavs to require that the boundary be pushed farther to the east within these intractable mountains.

CLIMATE

The climate of Bulgaria, like that of Yugoslavia, is transitional between that of continental eastern Europe and the mild climate of the Mediterranean. In a country as mountainous as Bulgaria there are necessarily sharp climatic changes over short distances. The principal mountain areas—the Balkan chain, the High Rhodope, and the Western mountains—in a sense make their own climate. They have a high rainfall of over 1,016 millimetres (40 inches) on their higher slopes, and over 762 millimetres (30 inches) on their lower. At the same time their winters are long and severe and snow is heavy. The highest parts of the Stara Planina, Vitoša and the Rila and Pirin plateaus usually retain a partial snow cover throughout most of the summer, and in winter the mountain roads are frequently closed.

Not only do these mountainous regions create their own climate, but, through the degrees of protection which they afford, they greatly modify that of the lowland regions of Bulgaria. Beškov distinguishes three major climatic types, the continental, the maritime, and an intermediate or transitional climate.

The whole of the northern or Danubian Platform, excepting only a narrow strip of territory along the Black Sea coast, is described as having a continental climate. Average temperatures for January, the

[1] The fourth was the Timok area, which lies on the margin of the Stara Planina.

coldest month, are a degree or two below freezing; Pleven has − 1·7°C (29°F) and Gabrovo slightly less. Summers are hot, with an average of 23·9°C (75°F) at Pleven, but temperatures are much reduced in the Balkan foot-hills. Rainfall ranges from 559 to 660 millimetres (22 to 26 inches) over most of the Platform, but sinks to less than 508 millimetres (20 inches) in some areas close to the Danube. It is predominantly a spring and early summer rainfall, with the heaviest monthly falls in May and June, and a secondary maximum in autumn.

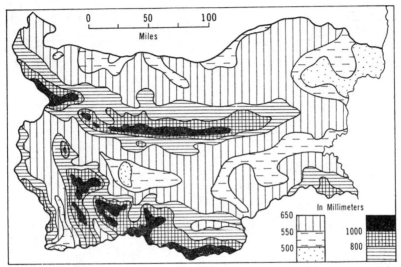

Fig. 13.2. Mean annual rainfall. After A. C. Beškov.

The Sofia Basin and the hills and basins around the headwaters of the Struma also belong to this region of continental climate, though temperatures are reduced somewhat in both winter and summer by the greater altitude and also by the tendency for inversions to occur in these upland basins.

The mountains have played an important role in modifying the climate. The region lying to the south of the Stara Planina is described by Beškov as having a transitional climate. Winters are markedly warmer and summers hotter. At the same time the mountains cut this region off from rain-bearing winds. It has less then 660 millimetres (26 inches) over the whole of its extent, and in the protected Plovdiv area this drops to under 508 millimetres (20 inches). As in the region of continental climate the heaviest rainfall is in early summer, but Mediterranean influences begin to show in a secondary autumn maximum. Winter frost is not usually severe; snow is of short duration, and the long, hot and moderately wet summers favour subtropical crops such as cotton and rice. A similar transitional climate is found in the upper Struma valley where the mountains also provide protection both from the northerly winds of winter and the rain-bearing winds from the west.

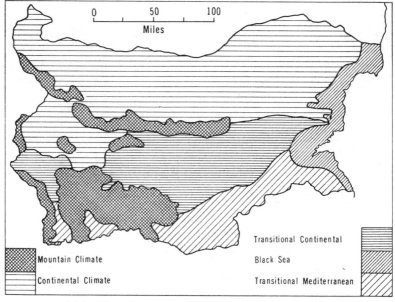

Fig. 13.3. Climatic regions of Bulgaria. After A. C. Beškov.

A maritime climate is experienced over a narrow belt of country which borders on the Black Sea and the Turkish boundary, and also in the lower Mesta and Struma valleys. Beškov distinguishes between the Black Sea maritime climate, with January averages above—sometimes considerably above—freezing but exposed to fierce winds from the north-east, and the Mediterranean maritime climate in which overall temperatures are somewhat higher and rainfall considerably greater and more concentrated in the winter months. Petrič, near the junction of the Strumešnica with the Struma, has the warmest temperatures recorded in Bulgaria together with a rainfall sufficient for agriculture, even if the specialised crops now being grown there do require it to be supplemented by irrigation in summer.

SOILS

The distribution of soil types shows a close adjustment to climate. Except in parts of the Danubian Platform and central lowlands, where loess has been laid down, the parent soil materials derive from the underlying rock and owe their qualities in part to this source. A *rendzina* thus occurs on certain areas of limestone in the Balkan Mountains; lithosolic soils, of negligible agricultural value, are found over parts of the higher plateaus, and along the valleys of the larger rivers are alluvial soils in which no characteristic horizons have yet appeared.

The northern platform and the lowlands along the Marica and Tundža, with their continental or transitional climates, have soils which may broadly be classified as chernozem. True chernozem occurs only in parts of the Danubian Platform, but degraded or poorly formed chernozems are more widespread. These may be taken to include the dark *smolnica* of the central plains. On the Danubian Platform the chernozems grade southwards into grey soils, produced by the leaching and erosion of chernozem, and these in turn into the grey and brown forest soils of the mountains. Encircling the region of degraded chernozem, which occupies much of the central lowlands, is a curving belt of chestnut soils and brown forest soils. These owe their origin to the hot dry summers and mild winters of this region, and thus also approximate to the chernozem type of soil. Similar soils are characteristic of most of the basins of the Rhodope region where very high summer temperatures are experienced and rainfall is reduced by the surrounding mountains.

Bulgaria may thus be said to have one region of superior soil, the Danubian Platform, and one of intermediate though very variable quality, the central lowlands. To these should be added the small but important mountain basins with generally brown forest or alluvial soils. These together make up almost three-quarters of the area of the country, and help to explain Bulgaria's agricultural pre-eminence among the countries of Eastern Europe.

There are few areas, however, where the productivity cannot be increased by irrigation, and some where it is positively necessary. The best of the soils, it must be remembered, are themselves the product of

dry, steppe-like conditions. Large-scale irrigation is a development of
recent years, and in most areas was made possible only by the collectivisation of agriculture. In the basins of the Balkan range and Rhodope
mountains the practice of irrigation is relatively easy, as the streams
have only to be controlled and guided downwards from the surrounding
hills. It is less easy in the central lowlands and almost impossible on
much of the Danubian Platform, where the rivers are deeply sunk
below the plateau surface. Nevertheless increasing use is being made of

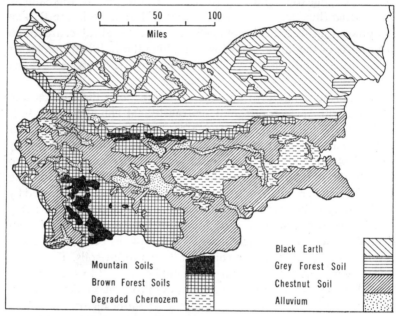

Fig. 13.4. Principal soil types of Bulgaria. After A. C. Beškov.

mobile pumps which lift the water from the rivers and feed it to the
fields by a system of sprinklers, which can readily be moved from one
site to another. Reference has already been made to the construction
of dams in recent years in the Balkan and Rhodope regions. A
strict limit, however, is set to this development by the paucity of
large rivers. The Danube is of little value in this respect except to
the alluvial tract along its banks; water is pumped from the Marica
but for water storage there is no alternative to a great number of
small dams built along the courses of the many small mountain
streams.

VEGETATION

Bulgaria is naturally a country of broadleaved, deciduous forest, in which the oak, beech and elm predominate on the lower and less well drained soils. Along the Danube valley, where the grey soils give place to chernozem, the forest became more open and passed into steppe. At the opposite extreme, the deciduous forests passed upwards into mixed forest in the Balkan and western mountains and in the Rhodope. Only at the highest levels in these areas did the broadleaved yield place entirely to coniferous, and only in the central Stara Planina and in the Rila are there today extensive forests of softwood.

In the south-east and in the Mesta and Struma valleys of southern Bulgaria Mediterranean influence begins to be reflected in the vegetation. The chestnut and southern evergreens make their appearance. Spring comes earlier here, with a typically Mediterranean richness of flora. Sometimes the hillsides may be pink with the redbud, and the meadows are carpeted with wild flowers.

Over much of Bulgaria both steppe and forest have given place to cultivation. Areas of northern Bulgaria, which once supported a tall grass-steppe, are now the country's chief wheatlands. And of the former broadleaved forests only small patches remain in the lowlands covering generally the steeper slopes, the areas of poorer soil, and the ill-drained alluvium along some of the watercourses. The mountains remain very extensively forested, and here are found most of the woodlands which still cover about a fifth of the area of Bulgaria.

POPULATION AND SETTLEMENT

The population of Bulgaria at the last census (1965) was 8,226,564. Its growth has been rapid during the present century, and the total is now almost three times as large as it was at the time of the formation of the modern Bulgarian state. This growth has been accompanied by a change from a predominantly rural population to one which is more than 40 per cent urban. This increasing urbanisation of the population may be expected to influence the total population growth adversely since the urban reproduction rate is markedly below that of the villages. Although 119 settlements are recognised as towns, over 40 per cent of the urban population was estimated in 1964 to be living in the five largest. The growth of these in recent years, with a vigorous programme of industrialisation, has been particularly rapid. In the smallest towns, known as 'agricultural towns', growth has been very

slight and their fraction of the total urban population has in fact
declined.

Population distribution

Urban growth, in general, has been in the fertile, well cultivated and
easily accessible regions, such as the Danubian Platform, the Black
Sea coast and the Marica valley, and has served to intensify the
contrasts which already existed in population density. Only the

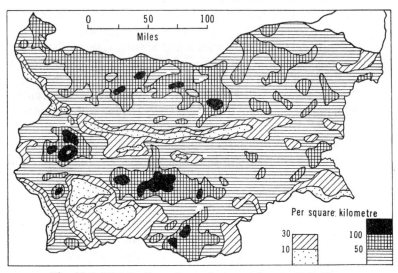

Fig. 13.5. Distribution of population. After A. C. Beškov.

Sofia Basin is in any sense an exception; here about a quarter of the
total urban population lives in an upland basin of no exceptional
agricultural value.

The variations in population density accord remarkably closely
with the landform regions that have already been examined. Two
areas of relatively dense population—over 50 and locally over
100 to the square kilometre—correspond respectively with the areas
of chernozem and closely related soils of the Danubian Platform, and
with the Marica valley. A secondary area of dense population, based,
however, more on manufacturing than on agricultural activity,
occupies much of the Sofia Basin together with the adjoining Samokov
and Pernik basins.

Other densely populated areas are of small extent. Along the Black

Sea coast they comprise the port-cities of Varna and Burgas and their immediate and now industrialised hinterlands, and include the Blagoevgrad and Petrič basins in the Struma valley, and the Arda valley of south-eastern Bulgaria.

The most thinly peopled regions are, of course, the mountains, and in this respect the population map reflects with remarkable accuracy the outlines of the contour map: the Stara Planina and parts of the Sredna Gora; the Rila, Pirin and Western Rhodope; the Western Mountains, and, occupying a narrow strip along the Turkish border, the Strandža hills, where the low density derives more from ardity and poor soil than from any great altitude.

Population structure

The population of Bulgaria is characterised by a birthrate which has been falling steadily for half a century, and is now at the relative low level of 16·1 per thousand. It is, as has been noted, somewhat uneven as between town and country, and may be expected to drop further with increasing urbanisation. It shows an excess of females of less than one per cent. The age structure of the population is more nearly normal than that of any other East European country, primarily because it has in fact not suffered significantly from warfare for the past fifty years, either in terms of casualties or of greatly reduced birth-rates.

Ethnic composition

The population of Bulgaria is ethnically more homogeneous than that of any other Balkan country, a consequence of the way in which peripheral and ethnically more diverse areas have been stripped away as a result of Bulgaria's unsuccessful wars. Recent figures show that about 88 per cent of the population can be classified as ethnically Bulgarian. Their language is one of the Slav group, but in syntax—notably in the use of a postpositional article and the elimination of most inflections—differs markedly from the others. But like most other Slav languages, it shows marked dialect differences, the most important of which is that between East Bulgarian, the source of the literary language, and West Bulgarian. The Macedonian dialect of the Struma region can be regarded as yet another variation of Bulgarian, though sometimes treated, primarily for political reasons, as a separate Slav language. It is estimated that about a million ethnic Bulgarians live outside the boundaries of their country. Most of these have been left by boundary changes and have not been repatriated. They form small, scattered communities in northern Greece, in Yugoslav Macedonia, in Romania, especially the Dobrudža, and even in Soviet Bessarabia.

Turkish and Muslim minorities. The Turks constitute the largest minority in modern Bulgaria, and were in 1956 estimated to number about 656,000, 8·6 per cent of the population. They are all that remain of a much larger Turkish community which settled mainly in the Marica valley and eastern Bulgaria during the centuries of Turkish domination. Most were settled agriculturalists; some owned estates which they cultivated with Bulgarian labour, and a few, who had practised a similar way of life in Anatolia, became nomadic pastoralists in the Rhodope. But with the exception of this last group, the Turks avoided the mountains.

Many Turks had left Bulgarian territory at the time of the formation of the modern Bulgarian state, and some 50,000 fled in the course of the Balkan wars. During the period between the two world wars, there was a further migration of Turks back to Turkey, conditions of which had been agreed upon in a Turkish–Bulgarian convention of 1925. In the late 1930s the number of Bulgarian Turks seeking to emigrate became so large that the Turkish government was obliged to limit the numbers admitted. According to Turkish sources, which are not wholly supported by Bulgarian, almost 90,000 Turks migrated at this time.[1] Migration was much reduced during the Second World War, and remained at a low level until 1950. Then the Bulgarian government, 'hoping to gain Turkish land for collectivization and seeing a chance to strain the Turkish economy, eased emigration restrictions.... On August 12, without forewarning, the government announced that within three months 250,000 Turks would be forced to immigrate to Turkey.'[2] The actual number expelled was in fact a great deal smaller than this, but nevertheless sufficient to cause great embarrassment to the Turkish authorities and untold suffering to the emigrés themselves.

Migration, both voluntary and forced, has thus more than halved the Turkish population of Bulgaria during the present century. Those who remain are distinguished by their language, though it is to be presumed that in religion also they differ from the predominantly

[1] See H. L. Kostanick, 'Turkish Resettlement of Bulgarian Turks 1950–1953', *University of California Publications in Geography*, **viii**, no. 2, 1957.

[2] *Ibid.*, p. 105.

Orthodox Bulgarians. They are found largely in the eastern half of the country, and still comprise a significant part of the population in the eastern third of the Danubian Platform, in the Burgas district, and in the province Kardžali, in Bulgarian Thrace. The Ludogorie, still known in many atlases by its Turkish name of Deli Orman, had long been a predominantly Turkish settled region, and the town of Shumen, now renamed Kolarovgrad, remains a centre of Turkish culture in this region. It is in Kardžali province that the Turks make up the highest proportion—about two-thirds—of the total population. There is a handful of Turks in the Marica valley, but almost none in the western provinces of Bulgaria.

Everywhere, however, are the visible symbols of the Turkish presence. Few towns are without their mosque, though many of these, especially in the west, have passed into disuse.[1] The familiar mosque in Dimitrov Street in Sofia is known locally as the 'Turkish Church'. Even more widespread than the mosque is the so-called 'Turkish' style of domestic architecture, the houses of two or more storeys, with window openings few and small on the ground floor, overhanging upper floors, and, wherever possible a courtyard or patio shielded from prying eyes. Only the most modern industrial town can show no specimen of Turkish architecture, and in some, such as Plovdiv, Trnovo and Shumen (Kolarovgrad) one can readily visualise the appearance of these cities when Turkish rule was entrenched.

The Bulgarian Turks are Turkish-speaking, but the Muslim Pomaks speak Bulgarian. Since their distinguishing feature is a non-linguistic cultural trait, they are not listed and enumerated as a national minority, and statistical data regarding them is not easy to come by. They are, like the Bosniaks of Yugoslavia, muslimised Slavs, whose ancestors were converted to Islam in the seventeenth century. So completely did they accept their new religion that they played an important role in the Turkish armies and earned their name—*Pomak*, or 'helper'—from this fact. They are said to number about 160,000, and are found chiefly in the hill country of the North-eastern and South-eastern Rhodope.

This discussion far from exhausts the category of Islamic peoples of Bulgaria. The Tatars, whose ancestors were brought to the Dobrudža a century ago from South Russia, now speak Turkish and

---

[1] The author remembers a ruined mosque in Stanke Dimitrov, a town which claims today to have no Turks. Before it was finally abandoned, it was made to serve as the local gaol.

accept Islam. The Gagaouz, however, a Turkic people from Central Asia, and now settled mainly in the Ludogorie and near Varna, have become assimilated at least to the extent of becoming Orthodox Christians. Both groups are small and are said together to number no more than 10,000.

The Gypsies. These constitute the second largest minority group. They are said to have entered Bulgaria with the Turks,[1] and some three-quarters of them are, at least superficially, Muslim. The remainder claim to be Orthodox and to have come more recently from Romania. They are said altogether to number about 150,000, the majority of whom are settled in the Gypsy-quarters of the towns, particularly in the eastern provinces. Here they live in conditions of great squalor; carry on certain occupations, which have become traditional amongst them, and supply unskilled labour. At the same time some members of the Gypsy community, notably those of Romanian origin, still retain in some degree their nomadic way of life, despite the attempts of the government to settle them and to absorb them into the Bulgarian community.

The Jews. Most members of the East European Jewry belong to the Russian or Askanazan community. These migrated slowly southwards towards the Balkans, but relatively few ever reached Bulgaria. Here the Jews are mainly of Sephardic or Spanish origin. Their ancestors left Spain with the Moors and found refuge within the more tolerant empire of the Turks. Thence they spread into the Balkans, where their descendants still speak a language—Ladino—which incorporates a good deal of Spanish.

The Jewish community was never large. Before the Second World War it is said to have numbered about 48,000. It suffered little at the hands of the authorities, and Bulgarian Jewry, alone among the Jewish communities of Eastern Europe, was larger at the end of the war than when it began. Over half lived in Sofia, and most of the remainder in the other large towns. This concentration of the Jews in the larger urban centres is said[2] to have been due in part to the spread of peasant cooperatives, which deprived them of their principal livelihood in the smaller towns. The Bulgarian Jews were primarily engaged in commerce, especially in the clothing and food trades. They did not dominate as conspicuously as in some other areas of Eastern Europe,

---

[1] See page 62 for a discussion of the East European Gypsies.
[2] Peter Mayer *et al.*, *The Jews in the Soviet Satellites*, Syracuse Univ. Press, 1953, p. 559.

largely because here they faced the competition of the Armenians and Greeks, both of whom showed no less aptitude for commerce. Anti-semitism was less obvious than in any other East European country; the pre-war Jewish community survived largely intact, and was in fact reinforced by a few refugees from the north. Nevertheless, the Bulgarian government showed a considerable distrust of Zionism after the war; certain restrictions were placed on Jews, and the majority of the community migrated to Israel as soon as it had the opportunity. There are considerable discrepancies in estimates of the numbers of Jews remaining in the country; the highest would place them at about 6,000, the lowest at only a third as many.

Other ethnic groups. The remaining ethnic minorities are very small. They include a small number of Russians, who came originally as refugees after the failure of the 'Intervention' policy towards the Soviet Union in 1919–20; a handful of Greeks who were left after the Greek–Bulgarian population exchange of 1920; a small Armenian colony, now much diminished by repatriation to Soviet Armenia or the Middle East.

Bulgaria formerly contained a number of romance-speaking Vlach communities. It appears, however, that these have migrated northwards into Romania, and their place has been taken by the similar Karakačans. Before the break-up of the Turkish empire in Europe these nomadic herdsmen were accustomed to wandering northwards into Bulgaria from Greek Macedonia, Thessaly and Epirus. Their language was basically Greek, as that of the Vlachs was romance. The establishment of modern boundaries cut short their wanderings, and those left in Bulgaria—and they number very few communities— take their flocks to the high pastures of the Stara Planina and Rhodope in summer and spend the winters in the nearby valleys or in the lowlands of Bulgarian Thrace.[1] These peoples now speak Bulgarian, with, it is said, some Greek vocabulary, and the government is gradually settling them in villages near their mountains.

In all, the minority peoples, even if the Pomaks are included, scarcely number a million. Some, like the Gypsies, unquestionably present a social problem, but none—not even the Macedonians and the Turks—can be said in themselves to create a political problem. Whether, however, they will again become pawns in other people's political games we cannot know.

---

[1] A map of both summer and winter quarters of the Karakačans is given in *Viehzucht und Hirtenleben in Ostmitteleuropa*, Budapest, 1961.

Rural settlement

The Bulgarian population is still, despite the recent trend towards industrialisation and urbanisation, a predominantly rural one. Most Bulgars live in the villages, and their conditions of life remain close to the land. Indeed, all except the largest towns are still in some degree agricultural, and the smaller are in function little more than large, diversified villages. The country's settlement pattern is dominated by the grouped but unplanned village, known sometimes as the *Haufen-dorf*. It is assumed that the original settlement of the Bulgars was in small communal family villages or hamlets, known as *zadruge*. As the family increased in size groups within it broke away and established their own clusters of houses in close proximity to the parent settlement. In this way the original hamlet grew into a very loosely agglomerated village. The process advanced less in the mountain regions than in the plains which offered greater scope for the extension of cultivation. The settlement pattern of the mountainous regions is thus still dominated by the hamlet, rather than by the village, and in some mountainous areas of the Stara Planina the isolated farmstead still predominates.

The Turkish invasion and conquest brought about considerable changes in the pattern of rural settlement. The insecurity which they brought about led to the abandonment of exposed settlements, such as those which lay along the routes regularly used by the Turkish armies, and an intensification of settlement within the protecting shield of the mountains. At the same time the Turks themselves established village settlements in the plains, especially those of the eastern half of the country. Sometimes villages came to be shared between the Bulgarian peasants and immigrant Turkish farmers. In these instances the villages were clearly divided, each community having its own quarter, distinct in style and in such cultural traits as church and mosque. Sometimes, especially in the north-east of Bulgaria, exclusively Turkish villages were established, while on the plains large estates passed into the hands of Turkish landowners, who cultivated them with the aid of serf-like Bulgarian peasants who were housed and closely supervised in a compound on the estate.[1] The Turkish village remains in north-eastern and south-eastern Bulgaria, but the *čiflik* has disappeared, and if its workers' compound has survived it is used only to stable animals and store equipment.

Bulgarian communities which shifted their settlement from the

[1] This čiflik settlement has already been described for Yugoslavia, see page 677.

plain to the hills were often obliged by the terrain and by the paucity of crop land to divide the village into a number of hamlets or even isolated settlements. At the same time they sometimes took over the mountain huts, or *kšsara*, of the transhumant pastoral people, who may have been Slav, but were more often Vlach or Karakačan.[1]

The defeat and withdrawal of the Turks has brought about a reverse movement. Bulgarian peasants have re-emerged from their protected upland settlements, and the Turkish landowner and much of the Turkish peasantry have disappeared from the plains. When protection from the Turk was no longer necessary, a secondary dispersal of settlement began to take place; compact settlements became more open, as new farm buildings were established around their periphery. The *zadruga*, which had proved so unifying a force among the Bulgarian peasantry, began to break down. The village community became less self-sufficing; growing population brought increasing pressure on the land, and its younger members succumbed to the lure of the towns. At the same time the government was urging the establishment of cooperatives for the marketing of farm products and the purchase of supplies. The movement from the patriarchal village towards the socialist community had already advanced far even before the Second World War.

The Bulgarian village, with its meandering dirt roads, its scattered peasant houses and farm buildings, and, all too often, its open sewers, had been the reverse of planned. The houses, usually single-storied, built of wood and plaster and roofed with thatch, stood amid their small gardens or lined irregularly the dusty village street. Even this changed. The layout of many a village was reduced to the semblance of a plan. Houses were rebuilt, often with masonry, and roofed with tiles. The quaintness went out of the village, and with it one of the factors in its poverty and backwardness. Change has continued at a faster pace since the Second World War. Everywhere the traditional Bulgarian village cottage is being replaced by a larger, more comfortable, more functional building, built generally of reinforced concrete and brick, with a tiled roof and scarcely differing in style from one end of the country to the other. The contemporary architects and planners have brought order and regularity to the new villages which they have created and to the older ones which they have rebuilt, to the immeasurable improvement of the level of human well-being if not also of the beauty of the landscape.

[1] See H. Wilhelmy, *Hochbulgarien*, 2 vols., Kiel, 1934–5.

Urban settlement

The urbanisation of Bulgaria is a recent phenomenon. As late as
1939, nearly 80 per cent of the population lived in villages and was
engaged mainly in rural pursuits. Cities had remained few and small.
In 1910 only Sofia exceeded 100,000, and in all only five cities had each
more than 25,000, and eighteen more than 10,000. During the years
between the two World Wars Bulgaria remained a predominantly

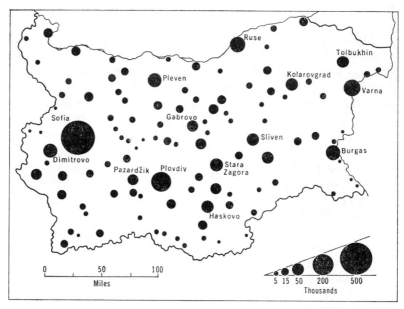

Fig. 13.6. Distribution of towns in Bulgaria. All towns of over 5,000 are
marked. Those of over 40,000 only are named.

agricultural and peasant state and the growth of cities was slow. Sofia
increased to more than a quarter of a million, and Plovdiv to 100,000,
but elsewhere the change was slight. When the Second World War
began more than three-quarters of the population was still rural,
notwithstanding the fact that Bulgarian statistics are unusually
generous in according the title of 'city' to communities whose functions remain largely agricultural.

The introduction in 1947 of a planned economy brought sudden and
sweeping changes. Between 1947 and 1965 the urban component of
the population has increased from 24·6 per cent to 43·9 per cent of a
greatly increased total. This has been achieved in part by the

population's natural increase, but primarily by migration from the rural to the urban areas. In the first ten years of planned development over half a million people left the countryside for the towns. The villages had unquestionably been overpopulated relative even to their pre-collectivisation level of technology. Collectivisation greatly reduced labour needs, as it was intended to do, and the government directed surplus labour into manufacturing, transport industries and building construction.

There were few existing towns that were not greatly expanded; the status of a number of village settlements was changed with the building of a factory, and some towns were founded on virgin sites to serve the social needs of specific factories opened in their vicinity. Many were renamed, either to remove some bourgeois connotation or to honour a hero of the Revolution. The spirit of Georgi Dimitrov should be as embarrassed as geographers are confused by the number of place-names that now commemorate him. Among newly created towns are the mining centre of Madan in the Rhodope; the booming industrial town of Dimitrovgrad, on the Marica, and the Black Sea resort of Zlatnipjasăci (Golden Sands). New industrial quarters have been added to old towns, like Sofia, Plovdiv and Gabrovo. The new building is readily distinguishable from the old. Though small, detached villas characterise the countryside, in the towns tall blocks of flats, in which the workers live in proletarian equality, are the rule. They are built within walking or at least cycling distance of the factories for which they serve as dormitories.

Current statistical sources enumerate 119 towns, among which the small town of less than 10,000 citizens is dominant. The following table shows the growth in the number and size of towns.

Table 89. Size and growth of towns in Bulgaria

	1926	1956	1963
Over 100,000	1	3	4
50,000–100,000	2	5	9
25,000–50,000	6	12	15
10,000–25,000	17	33	data not
5,000–10,000	29	37	available
Less than 5,000	38	22	
	93	112	119

Distribution of towns. In so far as it is possible to distinguish a geographical pattern in the distribution of towns, it is one of west-to-east zones. This conforms with the trend of the landforms and also with the dominant directions of movement. Thus we have the Danubian towns, the lines of towns which lie close to the northern and southern foot-hills of the Stara Planina, and that which follows the classical routeway up the Marica and through the Sofia Basin to the Nišava. There are, of course, others: the very small towns of the Dobrudža and Ludogorie; the ports and resorts of the Black Sea coast, and the towns that have grown up in the basins of the Rhodope region.

Penkoff has classified these towns into (1) industrial, transport and port towns, (2) industrial and trading towns, (3) agricultural and trading towns, and (4) agricultural towns. These categories are far from mutually exclusive, but provide nevertheless a useful framework for a discussion of the Bulgarian town. The first two categories include the sixteen largest towns together with a few of smaller size. Foremost amongst them are Sofia, Plovdiv and Varna, which deserve particular attention.

Sofia. In the heart of modern Sofia, ringed by government buildings and carefully sheltered and protected by the authorities, are the remains of a Roman bathing establishment, above which, more perfectly preserved is a Byzantine church. Nearby is the sixth-century church of St Sophia, from which the city derives its present name, and within a quarter of a mile are the Turkish mosque, the former palace of the kings of Bulgaria, and the headquarters of the Communist party—evidence of the continuity of the settlement and of its continuing importance for almost 2,000 years. The city lies on the terraces to the west of the Iskâr, near the point where the great road from the Marica valley to Niš and Beograd crossed it. To the south the slopes of Vitoša rise at first gently and then steeply; only a few miles to the north the Iskâr enters the foot-hills of the Stara Planina. South-east and north-west stretches the Sofia Basin, not quite level, nor affording the best conditions for agriculture, but smooth enough for the city, its factories and its railway yards to spread with ease, and fertile enough to supply a considerable part of the city's food supply.

The city was formerly known as Sredec, in reference to its central position in the Balkan peninsula. It has been a focus of routes for much of its history. Its main thoroughfare has always been the Marica–Nišava routeway, which at Sofia was joined by the route which, linking basin with basin along the western flanks of Vitoša and the Rila, reached the Struma valley and the Aegean Sea. Of less importance were the routes northward by the Iskâr gorge to the Danube; north-eastward by the Botevgrad pass to the older centres of Bulgar settlement at Trnovo and in the Ludogorie; eastward to the cities of the Tundža valley, and south-westward to Kjustendil and the passes which led to Macedonia.

In the early centuries of Bulgarian history Sofia was too peripheral for it to become the national capital, but its focal position contributed to its commercial importance throughout the Middle Ages. It declined under Turkish rule, and when in 1879 it became the capital of the modern state, its population was only about 20,000. Its growth has since been rapid, with the establishment here of the institutions of government, the building of a railway network and the foundation of modern industry. Sofia is today by far the most important industrial centre in Bulgaria, and in 1958 produced about 24 per cent of the crude industrial output of the country. The factories, which lie around the city on most sides except the south, are concerned primarily with metallurgy and engineering, textiles, chemicals, and a wide range of food and consumer goods industries. Indicative that not even Sofia has been able to escape from its agrarian past is the fact that the city contains eleven collective farms and one state farm. There is an abundant supply of low grade coal within a few miles (see below, page 795), and of water from Vitoša and Rila.

Sofia is in many respects one of the more attractive cities of the Balkans. Its wide streets, handsome buildings, numerous gardens and parks, and the distant views of Vitoša and the Stara Planina combine to give it a spaciousness and colour found in few others. Of course it has its drab working-class quarters and unkempt suburbs but these are less extensive and obtrusive than in those cities whose industrial growth began earlier and lasted longer. The current industrial growth of Sofia is represented by factories more streamlined than those of the past and by tall white blocks which have an austere charm.

Plovdiv. The second city of Bulgaria, with an estimated population in 1965 of about 206,069, lies almost 100 miles to the east, in the heart of the alluvial plain of the upper Marica. It is an older settlement than Sofia, and was founded in the fourth century b.c. by the Macedonian king to whom it owes its earlier name of Philippopolis. Its site was determined by the outcrop close to the south bank of the river of a number of granite masses which rise steeply to a height of a few

26

hundred feet above the alluvium of the valley floor. They provided an easily defended site, and commanded the valley crossing. Endowed with such a natural advantage, Plovdiv became in classical times and has since remained the chief urban and market centre of the western part of the Marica plain. It is a city of contrasts. On the summit of the most easterly of its hills lies the old town with narrow, picturesque streets and well-preserved domestic architecture of the eighteenth and early nineteenth centuries. At its foot lies the Plovdiv of the late nineteenth and early twentieth centuries, with streets of tall tasteless houses and small shops, and to the east and across the river to the north, the modern industrial and residential town.

Plovdiv has become one of the foremost textile manufacturing centres in Bulgaria. Many of the mills were built since the end of the Second World War, and their construction has been accompanied by that of tall blocks of workers' housing. Despite the broadening of its industrial base with the growth of machine and food-processing industries, Plovdiv continues to be the focus of the richest agricultural region in Bulgaria, serving as its market, manufacturing its fertiliser and farm equipment, and processing its food products.

Varna. The third largest city and the chief port is Varna, with a population of about 175,400. It lies at the head of a shallow bay, over-looked on the north by the Dobrudža plateau, up whose slopes the modern city climbs. To the west is Lake Varna (Varnensko ezero), the drowned valley of the Provadijska river, now closed by a sand and shingle bar. The modern port has been cut into these soft deposits, and is now able to handle large merchant ships. Varna owes its growth more to its harbour than to the productivity of its hinterland. North-east Bulgaria is, aside from the Rhodope, today the least industrialised part of the country, but Varna is itself being developed as one of Bulgaria's leading industrial centres. Ship-building is the dominant industry, but other metal-working as well as textile and chemical industries have been established. Eighteen miles to the west, and accessible by barge from Varna is the industrial town of Reka Devnja, a newly created industrial complex, with cement, fertiliser and basic chemical industries.

Burgas. With Varna it is natural to associate Burgas, similarly located at the head of a bay and between an estuarine lake and the sea. It lies 54 miles to the south of Varna, and is better situated in relation to the towns of the Marica valley. It was developed from a fishing settlement early in the present century as Bulgaria's foremost port, and retained this position until, in the 1950s, it was exceeded by Varna in the volume of shipping handled. Burgas now has a population of about 102,000. It has grown less quickly than Varna because its industrial expansion has been less rapid, but has very recently become the site of oil-refining and petrochemical industries. It has now become an important oil port, capable of handling tankers of up to 20,000 tons.

Ruse. The only other town with over 100,000 inhabitants is Ruse. It is the foremost Danube river port and has been in recent years one of the fastest growing of Bulgarian towns. This rapid expansion of the three ports is indicative of the increasingly important role of foreign trade in the Bulgarian economy. Ruse lies along the river, below the low bluffs in which the Danubian Platform terminates, and its docks have been dug from the soft alluvium. To the east of the town is the newly built 'Friendship' bridge, which combines the road and rail link between Sofia and Bucharest. Its industries which are mainly responsible for its growth, include the manufacture of agricultural machinery and fertilisers, light engineering and the processing of agricultural products.

To the same category of industrial towns belong a number of smaller urban centres, such as Pleven, Shumen (Kolarovgrad) and Tolbuhin in the Danubian region; the textile town of Gabrovo, in the northern foot-hills of the Stara Planina; the steel town of Pernik (Dimitrovo), to the south-west of Sofia; Kazanlâk, Sliven, Jambol and Stara Zagora in the Sredna Gora region, and Pazardžik, the new town of Dimitrovgrad, and Haskovo, in the Marica valley. In all of these and also in some smaller urban centres the population is engaged overwhelmingly in manufacturing industries and their ancillary transport services.

In the second group of towns the manufacturing functions are secondary, and the towns serve rather as market and commercial centres for their surrounding areas. They usually have a factory or two, engaged in processing local agricultural goods and manufacturing consumers goods. This category includes a number of Danube river towns, such as Vidin and Silistra; a line of towns along the northern edge of the Stara Planina, and a considerable number scattered over the central plain and along the Struma valley. It includes such familiar cities as Veliko Trnovo, capital of the Second Bulgarian Empire, set on its hills with its picturesque old quarter almost enclosed by the meanders of the Jantra. Asenovgrad, Harmanli,

Čirpan and Svilengrad, all of them on or close to the Marica, are
towns of this kind, as are Kjustendil, Stanke Dimitrov, Blagoevgrad
and Petrič in the Struma valley.

In Penkoff's last two urban categories industrial functions are
negligible, and towns are distinguished only by their small local
market functions. The agricultural towns have at least 80 per cent
of their population in agriculture, and many of them are actually
smaller than the larger villages, from which they are in fact almost indistinguishable. There are said to be 22 such towns, including Melnik,
the almost perfect town of the Ottoman period in the southern Pirin,
which, despite its renown, has less than 1,000 inhabitants. Such a
classification is necessarily fluid in a country with as rapid an economic
growth as Bulgaria. Many of the present industrial towns were only
villages 10 or 15 years ago, and agricultural towns could be as suddenly
upgraded by the decision of the government's planning authorities to
establish there a cement, a sugar, or a fertiliser factory.

AGRICULTURE

Despite the industrial growth of recent years, Bulgaria remains in
many ways a predominantly rural and agricultural country, and its
farming structure has probably suffered less than that of the other
countries of Eastern Europe. The contribution of agriculture to the
total national income, while increasing in the aggregate, has sunk
relatively from 57 per cent of the total in 1939 to 34 per cent in 1964.
Employment in agriculture remains about double that in manufacturing industries, even if the gross production of the latter has in
fact come greatly to exceed that of agriculture.

Land use
Despite the revolutionary changes in the structure of agriculture that
have taken place during the past twenty years, there has been little
change in the pattern of land use. For many years the extent of farmland has been about 40 per cent of the total, and technical developments of recent years have served to increase it to 43 per cent. This
serves to show that the dense rural population had long been making
the fullest use of its soil consistent with its technical equipment. The
generalised pattern of land use before the Second World War and at
intervals thereafter demonstrates this remarkable stability. Thus about
half the area is under forest, used industrially or for buildings, or

occupied by swamp, sand-dunes or high mountains, and is thus not agriculturally productive. Though small extensions are being made to the area of cropland, these proportions are unlikely to change significantly.

Table 90. *Land use in Bulgaria, 1939 and 1964*
(*area in thousands of hectares*)

| | 1939 | | 1964 | |
	Area	Per cent	Area	Per cent
Total land area	11,056	100·0	11,056	100·0
Cropland	4,184	38·0	4,574	41·6
Meadow	276	2·5	} 1,198	10·9
Pasture	} 6,404	58·2		
Forest			3,608	22·8
Built-up and waste	—	—	1,713	15·0

Sources: *Yearbook of Food and Agricultural Statistics, 1948; FAO Production Yearbook, 1965.*

Crop-farming has always been more important than animal husbandry, and now accounts for almost two-thirds of the total value of agricultural production. There is a tendency for the share of animal products to increase very slowly, but in this respect also no great change is to be expected. Nor has the use made of cropland greatly altered, despite the revolution in the ownership and organisation of the land. Cereal crops predominate, as they always have done, though the area devoted to them has contracted in recent years and is now about three-quarters of the total. Their place has been taken by industrial crops, notably sugar-beet, sunflower and cotton, by fruit, vegetables and tobacco.

Cereal crops. Wheat is the most widely grown of the cereal crops, and is produced on about 26 per cent of all cropland. It is particularly important over the Danubian Platform, where it is sown in autumn and harvested in mid-summer. It is somewhat less intensively grown in the central lowlands. Total production has tended to increase, but in recent years a series of poor harvests has necessitated some wheat imports. Rye is grown on little more than 1 per cent of the cropland, most of it light, poor upland soil, unsuited to the wheat which is the preferred bread crop. Rice-growing covers an even smaller proportion of the cropland, most of it along the easily flooded lowlands which border the Marica and lower Tundža.

(a)   (b)

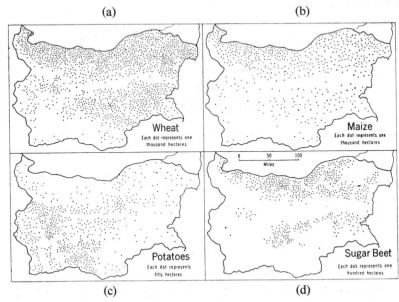

(c)   (d)

Fig. 13.7. Agriculture: distribution of (a) wheat, (b) maize, (c) potatoes, (d) sugar beet. After A. C. Beškov and E. B. Valev.

Table 91. Area and production of crops, 1964
(area in thousands of hectares;
production in thousands of metric tons)

	Area	Percentage of cropland	Production
Wheat	1,194	26·1	21,318
Maize	658	14·4	2,056
Rye	58	1·3	64
Rice	11	0·2	31
Barley	358	7·8	764
Oats	130	2·8	149

Source: *FAO Production Yearbook, 1965.*

Second in importance to wheat, however, is maize, grown primarily as fodder though milled and used also as human food. It is predominantly a crop of the Danubian Platform, and is relatively little grown in other parts of the country. Barley is probably the most extensively grown of all the cereal crops, and is met with in all regions except the mountains. Though used for malting, it is grown primarily as a fodder crop. Oats, lastly, occupy only small areas in the damp uplands of the mountain regions.

Millet is cultivated to a small extent and is mainly fed to poultry. Legumes, particularly white beans and lentils, are widely grown on the Danubian Platform, where their cultivation is associated in particular with that of maize.

Industrial crops. The expansion of the area under industrial crops has paralleled the industrial growth of the country as a whole. These crops had been greatly developed during the 1930s primarily to supply the German market; their production was further increased by some 50 per cent during the 1950s, and they now contribute about 16 per cent of the gross agricultural production.

In terms of area planted the oil-bearing plants are the most important. The sunflower, most colourful of all field crops, is widely grown throughout the Danubian Platform and central lowlands, and in 1964–65 was planted on 239,000 hectares. Flax-seed, rape-seed, poppy-seed and ground-nuts are grown to only a very small extent.

Tobacco is in terms of value one of foremost industrial crops. A high quality Turkish-style tobacco is produced, and a large part of the crop is exported. Cultivation is scattered over much of eastern and southern Bulgaria, but is intensive only in the Struma, Mesta and lower Marica valleys and over the lower and more easterly parts of the Rhodope. The chief centres of tobacco cultivation are Blagoevgrad and Kârdžali.

The cultivation of the sugar-beet has expanded with exceptional rapidity since the end of the Second World War, and is now found over most of the northern platform and much of the central lowlands. The area under beet has risen from 8,400 hectares (20,760 acres) in 1939 to 76,000 (187,800 acres) in 1964. Production is heavily dependent on the location of processing plants, and the recent construction of factories at Vraca and Reka Devnja, in areas where hitherto little sugar-beet had been grown, will inevitably lead to a greatly increased production. Already the production of crude sugar has risen to 244,000 tons, more than sufficient to satisfy the relatively low level of private demand and also the needs of the fruit industries.

Textile crops are the native European flax and hemp, and cotton, which was introduced by the Turks, but in fact was little grown before the 1930s. The area under cotton then grew sharply as German demands made themselves felt. After a wartime contraction, the area under cotton again expanded and reached 90,000 hectares (222,000 acres) about 1950. It has since declined owing to the difficulty of finding sufficient labour for harvesting, and was only 46,000 hectares

(a)   (b)

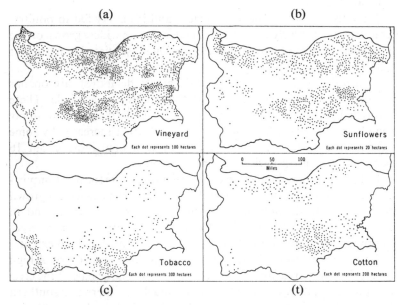

Fig. 13.8. Agriculture: distribution of (a) viticulture, (b) sunflowers, (c) tobacco, (d) cotton. After A. C. Beškov and E. B. Valev.

(113,700 acres) in 1964–5. Cotton remains an essential crop, and supplies most of the raw material for the expanding textile industry. Bulgarian cotton is not, however, of the highest quality and is supplemented in the mills by imported cotton of longer staple. Most of the Bulgarian cotton is grown in the central lowlands from Plovdiv eastwards to the Tundža valley. A smaller quantity is grown on the northern platform, where it has been introduced only recently, in the hinterland of Burgas, and in the Struma valley. An expansion is anticipated in cotton production, but for this it is likely that both irrigation and mechanical cotton pickers will be necessary.

Hemp is a product of the damp lowlands along the Danube and

Marica, and is grown for the manufacture of rope, sacking and very coarse fabrics. Flax, fundamentally unsuited to the Bulgarian climate, is less widely grown, and is met with only in the damp, cool valleys of the Rhodope.

Lastly, one of the least extensive but most famed of Bulgaria's industrial crops is the roses of the Kazanlâk Basin. Their cultivation was introduced from Iran by the Turks. Favourable conditions for them were found on the southern flanks of the Stara Planina, between Levskigrad and Kazanlâk, and here their cultivation continues to occupy from 5,500 to 8,000 hectares (13,600 to 19,800 acres), 'in small patches, like vineyards, . . . scattered amidst the fields of wheat, barley, corn (maize) and other crops.'[1] The industry has failed to recover from its neglect during the war years, and is now much less important than formerly. The rose petals, harvested in May and June, are soaked to extract their oil, which is then isolated by evaporation to yield the *attar*, which is a basis of many scents.

Fruit and vegetables. The Bulgars are born gardeners, and the more intricate and painstaking the agricultural work, the better they perform it. The area under vegetables, particularly such vegetables as leeks and onion, paprika and squash, tomatoes and beans, has increased threefold during the period of planned development. Such cultivation is suited to the aptitudes of the Bulgarian peasant; it demands a great deal of labour, in a country in which peasant labour remains abundant, and it provides export goods which can be despatched by lorry and marketed in Central Europe.

The chief areas of intensive market gardening are, first and foremost, the Marica plain from near Plovdiv westwards to Pazardžik. Here it is not unusual, according to the season, to see acre on acre of the rich alluvial soil covered with small cloches, made of glass or of cotton fabric, and armies of workers, the majority of them often women, transplanting and weeding the tender plants. At the opposite end of the production cycle are the large lorries and trailers, painted a bright blue and clearly marked 'Bulgaria', which carry the fruit and vegetables across Yugoslavia and Hungary to their distant markets. Other prominent areas of market garden cultivation are on the northern platform, especially near Trnovo, Vraca and Mihajlovgrad, and around Sofia, where it serves primarily the local city market.

The potato came late to Bulgaria, but the area cultivated has increased considerably in recent years. It is still grown more as a garden

[1] Henry J. Bruman, in *Econ. Geogr.*, **xii** (1936), 273–8.

26*

than as a field crop, and is still almost restricted to the lighter soils and the mountains and hills.

Fruit cultivation recommends itself for the same reasons as that of vegetables, and the area under fruit gardens, orchards and vineyards has increased no less sharply. They have been developed primarily around the margins of the hilly regions, where shelter from the winds and greater exposure to the sun can be obtained. Fruit trees and bushes are grown almost everywhere, but the areas of most intensive cultivation are the upper Tundža valley, the northern foot-hills of the Stara Planina, the hilly borders of the Marica valley, and parts of the Struma valley. In spring the slopes are flecked with the white of fruit blossom, sometimes contrasted with the pink of redbud, which grows here as a hedgerow tree. Apples, plums and cherries are the most common, but there is no lack of apricots, peaches and soft fruits. Much of the fruit is exported fresh or as tinned fruit or fruit juice.

The grape vine is the most important of the fruit plants, and vineyards are now found in all parts of the country except the mountains (Fig. 13.8a). The most intensive viticulture is in the upper Marica valley, along the margin of the Sredna Gora and on parts of the Danubian Plateau and Black Sea coast. Bulgarian viticulture, like that of Western Europe, has had its problems. Large areas of vineyard were lost through disease, and only after the introduction of American vinestocks did the industry make much progress. Even so, the area under vines has increased less sharply than that under vegetables and other fruit. Most of the vineyards produce wine-grapes, though Bulgaria has long been noted for the quality of its dessert grapes which are exported in considerable quantities. The quality of Bulgarian wine has been improved, and the red 'Gamza' and white 'Misket', as well as other varieties, are on sale in most of Eastern Europe and, one hopes, will soon make their appearance on the Western market.

Animal husbandry. Bulgarian agriculture has always leaned heavily in favour of crop-farming, and though the contribution of animal farming to the total farm income has recently risen somewhat, in few years does it exceed 35 per cent. For this both the climate and the social structure are in part responsible. The hot and rather dry summers restrict the growth of pasture, and green fodder crops do not in general do well. The rural overpopulation, secondly, has meant that little land has been available for grazing and fodder. The most numerous animals by far are the sheep, which graze the mountain pastures in summer and are the least exacting in their food. Goats were formerly numerous for the same reason, but are today much fewer than before the Second World War. Both sheep and goats are distributed generally throughout the country, with, however, a certain tendency to be relatively more important in the hilly regions.

The distribution of pigs, which in number come second to sheep, tends to be the converse: relatively numerous in the best agricultural areas and few in the hills, thus reflecting the occurrence of their basic food, which is mainly maize and vegetable waste. Cattle are relatively few, though widely distributed; they yield only small amounts of milk, and dairying is of slight importance. Any attempt to increase the importance and productivity of dairy-farming will certainly be hindered by the shortage of land and even greater scarcity of irrigation water for the production of fodder. Much as an increase of animal protein is needed in the diet, it would not appear that this can be best achieved through an increase in the domestic dairy industry.

Collectivisation has greatly reduced the need for draught animals. Bullocks, cows, horses and, in the hot plains, water buffalo have been used, but they are everywhere being replaced by the tractor. In the mountains, especially in the Rhodope, the donkey and the mule come into their own, and on the rough, hilly terrain, animals are less easily displaced by machines than on the plains.

The structure of agriculture
Before the socialisation of agriculture Bulgaria was the European peasant country *par excellence*. The destruction or expulsion of its landowner class, which was mainly Turkish, and the distribution of the estates among those who worked them had produced an equality rarely found in a peasant society. The land reform of the immediate postwar years called for a maximum farm holding of 20 hectares (49·4 acres), and the distribution of land in excess of this limit. A higher limit was permitted in the dry north-east of the country. This had, however, only a minute influence on the structure of agriculture, because only 0·9 per cent of the holdings, with 5·4 per cent of the agricultural land, in fact exceeded this limit. At the opposite extreme, however, there were far too many very small farms. Prewar statistics showed that 14 per cent of all holdings had under one hectare, and 42·6 per cent had less than three. At the same time, agriculture was grossly undercapitalised, farms were severely fragmented, and the farm population was far too large. The remedy lay not in land reform in the generally accepted sense, but in a drastic programme of merging

farms and absorbing surplus labour into more productive employment.

Collectivisation. The programme of collectivisation was initiated in 1945. It met with some resistance, but was completed sooner than in any other East European country. By 1950 about half the agricultural land had been collectivised. During the next five years little progress was made, and then, between 1955 and 1960, the remaining agricultural land passed under social control. Reasons for this relatively smooth implementation of the programme probably lie in the peasant cooperatives, whose success had already predisposed many of the peasants to accept communal organisation and control of their lands; in the absence of rich peasants, and the low standard of living of the majority who were not indisposed towards change, and in the government's more sympathetic attitude towards agriculture and the peasant.

By 1958, almost the whole extent of agricultural land was organised in over 3,000 cooperatives. Their average area was about 1,200 hectares, but they varied greatly in size and efficiency. There were poor collectives, as previously there had been poor peasants. For many of the land reclamation and land development projects, particularly those involving water-storage and irrigation, the collective farms seemed far too small. In consequence their number was in 1959 drastically reduced by merging groups of neighbouring farms.[1] Since this meant in many instances the merging of rich and prosperous with poor collectives, it tended to be resisted by the farmers. It resulted, however, in a reduction of the number of collectives to 945 in 1964, with an average area of over 4,000 hectares.

Capitalisation of agriculture. Farm labour, as has been noted, was greatly reduced, and machines are increasingly being used. The number of tractors had risen to about 13,650 by 1964, and there has been a commensurate increase in the numbers of other types of farm machinery. The results of collectivisation have become no less conspicuous in the great extension of the area under irrigation. It reached 900,000 hectares (2,200,000 acres) in 1963, and it is claimed that by 1965 over a third of the agricultural land would be in some degree watered artificially. Although this objective has clearly not been reached, the expansion has been very great, and is reflected in the greatly increased areas under vegetables, soft fruit and such crops as

[1] This process is described for an area in the Sofia Basin by M. Billaut, 'La collectivisation agraire en Bulgarie', *Annls Géogr.*, **lxix** (1960), 484–92.

cotton. To some extent irrigation is provided by pumps established along the river banks, which force water up to movable systems of sprinklers. This method is effective only in rivers where there is a good summer flow, and in many Bulgarian rivers there is in fact very little at this time of the year. The alternative is the construction of dams in the mountain valleys to conserve water when the snow melts or the rains come. Foremost among the dams completed is the Iskâr series to the south of Sofia; the Dimitrov dam on the Tundža; the Stambolijski dam on the Rosica, a tributary of the Jantra, and the Batak dam in the Western Rhodope. There are, however, many smaller works, and the Arda river in the Eastern Rhodope has been turned into an almost continuous lake.

The most extensive areas of irrigated land lie close to the Danube, where the supply of water is limited only by the available pumping equipment, and downstream from existing reservoirs (see above, page 760). This means, in effect, the Sofia Basin and the valleys of the Marica, Tundža and Rhodope rivers. Little irrigation is practised, and little is possible in the eastern third of the country, where agriculture is likely to continue to be based mainly on wheat, maize and other field crops for which nature provides sufficient moisture.

Bulgarian agriculture had been notable for the low level of its yields. Poor strains were grown, and little or no fertiliser was used. Conditions have improved in both respects. Domestic production of fertiliser is increasing, and, although the use of the basic chemical fertilisers is far below the European average, it has made considerable advances. In consequence the yield of field crops has increased, in the case of maize by 50 per cent, over the prewar level, and by smaller amounts in that of wheat and other crops.

Future trends in Bulgarian agriculture have been foreshadowed by the developments of recent years: the increasingly intensive use of the land, greater employment of irrigation and application of larger quantities of fertiliser, and the growing export of tobacco, wine, vegetables and fruit, both fresh and preserved. The increasing speed and ease of transport are now placing the growing Central European market within reach of these goods.

MANUFACTURING INDUSTRIES

The growth of manufacturing industries, before the current period of planned growth, was held back by lack of both capital and of domestic purchasing power. It was in the interest of certain outside powers, notably of Germany, to keep Bulgaria in an agricultural and economically dependent position. Under Turkish rule manufacturing industries had made some progress; a few factories—chiefly textile—were established, but this development was checked with political independence, and even by 1940 they had reached only a very rudimentary level. At this time factory industry contributed only about 9·5 per cent of the gross national product, and handicrafts a further 6·5 per cent.

No important addition was made to the industrial structure of Bulgaria during the war years, and when hostilities ended industrial equipment, though undamaged by fighting, was in a very poor condition. At the end of 1947, almost all industrial undertakings were nationalised, and the government instituted a Two-Year Plan to restore industrial production to its humble prewar level. The first Five-Year Plan was instituted in 1949, and was fulfilled in great haste and ahead of time. It followed the Soviet pattern as closely as was possible, and emphasised heavy industry almost to the exclusion of other branches. Much as Bulgaria needed capital goods industries, this expansion was unbalanced and ill-conceived, and was adapted more to Soviet demands than to the real needs of Bulgaria. A second Five-Year Plan, following not dissimilar lines, was designed to run from 1953–57, but before it was really brought into operation Stalin died, tensions were relaxed, and Bulgaria was emboldened to modify the plans which had previously received his approbation. Nevertheless, heavy industry continued to receive a disproportionate amount of the total investment, and the consumer goods industries too small a share. The third and fourth Five-Year Plans, which followed with a monotonous regularity, have continued to stress heavy industry and capital goods, but they have provided for greater expansion in the consumer goods sectors and also, as has been seen, for a carefully thought-out expansion of agriculture.

Fuel and power industries
One of the major problems faced by the earlier and less well-conceived economic plans was the inadequacy of the fuel and power industries. Although this situation was in some measure remedied by the later plans, shortages in the supply of industrial power are more likely than any other factor to inhibit industrial growth.

The mineral fuels. In Bulgaria, as in Yugoslavia, there are many deposits of coal, all of them small and most of them low grade.

Some 20 such basins are known, though most are not exploited.[1] They range in geological age from the Upper Carboniferous to the Upper Tertiary and in quality from anthracite to the poorest lignite. The better quality fuels, anthracite and bituminous coal, occur in only very small quantities and primarily in the Stara Planina north of Sofia and near Sliven. The latter deposit contains a coking coal, but quantities are believed to be very small. The total production from these fields has only in recent years begun to exceed 500,000 tons annually.

Most of Bulgaria's fuel reserves are of lignite and brown coal, and it is these which must continue to supply the fuel base of Bulgaria's industrial growth. Earliest to be developed was the Pernik (Dimitrovo) Basin, which has supplied the bulk of Bulgaria's fuel for many years and now supports one of the two integrated iron and steel plants. The seams occur in one of the Tertiary basins which lie around the head of the Struma. Down the valley from Pernik lie the similar though apparently much smaller brown coal basins of Bobovdol, near Stanke Dimitrov, and Brežani—sometimes called Pirin-Struma—to the south of Blagoevgrad. A further brown coal basin encircles the city of Burgas on the Black Sea coast, and is being used to supply its industries.

The largest reserves, however, are of the even lower grade fuel, lignite. A very extensive deposit underlies the Marica valley to the north-east of Dimitrovgrad, and is now being worked in several very large open-cast pits. The fuel is briquetted, and, in addition to providing fuel for thermal-electric stations, is beginning to be used for the distillation of its chemical by-products. The Marica Basin has already taken over first place from the Pernick Basin, and is likely in the near future to support one of Bulgaria's major industrial concentrations. Other large lignite fields underlie parts of the Sofia Basin and occur in the lower Struma and Mesta valleys. The Sofia Basin is likely to gain in importance, as the Pernik reserves near exhaustion.

Coal production has increased greatly since 1948, though the growth has been largely in brown coal and lignite. In 1964 output of all varieties reached 24·4 million tons, but the objective for 1965 of 28·7 was not realised, and production was in fact 552,000 tons of bituminous coal and 24,490,000 tons of brown coal and lignite.

Petroleum and natural oil resources were discovered early in the

[1] These are tabulated and their resources assessed by Victor H. Winston, in *Bulgaria*, ed. L. A. D. Dellin, New York, 1957, pp. 44–7.

period of planned development near the Danube in north-western Bulgaria and in the hinterland of Varna. The extent of these deposits is far from clear, though the Bulgarian government is building several refineries in anticipation of a large output of crude oil. Production rose to 247,000 tons in 1956, but has since declined steadily to 160,000 tons in 1964. Early expectations may have been too sanguine, though it is claimed that large reserves have recently been discovered near Pleven. Deposits of oil-bearing shale have been prospected in western Bulgaria and represent a potential source of fuel of perhaps considerable importance.

Electric power. It is as electrical power that most energy is now consumed, and, with the construction of a number of thermal- and hydro-electric stations, the installed capacity has increased from 170,000 kilowatt/hours in 1948 to 2,155,000 kilowatt/hours in 1965. Of this more than three-quarters is derived from thermal plants, which burn brown coal or lignite. The largest of these have been built on the Marica lignite field, where their tall smokestacks and plumes of smoke break the skyline to the north-east of Dimitrovgrad. The Pernik, Sofia and Burgas fields also support thermal-electric stations.

Bulgaria has no major source of hydro-electric power, and has been obliged to construct a number of small generating stations on the rivers which discharge from the Rhodope and Stara Planina. The largest, including the Batak, Arda and Iskâr systems, are in the Rhodope massif, where there is scope for the further extension of the region's hydro-electric capacity.

Metallurgical and metal industries

The development of the metallurgical industries was an essential part of the earlier Five-Year Plans for idealogical rather than practical reasons. Before the Second World War there had been no important metallurgical—i.e. smelting and refining industry, and the metal-using industries had been of a primitive order.

In 1949 work was begun on the construction of an integrated iron and steel plant at Pernik, where there had previously been a small iron-works, and by the time that the Second Plan had been completed, it had two small blast furnaces, three open-hearth furnaces and a rolling mill for rails and shapes. It derived its fuel from the Soviet Union and also from local brown coal basin, and its ores, came primarily from the deposits of Kremikovči, north-east of Sofia, and Krumovo, in the lower Tundža valley.

The fourth Five-Year Plan called for the construction of a second integrated iron and steel plant at Kremikovči in the close vicinity of the ore deposits; its first stage is now completed, and is expected to produce 1,120,000 tons of pig iron and 1,250,000 tons of steel a year by 1970.

It may be questioned whether the Bulgarian raw material base is adequate to support two iron and steel works even of the moderate size of those of Pernik and Kremikovči, though the country is well able to absorb their output. The iron-ore base consists essentially of the two ore bodies already mentioned. That of Kremikovči, which is variously estimated to contain from 200 to 250 million tons of ore, is mainly limonite with some siderite and haematite. It is of low grade, but is said to be shallow and easy to mine. The Krumovo ores are magnetite and of much higher grade, and are thus better able to stand costs of transport, but are of very much smaller extent. There are several other ore deposits—in the Strandža mountains, in the western Stara Planina, and at a number of sites in the Rhodope, but none of them remarkable, it appears, either for their quality of their size.

If the ore reserves are adequate, this cannot also be said of the fuel. Bulgaria has little bituminous coal and even less coking coal. The Kremikovči works are to make the most of the small field in the central Stara Planina, but an increasing dependence must inevitably be placed on brown coal and on imported coking coal and coke.

Non-ferrous metals. The geological structure of the southern half of Bulgaria—Palaeozoic rocks intruded by igneous—makes the occurrence of metalliferous ores at the least very probable. The Rhodope Massif has a varied range of economic minerals, foremost among which are lead, zinc, and copper, with smaller reserves of chrome, molybdenum, manganese and gold. A second relatively highly mineralised region occurs in the western Stara Planina, and a third in the immediate hinterland of Burgas, where its resources consist mainly of copper.

Non-ferrous mining was well established before the Second World War, but the earlier plans provided for a large expansion of mining and the construction of smelters. The most productive mines are the lead and zinc workings at Madan and Rudozem, in the south-eastern Rhodope. The ores are concentrated near the mines and are then sent to smelters in Plovdiv and Kârdžali, while by-product sulphides go to the chemical complex at Dimitrovgrad. Other lead and zinc workings are found at Ustrem, in the Sakar hills, and in the western Stara

Planina. The former sends its concentrates to Kârdžali and Plovdiv, and the latter to a smelter in Sofia. Most of the copper ore is mined in the western Stara Planina and near Burgas; it is concentrated locally, and is then sent to one of the three new electrolytic smelters. These are Pirdop, near the eastern margin of the Sofia Basin, Elisejna, a small integrated plant in the Iskâr valley to the north of Sofia, and the large Medet complex, near Panagyurište. A little gold is obtained from a mine close to the Yugoslav border in western Bulgaria, but other non-ferrous metals are not mined except in conjunction with the ores of the more important metals.

The production of non-ferrous metals has increased sharply with the recent completion of several large smelters. Bulgaria has ambitious plans for the extension of non-ferrous mining and smelting, but the quality of the ore being produced is deteriorating, and output of metal may not go much above the current production. Table 92 shows, however, how rapid has been its growth.

Table 92. Production of non-ferrous metals (in thousands of tons of metal content, and in thousands of tons of refined metal)

	1948	1955	1960	1965	Percentage of world production
Copper ore	1·2	5·0	11·0	29·9	0·7
Lead ore	12·9	51·7	94·8	100·1	4·6
Zinc ore	9·7	41·2	77·0	79·6	2·1
Copper, refined	—	3·8	7·8	25·2	0·5
Lead, refined	—	1·4	16·9	93·4	4·5
Zinc, refined	2·1	5·1	40·4	65·8	2·1

Source: *UN Statistical Yearbooks, various dates.*

Metal-using industries. The mechanical construction and engineering industries were only very weakly represented in Bulgaria in 1948, and most of the present undertakings have been established since that date. Their rapid advance in recent years has been the chief reason for the establishment of the second integrated iron-and-steel plant at Kremikovči. Bulgaria has tended to specialise within the general framework of Comecon on certain of the lighter types of metal goods. No attempt has been made to produce the larger and more complex forms of capital equipment, except ships of 4–5,000 tons; not even railway locomotives have been built, and Bulgaria is only now beginning to construct lorries at a plant at Kolarovgrad. An automobile factory is about to be built at Loveč, which will manufacture the Soviet-type 'Moskvič' car.

There has, however, been considerable emphasis on the manufacture of agricultural machinery, very necessary in a country in which there had until recently been almost none. Small equipment for the bulk handling of goods, such as fork-lifts, hoisting equipment, and light automated trolleys, are being made in large numbers, and machine tools, lathes, and drilling and boring equipment have become Bulgarian specialities. Ship and barge construction has been established at Varna and at some of the Danube river ports, and pumps and electric motors are also made.

The most important centre by far for this varied range of production is the Sofia region, including Pernik. Plovdiv, Ruse, Varna and Burgas are also important, and single branches of metal fabricating industries have been established in many of the smaller towns of the central lowlands and northern platform, such as Vidin, Gabrovo, Čirpan and Drjanovo.

Chemical industries

This group of industries with their wide ramifications is of great importance to a developing and mainly agricultural country. On it depends the supply of fertilisers, essential to the fulfilment of the agricultural programme. Before the initiation of the Five-Year Plans, chemical production was restricted to a few elementary commodities, such as soap, and to the products of the small oil refinery at Ruse. The plans have emphasised the manufacture of the basic chemicals: caustic soda and the common acids. From these a number of large chemical combines have moved to the production of nitrogenous fertilisers, superphosphates, and more recently cellulose, organic compounds, synthetic fibres and rubber.

The chemical industries are highly concentrated, with the production of the basic acids and alkalis, and of fertilisers, cellulose, and other relatively simple derivatives located mainly in the areas around Plovdiv, Stara Zagora, Dimitrovgrad and Varna. The manufacture of those chemicals which are oriented more towards the consumer, such as soap and cosmetics, paints and varnish, drugs and medications, is strongly concentrated in the Sofia region, where a large part of its market is to be found. A fertiliser factory is now being built at Vraca, evidently to supply the agricultural region of north-west Bulgaria, and the manufacture of synthetic fibre is now established at Vidin, Svištov and Jambol.

The expansion of oil-refining and the establishment of petrochemical industries has been encouraged by the recent discovery and exploitation of reserves of crude oil and natural gas in north-western Bulgaria as well as around Varna and in the shallow water offshore. In addition to the original prewar refinery at Ruse, new and larger works have been built at Burgas and Varna, and others are either planned or under construction at Vraca and Dolni Dâbnik, near Pleven.

Building construction industries

The building materials and construction industries are basic to the expansion of all others, and the change in domestic building from an essentially wooden construction to one of concrete and brick has placed further demands on this branch of industry. Cement manufacture has expanded the most rapidly, from 370,000 tons in 1948 to 880,000 tons on the completion of the second Five-Year Plan in 1957, and to 2,681,000 tons in 1965. The location of cement plants is determined by that of its raw materials, limestone and clay or marl, and this greatly restricts their distribution. The large modern cement works have been built in Dimitrovgrad, and also at Temelkovo, near Pernik; at Pleven, Vraca, and in the new industrial complex at Reka Devnja, near Varna.

The manufacture of bricks and tiles calls for a smaller range of materials. The ratio of their value to bulk is low and every attempt is made to manufacture them as close as is practicable to where they will be used. The result is a very large number of relatively small brick and tile kilns. Larger brick works are to be found near Sofia, Varna, and at several places in the central lowlands and northern platform.

The ceramic industry is related to the brick in that both require basically clay and fuel. Although there are numerous potteries, the industry consists still of small works designed to serve mainly local needs. Glass manufacture has been somewhat more developed, because it is essential for both market-gardening and the electronics industry, and its chief centre is at Beloslav, near the Reka Devnja industrial complex.

Textile and clothing industries

The manufacture of textiles is the oldest factory industry in Bulgaria, and was established under Turkish rule considerably more than a century ago. It continued to grow slowly in all its branches through the nineteenth and early twentieth centuries, and has been greatly expanded under the industrial plans. Bulgaria must be the only European textile producer which can itself supply a large part of

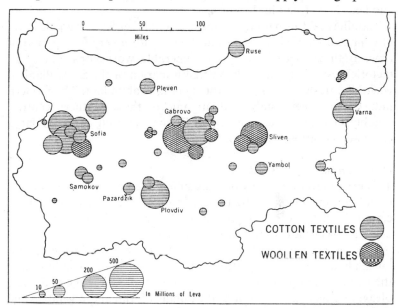

Fig. 13.9. Distribution of textile manufacturing in Bulgaria 1959. After A. C. Beškov and E. B. Valev.

all its raw materials. Although the earliest textile industry was based on wool, the spinning and weaving of cotton now occupies the greater part of the labour force, and the domestic cotton crop has now to be supplemented by a comparable volume of imports.

The textile industry was from the first important in eastern Bulgaria, and this area has retained a relative advantage. The chief centres of the cotton industry are Varna, Ruse and Gabrovo, as well as in the large centres of Sofia and Plovdiv, which lie nearer to the chief consuming areas. The quality of cotton fabrics is said to be low, and the planning authorities have recently announced their intention to raise the level and to increase the already considerable export of fabrics.

The woollen industry began in Sliven, and this remains one of its most important centres; others are Gabrovo, which has over 40 per cent of the industry, and Sofia. Other branches of the textile industry are relatively unimportant. Raw silk is produced and woven along the lower Marica valley; hemp is spun and woven into coarse fabrics at Pazardžik, Varna and Ruse; there is a hosiery industry in Sofia, Plovdiv and Varna, and carpets are made at Sliven, as well as in and near Sofia (see Fig. 13.9).

Tanning and the making of footwear and other leather goods have, of course, been craft industries in Bulgaria for a very long period of time. Both are carried on in innumerable workshops and small factories, especially along the northern margin of the Stara Planina, where the fresh water needed for tanning is abundant. The modern industry has been established in some of these northern centres, notably Gabrovo, Ruse and Stara Zagora, as well as in the large consuming centres of Sofia and Plovdiv.

Other consumer goods industries

This broad group of industries has suffered from the demands made on labour and materials by the expanding basic industries. Only in certain branches of food processing, for which there is an export demand, has production greatly increased.

Food processing. Food industries are concentrated in the central lowlands and northern platform. In addition to flour-milling and the extraction and processing of oil from sunflower, rape and other oleaginous plants, these include the tinning of fruit and vegetables and the preparation of purées and conserves.

Sugar-beet is a crop primarily of the northern platform, and most of the processing factories are distributed across this region from Lom in the west to Reka Devnja in the east, with the largest at Gorna Orjahovica. The production of refined sugar has increased from 67,000 tons in 1948 to 244,000 in 1964.

Tobacco. The preparation of tobacco was formerly carried on mainly in the houses and small barns and workshops close to the fields where it was grown. Now the drying and curing of the leaves is performed in a number of centrally placed establishments in the Rhodope region and the lower Marica valley, and the final stages of manufacture are concentrated in a number of factories situated in the larger towns, including Plovdiv, Sofia, Pleven and Stara Zagora.

Woodworking and paper manufacture. These branches of industry derive their raw materials primarily from the forests of Bulgaria. Sawmills are found mainly within the Rhodope and Stara Planina; pulp and paper mills around their margins, and the manufacture of furniture and of other domestic equipment and appliances, in the larger cities.

Industrial regions

In 1959 Bulgaria was divided into 30, later reduced to 28, districts, or *okruzi*, for purposes of administration and planning. These replaced the thirteen rather arbitrary *okruzi* which had previously served. The

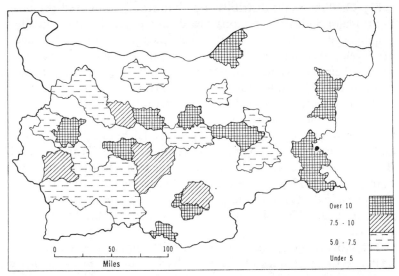

Fig. 13.10. Distribution of industry in Bulgaria as shown by the percentage of the population in manufacturing. After A. C. Beškov and E. B. Valev.

purpose of the new organisation was allegedly to permit a greater participation by the workers in regional planning and the assumption of greater responsibility for the results. Three of the *okruzi* are urban— Sofia, Plovdiv and Varna. The rest accord only in the very broadest sense with landform regions, but do nonetheless reflect the individuality of the Danubian Platform and the central lowlands. Their role is primarily economic, and each focuses on a significant industrial centre from which it derives its name. The thirty *okruzi* are sometimes grouped into six regions,[1] each having a distinctive economic character.

[1] For example, by A. Beškov and Ignat Penkow; see bibliography.

The north-western and the north-eastern, with the exception of the towns of Varna and Ruse, together with the south-eastern, are all relatively non-industralised. The north-central region, despite a considerable development of light industries in the northern foot-hills of the Stara Planina, also remains a mainly agricultural region. The south-western and south-central regions with respectively 33·3 and 25·65 per cent of Bulgaria's total industrial production in 1958, are by far the most heavily industrialised, and present develop-ments do nothing to threaten the overwhelming supremacy which these regions have established.

Fig. 13.10 shows the distribution of industrially employed persons. Four major industrial regions are distinguished by their greater employment in manufacturing. They each have the advantages of developed transport facilities, natural resources for at least part of their needs, and adequate power resources, and these advan-tages are tending now to attract new industries, so that the relative im-portance of these regions is likely to increase.

The Sofia industrial region spreads over not only much of the Sofia Basin, but extends southwards up the Iskâr valley to Samokov and south-westward to Pernik. It contains a significant part of Bulgaria's brown coal and lignite, all of the iron and steel, and much of the metal-working and mechanical engineering industries. It is also prominent in the textile, chemical and consumer goods industries, and is the most varied in its industrial structure as well as the largest of the regions.

The Plovdiv region occupies much of the upper Marica plain. It lacks the fuel resources of the Sofia Basin, but has in its intensive agriculture the basis of an important food-processing industry. It is important for its textile and non-ferrous metallurgial industries, but is less diversified than the Sofia region.

Dimitrovgrad is the newly built focus of a more specialised industrial region, which lies around the junction of the Sazlijka river with the Marica. Its basis is the abundant local reserves of lignite, and its manufactures—basic chemicals and fertilisers, cellulose and cement —make heavy demands on the thermal-electric power generated here. This region includes smaller centres of light industry, such as Haskovo and Harmanli, but it differs from Sofia and Plovdiv in comprising a newer and narrower, but more integrated group of industries.

The last industrial region comprises Varna, with its shipyards, refineries and textile mills, and the newly developed industrial complex at Reka Devnja and around the head of Lake Varna. The latter is broadly similar to Dimitrovgrad in its concentration on chemicals and cement.

These industrial regions are obvious, however they may be delimited on the map. The list of other industrial centres must, in the absence of statistics of employment and production, be in some measure subjective. Burgas and Ruse have clearly an important and varied industrial structure. Gabrovo and Sliven, though more specialised, are only a degree less important. Pleven, Kazanlâk and Stara Zagora have each a broad industrial base, and Vraca is becoming the industrial focus of the north-western region. Then there are the numerous smaller towns, each with a factory or two, and some with specialised and highly important undertakings, many of which have been noted in the foregoing pages. They include Tolbuhin, Razgrad and Kolarovgrad, Gorna Orjahovica and Loveč, Kârdžali, Blagoevgrad and Stanke Dimitrov.

Industrial production

The industrial revolution of the past 20 years has transformed Bulgaria from an overwhelmingly rural and agricultural country into one in which the gross value of manufactures has begun to exceed that of agriculture. The gross national product has risen sharply and continuously since the inauguration of the first of the national plans in 1949. After correcting the figures to eliminte the results of inflation, the national income is seen to increase in Table 93.

Table 93. Increase in Bulgaria's national income since 1954
(in millions of leva)

1953	2,779·8
1955	2,820·3
1956	2,744·7
1959	4,219·8
1962	5,158·2
1964	6,203·7
1965	6,635·6

Source: *UN Yearbook of National Accounts Statistics, 1966.*

A breakdown of the gross material profit by sectors shows (in Table 94) above all the expansion of the mining and manufacturing sector, and the contraction of that devoted to 'trade', which here includes not merely retailing, but also handicrafts. The value of industrial production appears to have increased some ten- or twelve-fold since the beginning of the Five-Year Plans. During this period, manufacturing industries have received about 40 per cent of all investment capital.

Table 94. Breakdown of the gross material profit, by percentages

	Agri-culture	Mining and manu-facturing	Building con-struction	Transport and commerce	Trade	Others
1955	30	34	8	5	20	3
1957	34	41	7	3	12	3
1959	33	43	7	4	11	2
1962	33	44	7	4	9	2
1964	34	45	7	4	8	2

Source: *UN Yearbook of National Accounts Statistics, 1965.*

The composition of the industrial share of the national income has also undergone considerable changes. The food industries, which formerly contributed almost a half, now account for only a quarter, while the contribution of the metallurgical, and chemical engineering industries has greatly expanded.

COMMUNICATIONS AND TRADE

The main thoroughfare of Bulgaria has always been, from the days of the Caesars to those of the Kaiser's *Baghdadbahn*, the route which leads up the Marica valley, through the Sofia Basin, and down the valley of the Nišava. Other roads and routes have been little more than feeders to this main highway. Along it grew up the chief cities of antiquity—Adrianople, Philippopolis, Serdica, and although, with the coming of the Bulgars, the centre of political life was shifted to the more easterly parts of the Danubian Platform, economic life continued to focus on the great routeway. It was almost inevitable that much of the economic development of recent years should have taken place along this axis, not so much because of the relative ease of transport and communications as because the route itself links together a series of Tertiary basins in which are found both deposits of solid fuel and areas of good soil.

Road system. Bulgaria claims to have a road system of about 17,500 miles, of which about a tenth can at present be described as smooth-surfaced motor roads. The rest are of the kind which in the Balkans is called 'macadam'. It is rough, dusty and muddy according to the season, but is nevertheless regularly used by the buses and lorries, not to mention the peasants' carts, which still form the chief means of conveyance in much of the country.

The chief roads lie approximately from west to east, following the trend of the mountains and rivers. Very broadly, three routes stand out: first, that which takes an irregular course, with numerous branches and detours to link up the many scattered towns, across the northern platform from Vidin to Varna; secondly, the route which traces the narrow depression along the southern margin of the Stara Planina, and carries the route from Sofia to Burgas, and lastly, the great road itself from the Nišava to Edirne and Istanbul. This last is obliged to cross the mountains which enclose the Sofia Basin. This it does by the low Dragoman Pass at about 2,360 feet, between the Nišava valley and that of the Iskâr, and by the less clear-cut but no less easy route through Ihtiman from the Sofia Basin to the headwaters of the Marica.

These west to east routes are linked together by a number of shorter but usually more difficult routes. A number of roads cross the Stara Planina and Sredna Gora, but roads across the Rhodope are few, difficult and liable to be closed by snow in winter. The most important through road in the whole Rhodope region is clearly that which follows the course of its largest river, the Struma, and links Sofia with Blagoevgrad and the Greek border near Petrič.

Railway routes. The railway system of Bulgaria follows closely the geographical pattern established by the roads. The earliest railways were built under Turkish rule. They were conceived primarily for strategic reasons, and ran from the Black Sea coast at Varna to Ruse, on the Danube, and up the Marica valley to the edge of the mountains. It was not until after the establishment of the modern state of Bulgaria that this rudimentary network was extended, and the principal west-to-east route—the Orient Express railway—was completed in 1888, and brought into regular use by through trains shortly afterwards. When the Second World War began Bulgaria had a railway network which served to link most parts of the country with Sofia. All were single track and some were narrow gauge. Since the initiation of the economic plans a number of branch lines have been built, of which the most important is that to Silistra, on the Danube. The Tundža valley railway has been linked directly with Sofia; the Struma valley line has been converted from narrow to standard gauge, and the line from Sofia to Plovdiv double-tracked. A beginning has been made with the electrification of the Bulgarian railways, and two of the most used lines—those from Sofia across the Stara Planina to Mezdra, and that from Sofia to Plovdiv—are now electrified, as well as that from Ruse to Gorna Orjahovica.

The length of the Bulgarian rail network is 3,578 miles, of which 210 are still (1964) narrow gauge. In general the main lines appear to be intensively used, though traffic is light on some of the less important branches. Brown coal and lignite, cement and other building materials, metalliferous ores, sugar-beet and grain are reported to make up the greater part of the goods carried.

River navigation. The only river regularly used for navigation is the Danube. Since the Second World War Bulgaria has built up a small fleet of river barges. The Danube, because of its peripheral location, can do little to help the internal traffic flow of Bulgaria. Goods are however distributed between the eight river ports which are almost equally spaced along the Danube from Vidin down to Silistra. Some handle part of Bulgaria's foreign trade, and Ruse has recently become the foremost port in terms of the volume of goods handled.

Air transport. Internal airlines are poorly developed, and, in fact, only serve, with intermediate stops, to link Sofia with the three main ports. Sofia itself has the only regularly used international airport, and is linked by regular if not frequent flights with the capitals of neighbouring countries.

Seaports and shipping. Bulgaria has two important ocean ports, Varna and Burgas, and one inland port, Ruse, which nevertheless handles a good deal of foreign commerce. The situation of the two Black Sea ports, each at the head of its deep and fairly sheltered bay, has already been described. Both were of minor significance until, early in the present century, harbour works were constructed. These have been extended under the recent economic plans. The approaches to Burgas are narrow, and only vessels of relatively shallow draught can reach the harbour. Varna is less encumbered, and has grown more rapidly. Docks have been excavated in the soft deposits which lie between the bay and Lake Varna, which serves as an inland extension of the harbour. The volume of goods handled in both ports has increased sharply in recent years, and in 1963 reached 2·7 million tons at Varna and 2·2 at Burgas. Part of this is transit traffic from other Balkan and Danubian countries; much consists, however, of the developing trade of Bulgaria itself.

Foreign trade
The volume of foreign trade carried on by Bulgaria has grown in step with the economic expansion of the country. The total turnover, which is roughly equally divided between exports and imports, multiplied nearly six times within the period 1953 and 1965. At an estimated value of 2,340 million dollars in 1965 this represents a per capita foreign trade of about 28 dollars.

Table 95. Bulgaria's foreign trade—by commodity (in millions of leva)

1964	Imports	Exports
Live animals	0·9	0·0
Foodstuffs	56·2	415·4
Raw materials for the food industry	42·2	84·6
Other raw materials of vegetable and animal origin	139·5	186·7
Fuels, minerals and metals	367·3	108·7
Chemicals, fertilisers, rubber	88·7	30·2
Building materials	13·0	22·2
Machinery and mechanical equipment	600·9	240·8
Consumer goods of industrial origin	69·2	187·1
	1,377·9	1,375·7

Source: *UN Yearbook of International Trade Statistics, 1965.*

Agricultural products still dominate Bulgaria's exports, and make up more than half of the total by value. It is not possible to derive the value of the separate items, but it is clear from the tonnages reported that tomatoes, grapes and other fresh fruits, followed by vegetables and maize make up most of it. Machinery and mechanical equipment has been of increasing importance, and in 1965 accounted in value for about a quarter of the whole. This was followed by consumer goods of industrial origin, and fuels, minerals and crude metals; other goods were relatively insignificant. The pattern of imports is distorted to a similar degree in favour of machinery and mechanical equipment, which account for 43 per cent of the total. This is followed by fuel—chiefly petroleum—minerals and crude metals, and foodstuffs and other vegetable products, including raw cotton.

Direction of trade. The foreign trade of Bulgaria is even more narrowly oriented than that of most other East European countries. The earlier concentration on the Soviet Union and the other countries of the Eastern bloc had in 1965 still not been relaxed. Of the total trade 53 per cent is with the Soviet Union, and about 23 per cent with the other socialist countries of Eastern Europe. East Germany, Czechoslovakia and Poland are Bulgaria's major trading partners within the bloc. Outside the bloc the greatest volume of trade was carried on with West Germany, France, Italy and Austria, and outside Europe, Canada and Cuba. It is noteworthy that in the case of a number of capitalist countries—particularly Canada—trade was unbalanced to a high degree. This can only be understood in terms of the large credits allowed to Bulgaria to pay for the unrequited imports from these sources.

Table 96. Bulgaria's foreign trade—by countries (in millions of leva)

1964	Imports	Per cent	Exports	Per cent
USSR	656·2	52	609·2	53
Eastern Europe[1]	261·3	21	279·5	25
Rest of the world	325·5	27	257·5	22
	1,243·0	100	1,146·2	100

[1] Including Yugoslavia and Albania.

Source: *UN Yearbook of International Trade Statistics, 1965.*

Bibliograhy

General

BEŠKOV, ANASTAS, *Volksrepublik Bulgarien*, Verlag die Wirtschaft, Berlin, 1960.

BEŠKOV, A. C. and E. B. VALEV, *Geografiia na Bulgariia*, Bulgarian Academy of Science, Sofia, 1961.

Background Notes: Bulgaria, U.S. Department of State, Washington, D.C., 1965.

DELLIN, L. A. D., ed., *Bulgaria, East-Central Europe under the Communists*, London, Stevens, 1957.

GELLERT, J. F. *Mittelbulgarien*, Berlin, 1937.

RINKA, ERICH, *Bulgarien*, Dresden, 1956.

WILHELMY, HERBERT, *Hochbulgarien*, 2 vols., Kiel, 1935–6.

Physical Geography

BEAVER, S. H. 'Bulgaria: A Summary', *Geography*, **25** (1940), 159–69.

JARANOFF, DIMITRI, 'Les zones morphologiques dans les parties centrales et orientales de la péninsule Balkanique', *C.r. du IVe Congrès des Géographes et Ethnographes Slaves, 1963*, Sofia, 1938, 78–82.

POPOV, V., D. DIMITROV, I. IVANOV, M. GEORGIEV, P. PENEV, *Bŭlgariia: Khristomatiia po fizicheska geografiia*, Sofia, 1963.

Historical and Political

'Bulgaria–Greece Boundary', International Boundary Study, No. 56, October 1965, Washington, D.C., Department of State—Bureau of Intelligence and Research.

LOGIO, G. C. *Bulgaria: Past and Present*, Manchester, Sherratt & Hughes, 1936.

MACDERMOTT, M. *A History of Bulgaria, 1393–1885*, London, Allen & Unwin, 1962.

RUNCIMAN, STEPHEN, *History of the First Bulgarian Empire*, London, Bell, 1930.

SETON-WATSON, R. W. *Rise of Nationality in the Balkans*, London, Constable, 1917.

Population and Settlement

'Le développement de la population en Bulgarie', *Population*, Paris 1959 (14th year), 339–44.

'La population et l'économie de la République Populaire Bulgare', *Notes et Études Documentaires*, No. 2787, Paris, 1961.

BACZWARON, MARIN and MICHAIŁ MICZEW, 'Stopień urbanizacji Bułgarii', *Przegl. Geogr.*, **37** (1965), 599–616.

HOFFMANN, GEORGE W., 'Transformation of Rural Settlement in Bulgaria', *Geogr. Rev.*, **54** (1964), 45–64.

— 'Die Umwandlung der Landwirtshaftlichen Siedlungen in Bulgarien', *Geogr. Rdsch.*, **17** (1965), 352–61.

KOSTANICK, HUEY L., 'Turkish Resettlement of Bulgarian Turks 1950–1953', *University of California Publications in Geography*, **8**, No. 2, 65–146.

MEYER, PETER, *et al.*, *The Jews in the Soviet Satellites*, Syracuse University Press, 1953.

PENKOFF, IGNAT, 'Die Siedlungen Bulgariens, ihre Entwicklung, Veränderungen und Klassifizierung', *Geogr. Ber.*, **5** (1960), 211–27.

Economic Geography

Analysis of Bulgarian Foreign Trade, Washington DC, U.S. Department of Commerce, World Trade Information Service, 1961.

BATAKLIEV, IVAN, 'La culture du Tabac en Bulgarie', *C.r. du IVe Congrès des Géographes et Ethnographes Slaves, Sofia 1936*, Sofia (1938), 191–4.

BATAKLIEV, IVAN, 'Viticulture in Bulgaria', *Geography*, **24** (1939), 85–94.

BEŠKOV, ANASTAS, 'Tobacco in Bulgaria', *Econ. Geogr.*, **16** (1940), 188–94.

BILLAUT, MICHELINE, 'La collectivisation agraire en Bulgarie: l'exemple du village de Petartch', *Annls Géogr.* **69** (1960), 484–92.

BLANC, ANDRÉ, 'Aspects et problèmes de l'agriculture Bulgare', *Revue Géographique de l'Est*, **4** (1964), 301–13.

BLOCHKOW, ANASTAS, 'Wirtschaftliche Einteilung Bulgariens', *C.r. du IV^eCongrès des Géographes et Ethnographes Slaves*, Sofia, 1936.

BRUMAN, HENRY J., 'The Bulgarian Rose Industry', *Econ. Geogr.*, **12** (1936), 273–8.

'Bulgaria', *European Conference on Rural Life*, League of Nations, Geneva, 1950.

BYCZWAROW, MARTIN, 'Hutnictwo żelaza i metali nieżelaznych w Bułgarii', *Przegl. Geogr.*, **34** (1962), 333–49.

COUSENS, S. H. 'Changes in Bulgarian Agriculture', *Geography*, **52** (1967), 12–22.

DOUKAS, KIMON A. 'Bulgaria's Modes of Transport', *Econ. Geogr.*, **19** (1943), 337–46.

GEORGE, PIERRE, 'Bulgarie', *Annls Géogr.*, **72** (1963), 122–3.

KAYSER, BERNARD, 'Les problèmes de l'agriculture bulgare', *Études Rurales*, No. 4 (1962), 5–23.

KHRISTOV, TODOR, *Geografiia na promishlenostta v Bulgariia*, Sofia, 1962.

KOSTROWICKI, J. *et al.* 'The Collective Farm of Petărch in the Suburban Zone of Sofia', *Land Utilisation in East Central Europe: Case Studies*, Geographia Polonica, **5**, Warsaw, 1965, 345–72.

— 'The Collectivised Village of Dermantsi in the Northern Foothills of the Balkan Range', *ibid.*, 373–406.

LIJEWSKI, TEOFIL, 'Powojenne prezemiany transportu w Bulgarii', *Przegl. Geogr.*, **33** (1961), 679–89.

MARINOW, VASIL, 'Die Schafzucht der nomadisierenden Karakatschanen in Bulgarien', *Viehzucht und Hirtenleben in Ostmitteleuropa*, Budapest, 1961, 147–96.

'The party and the Peasant: III, Bulgaria', *East Europe*, January 1958, 34–6.

'La population et l'économie de la République Populaire Bulgare', *Notes et Études Documentaires*, No. 2787, Paris, 1961.

PENKOW, IGRAT, 'Rozwoj i geograficzne rozmieszczenie produkcji w Bulgarskiej Republice Ludowej', *Przegl. Geogr.*, **32** (1960), 289–302.

RADOJKOW, W. 'Einige Veränderungen in der sozialökonomischen Geographie Bulgariens', *Z. Wirtgeogr.*, **9** (1965), 175–9.

SEVERIN, R. KEITH, 'Bulgaria's Agricultural Economy in Brief', *Foreign Agriculture Economics*, Washington, DC, U.S. Department of Agriculture, 1965.

STRASZEWICZ, LUDWIK, 'Bułgarski przemysl lokienniczy', *Przegl. Geogr.*, **33** (1961), 663–78.

WARRINER, DOREEN, ed., *Contrasts in Emerging Societies*, Indiana University Press, 1965.

ZAGOROFF, S. D. *et al.* *The Agricultural Economy of the Danubian Countries 1935–45*, Stanford University Press, 1955.

CHAPTER FOURTEEN

Albania

The last, smallest and least developed of the countries of Eastern Europe is Albania. It lies on the coast of the Adriatic Sea, between Yugoslavia and Greece. It spans the southward continuation of the Dinaric Mountains from the narrow belt of coastal lowlands eastward to the basin-plains of Macedonia. Despite the extraordinary ruggedness of its terrain and the difficulties of travel across the north to south strike of its mountain ranges, the location has been throughout historical times one of exceptional strategic value. At its narrowest the Strait of Otranto, which separates the Albanian coast from the opposite shore of Italy, is only 47 miles wide. On a very clear day it is possible to see the Albanian mountains from Apulia, and the crossing has been made in frail boats since prehistoric times. The classical Greeks, in their voyages from Greece to Magna Graecia and Sicily, regularly sailed up the Albanian coast until they could make the shortest crossing of the strait, and then followed the coast of southern Italy.

Greek colonies, notably Epidamnos, on the site of the modern Dürres, and Apollonia, were founded along the Albanian coast, from which the Greeks must have carried on some business with the fierce mountain people of the interior. In time these too acquired a political organisation that was broader-based than the tribes of Hellenic times. In the third century B.C. these tribesmen, disciplined and equipped after the Hellenistic model by their king, Pyrrhus, actually invaded southern Italy, where they inflicted serious defeats upon the Roman armies.

Although the Albanian tribesmen gained no permanent foot-hold in Apulia, their ships preyed on Roman commerce, and a state of no mean power was beginning to take shape with its capital at Scodna, the modern Shkodër. The Romans felt obliged to intervene, and in 228 B.C. subjugated and annexed the narrow coastal lowland. The safeguarding of this foothold beyond the Strait of Otranto was found to necessitate the subjugation of the mountainous country of the interior, and the protection of the latter in turn made necessary the conquest of Macedonia and intervention in Greece. In this way the Romans were led on through Thrace to Asia Minor, unable to draw a line that was strategically defensible and tactically strong. Late in the second century B.C. the Romans built the Via Egnatia across Albania, Macedonia and Thrace, to the site of the future Constantinople. Its western termini were at Dyrrhachium, the modern Durrës, and Apollonia. These two branches then joined and the road followed the Shkumbî valley to the Ohrid basin, and thence, through Macedonia to Thessaloníki and Thrace. Along it moved Roman legions and Greek merchants, but they seem to have had strangely little influence on the mountain tribes through whose territory they passed.

These tribes were part of the Illyrian people, who had occupied the whole Dinaric–Píndhos mountain system and had spread possibly as far north as the Vistula basin (see page 46). They were settled in the Albanian region before the coming of the Greeks, and retained their language through the long period of Greek and Roman penetration of their country. The Albanian dialects absorbed elements from Greek and Latin, as they also did from Slavic, but the language of present-day Albania and of Albanian communities beyond its borders is considered to be basically the ancient language of the Illyrians.

The Albanians adopted Christianity, in both its Latin and Eastern forms, more readily than they did the Latin and Greek languages. Very broadly, Latin Christianity, or Catholicism, came to prevail in the more northerly and mountainous parts of the Albanian region, and Orthodox in the more southerly, through which ran the road from Constantinople.

There was little political cohesion under Roman rule, and none thereafter. The tribal structure, which had never been suppressed, even in the more accessible parts of southern Albania, again came to the fore. It is from one of the tribes which inhabited northern Albania at this time, the Albanoi, that the region as a whole derived its popular name.

In the middle years of the sixth century the Slav tribes crossed the Danube. During the following years they pressed into the Illyrian-held regions of the Balkans. In most of this area the Illyrian language, in so far as it had survived Roman conquest and occupation, disappeared before the Slav languages. Only in the region currently known as Albania did it survive. In general it was the rugged relief which, at the same time, increased the difficulties of overrunning

Albania and diminished the rewards of conquest. A long and little-known struggle was fought between the north Albanians and the Slavs of Montenegro, in which the former succeeded in holding not only the Prokletije, or North Albanian Alps, but also the Shkodër basin. Later, with the rise of the Serbian state, Slav pressure against this area increased, and the Metohija, Tetovo and Ohrid basins (see page 644) passed from Albanian to Slav control.

The area remained during the following centuries in theory part of the Byzantine Empire, but only the strongest of the emperors, like Alexios I Comnenos, ever succeeded in making the imperial power felt amongst the tribesmen. For a period in the late eleventh and early twelfth centuries the Norman rulers of southern Italy and Sicily established control over the coastal plain of Albania, emphasising yet again the ease with which the opposite shores of the Strait of Otranto could be linked politically. In the thirteenth century, it was Venice which secured control over the Albanian coastland, while much of the area from Albania southward to the Gulf of Corinth was temporarily united under a native ruler as the Duchy or Despotate of Epirus. The ties of this petty state were also westward with the south Italian Duchy of Naples, and in 1272 much of south Albania and Epirus was occupied by the Neapolitans under their prince, Charles I of Anjou.

The Angevin kingdom of Albania and Epirus lasted for almost a century, and was then replaced by the overlordship of Serbia. The conquering Serb ruler, Stefan Dušan (1331–55) drove southward through Albania, Epirus and Thessaly. The Greeks fled before his advance and their lands were occupied by the Slavs or the Albanians, who formed a considerable part of his army. It was at this time that Albanian communities settled in the Peloponnesus and on some of the Greek islands. But Serb hegemony was short-lived. Stefan Dušan was the last of the powerful Serb leaders, and within a generation of his death Serb power had been destroyed on the battlefield of Kosovo by the invading Ottoman Turks.

The Albanian tribes were again without unity or cohesion at the time of the Turkish invasion which began in 1385. Local resistance and isolated revolts marked the following years, but much of Albania passed under Turkish control. Many Albanians who had never allowed their religion to weigh heavily upon them, were converted to Islam. In this way they were allowed to keep their lands and were exempt from some of the taxes which the Turks imposed on the infidel. Often they made the best of both worlds, both circumcising and baptising their children and giving them both Muslim and Christian names. It was at this point that the Albanian people were rallied by the greatest of their national heroes, Gjergj Kastrioti Skënderbeg, known more widely as Skanderbeg. Prompted by a defeat of the Ottoman armies at the hands of the Hungarians, Skënderbeg in 1443 led a revolt in southern Albania. He was supported by the Republic of Venice, by Italian princes and by the Pope, and until his death 25 years later Albania was for practical purposes independent.

The end of Skënderbeg's resistance was followed by the gradual reassertion of Turkish control. Many Albanians left the country, migrating this time across the Strait to Italy, where there long remained Albanian communities, many of them Orthodox or Uniate in religion. Most of those who remained were converted to Islam. Albanians served in the Turkish armies and played a noteworthy role in the Ottoman administration. But in Albania they were quiescent, enjoying what amounted to autonomy under Ottoman overlordship.

The making of the Albanian state. For centuries the Albanians lived to themselves. Life within the mountains was far from quiet or uneventful, but it was disturbed only by tribal feuds and sporadic risings against Turkish rule. Power lay in the hands of pashas and beys. Some of these, like the Bushatis in northern Albania and Ali Pasha Tepelena —the Lion of Ionanina of the eighteenth century—in southern Albania and Greek Epirus, became virtually independent of the Sultan. But both were in time subdued by the Ottoman armies. So things remained until Russian armies came into the Balkans and at San Stefano in 1877 established the state of 'Great Bulgaria'. Throughout these years Albania was the least progressive part of the backward European provinces of the Ottoman Empire.

In 1878, however, a group of Albanian leaders met at Prizren to discuss the future of Albania, while at the same time a more notable assembly was meeting in Berlin to arrange the future of the Balkan peninsula itself. The Albanians feared that the alternative to a continuance of Turkish rule in the southern part of the Balkans was the partitioning of the area between Greece and the Slav states. Unless they could secure autonomy for themselves they preferred to continue in their present status. They formed the Albanian League for the Defence of the Rights of the Albanian Nation, and very soon had an opportunity to demonstrate that their claim to 'resist until death' any encroachment on Albanian territory was no idle boast. The League first protested against the boundaries established at Berlin, and then proceeded to prevent by force the Montenegrins from taking over the areas of Podgorica—the present Titograd—and Antivari, or Bar. In the end it was necessary for the powers to persuade the Porte to compel the Albanians to desist and allow the Montenegrins to take what the Berlin Conference, in order to maintain a balance of power, had awarded them.

The foundation of the League and the encroachment of Montenegro marked a turning point in the development of the Albanian nation and state. Henceforward it was impossible to count with any assurance on a policy of autonomy within the Turkish Empire. The Turks obviously had neither the power to resist the resurgence of Greece and the Slav states, nor the desire to see the forces of Albanian nationalism strengthened. They feared, and probably rightly, that autonomy would be merely a half-way stage to independence; they reverted to their old restrictions on Albanian schools and on the use of the Albanian language. Even the Greek Patriarch became apprehensive and threatened with excommunication any of the Orthodox faithful who read or wrote in Albanian. But all to no avail; the Albanians had always taken their religions lightly, and the patriotic literature which began to come from presses, generally in Italy, urged the superiority of national to merely sectarian allegiance. In most of the countries of Eastern Europe, a church, more or less national in its scope, had borne the torch of nationalism, and its priesthood, whether Orthodox or Catholic, had helped to shape national traditions and, in some instances, even national policy. In Albania it served no such purpose. Three churches shared the allegiance of the people; none identified itself clearly with the national cause, and all were discredited.

The national awakening in Albania came late, but when it struck it had the force of a tidal wave. The last quarter of the nineteenth century and the first decade of the twentieth was a short period in which to create a literature and a tradition and to educate a nation, and the result bears signs of the haste with which it was done. Turkish opposition to Albanian nationalism intensified, and the Albanians retaliated by a sequence of scattered risings against the Turks. They were suppressed with increasing difficulty. Then, in the summer of 1912, a revolt broke out which the Turks were quite unable to suppress. The intention of the rebels was clearly to serve notice on the Balkan League that their country was not for partitioning among its members. The Ottoman government yielded to the Albanian demands, and agreed to the creation of a separate province from the four vilayets, Shkodër, Kosovo, Ionanina and Monastir (Bitola), in which most of the Albanians lived, and to the recognition of Albanian as its official language. During the following months the complete and unexpected military success of the Balkan League made it clear that there would no longer be an Ottoman Empire in the Balkans, and the Albanian policy of seeking autonomy within it was no longer practical. The Albanian leaders therefore turned to one of seeking complete independence, and in November 1912 proclaimed the Republic of Albania and appealed to the powers for recognition and protection.

That Albania ultimately received the recognition which it demanded had nothing to do with the merits of the case. The powers were deeply divided; each had some strategic stake in Albania, and the territory became a pawn in the European game of politics. Serbia, Greece and Montenegro objected strongly to an independent Albania. The first had long cherished the ambition to open up a commercial route by way of either the Drin or Shkumbî valley from Old Serbia to the sea. Greece expected to incorporate southern Albania, in which there was a considerable Orthodox population, and Montenegro still hoped to nibble away at northern Albania. Outside the Balkans, feelings were no less divided. Italy favoured an Albanian state across the Strait of Otranto, and hoped that it might itself come to dominate it. Austria–Hungary had no desire to see a Serbia with increased territory and its own outlet to the sea, while France and Russia, ranged against Austria–Hungary in the European system of alliances, for the same reason favoured an independent Albania.

The treaty which ended the First Balkan War left the future of Albania with a Council of Ambassadors of the great powers. This council met in London, with Sir Edward Grey, the Foreign Minister, acting, like Bismarck at Berlin in 1878, as 'honest broker'. It was decided to recognise an independent Albanian state, to delimit its boundaries, and, by way of bringing it into line with western culture, to give it as its king a nonentity from a petty German princely family.

We are not concerned with the politics *per se* of Albania; it is enough to say that this prince, Wilhelm von Wied, was politically naive and inexperienced, personally foppish and irresolute, and altogether distasteful to the rough Albanians. He was forced to leave the country after a brief sojourn of only six months. By this time the First World War had begun, and the powers had more pressing obligations than sorting out the affairs of Albania. The country relapsed into anarchy, as it had done so many times in the past. The Serbian army retreated across Albania to the sea, tracing out one of the routes along which the Serbs had formerly hoped to build the railway to the coast. They were followed by the Austrians, who occupied part of Albania for the rest of the war. Italians landed on the coast and occupied the ports and coastal plain, and the French, operating from their base in Thessaloníki, advanced into southern Albania.

The events of the previous years had done little to convince the powers that Albania could possibly become a stable and independent state. Italy, in traditional fashion, aimed at some kind of protectorate over Albania, and even concluded in 1919 an agreement with Greece for the partition of the country. That such was not the outcome was due both to the vigorous reaction of the Albanians and to the intervention of the American President. At the beginning of 1920 the Albanian leaders gathered a hastily elected group of representatives at Lushnjë. This body protested vigorously against what was happening in Paris; demanded independence 'within its ethnic and natural frontiers', and formed a provisional government. Soon afterwards the Italian forces were expelled, and Italy, in August 1920, recognised the sovereignty and independence of Albania, though retaining the small island of Sazan (*It.:* Saseno), which lay off the south Albanian harbour of Vlorë (*It.:* Valona).

The boundaries of the new state remained in dispute. Those of 1913 had never been demarcated, and Albania claimed territory beyond them, in the Kosovo–Metohija region of Yugoslavia, while both Yugoslavia and Greece claimed territory which the Council of Ambassadors had in 1913 assigned to Albania. In 1921, however, the representatives of the great powers re-affirmed the boundary of 1913, which was subsequently demarcated by a mixed boundary commission. The boundary was of the kind commonly described as 'natural'. No attempt was made to separate ethnic groups, and the boundary line was drawn wherever possible along the crests of the often narrow and steep-sided mountain ranges.

We are not concerned with the internal political events by which Albania progressed from the anarchic rule of the Republic to the almost oriental despotism of King Zog, nor, at this moment, are we concerned with Italian economic penetration of the country. In April 1939 the government of Zog collapsed; the Italians landed on the coast and took over the reins of government. The Italians posed as the champions of Albanian irredentism, and when they attacked Greece in October 1940, were supported by at least a part of the Albanian population. It is well known that the Italians fared badly in this campaign, and were in fact rescued by the Germans after the latter had overrun Yugoslavia. Albania, now a puppet state under Italian rule, was rewarded for its unwilling participation in the war by being allowed to incorporate Yugoslav Kosovo–Metohija (see page 643).

The defeat and surrender of Italy in 1943 was followed by the withdrawal of the Italian forces from Albania. Their place was taken by the Germans, who were in their turn obliged to pull out during the following year. In the meantime, partisan activities in Albania had been intensified and had acquired a strongly Communist orientation. For this the Yugoslav Partisans of Tito were largely responsible. Yugoslav agents had organised the underground Communist party and had planned its guerrilla activities. When the Germans withdrew, the Communist Partisans, under predominantly Yugoslav leadership, were the only group capable of taking over the government, all others having been liquidated or reduced to impotence by the activities of the Italians, the Germans and the Partisans themselves. The territorial claims of both Albania and her neighbours are so closely entwined with Albania's internal politics during the following years, that a brief account of the latter must be given.

A Communist government, with Enver Hoxha as premier, was established at Tirana in November 1944. His mentors were the Yugoslav advisers who had now been with the Albanian Communists for about three years. In 1945 a new constitution was devised, and at the beginning of 1946 Albania proclaimed itself a 'People's Republic'. At the same time ties became yet closer with Yugoslavia. A Treaty of Friendship and Mutual Assistance was signed by the two countries; it was planned to merge their currencies and economies, and it was even proposed that Albania should become a constituent republic of the Yugoslav People's Federal Republic. Considering her political and economic condition Yugoslavia furnished a surprisingly large amount of economic aid to Albania, and this, together with UNRRA help, played a large part in overcoming the destruction of five years of war.

With the retreat of the Germans, Kosovo–Metohija was restored to Yugoslavia, and the Yugoslav-dominated government of Albania made neither protest nor counterclaim. Indeed, for a year or two the Albanians of Kosmet, whose fate had previously caused so much indignation in Albania itself, seemed to have been forgotten. At the

27*

same time, however, southern Albania and northern Epirus came again into dispute. Previous Albanian claims had extended south as far as the former Turkish vilayet of Ionanina. On the other hand, the Greeks had laid claim to southern Albania, particularly the provinces of Korçë (*Greek*: Koritsa) and Gjirokastër (*Greek*: Argyrokastro). The issue was clouded by uncertainty regarding the ethnic affiliations of southern Albania and by the fact that it was used as a base for guerrilla forays into Greece.

For nearly four years the government was dominated by Yugoslavia, and Albania was in fact a 'satellite's satellite'. Protest against the government and its policies was rigorously suppressed, but it is nevertheless clear that many Albanians would have preferred to have fought Yugoslavia to regain the Kosmet, rather than to become a Yugoslav protectorate. A change, however, came in 1948. In June of that year Stalin, who had resented its independent attitude, expelled Yugoslavia from the Cominform. Albania was called upon to choose its position, and chose to go with the Soviet Union. Almost immediately, treaties and agreements with Yugoslavia were denounced; Albanians made raids across the boundary into Kosmet, and almost overnight Albania and Yugoslavia resumed their normal relations of hostility to one another. A break so sudden and so complete must have been basically acceptable to the Albanians, or it could not have been carried through with so little repercussion at home. It is probable that the proud Albanians resented being placed in a position of dependence on the Yugoslavs whom they detested; it is certain that one of the aims dearest to their hearts was to incorporate the Kosmet.

Russian advisers replaced Yugoslav in Albania, and Russian technicians continued the projects that had been begun by the Yugoslavs. Albania had at least been promoted from the rank of satellite's satellite to that of satellite. Albania's usefulness to the Soviet Union was, however, severely limited; access was difficult; Albania's location lost much of its strategic value when the guerrilla war against Greece was called off, and the country was too backward to have much economic value. Soviet aid to Albania was relatively small, and, furthermore, the overall lessening of hostility between the Soviet Union and Yugoslavia led the Albanians to wonder whether the former was after all their most reliable ally against their archenemy, the Yugoslavs. In the late 1950s Soviet–Chinese relations began to worsen, and in the debates, both public and private, which accompanied this deterioration, Albania usually found herself ranged with the Chinese and against the Warsaw-Pact countries. No doubt this change in Albania's political leanings was prompted by pragmatic considerations: the Soviet Union would not support Albania against Yugoslavia and provided only slender economic and military aid, whereas expectations from China appeared greater. But this pragmatic course was soon supported by ideological and theoretical arguments. Albania echoed Chinese condemnations of revisionism, held close to the Stalinist line, and espoused the most militant form of Communism. All this theorising was laced with abuse of Yugoslavia; it was 'a mixture of crude dogmatic Marxism and extreme nationalism, with the latter ingredient predominating'.[1]

At the end of 1961, Albania formally broke diplomatic relations with the Soviet Union, and Soviet advisers and technicians returned home, just as the Yugoslav had done twelve years earlier. Chinese technicians appeared in their place, and a small number of factories were begun in 1963 with Chinese aid. Chinese technical and economic aid has continued to flow into Albania, though its amount is not clearly known. Albania left Comecon in 1963, broke diplomatic relations with the Soviet Union, and has become an even stronger exponent of the Chinese line than China herself. On the other hand, there has been in recent years, with the loosening of the political and economic structure of the Communist bloc, a renewed attempt to negotiate commercial agreements with other East European countries.

LANDFORMS

A few miles south-east of the boundary with Yugoslavia the coast changes direction, from north-west–south-east to north–south. For 105 miles this latter direction is maintained until in southern Albania the prevailing north-west to south-east trend is resumed. The major landforms of Albania, however, tend to preserve their Dinaric trend, and to continue the direction of those of Yugoslavia. The coastal plain of Albania is dissected by hilly ridges. These, in consequence, lie obliquely, rather than parallel to the coast, and run out to sea in a series of low headlands. The mountains of the interior are broadly similar in structure and landforms to those of Yugoslavia, whose directions they continue, and they are, in turn, continued in those of Epirus and western Greece.

[1] *The World Today*, **17** (1961), 199.

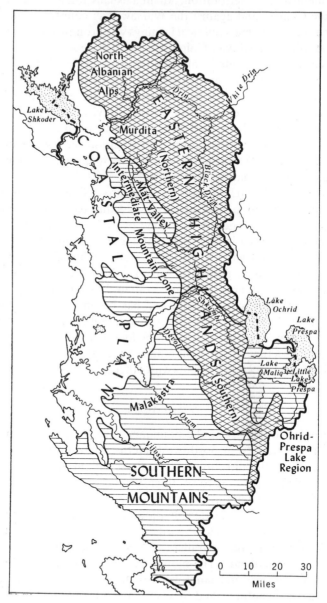

Fig. 14.1. Landform regions of Albania.

We have already seen (page 633) how the Karst of Montenegro narrows towards the Albanian border. Rocks lower in the geological series come to the surface along the coast, while to the north-east Palaeozoic rocks give rise to the rugged Malsi e madhe (*Slav.*: Prokletije), along whose summits lies the present boundary of northern Albania with the Montenegrin republic. Within Albania these beds are extensively intruded by basic igneous rocks, among which gabbro and serpentine are prominent. The resulting relief is probably the most rugged in the whole Balkan peninsula. These structures extend south-eastward, conforming with the Dinaric trend, through the Jablanica Mountains, lying to the west of the Ohrid Basin, to the Grámmos and Píndhos Mountains of northern Greece.

Along the south-western margin of this region of older and harder rock and very strong relief lies one of younger rocks and somewhat gentler landforms. This is a continuation of the coastal and karstic regions of Yugoslavia. Towards the north it consists of no more than a narrow belt, some 5 miles in width between the highlands and the coastal plain. It broadens south-eastward, and south of the Shkumbî river extends to the coast. There are thus three major landform regions: the coastal plain, the intermediate region of mountain ridges and intervening valleys and lowlands, and, lastly, the highlands of the north and east (Fig. 14.1). Each of these regions will be examined later.

Drainage

The drainage pattern of Albania stands in sharp contrast with that of the Dinaric region of Yugoslavia. A large number of rivers rise near or beyond the eastern and southern boundaries of the country and flow to the Adriatic Sea. Their courses lie mainly in a south-east to north-west direction, between the parallel ranges of the Dinaric system. Some of the larger, particularly the Drin, Mat and Shkumbî, break across one or more of the ranges by gorges and deep valleys which are probably antecedent to the mountains, and all take a more irregular course across the coastal plain.

The largest and most important of Albanian rivers is the Drin. Its main course, the Black Drin or Drin i zi (*Serbo-Croat*: Crni Drim), has its source in Lake Ohrid. Its upper course, which lies partly within Yugoslavia, is northerly or north-westerly, between the Jablonica and Korab mountains. At Kukës it is joined by the White Drin or Drin i bardhë (*Serbo-Croat*: Beli Drim), which drains the Metohija basin

(Kosmet), and flows by one of the few gaps across the boundary ranges. Below Kukës the Drin flows across a small basin, and then plunges into a deeply incised gorge tract which extends for some 25 miles. At its exit from the gorge, on the margin of the low and marshy coastal plain, the main river divides. One branch flows westward to enter Lake Shkodër; the other by a yet more tortuous course southward across the alluvium to the sea. A radial pattern of short rivers drains the Prokletije, many of them dropping steeply to the Drin.

Within the great curve formed by the Black and lower Drin flows the Mat. Its course lies between the gentler ranges of the intermediate zone, before cutting across the most westerly of the latter to reach the sea. The chief rivers of central Albania are the Shkumbî and Devoll. The former rises within some 4 miles of Lake Ohrid, separated from it only by the low Mokra Planina (*Alb*: Malet e Mokrës). Its course is north-westward; then westward across the mountains to the sea. The Devoll has its source within the Ohrid Basin, and must at one time have served as one of the outlets of the lake. The Black Drin probably deepened its course more rapidly than the Devoll and in time came to take the whole of the Ohrid drainage. The course of the Devoll is a twisting one, flowing alternately parallel to the mountain ranges and transversely across them. The evidence of the topographical maps is strongly suggestive of river-capture by the Shkumbî at the expense of the Mat, and of the Devoll from the Shkumbî.

The rivers of southern Albania are, like the structure and relief, simpler than those of northern Albania. Their main courses lie parallel with the ranges which here lie in a south-east to north-west direction. The Osum rises in the Grámmos Mountains on the Greek border, and the Vijosë and several of its tributaries actually within Greece. There has been a certain amount of river-capture, and one finds several water-gaps across the ridges of this region.

Albanian rivers are merely torrents in many places, difficult or even impossible to cross in autumn, winter and spring, and almost dry in summer. They present simple, almost exaggerated examples of the characteristic Mediterranean river-regime. The transition from mountain course to the low-lying plain is abrupt. Their speed of flow is immediately reduced. They break up into braided streams, flood, and deposit their heavy burden of sand and silt. Aerial photographs show immense deposits of sand along their lower courses, the sinuous lines in which show how frequently the rivers have changed their courses. In all instances their plain courses are sharply meandering, bordered by natural levées, and flanked by malarial marshlands which dry out in the hot summer.

Landform regions

On the basis of the structure and relief briefly outlined above it is possible to define three major regions of Albania, each with subdivisions.

Coastal Plain. The coastal plain of Albania extends from the shores of lake Shkodër in the north to the Gulf of Vlorë in the south, a distance of about 125 miles. Its width varies greatly. At its narrowest, near the mouth of the Drin, the mountains are cut off from the coast by only about 4 miles of marshy plain. Some 50 miles farther south, the plain extends inland for over 30 miles. Yet farther to the south the mountains of the interior again advance towards the coast, and, though the lowland extends up the valleys of several of the rivers, the plain itself tapers southward, and ends just outside Vlorë. North of the Shkumbî it is known as the Karajë; to the south as the Myzegë.

The plain itself is over most of its extent very flat, and rises only a few feet above sea-level even many miles from the coast. It is underlain by Tertiary deposits, but these are largely obscured by thick deposits of Recent sand and alluvium, laid down by the rivers which flow across it from the mountains of the interior. The rivers themselves, as has been noted, meander across the plain. Their channels in many places divide and subdivide; frequently they are bordered by marshes and small lakes, which form the breeding places for malarial mosquitoes. A heavy load of alluvium reaches the sea, and several of the rivers have small cuspate deltas. Silt is carried along the coast by the slow, northward flowing current, and forms spits and bars. These in turn cut off inlets which become in time marshes studded with small lakes, and finally evolve into winter grazing land. The coast is thus prograding, and is estimated to have advanced in some places up to 3 miles since classical times.

The surface of the plain is broken by a number of hilly ridges, composed of Tertiary beds, and rising in many places to more than 1,000 feet above the plain. These hills occur to the south and west of Tiranë as a series of roughly parallel ridges; elsewhere they survive only as isolated hills, showing by their direction that they once formed part of a more extended and continuous hill system. Both the hills and ridges of the plain and the mountains which enclose it on the east emerge very steeply from the diluvial and alluvial deposits by which their lowermost slopes are covered.

The plain has considerable agricultural potential. Much is under cultivation; large areas provide winter grazing for the animals, mainly sheep and goats, which move up into the highlands for summer. Summers are hot in the plain, and with irrigation sub-tropical crops can be grown. There is, for instance, an extensive cultivation of rice and cotton, but this is the season when the rivers deliver least water, and the volume of irrigation water available remains restricted in the absence of engineering works along the upper courses of the rivers. It is, however, difficult to conceive of any terrain better suited for the building of storage dams than the hill-country of the interior. So far no progress has been made in this direction. Some areas of coastal marsh have, however, been reclaimed in recent years, and the danger from malaria has been reduced.

The plain has few human settlements over much of its extent. The towns lie either on the coast, like Durrës and Vlorë, the chief ports of Albania, or close to the meeting place of mountain and plain. It is in such situations as the latter that one finds most of the larger towns: Shkodër, Tiranë, Elbasan, and Berat. Between are only small villages, widely scattered, and the isolated huts of the transhumant shepherds.

Intermediate mountainous zone. Inland from the coastal plain lies a belt of mountains which form a direct extension of the coastal mountains of Yugoslavia. They are built of sedimentary deposits— sandstones, shales and limestones—of upper Secondary and lower Tertiary age. They were folded into a tight sequence of syncline and anticline during the Alpine mountain building. In part they consist of *Flysch*, derived by denudation from the concurrent uplift of the mountain mass. Limestone, relatively resistant to erosion, tends to give rise to steep ridges; the sandstone has often been eroded to rounded hills, and the softer shales and clays are in many localities heavily eroded and present today a 'badlands' surface. Limestone is very much less extensive than in the Karst region of Yugoslavia, and karstic landforms are only feebly developed.

In the northern half of Albania this intermediate mountain belt is generally little more than 15 miles across, and often a good deal less. It consists of two or three ill-defined ridges of harder rock, with softer and heavily eroded beds lying between them. The Mat flows between such ridges and drains a basin, fault-bounded and partially filled with alluvium. The Shkumbî cuts across the ranges by a series of gorges or water-gaps, of diminishing size as the ranges themselves become lower and narrower towards the west.

South of the Shkumbî, this region of alternating mountain ridge and deep, steep-sided valley broadens, extending westwards to the coast of southern Albania. Its breadth increases at most to some 50 miles. On the topographical map one can count some eight separate, though not always continuous ridges. Many are anticlinal, and have a core of upper Secondary—generally Cretaceous—limestone. Toward the east, particularly in the Malakastra country between the Vijosë and Osum rivers, this limestone outcrops along the crests of the ridges, and is flanked by softer and severely eroded Tertiaries (see Fig. 14.1) Most of these ridges are steep and high. The Nëmerçkë, between the Vijosë river and its tributary, the Drin, rises to 8,157 feet, and most ridges rise at some point to over 5,000 feet.

Between the ridges are valleys. Towards the north-west they open towards the Coastal Plain; to the south-east, some terminate against the granitic massif of the Grámmos Mountains, but several extend across the international boundary into Greek Epirus. These longitudinal valleys alternately contract between the towering mountains and broaden into small elongated plains with extensive alluvial floors. It is in such locations that the small towns of southern Albania are found. The largest of these basins is that of the *southern* Drin, a tributary of the Vijosë, and in it lies the most considerable town of the region, Gjirokastër. Other towns in similar locations are Këlcyrë, Tepelenë, and Berat.

In consequence of the structure and relief, therefore, the mountains of southern Albania are open and accessible. Movement has never been difficult, even if today it is infrequent, along the valleys between the Albanian plain and those of the southward flowing rivers of Greek Epirus. By contrast the mountains in northern Albania rise wall-like between the plain and the hinterland as if daring coastal peoples to press into the interior. A consequence of these differences between landforms in the northern and southern halves of the country is the contrast in historical development, and in language and culture between the two parts of the country. To this contrast we turn later in this chapter.

Highland Albania. The intermediate zone of hills of central and southern Albania merges gradually and in some places almost imperceptibly into a region of stronger relief, greater altitude and, in general, older and harder rocks. The ridge and valley sequence gives place to high, plateau-like uplands, formed in rocks of greater age and hardness. These are trenched by the valleys—generally extremely deep, steep-sided and narrow—of the Drin and its many tributaries, of the upper Shkumbî, Devoll, and Osum. Highland Albania forms a belt of country which lies along the whole of the east of the country. It is broadest in the north, where it extends for some forty miles from the precipitous margin of the Shkodër plain eastwards to the Yugoslav border. It narrows towards the south, around the headwaters of the Shkumbî and Drin, but again broadens towards the Greek border.

The region is one of great structural complexity. Much of its surface is made up of Secondary rocks from the Triassic to the Cretaceous. Limestone is prominent among these beds, but does not occur on as massive a scale as in the Karst of Yugoslavia. Many of the most rugged summits in the so-called North Albanian Alps are however developed in limestone. Underlying the Secondary beds is a foundation of Palaeozoic. The latter outcrops over small areas in the extreme north of the country, and more extensively on both sides of the upper Drin, where they are a continuation of the Šar massif of Macedonia. Over large areas, however, the sedimentaries are interrupted by outcrops of basic igneous and metamorphic rock of very varied character, among which gabbro, peridotite and serpentine predominate.

Highland Albania is at its highest and most rugged in the extreme north. There a complex mass of hard limestone and other sedimentary rocks, the Malsi e madhe, commonly known as the North Albanian Alps, has been dissected by a radial pattern of short rivers into a number of separate masses, whose bare rocky summits rise to over 8,000 feet. The valleys are deep, narrow and constricted at many points by the limestone crags. These highlands, though small in area, are remarkably difficult of access, with consequences that will be noted later. Their higher surfaces provide only summer grazing, but the valleys continue to be inhabited by the Gheg tribesmen.

South of the east–west section of the Drin landforms are somewhat lower and considerably gentler. They constitute in effect a dissected plateau, the Murdita, rising to heights from 5,000 to over 7,000 feet, and formed largely in the intrusive igneous rocks. The valleys of this region are broader and more accessible than those of the North

Albanian region, and the flanks of the mountain masses drop more gently to the Drin, Mat or Shkumbî. East of the upper Drin, the Korab Mountains, which carry the boundary with Yugoslavia, rise to heights which exceed even those of the North Albanian Alps, and are equally rugged. They consist in general of intensely folded and highly metamorphosed rocks of Palaeozoic age, and are, in effect, an extension of the structures of the Šar Mountains.

The deep valley of the Black Drin is made up of alternating gorge tracts and small plains, eroded where the river flows across outcrops of softer rocks. The rivers discharging westward from the Korab Mountains, which have proved unusually susceptible to soil-erosion, have built enormous alluvial cones. These in some places almost close the valley, and force the river across to its western side. No modern road follows the Drin, the difficulties presented by its gorges and marshes having proved too severe an obstacle.

The Shkumbî valley marks a change in the landforms of the Highland region. To the south of this line Palaeozoic rocks occur towards the east, igneous and metamorphic to the west, with extensive areas of Tertiary *Flysch*. The latter yield a gentler relief than is to be found in the mountains to the north of the Shkumbî, and it has been eroded, particularly round the headwaters of the Shkumbî and south of Lake Ohrid, to form upland basins of some limited fertility. This southern part of Highland Albania is, furthermore, drained by a series of transverse rivers, which have opened up routeways from the Ohrid region westward to the coastal plain.

A distinctive part of Highland Albania is the Lake Region, which is shared with Yugoslavia. Here a series of faults, predominantly north-to-south in direction, has led to the formation of basins, similar in all respects to those already met with in Macedonia (page 646). Albania contains part of Lake Ohrid and the south-western extremities of Lake Prespa and Little Lake Prespa. All were formerly far larger than they are today, and, as evidence of their earlier extent, an alluvial plain, dotted still with marshy areas and small relict lakes, like Liqeni i Maliqit (*Serbo-Croat*: Malig), spreads southward from Lake Ohrid for some 30 miles, almost to the foot-hills of the Grámmos Mountains. The area around its market centre of Korçë is in fact one of the more intensely cultivated and densely settled areas of Albania. A similar basin lies to the south of Lake Prespa, with its local centre at Bilisht.

The south-eastern boundary of Albania follows the crest of the

Grámmos Mountains, a high, rugged massif of Tertiary (*Flysch*) sandstones, which strikes from north to south, against the prevailing Dinaric trend.

CLIMATE, VEGETATION AND SOILS

The climate of Albania differs little from that of the adjoining coastal region of Yugoslavia. Temperatures are a degree or two warmer in winter over the coastal lowlands, but there is little sensible difference between the summer temperatures of lowland Albania and those of the Yugoslav coast. Winters are mild; January averages more than 7·2°C (45°F) over most of the plain but there is considerable difference between stations in the north and those in the south. Summers are hot, with averages rising to over 23·9°C (75°F) in the south. The summer drought is strongly marked, especially in southern Albania. The wet season begins in September or October and lasts into early spring. At this time rains are frequently torrential; on the other hand less than 5 per cent of the total rainfall comes in the summer months. The total rainfall in the plain is rarely less than 1,016 millimetres (40 inches) a year, and in the foot-hills of the mountains this increases to over 1,778 millimetres (70 inches).

In the hills of the interior temperatures are very much lower. The sub-tropical plants of the coastal region begin to disappear in the foot-hills. Information is scanty on temperature conditions in the mountain valleys. January averages in the Drin valley are little above freezing, and the unrecorded temperatures in the mountains are very much lower. Summer temperatures are modified by the greater altitude, but increasing distance from the sea prevents the reduction from being as great as might otherwise have been the case. Some of the inland basins are intensely hot during the daytime in summer, but, as is usual in a mountain setting, the nights usually cool off.

Data are not available on the amount and seasonal distribution of rainfall in the mountains. We know only that it is relatively heavy, and that its concentration in the winter months becomes less pronounced. As the Yugoslav boundary is approached a secondary rainfall maximum appears in late spring and early summer. Much of the winter precipitation is as snow over the higher ground, and snow may linger on the high mountains until summer.

The Albanian Plain shares with the coastal region of Yugoslavia an exposure to winds of great violence. The *bura* may sweep down from the mountains, especially in winter, when it brings chilling temperatures to the plain. No less characteristic of at least southern Albania is the *sirocco*, a moist, warm wind, which is drawn in toward the front of depressions which move eastward across the Mediterranean.

Vegetation. The vegetation of Albania is no less characteristic of the Mediterranean than is the climate. The effects of the long summer drought, which prevails over all except the mountains of Highland Albania, are accentuated by the sandy, permeable rocks and the almost bare limestone surfaces, which cover large areas of the country.

Lowland Albania, except where some form of agriculture is practised, is covered with a low-growing evergreen scrub—the so-called *maquis*. It varies greatly both in plant type and in the thickness of the vegetation cover; it extends upwards to a level of from 600 to 1,000 feet, but is interrupted, not only by cultivated land and land partially cleared to make rough grazing, but also by salt marshes close to the coast. Above the level of the *maquis* is oak forest, in which various evergreen species predominate. It has been extensively cut over, and has suffered greatly from the depredations of grazing animals. Above about 3,000 feet the oak forest passes into beech forest, interspersed in places with conifers. The higher mountains rise above the tree-line, and bare rock predominates, with only a thin scatter of Alpine plants and patches of grass. In all parts of Albania, however, both mountain and plain, there are broad areas where the vegetation is of the scantiest: the severely eroded *Flysch* of the foot-hills, the spread of sand and gravel in the lowlands, the exposures of bare limestone rock, and the steep mountain slopes from which the forest cover has been removed.

Soils. The agricultural resources of Albania are small even for a country as mountainous as this. On the limestone the soils are at best thin, and over large areas are wholly lacking. The basic igneous rocks yield generally only a reddish clay of little agricultural value, and over the plain the alluvial deposits are damp and poorly drained, and the sandy and gravelly soils are both dry and infertile. Agriculture is practised chiefly where the small extent of alluvial soil can be irrigated during the hot dry summers, and this is chiefly a narrow strip of land lying from north to south between the foot-hills of the Albanian mountains and the coastal marshes. The valleys—particularly the more open valleys of southern Albania—are floored by alluvial deposits, and are usually cultivated. In the more northerly valleys, however, the alluvium is narrow and intermittent, often obscured by the stony deposits that have been washed down upon it, and so cut into valley terraces by the river's action that its agricultural value is negligible. Within the mountains, however, lie upland basins, such as the Mat valley, the plains of Ohrid and Korçë, and the Debar and Kukës plains along the upper Drin. Here the alluvial soils, made up in part at least of the deposits which accumulated in former lakes, give rise to soils of above average quality, but such cover only a very small proportion of the total area, perhaps no more than five per cent.

POPULATION, SETTLEMENT AND AGRICULTURE

It is now generally held that the Albanian people derive both their ancestry and their language from the Illyrian people who inhabited the Dinaric region in classical and pre-classical times. Their racial stock has, however, absorbed elements of many peoples: Greek, Italian, Slavic and Turkish, who have penetrated and settled in this region. At the same time, however, in the remote and inaccessible mountains of northern Albania the original racial traits have been intensified by inbreeding, so that here one finds today the most extreme examples of the Dinaric physical type. The Albanian language has also survived from pre-classical antiquity, though absorbing elements of Greek, Latin and Slavic, with which, as an Indo-European language it was in any case related. It has certain resemblances to Romanian, which is derived in part from the similar Thraco-Illyrian language of Dacia.

Albanian in all its dialects remained a spoken rather than written language for very many centuries. Albanian literature did not begin until the sixteenth century, and remained of minute proportions until the late nineteenth. In so far as Albanians were literate at all, it was in Greek. We have already noted (page 818) how the Orthodox attempted to maintain the Greek monopoly on literacy, at least in southern Albania, where they were powerful, until late in the nineteenth century. It follows that the Albanians had no alphabet in which to express the sounds of their language. In the last few years of the nineteenth century several attempts were made to devise a set of convenient symbols, and, as one might have anticipated, the choice was in reality between one deriving in the main from Roman characters, and one based upon the Greek. Very broadly the former was favoured in northern Albania, where Roman Catholicism was strongest, and the latter in southern, which was most under the influence of the Orthodox Church. It was not until the first decade of the present century that agreement was reached to use a Latin alphabet. The controversy is said to have been resolved only when it was demonstrated that the Latin alphabet lent itself more readily to mechanical reproduction.

A common alphabet has not, however, brought with it a common language. The small dialect differences between tribe and tribe are trifling beside the important gulf which separates Gheg from Tosk. These two languages are close enough to be mutually intelligible, but differ considerably in syntax and to some degree also in vocabulary. Gheg is spoken over northern Albania and extends as far south approximately as the Shkumbî river. Before the Second World War standard Albanian was generally recognised to be the dialect spoken around Elbasan, in the southern part of this region. More recently Tosk, which is spoken over Albania south of the Shkumbî, has emerged as the dialect favoured by the Party and the government, most of whose leaders have been Tosks. It would appear that the Ghegs comprise somewhat over half the total population of about 1,865,000 Albanians. It is somewhat difficult to estimate the number of Albanians living outside Albania. Albanian sources claim about 900,000 Albanians—almost all of them Gheg—in Yugoslavia, while Yugoslav sources admit to only 754,000. Albanians living in Greece are variously estimated at from 30,000 to 60,000, all of them Tosk. The Albanian colonies in southern Italy are also mainly Tosk, having migrated thither mainly in the later Middle Ages in the face of the Turkish invasions.

Although the large majority of the population of Albania is either Gheg or Tosk, there are nevertheless two significant minority groups, Greek and Slav. In the south is a Greek minority which constitutes the basis of the Greek claim to southern Albania. There are wide differences in estimates of its size, with Greek sources tending to magnify it. They range from 35,000 to 150,000, and the reality probably lies very much closer to the lower than to the higher limit. The number is difficult to estimate because, it is said, most Greeks also speak Tosk, and are counted among the latter by Albanian authorities. There has undoubtedly been some migration of the Greek-speaking population into Greece during and after the Second World War.

The Ohrid region was, as has been noted, claimed by Bulgaria during the nineteenth century, and the validity of this claim is supported by the existence here of a very small group of Bulgars. These are, however, mixed and confused with Macedonians and with Serbs who migrated into this area, mainly from Bosnia, a half century ago. The total

Slav-speaking population of south-eastern Albania numbers only a few thousands. There is in additon a handful of Serbs and Montenegrins in the area of Shkodër.

The only other linguistic minority of consequence is the Aromanian, or Vlach, group of southern Albania. This is, in reality, only the northern fringe of the larger Vlach group which inhabits the Grámmos and Píndhos mountains of north-western Greece. The Vlachs remain transhumant pastoralists, though there has long been a tendency for numbers of them to settle and become agriculturalists. When this happens they very quickly become assimilated to the local settled population, whether Albanian or Greek. Their numbers are not easy to estimate, but have been put at from 10,000 to 20,000. To these must be added the yet smaller Turkish-speaking population which has remained here since the period of the Turkish occupation, and the Gypsies or Tziganes, who still pursue their semi-nomadic crafts here as throughout the Balkans.

Religion. Albania is today a predominantly Muslim country, with significant Christian minorities, both Orthodox and Catholic. Before the end of the Roman Empire much of the country had been converted to Christianity, but with the schism between the Western and the Eastern Churches Albania came to be divided in its allegiance. In this, just as in the matter of language and dialect, the division was primarily between north and south. Southern Albania adhered to the Eastern Church and remained subject to the Patriarch of Constantinople. This was primarily a matter of ease of communication. Southern Albania is readily accessible to Epirus and northern Greece, and the Ohrid–Prespa region not only has easy routeways leading into Macedonia and Thrace, but also the Roman Via Egnatia, the course of which continued to be used from the Albanian coast to Constantinople.

By contrast, the more mountainous and less accessible regions of northern Albania remained in allegiance to Rome. Albanians, however, seem never to have held tenaciously to either creed, and when the Turks came very many, attracted by the freedom from taxation and the privilege of holding land which belonged to the Muslim, were converted. The land-owning *beys* of more recent times were mostly descendants of indigenous Albanians who had become converted to Islam. Today Muslims predominate throughout central Albania, and are mixed with Catholics even in the Shkodër region. It is difficult to reconcile the estimates given of the size of the religious communities. It seems probable, however, that almost 70 per cent of the population considers itself Muslim, most belonging to the Sunni sect, with, in southern Albania, a large community of the tolerant and industrious Beklashis. About 20 per cent belong to the Auto-cephalous Orthodox Church, which is headed by the Metropolitan of Tiranë, and less than 10 per cent is Roman Catholic. These latter are able to maintain only the most slender contact with the Church of Rome, and are for practical purposes independent of all authority except that of the Albanian state.

Social organisation. In terms of social organisation and manner of life the Albanians must be among the most, if not the most primitive people in Europe. In this respect, however, as in so many others, there is a marked contrast between southern and northern Albania. Only in northern Albania, among all the countries of Europe, is a tribal organisation of society maintained. The tribes are groups of families which claim descent in the male line from a common ancestor. The marriage customs and prohibitions, designed to maintain the purity of the tribal stock, are still practised. They contribute also to a consider-able degree of in-breeding. In general, a tribal area consists of a single large mountain valley. The high ridges and plateaus serve as 'frontiers' between the tribes, and are grazed in summer by the animals from both sides, though the rights of each are rigidly determined by tribal custom.

Life has always been hard in the mountains of northern Albania. The limits of the local economy are inelastic, and population pressure severe. Under these conditions, as Carleton S. Coon has shown,

> Warfare was almost continuous. The underlying cause was of course population pressure. The overt causes were seduction, theft of women, elopement, cattle-stealing, and general raiding. It did not take much to give offense, particularly in the late winter, when food was scarce. Even a man who had almost enough to eat himself would be under severe tension, because of the general nervous strain of his kinsmen and dependents, and consequent maladjustments within the household.[1]

From this condition of endemic warfare sprang the blood-feud, of which Albania has long been the most notorious and remains almost the only European practitioner.

[1] Carleton S. Coon, *The Mountains of Giants*, Papers of the Peabody Museum of American Archaeology and Ethnology, Harvard University, **23**, no. 3 (1950) 32.

This seemingly lawless practice could develop and survive only in a country where the public authorities were unable to see that justice was done. In most of Albania the Turks were not greatly interested in securing the peaceful settlement of disputes, and in its northern highlands they were unable. The task devolved therefore upon the local communities and, in particular, upon the kin of every person who was wronged. Its pursuit was governed by precise rules which are in sharp contrast with its apparently lawless character. It appears to have died out in south and central Albania, and survives today, perhaps on a diminished scale, only in the Highlands of Northern Albania, an area which is ironically mainly Roman Catholic.

Not only the blood-feud, but many other aspects of social life are governed by the same unwritten code of tribal and social conduct. Traditionally this code derives from Lek Dukagjin, and is commonly known as the 'Law of Lek'. It is interesting that it arose during the later Middle Ages, when the Turks were overrunning much of Albania. It served to hold the Albanians together and to govern their relations among themselves at a time when their country was under Turkish domination.

Settlement. The settlement pattern and even the style of the houses themselves reflect the social conditions amid which they developed. Settlement usually takes the form of small and rather loosely grouped villages, not unlike those of Yugoslavia. In most parts of the country the terrain and soil are such that a large village could not be supported by its own agriculture. Topographical maps and air photographs show that villages are in general somewhat larger in the plain than in the hills. On the other hand, isolated settlements are rare, probably because they would be too insecure. Where they occur they are commonly found to be the seasonal houses of transhumant shepherds and cowherds.

The house itself is simple in the extreme, one or two rectangular rooms, with few window openings and a strong door. In most parts of Albania it is built of rough stone carried up from the nearest stream and set in mud. Wood suitable for building construction is scarce in much of Albania, and quarried and squared stone demands too much labour. Roofs are of wooden shingles, stone shingles, pantiles or thatch, according to what is locally available. The house expands by adding a room or a lean-to, as the family grows.

In some parts of Albania, notably the north, the simple one- or two-roomed house is interspersed with the more formidable *kullë*, or tower. This is a fortified house which rises sometimes as many as four storeys. On the ground level, which has a doorway, but no windows, the animals are usually stabled; above it, reached by an inside ladder that can be quickly withdrawn, is the living-room, and above this again may be bedrooms. Windows are few and small; machicolations may overhang the entrance, and the roof may have a battlemented parapet. The whole is designed for security in a region of inter-tribal warfare and to protect those within from any marksman bent on a blood-feud. Such *kullë* are found most frequently in the parts of Albania where the tribal structure of society survives with the least alteration, but they were widely built by the *beys* or rich landowners of central Albania more to overawe their servile tenants than for protection from one another.

The houses of the village are built without order. The farmer builds anywhere on his own land, and the unwritten law requires that it be not too close to the boundary of his property. Other laws, obeyed rather in the towns than the villages, forbid the cutting of windows that might look down into the house or yard of another. This jealous preservation of privacy is, however, a Muslim rather than specifically Albanian trait. The Albanian house is functional rather than beautiful. It lacks the decoration and the charming detail that make peasant houses in many parts of Eastern Europe into works of art. Margaret Hasluck wrote:

> On planning his house, the Albanian householder sought chiefly shelter from the elements and his enemies, and took no thought for beauty. When villages are picturesque, as many are, it is always for such extraneous reasons as their site, the line of their roofs against a lightly clouded sky, and the greenery surrounding them, rather than for the architecture of their individual houses.[1]

Urban development. Albania is probably the least urbanised country in Europe. In 1961, only about 31 per cent of its population lived in settlements that Albanian statistical sources listed as urban. Many of these were however very small (see Fig. 14.2), and it is difficult to make any clear distinction between the small towns, in which agriculture remains important, and the larger villages, in which crafts are pursued and some marketing carried on. The towns tend to lie, as has been noted in the regional section of this chapter, either on the coast or along the junction of mountain and plain, with a few of the smaller

[1] Margaret Hasluck, *The Unwritten Law in Albania*, Cambridge, 1954, p. 19.

towns serving as market centres in the larger and more fertile basins of the interior.

In recent years the size of towns has increased, and it seems possible that the total population of the six largest may have increased almost threefold since the period of the Second World War. Tiranë, the capital

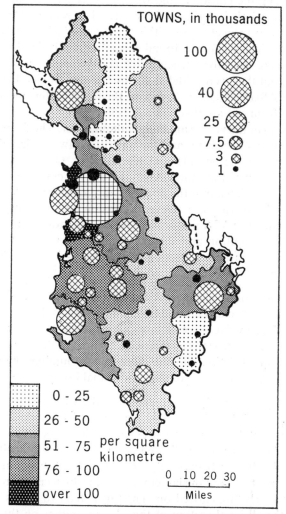

Fig. 14.2. Distribution of population and of cities in Albania. Data from *Anuari Statistikor i Republik es Popullore l'e Shgiperise*, Tirane, 1962.

and largest city, is now probably about four times its prewar size, owing in part to the growing bureaucracy, but also to the expansion of factory industries. The towns of Albania remain more oriental in appearance and function than those of any other part of Eastern Europe. They 'are essentially bazaars, usually protected by a fortress, and dealing in local products of pastoral and agricultural life'. In them crafts in wood, leather, silk, woollens and metals are carried on; they serve as meeting-places for the peasantry of their surrounding regions, and as centres for the collection of taxes and the dissemination of news and rumours. In general, they are low-built, with one-, or at most two-storied buildings predominating. Their streets are narrow and poorly paved, if paved at all. Only the larger and more sophisticated have a piped water supply and a system of sewers. In some parts, particularly of the smaller towns, open sewers run down the streets and water is drawn from wells or nearby streams. This state of affairs, it must be emphasised, is changing. Before the Second World War modern quarters were built under Italian influence in the larger towns, and since the war the Albanians have made further progress, which would in all probability have been greater if they had not hitched their political destinies to China.

Tiranë, the largest city with an estimated population of about 152,500, lies on the inner margin of the coastal plain, overlooked by the limestone ridge of Mali i Dajtit. It lies beside the Lanë, more a torrent than a river, and is surrounded by a region of good soil derived from either recent alluvium or Tertiary sands and marls. It is a loosely built town; many of the houses stand in their own grounds, surrounded by greenery, which gives it the air of a garden-city. Near the centre, where are clustered the governmental and other public buildings, the streets are wide and attractive, but they degenerate into narrow lanes towards the periphery.

Tiranë is now the most industrialised of Albanian cities, and the only one to constitute an administrative *rreth* (circle, *Kreis*), the Qyteti i Tiranë. Almost a half the light industries of Albania are in Tiranë, together with more than half the productive capacity in the metal-using industries.

Shkodër appears to be the second largest city, with an estimated population of about 46,000. It lies a short distance to the east of Lake Shkodër (Liqeni i Shkodrës) and on the narrow plain which separates the lake from the foot-hills of the northern highlands. It lay on a north–south route from Montenegro into Epirus, and also near the

Buenë river (*Serbo-Croat*: Boyana) which carries the discharge of the lake into the Adriatic Sea, and still allows shallow-draught vessels to reach the town from the sea. Shkodër, however, is in no sense a port and the little shipping which frequents it is barge-traffic from the port of Shëngjin.

Elbasan and *Berat* appear to be only a little smaller than Shkodër. Both lie within mountain valleys, where the latter open towards the plain. Elbasan lies some distance from the north bank of the Shkumbî. It is said to have a population of about 35,000, having approximately doubled in size since the prewar years. It is predominantly a Muslim town; the Turkish-style house is common, and minaret and mosque are conspicuous features of its landscape. Its industries have recently been expanded with the establishment of a metallurgical works. Berat, 30 miles to the south, lies in a very similar location, on the Osum river and·dominated by high mountains. The old town, still girt by its medieval walls, built by the Byzantine emperors, lies on a steep-sided, flat-topped hill; the more modern lower town has spread out at the foot of the hill over a small plain. The lesser towns of the Albanian plain include Lesh, on the river Drin between the northern highlands and the coastal marshes; Leshnjë and Fier, both in the southern part of the plain.

Korçë is the largest of the mountain cities, and is the urban focus of the most extensive of the upland basins, that of Lakes Ohrid-Malig. It is said now to have a population of about 43,500, and has in very recent years become the centre for metalliferous mining and petroleum drilling. Among the towns of the mountain valleys and intra-montane basins is *Gjinokastër* (*Greek:* Argyrokastro), lying in the valley of the Dhrino, or southern Drin; its valley is continued into Greece, with which communication is easy. Greek influences have always been strong, and the city contains today a large Greek community.

The chief ports of Albania are Durrës and Vlorë, both of which were developed in classical times and have since remained of some commercial importance. Of very minor importance are Shëngjin, on the northern edge of the Drin delta, and Sarandë (*Ital.* Santi Quaranta) lying at the northern entrance to the Corfu Channel in southern Albania.

Durrës, the Durazzo of the Italians, the Dyrrhachium of the Romans, and the Epidamnos of the Greeks, lies on the northern shore of the shallow Durrës bay, protected from the westerly winds by a projecting headland. It is the best harbour on the Albanian coast, and became in turn the base from which all invaders from the west penetrated the country. Details are not available of the extent of its present development, but it appears to serve the needs of much of Albania's present foreign trade. It has the best inland communications of any place on the Albanian coast and has a standard-gauge railway link with both Tiranë and Elbasan. Its population is about 46,000.

Vlorë or Vlonë (*Ital.*: Valona) (45,000) lies on the west-facing shore of Valona Bay. It is less protected by nature than Durrës, and the city itself lies a couple of miles inland, with a small port-settlement, not unlike a Greek *skala*, on the coast. A narrow-gauge railway runs a few miles into the hinterland, but does not at present reach any of the major inland towns of the country.

ECONOMIC DEVELOPMENT

Albania has always been a predominantly agricultural country. Nearly three-quarters of its population remains rural, and in 1956 it was estimated that 56 per cent of its net material product derived from agriculture. By 1958, it is claimed, this had dropped to 43 per cent owing to the rapid expansion of manufacturing. So sudden a change is inherently improbable, and it may well be that fully a half of the material product still derives from the land. Nevertheless, the importance of manufacturing has clearly increased in recent years. Albania still lags very far behind all other countries of Eastern Europe, but is planning expansion and emphasising capital-forming industries. Its progress would probably have been faster if it had not changed its political allegiance so frequently, and it would appear—though data are very scanty—that economic plans have not be fully realised.

Agriculture
Before the Second World War, 80 per cent of the population was engaged in agriculture. Most cultivated small agricultural holdings, which are said rarely to have exceeded 4 hectares (10 acres) in the more fertile parts of the country. Many were tenants on the estates of Muslim *beys*, cultivating their inadequate farms on a share-cropping basis. Attempts, associated particularly with the name of Fan Noli, a political leader of the early 1920s, to reform the structure of agriculture, failed lamentably. With the accession of Ahmet Zogu to power the rich landowners became so influential in the government that a

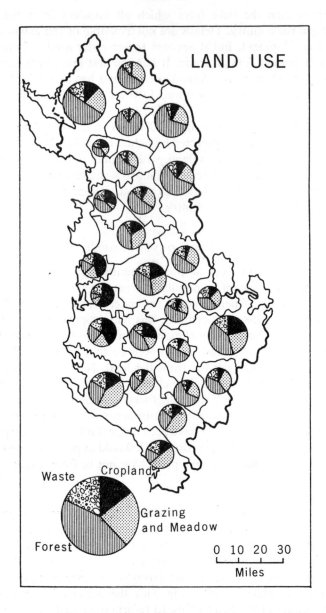

Fig. 14.3. Land use in Albania. Data from *Anuari Statistikor i Republik es Popullore l'e Shgiperise*, Tirane, 1962.

true land reform was impossible. The agrarian reform law of 1930, which set upper limits to the size of estates, was largely ignored in practice.

Table 97. Land use in Albania

	Acres	*Per cent*
Arable	408,000	6
Vineyards, olive-groves	400,250	5
Pasture	1,109,550	31
Forest	2,449,800	36
Potentially productive	748,550	11
Unproductive	748,550	11

The total area of Albania is about 10,629 square miles (27,500 square kilometres). Its land use in 1938 is shown in Table 97. Agricultural production barely sufficed for the needs of the country, and the level of human welfare was one of the lowest in Europe. The available statistics indicate that a tenth of the whole country was unproductive, but capable of being brought under some form of agricultural land use. Much of this unproductive land lay in the coastal plain, and consisted of marshes which provided seasonal grazing but were infested with malarial mosquitoes. Some progress had been made before the Second World War in reclaiming the marshes, chiefly by the Rockefeller Foundation and by Italian agricultural enterprises.

The practice of agriculture was primitive in the extreme. An ox-drawn plough, which showed little advance on that of classical times, was still widely used. Grain was harvested with the sickle and winnowed in the wind. Little use was made of manure, and artificial fertilisers were unknown in much of the country. Crop yields were the lowest in Europe. The peasantry did not have the knowledge, money and initiative to improve agriculture, and the *beys* had little desire to do so.

Heavy winter rains, soil-wash on the steeper slopes, and floods on the more level land restricted the area under crops. Autumn-sown grains were excluded by these physical conditions, and the cultivation of spring-sown crops in some parts of the plain was impossible without irrigation during some part of the summer. Wheat is an important crop only in drier regions of the interior and of the south. Elsewhere,

28

the most widely cultivated crop is maize, which can be planted in spring, and provides the staple food of the Albanian peasant. Barley, oats and rye are grown in the mountains, since they can tolerate poorer soil and cooler growing conditions. Vegetables are grown around most peasant houses. Vines are planted widely, but wine—generally said to be of poor quality—is made and drunk only by the Christians. Olive groves are numerous on the coastal plain, but much of the fruit was formerly sent to Italy for the extraction and refining of the oil. Rice is grown in parts of the plain where irrigation can be practised in summer.

Industrial crops are grown on only a very small scale, partly because of undeveloped transport facilities and lack of processing equipment, partly because the land cannot be spared from food production. Sugar-beet is grown in some of the interior basins, and sugar-cane in parts of the coastal plain. A little cotton is produced along the lower Shkumbî valley, and tobacco is grown, not only to be cured by the peasants for their own use, but also to supply cigarette factories in the towns.

The agricultural revolution. Such was the agriculture of Albania when the country was invaded by the Italians. The postwar years have seen important changes. Agriculture is collectivised. Some progress has been made in introducing better tools and mechanical equipment. The area under crops has been greatly extended, and perhaps the yields improved. At the same time, however, the number of mouths to be fed has increased by almost 70 per cent, and hunger looms as strongly today as it ever did.

In 1945 a more thorough-going land reform than that of the 1930s was introduced. The large estates were drastically reduced in size and peasant holdings either created or enlarged. But forced collectivisation came soon after, and was intensified after the break with Yugoslavia. Then followed a softer policy, as if the Albanian leaders realised how unsuitable was their country and inadequate their technical equipment for collectivised agriculture. By 1955 there were a few state farms, but only about 15 per cent of the cropland was in collectives. After 1956 collectivisation was pressed more vigorously. By 1958 the socialised sector embraced almost 80 per cent of the cropland, and by 1961, 93·3 per cent.

The area under some form of agricultural use has clearly been increased very greatly, and reports speak of an increase in the cultivated area of 93 per cent above the level of 1938. In 1961 almost 17 per cent of the total area was under crops and orchards; over 26 per cent under meadow and pasture, and about 45 per cent under forest. At this date the total area neither used agriculturally nor under forest was about 13 per cent of the whole area. It is evident that the area of potential but unused cropland had been reduced to quite small proportions.

It is very difficult to compute the increase in production of grain and other crops. In 1940–41, total grain production, including that which was in all probability used for fodder, was about 192,000 tons. In 1963, the production of bread-grains amounted to over 270,000; the increase in production of the latter must have been at least 40 per cent. On the other hand, not all harvests have been as good as that of 1963. Reports coming out of Albania during the last two years speak of very large increases in agricultural output: a production in 1965, for example, 40 per cent above that of 1960. It is evident that much of this increased production has been in industrial crops: cotton, sugar-beet, tobacco, sunflowers, flax and hemp, some of which was destined for export. The tobacco crop is said to have grown to eight times its prewar size, and that of fruit, including olives, to four times. The irrigated area is now reported to be five times that of 1938. The most optimistic claims for food crops, however, do not suggest an expansion as great as the known increase in population.

Forestry. Albania was at one time a richly forested country, but the destruction of its woodland cover began at an early date. The oak woods which were once extensive on the intermediate mountain slopes have been very largely destroyed for charcoal, for construction timber and to provide material for shipbuilding. The Republic of Venice, for example, obtained much of its ships' timbers from the Dalmatian Coast and Albania. Forests are extensive today only in the mountains north of the Shkumbî valley and in the northern Highlands, precisely because these areas are too difficult of access to have been worked over. Forests are said today to occupy about 910,100 hectares (2·25 million acres), of which almost two-thirds is second growth. It has been forcefully argued that this is inadequate to supply normal needs for fuel and building timber without seriously depleting reserves, and that widespread reafforestation is desirable. The government is said to be coping with this problem and to have already replanted some 18,200 hectares (45,000 acres). The severe soil erosion in many parts of the country, but especially in the Tertiary foot-hills bordering the plain, makes re-afforestation of these areas all the more necessary.

28*

Manufacturing industries

Albania has always been the least industrialised country of Europe, and despite the changes of recent years remains so. Yet it is not without considerable advantages and natural resources for industrialisation. Its metalliferous mineral resources are considerable; its hydro-electric power potential is significant; it has resources of mineral fuels, and is capable of producing certain industrial raw materials of vegetable origin. Yet real progress up to 1939 had been made only in metalliferous mining and the extraction of petroleum.

Metalliferous mining. The mountains of Albania, like the Dinaric system of Yugoslavia, contain a wide range of metalliferous minerals. Deposits, it is said, are not large, but they contain certain ores which are in regular demand, especially chrome and copper. Chromite (Cr_2O_3) occurs widely in Albania in close association with the intrusive masses of serpentine and of other basic igneous rocks. The largest and most easily worked deposits are in the mountains south-west of Lake Ohrid; in the middle Drin valley, near Kukës; in the extensive serpentine massif, the Murdita, south of the Drin, and in the mountains of the extreme north-east (see Fig. 14.4). Output of chrome ore rose under the Italian management of the mines, to about 36,000 tons in 1942; declined during the later years of the war, and again increased in the 1950s. The mines, nationalised in 1945, are being expanded and mechanised. An objective of 120,000 tons of ore was set for 1955, and output is said to have reached 122,094. It rose to 289,075 tons in 1960, but in 1961 amounted only to 232,458.

Copper reserves in northern Albania are said to be large, but most consist of low-grade sulphides. The ores are said to have been worked in ancient times, but modern mining did not begin until the late 1920s when an Italian firm gained concessions. The Italian enterprise remained quite small, but the industry has been greatly expanded since being taken over by the state in 1945. Most of the mines lie between the Drin and the Mat valleys, and that at Rrubik, in the hills behind Lesh, has been expanded and a new refinery has been built. Output was expanded from 24,465 tons in 1955 to 81,477 in 1960, but in 1961 dropped to 80,491. An electric wire and cable factory has been built at Shkodër, and Albania is using copper and copper products to help pay for its mounting import of capital goods.

Iron-ore deposits appear mostly to be not only uneconomically small, but also of a grade so low that in most parts of the world they would not be used. The largest lie in the highly mineralised regions

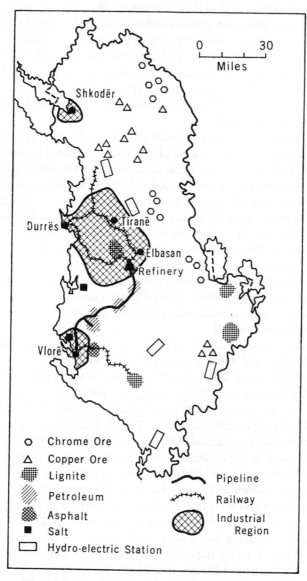

Fig. 14.4. Distribution of fuel and mineral resources in Albania, and the location of the principal industrial regions.

west of Lake Ohrid and in the Drin valley. The only really good ores
are found near Pogradec, at the southern end of Lake Ohrid. Iron ore
was mined before the Second World War and was exported to Italy,
but transport difficulties were acute, and the ores are said not to have
been worked since. The Albanian government has, however, formu-
lated plans for the building of a ferrous metallurgical plant near
Elbasan, for which the Pogradec ores would doubtless be brought
down the Shkumbî valley.

A number of other ores of economic value are known to occur, and
prospecting which is now taking place may be expected to yield more.
A nickel-iron deposit has been discovered in the Pogradec area;
bauxite occurs in the hills of the coastal region; magnesite is found at
several places, and is known to have been worked on a small scale, and
rock salt is mined near both Durrës and Vlonë. Expansion of mining is
dependent above all on improvements in transport and communications, without which the ores cannot possibly be marketed or moved
to the refineries.

Mineral fuel. Albania's reserves of mineral fuels do not appear to
be commensurate with those of metalliferous ores. Bituminous coal is
lacking; there are small deposits of lignite, and petroleum is the only
significant source of fuel.

The most extensive lignite deposits occur in the Krrabë plateau, to
the south of Tiranë. Others are found in the Vijosë valley of southern
Albania, in the Korçë Basin, and in the hills east of Tiranë. Most are of
upper Tertiary age, and their quality is reported to be good. Total
reserves are not large, and may not greatly exceed 15 to 20 million
tons. Mining began after the First World War, but remained very
small until after the Second. Output increased fairly rapidly during
the 1950s, and by 1954 reached 116,000 tons. Production has recently
been said to have reached 350,000 tons a year. The fuel appears to be
used mainly domestically and for power generation. There is no
evidence that it will serve any metallurgical purpose, a factor of some
importance in view of plans to develop ferrous metallurgy.

The most valuable fuel resource of Albania is its petroleum. It
occurs in the Tertiary deposits along the inner edge of the plain;
particularly between Elbasan and Vlonë. Reserves have been put at
up to 15 million tons, but it is probable that more recent prospecting
has greatly increased the estimate. Exploitation was begun in 1918,
but until the outbreak of the Second World War, output remained
at less than a million barrels (about 150,000 tons) a year. The petroleum

has an asphaltic base, which makes it relatively difficult and costly to refine. Partly for this reason it was at first shipped out to Italy. The Italians constructed a pipeline along the Devoll valley which connected

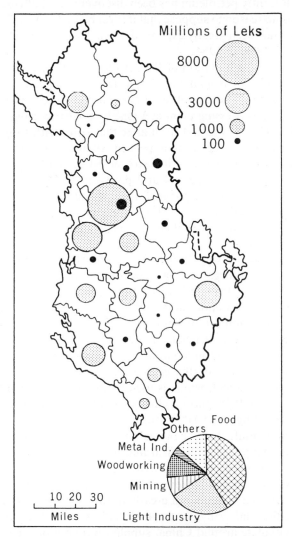

Fig. 14.5. Distribution of manufacturing in Albania, as measured by the value of the products. Data from *Anuari Statistikor i Republik es Popullore I'e Shgiperise*, Tirane, 1962.

with the major oil wells, and delivered the oil to storage tanks on the Gulf of Vlonë. During the 1950s this pipeline was repaired and extended, and a refinery built at Çerrik, its northern terminus, near Elbasan. Recently petroleum has been discovered in the Korcë Basin, but there is no reason to suppose that it is yet being worked. Petroleum production has been greatly expanded, from 208,078 tons of crude oil in 1955 to 764,000 in 1964.

Near the southern margin of the petroleum field, at Selenicë is an important source of asphalt bitumen, which was known and exploited in classical times. The asphalt continues to be worked today, and is sent down to a processing plant at Vlonë by a narrow-gauge railway.

Manufacturing. It was not until after the treaty with Italy of 1926 that modern industry began to appear in Albania. By the time of the Second World War it was still restricted to sawmills and factories for processing the local agricultural products and for making such simple necessities as soap, paper, furniture and handtools. Nor was much progress made in establishing industry until after the breach with Yugoslavia, and even then it appears that the plans were in general not fulfilled.

Handicrafts have always been important in Albania, and handicraft workers have been organised in cooperatives and allocated quotas. In the absence of adequate industrial power and factory equipment, the economy has to continue to rely heavily on handicrafts. They continue to be an important source of textiles, of articles in wood and of farm equipment, and much of the agricultural produce, such as tobacco, olives and cotton, continues to be processed by hand.

A striking measure of the expansion of factory industry is the manufacture of cement, which is used mainly in large-scale building construction. By 1965 output, chiefly from Shkodër and Vlonë, had risen from nothing to 150,000 tons. A similar expansion has taken place in the manufacture of bricks and tiles. Growth in the metal-lurgical, mechanical and chemical industries, upon which the future of the country must depend heavily, is contingent upon supplies of the basic capital goods from abroad. It does not appear that the Soviet Union ever contributed greatly to the development of its very minor satellite, and even after the latter had changed its orbit and had begun to circulate around China, supplies were not on a particularly generous or lavish scale.

The smelting capacity of the two important metalliferous ores— chromite and copper—has been expanded. The Çerrig oil refinery and the Vlonë asphalt plant are probably capable of handling most of the crude product. More recently the manufacture of the basic chemicals has commenced: of caustic soda at Vlonë and of sulphuric acid and superphosphate at a site described as 'in western Albania' and probably in the Tiranë–Durrës area. Emphasis appears to be placed on the manufacture of agricultural fertilisers.

Ferrous metallurgy appears still to be limited to foundry work, but there are plans for the establishment of an iron-steel complex at Elbasan. Ore would probably be supplied from Pogradec, and fuel would be imported unless a technique is used which can employ natural gas or petroleum for the reduction of the ore. Several mechanical engineering works have been established to use imported crude metal. These are engaged mainly in the manufacture of mining and agricultural equipment. It is claimed that a tractor factory is being built, which will ultimately have a capacity of 10,000 tractors a year, not only an unrealistic but also an unduly ambitious objective.

Other factories that have been built recently are engaged in the manufacture of paper, at Lushnjë; of cement, at Krujë; of textiles, at Tiranë, and of cigarettes, beer and other consumer goods, and in the preparation and preserving of foodstuffs in several of the towns.

It is difficult to measure the expansion of manufacturing during the last two decades. In 1955 mining and manufacturing are said to have contributed 28 per cent of the net material product of Albania. By 1958, this had risen to 38 per cent, and is now certainly more than 40 per cent.

It is difficult to speak of industrial regions in a country in which industry is so little developed. It is nevertheless clear that a rudimentary manufacturing region is in process of developing in the central part of the Albanian plain. Its foci are Durrës on the coast and Tiranë, 20 miles inland, and it may be said to extend southward to include Lushnjë, and northward perhaps to Krujë. Within this area are most of the mechanical engineering, chemical and consumer goods industries, part of the cement industry and the only oil refinery. Furthermore, this region contains most of the country's railway mileage, and most of the industrial plans of which we have knowledge appear to relate to this area. Second in importance is the Vlonë area in southern Albania. It lies close to the oil fields, has in the past been the shipping point for crude oil, and has an asphalt plant and the rest of the chemical industry.

Shkodër has fared less well in recent plans for industrial development. Reasons for this may lie in the fact that for a port it has only the poor harbour of Shëngjin; that it has no railway, and is poorly connected by road with the rest of the country. The planners, furthermore, can surely not have overlooked the fact that it is in sight across the lake of Yugoslav territory. The same objection probably holds true for Korçë, which has a considerable fuel and mineral endowment, but lies less than 20 miles from Yugoslavia and even nearer the Greek boundary.

Industrial power. The provision of power for the developing industries of Albania and also to provide services for its cities has been a matter of both urgency and difficulty. Before the Second World War some power had been generated thermally in the larger towns, and the Italians had begun work on a hydro-electric project near Tiranë. This was not completed until 1952, and four other hydro-electric stations have since been constructed. The older thermal electric stations are presumably still being used, but their capacity is small. In 1964 the production was 491 million kilowatt/hours, of which nearly half was hydro-electric. Fuel supplies, both lignite and petroleum, would appear to justify some expansion in the thermal electric capacity, but reliance must clearly be placed primarily on hydro-elecric power. The potential here is large, and estimates have placed it as high as 2·5 million kilowatts.

TRANSPORT AND COMMUNICATIONS

The chief obstacle to economic development, apart from the foolish and opportunistic policy of the government, has been the lack of an adequate, modern network of transport and communication. Development has of necessity been concentrated in the region, defined on page 853, where communications have been the most strongly developed. In the mountainous interior the opening up of known mineral resources has had to be postponed until road or railway has been built.

Road system. The Romans had built a road from the coast at Dyrrhachium (Durrës) up the Shkumbî valley to Lake Ohrid and on through Macedonia and Thrace to Constantinople. This was a well-engineered road. It was maintained in a somewhat perfunctory fashion as long as the Byzantine Emperors retained control of the area, but through the long period of the Turkish occupation nothing was done, and it was left for the Austro-Hungarian authorities during the First World War to initiate the modern road system. They built over 400 miles of motor road and laid down some 300 miles of narrow-gauge light railway track. The latter scarcely survived the war, but the roads remained as the nucleus of the later Albanian system. The latter was built in part by a system of *corvées* imposed upon the local peasantry. The quality of construction was not high and the roads do not appear to have stood up well under heavy use. During the Second World War the Italians, like the Austrians in the First, embarked on a programme of road-building, which was largely undone during the guerrilla fighting which followed. After the Second World War the government rebuilt, repaired and extended the road system, but again relied heavily on unskilled and unpaid labour. There is now a network of all-weather but not generally asphalted roads, but a great many supplementary roads remain to be built.

A major problem of road travel is the provision of bridges. A number of very handsome high-arched packhorse bridges had been built during the Turkish period. Some were destroyed during the fighting; others are ill-suited by their architecture and location for modern lorry traffic. In all parts of Albania great reliance has to be placed on ferries, though a few modern steel and concrete bridges have been built on the more vital roads.

Railway system. It has been noted that the Serbs had hoped to build a railway through Albania to the sea. They failed—primarily for political reasons, and there is still no railway across the country. The Austrian-built light railways did not outlast the First World War, and it was left for the Italians to commence the building of a standard-gauge railway. Their undertaking, left unfinished when they withdrew in 1943, was taken up by the Yugoslavs, and after 1947 was continued with Soviet help. In this way two lines were built from Durrës to Tiranë and Elbasan respectively. The two latter have been linked, and branch lines built to the Çerrik oil-refinery, to Milot, on the Mat river, and to Kashar. More recently two lines have been built into the interior from Vlonë, to Memaliaj, an important lignite mining centre in the Vijosë valley. There are now about 110 miles of standard-gauge railway, all of it built since 1947, but still restricted in effect to the plain. No doubt the railway network will be extended in the plain by constructing a line northward to Shkodër and by linking the Vlonë and Durrës systems. It is doubtful whether railways into the mountainous interior could be either successful or profitable, owing to the

28**

exceptionally rugged terrain. It is likely that reliance here will be placed upon improved, all-weather roads, and for this the government needs to employ something more effective than the unskilled *corvée* of the local peasantry.

FOREIGN TRADE

A country as undeveloped, as rural and as self-sufficing as Albania cannot be expected to carry on a large foreign trade. Until after 1926 Albania cannot be said to have had any foreign trade, and its primitive self-sufficiency was untouched by outside influences. Thereafter the import trade mounted with Italian investment and development in the country; exports, however, consisting mainly of agricultural products, remained small. The trade of Albania during the years before the Second World War was primarily with Italy and almost wholly by sea. In the period immediately following the war it was, aside from imports of food and equipment provided by UNRRA, almost entirely with Yugoslavia. After 1948 trade developed with the Soviet Union and with the bloc countries of Eastern Europe, and during the 1950s trade with the non-Communist world was of negligible importance. Following the appearance of the Sino–Soviet rift, commerce with the Soviet Union declined and then ceased, but trade has been maintained and is apparently now being intensified with other countries of Eastern Europe, including Yugoslavia. The People's Republic of China has taken the place of the Soviet Union in the foreign trade of Albania, and two-thirds of the total trade is said now to be with the Communist countries of Asia, and most of the remainder with the countries of Eastern Europe.

The trade of Albania is, and indeed has always been, highly un-balanced. Even before the Second World War the value of Albanian exports never really rose to more than half that of the imports, and the balance was made good by loans and foreign investment. This situation has continued since the war, with Albania apparently able to raise credit with most of the world's Communist governments. One can be confident that Albania is not paying with current exports for the considerable imports of capital equipment now being received from China. In 1964, exports amounted to only 61 per cent of the value of imports. Nevertheless, the expansion in the volume of trade, even when all allowance is made for inflation, is truly remarkable.

Albania's exports are made up almost entirely of the minerals and metals from its mines and agricultural products of which tobacco is the most considerable. In 1961 these comprised about 95 per cent by value of all exports. Imports were similarly dominated by machinery, metals, and chemicals, but foodstuffs were of lesser importance.

Bibliography

General Works

Albania Basic Handbook, Great Britain, Foreign Office, 1943.

Albania, British Naval Intelligence, 1944.

ALMAGIA, R. *L'Albania*, Rome 1930.

DURHAM, M. E. 'ALBANIA', *Geography*, **26** (1941), 18–24.

LOUIS, H. *Albania: eine Landeskunde vornehmlich auf Grund eigener Reisen*, 1927.

NEWMAN, BERNARD, *Albanian Journey*, London, Pitman (1938).

SKENDI, STAVRO, ed. *Albania*, London, Atlantic Press, 1956.

Historical and Political Geography

BOWMAN, ISAIAH, *The New World* (Chapter XVIII), London, Harrap, 1929.

C.H.G. 'Greek Claims in Southern Albania', *The World Today*, **2**, 1946, 488–94.

F.N-B. 'The Albanian Mystery: Russia's Least-Known Satellite', *The World Today*, **8**, 1952, 466–73.

GEGAJ, ATHANASE, *L'Albanie et l'Invasion turque au XVe siècle*, University of Louvain, 1937.

HAMM, H. *Albania: China's Beachhead in Europe*, trans. V. Andersen, London, Weidenfeld & Nicolson, 1963.

LOGORECI, ANTON, 'Albania: A Chinese Satellite in the Making?' *The World Today*, **17**, 1961, 197–205.

NICOL, DONALD M., *The Despotate of Epirus*, Oxford, Basil Blackwell, 1957.

SKENDI, STAVRO, *The Albanian National Awakening*, Princeton Univ. Press, 1967.

— 'The Northern Epirus Question Reconsidered,' *Journal of Central European Affairs*, **14** (1954), 143–53.

— 'Beginnings of Albanian Nationalist and Autonomous Trends,' *American Slavic and East European Review*, **12** (1953), 219–32.

STICKNEY, EDITH P. *Southern Albania or Northern Epirus in European International Affairs*, 1912–23, Stanford University Press, 1926.

SWIRE, J. Albania, *The Rise of a Kingdom*, London, Williams & Norgate, 1929.

— *King Zog's Albania*, London, Robert Hale, 1937.

V.R. 'Albania: A Balkan Bridgehead', *The World Today*, 6, 1950, 73–83.

VON THOLLÓCZY, LUDWIG, ed., *Illyrisch-Albanische Forschungen*, Munich, 1916.

WOLFF, ROBERT LEE, *The Balkans in Our Time*, Harvard University Press, 1956.

Physical Geography

NOWACK, ERNEST, 'A Contribution to the Geography of Albania', *Geogrl Rev.*, **11**, 1921, 503–40.

WILGAT, TADEUSZ, 'Régime des cours d'eau d'Albanie', *Przegl. Geogr.*, **34**, 1962, 25–74.

Social and Economic Geography

Anuari Statistikor, Republikes Popullore t'e Shgiperise 1961, Tirane, 1962.

BLANC, ANDRÉ, 'Naissance et évolution des paysages agraires en Albanie', *Geogr. Annlr*, **43** (1961), 8–16.

— 'L' évolution contemporaine de la vie pastorale en Albanie méridionale', *Revue de Géographie Alpine*, **51** (1963), 429–61.

COON, CARLETON S. *The Mountains of Giants*, Papers of the Peabody Museum of Archaeology and Ethnology, Harvard Univ., **23**, No. 3, 1950.

DURHAM, M. E. *Some Tribal Origins, Laws and Customs of the Balkans*, London, Allen & Unwin, 1928.

— *High Albania*, London, Edward Arnold, 1909.

HASLUCK, MARGARET, *The Unwritten Law in Albania*, Cambridge University Press, 1954.

LAMANI, DHORA, 'Albania w drodze rozwoju', *Przegl. Geogr.*, **32**, 1960, 125–28.

La République Populaire d'Albanie: évolution économique et sociale, Notes et Études Documentaires, No. 1845, Paris, 1954.

Les Minorités ethniques en Europe Centrale et Balkanique, Institut National de la Statistique et des Etudes Economiques, Etudes et Documents, Paris, 1946.

CHAPTER FIFTEEN

Conclusion

This book has been conceived and written within the framework of the political boundaries that were established during and after the Second World War. It has, however, been emphasised that three of the countries discussed occupied before 1939 more extensive territories than those which they now possess, extending eastward into the lands of the Soviet Union, and that their economic development took place, in part at least, in a broader framework than that of the present.

These three countries, Poland, Czechoslovakia and Romania, lost territory to the Soviet Union. The recovery of this territory is not imminent, and indeed, it is impossible to conceive at present of political conditions that would make its restoration possible. None of the governments concerned has made any formal claim to it, and only in Romania is there at present open discussion of the possibility of regaining part of it.

To the south of the countries dealt with in this book there also lies a belt of territory extending from the Bosporus to the Adriatic, in which at some time or other the Balkan countries of Bulgaria, Yugoslavia and Albania have either made claims or established temporary occupation. Again, no formal claim is made, if one excludes that of Albania on Greek Epirus, but the history of the Balkans is so intimately bound up with that of European Turkey and northern Greece that these regions cannot be entirely excluded from discussion in this book. It seemed desirable therefore, to survey briefly the provinces and regions which border Eastern Europe in the narrow sense used in this book on the east and south.

The retreat of the boundaries of Eastern Europe has been most marked in Poland, where they had previously extended very much farther than was warranted by the ethnic situation, and least so in Czechoslovakia which in 1945 surrendered the small, Ruthenian-occupied territory of Sub-Carpathian Russia. In 1940 Romania was obliged to surrender the province of Bessarabia to the Soviet Union, whose claim to it on historic and ethnic grounds was no better than her own. In all an area of about 96,500 square miles (249,800 square kilometres) passed from the control of East European countries to that of the Soviet Union between 1939 and 1945. Closely related to the Soviet occupation of the former eastern provinces of Poland was her annexation of the Baltic States, especially of the Republic of Lithuania, in 1940 and of the northern part of the former German province of East Prussia in 1945.

The eastern borders of Poland

The state of Poland has been created in large measure by an eastward movement of conquest and settlement from the original core-area of the Polish state of Wielkopolska. This expansion took the Poles into areas settled by White Russians and Ukrainians, by Lithuanians and by the Borussi or Prussians. Polish policy and achievement differed between these different areas, but in none of them, with the possible exception of parts of Prussia, was Polish settlement dense or the Polish cultural impact particularly great.

Prussia. The Prussians, linguistically akin to the Lithuanians, proved at first to be the most intractable of Poland's neighbours. Their numbers were probably small, but they occupied the region of terminal moraine, marsh and lake which has since borne the name of Prussia. Here nature gave them protection, and from this region in the earlier middle ages they raided the Polish settlements of Kujawy and Mazowsze. It was to protect himself from these raiders that Conrad of Mazowsze, in 1226, called in the German Knights to his aid, and thus contributed to the formation of the German province of East Prussia. The Prussians were thus eliminated and the Poles who had intruded into this area were subjugated and in part germanised.

The area of German occupation assumed by the mid-fifteenth century the approximate shape which it was to occupy until 1945. It embraced, in addition to the vanishing Prussians, communities of Poles towards the south and of Lithuanians to the east and north, all of them undergoing a process of forced germanisation, especially during the nineteenth century. After the First World War a small area in the north of Prussia, including the port of Memel was added to Lithuania, and another in the south to Poland. It was not until 1945, however, that East Prussia, partitioned between Poland and the Soviet Union, disappeared from the map. The Protocol of the Potsdam Conference confirmed that the area lying to the north of a line drawn from 'a point on the eastern shore of the Bay of Danzig . . . to the north of Braunsberg (Braniewo)—Goldap (Gołdap)' should be incorporated within the Soviet Union. It was not added to the adjoining SSR of Lithuania, but was constituted an exclave of the Russian SFSR The reason for this probably lay in the degree of distrust felt by the Russians towards the Lithuanian SSR and the critial importance which now attached to this most westerly extension of the Soviet Union and to its port of Königsberg, now renamed Kaliningrad.

The area of the former East Prussia lying south of the line of partition has already been described (see page 307). That which lies to the north is in many ways similar. It lies within the belt of terminal moraines which constitute the most significant landform feature of East Prussia, and its surface consists of ground moraine and the alluvium which has been deposited in post-glacial times by the rivers which drain the morainic hills. The drainage is principally to the Pregel and Niemen. The former flows westward to enter the Frisches Haff below Kaliningrad, and the latter takes a longer and more circuitous course from the marshes of Belorussia, across the zone of terminal moraines to the Kurisches Haff. The highest parts of the moraine lie within the present boundary of Poland, and northern Prussia is a region of gentle relief. It is typical ground moraine country, with only a few fragments of sandy terminal moraine. Soils are heavy and along the valleys are far from well drained. The long, severe winters and short summers combine with the general poverty of the soil to restrict agriculture. Forest, mainly broadleaved and coniferous, is extensive, especially upon the poorer soils, and along the valley floors is damp meadowland. The chief cultivated crops are rye, potatoes and fodder crops.

Towns are few and small; only Kaliningrad has attained more than modest size. It lies six miles up the Pregel, and was developed under the Teutonic Knights as a German port. It became the capital of East Prussia, and the chief commercial outlet of the province. Its trade, however, ended with its partial destruction during the Second World War.

The chief town of the Niemen Valley is Sovetsk (Tilsit), lying on the south bank of the river and at the head of the not inconsiderable delta. It is a much smaller city than Kaliningrad, but, like the latter, was founded by the German traders and settlers during the Middle Ages. North of the lower course of the Niemen, which is sometimes known as the Memel River, lies the Memelland, the area of the former East

Prussia, which together with its port of Memel (Klaipeda) became part of the Lithuanian republic in 1923.

Lithuania. Poland's relations with Lithuania were very much closer than those with the Prussians. The Lithuanian state, expanding south-eastwards from its early core in the Niemen valley, blocked Poland's expansion to the east. After 1386, when the Polish heiress Jadwiga married Jagiełło, Prince of Lithuania, Poland and Lithuania had a common ruler and shared the same destiny in the forests of White Russia and the plains of the Ukraine. The nobility of the two countries established a sort of blood brotherhood with one another; Lithuanian political institutions came to be modelled on those of Poland, and in 1569, by the Union of Lublin, the two countries were merged, though certain institutions of government remained separate and distinct. Until its extinction in the Third Partition (1795) the kingdom of Poland continued to be a joint Polish-Lithuanian state.

Even though many of the great landowners and statesmen—prominent among them the Radziwiłł—had been Lithuanian, cultural and political leadership rested with the Poles. The Lithuanian nobles were assimilated to the Polish; Warsaw became, especially in the eighteenth century, their principal cultural focus. Poles, and later Jews, became the dominant ethnic element in the small towns of Lithuania, and an ethnic stratification emerged in which the peasantry remained Lithuanian in speech and culture, while the land-owning class and small bourgeoisie was assimilated to the Poles. The Poles acquired, and have since retained a deep emotional attachment to the Lithuanian capital of Vilna. Though it had in July 1920 been handed over by the retreating Russians to Lithuania, it was nevertheless seized four months later by the Poles, and was retained until 1939, at the price, however, of alienating the Lithuanians, who rightly regarded it as the historic capital of their state.

In other respects also Lithuania has left a deep impression on the Poles. It became *their* country, and when Mickiewicz in exile wrote his patriotic epic poem, *Pan Tadeusz*, he set it, not in Great Poland, as one might have expected, but in Lithuania.

The area thus immortalised in Polish literature lay beyond even the pre-1939 borders of Poland. In 1921 Poland was able to annex a broad corridor extending north-eastwards to the Dvina River. Its western boundary followed very approximately the higher ground of the Baltic end-moraine—the Suwałki Heights. Much of this region was covered with older boulder clay and strewn with outwash from the newer. It is drained by the Niemen and by its major tributary, the Wilja, and, in the north, by the Dvina. It is a region of gentle relief; much of it is poorly drained, and along the valleys are extensive areas of damp woodland and meadow and of fenland or *Moor*. Climate is more severe even than in East Prussia, and crop farming is less developed.

The largest town is Vilna (*P*: Wilno, *Lith*: Vilnyus), situated on the Wilja, where a low platform extends towards the river from the direction of White Russia, thus facilitating movement across the damp valley floor. Vilna was the medieval capital of Lithuania, but became partly polonised, and was regarded by the Poles as one of their historic cities.[1] After its occupation by the Poles in 1920, the Lithuanians, for whom it also had powerful historical association, were obliged to move the seat of their government to Kaunas (Kovno) on the Niemen and 60 miles to the west.

The only other city of significance in this part of Lithuania is Grodno, also on the Niemen, where the highway from Warsaw to Vilna crosses the river.

White Russia and the Ukraine. As the Polish and Lithuanian nobles extended their control eastwards and south-eastwards they passed into a region thinly settled by peasants who spoke a Russian dialect and belonged to the Eastern or Orthodox Church. In Lithuania there was a linguistic barrier between the upper and middle classes and the peasantry. In White Russia and the Ukraine the linguistic difference was further emphasised by a contrast in religious affiliation. The peasants thus had their own particular organisation, with its own leadership, to which the Catholic Polish-Lithuanian aristocracy could not possibly belong. The latter distrusted an organisation which excluded them, while the Orthodox Church itself came gradually to focus the anti-Catholic and anti-Polish feelings of the peasantry.

The Poles themselves had attempted to bridge this gap between themselves and their Ruthene peasantry by forcing the latter to belong to the Uniate Church, which retained the Orthodox ritual and local organisation but accepted Catholic doctrine and dependence on the Polish bishops and hierarchy. The experiment achieved no great success, though a number of uniates, perhaps as many as a million,

---

[1] Mickiewicz, in *Pan Tadeusz*, specifically mentions the Ostra Brama (Narrow Gate) of Vilna along with the Jasna Góra at Częstochowa as the foremost national monuments of Poland.

remained in the former Polish eastern provinces, until they were forcibly reabsorbed into the Orthodox Church. The rift between the Catholic aristocracy and the mainly Orthodox peasantry of eastern Poland was one of the more important sources of weakness in the earlier Polish state and was the major factor in its dissolution in the Partitions.

During the period of Russian occupation, from 1796 to 1918, the position of the Polish landowning class in these eastern lands was greatly weakened both numerically and in its political and economic influence. Nevertheless, they remained numerous enough to give some appearance of legitimacy to the extreme Polish claims in this direction. The delimitation of Poland's eastern boundary did not, as has been seen (page 101), lie within the competence of the Paris Peace Conference in 1919. Instead it was left for the two claimants to settle the matter by war, with only the advice of the Western Powers, which was unsolicited, unwelcome and generally ignored.

The treaty of Riga (March 1921) gave Poland a boundary which included a White Russian and Ukrainian majority and about 75,000 square miles (194,000 square kilometres) of territory more than had been recommended in the Curzon Note. During the years between the First and Second World Wars Poland encountered opposition and hostility from her non-Polish subjects. It was as if the disputes and quarrels of the eighteenth century, Ukrainian peasant versus Polish landowner, had been resumed after an interval of a century and a half. In 1939 the dispute was ended by the 'Fourth Partition' of Poland. The eastern provinces were taken by the Soviet Union, and her possession was confirmed, subject to minor boundary changes, by the Protocol of the Potsdam Conference. The new boundary followed in general that which had been recommended by the Spa Conference in the so-called Curzon Note.

The Eastern Provinces, which were in the possession of modern Poland for only 19 years, constituted a thinly peopled region, whose resources lay mainly in its croplands and forests. It represented an eastward extension of the principal landform regions of present day Poland (see pages 308 to 312), but was drained mainly by the Niemen and the Black Sea rivers.

The areas of inter-war Poland which are at present within the boundaries of White Russia and the Ukraine may be said to form three distinct landform regions: on the north the lowland region of the Pripyat (*P*: Prypeć) Marshes; to the south of it the rolling uplands of Podolia and Volhynia, and lastly the Carpathian foot-hills and mountains in the south.

Pripyat region. South of the Niemen valley, the land rises to a low platform—the Belorussian plateau, which rarely exceeds 1,000 feet in altitude and then sinks imperceptibly to the basin of Polesie (*R*: Polesye). This is a vast, level and poorly drained region, much of whose surface remains today, despite attempts to drain it, an expanse of peat fen. It is one of the most distinctive regions in the whole of Eastern Europe. The gradient of its principal river, the Pripyat, is so slight that it drops only 58 feet in a distance of over 80 miles. It has been a barrier to both settlement and movement. It remains one of the least densely settled areas of Europe, and the flow of commercial and military movement has been obliged to take either the routeway to the north, which passes through Minsk and over the White Russian plateau, or to the south through Podolia. Within the region itself settlements occupy the small 'islands' in the prevailing fen, or are clustered around its margin. The largest of them is the town of Pinsk, which in 1938 had a population of only 36,700. It fulfilled nevertheless the role of 'capital' of the Pripyat region.

Podolia and Volhynia. The rise of the land surface to the south of the Pripyat Basin is as gentle as on the north, but in its quality it differs greatly. This is a rolling, upland country, which in the Podolian Plateau rises to heights of more than 1,200 feet. It lay beyond the limit of all except the earliest glaciation; the layer of boulder clay which may once have covered parts of it has been stripped away and in its place the wind has laid down beds of loess. This rounds the hills, gives a plastic quality to the landscape, and immeasurably enriches the soil.

The drainage is predominantly towards the south-east by the Prut and Dnestr, though there is evidence, especially in the north of the region, of east–west valleys cut by escaping melt-waters early in the Ice Age. It was a lightly wooded region at the beginning of human history, but the woodland has now been largely cut to make room for farmland. The climate, despite the severity of the winter months, is more genial than that met with to the north of Polesie. Summers are longer and hotter, and the duration of sunshine very much greater. This is, in general, good cropland, and long served to provide Western Europe with wheat.

Podolia also provided a routeway of incalculable importance between Central Europe and both Russia and the Black Sea. Along this route came invaders from the east, notably the Tatars, and within it Poles and Turks fought their long sanguinary struggle (see page 552).[1] In consequence, the high economic promise which this region held has been nullified by its own insecurity and instability.

The higher degree of urbanisation reflected the greater wealth of this region. Its largest city since the Middle Ages has been Lv'ov (*P*: Lwów; *G*: Lemberg). Founded by the Poles, it served for centuries as a Polish fortress on the road from the east. Like Vilna, it played a highly important role in Polish history, and its loss to the Soviet Union in 1939 has been the source of much bitterness. Other agricultural and commercial towns of this region are Tarnopol and Stanisławów, though others, no less famous in Polish history and literature— Chotin (*P*: Chocim) and Kamenets Podol'sky—lay beyond the 1921 boundary of Poland.

Carpathians. Podolia is bordered on the south by the Carpathians, which here comprise a series of short, parallel mountain ranges, lying one behind the other and separated by the valleys, in turn longitudinal and transverse, of the upper Prut and of the tributaries of the Dnestr. The region is densely forested and thinly peopled. Agricultural land— predominantly meadow and grazing—is found mainly along the valleys. Although petroleum and natural gas have long been important, especially near Borisław and Drohobycz on the northern edge of the mountains, urban and industrial development have been of negligible importance.

Sub-Carpathian Russia

At a meeting held in Pittsburgh, in 1918, a group of emigrés from the mountainous region which lies between Slovakia and Romania took it upon themselves to speak for the native inhabitants of their homeland. These were Ruthenes, members of that branch of the Slav peoples who have elsewhere in this book been called Ukrainians. Their ancestors had filtered through the several low and easily negotiated passes of the Carpathian Mountains from the adjoining regions of Volhynia and Podolia into the drainage area of the Tisza. There they occupied the mountain valleys, and their area of settlement extended, like that of the Slovaks, down to the borders of the Hungarian Plain.

To the west lived the Slovaks; to the east were Romanians and to the south Hungarians; all had been under Austrian rule since the later years of the seventeenth century. Close proximity to the Hungarians

[1] For a highly romanticised account, see H. Sienkeiwicz, *Pan Michał.*

had even led some of them into the Roman Catholic Church. Though the mountains which separated them from the Ukrainians of Podolia and the Ukraine constituted no great barrier to communication, the Ruthenes of the Carpathians did not establish particularly close ties with the rest of the Ukrainian peoples. They remained a poor, and backward peasant society, whose petty commerce was in the hands of the Jews and who lacked almost all power to influence their own political future.

Thus it was that a group of Americans of Ruthenian origin, more articulate and politically more sophisticated than their kinsfolk in Ruthenia, were able to influence the fate of their homeland. They appealed for the inclusion of Ruthenia within the boundaries of the Czechoslovak state, and Masaryk, not without misgivings, accepted their overtures. The effect was to add yet another minority—some 600,000—to the already complex population of Czechoslovakia, and to complicate yet more the already acute problem of communications within the country. At the same time, however, the incorporation of Ruthenia was seen as giving Czechoslovakia physical contact with Romania and as completing the ring of states encircling Hungary.

Ruthenia was an area of about 4,870 square miles (12,610 square kilometres). In terms of relief it consisted of the roughly parallel ranges of the Carpathian system, together with the small areas of lowland which bordered these mountains on the south or formed small basins within them. The mountains resemble those on the Podolian side of the boundary; they are forested, with extensive areas of mountain grazing and meadow and cropland along the valleys. The plain of southern Ruthenia makes up about a quarter of the whole. Much of it, however, is either sandy or poorly drained, and, except in the most fertile areas of loam soil, population is sparse. Where the more important mountain valleys open into the plain are small market towns (see page 438), the most important of which are Uzhgorod (*C-s*: Užghorod; *H*: Ungvár), Munkachevo (*Sl*: Mukačevo; *H*: Munkács) and Khust (*C-s*: Chust; *H*: Huszt).

The Romanian East
The Austrian province of Galicia had until 1919 extended beyond the new eastern boundary of Poland to meet the territories of both Tsarist Russia and Romania. Its easternmost part was added to Romania in 1919, largely on ethnic and cultural grounds.

Bucovina. This small region of about 3,400 square miles (8,700 square kilometres), lies mainly within the Carpathian foot-hills. It is a hilly and forested region in which, as its name suggests, the *buk*, or beech is widespread. Comparatively little of its area is farmland, though it does extend on the north into the plains of Podolia. It lay across the dividing line between predominantly Ukrainian culture and Romanian. The latter tends to predominate in the more hilly south of Bucovina, and the former in the northern part which lies open to the Ukraine. The chief town of the region, Chernovtsy (*Rom*: Cernăuţi; *G*: Czernowitz) lies within the northern part of the area, but, like so many small towns of this region, was in the main Jewish-settled.

In 1947, by the terms of the treaty of peace between Romania and the Allies, Bucovina was partitioned. The northern part was added to the Ukrainian SSR, with which its cultural ties were indeed closest. The southern part, with its chief town of Suceava and its numerous Romanian monasteries and cultural monuments, remains part of Romania.

Bessarabia. The province of Bessarabia is very much larger—about 13,000 square miles (33,670 square kilometres)—and ethnically a great deal more complex. It lies between the Prut and the deltaic tract of the Danube on the south-west and south and the Dnestr on the north-east, and extends from the borders of Podolia to the shore of the Black Sea. It is an undulating and, in places, a hilly region, to which the veneer of loess had given a smoothness of contour like that of Podolia itself. It is drier and warmer than other parts of Eastern Europe's borderland; its soils in general are fertile, and it is a region of great agricultural importance.

Its tangled history has, however, prevented until recent years the full development of its resources. Its name is derived from that of the medieval Basarab princes of Walachia, who for a time controlled it. Lying between the Ukraine, Podolia and the lower Danube, it proved to be a battle ground between peoples from all three, and its population, made up of Turks and Tatars, Romanians and Russians, Ukrainians and Jews, is ethnically one of the most complex in all Eastern Europe.

Until early in the nineteenth century, it had been part of the Ottoman Empire and loosely attached to Moldavia. On several occasions during the eighteenth century, the Russians attempted to take over the province. In 1812 they occupied most of it, and in 1829 extended their hold as far as the deltaic tract of the Danube. In 1856, at the end of the Crimean War, southern Bessarabia was restored to Moldavia and was subsequently included in Romania. Pro-Romanian sentiment developed in the part of Bessarabia which remained under Russian rule, and came to a head early in the twentieth century. Early in 1917, a National Moldavian Committee was set up in Bessarabia, and demanded at first autonomy within Russia. At the end of the year the Bessarabian leaders called upon Romania for help to drive out the Bolshevik forces. Thereupon the complete independence of Bessarabia was proclaimed. When, however, it became apparent that Bessarabia would have difficulty in maintaining this position its leaders voted for union with Romania, a step which was recognised by the Paris Conference.

For over 20 years Bessarabia was a neglected province of Romania. Russian claims to it had been suspended, not abandoned, and fear of their revival checked whatever desire the Romanians might have had to develop the province. Its agricultural products would have competed with those of the rest of Romania, if roads and railways had been improved. So Bessarabia remained the most backward part of a generally underdeveloped country. In June 1940 the Soviet Union demanded the retrocession of Bessarabia along with northern Bucovina. The Romanian government had no alternative but to comply. Soviet occupation took place at once, and, though interrupted during the German invasion of Russia, was formally recognised in the treaty of peace of 1947.

Most of Bessarabia is now included in the Moldavian SSR, with its capital at Kishinev, but the coastal and deltaic region of southern Bessarabia have been included in the Ukrainian SSR. The Moldavian SSR, which also includes a small area to the east of the Dnestr, has a population of about 3·4 million, two-thirds of whom are Moldavians (Romanians) and most of the others Russian or Ukrainian. The population of Bessarabia, which is thus no longer an administrative unit, must be of the order of four millions.

The chief towns are Kishinev, whose population has in recent years grown to about 289,000; the port city of Belgorod Dnestrovskiy (*Rom*: Cetatea Albă; *G*: Akkerman) and the much smaller towns of Bendery and Tiraspol on the Dnestr, and Beltsi in northern Bessarabia. The Soviet Union has profited from the great agricultural wealth of the region, which is now not only an important source of grain, but a leading producer of wine and tobacco. Industrial development, which has been rapid, is concerned mainly with food preservation and processing farm products.

The southern borderland

From the summits of the Rhodope in southern Bulgaria it is possible to see the Mediterranean Sea—the 'White' Sea, as it is called in all the southern Slav languages. The distance may be no more than 50 miles, but within that short distance one passes from a Slav culture into one that derives in many respects from the classical civilisations. We have, across the southern Balkans from Epirus in the west to European Turkey in the east, a belt of territory distinguished not so much by shifting boundaries and territorial claims—though these have not been absent—as by the fact that from here came many of the cultural influences that have shaped the Balkans. The latter cannot be studied apart from Greece and Turkey, though the exigencies of text-book organisation require that a line be drawn to separate the People's Democracies from the present totalitarian regimes to the south.

From Greece came the Cyrillic script and the Orthodox faith; from Turkey, the Islamic. From Greek ports, notably Thessaloníki, the earliest road system penetrated the Balkans. The present urban pattern is still basically that created by the Hellenistic Greeks and Romans. Architectural styles, both domestic and religious, and many aspects of folk-life have been deeply influenced from the direction of the Mediterranean.

The cultural divide between Albanian and Slav on the one hand and the Greek and Turk on the other is not so clear-cut that there can be no territorial claims of one side against the other. The Slav peoples, furthermore, have looked on southward expansion as a means of establishing an outlet to the Mediterranean and a freer access than was available by other routes to the markets of the world. The record of Yugoslav and Bulgarian expansion towards the Aegean Sea and the Sea of Marmara has already been outlined (see page 94). Pressure was renewed at the end of the Second World War, but, if peace and harmony are not altogether conspicuous along the boundary in Macedonia and Thrace, a *modus vivendi* has at least been achieved and war no longer threatens.

This southern borderland is for convenience divided, from west to east, into (1) Epirus and the Píndhos Mountains, (2) Macedonia, (3) Greek Thrace, and (4) European Turkey. The principal geographical features of each are summarised.

Epirus and the Píndhos Mountains. This region of high mountains, deep valleys and occasional fertile lake-basins, is in fact a southward continuation of southern Albania and south-western Yugoslavia. At many points rivers flow from the one to the other, and human inter-action has taken place *along* the valleys, with the consequent mingling of Greek and Albanian and Greek and Yugoslav communities. Classical civilisation made the smallest impact on this region, except in the coastal and lowland settlements of Epirus.

Epirus, the more westerly part of the region, is made up of north-west to south-east trending ranges, with broad and locally fertile valleys between them. There are a number of small towns, of which Ioánnina is the largest and best known. Along the coast is a discon-tinuous strip of lowland, where large villages and small towns derive in many instances from the settlements of the classical Greeks. The Píndhos, by contrast, is a rugged massif of very varied geological composition. It is trenched by the deep gorges of the rivers which rise within it, and is extremely difficult to penetrate. There are no towns; only the villages of the Greek peasants in the valleys and of the transhumant Vlachs at higher altitudes. Climate is severe in the high-lands. Rainfall exceeds 2,032 millimetres (80 inches) a year in most parts and deep snow accumulates in winter.

Macedonia. The province of Macedonia (*Gr*: Makedhonía) extends from the eastern margin of the Píndhos to the river Mesta, a distance of almost 200 miles. It is a region of varied relief and landscape. To the west it is a region of alternating mountain range and broad valley, lying parallel with the Píndhos, but drier, more open and more densely settled than in the regions farther west. Here the Aliákmon river and its tributaries create a corridor into the highlands opening up the several fertile and well settled lake basins of the interior (compare Yugoslav Macedonia, page 647).

To the east lies the plain of the lower Axiós (Vardar), and Kambanía. This is, in fact, a large area, more than 30 miles in each direction, made up of alluvium, and it consists in part of the bed of Lake Yiannitsa, which has only recently been drained and brought under cultivation. Around the margin of the alluvium Tertiary sands and clays give rise to a somewhat stronger relief and beyond these rise the mountain ranges, most of them of limestone, but some carved from metamorphic and igneous rock.

This plain, with its frontage on the Thermaic Gulf (Gulf of Thérmai), has always been the heart of Macedonia. Near its centre lay Pella, capital of Philip and Alexander in the fourth century B.C. On its south-eastern margin lies the city and port of Thessaloníki, which has served since classical times as the chief gateway to the Balkans. To the north the Vardar (Axiós) has opened up a routeway into the heart of the Balkans; to the north-east, the Strimón (Struma) valley puts Thessaloníki in touch with the Sofia basin, and towards the west the rivers and lake basins already mentioned open up the routeway along which the Romans built their *Via Egnatia* from the coast of the Adriatic Sea. Thessaloníki (*S-C:* Solun) is, indeed, the focus of the southern Balkans, and for long it was the ambition of Serbs and Bulgars to possess it (see page 94). At present the port serves as a commercial outlet for Yugoslavia, which has a 'free zone' within it.

A line of hills, which extends southwards and culminates in the three-pronged peninsula of Khalkidhikí, separates the plain of Kambanía from the smaller plain of the Strimón, and more hills— spurs of the Pirin massif of Bulgaria—separate the Strimón Basin from that of the Néstos (*Bulg*: Mesta). Along the coast, which consists of alternating headlands and flat alluvial and marshy plains, lay a succession of *poleis* in classical times, and contemporary sources witness to their former prosperity. Of some only a mound remains, and not even the site of others is known precisely. Only Kaválla retains any importance as a city and port. For this decline and decay it is usual to blame the invasions and wars that have disturbed the region from the time of the Germanic and Slav invasions of the Roman Empire until that of the troubles following the Second World War. But to the destruction of war must be added the long periods of neglect when the lowlands gradually turned themselves into swamps and wash from the hills spread in huge alluvial cones over the plain.

Thrace. This term is sometimes used to indicate the south-eastern part of the Balkan peninsula, including European Turkey and parts of Bulgaria. Its connotation is even less precise than that of 'Macedonia'. Greek Thrace is the small tract of land lying between the Rhodope and the Aegean and extending from the Néstos river to the Évros (Marica). It resembles eastern Macedonia in its general features, but the lowlands are more extensive. Along the north lies the crest of the Eastern Rhodope, and to the north-east a protruding finger of Greek territory extends around its foot-hills to the vicinity of Edirne (Adrianople), which remains in Turkey. The coast is, in general, straight, flat and harbourless. The bay of Porto Lágo, the only considerable indentation of this coast, is unsuited for shipping, and Alexandroúpolis (Dedeagach), a port with no physical advantages whatever, handles a little coastal trade and served for a time as the maritime outlet of Bulgaria (see page 95).

European Turkey. This area of 9,156 square miles (23,580 square kilometres) is all that remained after the First World War of the former Ottoman Empire in Europe. It is roughly triangular in plan, with a broad base along the lower Marica (Évros) and the Bulgarian border. To the north-east is the Black Sea; to the south-east, the Sea of Marmara, and Dardanelles. On the north lie the Istranca (*Bulg.* Istrandźa) Mountains, which reach heights of over 3,000 feet. On the south lie the lower Tekirdağ hills, grass- and scrub-covered and re- sembling those of Macedonia and Greek Thrace. Between lies a depression drained towards the Mariç (Marica) by the Ergene and its tributaries. This is a steppe-like region, with clustered villages generally along the watercourses. At its western end lies Edirne (Adrianople), now only a ghost of its former self, though dominated still by the splendid sixteenth-century mosque of Selim II; at the eastern, over a hundred miles away, is Istanbul (Constantinople), and between lies nothing larger than a big village.

Istanbul, the Greek Byzantium, city of Constantine and Justinian, of the Comneni and Palaeologi, and of Suleiman and the Turkish sultans, throughout its history exerted the strongest influence on the Balkans. It was at once a pole of attraction to Slavs, Tatars and Russians, none of whom in fact ever took it; it was an inspiration to the tribal kingdoms of Eastern Europe, whose rulers in varying degrees modelled their courts and administration on the Byzantine. It protected south-eastern Europe from the Turks until, weakened by the depredations of its Christian 'allies', it succumbed to both. There- after it became the source of Ottoman and Islamic influence in south- eastern Europe, until the Ottoman Empire came to an end and Turkey was in 1923 reduced to its present boundaries.

The ancient city lies across a triangular promontory between the Sea of Marmara and a small estuary known as the Golden Horn. On the highest part of this area stands Aya Sofiya (St Sophia), church, mosque and now museum, epitomising the history of the city. Only a few yards away is the Topkapi palace—from which the Sultans once ruled Hungary and Romania, and on the slope down towards the Golden Horn lies the 'Sublime Porte'—there is nothing 'sublime' about the squalid buildings that survive—from which the policy of the Turkish Empire was directed.

Today Istanbul and European Turkey have little significance to the countries of Eastern Europe, where Turkish minorities are small and almost forgotten, except when Bulgaria temporarily revives its old feud and expels a few of them. Yet Turkey is important, if only because within its territory lie the Bosporus and Dardanelles, through which the seaborne shipping of at least Bulgaria and Romania must pass to reach the Mediterranean. With the completion of works now in progress to improve navigation on the Danube the significance of the Turkish Straits is likely to increase rather than diminish. Fortunately, the Treaty of Montreux of 1936 guarantees freedom of navigation for commercial shipping, though it places certain restrictions on the passage of military vessels.

Bibliography
Eastern Poland
BRZENK, ELEANOR T. 'Poland East of the Curzon Line', *Malcolm Jarvis Proudfoot Memorial Volume*, Northwestern University Studies in Geography, No. 2, Evanston, 1957, 55–70.
BOYD, LOUISE A. 'The Marshes of Pińsk', *Geogrl Rev.*, **26** (1936), 376–95.
Collectanea Acta Geographica Lithuanica, Vilna, 1960—contains useful articles on the chief cities, including Vilnius, Klaipéda, Kaunas and on hydrology and landform regions.
CONZEN, G., 'East Prussia: Some Aspects of its Historical Geography', *Geography*, **30** (1945), 1–10.
FRENCH, R. A. 'Drainage and Economic Development of Poles'ye, U.S.S.R.', *Econ. Geogr.*, **35** (1959), 172–80.
GEDDES, ARTHUR, 'Economic Prospects in the Soviet-Polish Borderlands: a Review', *Scott. geogr. Mag.*, **56** (1940), 28–33.
KONDRACKI, JERZY, 'Z morfogenezy doliny dolnego Niemna', *Przegl. Geogr.* **21** (1948), 11–36.
LENCEWICZ, S. and S. PAWŁOWSKI, 'Polesie et Białowieża', *Congrès International de Géographie, Excursion Handbook*, Warsaw, 1934.
LIMANOVSKI, M., 'Nord-est de la Pologne, bassin du Niemen et de la Dźwina', *Congrès International de Géographie, Excursion Handbook*, Warsaw, 1934.
MORTENSEN, H., *Litauen: Grundzüge einer Landeskunde*, Hamburg, 1926.
Polish Encyclopaedia, **2**, part 5, 'The Eastern Polish Marches', 783–945.
RUSSELL, SIR JOHN, 'Reconstruction and Development in Eastern Poland, 1930–39', *Geogrl J.*, **98** (1941), 273–91.
SENN, A. E. *The Emergence of Modern Lithuania*, Columbia University Press, 1959.

VAN CLEEF, EUGENE, 'East Baltic Ports and Boundaries', *Geogrl Rev.*, **35** (1945), 257–72.

ZWEIG, FERDYNAND, *Poland Between Two Wars*, London, Secker & Warburg, 1944.

ZIERHOFFER, AUGUST, and JULJAN GZYŻEWSKI, 'La Podolie, les Karpates polonaises orientales et leur avant-pays', *Congrès International de Géographie, Excursion Handbook*, Warsaw, 1934.

Ruthenia

ALLEN, W. E. D., *The Ukraine, a History*, Cambridge University Press, 1941.

ARMSTRONG, JOHN A., *Ukrainian Nationalism, 1939–1945*, Columbia University Press, 1955.

FREDERIKSEN, O. J., *A History of the Ukraine*, Yale University Press, 1941.

SHUTE, JOHN, 'Czechoslovakia's Territorial and Population Changes', *Econ. Geogr.*, **24** (1948), 35–44.

YUHASZ, MICHAL, *Wilson's Principles in Czechoslovak Practice*, Homestead, Pennsylvania, 1929.

The Romanian Borderland

BABEL, ANTONY, *La Bessarabie*, Paris, 1926.

CLARK, CHARLES U., *Bessarabia*, New York, Dodd, Mead, 1927.

The Southern Borderland

ANCEL, JACQUES, *La Macedoine*, Paris, 1930.

DAMASKENIDÈSS, N. 'La riziculture dans la vallée du Vardar', *Annls Géogr.*, **64** (1955), 54–6.

HAMMOND, N. G. L. *Epirus*, Oxford University Press, 1967.

HOFFMAN, GEORGE W., 'Thessaloniki: the Impact of a Changing Hinterland,' *East European Quarterly*, **2** (1968), 1–27.

PRENTICE, ANNE, 'Livestock and Forage Production in Central Macedonia', *Scott. geogr. Mag.*, **73** (1957–8), 146–57.

TOURRATON, JEAN, 'La centrale hydroélectrique d'Agra (Macédoine) et le programme de l'électricité en Grèce', *Annls Géogr.*, **64** (1955), 293–5.

ULLYOTT, P. and O. ILGAZ, "The Hydrography of the Bosporus," *Geogrl. Rev.* **36** 1946, 44–66.

VOURAS, PAUL P. 'Northern Greece in Our Times', *Balkan Studies*, **1** (1960), 33–48.

APPENDIX

A number of East European place-names assume an embarrassing variety of forms. The names of all the larger towns, as well as many river and regional names, have, in addition to their local forms, different spellings and pronunciations in other European languages. The list of such forms is almost limitless. The following table lists only the variant spellings most likely to be met with of the more important place and regional names.

The following abbreviations are used:

Alb	Albanian	*Maced*	Macedonian
B	Bulgarian	*P*	Polish
C-s	Czechoslovak	*Rom*	Romanian
Eng	English	*Rs*	Russian
Fr	French	*S-C*	Serbo-Croat
Gn	German	*Slov*	Slovenian
Gk	Greek	*Turk*	Turkish
H	Hungarian	*Ukr*	Ukrainian
It	Italian	*Cl*	Classical
Lith	Lithuanian		

POLAND

Polska (*P*) Polen (*Gn*) Pologne (*Fr*) Polsko (*C-s*) Poland (*Eng*)
Lengyelország (*H*) Pol'ša (*Rs*)

Towns

Białystok (*P*) Bielostok (*Rs*)
Brześć Litewski, Brześć nad Bugiem (*P*) Brest Litovsk (*Rs*)
Bydgoszcz (*P*) Bromberg (*Gn*)
Bytom (*P*) Beuthen (*Gn*)
Cieszyn (*P*) Těšín (*C-s*) Teschen (*Gn*)
Częstochowa (*P*) Czenstochau (*Gn*) Chenstochov (*Rs*)
Dąbrowa (*P*) Dombrau (*Gn*)
Elbląg (*P*) Elbing (*Gn*)
Gdańsk (*P*) Danzig (*Gn*)
Gdynia (*P*) Gdingen (*Gn*)
Gniezno (*P*) Gnesen (*Gn*) Hnězdno (*C-s*)
Gliwice (*P*) Gleiwitz (*Gn*) Hlivice (*C-s*)
Jelenia Góra (*P*) Hirschberg (*Gn*)

Katowice (*temporarily* Stalinogród (*P*)　　Kattowitz (*Gn*)
Kołobrzeg (*P*)　　Kolberg (*Gn*)
Kostrzyn (*P*)　　Küstrin, Cüstrin (*Gn*)
Koźle (*P*)　　Cosel, Kosel (*Gn*)
Kraków (*P*)　　Cracow (*Eng*)　　Krakau (*Gn*)　　Krakowie (*Fr*)　　Krakov
　(*C-s*)　　Krakkó (*H*)
Kłodzko (*P*)　　Kladsko (*C-s*)　　Glatz (*Gn*)
Łódź (*P*)　　Littmanstadt (*Gn*)　　Lodz' (*Rs*)
Malbork (*P*)　　Marienburg (*Gn*)
Olsztyn (*P*)　　Allenstein (*Gn*)
Opole (*P*)　　Oppeln (*Gn*)　　Opolí (*C-s*)
Oswięcim (*P*)　　Auschwitz (*Gn*)
Poznań (*P*)　　Posen (*Gn*)
Pszczyna (*P*)　　Pless (*Gn*)
Racibórz (*P*)　　Ratibor (*Gn*)　　Ratiboř (*C-s*)
Sandomierz (*P*)　　Sandomir (*Rs*)
Sosnowiec, Sosnowice (*P*)
Świdnica (*P*)　　Schweidnitz (*Gn*)
Swiętochlowice (*P*)　　Schwientochlowitz (*Gn*)
Szczecin (*P*)　　Stettin (*Gn*)　　Štítina (*C-s*)
Toruń (*P*)　　Thorn (*Gn*)
Wałbrzych (*P*)　　Waldenburg (*Gn*)
Warszawa (*P*)　　Warschau (*Gn*)　　Warsovie (*Fr*)　　Varšava (*C-s*)
　Warsaw (*Eng*)　　Varsó (*H*)
Wolin (*P*)　　Wollin (*Gn*)
Wrocław (*P*)　　Breslau (*Gn*)　　Vratislav (*C-s*)　　Boroszló (*H*)
Zabrze (*P*)　　Hindenburg (*Gn*)
Zgorzelec (*P*)　　Görlitz (*Gn*)　　Zhořelec (*C-s*)
Zielona Góra (*P*)　　Grünberg (*Gn*)

Regional names
Karkonsze (*P*)　　Krkonoše (*C-s*)　　Riesengebirge (*Gn*)
Mazury, Masury (*P*)　　Masurien (*Gn*)　　Mazuria, Masuria (*Eng*)
Pomorze (*P*)　　Pommern (*Gn*)　　Pomořany (*C-s*)　　Pomeranie (*Fr*)
　Pomerania (*Eng*)
Śląsk (*P*)　　Schlesien (*Gn*)　　Slezsko (*C-s*)　　Silésie (*Fr*)　　Silesia (*Eng*)
Wielkopolska (*P*)　　Grosspolen (*C-s*)　　Velkopolsko (*C-s*)　　Great(er)
　Poland (*Eng*)

River names
Bóbr (*P*)　　Bober (*Gn*)　　Bobr, Bobrava (*C-s*)
Noteć (*P*)　　Netze (*Gn*)
Nysa (*P*)　　Neisse (*Gn*)　　Nisa (*C-s*)

Wisła (*P*) Vistula (*Eng*) Visla (*Rs*) Weichsel (*Gn*) Vistule (*Fr*)
Warta (*P*) Warthe (*Gn*)
Odra (*P, C-s*) Oder (*Gn*)
Prypeć (*P*) Pripet (*Eng*) Pripyat (*Rs*)

CZECHOSLOVAKIA

Československo (*C-s*) Czechoslovakia (*Eng*) Tschechoslovakei
(*Gn*) Čehoslovačka (*S-C*) Csehszlovakia (*H*)
Czechosłowacja (*P*) Tchécoslovaquie (*F*)

Towns

Aš (*C-s*) Asch (*Gn*)
Banská Bystrica (*C-s*) Neusohl (*Gn*) Besztercebánya (*H*)
Bohumín (*C-s*) Bogumin (*P*) Oderberg (*Gn*)
  Banská Štiavnice (*C-s*) Schemnitz (*Gn*) Selmec (*H*)
Bratislava (*C-s*) Pressburg (*Gn*) Pozsony (*H*)
Brno (*C-s*) Brünn (*Gn*)
České Budějowice (*C-s*) Budweis (*Gn*)
Cheb (*C-s*) Eger (*Gn*)
Chomutov (*C-s*) Komotau (*Gn*)
Čierna nad Tisou (*C-s*) Csernö (*H*)
Domažlice (*C-s*) Taus (*Gn*) Tusta (*H*)
Frýdek-Místek (*C-s*) Friedek (*Gn*)
Hlučin (*C-s*) Hultschin (*Gn*)
Hradec-Králové (*C-s*) Königgrätz (*Gn*)
Gottwaldov, *formerly* Zlín
Jablonec (*C-s*) Gablonz (*Gn*)
Jáchymov (*C-s*) Joachimsthal (*Gn*)
Jihlava (*C-s*) Iglau (*Gn*)
Karlovy Vary (*C-s*) Carlsbad, Karlsbad (*Gn*)
Karviná (*C-s*); Karwin (*Gn*) Karwina (*P*)
Kežmarok (*C-s*) Käsmark (*Gn*) Késmárk (*H*)
Košice (*C-s*) Kassa (*H*) Kaschau (*Gn*)
Kremnica (*C-s*) Kremnitz (*Gn*) Körmöcbánya (*H*)
Kutná Hora (*C-s*) Kuttenberg (*Gn*)
Levoča (*C-s*) Leutschau (*Gn*) Löcse (*H*)
Liberec (*C-s*) Reichenberg (*Gn*)
Litomyšl (*C-s*) Leitomischl (*Gn*)
Litoměřice (*C-s*) Leitmeritz (*Gn*)
Mariánske Lázně (*C-s*) Marienbad (*Gn*)

Martin, Turčiansky Svátý Martin (*C-s*)　Turóczentmárton (*H*)
Mladá Boleslav (*C-s*)　Jungbunzlau (*Gn*)
Most (*C-s*)　Brüx (*Gn*)
Nitra (*C-s*)　Nyitra (*H*)　Neutra (*Gn*)
Olomouc (*C-s*)　Olmütz (*Gn*)
Opava (*C-s*)　Troppau (*Gn*)
Ostrava (*C-s*)　Ostrau (*Gn*)　Ostrawa (*P*)
Pardubice (*C-s*)　Pardubitz (*Gn*)
Plzeň (*C-s*)　Pilsen (*Gn*)
Poprad (*C-s*)　Poprád (*H*)
Prague (*Fr, Eng*)　Praha (*C-s*)　Prag (*Gn*)　Prága (*H*)　Praga
　(*P, Rs*)
Prešov (*C-s*)　Eperjes (*H*)　Eperies (*Gn*)
Ružomberok (*C-s*)　Rosenberg (*Gn*)　Rózsahegy (*H*)
Slavkov u Brna (*C-s*)　Austerlitz (*Gn*)
Sokolov *formerly* Falknov, Falkenau (*Gn*)
Spišska Nová Ves (*C-s*)　Igló (*H*)　Neudorf (*Gn*)
Svitavy (*C-s*)　Zwittau (*Gn*)
Teplice (*C-s*)　Teplitz (*Gn*)
Těšín (*C-s*)　Cieszyn (*P*)　Teschen (*Gn*)
Trenčín (*C-s*)　Trentschin (*Gn*)　Trencsén (*H*)
Trnava (*C-s*)　Nagyszombat (*H*)　Tyrnau (*Gr*)
Ústí-nad-Labem (*C-s*)　Aussig (*Gn*)
Znojmo (*C-s*)　Znaim (*Gn*)
Žilina (*C-s*)　Sillein (*Gn*)　Zsolna (*H*)
Znojmo (*C-s*)　Znaim (*Gn*)

Regional names

Čechy (*C-s*)　Bohemia (*Eng*)　Böhmen (*Gn*)　Bohême (*Fr*)
Karpaty (*C-s*)　Carpathians (*Eng*)　Karpathen (*Gn*)　Carpathes (*Fr*)
　Karpaty (*H*)　Karpati (*S-c*)
Krušné hory (*C-s*)　Ore Mountains (*Eng*)　Erzgebirge (*Gn*)
Krkonoše (*C-s*)　Karkonosze (*P*)　Riesengebirge (*Gn*)　Giant
　Mountains (*Eng*)
Moravia (*Eng*)　Morava (*C-s*)　Morvaország (*H*)　Morawy (*P*)
Ruthenia, Ruthenian Ukraine (*Eng*)　Podkarpatská Rus (*C-s*)
Slovensko (*C-s*)　Slovakia (*Eng*)　Slovakei (*Gn*)　Słowacja (*P*)
　Slovaquie (*Fr*)
Šumava, Český les (*C-s*)　Böhmerwald (*Gn*)　Bohemian Forest
Tatra (*Eng, Gn*)　Tatry (*C-s, P*)　Tátra (*H*)
Spiš (*C-s*)　Zips (*Gn*)　Spisz (*P*)　Spis, Szepesseg (*H*)

River names

Labe (*C-s*) Elbe (*Gn*) Elba (*H*) Laba (*P*)
Hornád (*C-s*) Hernád (*H*)
Hron (*C-s*) Garam (*H*) Gran (*Gn*)
Ipel' (*C-s*) Ipoly (*H*)
Morava (*C-s*) Morva (*H*)
Nitra (*C-s*) Nyitra (*H*) Neutra (*Gn*)
Odra (*C-s, P*) Oder (*Gn*) Odera (*H*)
Ohře (*C-s*) Eger (*Gn*)
Tisa (*C-s*) Tisza (*H*)
Váh (*C-s*) Vág (*H*)
Vltava (*C-s*) Moldau (*Gn*) Moldva (*H*) Wełtawa (*P*)

HUNGARY

Magyarország (*H*) Ungarn (*Gn*) Maďarsko (*C-s*) Madžarska,
Ugorska (*S-C*) Węgry (*P*) Vengrija (*Rs*) Hongrie (*Fr*)
Macaristan (*Turk*) Hungary (*Eng*)

Towns

Budapest, Obuda Ofen (*Gn*)—(Buda only) (*H*) Budimpešta (*S-C*)
  Budapeszt (*P*) Aquincum (*Cl*) Budapešt (*C-s*)
Debrecen (*H*) Debreczin (*Gn*) Debrecín (*C-s*)
  Dunaujvaros, *temporarily* Sztalinvaros
Eger (*H*) Erlau (*Gn*)
Esztergom (*H*) Ostřihom (*C-s*) Gran (*Gn*) Strigonium (*Cl*)
Györ (*H*) Raab (*Gn*) Ráb (*C-s*) Arabona (*Cl*)
Komárom (*H*) Komárno (*C-s*) Komorn (*Gn*)
Mohács (*H*) Mohatsch (*Gn*)
Miskolc (*H*) Miškovec (*C-s*)
Pécs (*H*) Fünfkirchen (*Gn*) Pečuj (*S-C*) Pětikostelí (*C-s*)
Szeged (*H*) Szegedin (*alt. form*)
Székesfehérvár (*H*) Stuhlweissenburg (*Gn*)
Sopron (*H*) Ödenburg (*Gn*) Šoproň (*C-s*) Šopron (*S-C*)
Szombathely (*H*) Steinamanger (*Gn*)
Vác (*H*) Waitzen (*Gn*) Vacov (*C-s*)

Regional names

Bácska (*H*) Bačka (*S-C*)
Bakony (*H*) Bakonjska Šuma (*C-s*) Bakonywald (*Gn*)
Balaton (lake) (*H*) Plattensee (*Gn*) Blatenské jezero (*C-s*)
Baranya (*H*) Baranja (*S-C*)
29

River names

Dráva (*H*) Drava (*S-C*) Drave (*Fr*) Drau (*Gn*)
Hernád (*H*) Hornád (*C-s*)
Ipoly (*H*) Ipel' (*C-s*)
Körös (*H*) Criş (*Rom*)
Maros (*H*) Mureş (*Rom*)
Rába (*H*) Raab (*Gn*)
Szamos (*H*) Someş (*Rom*) Samoš (*C-s*)
Temes (*H*) Timìş (*Rom*) Tamiš (*S-C*)
Tisza (*H*) Theiss (*Gn*) Tisa (*Rom*) Tisa (*C-s*)

ROMANIA

Romania (*Rom*) Rumania, Roumania (*Eng*) Rumanien (*Gn*)
Rumunsko (*C-s*) România (*H*) Rumunjska (*S-C*) Roumanie (*Fr*)

Towns

Alba Julia (*Rom*) Gyulaferhérvár (*H*) Karlsburg (*Gn*)
Baia Mare (*Rom*) Nagybánya (*H*)
Braşov, *formerly* Oraşul Stalin (*Rs*) Brassó (*H*) Kronstadt (*Gn*)
   Brašov (*C-s*)
Bucharest (*Eng*) Bucureşti (*Rom*) Bukarest (*H*) Bukurešt (*C-s*)
   Bukurest (*S-C*)
Cîmpulung, *formerly* Câmpulung Kimpolung (*Gn*)
Cluj (*Rom*) Kolozsvár (*H*) Klausenburg (*Gn*) Kluž (*C-s*)
Constanţa (*Rom*) Constantz (*Gn*) Kustenje (*S-C*) Kjustendža
   (*B*) Tomis (*Cl*)
Galaţi (*Rom*) Galatz (*Gn*)
Giurgui (*Rom*) Giurgevo (*B*)
Haţeg (*Rom*) Hatzeg (*Gn*)
Iaşi (*Rom*) Jassy (*Eng*) Jaszvasar (*H*) Yaş (*Turk*)
Oradea (*Rom*) Grosswardein (*Gn*) Nagyvárad (*H*) Velký
   Varadín (*C-s*)
Orşova (*Rom*) Orsova (*H*) Orsowa (*Gn*)
Petroşeni (*Rom*), *formerly* Petroşani
Ploieşti (*Rom*), *formerly* Ploeşti
Satu Mare (*Rom*) Sathmar (*Gn*) Szatmar, Szatmárnémeti (*H*)
Sibu (*Rom*) Hermannstadt (*Gn*) Nagyszeben (*H*) Sibiň (*C-s*)
Timişoara (*Rom*) Temesvár (*H*) Temeschburg (*Gn*)
Tirgu Mureş (*Rom*) Neumarkt (*Gn*) Marosvásárhely (*H*)

Regional names

Ardeal (*Rom*) Transilvanija (*S-C*) Transylvania (*Eng*)
  Transylvanie (*Fr*) Erdély (*H*) Siebenburgen (*Gn*) Sedmihradsko
  (*C-s*)
Basarabia (*Rom*) Bessarabia (*Eng*) Bessarabie (*Fr*)
Bucovina Bukovina (*Rom*) Bukowina (*Gn*) Bukovine (*Fr*)
Dobrogea (*Rom*) Dobrudža (*B, S-C*)
Moldova (*Rom*) Moldavia (*Eng*) Moldva (*H*) Moldavija (*S-C*)
  Moldau (*Gn*) Moldavya (*Turk*)
Muntenia (*Rom*) Muntenija (*S-C*)
Oltenia (*Rom*) Oltenija (*S-C*)
Walachia, Wallachia (*Rom*) Walachei (*Gn*) Valašsko (*C-s*)

River names

Criş (*Rom*) Körös (*H*) Kriš (*C-s*)
Iza (*Rom*) Tisza (*H*)
Mureş (*Rom*) Maros (*H*)
Prut (*Rom*) Pruth (*Gn*)
Olt (*Rom*) Alt (*Gn*)
Somoş (*Rom*) Szamos (*H*)
Timiş (*Rom*) Temes (*H*) Tamiš (*S-C*)

YUGOSLAVIA

Jugoslavija (*S-C*) Juhoslávia (*Slovene*) Yugoslavia, Jugoslavia
  (*Eng*) Jugoslawien (*Gn*) Jugoszlavia (*H*) Jugoslavie (*Fr*)
  Jugoslávie (*C-s*)

Towns

Bar (*S-C*) Antivari (*It*)
Beograd (*S-C*) Belgrad (*Gn*) Belgrád (*H*) Belgrade (*Eng, Fr*)
  Bělehrad (*C-s*)
Bitola (*Maced*) Botolj (*S-C*) Monastir (*Turk*)
Celje (*S-C*) Cilli (*Gn*)
Dubrovnik (*S-C*) Ragusa (*It*)
Koper (*S-C*) Capodistria (*It*)
Karlovac (*S-C*) Karlstadt (*Gn*)
Kotor (*S-C*) Cattaro (*It*)
Kranj (*S-C*) Krain (*Gn*) Carniola (*Eng*)
Ljubljana (*Slov, S-C*) Laibach (*Gn*) Emona (*Cl*) Lublaň (*C-s*)

Maribor (*S-C*)   Marburg (*Gn*)
Novi Pazar, Novipazar, Novibazar (alt. spellings)
Novi Sad (*S-C*)   Újvidék (*H*)   Neusatz (*Gn*)   Nový Sad (*C-s*)
Niš (*S-C*)   Nish (*Eng*)   Nisch (*Gn*)
Ohrid (*Maced*)   Ochrid (*S-C*)   Ochrida (*Gn*)   Ohrit (*Alb*)
Osijek (*S-C*)   Eszék (*H*)   Esseg (*Gn*)   Mursa (*Cl*)
Pančevo (*S-C*)   Panchevo (alt. spelling)   Panscova (*H*)
Peč (*S-C*)   Pech (alt. spelling)   Ipek (*Turk*)   Pejë (*Alb*)
Petrovaradin (*S-C*)   Peterwardein (*Gn*)
Prilep (*S-C*)   Perlepe (*Turk*)
Priština (*S-C*)   Prishtina (alt. spelling)   Prishtinë (*Alb*)
Ptuj (*S-C*)   Poetovio (*Cl*)   Pettau (*Gn*)
Pula (*S-C*)   Pola (*It*)
Rijeka (*S-C*)   Rjeka (*Slov*)   Fiume (*It*)
Sarajevo (*S-C*)   Sarajewo (*Gn*)
Šibenik (*S-C*)   Sibenico (*It*)
Sisak (*S-C*)   Siscia (*Cl*)
Skopje (*Maced*)   Skoplje (*S-C*)   Üsküb, Uskub (*Turk*)   Scopia,
   Scupi (*Cl*)
Slavonsky Brod (*S-C*)   Bród (*H*)
Smederovo (*S-C*)   Szendra (*H*)
Sombor (*S-C*)   Zombor (*H*)
Split (*S-C*)   Spalato (*H*)
Subotica (*S-C*)   Szabadka (*H*)   Maria-Theresiopel (*Gn*)
Titograd, *formerly* Podgorica (*S-C*)
Tetovo (*S-C*)   Tetovë (*Alb*)   Kalkandelen (*Turk*)
Ulcinj (*S-C*)   Dulcigno (*It*)   Olcinium (*Cl*)
Varaždin (*S-C*)   Varasd (*H*)
Vrsač (*S-C*)   Versec (*H*)   Werschetz (*Gn*)
Zagreb (*S-C*)   Zágráb (*H*)   Agram (*Gn*)   Záhreb (*C-s*)
Zemun (*S-C*)   Semlin (*Gn*)   Zimony (*H*)
Zrenjanin (*S-C*)   Nagybecskerek (*H*)

Regional names

Bačka (*S-C*)   Bácska (*H*)
Baranja (*S-C*)   Baranya (*H*)
Bosna (*S-C*)   Bosnia (*Eng*)   Bosnien (*Gn*)   Bosznia (*H*)
Crna Gora (*S-C*)   Montenegro (*It, Eng*)   Černá Hora (*C-s*)
Hercegovina (*S-C*)   Herzegovina (*Gn*)
Hrvatska (*S-C*)   Croatia (*Eng*)   Croatien (*Gn*)   Chorvatsko (*C-s*)
   Croatie (*Fr*)
Istra (*S-C*)   Istria (*Eng, It*)   Istrien (*Gn*)   Isztria (*H*)
Karavanke (*S-C*)   Karawanken (*Gn*)   Karavankák (*H*)

Makedonija (*S-C, Maced*)   Macedonia (*Eng*)   Makidonya (*Turk*)
Srbja (*S-C*)   Serbia (*Eng*)   Serbien (*Gn*)   Serbie (*Fr*)   Srbsko (*C-s*)
Slovenija (*S-C*)   Slovenia (*Eng*)   Slowenien (*Gn*)
Šumadija (*S-C*)   Schumadija (*Gn*)
Slavonia (*Eng*)   Slawonien (*Gn*)
Srem (*S-C*)   Szerém (*H*)   Syrmien (*Gn*)

River names

Boyana (*S-C*)   Buenë (*Alb*)
Drava (*S-C*)   Drau (*Gn*)   Dráva (*H*)
Drin (*S-C*)   Drim (*Alb*)
Mura (*S-C*)   Mur (*Gn*)
Neretva (*S-C*)   Naretva, Narenta (alt. forms)
Strumica (*S-C*)   Strumitsa (alt. spelling)   Sztrumesnica (*H*)
   Strumešnica (*B*)
Sava (*S-C*)   Save (*Gn*)   Szava (*H*)
Soča (*S-C*)   Isonzo (*H*)
Vardar (*S-C*)   Axios (*Gk*)

BULGARIA

Blagariya (*B*)   Bugarska (*S-C*)   Bulgarien (*Gn*)   Bulgarie (*Fr*)
   Bulharsko (*C-s*)   Bulgaria (*Eng*)

Towns

Burgas (*B*)   Burgaz (alt. spelling)   Burgasz (*H*)
Blagoevgrad, *formerly* Gorna Dzhumaya
Botevgrad, *formerly* Orchanie
Haskovo (*B*)   Chaskowo, Haszkovo, Khaskovo (alt. spellings)
Kazanlik (*B*)   Kazanlâk (alt. spellings)
Harmanli (*B*)   Charmanli, Kharmanli (alt. spellings)
Kjistendil (*B*)   Kyustendil, Keustendil (alt. spellings), Kjusztendil (*H*)
Pernik, *temporarily* Dimitrovo
Plevna (*B*)   Plewen (*Gn*)   Pleven (alt. spelling)
Plovdiv (*B*)   Plowdiw (*Gn*)   Philippopolis (*Cl*)   Filibe (*Turk*)
Ruse, Russe (*B*)   Rusze (*H*)   Ruschuk, Ruščuk (*Turk*)
Shumen, *formerly* Kolarovgrad
Silistra (*B*)   Silistria (alt. spelling)

Sofia, Sofija (*B*) *formerly* Sredets   Szofija (*H*)   Serdica,
   Sardica (*Cl*)   Sofya (*Turk*)
Sliven (*B*)   Slivno (alt. form)
Stanke Dimitrov, *formerly* Dupnitsa
Trnovo (*B*)   Trnowo (*Gn*)   Tirnovo (alt. spelling)
Varna, *temporarily* Stalin (*B*)   Warna (*Gn*)
Vraca, Vratca (*B*)   Vrattsa (alt. spelling)

Regional names

Dobrudža (*B*)   Dobrudja (alt. spelling)   Dobrogea (*Rom*)
Istrandže (*B*)   Istranca, Strandža (*Turk*)
Rhodope (*Gk*)   Despoto Planina (*B*)   Dospad Dagh (*Turk*)
Thrace (*Eng*)   Thracia (*Cl*)   Thrake (*Gk*)

River names

Iskâr (*B*)   Isker (alt. spelling)   Iszker (*H*)
Marica, Maritza (*B*)   Meriç (*Turk*)   Évros (*Gk*)
Mesta (*B*)   Néstos (*Gk*)   Kara Su (*Turk*)
Struma (*B*)   Strimón (*Gk*)   Strymon (*Cl*)
Tundža, Tundja (*B*)

ALBANIA

Shqipni, Shqipri, Shqipëria (*Alb*)   Albania (*Eng*)   Albanie (*Fr*)
   Albanien (*Gn*)   Albanija (*S-C*)

Towns

Bilisht (*Alb*)   Bilsht (alt. form)
Dibër (*Alb*)   Dibra, Debar
Dürres (*Alb*)   Durazzo (*It*)   Dyrrhachium, Epidamnos (*Cl*)
   Drač (*S-C*)   Diraç (*Turk*)
Elbasan (*Alb*)   Elbasani (*It*)
Gjirokastër (*Alb-Tosk*)   Gjinokastër (*Alb-Gheg*)   Argyrokastro,
   Argyrocastro, Agirocastro (*Gk*)
Korçë, Korrcë (*Alb*)   Korcha, Kortcha (*Gn*)   Koritsa, Korytza,
   Korytsa (*Gk*)   Corizza (*It*)
Krujë (*Alb*)   Croia (*It*)
Lesh (*Alb-Tosk*)   Lezhë (*Alb-Gheg*)   Alessio (*It*)

Ohrıt (*Alb*)   Ohrid (*Maced*)   Ochrid (*S-C*)
Sarandë (*Alb*)   Santi Quaranta, Porto Edda (*It*)
Sazan (*Alb*)   Saseno (*It*)
Shëngjin (*Alb*)   Shën Gjin (alt. form)   San Giovanni di Medua (*It*)
Shkodër (*Alb*)   Skadar (*S-C*)   Scutarì, Skotari, Scutari d'Albanie
   (*It*)   Scodra (alt. form)
Tiranë (*Alb*)   Tirana (*Eng*)   Tiran (*Gn*)
Vlorë, Vlonë (*Alb*)   Valona (*It*)

Regional and River names

Buenë (*Alb*)   Boyana (*S-C*)
Drin i zi (*Alb*)   Drin, Black (*Eng*)   Crni Drim (*S-C*)
Drin i bardhë (*Alb*)   Drin, White (*Eng*)   Beli Drim (*S-C*)
Epirus (*Cl, Eng*)   Epeiros (*Gk*)   Epir (*S-C*)
Liqeni i Maliqit (*Alb*)   Malig jezero (*S-C*), Lake Malig (*Eng*)
Liqeni i Shkodres (*Alb*)   Skadarsko jezero (*S-C*)   Lake Skadar (*Eng*)
Malet e Mokrës (*Alb*)   Mokra Planina (*S-C*)
Malsi e madhe (*Alb*)   Prokletije (*S-C*)   North Albanian Alps (*Eng*)
Shkumbî, Shkumbi (alt. spellings)
Vijosë (*Alb*)   Voyoussa, Voyutsa, Viosa (alt. forms)

OTHER PLACE-NAMES AND RIVER AND REGIONAL NAMES (INCLUDING

GERMAN)

Adriatic Sea (*Eng*)   Jadransko more (*S-C*)   Deti Adriatik (*Alb*)
   Adriatické moře (*C-s*)   Adriatico (*It*)
Baltic Sea (*Eng*)   Bałtyk (*P*)   Ostsee (*Gn*)   Baltské moře (*C-s*)
   Baltiyskoe More (*Rs*)
Bamberg (*Gn*)   Bamberk (*C-s*)
Bautzen (*Gn*)   Budyšín (*C-s*)
Bavaria (*Eng*)   Bavorsko (*C-s*)   Bayern (*Gn*)
Bavarian Forest (*Eng*)   Bavorský les (*C-s*)   Bayerischer Wald (*Gn*)
Belgorod Dnestrovskij (*Rs*)   Cetatea Alb (*Rom*)   Akkerman (*Gn*)
   Tyras (*Cl*)   Bilhorod Dnistrov'skyj (*Ukr*)
Belorussia, Byelorussia, White Russia (*Eng*)   Belorusskaja (*Rs*)
   Běloruská (*C-s*), (*P*)
Beltsy, Bel'cy (*Rs*)   Bălţi (*Rom*)
Bucovina, Bukovina (alt. forms)

Brandenburg (*Gn*)   Braniborsko, Branibor̆ (*C-s*)
Chernovtsy (*Rs*)   Cernăuţi (*Rom*)   Czernowitz (*Gn*)   Černovice (*C-s*)   Černivci (*Ukr.*)
Danube (*Eng*)   Donau (*Gn*)   Duna (*H*)   Dunareă (*Rom*)   Dunaj (*C-s, S-C*)   Dunav (*B*)   Ister (*Cl*)
Dede Agach, Dedéagach (*Turk*)   Alexandroúpolis (*Gk*)
Dnepr (*Rs*)   Dniepr (*P*)   Dněpr (*C-s*)   Dniepras (*Lith*)   Dnipro (*Ukr*)   Borysthenes (*Cl.*)
Dnestr (*Rs*)   Dněstr (*C-s*)   Nistru (*Rom*)   Dniestras (*Lith*)   Tyras (*Cl*)   Dresden (*Gn*)   Drázďany (*C-s*)
Edirne (*Turk*)   Adrianople (*Eng*)   Adrianopolis (*Cl*)   Odrin (*B*)
Germany (*Eng*)   Německo (*C-s*)   Niemcy (*P*)   Deutschland (*Gn*)   Germanija (*Rs*)   Allemagne (*Fr*)
Graz (*Gn*)   Stýrský Hradec (*C-s*)   Gradec (*Slov*)
Grodno (*P*)   Gardinias (*Lith*)   Hrodna (*White Rs*)
Ioannina, Ioánina (*Gk*)   Janina (*S-C*)   Yanina, Joannina, Yannina (alt. forms)   Yanya (*Turk*)
Istanbul (*Turk*)   Constantinople (*Eng*)   Stamboul (*Fr*)   Car̆ihrad (*C-s*)   Carigrad (*B, S-C*)   Konstantinopel (*Gn*)   Byzantion, Byzantium (*Cl*)
Kamenets Podol'sky (*Rs*)   Kamieniec Podolski (*P*)
Kaliningrad (*Rs*)   Königsberg (*Gn*)   Královec (*C-s*)
Karl-Marx-Stadt, *formally* Chemnitz. Kamenice (*C-s*)
Kaunas (*Lith*)   Kovno (*Rs*)   Kowno (*P*)
Kavalla, Kaválla, Kawalla (alt. forms)
Khalkidice, Chalcidice (alt. forms)
Khotin, Chotin (*Rs*)   Hotin (*Rom*)   Chocim (*P*)
Klaipéda (*Lith*)   Memel (*Gn*)   Klaipeda (*P*)
Khust (*Rs*)   Chust (*C-s*)   Huszt (*H*)
Klagenfurt (*G*)   Celovec (*S-C*)
Kishinev (*Rs*)   Chişnău (*Rom*)   Kischinew (*Gn*)
Leitha (*Gn*)   Lajta (*H*)   Litava (*C-s*)
L'vov (*Rs*)   Lviv (*Ukr*)   Lwów (*P*)   Lemberg (*Gn*)   Ilyvó (*H*)   Leopolis (*Cl*)
Magdeburg (*Gn*)   Magdebourg (*Fr*)
Píndhos (*Gk*)   Pindos, Pindus (*Eng*)   Pind (*S-C*)
Leipzig (*Gn*)   Leipsic (alt. form)   Lipsko (*C-s*)
Mukačevo (*C-s*)   Munkács (*H*)   Mukachevo (*Rs*)
Pripet (*Eng*)   Prypeć (*P*)   Pripyat, Pripjat (*Rs*)   Pripet' (*C-s*)
Prussia (*Eng*)   Preussen (*Gn*)   Prusy (*C-s*)
Podolia (*Eng*)   Podolsk (*Rs*)
Sovetsk (*Rs*)   Tilsit (*Gn*)

Sub-Carpathian Russia, Carpathian Ruthenia, Carpatho-Ukraine
(*Eng*) Podkarpatská Rus (*C-s*) Zakarpatskaya (*Rs*)
Thessaloníki (*Gk*) Thessalonike, Saloniki (alt. forms) Salonika,
Thessalonika (*Eng*) Therma (*Cl*) Solun (*S-C, B*) Soluň (*C-s*)
Selanik (*Turk*)
Uzhgorod, Ushgorod (*Rs*) Užhorod (*C-s*) Ungvár (*H*)
Vienna (*Eng*) Wien (*Gn*) Vienne (*Fr*) Vindobona, Vindobna (*Cl*)
Beč (*S-C*) Vídeň (*C-s*) Bécs (*H*)
Villach (*Gn*) Beljak (*S-C*)
Vilna, Vilno (*Rs*) Vilnyus, Vilnius (*Lith*) Wilno (*P*) Wilna (*Gn*)

Index

Adam style, origin of, 689
Adriatic Sea, 9, 17, 94, 18, 23
  coasts of, 44
Agricola, Georg, 162, 258
Agriculture, 145–50,
  in: Albania, 843–7; Czechoslovakia, 439–47; Bulgaria, 784–93; Hungary, 509–14; Poland, 360–8; Romania, 576–87; Yugoslavia, 690–702
  employment in, 122–3
  mechanisation of, 268–9, 367
Airlines, 284, 385, 466
Ajka, 485, 507, 518
Albania, 3, 9, 75, 83–4, 87, 91, 94, 110, 112, 116, 117, 174, 180, 672, 737, 814–57
  agriculture in, 146, 843–7
  boundaries of, 112, 819–20, 831
  and China, 822–3, 841
  climate of, 832–3
  creation of, 94–5, 817–20
  drainage of, 825–7
  fuel resources of, 158, 850–2
  languages of, 60, 818, 834–6
  manufactures in, 848–54
  plain of, 827–8
  peoples of, 40, 44–5, 55, 60–1, 68, 110, 814–17, 830, 834–7
  population of, 61, 834–5
  relief of, 16, 823–32
  soils of, 833–4
  trade of, 182–3
  urbanisation of, 839–43
  vegetation of, 833
  and Yugoslavia, 820–3
Alexander of Yugoslavia, 670
Alföld, Great, 14–15, 480–1, 485, 487–93, 498, 500, 502–3, 504, 505, 512–13, 515
  towns of, 508–9, 522
Alföld, Little, 14–15, 480, 483–7, 502, 503, 512–13, 522
  See also Hungarian Plain
Aliákmon River, 871
Ali Pasha, 817
Aller River, 197, 203, 204, 209

Alliances, in Eastern Europe, 115
Almásfüzitö, 518
Alphabet, cyrillic, 59, 668
  in Albania, 834–5
Alpine mountain system, 6, 7–9, 13–17. *See also under separate countries*
Altmark, 204, 226, 232
Aluminium industry, 518–19
Andrychów, 360, 379
Animal farming, 252–4, 367–8, 445–7, 585–6, 513–14, 700–2, 790–1
Aquincum, 40, 506
Arad, 575, 598, 602
Arda River, 760, 796
Argeş river, 550, 592
Armenians, in the Balkans, 775
Aš, 459
Asenovgrad, 783
Ashkanazim Jews, 52–3, 69
Aurelian, Emperor
Ausgleich, 97, 394, 475, 685
Augustów Canal, 384
Austria, 8–9, 20, 72
Austro-Hungarian Empire, 1, 2, 72, 82, 84, 92–3, 95, 96–7, 98, 108–9, 296
Avars, 42, 47, 75, 77
Axiós, 871
Azov, Sea of, 90

Bacău, petroleum region at, 591–3, 598
  industrial region of, 605
Bačka, 135, 655–6, 664–6, 667, 673, 674, 691–2, 723
  urbanisation of, 681
Bačkovo monastery, 761
Bácska, 489, 512. *See also* Bačka
Baghdad Railway, 93
Baia Mare, 571, 597, 606
Baja, 489, 524
Bakony Forest, 6, 15, 126, 160, 473–474, 478–9, 485–6, 496–8, 501, 511, 515, 517
Balaton, Lake, 479, 485
Balkan Entente, 115